Contemporary Literary Criticism

Guide to Gale Literary Criticism Series

When you need to review criticism of literary works, these are the Gale series to use:

If the author's death date is:	You should turn to:
After Dec. 31, 1959 (or author is still living)	***CONTEMPORARY LITERARY CRITICISM*** for example: Jorge Luis Borges, Anthony Burgess, William Faulkner, Mary Gordon, Ernest Hemingway, Iris Murdoch
1900 through 1959	***TWENTIETH-CENTURY LITERARY CRITICISM*** for example: Willa Cather, F. Scott Fitzgerald, Henry James, Mark Twain, Virginia Woolf
1800 through 1899	***NINETEENTH-CENTURY LITERATURE CRITICISM*** for example: Fedor Dostoevski, Nathaniel Hawthorne, George Sand, William Wordsworth
1400 through 1799	***LITERATURE CRITICISM FROM 1400 TO 1800 (excluding Shakespeare)*** for example: Anne Bradstreet, Daniel Defoe, Alexander Pope, François Rabelais, Jonathan Swift, Phillis Wheatley
	SHAKESPEAREAN CRITICISM Shakespeare's plays and poetry
Antiquity through 1399	***CLASSICAL AND MEDIEVAL LITERATURE CRITICISM*** for example: Dante, Homer, Plato, Sophocles, Vergil, the Beowulf poet *(Volume 1 forthcoming)*

Gale also publishes related criticism series:

CHILDREN'S LITERATURE REVIEW

This ongoing series covers authors of all eras. Presents criticism on authors and author/illustrators who write for the preschool through high school audience.

CONTEMPORARY ISSUES CRITICISM

This two volume set presents criticism on contemporary authors writing on current issues. Topics covered include the social sciences, philosophy, economics, natural science, law, and related areas.

ISSN 0091-3421

Volume 45

Contemporary Literary Criticism

Excerpts from Criticism of the Works of Today's Novelists, Poets, Playwrights, Short Story Writers, Scriptwriters, and Other Creative Writers

Daniel G. Marowski
Roger Matuz
EDITORS

Robyn V. Young
ASSOCIATE EDITOR

Gale Research Company
Book Tower
Detroit, Michigan 48226

STAFF

Special thanks to Carolyn Bancroft and Sharon Hall
for their assistance on the Title Index.

Library of Congress Catalog Card Number 76-38938
ISBN 0-8103-4419-X
ISSN 0091-3421

Computerized photocomposition by
Typographics, Incorporated
Kansas City, Missouri

Printed in the United States

Contents

Preface

Literary criticism is, by definition, "the art of evaluating or analyzing with knowledge and propriety works of literature." The complexity and variety of the themes and forms of contemporary literature make the function of the critic especially important to today's reader. It is the critic who assists the reader in identifying significant new writers, recognizing trends in critical methods, mastering new terminology, and monitoring scholarly and popular sources of critical opinion.

Until the publication of the first volume of *Contemporary Literary Criticism (CLC)* in 1973, there existed no ongoing digest of current literary opinion. *CLC,* therefore, has fulfilled an essential need.

Scope of the Work

CLC presents significant passages from published criticism of works by today's creative writers. Each volume of *CLC* includes excerpted criticism on about 45 authors who are now living or who died after December 31, 1959. Nearly 1,900 authors have been included since the series began publication. The majority of authors covered by *CLC* are living writers who continue to publish; therefore, an author frequently appears in more than one volume. There is, of course, no duplication of reprinted criticism.

Authors are selected for inclusion for a variety of reasons, among them the publication of a critically acclaimed new work, the reception of a major literary award, or the dramatization of a literary work as a film or television screenplay. For example, the present volume includes Howard Moss, who won the Lenore Marshall/Nation Poetry Prize for his *New Selected Poems;* Richard Condon, whose novel *Prizzi's Honor* was adapted into an acclaimed film; and Delmore Schwartz, whose posthumous publications *The Ego Is Always at the Wheel: Bagatelles* and *Portrait of Delmore: Journals and Notes of Delmore Schwartz, 1939-1959* received significant critical attention. Perhaps most importantly, authors who appear frequently on the syllabuses of high school and college literature classes are heavily represented in *CLC;* John Steinbeck and Tennessee Williams are examples of writers of this stature in the present volume. Attention is also given to several other groups of writers—authors of considerable public interest—about whose work criticism is often difficult to locate. These are the contributors to the well-loved but nonscholarly genres of mystery and science fiction, as well as literary and social critics whose insights are considered valuable and informative. Foreign writers and authors who represent particular ethnic groups in the United States are also featured in each volume.

Format of the Book

Altogether there are about 700 individual excerpts in each volume—with an average of about 14 excerpts per author—taken from hundreds of literary reviews, general magazines, scholarly journals, and monographs. Contemporary criticism is loosely defined as that which is relevant to the evaluation of the author under discussion; this includes criticism written at the beginning of an author's career as well as current commentary. Emphasis has been placed on expanding the sources for criticism by including an increasing number of scholarly and specialized periodicals. Students, teachers, librarians, and researchers frequently find that the generous excerpts and supplementary material provided by the editors supply them with vital information needed to write a term paper, analyze a poem, or lead a book discussion group. However, complete bibliographical citations facilitate the location of the original source and provide all of the information necessary for a term paper footnote or bibliography.

A *CLC* author entry consists of the following elements:

- The **author heading** cites the author's full name, followed by birth date, and death date when applicable. The portion of the name outside parentheses denotes the form under which the author has most commonly published. If an author has written consistently under a pseudonym, the pseudonym will be listed in the author heading and the real name given on the first line of the biographical and critical introduction. Also located at the beginning of the introduction to the author entry are any important name variations under which an author has written. Uncertainty as to a birth or death date is indicated by question marks.

• A **portrait** of the author is included when available.

• A brief **biographical and critical introduction** to the author and his or her work precedes the excerpted criticism. However, *CLC* is not intended to be a definitive biographical source. Therefore, *cross-references* have been included to direct the reader to these useful sources published by the Gale Research Company: *Contemporary Authors,* which includes detailed biographical and bibliographical sketches on more than 88,000 authors; *Children's Literature Review,* which presents excerpted criticism on the works of authors of children's books; *Something about the Author,* which contains heavily illustrated biographical sketches on writers and illustrators who create books for children and young adults; *Contemporary Issues Criticism,* which presents excerpted commentary on the nonfiction works of authors who influence contemporary thought; *Dictionary of Literary Biography,* which provides original evaluations and detailed biographies of authors important to literary history; *Contemporary Authors Autobiography Series,* which offers autobiographical essays by prominent writers; and *Something about the Author Autobiography Series,* which presents autobiographical essays by authors of interest to young readers. Previous volumes of *CLC* in which the author has been featured are also listed in the introduction.

• The **excerpted criticism** represents various kinds of critical writing—a particular essay may be normative, descriptive, interpretive, textual, appreciative, comparative, or generic. It may range in form from the brief review to the scholarly monograph. Essays are selected by the editors to reflect the spectrum of opinion about a specific work or about an author's literary career in general. The excerpts are presented chronologically, adding a useful perspective to the entry. All titles by the author featured in the entry are printed in boldface type, which enables the reader to easily identify the works being discussed.

• A complete **bibliographical citation** designed to help the user find the original essay or book follows each excerpt.

Other Features

• A list of **Authors Forthcoming in *CLC*** previews the authors to be researched for future volumes.

• An **Appendix** lists the sources from which material in the volume has been reprinted. It does not, however, list every book or periodical consulted during the preparation of the volume.

• A **Cumulative Author Index** lists all the authors who have appeared in *CLC, Twentieth-Century Literary Criticism, Nineteenth-Century Literature Criticism,* and *Literature Criticism from 1400 to 1800,* along with cross-references to these Gale series: *Children's Literature Review, Authors in the News, Contemporary Authors, Contemporary Authors Autobiography Series, Contemporary Authors Bibliographical Series, Dictionary of Literary Biography, Something about the Author, Something about the Author Autobiography Series,* and *Yesterday's Authors of Books for Children.* Users will welcome this cumulated author index as a useful tool for locating an author within the various series. The index, which lists birth and death dates when available, will be particularly valuable for those authors who are identified with a certain period but whose death date causes them to be placed in another, or for those authors whose careers span two periods. For example, Ernest Hemingway is found in *CLC,* yet a writer often associated with him, F. Scott Fitzgerald, is found in *Twentieth-Century Literary Criticism.*

• A **Cumulative Nationality Index** listing the authors featured in *CLC* alphabetically by nationality, followed by the volume numbers in which they appear, is included in alternate volumes of *CLC.*

• A **Cumulative Title Index** listing titles reviewed in *CLC* in alphabetical order from Volume 1 through the current volume is included in alternate volumes of *CLC.* Titles are followed by the corresponding volume and page numbers where they may be located. In cases where the same title is used by different authors, the author's surname is given in parentheses after the title, e.g., *Collected Poems* (Berryman), *Collected Poems* (Eliot). For foreign titles, a cross-reference is given to the translated English title. Titles of novels, novellas, dramas, films, record albums, and poetry, short story, and essay collections are printed in italics, while all individual poems, short stories, essays, and songs are printed in roman type within quotation marks; when published separately (e.g., T.S. Eliot's poem *The Waste Land*), the title will also be printed in italics. A separate offprint of the Author, Nationality, and Title Indexes is also available.

Acknowledgments

No work of this scope can be accomplished without the cooperation of many people. The editors especially wish to thank the copyright holders of the excerpted essays included in this volume, the permissions managers of many book and magazine publishing companies for assisting us in securing reprint rights, and the photographers and other individuals who provided portraits of the authors. We are grateful to the staffs of the Detroit Public Library, the Library of Congress, the University of Detroit Library, the University of Michigan Library, and the Wayne State University Library for making their resources available to us. We also wish to thank Anthony Bogucki for his assistance with copyright research.

Suggestions Are Welcome

The editors welcome the comments and suggestions of readers to expand the coverage and enhance the usefulness of the series.

Authors Forthcoming in *CLC*

To Be Included in Volume 46

Alice Adams (American novelist and short story writer)—In her fiction, Adams often explores the emotional lives of upper middle-class professional women. Her recent works include a novel, *Superior Women,* and a short story collection, *Return Trips.*

Louise Bogan (American poet, critic, editor, translator, and autobiographer)—A distinguished figure in twentieth-century American literature, Bogan wrote classically structured poetry that passionately explores the extremes of experience. Her collections of verse have been complemented by the publication of *Journey around My Room: The Autobiography of Louise Bogan.*

Len Deighton (English novelist, short story writer, nonfiction writer, and scriptwriter)—Deighton is a highly popular author of spy thrillers who delighted critics and readers with the parodic elements in his first novel, *The Ipcress File.* Recent works to be covered in his entry include *Mexico Set* and *London Match.*

Jean Genet (French dramatist, novelist, and poet)—Described by Jean Cocteau as France's "Black Prince of letters," Genet was a controversial author who sought to replace Western values with his own system of antimorality. Among his most respected writings are the plays *The Maids* and *The Balcony* and the prose works *Our Lady of the Flowers* and *The Thief's Journal.*

Ken Kesey (American novelist, essayist, and short story writer)—Best known for his experimental novel *One Flew Over the Cuckoo's Nest,* Kesey has ended a long publishing hiatus with *Demon Box,* a collection of vignettes and short stories.

John Montague (American-born Irish poet, short story writer, and editor)—Montague's recent volumes of verse, *Selected Poems* and *The Dead Kingdom,* have secured his reputation as one of contemporary Ireland's leading poets.

Alberto Moravia (Italian novelist, short story writer, essayist, critic, dramatist, and scriptwriter)—Regarded as one of the foremost twentieth-century Italian literary figures, Moravia often presents a world of decadence and corruption in which his characters are guided primarily by their senses and by sexual obsession. Recent works to be covered in his entry include *Erotic Tales* and *The Voyeur.*

Vladimir Nabokov (Russian-born American novelist, poet, short story writer, essayist, dramatist, and critic)—Considered one of the greatest stylists of twentieth-century literature and renowned for his experimentation with language, Nabokov has gained renewed attention with the posthumous publication of his novel *The Enchanter.*

John Cowper Powys (English novelist, poet, autobiographer, essayist, and critic)—A prolific author in several genres, Powys is admired for the depth of imagination, ornate prose style, and philosophical beliefs displayed in such novels as *Wolf Solent, A Glastonbury Romance,* and *Weymouth Sands.*

Bernard Slade (Canadian-born dramatist and scriptwriter)—A popular Broadway dramatist best known for *Same Time, Next Year, Tribute,* and *Romantic Comedy,* Slade combines humor with emotionally affecting situations in plays about marital and familial love.

Alice Walker (American novelist, short story writer, poet, and essayist)—Walker writes powerful, expressive fiction depicting the black woman's struggle for spiritual wholeness, sexual freedom, and political autonomy. Criticism in her entry will examine her controversial Pulitzer Prize-winning novel, *The Color Purple.*

Anzia Yezierska (Russian-born novelist and short story writer)—Yezierska is best known for her fiction detailing the experiences of female Jewish immigrants in the United States at the beginning of the twentieth century. Since her death in 1970, several of Yezierska's works have been reissued, prompting renewed critical interest in her writings.

To Be Included in Volume 47

Louis-Ferdinand Celine (French novelist, essayist, and dramatist)—Best known for his novels *Journey to the End of the Night* and *Death on the Installment Plan,* Celine combines fractured syntax, Parisian argot, and obscenities to portray the chaos of Europe during World War I. The posthumous publication of *Conversations with Professor Y* has renewed critical interest in this controversial author.

James Dickey (American poet, novelist, critic, and essayist)—Widely acclaimed for his novel *Deliverance* and his National Book Award-winning poetry collection *Buckdancer's Choice,* Dickey has garnered critical attention for his recent novel, *Alnilam,* which details a blind man's search to learn the truth about his enigmatic son, who died in an airplane crash.

Michael Frayn (English dramatist, novelist, journalist, and scriptwriter)—A satirist of human foibles and contemporary society, Frayn is best known for his farcical play *Noises Off,* in which he examines the dichotomy between art and reality. Recent dramas to be covered in his entry include *Wild Honey,* adapted from Anton Chekhov's *Platonov,* and *Benefactors.*

Sheila Fugard (English-born South African novelist and poet)—A respected author who examines life under apartheid in South Africa, Fugard combines feminism and the Gandhian concept of nonviolent resistance to address her country's social problems in her recent novel, *A Revolutionary Woman.*

Ellen Gilchrist (American short story writer, novelist, and poet)—Gilchrist is best known as the author of the short story collection *Victory over Japan,* for which she received the American Book Award in fiction. Her recent volume of short fiction, *Drunk with Love,* has elicited significant critical attention.

John Masefield (English poet, novelist, short story writer, autobiographer, and dramatist)—The Poet Laureate of England from 1930 until his death in 1967, Masefield gained notoriety with his long narrative poems containing epithetic, colloquial language and vivid descriptions of the sea.

Marianne Moore (American poet, critic, essayist, and dramatist)—A prominent figure in twentieth-century American literature, Moore wrote poetry characterized by her technical and linguistic precision, acute observations, and detailed descriptions. Recent collections of her works to be covered in this entry include *The Complete Poems of Marianne Moore* and *The Complete Prose of Marianne Moore.*

Elsa Morante (Italian novelist, short story writer, essayist, and poet)—Best known for her novels *Arturo's Island* and *History,* Morante often focuses upon Marxist and Christian themes in her works. Criticism of *Aracoeli,* a novel published shortly before her death in 1985, will be featured in this entry.

R. K. Narayan (Indian novelist, short story writer, and essayist)—One of India's most celebrated contemporary authors, Narayan is noted for his creation of Malgudi, a mythical town in southern India which provides the setting for much of his fiction. Criticism of his recent novel, *Talkative Man,* will be included in Narayan's entry.

Walker Percy (American novelist, essayist, and critic)—Percy's philosophical novels often depict Southern characters who attempt to rise above the deadening routine of modern existence and attain spiritual happiness. In his recent best-selling work, *The Thanatos Syndrome,* Percy uses elements of the thriller to explore the moral implications of social engineering.

Tristan Tzara (Rumanian-born French poet, dramatist, and essayist)—Tzara was the founder of Dadaism, an intellectual movement of the World War I era that espoused intentional irrationality and repudiated traditional values of art, history, and religion. Tzara's nihilistic precepts continue to influence contemporary artists of all genres.

Yevgeny Yevtushenko (Russian poet and novelist)—Among the most outspoken and controversial poets to emerge in the Soviet Union since the death of Stalin, Yevtushenko has written two recent novels, *Wild Berries* and *Ardabiola,* in which he expands on the personal themes of his poetry.

Kathy Acker

1948-

(Has also written under pseudonym of The Black Tarantula) American novelist, scriptwriter, and librettist.

Acker is probably the most celebrated writer of what some critics have labeled "punk fiction," a genre marked by rejection of literary conventions and assault on bourgeois mores. Incorporating pornography, plagiarism, fragmented narrative, and autobiographical detail in a manner similar to William Burroughs's cut-up technique, Acker integrates into her own texts portions of works by Marcel Proust, Charles Dickens, the Marquis de Sade, and more obscure authors in an effort, in her words, "to attack any central, moral voice." Acker's work is characterized by an emphasis on the sensuality of language and by sudden shifts in time, space, subject, narrative voice, and the gender and identity of her characters.

Acker's early novels were published by small presses and received little critical attention. *The Childlike Life of the Black Tarantula* (1975), *The Adult Life of Toulouse Lautrec* (1978), and *I Dreamt I Was a Nymphomaniac: Imagining* (1980) demonstrate her preoccupation with sex, violence, and childhood and reveal her concerns with the stifling qualities of middle-class American society, relationships with men, and male sexism. Some critics contended that Acker's exaggerated depictions of sex and violence were numbing and that her plots were meandering and incomprehensible. Several others, however, defended Acker as a radical experimentalist who creates new categories of characterization, syntax, and narration and exceeds acceptable sexual and emotional boundaries as a means of exploring her characters' identities and desires.

With *Great Expectations* (1982), Acker gained substantial critical attention. The fragmentary, chaotic structure of the book alienated many reviewers, but some critics lauded Acker's impressionistic style. Michael Duff commented: "[Acker's] satire of the chaos and greed which mark our culture is trenchant. She is a serious moralist who calls into question our . . . hierarchical and moral reasoning." *Blood and Guts in High School Plus Two* (1984) was generally dismissed by critics, who found the novel degrading to women, outmoded in its social commentary, and excessively violent and obscene. In *Don Quixote* (1986), Acker transforms Miguel de Cervantes's protagonist into a contemporary radical feminist who attempts to subdue the worldwide spread of right-wing American policies. With a talking dog as her Sancho Panza, Acker's Don Quixote undertakes a heroic excursion into a mythical world run by two "power-mongers," Niccolò Machiavelli and Jesus Christ. Although some critics contended that *Don Quixote* is aimlessly plotted, Anne Haverty praised Acker for her "presentation of America [as] gruesomely clever and subversive," and Tom LeClair commended Acker's "scarified sensibility, subversive intellect, and predatory wit." Acker has also written the script for the film *Variety,* the play *Lulu Unchained* (1985), and the libretto for the opera *The Birth of the Poet* (1985).

(See also *Contemporary Authors,* Vol. 117.)

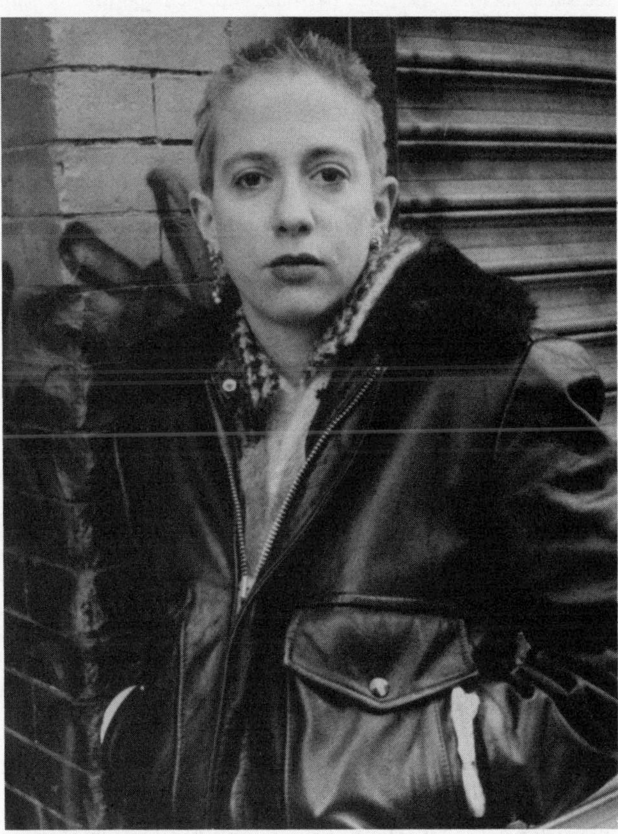

© *Jerry Bauer*

SALLY O'DRISCOLL

In Acker's writing, pornography, plagiarism, autobiography, and narrative fragments are slotted together to create a texture and a mood rather than plot or character. She has a poet's concern for the power of language, and for the dislocation that occurs when content suddenly switches from violence or pornography to childhood memory or historical fact. But these books aren't academic exercises: her experiments produce an authentic voice, which is a rare commodity in modern fiction. There is a persona in her work who uses anything at hand—fantasy, dream, sex, film synopses—to express itself and explore the edges of vulnerability. This persona has something in common with Genet's—both ignore acceptable sexual and emotional limits to pursue a feeling, an identity. Acker and Genet also use autobiographical details and transform them in the narrative—a risky process, but it adds punch to the authenticity of the voice.

I loved Kathy Acker's books as soon as I discovered them because of a gut reaction to this persona. Here was somebody who could exist—the voice of a vulnerable, fucked-up, adventurous person who would take any risks and go as far as possible to find sensation, without judgments; yet it is also a self-conscious persona with no illusions. This voice is a literary creation that transcends the author's personal experiences. It's a female voice that goes beyond feminism, artistic freedom turned into a free lifestyle. Whether or not Acker's persona could be acted out in a real life, the fact that she creates it on the page gives it power and touches off feelings about what is emotionally possible, though maybe not probable.

There is a continuity in Acker's books: they are concerned with the same themes, the same persona, and she experiments with the same techniques. But there is also a progression: in her first book, ***The Childlike Life of the Black Tarantula,*** she uses characters and situations from other people's books and changes them to fit her persona; in her latest, ***Great Expectations,*** these other texts have *become* her book—rewritten, it's true, but Acker's development to the point of almost abandoning the act of writing is radical.

In ***The Childlike Life of the Black Tarantula,*** each chapter explores a different part of Acker's persona—childhood, sex, murderous rage, etc. The chapter titles show how she uses the books she reads. . . . At the end of each chapter she identifies the books she used ("All events are taken from *Therese and Isabelle* by V. Leduc, my past, and my fantasies") so that whatever other writing she uses is separate from her own, even though the characters all become part of ***Tarantula*** and names and dates and places are freely switched around.

The writing in ***Tarantula*** is poetic and powerful. Acker uses short sentences that flow into each other, but she can slide into a paragraph, build up tension, and then drop off into a sharp change of mood with the next paragraph. Her style reflects the effect she gets when she intersperses the fragments from other books with her own narrative. It's an almost physical manipulation of language, an undulating series of up-and-down rhythms.

In ***Tarantula,*** Acker uses only three *kinds* of writing—pornography, factual events (as in the lives of the murderesses), and the narration of her own thoughts. She writes about these different contents in the same style, and uses only the internal rhythms of that style to structure the book. In a later book, ***The Adult Life of Toulouse Lautrec,*** she starts matching style to content so there's a *structural* tension when different fragments clash. She uses all sorts of styles in this book: detective-novel clichés, a mythic folk tale, gangster-novel jargon, plus pieces of what looks like a college term paper on corporate capitalism and a synopsis/commentary on *Rebel Without a Cause*. Sometimes the experiment works and the joining of one fragment to the next seems significant; in most of ***Toulouse Lautrec,*** though, the mixture of styles is arbitrary, even coy.

[***I Dreamt I Was a Nymphomaniac: Imagining*** is] about the desire to write, the rhythms of desire, merging identities with another person, and how hard it is to hold on to desire in real life. Instead of using the technique of jumping from one narrative fragment to another, it starts with dreamy sexual fantasies, moves into more surreal daydreams, then describes an imagined revolution, and closes with excerpts from case histories of injustices in American prisons. At the beginning, desire seems easy, simple to describe and to write about, but then an anxiety-filled fantasy is repeated over and over until it becomes scary, as though Acker were trying through writing to hold on to a moment of desire that is about to disappear. . . .

Nymphomaniac is the dreamiest and most surreal of Acker's books, and also one of the more overtly "political." Politics—an awareness of social conditions that her persona runs up against—is a theme that runs through all of her work. Even when it's not explicit, it's there in her deliberate attempt to think beyond the acceptable, not to be constricted by moralism or emotional safety. Acker tries to integrate that awareness into her other themes—sex, making a living, relations between men and women, between the straight world and the "bohemian" world—but since politics has to do with power and Acker's work is a pursuit of desire and sensation, not power, politics is symbolized by circumstances that thwart desire. ***Nymphomaniac*** is about the loss of desire: the book progresses from personal to political, from soft to hard, from desire realized in fantasy to desire thwarted by imprisonment.

Occasionally, Acker has experimented with more traditional narrative. ***Kathy Goes to Haiti*** is probably her most accessible book, the story of a passionate holiday love affair. Although the locale is more exotic and the narrative line straighter than in her other books, Acker's protagonist still has her emotional intensity and a vulnerable edge, and since there's a stable cast of characters and room here to expand into dialogue, some of the feelings that are expressed in impressionistic flashes in the other books are fleshed out in this one. Kathy sits on the beach for hours talking to beggar boys; she talks to her lover and his friends, to taxi drivers, to anyone—most of the book is dialogue.

In all of Acker's books the protagonist is alone, reaching out, but this is the only one where you can see this happen, in the speech. Acker still produces that physical feeling from her writing. . . . (p. 14)

Great Expectations is in the same style as Acker's other books, but it takes them further—it's her most accomplished experimental work. Nearly all of the writing is taken in fragments from other books, rewritten, and layered. The back cover lists Dickens, Proust, Flaubert, Réage, Victoria Holt, and Keats as sources: there are also reworkings of Propertius, Madame de Lafayette, and probably several others as yet unidentified, though none of the texts is taken verbatim. The plagiarized texts are interspersed with her own narrative, and some of the autobiographical facts that came up in the earlier books are here in more detail.

Nymphomaniac only used other texts near the end of the book, when holding on to desire and writing about it seemed to become impossible: ***Great Expectations*** takes that conclusion as its starting point. In one place, Acker says, "It's a common belief that something exists when it's part of a narrative. Self-reflective consciousness is narrational": trying to reconcile the need for narrative with the difficulties it causes, Acker deprives other narratives of connotation and puts them into a context where the fact that they are narrative becomes more important than their original content. It's the opposite of what Roland Barthes did in *S/Z*—he read a Balzac short story piece by piece and drew out every possible meaning the words could have in their context. Acker takes away most of the context so that the language only has power as language. The result is a different kind of pleasure of the text.

That type of analysis shows just a part of what goes on in Acker's books, though. She deals with the problems of art on much more concrete levels too, especially in ***Great Expectations,*** where she describes the politicking that goes on in the art world. Acker has been involved with the downtown New York art scene for years, and in the earlier books she would sometimes give her characters the names of artists she knew (not always flatteringly); in this book she's especially caustic about the power plays that make it impossible to live as an artist—no money without fame, no way to produce work without money. Acker herself knows plenty about the problems of making a living while trying to write. In her books she sometimes sounds like one of those half-crazy women you meet in bars who'll give you 10 different versions of their life-story over the course of a few drinks, but in Acker's case a lot of it is true. . . .

Acker has an ambivalent relationship to the Soho art world: that's where her friends are, and her own work reflects some of the attitudes of that scene, but she criticizes it in her books. It's an ingrown world, protected by money and mystique, and as a result a lot of the art created in that environment seems less than relevant, done almost as a hobby: Acker talks about her writing in the same way, as if it were fun, and that feeling is in her books too—a kind of unseriousness. At the same time, her work has none of the exclusiveness of Soho. She uses the art world as a rich source of material about people living as artists, being concerned with how to get fame and what it means, competitiveness and back-stabbing. But her writing also encompasses everything she has seen or done or imagined, and she doesn't hold back. Acker's writing has a completeness and a passionate involvement, while "serious" writers like Ann Beattie or Jayne Anne Phillips produce a circumscribed and constrained vacuum—they seem emotionally crippled.

Of all writers to compare Kathy Acker to, William Burroughs is the obvious choice. She says he's one of her favorites, and ***Black Tarantula*** and ***Toulouse Lautrec*** especially borrow a lot in style from his cut-up collages of autobiography, drugs, and sex. Like Burroughs, Acker uses those themes as take-off points for explorations of the sensuality of language. Burroughs's books are pieces of narrative that suddenly disintegrate into unrelated fragments of pure poetry. Although Acker is close to that style in her early books, she has moved in a different direction: she still retains Burroughs's general idea of how to make language sensuous, but in ***Great Expectations*** she finds rhythms that are more distinctively her own.

Pornography and sex are an important part of Acker's work, as they are for Burroughs. But it isn't easy for a woman to write about sex the way she does, at a time when pornography is defined by some feminists as violence against women. Whether one agrees with that or not, it's hard to go against the moral climate; yet written pornography is also a genre, with its own special literary virtues. It derives power from its purpose as well as its content—it's written deliberately to excite, and Acker uses pornography to express that excitement in all her writing: she exploits the *language* of sex.

Because all of Acker's technical experiments are at the service of achieving a physical, sensual presence in her writing, there is always a gut-level emotional feeling to her work. As she says in ***Great Expectations,*** "A narrative is an emotional moving." It should be, but she's one of the few people writing today who manage to blend that kind of warmth, gutsiness, and skill. (p. 15)

Sally O'Driscoll, "Professor of Desire," in VLS, *No. 4, February, 1982, pp. 14-15.*

CHARLES SCHLOTTER

When is an experimental novel unexperimental? When it weakly imitates every other experimental novel. Acker's ***Great Expectations,*** not to be confused with Dickens', is composed of all the time-honored gimmicks that were considered avant-garde sixty years ago! The result is a book that, far from being daring or shocking, is just as formula-ridden as any gothic potboiler.

Here is the recipe: First, create a narrator with multiple identities and sexes. Then place his/her/its disjointed narrative in a loose framework of shifting time and space. Be sure to include several deliberately mangled literary pastiches—this will give the graduate English faculties something to analyze. Interrupt the occasional wisps of a plot with unconnected scenes of rape and disembowelment, cribbed from Celine. . . .

Harp on suicide, deviate sex and excrement to give your novel depth. One of your narrator's identities should be a prostitute. Copy every known hooker cliche—twice!

Throw in a paragraph or two of unconnected historical data, distorted if possible—this will give the graduate History faculties something to analyze.

Throw in a poem. . . .

Into the stream-of-consciousness insert arbitrary capital LETTERS, like that. Add a heaping tablespoon of self-conscious special pleading for True Art and Artists, maybe ironic, maybe not, who cares? End abruptly.

Charles Schlotter, in a review of "Great Expectations," in West Coast Review of Books, *Vol. 10, No. 1, January-February, 1984, p. 38.*

NEVILLE SHACK

These plain tales [published in Great Britain as ***Blood and Guts in High School Plus Two***] have been expelled from the bunker of punk sensibility; now they must negotiate a way around the landmines of the real world. Unfair perhaps, because Kathy Acker is a sectarian writer. Her prose is programmed to serve certain recurring themes: priapic, vulvar, scatological, sexually exploitative in general. Some would use the shorthand description, pornographic. Yet the object is usually to disgust, not titillate.

Genital fantasias are almost invariably boring. Their range of metaphors and images is quickly exhausted. In this particular case, a strident anti-humanism grants the writer licence to convert people into the instruments of their private parts; fear and loathing in the erogenous zones.

Janey, the central character of ***Blood and Guts in High School*** (the first of three pieces collected here), is an anti-anti-heroine to such a degree that she ends up being abused by Jean Genet, who appears in a cameo rôle. For her sins, they knock about in North Africa together. Through the horrors of her adolescence she has assured us that human emotions are mostly garbage, and even more worthless. There is a kind of effect in the combining of a shrill tone with some recognizable conventions of a picaresque story.

But does this limited energy do much to heighten the power of the material? Not really. For all its nodding to the forms of experimental writing, the content here gets progressively jaded. The book as a whole leads us to expect startling and radical reinterpretations of reality. There are some isolated passages where the libido breaks through subversively. There are others where the depiction of sickness in society rings true. But, by the end, Acker's failure to provoke you fully into any reaction whatsoever is more surprising than this or that detail in the book. She does not rise to her own challenge as a visceral writer. Picturing the ways in which the self can be degraded, she is content to highlight the banalities of a small corner of experience—in neon. It induces more stupor than retching. . . .

The second story, ***Great Expectations*** (more spleen than spoof as far as Dickens's example goes), continues trading from a view of the world as an emporium of mindless sex. Allowances are made for romance as a notional American commodity, but paranoia and the reduction of men to sexual tyrants interrupt. . . .

In the final story there might or might not be a homage to the late Pier Paolo Pasolini. There *is* topical social comment, like the suggestion that President Reagan is using AIDS to control the American populace. . . .

Kathy Acker, like many "shocking" writers, maintains a high profile. . . . Robert Mapplethorpe, one of the most voguish of homoerotic photographers, has recorded her on the back cover shielding exposed breasts with her elbows. The pose works very well, containing a totally natural charm. In her own work she is said to see herself standing against "poseur nihilism". The hazards are obvious, notwithstanding. True, she can't really be accused of fey pretentiousness; but the dividing-line between specific areas of nihilism is thin. Ultimately, if not before, the subject-matter rebels against the writer's control, and the reader might well have given up.

Neville Shack, "Nihilism, Inc.," in The Times Literary Supplement, *No. 4219, February 10, 1984, p. 136.*

COSMO LANDESMAN

It takes two pages of Kathy Acker's [***Blood And Guts in High School Plus Two***] to realise that the American innocent is dead. From the ashes of the sixties a crippled phoenix has emerged preening its conspicuous corruption for all the world to see.

Janey, the protagonist of the first of these three stories is a modern American girl. She is violent, sado-masochistic, psychopathic, self-destructive, neurotic, obsessive, paranoid and is involved with incest, buggery, rape and only ten years old. A case of too much too soon? No. Unable to find the life affirming love she seeks she settles for the life destroying delights of sado-masochism. She says, "Death is the only reality we've got left in our nicey-nicey-clean ice-cream T.V. society so we better worship it. S&M sex and Punk Rock". For Janey being the victim is the means of victory over society.

Reading ***Blood And Guts In High School*** it is tempting to conclude that Kathy Acker—the current darling of the American avant-garde—was a casualty of poor toilet training as a child and too much symbolist poetry as an adolescent. Resulting in compulsive taboo breaking and the notion that to be a real artist it is de rigueur to be mad, bad and dangerous to read.

Acker is at war with Bourgeois culture and society. But unlike her heroes, Genet or Burroughs, Acker is as articulate and imaginative as a punk rocker whose brain has been marinating in glue since the days of the Sex Pistols. Scene after scene of violence and brutality are the shock tactics she uses to shock all of us brain-washed middleclass people. Beneath its high artistic ambitions is the low sensationalism of the video nasty. If you can imagine the gothic perversity of Lautremont mixed with the glory and the gore of the Texas Chainsaw Massacre you will have an idea of whats in store.

But what is so odd about this book is that Acker's view of society is so dated. Its the same old American whine—Mommy and Daddy never loved me, its the materialistic society that fucks you up from the Sixties. How about this for a bit of Hippie-Anarcho logic—"Everything in the materialistic society is the opposite of what it really is. Good is bad. Crime is the only possible behaviour". Now that's a bit of Living Theatre diatribe 1969. Someone should tell Kathy Acker that if you are losing your mind you don't need a literary agent you need help. For the book suggests in classic hippie fashion that madness is beautiful. (p. 34)

Cosmo Landesman, in a review of "Blood and Guts in High School Plus Two," in Books and Bookmen, *No. 342, March, 1984, pp. 33-4.*

BERTHA HARRIS

Kathy Acker's novel ***Great Expectations*** is the autobiography of ambition itself. Its title leads us to expect an orphan with problems of identity—but that expectation is baffled. Without warning the orphan becomes many voices all speaking at whim. And Miss Acker abruptly deserts one style for another, and then still another. Problems of coherence and intent are deliberately left to the reader's imagination.

In her opening section, "Plagiarism," Miss Acker lures us with a joyful perversion of Dickens: "My father's name being Pirrip, and my Christian name Philip, my infant tongue could make of both names nothing longer or more explicit than Peter. So I called myself Peter, and came to be called Peter."

Not "Pip," but Peter. The change signals the whole world of disoriented differences that follows. Peter is at first a homosexual consulting the tarot for new boyfriends. Later, he is the lover of a woman called "Kathy." But after he becomes "rich and famous" as an artist, he leaves her for other, possibly more glamorous, women; one is "a Mafiosa."

Kathy's ambition is to be a rich and famous artist like Peter, but because she is female, she is an orphan in the art establishment. The female artist, Miss Acker seems to be saying, needs a "father" to legitimize her claims to great expectations. To help the female artist, Peter obligingly multiplies himself into other art-world stereotypes; and in the unconfined reaches of Miss Acker's punk hallucinations, all these different manifestations of Peter travel through time, history, space, sex and literature.

As "Sarah," Peter becomes the victimized heiress girlfriend of two New York painters, "Clifford Still" and "Jackson." Sarah, a hopeless romantic, indicts big business and Government for a conspiracy whose aim in part is to keep fatherless female artists like Kathy out of the action. . . . But Sarah has her practical side and advises Kathy to "put lots of porn" in a book she is writing.

To organize the pornography, Peter becomes "Rosa," a prostitute and terrorist. Rosa is also a prolific letter-writer. On behalf of "the female artist," her approach is blunt: "Dear Susan Sontag, Would you please read my books and make me famous?" . . .

When Peter is not in New York with his mother, in one or another of his manifestations he may be in Egypt with Anwar Sadat or in 9th-century Paris with Charles the Simple. Occasionally he commits art criticism ("Cézanne allowed the question of there being simultaneous viewpoints. . . . The Cubists went further. They found the means of making the forms of all objects similar"). The many characters he assumes conduct search-and-seizure raids on World Literature. They linger in a pastiche of Millerish sex shows, replete with allusions to *The Story of O;* they have moments of narrative and lyric bliss with Melville, Keats, Woolf, Djuna Barnes, Propertius.

It is all in vain; none of them finds a father for their orphan, Kathy. The paternal affection and preference "the female artist" yearns for—a doomed romance as old-fashioned as Freud—is too completely hidden by Miss Acker's *trompe l'oeil* travesties. Or maybe not. The "romance" could be simply another literary joke, this one played on the Gothic sensibility. Miss Acker hints at that. . . .

It's interesting to meet a "female artist" with a lot of nerve; but there's more nerve than artistry to ***Great Expectations.*** Kathy Acker's writing is limp and glassy-eyed, without the persuasive courage of conviction this kind of outlaw fiction requires. The result, possibly intentional, leaves the reader as disoriented as the characters.

Bertha Harris, "Looking for Mr. Goodart," in The New York Times Book Review, *March 4, 1984, p. 30.*

BRIAN MORTON

[The] *idea* of Kathy Acker is a dangerous one. A punk novelist, an ex-sex show starlet, on the edges of the New York drugs scene, viciously spoofing (this is the Grundy view) Charles Dickens, making play with Pasolini's appalling murder, cashing in on a taste for violence and anarchy, someone with a closer affinity for rock bands like New Order and rock's hangers-on like Sid Vicious and Nauseating Nancy Spungen than for any other writers, except perhaps notoriously dodgy types like Kerouac and William Burroughs. . . .

The deliberate plagiarisms and stylistic effects of ***Blood and Guts in High School*** and the two other texts in the volume, ***Great Expectations*** and ***My Life, My Death by Pier Paolo Pasolini*** constantly betray the thinking that lies behind them. The punk inarticulacy and violence fail to mask or to blend with the graduate school experimentalism that is already well out of date, 25 years if you date it from the Beats, 60 if you give Surrealism the credit. Monotonously repeated obscenity quickly becomes irritating. Uninflected sex and violence rapidly lose interest even as pornography; nihilism has a poor shelf life and Johnny Rotten, Sid'n'Nancy did it better anyway.

The idea of pillaging *Great Expectations,* or examining the mystery and ambiguity of Pasolini's fate is an interesting one. But the intention isn't clear. If it is, after all, to shock and to kick down convention, then Acker is swinging at targets that are no longer there. ***Blood and Guts*** isn't shocking enough; as satire, it's targetless, as sensibility, it's too abstract, as fiction, it's too drab. Shock value is the most inflatable of currencies and the quickest to crash.

Brian Morton, "Shockwave," in The Times Educational Supplement, *No. 3541, May 11, 1984, p. 29.*

MICHAEL DUFF

[***Great Expectations***] is a short obsessive novel. As a chronicle of despair, the book explores the lives of different but interchangeable heroines lost on the fast track of life. Reader beware: Acker is strong stuff. If you are dauntless and willing to venture into risky narratives which challenge your assumptions, ***Great Expectations*** will be rewarding as well as disturbing.

The plot is convoluted and almost unintelligible, but the fragmentation of the narrative perfectly suits the cracked psyches of the players. There are a series of narrators: Rosa, Cynthia, Natalie, Sarah, Kathy, and O. Each exists in extremis and lacks any distinguishing characteristics other than intense self-loathing. "I am separating women into virgins or whores," she states, but her women are all victims here. Only tangentially, through obsessive monologue, does the reader infer that a revered/detested mother (of Rosa) has died; incest occurred (between O. and her father); money has been inherited; trips planned and taken (Cynthia); lovers discarded (Rosa's Peter and Sarah's Clifford); fame sought (Kathy), and security needed by all but never found. The concerns are traditional. The treatment is not.

Acker's approach is non-narrational. Consequently, we are constantly losing the characters. They revolve into themselves and away from the reader. Acker attempts to displace the logical progression of plot development with her circular reasoning. The narrative becomes a whirl of intuitions and pieces of incidences made real by her use of language. . . .

For [Acker], logic is equated with falseness. "I have never been able to perceive how anything can be known for truth by consecutive reasoning." Logic is a hierarchical—hence male—construct. The only choice then, being a woman, is to "commit yourself to not knowing." The result is a highly charged, impressionistic prose that defies traditional analysis, since coherence, character development and plot progression do not exist.

Sexuality is the one aspect of human behavior least susceptible to the restraints of reason, and it is on sexuality that Acker concentrates. She has been attacked for this and accused of being a pornographer. There is nothing pornographic here. The sexual descriptions, though blatant, lead to disgust and revulsion, the very opposite of the easy titillation of true pornography. . . . It is startlingly brilliant how she reveals our sexual practices as being symptoms of our own degradation and despair and not of our liberation.

The artistic problems inherent in this work are large. She is only partly capable of solving them. Nonetheless, hers is a heroic if doomed effort to reorder patriarchal reality and narrative forms into a new feminine and intuitive order. Her satire of the chaos and greed which mark our culture is trenchant. She is a serious moralist who calls into question our narrative conventions, and consequently, our hierarchial and moral reasoning.

"Writing is not a viable alternative anymore," she states. However, she continues to follow her harrowing muse. The slick, commercialized surface of American culture is jettisoned. The danger, and indeed the danger in any so solipsistic a work, is that it begins to unintentionally parody itself, losing in the process its considerable moral power.

Michael Duff, in a review of "Great Expectations," in The Small Press Review, *Vol. 16, No. 8, August, 1984, p. 8.*

ROY HOFFMAN

Playing with elements of profanity, pornography and lewd illustration, Kathy Acker [in ***Blood and Guts in High School***] attempts to piece together the beaten-down life of a girl named Janey, who starts out in a bizarre incestuous relationship with her father that is described in an oddly breezy manner. She winds up, after a sojourn through crime, wild promiscuity and slavery to a Persian master, in the Egyptian desert at the side of Jean Genet. The novel, willfully "innovative" in its assemblage of literary and not-so-literary forms—poetry, dramatic script, dream map, grammar book—has the cool, hip, matter-of-fact vulgarity of the old Zap Comix, a cartoon that combined sex, violence and drugs in a picaresque rendering of the down and out. At times, Miss Acker does manage to open up the desperation of Janey, whose moral sphere becomes so inverted that reasonably human conduct seems beyond her grasp. . . . [There's] a deep moral dislocation in ***Blood and Guts in High School;*** the novel, which devotes thousands of words to depicting the cruelty inflicted on Janey and on women in general, is itself abusive toward women. There are beatings, rapings, psychological torture, and more energy is spent laying out these abuses than in defusing or counteracting them. And Janey's descent, as victim, into becoming the perfect image of all her oppressors want her to be is not so much harrowing as pathetic. By the time four judges visit Janey and make pronouncements like, "You're a woman. You whine and snivel. You don't stand up for yourself. . . . You have every vice in the world," the accusations seem to be the very argument of this book—not the parody of that argument, as, we can only presume, the author intended them to be.

Roy Hoffman, in a review of "Blood and Guts in High School," in The New York Times Book Review, *December 23, 1984, p. 16.*

ANNE HAVERTY

[Kathy Acker's] female Don Quixote is no mere commentator. She participates in experience, in corruption, in the receiving and inflicting of love.

This Don Quixote has an abortion which makes her mad but liberates her into her knighthood—"Because to Don Quixote having an abortion is a method of becoming a knight and saving the world. This is a vision . . .". [***Don Quixote***] is a meditation on her (k)night-time journey. It is a loosely structured succession of surreal images and unreal events, interleaved occasionally with other texts, as is Acker's habit—in this case passages from political history. ***Don Quixote*** has the qualities of a dream, sometimes the intensities of one, and sometimes the brutal persuasiveness of nightmare. Its narrative thread is tenuous, its locations timeless and shifting. Its characters come and go: talking dogs, a Prince, God, pirates. Don Quixote herself, more concerned with the varied problems of love than with windmills, metamorphoses into an unsuccessful Don Juan. Her tilting is expressed in her madness and her irreverence. The enemies this Don Quixote must subdue are her obsessive need for love, which nullifies her sense of self, and her political enemies—"the evil enchanters of this world such as the editors of *TLS* and Ronald Reagan". If theirs are the voices of orthodoxy, hers is the voice of anarchy, lyrical and crass by turns. Her words are the absolute words of romance: hope, despair, love, death, devastation and creation.

On her night journey, Don Quixote has many adventures, mostly sexual and largely painful. She enacts her fantasies and acquires knowledge: that ecstasy no longer resides in rejection, that God is imperfect—"you can't turn to Me. Turn to yourself". She awakes, appeased, to the world of the morning. She has travelled into and emerged from the Acker blackness of memory and experience where anarchy reigns.

This intractable novel is required too often to serve as a dumping-ground for its author's many random musings and aphorisms, which gives an impression of self-indulgence and often makes it tedious to read. It has some of the worst qualities of dream-literature: a cluttered opacity, the relentless recounting of haphazard events, the lack of a centre in the mutant character of Don Quixote. These might be accommodated if the prose was as consistently beautiful as it sometimes is, but Acker is too often undisciplined and toneless.

And yet, for all its tediums and jarring rhythms, ***Don Quixote*** is a significant addition to the too thin body of experimental writing in English. Acker speaks from a level that is both above and below the urbanity of daily life, from the complex world of misery and exploitation that yet fears annihilation. And she does so with a voice of natural sophistication, strikingly remote from the bourgeois canon. She is also very funny. Her presentation of American history, and the chapter "An Examination of What Kind of Schooling Women Need" are gruesomely clever and subversive. ***Don Quixote*** is also, thematically at least, a development for Kathy Acker. Here, the personal complement the political concerns, and her perspectives on both escape banality. Her raw and direct responses make this mistress of the obscene a writer of admirable purity.

Anne Haverty, "In the (K)Night-Time," in The Times Literary Supplement, *No. 4338, May 23, 1986, p. 554.*

TOM LeCLAIR

Kathy Acker's ***Don Quixote*** is a literary trash compactor, collapsing with hammer thumps and electronic whine the fictional containers—the genres, stories and characters—from which we take nourishment and, Ms. Acker says, sup poison. Cervantes constructed his two-volume landfill of medieval rubbish and Renaissance life over two decades. Ms. Acker's 207-page version is the product of the "new era" one of her characters in her last novel, ***Blood and Guts in High School,*** describes as an age when "people will have to grapple with all sorts of difficult problems, leaving us no time for the luxury of expressing ourselves artistically."

The novel begins with Don Quixote, now a 66-year-old contemporary woman, having an abortion, which maddens her: "She conceived of the most insane idea that any woman can think of. Which is to love." This ideal is crazed, we learn later, because most women are too intelligent to believe in romantic love but have been persuaded by men and literature that love is woman's function and tragic triumph. Cervantes showed what courtly love could do to a man. Ms. Acker sketches 350 years of sentimental history and illustrates the cumulative effects of romantic madness with Ms. Quixote's wanderings through the gender wars of today's London and New York, her Sancho Panza a talking dog named St. Simeon.

Like Cervantes' book, Ms. Acker's collects adventures, authorial addresses, reportage, other texts, anecdotes and hallucinations. Subtitled *Which Was a Dream,* ***Don Quixote*** has the three-part structure of the mythic heroic journey. "The Beginning of the Night" is also the knight's departure, her futile and often funny sallies into a world controlled by two "power-mongers," Machiavelli and Christ. In the second part, "Other Texts," Quixote has to read works by four male writers who create or unwittingly perpetuate harmful stereotypes of women. These works—Bely's *Petersburg,* Lampedusa's *Leopard,* Wedekind's *Lulu* plays and an anonymous science fiction story—Ms. Acker bashes with broad parody and grotesque revision. In the third part, "The End of the Night" (and knight), Quixote returns from literature to save America from "evil enchanters" such as Richard Nixon, Henry Kissinger and New York City landlords. . . . "Economic and political war or control," Quixote comes to believe, are now "taking place at the level of language or myth." She also knows about "the later semioticians . . . Derrida . . . Foucault." But Ms. Acker is no academic deconstructor. Not even a maker of Donald Barthelme collages or Angela Carter rewrites. . . . What is evident in ***Don Quixote,*** as well as in ***Blood and Guts*** and another earlier novel, ***Great Expectations,*** is a punklike reductiveness of lexicon and texture, a combination of the early Sex Pistols' raging repetition and the drugged synthesizer tonalities of Laurie Anderson's mantric songs.

The original Quixote complained that his story was told by "some ignorant chatterer who set himself to write it gropingly." Despite the Cervantean precedent, Ms. Acker's stylistic choices are, I think, at unfortunate odds with the sophistication of her materials. The novel is eccentrically learned; quite carefully constructed, though it appears haphazardly plotted; in control of its double and triple ironic inversions; canny in its feminist critique of male and female fictions, including feminist mythologies; and often acute in its overheard voices. But ***Don Quixote*** is much too frequently composed of banal language, the stilted and formulaic high-school passion I thought Ms. Acker had disposed of in ***Blood and Guts.*** How to separate the trash compactor from the trash? This is the challenge Ms. Acker does not manage with a craft equal to her cultural range.

Like most postmodern experimenters, Ms. Acker includes within her novel several defenses of its alienating methods. "Masochism is now rebellion" might explain her "messed-up language." Ms. Acker also likes to play authorial hide and seek. Toward the end of ***Don Quixote*** she implies that it, as well as other novels, are symptoms of trauma, the howl of guilt and anger inflicted by the suicide of a mother dominated by male notions of femininity. Whether autobiographical fact or not, this experience of self-destructiveness supplies a powerful cause of Quixote's abortion-madness and a motive for Ms. Acker's self-imploding prose. Her scarified sensibility, subversive intellect and predatory wit make her a writer like no other I know.

Tom LeClair, "The Lord of La Mancha and Her Abortion," in The New York Times Book Review, *November 30, 1986, p. 10.*

C. CARR

Don Quixote is now a theoretical girl, a female character marching forth on the spindly legs of poststructuralism; that is, she can tell you what it means to be a cunt. Thus Kathy Acker updates another classic. Better known for her image as a big bad mouth than for her eight books, Acker's often labeled a "punk" writer—which is certainly to judge a book by its haircut.

In its cleverly concealed didacticism, her ***Don Quixote*** shares something with the original. Cervantes hoped that readers would learn to "abhor the false and foolish tales of chivalry" which had driven his knight-errant mad. The Quixote of yore believed every fiction and so perceived his shabby world as a landscape of monsters, enchantments, and lovesick princesses. Acker's Quixote believes nothing. She knows that she's roaming in a world of lies and fakes, that identity itself is an internalized fiction.

Even so, she has also gone mad, because she's about to have an abortion. As the girl-narrator puts it in an earlier Acker book, ***Blood and Guts in High School:*** "Abortions are the symbol, the outer image, of sexual relations in this world. Describing my own abortions is the only real way I can tell you about pain and fear . . ." Her abortion gives Quixote "the most insane idea that any woman can think of. Which is to love." So this nothing-errant will tilt at love like the old Don at his windmill, for in the world of Acker's novels, there *is* no love. Certainly no romantic love.

In all her books, Acker is obsessed by her relationships to men and to (male) language. Failure may be inevitable, but she's compelled to keep trying. Failure, in fact, makes intellectual sense. She's part of that century-long tradition of writers—from dadaists to deconstructionists—who've railed at the limits of the Word. And she's certainly absorbed poststructuralist theories about the death of the Author (of originality), the end of humanism, the impossibility of truth. As one of the girl-narrators in ***Don Quixote*** explains to a friend, these philosophies provided "a language with which I could speak about my work," which then "allowed me to go one step further in my work." And so ***Quixote*** does, for Acker deconstructs gender in this book as she never has before. A writer who feels more at home in the art world than in the literary one, Acker addresses the same issues of sexuality and representation that we see in the work of visual artists like Barbara Kruger, Sherrie Levine, and Cindy Sherman. I can't think of many other women novelists facing these tough questions so directly.

Sometimes, though, I'm more intrigued with the "project" than with the on-again off-again pleasures of an Acker text. ***Quixote*** is much like her other stuff in style. It refuses to behave like a good read. Sure, it has its Graphic Sex and Violence, but that doesn't make it fun. Narrators mutate, and narratives dangle or implode into filthy wacky little fragments. Acker almost always appropriates Great Novels or Great Dramas, though she generally throws out the plot. She wants the characters—or maybe just the title, as in her definitely post-Dickensian ***Great Expectations.*** The old novel is there like a ghost in the reader's mind. Just as the Great Artists or political figures who occasionally have roles (Kissinger, Genet, et al.) already carry symbolic baggage through our brains. . . .

Typically, Acker won't say what anything means, only that "language is more important than meaning." The reader enters a conundrum in her books. Often Acker's tone is so cynical, her content so contradictory, her structure so apparently haphazard that it's hard to tell where *she* is in the resulting chaos. She's a camouflaged writer creating the sort of work Barthes describes in *Image-Music-Text:* "a text is not a line of words releasing a single 'theological' meaning (the 'message' of the Author-God) but a multi-dimensional space in which a variety of writings, none of them original, blend and clash."

With no narrative-drug to hook us, no coherent voice to guide us, no emotional thread to pull us through it, Acker's text practically dares us to make something of it. . . .

Acker's books don't have living, breathing plots, but they have their motifs, their recurring nightmares: the mother dead by suicide, the girl abandoned by her father (husband) (friend), the girl captured by white slavers or involved with a very old man, and, of course, the attraction born as much in hatred as in love. One problem I've always had with Acker's work is her refusal to move her girl-narrators out of their victim postures. They are despised, used, abused—and they take it, thinking this will get them love. . . . They never quite connect with the rage that could make them powerful. "Look what you did to me," they seem to say. But then, they *are* nothings. "Nothing matters so I can do what I want," they seem to say, as if nihilism bred spoiled brats.

Acker steps back from acting the victim in ***Quixote,*** however. The knight-narrator has moved to a whole new level of alienation, where she doesn't even believe the myth of her own masochism. . . .

In the middle section of the book, called "Other Texts," Don Quixote does not appear, having "died" at the end of Part One. (In Acker's writing, "death" often means that there's no hope of getting what you want—as it does here. Or death is death, "the one Absolute, the one thing knowable.") "Other Texts" turn out to be Ackered variations on the likes of Wedekind's *Lulu,* full of incidents that might have fit in earlier Acker books: a woman slitting her wrists as a man tells her "no man will ever love you"; a woman asking "how does my body feel pleasure?" and responding with what gives her boyfriend pleasure. But the entire section has been prefaced with a reminder that Quixote, being dead, can't speak. "All she could do was read male texts which weren't hers." Knowing this, she avoids being a victim, but won't succeed in becoming a victor either. Such behavior would emerge from some place where she's never been. She's in limbo, wandering through the shadows of New York and London and apparently through time as well, hoping to defeat the evil enchanters that prevent self-knowledge and make love impossible: poverty, alienation, fear, inability to act on desire, inability to feel. She understands herself to be picaresquing in a male, thus alien, land.

She decides that being part male may be the only way to go. So Quixote declares herself a "female-male or night-knight" after changing her names to "catheter" and "hackneyed"—long male names, as she puts it. And for perhaps the first time in an Acker novel, the narrator has a series of companions—her Sancho Panzas—instead of lovers. The first of these, Saint Simeon, disappears early on only to come back a few pages later as a talking dog. Together, knight and dog encounter a Leftist "who always had to explain the world to everyone," some monks who ask to be beaten, and the madam of a brothel, but as usual these are like incidents seen through gauze, told by a narrator more interested in her own mind than in making us some stories. (p. 9)

It's apparent from the language and scenarios in ***Don Quixote*** that Acker has found a brand of feminism she can live with—something wild and "post-Lacanian." Lacan's phallocentrism, like Freud's, dismissed women as impotent, defined by their "lack," defined by a whole vocabulary of negativity. In ***Don Quixote,*** the knight so aware of being "object," "mirror," and "endless hole" realizes that part of her problem is with definitions and who gets to define. "I wanted to find a meaning or myth or language that was mine, rather than those which try to control me," Quixote reflects near the end of the book, knowing that she's failed. The post-Lacanian postfeminists assume that women have a different relationship than men do to both desire and language—a difference they are still struggling to understand, as Acker is. (pp. 9-10)

Acker's female characters find their only truth in the body, in sexuality. "I want your cock inside me!" becomes a first intimation of self-discovery for the nothings (cunts) who've been told what they are through the ladylike centuries. As one of her female dog-companions tells Quixote: "My physical sensations scare me because they confront me with a self when I have no self." This dog could easily be Quixote herself. The female narrators in Acker's texts always seem interchangeable, different names tagged to the sound of one voice raging—obscene, cynical, bewildered, and demanding to fuck. . . .

In Acker's work, every connection with some possible love seems doomed. . . . In ***Quixote,*** one of the dog-companions tells a long convoluted tale about the beginnings of a relationship. The dog's neuroses and those of her lover seem to align in such a way that This Could Be Love (possibly). First the dog had resolved to be a lesbian because men treated her so badly, but "being with another woman was like being with no one, for there was no rejection or death." For the dog, sexuality was rejection. Finally she'd met a girlish man, De Franville, who saw her as a boyish woman, his mirror. De Franville had to control his lovers to make sure they didn't get too close, even though he despised control, while the woman (dog) could only love if she feared. One night De Franville went to a party dressed girlishly to attract the woman who had come dressed as a man (a Nazi captain, in fact). Because she wanted girls. Because she couldn't love them. Naturally, she and De Franville fell in love. From here on the dog who is telling this tale speaks sometimes as the woman (dog), sometimes as the man, but always refers to the other as she(he) or he(she). . . . They fell immediately into an s&m relationship which allowed them the control and the rejection they needed, and "Don Quixote was disgusted that human heterosexuality had come to such an extreme end, even though the dog wasn't human, only female."

This master/slave dialectic recurs throughout the book and throughout Acker's work—the all-purpose metaphor for a society dependent on unequal power relations. . . . In Part Three, Don Quixote is doing battle with the Nixon administration. Apparently. It's sometimes hard to know what the hell is going on in a text this perversely dissociated. After many pages of the Angel lecturing on dualism, the dog-eat-dog of relationships, and so on, Acker suddenly tells us, "Don Quixote got rid of Nixon." She doesn't say how. The sentences refuse to build into a climax, the complicated ideas appear in Dick-and-Jane simplicity, and the ideas and events continue to contradict each other (because, says our narrator, contradiction is part of a dualistic world). I feel my mind slip over the opaque surface of it all. Is that, finally, the point? As Quixote put it to a character identified only as the old male creep, "Being female, I'm not used to points." . . .

It's odd that someone who finds her only truth in desire seems to write less out of her emotions than her intellect—all those theories of posteverything. Sometimes I think they just get in her way. But then Acker questions her emotion too. What is it, anyway? And how connected to her consciousness? There is a pervasive sadness and longing in Acker's books. Sometimes, as she writes (at the end of ***Great Expectations***), "wants go so deep there is no way of getting them out of the body, no surgery other than death." To me, this describes a desire beyond language that wipes out any narrative or character or meaning in its path. ***Don Quixote*** ends with the death of God.

Which I read as the death of the Author, since this God tells Quixote "there are no more new stories, no more tracks, no more memories: there is you knight." In the last few paragraphs, this Author-God—whom Quixote calls "my master"—sets the knight free, after asking her why she thinks She is Male. The knight then wakes to the world before her, where she won't have an Author, a role, or a meaning. I found this moving—which, "God" knows, might even be an inappropriate response to an Acker work. Certainly for anyone who's always been an object, the goal is not to mean (or move) something, but to *be*. (p. 10)

C. Carr, "Text and Violence: Kathy Acker Strikes Again," in VLS, *No. 53, March, 1987, pp. 9-10.*

Louis (Stanton) Auchincloss

1917-

(Has also written under pseudonym of Andrew Lee) American novelist, short story writer, critic, essayist, editor, and dramatist.

© 1987 Thomas Victor

A prolific writer, Auchincloss is best known as a novelist of manners and is considered by many critics to have succeeded Edith Wharton as chronicler of the New York aristocracy. His background as an attorney and a member of an upper-class New York family provides material for many of his works. Following the genteel tradition, Auchincloss's fiction is peopled with bankers, trust officers, corporation executives, lawyers, and their spouses and children. He shows them at work and at leisure while depicting the fading power of their collective class. Auchincloss's most frequent setting is the legal world of Wall Street, and his themes revolve around ethical dilemmas and moral choices. Critics have consistently praised Auchincloss for his informed and illuminating presentations of this exclusive circle. Auchincloss's prose is characteristically elegant, confident, and smooth, with a tone of ironic wit. His works have widely varied narrative structures: some alternate between first- and third-person narration, others are developed as memoirs, diaries, and biographies, and the narratives of several alternate between two characters. Some critics disapprove of Auchincloss's chosen milieu, contending that it is too narrow and suggesting that his penchant for the traditional has become obsolete. However, many others consider him an astute social observer and historian and commend his humor, insight, and ability to evoke a relatively sequestered social environment.

Auchincloss's first novel, *The Indifferent Children* (1947), written under the pseudonym of Andrew Lee, elicited favorable comparisons to Edith Wharton and Henry James and established him as an astute observer of America's elite. The protagonist of this novel, a young, upper-class World War II soldier, possesses a sympathetic and ironic sensibility which has become a standard of Auchincloss's characters. Two of Auchincloss's early novels, *Sybil* (1952) and *A Law for the Lion* (1953), depict the lives of dissatisfied New York society women, the psychological reasons for their unhappiness, and their quests to discover their identities. *Sybil* concerns a shy, insecure upper-class woman who undergoes self-evaluation and gains the confidence she needs to live in a social milieu which does not allow for individualism. In *A Law for the Lion,* Auchincloss concentrates on the unsuccessful marriage of his central character. The female protagonist of *The Dark Lady* (1977) is stronger and more ambitious than Auchincloss's earlier heroines. This book focuses on the rise of Elesina Dart from alcoholic actress to member of Congress and depicts the people she manipulates and victimizes.

With *The Great World and Timothy Colt* (1956), Auchincloss introduced into his fiction a character type which recurs in several of his subsequent works: an affluent individual who does not conform to his socially prescribed role and is eventually driven to self-destruction. Timothy Colt, a lawyer who sees good and evil only in clear-cut terms, confesses to a minor indiscretion because he feels guilty for having abandoned his legal idealism and wants to be punished. *Venus in Sparta* (1958) depicts a man whose failure to live up to the expectations of his mother and his employers results in his suicide. In *I Come as a Thief* (1972), the religious conversion of the protagonist serves as the catalyst which allows him to escape the torment of his past. In *The Country Cousin* (1978), a lawyer conceals his wife's destruction of the codicil to a will despite his high ethical standards. Unlike Auchincloss's other works dealing with moral conscience, *The Country Cousin* is light in tone and intentionally sardonic.

Several of Auchincloss's novels are multigenerational sagas which concentrate on psychological and social characteristics of the American elite. *The Pursuit of the Prodigal* (1959) serves as a transition from Auchincloss's novels about Wall Street law firms. This book, which examines the erosion of social position among prominent families, centers on an eccentric, nonconformist lawyer who rebels against his wealthy family. In *The House of Five Talents* (1960), Auchincloss depicts the rise of a middle-class family to aristocratic status between 1875 and 1948 and the effects on the family of its newfound affluence. *Portrait in Brownstone* (1962) chronicles the Denison family from the beginning of the twentieth century to 1951 and recounts the emergence of Ida Denison Trask from shy young intellectual to family matriarch. *The Rector of Justin* (1964) is considered one of Auchincloss's best works. This novel reconstructs the life of a recently deceased headmaster of a preparatory school through the recollections and impressions of several characters, each of whom had known a different side of his personality. The narrative form of *The Rector of Justin* allowed Auchincloss to explore more fully the complexities of human character. The self-satisfied hero of *The House of the Prophet* (1980), who is more respected by the public than by his family, is presented in much the same manner as the protagonist of *The Rector of Justin*. In this novel, journalist Felix Leitner's life is traced from childhood to death by a friend and admirer.

Some of Auchincloss's works are categorized as conventional historical novels. In *The Cat and the King* (1981) and *Exit Lady Masham* (1983), Auchincloss fictionalizes the lives of European royalty. Set in the court of Versailles, *The Cat and the King* is a recreation of life under the reign of Louis XIV based on the memoirs of Louis Rovroy, the second Duc de St. Simon, a famous historian of that period. *Exit Lady Masham* is a fictional memoir of the English court of Queen Anne as narrated by Abigail Hill Masham, an influential attendant to the Queen. *Watchfires* (1982) is a novel about marriage, duty, and liberation during the American Civil War era. Auchincloss presents his most optimistic view of marriage in this work, as he depicts a union which survives infidelity and becomes stronger and more trusting.

In two of his novels, *The Book Class* (1984) and *Honorable Men* (1985), Auchincloss recreates his childhood experiences. *The Book Class* revolves around a literary discussion group composed of upper-class women and explores the hidden power of the seemingly unliberated females of his mother's generation. The novel's narrator is the son of one of the women who had participated in the group. *Honorable Men,* which explores the strain of puritanism embedded in upper-class Easterners of Auchincloss's generation, centers on a character whose burdensome sense of duty is the result of his family's position in the community. With *Diary of a Yuppie* (1986), Auchincloss addresses a more contemporary topic. The protagonist of this work is a thirty-two-year-old lawyer who quickly rises to the top of his profession and eventually establishes his own law firm specializing in corporate takeovers by stealing clients from his former employers.

Auchincloss is also a prolific short story writer. Many of his collections are constructed as unified works and are set in the same milieu as his novels. *The Injustice Collectors* (1950) is a volume of psychological studies of neurotic and masochistic characters. Each story of *The Romantic Egoists* (1954) shares a common narrator, and one piece served as the basis for the novel *The Great World and Timothy Colt*. The pieces in *Powers of Attorney* (1963) revolve around the partners and employees of a large Wall Street law firm. *Tales of Manhattan* (1967) contains Auchincloss's usual brand of fiction and also includes a play, *The Club Bedroom*. In *Second Chance: Tales of Two Generations* (1970), Auchincloss examines the generation gap and the relationships between contemporary and past values. *The Partners* (1974) is regarded as Auchincloss's most unified collection of short fiction. The central character of this volume appears in almost all of the stories and emerges as a fully developed protagonist. *The Winthrop Covenant* (1976), inspired by the American Bicentennial, spans over three centuries and details the lives of the Winthrop family. Each of the stories in *Narcissa and Other Fables* (1982) explores the moral confusion which has resulted from the decline of conventional values. Also included in this collection are twelve page-long sketches revealing ironies and shortcomings of contemporary times.

Auchincloss is highly regarded for several scholarly works of criticism. These books include *Edith Wharton* (1961), *Reflections of a Jacobite* (1961), *Ellen Glasgow* (1964), *Pioneers and Caretakers: A Study of Nine American Women Novelists* (1965), *On Sister Carrie* (1968), *Motiveless Malignity* (1969), *Henry Adams* (1971), and *Reading Henry Adams* (1975).

(See also *CLC,* Vols. 4, 6, 9, 18; *Contemporary Authors,* Vols. 1-4, rev. ed.; *Contemporary Authors New Revision Series,* Vol. 6; *Dictionary of Literary Biography,* Vol. 2; and *Dictionary of Literary Biography Yearbook: 1980*.)

B. V. WINEBAUM

[In ***The Indifferent Children,*** Andrew Lee] has had a try at high society, and has come uncomfortably close to setting [its members] down as they probably exist.

For all his understanding, Mr. Lee's socialites will be unrecognizable to many of his readers, trained as they have been over the years to accept other, less accurate symbols as the genuine thing. In an introductory blurb, Mr. Harry Bull, recent factotum of *Town and Country* magazine, announces, "Since Henry James and Edith Wharton I know of no novelist who has been able to handle the highest stratum of American society with the subtlety and detachment of Andrew Lee." High praise, indeed, from a man who has made the worlds of fashion and wealth his province, if not his stratum—and I believe that in one regard, at least, Mr. Bull's uncondescending yea is justified. Though they are remote, aloof enough to be virtually unbelievable, the social characters of this first novel are representative of the highest by-ways of what is now unblushingly labeled "The American Aristocracy," an isolated, self-excluding set to whom the Social Register is no more than a convenience, a supplementary telephone directory, a document scarcely worth mention, although, of course, one permits listing of the family name and residences there. These types exist, but how mercifully rare!

The implicit comparison with James and Wharton, however, will not bear inspection. Mr. Lee, who has quaintly hidden his true identity beneath a pseudonym, has a long way to travel and observe before he approaches the psychological magnitude of James or the trenchancy of Wharton. He does have an eye for style and a sense of taste as (and when) it exists in his circumscribed circle. He is able, with ease, to differentiate the closely merging caste lines between his aristocrats and the Army and Navy brass hats with whom they are forced to associate during the late emergency. And between the very rich and the simply well-bred of the society group, he has managed a balance that is heartless as it is exact.

One may find sympathy for the characters if not understanding, or perhaps a gentle revulsion hardly warm or intense enough to be hate. These are the qualities of the polite novelist, the recorder of trivialities rendered as essentials. But Mr. Lee is potentially a better writer than this: and ***The Indifferent Children*** pretends to do more than amuse or divert. It offers, apart from the trimmings and the behind-the-scene views of embassies and estates, a completely individual picture of the over-civilized man in wartime and his ultimate defeat. The central character of Lieut. Beverly Stregelinus, rigid and frigid, is far too consistent and elaborated to be explained away by the fatalistic melodrama of the epilogue. Nor does the violence of the final sections, climaxing in the suicide of Stregelinus' fiancée, seem justifiable. Here the echoes of E. M. Forster, not James or Wharton, are evident. The novel's development suffers the autobiographical overseriousness of first novels—a desire to exhaust the material rather than the reader's sensibility.

The influences, like the pedigrees of the characters, are both good and acceptable. The intentions of both author and hero are honorable. The result is a serious, readable book about a strangely removed world within the world. . . . Unlike so many current works of fiction, ***The Indifferent Children*** is a true novel, not an expanded short story or a series of disjointed incidents thrown under one cover. Having granted the premises of its subject, one cannot quarrel with its effect, which is more knowing than any single portrait in the book—a tribute to Mr. Lee's skill as a true creator of fiction.

B. V. Winebaum, "An Isolated, Self-Excluding 'Aristocracy'," in The New York Times Book Review, *June 1, 1947, p. 13.*

VIRGILIA PETERSON

Although Louis Auchincloss, the author of these eight stories gathered under the title of ***The Injustice Collectors,*** is a practising lawyer and only a writer by avocation, his writing is in no way amateurish. He must, therefore, be measured as a professional. Since he chooses to write about the thin slice of the privileged rich in American society—at a time when so few of our novelists are concerned with this almost anachronistic group—a comparison with John Marquand as satirist is almost inevitable.

By its very title, ***The Injustice Collectors,*** Mr. Auchincloss's book shows a degree of sympathy for his leading characters which Marquand rarely allows. In each of these stories it is possible, without too much stretching of the reader's imagination, to be sorry for the man or woman around whom events unfold. . . .

With the exception of one wartime story . . . , these tales are set in rich houses in New York or in the resort of Anchor Harbor, Maine. Here are egocentric old ladies, bitter daughters, cold daughters-in-law, a poor, foolish Mama's boy, a rich widower with a spoiled son, an empty shell of a girl who blooms into power not through love but through social work, and two different unmarried maidens whose pale personalities come to dominate the inner drama of the lordly-seeming families with whom they are employed—all characters conspicuous for their concentration on themselves. But instead of the fanatical gall of the inspired satirist, you find in Mr. Auchincloss the kindly impatience with human nature of a worldly moralist. Despite his always smooth and sometimes neatly aphoristic writing, despite his knowledge of the narrow circle he draws with all its implicit materialism and imitative aristocracy, Mr. Auchincloss has too little impact as a critic of man's ways. Whereas the well-bred, fastidious irony of an Edith Wharton fitted the times of which she wrote, this kind of satire applied to our day seems as anachronistic as the society it depicts. For all its merits, it is out of context today, and as such, curiously lacking in passion and in the power to move.

Virgilia Peterson, "In a World without Passion," in New York Herald Tribune Book Review, *October 1, 1950, p. 12.*

SARA HENDERSON HAY

The title of this book [***The Injustice Collectors***] derives from Dr. Edmund Bergler's *The Battle of the Conscience,* where the phrase is used to describe neurotics who continually and unconsciously construct situations in which they are disappointed or mistreated. . . .

This is the theme which Mr. Auchincloss engages in his collection of short stories. The injustice collectors who move through these pages are not the underprivileged, the social outcasts, or those loosely termed unfortunates; the milieu of which he writes is that of wealth and leisure and caste; these are nice people, often charming people, stuffy people, expensively provincial people of Anchor Harbor, Maine; of Park Avenue and Long Island and Florida and the Riviera in winter. His stories are the more subtly penetrating because they are not melodramatic nor dismally sordid; the neurotics, the maladjusted, the self-punishers who in these eight excellent portrait studies work out their own destruction and defeat seldom realize that they are either destroyed or defeated. Mr. Auchincloss points no moral, nor suggests any alternatives for his characters. He is not concerned with analyzing the reasons why they behave as they do; he contents himself with symptoms rather than causes.

He is wonderfully adept at showing the conflicts between personalities; at exposing the tyrannies, the dominations, the iron fingers in the velvet gloves of courtesy and social convention and family relationships; he can draw a devastating picture in a few brief lines. . . .

The story **"Maude"** is one of the most effective in the book. "All Maude's life it had seemed to her that she was like a dried-up spring at the edge of which her devoted relatives and friends used to gather hopefully in the expectation that at least a faint trickle would appear. . . ." Maude so resented what she conceived of as the obligation to feel and be like other people that she negated and denied her own honest reactions, finding in her frustration of herself both justification and penance, taking an unconscious satisfaction, even, when her lover's death prevented the emotional release which she desired but did not want to desire. This story is a penetrating and expert portrayal of a neurotic refusal to meet life, of a clinging to a fancied independence which was in fact only a fear of emotional involvement. (p. 37)

[In **"Maude"** and the other stories in this collection] Mr. Auchincloss explores some of the various paths of defeat which people can unconsciously pursue. His style is fluent, cultivated, urbane. In spite of the inherent tragedy in the situations and the people involved, there is much that is deftly humorous. He has wit and irony; he has also a real understanding of and pity for the seekers of their own hurt.

The Injustice Collectors is the work of an extremely skilful and observant writer. These are not clinical case histories, but with the device of fiction Mr. Auchincloss puts his finger on fact. It is a tribute to the impact of these stories that one begins to speculate upon one's own propensities as a collector! (pp. 37-8)

Sara Henderson Hay, "Seekers of Hurt," in The Saturday Review of Literature, *Vol. XXXIII, No. 41, October 14, 1950, pp. 37-8.*

NANCY LENKEITH

A girl of 21 who hates parties, loves books and marries a rake is a fair subject for comedy: but it is not as a comic subject that Louis Auchincloss takes Sybil or the Long Island tribe against which she rebels. . . . The title of his previous book—***The Injustice Collectors*** . . . gives a clue to his view of Sybil's misfortune. The result is [***Sybil***], a serious, solid, sensitive . . . novel, much in the manner of Edith Wharton.

At one of those subscription dances which are "the minimum course from crushes to matrimony," horsy Philip Hillyard cuts in on Sybil and is stopped short by her fierce innocence. Immediately, he sets out to tame the grim, willowy girl who scorns both the dutiful gentility of her own family and the noisy smartness of his; and she, with equal determination, decides to test him by her bookish notions of what love should be. They get married: she has a child in New York and he a wartime affair in San Francisco, then another closer to home, which leads them to consider a divorce. . . .

Though Mr. Auchincloss is at his poignant best in the portraiture of Sybil's despair, she is no Griselda in his mind, in the reader's or even in her own wild lucidity. After a summer separation, she sees clearly that it is her stubborn pride that has made her unhappy, that she cannot deny the complexity of life and of people, that if she loves Philip she must accept him as he is—a man of much spark and no warmth.

Mr. Auchincloss has the good taste to keep Sybil out of the dissecting-room. He has her explained by the secondary characters in the story, all quite merciless in their efforts to rescue her from herself, all very much alive in their beneath-the-surface Long Island existence. Though it may lack style and humor, [***Sybil***] reveals a sureness and shrewdness of intention missing in much recent fiction.

Nancy Lenkeith, "The Burden of Pride," in The New York Times Book Review, *January 6, 1952, p. 5.*

JOSEPHINE LAWRENCE

It is frankly exasperating not to be able to warm up to Sybil in her role of heroine [in the novel ***Sybil***]. The sense of frustration is due in part to a peculiar vague quality that washes out definite impressions. Mr. Auchincloss is writing against a New York and Long Island backdrop, but city and shore alike lack authentic atmosphere. Similarly . . . except for a brief interlude allowed the war, time may be said to stand still. Sybil, in spite of her fondness for bars, refuses to emerge as a modern young woman; in the world of Edith Wharton she would be more at home. (p. 31)

Josephine Lawrence, "Society Heroine," in The Saturday Review, *New York, Vol. XXXV, No. 4, January 26, 1952, pp. 12, 31.*

R. D. CHARQUES

Though nothing is duller than a novel without a love interest, it is surprising how much more needs to be added to a love interest before a contemporary novel becomes really absorbing. . . . This, to start off on a serious or over-serious note, is a fair criticism of ***A Law for the Lion,*** which has a narrow range but is otherwise an active piece of work, nicely observed and decorated with taking passages of comedy. There is not a lot to say about it, however, except that it is often, in spite of weak moments, cleverly and entertainingly done.

If more is to be said, it may be noted that Mr. Auchincloss, an American writer, who is still inclined to fumble with a polished and witty talent, spreads himself thinly in this new book of his over the story of a divorce in a prosperous professional New York setting. He makes his point about his heroine's liberation from the mere habit of matrimony with intelligence and an alert narrative irony, more particularly in the later chapters, but so far as a realist's sense of things contemporary is concerned it is plain that even the best of divorces does not take us very far. The trouble in part may be that Eloise Dilworth takes a long time to acquire a face and features. In her thirties, married to a respectably go-getting lawyer and with two children, until three parts of the way through she remains a vaguely charming nullity of a woman, so that there is no apparent reason why her *demi-vierge* pursuit of a wild young man in Greenwich Village should carry her beyond the margin of safety. Indeed, bore though he is, it is her husband George rather than the too filial Eloise who deserves our sympathy, since he establishes his own moral claim to a divorce by suffering the visitations of a maddeningly maladroit—does Mr. Auchincloss realise how maladroit?—mother-in-law. Still, reviewers, like politicians, should never argue, and ***A Law for the Lion*** is lively and amusing and contains many good things.

R. D. Charques, in a review of "A Law for the Lion," in The Spectator, *Vol. 191, No. 6532, September 4, 1953, p. 254.*

SARAH HENDERSON HAY

Louis Auchincloss's new book, ***A Law for the Lion,*** is a sensitive and searching novel about ethics and morality, as practised in the segment of society with which he has dealt in his previous work—that little world of established wealth and position, the ultra-respectable reactionaries, the "Proper New Yorkers" and frequenters of the proper Long Island summer retreats. As in his earlier novel, ***Sybil,*** Mr. Auchincloss reveals the cynicism behind the respectability, the hypocrisy beneath the rectitude, the stuffy provincialism which observes convention for convention's sake. . . .

A Law for the Lion explores the matter of ultimate morality; its climax and its resolution hinge on adultery and divorce. In it Mr. Auchincloss strikes some telling blows for the cause of a uniform divorce law, and against the accepted perjury of a Nevada "residence." And subtly, but no less relentlessly, he exposes those who while professing the highest moral principles are really guided by the most venal and materialistic expediency.

The focal point on which these issues are brought to bear is the case of Eloise Dilworth, whom the law judges unfit to rear her children because she has upon one occasion been unfaithful to her marriage vows, and who will not testify in her own defense as to the emotional emptiness of her thirteen years of wedlock, nor state unequivocably that she believes the ultimate rightness or wrongness of any individual's conduct can always be decided by an inflexible code. . . .

A Law for the Lion is a compassionate, honest, and very moving story, but I think that, in the earnestness of his conviction, Mr. Auchincloss has sacrificed something of the leisurely elegance and urbanity of style which lightened but did not detract from the seriousness of his earlier work.

There are somewhat fewer of the witty, mischievous, devastating excursions into the general landscape of the Old Guard, less of that deft satirizing of upper-upper-class Society which he can so neatly and skilfully evaluate. There are so few contemporary writers who can afford, as Mr. Auchincloss can, to use two words instead of one and still not be verbose. I wish he had allowed himself more indirection to make his direction plain.

Sarah Henderson Hay, "Poor Sinner in a Labyrinth," in The Saturday Review, *New York, Vol. XXXVI, No. 40, October 3, 1953, p. 28.*

SARA HENDERSON HAY

The problem of convention and revolt is a subject which has engrossed Louis Auchincloss in several books. It engrosses him once again in ***The Romantic Egoists***. . . .

His principal character this time is Peter Wescott, an inhabitant of that Proper World of Boston and New York and Long Island, a product of the Proper Schools, on his way up as a junior member of a law firm of impeccable propriety and stature. But Wescott always finds himself drawn to the dissenter, the rebel, the non-conformist. In a series of chronological memoirs, he recalls eight people whose lives, more or less briefly, have crossed his own. All of them, in one way or another and with varying degrees of success, have run counter to the accepted pattern. All of them, in their fashion, bear witness to the intrinsic dignity of that egoism which must sustain even the most pathetic and misdirected efforts to be one's true self.

It is a considerable technical triumph for an author to be able to make plain, in a first-person narrative, an image of what the narrator himself is not fully aware. Through implication and understatement, Mr. Auchincloss shows clearly, in Wescott's recollection of his eight friends, the reflections of qualities in Wescott himself which drew him to the non-conformists.

Without moralizing, Mr. Auchincloss points out essential moralities; he has both ironic wit and sympathy, and he is, in addition, the master of a clean, cultivated, articulate literary style which . . . is an esthetic delight.

Sara Henderson Hay, "Instinctive Non-Conformist," in The Saturday Review, *New York, Vol. XXXVII, No. 28, July 10, 1954, p. 35.*

ANGUS WILSON

The Romantic Egoists has a strict social framework and a convinced social standpoint. . . . I find the creed most distasteful. Mr. Auchincloss is an arrogant neo-aristocrat and his convictions make him, I think, cocksure, lacking in compassion, and, on occasion, deficient in good taste. Nevertheless, he is a very clever and subtle student of human social behaviour in the widest sense and one is led from one story to another by the unity of mood and viewpoint to a very rewarding total effect which goes far deeper than any subtle momentary flash or exact recapture of evanescent sensibility. (p. 402)

Angus Wilson, "The Short Story Changes," in The Spectator, *Vol. 193, No. 6588, October 1, 1954, pp. 401-02.*

JOHN BROOKS

People who have followed the writing career of Louis Auchincloss, the only living novelist who practices law at 67 Wall Street, have been waiting for some time for him to tackle the downtown legal world head-on in a novel. . . . Now, with ***The Great World and Timothy Colt,*** he has done it, and has done it well, bringing to this task the qualities that were to be found in almost all of his earlier work: a limpid style, an easy skill at letting his characters come alive through dialogue, a willingness to deal with important issues and an ability to dramatize them in human terms. But perhaps his most distinctive characteristic is his interest in contemporary manners and his belief—shared with Fielding, Jane Austen and Thackeray, but with few enough contemporary American writers—that small differences in social behavior cannot only reveal character, but affect destinies.

Consider the pivotal scene of ***The Great World and Timothy Colt.*** Timothy, great grandson of a rector of Trinity Church and a destined partner of the firm of Sheffield, Knox, Stevens and Dale, goes to a party thrown by George Emlen, a bumptious client with whom he does not get along at all well, and, after too many drinks and considerable goading in public by Emlen, Timothy insults the client by toasting him as "his own financier, his own lawyer, his own accountant, and if there's any justice in the after-life, which I very much doubt, his own hell!"

Now, by the standards of many contemporary writers, that would be such a mild imprecation that an antagonist would consider it suitably answered with an obscenity or two. It must be just about the most genteel, and grammatically the most complex, insult to have been hurled in American fiction since Henry James. But it turns out to be the turning point of Timmy's career. As a result of it, he quarrels with his wife (who feels Timmy should apologize to Emlen, which he does, under pressure), quarrels with his sponsor at the firm, and finally, having decided that there is no middle ground between his ideals and the great world, leaves his wife and children, takes up with Emlen's first cousin, a worldly and charming girl, and begins practicing law as ruthlessly and cynically as he can. He comes a cropper, of course, because he does not know how to be tough at the right times, and after his conscience has gnawed at him for a while about a rather shady distribution of a trust, he quite unnecessarily confesses in court to malpractice, and fades out under the shadow of possible disbarment.

In essence, this is the familiar comedy of the boy from the provinces being debauched by the city slickers—although, with a telling stroke of irony, Mr. Auchincloss makes his innocent one the boy brought up in the city, while the adopted New Yorkers, restless and ambitious, are the worldly ones. But Timmy is so ironbound in his initial idealism, so abandoned in his overnight defection to legal and social opportunism, and in general so impulsive in his reaction to every situation that one is perhaps inclined to laugh at him more than Mr. Auchincloss has intended. He is entirely real, though, and in spite of his erratic behavior he is likable. (pp. 4, 50)

Apart from his knowledge of the law, Mr. Auchincloss probably knows more about traditional New York City society than any other good novelist now working. Furthermore, he seems to believe in the continuing importance of what is left of such society, and the values it attempts to preserve and hand down. It is precisely the background presence of such belief that makes his satirical jibes so entertaining, and makes the rather neat, foursquare world of his books so comforting to read about. ***The Great World and Timothy Colt***—appeals in part, perhaps unintentionally, to the escapist impulse; but it also shows how traditional writing methods and social attitudes can throw a refreshing light on parts of the contemporary scene. (p. 50)

John Brooks, "Ideals on Trial," in The New York Times Book Review, *October 21, 1956, pp. 4, 50.*

ISABEL QUIGLY

Few novels apart from the avowedly realist take much notice—much specific, practical notice, that is—of things like jobs and money; still less of, say, intrigues over work, professional morality, skill at a job and the pleasure it gives, the pattern of a lifetime in terms of work: all of which is the stuff of ***The Great World and Timothy Colt,*** a novel in which the public side of a man sweeps up his private morality, and where we are shown, in the involved internal affairs of a large New York office, the graph of a soul. Souls, though, are not ostensibly—only by implication—the point: it is social behaviour we are brought to watch, action and inter-action in a crowded world, but on so large and complex a scale that it embraces even the very private and subterranean, and we see public action in terms of character and personal motive. . . . Mr. Auchincloss's scope and subtlety together, the piercing exactness of his observation, the sustained excellence of his style, above all the weight of personality—that indefinable but measurable quality—all set him far beyond, say, Marquand, whose world and method he perhaps at first sight recalls. It is hard, in fact, to think of any living fellow-countryman of his with whom to compare him; and among the dead the only one that comes to mind as a possible source of comparison—not, I hope, too extravagantly—is James. (pp. 90-1)

Isabel Quigly, in a review of "The Great World and Timothy Colt," in The Spectator, *Vol. 198, No. 6708, January 18, 1957, pp. 90-1.*

GEORGE P. ELLIOT

[Within] the fictional comedy of manners, which pretty much is [Auchincloss's] chosen form, he is the best since the early Marquand. He sees the world of the New York rich with a satiric and meticulous eye; he is a real pro at the difficult craft of constructing and developing a plot; he controls his characters and their actions with a firm, steady hand. ***Pursuit of the Prodigal*** is nearly first-rate of its kind, though not quite. The protagonist moves from the old-fashioned, staid, respectable world of his Long Island family and his first law firm to Greenwich Village and a law firm which seems to him not hypocritical in its chicaneries; then, through remarriage, he moves halfway back to his origins. He hurts others and is hurt; he discovers as much of himself as he can, he is defined, within a society which he is intimately a part of, a recognizable and in some ways fairly important segment of actual American society.

But such a form demands of its author an absolutely, unrelentingly firm discipline, cold, impartial, morally right; and rather more often than is good for his book, Auchincloss relaxes into such shoddinesses as spite against a character (especially the protagonist's first wife) and a certain banality of style (especially in some of the social conversations). It seems to me that all he lacks as a novelist of manners is adequate control over the form he has chosen, a difficult form, it is true, but proved to be sound. (pp. 349-50)

George P. Elliot, "Real Gardens for Real Toads," in The Nation, *New York, Vol. 189, No. 16, November 14, 1959, pp. 345-50.*

RONALD BRYDEN

Louis Auchincloss's novels are what good *New Yorker* stories would become if they grew up, and I mean that mostly as a compliment. [***Pursuit of the Prodigal***] is about a successful second marriage, and bears as little relation to *Rebecca* as you can imagine. . . . Mr. Auchincloss works this out with his usual subtlety and concreteness. The mantle of Edith Wharton, or whatever she wore, is now firmly his, and only these two have made New York so real a place, with its core of nineteenth-century provincialism—the Jacobethan-panelled banks and offices, the whisky-advertisement clubs, the old brown houses which are still the tissue holding up that gleaming spine of towers. I'm not sure why his brilliant parochialism irks me slightly this time. There's no good reason why Manhattan shouldn't provide as deep a microcosm as Faulkner's Yoknapatawpha. But it's harder to accept the wildness of soul which drives a man to take his girl on Sundays to 'remote areas, to Staten Island and Hell Gate Bridge, and the upper limits of the Bronx.'

Ronald Bryden, "Childe Colin," in The Spectator, *Vol. 204, No. 6871, March 4, 1960, p. 329.*

VICTOR CHAPIN

A writer like Louis Auchincloss, who produces a novel on the average of one a year, might be tempted through his great energy and facility to forego the subtlety of which he is capable for the sake of the great popular success which, in his case, has always remained just out of reach. In writing his latest novel, ***The House of Five Talents,*** it would have been so easy to add a lacing of sentiment and a dose of melodrama to a good plot and settle back to watch the best-seller list. To Auchincloss' credit (and to his publisher's sorrow, perhaps), he has resisted a dozen opportunities for the kind of acceptable hokum that would set the pulses pounding and tears flowing.

This is a long novel that, as its heroine tells us, is not so much the story of a family as of a family fortune. It is narrated by Augusta Millinder, a luckless and apparently lackluster spinster, who in her long life has watched the progress of her family's great fortune through five generations. At the age of 75, she has set herself the task of writing an honest account of the relationships between herself and the others in her family, their relationships with one another and, most importantly, the relationship of all of them to the money. . . .

It is a bold device on the part of a male writer to adopt the method of writing in the first person from a woman's point of view, but Auchincloss has brought it off. He has been wise enough to present his heroine first in her old age, and to tell her story from the vantage point of her latter-day wisdom and self-knowledge. As a novel, Gussie's story is essentially picaresque, a series of episodes involving characters who play their parts and then disappear. But Gussie is the pivot. (p. 24)

Once settled into spinsterhood, with her share of the fortune and in possession of the family mansion on Fifth Avenue, Gussie turns to good works and the contemplation of family problems. Conveniently, the cousins, aunts, uncles and nephews come to her, and she is witness to many family dramas as she is taken up (then usually dropped) first by one branch and then another. There are memorable scenes: Uncle Josiah Hoyt, a prurient puritan who has always tyrannized his family, loses his hold over them when he loses his hold on their money; Gussie rescues a cousin from disgrace and then, in a sentimental moment, undoes her own good deed. Everywhere we are amused; but we are shaken, too, for which of us has not romanticized the rich?

Auchincloss is writing a social comedy and he is unsparing in his development of the irony implicit in his situations. But this irony is always exploited through people who, though they may be foolish, are always believable. We laugh at poor Gussie when she finds that she has precipitated the very adultery she was trying to prevent—but we feel for her, too. She is the captive of her own people and of the wealth they share and so she remains to the end, even though she comes to know them all for exactly what they are.

In the end, the fortune has dwarfed all those who share in it and, rather than being fortunate in their wealth, some of these people at least would have been better off without it. We find ourselves admiring most the people of the second generation, who did not have to earn the money and could devote themselves to making a display of it. Eliza Millinder, Gussie's mother, is a cold woman and, at times, even a cruel one, but she is the dominant character in the novel; hers, I think, is a great portrait. She is one of those characters you cannot like and who would not expect you to like her; but you are forced to admire her and, just as if you had known her in life, you will never forget her. She alone of all the Millinders gives the fortune a good run for its money. To her it presents a challenge which she makes every effort to meet. She wants the power she knows money provides and she finds it at last in the passion for collecting. She, too, is ultimately defeated; but her defeat is more interesting and appears less futile than that of Millinders in subsequent generations, who don the protective coloring of conformity and conceal their wealth and ignore its power behind philanthropic foundations and a concern for public relations. The originals in Eliza Millinder's day had a chance. Those of the present day come to grief anonymously.

The House of Five Talents is a masterful novel and, I think, just misses being a great one. It withholds that ultimate satisfaction that great novels give, yet it is difficult to tell why this is so. Perhaps it is because this novel stirs the intelligence but not the imagination. It is perceptive, instructive, amusing, revealing; but it moves us only briefly. Can it be that this is because Auchincloss has been both courageous enough and foolish enough to take for his subject the hardest, most intractable and, perhaps, most distressing fact of life?

That fact, of course, is money. (pp. 24-5)

Victor Chapin, "What the Rich Can't Buy," in The New Leader, *Vol. XLIII, No. 42, October 31, 1960, pp. 24-5.*

PATRICIA KANE

A pat declaration of faith in mankind and the bar is among the inevitable platitudes of lawyers' public speeches, according to a Louis Auchincloss lawyer. Just as the character only amuses himself with wistful and whimsical thoughts about delivering any but the expected oration, Louis Auchincloss' fiction only hints a doubt about the rightness of the world created and maintained by Wall Street law firms.

The cautious and correct lawyers of Auchincloss are not the hierophants that Alexis de Tocqueville once found American lawyers to be. They are practicing a well-known profession, not participating in a mystery—to paraphrase Oliver Wendell Holmes, Jr. (p. 36)

Mr. Auchincloss could tender impeccable credentials as an interpreter of this downtown world; he is a partner in a Wall Street law firm of twenty partners whose practice is largely in estates and tax law. Although as a novelist he admittedly lacks the stature of a Henry James, he is a facile writer who presents with dispatch and lucidity an insider's view of a world nearly as bizarre for most readers as Samarkand. Many American novelists have written about lawyers, but no writer of consequence has written with such authority of the distinctively twentieth-century climate of finance in legal practice.

Auchincloss writes about downtown not just because it is the world he knows and can report, but because its hierarchy admirably suits a literary form that attracts him. In an essay called **"The Novel of Manners Today,"** Auchincloss remarks, in an unconscious echo of Hawthorne's preface to *The Marble Faun,* that while as a citizen he has no nostalgia for the old ways, as a novelist his eyes might "light up at the first glimpse of social injustice" because a novel of manners loses significance in a classless society. While Auchincloss locates nothing that could be called social injustice, he does find a stratified society in huge Wall Street law firms, an attendant snobbishness about other firms engaged in other kinds of practice, and a perspective from which to view the rich, both old and new.

Auchincloss' fiction differs in several particulars from that of others who have portrayed lawyers. He brings to the structured world that he knows intimately no Populist prejudice against city lawyers, no nostalgia for the less organized life of a small-town practitioner, and almost no interest in courtroom advocacy. While he takes for granted the necessity of the Wall Street world, he brings to his fiction a quality of detachment, even of irony, that produces readable novels, which contain comic and witty moments. He does not satirize lawyers, however, as did James G. Baldwin in *Flush Times in Alabama and Mississippi* or Mark Twain in *Roughing It.* Auchincloss' lawyers are neither the uneducated swindlers nor the pompous buffoons of those frontier tales. Nor are they secular priests in the style of a lawyer created by William Faulkner in such works as *Requiem for a Nun* or by William Dean Howells in *The Leatherwood God.* Certainly not the contemptible pawns of financiers found in Theodore Dreiser's *The Titan,* neither are they saviors of civilization in the pattern of the judge in James Fenimore Cooper's *The Pioneers.*

Auchincloss's laywers have as clients those with money and power. They have no sense of calling or responsibility to society as distinct from their clients. Expending no energy serving or preserving law, they look for loopholes in the statutes that will help their clients' prosperity. Unlike the sanctimonious lawyers of James Gould Cozzens' *By Love Possessed,* they seldom delude themselves or others by pretending that they have other dedications. Indeed they may see their role as contributing to the general welfare in that they work out the relationship between government and industry and have a "glory" as "architects of society." If they have any literary antecedent, it is Cooper's ideal lawyer who allied himself with the agrarian aristocracy of that day. In temperament they are not unlike the New York lawyer in Cooper's *The Ways of the Hour* who was so governed by his sense of decorum that he deigned to employ an emotional appeal to a jury, but their sense of decorum would necessitate rejecting as pretentious and undescriptive Cooper's choice of *votaries* as an appellation for lawyers.

Auchincloss' lawyers of a given position in a firm not only resemble each other sufficiently to make possible generalizations about them, they have few qualities that one could call distinctively those of a lawyer. They are virtually interchangeable with their counterparts in the trust department of a bank. If, as seems likely, this interchangeability—unremarked by

Auchincloss—accurately reflects reality rather than the novelist's inability to imagine more than one kind of character, it reveals on another level the union of finance and law shown in the stories. Despite the details of the law of trusts, estates, taxation, and the like, and although the moral crisis for a character may turn on a decision within the maze of such law, Auchincloss does not convey a clear association between character and occupation. Indeed he has disclaimed a connection in a remark about the protagonist of ***The Great World and Timothy Colt:*** "He is not a man who finds it hard to be honest in a New York firm because of his milieu." Auchincloss' lawyers are less men of the law, which for good or ill the lawyers in most novels by American writers are, than they are men of the world of finance who specialize in the law of finance.

In the legal establishment of the world of finance a writer of Auchincloss' perceptions can find many elements to make the novel of manners a viable form. The structure of the firm contains clear gradations. Any suggestions of a more fluid organization, such as an open door to the senior partner's office, does not camouflage for those in the group what the lines are. Among the ingredients of such a firm and its members are conventions, prescribed amenities, definable manners, exclusiveness, and pride. Toward outsiders the expected responses range from scorn for the "uptown bar" and its divorce practice to courtesy toward clients, whatever one's personal feelings or however gross and insulting the client. In chronicling the adventures of members of this society, Auchincloss' tone often resembles that of high comedy although it also has something in common with that of Faulkner's comic tales. Auchincloss avoids the vice that he deplores in "most novels that deal with society": they "take on some of the meretricious gaudiness that it is their avowed purpose to deplore," and their "authors become guilty of the snobbishness and triviality of which they accuse their characters."... Not an apologist for the manners he observes, neither is Auchincloss a reformer. His analysis evokes laughter more likely to be thoughtful than derisive because he finds moral values to reside within the conventions and disciplines of the class-like organization of a law firm.

At the top of a Wall Street firm resides the eminence of a senior partner. In an Auchincloss novel the senior partner is not only successful and respected, he is likely to be a talented and well-mannered man, satisfied with the world he has helped to create. But unlike Faulkner's Gavin Stevens, he would not become a district attorney, defend an unsavory murderess, or devote himself to stemming the rise of a clan of plutocrats. Nor would he enter a courtroom to establish truth and solve a murder as does Mark Twain's Pudd'n-head Wilson. His occasional courtroom appearance is undertaken only in behalf of a valued client and friend. His demeanor there might be more suitable to "a legal discussion over an after-dinner brandy than an argument in court," and his treatment of the opposing lawyer reflect "the good manners of a clubman to a fellow member's guest who is misbehaving himself."... (pp. 36-9)

The other partners resemble the senior in most particulars, but they are sometimes lesser men in talent or ethics. Some incompetents remain in their jobs because of family connections or long association with the firm. One such person (in ***Powers of Attorney***), theoretically the authority on property law, devotes his life to studying Plantagenet law. In his reverence for principles of law removed from the facts of present practice he resembles the "new judge" in *Adventures of Huckleberry Finn* who awards custody of Huck to his drunken father because of the legal principle that families should not be separated. Auchincloss' tone is gentler than Twain's, and his lawyer does no actual harm, but the comic portraits are of similar mentalities. (p. 40)

Below the partners are the associates, the bright young men, most of whom led their classes at the best law schools, who yearn to move up. They are expected to move with ease in the world of the rich, not to be what Auchincloss describes in another connection as "wide-eyed Scott Fitzgeralds, bareheaded before the refracted gleam of gold."... An associate's pride in his present status and his expectation of success stem from the kind of law he practices. For example, when one is asked by his son about being a mouthpiece, he stuffily and peevishly retorts that he does not argue in court and is "not that kind of lawyer."... Most associates work hard to improve their position, but some lack the requisites for promotion, and occasionally a rebel may leave voluntarily. Those who continue the climb work in the approved section of the firm, usually securities rather than litigation or real estate, under the direction of the senior partner. Auchincloss describes their devotion to the senior, with characteristic mild irony, as like that of "acolytes at an altar" as they move "silently to and fro with absorbed, preoccupied faces, conscious only of their high priest and his ministrations."... (p. 41)

The values of downtown lawyers are less vulnerable to threats from . . . occasional outsiders, however, than they are to deviations by one of their own. Consequently their disapproval and censure act to correct the situation or to dissociate the establishment from the lapsed member. An example of such opinion, which also illuminates attitudes toward law itself, emerges in the wake of a novel about divorce, ***A Law for the Lion.***

The righteous and literal standards of a successful lawyer lead him to disregard the understood way of doing things and result finally in his having to practice law in a smaller and lesser firm. George Dilworth is the sort of person who likes to use unfashionable words like *disreputable* "to underline his conscious self-identification with an earlier day of more rigid principles."... When he discovers that his wife has been unfaithful, he decides to divorce her in New York, charging adultery and demanding custody of their children. His closest friend, another partner named Henry Hamilton, encourages him and acts as his attorney. The senior partner disapproves of Dilworth's behavior, questioning the taste of one who applies broad moral rules to individual problems. Auchincloss astringently describes the senior's attitude: "He professed many principles himself; few people, indeed, professed more; that was the way one lived, it was the secret, perhaps, of civilization. But to premise one's conduct on their absolute relation to reality, well, that was being childish, and being childish was something that the son of a famous judge had little or no time for."... When the senior partner feels that the firm will not be jeopardized by the loss of two able partners, and when other lawyers and even clients are shocked at the violence and vengefulness of the divorce suit, he asks both Dilworth and Hamilton to leave.

Lawyers generally disapprove of Dilworth's suit and Hamilton's method of presenting it. The "uptown lawyer" who represents Mrs. Dilworth would not "file a smutty petition like that in court for anything in the world."... More compelling in disciplining Dilworth is the view among the "better informed of the downtown bar" who are shocked at his seeking "so public and scandalous a redress even for what they conceded was a serious wrong'' when Reno exists to keep the ''delinquencies of the respectable from prying eyes.''. . . More than that, they feel that his case is bad for the profession because the court (to the disquiet of the trial and appeal judges) must find as a matter of law that Mrs. Dilworth is an unfit mother. Their reasoning is that the widely-publicized Dilworth case reveals flaws in statutes by showing how harshly they can operate. The downtown bar feels that the laws should not be broadened and for someone in the position of Dilworth ''to allow his personal pique to induce him to tamper with the precarious set-up as to make justice seem tyrannical and morality antiquated was little short of outrageous.''. . . Those who betray the group can win only a pyrrhic victory.

As Dilworth's story illustrates, Auchincloss exposes with the same precision lawyers who enforce or follow understood principles of behavior and those who become indiscreet violators. In short, he is not over-awed by lawyers. (pp. 42-4)

Auchincloss' refusal to be awed by lawyers combines with his admiration for them to produce his characteristic tone of detachment. A delightful example is the mocking, yet loving, look at a hero in the moment when he comes into the clubhouse after playing golf and sees a partner and several associates sitting in the bar:

> As Tilney paused now, . . . his sweater and flannels a reproach to their urban darkness, . . . there was in Tilney's gaze, unconcealed by his perfunctory grin, some of the sternness of Abraham contemplating Sodom. . . . To his surprise and indignation he found himself surveyed as if he were something quaint and ridiculous, a sort of vaudeville character, vaguely suggestive of Edwardian sports and fatuity. . . .

The humor of this passage lacks the bite of a Faulkner tale in which a sardonic friend says of the lawyer hero that he misses the point entirely because ''if it aint complicated it dont matter whether it works or not because . . . it aint right.'' But both writers mock as friends.

Despite the rueful awareness of Auchincloss' heroes that life in ''green goods'' (the insider's terms for securities practice) in a downtown firm is not paradise, and despite their attraction to occasional mavericks who make them briefly dissatisfied with their lot, they content themselves with a secure life that is familiar and respected. Although even a senior partner can be tempted at the thought of life as a college president, when he discovers that the offer is a ruse engineered by an ambitious younger partner, he can return with real pleasure to ''weighing the chances of winning a directed verdict'' in a securities case, laughing at his dream of being ''whimsical and philosophical, entrancing his disciples under the crab-apple trees,'' and insisting that ''all is for the best in the best of all possible worlds.''. . . The character and Mr. Auchincloss know how platitudinous that last phrase is, but platitude or not, they believe in mankind and the bar. (p. 45)

Patricia Kane, ''Lawyers at the Top: The Fiction of Louis Auchincloss,'' in Critique: Studies in Modern Fiction, *Vol. 7, No. 2, Winter, 1964-65, pp. 36-46.*

BROM WEBER

The majority of the stories [in ***Second Chance: Tales of Two Generations***] deal with individuals who, after contemplating or launching a new life on the sea of emotional or social possibility, forgo their adventure or conclude it by foundering badly. Defeat occurs most often because of indecision about the propriety or desirability of a new life. The individual then recedes into his habitual pattern despite its inadequacies. Frequently, nonheroic reactions such as lethargy and fear of novelty are concealed behind transparently irrelevant moral excuses.

In several stories, however, a character recognizes quite clearly that a projected change is either meretricious or incapable of realization. These particular fictions reach beyond mere depiction of the travail of a social class that sometimes senses it is obsolescent and corrupt or is accused of being so. In these stories Auchincloss by implication prescribes values and attitudes which, in his judgment, justify the survival of those guided by them.

In both types of story, strangely enough in view of Auchincloss's intention to probe an ''identity crisis,'' there is no intermingling of social classes. Messages of discord or change from without are generally delivered by children or grandchildren rather than by interlopers. When the latter do appear—Jews in **''Second Chance''** and **''Suttee,''** an Italian immigrant's son in **''The Prince and the Pauper''**—they turn out to be incorporated members of the Establishment. Furthermore, young family emissaries of alien concepts are not particularly effective champions of the ''socialism'' and ''liberalism'' they urge upon their elders. (p. 24)

Since the problem of identity is not merely psychological but sociological as well, the social insularity of almost all the characters in these stories prevents them from developing a significant segment of whatever identities they possess or might create. Indeed, the relegation to offstage of the social conflict and turmoil so prevalent in our time establishes a dreamlike pall around the characters that hampers any genuine search for their identities.

The fictionist of manners may, if he wishes, flesh out the being and world of a character by concentrating upon personal depth rather than social breadth. Henry James, for example, so complicated and intensified the emotional, physical, and intellectual experience of his characters that in his pages a paralyzed, isolated creature will appear to be electrically charged, connected by hot wires to a myriad invisible yet tangible people, his social existence taking form quite miraculously.

Just that kind of rich creation is to be found in **''Black Shylock,''** the initial and also most successful story in ***Second Chance.*** Powerfully, dramatically, Auchincloss shows that perversity of spirit raised to high art may produce apocalyptic revelation, yet is essentially socially delusive and personally nonsustaining. This fictional argument against pure negation and for moral responsibility achieves its victory because the central character is permitted to develop his paranoid fantasies without visible restraint on the part of his creator.

There are, of course, other good stories in ***Second Chance,*** but none achieves the strength and magic pervading **''Black Shylock.''** One admires Auchincloss's delicate wit, firm language, knowledge of contemporary events and catchwords, and admirable distaste for vulgarity and mendacity. Yet all too often he does not put his gifts to full use, seemingly hesitant to risk marring the polish of his fiction by exposing it to unknown strains. In this he may well be one of his own characters, still not aware of the range of his own identity.

The concluding story in this collection, **''The Sacrifice,''** suggests that the end of the search for identity is to be found in a willingness to abandon the search. Judge Platt discovers, to his horror, that he hates the violators of "law and order." Recognizing that hatred, like rudeness and murder, is a human phenomenon, he frees himself of human ties and thus can experience the love inherent in the "peace of God." ***Second Chance,*** then, appears to be saying that spiritual transcendence is all that remains for its characters.

The answer is much too simple, as simple as the belief that the absence of "general agreement" is a phenomenon of the 1970s. It may well be that the exclusiveness, the naïveté, the complacency, and the inertia of the twentieth-century heirs of the genteel tradition have rendered them irreversibly anachronistic. Perhaps they are fated to vanish wholly. Auchincloss's authority is such that one hesitates to reject his conclusion. He probably has good sociological support for it. Nevertheless, not having plumbed the regenerative powers of his characters sufficiently in these stories, he has not established his conclusion's validity artistically. (pp. 24-5)

Brom Weber, in a review of "Second Chance: Tales of Two Generations," in Saturday Review, *Vol. LIII, No. 35, August 29, 1970, pp. 24-5.*

RICHARD FREEDMAN

This collection of short stories [***Second Chance: Tales of Two Generations***] is like a twelve-course dinner in a Chinese restaurant. Each story is delicious as it slithers down, but an hour later you're hungry again for some Chekhov or James.

The monosodium glutamate flavoring it all is the "generation gap," about which Auchincloss is wryly sensible, as befits the Homer of the Wall Street investment lawyers. . . .

In some of the stories there are *three* generations, all abrading one another's sensibilities like billiard balls. As one compromised Establishment grandfather asks his militantly pure grandson, "What are the mere fifty-five years that separate us in the six thousand of recorded history?" What indeed, except that in Auchincloss's world the old seethe with self-destructive hatred for the intellectual shoddiness and moral pretentiousness of the young, who can carry on as they do because they are "simply waiting for the inevitable enfranchisement of time."

Since youth has time on its side, it can afford to scrutinize with beady-eyed objectivity the failures and eccentricities of the old, while the old merely go dottier every day. Both are consumed with selfishness, and it is a rare victory when some dotard has sufficient dignity left to renounce a late, self-serving marriage, or make out a reasonable will. . . .

These stories are so intelligently conceived and mellifluously written that they ought to be better than they are. Unfortunately, after nineteen highly professional books, Auchincloss seems to have reached his level and won't try for anything higher. His characters are temporarily arresting but really paper-thin, often nothing more than one-dimensional "humors." For the logical heir to Edith Wharton, this is simply not enough.

Richard Freedman, "More Tales from the Homer of Wall Street," in Book World—The Washington Post, *September 20, 1970, p. 4.*

LINDSAY DUGUID

Louis Auchincloss's latest novel [***The Cat and the King***], set in France at the time of Louis XIV, is dedicated to "Jacqueline Kennedy Onassis who persuaded me that Versailles was still a valid source for fiction." . . .

The Cat and the King is the Duc de Saint-Simon's personal history, "a record of the thing above all else I had resolved to keep out of my memoirs—namely myself." It purports to be the true record of what lay behind his more famous chronicle of the reign of the Sun King and it is presented as an informal self-portrait which incidentally sheds light on the known facts of history somewhat in the manner of Mary Renault's novels (or, more recently, Gore Vidal's *Creation*). There is some play with the leather chest in which the memoirs are to be stored but the book does not have any sort of false "editor's note" explaining how the Duke's papers came to be found. Little time is wasted on any historical preamble and Saint-Simon introduces himself as a fussy, venal aristocrat, replete with power and concerned with the preservation of hierarchy. One of his reasons for writing has been a desire to preserve a memory of the old order. . . .

This faintly homespun courtier . . . picks his way skilfully through the factions and alliances at court in order to obtain status and sinecures. He is helped by his wife Gabrielle, who provides the motivating power and some disconcertingly acute observations. The action turns on issues such as the legitimization of the royal bastards, the advisability or otherwise of proposed marriages, and the conduct of some very offstage foreign wars. These provide the material for Saint-Simon's doubts about the sovereignty of the royal house and the fallibility of the king. There are also many minor plots, intrigues and pieces of gossip concerning such figures as Monsieur, Monseigneur, Conti, Madame de Montespan and the Duc de Savonne who are known to us from the history books but who are here described with a mixture of respect and cynicism which nicely points up the strange combination of rigid etiquette and gross familiarity which characterizes the court.

Louis XIV himself is portrayed as an effigy of regal dignity and power, whose authority almost justifies the hysterical deference paid by Saint-Simon and the court. He is a great man with no apparent personality who induces awe by virtue of his kingship. . . . The *levées* and *couchées,* even the *chaise percée* of this figure, make an admirable centre for the eddies of gossip and intrigue which swirl round him.

Another factor which saves Saint-Simon's concerns from seeming altogether ludicrous is the palace of Versailles itself. The glittering splendours are not described in detail, but there is an impression of myriad apartments, of endless corridors and, above all, of the great formal gardens which provide an image of civilization and its discontents. . . .

This is really as far as Auchincloss goes in evoking the era, and he has made a decision to have the characters speak in modern demotic American ("Madame de Maintenon dropped her like a hot potato as soon as she picked up the first whiff of her ill-favour" "Order, order, order—like those goddam gravel walks out there") which sometimes approaches the ridiculous. The family rows, parties and weekends (Marly is described as though it were an exclusive New England country club), and the ladies with bad reputations familiar from Auchincloss's earlier novels, recall the Cabots rather than the Bourbons. But perhaps because Savonne is so clearly the Harvard room-mate and the throne room the Oval Office, the politicking comes through strongly. In the end Auchincloss appears to have taken little advantage of the setting so kindly suggested by Mrs Onassis. His interest is in the more universal workings of ambition: and, ignoring historical colour, he uses his undoubted skills to make the concerns of the characters worth taking seriously on their own terms.

Lindsay Duguid, "A Version of Versailles," in The Times Literary Supplement, *No. 4093, September 11, 1981, p. 1038.*

DAVID BLACK

[Readers] have often misperceived [Louis Auchincloss]. His virtues—like his understanding of the class system in America—have been damned as faults. And his faults—like his slack style—have been praised as virtues. He was a postwar writer with what seemed to be a pre-war sensibility. And the one quality that set him apart from the rest of his literary generation—his career as a lawyer—seemed to have nothing to do with literature: He became marked in the public mind as the novelist with the double life; and this double life, like the twin images in a badly focused camera's range-finder, has tended to blur Auchincloss's achievement.

But ***Watchfires*** . . . is so strong, and in significant ways so different from his earlier work, that it is no longer possible to misperceive his achievement. ***Watchfires*** is warmer, more intense, more intimate than any book he has written previously. As a writer, Auchincloss seems newly open and vulnerable. Moreover, his characters all find some sort of liberation.

Watchfires is set at the eve of the Civil War. Dexter Fairchild, a New York lawyer like many of Auchincloss's characters, frees himself from the suffocating confines of tradition and duty through what he sees as a pagan love affair with his brother-in-law's wife. Dexter's wife frees herself from the confining and traditional role as Knickerbocker mother through her involvement with the Underground Railway. Dexter's mistress frees herself from her role as a Knickerbocker mother through her bohemian sexuality. The South tries to free itself from the North, and the North from the South. Slaves free themselves from their masters. And the country frees itself from the past. The book's plot is a masterpiece of reflecting themes, the kind of mirror-play that suggests, at last, the artistic confidence of a fully matured talent.

Watchfires works out its theme of liberation with such single-minded success that it carries Auchincloss out on the other side of what seems to have been a personal and artistic obsession that has consumed him ever since he started writing as a child. (p. 24)

David Black, "Louis Auchincloss Reconciles His Two Worlds," in Saturday Review, *Vol. 9, No. 4, April, 1982, pp. 24-6, 28.*

ANNE TYLER

In 1976, in a collection of his stories entitled ***The Winthrop Covenant,*** Louis Auchincloss included a tale about a New York lawyer living in the days just before the start of the Civil War. This lawyer, though opposed to slavery, believed in keeping the Union together at any cost, and he disapproved of the Underground Railroad because it violated private property. After expounding on these issues, he went off to deal with a beautiful young sister-in-law discovered on the verge of adultery. He patched up at least the exterior of her marriage, although neither husband nor wife seemed all that interested in it, and then proceeded so singlemindedly to disgrace her would-be seducer that he himself, saying his prayers later, had some doubts about his motives.

The story ended there, with the lawyer's uneasy night thoughts. Now, in ***Watchfires***, . . . the two threads of the plot are picked up again and woven more tightly together. The first part of the novel contains great chunks of the short story, with flashbacks and digressions interspersed. Then the lawyer, Dexter Fairfield (only his name has been changed), does after all succumb to the charms of his sister-in-law, and his wife overlooks their extended affair because he's bought her off—contributed financially to her work with escaped slaves.

It's a tidy bit of weaving, all right, but maybe too tidy. The short story had a subtlety lacking in the novel; Dexter was more complex and more interesting as a tortured sinner of the imagination. In his present guise, he adjusts to his fall a little too glibly. And his wife, who emerges in the novel as a solid, endearingly earnest woman, doesn't seem the type to make such an easy compromise.

As if realizing that, Louis Auchincloss veers to other subjects. Dexter's affair ends without much real effect. The Civil War begins, posing some difficult questions. Is war being waged out of love for the slave or out of hatred for the slaveholder? Is private duty (caring for an ailing husband) more important than public duty (nursing wounded soldiers)? Suddenly, we skate right past the war and end up in the Erie Railroad stock scandal, with Dexter's wife campaigning for women's suffrage.

"Skate," in fact, is the operative word throughout. The prose is elegant, the manners faultless, the ebonized rosewood chairs meticulously detailed; but whenever the characters really come face to face, either hashing out their differences or arriving at some new accord, the author glides us past the moment as unobtrusively as possible. We move abruptly to a less troublesome scene—even, once, to a less troublesome decade—like people on a floor too highly polished.

On the other hand, elegant prose is rare enough these days to make ***Watchfires*** pleasant reading. From the very first chapter, with its crisp declaration of the issues troubling Dexter Fairchild, we sense we're in the hands of a writer who knows where he's headed. And the atmosphere comes across vividly, whether it's that of a glamorous party, an ornate drawing room, or a city fizzing with wartime excitement. (p. 12)

Long recognized as our most observant and perhaps our only novelist of manners, Louis Auchincloss is at his best here wryly chronicling society's attempts to gloss over vulgar reality. "The slavery question had destroyed all good conversation," Dexter reflects at a family gathering. His father-in-law, upon learning that a beloved grandson has been killed in a train wreck, mourns that "there would be no more dinner parties that season." And one of the most stunning scenes in the book occurs when the upper class sets out with champagne buckets, picnic hampers and parasols to watch a Civil War battle. The Union soldiers are unexpectedly defeated and scattered, the socialites' carriages stampede in all directions, and the full impact of the war hits Dexter . . . .

Watchfires lacks the depth that makes a book stay on in the reader's mind, but it's nonetheless accomplished and graceful. It shows Louis Auchincloss to be a slightly skewed Jane Austen—equally intrigued by romantic alliances but less perceptive in divining their undertones, equally concerned with financial matters but more knowledgeable about their mechanics. (p. 34)

Anne Tyler, "The Civil War and Elegant Parties," in The New York Times Book Review, *May 2, 1982, pp. 12, 34.*

FRANCES TALIAFERRO

"The tragedy of American civilization is that it has swept away WASP morality and put nothing in its place." So speaks a rueful character in one of the moral "fables" collected in Louis Auchincloss's 25th work of fiction [***Narcissa and Other Fables***]. Perhaps traditional WASP morality made the unexamined life worth living, but in none of these short stories does that code flourish unchallenged. Mr. Auchincloss shows us something more interesting: a changing society in which conventional morality has not vanished but has gone underground, its honorable certainties turned quirky and countercultural.

In **"The Tender Offer"** we meet Valerian Shaw, a decent chap in his 60's who takes pleasure in his books, his "collection of New York iconography" and his peaceable hobby of the city's history. He earns his living as the anachronistically old-fashioned partner in a relentlessly fast-paced Manhattan law firm. Inevitably, Val is superseded when his longtime client, a small bank, is "merged, taken over, consumed, raped."

Val is uncomfortable with corporate takeovers: "Even the vocabulary gets me down. Terms like 'bear hug' and 'blitzkrieg' and 'shark repellent'!" When he is asked to assist legally in the corporate rape of a respected publishing house by a thuggish conglomerate, his moral choice is clear: He warns his old friend at the publishing house. Val's reward is desertion by the friend and outrage from his own firm; he is charged with violating "the most sacred of the canons of ethics." Val, the defender of old loyalties, is an outlaw in a culture governed by the rapacious.

Mario Fabbri of **"The Fabbri Tape"** is the child of Italian immigrants, a classic New York success who has married a well-connected WASP and become managing partner of an eminent law firm. When one of his close friends, a judge, reveals that he has taken bribes, Fabbri chooses to help his friend and participate in a cover-up. In the ensuing scandal Fabbri is disgraced, but at heart he remains a first-generation idealist: "Who knows how many of the heroes and inspiring events of our history do not owe some of their luster to cover-ups? . . . Supposing—just supposing—it had been possible to cover up the Watergate break-in and spare the world a knowledge that has disillusioned millions with the very concept of democratic government. Would you not have done so?" In context, the possibility sounds surprisingly attractive.

Not all these stories deal with questions of private versus public ethics. As always, Louis Auchincloss is a worldly philosopher who writes with confident authority of the law office and the board room, but he is also a social historian and an amused observer of the prosperous at play. The venue may be a cruise ship or a minor stately home in Virginia, an urban chateau on Fifth Avenue or a great bibliophile's private library overlooking the East River. His characters tend to be "tribal creatures" who pay lip service to social taboos but who live by the laws of self-interest . . . .

The [heroine of **"Narcissa"**], Elise Marcy, is a rich woman who dabbles in painting and plays "queen of the Village in Fifth Avenue and queen of Fifth Avenue in the Village," depending on her current level of boredom. Imperious Elise, who has been painted in a succession of fashionable costumes by a succession of fashionable artists, is held in awe by most of her circle. Only Perry St. Clare, a brilliant and disagreeable painter, understands Elise's narcissism: He knows intuitively that she is titillated by the thought of being seen naked in public, and when he asks her to pose nude for him as the courtesan Diane de Poitiers, he panders to her most thrilling private fantasy.

Most of these stories have something to do with fantasy and exposure of one sort or another. These themes must fascinate the novelist of polite society, who has particular reason to ponder the discrepancies between reputation and reality. They make a fine subject for the ironic observer. "Fable" is a misnomer for these stories, for here one finds no talking animals or cautionary tag-lines, but Mr. Auchincloss has the fabulist's powers of penetration and compression as well as the novelist's ability to adorn a tale.

Frances Taliaferro, "Old Values Gone Underground," in The New York Times Book Review, *April 3, 1983, p. 6.*

CHRISTOPHER RICKS

Louis Auchincloss's ***Exit Lady Masham*** is wonderfully lucid and a mystery. It tells the story of Abigail Hill, her rise as a confidante of Queen Anne and her part in the intrigues (involving blackmail) against Marlborough on behalf of the peace party, Robert Harley, Oliver St. John and Jonathan Swift. The telling is shrewd, and there are some vinegary vignettes. But the mystery remains. What peace does Mr. Auchincloss believe he can effect between the warring styles within his book? Sometimes we are in the world of "Tush, tush" and "I had no wish to be aught than an observer." Then we find ourselves in the world (still with the same narrator, dear Abbie) of "It was curious to me that a man with such a tin ear for poetry. . . ." Mr. Auchincloss does not have a tin ear, so how does he expect us to hear this?

The serious subject here is the succession to the English throne, the fate of the Jacobite cause and of the Pretender. Mr. Auchincloss is the author of ***Reflections of a Jacobite***—by which term he meant he loves Henry James. The late James, with his amazing style, has been dubbed the Old Pretender. In this book, with its amazing style of anachronistic insouciance . . . , Mr. Auchincloss, the old hand, is something of an old pretender himself.

Christopher Ricks, "The Don, the Doctor and the Duke," in The New York Times Book Review, *January 1, 1984, p. 24.*

JONATHAN YARDLEY

That [Auchincloss] has somehow found time in [his] busy professional life to turn out so many books as he has suggests that he is possessed by a compulsion to write, a suggestion that is given heightened credibility by the books themselves; if some of them are exceptionally artful and resonant, too many others are flat and routine, as though they had been written merely to keep the machine running. ***The Book Class,*** unfortunately, is one of these.

It is the story, although there is no real story to it, of a dozen women of the Manhattan upper class. This world has always been Auchincloss' principal subject, no matter where a particular book may be set, and in the best of his novels . . . he has accomplished a principal obligation of the novelist of manners:

to find universal meaning in a world that at first glance seems privileged, exclusive and forbidding. But in the novels in which he has relatively little to say he has tended to fall back on mere description and evocation, which makes for reasonably diverting reading—Auchincloss is always an intelligent writer, and usually a graceful one—but which fails to make any connections with the reader who lives outside the class about which he writes.

No connections are made by ***The Book Class.*** It is indeed intelligent, graceful and witty, but it is also irrelevant; although it has characters, incidents and the semblance of themes, it is difficult to see what Auchincloss hoped to say or do in the writing of it. Its women are "the wives and daughters of the managers of money and industry in New York City, what is sometimes called 'society,'" a dozen of whom formed their Book Class "as debutantes in 1908 and met every month (except, of course, in the torrid summertime) to discuss a selected title, old or new, until the death of Cornelia Gates sixty-four years later." They are women of wealth and station. . . .

Since the novel is informed by contemporary sensibilities, questions of the role and status of women predictably arise. One member of the group, looking back on her life and the men to whom she had been attached—through whom, some might say, she had lived—speculates that "I may not have been quite so subservient as I imagined, that there may be elements of aggression behind a woman's need to support a man." Another member, wondering whether the women would have been happier if they'd been born a half-century later, says: "Let's put it that none of them was a rebel. Yes, they accepted the status quo. But they accepted it critically. It was, after all, a men's status quo, and I think every one of them believed that, given the opportunity, she could have made a better job of it." Whatever the limits imposed on them, they were serious people who took their obligations responsibly and tried, however fallible they may have been, to be good.

They get affectionate and clear-eyed tribute in ***The Book Class,*** but Auchincloss never manages to make the reader care about them; they never seem to matter, to be of real consequence, and thus in the end neither does the book. Intelligent and craftsmanlike though it is, ***The Book Class*** is Auchincloss going through the motions, sticking to his last. Such dogged fidelity to a writer's calling is honorable and admirable, but it increases the risk that the writer will put his ordinary side on public display. Ordinary, by contrast with his best work, is what ***The Book Class*** most certainly is.

Jonathan Yardley, "Readers of a Gilded Age," in Book World—The Washington Post, *July 22, 1984, p. 3.*

ABIGAIL McCARTHY

At first thought, it seems an unlucky blow of chance that this slight, spare, skillful novel by Louis Auchincloss [***The Book Class***] should appear in the same year and so soon after 88-year-old Helen Hooven Santmyer's life work, . . . *And Ladies of the Club*. Both novels use a woman's literary group as framework—Mrs. Santmyer to give us a history of a small Ohio city through the stories of its dominant families and Mr. Auchincloss to limn the lives and influence of women in the segment of American life he has made his own, New York society. Mrs. Santmyer's seems the weightier and more important book.

On second thought, one realizes the two books should not be compared. They are for different readers. In crass market terms, . . . *And Ladies of the Club* is for supporters of the best-seller list, with their appetite for historical detail and "the big read"; Mr. Auchincloss's novel is for the young and upwardly mobile (who are said to like short books) and those who fancy, in their imagination at least, a world of class and status built on wealth and family. . . .

The narrator is that favorite of the author's—the somewhat effeminate misfit who is of that world but just enough of an outsider to be a good observer. In ***The Book Class,*** he is Christopher Gates, an elderly decorator, driven to desperation by "the lawyer in menacing black sequins, the surgeon in blood red *crêpe de Chine,*" who harangue him about sexual discrimination at dinner parties. He makes a claim in a television symposium that women's liberation has cost women most of the domestic, economic and political power it took their ancestors 2,000 years to achieve. In consequence, he says plaintively, "I have every woman's libber in the city down on me." He decides to justify himself by making a sober appraisal of just what power the wives and daughters of the managers of money and industry did hold and uses the members of his mother's book discussion group for his study.

These women are alike in being serious about the lives they lead and, except in one case, their refusal to use feminine wiles to attain their ends. "They use tribalism instead," Christopher Gates says in summing them up. Collectively, they had impressed him as a young man with the idea that women are intellectually and intuitively superior to men but not "nicer." . . .

They are busy, these women, running households, presiding at charity board meetings, shopping, lunching, entertaining—but their lives seem peripheral to the lives of the men in their world.

From the beginning, Christopher Gates admitted that the women to whom he had attributed power had no real political or economic clout. After examining their lives, he asks himself, "Just what was the 'power' of the Book Class? . . . Was it a figment of my imagination?" In the end, he can make only one small affirmation: "Those women continued to occupy an unduly large space in the reflections and fantasies of their surviving children." The reader must ask why.

The only surviving member of the Book Class insists that these women did not waste their lives. They accepted their world and their position and believed they had a duty to maintain both. They knew they were privileged and felt under an obligation "to be good" and, one infers, to do good.

It is Mr. Auchincloss's achievement that, although, as one of his characters asserts, the world and society of the Book Class is as long gone as Imperial Rome, he makes even its peripheral characters interesting and in so doing raises questions for our own era. Would these women have been happier now—"with careers and divorces"? As he has the last of them answer, it's hard to say.

Abigail McCarthy, "Tribalism, Not Feminism," in The New York Times Book Review, *August 12, 1984, p. 12.*

JOHN GROSS

[At] one level Louis Auchincloss's new novel [***Honorable Men***] is a study in the way destructiveness can wrap itself up in idealism and a sense of duty. It follows the fortunes of Chip Benedict, the scion of a glass-manufacturing dynasty that lords it over a small town in Connecticut, from his prep school days in the 1930's to the moment of conscience-searching during the Vietnam War when he resigns his post as special assistant to the Secretary of State in the Johnson Administration. An honorable man, beyond a doubt, but by the end of the book, we have learned a good deal about the price he pays for living up to his standards, and still more the price he exacts from those around him.

On the face of it, the cards are stacked heavily in his favor. He is intelligent, good-looking, debonair; he flourishes at Yale, marries the beautiful Alida, the debutante of her year, fathers two children (one of each sex, it need hardly be said), and serves with distinction in the Navy during World War II. When he assumes command of the family business, he wins praise from Fortune and Forbes for the way he runs it, and when it is taken over after a proxy battle, he moves to New York and soon becomes a valued board member of all the best philanthropic institutions.

None of this insures automatic happiness. As a young man, Chip is haunted by the sense of being a fraud; a residual puritanism fills him with dark thoughts about his own unworthiness (and most other people's as well). But his technique for coping with such feelings is every so often to enforce an inhumanly rigid code of honor, insisting on fine moral points without being able to admit to himself how much they serve his own interests. ''Ethics,'' says an embittered former friend, ''are his stock-in-trade''—and the same friend paints a disturbing picture for Alida of how much deliberate damage Chip has accomplished in the name of ethical scruples.

The indictment, fueled as it is by a rankling personal grievance, goes too far, but Alida, who is herself one of the victims of Chip's urge to undermine and subjugate, is forced to recognize that there is a good deal of truth in it. So is the reader—it is not only the antiwar politics of his children that have turned them against him, for example, and it is no accident that he has managed to alienate them so thoroughly.

At the same time, his estimable qualities are genuinely estimable. He is no simple self-deceiver, any more than those who suffer from his high-minded ruthlessness are plaster saints. Mr. Auchincloss displays both shrewdness and realism in the complicated distribution of moral qualities among his characters, just as he does in the often ironical assignment of rewards and punishments.

Is there some wider moral about America and American politics that is meant to be floating around the novel? Possibly, but if there is, it has not been very effectively realized. The true strength of ***Honorable Men***—Mr. Auchincloss's characteristic strength—lies in its delineation of manners, its feeling for social texture, the way it satisfies our curiosity about the customs and furnishings (including the mental furnishings) of the not-insignificant corner of the world with which it deals.

John Gross, in a review of ''Honorable Men,'' in The New York Times, *September 13, 1985, p. C25.*

A. R. GURNEY, JR.

Louis Auchincloss is one of the few remaining heirs to what has been called the ''genteel tradition'' in American fiction, and no one is more aware of his literary predecessors than Mr. Auchincloss himself. His latest novel, ***Honorable Men,*** resonates with echoes of his distinguished ancestors; it even occasionally gives an explicit bow in their direction. . . .

[To Louis Auchincloss] as to Mark Antony, ''honorable men'' for all the right reasons can do all the wrong things. In the course of his ostensibly upright career, Chip Benedict manages to betray a friend, destroy his father, sell out his family's company, ruin his marriage and send his children reeling into desperately puritanical protests of their own. As a naval officer in World War II, he temporarily finds a kind of simplified moral universe where he can feel most in tune with himself; in the heroic act of helping to rid his ship of an undischarged bomb, he feels a brief relief from the explosive pressures within his own soul. Peacetime muddies the moral waters again, but when, in his yearning for redemption, he offers his services to the State Department in support of the Vietnam War, the grim legacy of the Puritan heritage becomes apparent in all its perversity. . . .

Chip is commissioned ''Special Assistant to the Secretary of State, with the particular mission of engendering support for the American cause in Vietnam among the nations of Southeast Asia.'' He leases a house in Georgetown, works hard, travels to Asia, separates from his wife, initiates an affair with his secretary and ultimately resigns from his job with the same stoic setting of his jaw that has carried him through the other grim decisions in his life. He may have ''seen the light,'' but it is a pallid, godless flicker. Whatever guilt or anguish he may feel about his participation in the Vietnam War is submerged in his psyche. . . .

Oddly enough, in these latter sections of the novel, when his hero moves to Washington and his Puritan convictions would seem to have the most serious and destructive repercussions on the country at large, the author turns away as if in distaste from the political arena to focus once again on the domestic and the personal. Mr. Auchincloss knows more than most of us about the corridors of power, but in this book he's not particularly interested in leading us down them.

There are other problems with ***Honorable Men.*** Half the narrative burden is in the hands of Chip's wife, Alida, who seems to lose shape and spine as she tells her side of it. She admits as much, by describing herself as ''the worn-out garment that I turned myself into for his adornment.'' The trouble is, old clothes aren't terribly exciting, and Alida doesn't bring much life to the story. Indeed, there is a tendency toward stuffiness in the writing that can occasionally settle over the book like dust. . . .

But in his attempt to come to grips with a long-standing American obsession—how the values, if not the beliefs, of our Puritan forefathers still permeate some of their descendants, and what is won and lost by adhering to them—Mr. Auchincloss adds a significant work to his long and considerable canon. Chip Benedict's struggle to reconcile a Classical concern for public reputation with his Christian thirst for personal righteousness is memorable. Moreover, it is a struggle that could only occur in this country, under our special heritage, and as such it illuminates our sense of ourselves as Americans. Finally, in its descriptions of upper-class life . . . ***Honorable Men*** ushers us into a rare world in prose as smooth and burnished as well-oiled furniture.

A. R. Gurney, Jr., ''Overburdened by His Virtue,'' in The New York Times Book Review, *October 13, 1985, p. 3.*

VERNON BOGDANOR

Honourable Men epitomises the genre which Louis Auchincloss has made so much his own—the novel of manners. Chip Benedict is the *beau idéal* of the corporate executive, yet desperate to escape from the moral burden of his puritan upbringing, something which he carries around with him like ball and chain making him a living warning against the domination of ethics. Marrying in a vain attempt to emancipate himself, Chip finds that he is freed from one set of role expectations only to be embraced by another, equally oppressive. . . . Auchincloss treats this familiar theme with a spare and ironic vigour. His prose style is that of a skilled surgeon wielding a very elegant scalpel, and ***Honourable Men*** is a novel full of disturbing implications, no less so for remaining concealed behind a tasteful formal framework. (p. 29)

Vernon Bogdanor, "In or Out?" in The Listener, *Vol. 115, No. 2956, April 17, 1986, pp. 28-9.*

JOHN JAY OSBORN, JR.

Louis Auchincloss's ***Diary of a Yuppie*** is the story of Robert Service's quick rise to the top in the world of New York law. Service's father was a permanent associate—that is, as a young attorney he was passed over for promotion to partner but remained with his firm in a lesser role. Service is ashamed of his father's failure and intends to succeed. As the novel opens, he is a specialist in corporate takeovers and about to be made a partner at Hoyt, Welles & Andrew, a law firm with 36 partners and a hundred clerks. But Service worries that it is too pedestrian, aristocratic and moralistic to be competitive in the long term. Sensing that decay has set in, he establishes a rival firm, stealing both business and the best associates away from Hoyt, Welles. As he expands his new firm, he deals harshly with rivals and obsequiously with clients. His ethics disturb his wife, who leaves him. After an infatuation with Sylvia Sands, a beautiful, viperish widow, Service manages to win back his wife, all the while keeping his mind on business and opportunistically picking up clients when he can.

Diary of a Yuppie is more than an ordinary story of ambition because of the moralists Service confronts along his way. . . . These characters explicitly deal with issues such as the difference between family values and business values, responsibility to self versus responsibility to others and the constraints that friendship imposes on ambition. They are given to intelligent self-examination and are concerned with how well they did something, not how well they did. When Service is dealing with their criticisms, ***Diary of a Yuppie*** is absorbing and fun.

Mr. Auchincloss's style is well suited for detailing all these moral preoccupations but less successful in creating a fictional world. . . . Action is described in a few sentences, then mulled over for pages. The characters ignore their environment. They are self-absorbed, unconscious of their surroundings. We never see Wall Street or midtown. The novel could be set in any large city. The characters may be upwardly mobile, but they're uninterested in spending money (isn't shopping an important yuppie sport?), in trends, fashion, art. They talk in a forced, old-fashioned, pedantic manner without a trace of business school/law school/Wall Street slang. They refer to their "elders and betters," to "thee and me.". . . And Service rarely turns his attention to the law he practices. His big takeover coup results from examining the trash of an adversary. . . .

One assumes that the limited scope of ***Diary of a Yuppie*** is intended. Mr. Auchincloss must want to throw the moral issues into relief by suppressing the story's background. The result can be monotonous.

But any summary of the debits and credits of ***Diary of a Yuppie*** comes out in the black. The novel's limitations may annoy the reader, but it is refreshing to find characters who are willing to discuss the spiritual dimensions of their business decisions, the ethics of their trade.

John Jay Osborn, Jr., "People Who Sniff at Success," in The New York Times Book Review, *August 31, 1986, p. 6.*

RICHARD T. MARIN

Twenty years ago Auchincloss's novels must have come as something of a breath of fresh air amid what many reviewers regarded as the fetid literary atmosphere of the day. His fiction did not eulogize unclean highway heroes or detail the passions of sniveling transvestites in Brooklyn. He shunned *les bas fonds* and never learned, as Auden said, "how to be plain and awkward . . . among the Filthy filthy too." He inhabited not the lowlife, but the highlife; the world of high finance and high society. While other novelists panted after the sordid pleasures of drugs, sex, and violence, Auchincloss carefully traced figures in the carpet, spinning Jamesian yarns in tasteful, decorous prose. A reviewer of Mr. Auchincloss's ***Tales of Manhattan*** called him the "Mr. Clean" of contemporary literature, because his writing contained "no smells, no grime, no crummy sex." That was in 1967. Little has changed. . . .

Auchincloss has written with grace and ease (in ***The Rector of Justin***) of New York society in the 1890s. But his fiction seems hopelessly antiquated in the 1980s. It was once said of his novels that they represented a museum of all that American writing valued before World War I. His characters have always inhabited drawing rooms, not living rooms. Living rooms, for one, have televisions—an apparatus that Auchincloss ignores with silent contempt [as is evident in ***Diary of a Yuppie***]. Are we to believe that the lifestyles of today's rich and famous do not include a few private moments with Pat Sajak, or Alistair Cooke?

If nothing else, the yuppies will at least command a sentence in the history books as the world's first generation of vidiots. Even Auchincloss's newly found liberal sensibility (he votes Democrat now) seems oddly out of synch with the times. . . . One wonders if this conversion took place at his Wall Street office, his Park Avenue apartment, or his summer retreat in Bedford? A *conservative* attack on the New Breed, from the ranks of the Old Monied, would have made for a much gamier read.

Richard T. Marin, in a review of "Diary of a Yuppie," in The American Spectator, *Vol. 19, No. 11, November, 1986, p. 53.*

ROBERT TOWERS

The yuppie of [***Diary of a Yuppie***] is Robert Service, a thirty-two-year-old associate in the respected law firm of Hoyt, Welles & Andrew, who is on the point of being promoted to a partnership. His mentor and conscience within the firm is Branders Blakelock, a famous trial lawyer of the old school, a clubman and golfer whose interest in the boyishly good-looking young man may well, Service suspects, contain an unconscious element of homoeroticism. His moral conscience at home is his wife Alice, who has known him since they were children. At issue in the takeover in which Hoyt, Welles is currently engaged is a shredded memorandum, pieced together, which has been surreptitiously obtained from the wastebasket of the president of the "targeted" company—a personal memorandum so potentially damaging to the company president that it might be used to force a settlement or to launch a stockholder's suit to unseat him. Should this piece of what is euphemistically termed "abandoned property" be put to such use? Service can hardly wait to do so, but Mr. Blakelock, who finds such tactics obscene, won't hear of it.

At home, Alice Service also questions her husband's advocacy of such dirty tricks. Here is Service's defense:

> The trouble with you and Blakelock is that neither of you has the remotest understanding of the moral climate in which we live today. It's all a game, but a game with very strict rules. You have to stay meticulously within the law; the least misstep, if caught, involves an instant penalty. But there is no particular moral opprobrium in incurring a penalty, any more than there is being offside in football.

After their client loses, Service begins to wonder if he is with the right firm after all. Soon he is plotting to start a firm of his own, taking with him the most promising young lawyers from Hoyt, Welles & Andrew. This plot succeeds, Mr. Blakelock disowns him, and Alice asks for a separation.

Dismayed but undeterred, Service pursues his ruthless course, ridding himself of his most troublesome rival and "reorganizing" his social and sexual life. He takes up with a counterpart in greed, a well-connected young widow, Sylvia Sands, who provides him with an entree into what is "obviously the highest" society in New York. More elaborate temptations are in store for him in this exalted sphere. Meanwhile, Alice, like some disconsolate heroine in a late-Victorian morality play, waits in the wings. ***Diary of a Yuppie*** ends in a flurry of ambiguities, chief among them being Service's "semiconversion" and Alice's accomodation to what may or may not be "a new Bob Service."

On its face, there is no reason why the fictional exploration of such material should not result in a solid, interesting novel worthy of the author of ***The Great World and Timothy Colt*** and ***The Rector of Justin.*** Unfortunately, ***Diary of a Yuppie*** carries still further the perfunctoriness of treatment that has marred so much of his recent work. The admirer of Henry James and champion of Edith Wharton seems to have become bored with the dilemmas that once inspired him. Having set up the device of a diary or journal, Auchincloss does little to make it credible—and indeed seems to forget all about it for most of the book. Nor does he make any effort to suggest the speech of the class of young professionals to which Service ostensibly belongs. One wonders if Auchincloss has ever talked with a real, live yuppie. He resorts to stagy dialogue of a sort—full of exclamation points and rhetorical questions—that might have been appropriate to a soap opera (had such existed) of 1895. . . .

Service himself is a thoroughly unconvincing confection, a former English major at Columbia who lards his speech with references to "Mr. James" and claims Walter Pater is his favorite writer. While given to the rhetoric of passion, he comes across as singularly passionless. . . . His constantly reiterated moral position—right up to his "semiconversion"—is the old cynical refrain that we all have our secret meannesses, lusts, and greed but that only a few of us are honest enough to admit them, even to ourselves. The improbabilities of his characterization and the fatuousness of his confessions are such that we can never be sure whether Auchincloss intends Service as a moral monster, a pathetic bundle of self-delusions, a pretentious phony, or a misguided but redeemable young man. (p. 29)

Robert Towers, "The Wild Blue Yonder," in The New York Review of Books, *Vol. XXXIII, No. 20, December 18, 1986, pp. 29-30, 32-3.*

Paul Bailey

1937-

English novelist, dramatist, biographer, critic, and scriptwriter.

Bailey is considered one of the most skillful novelists to emerge in England during the 1960s. His novels, which are often brief, are regarded as distinctly British in setting and characterization and remain relatively unknown in the United States. Bailey's fiction is influenced by three factors in his life: the death of his father when Bailey was eleven years old; the kindliness of an elderly couple who cared for him while his mother worked; and his homosexuality. These circumstances instilled in Bailey a pessimistic but profound belief in the essential loneliness of human beings and a compassion for the problems of the aged and mentally infirm. The major focus of Bailey's fiction, according to James Brockway, is "the denial of human fellowship, of love." Bailey's protagonists often live in emotional isolation, oblivious to normal human relationships, until a poignant incident prompts memory and reflection, leading to grief, suicide, suffering, death, or, occasionally, acceptance. These feelings are usually rendered in a compressed, fragmentary prose style which lends complexity and obliqueness to Bailey's fiction.

Alan Ross reflected critical consensus when he deemed *At the Jerusalem* (1967) "probably the most original, and certainly the most accomplished, first novel of the year." In this essentially traditional book, Bailey follows the gradual decline of Mrs. Gadny, who is unable to adapt to life in a nursing home. She attempts to defend her privacy and identity against the crude but well-meaning friendliness of the residents and staff but is eventually ostracized and is committed to an asylum. Through the novel's objective, dispassionate observation, Bailey avoids sentimentality and moral judgments; Martin Seymour-Smith expressed doubt that life in a rest home "has been [depicted] more fairly or evocatively or tragically than in this excellent short book." Estrangement is also the central theme of *Trespasses* (1970), an ambitious novel focusing on a man's guilt and psychological disintegration following his wife's suicide. In this work, Bailey employs the terse, first-person monologues of supporting characters to disclose motives and events, which combine to create a wholly realized portrait of a disordered mind. Most critics praised Bailey's realistic recreation of dialect and contended that his narrative technique effectively mirrors the protagonist's mental state.

A Distant Likeness (1973) is similar to *Trespasses* in its fractured narrative style but exhibits a greater complexity and a distinctive minimalism. This novel centers mainly on the first-person observations of police inspector Frank White, whose wife has left him for another man. The story shifts between past and present and blends factual reportage and stream-of-consciousness techniques. Frank discovers parallels to his domestic life while investigating the case of a wife-murderer whose "distant likeness" leads Frank to suspect what Camille LaBossière called "the palpable truth of metaphysical evil independent of moral choice." Several critics found Bailey's narrative technique confusing or inappropriate to his subject matter. Bailey's next book, *Peter Smart's Confessions* (1977), is more traditional in form and humorous in tone. A *bildungsroman* describing the life of a boy who is tormented by his

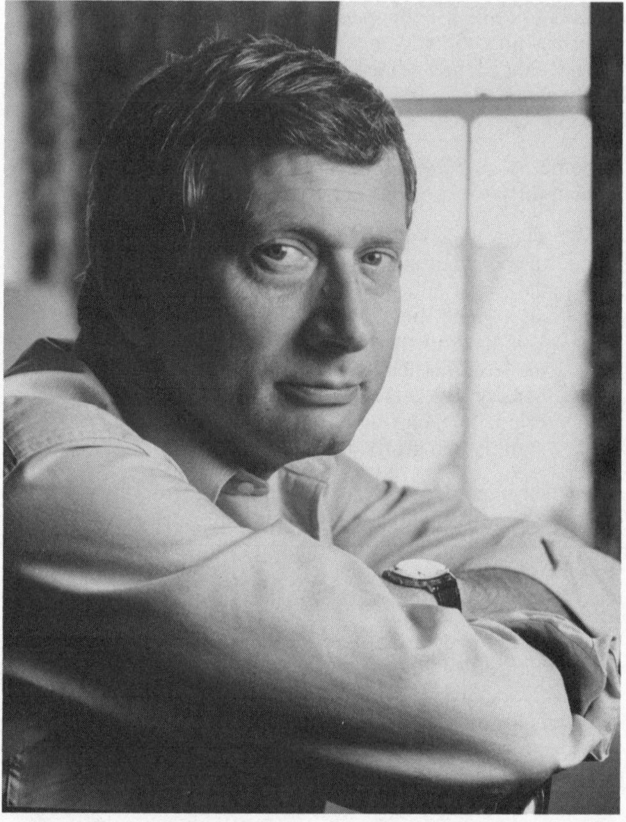

Photograph by Mark Gerson

intolerable mother and the death of his father, the novel centers on Peter's attempts to become an actor and escape the pain of his true identity. Much of the book's humor derives from the eccentric people Peter meets in theatrical circles, his somber, self-deprecating attitude, and his failed attempts at suicide.

Bailey returns to concerns of the elderly in *Old Soldiers* (1980). The novel's two aged characters, Victor Harker and Harold Standish, possess vivid memories of World War I and function as dramatic opposites. Victor, who has fled from London after the death of his wife, is evoked through descriptions of his memories as he roams the graveyards and churches of his troubled childhood. Harold, whom Victor meets in a church, cultivates three distinct personalities to escape his real identity as an army deserter and to deny his own mortality. Although some critics faulted Bailey's explanation for Harold's insanity and eventual suicide, the novel drew generally favorable reviews, and Nicholas Shrimpton praised it as "a marvellously skilful book, deftly constructed and full of incidental delights." *Gabriel's Lament* (1986) explores a young boy's psychological torment after his mother suddenly leaves home. Raised by his irascible but affectionate father, Gabriel does not learn the reason for his mother's disappearance until he is approaching middle age, when he opens a box containing her letters after his father's death. Although it causes him suffering and suicidal frustration, Gabriel's discovery inspires him to write his "lament'' and to purge his long-repressed emotions. Hermione Lee called *Gabriel's Lament* ''a powerful study of bereavement as obsession and of the consolations of comic art.''

Bailey has written several dramas, including *Crime and Punishment* (1978), based on Fedor Dostoevski's novel, and a biography, *An English Madam: The Life and Work of Cynthia Payne* (1982). He has also contributed articles and reviews to numerous English periodicals.

(See also *Contemporary Authors,* Vols. 21-24, rev. ed.; *Contemporary Authors New Revision Series,* Vol. 16; and *Dictionary of Literary Biography,* Vol. 14.)

MARTIN LEVIN

Faith Gadny, 70, newly admitted into a home for the aged, tries to hang on to her sanity. (''She would try to keep her mind empty—it was the sensible policy.'') ***At The Jerusalem*** . . . translates Mrs. Gadny's struggle against present and past into a compressed mixture of dialogue and reverie. The void of the Jerusalem, a London ex-workhouse, is filled with aimless nattering, institutional routine and a sense of finality. It is this last that keeps pressing in the author's pensioner and transforms the mundane into the monstrous. The chattering of Mrs. Capes, a well-meaning housemate, becomes unbearable; the memory of being an alien in her daughter-in-law's home is knife-sharp in retrospect. Mr. Bailey, an old party of 30, describes the demons of old age with amazing preciosity.

Martin Levin, in a review of ''At the Jerusalem,'' in The New York Times Book Review, *May 21, 1967, p. 42.*

MILES BURROWS

[***At the Jerusalem***] concerns the residents of an old people's home called the Jerusalem, and the experience of a Mrs Gadny who enters it after the death of her daughter and the failure of her attempts to live with her stepson's family. . . . At the Jerusalem she is suddenly thrown into mess life or 'community living,' and strives to preserve her own privacy, gentility and individuality against the assault of confrontation with the senile, coarse or over-friendly old 'ladies', and the unconscious 'double-binding' techniques of the staff. . . .

Mr Bailey's social comment is precise and made with an enviably light touch while never failing to be serious. His style is uncontaminated by Beckett or by Muriel Spark's fey delight in the macabre, but rather seems to warn us against such a mood in the character of Henry the stepson, who has a cold passion for photography and the collection of murder news-cuttings which he pastes into a scrapbook. Henry seems to incarnate not only the guilt of filial impiety but also the guilt-feeling of the novelist himself in appearing to stand aside and coolly photograph the scene for his hypocrite readers. But apportioning blame is no part of Mr Bailey's task: non-communication may be as much a feature of senility itself as of the surrounding institution. The matron and nurses, dominated by their roles, are depicted as kind people, not as monsters. He raises by implication the question: what kind of old people's home are we preparing for ourselves? . . .

Moralising is avoided by this svelte novel, which is the more painful in effect for being non-satirical. Paul Bailey trained as an actor and has a nice ear for the vocabulary and speech rhythms of the working class, which he does not romanticise. He delicately exposes the group dynamics which lead first to the cautious acceptance of the reserved Mrs Gadny, then to her extrusion into the role of 'Dotty Faith', and finally (amid the doubtful gaiety of the birthday party of a moribund nonagenarian) to her utter rejection.

Miles Burrows ''Mess Life,'' in New Statesman, *Vol. 73, No. 1890, June 2, 1967, p. 765.*

MARTIN SEYMOUR-SMITH

Paul Bailey's ***At the Jerusalem*** is a laconic, merciless, appallingly accurate description of life in an old people's home. The predicament of old people thrust by their families (perhaps unavoidably) into homes is well known and has been made the theme of a number of novels and more TV plays. However, I doubt if it has been done more fairly or evocatively or tragically than in this excellent short book. Everyone and everything is presented with complete detachment. . . . This is the very simple tale of how Mrs Gadny is rejected by her family, enters 'The Jerusalem,' hates it and withdraws from it into herself, and is sent away to a mental hospital. It is so well done that it is often not bearable—which adds up to a most promising début for Mr Bailey.

Martin Seymour-Smith, ''Grey Days,'' in The Spectator, *Vol. 218, No. 7249, June 2, 1967, p. 649.*

MARY SULLIVAN

[The word compassionate] may fairly be used of Paul Bailey's ***At the Jerusalem,*** for he feels with all the inmates of the old people's home 'The Jerusalem', and doesn't use them merely as instruments of the misery of his central character, Mrs Gadny. No distinction is imposed on her for the sake of the plot; she is not cleverer or more interesting than the rest; her difference is only that she can't adjust to the well-meaning brutality of institutional life. She escapes by wrecking the oldest inhabitant's birthday party, and then only for another, grimmer, Home: 'More modern. In the country. For a holiday'. The novel is written almost entirely in dialogue, which drifts to and fro between Mrs Gadny's memories of her dead husband and daughter, and present reality. It catches the tops of conversations and shores them up with her muddled but relevant thoughts. It is accurate, kind, funny, and very sad.

Mary Sullivan, ''Gerontophile,'' in The Listener, *Vol. 78, No. 1997, July 6, 1967, p. 25.*

THE TIMES LITERARY SUPPLEMENT

Mr. Paul Bailey's award-winning first novel, ***At the Jerusalem,*** combined mature understanding with immense control and accomplishment, in a manner suggesting exceptional promise. With ***Trespasses,*** he establishes a firm place among the best of the young novelists. Once more, as in the earlier book, his principal strength lies in the way he causes a small world to radiate wider and graver implications; ***Trespasses,*** again, is brief and self-denyingly economical; yet it manages to encompass, in a hauntingly perceptive and compassionate way, a large range of attitudes and situations.

Its theme is estrangement: the subtle inevitable processes by which parents and children, men and women, draw tragically and uncomprehendingly apart from one another. Ralph Hicks's way of piecing together his disintegrated world during a breakdown after his wife, Ellie's suicide is to write down the associations suggested by a number of small, significant words. . . . The narrative proceeds largely in a series of very short passages, tracking to and fro in time, gradually building up by cross-reference, amplification and repetition a clear and full picture of where things went wrong (there are intervals where he adds to this scheme by speaking with the voices of other characters).

The apparent piecemeal casualness of this technique suggests another deceptively simple novel where the reader has to learn the truth by making his own moral judgments: Mr. William Golding's *The Pyramid*. Mr. Bailey lacks as yet the ease with which Mr. Golding there offers an insistent horror under calm surfaces; but his sense of the crippling alienation and waste in some human situations is already almost as sure. . . .

Mr. Bailey's one failing may be in giving us, in Ralph's case, the problems without a complete sense of the person. But the treatment of his minor characters is vigorous and thorough, and their message clear: understanding and tolerance given in a degree which approaches love . . . is the only answer. Ralph has to learn to reconstruct his world as "Man", and acquire these qualities of human sympathy at the same time. Mr. Bailey's avoidance of gimmickry or pretentiousness in his very original experimental technique, his fine, trenchant way with an old friend, the sensitive young hero, his mature skill with dialogue, and his unerring social sense, enable him to write a novel that both moves and excites.

"The Habit of Withdrawal," in The Times Literary Supplement, *No. 3555, April 16, 1970, p. 401.*

MARY BORG

Paul Bailey's first novel, ***At the Jerusalem,*** was justly praised when it appeared in 1967. ***Trespasses*** takes up some of the themes introduced in that novel and expands them: his concern is with charity and care, with self-involvement and people's attempts to break out of it, with their blind claims on the attention of others. He takes as his theme a quotation from George Eliot: 'The beginning of compunction is the beginning of a new life.' His central character, Ralph, could almost be the grown-up version of the old lady's stepson in ***At the Jerusalem:*** a withdrawn, remote child, apparently unable, or unwilling, to make the effort to be sociable and friendly. Ralph has always been unable to display 'proper' human feelings, either to his mother, his grandmother, the children he teaches, his wife's queer friend, Bernard, or, above all, to his wife, who kills herself because of him.

The book is technically adventurous and fragmentary, written to a very formal, involved schema of flashbacks which come full circle with Ralph in a mental home starting the painful process of coming to terms with himself. There is an even greater subtlety in that the first-person narratives of the supporting characters—all of them also concerned with selfishness and compassion—turn out to have been 'written' by Ralph himself as a way of making contact with the lives of others. It's extremely accomplished and Paul Bailey yet again shows a sad wit, deep observation of the plight of the lonely and the old. Like Mrs Gadny in ***At the Jerusalem,*** Ralph's mother is an uprooted country girl struggling with the inhumanity of cities. Some of the episodes, especially those involving the humane Bernard, are on a level with the very best of Angus Wilson: indeed, the same humanity informs both these writers' work. But I feel, sneakingly, that Paul Bailey has slightly overreached himself this time: a not uncommon fault with a second novel. The book lacks the complete economy and control of ***At the Jerusalem,*** and, in places, looks dangerously like a case of special pleading: it never quite fulfils the wide promise of the George Eliot quotation. Nevertheless, it is churlish to cavil at someone for setting his sights that high. It remains a distinguished near-miss.

Mary Borg, "Unpindownable," in New Statesman, *Vol. 79, No. 2040, April 17, 1970, p. 558.*

MAGGIE ROSS

One of Paul Bailey's greatest strengths is the authenticity of the voice with which he speaks. His is the voice of that class of inarticulate, repressed people for whom outward gentility is everything; for whom there is no escape from inherited repressions. Utterly rooted in England's system of class (and what English novelist can avoid the subject?), his characters, frantically struggling in the trap of loneliness and non-understanding, are painfully recognisable. The method by which he has chosen to present them in his second novel, ***Trespasses,*** seems at first sight to be too restricting. Within the seeming inflexibility of a series of unconnected formal headings such as 'Then', 'Before', 'Black', 'Here', 'Boy', written by by the main character Ralph in order to purge his past and come to terms with his present, he manages to bring together with great coherence the separate sad lives of these frustrated victims.

There is truth and compassion in the slow knitting together of the threads of those Ralph has failed to love: his weak mother, his grandmother, his wife's homosexual friend Bernard (who could so easily have been mere caricature), and his wife Ellie—a liberal crusader, warm-hearted and foolish, whose mistaken supposition that her love can break through repression leads to tragedy. There is real humour in the portrait of Mrs Goacher the landlady, with her never-ending stories of her randy daughter's goings on, a character of whom Ralph says: 'She's like a rock; she's there. She has no doubts. I feed her with questions and she always supplies the answer I expect.' Thus illustrating his own self-absorption. Ralph is full of self-pity of a kind which is all too familiar.

To say that some of the fragments—and there is great variety in the juxtaposition of dialogue, narrative, letters and dreams—add too little to one's comprehension of Ralph's present condition is merely to wish a good novel better. This is Paul Bailey's choice, and the writer has the options. What mars the novel for me is that he felt it necessary half-way through to include two long sections written with the voices of Ralph's mother and Bernard. Ralph's own answer is 'I am so truly sick of myself that it will be pleasant to be Bernard Proctor,' but with this a new pattern is introduced, in which it is suddenly possible for him to see more clearly than the remaining fragments of the novel suggest into the lives of these two. The last thing Paul Bailey has to fear is that he is incapable of sustaining a courageous technique. He is too good a writer to have to elucidate what is already clear.

The world of ***Trespasses*** is the authentic extension, and the cause, of the world he portrayed so movingly in his first novel ***At the Jersualem.*** This time he takes from George Eliot the more hopeful theme that 'the beginning of compunction is the beginning of a new life.' Perhaps in his next work he will get even closer to his intention.

Maggie Ross, "Painfully Recognisable," in The Listener, *Vol. 83, No. 2144, April 30, 1970, p. 592.*

KENNETH GIBSON

[***Trespasses*** deals] . . . with the strangeness, the *otherness,* of life. Even when the antagonist-hero of ***Trespasses*** mocks himself as an "Alienated Man," he is unconvincing in his rejection. For it is Bailey's stratagem to present Ralph Hick's dilemma as a series, first of labelled incidents, like file-cards; then as monologues from correlative characters who know of, or have watched Hicks' disintegration following his wife's suicide; and finally as a capitulative narration connecting the labels and asserting his gradual claim to the title of *a man* and not a psychic jigsaw. Hicks' fear of life is aimed at his wife Ellie, she of the "cow's eyes." It's as if he has heaped on her all his memories—she *becomes* them—of his past: his clever successes as "Mummy's Ralphie;" his Prize Boy mask; and always, always, his hideous view of sexuality as aligned with madness. . . . and with death, of the heart, of the flesh. (p. 311)

Bailey's techniques may not be radical, but, quite simply, his novel is magnificent. The two unformed and unfocused people in the centre are hemmed about with characters brilliantly "there"; yet it is their sense of life, however painful, crude or self-absorbed, that pushes Ellie towards death and Ralph into madness. . . . It is only the ending—

> My Name is Ralph Hicks and I hope I will become a man. It is a beginning.

which does not ring true; the strategy fails. One probably can't accuse Mr. Bailey of anything more than a slackening of grip, given the structure he's built. His fictive reach is still within his grasp. Meanwhile, he can write most of the younger authors in the room under the table, if this spare, often-hilarious, and moving novel is any evidence. (p. 312)

Kenneth Gibson, in a review of "Trespasses," in The Canadian Forum, *Vol. L, Nos. 598 & 99, November & December, 1970, pp. 311-12.*

JOSEPH CATINELLA

[***Trespasses***] is a dim compound of dreams and memories, stirred by a spectral hero. Reviewing his past from a mental hospital, where his problems but not his clichés are treated, Ralph writes: "I am an Alienated Man, you know me well, I am oh such a familiar specimen." He is, but that doesn't deter him from recording his "trespasses" against others—an exercise in literary therapy organized under headings like "Then," "After," "Here," "Him," and "Her."

Hollow. Ralph's major trespass is that he's a fictional cipher, chilled by his landscape and numbed by all human encounters. In what might be called an English novel of insensibility, Mr. Bailey would have us believe that Ralph's alienation from people was caused by the death of his father—a man so vaguely drawn that even Ralph can't remember him. . . .

Before he entered the hospital, Ralph never surmounted this difficulty. He was cold to his mother and distant to his pupils. (Ralph was "the one master the children feared.") After marrying an upper-class girl named Elspeth, he bought a screen behind which he could hide from her. . . .

In a novel where few motives are clarified, the reader gathers that Ralph may have been attracted to her "cow's eyes." "It was my only term of endearment," he notes. But Ralph soon began to ignore her, and Elspeth, an untidy housekeeper interested in undefined social causes, committed suicide. He found her blood-splattered remains in their bathroom: "Even her death was a mess. Nothing comparatively subtle like drugs or gas. She had to hack, hack, hack."

All of this verges on parody because Mr. Baily treats alienation as a concept; he fails to dramatize it in significant human terms. His style, moreover, flirts with stream-of-consciousness though its heart belongs to exposition: Ralph's present desire to "become a man" is spelled out with a bluntness that might have pleased H. G. Wells, if not Virginia Woolf. The imagery, more liquid than lyrical, would have displeased both writers; "How I wanted, in private, to squeeze out one tear of genuine sorrow, to exchange it for all those automatic gallons I had shed in the busy street."

At one point in the book Ralph tires of recording his trespasses and writes through the person of Bernard, a homosexual friend of Elspeth. Unfortunately, the Ralph-Bernard collaboration ranges from plagiarized wit ("'Only Disconnect' became my motto") to low-camp facetiousness ("The mere thought of my years at Oxford—oh, them gleaming spires!—makes me shudder."). After this passage, it's almost with relief that a reader returns to Ralph's private nullity.

Joseph Catinella, in a review of "Trespasses," in Saturday Review, *Vol. LIV, No. 10, March 6, 1971, p. 37.*

SUSAN HILL

Paul Bailey makes his readers work hard. What you get out of his novels is in direct proportion to what you are prepared to put into them. There are no signposts or bridging passages; he never plods anxiously from A to B. Reading ***A Distant Likeness*** is like doing a crossword into which you must fit not only words but the black squares between. His last, excellent novel, ***Trespasses,*** which had little spare fat on it, revealed him as a most impeccable craftsman and an innovator, but one with something profound to say, too. The new book is very short and contains not a superfluous or misplaced word. We move to and fro in time; several stories are interwoven; people are laid bare in a single descriptive phrase, a snatch of dialogue.

Frank White is a policeman, a hunter. His Italian father changed his surname, to prove he was as 'English as roast beef', but boys still called Frank a wop. His marriage has broken down and his wife wants a divorce, to marry Alec [Belsey] who has made her pregnant, when White could not. Alec is ghosting White's memoirs for a popular newspaper. . . . They will be avidly read. White is famous as the tracker-down of mass murderers, like the notorious child-killer Albert Hawker. . . . Now he has caught Belsey, who axed his wife and son and 'has done with words'. Even White can't prise his mouth open. He delves into Belsey's past, chats up his old, eccentric father, is insulted by his alienated, hippy daughter. White has an image of himself as a strong, lean man, 'in control', dedicated to the extermination of criminals, a custodian of the safety of ordinary people—a fanatic. As he tries to break down Belsey, he himself is breaking both down and then out, into violence.

Susan Hill, "Bailey's Bridgelessness," in The Listener, *Vol. 89, No. 2307, June 14, 1973, p. 808.*

THE TIMES LITERARY SUPPLEMENT

The psychopathic killer in Paul Bailey's [***A Distant Likeness***] will not break silence in his police-station cell. Handed a notebook and pencil on the fifth page of this very short book, he writes: "No More Words." There is a significant and intended reference here to a problem which is patently besetting Mr Bailey, though he may himself see it less as a dilemma than as a challenge: how to say as much as possible in an ever-contracting space. ***A Distant Likeness*** is written almost entirely in tiny, cryptic paragraphs collected in short batches separated by blank pages. The narrative is in the mind of one man, Inspector Frank White, but it flickers bewilderingly between past and present, from one scene and character to another, sometimes even in the same ten-line section. In ***Trespasses,*** Mr Bailey's last book, this terse, allusive technique seemed justified by the situation: his hero was striving desperately to reintegrate himself, to piece thoughts and words together, after a breakdown. Here, with the extension of this method to the point where reading becomes a case of mere "puzzling out", it seems wilful and precious. It is disappointing to watch a novelist of Mr Bailey's talents flexing tiny muscles with such calculated fastidiousness.

The "likeness" of the title—something which cries out for an amplification which the author ruthlessly avoids—is that between Inspector White and his silent prisoner. White is a tough, efficient policeman but a failure in human terms. . . . Like the criminal who is also outwardly a "success", White has made a mess of life, or had a mess made of it for him. His wife has left him for the man who purports to be ghost-writing his views on crime and punishment as the policeman who brought a notorious child-murderer to justice. His parentage was bizarre, his childhood and adolescence unsettling. This past pursues him through his thoughts and nightmares as he struggles to force some sort of utterance out of the psychopath. . . . In the end, for all his toughness, his attempt fails. The killer will not speak. When he hands him a knife in a moment of self-hatred, hinting that the man might like to kill himself also, the criminal nearly kills a warder.

Such an idea has its possibilities, but Mr Bailey has let them drain away through the spaces between his neat, minimalist paragraphs. There is a point, exactly the one the novelist did *not* intend to reach, at which a finely pared-down economy, reticence and suggestiveness results in something approaching cliché. Tiny cinematic "shots" of Inspector White's uneasy childhood (bathing with his mother), bits of easy adolescent murkiness, minor characters who ought to be vivid and authentic but remain caricatures, all suggest, sadly, the kind of trap which he was most strenuously exercised to avoid. No amount of ingenuity in the deployment of symbols, the details which echo meaningfully across the pages, the nice attention to minuscule portrayals of settings, can compensate for the final absence of the full-blooded novel which Mr Bailey's skills might have provided. ***A Distant Likeness*** is thin stuff unless one is gullibly willing to fill it out with all that it does not contain.

"Buttoned Lips," in The Times Literary Supplement, *No. 3721, June 29, 1973, p. 737.*

PIERS BRENDON

There is a good deal of space separating the lines of this attenuated novel [***A Distant Likeness***] and Paul Bailey wants us to read between them. We are becoming increasingly accustomed to such tasks. From Beckett's verbal velleities to Pinter's pregnant pauses we have been taught to scratch for significance in the interstices of dialogue. We have learnt to glean insight from the most mundane sources, here an Eccles cake, there a pair of shoes. Mr Bailey counts on this imaginative education. He assumes our understanding of these intimation-via-hiatus, hint-via-humdrum conventions. He has pared down his style to the bones and left the reader to clothe them as best he may. His characters speak in a series of bare exclamations. . . . Or they utter portentous banalities. . . . What does it all add up to, and how does Mr Bailey's new novel compare with his highly praised ***At the Jerusalem***?

In a word, ***A Distant Likeness*** is a disappointment. It tells the story of the psychological disintegration of a policeman. Inspector Frank White's childless marriage has collapsed and he is trying to extract a confession from a particularly brutal murderer who refuses to speak at all. White is a copper of the old school, a man to warm the cockles of the *Daily Express*'s heart—'the sooner we stop glorifying thugs and villains the better.' . . . But White's recollections of the various traumatic cases he has handled begin to haunt and disorientate his mind. Scenes from his childhood recur obsessively. He gets drunk and has a totally uncharacteristic homosexual encounter (beautifully described). Finally, his methods with the murderer he is interrogating lead to disaster.

There are, indeed, some excellent scenes and some vivid snatches of dialogue in the book. . . . But in general the technical expedients to which Mr Bailey resorts impede the reader's enjoyment and at times his comprehension. The story is a number of fragments, like reflections in a broken mirror. No doubt this is intended to symbolise the dislocated apprehensions of Inspector White himself. But the constant fluctuation (it sometimes looks like capricious experimentation) between straight reportage, stream of consciousness, snippets of letters and memoirs, flashback and dream conveys a superfluity of confusion. Mr Bailey's prose is often too economical, even parsimonious, to rescue the reader from complete bewilderment.

Still, there is just enough in ***A Distant Likeness*** to convince us (if we need convincing) that Mr Bailey is a novelist of considerable talents though we may wonder why he did not put them to better use in this particular book.

Piers Brendon, in a review of "A Distant Likeness," in Books and Bookmen, *Vol. 19, No. 1, October, 1973, p. 104.*

JANE MILLER

Paul Bailey has always given his novels evasive narrators who are oddly unwilling to encourage reliance on their judgment. A director in [***Peter Smart's Confessions***] is mocked for his need not just to give *Hamlet* some improbable new meanings but to demonstrate his control of the performances his direction elicits. That Peter Smart's "definitive Reynaldo" in that production should be so lengthily admired by a Sunday paper is a joke, of course; yet when Peter casts himself as victim, stooge or sounding board in remembered encounters with people who have been allowed to overwhelm him he may only seem to present himself as bit-part actor, disingenuous recorder or mimic. For his confessions are made to follow on the most nearly successful of a series of suicide attempts, and his holding back in the relationships he describes is not meant to distract us from the despair which has dictated his selection of memories and moments. Even his death-wish is made comical by the exasperation it occasions in other people, by its repeated failure to achieve itself and by his habit of taking his inspiration from real-life or literary suicides. A postscript announces that Peter Smart has managed to die at last, from cancer; another joke at his expense, likely to remind us of his lifelong inability to pick appropriate models for himself. The self-deprecating humour, like the mimicry, is there as source and expression of the narrator's dilemma.

Paul Bailey organizes this novel in short scenes, as he has done before. In ***Trespasses*** their telling was shared between characters whose connection was established only gradually and from internal evidence. Here, the scenes and their protagonists cohere through the narrator's highly problematic presence in them. . . . The history he writes for himself is composed of the sounds of voices, obsessional, lunatic and monotonous ones, often wonderfully funny and idiosyncratic, and always impervious to his own. . . . [Peter's] talent (like one of Paul Bailey's) is for parody, it turns out, and his confessions are built round teasing imitations of art journalism, popular novels of romance and violence, the language of portentous autobiography and some hectic verse drama. As a boy he is better at reviewing his own masterpiece as it might be by Cocteau than at writing it. A gap in his memoirs might be explained by the discovery that his talents and interests in writing have foundered, for he reappears as an actor, employed but no good at it. A moving conversation with a gifted actor who despises his own talent and wants only to fly planes again confirms Peter's sense of writing and acting being alternative kinds of mimicry, no more than outlets for the mutilated. Such pessimism is countered, though, by his exuberant delight in speech, in what it suggests of character and in what it hides. The banalities of his characters' dialogue can hold hints of desertions, rejections, betrayals and disappointments, so elaborately disguised in linguistic accretions that Peter usually realizes too late that a dismay like his own might lurk within his tormentors.

There are moments when Paul Bailey lets his listening narrator forget his own purposes, when the camp bickering of actors, for instance, seems there for its own sake, the reason for remembering scenes or conversations forgotten or become almost obtrusively tenuous. At its best, though, this is black and serious comedy, of a kind Paul Bailey has always known how to write, and which here is able to inform and explain a complex account of a life.

Jane Miller, "Pretend I'm Not Here," in The Times Literary Supplement, *No 3924, May 27, 1977, p. 644.*

PADDY KITCHEN

Paul Bailey's ***Peter Smart's Confessions*** contains a mother of apparently total malevolence, and whenever she was on stage, I capitulated. But when other people are in the spotlight (there is so much dialogue, it often seems like a play), the jokiness tends to become tedious. The book's construction is very deliberate, and this perhaps squeezes some life out of the narrative. It opens with Peter Smart recovering from a suicide attempt: he has by mistake swallowed his hated wife's hated Pekingese's tranquillisers, instead of the Nembutal. He decides to write his autobiography, relying heavily on the dialogue of his motley and intermittently splendid cast of relations, friends and employers. Letters, reviews and pontifications are also grist to Paul Bailey's mill—anything, it would seem, to pin down authentic voices. Bailey does allow Peter Smart some introspection and development, though not very much.

Irony and humour are not unwelcome in tragedy, but too often here they deteriorate into long-drawn-out badinage. However, there are some brilliant passages, particularly in the childhood section. Here, the dreadful mother dominates, silencing the father with her coughing to conceal her farting, and always addressing Peter as 'You'. (p. 730)

Peter has too little experience of love or friendship on which to build his personal life. He gets involved with a would-be suicide who is even less capable of coping with relationships than he is, and misery is bleakly compounded. They unintentionally have a child which the woman can not love, and Peter sinks to becoming a desolate drunk on the Grassmarket. (p. 731)

Paddy Kitchen, "Pass Marks," in The Listener, *Vol. 97, No. 2511, June 2, 1977, pp. 730-31.*

PETER ACKROYD

[Paul Bailey] has taken off from Dickens, bypassed the mediocre heavies like Orwell and Priestley, glanced against Firbank and Angus Wilson, and eventually landed in that twilight world where parody, satire and fantasy are effortlessly aligned. ***Peter Smart's Confessions*** is a sport, a game constantly threatening to get out of hand as Bailey swoops with horrid glee upon each of his characters as they alternately fumble, strut and moan through their lives. Among them Peter Smart himself shrinks to a cipher (he is a self-confessed Hamlet, but in this case without a proper stage), a barely acknowledged object which the monsters sweep around and occasionally, just occasionally, knock against. It is as if Paul Bailey were permanently fixed with the vision of a child, seeing the world from knee-height and understanding very little of it. So he leaves everything to his characters, and the novel echoes with their voices.

There is Doris Hedley (Miss): 'She is not her lively old self at all. She had the last of her teeth out on Tuesday and a new gas cooker put in. You should have seen the mess but that's British workmen.' There's Mother: 'Your father will run a bath for you when he can summon the energy to get up out of that chair. The war will probably be over by the time that happens. Oh look, he's taken the hint. Wonders will never cease.' There's Granny Smart, reading her *Dead Flesh for Sale* and *She Slashed for Love:* 'Don't you go growing up breaking women's hearts, our Pete. Life's best when it runs easy and natural.' There's Dr Cottie, the author of *With Stethoscope and Scalpel:* 'The small amount of food I take each day is made to do its work. My wheels, so to speak, run smoothly. They do not grind to a halt.' Monologues like these bristle through the novel, as Bailey's characters address the world about themselves, ferocious and furious, helpless and merciless in turn, lying and hesitating. Bailey is overwhelmed by their mannerisms, by those ridiculous gestures which always give them away but which draw them to him. It can go a little too far, but it's fascinating to watch.

And, like all good comedy, pathos is just around the corner—the joke handkerchief is always stiff with dried tears. It becomes quite clear that all of these mannerisms, all of the clichés and the circumlocutions and the homely phrases, are simply ways in which Bailey's characters can hide themselves from the light. They are concealed by their own outrageousness. But it is not as if they were hiding any nasty or ungainly impulses.

No one in the book means any harm to anyone except himself. Bailey's world is actually populated by kind and generous souls whose feelings have, somehow or other, stopped short at the source. So when he dwells upon a character, playing with a neurosis here or a nervous habit there, embroidering a little, encouraging them to send themselves up, he is actually adding to the enormous carapace which they seem to have carried since birth. And this wilful and witty book carries one too. Despite his mockery and his distance, Bailey actually writes very mournful novels. If you listen closely enough, like a child, you can actually hear the sadness breaking through: 'I grabbed my aunt's hands, to still them, and to give myself support as well—I had sensed, on the way to the station, that something more than two women was leaving me. They were taking my childhood away with them.' (pp. 22-3)

Peter Ackroyd, "The Limit," in The Spectator, *Vol. 238, No. 7770, June 4, 1977, pp. 22-3.*

JAMES BROCKWAY

In his fourth novel—his fourth in ten years—Paul Bailey has turned to comedy. Since, however, ***Peter Smart's Confessions*** is Paul Bailey writing comedy, the book begins with Peter in a hospital bed, dreaming he is entering heaven, a condition induced by his latest attempt to commit suicide, and ends with his dying of cancer, all his attempts to leave this earth voluntarily having failed.

The irony of this final situation is an irony with which the entire novel is charged, with which, indeed, all Paul Bailey's writing is charged. It is the irony of life itself, of which this author is more aware than most others, and it is this ingredient of his style which makes reading him such a pleasure—even more than his impatience with all trimmings, than his ability to say so much in so few words about the sheer, but sometimes comic, awfulness of life. Again since it is Paul Bailey writing comedy here, his novel encompasses a countless number of deaths. (p. 62)

To write, using this lugubrious material, a humorous novel which is consistently entertaining, exciting and compelling, one has to be Paul Bailey. His ability to bring it off was, however, evident in his very first novel, ***At the Jerusalem,*** of 1967, the story of Faith Gadny, an intelligent old lady with a mind of her own, who is driven into a psychiatric clinic by the 'normal' behaviour of staff and inmates of an old people's home. It is true that Mrs Gadny's fate is tragic and that comedy hardly plays the same role in this first novel as it does in Peter Smart's story, except in some of the characterisation via dialogue. Yet the writing is so sprightly and so just right that its effect is exhilarating, despite the theme. ***At the Jerusalem*** is the only novel I really did read 'at one go.' . . . I wanted to know what would happen to Mrs Gadny, but what really held me was the narrative technique, the dialogue, the brilliantly accurate characterisation through this dialogue and the mosaic structure of brief episodes switching to and fro in time and space, which Bailey was to use more cunningly and elaborately still in his second novel, ***Trespasses,*** of 1970.

By 1973, in his third, ***A Distant Likeness,*** which also begins with the leading character waking from a dream of dying, he had taken this structure so far and was applying it so stringently that several 'episodes' had been reduced to a single sentence: 'The smile would vanish'; 'He would sleep on the sofa', while one consisted of just two words: 'More warmth'. The reader was left to fit the pieces into the pattern himself.

In ***Trespasses,*** which tells of Ralph Hicks's fatally inappropriate marriage, leading to his young wife's suicide, and which shows us his gradual regeneration, this 'fitting the pieces together' technique was a superbly well-chosen instrument, superbly handled, to show how the young husband gets his ideas about himself and his behaviour gradually sorted out and gradually evolves some hope of becoming a real person. Superbly well-chosen, because the reader's experience parallels Ralph's—the psychological situation gradually becoming clear to him as more and more pieces fit. In ***A Distant Likeness,*** however, in which the police inspector tracking down a sadistic sex-murderer begins, step by step, to look more and more like his quarry, the technique has been applied so drastically that there is a sense of its being forced on the material and given precedence over it. It is as though Bailey is saying: 'Now I'll show you how to do it, using the absolute minimum of words, giving you the absolute minimum of clues. You will have to work very hard indeed'. It is true that this ruthlessness of technique echoes that of the material, crime, *ie* the way human beings too often treat other human beings. Yet, for all its cleverness, the novel suffers from seeming too self-consciously a *tour de force*.

In ***Peter Smart's Confessions,*** scenes from the life of a small-part actor who thinks himself a 'shit' and refers to his confessions as a 'trivial account of a trivial life', the same technique is employed but now in far more relaxed and expansive a form. The episodes—sometimes as long as four pages—still have a tendency to be mixed up chronologically, their order residing in what is happening to shape Peter's thinking and personality. Now, however, Bailey lingers so lovingly on Peter's childhood years—despite the mental cruelty they involve, the being acquainted at too young an age with death—that we are far through the novel when we realise that the author is far from being far through Peter's life. In order to avoid the cardinal error of writing a long novel, Bailey then puts on the screws again, condensing Peter's adult life into savagely brief episodes—his marriage is treated with a brevity which does not fall short of contempt—and finally polishing Peter off, thus leaving an actor friend to tie up the loose ends in less than five (excellently written) pages of six résumés, one per main character. Yet Peter is by then a father, old enough to have a son he last sees with 'head shaved; face decorated with streaks of white paint; dressed in a saffron robe and sandals—selling *Back to the Godhead* in Oxford Street'—a sight fit to drive far more stable-minded fathers than Peter to suicide. It ought not to work. But it does. In fact, Bailey even finds room to insert a number of parodies and pastiche pieces—a ludicrous producer's new angle on *Hamlet,* buttocks jerking away on Mother Gertrude's bed; lines from a verse-play, a kind of Fryed Eliot; poems by a Sister Evangeline; and the unreadable works of F Leonard Cottie, whose titles are more than enough.

How does he do it? How does he manage to cram a life into one hundred and eighty-odd pages, an account which at times—in the childhood scenes—gives one the sensation of being immersed in a six hundred and eighty page novel by Dickens or one rather less than that size by Laurence Sterne? . . . Bailey accomplishes it by means of the pregnant sentence. Every one of his seems charged with meaning (even the 'More warmth' one I quoted above from ***A Distant Likeness***). The ones that aren't so charged he has already chucked out—so each one left in makes its impact. Poking fun at David Storey, Bailey mentions a terrible play Peter acted in, entitled *The Construction:* 'a dramatic entertainment—it will be remembered by those who endured it—in which a council house is built, brick by brick, on stage'. He himself employs the same technique, building his novels sentence by sentence, but there is no question of 'endurance' for the reader. For one thing, because of his tragic view of human imperfection he remains a humorist and also an actor who exists by the grace of dialogue and eccentric characters. Everything here is taut and exciting, because everything is charged with intelligence and wit, and with, oh God, yes, with feeling. Thinking of his dead, Peter remarks of his father and his Aunt Hilda, both unlucky in love: 'She had cried out for Edward. My father had cried out for Alice. Silence, then darkness, had answered them.' This is what this novel, indeed all Bailey's work, is about: people answering other people with silence. The denial of human fellowship, of love. All through his childhood, Peter appeals surreptitiously to his mother for one kindly response, for one sign of human solidarity. He gets none. 'Why, mother?' 'That's the twenty-fifth letter'. All through, she addresses him as 'You', refusing to use his name.

Which brings me to end this sadly inadequate account of a sad, funny book by saying that the portrait of Peter's mother (all 'mouth and trousers') is the finest achievement in a novel which contains several memorable portraits—of the grandmother, of a fellow-actor, and of Dr F Leonard Cottie, physician-author of books fated to be used as door-stops. It is he who provides the novel's final irony, for long after his death his awful memoirs are serialised on television and earn and earn. By then, however, his heiress 'cannot appreciate her wealth since—at the age of ninety-seven—she is all but gaga in a Home'. (pp. 62-3)

James Brockway, "Memento Mori," in Books and Bookmen *Vol. 23, No. 2, November, 1977, pp. 62-3.*

NICHOLAS SHRIMPTON

Old Soldiers [is] a book of delicate and elusive design which conceals its central interest for more than half its length. One does need to say more, a great deal more, if the cunning processes of distillation here at work are to be properly saluted.

Bailey's hero, Victor Harker, is a recently widowed former bank-manager who returns to his native London after 50 years away. He does not like the city, but he cannot bear the memories of his wife which their home now forces on him. So, in his brisk old-soldierly way, he marches out of King's Cross Station to seek distraction and repose.

Such a scenario combines madness with a faint hint of the grotesque, and the latter element is powerfully reinforced by Harker's first metropolitan encounter. Gazing up into the dome of St Paul's, he is approached by a free-lance tourist guide called Harold Standish. Harker realises immediately that Standish is a fraud. But he is alone in London and the two men share some memories of the first world war. They agree to meet for dinner.

What Harker cannot realise is the bizarre extent of Standish's fraudulence. He is not, in the traditional sense, a con-man. But he does rotate three distinct personalities, changing his clothes and dentures in the lavatories of London's railway terminals. For a few days at a time he will be Captain Standish and live in an old flame's guest house near Victoria Station. Then he will transform himself into Tommy, a pious tramp much cherished by the female superintendent of an East End mission hall. Finally he will don sandals and purple fedora to become Julian Borrow, an unpublished poet with a room in Islington and a stand at Hyde Park Corner. Set against the conventional dignity of Vincent Harker, this exotic creation offers a rich and obvious vein of eccentric humour.

For its first three chapters ***Old Soldiers*** seems precisely that, a polished comic automation fuelled by Spirit of Ealing and Essence of Pickwick. Only slowly does it become clear that this is actually something quite different. Beneath his jocular surface Paul Bailey is offering a meditation upon mortality and he conducts it, discreetly but appropriately, in a setting of tombs. Harker's wanderings are not random. He visits his parents' grave, in what I take to be Tower Hamlets Cemetery, and then tours Wren's City churches. His reconciliation with his wife's death, in other words, is achieved by the sustained contemplation of a series of funeral monuments. Standish's frantic progress from one personality to another is equally deliberate. He is in flight from death, as he has been ever since a moment of military panic in 1916, and seeks to evade in one identity what might at any time seize him in another.

I was not entirely persuaded by Paul Bailey's literal explanation of how Standish's protean obsession began. But in other respects this is a marvellously skilful book, deftly constructed and full of incidental delights. (pp. 324-25)

Nicholas Shrimpton, "Flight from Death," in New Statesman, *Vol. 99, No. 2554, January 29, 1980, pp. 324-25.*

ELAINE FEINSTEIN

Intimations of mortality are among the most sobering of human reflections; and to bring us into the presence of the dead and dying and then, without the slightest precautionary numbing of ordinary emotions, bewilder us into laughter is a remarkably difficult manoeuvre. Paul Bailey's [***Old Soldiers***], however, does just this, and gently, without a taint of black farce. Victor Harker, retired and recently widowed, is on a visit to London (which he hates) in flight from memories of domestic happiness in Newcastle. London is no solace to him. On the contrary, it wakes all the bitterness of years long past: dreams of his dead father's whining and weakness and "Longing to cease being Billy Harker" and, more persistently, visions of friends blown to pieces in the First World War. Worst of all, because he is lonely, and Captain Hal Standish can claim to be an old soldier of the same generation, Victor finds himself entangled with a man he knows is a sham. And Standish takes his place at the surreal periphery of Victor's London experience; in so far, that is, as Hal Standish himself can be said to have an existence at all. For he is only one of three interlocking impostures linked by the Euston Left Luggage Lockers where the appurtenances of each rôle are stashed in turn. . . . Each part brings its own perks, but who precisely sits concealed behind these three bizarre faces?

Victor Harker, conned into taking whoever-it-may-be in his Standish incarnation for an expensive meal, grows more and more irritated at the crudity of the disguise, and although he remains icily polite through grotesque behaviour, can hardly wait to be rid of him. And yet as the book moves to its close, it turns out that the two men have unexpected ghosts in common.

Elaine Feinstein, in a review of "Old Soldiers," in The Times, *London, February 28, 1980, p. 13.*

PETER LEWIS

In ***Old Soldiers,*** his fifth novel and his most completely satisfying one since ***At the Jerusalem,*** Bailey returns to the subject of old age and concentrates on two sharply contrasting men in their seventies, both with unforgettable memories of the First World War. The retired banker, Victor Harker, and the bizarre chameleon, Eric Talbot, whose real identity is revealed only at the end, are old soldiers in the metaphorical sense, too, although beneath their superbly maintained facades both are essentially vulnerable and fragile. Bailey's two-word title manages to be both ambiguous and ironic.

The narrative turns on the chance encounter of the two old men in St Paul's Cathedral. The respectable, conventional, superficially dry-as-dust Victor, whose much younger wife has recently died, returns to London after more than fifty years in Newcastle so as to escape from an almost unendurable loneliness and numerous associations of past contentment. Even the hated London of his childhood seems preferable to the city where at the age of forty he unexpectedly found happiness with a woman he loved but did not expect to love him. The man he meets in London has been running away from reality for much longer—since the First World War in fact—and has concealed his self behind three different personas: the military man, the tramp, the bohemian poet.

In many ways the two men are opposites and do not even like each other, yet they are drawn together because each supplies a crucial need for the other. To his astonishment, the discreet, guarded Victor finds himself talking freely about his life, marriage and grief to a man he does not trust at all, while Eric finally reveals his true self and his long-buried secret to Victor, thus liberating himself from his past and from his masks; having done so, he cannot continue living since he has effectively murdered his three fabricated selves, and like his father before him he commits suicide. There is something of Conrad's Lord Jim in Eric, a man who has a romantic and heroic conception of himself and who fails at the moment of crisis so that his subsequent life is an attempt to hide from the consequences of his failure. Yet this side of Eric is not revealed until the end of the novel, and then only cryptically.

Another literary parallel that tentatively suggests itself is *Mrs Dalloway,* in which two very different characters briefly cut across each other's paths in London, one of whom, a shell-shocked First World War victim, commits suicide, while the respectable Clarissa Dalloway discovers an unlikely affinity between herself and the disorientated Septimus Warren-Smith. ***Old Soldiers*** is not derivative, but the way in which Bailey traces the independent existences of his two central characters during the short time-span of the novel is reminiscent of Virginia Woolf's treatment of her two principal figures. Victor and Eric have more contact and more impact on each other than Clarissa and Septimus, but for much of the novel Bailey shows them apart, not together, and he therefore interweaves two narrative strands between their initial meeting at the opening and their second proper encounter two thirds of the way through the book. One strand follows Eric's life with its radical transformations and its revelations of three totally different life-styles strangely embodied in this one man. The other strand follows Victor through a chain of memories, dreams, nightmares and dashed hopes as he wanders in London, revisiting places associated with his childhood.

Like several of Bailey's novels, ***Old Soldiers*** is characterized by extreme compression in an attempt to produce great poetic intensity. . . . After the relatively expansive fourth novel ***Peter Smart's Confessions*** (1977), ***Old Soldiers*** marks a return to the brevity and imagistic density of ***A Distant Likeness,*** but without the sense of strain and overpurification which somewhat marred that highly ambitious novel. ***Old Soldiers*** may not be aspiring so high, but it is more consistently successful. On the first page, for example, Bailey succinctly communicates a great deal of information about Victor, including an important flashback, as well as transporting him from a train arriving at King's Cross to his London hotel. Many novelists would need a chapter, not a page, to accomplish so much. And several chapters could have replaced the space between the penultimate sentence and the final one abruptly announcing Victor's death. Bailey's bold leap is, however, absolutely right and absolutely chilling. He is the least prosy of prose writers, and for all his avoidance of obvious poetic effects he is one of the most genuinely poetic of our novelists.

Bailey's writing is marked by elision, producing an effect that can resemble collage but without the randomness usually associated with the technique. The control is evident in the way in which every detail, even the seemingly inconsequential one, is made to count, often preparing for further instances that add up to a pattern of significance. . . . Bailey makes even more extensive use than in ***Peter Smart's Confessions*** of repeated words and phrases, which gradually become loaded with implications: "dust" is linked with Victor; whether the cognac glass is warmed or unwarmed becomes significant; and the words "glorious future" on the last page are especially ironic in the light, of "the bright future . . . bright past" of the first page.

Yet Bailey's symbolist methods, although obvious, are far from being ostentatious or indulgent. Even the noise of the wind in the trees, which towards the end of the novel is repeatedly linked with the death-rattle and so with Eric's fear of death as he senses its imminence, is not excessively exploited, although it could easily degenerate into melodrama. . . . Bailey is careful not to overdo such devices, but there is certainly a danger they will become mannerisms if allowed to proliferate any further.

It goes without saying that Bailey's vision is pessimistic, but there is a world of difference between his Conradian pessimism and the facile absurdism with which we have been inundated since the heyday of Existentialism. Bailey once said of Conrad that no novelist depicts so well the essential isolation of human beings, the way in which we all live alone and die alone; and this is what Bailey also excels in. He exposes the vulnerable core at the heart of all individuals, the strategies by which people try to disguise their vulnerability and to protect themselves from the daily assault of reality, including the inevitability of death.

Among the reasons why Bailey writes about old people, and writes about them so well, is that he recognizes how especially exposed they are and how they cannot take refuge in a fantasy world nearly so easily as the young. Eric is such an extraordinary creation because he is an old man still trapped in the fantasy he established for himself when young. Yet if Bailey peels away the deceptions and self-deceptions, the masks and pretences, by which his characters live, he does so with enormous sympathy for their predicament. "Compassion" is an easily spoken word, especially by critics, but it is entirely appropriate to use it about Bailey's presentation of his characters. . . .

Yet there are ways in which Bailey's very restraint works against such positives. To achieve intensity he does make sacrifices, and in deliberately eschewing the richness of character and detail of the traditional realistic novel he is also abandoning possibilities of warmth. He might even be leaving himself open to the charge that he is selling human experience short. Bleakness is certainly not all in Bailey, although he has been accused of this, but the reticence and formal concision of this book could give that impression. The Dickensian side of his considerable talent, which was so evident in ***Peter Smart's Confessions*** and made the first half of that novel a new departure for him, is much more muted here, although ***Old Soldiers*** is not lacking in humour.

Peter Lewis, "In the Dry Season of Age," in The Times Literary Supplement, *No. 4014, February 29, 1980, p. 228.*

FAY WELDON

There is a kind of casual magic in Paul Bailey's prose: a silkiness of effect that is hard to define or analyse. I think he is one of our very best male novelists. He writes short sentences, short paragraphs, short books: they wring the heart; let me quote:

> "Prayers were said at the Mission for the soul of Tommy, who had disappeared, as many of Sergeant Marybeth's strays had done. How could people vanish so? It was a constant mystery. It was as if they dug holes in the earth and tunnelled themselves out of sight."

Tommy, the tramp in Paul Bailey's ***Old Soldiers,*** is the same as Captain Hal Standish is the same as Julian Borrow the poet: between them a man of action who lost his childhood at the battle of Somme, and spent a lifetime since inventing other people. Paul Bailey deals with the pain of experience with a kind of sleight of hand, juggling the pain against the pleasure of feeling it. Writing novels is more, of course, than the filing of bad dreams: it is an act of generosity, the handing over of experience from one to the many. The ability to conceive of the sheer dreadfulness of the dream, and transmute it into pleasure for the benefit of others, is a rare quality, and one that always glitters and shines through Paul Bailey's work. (p. 442)

Fay Weldon, in a review of "Old Soldiers," in Punch *Vol. 278, No. 7273, March 12, 1980, pp. 441-42.*

VICTORIA GLENDINNING

One day in 1950, when Gabriel is 12, his pretty young mother leaves a fish pie ready for supper, and goes out. She does not come back. This is every child's nightmare; and ***Gabriel's Lament,*** Paul Bailey's most complex novel so far, seems to me a sad story, though it can be read as a funny one. It's a book worth reading twice. Its point is that the hells of grief and shame and lost love are preferable to the grotesque pretences that people construct to deny them.

Gabriel is left with his old father, who prevaricates: Mummy is on holiday, or has telephoned while he was at school. Finally, he announces she has found a younger man and will never come back. Gabriel, doggedly expecting her home day after day, becomes disturbed and physically retarded, "my body expressing the grief my mind was unaware of". Not until he is middle-aged does Mummy stop haunting him when, after a breakdown, he opens the box that was his father's only legacy and learns the truth.

Then, Gabriel writes his life-story, this "lament". He knows now what happened to Mummy but we don't, until the end. The cleverest writing here is in the way Bailey directs the reader's imagination (but not romantic Gabriel's) into horrid assumptions about the "terrible knowledge" about her fate that Gabriel's father conceals.

The novel stands or falls on the figure of Father. Gabriel's breakdown happens in America, where he is lecturing on itinerant preachers, about whom he has written a book that has made him rich. It is because of his father that he is fascinated by cranks and visionaries, fantasists, fanatics, and charlatans. . . . He is "the great Dissimulator", hiding pitiful truths about his wife and his own secret shames behind a wordy barrage of boasts, anecdotes, cruel facetiousness, and hectoring homilies. . . .

This is a book packed with "characters", neurotics and obsessional talkers. It is touch-and-go whether Father himself is a great comic creation or a bore, just as it is touch-and-go whether Gabriel is a seeker after love, truth, and "the commonplace history of life as it is lived", or just a bit of a wimp. But the points are forcefully made, and the novel, like all Paul Bailey's books, is most cunningly constructed. His writing is calm and fastidious even when his subject matter is anything but.

Victoria Glendinning, "Searching for Mummy," in The Times, *London, September 25, 1986, p. 14.*

GALEN STRAWSON

Gabriel Harvey is a man alone in a room in a fine house in Chiswick. He is writing a lament, writing down his life in order to be able to understand it—or simply stand it. He uses all his wit and clarity, and having a great deal of both, he succeeds as well as anyone could. The by-product of his solitary therapy is an impressive if overlong novel, a book freighted with suppressed emotional intensity. It is a record of suffering, suffering at first concealed for three decades; then engulfed in a greater grief; and finally calmed in the backlash of moral reversal.

Gabriel's Lament is a study in deferred mortification. At bottom it is a tale of two snobs and their victim. But there is a great deal not to say about it in a review, since it depends for its final effect on the misapprehensions it creates. It begins in 1949, when Gabriel Harvey is twelve, living in London in a tiny rented terrace house south of the river. His mother Amy is thirty-one, his affectionate, cantankerous father, Oswald, sixty-six. Amy works to support them. Oswald curses and pontificates, and holds court in The Prodigal's Return.

And then everything changes. Oswald inherits a lot of money from a baronet he once served. (Why? One's suspicions are finally confirmed.) He buys a villa in Clapham. His wife [Amy] must no longer work. And she must have a kitchen "that Escoffier himself would be proud of". . . .

Amy hates this change. (Why does she hate it so much? One finds out only at the end.) She says that Escoffier is welcome to the kitchen, and feels she is losing touch with her old husband. And so she leaves for a short holiday, which she prolongs—and then prolongs. She cleans behind Gabriel's ears, dispatches him briskly to school on February 1, 1950, and he never sees her again.

Gabriel is confident. She will certainly come home for his birthday in March; or at least for her own. He waits in his love and in his hope, in the beginnings of his new religious faith—that one day she will come. Meanwhile anxiety goes to work in one of its favourite locations. He starts wetting his bed. He becomes young "Piss-a-bed", goaded by his increasingly irritable father, humiliated by a rubber sheet. His outstanding schoolwork goes to pieces. . . .

Five years later he finally leaves home; he escapes his father at the age of seventeen, working first as a letter-sorter at Mount Pleasant, then for nine years as a factotum skivvy in the Jerusalem, a home for the elderly and dying (the Jerusalem to which Paul Bailey devoted a whole short novel [***At the Jerusalem***] in 1967), then in an ironmonger's shop. He is a small and very "pretty" man with a passion for music. At twenty-seven he has no need to shave. He has no sexual life. He buys a Moygashel frock like his mother's, and wears it in her memory on her birthdays, sitting in perfect quiet, alone in his room. . . .

In his spare time he writes a book called *Lords of Light* about a series of preachers, mostly itinerant, some charlatans, some sincere, some mad, some inspired. After twenty rejections, an obscure publisher takes it on, Hollywood turns part of it into a highly successful item of inspirational *schlock* called *Mersey Messiah,* and Gabriel ends up well off.

That's the shilling life—and a bit more. What it leaves out is most of the book: the people Gabriel meets as he moves to the lonely, crowded margin of 1950s and 1960s London, and becomes another eccentric human detail in a squalid boarding-house room, suffering the past that curls back in his parents' phrases. . . .

As Gabriel says, he keeps the company of talkers, porpoises in language. Bailey's ear is very good and is matched by his invention. He captures and creates a remarkable spectrum of idiolects, each with its own quirks and lapses, its own delicacies and metaphorical predilections, its own pattern of directness and indirectness and special modes of humour.

There is perhaps too much of this (the short story occupying pp 222-239 could be dropped from the novel without loss); there are moments when ***Gabriel's Lament*** risks becoming a kind of Emporium of Characters, a container for set pieces. And Bailey's characters are sometimes too informally unhesitating in their speech, too similar in their graphic aplomb, too precise to be wholly believable. But this is a very modest use of poetic licence; a fading vernacular of such richness deserves a dramatic record of this sort, so vivid with humour and charm in the grip of reality.

The biggest talker of them all is Gabriel's father, whom Gabriel continues to see only because it was his Swedenborgian aunt's last wish. Oswald is condemned to repartee, unable not to speak, a chippy British pub philosopher given to rumbustious tmesis with a single infix ("inbloodysatiable", "unbloody-slakable", "rehabloodybilitate"). . . .

And yet he mixes his streaming linguistic vulgarity and torrents of universal racial prejudice (Scots excepted) with unmistakable evidence of finer feeling and discernment; with witty, pungent images and a grandiose roaring coarseness that has nothing to do with vulgarity. . . .

He keeps it up until he is ninety-four and legless. And when he dies he leaves his son a box. And in the box Gabriel finds the multiplication of his suffering, a motive for suicide, and the first chance of emotional progress that he has had for thirty years. There is a time when he hates his father, and a time when he hates his mother. But most of the emotion in families is just intensity of feeling before it is anything else, intensity which shifts from light to dark without fixing finally in love or hate. And when both his parents are dead and known to be so, when the scales have settled in the slow balance of time, Gabriel finds that he still loves them both—as he did at the beginning, in the tiny terraced house south of the river.

Galen Strawson, "Cursèd and Loving," in The Times Literary Supplement, *No. 4356, September 26, 1986, p. 1058.*

HERMIONE LEE

> Comforters, dispensing balm—in jokes and ballads, in sketches and songs, in novelty acts as grotesque as they were macabre. Comforters with lived-in faces, singing of . . . a vast assortment of everyday scoundrels. Comforters, lightening the pain of the here-and-now with mockery—for they were veterans when it came to distress.

Paul Bailey's narrator, Gabriel Harvey, himself much distressed and in need of comfort, is speaking here, in typically plush and plaintive style, about the music-hall. It's a key to [***Gabriel's Lament***]. The music-hall is old London, seedy, cruel, humorous and Dickensian, Gabriel's refuge and inspiration. The music-hall is democratic: it acts out Gabriel's belief in the equality of all including the grotesques, the scoundrels and the distressed. And, as with this inventive, mannered, garrulous novel, whose playfulness labours to assuage a chronic sense of pain, the art of the music-hall is improvisation and impersonation.

Gabriel's leading impersonation, his 'star turn,' is his monstrous old father Oswald, raconteur, racist, bigot, bully, class-traitor and liar, who is 54 when his son is born and doesn't die until he's 93, with one leg gone. Oswald's sayings are—to excess—the book's *tour de force*. . . .

Not surprisingly, offensive Oswald is a lonely old sod, left by all three of his children and by his young third wife, Gabriel's 'beloved Mummy,' who walks out when Gabriel is 12. But the novel's grief is not Oswald's but Gabriel's, whose mourning for his mysteriously vanished Mummy, and hatred for his all-too-present father, take the casebook forms of bedwetting, self-soiling, stunted growth and wearing a dress in secret. Even his outbursts of hate against Oswald are hidden inside resentful, costive parentheses.

Gabriel is not an engaging narrator, but Paul Bailey's great strength is his sympathy for people who, in Oswald's terms, would be written off as deviants, social cripples disabled with oddness. . . . Like father and son, they are all damaged or bereaved, and hiding shameful secrets.

Gabriel's feeling for the 'commonplace history' of oddities finds expression in the history he writes of obscure 'cranks and visionaries,' which, thanks to a Hollywood adaptation (unconvincing, this), makes him rich and successful. But, aged 40, lecturing on his book to friendly Americans in Sorg, Minnesota, Gabriel has still to learn the truth about his mother, and to vanquish and understand his dead father. He does so, in the end, by writing his 'lament': an alternative to suicide. For all its loquacious indulgences and whiffs of the maudlin, this is a powerful study of bereavement as obsession and of the consolations of comic art.

Hermione Lee, "The Talking Wounded," in The Observer, *September 28, 1986, p. 27.*

FRANCIS KING

It is through ridicule that Gabriel in Paul Bailey's ***Gabriel's Lament*** cuts down his father Oswald, in revenge not merely for the mysterious loss of his mother but for innumerable humiliations callously inflicted. On the first page Gabriel, now in his forties, visits the nonagenarian Oswald on 'what I hoped would be his death-bed.' The interview terminates abruptly, still on the first page when Oswald, 'his hands . . . suddenly restless, pummelling the eiderdown', hisses: 'Signs of life, signs of life. Yes, there is definite activity below. I feel a turd worming its way out.' The incident reveals the dying man in an ignominious situation that, to Gabriel, can only be satisfying, since Oswald, in the past, has so often taunted him with his own adolescent bed-wetting. It is also symbolic of the actions of a man who has, in effect, been unable ever to refrain from shitting on those with whom he has come into contact.

But if, like Sir George Sitwell in Osbert's unfilial reminiscences of him, Oswald is presented as a monster, he is, also like Sir George, a monster who keeps one constantly amused, in a way that saints often fail to do. Raffish, philistine, bullying, disloyal, dishonest, a liar: Oswald has no redeeming quality, unless it be the cockiness with which his head persists in bobbing up above the waves that constantly threaten to close over it. To his son, while he is still growing up, he delivers a series of opinionated lectures, which provide the book with some lovely set-pieces. (p. 30)

The disappearance of Gabriel's mother, Amy, is the pivot of the book. Oswald keeps up a pretence to the boy that one day Amy—who, Oswald at first maintains, has taken herself off on a holiday—will come back to them. What in fact has happened to her is revealed only at the close, when Gabriel inherits from his father, as a sole legacy a box containing his mother's letters. At the nature of this revelation I guessed wrongly, imagining something far more melodramatic.

The book differs radically from Mr Bailey's five previous novels. . . . Whereas, the previous novels are spare, austere and essentially tragic, this one is rich, ebullient and essentially comic, as Gabriel moves on from 'Blenheim' to a series of dingy lodgings filled with colourful characters and to a series of deadly jobs redeemed by lively fellow employees. At one point, Gabriel describes one of the people whom he meets as 'another performer into whose play I find myself suddenly propelled.' There is a larger-than-life and therefore theatrical air about most of these people, grandiloquently, volubly and unashamedly revealing their eccentricities. This air suggests Priestley at his robustly humorous best.

I have a few quibbles. It seems to me unlikely that Gabriel's study of itinerant preachers *Lords of Light* would be bought by Hollywood for a movie, and even more unlikely that the proceeds would enable him to acquire a Georgian Thames-side house at Strand-on-the-Green. It also seems to me odd that Mr Bailey should be under the impression that 'clap' means syphilis. The word he wants is 'pox'. But the book had me laughing repeatedly at such splendid characters as Gabriel's first landlady, her hair present in everything she cooks or serves up, his fellow-lodger Countess Bolina, an impoverished white Russian, . . . and the inhabitants of the Jerusalem, the old people's home (there is a reverberation here from Mr Bailey's first novel ***At The Jerusalem***) at which Gabriel finds employment. Gabriel himself—a waiflike child-man, in constant search of the mother who abandoned him . . .—is, in contrast, a profoundly saddening character, even though his gallantry prevents him from being a sad one. . . . [***Gabriel's Lament***] is one of the half-dozen most enjoyable [novels] to have come my way this year. (p. 31)

Francis King, "Fathers and Sins," in The Spectator, *Vol. 257, No. 8256, October 4, 1986, pp. 30-1.*

Charles Baxter

1947-

American short story writer, poet, and critic.

In his two volumes of short stories, *Harmony of the World* (1984) and *Through the Safety Net* (1985), Baxter employs precise language and imagery and ironic humor to depict mundane characters whose identities are threatened by the underlying tensions in their lives. In the acclaimed story "Harmony of the World," for example, a competent but uninspired pianist is consistently frustrated in his attempts to fulfill his artistic ambitions due to his failure to recognize the discordant qualities in music and life. Several of Baxter's characters strive to achieve or maintain order and harmony in their existence but are demoralized by seemingly random chaotic events. Michiko Kakutani commented: "Just beneath the surface of [the real world] . . . , Mr. Baxter implies, lies another world impervious to the assaults of intelligence and human logic, and he gives his characters—and his readers—intimations of that world in quick, spinning glimpses of both beauty and danger."

(See also *Contemporary Authors,* Vols. 57-60.)

Photograph by Robert Chase. Courtesy of Charles Baxter.

FRANCOIS CAMOIN

[In ***Harmony of the World***] Baxter's prose is vigorous, lively and precise. Words and sentences wheel and turn with the certainty of a well-trained marching band. I read this collection in manuscript . . . , and it stood out from the other manuscripts I was reading—here was someone who knew what to do with the language. Here is the opening of **"Weights,"** a story about an unemployed young man who becomes obsessed with his own body:

> When Tobias slipped open his usual locker, he saw someone else's white sock inside, soaking wet. It smelled of sweat, or of living matter washed up by the ocean. Instead of picking it up and putting it on the floor, he moved down to the next locker, number fifty-eight. The Y didn't assign lockers, but Tobias thought of number fifty-six as his, territorially.

The rhythms are uncommon, harsh, eccentric; the narrative voice makes up the world as it goes along. Here is no Keplerian faith in the harmony of the world, or of the word, for that matter. "Territorially," when the sentence had already come to a conclusion: like a correction, an afterthought, a brassy note, more Bartok than Beethoven.

A world where discord rules. The title of the collection is ironic; the subject of [**"Harmony of the World"**] is Paul Hindemith's failed attempt to write an opera based on Kepler's life, inspired by Kepler's *De Harmonice Mundi,* in which the astronomer "set out to establish the correspondence between the laws of harmony and the disposition of planets in motion." The work is a failure; Hindemith's opera is a failure, as is the central character's attempt to forge a career as a concert pianist. If there's a point to the story, it's the impossibility of merging form and content, except through a touch of madness, which is, we are told, just what this narrator lacks.

Well, irony is a fashionable thing in contemporary fiction, perhaps because it's one of the few possible responses to a world in which harmony is not possible unless we cheat, ignore the pervading discords, spend our days listening, like some of Baxter's characters, to Percy Faith on the beautiful-music stations. Irony can be the easy thing, as easy as lyricism. Or it can, as in this collection of stories, be earned. If there is morality in fiction at all, it consists of this: the refusal to embrace form until it *becomes* inevitable. There are no easy effects here, just the hard narrow line of prose followed to a conclusion which becomes inevitable only after the story is finished. (pp. 355-56)

Francois Camoin, in a review of "Harmony of the World," in Western Humanities Review, *Vol. XXXVIII, No. 4, Winter, 1984, pp. 355-56.*

PERRY GLASSER

Charles Baxter does not write film software, though ***Harmony of the World,*** the sixth winner of the AWP [Associated Writing Programs] Award Series in Short Fiction, indeed exhibits the cinematic qualities of a documentary. Nearly all ten of these stories are written in short takes, motes of prose separated from each other by blank lines where we irresistibly mentally insert CUT TO. The style fights our sense of time and space; nevertheless we are left with a kind of pure narrative that moves as rapidly as film. As readers we compulsively supply the "narrative glue" that Baxter deliberately omits, and consequently reading Baxter becomes a rich experience, one that requires us to be active participants in the fiction, rather than passive members of an audience.

Baxter entertains us by the compassion and wisdom with which he draws characters so many of us know. In **"Xavier Speaking,"** Arthur and Carrie, who "read Fanon, Norman O. Brown, and Cleaver to each other . . . , listened to music, smoked first dope, then hash, then, sitting on the bank of the Mississippi River on the St. Paul side, dropped LSD," move to a farm in Wisconsin because, "Good dirt is a drug." Some years later, a Charles Manson-ish Vietnam vet, Xavier, shows up.

> "Sure, he's a psychopath," Carrie admitted.
>
> "Then why do you want to sleep with him?"
>
> She paused. "I want . . . to put my fingers on whatever is producing all that heat. I want to touch that furnace."
>
> "You'll be burned."
>
> "I'll be changed."

That lovely bit of dialogue floats alone, a discrete passage independent of description of time, place, or even notice of a facial expression. The stories proceed less by the accrual of detail than by the accrual of crucial moments, a cinematic technique that in print makes a very pleasing kind of magic. Baxter at his best, as in **"Harmony of the World," "A Short Course in Nietzschean Ethics," "Weights,"** and **"Xavier Speaking,"** flashes us through his characters' lives and creates stories that are engrossing and provocative. Unfortunately, some of Baxter's stories do not so much conclude as taper off. The short cinematic takes work less well in **"Horace and Margaret's Fifty-second"** or **"The Would-be Father,"** because these otherwise satisfactory stories end not with action or a gesture, but with a character meditating on the perceived world. It is as though entire stories had been constructed to reach a devastating culminating image, but in fact the image is a static lifeless abstraction. Despite that evenness, ***Harmony of the World*** deserves a wide readership. (pp. 63-4)

Perry Glasser, "Literary Intimacy," in The North American Review, *Vol. 269, No. 3, September, 1984, pp. 63-5.*

W. C. HAMLIN

No harmony here—not in [***Harmony of the World***], not in these stories—but there is a world of discord and pain and terror. Actually what Baxter has done is this: he has combined his considerable talent, superb craftsmanship, and devilish humor to create ten wonderful horror stories. The thread of humor is important in that it makes bearable the experience of viewing the people in his stories as they, one by one, become victims of the unaccountable pranks of the universe. Baxter employs a lean, no-frills style; he has a fine ear for dialogue; he knows the effectiveness of precise detail and fresh imagery. He is a good writer, and ***Harmony of the World*** is recommended for all those addicted to the short story.

W. C. Hamlin, in a review of "Harmony of the World: Stories," in Choice, *Vol. 22, No. 2, October, 1984, p. 265.*

PUBLISHERS WEEKLY

[In the eleven stories collected in ***Through the Safety Net***], Baxter reveals bright flashes of unmistakable talent, but the collection is flawed by a fondness for excessive detail, implausible turns and mere trickiness. In [**"Stained Glass"**], when Donna decides the "relationship" has run its course, Bobby goes wild. He sends roses and chocolates, pleads, behaves strangely. She changes the phone number, the locks. In desperation, Bobby sends her an image he has made of her on stained glass—and we are given to understand that, at last moved by his adoration, Donna will fly into his arms. We are not convinced. . . . Baxter's explorations of middle-class characters in danger-fraught situations have a zany insanity that some may find engaging.

A review of "Through the Safety Net," in Publishers Weekly, *Vol. 227, No. 21, May 24, 1985, p. 63.*

MICHIKO KAKUTANI

[Mr. Baxter's characters in ***Through the Safety Net***] are afraid of falling, afraid that the flimsy constructions of love and art that they have built against the dark outside will suddenly collapse. Evil is ordinary, as Auden once observed, and disaster always seems to take place while "someone else is eating or opening a window or just walking dully along." Indeed, the precautions that Mr. Baxter's characters take—they check the doors and windows at night, they lock the kitchen cabinets so their children won't eat the ElectraSol, drink decaffeinated coffee and wear seat belts when they drive—prove ineffectual in warding off the unexpected perils of daily life: "falls from ladders while putting up storm windows, falls on icy sidewalks, traffic accidents, drownings in four feet of water, heart attacks, strokes, cancers.". . .

Just beneath the surface of "the real world that made Plato so unhappy," Mr. Baxter implies, lies another world impervious to the assaults of intelligence and human logic, and he gives his characters—and his readers—intimations of that world in quick, spinning glimpses of both beauty and danger. The lovely angels that a failed doctoral student meets in his drunken dreams; the monster with three green eyes and a cigar that haunts a child's nightmares; the hideous face, frozen in an Edvard Munch-like scream, that unwittingly appears in a Sunday painter's pretty nature scene—all are reminders that the nicely ordered domestic world of name-brand household products, piano finger exercises and Scrabble games is also a highly precarious and provisional one, that what we love and know is subject to slippery accidents of luck and fate.

An extraordinarily limber writer, Mr. Baxter makes his characters' fears palpable to the reader by slowly drawing us into their day-to-day routines and making us see things through their eyes. Although one story (**"Media Event"**), narrated by a desperate publicity-seeker, reads like a creative-writing exercise in the use of point of view, and another (**"Stained Glass"**) features a pair of oddly caricatured lovers, most of the tales in this volume attest, elegantly and succinctly, to Mr. Baxter's gift of sympathy, his ability to write from inside his characters' hearts and minds.

He is adept not only at portraying them in extremis—coping with a death in the family, with the breakup of a relationship—but also at delineating the texture of their daily lives; the incalculable shifts, moment to moment, of their emotions; their tendency to turn romance into negotiation, their deeper yearnings for connection. One story, **"A Late Sunday Afternoon by the Huron"**—which recalls Stephen Sondheim's musical *Sunday in the Park With George*—simply works an improvisation on Delmore Schwartz's poem "Seurat's Sunday Afternoon Along the Seine" (itself an improvisation on the painter's famous canvas), to create a shimmering, impressionistic picture of a small Michigan community enjoying itself at the park, on "the day of forgiveness."

Many of Mr. Baxter's characters happen to be members of the "Big Chill" generation—they drink low-caffeine cola, listen to jazz on tape decks in their cars and talk about different "neurotic styles," "meaningful work" and the way the "country is falling into the hands of the rich and stupid." Many have eschewed the more conventional, upscale lives espoused by their parents and wives, choosing instead to teach high school in a small town, work on a doctorate on an obscure subject, or hole up in a cabin to write. But what they refer to, tongue-in-cheek, as their "idealism" often turns out to be more a case of aimlessness or disaffection—an unwillingness to grow up.

"In any university town," writes Mr. Baxter,

> there are hundreds of men like Harrelson, out late at night buying pizzas, sitting at bars sipping their beers quietly, or roaming the streets in their old clunkers. They are all afraid of going home, afraid of looking again at the sheets of clean typewriter paper and the notebooks bare of written thought. They are afraid of facing again their sullen wives and lovers, their tattered and noisy children, if they have any. Against the odds, they refuse to succeed.

It is one of Mr. Baxter's achievements in this fine collection that he refuses to simply turn Harrelson—or for that matter, any of his characters—into a representative figure; that he instead finds in the ordinary, yet altogether peculiar, facts of his life, broader and more resonant echoes.

Michiko Kakutani, in a review of "Through the Safety Net," in The New York Times, *Section III, June 26, 1985, p. 23.*

ROBERT MURRAY DAVIS

None of the stories in [Charles Baxter's ***Harmony of the World*** or William Ferguson's *Freedom and Other Fictions*] reaches the metafictional fringe, but all come with the proper credentials for serious academic fiction. Baxter and Ferguson are professors; . . . and Baxter's is "the first-place winner of the sixth annual AWP . . . Award Series in Short Fiction." Baxter's title story was chosen for a Pushcart Prize volume and for *Best American Short Stories 1982*. . . . (p. 358)

Charles Baxter finds only terror and confusion in old age, and he finds little consolation in any kind of process or ritual. These can be stays against madness and violence, as is the manic workouts in **"Weights"** or the anonymous telephone calls to strangers in **"The Crank"** or the faked horoscopes in **"The Would-Be-Father,"** but the violence is suppressed rather than contained or dissipated, and the characters know that what they would deny inside them will break loose. Because he begins with real or readily imaginable situations, his stories are more convincing and more disturbing than those by Ferguson, which depend on a terror that is largely literary.

Even when Baxter's material derives from research rather than from experience, it is carefully integrated into the story. **"Harmony of the World"** is, like [Ferguson's] "Morrissey," about a musician who fails because he lacks the passion or madness required. Unlike Morrissey, however, the unnamed narrator has a past. He leaves his small and complacent Ohio town, where playing too well "would have been faintly antisocial," for music school, where he is forced to recognize his lack of passion or fanaticism by the brutal kindness of a teacher. He takes a job as a not too dishonest music critic in a medium-sized town and becomes fascinated with Hindemith's "Harmony of the World," which is to be performed in his "anonymous city," at the same time that he becomes accompanist for and lover of an amateur singer whose lack of control makes him wince. The affair and the research progress at the same time, and after the failure of the symphony and of the vocal concert, the narrator tries to jolt his lover as he had been jolted by his teacher into realizing shortcomings and abandoning futile pursuit of a career. Seeking order as Hindemith did, with conviction but without passion, he succeeds only in alienating his lover and discovering his own sterility, seeing, as Hindemith insisted that he saw, "doubles and reflections and wave motion everywhere. There is symmetry, harmony, after all"—in life as well as in music. But the realization does him no good; he can only liken himself to Dante's souls in limbo. . . . Among the obvious differences between Baxter's story and "Morrissey" are the character's knowledge of his plight and of his responsibility for it; his fatal attempt to use—in imitation and stubbornness rather than in passion and fanaticism—the lesson given by his master; and the return, in spirit if not in body, to the small town whose deadness he feared and whose minor graces he could not learn. There is a motivation, a progression, and a structure to the story which neither "Morrissey" nor any of Ferguson's other stories have.

If one has to choose, then, Baxter rather than Ferguson because he observes more sharply; because he depends less upon mere writing; and because by any standard he is a very talented writer. (pp. 359-60)

Robert Murray Davis, in a review of "Harmony of the World," in Studies in Short Fiction, *Vol. 22, No. 3, Summer, 1985, pp. 358-60.*

RICHARD EDER

The last story in **[*Through the Safety Net*], "A Late Sunday Afternoon by the Huron,"** records moment by moment the activities of a dozen picnickers spending the day in a Michigan community park.

A family eats and minds its children. A few young men, just out of school and starting factory jobs, drink beer and horse around. A couple make love behind the trees. Everything is meticulously normal and made oppressive by the unsparing detail of the narrative. It is lab notes of an experiment to drain the oxygen out of a human setting.

Charles Baxter finds in his characters nothing but the clay of which they're made. In Genesis, God blew on the clay. For Baxter, modern life sucks that breath away. "What a relief it is, sometimes, not to have to tell a story about these people," he writes in one of his picnic lab notes.

We sense his refusal all through **"Late Sunday,"** and it quite takes our attention away from its inert characters. It is like hearing someone tell a story in a heavy stammer, and suddenly realizing, while trying to hear beyond the stammer, that it is not natural but deliberate.

Baxter, like a number of other contemporary short-story writers, writes about the anomie of our life. Listlessness pervades the world. Raymond Carver, at his best, transcends such listlessness by the energy of his art; Frederick Barthelme, by the skillful and insidious starvation of his narrative.

Even when presented most artfully, listlessness is a fragile subject. It is something like working a nearly worked-out mine. Baxter's solution—except in the last story, where he resigns—is to insert a touch of melodrama, of extremity into his plots and emotions. The author gives his receding characters an extra kick downhill. . . .

In **"Surprised by Joy,"** a couple are devastated by the death of their 3-year-old daughter, graphically and pitifully recounted. The wife gradually heals; the husband clings to mourning, and their divergence is like a second death. . . .

The best of the stories is **"Saul and Patsy Are Getting Comfortable in Michigan."** A young couple from Chicago move to a small Michigan town to get away from the urban rat race; and he becomes a teacher in the local high school. The story is a delicate and ferocious tale of estrangement. Hemmed in by the prairie distances, they huddle together playing a lot of Scrabble and making a lot of love just to keep out the cold.

They tell themselves that they like peace and quiet and the "indifference" of neighbors who are friendly enough, but lack the urban compulsion for intimacy. But things gnaw at them. The husband, who is Jewish, construes all kinds of suspicions out of his barber's remark that his hair is kinky; and out of a glaring neighbor, who turns out to have Alzheimer's disease. Finally, monotony languishes them; driving home from a party, he falls asleep at the wheel. There is a shivering sense of menace and despair throughout the story, and Baxter's description of the prairie car wreck is masterful. . . .

There is terror here; and once in a while, in the other stories, there is a similar flash of emotion rendered with a chill precision that makes it memorable. Mostly, though, Baxter doesn't go beyond establishing the smog in which his characters move, and he uses a kind of white light upon it that, instead of penetrating it, magnifies it.

Richard Eder, in a review of "Through the Safety Net," in Los Angeles Times Book Review, *August 11, 1985, p. 7.*

RON HANSEN

[*Through the Safety Net*] opens with a harrowing and knowing story about a couple splitting up. It ought to have been simple: Donna would point out that "this *thing,* their relationship, wasn't going anywhere," and Bobby would give her up. Instead, Donna finds roses dropped at her door, boxes of chocolates placed on her desk at work, daily pleas and complaints in her mailbox, Bobby staring up at her from the apartment courtyard when she opens the living room curtains. **"Stained Glass"** is about the compelling nature of worship and mad persistence. Bobby's only appeal is his overemphatic passion, but in a plain world of the predictable and commonplace, passion is irresistible.

With **"Media Event"** Mr. Baxter ups the ante, creating a powerful, arresting written testament of a psychopath who believes "there is only one story in America, and that is the story of how to become famous.". . .

Of the 11 stories in ***Through the Safety Net,*** eight have to do with outsiders and interlopers, with people estranged from life. One couple is incapacitated by the death of their child; a perpetual graduate student bumps his way through "the real world that made Plato so unhappy"; a real estate developer takes up painting and is surprised to learn he has put a ghost in a green pasture, a screaming man in the Minnehaha Creek, and promptly gives up his attempts at art and its intimations of mortality.

Possibly the best story in the book explores a 5-year-old's complex reactions to his grandmother's dying. **"Talk Show"** could have been precious, sentimental or overly shrewd, but craftsmanship and discipline have made it as accurate a depiction of a complicated, passionate and deeply puzzled little boy as I've seen since J. D. Salinger's "Teddy."

Mr. Baxter's stories are intelligent, original, gracefully written, always moving, frequently funny and—that rarest of compliments—wise.

Ron Hansen, "Web-footed Babies and People in Extremis," in The New York Times Book Review, *August 25, 1985, p. 18.*

JOHN SAARI

The safety net Baxter writes about in his second collection of short stories **[*Through the Safety Net*]** is psychological and its failure inescapable—nothing can prevent one from falling through it. He repeatedly intertwines doubt and belief, revealing the difficulty of ascertaining truth. Many of the stories are set in Michigan, and the characters have a recognizable familiarity but are free of the trendy Yuppie values found in the *New Yorker*.

To summarize a philosophical message from these stories is to do them a disservice—their meanings are pleasingly ambiguous. But to describe Baxter as a casual nihilist is to ignore the fluid beauty of his style. He writes about a world of chance, risk, and unexpected death. His stories are emotionally unsettling and mentally jarring.

At a time when children have just about disappeared from fiction or exist as obnoxious adults in little bodies, Baxter writes about them with sensitivity and perception. Louie, a small boy in **"Talk Show,"** spends his time recording his daily experiences on tape and comes to learn about death when his grandmother gets cancer. He speaks into the mike: "This is the talk show for today. How is Grandma? She's not worse, she's not better, she's dead."

Many writers today feel no depth of compassion for their characters. Baxter, in contrast, is adept at portraying his characters as human beings, even when some of them are not the best examples. Two stories, **"Winter Journey"** and **"The Eleventh Floor,"** rival the best of John Cheever at catching flawed but fascinating men at the edge of disaster.

John Saari, in a review of "Through the Safety Net," in The Antioch Review, *Vol. 43, No. 4, Fall, 1985, p. 498.*

Alan Bennett

1934-

English dramatist, scriptwriter, and nonfiction writer.

Bennett first gained recognition, along with Jonathan Miller, Peter Cook, and Dudley Moore, as a member of the English comedy revue *Beyond the Fringe* (1960). Noted for its revolutionary approach to traditional music-hall shows, *Beyond the Fringe* featured extended sketches and topical humor inspired by the work of such socially conscious American comedians as Lenny Bruce and Mort Sahl. Much of Bennett's work as a dramatist retains the wit of *Beyond the Fringe* but focuses upon what he perceives to be the decline of British culture since World War II. Bennett's plays reveal his talent for extravagant wordplay, including puns, malapropisms, and litotes.

Bennett was a lecturer in medieval history at Oxford University when he was asked to join the cast of *Beyond the Fringe*. Unusual for its time in that it presented an irreverent English outlook on nuclear holocaust, the cold war, and religion, *Beyond the Fringe* enjoyed enormous success both in England and the United States. Bennett's first play, *Forty Years On* (1968), resembles *Beyond the Fringe* in structure but differs in its nostalgic tone. Set in a boy's school that serves as an allegorical representation of contemporary England, *Forty Years On* revolves around the school's departing headmaster and his younger, more progressive replacement. *Forty Years On* also includes a variety show presented by the school's students which parodies such literary figures as Oscar Wilde and Virginia Woolf. In *Getting On* (1971), Bennett portrays a curmudgeonly member of Parliament who expresses his disenchantment with post-World War II British culture through scathing wit and adherence to traditional values. *Habeas Corpus* (1973) is a farce of English sexual attitudes involving an adulterous doctor and his lascivious wife. The plot of *The Old Country* (1977) centers on a traitorous British diplomat and his wife who have defected to the Soviet Union. The couple, who have retained their British mannerisms, receive visitors from Cambridge who convince them to return to an England they will no longer recognize. In similar fashion, *Enjoy* (1980) depicts an English family who live in the last remaining home of a neighborhood under demolition. In his recent work, *Kafka's Dick* (1986), Bennett satirizes literary biographers, whom he portrays as more interested in biographical trivia than in the writings of an author. This play concerns Franz Kafka, who, with his father and his executor, materializes in the home of a contemporary insurance agent. Anxious to stake a literary reputation, the opportunistic agent plots to discover and reveal the true size of Kafka's phallus.

Bennett is also known for his scripts for television and film, many of which have been published in book form. *Office Suite* (1978), *Objects of Affection and Other Plays for Television* (1982), and *The Writer in Disguise* (1985) collect his plays that were produced for British television. Bennett's film credits include the scripts for *A Private Function* and *Prick Up Your Ears*.

(See also *Contemporary Authors*, Vol. 103.)

Photograph by Mark Gerson

ROBERT COLEMAN

As you must know by now, ***Beyond the Fringe*** is a British—veddy British—revue by and with four clever young satirists: Alan Bennett, Peter Cook, Jonathan Miller and Dudley Moore. They hit their topical targets with unerring accuracy. All may not agree with their viewpoints, but we doubt that any will deny their showmanship.

The quartet is the epitome of versatility. It spoofs Prime Minister Macmillan, the royal family, religion, pompous academicians, concert pianists, Shakespeare, folk singers and war. Its needle-pointed jibes would seem to indicate they cast their ballots for Laborites rather than Conservatives.

We found some of their material in dubious taste. For us, God and religion are not subjects for levity. Neither are racial groups nor our policy toward Cuba. And we find it difficult to chuckle at the plight of a prisoner about to be hanged and comic dissertations on the atom bomb. . . .

Beyond the Fringe is aimed at a sophisticated audience. Its four stars are adroit at characterization, have a lethal sense of humor, and can even garner howls with the macabre. It is way-out fun for the knowing. We suspect, however, that the intimate revue will have a limited appeal.

Robert Coleman, "'Beyond Fringe' a 4-Star Howl," in New York Mirror, *October 29, 1962. Reprinted in* New York Theatre Critics' Reviews, *Vol. XXIII, No. 19, Week of November 5, 1962, p. 219.*

ROBERT BRUSTEIN

[*The essay excerpted below was originally published in* The New Republic, *December 15, 1962.*]

In an article entitled "Sicknik Time," Benjamin DeMott anatomizes the satire of the so-called "sick" comedians, which he finds irresponsible, unclarified, and socially ineffectual. To illustrate this, Professor DeMott lumps together such diverse sources of humor as Nichols and May, Lenny Bruce, Jules Feiffer, Pinky Lee, Joe E. Lewis, and *Mad* magazine, all rendered into the same unappetizing bowl of sour farina. This reductive method tells us little about the specific style and attack of the individual comics, but it is DeMott's intention to consign them all to a generalized sociological category; and the most impressive part of his essay catalogues the themes and conventions which sick comedy usually assails: racial subjects, bourgeois domesticity, commercialized religion, politics, public relations, and cultural improvement. (p. 190)

I bring this up in order to introduce a discussion of ***Beyond the Fringe,*** the first British equivalent of American-type satire to reach our shores. This scorching review has all the qualifications of sick comedy as defined by DeMott. It roasts all his categorical turkeys, it has no firm moral center, it is immoderate, irresponsible, and totally destructive, it affirms no changing world, and—if I may be permitted an unDeMottian judgment of value—it is violently funny. The sketches certainly contain echoes of Jules Feiffer and Nichols and May, even occasional hints of Lenny Bruce, along with that rebellious tone and contempt for authority which one associates with the work of Amis, Osborne, and J. P. Donleavy. ***Beyond the Fringe*** has not yet been identified with sick comedy, perhaps because the community it attacks is not our own; but even now, I suspect, English critics are expressing sociological disapproval over its anti-social behavior.

The review's title suggests its stance: that posture of disaffiliation from the system which DeMott seems to deplore. Beyond the fringe are four extremely talented and alienated young men; within the fringe are all the pieties, platitudes, and prejudices of the last English generation; and the sketches consist of venomous darts hurled over the boundary line. The major political target is Prime Minister Macmillan: one episode finds him, ancient and confused, describing the youthful vigor of Kennedy, while pawing, arthritically, at a globe of the world; another represents a duel between a Russian and a Briton, the weapons a chorus of raspberries for their respective leaders. Commercialized religion also gets the Bronx cheer as a TV theologian, who bubbles like a social worker, speaks of channeling juvenile violence toward God (a later sketch shows a vicar explicating a passage from the story of Jacob in terms of class distinctions). The English worship of royalty is assailed; play censors and censors of pornography are identified with the perversions they would suppress; an African statesman is made to look as venal, corrupt, and self-serving as his European counterparts. Four homosexuals admire one another's hair and clothing before launching into a singing commercial for a man's cigarette; two linguistic philosophers trade "how questions" and "why questions" with examples from "real life"; a Beaverbrook journalist and an adman discuss ways to express dissent (the journalist titters at the boss behind his hand). (pp. 191-92)

The first act finale, "After-myth of War," satirizes the blood-and-beaches attitudes of the English under Churchill, complete with stiff upper lips, unending cups of tea, and futile sacrifices, finally collapsing into utter desperation as the war generation hands the world over to the youngsters. And the funniest sketch of all satirizes Shakespearean productions (especially Olivier's *Henry V* and the current Old Vic), and even Shakespeare himself—reducing the clown scenes, duels, and choral speeches to bluster and bombast, and the blank verse to absolute nonsense.

If all these subjects lie within the fringe, there is one subject that extends beyond: the H-bomb—and it is under the shadow of this monstrous birth that the entire review is played out. The evening is studded with nuclear references, and two sketches deal with the bomb directly: in the first, a panel group, addressing itself to the question "Kill or Be Killed—or Both," prescribes brown paper bags as a defense against radiation, thus suggesting the absolute idiocy of civil defense; in the second, and final sketch, "The End Is Nigh," a group of fundamentalists are revealed, sitting on a mountaintop, awaiting apocalypse. It is this expectation of nuclear annihilation which accounts for the fury and savagery of much of this review, as it partly accounts for the extravagance of our own sick comedians. For if the young seem negative and irresponsible, then this may be because their positive and responsible elders have left them such a poisoned inheritance. And it is a measure of health, not sickness, that their inevitable anger and resentment can still be disciplined within a witty, sharp, and purgative art. (pp. 192-93)

Robert Brustein, "The Healthiness of Sick Comedy: 'Beyond the Fringe'," in his Seasons of Discontent: Dramatic Opinions, 1959-1965, *Simon and Schuster, 1965, pp. 190-93.*

IRVING WARDLE

[***40 Years On***] is a first play that will surprise nobody who remembers the author, Alan Bennett, as the parsonical satirist in the ***Beyond the Fringe*** team.

Ever since that show we have been waiting for a full-scale mock-heroic pageant of modern British myth, and Mr. Bennett has now supplied it. In outline, his comedy concerns a parents' day at which the incoming liberal headmaster stages a school play for the benefit of the retiring traditionalist. In the ensuing battle between the old order and the new it becomes clear that we are meant to take the school as an image of Britain at the crossroads, an image that it signally fails to project.

But if Mr. Bennett is defeated in the larger purpose he is brilliantly successful in the smaller: both in juggling with the formal and informal aspects of the situation, and in using it as the framework for a lethally witty series of parodies.

Irving Wardle, "Gielgud Is Starred as '40 Years On' Starts London Run," in The New York Times, *November 5, 1968, p. 53.*

CLIVE BARNES

40 Years On, with its title taken from an English public (meaning private) school ditty, is defiantly English. So English indeed that I suspect it might well make its strongest appeal to

American tourists anxious to identify with Big Ben. But the reason I feel it might fail in New York is not that it is so English, but that fundamentally it is so cheap and nasty.

The story, such as it is, is set in a very minor public school. The headmaster . . . is retiring, and his successor has arranged some kind of entertainment intended to paint a picture of the past seen through the hindsight of today.

Mr. Bennett's jokes (one or two of them are passable, but fewer are original) favor slickness and prep-school facetiousness rather than humor. He confuses irreverence with relevance and constantly ends up in the position of the bold boy who has scrawled a moustache on a reproduction of the Mona Lisa. He has that typically English tendency toward naughtily scatological humor and also gets some mileage out of anti-homosexual gibes that in the circumstances appear mildly inappropriate.

Mr. Bennett, with donnish cynicism, weak-hearted puns, attempts at simulated nostalgia, gallant pot shots at dead targets and enthusiastic attacks on men and events that make Mr. Bennett appear callously trivial, has ironically produced a perversely illuminating evening. I can only presume that most of the critics who heralded it so sweetly are probably living further in the past than Mr. Bennett himself.

It is not, I suggest, the Englishness of ***40 Years On*** that is likely to make it unacceptable to a Broadway audience, but rather its pretentiousness and ineptness.

Clive Barnes, in a review of "40 Years On," in The New York Times, *July 26, 1969, p. 14.*

JULIUS NOVICK

[***Forty Years On***] offers a somewhat impressionistic account of the last eighty years or so of English history, in the form of an end-of-term extravaganza, with songs, presented by the boys at an English public school on the occasion of the retirement of their headmaster.

Mr. Bennett, the author, was a member of the famous quartet who wrote and performed ***Beyond the Fringe.*** His new work, too, is a sort of revue, a series of sketches set (this time) into a framework. Much of it sounds rather like ***Beyond the Fringe,*** only, if anything, funnier. ***Beyond the Fringe*** was not exactly guerrilla theatre but it was distinctly skeptical about established authorities, and it could scarcely be viewed as Conservative Party propaganda; in ***Forty Years On*** the retiring headmaster, who speaks for the past, is a running fount of marvelous fatuities: "Doubtless, the future will see many changes. Well, perhaps that is what the future is for." "God is not mocked, and if He is, I'm not." "I'm all in favor of free expression so long as it is kept under control."

But oddly enough, the nostalgia in ***Forty Years On*** seems to be essentially genuine. Like so many of the insurgent British writers of the late 1950s or early 1960s, Bennett seems to have mellowed, or soured, into something of a conservative; he seems half-inclined to agree with Max Beerbohm that those whom the gods loved died in August 1914. Some of the evocations of past glories and delights are sincerely done, and quite touching. Like John Osborne and others, Bennett seems to be disgusted with the shoddy, small-souled, gracelessness he finds in postwar England.

This of course is a partial view. But even the most comfortable among us, nowadays, in America even more than in Canada or Britain, seem to be aware that something is missing from our shiny modern lives; perhaps a sympathetic look at the past—even other people's past—even, or especially, an idealized past—will help to give us some idea of what it is we're missing. In ***Forty Years On,*** moreover, there is plenty of satire, parody, and miscellaneous buffoonery to keep the nostalgia from becoming maudlin or pompous.

Julius Novick, in a review of "Forty Years On" and "Beyond the Fringe," in The Nation, *New York, Vol. 211, No. 6, September 7, 1970, p. 190.*

BERNARD LEVIN

Alan Bennett was the least extrovert and most individual of the four members of the ***Beyond the Fringe*** team which had so startled theatre-going London at the beginning of the Sixties, and which had signalled the beginning of so many of those changes in manners and morals, attitudes and expectations, that had taken place by the time the decade ended. For some years after its spectacular success he had lain fallow; some television comedy-programmes, a little writing, had come from him; but all the while, within his fertile, perceptive mind, the definitive comment of the wiser heads of his generation on the England of their fathers was gestating. At the end of 1968 it was born, and it was seen that he had been hatching vipers. ***Forty Years On*** was widely misunderstood and dismissed, many being deceived by its brilliantly funny surface polish, as a trifle, or—others being no less deceived by the author's previous reputation—as nothing more than a series of revue sketches. In truth, however, it was much more, and properly understood offered small comfort to anybody, for it managed with astonishingly sure-footed skill the exceptionally difficult task, one which was achieved successfully by almost nobody else in the decade, of facing both the future and the past calmly, with understanding and without self-deception. In the Sixties, in Britain as elsewhere, one world was dying and another being born, and it is a measure of Bennett's achievement that in ***Forty Years On*** he says clearly that although it is inevitable that this should be so, and that the new world must be welcomed, if only because it will come whether it be welcomed or not, nevertheless the old world had value and substance too, and in losing it for ever England was losing something she could ill spare. . . . [Bennett] could see, and say, clearly, that it is perfectly possible, and even proper, to regret the passing of something that it is necessary should pass.

From this point of departure, he galloped off; his allegorical devices, of using a minor public school to represent England, and of setting it at the moment the old, conservative headmaster is retiring and being succeeded by a young radical one to represent the decade, both worked perfectly. What was so extraordinary about such a play from a man of Bennett's age (he was thirty-three when it appeared) was that he had put his finger unerringly on the point at which Britain had finally been forced to decide which way she would go, though she had spent the entire time since—Bennett's lifetime—desperately trying not to admit as much, and only now, in the Sixties, had begun consciously to face the reality that had been staring at her since 1940. It is Neville Chamberlain who dominates this play, which has within it another play, turning on the narrative of an anti-Munich Conservative M.P. (Bennett actually quotes Harold Nicolson's *Diaries* in the course of it) through whose eyes the Second World War is seen, interspersed with sharply pointed comments (which in turn are interspersed with episodes of great beauty and poignancy) on the passing years from the

Boer War to T. E. Lawrence and from the slaughter of the trenches in the First World War to Virginia Woolf. (pp. 358-60)

Bernard Levin, "Brief Chronicles," in his The Pendulum Years: Britain and the Sixties, *Jonathan Cape, 1970, pp. 350-65.*

CLIVE BARNES

In London ***Habeas Corpus*** seemed slight and boring—[in New York] it is slightly less boring, but no less slight. It is, of course, very difficult to write a Feydeau farce if you are not a Feydeau, and Mr. Bennett exhibits little sense of construction or even purpose in this episodic and facetious rigmarole about a philandering doctor and his predictably tedious ménage. . . .

[Mr. Bennett] does not write badly. Indeed it is one of his problems that he very occasionally writes tantalizingly well, but, and it is the nature of his art to provoke parody even in criticism, he might be said to be "jumping, often with a certain modest brilliance, into chasm after chasm of triviality." Mr. Bennett does not really write plays—he offers extended revue sketches that lend themselves to eccentricity but terrifyingly little else.

The action here takes place in Hove, a suburb of the English seaside resort of Brighton. The hero, Arthur Wicksteed, is a general medical practitioner given over to practices with his female patients that are often more general than medical. He has a wife, sailing full-sail through menopause undaunted by the waves, and a spinster sister who has been unendowed by nature but is engaged to a Church of England canon, celibate enough but appearing to have had some warm friendships with choir boys, and, presumably, the like. There is a cleaning woman—there always is—a somewhat doused leading light of the medical profession, and a Lady Rumpers, described in the program as a pillar of the Empire, who has a daughter, Felicity, almost designed by God to end up in her bra and panties. Other characters intrude.

If one can see little method in Mr. Bennett's madness, one can, at least, sometimes discern a theme. He appears to be celebrating—perhaps in a waspish fashion—human carnality and sexuality. "Show me a human body," his doctor at one point observes with righteous irony, "and I will show you a cesspool." Mr. Bennett's jokes are often better than that, but I will abstain from quotation not wishing to spoil an audience's fun and an author's one thin advantage during a comparatively, from a dramatic viewpoint, disadvantageous evening. Nor shall I recount the plot—partly because this was difficult to notice, and why should a critic work harder than a playwright?

Clive Barnes, "A Parade of Wit for 'Habeas Corpus'," in The New York Times, *November 26, 1975, p. 12.*

GINA MALLET

Can even a farce rest only on a pair of falsies? It is true that in the course of ***Habeas Corpus*** (which means, appropriately, let's have the body) a couple of sets of real female breasts are fondled and pummeled, and one or two actors lose their trousers, but the evening's focus is on the pair of "the Rubens, made of sensitized Fablon as used on Apollo space missions." The breastworks are delivered to one Connie Wicksteed, who looks so like a choirboy that the errant local curate has fallen in love with her. Connie lives in the genteel resort town of Hove with her brother Arthur, a G. P. specializing in lechery, his wife Muriel, a lady endowed with Jane Russell proportions, and a cleaning woman who is a victim of overexposure to modern communication: "I'm now going into the lotus position." By the time a salesman arrives to make sure the falsies fit, Connie has gone Girl Scouting, but several other stock characters—including Muriel's former lover, the minuscule Sir Percy Shorter, and a mindless sexpot, Felicity Rumpers—have joined the seedy Wicksteed household for the game of "Who's got them on?"

What follows is entirely predictable and unabashedly vulgar. Inhibitions must be left at the door. Alan Bennett, . . . has constructed no more than a sloppy farce. . . . The Wicksteeds live in a world still superficially Victorian, but underneath there rage fires of frustration fed by the characters' anxiety that if an opportunity arises, their sexual equipment may be unequal to the occasion. Thus every double-entendre is not merely dirty but wistful.

Gina Mallet, "False Premises," in Time, *New York, Vol. 106, No. 23, December 8, 1975, p. 91.*

HAROLD CLURMAN

I found a good deal of [***Habeas Corpus***] funny and two or three scenes hilarious. . . .

An appreciation of the show depends on one's disposition and momentary mood. If one is not prepared to lend oneself to its kind of fun one is apt to find it wearisome. But something more should be said about it, whether it is accepted on its own terms or rejected as foolish fluff. For Alan Bennett . . . is anything but a fool. He has a canny grasp of the contemporary English temperature.

While American audiences often relish bedroom shenanigans through a reverse puritanism—as an escape from unavowed repression—there is something more to it than that in England, where a widespread skepticism obtains about everything. The economic, social, political standstill has created an all-pervasive uncertainty. The stalwart pride of the inherited past is breaking up; everyone realizes this but is loath to admit it—except as a joke. Very little is left to believe in or to hold on to. "If we laugh at our dismay," the English seem to be saying, "we are being candid without giving ourselves away. Perhaps only the pleasures of the flesh are left to us." But it is not a frank and healthy lust, a joy of the senses. It has become a grimace—in some instances painful, in others angry, in still others, jeering. Alan Bennett ducks all such attitudes: he invites his (English) audience to regard the situation as a spoof, a poke in the ribs, something to be laughed at and then forgotten. It is not satire; it is frolic, hence safe.

The clergyman in ***Habeas Corpus*** who sways from the asexual to the ambisexual as he plunges into a moment of grotesque abandon hoots that he is now in "the forefront of Anglican sexuality." And the refrain throughout the play's high jinks is, "I suppose this is what is meant by the permissive society." There is, in short, a direct line from the turbid ambiguities of Pinter's *The Lover* to the harum-scarum of Orton's *What the Butler Saw,* ending in ***Habeas Corpus*** as a burlesque blowup. The play assumes no "position" but sets itself forth without care as a grinning symptom.

Harold Clurman, in a review of "Habeas Corpus," in The Nation, *New York, Vol. 221, No. 20, December 13, 1975, p. 638.*

GILBERT CANT

The Old Country is a riddle wrapped in a mystery inside an enigma—inside cellophane. The setting is a seedy, book-infested cottage in the woods. Hilary . . . and his wife Bron . . . potter around, she arranging flowers and he devising puzzles. If they did not know where they were, he asks, where might they be? Scotland? Almost anywhere, he decides, including where they are: Hilary, a former high official of the British Foreign Office, is a traitor, and they are in a Russian dacha.

Yet the spiritual setting of this spare new comedy by Alan Bennett . . . is England and the foibles of the English. Despite their exile, Hilary and Bron are more English than those who stayed behind. She shuffles around in hearty tweeds; he frets over the decline of Lyons Teahouses.

Into this peculiar household come visitors, his sister Veronica . . . and her husband Duff . . . , a government official who tries to persuade Hilary to come back. He will have a short prison term, but his memoirs will make him rich. From that basic script Bennett unwraps his verbal puzzles. . . .

Bennett makes a pleasant afternoon outside Moscow into an amusing evening at the theater. Yet it is hard to like ***The Old Country*** more than just a little.

Gilbert Cant, "The Puzzler," in Time, *New York, Vol. 110, No. 14, October 3, 1977, p. 89.*

CHOICE

[In ***The Old Country,*** Alan Bennett] has created a play that manages to live and speak even when confined to the printed page. The comparative lack of movement indicated for the play's performance is perhaps consciously balanced by a playfulness and quickness of the dialogue. There is a rejoicing in language for its own sake, which is something of a mixed blessing inasmuch as motivation and psychology are not given the prominence probably needed to give the play more substance. However, the treatment of a British civil servant in exile in the Soviet Union (for homosexuality-linked security violation?) and haunted by nostalgia for home is engrossing.

A review of "The Old Country," in Choice, *Vol. 16, Nos. 5 & 6, July & August, 1979, p. 662.*

THOMAS E. LUDDY

Bennett, well known for ***Habeas Corpus,*** turns his keen ear for realistic comic dialogue to examining the passing of the neighborhoods and generations in ***Enjoy,*** a comedy that is light on the surface, but beneath, dark indeed. Set in Leeds, ***Enjoy*** places a late-middle-aged couple in the last house in a neighborhood under demolition. They are watched by silent and sinister observers recording their normal life for posterity. But no normal life occurs. The comic development is wonderfully funny and touching. Yet the end of the play slides into expressionistic revelations of the severity of the theme. A most successful play.

Thomas E. Luddy, in a review of "Enjoy," in Library Journal, *Vol. 106, No. 6, March 15, 1981, p. 676.*

DONALD CAMPBELL

There is a curious inconsistency in Alan Bennett's drama. As long as he is content simply to create characters and set them in an environment where they cannot fail to speak for themselves, he is brilliantly original as a comic observer of the eccentricities of contemporary English life. His plays are as arresting in their impact as they are unfailingly funny in their execution. It is only when he tries to make his drama do something—or, rather, *say* something—that Bennett comes unstuck, almost as if his writing had suddenly run into a brick wall. Largely, one feels, the problem is simply a matter of form, Bennett being much more of a television writer than a stage playwright. Given the facts that his first play was a theatrical triumph in every sense of the word, this may seem an odd claim to make but, on the evidence of the two volumes under review [***Forty Years On, Getting On, Habeas Corpus*** and ***The Writer in Disguise***], one is left with the impression that ***Forty Years On*** is the exception that proves the rule.

Forty Years On is certainly a very fine piece of work. This parodic evocation of English middle-class life during the first forty years of this century, set within the context of a present-day school play, rattles along uproariously, yet is entirely lacking in that quality of rawness one often finds in first plays. No speech is too long, not one single line seems out of place, the explosive irreverence of the satire is contained within a superb theatrical craft. Reading it alongside the other two plays in the volume, however, one can scarcely believe that all three plays had been written by the same author. ***Getting On*** is one of those 'disillusioned Labour MP' plays that writers of Bennett's generation and background apparently feel obliged to write. It is seriously over-written and is entirely unsuccessful in engaging any real sympathy with its theme. As for ***Habeas Corpus,*** the best that can be said of it is that it is an unremarkable, if moderately funny, black farce which relies far too heavily on the stock clichés of the genre.

Turning to the television plays contained in ***The Writer in Disguise,*** one finds an entirely different state of affairs. Television seems to suit Bennett's writing in two important ways; the variety of location liberates his imagination and the necessary economy of television dialogue brings a focusing restraint to his over-facile sense of humour. Four of the plays in this volume succeed by virtue of their sheer authenticity. They are full of convincingly human, painfully recognizable characters, drawn with great perception, wit and a totally undisguised sense of delight. The sole exception is ***The Old Crowd,*** a rather baffling piece about a party in an unfurnished house. . . . In ***The Old Crowd*** the characters do not live in the imagination, they blur into each other, making the text virtually unreadable. For all that, the need to move in a new direction is always a praiseworthy quality in any serious playwright, even when the attempt to do so fails.

Donald Campbell, in a review of "Forty Years On, Getting On, Habeas Corpus" and "The Writer in Disguise," in British Book News, *June, 1985, p. 368.*

MICHAEL RATCLIFFE

[***Kafka's Dick***] is a kind of leisurely vaudeville about the tormented Kafka of litcrit and biographical legend and the kind of people who have kept him and his brute father . . . in torment: the historical Brod, the writer, critic, executor and friend who refused to burn the manuscripts as instructed in Kafka's will, and the Bennett-imagined Sydney . . . , a fatuous insurance agent who indulges an amateur passion for Kafka today despite the exasperation of his supposedly dim wife Linda. . . .

At the start, the dying Kafka dreams himself and Brod forward 65 years into Sydney and Linda's lounge. Sydney is brooding over the latest item of scholarly marginalia (something to do with Kafka's sexual endowment); Linda is Hoovering round the three-piece suite.

Enter Max Brod through the windows, having peed over the tortoise on the lawn. The outraged Linda washes, then kisses, the tortoise which turns into Franz Kafka. The man who woke up one morning as a beetle has come back to life as a tortoise and once again been pissed upon by the disobedient executor Brod. The joke and the metaphor suggest the Stoppard of *Travesties* and *Jumpers,* but Bennett's touch is neither so logical nor so secure.

Sydney is by turns enchanted, proprietorial, vindictive. Linda makes the journey more positively, in reverse: from outrage to flirtatious amusement, and finally affectionate concern. It is in the growing friendship of Linda and Kafka that the play's optimism alone lies. . . .

The play remains a paradox in itself: a mordant attack on twentieth-century trivialisation and barbarity by a playwright who cannot resist blunting the force and intensity of his attack by a constant stream of gags, some of which are very good, but many of which are surprisingly cheap and feeble from one of the funniest and most fastidious writers working in England today.

Michael Ratcliffe, "Franz Agonistes," in The Observer, *September 28, 1986, p. 23.*

JIM HILEY

Alan Bennett is well liked and has no doubt earned a bob or two to garnish his drama awards. But unjustly, you'll seldom find him registered among the best British scribes. What's his offence? He collides with the class systems of both theatre and nation. As a playwright, Bennett is difficult to categorise, and compounds that by messing frequently with television. In his chronicles of ordinary life, he prefers comic elegance to the more familiar, more demeaning rough strokes. He knows all about the parish pump, but refuses to be parochial.

Not unlike ***The Insurance Man,*** its brilliant companion piece for television, ***Kafka's Dick*** . . . exists atmospherically between Prague 70 years ago and a timelessly hide-bound England. As in other work, too, Bennett can be seen gibing at domestic confines and a single tone.

But whereas Stoppard, say, erects fanciful structures for cold philosophising, Bennett expresses a kind of humanistic anxiety. This is appealing—at times naive, in the best sense, for all the technical audacity. Yet it also pinpoints Bennett's principal shortcoming. On the one hand, he tilts at what Englishness stifles. The suburban insurance man in ***Kafka's Dick*** describes a country where titbits—like the fact that Auden never wore underpants—'pass for culture'. Sydney . . . adds: 'Gossip is the acceptable face of intellect.' But Bennett himself refuses to get 'too' serious. He perches fretfully on the fence. Where passion is called for, he exhibits concern. Even so, ***Kafka's Dick*** provides a rewardingly inventive, provoking, often hilarious night out—a nutritious confection with pins in the cream.

Most of the action occupies the grey drawing-room . . . of Sydney, a spare-time Kafka scholar who would 'rather read about writers than read what they wrote'; Linda . . . , his repressed, disgruntled wife; and Sydney's father . . . , a codger fenced into a walking-frame who lives in fear of being bundled away. (pp. 31-2)

From Sydney's tortoise, Kafka himself . . . metamorphoses—an edgy, whining depressive, who grows jealous easily (particularly of Proust) and finds himself plunged into a succession of trials.

First is the discovery that Brod did not, as pledged, destroy Kafka's manuscripts after his death, but published them and so secured celebrity for the author who craved a 'small name'. Next is a humiliating encounter with his bowler-hatted, bull-dozing father . . . , who threatens to reveal the size of the eponymous organ—another titbit—unless Kafka will testify that his dad is no tyrant. Sydney seizes on this as a chance to rewrite literary history and so make *his* name. Kafka is then arraigned on the charge that ordinary folk are 'eradicated' by illustriousness such as his. And Sydney ponders the fairytale function of artists' lives: whatever the individual's fate, his story always ends happily—in fame.

Here Bennett might have risen to another dimension of ideas and feeling. Instead, he deposits us in a skittish heaven, where Betty Hutton hobnobs with Wittgenstein, and a partying, avuncular God . . . tells Gandhi to 'go easy on the cheese straws'.

Bennett does, though, give Linda a speech about how every woman is familiar with the non-status the men complain of (and Kafka desires). But this feels embarrassingly like track-covering, since Linda has so far been depicted with a sexist archness spectacularly at odds with the rest of the play. There are crudities to enjoy, however, among the usual quota of ripe lines. (p. 32)

Jim Hiley "Culture with a K." in The Listener, *Vol. 116, No. 2980, October 2, 1986, pp. 31-2.*

VICTORIA RADIN

Having just survived a Kafkaesque experience, I was in good mettle to enjoy Kafka's dick, or any of his parts. But ***Kafka's Dick,*** like the original member, apparently, is smaller than one hoped. It's not that it's short or unremarkable. It's absolutely gnarled with *richesses,* a veritable *embarras* of them, as Sydney . . . might say. But its desire to do so many things with itself makes knowing it a bit disappointing. . . .

[Bennett's] play is poisonous about biographers (a tribe to which he must now admit some allegiance) and kindled by farce. Much of this bumpy, funny and far too intellectualised comedy of mistaken (and lost) identities (animal and human) is *après* Orton. But then it would be fair to say—if my lit-crit impulses hadn't been beaten up and etherised upon a table—that there are basic similarities between Orton and Kafka. Both share a profound hatred of authority, particularly when it is invested in men. In Bennett's play, the bestial and indeed Freudianly-castrating father-figure does, so to speak, his nut.

But before we go for the red herrings let's get to the tortoise. Bennett's premise is that Kafka, having wrung from his pal Max Brod the promise to burn all his manuscripts and papers, falls into a feverish dying sleep and dreams what in fact really happened—that Brod not only published them but with his own biography released a flood in which every one of his dead friend's private parts, including the titular one, have been picked and pawed over. . . .

But to the tortoise. Kafka is born again out of one—metamorphosed, as it were. Kafka's Dad, the horrible Hermann, materialises as a cop (later, in paradise, when Bennett loses his grip, as God) who owes a lot to Père Ubu; and his mother comes on as . . . mum. One of Bennett's points, in his rather double-edged battle with misogyny, is that women have no identity outside their relationship to a man. The Ks turn up at the house of Linda, dim and lusty, and Sydney, who happens, like guess-who, to be in insurance and is writing an essay on you-know-who. It is also the home of Sydney's elderly father, who thinks each one is a 'Them' or authority-figure come to cart him off to a home. (They aren't but he is. Going to be.) Bennett gives some of his best lines to this initially merely cruelly-written figure, who gradually becomes sympathetic as he tries to evade incarceration by arming himself with facts about our K.

He becomes, in what is effectively one of the play's two Trials, one of Us rather than one of Them. And who are We and They? The vulgar or merely spiritually bankrupt, or bullying, or second-rate Philistine (as opposed to the exploited creative artists) keep falling out of the farce, like a skeleton from a closet, despite what may be Bennett's own attempts at self-parody in the (partly) craven K. But the demarcations constantly shift. Sydney claims that in Britain 'gossip is the acceptable face of intellect'. This goes down rather oddly in a play in which the author gives his audience points for every name he drops. . . .

The problem with ***Kafka's Dick,*** whose audacity and high spiritedness I applaud but whose pretensions I deplore is that characters are made too inconsistently to grease the wheels of what is a vastly cumbersome plot.

Victoria Radin, "Bounced Czech," in New Statesman, *Vol. 112, No. 2902, November 7, 1986, p. 25.*

Eric Bogosian

1953-

American performance artist.

Bogosian is regarded as a leading performance artist. Performance art is a loosely defined theatrical form that encompasses drama, dance, comedy, music, impressions, improvisations, and monologues in various combinations as a means for surprising an audience. After having worked in small theaters and off-Broadway productions, Bogosian attracted significant critical attention for *Drinking in America* (1985), a series of dramatic monologues. In this satirical work, Bogosian examines the psyches of several obsessed males by assuming such identities as a manic Hollywood agent, a teenaged drug addict, a zealous television evangelist, and an unprincipled salesman. Each impersonation is linked to the theme of the lust for power—financial, sexual, or political, among others—and its intoxicating and corrupting capabilities. John Howell remarked: "*Drinking in America*'s literate and authoritative portraits make a . . . simple, devastating comment, with an '80s twist, on the sources and reasons behind the exercise of uninhibited power in a morally scattered society." Through his biting social commentary, Bogosian hopes to provoke his audiences into reevaluating their moral standards. Bogosian's talents as a writer and performer, particularly his ability to recreate various American idioms, have led critics to compare him with Lenny Bruce and Richard Pryor.

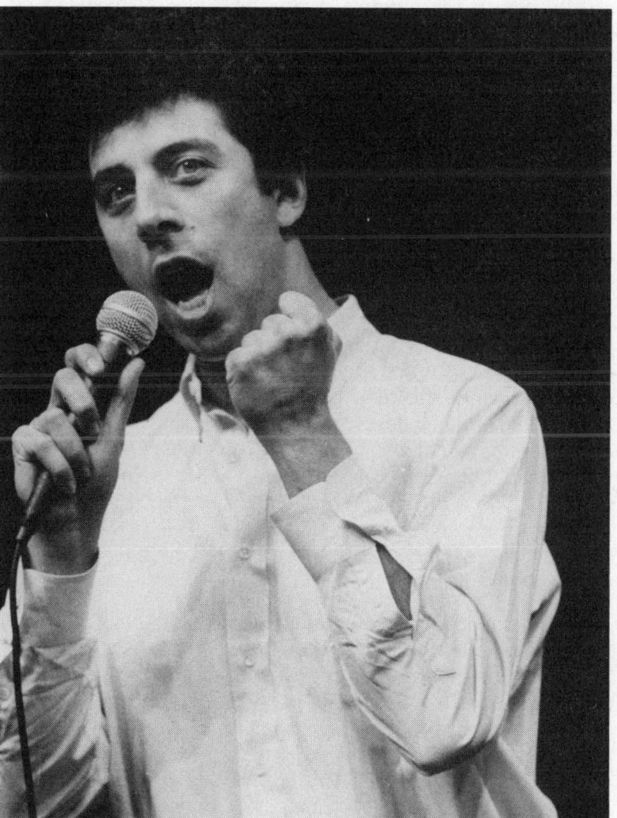

Sara Krulwich/NYT Pictures

JOHN SIMON

[Eric Bogosian] has imagination, wit, some histrionic variety, and a good ear for the rumblings of society's underbelly and the burblings of our brain-damaged media. In skit after skit [in ***Funhouse***], he mercilessly belabors everything from bums, hoodlums, murderers justifying themselves on television, and rock freaks to necrophiliac disc jockeys, ghoulish life-insurance salesmen, cancer victims and their heartless doctors. If there were nightclubs for misanthropes, Bogosian would have his life's work cut out for him. As it is, this doomsday catalogue charily leavened with gobbets of gallows humor quickly wears out itself and us.

John Simon, in a review of "Funhouse," in New York *Magazine, Vol. 16, No. 43, October 31, 1983, p. 60.*

KEVIN GRUBB

Performance artist Eric Bogosian is a hard man to categorize. Though he is credited with establishing a contemporary dance program at Soho's progressive Kitchen, he is not a dancer by standard definition. One is tempted to label him an impressionist, though his characters, largely drawn from society's seamier crevices, are not cut from the fabric of, say, Rich Little or Charles Pierce. Neither does he fit into a mime niche, since his blue-tongued soliloquies immediately call forth stand-up comics like Lenny Bruce or Richard Pryor. By combining several expressive techniques, Bogosian has arrived at an engrossing, though difficult-to-digest, brand of performance art.

Bogosian's ***Funhouse*** . . . provided an opportunity to watch this high-strung acrobat in a sixty-minute . . . one-man show choreographed with the precision of a ballet. . . . Bogosian gingerly picked at societal maladies: cancer, anorexia, sexual hysteria, and death. In one of his impersonations, Bogosian was an old man on the street, barking to anyone nearby: "We live in a toilet. . . . Flush the toilet, that's what I say." (p. 80)

Alienated from human touch, ***Funhouse***'s characters clung to artificial substitutes. When they did manage to connect, it was often a disappointing—sometimes tragic—encounter. In one of the more poignant and harrowing scenes, Bogosian played a former war-veteran-turned-alcoholic lying on the sidewalk, arm extended. His drunken stupor was conveyed in convulsive movements, perhaps from the d.t.'s, perhaps because he was uncertain to whom he was reaching. He asked a passing business executive carrying a *New York Times* to help him to his feet. When the man scornfully turned away, the vet yelled, "I helped save this country from communism. Doesn't that mean anything?" The silence that followed was deafening.

Bogosian demonstrated that insanity and perversity are not remote conditions afflicting only the unfortunate and depraved.

We are all equally vulnerable. It is only by accident that some people escape the fate of the street and the need to resort to whatever means are available to survive one more day. Despite its doom and gloom, Bogosian's nightmarish funhouse never became solemn. Though brooding and pessimistic, ***Funhouse*** was not so caught up in presenting life's cruelties that it could not cast a wry glance at our varied methods of coping with catastrophe in the eighties. Bogosian neither trivialized nor embellished, but presented the facts with all their inherent horror and humor. It is this clear-eyed vision that makes him one of our most important performing artists. (p. 81)

Kevin Grubb, in a review of "Funhouse," in Dance Magazine, *Vol. LVIII, No. 1, January, 1984, pp. 78-83.*

JOHN HOWELL

Right now there's a proliferation of solo caricaturists—performers who create an entire portrait gallery of characters—but Eric Bogosian is the only one who works "cold"; he uses no props, no costumes and doesn't mix media. Dressed typically in a white shirt and black jeans, Bogosian works with his flexible, highly developed voice and with nuanced body movement to invent his personas. What's more, Bogosian presents several characters in each show under a single thematic umbrella. It's a difficult format—and one that has worked in a hit-or-miss way in his earlier shows. But in ***Drinking in America,*** 1985, every shot was a bull's-eye, creating a singular, serious work of comic drama.

In earlier performances, Bogosian mimicked his characters perfectly. ***Voices of America,*** 1982-84, worked over the aural schizophrenia of pop radio with hilarious, if stereotypical, results, and ***Men Inside,*** 1982-84, served up individual portraits of the male psyche that were sometimes funny, sometimes chilling, sometimes confusing. But Bogosian didn't always fully inhabit these earlier characters. . . . In ***Drinking in America,*** Bogosian was no less showy, but he was so deeply and consistently inside his personas that it was almost magical to watch him disappear into them, with no theatrical hocus-pocus.

Some of this newly concentrated punch was due to a pared-down roster. . . . The new force was also traceable to a more focused theme: intoxication. . . . The intoxicants examined in ***Drinking in America*** weren't limited to alcohol. The performance opened with an informal reading from Bogosian's '70s journal about taking LSD and the subsequent "truths" discovered with its help. This "forgery" (it was a recent piece of writing) and Bogosian's casual, overly earnest manner were persuasively disarming; they set up the audience to believe, in a wonderfully impure way, in a hazy DMZ between Bogosian and his characters. . . .

Drinking in America then offered a gallery of perfectly limned drunkards: a staggering, gravel-voiced wino who railed against God; a manic, coke-snorting Hollywood agent; a strutting heavy-metal musician (who lip-synced a Scorpions' tune); a vicious, Jimmy Swaggart-like preacher; and a thrill-seeking Jersey teenager strung out on every drug possible. Bogosian moved precisely through each scene, keeping each character's monologue true to its individual vocabulary and to the general point of the whole show: the attitudes unleashed by intoxicants. There was a lot of moralizing in Bogosian's slice-of-life clichés, moralizing of the self-justifying sort (he writes his own scripts), but Bogosian never patronized these lost souls. His moral was appropriately double-edged: aren't these people weird? said his material, and isn't there something of them in you and me? asked his all-out performance. . . .

Drinking in America's literate and authoritative portraits make a . . . simple, devastating comment, with an '80s twist, on the sources and reasons behind the exercise of uninhibited power in a morally scattered society.

John Howell, "Eric Bogosian, 'Drinking in America'," in Artforum, *Vol. XXIV, No. 3, November, 1985, p. 108.*

FRANK RICH

There are few theatrical experiences more exhilarating than watching a talented young artist fulfill his promise. . . . Eric Bogosian . . . has put together an airtight 80-minute show in which his gifts for acting and social satire collide to their most incendiary effect yet. ***Drinking in America*** . . . , like such past Bogosian efforts as ***Funhouse*** and ***Men Inside,*** . . . is a breakneck, hair-raising comic tour of the contemporary American male psyche, with its creator playing all the roles. But if this is the funniest and most shapely of Mr. Bogosian's shows, the edges of his humor have not been smoothed out. ***Drinking in America*** leaves a hangover of outrage that a theatergoer can't easily shake.

The demographically diverse men on view include, among others, a grasping show-biz hustler, a latter-day Willy Loman on the road, a ghetto junkie, and a gyrating heavy-metal rock star. While many of the characters are indeed intoxicated—on cocaine, Quaaludes or heroin as well as alcohol—***Drinking in America*** charts a more pervasive spiritual malady. The men we meet are gluttons for power, money and sex as well as for chemical stimulants; they have pigged out on the American way. Although Mr. Bogosian hardly approves of a neo-Nazi television evangelist who appears late in the show, he does seem to share the preacher's conviction that "the Devil seduced us with a life of plenty and invited us into hell."

Such is the ecumenical nature of Mr. Bogosian's harsh indictment that he mocks not only the self-satisfied affluent but also the self-indulgent have-nots. The narcoticized derelicts of ***Drinking in America*** proselytize for "having it all" as ferociously as those characters who do live the good life. From the gutter, the addicts gleefully endorse the virtues of big cars, compliant women and other supposed rewards of the success ethic. Nor does Mr. Bogosian spare himself from attack. In one bit, a performer named Eric records a voice-over for a smarmy commercial hawking an imported beer to the upwardly mobile. . . .

Mr. Bogosian's writing . . . reveals his uncommonly sharp ear for all kinds of American voices. He is equally adept at capturing the language of an ethnic coffee-shop owner, a slickly hypocritical rock disk jockey and a young urbanite employed in a "semi-creative job with very little pressure to perform." Yet the writing is not merely jokey, and at times it can lift off into extravagantly surreal flights. In what may be the tour de force of ***Drinking in America,*** a blue-collar hood regales a buddy with an account of an all-night booze-and-acid binge of "partying" that escalated into a violent crime spree. The events are described in vivid subliterate vernacular, and, like a car pileup on a highway, they are grotesquely slapstick. But even as we laugh, we are terrified by the cruelty of a hooligan whose manic giggles and cracker-barrel storytelling style cannot hide a complete absence of conscience.

If there are several such high points in ***Drinking in America,*** there are no real valleys. . . . Mr. Bogosian has for the first time edited his material and his performance to the quick. ***Drinking in America*** rarely slows down, and it has been cohesively assembled to achieve a cumulative effect.

The show even has a beginning and an end. At the outset, Mr. Bogosian reads from a composition book containing a journal he purports to have written while attending Boston University in 1971. A hilariously accurate parody of the period's LSD-induced, messianic flower-child rhetoric, the diary contains such entries as "There's no point to a liberal-arts degree now" and "I want to change the world, and I know I can do it." At the end of ***Drinking in America,*** Mr. Bogosian indicates how little progress he thinks the world has made: He appears as a heavy-lidded, slurred-voiced panhandler, hustling the audience for quarters from the stage edge.

Striving to be obsequious, the bum reassures his potential donors by saying, "You should just get rid of me, forget about me." But even though this threatening, feral apparition weaves away into the dark night soon after, Mr. Bogosian, still eager to change the world, has seen to it that we cannot forget.

Frank Rich, in a review of "Drinking in America," in The New York Times, *January 21, 1986, p. 15.*

JOHN SIMON

In ***Drinking in America,*** [Bogosian] has interwoven monologues from all walks and staggers of life as connected by the thread of alcohol, drugs, and, occasionally, stone-cold-sober self-delusion. Cleverly written and most skillfully acted—with a large and accurate gallery of faces, bodies, and voices—these agents, salesmen, disc jockeys, rock singers, medium and small businessmen, panhandlers, punks, and whatnot are presented with seamless transitions and suggestive contrasts or parallels. A couple of skits (the upper-middle-class man with his "semi-creative job" and the merely photographic rock singer) fail to score, but the others are precise, sharp, witty, and disturbing. Bogosian is flexible and various, and never prolix. To me, this is still something less than theater—nightclub or cabaret—but it is sardonic and uncompromising social commentary. . . . [It] sinks its teeth deep into America and gives *us* something to chew on.

John Simon, in a review of "Drinking in America," in New York *Magazine, Vol. 19, No. 5, February 3, 1986, p. 57.*

BRENDAN GILL

Bogosian propels us through several levels of contemporary American life, from the depths of a Manhattan slum to whatever not very lofty height may be thought appropriate to a brash, money-grubbing Hollywood agent. He calls his rapidfire series of dramatic monologues ***Drinking in America,*** but it might just as accurately be called *American Inferno,* since the alcohol and drugs that Bogosian's characters depend upon to get them through their dreadful nights and days are not causes but symptoms. So forcefully does Bogosian drive his point home that even the one apparently happy character he impersonates strikes us as a repellent freak: he is content with his job, his family, his friends, and his prospects, and we laugh at him for his vacuous benignity.

Laugh? Yes—for, hard as it may be to believe, continuous laughter is the response the audience makes to Bogosian's portrayal of rogues, dolts, hacks, and down-and-outers. (Intellectuals are among the few frequently encountered figures in our society who fail to find a place in his inverted pantheon.) Writing his own epitaph, Swift noted that in death savage indignation could no longer lacerate his heart; Bogosian is an artist as well as a scourge, and his indignation, which is certainly savage, is tempered by the skill of his clowning. A drugged punk terrorizing an old couple in a country cottage, a revivalist preacher threatening us with hellfire, a rock star faking sexual ecstasy—why should these Goya-like monsters give us delight instead of providing us with the occasion for nightmares? That is Bogosian's secret in ***Drinking in America*** . . . , and he does well to keep it.

Brendan Gill, "Winning Losers," in The New Yorker, *Vol. LXI, No. 50, February 3, 1986, p. 85.*

CATHLEEN McGUIGAN

Bogosian, an intense 32-year-old with burning eyes and a voice like a double bass, is one of a small but growing band of avant-garde performers—part satirist, part actor—who are being swept out of downtown Manhattan lofts and into the mainstream world of TV, film and theater. . . .

In Bogosian's [***Drinking in America***], he deftly assumes more than a dozen roles—from a Bowery bum to a Texas industrial-tile salesman to a heavy-metal rocker to a manic Hollywood agent fueled on Jack Daniel's whisky and cocaine. All are loosely linked by the theme of addiction and the corrupting power of the American dream. As a writer and vocal mimic, Bogosian has a terrific ear for the way people talk. Still, the impact of these characters isn't quite unsettling enough; he lets the audience stay at a laughing, comfortable distance. A hyped-up punk's tale of a night of joy riding—inspired by the tough guys Bogosian grew up with in Woburn, Mass.—is a tour de force of comic terror. But a black heroin junkie, sitting alone and justifying his habit, isn't convincing—perhaps because, unlike other Bogosian rogues who address unseen characters, we have no sense of whom he is talking to or why he's explaining himself at all.

Cathleen McGuigan, "From Fringe to Uptown," in Newsweek, *Vol. 107, No. 12, March 24, 1986, p. 69.*

PATRICK AMOS

Eric Bogosian, in keeping with the tradition of titling performance work in such a way as to lay claim to the national character—as in Laurie Anderson's *United States* or Tim Miller's *Democracy in America*—calls his latest one-person performance ***Drinking in America.*** Bogosian's work, more modestly scaled than these other all-American efforts, consists of a quick succession of isolated character studies delivered with few props and lots of acting ability. . . .

Bogosian's dark humor is based on logical inconsistency and contradiction: a salesman who says he is successful because he "cares about people" coaches a prostitute to both continue her education and give him his money's worth; another guy claims he is happy while busily proving himself unable to grasp the concept; a bum conjures up images of luxury while lying on the sidewalk. This complacency-in-contradiction could be summed up by one character's line: "Of course it's ironic,

Arty. Of course it's ironic.'' What is lost after the introduction is where Bogosian stands in all this: he crafts his clichés but never leaves them or positions himself relative to them or even one to another.

As an actor, Bogosian has mastered his characters, their mannerisms, their many voices. Still, there is something insidious about how the work proceeds. The renditions are often moving but, because the characters are always played toward the grain and the audience's expectations, we are moved in directions we are already too willing to go. Our sympathies are liberally solicited for the junkie whose wisdom is of course hard won and heartrending, while the media evangelist is a ludicrous ass we can safely love to hate. The performance ingratiates itself by manipulating our sentiments: Bogosian picks us up with a raucous and wholly gratuitous lip-synch rock performance only to better pull us down with the final quiet poignancy of a street drunk's ''just forget about me'' soliloquy. He doles out artificial highs and lows with finesse, exercising the sort of control over the audience that the characters seem to lack over their own lives.

His characters often talk about power and almost always lack it, whether sexual, financial or political. But the theme of power and its abuse is carried most strongly by Bogosian's marshalling of his acting skills to keep his characters tightly reined. For all their loose-tongued willingness to talk, there is little narrative straying that the performer doesn't collect on immediately. Only the hung-over teenager's recounting of his previous night's exploits suggests what Bogosian is really capable of. . . . This sketch, like the introduction, is a story told, enlisting the power of narrative to take us somewhere unexpected. The distended tale only hints at the real wildness Bogosian could achieve if he let his scenes last more than five minutes, if he introduced his characters to each other, if he let their worlds overlap.

Drinking in America functions finally as an ''actor's showcase,'' a low-budget, self-scripted theatrical work whose prime if not expressed purpose is to give the actor an opportunity to demonstrate his acting talents. It does that. At least in this respect, Bogosian's piece is reminiscent of Whoopi Goldberg's Broadway solo last year. Both Bogosian and Goldberg come from performance space if not performance art backgrounds, both rely on dark comedy and characterizations, and both seem destined for more traditional acting careers. (pp. 189-90)

Patrick Amos, ''Eric Bogosian at the American Place Theater,'' in Art in America, *Vol. 74, No. 4, April, 1986, pp. 189-90.*

KEVIN GRUBB

More a performance artist than a stand-up comic, Bogosian's fascination long has been with humanity's darker side: necrophiliacs, torturers, Times Square hawkers, the hopelessly addicted. It is with this last group that ***Drinking in America*** concerns itself. Intoxicated with power, Bogosian's menagerie of coke-heads, alcoholics, sexual compulsives, and thrill-seekers offers a brooding meditation on a deteriorating America.

Bogosian opens the show by reading an excerpt from a journal entry he wrote in 1971 while he was an idealistic college student. Written while he was on acid, the entry becomes a startling stream-of-consciousness monologue when read. In its naive appraisal of love, politics, success, and other on-the-threshold-of-adulthood concerns, this opening scene provides an appropriate backdrop for all that follows. . . .

Drinking in America offers the blackest humor of any Bogosian work so far. His ear for dialects, gift for capturing movements that reveal character, and, most importantly, insight into a decaying American Gothic make us shiver even as we laugh.

Kevin Grubb, in a review of ''Drinking in America,'' in Dance Magazine, *Vol. LX, No. 5, May, 1986, p. 104.*

Ben(jamin William) Bova

1932-

American novelist, nonfiction writer, essayist, short story writer, and editor.

Bova's speculative fiction is distinguished by its credible projections of social disintegration and its convincing arguments for increased technological research and continued space exploration. As a writer of both science fiction and nonfiction works, Bova maintains a consistent viewpoint: that technology is the answer to humanity's present problems and to its future survival. He believes that the migration of people to space colonies throughout the universe is a viable solution to overpopulation and the mismanagement of the earth's natural resources. Bova has advanced these opinions through both his literature and his editorial positions at *Analog Science Fiction/ Science Fact* and *Omni* magazines.

Bova has published over fifty titles, including works for young adults, during the past two decades. His most notable early adult novels are *The Multiple Man* (1976), a speculative tale about a United States president who disappears and is replaced in office by a genetically-engineered clone; *City of Darkness* (1976), a story of racial unrest in a near-future Manhattan in which a domed, maximum-security prison is opened to the public once yearly as a tourist attraction; and *Colony* (1978), an examination of space colonization as an alternative to life on an overpopulated earth in which three international groups vie for world dominance. While some reviewers faulted Bova for stock characterizations and didactic tendencies, most praised his concise style and scientifically plausible plots.

Bova's recent fiction combines themes relating to geopolitical intrigue and the effects on humanity of extraterrestrial contact. *Voyagers* (1981), one of Bova's most accessible novels, concerns the discovery of extraterrestrial life in orbit near earth and the attempts of the United States and the Soviet Union to intercept the alien spaceship. Although some critics cited Bova's reliance on conventional characterization and plot, Spider Robinson considered *Voyagers* "the book to give to that friend . . . who thinks SF is escapist fantasy." *Privateers* (1985) is a precautionary tale about the dangers Americans may face if the Russians gain control of outer space. Some critics suggested that Bova wrote this book in support of the Strategic Defense Initiative—the "Star Wars" system advocated by President Ronald Reagan. *Voyagers II: The Alien Within* (1986), a sequel to *Voyagers,* focuses on Keith Stoner, an American astronaut who made contact with the alien vessel in the first book. Stoner is revived from a twenty-year state of suspended animation and is later revealed to have absorbed the alien's technological and mental capabilities. While this novel was considered less successful than its companion volume, Bova was praised for his realistic presentation of the possible existence of other intelligent life forms in the universe.

Bova's canon also encompasses such diverse material as *THX 1138* (1971), a novelization of a screenplay by George Lucas and Walter Murch; *Survival Guide for the Suddenly Single* (1974), a lighthearted examination of divorce; and *The Starcrossed* (1975), a satire of a short-lived television series on which Bova worked with Harlan Ellison. Prominent among his books for young adults is the Exiles trilogy—*Exiled from Earth* (1971), *Flight of Exiles* (1972), and *End of Exile* (1975)—which traces the lives of two thousand scientists and their descendants who have been banned from earth.

Photograph by Jay Kay Klein

(See also *Children's Literature Review,* Vol. 3; *Contemporary Authors,* Vols. 5-8, rev. ed.; *Contemporary Authors New Revision Series,* Vol. 11; *Something about the Author,* Vol. 6; and *Dictionary of Literary Biography Yearbook: 1981.*)

ROBERT BERKVIST

The level of imaginative thinking is not terribly high in ***The Star Conquerors,*** but Ben Bova has written a deft, well-paced war story dealing with an unoriginal theme (earth menaced by a far older, seemingly irresistible civilization). Jeff Knowland, earth's knight in shining space armor, is too thinly drawn to cast much of a shadow, for all his limitless capabilities. The supporting cast, too, is composed of mere sketches, but is adequate to the task of convoying Jeff and humanity's fortunes across the galaxy to the lair of the merciless Masters. Although the route is a well-traveled one, it need not be dull with a competent driver at the wheel; Mr. Bova is that.

Robert Berkvist, "Probing the Galaxies," in The New York Times Book Review, *January 31, 1960, p. 32.*

P. SCHUYLER MILLER

[***The Star Conquerors***] is a notch or two above the average for the series, and introduces a new writer—a neighbor of Isaac Asimov's—with a nice hand at interstellar war. (p. 163)

Narrator is a young humanoid observer with Earth's Star Watch, in the war against the mysterious Masters for domination of one segment of the galaxy. The Masters never appear; their forces are the reptilian Saurians, by whom Alan Bakerman—properly Ahgh'loun B'khrom'mnin—was brought up, and a variety of other humanoid mercenaries. Some of the Star Watch, quite naturally, are a bit suspicious of Alan's own real loyalties.

In lively action that shuttles from the stars back to Earth, then to the stars again, and at last corners the Masters, we get a vivid impression of the immenseness of the galaxy. The characters are nicely complicated, and there is a Pyrrhic twist to the final victory. While never pretending to be more than a fast-moving adventure yarn, the book manages to be more adult than all but the very best of . . . [the] teen-age science-fiction novels. (pp. 163-64)

P. Schuyler Miller, in a review of "The Star Conquerors," in Analog Science Fiction/Science Fact, *Vol. LXV, No. 5, July, 1960, pp. 163-64.*

ROBERT BERKVIST

Ben Bova's ***Star Watchman*** . . . is standard, but very readable fare. Emil Vorgens is an interstellar policeman of sorts. A rebellion is under way on an outpost of the Terran Empire. Vorgens's orders: Put out the fire. Never a dull moment.

Robert Berkvist, "Other Places, Other Planets," in The New York Times Book Review, *March 7, 1965, p. 26.*

P. SCHUYLER MILLER

[***Star Watchman***] is, in a sense, a sequel to ***The Star Conquerors***. . . . It dips into the same future universe about a hundred years later than the earlier book, and shows some of the problems arising from the victory of the Terran Empire over the Masters. On another level, it is a pretty straightforward parallel to our present world situation. (p. 158)

For the United States and Russia, former allies against a common enemy now standing each other off in a cold war, take the Terran Empire and the humanoid Komani. In place of Viet Nam, or Korea, take the frontier planet Shinar, reft by civil war and occupied by a Komani force, with religious complications, tribal customs, Armed Forces infallibility, State Department inertia and fug-headedness . . .

Emil Vorgens, young Star Watch officer, is sent to Shinar to negotiate a truce with the Komani. Instead, he finds himself dragged into a kind of Custer's Last Stand of an encircled force of Imperial Marines and up to his ears in local politics. (p. 159)

P. Schuyler Miller, in a review of "Star Watchman," in Analog Science Fiction/Science Fact, *Vol. LXXV, No. 4, June, 1965, pp. 158-59.*

PETER J. HENNIKER-HEATON

[In] ***The Weathermakers*** [Ben Bova takes us] back to Earth, to Boston. Boston as it is today, except that by some aberration sailing boats on the Charles Basin see the late April sun setting behind the towers of Back Bay! Ben Bova has built a really thrilling tale out of how a young businessman and his associates make a bid to control the weather for the benefit of his father's business and business in general.

The story swings out into the Atlantic, up and down the east coast, crosses American skies to Hawaii, and backs again to Boston, taking rain and sunshine, hurricanes and political storms in its stride. This book, if widely read, may result in meteorological courses being somewhat overcrowded in a few years' time; for who isn't tempted by the possibility of bringing the weather to heel?

Peter J. Henniker-Heaton, "Identity Crisis—Sci-Fi Style," in The Christian Science Monitor, *May 2, 1968, p. B8.*

RAYMOND W. BARBER

When the Cobra, a supersonic fighter plane, falls to pieces over the Arctic Ocean, Paul Sarko, who designed the special alloy used for the plane, is called in to determine the cause of the accident. What follows [in ***Out of the Sun***] is a mixture of spies, scientific investigation, and air combat with a little romance thrown in. . . . [This] title's rapid pace, high interest level, sustained mood, and suspense-filled plot make this an attractive title. . . .

Raymond W. Barber, in a review of "Out of the Sun," in School Library Journal, *Vol. 15, No. 1, July, 1968, p. 197.*

PUBLISHERS WEEKLY

Set in the future where galaxies are inhabited and peace is kept by a universal police force and a new machine that enables people to release their hostilities in a harmless way, [***The Dueling Machine***] combines excitement, scientific accuracy and credibility to provide thought-provoking and enjoyable reading.

A review of "The Dueling Machine," in Publishers Weekly, *Vol. 196, No. 16, October 20, 1969, p. 61.*

ELIZABETH HAYNES

[***The Dueling Machine*** is a] fast-moving, thoughtful SF novel set in the far future. Man has spread outward to the stars, but the inhabited planets are comparatively few and very crowded. To relieve the psychological tensions resulting from close living, Dr. Leoh invents the dueling machine—a device that amplifies the imagination and enables men to fight a duel to the death without actually being harmed physically or mentally. However, one high-ranking official goes insane and another really is killed during a duel. . . . Fans of the author's ***The Weathermakers*** . . . will find this new book very different, and perhaps not as enjoyable. Still, it is entertaining, above-average science fiction.

Elizabeth Haynes, in a review of "The Dueling Machine," in School Library Journal, *Vol. 16, No. 3, November, 1969, p. 126.*

THE CHRISTIAN SCIENCE MONITOR

At 16, Danny Romano has already spent half his life in reformatory institutions. Now he's imprisoned again, but in a futuristic reeducation center watched over by a near-infallible computer. The center is designed to reform its teen-age patients and release them as soon as they are ready to progress into the world and upward through it.

Danny doesn't want to progress. Burningly, unceasingly, he wants—and tries—to escape. How the institution turns that fierce determination to Danny's advantage is clearly told in Ben Bova's ***Escape!*** . . .

Utopian, constructive, kindly, optimistic. Boyish and mannish. Highly readable.

N. M., "Thud-and-Blunder Stuff," in The Christian Science Monitor, *May 7, 1970, p. B6.*

GILBERT MILLSTEIN

[***Escape!*** is] the story of Danny Romano, convicted of attempted murder and sent for therapy to a very special juvenile center—which, unfortunately, soon becomes more important to the author than Danny. The center is operated by a man of endless good-will (himself, a classic cliche) assisted by a computer programmed for the future and able to speak when the occasion demands dialogue. One gathers that all this is part of Mr. Bova's wish-fulfillment, his hope that such a combination of forces will solve the problems of tomorrow's Danny Romanos. I found the demonstration unconvincing.

Gilbert Millstein, "Boys on the Run," in The New York Times Book Review, *Part II, May 24, 1970, p. 20.*

ELIZABETH HAYNES

[***Exiled from Earth*** is an] absorbing, chilling SF picture of what the earth could be like in the not-too-far-off future. Computer specialist Lou Christopher, absorbed in his work on a genetic engineering project, is abruptly arrested and told that he and all the other scientists on the project are to be permanently exiled from earth. The world government considers the project a threat to the tenuous stability and peace of the overcrowded earth. Lou escapes, is recaptured, helps thwart a plot against the government—all to no avail. In the end he and the others turn their faces to the stars rather than stagnate in exile. . . . Another good story by the author of ***The Weathermakers.***

Elizabeth Haynes, in a review of "Exiled from Earth," in School Library Journal, *Vol. 18, No. 1, September, 1971, p. 171.*

DONALD GODDARD

[***Flight of Exiles*** is] an episode in a stellar odyssey, this time by 20,000 Earthlings looking for a new home in the galaxy. But here is all the space gadgetry, mock-technological detail and cardboard characterization we have grown accustomed to. Will Larry the leader outwit Dan the psychotic and save his precious cargo of deep-frozen humanity? After a voyage of 40 billion kilometers, can the crew resist the lure of the golden planet beneath them and journey on another 50 years to more hospitable climes? Of course they can. But if short on suspense, the story is never less than interesting.

I can forgive Mr. Bova almost anything for his splendid idea of loading all the world's genetic scientists aboard a space ship to experiment on each other—and then dispatching the whole lot to Alpha Centauri.

Donald Goddard, "Twists, Turns," in The New York Times Book Review, *November 26, 1972, p. 8.*

RUTH ROBINSON

Larry Belsen and Dan Christopher, sons of the scientists in ***Exiled from Earth*** . . . , both fall in love with the same girl [in ***Flight of Exiles***] and are also rivals for leadership of the exiles who have been in space for 50 years. A fire, which could be sabotage, and a death, which could be murder, add to the crisis brought on by the discovery that the planet where they intend to settle is unsuitable. Deciding whether a new generation should be genetically altered to live there or another 50-year journey to a more favorable world should be attempted is left to Larry and Dan—and one of them is psychotic! While the love interest may irritate some SF fans, . . . the undemanding story is a good steppingstone to Heinlein's more complex *Orphans of the Sky*. . . .

Ruth Robinson, in a review of "Flight of Exiles," in School Library Journal, *Vol. 19, No. 5, January 15, 1973, p. 266.*

PUBLISHERS WEEKLY

Alex Morgan [the hero of ***When the Sky Burned,***] is a young man with an Oedipal problem—his mama, who is head of the moon colonists who survived the holocaust which blew Earth up, wants him to go back down to Earth (now more or less free from nuclear pollution) to find and kill his daddy. . . . Alex finds his father, but doesn't kill him, goes through a series of grueling adventures (which we find out later are "tests"), meets a pretty Earth girl, combats a malevolent rival from the moon colony who is after his mother (more of that Oedipus stuff) and finally elects to join the Earth people—for the ultimate sake of the moon people who must learn to re-establish their connections with Earth on a peaceful basis. All this is on the level of simple-minded action-adventure; the only concession to an adult audience is a four-letter word or a reference to sex scattered here and there.

A review of "When the Sky Burned," in Publishers Weekly, *Vol. 203, No. 26, June 25, 1973, p. 70.*

ROBERT L. MIDDLETON

[***When the Sky Burned*** is] a rousing adventure story in which the society of the future is suggested rather than delineated. Its relentless pace gives the reader no time to notice the flimsiness of the scenery and the props. Recommended. . . .

Robert L. Middleton, in a review of "When the Sky Burned," in Library Journal, *Vol. 98, No. 15, September 1, 1973, p. 2466.*

DENISE M. WILMS

[In ***End of Exile,*** a group of young people] must decide whether to go against their established taboos and repair the ship's instruments to save themselves, or cling to the old directives left to them as children, forbidding them to tamper with any devices. The catalyst for change is Linc, who knows he could try to repair some of the deterioriating machines; when he successfully fixes a vital pump, a power struggle begins with Linc opposed by the maniacal cripple Monel. The conflict escalates to life-and-death proportions as the ship heads for oblivion unless its instruments can function to chart the craft down to its target planet. Bova plays the suspense down to the last pages, and readers coming along for the excitement can also ponder the prominent theme of tradition versus social change.

Denise M. Wilms, in a review of "End of Exile," in The Booklist, *Vol. 72, No. 4, October 15, 1975, p. 297.*

DAN MILLER

[In ***The Starcrossed,*** Bova] weaves a witty satire around the late and unlamented science-fiction television series "The Starlost." There are guffaws aplenty as Bova unmercifully dissects the Hollywood TV world that produced a series embarrassing to its actors, writers, producers, and SF fans alike. . . . The first-rate story romps around [Ron Gabriel, the "starcrossed" author based on Harlan Ellison, and his] struggle to protect his artistic integrity from the rapacious claws of futuristic commercialism and incompetence. Bova forsakes subtlety for burlesque toward the conclusion, but somehow it doesn't matter. The laughs keep coming.

Dan Miller, in a review of "The Starcrossed," in The Booklist, *Vol. 72, No. 9, January 1, 1976, p. 615.*

PHILLIP H. SCHNEE

[***The Starcrossed***] is Science Fiction, the time is about thirty years in the future, and Bill Oxnard, an engineer, has just invented 3-D television. The problem is to get together a show and some backers for the first 3-D series.

They come up with the idea of a Science Fiction "Romeo and Juliet." The putting together of this show is what the story is really about. It is a satire of the television industry. . . .

Of course the show is a flop and the blame is put on the writer even though the final product is nothing like his original concept. I think it fitting that Science Fiction be the scene for this debacle, since Science Fiction has never gotten a fair shake from television.

This book is enjoyable. . . .

Phillip H. Schnee, in a review of "The Starcrossed," in Best Sellers, *Vol. 35, No. 12, March, 1976, p. 366.*

GERALD JONAS

[***End of Exile***] is a fresh, vigorous and altogether successful reworking of one of the classic themes of science fiction. A huge spaceship, bound for a distant star with a cargo of would-be colonists, suffers a terrible disaster en route. The leaders of the expedition are killed; much of the ship is wrecked. The survivors gather in those areas where the life-support systems are intact. Their minds benumbed by tragedy and by the struggle to stay alive, they gradually revert to a primitive existence. In time they forget about the original purpose of the voyage; they forget they are on a voyage at all; they come to think of the ship as the universe itself.

In ***End of Exile*** the survivors are all children. As infants, they were cared for by an old man named Jerlet. Then Jerlet went away, leaving behind taped instructions that the children still obey as if they were the Ten Commandments: No violence, no tampering with machines, etc. But a boy named Linc learns the truth. Jerlet's commandments were safety-precautions for the very young. Unless the children take control of the ship and change its course, it will soon plunge into a yellow sun. Linc confronts his friends with a clear choice: Grow up and accept responsibility, or die. . . . The conflict, as Bova describes it, is taut with suspense; every move that each young person makes is treated with the utmost seriousness. ***End of Exile*** is the third book in a trilogy, but it stands alone as a story. . . .

Gerald Jonas, in a review of "End of Exile," in The New York Times Book Review, *March 7, 1976, p. 18.*

ROBERT BERKVIST

[In ***City of Darkness***] Ben Bova, a practiced hand at science fiction, takes a down-to-earth look at New York in the indeterminate future and finds it has become a maximum-security prison for undesirables. The city is enclosed in a dome, open to visitors from the Outside only during the summer months. Then, sanitized suburbanites from the super-healthy but boringly regulated Tracts, where even the weather is controlled, come to New York as to some down-and-dirty Disneyland. . . . Warring gangs roam the filthy avenues, the shadows hide poverty, fear and death.

Into this forbidding world steps Ron Morgan, a Tract teen-ager rebelling against his dictatorial father. In the city for a fling, on the eve of having to choose his "career vector," Ron is trapped inside the dome. . . . He buys survival by putting his mechanical skills at the service of one of the gangs. He even acquires a family of sorts. When racial warfare erupts, Ron is captured by the Muslims, a highly disciplined black group intent on a breakout. The Muslim leader, Timmy Jim, tells Ron why the city was closed: "They took out the whites, all right. Rich and poor . . . but they kept *us* inside. . . . Wrote off all the welfare cases. Left us to be rat bait." Then Timmy Jim sets Ron free. "Go on Outside," he says, "tell 'em all about us. . . . We'll be comin'." Ron leaves the city determined to be an instrument of change. . . .

Mr. Bova is a good storyteller, and ***City of Darkness*** is a tingling adventure until its closing chapters. The desolate dome city is beautifully evoked, the action fiercely realistic. But all this believability crumbles under an overload of portentousness. When Mr. Bova insists on turning his sprightly cautionary tale into a heavy-handed morality play, that dome is soon awash in stereotypical nonsense.

Robert Berkvist, in a review of "City of Darkness," in The New York Times Book Review, *April 11, 1976, p. 10.*

CELIA BETSKY

[The ten stories in ***Forward in Time***] were written over a period of 10 years, and the time periods they cover range from the near to the far distant future. In **"The Next Logical Step"** a warlike CIA man is introduced to a computer that is the last word in wargames simulators, and he ends up slightly pacified. **"Zero Gee"** features the series character astronaut Chester Kinsman, who looks forward to a three-day earth orbit with a lovely lady journalist, then learns that she is to be chaperoned. In **"The Perfect Warrior,"** a long segment from a novel about interplanetary warfare, differences are settled with a sophisticated dueling machine, which is supposed to leave both combatants unharmed, but doesn't always work that way.

Celia Betsky, in a review of "Forward in Time," in Saturday Review, *Vol. 3, No. 14, April 17, 1976, p. 33.*

HENRI C. VEIT

[***The Multiple Man***] is an excellent political thriller welded to sf elements, fascinating and all too plausible. The United States is involved in a Middle East crisis and high unemployment has led to riots. The President's press secretary is called in to cover up the death of what appears to be an exact duplicate of the President, found murdered in a Boston alley. . . . The denouement is splendidly built with pulsing excitement.

Henri C. Veit, in a review of "The Multiple Man," in Library Journal, *Vol. 101, No. 11, June 1, 1976, p. 1312.*

SALLY C. ESTES AND STEPHANIE ZVIRIN

Inconsistencies in the story line, unfortunate stereotyping, and insufficient character motivations weaken . . . [the] already overburdened plot [of ***City of Darkness***]. Nevertheless, Bova's grim futuristic setting and graphic style plus the contemporary theme of youthful gangland violence should make this popular. . . .

Sally C. Estes and Stephanie Zvirin, in a review of "City of Darkness: A Novel," in The Booklist, *Vol. 72, No. 21, July 1, 1976, p. 1521.*

RICHARD E. GEIS

The intriguing problem for the reader of ***The Starcrossed*** is to try to divine how much of this story of a betrayed, undermined, misguided sf television series is masked truth, how much slightly distorted for effect, how much is plot-romance, and how much is highly relished, malign satire.

Ben Bova was the science advisor for the one-season disaster of a sf series, "Starlost." Harlan Ellison was the originator of the idea, did work like a trojan to get it off the ground, did write the opening scripts (which were butchered, beyond his control) and the abortion was produced in Canada.

Harlan has detailed this hellish experience in his oft-reprinted article, "Somehow, I Don't Think We're in Kansas, Toto."

But is/was Harlan really the irrepressible, aggressive, talented, woman-chasing, hard-driving man Ben Bova describes in the character named Ron Gabriel? Was there so much incredible backbiting, scheming, lying, cheating, etc. etc. etc. as revealed in this novel? Were Canadian highschool students recruited to produce the script ideas for "Starlost"? (To save money.) Were the Canadian artists and craftsmen so dismally dumb! and stubborn? Were the actors so untalented and miscast? Was the producer such a misbegotten cretin? Was the director really an acid-freak on the skids? We may never know. It's marvelous fun to guess, though.

Richard E. Geis, "Starschlocked," in Science Fiction Review, *Vol. 5, No. 3, August, 1976, p. 48.*

NEWGATE CALLENDAR

Ahead of our time is ***The Multiple Man*** by Ben Bova. . . . It takes place in a future America that has the most popular President since Kennedy; an America that has a Jewish Vice-President and a press secretary very much on the ball. In Boston, while the President is making a speech, a body is found—the exact double of the President, even to fingerprints. This has happened once before. Who is in the White House? The real thing? A clone? A *something*?

Part science fiction, ***The Multiple Man*** has a solution that surpasses belief. But in its comic-strip manner it is a lot of fun. (p. 21)

Newgate Callendar, in a review of "The Multiple Man," in The New York Times Book Review, *August 29, 1976, pp. 21-2.*

JOANNA RUSS

[***Millennium*** is] a slick, optimistic replay of 1776 in which a predictably humane-and-decent society on the moon revolts against a predictable dystopia on earth. The moon society is half American and half Russian, which gives the author a chance for a lot of International Understanding (there are, luckily, no Maoist Chinese practicing self-criticism in the corridors) with a lot of sloppiness in the beginning, great wedges of exposition, and some Sears Roebuck eroticism that annoyed me until I realized the author was simply trying to trot out his characters as fast as possible. . . . The story that unrolls after this, however, is slick enough to be fun, and even moving if you can forget that its assumptions are more-than-twice-told tales. I'm tempted to call the novel *Executive to the Stars* but that only pegs the school to which it belongs, and however stodgy the school (and the ideas thereof) the book is an OK, intelligent workout for an idle hour or for people who are terrified of live books. (p. 70)

Joanna Russ, in a review of "Millennium," in The Magazine of Fantasy and Science Fiction, *Vol. 51, No. 5, November, 1976, p. 70.*

T. A. SHIPPEY

A Novel about People and Politics in the Year 1999: this is the subtitle of Ben Bova's ***Millennium,*** but like most such authorial promptings it contains more piety than truth. The politics of 1999 are those of 1776, with the twin cities of Selene (Lunagrad and Moonbase) seceding from their parent states just like the thirteen colonies; it is not a new idea and Mr. Bova feels no need to explore it. As for the people, their roles naturally divide into George Washingtons and Benedict Arnolds, while what individualities they have look customized: one is black, one crippled, one has a family Earthside, one comes from an ethnic minority in the USSR, and so on—one "feature" to each character to provide a handle for motive/manipulation.

If ***Millennium*** really was a novel about people and politics, one could say little good of it. But of course its true subject is things: the networks of laser-armed satellites which USA and USSR are rushing into service, the projections which show that the side to finish first will have total world domination, the statistics which call for the losing nation to launch a pre-emptive strike just to keep a percentage of itself in being. The strength of science fiction of the kind Mr Bova writes is that it recognizes and communicates the strength of non-human causality. That is how things are, it insists, not just how they might be in the millennium.

T. A. Shippey, "The Things Things Can Do," in The Times Literary Supplement, *No. 3957, January 27, 1978, p. 82.*

ORSON SCOTT CARD

Set in the same universe as ***Millennium*** (but using none of the plot lines from that book), [***Colony*** is] a typical bestseller-type novel which follows a newswoman, a black revolutionary, an Arab revolutionary, and the result of genetic manipulation experiments through the vicissitudes of an attempt by big corporations to take over the world, even if it means destroying it in the process.

But beyond that, there's nothing in it typical of the normal bestseller, whose highest aspiration is to reach the level of junk. Ben can *write,* you see, and furthermore his sole objective is *not* just to sell books—he also intends that his book say something that will linger in the mind. The reporter, Evelyn, learns about the real world and grows up in the process of the novel (What? A bestseller with character development?); colony head Dr. Cobb, who at first seems all-wise and all-powerful, turns out to have been blinded by his own vision of what the universe *should* be, and it takes more down-to-earth minds to solve some of the immediate problems; corporate megalomaniac Garrison, thoroughgoing bastard though he is, is also shown to be somewhat loyal and inventive and clever. . . .

While avoiding the shallowness of the bestseller, Ben has also avoided some typical pitfalls of the sf writer. His L-5 colony is a marvelous thing, and it might have been tempting to milk it to death, but he resisted the temptation to gosh-wow us with this marvelous colony and set most of the action on earth, with only the climax of the book occurring on the colony. Furthermore, the solution to the crisis at the end has its groundwork laid in Chapter One; there is no cheating, but I doubt you'll guess what the resolution is until Ben wants you to.

Colony is a genuine thriller, a good science fiction novel and a fine piece of writing. My quibbles are minor: Maybe people *do* fall desperately in love at first screw, as Ben has Bahjat and Denny doing, but I found it hard to believe that a few ecstatic nights could make a woman like Bahjat go off the deep end as she did. Maybe a handful of corporate giants *could* meet fairly often without anybody knowing about it and without any of them stabbing the others in the back, but I doubt it. . . .

I enjoyed ***Colony.*** I was tired when I started reading it nearly at midnight—I was wide awake when I finished reading it at five a.m. But my guess is that I'm not the only sf reader who'll put . . . attempts by some of our best writers to tap the mainstream market on the back burner for a while. (p. 29)

Orson Scott Card, in a review of "Colony," in Science Fiction Review, *Vol. 7, No. 5, November, 1978, pp. 28-9.*

EDWARD WOOD

I'm sure I was not alone in being displeased when Ben Bova's ***Millennium*** failed to make it to the Hugo nominations for best novel of 1976. However, in ***Colony*** . . . Bova has written an even better novel which means it's his best to date. It has a small connection with ***Millennium*** in that we meet again, very briefly, Frank Colt, Emanuel De Paolo and Leonov. This is not their book. This is the book of David Adams, a genetically enhanced man born on Island One. Island One is a space colony akin to O'Neill Life Colonies but in the L4 position for reasons of economy (not specified) and aesthetics (specified).

The action of the novel covers the time period May 2008 to December of the same year and ranges from Island One to the Moon to various portions of Earth. A world government is trying to feed and obtain energy for eight billion people while the Five Corporations own everything of value on Earth and in space and are content to keep it that way. They secretly supply arms and money to the People's Revolutionary Underground (PRU), a very large international, terrorist organization, that believes national governments can handle the world's problems more efficiently and with greater urgency than the world government. To keep the pot boiling, the Five Corporations start a few famines here and there with their control of the weather. Much of the action is on Earth. . . . It is a fast moving story that gives a very convincing picture of the future. Bova has written a story that makes the reader want to read more and more after finishing the last page—that's a true victory of the writer's craft.

But it is not a perfect book. Bova believes corporations are much more efficient than I do. Also I don't understand how David Adams is genetically manipulated after being saved from his mother's womb (she was a worker killed during the construction of Island One) as a fetus of two months. That's a lot of cells to change, even in groups. Also terrorist movements that are small can remain fairly secret but large movements invite infiltration and counter action.

It is not the prerogative of a reviewer to tell a writer what to do but ***Colony*** and ***Millennium*** could be the beginnings of a joyous romp across the 21st century with a book per decade per planet/satellite, so by 2100 A.D. mankind would be fairly close to Pluto. (pp. 166-67)

Edward Wood, in a review of "Colony," in Analog Science Fiction/Science Fact, *Vol. 99, No. 3, March, 1979, pp. 166-67.*

HAL W. HALL

Set in the framework of the Terran Empire (the same setting as his ***Star Conquerors*** [1959]), . . . [***Star Watchman***] is the story of Emil Vorgens, a junior officer of the Empire's Star Watch, on his first—and minor—assignment to a planet called Shinar. As is often the case, the simple becomes complex and dangerous, and Vorgens is faced with a hostile alien force, a rebellious internal faction among the Shinar natives, and an attractive girl. There is a clear subplot of a vigorous young man rebelling against his father, an element which will provide a point of ready identification for many young people. The other major characters are both youthful and successful, and the story is well paced. It can be read with enjoyment by young and old alike. (pp. 32-3)

Hal W. Hall, in a review of "Star Watchman," in Science Fiction & Fantasy Book Review, *Vol. I, No. 3, April, 1979, pp. 32-3.*

KIRKUS REVIEWS

[Chet Kinsman] is the brightest star in the fledgling Air Force space corps until the emergency reconnaissance mission in which he murders a Russian woman cosmonaut. Trying to pick up the pieces of his life and career, he hits on the idea of a permanent non-military "Moonbase," and manages to make the dream reality at the cost of horrific moral and political compromises. Despite occasional pretensions to moral complexity, [***Kinsman***] betrays its origin as a handful of shorter pieces; the episodes remain perfunctorily linked, and such recurrent motifs as the shifting NASA-Air Force rivalries are not really brought into focus. Competent but disappointing.

A review of "Kinsman," in Kirkus Reviews, *Vol. 47, No. 12, June 15, 1979, p. 713.*

THOMAS D. CLARESON

[In ***Kinsman***] Bova's protagonist enters the present Air Force Academy, hoping to become an astronaut, even though he is a Quaker who must break with family tradition to achieve his ambition. In the course of his career, he is forced to kill a Russian cosmonaut during hand-to-hand combat in space, is threatened with grounding as a result of his reactions and must undergo therapy. His major achievement comes, however, when he is instrumental in persuading American businessmen and congressional legislators to finance Moonbase—and have that colony be something other than simply a military base. . . . [Bova] again voices that dream of reaching outward to the stars which has so deeply motivated the American space program.

Thomas D. Clareson, "Galaxy of Tomorrow's Tales," in Book World—The Washington Post, *September 23, 1979, p. 7.*

EDWARD BRYANT

The theme [of ***Voyagers***] is the long- and well-used one of first contact between human beings and extraterrestrials. . . .

I had the feeling, reading ***Voyagers,*** that there was some auctorial intent to aim this novel at the general, non-sf audience. I'm afraid that much of the material will appear tired and overused to the reader familiar with similar stories.

The novel centers around the discovery that an object, probably an alien starship, is heading from the vicinity of Jupiter toward Earth. Astrophysicist and one-time astronaut Keith Stoner knows it's of paramount importance that the human species *do* something about this—recognize and accept the existence of extraterrestrial intelligence, and mount a manned expedition to intercept the interstellar vehicle.

At first the authorities keep the revelation a secret. Stoner finds himself whisked away by Naval Intelligence. Meantime, both the American and Soviet governments start gearing up plans to capitalize politically, militarily and technologically on whatever goodies the alien phenomenon may provide.

In true best-seller style, the book introduces a broad cast of stock characters: The tough, party-line female KGB agent; the tired English double-agent she controls with tiny electrodes planted in his brain; the gay Nobel-laureate cosmologist who is recalled from monastic retreat by the Vatican to check out Catholic interests in the man-is-not-alone-anymore affair; the unstable Dutch astronomer zonked out on PCP; the randy Russian language expert who puts personal friendship and the spirit of scientific inquiry above national interests; the lucky female grad student who is the middle-aged, middle-class male's interpretation of a liberated woman, and so forth.

Most of the book is taken up with the mechanics of first coping with the idea of ET contact, then getting ready for a combined Soviet-American space mission, finally sending Keith Stoner and a Russian cosmonaut to check out the alien spacecraft. It's neither good nor bad—just standard stuff. Competent is probably the word I should use here. Despite desultory pokes at making the characters fully-dimensional people, the focus remains on the uncomplicated, linear plot.

Excitement finally comes after the exploratory probe launch when Stoner and his partner reach the intruder. This is where the oft-cited sense of wonder in science fiction comes into play. Ben Bova felt wonder when he visualized that spaceship. He could empathize with Keith Stoner when the scientist jet-packed across the void between Earth ship and ET. As readers, we feel wonder too, the awe at making contact with something from beyond. . . . And that's what contemporary science is all about. (p. 14)

Edward Bryant, "Man and Superman: Beyond Human Limits," in Book World—The Washington Post, *September 27, 1981, pp. 10, 14.*

ALGIS BUDRYS

Voyagers combines the realism of near-future technological stories and international-intrigue novels with the almost uniquely science-fictional sense of the brooding majesty of the Universe. It is, in other words, an intelligent practitioner's deliberate attempt to translate science fiction into the bestseller marketplace. . . . (pp. 51-2)

Bova postulates a situation in which an alien spacecraft enters the Solar System, eventually approaches Earth just closely enough to be reached if a joint U.S./U.S.S.R. effort is made at crash priority, and then is reached at the very limit of feasibility by one astronaut who has very little time in which to study it and its enigmatic contents. The bulk of the wordage is procedural; on this simple skeleton, Bova erects subplot after verisimilitudinous subplot and scene in which we get a very convincing sense of what this would mean to the U.S. space establishment and government, within big-time research academe, within the Kremlin, and within the Vatican as well as in the Bible Belt. It is essentially a scenario in response to the simple question What would happen to our society if we, in our time, were faced with incontrovertible proof there were other civilized races out there somewhere?

No more than that. But that's quite a bit. And Bova—who has not always been my favorite SF writer, . . . has produced some excellent, compelling prose to carry it onward. It's the very best fiction writing I've ever seen from him. More important, it is a full grade beyond the necessary or usual in this kind of book.

There are *some* cardboard characters among the principal cast, and I think they would still have been there if all the sub-plots had been preserved, since the she-loves-me, she-loves-me-not exchanges between the hero and the heroine are stereotyped *per se*. But this is not true of all the characters, particularly the very well-drawn Russians, and most particularly the ponderous KGB functionary.

Bova has done a bang-up job on that aspect of his book, and a very good job on most of the others. For readers, there are only slight glitches—missing bridges; characters sometimes depart to perform some crucial task in which they might fail, but succeed—or fail—offstage. A fair number of recent SF novels have been accepted and rewarded as major works while containing exactly similar discontinuities, whether for the same reason is not important here. What is important is they obviously don't constitute major deterrences to pleasure. (pp. 52-3)

Algis Budrys, in a review of "Voyagers," in The Magazine of Fantasy and Science Fiction, *Vol. 61, No. 5, November, 1981, pp. 51-3.*

SPIDER ROBINSON

I think Ben Bova is one of the most moral, most socially responsible, and most criminally underrated writers in science fiction. (p. 116)

Ben Bova, since he took over *Analog* and began one of the most brilliant careers in SF editing nine years ago, has produced several science fact books, a manual on selling SF, a survival guide for the suddenly single (in collaboration with Barbara Berson), a couple of superior juveniles, several story collections, and at least four major SF novels.

Voyagers is the latest and the biggest and, I think, the best of these latter, a work whose maturity and skill are as massive as its sheer physical bulk. . . . It is one of those rare books which are accessible to the most ignorant non-reader-of-SF, without being so watered down as to insult the intelligence of the faithful.

I began this by describing Ben as moral and responsible. ***Voyagers*** may serve to demonstrate what I mean: Ben's insistence on tackling themes and topics of genuine importance and immediate relevance. His books tend to take place in near-future fictons which are more or less straight-line "If this goes on—" extrapolations of present-day reality, and to focus on crises whose roots are clearly discernible in the here and now. His books always leave you with the feeling, "Yes—that is the way it might happen." Again and again he returns to the question of racial survival vs. nuclear holocaust, and to the theme of personal heroism. In ***Kinsman*** and especially in the magnificent ***Millennium,*** Ben examined the continuing Cold War and demonstrated that if there is any hope for survival, it lies in individual acts of intelligent heroism, of personal ethical behavior at the gravest of personal expense. ***Colony*** studied the political and economic effects of space colonization, and again maintained that men and women of integrity and courage can make a difference.

Now, in ***Voyagers,*** Ben returns to a Cold War setting, so near-future that Carl Sagan and Walter Cronkite are still alive and working in it, and adds one science fiction whammy: ETI. An American astronomer and ex-astronaut named Keith Stoner picks up a series of precisely timed radio pulses from Jupiter. Are they patterned? Are they *language*? When he tries to alert the world scientific community, he soon finds a government zipper on his mouth and invisible shackles on his feet. If the pulses *do* represent Extra Terrestrial Intelligence, it is obviously possessed of superior technology—which must not be allowed to fall into the hands of them evil Roosians. Meanwhile, in Mockba, the Russians also have detected the signals, and a linguistics genius named Kirill Markov, whose wife is a KGB major, finds himself drafted to try and decipher the signals—in secret, of course, since the superior alien technology must not be allowed to fall into the hands of those evil Americans. . . .

Thus begins the most plausible and convincing account I have ever read of how the human race might really react to First Contact if it took place in-system in the next decade or two. And while the two giant bureaucracies grapple for position, individual heroes and heroines make personal choices based on a higher loyalty than nationalism or even romantic love, and bring about a startling resolution. Beneath it all lies the message that an intelligent species need not necessarily destroy itself, that the stars are within our grasp. And that individual intelligence and courage are the only things that will get us there. Refreshing to hear in these dark times. (pp. 116-17)

This is the book to give to that friend of yours who thinks SF is escapist fantasy. He or she will have such a good time that they'll be done with the book before they realize that they've been cajoled into thinking. Ben is one of SF's very best ambassadors to the general public, and this is one of his very best efforts. (p. 117)

Spider Robinson, in a review of "Voyagers," in Analog Science Fiction/Science Fact, *Vol. CI, No. 12, November 9, 1981, pp. 116-17.*

JAMES CAMPBELL

A lecherous astronomer stands next to a young female graduate student, on the porch of an observatory, planning her seduction. The nightsky whitens as a massive solar flare burns off most of Asia and Europe. Some few surviving Russians in a command bunker deep in the Urals push the button sending the surviving missiles in the mistaken idea the US is to blame for the death of their nation. On the large, permanently manned space platform all are killed by sleeting solar radiation. The plot [of ***Test of Fire***] hinges on the assertion that the moon colony is not self-sufficient genetically, as well as in other ways. One man in the moon sees this and dedicates himself to the reconstruction of the Earth's civilization and technology as the only way to save the moon colony. He is misunderstood by most on the moon. He leads an expedition to Earth to retrieve fissionables for the moon's reactors. The action moves forward twenty years. The only reason I could see for this is to give the man's son, whom he never saw, time to get old enough so it would be plausible he could lead the major expedition to recover the fissionables. Bova writes well. However, the plot creaks mightily.

James Campbell, in a review of "Test of Fire," in Voice of Youth Advocates, *Vol. 5, No. 6, February, 1983, p. 42.*

THOM DUNN

In the not-too-distant future, the sun flared for a period of several hours, destroying Europe, Asia, and Africa. Before The End, Russia, presuming an atomic attack, launched its entire arsenal, destroying cities and technology in North America. The world sank into barbarism except for a lunar colony of some 500, who make periodic raids upon Earth for fissionable fuel materials. But one man with foresight returns to Earth to hold the fissionables hostage in order to force the Moon out of its isolation.

After developing this premise in skillful if necessarily superficial fashion, Bova settles down [in ***Test of Fire***] to narrate 150 pages of commando-style warfare in the wilds of post-cataclysmic North America. Here, then, is an entirely competent, straightforward, "Golden Age" adventure SF novel, a revision and expansion of ***When the Sky Burned*** (1973), which results in a simpler and more lyrical narrative. But if this is not "new wave" fiction nor contains unusual elements of plot, character, or style, it is still to be recommended highly for use in science fiction classes. . . . There are many topics for discussion here, including techno-primitive warfare (laser guns and no gasoline), technological outposting for cultural survival, and yet another argument against nuclear weapons proliferation. Basic character types of heroic fiction wrestle with questions of loyalty and self-worth, and some readers may argue that Bova's male-female role distinctions are old fashioned. In short, ***Test of Fire*** will serve well in an SF class unit on post-holocaust fiction, contrasting in interesting ways with Russell Hoban's *Riddley Walker* (1980) or Pat Frank's *Alas, Babylon* (1959).

Thom Dunn, in a review of "Test of Fire," in Science Fiction & Fantasy Book Review, *No. 12, March, 1983, p. 25.*

KEITH SOLTYS

[***The Winds of Altair***] is an expansion of the 1973 . . . novel, which I haven't read. The setting is a couple of centuries hence. A horrendously overpopulated Earth is under the control of the universal Church of Nirvan. Only the infusion of extra-terrestrial resources and the promise of emigration to colony planets is keeping the system from breaking down. One of the Church colony groups has picked a planet around Altair to terraform. But the planet has life, life that terra-forming may kill, and the colonists are faced with a terrible moral choice, genocide or their own death.

Typically this kind of novel hinges on the rebellion of the young hero. In this book the repressive Church dominated society and the overriding moral questions provide good reason for that rebellion. The background details are well thought out and the plot moves along smoothly, making the ***Winds of Altair*** an entertaining read. Though the story was expanded, it doesn't seem padded; if anything the opposite is true. Things move along a little too easily. There isn't enough depth to provide a real sense of drama.

Keith Soltys, in a review of "The Winds of Altair," in Science Fiction & Fantasy Book Review, *No. 18, October, 1983, p. 17.*

ROLAND GREEN

Bova's fiction [collected in ***Escape Plus***] is not up to the level of his futurist and space-advocacy writings, but it is respectable, intelligent, and interesting in what it reveals about one of the major figures in the history of modern sf. Recommended for collections with a strong audience for Bova or hard-science sf in general.

Roland Green, in a review of "Escape Plus," in Booklist, *Vol. 81, No. 11, February 1, 1985, p. 756.*

KEITH SOLTYS

Readers who are only familiar with Ben Bova through his novels ***Millennium*** and ***Kinsman*** may find ***Escape Plus*** a bit of a surprise. The eleven stories in this collection show that Bova has a wider range than his novels might indicate. They range from his first published story in 1960 through 1981.

"Escape," originally published in 1970 as a separate novella is about the rehabilitation of a juvenile delinquent in a high tech prison, while **"Blood of Tyrants"** shows the other side of the coin, what might happen when rehabilitation fails. There are several light, "one punch" stories as well as others, like **"The Last Decision"** and **"The Shining Ones"** that show more depth and pack a real emotional punch.

This is a good, well balanced collection that should appeal to a wide range of readers.

Keith Soltys, "Bova's Short Fiction: A Balanced Collection," in Fantasy Review, *Vol. 8, No. 3, March, 1985, p. 12.*

LAWRENCE I. CHARTERS

When you read a "major" novel and come away thinking "unbelievable," something is wrong. Part of this feeling may be due to timing; reading ***Orion*** after reading some of Poul Anderson's time travel stories and before a couple of Roger Zelazny fantasies puts the novel up against some stiff competition. Yet Bova is hardly a lightweight author; ***Kinsman*** and ***Millennium,*** for example, displayed very tight plotting, crisp action, and memorable characters. ***Orion,*** in spite of its length (expanded from **"Floodtide"** in *Analog*), lacks any of these characteristics.

The title character, Orion, has been created by Ormazd, a god-like being, to destroy Ahriman, the Dark Lord. Given this fantastic premise, loosely based on ancient myths, the reader might expect a fantasy. Instead, Orion lives backward in time, reborn again and again at earlier stages in human history, starting in the near future and ending ten thousand years ago. Orion is greatly confused by all this, and the predictable, tedious dialogues which patch together the four main sections do little to help matters.

Where Anderson may have made the Mongols come alive with some interesting tidbits on everyday life, plus a few well-rounded character sketches, Bova's Mongols are textbook bland. An interesting variation on the Biblical story of the great flood, instead of inspiring some Zelazny-like poetic prose, reads more like a high school student complaining about his poor love life. As for the conclusion—well, it is about as satisfying as a thoroughly predictable plot and poor characters will allow: it is unbelievable.

Lawrence I. Charters, "Predictable but Unbelievable," in Fantasy Review, *Vol. 9, No. 6, June, 1985, p. 16.*

ELTON T. ELLIOTT

Despite the necessarily episodic nature of the book, ***Orion*** hangs together beautifully as a novel. It is similar in tone to Bova's marvelous short story, **"Stars Won't You Hide Me."**

Bova seems to be at his best when he's dealing with material which has strong mythic overtones. I've enjoyed his other material but ***Orion*** has the magic. The narrative deals with a man, John O'Ryan, who attempts to save the human race from death at the hands of its most hated enemy, Ahriman. He is aided by a god-like being, Ormazd, and a woman who helps him through the ages.

Bova fuses the time-travel notion with a revenge motif, adds a touch of ancient Persian mythology, and all in all has created quite a delightful, smooth, yet intense novel.

Elton T. Elliott, in a review of "Orion," in Science Fiction Review, *Vol. 14, No. 3, August, 1985, p. 16.*

ROBERT A. PARSONS

Privateers is a Sci-Fi novel of thesis set in the early twenty-first century that unabashedly espouses a twentieth century partisan political position. Sometime in the late twentieth century, the United States lost its will to compete in the race for space. The Soviet Union now dominates all extraterrestrial exploration and exploitation and, from a position of absolute military superiority, monopolizes the world economy and manipulates global politics to its own advantage. The United States, under the administration of its first female president (who just happens to be the ex-lover of the macho multi-billionaire hero Dan Randolph), has been reduced to a third-rate power with crippling political and economic problems. A group of semi-independent third-world nations control the earth's natural resources, and their collective power and political influence is far greater than that of the United States. . . .

I have a number of problems with ***Privateers.*** First, like all novels of thesis, it suffers from restrictions imposed on both plot and character development by the predetermined position taken by the author. Second, Randolph, a space-age version of John Wayne, is not a character I find particularly appealing. Third, I vehemently disagree with the novel's explicit thesis that any retreat on the part of the United States from the nuclear arms race and the space program will inevitably lead to a nefarious era of Soviet world domination. A more cynical reader than I might even question the objectivity of Bova, the current president of the National Space Institute. Yet despite these literary and attitudinal objections, I am forced to admit that ***Privateers*** is exciting adventure literature, although it falls somewhat short of the imaginative standards I prefer in Science Fiction. It held my attention and I found myself peeking into the next chapter when I was too sleepy to read on at night. Any novel that does that meets my personal criteria for good recreational fiction.

Robert A. Parsons, in a review of "Privateers," in Best Sellers, *Vol. 45, No. 8, November, 1985, p. 295.*

ELTON T. ELLIOTT

Ben Bova's new novel, ***Privateers*** . . . is an emotionally supercharged story of what might happen if the United States loses the race for space supremacy with the Soviet Union. In this future world Russia rules, the U.S. has turned isolationist and one man, American multi-billionaire Dan Randolph, stands between the Soviets and total domination of the planet. He plans to bring an asteroid into earth orbit, but when the Soviets steal it, he turns to privateering, ripping off their ore shipments. The story also has a soap-operaish romance and other personal interplay between Randolph and a Russian functionary. It's interesting but not as compelling as the political machinations. I felt that the ending is too easy. . . . Overall, ***Privateers*** is Bova's best work to date. The future world that he creates is all too believable. . . . The reactions of the American president ring true as does Randolph's extreme anger at the Soviets and the idiots ruling America. This book has superb characterizations and with it Ben Bova joins the top rank of overt political novelists like Arnaud de Borchgrave and Robert Moss.

Elton T. Elliott, in a review of "Privateers," in Science Fiction Review, *Vol. 14, No. 4, November, 1985, p. 32.*

TOM EASTON

More and more, Ben Bova's stories remind me of Poul Anderson's. The latest such is ***Privateers,*** which echoes strongly of *Star Fox*. The resemblance is far from total, however, for though Bova has a hero acting as a pirate, the circumstances, the issues, and the consequences are his own.

In Bova's future, premised on the nightmares that must have plagued him when he was writing his Star Wars book [***Assured Survival***], the US has let the Soviets build an orbital defense first. As a result, it was forced to bow to Soviet demands for disarmament, abdicate space entirely, and let the USSR get the UN license to mine the Moon. Yet not all US citizens took the defeat of dreams quietly. Astronaut and capitalist Dan Randolph moved to Venezuela and set up his own space center and orbital industrial facility. Similar capitalists have established national toeholds in space for Zaire, Japan, and a few other nations. Yet the Soviets dominate all. They have the lasers that can shoot down anything. They also have the monopoly on lunar ores and can charge what they like, and they do, aiming to force everyone else out of space.

Randolph's solution is to mount an expedition to capture an asteroid, to bypass the Moon and the Soviet monopoly. But the ironically wicked monopolists capture the ship and samples and jail the crew for trial as pirates. Randolph leads a mission to free them and then undertakes to hijack the Soviet ore carriers—for though the Soviets own the right to mine the Moon, they do not own the ore; that belongs to all mankind.

The Soviets are outraged, especially since the other space groups begin to imitate Randolph's success, especially since Randolph has seduced and besmitten the Soviet space chief, Malik's, Venezuelan fiancée, especially since Randolph loves to rub Malik's nose in every insult. The Soviet response is predictably violent. Its defeat, on the other hand, seems highly unlikely. It doesn't hurt when Randolph gets the girl, but when the Third World and the free spacers unite to force the Soviets to eat crow, and the future seems suddenly more promising, I catch a strong whiff of pollyanna.

The book is a novel, yes, and an excellent one, a good yarn and a thrilling adventure. But it is far more a cautionary tale, intended to sway the public's supposed mind in favor of a technophilic future. And it has the faults of such propaganda tales, which too often force their stories to bow to their messages. This is most blatant . . . where Bova has Randolph step egregiously out of character.

On the other hand, what Bova cautions us against seems all too possible. Read the book, consider that his premise is not so easily escapable, and weep. (pp. 178-79)

Tom Easton, in a review of "Privateers," in Analog Science Fiction/Science Fact, *Vol. 106, No. 1, January, 1986, pp. 178-79.*

BILL COLLINS

Bova's new novel [***Voyagers II: The Alien Within***] is a sequel to ***Voyagers,*** but prior knowledge of the earlier book is not required. In fact, his gradual revealing of the plot of [***Voyagers***] as it influences what goes on in [***Voyagers II***] shows his craft at its best, without, I think, annoying those who have read the first volume. It was a thriller set in the near future, juggling personal, political, and patriotic tensions—the kind of theme Bova does best. At its close, the protagonist, Stoner, had gone into suspended animation on an alien spaceship so that a divided earth would not lose its technology because of sabotage to the joint US-USSR mission Stoner commanded.

Stoner's gamble has succeeded. Earth could not abandon him to the void, and private enterprise, in the form of multinational Vanguard Industries, has rescued both him and the alien ship. To complicate things, Vanguard's boss, Everett Nillson, has married Stoner's ex-lover, Jo Camerata. He has a vested interest in reviving Stoner, as the development of a successful cryogenic system would benefit both him and Vanguard. But is Stoner the first successfully unfrozen human, or has he become something else during his years aboard the alien ship? He never sleeps, and he can persuade people to do almost anything, from giving him free plane tickets to ending a war. He escapes from Vanguard's Hawaiian headquarters, is trailed both by Jo and her husband (for different reasons), hooks up with a beautiful Eurasian documentary filmmaker whose boyfriend is a covert terrorist, resolves a central African war, and ends up in a wing-ding confrontation aboard one of Vanguard's artificial satellites with Jo's crazed husband and the surprise arch-villain behind him. . . .

Though [Bova] has a political message to deliver, he doesn't batter the reader with it as do Heinlein and Pournelle; he's no prose stylist, but he's nowhere as unreadable as James P. Hogan or Robert L. Forward; his characters are basically stereotypical but he does give them some quirks and glitches that manage not to seem contrived. He's aware of sexuality and sexual politics in a way that many hard-sf writers aren't (how long has Campbell been dead?), though I think that if I were a woman I'd finally find him a chauvinist.

Bill Collins, "Bova's Latest—Predictably Upbeat," in Fantasy Review, *Vol. 9, No. 3, March, 1986, p. 16.*

RICK OSBORN

The Astral Mirror reads like an issue of *Omni,* not surprisingly, since Bova is its former editor. Like *Omni,* it combines non-fiction and fiction, with the former better written than the latter. The non-fiction highlights are **"Science Fiction,"** an insightful history of the genre and **"The Future of Science: Prometheus, Apollo, Athena,"** an overview of scientific progress. Bova is a literate and enthusiastic spokesman for the future, but this enthusiasm sometimes pushes him into such melodramatic statements as: "We stand poised on the brink of godhood."

For the most part, the fiction attempts—unsuccessfully—to be topical and humorous. The exceptions are **"Cement,"** a clever parody of anthropological research, and **"The Perfect Warrior,"** a serious novella that stands above the rest of the collection.

The Astral Mirror is recommended only for Bova enthusiasts.

Rick Osborn, "On the Brink of Godhood?" in Fantasy Review, *Vol. 9, No. 4, April, 1986, p. 20.*

TOM EASTON

Ben Bova's ***The Astral Mirror*** is a collection of 18 essays (two of them on SF) and stories intended as a visionary reflection of the future. It may even succeed for the non-fan reader, but fans will find the book a comfortable array of familiar ideas. There is material here from *Analog,* and from *Omni,* and from elsewhere. My favorite may be the scurrilous **"The Secret Life of Henry K,"** companion to the cockeyed optimism of **"The Angel's Gift,"** which reveals the *real* reason behind Watergate. The previously unpublished **"Amorality Tale"** presents a delightful obverse of the Lysistratan answer to war. None of the stories may be major artistic triumphs, for Bova is not the kind of writer who makes that kind of impression, but most are competent, thought-provoking entertainment. . . .

Tom Easton, in a review of "The Astral Mirror," in Analog Science Fiction/Science Fact, *Vol. 106, No. 5, May, 1986, p. 187.*

GENE DEWEESE

At the end of the original ***Voyagers,*** astronaut Keith Stoner reached a derelict alien spacecraft passing through the solar system and elected to stay behind, frozen with the long-dead alien pilot, when the rest of the expedition returned to Earth. Now, eighteen years later, the spacecraft has been towed into Earth orbit and Stoner has been thawed and revived. Meanwhile, the science found aboard the spacecraft has changed Earth greatly, not always for the better.

Stoner himself has also been transformed, sharing his mind with that of the dead alien and possessing gradually increasing mental powers, including forms of telepathy and psychokinesis. Once it is learned that he is awake, virtually every major power on Earth, both political and industrial, is after him, but Stoner apparently has goals of his own in mind.

[***Voyagers II: The Alien Within***] shares some of the pacing and action that made the orignal ***Voyagers*** the page-turner that it was, but the story seems more disjointed this time, even contrived. There's enough suspense to keep you going to the end, but the characters too often lapse into political lectures, and the seemingly endless revelations of who is really controlling whom become a bit much before the ultimate power finally steps out from behind the throne.

Gene Deweese, in a review of "Voyagers II: The Alien Within," in Science Fiction Review, *Vol. 15, No. 2, May, 1986, p. 45.*

TOM EASTON

In ***Voyagers,*** Ben Bova gave us a visiting starship that was actually a sarcophagus, bearing a dead alien with its gift of technology and vision. American and Soviet astronauts went up to meet it, but events conspired to make it likely that Earth would pass up the gift entirely. To make that less likely, Keith Stoner stayed on the alien craft when the others returned to Earth, opening his suit to the cold of space and trusting that his sacrifice would bring humanity back to get him, and the ship.

In ***Voyagers II,*** we see how right he was in his expectations. It took the girl who loved him, Jo Camerata, six years to raise to sufficient corporate power to mount the necessary expedition. Then, while he waited in cryogenic splendor for Vanguard Industries' scientists to figure out how to wake him, Vanguard looted wonders from the alien ship. It was another twelve years before Stoner woke, and in that time Vanguard, under the paranoid leadership of Jo's husband, Nillson, came to dominate the world, owning governments and egging on both sides in wars small and large.

Voyagers II begins with Stoner's waking. We soon learn that something is amiss, for he seems to have an extra presence—the "soul" of the alien—in his head, imprinted there during his long sojourn in space. The alien seems to be an observer, but it is also a controller, governing Stoner's emotional responses. Yet to it Stoner may owe his life, for he is the first and only to awaken successfully from freezing. Tests on volunteers have produced only gruesome deaths.

In due time, Jo and Stoner meet and we see signs that their old love would revive if allowed. But corporate politics and alien goals both interfere. Stoner escapes the Vanguard grip to wander the world, ducking death at every turn while he explores the nature of the human madness. The focus here is on the war in Africa, and we see something of the alien's drives in Stoner's delusion that he can stop the war. Or is it a delusion? His hypnotic power to make people do what he wishes brings success closer and closer.

Bova's concern here is war and peace. Repeating his argument in ***Assured Survival,*** he shows us the International Peace Enforcers in action, though without much success. That comes only when Stoner gets the leaders of the various factions together to discover that peace is possible after all. My reaction is that such a process might work, but it never has. Bova is far too sanguine. Worse yet, though his tale is well crafted and interesting, it does limp under the burden of too heavy a pot of message.

Tom Easton, in a review of "Voyagers II," in Analog Science Fiction/Science Fact, *Vol. 106, No. 6, June, 1986, p. 183.*

G(uillermo) Cabrera Infante

1929-

(Has also written under pseudonym of G. Cain) Cuban-born novelist, short story writer, essayist, critic, scriptwriter, editor, journalist, nonfiction writer, and translator.

Cabrera Infante is considered one of Latin America's most original and influential writers. Although he has lived in exile from Cuba since the mid-1960s, much of his fiction is set in Havana, where he was raised, and details the repressive and violent social and political climate during the Fulgencio Batista y Zaldívar regime prior to the Cuban revolution. Cabrera Infante relies heavily on playful use of language, and he abandons traditional literary forms, creating pieces that are loosely structured and nearly devoid of plot. Cabrera Infante's satiric, inventive prose has been compared to the works of Lewis Carroll, James Joyce, Jonathan Swift, and Laurence Sterne.

Cabrera Infante began his literary career during the 1950s by writing short stories, many of which were published in *Bohemia* and other Cuban periodicals and later collected in *Así en la paz como en la guerra* (1960; *In Peace as in War*). Written in the mode of social realism, these early pieces convey Cabrera Infante's contempt for the Batista dictatorship. When Fidel Castro seized power in 1959, Cabrera Infante became involved with the new government, serving on the Bureau of Cultural Affairs and later becoming cultural attaché to Brussels. He also acted as the director of *Lunes de Revolución,* the literary supplement to the pro-Castro newspaper *Revolución*. Castro disbanded the journal in 1961 when its editors embarked on a campaign protesting the censorship of a documentary film directed by Cabrera Infante's brother, Saba Cabrera Infante, which depicts Havana's nightlife during the height of Batista's rule.

In *Tres tristes tigres* (1965; *Three Trapped Tigers*), the novel that established him as a major literary figure, Cabrera Infante abandons social realism in favor of a humorous narrative developed through a series of monologues. This work, which chronicles Havana nightlife on the eve of Batista's fall, abounds with puns, parodies, and wordplay. Written primarily in Cuban street vernacular and narrated by several characters, *Three Trapped Tigers* depicts a society devolving into physical and spiritual confusion. Within this society, language becomes grotesque and is reshaped by people struggling for new means of communication. Raymond D. Souza noted that Cabrera Infante's characters search for "order in chaos, permanence in a realm of change, infinity in a world of limitations." Although critics generally regard *Three Trapped Tigers* as one of the most important contemporary novels to emerge from Latin America, it was banned in Cuba and led to Cabrera Infante's disillusionment and eventual dissent with the Castro government.

Cabrera Infante left Cuba in 1965 to live in Europe and eventually settled in London. In his first book written after leaving the country, *Vista del amanecer en el trópico* (1974; *A View of Dawn in the Tropics*), Cabrera Infante again explores pre-Castro Cuba. A compendium of over one hundred short sketches, the book traces Cuban history and is similar in structure to *In Peace as in War*. Comparing it to his earlier writings, however, reviewers found *A View of Dawn in the Tropics* austere and

pessimistic. Jorge H. Valdes contended that the collection depicts Cuban history "as a repetitive and often accidental course of events always leading to an unhappy ending." Cabrera Infante's next novel, *La Habana para un infante difunto* (1979; *Infante's Inferno*), chronicles the sexual initiation of a youth who bears many autobiographical traits. Because of its abundant wordplay, this work was frequently compared to *Three Trapped Tigers,* but many critics were not as appreciative of Cabrera Infante's imaginative linguistics. *Holy Smoke* (1986), the first book Cabrera Infante has written in English, is a factual account of the history of the cigar and contains an anthology of famous smoking scenes from literature and film. Like his previous work, *Holy Smoke* bristles with puns and wordplay. John Gross noted: "Conrad and Nabokov apart, no other writer for whom English is a second language can ever have used it with more virtuosity." A film enthusiast since childhood, Cabrera Infante has published two collections of film criticism—*Un oficio del siglo XX* (1963), under the pseudonym of G. Cain, and *Arcadia todas las noches* (1978). He has also written screenplays for the films *Wonderwall, Vanishing Point,* and *Under the Volcano*.

(See also *CLC,* Vols. 5, 25 and *Contemporary Authors,* Vols. 85-88.)

ENRIQUE FERNÁNDEZ

Cabrera Infante has made the hyperbolic claim that [***Infante's Inferno***] is the first erotic novel to be written in Spanish, a bravado statement, no doubt, but with a kernel of truth. Hispanic letters can be very sexy, but there has always been an inviolable prudery, a boundary past which no one ventures. Even writers who try to break down this barrier, like Goytisolo does in *Count Julian,* fail to reach the nakedness that Anglo-American letters passed long ago, when writers drop all modesty and begin to level with their readers, to reveal as much as they really know. Cabrera Infante's attempt to be out front about his sexuality may come from his therapeutic experience, an experience common in modern culture; in any case, his candor meets the needs of contemporary readers. When I first read his book three years ago in Spanish, I felt relieved to find, at last, a text that was real about sex, that spoke of feelings I recognized, that told stories I told or heard but never read in Spanish, that used the language of the dirty joke to talk about getting dirty.

For what both charmed and bewildered me about this book, whose Spanish title is ***La Habana para un infante difunto*** (a multilingual musical pun that would take too long to explain), is its language. This isn't the self-conscious textuality of ***Tres Tristes Tigres,*** or the cinematic economy of ***Vista del amanecer en el trópico,*** or the dandified critical prose of his satirical writings, or the streetjive Cubanism of my favorite riffs. If anything, ***La Habana*** resembles the author's journalistic writings, except the tone is even more conversational. It's an everyday Cuban voice, unaffected, untrammeled, authentic, almost painfully close to my own. Were it not for a sprinkling of literary tricks that point to the method in the madness I would have sworn there had to be something wrong with it; nothing could ring so true and be okay. Now that I've read the translation, I'm convinced that the language of ***La Habana*** is perfect.

Cabrera Infante himself favors the English version. It's aimed at a more literate reader, he argues, and it's free to be allusive where the Spanish original had to be referential. Judging from the texts, the English version has gained weight in puns, as did the English translation of ***Tres Tristes Tigres,*** published as ***Three Trapped Tigers*** in 1971. English, that most word-populous language, is the perfect vehicle for word-play. A pun can bounce along both the Anglo-Saxon and Latin corridors of the language, whereas less syncretic tongues are condemned to monovalence. Joyce is only possible in English. In ***Tres Tristes Tigres*** Cabrera Infante found the Hispanic equivalent of Joycean English—Havana's militantly ludic Spanish, a language where, as Roberto González Echevarría has pointed out, the speaker must announce a serious intention before words can be taken at face value. But that was in another country and besides, La Habana, for Infante, is dead. It doesn't surprise me that the writer now prefers his texts in English. I don't. . . .

The English version lacks the original's air of artlessness, that freedom from affectation that provoked and disturbed me when I first read ***La Habana.*** It's a more literate but less direct book, in which Cabrera Infante the punster nearly outshines Cabrera Infante the sexual memoirist. Nearly. The translation preserves most of the original's frankness about sexual obsession as we follow the author from his moments of sexual awakening in that very Latin American hotbed of promiscuity that was the Havana tenement, the *solar*. . . . The population density—entire families in one room—meant a cornucopia of carnality. Women of all sizes, colors, ages fill the author's eyes and his desires, even before he has a chance to know what sex is about. They come singing a bolero on the way to the shower, or grab him unexpectedly in outbursts of horniness, or tease and play with him—but only according to their rules—or lie naked before him in full tropical majesty. The *solar* is the birthplace of an obsession: women, sex with women, all that's sex about women. . . .

Nothing is spared in the narratives. As in love affairs, the aim is to reach some final nakedness, some absolute carnal knowledge. The women undergo transformations in the author's eyes, and if sometimes they appear evil or ridiculous (or both), so does Cabrera Infante, who portrays himself as he was, green and silly at first, jaded and calculating as he gains experience, physically unenchanting though curiously attractive to women. . . .

The book is filled with sexual safaris in moviehouses, and it concludes with one of the two full-blown surrealistic episodes that disrupt the confessional realism of the narrative. The author, already a serious film buff and a professional reviewer, goes to the theater in search of Arcadia. In this final episode Cabrera Infante gets his comeuppance for his womanizing, for his adulterous carryings on, for his succumbing to the flesh and betraying the movies. I'll leave it to the reader to find out the details; I'll just say that he fashions a nice conceit and points to the eschatological fears of the sexually obsessed. Even in its moments of highest fancy, ***Infante's Inferno*** is an honest *saison en enfer*.

Obviously, I identify deeply with this writer. A coincidence of background and obsessions has impelled me to follow his career and occasionally try to share my fascination with others. (I must have made some small contribution to the sale of ***Tres Tristes Tigres*** by seizing every opportunity to include it in the reading for courses I've taught.) ***Infante's Inferno*** guided me through an era I regard as some kind of technicolor dream, when only those who lived before the revolution know how truly sweet life can be. (p. 12)

Enrique Fernández, "Blame It on the Cha-Cha: Cabrera Infante's Carnal Knowledge," in VLS, *No. 25, April, 1984, pp. 10-12.*

MICHAEL WOOD

"He didn't understand," the writer in ***Three Trapped Tigers*** says of a friend's response to a story. "He didn't understand that it was not an ethical fable, that I told it for the sake of telling it, in order to pass on a luminous memory, that it was an exercise in nostalgia. Without rancor towards the past." . . . [This phrase] is a clue both to the particular qualities of [Cabrera Infante's] longer works of fiction (***Three Trapped Tigers*** and ***Infante's Inferno***) and to the pleasure that reading them provides. Both seem aimless and unstructured, the second even more so than the first, but they don't produce the irritation or boredom such appearances often promise. This is partly a matter of the frantically active language . . . , but it is also a matter of the tone of remembrance, the way in which the imagination is used to animate old places and distant people.

Rancor towards the past is very common, and if we feel it we either can't talk about the past or can't look at it straight, can't stop rewriting it. Sometimes we are in love with the past, as Proust was, but then we almost need to be Proust in order to prevent it from slipping through our over-eager fingers. Cabrera is not anxious about his past, and he has nothing against it.

His impulse is not exactly nostalgia, even though that is what his character in ***Three Trapped Tigers*** claims. His attention to the past is brighter and more energetic than nostalgia usually manages to be. He treats the past simply as if it were the present, as if it had never been away. . . . His master is surely not Proust but Nabokov—"odor or ardor," Cabrera wisecracks at one moment on the subject of his difficulties with loved women who give off too high a smell—for whom the past came when it was called, obedient, more than presentable, all its magical details intact. "The Past," Van Veen writes in *Odor,* or *Ada,* "is a constant accumulation of images. It can be easily contemplated and listened to, tested and tasted at random. . . ." And without rancor.

This kind of tender, circumstantial recreation is even more a feature of ***Infante's Inferno*** than of ***Three Trapped Tigers.*** "She flew away," Cabera writes of one girl, "and into my memory"; and of another he says, "It wasn't the last time I saw her—it's never the last time one sees anybody.". . . [***Infante's Inferno***] is very well written, the work of a stylist; we may get a faint whiff of rancid Conrad in the prose ("Only the young have such moments," he says in *The Shadow Line*). . . . Its focus is a personal past, historical in the widest sense, but likely to bear only tangential, or accidental, resemblances to what we usually call history. Carlos Franqui appears frequently, for example, as an old friend of Cabrera's, and a great mover in his Havana circle, but the overlap between this character and the political activist is very slim. The book's main character is a boy from the provinces, dazzled by the big city, and we learn before long that he will always be dazzled by it, is dazzled even now as he writes, and that if the city is no longer the heroine, as it is in ***Three Trapped Tigers,*** it is still a major character. "The city spoke another language," the boy thinks. "The streetlamps were so poor back home that they couldn't even afford moths."

Infante's Inferno—the title is a new gag to replace the untranslatable ***La Habana para un Infante Difunto,*** which relies not only on Ravel but on the similarity between *pavane* and Havana, and the fact that the French for *infanta* is *infante*—presents the discursive erotic memoirs of a character much like Cabrera himself, a Cuban Casanova, at least in longing and memory, and occasionally, it seems, in practice. This resemblance, Cabrera would no doubt say, is not accidental, but it is not crucial either. He is remembering and inventing, not confessing. He is twelve when he arrives in the tenement with the imposing staircase, in his twenties and married by the end of the book. Cuba still belongs to Batista. Cabrera encounters girls and women among his neighbors, discovers surprising homosexual inclinations in a respectable man, glimpses sexual paradise in a window across a passage, thereby anticipating a later career as a (near-sighted) voyeur. He writes lyrically of masturbation, comically of his first fiasco in a brothel, associates Debussy with various dreams of seduction, describes in baroque and at times moving detail his pursuit of women in cinemas, his high hopes of clutches and nudges in the conspiratorial dark. . . . [The] book ends with a brilliant fantasy on the subject, a mixture of Rabelais, Jules Verne, and a schoolboy joke. Groping in the lower depths of a woman in the appropriately named Fausto Theater—a free-ranging exploration, unlike many other "sour gropes," as Cabrera calls them—he loses first his wedding ring, then his watch, then his cuff links. They have fallen into the well of loneliness, and Cabrera, flashlight in hand, goes in after them, Gulliver in another country, a journey to the center of the birth, and wakes from his dream, if it is a dream, with that old moviegoer's cry: "Here's where I came in."

Cabrera and his Havana friends, once out of adolescence, were "crazy for culture," he says, and always making puns, "suffering insufferably from paronomasia as not only an incurable but contagious disease . . . mad echolalia." The disease is clearly permanent with him, and he unrepentantly mangles language and hops from one tongue to another like a frog released from the throat. Some of these jokes are so terrible that they seem heroic, make S. J. Perelman a sedate defender of the dictionary. "There was an old saw back home that said, 'The grass is where it's green.' It must be a rusty saw by now because I haven't heard it in ages (perhaps because I haven't been home in a coon's age) . . .": Groucho Cabrera Infante. . . . Others are so cumbersome, so fiendishly worked for, that the noise of grinding machinery deafens all chance of laughter. He admires Alida Valli, and finds a young girl who resembles her. This permits him to say "How green was my Valli." He likes the proximity of *glance* and *glans* so much that he mentions it twice. The "aisle of Rite" will perhaps be intelligible to people who have looked at maps of the south coast of England recently, and "a *coup de data* to abolish chaff" depends on Mallarmé's "*Un coup de dés jamais n'abolira le hasard*" turning into English (abolish chance) halfway through.

Still other gags seem wildly compulsive, a form of fiddling with the text, a buzzing that can't let things be, and they are a genuine distraction then. Why would we want to think of a "baptism of pale fire," or associate vacillation with Vaseline? At other times the gags make wonderful, surprising sense, and whole worlds come tumbling down on top of each other, as they always do in the best of puns: "pathetic fellacy," "a fugitive from the gym gang." It is as if Humbert Humbert had got hold of all Nabokov's prose and wouldn't let go. This means that Cabrera Infante can't achieve Nabokov's irony—"you can always count on a murderer for a fancy prose style"—and must at times seem like a *précieux ridicule* rather than a ridiculer of preciosity. The trouble with dropping names, however frivolously, is that you have to pick them up in the first place.

But the book is a mixture of passionate memory and reckless spinning in the echo chamber of language, time regained in an avalanche of associations. "Our works," Carlos Fuentes wrote, thinking of Cabrera Infante and one or two contemporaries, "must be works of disorder: that is, works of a possible order, contrary to the present one." Cabrera Infante's disorder is that of the intelligence overwhelmed by gags that go to the head like drink; his possible order is that of the evoked past, a period that comes so thoroughly alive that its squandering by the present is itself a judgment on the reigning power, the reproach, without rancor, that literature makes to history. (pp. 21-2)

Michael Wood, "Odor and Ardor," in The New York Review of Books, *Vol. XXXI, No. 11, June 28, 1984, pp. 21-2.*

GREGORY RABASSA

Guillermo Cabrera Infante bills himself as the only British subject to write in Spanish, but with [***Infante's Inferno***] we can see that he is also adept in the language of his adopted raj. More than a translation, it is a rewriting of ***La Habana para un infante difunto***. . . . The translation into English, by Suzanne Jill Levine abetted by the author, is so well done that the expressive possibilities of the two languages are quickly contrasted; and English seems to come off best as a medium for puns and for what the authorities used to call lewd and lascivious expression.

One is hard put to define this book within the gamut of hallowed genres. The qualities it displays are typical of much of the writing that has come out of Latin America of late. It is autobiographical with real people (such as Carlos Franqui) turning up, and the mise-en-scène is certainly authentic. But the unnamed protagonist and narrator is not Cabrera Infante at all times, just as the Marcel of *Remembrance of Things Past* is not always to be taken as Proust, and Stephen Dedalus is not always taken to be young Joyce, but young Joyce as adult Joyce thought he must have been. In this last sense we will not learn all that much about the young Cabrera Infante; we will learn quite a bit, however, about the adult one and also about what he now thinks it was like to grow up in the tumultuous Havana that preceded the Revolution.

Readers who are stuffy enough not to enjoy puns will be turned off rather early in the game. Those who disdain frank sexuality should not even attempt the book. How often it is that the outsider can sense the near absurdities of a language better than the native, who really lets words pass over him and only extracts the practical cogency of the moment: Cabrera shows this to be true as he works with English. It is easy to gather that he is an addicted punster who cannot help himself when faced with a possibility and who brings on the dutiful groan of the less perceptive. In this way he opens up words as much as in any etymological inquiry. Indeed, he comes rather close to what Joyce was laying bare in *Finnegans Wake*. The difference here is that there is less control as Cabrera runs on with his puns, only occasionally giving his expressions the synthesis found in Joyce's wordplay.

Interwoven by means of these puns, however, is a thread of pop culture. It is remarkable how much of North America's crust and how little of its magma have attracted Latin America. (pp. 31-2)

The theme of this novel (let us call it that) is coming of age in Havana, the Inferno of the title. . . . The sexual emphasis reminds us that the tropics have long been considered a prime mover of sensuality by those in colder climes. Hispanic *machismo* has fed greedily upon this myth. The narrator here dwells more upon the breakthrough into adolescence than the following of any uncontrollable urge. Cabrera Infante leads the narration so relentlessly along these lines that it becomes wearisome at times, saved only in part by the ever-present puns. In keeping with the character's years, however, there is a kind of autovoyeurism here, coupled to the scabrous words that go with it. This is where the book succeeds in holding itself together, where language and leer make a kind of counterpoint, giving adolescence its rhythm. Sex becomes a logorrhea of forbidden words. . . .

There is another side to the book that might be obscured by the overwhelming presence of so much sexual and linguistic play. It is the effect upon a sensitive adolescent's psyche of the amorphous hell that the Latin American city has become. The same period that brought forth a great flowering of Latin American novels also saw the burgeoning of great metropolitan areas as people flocked from the countryside to the cities, ultimately destroying both areas as places worth living in. The story begins with the move by the narrator's family, quite close in description to Cabrera's own, from small town to city, where they are forced into extremely crowded quarters. The solitude offered a growing boy in the country here must become a solitude of the mind, an invention, an art. It is the adjustment of so many Latin Americans who abandon their villages for life in the city and even in foreign countries. . . .

People will inevitably compare this book with Cabrera's earlier novel ***Three Trapped Tigers,*** where he established himself as the punmaster of Spanish-American literature. This novel, however, is more introspective. Although the first book would seem to be a broader picture of Havana during a particularly infernal period, no one comes close to the narrator of this one both as a symptom of the period and as an odd man out. (p. 32)

What is bothersome about this novel is the seeming waste of so much good material. As a collection, or a collector's item, it is chock full of material that might have been given more shape. Too many puns go undeveloped; it should have been possible to have had more of a chain (or a chain reaction) with them. Even though Cabrera suggests that an escape from this inferno is as hopeless as from Dante's hell (either that of the Florentine or that of Stephen Dedalus's great-aunt), the circles might have been better defined so that we could recognize them again as we sit through the display a second time. It could have been based on parody, so effective in the hands of Cervantes or Swift and more recently in Gilbert Sorrentino's *Blue Pastoral,* where the same essential material has led the author to even more outrageous romps with language, but within a sturdier frame.

The narration here has been concerned with the rites (or the rights) of passage, both what the narrator has passed through and, more importantly, what has passed through him, taking shape according to the alembic of his mind, and been passed on to us. If this sounds fecal, it is nonetheless within the bounds of the book, and within the bounds also of Freudian myth. The puns are weaponry, just as was Luther's inkwell or the baby's handful in emulation of the folkloric Chinese sage Hu Flung-dung. This passage into adolescence out of a crowded and disorganized childhood might well mirror what is going on in Latin American writing, caught between community and solitude and attempting to escape the temptation of a second go-around and to spin off into a higher orbit. (p. 33)

Gregory Rabassa "Our Man from Havana," in The New Republic, *Vol. 191, No. 2, July 9, 1984, pp. 31-3.*

DAVID GALLAGHER

The blurb of [***Infante's Inferno***] refers to its 'shades of Henry Miller, Frank Harris and even Woody Allen,' and no doubt the shades of all three are there. What else? ***Infante's Inferno,*** like Cabrera Infante's remarkable first novel ***Three Trapped Tigers*** (1971), is also an exercise in nostalgia, an attempt, as he put it there, quoting Lewis Carroll, to 'fancy what the flame of a candle looks like after the candle is blown out.'

The book endeavours to reconstruct, and to rescue from oblivion, the minutest details of Havana at the time: the exact location of a bar, the unique shape of a leg, the precise tone of a voice. Yet the act of writing up memories itself transforms them: the literary result is treacherous to the distant event because the forgotten detail is magnified out of all proportion. Cabrera Infante, like Joyce, is at his best turning a passing erotic detail into a slow-motion epic of language, full of cultural reference and allusion, and of cosmic humour. . . .

This is a wilfully playful book, whose metaphysical overtones are unobtrusive and serve merely to enrich the wealth of erotic detail. It is also defiantly apolitical, though readers' minds will inevitably turn to totalitarian Cuba as they read it, particularly if they know that the Castro regime has intermittently deployed an Orwellian Sex Police over the years, to stamp out un-Cuban sexual activities, in particular homosexuality. Totalitarian regimes always endeavour to reduce the scope of private life, and even if that is not at all its point ***Infante's Inferno*** is, last but not least, a mammoth political statement on behalf of individual freedom. It should help Cabrera Infante to be recognised here as one of the three or four finest novelists from Latin America.

David Gallagher "Our Man in Havana," in The Observer, *September 2, 1984, p. 21.*

NEAL ASCHERSON

Cabrera Infante is a fanatical punner. He puns in his political writing, at a tolerable level, but in [***Infante's Inferno***] the passion for 'scintillating wordplay' soars aloft and spatters everything. It starts as fun, but is soon unfunny. It is illuminating at first, but to read every other word in 3-D soon produces a blinding headache. The punning gets much more intense, too, in the second part of the novel as Cabrera Infante treats us to three serious and tenderly recorded sexual affairs. The wordplay has a purpose—to heighten and simultaneously distance the reader's response, through a grand shimmering of associations—but the author's thumb gets jammed on the spraycan button and everything ends up clogged with glitter. And the punning, which as a mere feat is fiendishly acute and inventive, raises the question of exactly whose thumb this is, for the novel is a translation (in Spanish entitled ***La Habana para un Infante Difunto***—'Havana for a Defunct Infant') and the puns—naturally—and the constant alliteration are in English. The title page says 'translated from the Spanish by Suzanne Jill Levine with the author'. In a world which never had as many writers in political exile as it does today, this sort of collaboration, which raises translation to a new level of creativity, is essential; several Czech novelists, for instance, now write only rough drafts in their own language and produce the final version in another language with the help of an intimate translator. Cuban literature owes Ms Levine some kind of prize, but she is unlikely to receive it in Havana. (p. 5)

Neal Ascherson, "Rumba, Conga, Communism," in London Review of Books, *October 4-17, 1984, pp. 3, 5.*

JOHN BUTT

Tres tristes tigres revealed [Cabrera Infante's] linguistic awareness; in ***Infante's Inferno*** that awareness has become acute glossomania. The novel has two themes, language and sex, both pushed about as far as they can go. The Spanish original (***La Habana para un infante difunto,*** 1979) reads as if made of words which, from too much cosseting, have grown out of control and become less a medium for saying things than a sort of exotic carnival din. The narrator/author is in love with Havana idiom ("so vulgar", the hero says, "so alive, and I miss it so"). But as well as a linguist he is also a punitive punner, and the result is a prose so overblown, empurpled and word-bound, so maddeningly alliterative, so riddled with groan-making gags of the sort that would clear a taproom in seconds, that the book is what the narrator, in his inimitable way, would probably call a manual of mauvais goo. . . .

The story, of a young erotomane's initiation in *ancien régime* Havana, is in the same spirit, a hilarious catalogue of what he calls *coups de foutre,* though his machismo is undermined by his tendency to be distracted on the job by some lexical oddity or phonetic quirk of his partner, or by the chance of a quick pun. The picture of pre-Revolutionary Havana corresponds to the late-capitalist Sodom and Gomorrah of Castroite lore, except that the streetwalkers are a scream and life is fun and amazingly free. But there is a deafening silence about what came after which must make us read this celebration of old Havana as a comment on the new. Just as Havanese is now "a dead language (or language of the dead) gone with the hurricane of history hurrying over cane fields", gone too are the dives and cathouses, turned over to crèches, literacy centres or houses of Soviet-Cuban friendship, the go-go girls now ageing in Miami or quite abandoned to high-mindedness and socialist endeavour. You feel that every dirty joke and every triumphant conjugation is really an unspoken indictment of the dreary Castroite world to come.

It is good that this Caribbean Alexandria has its Durrell. It is also true that a few days of Eastern-bloc "culture" can convince westerners that where there is no pornography there is no freedom, but the argument is of uncertain efficacy and best suppressed. Anyway, the hero confesses that "I was young then and the young always blow everything out of proportion", so we can go on suspecting that the new Havana is not as respectable, and the old was not as exhilarating as he suggests.

John Butt, "Mauvais Goo in Old Havana," in The Times Literary Supplement, *No. 4254, October 12, 1984, p. 1166.*

JOHN GROSS

The Cuban novelist G. Cabrera Infante was born in Gibara, a town in the northeast of the island built on the site of the village where Europeans first encountered Indians using tobacco. Columbus, taken there by one of his crew whom he had sent on ahead, virtuously declined the offer of a native cigar—thus becoming, as Mr. Infante says, "the first declared non-smoker on record"—but it is hard to picture Mr. Infante himself doing the same. He is an aficionado for whom a cigar is not merely a cigar but "a burning passion," and in ***Holy Smoke*** he has produced a rich compendium of cigar lore and literature.

It is a learned book, but learned with the spontaneous overflow of some inspired antiquarian of the past, rather than in the cut-and-dry spirit of modern scholarship. Mr. Infante weaves his way from one theme to another, as though in a tobacco trance, turning aside to follow an idiosyncratic fancy, gliding back to his starting point. Everything reminds him of something else, and everything else reminds him of a cigar.

There is a vein of poetry in the book, too. Mr. Infante now writes in English, and, Conrad and Nabokov apart, no other writer for whom English is a second language can ever have used it with more virtuosity. He is a master of idiomatic echoes and glancing allusions; he keeps up a constant barrage of word-play, which is often outrageous, but no more outrageous than he intends it to be.

For all the swerves in his narrative, he also manages to convey a great deal of solid historical and technical information. . . .

There is a fascinating account of the Cuban custom of reading novels aloud to the workers in cigar factories—in the 19th century, the works of Victor Hugo and Alexandre Dumas above all (whence the name of one famous brand, the Montecristo). There is also an up-to-date report on the cigars being turned out in the post-Castro Cuban diaspora, with particularly high praise for a brand called the May Rosa that is made in Manhattan, just off Union Square.

Mr. Infante, an exile himself—he left Cuba in the 60's, and now lives in England—has some entertaining first-hand anecdotes about Castro, of a generally unflattering nature. But while he deplores the way in which the revolution wrecked the tobacco industry he also concedes that the Cuban cigar, "as if of rubber," has come bouncing back. Today the island produces one brand, the Cohiba, that he roundly designates "The Best Cigar in the World."

If Cuba remains at the heart of the story, Mr. Infante also ranges far and wide. He discusses everything and everyone from Sherlock Holmes's pioneering monograph on the difference between various types of cigar ash to the evenings in Vienna when Freud and his original disciples gathered "to smoke in friendship and to fume at enemies." . . . He also touches on the danger of cancer—rather too lightly, even if he is concerned with cigars rather than cigarettes.

One field where his expertise glows as brightly as the tip of a Corona Corona (though he insists that, strictly speaking, such a category of cigar doesn't exist) is the movies. Movie references are dotted throughout the book, but there is also a sustained passage of some 60 pages about significant smoke-filled moments on the screen, a tour de force that takes in Lubitsch, Edward G. Robinson, Charles Coburn, Charles Laughton and a cast of thousands. Mr. Infante is both catholic and scholarly in his tastes: he finds room for the Three Stooges—commended for displaying "the best squashed cigars in showbusiness"—as well as the inevitable Groucho. . . .

Literature, as you might expect, is an even more pervasive presence, and the book concludes with a miniature anthology of passages from great and moderately great authors who have written about smoking—Ben Jonson, Thackeray, Chekhov, Mallarmé, P. G. Wodehouse and many others. Apart from being intrinsically interesting, these passages have the benefit of Mr. Infante's quizzical passing comments and, as always, his puns—a Balzacian dismissal of nouvelle cuisine, for example, as "la cuisine bête."

Not all the compulsive punning is as neat as that; some of it can be a positive problem. (At one especially dire moment a meal is described as "a beef encounter.") Still, there are some very good turns (or twists) of phrase—the devil as "the smiler with a pact under his cloak," for instance—and some happy disclosures, such as the revelation that every time Tom Stoppard signs himself with just his initials, as in a prologue, Mr. Infante's first reaction is to think, "There's Eliot being coy again." And even the bad jokes are a fairly small price to pay for the author's exuberance. ***Holy Smoke*** is a delightful book—a bit mad, perhaps, but then who would want to read a wholly sane book devoted entirely to cigars?

John Gross, in a review of "Holy Smoke," in The New York Times, *Section III, February 7, 1986, p. 31.*

ENRIQUE FERNÁNDEZ

Holy Smoke is the first book by a major Latin American author that has been written in English, not translated. It was inevitable. The literary bond between Latin and Anglo America is tightening. Some Latin books appear almost simultaneously in English and Spanish. Some are actually published in English first. And a growing number of Latin writers spend much if not most of their time in the English-speaking world. Cabrera Infante is one of them. He has lived in London for many years and is now a British subject. And he's often in the United States, lecturing, teaching or doing writer-in-residence gigs. (p. 43)

He writes in an English that is also a subtle variant of Spanglish, not the usual street jive, but a jive all his own, cultivated and strange. The sprinkling of Spanish words is the least of it. His syntax is shaped by Spanish, that most flexible of tongues. While English is word-promiscuous, it stiffens puritanically if you try to bend and twist and knot it. Spanish, on the other hand, is a circus acrobat: You can arrange the words in almost every possible combination and it'll make sense. In fact, the sense depends on the word order.

Cabrera Infante must be a nightmare to his editors, for he insists on his right to commit unnatural acts with English syntax. I mention this because his readers may be tempted to think he is the worst run-on-sentence delinquent of all time, e.g. "For Dickie Moore confessing his sins not to a priest but to sexy Signe Hasso in *Heaven Can Wait,* adulthood is one of the stages to hell." The sentences are not illogical, just oddly shaped, as is the book; even more than ***Infante's Inferno*** it meanders through time and memory, stopping almost at random to speculate or instruct. ***Holy Smoke*** is an "anatomy," in Frye's sense—its models are those hard-to-catalogue texts of the 18th century. And like those models, its tone is playful.

The puns run wild. . . . Unless it's enriched by English, as in Cabrera Infante's text, Spanish is not so punny. It's no pun at all. English, with its fusion of two language families and its multiplicity of foreign influences, lends itself to plays on words.

Cabrera Infante is like a deprived child let loose in this linguistic candy shop and, once again, the reader may conclude that many of his puns are nonsense. To which I say: Nonsense! This is English passed through several filters. First, Hollywood. He learned it at the movies. . . . Then, there's London, where the writer has lived in exile, in madness, and in the company of his favorite texts, the 18th century English satirists. All of it cast into a Spanish mold. Cuban Spanish.

Under the surface ***Holy Smoke*** is a bilingual book. The incompatibilities of the two languages give the text its peculiar flavor and humor. Some of this bilingualism is explicit, as in the episode where the Cuban pronunciation of H. Uppmann sounds like *Ecce Homo* to a foreign visitor. But most of it won't tickle you right away—unless you're already as bilingual as the text. It's an acquired taste. (p. 44)

Enrique Fernández, "Havana Vice: A Cautionary Tale," in The Village Voice, *Vol. XXXI, No. 12, March 25, 1986, pp. 43-4.*

JOSH RUBINS

By the standards of almost any other writer, G. Cabrera Infante's [***Holy Smoke***] . . . is freewheeling, ardently frolicsome. Unfettered by chapter divisions or other organizational fiddle-faddle, the Cuban expatriate writer (himself a beatifically complacent cigar smoker) celebrates tobacco in a blithely disjointed monologue: the ramblings of a cheerful Pooh-Bah who is scholar and groupie, poet and stand-up comic and guru, all in one.

Sociological musings give way without warning to vaudeville acts and shards of memoir. Movie synopses and condensed literary anthologies are breezily interrupted for sour polemics (anti-Castro, pro-smoking). Indeed, while the book is formally dedicated to the author's father ("who at 84 doesn't smoke yet"), Cabrera Infante tells us that it was a photograph of aloof, anarchic Marcel Duchamp that inspired him, after considerable hesitation, to puff his enjoyment of cigars into a swirl of associations: "Things are in smoke, art is in the rings." And an even more prominent guardian angel is Cabrera Infante's favorite Marxist—Groucho, of course, whose sleeping figure (eyes closed but cigar at firm tilt) stretches with passive-aggressive élan around the book jacket of ***Holy Smoke.***

Not that the madcap structure and subversive spirit prevent Cabrera Infante from dispensing a goodly quantity of marginally plausible information, beginning with variant reports on Columbus's unenthusiastic discovery of smoking Indians and "this vegetal brown gold"—he was looking for the not-so-vegetal yellow kind—on the island of Cuba. After a small orgy of etymology, Cabrera Infante is at his most plain-spoken, even a trifle solemn, in following the Cuban cigar from weed to humidor. . . . On cigar bands, cigar boxes, cigar cutters, and London tobacconists (Dunhill's *vs.* Davidoff), Cabrera Infante is enlightening. On the metaphorical nature of smoking itself, he can be eloquent: "Every man who smokes . . . is, with a pipe, a cigarette or a cigar, while it lasts, a portable Prometheus, stealing fire from more permissive gods."

Still, it's the outrageous Cabrerian tilt, with its verbal tumult, that gives this book a certain nervy presence. "I like my writers," Cabrera Infante says, "excessive, rhetorical, baroque"—adjectives which unquestionably describe nearly all the most beguiling passages in ***Holy Smoke.*** Cabrera Infante delivers wisps of assertion as if they were pronunciamentos: "there are no ugly cigars"; pipes are "utterly phony"; Othello is "the only Shakespearean character who would smoke a cigar if he knew how." Literary criticism is nonchalantly reduced to cigar counting (Dickens is out-puffed by Thackeray), notwithstanding the acknowledged glories of Gogol's preoccupation with other forms of tobacco: *Dead Souls* is "*Vanity Fair* with snuff." And when Cabrera Infante's passion for American films intersects with his oral fixations, his prose can occasionally take on an almost abstract energy—in feverish impressions of movie smokers from Edward G. Robinson to W. C. Fields. . . . Just as one doesn't need to know the subjects of William Saroyan's bizarre show-business necrology to become enveloped in his indecorous *Obituaries,* one can safely remain in the no-smoking section while responding to the similarly intense rhythms of Cabrera Infante's fiercest free associations. . . .

While readers new to Cabrera Infante may be struck by his jokey abandon, those familiar with his works of autobiographical fiction—***Three Trapped Tigers*** (1971) and ***Infante's Inferno*** (1984)—are likely to be both mildly disappointed and faintly disturbed. Slapdash and unabashedly weightless, ***Holy Smoke*** is minor Cabrera Infante, and no cause for complaint as such. More worrisome is the fact that, by his own standards, Cabrera Infante's incorrigibly playful style is far less commanding—and far more earthbound—this time. Despite a few inspired bubblings, the stream of consciousness that brimmed over in ***Three Trapped Tigers*** and ***Infante's Inferno*** now seems oddly stagnant.

Part of the problem may be that, linguistically, the Cuban-born, London-based writer (now a British subject) is for the first time working without a net. His previous books have been written and published in Spanish, then refashioned into English with the help of a translator or co-translator. . . . The resulting texts, finding dazzling Anglo-American equivalents for elaborate Spanish double-entendres, have strongly signaled Cabrera Infante's mastery of his second language and its transatlantic idioms. And, written directly into English ("undoubtedly the language of smoking"), ***Holy Smoke*** confirms that Cabrera Infante can be witty and poetic, as well as fluent, in his adopted tongue. Nonetheless, there's also no uncharacteristic stiffness in much of the phrasing here, with hints that Cabrera Infante's unbuttoned muse is being subtly inhibited.

Furthermore, though Cabrera Infante's intertwined enthusiasm for cigars and American movies is unmistakably genuine (and sporadically infectious), these affinities are pale stuff when compared with the fevers and yearnings that underlie ***Three Trapped Tigers*** and ***Infante's Inferno:*** sexual nostalgia, political disillusionment, aching memories of Cuba before Castro. While the verbal frenzies of these novels are fueled throughout by autobiographical fervor, only a few vignettes in ***Holy Smoke*** (there's one about the young Guillermo's first cigar) benefit from the ardor of reminiscence. Similarly, the new book lacks the natural background, the built-in justification, that came with the setting in ***Tigers*** and ***Inferno***: Havana in the Forties and Fifties—multilingual, multicultural, soaked in Americanisms.

Cabrera Infante's compulsive punning, for example, though always uneven (and the source of considerable tut-tutting even from admiring critics), has usually seemed to be a legitimate mainspring for his verbal attack. All those puns have registered as an almost inevitable reflection of the possessed author's tragicomic vision, generating lyricism and intellectual complexity as well as fairly consistent laughs. . . . In ***Holy Smoke,*** on the other hand, the surfeit of puns seems to arise not from mania (not even Perelmania, one might say), but from a mere tic. Or, worse yet, from a computer program—mechanically thorough, deaf to crucial nuances in spoken English—that turns up similar-sounding phrases (more or less). To a far greater extent than ever before, in pun after pun, Cabrera Infante appears to be insensitive to the matching of speech rhythms and vowel colorations that can make even the most strained gag a low delight. . . .

Such lameness, however, is less persistently disheartening than the texture—limply reflexive, perfunctory instead of spontaneous—of the prose twitchings throughout ***Holy Smoke.*** Cabrera Infante's eclectic, side-of-the-mouth allusions can be refreshing in their indiscriminate embrace of low and high culture; more often they seem self-indulgent and pointlessly obscure. . . . A single wisecrack based on one of literature's most overparodied phrases—"a consummation devoutly to be wish'd"—might be tolerable; between pages 125 and 304 Cabrera Infante offers, out of laxness rather than any discernible pattern, four, none of them inspired, Groucho Marx very much *manqué.* Worst of all, many of these pages are thickened with pseudostylishness that's more word-fill than wordplay, derived less from Joyce than from what used to be known as TIME-ese. Relentless alliteration is one hallmark of this manner, along with enervating intimations of light verse. . . . Another is the bland, automatic sort of allusion that's too mild to be considered full-fledged punning: an Ottoman ruler is "a Turkish delight," and Pope Urban VIII promulgates "a raging Bull." . . .

Holy Smoke, of course, is nonfiction, a casual anomaly. So it's reasonable to expect that his future novels will return to the higher stylistic level of his best work. Flashes of prime Cabrera Infante—including some choice puns, most of them neat multilingualisms like "*ipso fatso*"—are plentiful enough to suggest that the move into translatorless English won't necessarily impair his verbal fireworks for very long (though comparisons to Conrad and Nabokov will probably continue to seem overgenerous).

But even allowing for the special nature of this improvisatory trifle, one has a recurrent sense that Cabrera Infante's reliance on linguistic play may be in danger of becoming more habitual than impassioned. And it's significant, perhaps, that by far the funniest sequence in ***Holy Smoke***—the one that most wittily cements the cigar/Hollywood connection—involves virtually no wordplay at all. Cabrera Infante, after repeated musings on *Citizen Kane* and the cigar-smoking Joseph Cotten, imagines a series of television commercials for a new brand of cigars: "Rosebud, the cigar that goes up in smoke forever!" The blend of satire and whimsy, reminiscent of Donald Barthelme or Max Apple, is both hilarious and darkly nostalgic. Without the constant intrusion of showoffy one-liners, the unfolding of comic ideas is relaxed yet serious—briefly introducing a Cabrera Infante who could turn out to be even better company than the dazzling, erratic performer.

Josh Rubins, "Puffs," in The New York Review of Books, *Vol. XXXIII, No. 8, May 8, 1986, p. 35.*

Tom Clancy

1947-

American novelist.

Clancy elicited critical attention with his first novel, *The Hunt for Red October* (1984). A highly popular naval thriller which earned plaudits from reviewers as well as from defense experts, the book describes a Soviet captain's attempt to defect to the United States with a thirty-thousand-ton Russian submarine, the *Red October*. The United States Navy, anxious to inspect the submarine, must locate the vessel and escort the captain to freedom while avoiding the Soviet search. While several critics maintained that Clancy sacrifices character development in favor of intricate descriptions of military operations, most praised his skillful narrative style, technical expertise, and ability to build suspense.

Clancy's second novel, *Red Storm Rising* (1986), describes a future world war fought between the United States and the Soviet Union with conventional weapons. When a group of Moslem fundamentalists destroys a Siberian oil operation, thus precipitating a Russian energy crisis, the Soviets stage a terrorist incident intended to neutralize the North Atlantic Treaty Organization (NATO) and invade Western Europe to gain access to Middle Eastern oil. Although some reviewers contended that threats of nuclear retaliation should have surfaced in the war, many praised Clancy's ability to realistically convey technological operations and to create a convincing and entertaining tale. John Keegan called *Red Storm Rising* "a brilliant military fantasy—and far too close to reality for comfort."

© Jerry Bauer

REID BEDDOW

Underneath the freezing seas of the North Atlantic, a giant Soviet submarine, the 30,000-ton *Red October,* many times larger than any American sub, glides through the deep. Armed with 26 solid-fuel missiles (each with eight 500-kiloton nuclear warheads) she is headed for the East Coast of the United States. In hot pursuit are 30 surface ships and 58 other submarines—the entire Soviet Northern Fleet.

So begins Tom Clancy's breathlessly exciting submarine novel, ***The Hunt for Red October.*** It may be the most satisfactory novel of a sea chase since C. S. Forester perfected the form.

Its startling premise is that the *Red October*'s skipper, Captain First Rank Marko Ramius, wants to defect to the West, taking his ship with him. That is why the Russians are chasing one of their own. Thanks to a spy, the U.S. Navy knows Ramius' intent. At the Pentagon they salivate at the chance to dismantle an intact Russian submarine of the latest design. But neither Ramius nor the Russians know our side knows. So the U.S. Navy must deploy to meet the Soviet fleet's appearance in force, while at the same time it attempts to track down the *Red October,* establish communication with Ramius, and escort his ship to a concealed anchorage.

The scene of the action shifts rapidly, from Moscow to Washington, from Murmansk to Norfolk, from ship to ship, and back again, the tension constantly building with gratifying unpredictability. . . .

Who will catch the quarry first, the Russians or the Americans? The double hunt climaxes in a series of lethal encounters as the NATO and Soviet navies converge and the world teeters on the edge of Doomsday. An attractive cast of strong characters—CIA spooks, political commissars, old sea dogs and young sailors—lends credence to the elegant plot.

Clancy's strong suit is his facile handling of the gadgetry of modern weapons systems. Readers who don't know the difference between Tomahawk or Harpoon missiles will lap up his depiction of a hide-and-seek world, one where killer submarines shadow missile-firing submarines above an ocean floor alive with electronic sensors flashing data to ultra-high-speed computers.

Clancy's revels in the high technology of the arms race never bore. His chilling description of what happens when a nuclear reactor melts down, condemning a submarine crew to not quite instant and horrible death, will cause armchair admirals to shudder. The metallurgical properties of submarine hulls, ultra-low-frequency radio—all is grist for the author's mill. . . .

This is engaging stuff, and just as we used to rejoice in C. S. Forester's technical descriptions of 200 tars scaling the rigging of a man-of-war to shorten sail, so we warm to Clancy's deft handling of modern naval armament. ***Red October*** makes the pigboat of the motion picture *Das Boot* look like a Model T.

No doubt some persons will deplore Clancy's enthusiasm for the superpowers' game of high-tech chicken in Davy Jones' locker. All that is another argument: ***The Hunt for Red October*** is a tremendously enjoyable and gripping novel of naval derring-do. Evidently submariners mean it when they say, "There are only two kinds of ships—submarines and targets."

Reid Beddow, "In Deep Water: A Thriller of High Tech Hide-and-Seek," in Book World—The Washington Post, *October 21, 1984, p. 8.*

JOHN R. ALDEN

"Red October" is a ballistic-missile submarine, the most modern in the Soviet fleet. Thus it is with some concern that Adm. Yuri Paderin reads a taunting letter from the boat's skipper revealing his intention to defect. Worse, the man plans to take his sub along as a little present for the Americans. Capt. Marko Ramius has challenged the entire Soviet navy to stop him, and he is already five days at sea.

This is the premise behind ***The Hunt for Red October*** . . . , an intriguing first novel by Tom Clancy. The Soviets have to sight their sub and sink it, the Americans need to figure out what is going on, and Capt. Ramius must play out his lonely, duplicitous game against the entire world. There is everything here for a fine thriller, from a complex but plausible problem to the potential for superpower conflict, and Mr. Clancy rewards us quite satisfactorily.

The success of this tale is largely due to its apparent authenticity. Naval jargon flows flawlessly, with officers requesting permission to come aboard, muttering mysterious acronyms and passing the conn (operational command of a ship) back and forth across the bridge. SOSUS listening devices monitor the G-I-U.K. gap (the line connecting Greenland, Iceland and the United Kingdom), and subs ping each other with active sonar. Real ships patrol the pages of this book, real tactical maneuvers are employed, and real weapons systems are brought into action.

A catalog of Cold War incidents that have leaked from various archives also adds realism to Mr. Clancy's story. A 1975 mutiny aboard a Soviet missile frigate, the mysterious problems of an attack submarine off Japan in 1960, and the Glomar Explorer's recovery of a sunken Soviet sub all occurred, and all are mentioned in appropriate places. This accurate reporting extends equally to the U.S. Navy, and Mr. Clancy can refer knowingly to "a horrifying accident" on the American submarine Chopper in 1969 or "that scare with Tullibee," another American boat. . . .

[The novel's technical descriptions of undersea warfare] can make things difficult for civilian readers. Technical terms, such as "cavitation" (vacuum bubbles generated by propeller turbulence), are explained, but it is several chapters before the uninitiated will learn that P-3s and Orions are one and the same—magneto-meter-equipped anti-submarine warfare aircraft. I sometimes had no idea what weapons were being pointed or what kind of equipment was being discussed until contextual clues made things clear. A glossary of military terms and acronyms would have made following the twists of Mr. Clancy's plot a lot easier.

No potential reader should forget, however, that beneath this frosting of technical accuracy there lurks a work of genre fiction. This is a thriller; so come prepared to suspend a certain amount of critical judgment concerning both plot and characters. The book's American protagonist, for example, is simply too good to be true. . . .

Virtually everyone in this book is a caricature. Some of the Soviets show occasional flashes of competence, but more often they are portrayed as hagridden nincompoops who would have trouble peeling a potato. The Americans, of course, are uniformly intelligent, imaginative, capable and disciplined. . . .

But who cares if it all seems improbable? ***The Hunt for Red October*** tells a gratifying tale. The plot is coherent, the reading easy and the matrix of encompassing detail almost frighteningly genuine. Mr. Clancy has done a terrific job describing the deadly cat-and-mouse games played by submariners, and in the end it seems irrelevant that this is not great literature. It is great fun and filled with fascinating lore. And in a thriller, that's enough for me.

John R. Alden, "The Cold War at 50 Fathoms," in The Wall Street Journal, *October 22, 1984, p. 28.*

JOHN SHERMAN

What we have [in ***The Hunt for Red October***] is a taut, fast paced Cold War thriller but there are some reservations. . . .

Clancy has a fascinating idea here and develops it well. It's just the thing Cold War thrillers are made of. His prose is crisp and tight, lending itself to the tension felt above the waves, and the fear felt below. His characterization is much better than average. As we learn more of Ramius' background we can believe he is the type of man to defect. In John Ryan we get the first CIA agent portrayed as a good guy in years.

But Clancy's most developed character, the most important character in the novel, is the technology and for anyone not familiar with naval and engineering terminology much of this book will be a mystery. The scenes are constantly shifting, with each change neatly labeled by a subtitle. This in itself is not bad, but when we're switching from CLINCLANT to SOSUS to F-14s to E-2C Hawkeyes one is likely to get a little confused.

Clancy goes into great detail explaining all the various technologies, how they work, why they do things a particular way, and even defines slang terms. His knowledge of the subject is not in dispute. What I question is the inclusion of so much technical data in what is, afterall, a novel.

Red October is a good book, particularly if your interest runs towards the nautical.

John Sherman, in a review of "The Hunt for Red October," in West Coast Review of Books, *Vol. 10, No. 6, November-December, 1984, p. 30.*

RICHARD SETLOWE

Between the dramatic sailing and docking, ***The Hunt for Red October*** often flounders but never sinks, working its way through a mine field of intrigues. . . .

At times, first novelist Tom Clancy almost scuttles his own literary vessel with an overload of subplots, technical data, cardboard characters and schools of red herrings.

But at his best, Clancy has a terrific talent for taking the arcana of U.S. and Soviet submarine warfare, the subtleties of sonar and the techno-babble of nuclear power plants and transforming them into taut drama. . . .

At times, myriad sidebar plots seem contrived merely to service research on war games and hardware that neither the editors nor writer had the heart to throw overboard.

The ostensible hero is a naval historian, a desk-bound CIA analyst named Jack Ryan, who is frightened to death of flying, gets seasick in a rowboat, yet finds himself bouncing about the North Atlantic from warship to warship on flimsy helicopters and Harrier jets, eventually boarding Red October 300 feet below the surface.

The sub's captain is the half-Lithuanian Marko Ramius, son of a high party official and one of the Soviet elite. But these two potentially fascinating protagonists are never really fleshed out; Ramius' motives for defection are merely sketched. This novel devotes 10 times the space to analyzing the submarine's power plant than it does to what makes the central character of the captain tick.

And we learn next to nothing about the other defecting Red naval officers, although there are six pages of background on an ex-Red army tank man three subplots away from the main action.

Neither characterization nor dialogue are strong weapons in Clancy's literary arsenal. The characters are conceived in basic black and white with all the non-defecting Russians heavies from the grade-B movies of the '50s and all the CIA and Navy men regular guys who get their kids Barbie Dolls for Christmas and have seen *E.T.* five times. No torturing psychological conflict or confusing shades of gray here.

Clancy is more skilled and convincing writing about machinery—the machinery of underseas warfare and intelligence—than about men.

Richard Setlowe, in a review of "The Hunt for Red October," in Los Angeles Times Book Review, *December 9, 1984, p. 2.*

CASPAR WEINBERGER

My usual taste is for classical nineteenth-century English and American novels, and I do not read much military fiction. I have settled, however, on a new novel that is now the talk of the United States and does seem to me to deserve to be better known elsewhere. . . .

[***The Hunt for Red October***] tells the story of the defection to the United States of a Lithuanian who has risen to the command of a Soviet nuclear missile submarine, despite his fierce hatred of the Soviet system and its military bureaucracy. . . . In fast paced point and counter point, the compelling narrative moves between the Soviets' attempts to block the loss of "The Red October" by the use of a large fraction of their total naval strength, and the combined efforts of the American and British navies, first to deal with what appears to be the beginning of a major naval attack by the USSR, and ultimately to help "The Red October" find safe anchorage in the United States.

The technical detail is vast and accurate, remarkably so for an author who originally had no background or experience. Critics who take themselves seriously will no doubt fault the characterization as weak and unrealized, but none except the most jaded will be anything but enthralled by the swift and expertly built crescendo of narrative excitement, the intricacy of the plot, and the chilling but wholly believable series of tightly-knit episodes that build, through many subclimaxes, to a most exciting and satisfying conclusion.

There are also many lessons here for those who want to keep the peace. This is emphatically not a work of propaganda. It is rather a splendid and riveting story that demands to be finished at one sitting.

Caspar Weinberger, in a review of "The Hunt for Red October," in The Times Literary Supplement, *No. 4307, October 18, 1985, p. 1183.*

CHRISTOPHER LEHMANN-HAUPT

[In ***Red Storm Rising***], a band of Moslem fundamentalists destroys a major oil complex in western Siberia, thereby creating a critical energy shortage for the Soviet Union. Desperate to replenish their supplies, the members of the Politburo decide they must seize the Persian Gulf. But before they can do so, they must devise a scheme to neutralize NATO's forces. Simple enough. Use Hitler's old ploy by blowing up a building in the Kremlin and pretending the West Germans did it. Then invade Western Europe with conventional forces and simultaneously seize Iceland's air bases to gain tactical dominance of the Atlantic seaways. Done and done. A third of the way into Mr. Clancy's blockbuster, the war is on. And nary a nuke has been rattled in anger.

Except, of course, it isn't Henry V's eloquence at Agincourt that gets the troops to engage. It's messages like this one: "Z0357Z15JUNE Fr: Saclant To: All Saclant ships top secret 1. Execute unrestricted air and sea warfare against Warsaw Pact forces. 2. Warplan Golf TAC 7. 3. Stout hearts. Saclant sends."

And that, one has to assume, is the thrill of ***Red Storm Rising.*** For if Mr. Clancy . . . used the arcana of naval technology to simulate authenticity in ***The Hunt for Red October,*** then he has far surpassed himself in his new book. For the battle is joined here in every theater from outer space to the inner chambers of the Kremlin. And if any gadget of modern warfare fails to function somewhere in ***Red Storm Rising,*** it is unlikely to have been dreamed of in the average reader's nightmares.

There are, to be sure, several other attractions to this superpower thriller. There is the comfortable notion that World War III will bear not a little resemblance to World War II. Indeed, to history buffs, ***Red Storm Rising*** may even offer a measure of nostalgia since a large part of its action depends on convoying American troops and materiel across a submarine-infested Atlantic. There is also the reassuring notion that a non-nuclear war would not necessarily be won by the Russians despite their reputed advantage in manpower and conventional weaponry; and that, moreover, if the threat of nuclear conflict ever did arise, there might be opponents to its use even at the very heart of the Kremlin establishment.

There are people as well as machines in Mr. Clancy's epic. Although I guess his story could just as well have been told from the viewpoint of an earth satellite or a radar transponder, there are vaguely human shapes in these pages who register more or less successfully as devious K.G.B. men, courageous sub captains and the like. . . .

Red Storm Rising at its best is the verbal equivalent of a high-tech videogame. If only it could be projected on a cathode-ray tube and read by scrolling its pages with a button or a joystick. Or maybe it could even be animated somehow. Though not, heaven forbid, by actually destroying an oil complex in western Siberia. No serious reader of this fantasy would ever want such an event actually to happen.

Christopher Lehmann-Haupt, in a review of "Red Storm Rising," in The New York Times, *July 17, 1986, p. C21.*

JAMES K. GLASSMAN

Red Storm Rising grew out of a computer war game that Clancy played with a friend—a "new Battle of the North Atlantic" between Soviet and NATO forces. "No one outside the Defense Department," writes Clancy, "had ever examined in adequate detail what such a campaign would be like with modern weapons."

The premise: Arab terrorists blow up a Siberian oil refinery, choking the Russian energy supply. To get oil, the Politburo plans to invade the Persian Gulf. To discourage NATO from stopping them, the Soviets launch a blitzkrieg against Germany. But U.S. and German forces respond better than the Soviets expect, and war expands.

Clancy concentrates on three theaters: Germany, where U.S. Stealth bombers elude the Russians' radar and neutralize their superiority in tanks; Iceland, which the Soviets seize in the first days of the war; and the North Atlantic, where helicopters chase Soviet subs, which chase U.S. convoys.

As in [***The Hunt for Red October***], Clancy tells the story in fine detail. You don't have to be a war buff (I'm certainly not) to appreciate the exciting and edifying high-tech tank battles, undersea chases and aerial dogfights.

But there are problems. The reason for the fighting is unconvincing—the Russians don't need to start World War III to get extra oil. The last 50 pages—complicated Kremlin intrigue—are confusing, disjointed and superfluous.

The obvious question is: Where are the nukes? Clancy argues that both sides believe that, once tactical (that is, battlefield) nuclear weapons are used, an escalation to strategic nukes is inevitable. So both are afraid to use tactical weapons. I think the real reason is that conventional warfare makes for a better story.

More serious is that Clancy tries to do far too much. There are too many battles (they get cloying after a while, like too much dessert) and too many characters. And, because he's so busy describing the trajectories of missiles, Clancy has little time to develop his people. With the exception of an Air Force meteorologist in Iceland, I really didn't care much about any of them.

Clancy would have involved the reader more if he had concentrated on a single location—probably Iceland, where the heroic weatherman survives the Russian assault and treks across the country to help a U.S. landing force recapture the island.

The writing itself is spare and unobtrusive, and, like military men, it's both macho and sentimental at the same time. . . .

The Hunt for Red October was a better book. But [***Red Storm Rising***] is just as fast and fascinating. . . . I only wish Clancy had been a little less ambitious.

James K. Glassman, "Tom Clancy Gets Fancy in 'Red Storm Rising'," in USA Today, *July 18, 1986, p. 4D.*

JOHN KEEGAN

[The war which Clancy describes in ***Red Storm Rising***]—with uncanny realism—unrolls in three dimensions, land, sea and air. At sea a great deal of the action turns on the form of operations in which he first demonstrated his extraordinary grasp of technicality: antisubmarine warfare. But his narrative of ship versus sub and sub versus sub tactics goes hand in hand with a dramatic depiction of carrier operations and of the fraught venture of running convoys through hostile waters.

His grasp of the complexities of modern air operations is equally acute. He maneuvers fighters against fighters, fighters against bombers, bombers against ground targets, missiles against all three and anything that will fly against electronic early warning aircraft with a sureness of three-dimensional touch that prompts the reader to wonder whether the Pentagon wouldn't be spending some of its millions better at employing him inside Cheyenne Mountain than letting his talents go to waste in mere best-selling authorship.

His land battle scenarios are set in widely separated and varied localities. The Soviet war plan requires that one of the Russian airborne divisions seize Iceland, as a flanking position from which to menace the reinforcement of Europe by transatlantic convoys. So Clancy has it landed by subterfuge with what proves to be outstanding success. The only effective survivors of its descent are a party of Marines and an Air Force officer who, between them, play a key role in keeping NATO intelligence informed of Soviet machinations.

Those bear directly on the fortunes of the NATO armies in Europe which, outnumbered as they would be in reality, can hope to stem the tide of the Warsaw Pact onslaught only with the help of major reinforcements from the United States and massive infusions of material from the same source. The author's depictions of tank battles and river crossings on what NATO calls the "Central Front" are particularly well done. Those who have read an earlier essay in the genre, General John Hackett's *Third World War,* which President Carter is said to have kept on his bedside table, will wonder why that effort won the plaudits it did. It bears the same resemblance to Tom Clancy's flights of imagination as a high school essay does to a PhD dissertation.

The author even manages to invest some of his characters—who play an essentially subordinate role to the machinery—with something like hot blood and real emotion. That is particularly so in the case of one Soviet commander who directs operations on the Central Front. It proves a successful device to tell the story of the Soviet attempt at breakthrough from the Russian rather than American point of view. "Pasha," as he is nicknamed, is quite a convincing warrior figure, whose value system harks back to the ordeal of the "Great Patriotic War," as Soviet citizens are taught to call World War II, and who therefore harbors essentially moderate views about the efficacy of nuclear weapons.

If the book has a flaw, it is that it presupposes cooler thinking on both sides than we can hope would be the case if a conventional war did break out for real on the Central Front. Time and again the reader finds himself thinking, "Surely this development must prompt the opposition to escalate." Clancy brings NATO perilously close to defeat without even hinting that Washington, the NATO high command or what would surely have been some terrified NATO ally might utter so much as a bleat of demand for "nuclear release." In reality—and if deterrence means anything—nuclear requests and nuclear threats would have been uttered long before the pass to which Clancy brings NATO.

These, however, are quibbles. There is now a long tradition of military futurology in Western literature, which includes such remarkable works as Jules Verne's *Twenty Thousand Leagues Under the Sea* and H. G. Wells' *The War of the Worlds*. ***Red Storm Rising*** will take its place with those two triumphs of bellicist admiration. It is a brilliant military fantasy—and far too close to reality for comfort. (pp. 1-2)

John Keegan, "Tom Clancy Hunts Again," in Book World—The Washington Post, *July 27, 1986, pp. 1-2.*

ROBERT LEKACHMAN

Success has increased Mr. Clancy's ambition. His new theme [in ***Red Storm Rising***] is nothing less than World War III. The conflict begins in western Siberia one starry night when a band of Moslem extremists ignite a huge oil refinery complex and eliminate a third of the Soviet Union's crude oil production for as many as three years. How is the Politburo to cope with this?

The answer is in the Persian Gulf. No serious military obstacle bars Soviet troops from cheap, abundant Saudi oil. It's there for the seizing. Trouble is, NATO would surely make armed reprisals against the Soviet Union at the hint of a Middle Eastern incursion. To the majority of the Politburo, the situation's logic is inexorable: NATO must be defeated before action in the Persian Gulf. In the hope of splitting NATO politically, the K.G.B. directs a massive disinformation operation, the centerpiece of which is a bomb plot supposedly designed by the West Germans to assassinate the entire Politburo. To lend the scheme credibility, a bomb actually kills a group of Russian children about to receive an award in Moscow. If the deception succeeds, NATO will disintegrate, leaving the West Germans unprotected and the route to oil open.

But NATO holds firm. The Politburo gambles and sends Soviet troops to invade Western Europe. The remainder of the novel deals with the ebb and flow of battle as seen on the American side by such representative figures as a nuclear submarine commander, the captain of a frigate, a gruff naval aviator and a young Navy meteorologist, code-named Beagle, who becomes a vital intelligence source in Soviet-occupied Iceland. The narrative cuts back and forth among military action in West Germany, the war at sea and in the air and Beagle's fortunes. For good measure, Mr. Clancy briefs us from time to time on Kremlin political deliberations and developments.

Although the writing is unduly prolix, especially in its loving treatment of submarine warfare, the story is well told. The many readers of Mr. Clancy's first book will enjoy ***Red Storm Rising***. His is an oddly comforting version of World War III. Neither nuclear nor chemical weapons are employed by either side, although the Kremlin hard-liners come perilously close to resorting to them when the tide of battle in West Germany and at sea begins to turn against the Soviet forces. But not even conventional bombers are unleashed against civilians. Just as in World War I, almost all the victims are in uniform. (pp. 7-8)

Mr. Clancy's undistinguished prose is serviceable enough not to impede the flow of his narrative. His characterizations are on a Victorian boys' book level. All the Americans are paragons of courage, endurance and devotion to service and country. Their officers are uniformly competent and occasionally inspired. Men of all ranks are faithful husbands and devoted fathers. As when knighthood was in flower, the enemy is almost equally virtuous. Russian submarine commanders and generals are skilled in the lethal arts. Enlisted personnel fight as valiantly as the Americans and West Germans. The bad Russians are the Politburo Stalinists and the K.G.B. political officers who shadow and sabotage military commanders.

Don't get me wrong. Occasional *longueurs* aside, I enjoyed this rattling good yarn for the same reasons I used to curl up with one of C. S. Forester's Horatio Hornblower adventures. Lots of action. Good men in tight spots. The comforting certainty that our side will win. Mr. Clancy has left the world in sufficiently tidy shape so that, if he is so inclined, he can favor us someday with the story of World War IV. (p. 8)

Robert Lekachman, "Virtuous Men and Perfect Weapons," in The New York Times Book Review, *July 27, 1986, pp. 7-8.*

MARK ZIEMAN

Mr. Clancy's new-found status as the Pentagon's pet is both a blessing and a curse to ***Red Storm Rising***. Like the earlier ***Red October***, this thriller hinges on an almost disquieting aura of authenticity, which the author achieved through hard study. To research the novel, he drove and fired an M-1 tank, shipped aboard a Navy frigate and talked to well-placed sources including a Soviet defector. ***Red Storm*** sweeps the reader into the heart of battle, from a nighttime raid over Germany in the controversial Stealth fighter to a desperate submarine battle in the North Atlantic. No detail is spared. As Mr. Clancy puts it: "There's no such thing as a minor fact."

Or, it seems, an unimportant one. The weapon and defense acronyms—MIRVs, MiGs, MADs, FLIRs—that were scattered so enticingly throughout the shorter ***Red October*** simply get out of hand in the global war of ***Red Storm***. While Mr. Clancy's Navy buddies may be able to keep track of what's blowing up what, readers who can't and therefore have to count on the novel's character development to hold their interest may be disappointed.

With few exceptions, Mr. Clancy focuses strictly on the soldier in the field, ignoring the war's effects on such private citizens as the war-torn Europeans or even Washington officials. And too often those soldiers are cardboard stereotypes: Russian infantrymen rape the citizenry, tea-drinking British sea captains shout "Tally ho!" and scrappy American tank commanders crack jokes while defying deadly odds.

Still, ***Red Storm*** is bound to be another success for its author, if only because it's so much more authentic than books by such competitors as Robert Ludlum. Already the thriller is a runaway best-seller at the Pentagon's bookstore, say store clerks, and the U.S. Naval Academy in Annapolis will soon launch its own selling drive. President Reagan so far hasn't offered his opinion (he does have a copy), but Mr. Clancy shyly relates good initial responses from military men around the world, including a Soviet admiral who liked ***Red October*** so much that he stayed up all night reading a Russian-language translation.

Mark Zieman, "Pentagon Pet Lets the Soviets Have It Again," in The Wall Street Journal, *August 18, 1986, p. 18.*

Richard (Thomas) Condon

1915-

American novelist, scriptwriter, nonfiction writer, dramatist, and editor.

A prolific and popular author, Condon blends satire and suspense to create entertaining, often humorous novels that comment on contemporary society. Characterized by intricate plots and an abundance of factual information, Condon's fiction is concerned with paranoia, greed, and the exploitation of power, usually within a political context. Joe Sanders noted: "In Condon's novels, politics determines the shape of society, but politics is not a voluntary, cooperative activity, entered into for some common end; it is a device by which a few clever people manipulate many others to gain their selfish ends." Although critical reception of his work has varied throughout his career, Condon has maintained a large, loyal readership which is sometimes referred to as the "Condon Cult."

Condon's early novels, which include *The Oldest Confession* (1958), *The Manchurian Candidate* (1959), and *Some Angry Angel: A Mid-Century Faerie Tale* (1960), are his most critically acclaimed works. In these books, as in most of his fiction, Condon employs satire to attack contemporary culture and also parodies the suspense novel while working within the genre. In *The Oldest Confession,* businessman James Bourne, who views the world of finance as corrupt, leaves his job to pursue a more "honest" living as a thief. Critics lauded this novel for its blend of humor and suspense. *The Manchurian Candidate,* a psychological thriller satirizing the McCarthy era, is Condon's most popular early work. Set during the Korean War, this book details the capture of an American GI who is brainwashed by Communists and sent home to assassinate a Republican presidential candidate modeled after Senator Joseph McCarthy. Whitney Balliett found *The Manchurian Candidate* and *The Oldest Confession* "brilliant, highly individualistic, and hopelessly unfashionable demonstrations of how to write stylishly, tell fascinating stories, assemble plots that suggest the peerless mazes of Wilkie Collins, be very funny, make acute social observations, and ram home digestible morals." In *Some Angry Angel,* which was compared to Nathanael West's *Miss Lonelyhearts,* Condon chronicles the rise and fall of a gossip and self-help columnist.

Condon's novels of the 1960s and early 1970s met with less enthusiasm from critics, many of whom found his use of statistics and historical details to be burdensome. For example, Mordecai Richler described *An Infinity of Mirrors* (1964), which relates the experiences of a German colonel and his Jewish wife during World War II, as "a novel not so much to be reviewed as counter-researched." Several critics also faulted *The Ecstasy Business* (1967), a satire of the American film industry, and *Mile High* (1969), a fictional account of the Prohibition era, for their reliance on factual information. With the publication of *Winter Kills* (1974), Condon again received favorable critical attention. Set in the early 1960s, *Winter Kills* recounts the assassination of United States President Tim Keegan, a character based on John F. Kennedy. Leo Braudy described this novel as a "triumph of satire and knowledge, with a delicacy of style and a command of tone that puts Condon once again in the first rank of American novelists." Condon was also lauded for *Death of a Politician* (1978), a mystery about the murder of an American vice-president who bears many similarities to Richard Nixon.

© Jerry Bauer

In *Prizzi's Honor* (1982), a humorous yet poignant glimpse at a New York Mafia family, Condon relates the adventures of henchman Charley Partanna and his marriage to a freelance assassin. One of the numerous plot twists involves Charley's discovery that his new bride has been hired to assassinate him. Robert Asahina observed: "[Twenty] years after *The Manchurian Candidate,* it's nice to know that Mr. Condon is still up to his sly tricks." *Prizzi's Family* (1986) recounts Charley's formative years with the Mafia. While reviewers found *Prizzi's Family* entertaining, several commented that it did not match the quality of its companion volume. Condon has also written a play, *Men of Distinction* (1953), and several film scripts, including an adaptation of *Prizzi's Honor,* on which he collaborated with Janet Roach. Several of his other novels have been adapted for film.

(See also *CLC,* Vols. 4, 6, 8, 10; *Contemporary Authors,* Vols. 1-4, rev. ed.; *Contemporary Authors New Revision Series,* Vol. 2; and *Contemporary Authors Autobiography Series,* Vol. 1.)

QUENTIN REYNOLDS

Once again Richard Condon has proved that his typewriter generates brilliant sparks each time he plays it. His latest and third book, ***Some Angry Angel,*** is an absorbing novel of a drunken, talented horror named Dan Tiamat, who claws his way to fame and fortune as the country's number one gossip columnist. Like most of Condon's characters, Dan Tiamat carries the seeds of his own destruction. To describe his rise and fall in capsule form is virtually impossible: it is reminiscent of both the late Nathanael West's *Miss Lonelyhearts,* and Budd Schulberg's *What Makes Sammy Run?* . . .

In ***Some Angry Angel*** Dan Tiamat is despised by some, feared by others, loved by a few. He is the intimate of politicians, the confidant of gangsters and the more glamorous screen stars. He has a fierce hunger for celebrity and will stop at nothing to attain it. At the height of his fame his father-in-law (publisher of his newspaper) discovers that Tiamat is extravagantly unfaithful to a devoted wife. The worst punishment he can think of inflicting upon his errant son-in-law is to make him write a column giving advice to the lovelorn. The great man is humiliated and furious—but, under the terms of his contract, he has to comply. He tries to get his correspondents to face and accept the perverse truths of his cynical mind. Ultimately these answers bring tragedy to many of his pathetic supplicants. Eventually, of course, they boomerang to bring his own ruin.

This reviewer happens to be a charter member of the Richard Condon cult—a fast-growing group. It is his considered opinion that Dan Tiamat is one of the most extraordinary characters in modern fiction—and that ***Some Angry Angel*** is one of the most extraordinary books of the year.

Quentin Reynolds, "Hunger for Celebrity," in The New York Times Book Review, *March 20, 1960, p. 38.*

WHITNEY BALLIETT

Given the time and strength, Richard Condon, the fearless, indefatigable forty-five-year-old American satirical novelist . . . , may well impale every human failing in existence. His targets have varied remarkably in size and shape. In his first two books, he lanced such monoliths as American politics (Senator McCarthy in particular), New York City, and the military, not to mention such bubbles as pompous critics, momism, slick lawyers, and garrulous cabdrivers. His new book [***Some Angry Angel***], vilifies gossip columnists, lonelyhearts columnists, newspaper sensationalism, war correspondents, British majors, adultery, big-time hoodlums, and—again—New York City. Condon, who abhors the inept and commonplace, has taken the trouble to perfect his tools. He is a first-rate storyteller who almost always juggles suspense and plot with the ease of the Victorians; he is an extremely funny writer, in a bearish, out-of-my-way manner; and, concomitantly, he has a tough, unique mock-Mandarin prose, which lies in between the glistening plumbing of Hemingway and the baroque weather vanes of the Sitwells. Most important, Condon applies his equipment to his materials with a fury that, were it to get any hotter, would simply bring him to an apoplectic stop. . . .

Condon's anger, in fact, tends to shake ***Some Angry Angel*** dangerously out of shape, and he avoids complete chaos by sometimes falling back on such barefaced plot pins as coincidence and out-and-out nonsense. The lumpy characterization of the book's despicable hero, Dan Tiamat, is the principal cause of this awkwardness. The son of a poor Irish immigrant, Tiamat is weak, voracious, and self-centered. Fleeing from his background, he becomes a wealthy, alcoholic, internationally known gossip columnist. After a series of severe reversals, Tiamat, instead of merely dissolving, for which we have been prepared, suddenly turns into the epitome of vicious black arrogance—a ninety-seven-pound filament converted into an evil Charles Atlas. When this metamorphosis takes place, one book ends and another begins. But it doesn't matter. There are some memorable sequences, the best of which is a classic piece of slapstick writing, fifty pages long, that would have made W. C. Fields honk with pleasure. (p. 156)

Whitney Balliett, "The Voice from the Cabbage," in The New Yorker, *Vol. 36, No. 7, April 2, 1960, pp. 156, 158-60.*

GERALD WALKER

One could go on about Richard Condon's surrealist story lines, his laugh-out-loud satiric wit, and his inordinate ability to invent outlandish detail. But the key to reading the author of ***The Manchurian Candidate*** and ***Some Angry Angel*** correctly is to see him as a sophisticated Hans Andersen, a teller of sardonic fairy tales for adults.

Along the way in his new novel [***A Talent for Loving***], which is the Western to end them all, Condon follows his bent of inserting a measure of social commentary into neatly laced phrases. Thus: "Never among the savage peoples of history, excepting the white man, has there been any equal to the ferocity, the intelligence and the wanton destructiveness of the Apache Indians." But Condon's main aim is still to fascinate, surprise, entertain. And the reader is successfully dazzled into a page-turning trance, like a book-struck child.

The novel covers the years 1844-71, time enough for anything to happen. Anything and everything does. Major Patten, ex-professional gambler, stakes out a claim to the largest ranch in Texas. Then he marries the daughter of the hidalgo possessing the largest ranch in Mexico. Along with the extra acreage, however, comes an old Aztec curse placed upon the descendants of one of Cortes' more reprehensible followers:

"Every life born of your loins," ran the curse, ". . . shall be possessed with such a talent for loving that he shall grow insane for the need of love at the instant of his first carnal embrace!" Naturally enough, this results in certain problems in the upbringing of Major Patten's beautiful daughter Evaliña: one unchaperoned kiss leads to ruination as they used to say. (pp. 5, 26)

Since this is a novel by Richard Condon, [***A Talent for Loving***] ends with brilliantly eccentric symmetry as a war party of savage Injuns dash out to rescue the whites from a massacre by the cavalry. (p. 26)

Gerald Walker, "Aztec Curse, Open Skylight," in The New York Times Book Review, *July 23, 1961, pp. 5, 26.*

PATRICIA MACMANUS

With only three previous novels notched up, Richard Condon has already acquired something of a clique among our more fun-loving citizenry; and this reviewer, who had never read Condon before, wishes to be admitted to the brotherhood. This despite finding ***A Talent For Loving*** too long, too talky in spots, and a trifle too delayed in getting into its marvelously satiric stride. The compensations, however, of Mr. Condon's risible, rousing storytelling gifts far outweigh the lack of editorial blue-pencilling—which was all that was required.

What this salubriously irreverent writer has done is to take all the trappings of a Western-style historical novel, drape them over an uninhibitedly extravagant story, and produce what he terms a "non-historical comedy," set in the Texas-North Mexico region of the mid-nineteenth century. Hinging his satiric caper on the adventures of one Major Patten (his given name is "Major"), a dapper, shrewd, fearless, ambitious ex-professional gambler who parlays himself into the greatest landowner on both sides of the Rio Grande, Condon leaves no Western drama stone unturned; and in so doing he breathes comic life back into that TV-ridden form. Here, among the principals, are two of the handsomest, most dauntless cowboys, three of the most breathtakingly beautiful women, the suavest of haciendados, and—of course—the insouciant Major Patten. Here too are saloon brawls, Indian massacres, grand nuptial ceremonies à la Espanola, gun-duels between the fastest draws on two continents, rattlesnake-vs.-man contests, and a heap o' slumbrous sex . . . All of it capped by a red-headed heroine descended from a Mexican-Spanish family bearing an ages-old curse from Montezuma, to wit: an excessive, an almost insane talent for and need of loving from the moment of the first carnal embrace. . . .

Out of this melee, Love at last arises in Living Color, spreading benign wings over all the appropriate parties, and leaving the reader not only laughing, but caught up in a cracking good story.

Patricia MacManus, "Thataway, Pardners," in Books, *August 27, 1961, p. 15.*

MORDECAI RICHLER

Over the years, we have had a spate of ostensibly worthy but actually sensational, sexy films about the Hitler gang, an endless run of scatological articles about concentration camps in man magazines, and a flood of paperbacks about S. S. brothels. A more respectable but no less distasteful aspect of this traffic is the middlebrow documentary novel about the holocaust. Leon Uris, for instance, on the Warsaw ghetto. And now we have another novel by a more elegant writer, this one about the rise of Nazi Germany and Paris during the occupation, ***An Infinity of Mirrors*** by Richard Condon. . . .

An Infinity Of Mirrors begins innocuously enough, seemingly a novel not so much to be reviewed as counter-researched. To begin with, Mr. Condon informs us that he spent three years writing and researching his novel, and then he lists, in the manner of screen credits, some 46 source books that went into the making of it. Thoughtful conversations about Jewish history from, I suppose, *Basic Judaism* by Milton Steinberg, *What the Jews Believe* by Rabbi Phillip S. Bernstein and others; concentration camp detail from *Human Behavior in the Concentration Camp* by Dr. Elie A. Cohen and elegant homes furnished by Sacheverell Sitwell through his *Great Houses of Europe;* Eichmann's small talk, probably courtesy of that well-known writer of "additional dialogue," Hannah Arendt. There are no costume credits.

The early pages of the novel, set in Paris 1932, are heavy with documentary detail. In lieu of establishing shots, we are told (and I'm sure Mr. Condon is bang on) that "The National Lottery had just been introduced; Malraux had won the Goncourt; Mauriac had entered the Academy; Chanel had just launched the first of the dressmaker perfumes. . . ." (p. 4)

Elsewhere Mr. Condon's industry protrudes in conversations like essays. Here is Paul-Alain Bernheim, French Jew, and greatest actor of his time: "The origins of anti-Semitism are forgotten now, darling girl, but after we gave Saul of Tarsus the basic material from the life of one of our rabbis, Christianity spread across the world. . . ." Bernheim is not developed inch by inch as a character in a novel but is introduced by flat statement, film script style. "He was," we are told right off, "a Commander of the Legion of Honour. His prowess as artist, lover, duelist, patriot, wit, gambler, impresario, horseman, husband, feeder, rager, and fashion plate was constantly in the world press."

An Infinity Of Mirrors also has what film people call a strong story line as well as plenty of hotsy scenes. In fact the basic plot, like too many TV salesmen's faces, could move any product. It fits a western as well as a thriller. In this case, it just happens to be intercut with the holocaust. . . .

All the same, it's only fair to add that ***An Infinity Of Mirrors*** is very readable, fast-moving, and rich in romantic detail of the high life. In fact what Mr. Condon has succeeded in doing is to make the rise of Hitler seem glamorous and sexy. There is even a comic sub-plot about secret agents in the best British film tradition. My chief complaint, then, is not that Mr. Condon has written a bad novel, it is that he has written an immoral one. (p. 19)

Mordecai Richler, "A Captivating but Distorted Image," in Book Week—The Sunday Herald Tribune, *September 13, 1964, pp. 4, 19.*

DAVID DEMPSEY

Any novelist who conspires with history in writing a novel runs the obvious risk of letting history do too much of the work. Something like this has happened to Richard Condon in ***An Infinity of Mirrors.*** A note on the dust jacket tells us that the author spent three years researching and writing this book, and a bibliographical preface confirms the thoroughness with which this research has been done.

In a way, such conscientiousness is too bad; one suspects that this might have been a better novel if it weren't such good history—if Mr. Condon, that is, had been more willing to play with his characters as fictional creations in the way, for example, that Richard Hughes, using some of the same material, was able to do in *The Fox in the Attic.*

Set chiefly in Paris and Berlin, the story spans the period from the rise of Hitler to power in 1933 to the defeat of the German Army in France in 1944. It is told on two levels. One of these—the fictitious—concerns the marriage of a beautiful French Jewess, Paule Bernheim, to an officer of the Wehrmacht, Col. Wilhelm von Rhode.

The match is doomed when the couple returns to Germany just in time for Paule to feel the organized anti-Semitism fostered by the Nazis. An especially nasty personal experience drives her back to France with her German-born son, where she remains until she is reunited with von Rhode in the closing months of the war. (p. 52)

Condon treats both of his protagonists as victims of Nazism, but at the same time he sees them as morally weak and, finally, when their son has died in a roundup of Jews, as being corrupted by resorting to the kind of violence they are fighting against.

On a much broader level, the novel is documentation. Yet as matters stand, ***An Infinity of Mirrors*** is not a true *roman à clef,* since the keys to the story are passed out well in advance. Because Mr. Condon possesses a diverting style . . . , these keys offer admission to a kind of Playboy Club in which all the entertainment is in the Grand Guignol manner. Hitler is discovered to be the owner of the club, brooding and seldom seen, in an inner office. General Keitel is maitre d'hotel. Generals von Stauffenberg and Stuelpnagel are head waiters and SS officers act as bouncers. The club is bankrupt, the bunnies are mostly *hors de combat,* (if we may be permitted a fractured-French pun) and, as Mr. Condon states in his title, there are lots and lots of mirrors.

The trouble with these mirrors is that they reflect too many known events. The author uses them to flash messages from the sinking ship—almost every chapter. . . .

Whatever its faults as a novel ***An Infinity of Mirrors*** is certainly relevant to an age that is re-examining its guilt for the crimes of Nazism. Its chief merit is to explore once more the dilemma of those who opposed evil but were not strong enough to act on their convictions. (p. 53)

David Dempsey, "Too Real to Live," in The New York Times Book Review, *September 13, 1964, pp. 52-3.*

KURT VONNEGUT, JR.

[***Any God Will Do***] seems very middle-European to me. I hear echoes of Friedrich Durrenmatt, Max Frisch, *und so weiter*—and the theme, I take it, is the loss of identity by modern man. I might as well add the name of Thomas Mann, since a lot of the action takes place in a Swiss sanitarium, and since this is such a serious book (or I have been had again?). It is serious despite a plot rigged along the lines of low comedy. What could be more middle-European than that?

The anti-hero is looking hard for identity in Europe. He is Francis Vollmer, a New York City banker who has embezzled nearly half a million dollars and ditched his extremely nice wife. He seeks to demonstrate that he is the heir to a British title, though he is in fact the orphan of a pair of American circus dwarfs.

I should hedge some about Vollmer's representing modern man. Condon nowhere says that that's what he does, and Vollmer has his misadventures between 1919 and 1922. Perhaps this is as good a time as any to show how men started living as hollowly as they do today. Vollmer fills himself up with information about painting and music and cooking, but is unable to draw any nourishment from it. He is like a goat with a bellyful of jewelry. None of it will enter his bloodstream—and that is surely an apt comment on social climbers of all times who have pretended enthusiasm for the pleasures of persons higher up the social ladder, persons in all likelihood pretenders themselves. (p. 5)

The best parts of the book are its celebrations of food. Francis Vollmer becomes such a great cook even French chefs praise him. My guess is that Condon is almost that good himself, since he is able to write, for instance: "During this monologue, Francis had stripped the boiled chicken, covered its flesh with a layer of farce à quenelles à la panade and sprinkled truffles on top. He kneaded it into a firm lengthwise roll, having packed it with filets of tongue, chopped truffles and another layer of quenelles." Yummy.

The poorest parts of the book are its characters. The leading man, as has been said, is hollow and is supposed to be hollow, and the supporting players who put junk into him or take it out are cartoons. Consider the monologue that goes on while Vollmer is fixing the chicken, delivered by an old Frenchman who is discussing mistresses: "Sensibility, good health and a good disposition—these things combined with utter selfishness. That is what makes a great mistress." This may be true, but it is not fresh. Such Gallic outrageousness goes on for pages, and would bore anyone but Maurice Chevalier.

The book is an honorable failure—a failure because it is boring, despite many game and clever efforts on the author's part to bring it to life. It is honorable because it has tried to say some big things without a trace of meretriciousness. Condon has not solved a technical problem which may well be insoluble: how to write interestingly about a man who is truly empty. Kafka and other literary successes have wisely written about people who weren't truly empty, but only felt as though they were. That is probably as far as fiction can go, and still find readers.

Too bad. (pp. 5, 42)

Kurt Vonnegut, Jr., "The Fall of a Climber," in The New York Times Book Review, *September 25, 1966, pp. 5, 42.*

BERNARD BERGONZI

Mr. Condon, seeming to write with one eye on Stendhal and the other on the early Aldous Huxley and making a very neat link indeed, has produced [***Any God Will Do***], an amusing extravaganza about the adventures in Europe in the Twenties of Francis Vollmer, a New York banker, who is cunning, energetic, and pathologically snobbish. He wants above all to establish that he is a member of the British aristocracy, and is conned right and left while he is trying to prove it. I most enjoyed the early chapters, which show Francis, by a deft combination of good luck and unscrupulousness, rising in the banking world; but the whole book is immaculately "entertaining," if nothing more. (p. 30)

Bernard Bergonzi, "Updike, Dennis, and Others," in The New York Review of Books, *Vol. VIII, No. 2, February 9, 1967, pp. 28-30.*

THE TIMES LITERARY SUPPLEMENT

On the first page of Richard Condon's ***The Ecstasy Business*** Tynan Bryson, the hero of the book and the greatest film star of his generation, is described as

> . . . an unzipped fly in forever amber. Everything in his life was out of proportion. He owned 111 tennis rackets, sent to him by adoring fans after his triumph in *Sneaker* (retitled *Plimsoll* in the British Commonwealth) in which he had played alone to win the Davis Cup from the Australian doubles team.

Such a concentration of verbal humour on the first page is a bit like running the first mile of a marathon in four minutes. One wonders how Mr. Condon is going to keep it up and, if he does, whether reader and author alike may not be exhausted long before the end. This sort of wise-cracking comic writer is usually a sprinter rather than a distance runner; masters of the genre, such as S. J. Perelman, have generally stuck to shorter pieces.

But Mr. Condon is canny enough to be aware of the danger. Long before we have begun to tire of his verbal fireworks he is giving a brilliant comic picture of the film world that Bryson inhabits. . . . Bryson himself, frequently married to, and frequently divorced from, Caterina Largo, the most beautiful actress in the world, has a hot line to his analyst from whichever continent he may happen to be filming in, and *droit de seigneur* over the leading ladies in his films. He is also the first actor in history to be paid 100 per cent of the gross for a film.

Again, before the satire has a chance to pall, Mr. Condon has whipped his novel off in another direction, this time that of a weird comedy thriller. Bryson becomes the victim of repeated murder attempts, each preceded by a written threat which includes Yeats's words, "The visible world is no longer a reality, and the unseen world is no longer a dream". Illusion-and-reality is yet another theme of Mr. Condon's onion-layered novel. The first sentence of the book tells us that Bryson has an extremely weak grasp of reality, and as the murder attempts come closer to success his larger-than-lifesize life gradually becomes less distinguishable from the world of the films he acts in. . . . In this labyrinth poor Bryson is hopelessly lost. Mr. Condon, however, picks his way deftly through the complications of this urbane, very funny novel.

"Very Much a Laughing Matter," in The Times Literary Supplement, *No. 3423, October 5, 1967, p. 933.*

HERBERT MITGANG

Richard Condon, a cum laude graduate of the press agent's table at Lindy's, creates another of his Chinese-meal novels in ***The Ecstasy Business.*** You feel hungry an hour later, but all those sweet and pungent sauces tantalize you right up to the fortune cookie. Break it open after 300 pages of spare ribs and it reads: Look out for funny Hollywood novels. The Condon cult knows that he is an earnest man using every writing weapon from brass knuckles to Sioux pogamoggans against his fictional adversaries. His novels would be merely in the Max Shulman gag class except for the fact that he is deadly serious about the pollution of our atmosphere by sham and hypocrisy. . . .

Having once beaten the real-life drums for such modest, self-effacing producers as Cecil B. De Mille, Sam Goldwyn, Otto Preminger and Frank Sinatra, the author is eminently qualified to invent a cast of Hollywood characters who know whereof they speak—according to the expected script. . . .

One of Mr. Condon's . . . problems in ***The Ecstasy Business*** is his desire to construct a plot that touches reality occasionally instead of merely letting his inside Hollywood and show business patter carry the day. You turn the pages of the silly plot to get to the outrageous one-liners and winkle-pickers sprinkled through the book.

The director, for example, is "such a food snob that he not only favored Roquefort cheese, but refused Blue de Bresse and Danish Blue cheese because they were non-ewe." The psychiatrist in the story performs analysis by trans-Atlantic phone calls, insisting that the superstar couch down during the conversations, with the patient facing the Baltic and the doctor the Pacific. . . .

"If Shakespeare were writing today he'd be writing for the movies," one of Mr. Condon's characters insists. Certainly the author reveals himself as a true believer in the movies: "But reality in life is a bore, isn't that true? Is life scored with music?" And that is what finally may be unsound about the internal mechanism of ***The Ecstasy Business***—Mr. Condon has allowed himself to kid but not expose the motion-picture moguls.

He has momentarily forgotten Hollywood's first law: Scratch the tinsel and find the *real* tinsel beneath. Yet Condon is always the working entertainer. Even with a flop, he follows the Henry James dictum that the novel "amounts to never forgetting, by any lapse, that the thing is under a special obligation to be amusing."

Herbert Mitgang, "Hollywood-on-the-Rhine," in The New York Times, *December 30, 1967, p. 21.*

JULIAN SMITH

For a while it appeared there would be a Condon boom among our literati—*Time* came right out in February 1963 and included Condon in its list of *the* ten important new novelists, the other nine being Ralph Ellison, Joseph Heller, H. L. Humes, John Knowles, Bernard Malamud, Walker Percy, Philip Roth, David Stacton, and John Updike. Since then, only H. L. Humes, whoever he is, and Condon have been neglected by the people who get indexed in *PMLA*. For the time being the boom is over, probably because, in the words of an editor who denied even thinking about Condon, "he writes too rapidly"—which may be another way to say Condon prefers five ninety-five from an esthetically crippled reader to the kindest of words from Edmund Wilson and his friends. (p. 221)

Condon's novels are, nonetheless, worth reading, for he writes modern morality plays, horror tales of the natural, not the supernatural. And they are funny, a point frequently missed or forgotten by readers, reviewers, and Condon himself. His habit, in every novel, of making death comic is a good example of what endears him to the cult-joiners and disgusts our uptight literary establishment. In ***The Oldest Confession,*** Condon's first novel, the duke of Dos Cortes, a Spanish Gustave von Aschenbach, achieves death in Venice through "simple exhaustion" after renting a little boy in Hamburg. Not content to write tongue in cheek of a pederast's passing, Condon builds humorous conceit upon conceit. First, an American tourist points at the late duke, who is seated upright in an outdoor chair, and in the archetypal bad taste of the naive American confronting decadent old Europe blurts "'That old man looks dead.'" Then along come Katherine Hepburn and a film company to shoot a scene nearby; as a result, "his friends all over the world who saw the movie, two, three or four years later . . . were always surprised and delighted to see the old man rotting away in the background."

Sometimes Condon makes death comic to reinforce what is probably his chief preoccupation, the vanity of human wishes. In ***An Infinity of Mirrors,*** Paul-Alain Bernheim, one of Condon's most sympathetic characters, has a flat on his way to an evening of group sex. Getting out of the car, thinking all the while about the series of talks he must have with his daughter to dissuade her from marrying a German military attaché (the year is 1932, the Bernheims are French Jews), he is hit by a Citroën driven by James Cardinal Moran of Ludlow. The anticipated orgy, the pedestrian flat tire, the cardinal-executor, all make Bernheim's death ludicrous. . . . "Man's fate, as Condon sees it," said the perceptive *Time* reviewer of Condon's second novel, "is to work hard, sacrifice much, lead an intelligent, just, and fruitful life, and then show up at the Last Judgment minus his pants."

The Oldest Confession (1958), Condon's first novel, equates art fraud with more universal frauds and deceptions, particularly self-deception. The son of an industrialist and himself a once successful businessman, James Bourne has tried to make himself "honest" by becoming a criminal. That is, stealing money legally through capitalist finagling made him feel "clean, honest and integrated." This is self-deception of the most naive variety. . . . Bourne prides himself that he hurts no one by replacing with exact reproductions what he thinks are long forgotten paintings in dark corners of an immensely rich woman's castle. But because his plot is so successful, he attracts the attention of a superior criminal who murders two men and brings on his own murder, the life imprisonment of Bourne, the starvation of another man, the suicide of still another, and the ruined lives of Bourne's wife and the woman from whom he stole the paintings. (pp. 221-22)

Probably Condon's best known novel because of the excellent film version, ***The Manchurian Candidate*** (1959) opens with Raymond Shaw's return from Korea to receive the Medal of Honor at the White House. Another fraud, for Raymond won the medal not by heroism but because he and his patrol were captured, brainwashed, and sent back to their own lines believing Raymond had saved them. Actually, a team of up-to-date Fu Manchus has turned Raymond into a perfect killer—one who kills without question, memory, or remorse. His chief mission is to murder the 1960 Republican presidential nominee. . . .

Published during the first spasms of the actual 1960 campaign, ***The Manchurian Candidate*** was timely, and more than timely after the Condonesque events at Dallas and Los Angeles—there is even a "Manchurian Candidate" theory of the first Assassination. The novel's main trouble is that it tries too hard to be sensational: post-hypnotic suggestion, post-Pavlovian conditioning, and other fancy psychological gimmicks, political murder, agents provocateurs, secret agents, moronic politicians, asinine conservatives, incest, Communism, McCarthyism, Momism, matricide, step-patricide, uxoricide, suicide, and more. Condon tries to do so much that most readers probably miss the casually nasty humor. . . . (p. 223)

In some ways his best novel, ***Some Angry Angel*** (1960) is also his most disagreeable and least entertaining. Dan Tiamat, supposedly named for the Mesopotamian personification of chaos, works for the same paper, editor, and publisher as Raymond Shaw, and like Raymond dies violently in a convention hall on the last page. They are both despicable, blindly egocentric human machines, yet their very ugliness and weakness makes them attractive to Condon, makes them, as he says of Germans in [***An Infinity of Mirrors***], "beloved of God because they have always given Him so much to forgive." . . . (p. 224)

A Talent for Loving (1961) started as a cowboy filmscript and picked up the psychological embellishments of a novel, much as an altar boy might pick up a social disease. The result is a sometimes uncomfortable mixture of the maudlin and the absurd. Item: Jim Street never eats meat because he saw and smelled his mother's charred corpse after an Apache raid; the tragic cause has a comic effect when Street turns into a vegetarian cowboy who knows everything about a steer except how to eat one. To the extent that Condon is trying to purge sentiment, I applaud him; unfortunately, most of the sentimental passages exist on their own and are not torpedoed until much later in the novel.

After the trivial ***A Talent for Loving, An Infinity of Mirrors*** (1964) did nothing to further Condon's critical reputation; I agree with Orville Prescott that ***Mirrors*** "combines vulgar pretentiousness with blunt sensationalism," but I also think it is basically a good novel and could have been a really worthwhile one. Although Condon's criticism of Nazi Germany is what we've been reading for a generation now, the self-deception of the German army before and during the war is the kind of egocentric blindness Condon does best with. For instance, the heroine's husband, General Wilhelm von Rhode, becomes involved in a plot to kill Hitler not because Hitler is dangerous to society at large but because he is odious to the army. The same is true of Major Marco in ***The Manchurian Candidate:*** he destroys Senator Iselin not for trying to take over the government but for insulting the army in the process—Condon's great talent is his ability to make us like Marco and von Rhode and seduce us into applauding their actions while forgetting their motives. Von Rhode's moral and intellectual emptiness is dramatized when a friend suggests he wear a monocle to hide an empty eye socket: "'A monocle over a socket,'" marvels von Rhode. "'I like that. Conspicuous waste. Real ostentation. I could prop it in there, even if the muscles don't work.'" "'It would add a glittering sort of a deception,'" the friend agrees. . . . At first this may seem grotesque light banter meant to keep up von Rhode's spirits, but the next time we see him he has actually propped a monocle in the hole in his head.

The maimed von Rhode and Paule, his embittered Jewish wife, place all their hope for the future in the purity and innocence of their son, Paul-Alain. But the past (or is it the present?), in the form of SS Colonel Drayst, takes the boy away. Drayst's motive for having the child picked up in a Jewish razzia is banal (he wants to sleep with Paule) and horrifying (he wants to kill her afterwards). (pp. 225-26)

The most powerful scene in the novel is that in which Paul-Alain, dying from a ruptured appendix, is crowded into a bicycle racing arena with twelve thousand other victims. Though few of them can understand French, and though epidemics of diphtheria and scarlet fever break out, they are subjected to a loudspeaker "wild with outrage" endlessly playing the same message: "Attention! Attention! Walking on the board track while wearing shoes is strictly forbidden. Attention! Those who walk upon the board track with shoes on will be immediately and severely punished." (p. 226)

Not able to resist a slab of sentiment . . . , Condon has Paul-Alain live until his mother arrives so he can give her a last joyful cry and smile like your typical moribund Victorian child. Actually, I should not be overly critical, for the pathos of Paul-Alain's death is necessary to prepare us for his mother's transformation into a monster who uses the extermination camp machinery to destroy Drayst—pretending to submit to Drayst's passion, Paule agrees to come to his quarters but brings her husband who smashes Drayst's face with a rifle butt so he will not be recognized and systematically knocks out his teeth so he cannot speak. Then they treat his wounds so he won't die before the end of the line, dress him in civilian clothes, swathe his head in bandages, and deliver him with Jewish identification papers to a train headed for Auschwitz. Note the reversal of roles: Paule, the Jew, has become a Nazi; Drayst, the Nazi, has become a Jew. The point is that they are humans and that the capacity for cruelty and violence inherent in humanity, not in particular political creeds, is to blame for 1933-45. Paule sees this at the very end when Drayst is thrown into a boxcar; like the neurotic woman in *The Wasteland,* she cries "'What will we do. . . . For the rest of our lives, what will we do?'" "'We have killed a monster,'" says the uncomprehending von Rhode; "'We have become the monster,'" she answers. As the boxcar door is closed, Drayst's last sound is a "bleating cry"—he has become a sacrificial lamb, a scapegoat for Paule's own innate evil.

With ***Any God Will Do*** (1966), Condon shows signs of relaxing his obsession with cruelty and violence. Low key and oddly happy in its outcome, the story opens in 1919 literally with a bang, the self-foreclosure of a child-molesting bank president atop his mountain of money, and ends quietly in 1922, the year Eliot published *The Wasteland*. The coincidence in dates may be intentional, for Francis Vollmer, who would be a perfectly ordinary man were he not insane, combines the emptiness of Prufrock and the strawmen with the sensuality and cunning of Sweeney. His employer's suicide gives Francis the opportunity to steal the fortune he needs to become a gentleman worthy of his parents; an orphan, he believes himself the product of a politically-crossed liaison between members of two royal families, probably Queen Mary and Kaiser Wilhelm. In reality, Francis is the son of a dwarf circus clown, but when his wife Stacie tells him this, he flees to Europe to search for his "real" parents.

As usual, Condon mocks the vanity of human wishes: Francis' vain hope that his parents will reveal themselves, Lady Sian Recknell's vain wish to find happiness in protecting Francis from the truth, Stacie Vollmer's wish to punish Francis for deserting her because she wasn't "good enough." (pp. 226-27)

At the same time that he mocks human wishes, Condon insists upon their necessity. Consider the novel's epigraph:

> Interest is the key to life,
> Interest is the clue,
> Interest is the drum and fife
> And any God will do.

Condon means that if one has an interest, even in a delusion, one has the clue to existence, and any God, no matter which, will do. (p. 227)

Condon's latest novel, ***The Ecstasy Business*** (1967) is a combination film industry satire and suspense thriller that might have been subtitled *What Made Sammy Run Makes Condon Walk.* Though enjoyable, this is a pointlessly funny "entertainment," a white rather than a black comedy, in which self-delusion, Condon's most powerful theme, is reduced to the difficulty some Hollywood types have in distinguishing clearly between the real world and the reel world: Albert McCobb, the director of *Nowhere, Hopeless, Awful, Ghastly, Bull,* and other thrillers, is really an insane Yeats-quoting killer who works his murder plots into his film plots. Though it is little more than self-parody for Condon to transform his *danse macabre* into a *danse McCobb,* as long as he keeps reminding us of the fiends who roam through the world seeking the ruin of souls he has as much right as Graham Greene to relax occasionally and write a filmscript disguised as a novel. . . .

Not long ago, a Yale psychologist conducted a series of experiments demonstrating how easily well-intentioned, responsible, honest, ordinary men can be turned into machines for torturing other men. . . . When I discussed this experiment with my colleagues in the humanities here, they almost unanimously exclaimed not at the psychologist's findings, but at the fact that he made the study in the first place. Their reaction has a lot to do, I think, with the difference between the literary reputations of writers such as Faulkner and Ambrose Bierce. Both examine the grotesque in human nature, but Faulkner sugar-coats the pill and assures us that man will endure. Condon, like Bierce, makes the unpopular assertion that man will endure only in ignorance, cruelty, and perversity. (p. 228)

Half of Condon's value is that he does not affirm the goodness of man. The other half is his independence from currently "stylish" subject matter—while Updike, Malamud, Bellow, and their followers generally treat ordinary men and commonplace, dull, and "realistic" events, Condon writes of power politics, assassination, the world's largest ranch, its most famous movie stars and columnists, madmen, honest thieves—but rarely anyone we might know. For this reason, he is among the very few good writers who live on their craft without the help of foundations and universities. Translated into nineteen languages, he remains neglected by our literary opinion-makers, one of whom sniffed verbally in a letter to this writer: "He lives in another world from ours." Well, thank God he does live in that "other world," for "our" supposedly sane world is increasingly in danger from that other world. Dantes all, we need Virgils such as Condon to guide us through the new Inferno. (pp. 228-29)

Julian Smith, "The Infernal Comedy of Richard Condon," in Twentieth Century Literature, *Vol. 14, No. 4, January, 1969, pp. 221-29.*

PETE HAMILL

For some years now, Richard Condon . . . has been one of our supreme entertainers, a verbal tap-dancer whose ambitions usually have been limited to bedazzlement, fantasy and dark laughter. For the moment, he has abandoned vaudeville for a more serious stage. The result is [***Mile High,*** a] savage novel about the corruption of modern America.

In Condon's fictional world, the corruption touches every area of our lives, and infects all of our institutions. Wall Street, the churches, the major political parties, the universities, the courts, the police are all maggoty with greed, money and a lust for power. According to ***Mile High,*** it is not the Mafia that is moving into business; Condon's thesis is that the Mafia was the tool of "legitimate" business from the beginning, that the heroin pumped into our children's arms has been sent there by respectable American businessmen.

This would seem to be absurd, on the surface, but it is Condon's triumph in this novel that he makes the thesis plausible. He has presented us with the life of one Edward Courance West, a kind of baroque Gatsby, who is the child of an Irish ward-heeler and a Sicilian dancer. It is Eddie West who combines politics with mob muscle and forges an alliance with big business. Condon persuades us that West (a name that was certainly not chosen accidentally) understood from the beginning that greed was the basic motivation of businessmen, and that the chance for a big score would swiftly lead to a collapse of ethical standards. . . .

West gets away with everything in his private life, including murder, because he understands power. He grows older, but never changes his original estimates of the world. One son becomes a United States Senator. West himself sends money to Senator Joe McCarthy, builds a Citizen Kane hideout in the Adirondacks, ruins his marriage. At the end he tries to kill a second son's wife—because, though she is black, she reminds him of his mother.

The plot becomes more operatic as it goes along. One of the large weaknesses of the book, as fiction, is that we never feel anything about Eddie West himself, not even loathing. But Condon makes his opera believable, because he is the best of the practitioners of what might be called the New Novelism. If the so-called New Journalists have applied a veneer of fictional technique to factual stories, Condon applies a dense web of facts to his fiction. Eddie West walks corridors with Warren Harding; he meets frequently with Paul Kelly, one of the actual bosses of the early Mafia; he talks with Al Capone and Johnnie Torrio. Condon has a mania for absolute detail that reminds you frequently of Ian Fleming. . . .

There might really be two kinds of fiction: the fiction of sensibility and the fiction of information. Despite the cult that has grown up around Condon, he is not really a great novelist, and certainly makes no pretensions about the value of his work. But as a practitioner of the fiction of information, no one else comes close to him.

In ***Mile High,*** the technique has been melded with a large thesis. If much of the book remains thesis and exposition (and thus fails as fiction), the thesis itself is terrifying. He has written, with brilliance and style, an indictment that forgives nothing.

Pete Hamill, "For Eddie West, Power Was All That Mattered," in The New York Times Book Review, *August 31, 1969, p. 19.*

CHARLES NICOL

[In ***Mile High,*** Richard Condon has] moved toward the "straight" novel, but the characters who march behind him still seem to be suffering from advanced Pavlovian conditioning. Perhaps Condon is like Vonnegut's typical scientist: people aren't his specialty. He is a plotter and a plodder, and we may say kindly that he is indeed a craftsman, an artificer; his novel is an impressive *ballet mécanique*. Like a clockwork mouse, its life is solely in its style. No matted hairs cling.

Not that this style is particularly admirable, merely curious. Condon's sentences are sturdy rather than flashy, and rarely very lively. But his paragraphs are strange constructions, for Condon starts with a statement about his story, offering a reasonable bit of plot or character, and then forces that small item until it fits into place on top of his paragraph like a handle on a lunch bucket. The lunch bucket however, large, black, rusty, and unfortunately empty, is Condon's main concern: listing irrelevant, trivial facts, his characteristic paragraph grinds until it produces a footnote. (p. 115)

Facts are neither ideas nor things. When in *Hard Times* Mr. Gradgrind taught his students facts exclusively, Charles Dickens was careful to point out that Gradgrind's model pupil was stiff and bloodless, an educated zombie. Condon is so proud of having learned Facts that the title of his novel is a statistic, and after the title page comes a bibliography, an almost insurmountable feat of *kitsch*. If, as Dwight MacDonald pointed out, Americans are "fact-fetishists," Condon must be an ultimate American.

There are kinds of limited fiction where the facts, ma'am, are more important than the characters. The whodunit is the prime example: once we feed enough facts into the machine, all the characters come up lemons. Eventually, the whodunit becomes the howdunit, plotting replaces personality, the audience comes to respect only the technique of the planning, and it begins to seem unjust for the plotter to be caught.

Richard Condon is undoubtedly a master of such planning. In this novel, the Plan makes E. C. West one of the world's richest men. Starting with his father's share of Tammany Hall power, West singlehandedly invents Prohibition so he can accumulate the lion's share of the profits from bootlegging and the other organized crimes that come with it. Condon is actually able to make this grandiose (and highly impersonal) scheme seem convincing. Alas, it takes up only half the novel, and the second half features West as an older, lunatic millionaire, hiding in the Adirondack Mountains in an exact replica of an enormous Swiss hotel, trying to destroy his son's wife. The novel ends with West's last words, which, together with his reason for uttering them and other incidental scenery, constitute a gross, vulgar plagiarism of *Citizen Kane*.

Mr. Condon is that unique kind of writer who can make a list of automobile replacement parts exciting. Unfortunately, in ***Mile High*** he has tried a more ambitious project. (p. 116)

Charles Nicol, "Plotter and Plodder," in The Atlantic Monthly, *Vol. 224, No. 3, September, 1969, pp. 115-16.*

MICHAEL MEWSHAW

A synopsis of Richard Condon's [***Death of a Politician***] is bound to make it sound like still another *roman à clef* about power and corruption in Washington. But the plot, close to current events, is of tertiary importance. Style and characterization concern Mr. Condon far more immediately, and they show how a gifted writer can raise almost any material to the level of art.

Walter Slurrie, former Congressman from Texas and two-time Republican Vice President, is found murdered in a bathtub, sitting fully clothed on a velvet chair. Plenty of people wish they had pulled the trigger, and as the prime suspects give statements to the police, the reader learns why. . . .

Mr. Condon makes Slurrie more than a mere papier-mâché mannequin constructed of old newspaper articles. For all his quirks and weaknesses, for all the fun the author has at his expense, Slurrie eventually wins a measure of sympathy from the reader, who grows more interested in the man's life than in the cause of his death.

The other characters also have contemporary analogues whom they transcend. Eddie Cardozo, for instance, would, in the hands of a hack, have remained no more than a clone of Bebe Rebozo. But Mr. Condon finds a pitch-perfect voice for him and creates the complete small-time thug, oozing charm and Brilliantine.

True, the ending of ***Death of a Politician*** is forced, artificial, and arbitrary. But then a good part of Mr. Condon's brief seems to be that American political life is forced, artificial, arbitrary, and almost as frightening as it is funny. (pp. 10, 22)

Michael Mewshaw, in a review of "Death of a Politician," in The New York Times Book Review, *December 31, 1978, pp. 10, 22.*

THOMAS R. EDWARDS

[In ***Death of a Politician,*** Richard Condon] considers the murder, in 1964 at the Waldorf Astoria, of Walter Bodmor Slurrie, former congressman and senator, vice president of the United States from 1952 to 1960, unsuccessful Republican candidate for the presidency in the latter year, a hypocrite who's well known for his dirty campaigns, his anticommunism, and his love of properly laundered money. If Slurrie sounds just a little like what's-his-name, there are some other familiar types around too—Richard Betaut, pint-sized former crime-busting DA and governor of New York, twice defeated for the presidency but still a power in the party, in whose apartment Slurrie's body is found; Nils Felsenburshe, current head of the richest family in the world who may have political ambitions himself; David Arnold Dieter (''Dad'') Kampferhaufe, revered military hero and president who never let Slurrie come upstairs in the White House or get off the helicopter at Camp David; Horace Riddle Hind, reclusive billionaire from out West with a taste for actresses, plain food, old movies, and soothing drugs, who buys up Las Vegas and bankrolls Slurrie's excursions into corruption; Eddie (''Kiddo'') Cardozo, small-time Hispanic mobster from Miami who's Slurrie's guide, philosopher, and friend in many lucrative deals.

This is all bad enough, but Condon adds undreamed of horrors to what we knew or suspected about certain public figures. Slurrie got in with the Mafia by slipping them used tires when he worked in OPA, and they've directed his career ever since. Traumatized in his formative years by seeing his stern father copulating with a cow, Slurrie is helplessly impotent, and the ever-obliging Cardozo has had to beget his two sons. He won the vice-presidential nomination, despite Dad Kampferhaufe's loathing of him, because the Felsenburshes, Horace Hind, the Secret Police, and the Mob all wanted to have their man (he was *everyone's* man) at the center of things, where he could help organize or coordinate the Bay of Pigs, the Vietnam war, the assassination of the man who beat him in 1960, and the murder of Lee Harvey Oswald.

I'm not the first to observe that Condon's contempt for his readers almost matches his contempt for his characters. It's naughty of him to put the rise of Castro a decade too early, for example, just so that he can dump something else on the Kampferhaufe-Slurrie administration, and not all readers will find hilarious his insistence that Kiddo Cardozo sounds like Bill Dana playing ''Jose Jimenez.'' . . . And while some scenes are reasonably diverting . . . there's not much political analysis. But then Condon isn't an analyst but an exploiter of our need to believe the worst. He does it skillfully, but his books would be less fun than they are if one didn't suspect that he believes the worst too, that his pictures of a world of fools eternally at the mercy of knaves are also pictures of what, with anger and disgust, he takes to be the case. (pp. 35-6)

Thomas R. Edwards, ''Terror in Freedonia,'' in The New York Review of Books, *Vol. XXVI, No. 1, February 8, 1979, pp. 34-6.*

ROBERT ASAHINA

Charley Partanna, underboss of the Prizzi crime family, has a problem. He's just bumped off a traitor in Vegas who'd fleeced the organization to the tune of $720,000—and now he's discovered that his new girlfriend, Irene, was the dead man's wife. As if that weren't enough of a headache, Charley's also learned that she's been augmenting her income as a tax consultant by working as a freelance hitter, and that she's now been offered a contract by a family rival to ''do the number'' on *him*. . . .

What, another novel about the Mafia? Another fictional account of the ties between the *fratellanza* and entrepreneurial capitalism? Before pigeonholing ***Prizzi's Honor,*** however, the reader should be alerted: Richard Condon is not Mario Puzo; suspense, not the family saga, is his forte. And he winds the mainspring of the plot so tight that the surprise ending will knock your reading glasses off. Yet ***Prizzi's Honor*** is also a sendup of the prevailing sentimental picture of the underworld. To Mr. Condon, there *is* honor among these thieves—but it is precisely in the name of *omertà* that the *fratellanza* has been willing to ''cheat, corrupt, scam, and murder anybody who stands between them and a buck.'' The Prizzis have less in common with the Corleones than with the Borgias.

So it seems poor Charley has another problem, for he actually *believes* in the sanctity of the family, Sicilian style. ''He loved loyalty as a separate thing,'' Irene muses at one point, deciding she ''needed to take some kind of course on Sicilians,'' because they were ''too dumb to protect their money, then they went crazy for revenge as soon as somebody took it.'' Naturally Charley, known behind his back as ''the All-American Hood,'' has some difficulties dealing with a woman who thinks like that.

It's a tribute to Mr. Condon's considerable talents that his irony underscores, without undermining, the loony poignancy of Charley and Irene's ill-fated romance. . . .

Mr. Condon is an old pro at mixing satire and suspense. Twenty years ago, he began a novel with an outlandish comic premise: Since Joe McCarthy couldn't have done more for the Communists if he had been one himself, suppose he had been? His answer to that question, ***The Manchurian Candidate,*** the first of what has been a long string of best sellers for Mr. Condon, was one of the finest thrillers of recent times and perhaps the most darkly amusing look ever at the McCarthy era. ***Prizzi's Honor*** also involves a humorous variation on a real-life theme. What if, Mr. Condon wondered, the recent, well-publicized kidnapping of an Italian financier, widely believed to have been arranged by him (to take advantage of the tax deduction allowed corporations that have to pay ransom for the return of a kidnapped executive), actually had been part of a complex Mafia plot to take over his bank?

Rest assured, however, Mr. Condon never allows reality to be too great a burden for the reader. Charley and Irene, in different ways, are eventually undone by the author's delightfully preposterous and perverse plot complications, but throughout the novel, Mr. Condon's wicked sense of humor keeps the dealings and double-dealings in proper perspective. (p. 12)

Twenty years after ***The Manchurian Candidate,*** it's nice to know that Mr. Condon is still up to his sly tricks. In his case, at least, it's a pleasure that—as he tells us an old Sicilian proverb has it—''The less things change, the more they remain the same.'' (p. 37)

Robert Asahina, ''For Love and Money,'' in The New York Times Book Review, *April 18, 1982, pp. 12, 37.*

ALAN BOLD

To suspend disbelief long enough to accept the events described in [***Prizzi's Honor***] it is necessary to believe, first, that an abstract concept like honour can dehumanize the individuals who subscribe to it; and, second, that language can be reduced to a euphemistic rubble which these men of honour can deploy in place of conversation. Honour, in Condon's book, is a Sicilian defence of the family. For Charley Partanna, enforcer of the New York-based Prizzi family, this is an ethical obligation. . . .

Charley and his Mafia colleagues do not speak like other American citizens. They have their own colourful jargon and it enables them to operate on an Us versus Them basis. They think like a persecuted minority and members of the family know that "the environment" means the Prizzi organization, that to "zotz" means to eliminate, that a "hitter" is a hired killer and that "a little problem" involves a lot of bloodshed. Charley doesn't talk a lot but when he does he uses the jargon. When he thinks, which is often, he has his own way with words.

Charley's central role in the novel is to fall in love. . . . Although Charley has countless killings behind him he is still a sucker for a pretty face and falls in love at the first sight of Irene. Condon makes this clear in the tough-tender narrative style he uses throughout the book. . . .

By the time Condon springs his first surprise the reader has been set up for a series of violent incidents. Charley is in some difficulty since he can cope with homicide but finds romance a little strange. He discovers as the pivotal part of the plot, that Irene is just like him—a hitter, a person who zotzes other people, a hired gun (or knife or whatever). The difference is that he is a big man with a massive family behind him whereas she is the little woman operating on her own as a "classy woman contract hitter".

Condon's hyperbolic prose turns every event into an issue so that the novel is strung out tight on its own tension. Charley's understanding of the nature of Irene's work is traumatic, so Condon piles on the metaphorical effects: "The furniture of Charley's mind suddenly began to come loose, the pieces crashing into each other like unfastened objects aboard a ship at sea ploughing through a hurricane." If that sounds a trifle clumsy then it has to be said, in Condon's praise, that he consistently gives an impression of Charley as a blunt instrument or as an obstacle in a subhuman race. The reader is persuaded that if such men actually exist then Charley is an accurate representative of the species.

It is something of a challenge to a novelist to create a love interest in a story that pairs two ruthless murderers. Irene is presented as a colder fish than Charley—she has risen to the top of her profession on account of her ability to murder without remorse. She is as sound a psychopath as Charley. Condon suggests, however, that such creatures are capable of a great passion and Charley, for one, is sure that his love is the real thing. . . .

As the novel gets into its stride with Charley and Irene established as the perfect couple of killers, life looks odd to those inside "the environment". At a crucial moment Prizzi's sacred honour is at risk and Charley has to decide between Prizzi's honour and Irene. The choice is Charley's and the outcome of the novel depends on it. Condon's expertise ensures that suspense is sustained until the last page of the book which is an impressive example of a brutal genre and contains more shocks than most of its kind.

Alan Bold, "How to Zotz the Hitter," in The Times Literary Supplement, *No. 4132, June 11, 1982, p. 642.*

JOHN JAY OSBORN, JR.

The setting of Richard Condon's latest novel, ***A Trembling Upon Rome,*** is 15th-century Italy, which was not a time or place known for an enlightened political outlook. Self-styled princes and kings, today forgotten, murdered and pillaged in pursuit of meaningless titles such as Holy Roman Emperor. Piracy was an honorable profession; mercenaries had more business than they could handle. And for a time three popes ruled simultaneously, battling each other for the throne of St. Peter. Mr. Condon specializes in presenting a world that can most plausibly be seen in terms of conspiracy, treachery and betrayal. So this period may not provide his greatest challenge, but it does offer abundant opportunities for illustrating and confirming his vision of the world.

To Mr. Condon, everyone in the 15th century was in on some racket. . . .

The best scam of all, Mr. Condon suggests, was run by the Catholic Church. Nearly everything had been declared forbidden, but anything forbidden could be made legal and holy for a price. The church's bright young lawyers toiled into the early hours, seeking to increase the treasury by finding new activities to forbid. The game was so lucrative that eventually several popes competed for domination.

The contest to corner the market in absolutions, dispensations and indulgences—not to mention benefices and papal bulls—is at the heart of ***A Trembling Upon Rome.*** Mr. Condon's protagonist is Baldassare Cossa, son of Naples's best pirate and leading citizen. Cossa's father rightly figures that while piracy provides a steady income, his talented son's real chance for advancement in a growth industry is with the church. Cossa is sent to Bologna to study church law. His success while at the university . . . leads to a job on the Pope's staff. (p. 4)

Then comes the fateful schism; the Pope in France begins questioning the validity of the Pope of Rome, and it is very bad for business. The Medicis force the reluctant Cossa, who wants to concentrate on war and sex, into becoming their candidate for pope. All interested parties are lured to an elaborate conference at the city of Konstanz, where for four years popes and kings and a cast of thousands—knights, courtesans, gamblers, prostitutes, jugglers, pickpockets, bishops and dukes—dupe and murder one another until finally the church emerges united.

The betrayals and intrigues leading to Konstanz and the showdown at the conference itself are great fun, but it is difficult to get used to 15th-century nobles speaking like Chicago gangsters. And Mr. Condon's single-minded focus on intrigue forbids any discussion of how the population actually lived. Communication, transportation and all the details of daily life are ignored. This is probably deliberate, since these details might detract from the central thesis of the book: that the 15th century can best be understood as a reflection of our own worst tendencies. Mr. Condon may be right. The church may have had the racket of the century. But if people wanted to buy indulgences, it must have been because they believed in God and an afterlife. And the 15th century's great art (unmentioned) was not produced only to earn a fast buck. What cannot be explained as cynicism has been ignored. Nevertheless, Richard

Condon's idiosyncratic view of medieval Europe is hilariously wicked. (pp. 4-5)

John Jay Osborn, Jr., "Scam and Schism," in The New York Times Book Review, *September 4, 1983, pp. 4-5.*

DON G. CAMPBELL

[The] antihero of ***A Trembling Upon Rome*** came to the papacy with a most peculiar set of qualifications. Scion of a family of pirates, a lawyer, atheist, pimp, murderer, embezzler, womanizer and warrior, Baldassare Cossa was the final rash on the brow of a Catholic Church that had suffered more than 100 years of fever. . . .

But, for all of his villainy, Cossa has the Church in his debt for a single, unwitting contribution: He caused such a scandal that, following his deposition the horrible schism in the Church was finally mended.

Villain or not, Baldassare Cossa in novelist Condon's deft hands emerges as a likable rogue who drifted into papal politics almost accidentally and, in fact, turned down the papacy twice—not because he felt himself unworthy but simply because extortion possibilities were greater as the cardinal in charge of papal armies than they were as Pope.

Central to the theme is Cossa's coziness with the Medici family of Florence and its determination to gain the banking business of the Catholic Church. And, if there is a sly parallel here with a 1982 embarrassment linking the present papal hierarchy with another banking scandal, author Condon's tracking record for tying current events into his novels immediately makes coincidence suspect. . . .

Condon is in top form with this tongue-in-cheek, Rabelaisian political thriller that irreverently flaps a church's dirtiest linen right out in front of everyone. There is not so much "trembling" going on in Rome as a consequence of Condon's novel as there is wincing . . . just as many lesser families also wince at a mention of good old Uncle Sid, and that trouble down at the bank.

Don G. Campbell, "Laundering Historic Dirty Linen into an Unholy New Thriller," in Los Angeles Times Book Review, *November 6, 1983, p. 15.*

JOE SANDERS

Accompanying the development of both science fiction and fantasy, many books have appeared that contain enough fantastic content to be considered "borderline" fantastic literature. We see them scattered throughout bookstores, the wire racks in drugstores, and scholarly science fiction bibliographies. But even though it is impossible to ignore these novels, it also is impossible to look at them in quite the same way we look at works that are unquestionably fantasy or science fiction. Despite the similarities, there are significant differences. (p. 127)

Richard Condon is a well-established writer in this area of borderline fiction. (p. 128)

Condon's subject in most of his novels is political-social life in contemporary America. In novel after novel, he shows as much fascination with the world we live in as Dante did with Hell. In Condon's novels, politics determines the shape of society, but politics is not a voluntary, cooperative activity, entered into for some common end; it is a device by which a few clever people manipulate many others to gain their selfish ends. In some cases, it seems, they go on manipulating after any practically satisfying ends have been gained, out of unthinking inertia or the sheer joy of control. Each novel focuses on a device of control, a tool that a character in the novel has managed to systematize until it can be utilized with scientific precision: brainwashing in ***The Manchurian Candidate*** (and ***The Whisper of the Axe***), media manipulation to encourage frustrated impotence in ***Winter Kills,*** and bribery in ***Mile High.*** In this way, by their extrapolation in the soft sciences, these novels resemble science fiction.

Furthermore, if science fiction may be defined as a branch of literature that not only involves some significant extrapolation but the believes humanity will be able to understand or control the conditions of life, Condon's novels again very obviously border on science fiction. By depicting characters who are easily recognizable analogs of historical figures and by a carefully woven tapestry of invention and verifiable facts, Condon appears to be revealing the secret truth about the forces that control us. . . . Ben Marco, hero of ***The Manchurian Candidate,*** must fight his way through the thoroughly perfected brainwashing he has undergone before he can act. Meanwhile, a Senator Joe MacCarthy-analog lets himself be controlled by his ambitious wife who wants to make him president. And at the same time, Raymond Shaw, the Manchurian puppet of the novel's title, also brainwashed by the Communist Chinese, operates as the perfect, unknowing assassin controlled by a master secret agent planning to take over the American government. In ***Winter Kills,*** the hero must resolve mutually exclusive combinations of fact and interpretation to find out who killed his brother, a Kennedy-analog president, and he also must find out who is killing all the people who could help him answer that question. He is more hindered than helped by the information-gathering services owned by his Pa, which provide so much data that the hero is overwhelmed. Finally, the content of ***Mile High*** shows how American politics and idealism are manipulated and corrupted over the years by Edward West, while all the time he is becoming more murderously insane. Eventually, West's younger son must penetrate the illusions that his father has spun, in order to save his wife from West's plan to murder her.

In general, the extrapolation in these novels proceeds in a rather odd direction. Rather than working forward into the future, Condon works backward into the past. The main action is set in the present, or at the most perhaps a day or so in the future. Otherwise, although what he shows has clear implications for the future, Condon deals primarily with reinterpretations of the causes of present conditions. In each novel, his characters constantly are brought up short by the recognition that the past they have believed in is a lie, that the "truth" they are living by now is illusion, and that they must learn to see events from another angle. This reemphasizes the issue of "control," for the characters must become aware that they have been deliberately manipulated before they can act freely, gaining some control of their own lives.

[As John Clute suggests in *The Science Fiction Encyclopedia*], the novels thus have a strange, unsettling atmosphere. Deliberately so: To be settled is to be unaware of the many ways one is being controlled, living futilely according to unreal concerns; before one can *do* anything, one must become thoroughly unsettled in outlook. (pp. 129-30)

In Condon's novels nothing can be taken for granted. Every fact, every emotion, every relationship may be exactly what it seems—or it may be the opposite—or it may be something altogether different. One must learn to regard experience with dispassionate observation that makes possible sardonic humor at the recognition that there is an immense gulf between what things are supposed to be and what they actually are, but which also makes possible the satisfied recognition that the reader is not personally involved enough in matters affected by this discrepancy to be hurt. Normal experience becomes as alien a realm as anything described in science fiction, and this first step on the road to reliable understanding does strongly resemble science fiction. Condon even uses the language of science fiction from time to time, especially when describing characters who are unable to get past this stage of detachment in order to find reality in some facts, emotions, or relationships. (p. 130)

Although Condon's novels resemble science fiction in their concern with understanding and control, their extrapolation of conditions and "sciences" from the present, and their mood of (sometimes ironic) wonder, the first three discussed here nonetheless differ from science fiction in some major ways. The understanding and control in these novels tend to be illusory, or at least most characters stop short of the limited understanding and effectiveness the heroes achieve. The people in Condon's novels who achieve what looks like absolute mastery are actually absolutely vulnerable. The more they seem to understand the less they actually do understand; the more they appear to control, the less real control they have. In ***The Manchurian Candidate,*** Raymond's mother is simultaneously the senator's wife who manipulates American politics like a virtuoso, and the Communist master spy. She appears to control the situation completely, but, actually, since she is fixated on her childhood because of her incestuous affair with her father, she is out of rational control. Her private goal is to launch an atomic attack on the Communist nations the moment her husband enters the White House, in order to punish them for tampering with her son's mind—while at the same time, she orders her brainwashed son to make love to her because he looks like her father. In ***Winter Kills,*** Nick Thirkield's Pa owns everything he needs to live comfortably and makes lots of money; nevertheless, he must continue stealing more even if it means that he must engineer the murder of Nick's older brother, the president, so no one can slow him down. In ***Mile High,*** West actually wants to follow his mother's dream by becoming a dancer, "free of all restraint." . . . Instead, he devotes himself to accumulating money and power, while his thwarted desires emerge in his lifelong hobby of beating or killing women who remind him of his mother. These characters are all insane—brilliantly, successfully insane, to be sure. By the end of each novel, each of these master manipulators has gone berserk.

At the root of each central character's problems—and thus of the problems experienced by the world each dominates—is a crime by one generation against the next. In particular, the father of each character has succeeded in fixing his child's attention on some false or incomplete goal. The child is unable to progress past that fixation, and instead tries violently to impose the same goal on the next generation. That is why Condon's novels center on false, perverted family relationships. That is also why his novels do not show the future. Unless the people of the present generation can find the truth and destroy the older generation and the values it embodies, there will be no future. And, because their own family lives have been ruined, the older characters attempt to prevent their descendents from having any families; if they succeed, the next generation can never be born.

In looking for some touchstone strong enough to penetrate the lies that the older generation has had time and resources to construct, Condon's heroes cannot rely primarily on the "truth" of nature. Unlike characters in science fiction, . . . Condon's characters cannot appeal to objective reality and work out from there. The problem is not an unclear physical anomaly but a murderously confused society. So, in these novels, Condon's heroes are lucky enough to find some *person* in whom they can trust; outside facts are verified or rejected by comparison with the nature and perceptions of that friend or lover. Nothing else is reliable. In fact, in ***Winter Kills,*** a reader suddenly realizes that even the vividly convincing, fact-studded background scenes that appear to be the work of an omniscient author actually present contradictory accounts of the murder plot; like the hero, a reader is tricked and confused by an overload of irrelevant information, and like the hero the reader is forced to rely on the experience of one person—in this case the hero himself—to verify any fragments of reality. Only by accepting and trusting someone else, finally, can one learn to accept and trust himself. The alternative is the kind of brilliant insanity into which Edward West falls. . . . (pp. 131-32)

In their projection of that ultimate certainty that life is beyond human ability to understand and/or master unassisted, Condon's novels actually resemble fantasy more than they do science fiction. However, they fall on the borderline of that genre, too. There is no supernatural force in these novels. There is no "magic" except that provided by money or power—or demanded by human delusion; Raymond is not really the reincarnation of his father, Pa cannot really change facts at will, and West cannot really transcend time and space. These beliefs are merely sick illusions. Much as these novels feel "fantastic" because they disturb a reader's settled beliefs or his confidence that success comes from working straight ahead at given tasks, they are not quite fantasy. Ultimately, an order is restored in the novels, and the dangerously uncontrolled forces in the setting are brought into line. . . . The characters' attempted violations of nature, the impossible attempts to bend reality to their wills, are explained rationally; so, too, the novels return to a roughly patched together, though still disturbing reality.

Still, these three of Condon's novels remain uncommonly disquieting. Perhaps the most uncomfortable thing about them is that no extrapolation into the future is required, and that nothing in them is altogether impossible. The rearranging of historical perspective is hideous, but Condon's vision of America as nightmare is hard to dismiss. Another reason Condon's novels are not fantasy is that they do not transport the reader to a secondary world; instead, they are intended to produce a dreadful alteration of the way readers view *this* world.

With this purpose in mind, the most fascinating of the three novels is the one with the least fantastic devices but the most fantastic premise, ***Mile High.*** This novel very carefully and factually describes how Edward West was responsible for bringing Prohibition to America so that he could multiply his money and power by controlling the illegal sale of liquor and the political-social corruption that this industry necessarily entailed. It is Condon's most stunning depiction of how reality can be distorted, swung off course by selfish passion. West succeeds in restructuring the world to serve what is basically his own private, vicious fantasy. That a novel describing such an enterprise cannot be classified as "fantastic" shows much about the desperate/precarious sense of reality in these last years of twentieth-century America.

Overall, the popularity of Condon's novels shows the tendency to seek the security (if not always the optimism) of science fiction's belief in human ability to understand and control experience. It also shows how bedeviled readers must be by fantasies of dread. In Condon's novels, the public imposture of virtuous control at the highest levels of public life is revealed in practice to be a murderous frenzy. The heritage of the past is a treacherous illusion. Edward West is as tempted by his figurative demons as the central character of Mathew G. Lewis's classic Gothic novel *The Monk* is by his literal ones. But West is more dangerous than Ambrosio, for he controls the public conscience of society; no mob can rise to break in and reveal *his* crimes. West has successfully used the American dream to destroy the American dream. He has manipulated the naive notion of Prohibition to create a monstrous social and political organization. . . . (pp. 132-34)

Ultimately, here as in the other novels under initial consideration, Condon stops short of fully extrapolating this process into science fiction; he can sketch the direction of West's fantastic desires, but he is unwilling to imagine their concrete fulfillment. Ultimately also he shows that West's attainment of his objective only allows him to do the almost impossible, not to find the freedom he recognizes in his last, gasped words: "Volevo essere un ballerino"—I want to be a dancer. . . . Too late, too late.

Sometimes, however, the urgency of Condon's concerns does force him to look unflinchingly at the things he fears; what he then writes is unarguably science fiction. The enterprise described in ***The Whisper of the Axe*** is an especially extreme distortion of American values for personal satisfaction. The central character is another of Condon's insane master manipulators, described with the language of science fiction. Agatha Teel's anguished perception of herself as a gifted, pampered young black woman living in an America that exploits blacks, creates lasting alienation. . . . Teel has convinced herself that a healthy society can develop in America only after the present one that so confuses her has been totally destroyed. With help from the Communist Chinese and with massive financing from the drug trade that she knows is destroying ghetto dwellers, she organizes a new American revolution to begin during the bicentennial year, 1976. But while she relies on her assistants who have been brainwashed/trained by the Chinese, U.S. Army Intelligence relies on the more thorough brutality of its brainwashing to sneak an agent into the heart of the conspiracy.

This novel differs from Condon's more borderline novels in some important ways. Teel intends to start her insurrection in thirty American cities on the fourth of July, 1976—which was in the future when Condon's novel was written, published, and intended to be read initially. Moreover, the conspiracy is left essentially undamaged at the end of the book. (pp. 134-35)

Furthermore, while this novel shares the concerns of Condon's other novels, it also shows the fuller development of those concerns. ***The Whisper of the Axe*** does not lapse into the contrived, cop-out happy endings of the other novels. Instead, the characters live out their destinies, or at least what they have been accidentally or deliberately programmed to do. In this novel, Condon permits tendencies and trends to develop to their natural end, using the unsparing imagination of good science fiction.

The novel begins with Teel wounded, surrounded by corpses, after the escape of an enemy agent who may know enough to thwart her plans. She wonders "who would get to her first: his people or her people?". . . At the end, it turns out that the enemy agent, a U.S. Army officer whose identity has been in doubt throughout the story, delivers totally erroneous information to his superiors, as a result of which they will believe that the leader of the plot was one of those already killed. The officer has no choice. He *must* make this crucial mistake because of his obsessions, the way his intelligence has been reshaped and perverted by the society that controls him. This novel shows no trustworthy companions, no chance of discovering even a fragment of reliable truth, no healthy family relationships—and, above all, no secure future in which the disruptive social anomalies have been subdued. The older generation has built such a complex shield of delusions that its flaws cannot be seen. It cannot be destroyed by the younger generation, nor would there by anything to take its place if it could be. Insanity is blissfully triumphant at the novel's end. The U.S. agent is convinced that he is fulfilling his identity and saving his country at the moment he murmurs the wrong name and dies. . . . As in Orwell's *1984*, the characters demonstrate that total control means total surrender of self, the denial of the future. But no one seems to care. No one understands that it matters, even or especially at the novel's conclusion. Consequently, the reader is left to anticipate a future either of insane destruction or insane social-political manipulation. This is Condon's birthday greeting to America, intended more overtly than his more borderline novels discussed here to disturb readers while it actually confirms their unacknowledged dreads.

By looking at these four novels clustered on or near the borderline of fantastic literature, we can offer some comments on Condon's achievement and on the nature of borderline fantastic fiction. One obvious trait of borderline fiction is that it does not use very esoteric scientific or supernatural inspiration; rather, it is based on trends and fears already existing in the public mind. It also takes pains not to go too far out with whatever idea it does use; rather, it develops its idea a minimal distance into the future while still exploiting the interest and disturbance created by any departure from the norm. Finally, it tends to withdraw into the present, to return to familiar reality at its conclusion. These qualities mean that borderline fiction tends to be somewhat timid, unwilling to be truly daring in the speculation it involves. It also tends to be somewhat superficial if it limits itself to public concerns and to the degree of extrapolation the public mind will readily accept. It is easily gripping rather than deeply moving. Still, the ease with which it is accepted suggests that it does deal with genuine concerns, however transitory their surface features may be. In the case of Condon's novels, borderline fiction written with ingenuity, skill, and integrity of vision *can* be as unsettling as good fantastic literature. In particular, like science fiction, it can force a reader to contemplate change as a less horrible alternative than continuation of our present condition. (pp. 135-37)

Joe Sanders, "The Fantastic Non-Fantastic: Richard Condon's Waking Nightmares," in Extrapolation, *Vol. 25, No. 2, Summer, 1984, pp. 127-37.*

GARRETT EPPS

If, as Mario Cuomo claims, the Mafia is a myth, then Richard Condon is its Bulfinch. His randy, peckish, subliterate, brutal, bewildered mobsters are much more likable—and much more like the gods of classical mythology—than the solemn waxworks in Mario Puzo's books. Condon has been developing his mythos over the years, in novels like ***Mile High*** and ***Winter***

Kills. But he burst into Homeric glory when he invented the Prizzi family.

Prizzi's Family is what the movie trade calls a "prequel" to Condon's enormously entertaining 1982 novel, ***Prizzi's Honor***. . . . Pieced together from the outtakes of the first novel, ***Prizzi's Family*** would make a funny movie. As a novel, it is entertaining but rather thin.

Charley Partanna, underboss and enforcer for the crime family of Don Corrado Prizzi, was revealed in ***Prizzi's Honor*** to have had a star-crossed romance with Maerose Prizzi, Don Corrado's granddaughter. ***Prizzi's Family*** tells the story of that romance. (p. 1)

The disappointment of ***Prizzi's Family*** is that everything resolves itself so smoothly. In ***Honor,*** Charley could only survive by "doing the job" on his own wife, whom he loved to distraction—an irony worthy of the Greeks. No such choices are demanded here.

It must also be said that Condon has gotten a bit sloppy in putting the book together. The facts we learned in ***Prizzi's Honor*** don't mesh with what happens in ***Family.*** In the first book, Charley's true love was named Mardell Du Pont, and he was 20 years old when he did away with the stoolie. There are many similar conflicts.

But perhaps we shouldn't worry too much about the facts. This is mythology, after all, and gods need not be consistent. Even on an off day, Condon is one of America's wittiest popular writers, capable of creating a character in one urbane phrase. (Don Corrado's son Vincent is "a serious man with a face like a clenched fist and an attitude of barely controlled violence, as if one of Senor Wences' hand puppets had developed antisocial tendencies.")

Prizzi's Family is great reading for beach or airplane. I hope we have not seen the last of Charley and Maerose. (p. 2)

Garrett Epps, "The Life and Loves of a Hit Man," in Book World—The Washington Post, *August 24, 1986, pp. 1, 2.*

JIMMY BRESLIN

New York City Police Department Complaint Report, Uniformed Forces Number 61.

Jurisdiction: New York City Police.

Time of occurrence: Commencing at 2040 hrs., 9/9/86, and continuing until 1630 hrs., 9/12/86.

Time of Report: 0600 hrs., 9/28/86.

Victim's Name: Jimmy Breslin.

Actions of Victim Prior to Crime: He remained generally seated while reading the book ***Prizzi's Family*** in his home on West 67th Street and in his place of business on East 42nd Street, Manhattan.

Total Number of Perpetrators: One.

Perpetrator's Name: Richard Condon. Male, white, age 69, 6 feet tall, 190 pounds, gray hair, blue eyes, glasses, pink cheeks. Accent: Speaks cheerful English and in the past has written this language with a paintbrush that talks.

Direction of Flight: Bank.

Weapon Possessed: Typewriter.

Reconstruct Occurrence including Method of Entry & Escape. Include Unique or Unusual Actions: Defendant Condon is charged in that at the time and place of occurrence he did strike the complainant, Jimmy Breslin, repeatedly with a typewriter across the head and right hand, that being the one with which he turned pages, causing lacerations to both head and hand and a fracture of illusion, and thus Defendant Condon committed the charge of felonious assault, typewriter, a violation of criminal code 120.05. Defendant is further sought and charged in that at time and place of occurrence he did violate criminal code 155.65 in that in the publication of his new book, ***Prizzi's Family,*** he did commit an act of attempted humor.

Defendant also is charged with a gross violation of criminal code 155.40 in that he committed grand larceny with the publication of his book, ***Prizzi's Family.***

Complainant states that Defendant Condon, based on his remarkable ability and such successes as ***The Manchurian Candidate*** and ***An Infinity of Mirrors,*** did engage Complainant with ***Prizzi's Family.*** Defendant Condon said it was a "prequel," which Complainant Breslin suspected was a way for Defendant to cash in on the movie success of ***Prizzi's Honor*** by telling people what happened previously to the stars in the big hit movie made from his novel. Complainant states he was all for this, as he roots for all writers to be rich. At first the "prequel" seemed to be satire and then appeared to be heading toward spoof. Complainant waited to laugh and was surprised and disappointed when he did not. Complainant Breslin states that he is certain he heard Defendant Condon laugh. Defendant then delivered a felonious assault, using characters with no sense of reality to them who were involved in story lines that have more holes than a shooting victim. Defendant Condon probably will earn handsome pay and honors when they turn ***Prizzi's Family*** into a movie. But Defendant Condon did enter bookstores in disdain of criminal code 155.40 (grand larceny, first degree) in that he enticed people who trust his name and loved his past successes and that in doing so, he committed the crime of grand larceny, first degree.

Jimmy Breslin, "Charley and Maerose: The Early Years," in The New York Times Book Review, *September 28, 1986, p. 13.*

JULIE SALAMON

[Richard Condon's ***Prizzi's Honor***] was a best-seller and John Huston's marvelous film version, for which Mr. Condon wrote the screenplay, was a critical and financial hit.

This inventive and prolific wordsmith has an eye for cinematic structure; five of his 21 novels have been turned into films. . . . And, after the success of ***Prizzi's Honor,*** no wonder he began to think the way movie people do: If something's a hit, why not make a sequel? After all, didn't *The Godfather* spawn *The Godfather, Part II*—an even better movie?

In the case of ***Prizzi's Family,*** Mr. Condon has come up with a "prequel." This time around he's dropping in on the Prizzis in the '60s, filling in some of the background sketched out in the original. But Mr. Condon isn't all that interested in exposing family roots the way the second *Godfather* film did for the Corleones. He's out for satire and some fun, and he figured there was plenty more to mine out of the rich Prizzi lode.

He was right. This book is a good read and not just in the sense that it clips along, though it does that, too. Mr. Condon's puckish descriptive powers continue to be uniquely hilarious.

Vincent Prizzi, the middle-aged son in charge of the family's street operation (he decides who gets "zotzed," for example), had "a face like a clenched fist. . . . He had gout, high blood pressure, ulcers, and psoriasis because he was a resenter."

Mr. Condon takes gleeful delight in playing the paranoidal who sees America as corroded, its morals left in the hands of TV ministers-cum-politicians and mobsters. You get the feeling he approaches his morning newspaper chortling with anticipation at the headlines he can put to satiric use.

In general, his characters are either connivers or dupes who routinely accept corruption as a way of life. Here he sustains the sly joke of ***Prizzi's Honor;*** though they murder and steal, the Prizzis have an elaborate code of ethics and a rigid sense of honor.

The caricature doesn't become tiresome, though, because Mr. Condon isn't merely an ironic commentator on contemporary life, he's a storyteller. . . .

What makes Mr. Condon so much fun to read, though, is the way this sometime contributor to Gourmet Magazine comfortably mixes a highbred sensibility with streetwise smarts and crudeness. His characters have scatological nicknames whose derivation Mr. Condon explains at length. On the other hand, he describes Eduardo's WASPishly elegant apartment with an eye for rarefied detail such as the flowers "arranged in the nine parts of the Rikka style (Muromachi, fifteenth century) by an ikebana master."

If the movie would do justice to the book the way ***Prizzi's Honor*** did, this is one sequel I wouldn't mind watching.

Julie Salamon, "The Crazy Prizzis Revisited," in The Wall Street Journal, *October 1, 1986, p. 30.*

Evan S(helby) Connell, Jr.

1924-

American novelist, short story writer, essayist, biographer, poet, and critic.

In his novels and short stories, Connell explores complexities of human behavior through such themes as emotional isolation and the stultifying effects on individuals of social propriety and conformity. His protagonists are often devoted to preserving the status quo, and through them Connell demonstrates with humor and compassion the hollowness of such lives. Connell writes in an exacting, straightforward prose style, and he has been especially noted for his wide range of subject matter and his attention to detail.

Connell's first book, *The Anatomy Lesson and Other Stories* (1957), contains pieces that reflect his interest in the human spirit. Included in this collection is "The Beau Monde of Mrs. Bridge," which introduces the title character of Connell's first and best-known novel, *Mrs. Bridge* (1959). This book and its companion volume, *Mr. Bridge* (1969), comprise a series of vignettes which form a revealing portrait of an affluent midwestern family whose unfulfilled lives are dominated by social pretense. The semiautobiographical novel *The Patriot* (1962) is an initiation story about an idealistic young Navy cadet, and *The Diary of a Rapist* (1966) is a psychological study of a man's descent into insanity. Karl Muhlbach, another character first introduced in *The Anatomy Lesson,* is the central figure of the novels *The Connoisseur* (1974) and *Double Honeymoon* (1976). These books chronicle Muhlbach's search for happiness and his simultaneous rejection and acceptance of the socially prescribed role which is the source of his restlessness. Through his fiction, Connell gained a reputation as a writer of considerable insight into human conflict, desire, and motivation. Charles Thomas Samuels remarked: "[Like] a character actor who disappears into his role, Connell always has the potential for turning imitation into insight."

Throughout his career, Connell has displayed an interest in a variety of topics and literary genres. *Notes from a Bottle Found on the Beach at Carmel* (1963) and *Points for a Compass Rose* (1973) have been variously described by critics as novels, epic verse, and prose poetry. Both books consist of personal meditations and philosophical observations on ancient and contemporary themes. *A Long Desire* (1979) and *The White Lantern* (1980) are collections of essays; the former is a survey of world exploration, while the latter presents a spiritual and intellectual history of humankind. In *Son of the Morning Star: Custer and the Little Bighorn* (1984), Connell painstakingly investigates the people and events involved with the resounding defeat at the Little Bighorn of General George A. Custer and the Seventh Cavalry. Page Stegner stated that the book "makes good reading—its prose is elegant, its tone the voice of dry wit, its meandering narrative skillfully crafted."

(See also *CLC,* Vols. 4, 6; *Contemporary Authors,* Vols. 1-4, rev. ed.; *Contemporary Authors New Revision Series,* Vol. 2; *Contemporary Authors Autobiography Series,* Vol. 2; *Dictionary of Literary Biography,* Vol. 2; and *Dictionary of Literary Biography Yearbook: 1981.*)

ANNE CHAMBERLAIN

Unlike some of his contemporaries, Mr. Connell demonstrates in [***The Anatomy Lesson and Other Stories***] an impressive geographical, thematic, and stylistic range. He roams authoritatively across the continent; with a virtuoso's dexterity he explores theme and treatment, subject matter and attack, darting from the precious and the esoteric to almost legendary folk tales, laid in his native Midwest and in distant corners of America. This is a many-faceted writer and if, in a few of his experiments, he is less successful than in others, he must be credited with the verve and courage of a young artist unwilling to travel narrow channels.

[**"The Anatomy Lesson"**], which consists purely of a magnificent lecture on art by a dynamic old master, is an unforgettable tour de force. Interesting in contrast (as an example of the author's versatility) is the long and delicately symbolic **"Arcturus,"** a beautifully delineated study of a family faced by tragedy, and their guests of a winter evening. With classic ease the scenes unfold, weaving from child to adult, from grief to mordant humor, evoking a symphonic blend of mood and emotion.

A disturbing decadence, a world-weary and sardonic bitterness threads through much of this collection. **"The Trellis,"** for instance, consists of a curious dialogue between a police inspector and an eccentric, analyzing the suicide of a friend. The village and rural stories (one—**"I Came From Yonder Mountain"**—is a sheer prose poem) are pervaded with a dark mysticism, a hint of older, sadder worlds. Perhaps the least effective effort is **"The Beau Monde of Mrs. Bridge,"** a merciless dissection of a convention-bound matron; here is savagery without the necessary balance of compassion. . . .

Mr. Connell is very much his own writer; exciting and unique. To this challenging form he brings a surprising maturity, and a promise that in this very first volume often achieves rich fulfillment.

Anne Chamberlain, "Young Writer of Compelling Originality," in New York Herald Tribune Book Review, *May 26, 1957, p. 4.*

WEBSTER SCHOTT

[As evidenced in ***The Anatomy Lesson***], Evan Connell has written several good short stories, and I think there is reason to believe he is going to write some much better ones. He respects the English language and finds beauty in it. He knows how to make plots and what service to expect of them. He is committed to the idea that the business of the short story is to define human character.

All of which, of course, is not enough. An army of second-rate short-story writers from Somerset Maugham to Budd Schulberg could lay claim to such qualifications. No, the writer who tries to create art with the story must have something more. He must take a position: He must feel deeply (passionately, I suspect) about why the human beings he is telling us about operate as they do. It's not a matter of striking a pose or rising to a moral. It is a matter of finding motivation that prevails, getting at a piece of truth.

This is what makes Connell's short stories worth considering seriously. His people are captives within themselves. They are isolated—so isolated that one wonders whether Mr. Connell wouldn't like to make this isolation one of those "eternal verities.". . . For when Mr. Connell's characters reach out from their isolation to make contact with the world or its inhabitants, they are either rebuffed, entangled in the debris of other lives, turned further inward or simply destroyed.

In **"Arcturus,"** Connell's best story, the condition of isolation controls all of the action, even the behavior of children. Here the pitiful failure of the dying wife and mother to communicate with her husband, children, and former lover breaks an artificial dinner party into fragments of despair. All the husband wants is to feed on his own loneliness. . . . One could go on to examine how this idea of spiritual isolation shapes Mr. Connell's stories of an empty yellow raft at sea, ignorance and theology in Kansas, a neurotic's reminiscences of bohemian pleasures, the sterility of Mission Hills aristocracy in Kansas City. It is everywhere, including those stories in which Mr. Connell surrenders to the bizarre and startling. And in these stories, you can see what happens when an author who does view behavior consistently by the same light is trapped, consciously or otherwise, by characters chosen to represent the view. We want a writer's individual insight into the forces bearing on personality. But it must be found within characters who have substance and individuality of their own.

I suppose the writer who considers the little tragedies of loneliness to be a prevalent condition of our situation and who never finds more to say is headed for an unhappy fate as an artist. Although many have made good livings by repeating much less than this.

But Mr. Connell seems too dedicated to art to become his own victim. He has been writing practically full-time for eight years, has produced only eleven stories . . . and has experimented with the short story so continuously that he still has no consistent style. One thing more, the range of his stories, moving from upper-class to lower-class society, from East to West and settling several times on gritty Kansas, suggests a writer who is not comfortable in one place or one state of mind.

Mr. Connell is interested in the Midwest obviously because he was born and reared there. But apparently (since his later work is located elsewhere) he has decided there is nothing unique about Kansas except its plains.

Webster Schott, "Captives within Themselves," in The New Republic, *Vol. 137, No. 17, October 14, 1957, p. 20.*

FLORENCE CROWTHER

Mrs. Bridge is a wistful little book about a suburban wife and mother who goes through all the familiar motions (the P.T.A., the servant problem, the urge for expression and self-improvement) and yet is so detached from the emotional realities of all the people with whom she comes in contact that she is left at the end absolutely engulfed in loneliness.

In more than a hundred oddly truncated chapters, some of them only a paragraph in length, Evan Connell moves Mrs. Bridge from childhood to marriage, from parenthood to widowhood, while hardly rippling the air about her. . . .

On the brink of spinsterhood, she marries Walter Bridge, an ambitious lawyer, whose main preoccupation is the pursuit of success and wealth—in order to "give her everything."

He gives her a son and two daughters, whom she trains to be courteous, clean, honest, thrifty and considerate. When the training period is ended and there is nothing more to communicate, Ruth, the older daughter, takes up a promiscuous life in New York City while ostensibly working for a magazine; Carolyn makes a dismal marriage; and Douglas, the son, following the death of his father, writes her from the Army that what he really needed from his father was himself and not the things he bought for them. (p. 30)

Although ***Mrs. Bridge*** is easy reading—there is often a touch of humor, sometimes mild pathos—it is somewhat unconvincing. It's hard to believe that a lady from Kansas City with a house in the best residential section, one full-time maid, one mink coat and a Lincoln for her very own, should finish up as timorous and ephemeral as a lunar moth on the outside of a window. (p. 31)

Florence Crowther, "Stranded Matriarch," in The New York Times Book Review, *February 1, 1959, pp. 30-1.*

ROBERT GUTWILLIG

Anyone who has read Evan Connell's fine collection of short stories, ***The Anatomy Lesson and Other Stories,*** will not be so much surprised as gratified to learn that his first novel, ***Mrs.***

Bridge, is a good one. And if what I have to say in these succeeding paragraphs sounds as if my enthusiasm and regard were tempered or if I were hedging my bets, I can only murmur that after reading his stories and novel, I want a great deal more from Mr. Connell than he appears willing to give at this time. This, too, is meant as praise, for it seems to me that Evan Connell could become one of our best writers.

Mrs. Bridge, unfortunately, is not so much a novel as a series of episodes illuminating the lives of this constantly befuddled woman, her abstracted husband, their three children, and their Kansas City friends. There are a hundred and seventeen of these related, interrelated and unrelated little chapters; they stretch across more than fifty years and, in subject matter, embrace a truly stunning variety of actions and emotions between birth and death.

I have no idea why Mr. Connell chose to tell his lovely story in such a choppy manner. Perhaps he wanted to match his style and content together as closely as possible. Perhaps the book started as a short story or several stories. In any event, I think he made a mistake.

The Bridges are as vivid a family as I have encountered in modern fiction, and as individuals they are scarcely less immediate. But they are terribly, deliberately and predictably limited—for two reasons. First, we have met the Bridges many, many times before, both in life and in literature. . . . Mr. Connell does not want to make the ordinary extraordinary; he does not want to surprise and appall us; he merely wants to make the ordinary interesting and entertaining. He succeeds, but it isn't quite enough. Second, his method admits no irrelevancies or discrepancies, no real narrative or plot. It permits only the most ruthless selection. (pp. 525-26)

I once heard Frank O'Connor say that the first job of a real writer was to select, and if he was not ruthless in his selection, then he was not a real writer. Maybe so. But Mr.Connell knows so much more than he is willing to tell that he has failed us by remaining partially silent. This failure manifests itself in at least two ways. ***Mrs. Bridge*** ends rather badly; the characters and the book disperse, the protagonist is left physically and emotionally trapped in her car, and . . . and that is all. Again the ruthless selection. Also, one is constantly aware while reading the novel that the author feels pity for his characters, and consequently that was the only emotion this reader was able to summon up for them. Pity obviously implies a measure of condescension and superiority, and I hope that in his next novel Mr. Connell will write up to his characters and not down to them. (p. 526)

Robert Gutwillig, "Ruthless Selection," in Commonweal, *Vol. LXIX, No. 20, February 13, 1959, pp. 525-26.*

GRANVILLE HICKS

One of the notable first novels of 1959 was ***Mrs. Bridge,*** by Evan S. Connell, Jr., which had considerable popular as well as critical success. Its popularity is a little puzzling, since it tells no story in the ordinary sense of the word, but critical applause is understandable enough, for this is a brilliant performance. In more than a hundred brief passages Connell gives us a picture of a middle-class woman who is insulated from life and is dimly aware of the fact. . . . The skill with which Connell selects his details is impressive, and so is the assurance with which he maintains exactly the right tone towards his heroine.

Now Connell has published his second novel—***The Patriot*** . . . and, unfortunately, it is a long step backward. It is weak at exactly the points at which ***Mrs. Bridge*** is strong: that is, the author has not been selective enough, and he has failed to maintain a consistent tone.

The Patriot describes six or eight years in the life of Melvin Isaacs, who is seventeen when the novel begins, and has just enlisted as a Naval Air Force cadet. Approximately half the book is devoted to an account of Melvin's training—in Iowa, at Albuquerque, in Georgia, and finally at Pensacola. Connell himself was in the Naval Air Force, and it is obvious that he has made use of his experiences. Much of this material is in itself excellent, but there is more of it than is necessary, and the clutter of detail obscures the character of Melvin Isaacs, which is Connell's main concern. . . .

Melvin's errors and escapades often seem comic to his fellow-cadets, but Connell does not treat them humorously. Gradually we realize that Melvin is a misfit in a rather profound way; something deep within him balks at being adaptable. . . .

All of Melvin's doubts and fears come to a head in an implausible interview with an implausible officer, and, though he is on the verge of receiving his commission, he decides to quit the program. He makes a last flight, which turns out to be the maddest of all his exploits, and wrecks his plane. (Connell's description of the flight is quite splendid.) Inevitably he is washed out.

This might conceivably be the end of the story: what one of Melvin's comrades calls his "suicidal independence" seems to have done its work. But Connell is not finished with Melvin. He hurries him through his training as an ordinary seaman and on to a base in Texas, where his only job is to gather up the golf balls on the officer's driving range. . . . At last the war ends, and Melvin is discharged.

His ordeal, however, has not ended. Defying his father, who is a lawyer and wants his son to be one, Melvin goes to study art at the University of Kansas on the G.I. Bill. He joins a fraternity, and that, naturally, turns out badly, but his major misadventure is with his art. A bull he has fashioned out of a discarded baby buggy wins a prize at a student exhibit, and Melvin finds himself an object of flattering attention. Some of his abstract paintings are sold, and he begins to take himself seriously. . . .

Meanwhile he has married and his wife is going to have a child. Now, when his fortunes are at the lowest, he receives a notice that he is subject to the draft and is to report for a physical examination. Having spent a good deal of time in meditating on the futility of war, Melvin resolves to go to prison rather than engage again in military service. An ecounter with Sam Horne, who has stayed on in the Naval Air Force, strengthens his conviction.

At last Connell is ready to end the book—on a note of savage burlesque. Melvin's father, as we have seen from the beginning, is an ardent militarist. . . . Now he appears in Melvin's apartment, full of enthusiasm for "the forthcoming war between America and the godless despots of the Soviet Union," and bearing a garbage can stocked with items needed for survival in case of atomic attack. Melvin tells his father to leave, and to take the garbage can with him. He will not live underground, he says, and he will not fight in another war. "What will you do?'' his father asks. ''I don't know,'' he replies. ''But I know what I won't do.''

That, I suppose, is intended to sum up Melvin's character. But as a study of a dissenter the novel lacks coherence and point, for many of the episodes have no clear bearing on the theme, and only at moments is Melvin fully comprehensible. . . . Nor can the book be taken seriously as a sermon against war. For one thing, the chief exponent of militarism, Melvin's father, is made into a perfect fool in the closing scene. For another, we are never shown how Melvin's crucial decisions grow out of his experiences.

Connell is wholly in earnest, and many pages prove that he is a writer, but there would be little reason to pay attention to the book if it weren't for ***Mrs. Bridge.*** I can't help wondering if ***The Patriot*** wasn't in fact written before that book. That is what it seems like—a first novel, more or less autobiographical, well meant but fumbling.

Granville Hicks, ''Flyer out of Formation,'' in Saturday Review, *Vol. XLIII, No. 39, September 24, 1960, p. 16.*

DAVID DEMPSEY

The Patriot belongs to the class of war fiction typified at its best by Jaroslav Hasek's *The Good Soldier Schweik* (which is sadder) and Ludwig Bemelmans' *My War With the United States* (which is funnier). Mr. Connell's book is sad and funny enough—as a portrait of the warrior who fails to make the grade, yet survives his comrades to argue for a more rational world. His scenes of flying are fresh, convincing and wonderfully human. The entire section that deals with flight training, in fact, is a superb piece of descriptive writing.

But if Melvin Isaacs has a hard time staying up, so does the author. The novel tails into Melvin's post-war—and post-climactic—career as an art student on the G. I. Bill, his troubles with an improbable family, his marriage and final repudiations of the conventional trappings of success. In terms of much that is valid in Mr. Connell's point of view, this is troubling. One feels that he might have called his novel *The Self-Defeated,* for if success can spoil Melvin Isaacs, so can failure. ***The Patriot,*** beautifully and impersonally handled for the most part, ends in a strident repudiation of everything military. Courageous as this may have been in 1949, it is bound to seem a trifle naive in 1960.

David Dempsey, ''Reluctant Warrior,'' in The New York Times Book Review, *September 25, 1960, p. 50.*

WARREN BOWER

The first thing to be said about ***At the Crossroads*** is that there is good work in it, but that the stories included are less consistently effective than those in ***The Anatomy Lesson.*** It would seem to be a gathering of stories written since 1957, three of them a group built around a character named Muhlbach, who also appeared in the story **''Arcturus''** in the first book. These could have been a trial run for a novel, just as a number of the oddly brief ''chapters'' in ***Mrs. Bridge*** appeared in ***The Anatomy Lesson*** as a short story, **''The Beau Monde of Mrs. Bridge.''** The first piece in the Muhlbach group, **''St. Augustine's Pigeon,''** is a moving account of a widower seeking female companionship, being humiliated and cheated, and suffering a climactic indignity from a pigeon. Wholly successful in achieving a vivid sense of the pathos and pitiability of loneliness, it is easily the most rewarding and fully realized story in the book.

The third piece in the Muhlbach group, **''Otto and the Magi,''** is discontinuous, a mixed-up narrative in which Connell falls victim to his own facility with words and ideas and scenes. He seems to have set down what may well have actually happened, plus his comments upon the people involved, their motives, intentions, meanings; but it is all out of control, self-indulgent, without apparent concern for the reader. To be sure, Connell is no deviser of neat plots; his best stories flow in a rhythm of their own, with a high correspondence to what transpires within a subtle mind. His worst are without structure, and flow turgidly because of the heavy burden of private comment and extraneous detail carried by the stream of the narrative. . . .

The last stories in the volume comprise another triptych of tales under the general title of **''Leon and Bébert.''** In each of these two garrulous young men comment interminably upon whatever comes into their heads. There is no narrative interest; the talk goes on and on with no relevance to anything. What is accomplished is merely a fulsome demonstration of two shallow, chattering gossips. In a transparent effort to supply a reason for finding these dull sketches important, a blurb-writer in the publisher's office has applied the term ''surrealism''—as if a label that sounds impressive and esoteric could by itself furnish what is lacking in the sketches themselves. . . .

The title story, **''At the Crossroads,''** is a piece of undoubted surrealism, the scene ''the intersection of two empty highways in the desert.''

Mr. Connell is an interesting and resourceful experimenter with freer forms in the short story. In this volume he has widened his range, developed his freedom to bend form and structure to his own purposes. If there seems to be less return from these experiments than one could wish, it may well be that in more considerable works to follow the results of the present trials and occasional errors may reward writer and reader alike.

Warren Bower, ''Widowers and Wanderers,'' in Saturday Review, *Vol. XLVIII, No. 29, July 17, 1965, p. 37.*

MARCUS KLEIN

Connell has a talent for the bourgeois phrase or manner that will reveal the hollowness within. In his earliest stories and in his first novel, ***Mrs. Bridge,*** the chief mark of his fiction was a stretching forward, from mannered conventionalism, to freedom, lyricism, sensuosity. The hollow folk might be more or less aware, but they were engaged by an activity of apprehension. In Connell's second novel, ***The Patriot,*** the hero was an abused young man, a Navy flier, who secured heroism by rejecting all the disabling conventions of both war and peace. The rejection was comic and sometimes feckless, but it was not ironic. In the long narrative poem that Connell published after it, ***Notes From a Bottle Found on the Beach at Carmel,*** his note was an elegant, stately, strenuous reaching after a purity of illumination. More and more, except in these stories, he has avoided an easy assumption of higher wisdom, according to which of course all particularity of motive and passion and adventure and personality will be charming and potentially funny.

With just a couple of exceptions, the stories in ***At the Crossroads*** are charming and very funny. A story, **"The Corset,"** about a nice married couple who discovers an itch for sexual exoticism; a story, **"On the Via Margritta,"** about a little poet who converts all libido into his little poetry; the tales of Muhlbach and those of Leon and Bebert—all of these are done with exquisite nuance. Nothing is forced. The wit in the stories is sure and it is subtle. They might constitute the major triumph of a lesser writer. But all this fine knowledge of the hopeless ways of people is purchased at the price of a good will as static as it is infinite. Given such compassion, there is no participation. There is no possibility of pain, love, hatred, and despair. And Connell is better than all this majesty.

Marcus Klein, "Alert for the Pedestrian," in Book Week—The Sunday Herald Tribune, *August 29, 1965, p. 19.*

ROGER SHATTUCK

The Diary of a Rapist is Connell's sixth book. It follows two uneven collections of short stories, two novels . . . and ***Notes from a Bottle Found on the Beach at Carmel.*** (Everyone carefully refrains from calling this heavy-handed work a "long poem," even though the lines march down 250 pages arrayed as free verse. It might have fared better as naked prose.) After these five books in which Connell steadily widened his vision until it verged on the epic, he has chosen to reverse himself completely and limit his point of view to one obsessed mind as it reveals itself to us and to itself in a diary.

Earl Summerfield is twenty-six and married to a school teacher seven years older than he is. Four principal activities make up his existence. He sits all day in a state employment bureau as an interviewer; in the job he is dead to himself, invisible to his fellow victims, and exasperated by his anguish over a promotion that never comes. He reads the San Francisco *Chronicle* with a sensitized eye that picks out all stories on executions, crime, and violence (particularly with sexual overtones), and socially prominent beauties flaunting their charms. From the outset he finds his vicarious self in the ripest and rottenest items in print. At home, he locks himself in his room away from his wife, pores over his scrapbook, meditates on the strange and incomprehensible things that seem to be happening to him, and masturbates his way out of his fantasies. Weekends, sleepless nights, and vacations, he prowls—harmless bus riding and walking at the start. It becomes something more ominous in intervals of blurred consciousness during which he molests women and enters houses to leave his sexual or excremental "calling card." On July 4th an eloquent gap in the otherwise regularly kept diary tells us something has happened; we learn in due time that he has in fact raped Mara St. Johns, bathing beauty, socialite, Whore of Babylon, his Queen. He has had his eyes on her since a February appearance in the *Chronicle*. Apparently she does not go to the police in spite of his continuing harassment by telephone. At the end the way people stare at him makes Summerfield half aware of his own state of mind and, if I interpret the cryptic entries correctly, he acts on a deceptively casual remark that he should commit suicide.

The story builds with considerable suspense. The steady succession of entries conveys a sense of frightful change gradually eating away at a person beneath his outer shell. Yet Summerfield's monstrousness remains human, for none of his delusions or obsessions lies beyond our grasp. As he sinks deeper into madness, he also lives closer to a vision of truth: Society is corrupt; violence threatens at any moment; everyone, friend, foe, and official, lies to us constantly and shamelessly; we must undertake a sacred mission to punish the foulness and sin of the world. This novel, seemingly focused because of its form on the disintegration of a man's mind, is equally a social novel aimed back . . . at the hideous society that spawned the condition. The lunatic has a message and tells it with a surprising and perverse force. . . . There is no greater loneliness in a desert or a tower. We learn everything about him except what might be conventionally revealing—his past, his appearance, and what he does at the few crucial moments of his existence. Those very unexposed patches enhance the rest. Summerfield comes off as a kind of truncated *tour de force* who nevertheless remains fixed in one's consciousness.

My quarrel is with the way Connell handles the diary form. Every date in one calendar year has its entry except for July 4 and the last six days of December. Summerfield states repeatedly that he writes out of self-imposed discipline and that he has made previous attempts to keep a diary with less success. Above all, his life begins to mimic the compulsive printed format of the little book in which he forces himself to set down these "notes." He is living through a piece of time divided neatly on the page into days and weeks and months, but Connell comes close to overlooking the immediate physical aspect of his device. Summerfield too often sounds not like a twenty-six year-old victim of metropolitan *ennui,* but like a displaced sensibility with some real claim to superiority. And I cannot understand how, having introduced it, Connell can fail to make use of the scrapbook Summerfield is keeping. Newspaper clippings could have provided a fine stylistic contrast to the diary and a kind of cross check on points of obscurity that now confuse the story. The utterly frustrating ending might have been raised to a fine irony had newspaper stories been introduced as a kind of chorus. (pp. 23-4)

Roger Shattuck, "Fiction a la Mode," in The New York Review of Books, *Vol. VI, No. 11, June 23, 1966, pp. 22-5.*

STEPHEN ZOLL

The Diary of a Rapist is a pitiful journal recording a compulsive preoccupation with violence, scorn and hopelessness. . . .

As a novel, the portrait it gives of the rapist is little more than a conventional psychological case history in the terms of which the reader agrees to have more concern for the subject than his victim. But Connell has achieved far more than this convention. The rapist, Earl Summerfield, a name like buttermilk, is passive, depersonalized, paranoid, infantile, latently homosexual, anal, etc. The symptomatology is corroborated by convincing entries. Connell has produced a powerful fictionalized documentary the effect of which is extremely troubling; he has moved case history into autobiography and we experience the impersonal subject of the first as the feeling author of the second.

Imagine a novel with these limitations: a first-person narration by the one and only character; a point of view limited to that character's unjustified anger and destructive madness; nothing is probed or revealed of this character—it is all confessed—as the narrator is acutely self-aware that his personality is limited to obsequiousness, cowardice and false bravado; there are no literary devices—neither plot, irony, reversal, discovery, epiphany, etc.—only language that is inventive, flowing, disciplined and nevertheless convincing as the words of so limited a character. This is the cavil: Summerfield has no stature.

Even so, Summerfield is not used for violently confronting the reader with intimations of his own foibles magnified. . . . Connell's book is an exercise in pity and terror; the diary's power to make it impossible for the reader to keep from identifying with Earl Summerfield lies within its limitations: we are not manipulated or accused. We are made aware in Summerfield's greed of the weakness in our own faith that we can ever be satisfied. (p. 26)

Connell, I believe, would have the reader understand that this case history of aberration is not, narrowly, a psychological problem, but, perhaps, a religious one. On Christmas Day, Summerfield's last entry is, "In the sight of the Lord I must be one of the many." Leaving off his private diary, he has given up even vanity and disappeared into the scandal of public confession. Connell seems to be saying that recognition achieved finally by becoming one of the many is a theological madness, and that human hunger unsatisfied leads to greed so monumental that there can be no hope of satisfaction. Without hope there is neither faith, nor grace, nor salvation. Summerfield's obscene behavior is the best answer he can give his hunger; it is to save him from the abyss. Connell moves the reader because Summerfield suffers his mad logic and also disappears into the abyss from which his madness was to have saved him. (p. 27)

Stephen Zoll, "Violent Days," in The Nation, *New York, Vol. 203, No. 1, July 4, 1966, pp. 26-7.*

CHARLES THOMAS SAMUELS

Evan Connell makes things so difficult for himself that it is almost cruel to be critical. To begin with, he is austere in his choice of subjects. His first novel, ***Mrs. Bridge*** (1959), is the character study of a Midwestern clubwoman leading a dull, unfulfilled life, whose pathos she resolutely ignores. . . . ***Mrs. Bridge*** embodies its supererogatory theme (the emptiness of middle America) in a style, adhering strictly to the heroine's viewpoint, that precludes eloquence and, sometimes, pertinence as well. . . .

Everything Connell writes is competent, but none of his previous books is enough like another to persuade us that we must grant his subjects and dwell on his style. ***Mrs. Bridge*** is written in colorless prose, but [***The Diary of a Rapist***] recalls Celine. In his stories Connell moves from porno-baroque (in the Muhlbach tales from ***At the Crossroads***) to arch *New Yorker*. One of his books was so unexpected (***Notes from a Bottle Found on the Beach at Carmel***) that critics couldn't decide whether it was poetry or prose. . . .

Connell is ingenuous in disguising his inability to construct a tale. ***Mrs. Bridge*** is written in a series of very short chapters (some paragraph-long) that simply slice up the heroine's life, while ***The Diary*** employs the oldest and least convincing plot evasion known to literature. . . .

Evan Connell, then, is a novelist who can't construct stories about uninteresting or remote people told in characterless prose. Why give him any attention? Because in everything he writes, he is admirably serious and painstaking and because, like a character actor who disappears into his role, Connell always has the potential for turning imitation into insight. All he needed was a good part, which he has found in ***Mr. Bridge.***

Well, not precisely *found*. ***Mr. Bridge*** doesn't merely retell the Bridge saga from the husband's point of view; it makes use of the form and many of the earlier book's incidents in the way that a late-model car makes use of an earlier one's engine. The effect is not so much of Proustian refinement eventuating in discovery as of planned obsolescence. This is not deplorable, however, because the second ***Bridge*** novel is so much better than the first.

Most simply, it is better because it is about a man. Showing barrenness in the life of a woman—without job or children, self-scrutiny or spiritual movement of any vigor—is showing nothing that admits development or surprise. Because Mr. Bridge must make a living and engage the world, his inner life reflects more counterforce. Furthermore, in ***Mrs. Bridge*** absence of tension leads Connell to fill the void with TV situation comedy. By contrast, ***Mr. Bridge*** is grey and astringent, its rare comic moments laughter in the dark. In every way, Mr. Bridge is more complex than his wife and more representative of something fundamental in his country. (p. 21)

However, ***Mr. Bridge*** shares faults with its companion novel. The glimpse-of-life form produces redundancy, and Connell is not selective enough. Though the book is scrupulously realistic, melodrama occasionally obtrudes. . . . ***Mr. Bridge,*** which is laid in the thirties, strives, unlike the earlier novel, for a historical dimension, but despite the appearance of brand names and contemporary radio shows, the action, with its frequent emphasis on race relations and youthful rebellion, has the feel of the sixties.

These deficiencies are at least counterbalanced by a real artistic achievement. ***Mrs. Bridge*** is little but a series of *tableaux vivants;* ***Mr. Bridge*** makes this form incremental by exploiting the possibilities of cross-reference. I will cite only one example. In the book's funniest scene, Mr. Bridge is confronted by a robber on his way home from work. *Comme il faut,* the man appears, "one hand thrust into the slit pocket of a shabby trench coat," and orders Mr. Bridge to part with his cash, whereupon the hero says, "'Don't be ridiculous,'" and huffily departs. In a later chapter, when he is lecturing his son on prudence, he tells the boy never to resist a robbery because his grandfather lost his life by refusing to surrender his money to an armed bandit. What was merely comic is now a revelation about Mr. Bridge's obsession. Redundant, uneven, written in a prose that is seldom more than serviceable, ***Mr. Bridge*** nevertheless adds up to a moving portrait of a minor tragedy. (pp. 22-3)

Charles Thomas Samuels, "Dead Center," in The New Republic, *Vol. 160, No. 23, June 7, 1969, pp. 21-3.*

THE TIMES LITERARY SUPPLEMENT

There are 157 sections in ***Mr. Bridge,*** none of them related in any conventional narrative sense, yet combining to create something durable and fascinating to explore.

The continuity is provided only by the characters, who appear for a brief moment caught in some characteristic attitude, dissolve, and then reappear busily talking of some fresh small crisis or reacting to a new challenge. . . .

Walter Bridge is the kind of man E. M. Forster has always been so concerned about: he cannot connect. We see him mainly in a family context, and there is never warmth or humaneness in his relationships either with his wife or his son or his two daughters. He is never less than dutiful, never less than a generous provider, but what he provides is somehow always too solidly sensible ever to be fun. He gives his daughter, for example, some share certificates as a present, on the grounds that a portfolio must be better value than a handbag. He lives in Kansas City. He has been poured into the mould of American, Middle-west, ad hoc morality and he has set hard. Underneath the unyielding outer crust his lusts fitfully seethe, but never enough to force a crack.

With Mr. Connell commentary and criticism are always implicit. Is Bridge a monster? Or a joke? Or a model? Perhaps a bit of all three. But the final impression left with the reader of this subtle, most beautifully composed novel is that of a man stunted and pointlessly deprived.

"Dead Dutiful," in The Times Literary Supplement, *No. 3536, December 4, 1969, p. 1377.*

CELIA BETSKY

Evan S. Connell, Jr., likes to watch people figure-skating on the surface of time. They glide, they slip, they fall, try to move backward, plunge forward too fast, eventually realize they're out of their element. Karl Muhlbach, the hero of ***Double Honeymoon,*** is a man who not only feels he is in the wrong time (he prefers the 18th century), but who is also horrified to see time slipping away; it has left him a middle-aged insurance-company executive so boring he is not even likable. He performs the classic gesture of age sickened by itself: he has an affair with a younger woman. Why is it that when middle-aged men (authors?) face young girls, they lose all sense of reality? The clichés of plot, language, and style are embarrassing to read. . . . Connell's grasp of the situation is so frail that the answer can only be: so what?

Connell has tried his hand at New York in this book, but all he has come up with is an array of sleazy and interchangeable characters in search of a *New Yorker* cartoon. Cartoons are not his forte; he belongs with the severe drama of his Midwestern ***Mrs. Bridge*** or the sad dignity of ***The Connoisseur.*** Evan Connell is at his best when he shows the most mundane life being constructed as a conscious, even a self-conscious, work of art. Muhlbach is no artist. What does that tell you about his author?

Celia Betsky, in a review of "Double Honeymoon," in Saturday Review, *Vol. 3, No. 4, April 17, 1976, p. 33.*

WEBSTER SCHOTT

We first met Karl Muhlbach, a 45-year-old widower and New York fire insurance executive, in 1965 in Evan Connell's collection of stories, ***At the Crossroads.*** There in **"Saint Augustine's Pigeon"** the punctilious Muhlbach briefly abandons caution. Hungry for flesh he loses his billfold, gets drunk, and a pigeon defecates on his head. In another ***Crossroads*** story, **"The Mountains of Guatemala,"** Muhlbach attends a Christmas party and meets a mysterious and beautiful young woman, Lambeth Brent. He luxuriates in fantasy but says no. This story, slightly revised, becomes the first part of ***Double Honeymoon.*** All the rest is new. It's Muhlbach saying yes and running into trouble.

Lambeth is the sort of woman Tennessee Williams or Truman Capote might have found: intense, frivolous, cruel, childlike. Twenty years old, she has lived enough to be ninety. Her husband was killed in a plane crash at Pensacola. Lambeth says she is a model and a dancer, but she lies so much that finding her truths is impossible. Once she had an affair with an older woman. Perhaps a detective lover beats her up. Her telephone rings at odd hours of night, and the evening Muhlbach takes her to bed and bathes with her, there is a tapping at her door. She makes dates and breaks them. She steals clothing. She demands money and forgets it. She improvises a shifting nonreality. Long before Karl Muhlbach sees it, we know something serious is wrong with Lambeth.

Muhlbach senses it, because whatever Lambeth has, there's some in him too. His clocklike habits erode under the stress of lust. He flies after Lambeth like a wild bird. But an unbreakable line holds him to his desk at Metro Mutual, the kids and cook back at the townhouse. . . .

Lambeth is dead when ***Double Honeymoon*** ends. Like Hemingway's Lieutenant Henry, Karl Muhlbach walks away from the hospital in the rain. But he is the romantic as observer, not the romantic in action. He only tested the dream. He backed out of [a trip with Lambeth to] Connecticut. It was sweeter in fantasy, as he knew it would be, than in experience. Muhlbach puts up his umbrella. No trenchcoat. Then he disappears into the crowd, indistinguishable from the rest.

Like most of Evan Connell's fiction—especially ***Mrs. Bridge, Mr. Bridge,*** and his other Muhlbach novel, ***The Connoisseur—Double Honeymoon*** is more about a vision and characters within that vision than about the events of a plot. Connell sees a narrower world than we would wish. Chance for change occurs . . . but the unknown terrifies us. We retreat to the familiar. We're held in place—in Connell's world, anyway—by a social structure that controls the animal in us and provides little space to romp and play. Some go mad. Lambeth does. Others, like Muhlbach, make brief excursions and return.

I don't always share this vision. But when Connell shows it, I believe it. What he creates exists. . . . He observes like an owl. His oracular manner suggests the disengagement of nobility. He writes with irony, grace, precision. . . .

Connell, like Robert Frost, has a lover's quarrel with the world. It can't be resolved. It can only continue as he cooly lays down the mournful details of our unjust fate. We are such interesting creatures. We deserve to be free. If only we dared.

Webster Schott, "Testing the Dream," in Book World—The Washington Post, *June 6, 1976, p. H5.*

EDWARD HOAGLAND

Evan S. Connell's 11th book is one of those pleasure books of nonfiction that a good novelist will pause to write once in a while as a relief from the rigors of invention. ***A Long Desire*** is a survey of great feats of exploration, a compendium of a lifetime's reading of adventure, a book of wonders, florid history, provisional "facts" and catchy ironies, laconic heroism and scabrous villainies, cryptic deaths and other endings. It celebrates the glitter of a world newly created by God, yet nonetheless to be conquered for God, as Balboa did when he waded into the water at the Isthmus of Darien with a naked sword to take possession of the whole Pacific for Christ and Castile. (p. 12)

Mr. Connell wears his learning lightly, but this crème de la crème of world adventuring is possibly too thick a mix to read straight through. It is a book built on one man's uncommon enthusiasms, and so it is an antidote to the homogenizing modernism that, for example, recently led a social scientist to claim that cannibalism never even existed as a cultural tradition. A momentary antidote, as well, to the crushing of myths that goes with travel by airplane. Already by the 17th century, he says, many myths were fading, losing color, like those stiff tapestries from the Middle Ages that now and again we meet in the corridors of great museums. (pp. 12, 37)

[The final chapter focuses on Paracelsus, a sixteenth-century alchemist]. In Egypt, [Paracelsus] saw hippos and crocs "so fearful you would jump right back into your mother's womb." But besides obsessively shuttling about and trying to brew philosopher's stones, he wrote of gynecology, surgery, the occupational diseases miners suffered from and ideas precursory to the radio. Man's imagination "is like the sun, whose light cannot be touched and yet may set a house on fire," he said; and Mr.Connell affectionately relates him to the beginnings of the legend of Faust. (p. 37)

Edward Hoagland, "Far Away from Home," in The New York Times Book Review, *June 24, 1979, pp. 12, 37.*

WILLIAM PLUMMER

Connell is a master miniaturist, capable of delicate brushwork on the tiniest bits of ivory. So it's surprising to see him in ***A Long Desire*** working in what Sir Walter Scott called "the big Bow-wow strain."... In ***A Long Desire,*** the author turns his attention to "the singular person, inexplicably drawn from familiar comforts toward a nebulous goal, lured often enough to death—it is he, or she, whose peregrinations can never be thoroughly understood, who is worth noticing."

The book is a diadem of obsessions, each chapter a separate inlaid stone. . . .

Naturally, some chapters are better than others; several are sketchy and factitious, though on the whole, the deeds are outrageous, the personalities enthralling. Still I can't help wondering why Connell bothered.

He seems content merely to grease the machinery, to keep his narratives running pleasantly. His prose is precise, gentlemanly, at times exquisite, but I suppose my demurrer is a matter of scale and signature.

The only time his prose rises to his occasion, becomes agitated and idiosyncratic, is when certain Victorian lady explorers traverse the page. Says Connell: "Then there is May French Sheldon on the way to Kilimanjaro in a blonde wig, carrying a ceremonial sword, wearing a rhinestone-studded gown and a dozen Cleopatra bracelets. No. No, she must be the creation of a mad playwright." And: "But the mind cannot absorb Isabella Bird Bishop at the apex of her fame. . . . No, we say. No, no, I'll go along with Ibn Batuta or that Chinese whose name I can't remember, but this woman is too much."

It is imagining these women in the African wild that sets Connell adither; incongruity plucks his ironic string. "They give the impression of being mildly batty," he says, "these upright, energetic, innocent, valorous, polite, intelligent, prim, and condescending British females in long skirts." They are, in fact, quaint old biddies not so very different from Mrs. Bridge. It's no wonder that they are the ones to turn Connell's motor over. "The big Bow-wow strain" is not really his métier. (p. 56)

William Plummer, "Heroic Endeavors," in Saturday Review, *Vol. 6, No. 24, December, 1979, pp. 55-6.*

AUDREY C. FOOTE

Famous as Victoria's devoted prime minister, Benjamin Disraeli was also a fashionable novelist; in *Tancred* he limned a lady describing a new book which had caught, if not wholly held, her attention:

"But what is most interesting is the way in which man developed. . . . I think there were shells, then fishes; then we came. Let me see, did we come next? Never mind that; we came at last. And the next stage will be something very superior to us; something with wings. Ah! that's it; we were fishes, and I believe we shall be crows."

For those today whose grasp of evolution is similarly vague, Evan Connell is gracefully and tactfully instructive, on this and other historic matters, as Disraeli was with the queen. The first essay in [***The White Lantern***] is a stylish summary of man's theories about his origin and evolution, from 17th-century Archbishop Ussher's confident dating of the Creation at 4004 B.C. to 20th-century archeologist Louis Leakey musing over 2-million-year-old bones in the Olduvai Gorge.

Armchair explorer Connell is an urbane polymath, an amateur in the Victorian tradition. He is a connoisseur, not merely of pre-Columbian art like the hero of his last novel, but of everything arcane, exotic, ancient or bizarre; places, fauna, legends and feats, but above all personalities, especially quacks, cranks, heretics and heroic failures. Here, for example, he gives less space to Charles Darwin than to Charles Dawson, lawyer and antiquarian, who some 70 years ago perpetrated (probably) the greatest of all archeological frauds, the Piltdown Man.

The success of that fraud and the skepticism which had earlier greeted the Neanderthal Man indicate the difficulty of distinguishing between the genuine and fake, historic and mythic or even between astronomy and astrology, the theme of the last essay with its punning Latinate title, **"Abracadastra."** This survey of man's study of the stars begins with the pre-Socratic Thales and ends with Percival Lowell, a turn-of-the-century astronomer with impeccable credentials, both social and scientific, who became convinced that there were irrigation canals and pumping stations on Mars. . . .

Frauds, errors and losses divert the course of knowledge and discovery—and in these sprightly accounts, divert us. **"Vinland Vinland"** glances at the evidence for 11th-century Viking landings in North America; convincing, though some of the rusty little axes proposed as relics turned out to be souvenir plug tobacco cutters. . . .

Another discovery, another loss is the subject of [**"The White Lantern,"** an essay] on the Scott-Amundsen 1911-12 expeditions to the South Pole. "Victory awaits those who have everything in order. People call this luck," the Norwegian Amundsen remarked drily. "Defeat awaits those who fail to take the necessary precautions. This is known as bad luck."... His team not only reached the Pole first but luckily got back healthy, with food to spare. Captain Scott and his friends lost the race and their lives. Yet Connell reminds us—he hardly needs to—of the self-sacrifice of Edward Oates and the gallant understatement of his last words ("I am just going outside and may be some time") and of the stoic death of the charismatic Scott; he also comments that today the loser is often thought to have been the victor, and is remembered and honored as his successful rival is not.

The White Lantern is a companion piece to Connell's ***A Long Desire*** (1979): an essay on the Etruscans here parallels one on the Olmecs there, astronomers pair with alchemists, the South Pole with the Seven Cities of Cibola. The present volume is somewhat more concerned with history than with legend, but of course there have been as many myths about America as Atlantis, of primitive man as Prester John, and Connell writing of all these slyly reminds us of facts that turned out to be fables, fantasies that came true.

Audrey C. Foote, "Wanderers in a World of Wonders," in Book World—The Washington Post, *July 13, 1980, p. 4.*

RITA FINK

A year ago, in ***A Long Desire,*** Evan Connell beguiled us with the quest of those rare and unusual persons in history who sought the unknown and reached out to grasp the ostensibly unattainable. In the companion book, ***The White Lantern,*** Connell's text is man's compulsion toward the siren call of knowledge and how he goes about slaking his desire.

The dice were cast the moment someone in history started to worry about how many animals could fit in the Ark. Connell points up the cut-off of the age of darkness: "Science feels obligated to inquire, whereas the Church comes armed with infallible dogma." No wonder science can never be a god. Each time science embraces a truth, it will be simply a matter of hours until that truth is supplanted by new searches and findings. Can't have that happen to gods.

In the essay called **"Olduvai & All That,"** Connell recounts the classic story of the Piltdown man who came tumbling down. His wry conclusion is that the respected historian of today is the pathetic figure of tomorrow. In the search for knowledge, the options are wide open for all—the romantics, the skeptics, the believers and the seekers. . . .

With a startling degree of success the author rivets in the reader's mind the facts, as known, in each of the legions of the subject he presents. It is a dramatic display with an approach filled with respect, tinged with irony and skepticism and brushed with humor. . . .

In his seven essays, Connell warns that "one can be not only too guillible, but too skeptical," and one should avoid being overawed by the next authority. That puts us on a trembling rock, but who has a choice? The avalanche of curiosity is sweeping; it's too late in history to turn back. . . .

If I'm shipwrecked on a deserted island and can salvage but one book, that book will be ***The White Lantern.*** The theme is brilliant, the scope is sweeping, the writing is vivid and shot with humor. The presentation is dynamite; it explodes in the brain with the flashing light which urges: "Seek, Seek!" Evan Connell did.

Rita Fink, "Unending Search for Knowledge," in Pacific Sun, *Vol. 18, No. 29, July 18-24, 1980, p. 25.*

JONATHAN PENNER

"The author," so the jacket copy tells us, "is an assiduous collector of historical absurdities, coincidences, contradictions, artifices, outrages and insanities over which the protagonist ruminates mournfully while remaining partially paralyzed in the present—in short, contemporary man at an eternal crossroads seeking direction."

Accurate enough. But [***Saint Augustine's Pigeon***] has better to offer the reader than mournfully ruminating, partially paralyzed protagonists. And if any author can be summed up "in short," it would be better not to admit it—let alone actually tell us how.

The jacket copy might instead have praised what Evan S. Connell does best: see and write. (p. 5)

Connell can encapsulate a character wonderfully: "She was married to the mortician, an extremely tall man named Knopf who liked to underline trenchant phrases in the little books on Success that you buy for a quarter."

He can describe even dusk—"Chill as any stone, the sun sinks through cloudy folds, through antennae and chimneys"—as though no one had ever seen dusk before. And perhaps no one ever has, in exactly this way; but now some reader, somewhere, will. Here is the magic through which words ennoble our mute experience.

It's sad that this wonderful style so often sinks into pedantry and a kind of hypersensibility. "The sun obtrudes, strange fruit in the western quadrant, viable," is a strained way to suggest the approach of spring. A single story finds it necessary to employ the words *lentiginous, ferruginous, vesicant, bobbery, epicene, decoctions,* and *albify*.

The best of these stories are wonderful. **"The Fisherman from Chihuahua"** concerns a restaurant owner in California who develops a peculiar dependence on one of his patrons—a Mexican who howls. **"The Caribbean Provedor"** is set in a tropical port; the viewpoint character gets into trouble when he allows himself to be mistaken for an official investigator.

The people are real, the places are real. What happens is absolutely clear. But beneath their taut surfaces, both stories leave mysteries, letting their imaginary worlds run deep. One rereads them with added pleasure, and part of that pleasure is in not striking bottom.

Not so with others of these 16 stories. The jacket copy tells the truth, which it wrongly conceives as flattering: Many of the stories *do* invite interpretation "in short," and to this extent they are scarcely stories at all. Rather they are meditations on ideas.

Fiction can digest ideas. But the organ that absorbs them is character, and too often Connell cares more for the thought than for the thinker. Thus the protagonist will be assigned such a passage of analysis as this:

> I accept the madness of our time, he thinks. Each age does produce its folly—some scheme, project, or fantasy toward which the blood drains—economic, political, religious. Always. Panniers of mold from the hill of the Crucifixion, flagons of water from Jordan. There is testimony to the madness of an earlier age, but is ours more sapient?

Obviously, this is not real thought. It is not even plausible as stylized thought. It is sheer, barefaced writing, the thing that Connell does so well, and it doesn't belong inside his characters' skulls.

Consider [**"Saint Augustine's Pigeon"**], in which an intellectual widower named Muhlbach has a night on the town. Pursued by lust, meditating on Augustine's *Confessions,* he suffers a series of stock humiliations, ending with the splat of pigeon excrement on his hat. At the end, in a string of formally articulated thoughts, stubborn Muhlbach realizes that he has been acting the fool.

The heavily labored point is that his insight resembles St. Augustine's. The parallels fall into place obediently. But Muhlbach never becomes human. He is a man snapped together from modules: intellectuality, naiveté, lust. He is a head sowed with thematic thoughts.

The final piece is titled: **"A Brief Essay on the Subject of Celebrity: With Numerous Digressions and Particular Attention to the Actress, Rita Hayworth."** And an essay it frankly is. Its appearance in this volume of "selected stories" makes explicit the view of essay-as-fiction that the other stories so often imply. (pp. 5-6)

Jonathan Penner, "Anecdotes and Artistry," in Book World—The Washington Post, *February 15, 1981, pp. 5-6.*

FRED SHAFER

In the sixteen stories of ***Saint Augustine's Pigeon,*** Evan S. Connell's characters belong to a society in which the pressure to conform is strong. The stories are set, for the most part, in the United States during the fifties and sixties, when it seemed that scarcely anyone could escape social constraints. Many of Connell's characters are happy to embrace conformity, as part of what one of them calls "the responsibility of being human"; others, who think that they've freed themselves, have been influenced by the expectations of the community in ways they cannot imagine. As a storywriter committed to traditional forms but not to conventional values, Connell wants to know what happens to all of these people, particularly when they begin to see their lives more clearly.

The characters who accept conformity in Connell's stories tend to believe that they are following a system that has been established in their best interests. . . .

It helps their case that so many of the people who attempt to break the pattern end in failure, brought down apparently by influences on their personalities that they cannot overcome. No matter how hard they try, these characters continue to be the products of their upbringing, often remaining too innocent or naive to deal with new threats in an unfamiliar world. (p. 260)

The victories, when they come, tend to be small, and strange. One man finds a lover, but fails to see that she is even more domineering than the wife he wishes to divorce. The highlight of another man's life occurs when he persuades his wife to remove her corset and perform acrobatic tricks in their bedroom. Some people can only be witnesses of the success of others, as when a family from Iowa visits a restaurant in Santa Cruz and listens with awe to the wild, inspired cries of a fisherman. Seemingly, the most such characters can expect is to remain on the inside looking out; they aren't suited for escape.

The only real success in eluding conformity is the character J. D., who appears in two stories, a man regarded by his friends as "one of those uncommon men who follow dim trails around the world hunting a fulfillment they couldn't find at home." The statement suggests a special genius for breaking ties and disregarding influences; indeed, J. D. travels the world for years, seeking out the places where the tourists don't go, ancient villages in the mountains of Spain, windmills in Majorca, palaces remote in the provinces of India. The men who have stayed at home need to think that J. D. has wasted his life, becoming a "middle-aged man without a trade, without money or security of any sort," and with "no bona fide skills." When he returns home to live, however, they feel betrayed, admitting that "perhaps without realizing it we trusted him to keep our youth."

It would be easy to attribute such conformity solely to ignorance or a lack of imagination. Rather, the willingness to accept beliefs and forms prescribed by society, Connell suggests, may arise from a deep need for security in a troubled world. In a set of three stories, Muhlbach, a protagonist who recurs in Connell's novels, becomes obsessed with the fear of unknown forces when his wife dies. To protect himself and his two children from "evil . . . misery, destruction, violence, life without hope," he builds a bomb shelter. It doesn't matter that he has laughed at the government publicity on the value of shelters against nuclear attack. "I acquiesce in the name of prudence, which is a sort of wisdom," he contends, until his son attempts to shock him into recognizing his timidity. But Muhlbach accepts social restrictions in other ways as well, convinced that he must not exceed "the limits set for my nature." After attempting to meet a young woman in Manhattan, he decides to live "within my province," quietly and routinely. Like many of the other characters in these stories, he welcomes the comforts of a structured society.

To some critics, Connell might seem to contradict himself by examining social constraints while relying on established literary forms. He might even be accused of imposing conformity on the reader, who is required to stay within the boundaries of a carefully controlled text. Certainly this collection demonstrates that Connell is in charge of every element of his narratives and that he has been in firm control since his early publications more than thirty years ago. The stories are marked, however, by a dialectical play between the desire for freedom and the conformism of Connell's characters, which suggests the subtlety of his approach as a writer of short fiction.

Some of the most powerful effects of this struggle arise from what Connell leaves unstated. . . . When a character begins to discover the limitations of his or her life, Connell invariably draws back and lets the reader carry the implications forward. (pp. 260-61)

The freedom that Connell gives to some characters, he gives to the reader as well. By disguising the subtly subversive elements in his apparently traditional story-forms, he draws the reader into the panic of characters whose responsibility for their lives prompts the reader's responsibility to judge them. Connell is too crafty to judge them for us, but also too humane to allow us to condemn them without understanding their fears, which are ours. (pp. 261-62)

Fred Shafer, in a review of "Saint Augustine's Pigeon," in TriQuarterly, *No. 56, Winter, 1983, pp. 260-62.*

LORNA SAGE

Turning the pages of Evan S. Connell's novels about the Bridge family is like time travel. It has something of the effect of that autumnal Hollywood trick of training a fan on a loose-leaf calendar. ***Mrs Bridge*** (1959) and ***Mr Bridge*** (1969), now reissued simultaneously, are set in a prosperous suburb of Kansas City in the 1930s, and have a sly, painstaking exactitude that marvellously evokes a past style of all-American domestic life. That they have never been published in Britain before is surprising—though perhaps ironically apt, given that their central theme is American isolationism.

Mr Connell's technique for mapping out landlocked Middle America was nicely judged: a series of lightly sketched, teasingly brief encounters, seldom longer than a couple of pages each, in which his characters reveal the frightening versatility of their defences. . . . For the Bridges there is only one real world, and it's an extension of the nuclear family—a corporate, country-club organism that thrives on segregation (Jews, Italians, Irish, Negroes) and subordination (children, women) while at the same time, with magnificent inconsistency, assuming a universal doctrine of the sovereign individual and self-help.

Lightness of touch is all. Without it Mr Connell's relentless awareness of his people's bad faith would risk becoming complacent in its turn. However, he maintains a wry, dry, level tone. We overhear Mr Bridge and his business friends mouthing the clichés of intolerance. . . . But there are moments too of pure comedy of manners, as when Mrs Bridge's anxious good taste does battle with her Christian charity at the sight of

> a stucco bungalow with a lifesize cutout of Santa Claus on the roof, six reindeer in the front yard, candles in every window, and by the front door an enormous cardboard birthday cake with one candle. On the cake was this message: HAPPY BIRTHDAY, DEAR JESUS.
>
> 'My word, how extreme,' said Mrs Bridge thoughtfully. 'Some Italians must live there.'

It is of course clumsy, matronly, menopausal Mrs Bridge who most tellingly embodies the contradictions of this society, insulated as she is in prosperous, frustrated idleness, never daring to look too closely at her husband, her children, or her friends, for fear of lapsing into panic. In the sequel Mr Bridge, by contrast, can place work between himself and his family and conceal his uncertainties by giving them everything money can buy. On rare Sundays off, we're told, 'he would spend the morning in the yard with a can of snail poison.' Home has to be kept slightly out of focus, so that the doubts remain, as it were, in suspension, rather than settling into a muddy sediment of guilt. Not that he deceives his wife in the vulgar sense: it's characteristic of him that he has no sexual interest in his secretary, or his cook, though they perform the role of supernumerary wives. His cheat is that by banishing all that's alien, exotic, and different from his consciousness he's killed his libido. Like his wife, though less sadly, he's self-exiled from desire.

Mr Connell sees the Bridges as people who've sacrificed the pleasure principle to the reality principle, only to find that their sense of reality was on the blink. Friend Grace, who has the role of despairing chorus, says that their whole set are like 'those people in the Grimm fairy tale—the ones who were all hollowed out in the back.' They pose as realists, while inhabiting a myth. Doubtless, faced with a new generation of American conservatives born again into unreason, Mr Connell must feel that he was on to something. Certainly the republication of the Bridges novels has a timely feel, not least because Mr Connell is revealed as a percipient feminist out of fashion.

Lorna Sage, "Yesterday in Kansas," in The Observer, *July 17, 1983, p. 26.*

LINDA SPALDING

In 1959, Evan S. Connell published a book called ***Mrs. Bridge,*** written in tight abbreviated chapters—almost cartoons—describing the events of an entire life. Mrs. Bridge is a midwestern matron, an American old-girl, and the scenes of her life, the general environment and pace are as familiar to me as scenes from a neighbor's home movie. With David McFaddenesque wit that is underplayed and hilarious, Connell lifts the lid of American suburbia, releasing little episodes of family life with delicate detachment. This is the kind of book that wants to be read aloud. Its gentle, funny poignancy needs to be shared. Random reports, so simple and objective they seem impersonal, condemn Mrs. Bridge to mediocrity but, oddly, arouse our sympathies at the same time. . . .

Mrs. Bridge is familiar. I know her well enough to know where she buys her shoes and to imagine how her house smells. I know the way the crickets and leaves sound outside at night in her backyard. Because of this, I want to read about the comfort she provides. I want dilemma, mistakes and injustices exactly the way Connell gives them to me, without a word of judgement but, to be fair, I want the securities and kindnesses that must have been part of existence in that house where Mrs. Bridge's only role was to support everybody else. But Connell doesn't go that far. As if something about her eludes him, he never quite comes to terms with Mrs. Bridge. Like a piece of blotting paper, she absorbs every mood and opinion around her in a blotchy, second-hand way. . . .

The technique of summing up lifetime and character in small, synoptic chapters is wonderful. As readers, we flip through the story catching glimpses, tasting samples and finding flavour more important than plot. ***Mrs. Bridge*** is as picaresque as *The House at Pooh Corner,* with the same tone of 'I know better than anyone how silly this all is, but I'm giving it to you straight.' Because it is so silly, we all join in the fun.

Poor, shadowy Mr. Bridge is a man who deserves his own story and, ten years after the publication of ***Mrs. Bridge,*** Evan Connell obliges him. The pleasure of reading about the same set of events from another point of view is obvious. The surprise is that most of this history is made of different occasions. The biggest surprise is Mr. Bridge. This background figure in the life of Mrs. Bridge appears to be a man of lovable emotion, kindness and good humour. The whole environment has changed. Viewed from farther off, through hazier, more sympathetic reflections, Mr. Bridge is a man who's missed the boat but doesn't quite deserve his isolation. This is a McFadden character, but from the inside out, so that his story becomes painful to read. His life is divided between work and home, and he's aware of it. He lacks imagination and charm. But unlike Mrs. Bridge, who has given up her own reactions in favour of conditioned responses, Mr. Bridge feels all the alarm, doubt, satisfaction and concern we missed in the first book. His inability to express these emotions is what moves us. A man of convictions, he constantly falls back on them when everything else fails. (pp. 8-9)

What is it in these Bridges that makes us so sad? By the time Connell writes ***Mr. Bridge,*** he seems wearier, more depressed, less angry and, oddly, less detached. The second book is not as sharp and funny as the first one. Bits read aloud fall flat. Connell, growing softer, loses some of his edge and lets us believe in his characters. The most interesting, painful relationship in the second book, that of Mr. Bridge to his son, is the most fully written. Mr. and Mrs. Bridge still seem to have no sex, no laughter, no tears as if Connell, like a child, cannot imagine these things in adults. But the father and son are people he has been. The gulf between them as well as the pride and understanding are genuine.

Living through the dark days of a great depression and a great war, Mr. Bridge, careful and conservative, retains his social and economic position. What does he make of it? What do we? That these people are caught in expectations as ill-fitting as the cars they drive. That some breakdown in spontaneity is happening, to the detriment of family life. We read the stories and watch helplessly, wondering if such things are predetermined. (p. 9)

Linda Spalding, "Meet Mrs. Bridge," in Brick: A Journal of Reviews, *No. 20, Winter, 1984, pp. 7-9.*

JAMES ALEXANDER THOM

Lying in ambush for the writer of American history are all those amazing, amusing anecdotes and quaint details which, if used, would bury the story line, but which seem just too good to cast aside.

Evan S. Connell, in his new study of General George Custer's famous final fiasco [***Son of the Morning Star***], at first seems to be riding into just such an ambush. In his research, Connell has left no tome unturned—the bibliography lists some 400 sources—and in the writing he seems to have been unable to leave anything out: peccadilloes of the officers, their class standings at West Point, drinking habits of the Seventh Cavalry, profiles of salty scouts and individualistic Indians, a brief history of scalping, Custer's romance with wife Elizabeth and with a pretty squaw or two. . . . All this comes rushing forth while the reader anticipates a glimpse of Yellow Hair Custer at his so-called "last stand."

But the difference between this author and his subject is that there is method in Connell's madness. He, unlike Custer, knows what he is doing and what the result will be. . . .

Connell is, with this plethora of colorful details and no regard for chronology, putting together not a narrative but a mosaic of circumstances and personalities, placing Custer in context—political, military, cultural and psychological. The result is vivid and evocative. It leaves the reader astonished that such a man as Custer could ever have been worshipped as a hero. But his context is so well constructed that it is plain why he had to be. It was that kind of a country.

Connell does not set out to do a hatchet job (perhaps one should say tomahawk job) on Custer's reputation, but the facts speak for themselves. It is quite clear that Custer died for his own sins as well as ours. His included vanity, arrogance, fervid racism, stupidity and cupidity, love of killing, a casual disregard for the lives of his men, and plain silliness. (p. 1)

This handsome, flamboyant, cold-eyed cavalier may have become a romantic idol and a national martyr, but he was held in contempt by many of his officers and men. The name he fancied most was "Son of the Morning Star," bestowed upon him after he massacred Black Kettle's village by the light of Venus. His men, whom he punished for minor infractions by ridicule, lashing and branding, preferred such names as Hard Ass, Iron Butt, and Ringlets. The desertion rate from his western units was as high as 52 percent. (pp. 1, 14)

Connell, a novelist by trade, leaves the reader haunted by afterimages, absurd, poignant, pathetic, and horribly brutal: The stupefying tedium and disgusting rations in remote, dusty, windscoured army outposts. The seething antagonism among Custer and his subordinates Reno and Benteen. White soldiers robbing Indian graves and mutilating wounded squaws for fleshly souvenirs. Custer's column, accompanied by journalists, its full military band playing *Gary Owen,* charging a sleepy Cheyenne village early on a frigid morning. Crazy Horse as a brooding, aloof young warrior. Surrounded cavalrymen at Little Bighorn bawling in terror, shooting themselves and each other. A thirst-tortured, wounded soldier drinking blood from a vein of his dead horse. Corroded ammunition jamming in faulty rifles. Crow Indian army scouts sitting on the ground rocking, weeping and chanting after the first report of the Seventh's annihilation. Troopers' bodies bristling with so many arrows they look like hedgehogs. The discovery of Custer's obliterated force: hills strewn with bloated, pink, stripped, mutilated corpses and dead horses. Eyeballs and brains extracted and laid out on rocks, hearts impaled on poles. . . .

Connell understands that the truth of a conflict is best perceived, as in *Rashomon,* from all sides. He shows everything and everybody from every angle. Court-martial transcripts speak, and so does Black Elk, who was a youth at Little Bighorn. Sitting Bull, years later as a tame Indian, sums it up: "They tell me I murdered Custer. It is a lie. . . . He was a fool and rode to his death." Connell, knowing he is examining a tarnished idol, comments upon all this with a droll, mocking humor.

This is a vast mural of finely executed details. And it is, after all, the omission of such gritty, pungent, human details that makes standard histories so notoriously dull. This one is never dull. (p. 14)

James Alexander Thom, "Custer Rides to the Little Big Horn," in Book World—The Washington Post, *November 18, 1984, pp. 1, 14.*

PAGE STEGNER

Son of the Morning Star is impressive in its massive presentation of information, and in the conclusions it draws about the probable events that led to the fracas on the banks of the Little Bighorn. But its strength lies in the way the author has shaped his material. Whether or not one cares about Custer, ***Son of the Morning Star*** makes good reading—its prose is elegant, its tone the voice of dry wit, its meandering narrative skillfully crafted. Mr. Connell is above all a storyteller, and the story he tells is vastly more complicated than who did what to whom on June 25, 1876. Custer's life is surrounded by the personalities that helped define it. . . . It is surrounded by what one can only describe as the personality of an entire nation bent on expansion and more than willing to sacrifice dignity and honor to impulses born of greed and fear.

As such, Mr. Connell's narrative of the life and times of General Custer becomes a narrative of the conflict between two cultures, and the battle Custer fought at the Little Bighorn, insignificant in itself, a metaphor for all the self-righteous hypocrisy that characterizes Indian-white negotiations to this day.

Page Stegner, "General Custer, Immortal in Death," in The New York Times Book Review, *January 20, 1985, p. 10.*

WAYNE M. SARF

[Evan S. Connell, fascinated by the account of the battle of the Little Bighorn, immersed] himself in "Custeriana" and [emerged] with a best-selling work [***The Son of The Morning Star***] which John M. Carroll, one of Custer's most energetic defenders, calls "the best book ever written on the battle of the Little Big Horn." It is crammed with a wealth of vivid and fascinating detail.

Unfortunately, the "big story" often seems to elude Connell, who is obsessed with digression, flashback, and flashforward. Rather than telling the tale chronologically, Connell begins his crazy-quilt narrative with Custer's detachment already annihilated and the remainder of the Seventh under Reno and Benteen besieged by the Indians; but soon Captain Frederick Benteen is urinating against a tent within earshot of appalled ladies, as recounted at his 1887 court-martial. Before we really know who Marcus Reno is, we are already bombarded with opinions on his courage or cowardice; he dies on page 47 (complete with obituary) only to be resurrected later. The digressions are such that the narrative is almost indiscernible; it seems all potted biographies and discourses on subjects Western. Lost in Custer trivia, Connell even wastes more than a page on a temperance fanatic's destruction of a "Last Stand" lithograph put out by the Anheuser-Busch brewing company.

Connell does break with most popular authors in not vilifying Custer; absent is the Indian hater or incarnate fiend. But neither does he view Custer altogether favorably, and he sometimes repeats charges against him without applying the proper skepticism. . . . Connell's Plains Indians are refreshingly unsentimentalized (he unflinchingly details their love of war, the atrocities they committed, and the ecological havoc they wrought), yet he repeats the absurd charge that of Cheyennes slain at the Washita, 92 out of 103 were noncombatants. Evidence and simple probability dictate otherwise, especially since over 50 prisoners were taken. Perhaps most disappointingly of all, Connell attempts little systematic analysis of the Little Big Horn battle, preferring to bounce about facts and possibilities and leave the possibly bewildered reader to choose among them.

In one sense, Connell's lack of system could be said to reflect his view of Custer's complex personality. Rather than pinning Custer to any post-mortem psychiatric couch, Connell in effect marvels at his paradoxical magnificence. Ultimately, he seems to savor the mystery of it all; if his book has one grand theme, it is that much of the truth about Custer is beyond our grasp.

Perhaps one day what Bruce Rosenberg calls "the Custer of our dreams" will resemble a real person. (p. 74)

Wayne M. Sarf, "The Custer of Our Dreams," in Commentary, *Vol. 79, No. 3, March, 1985, pp. 71-4.*

Sandra Deer

1940-

American dramatist.

Deer's first play, *So Long on Lonely Street* (1986), is set at the Southern estate of the Vaughnum family, whose members have gathered to attend the funeral of their spinster aunt and to hear the reading of her will. Family secrets and scandals, including incest, suicide, and miscegenation, are revealed as the Vaughnums reexamine their relationships with each other and attempt to reclaim their lost heritage. Although most critics found her characterizations stereotypical and her dialogue clichéd, Deer, according to William A. Henry III, "created a clan of faded gentry who mingle the greed of the family in Lillian Hellman's *The Little Foxes* with the lubricious dementia of Beth Henley's *Crimes of the Heart*."

Courtesy of Sandra Deer

DOUGLAS WATT

So long, ***So Long on Lonely Street.*** Your heart's in the right place, but your mind is as scattered as birdseed.

It's fitting that the hero of the Sandra Deer comedy . . . should be a soap star, because the play itself unwinds like a soap opera, assuming daytime TV has long since exhausted permutations on the subjects of miscegenation and incest.

It is "late August at Honeysuckle Hill, a few miles outside a small Southern town," and a coffin in the living room of this run-down farmhouse on 25 barren acres contains the body of Aunt Pearl, the white half-sister of black Annabel Lee. . . . As things stand in the will left by Grandpa Big Jack, the spread passes on to his and his dead wife Beulah's one remaining "natural" child, which would be Annabel.

But King Vaughnum . . . , a cousin of the twin brother and sister born of Big Jack's late daughter, is scheming to take over the place and turn it into a shopping mall for Christian enterprises. However, if either Raymond . . . , the New York soap star, or his twin Ruth . . . , a local poet, should elect to move in with Annabel, the property will pass to Ray or Ruth on Annabel's demise.

But, oh hell, why go on?

This mushmouth play—actually, there are as many stabs at Southern drawl as there are players, except for New Yorker Ray—spends most of its time resembling a watered-down contemporary version of *The Little Foxes,* in which the mean Hubbards are squeezed into the person of King, with a little left over for his bigoted wife.

I'm always wary of onstage coffins, and I'm afraid it's not great fun when Annabel, who hasn't dared allow an undertaker near Aunt Pearl in the few days since she's passed away, raises the corpse to dress it properly for the funeral. . . .

[One] waits wearily for some genuine signs of life, even from the coffin, in this play with a name like a song title.

Douglas Watt, "He Ain't Never Goin' Back to That 'Lonely Street'," in Daily News, *April 4, 1986. Reprinted in* New York Theatre Critics' Reviews, *Vol. XXXXVII, No. 5, 1986, p. 336.*

CLIVE BARNES

Have patience. This really is going to be about the new play ***So Long on Lonely Street,*** . . . but before proceeding let me clear my throat, and brush out my mind.

There are times when reviewing plays that I force myself to think of Lawrence Welk. Or rather, of Lawrence Welk's music.

This music you may recall never received any large measure of critical acclaim—indeed it would scarcely be going too far to suggest that it was something of a critical laughing stock. Yet it was popular. Very popular. Even loved.

Now just as Welk would have done better with the kindness of strangers rather than the ministrations of critics, it seems to me that some plays, or at least their box-office potential, are more likely to be hindered than helped by critical attention.

For various reasons—too complex to enter into here—quite often general critical opinion is at variance with general popular taste. . . .

Back to ***So Long on Lonely Street.*** This is one of those Broadway plays . . . that audiences are probably going to like more than critics. If audiences ever get to see them.

I thought that ***So Long on Lonely Street*** was pure and preposterous hokum—Southern fried chicken without the chicken.

Imagine a satirical version of Lillian Hellman—not that poor Hellman would nowadays actually need a satirist—a family, an estate that has seen better days, a house that has known better nights, a death, a coffin, a will, a conniving cousin, a simpleminded black dependant, unexpected sins from a steamy Southern past, and a suggestion of new sins in an equally steamy Southern future.

Sandra Deer imagined just that, and acting on her imagination wrote a play about it. The play was first produced in Atlanta—Oh, Sherman where were you when we needed you!—and elsewhere, and now comes to New York.

And the charming matinee audience I saw it with—I suspect Lawrence Welk lovers to a man, or woman—really loved it.

They loved its predictability, its corniness, its little frissons of carefully controlled shock, its coy revelations and its cosy comeuppances. . . .

Who am I to say they were wrong? Although, for the record, I must say it. But I didn't like Lawrence Welk, did I? And I don't like Col. Sanders. Dammit—I don't even like Lillian Hellman. So watch out—preferably, watch out for yourself.

Clive Barnes, "So Long, Lawrence, It's a Lonely Street," in New York Post, *April 4, 1986. Reprinted in* New York Theatre Critics' Reviews, *Vol. XXXXVII, No. 5, 1986, p. 334.*

FRANK RICH

In Sandra Deer's ***So Long on Lonely Street,*** . . . an eccentric Southern family gathers at its faded homestead, Honeysuckle Hill, for the funeral of its spinster Aunt Pearl and the reading of her will. A lot is at stake. To some members of the extended Vaughnum family—especially Raymond, a New York soap-opera heartthrob who is described as "the prodigal son returned"—the old estate may be "a heritage" worth preserving. To others—especially King, the good ole boy who is described as "greedy" and "conniving"—the manor is prime real estate that might be cleared for a shopping mall. Still another putative heir—Ruth, a rebellious poet who is described as not having "much use for her heritage"—doesn't even care what happens to Honeysuckle Hill. Do you?

If so, perhaps you'll enjoy waiting two hours to hear the reading of the will—and then waiting a little longer for someone to retrieve a long-suppressed birth certificate that must also be recited before probate can really heat up. (The birth certificate, praise be, arrives by motorcycle.) Lest anyone be driven crazy by the suspense, Miss Deer makes sure that there are other revelations to distract us while we wait to hear Pearl's every last codicil. Various Vaughnums, we're told, have committed a drunken murder or suicide, been killed by a tractor or at war. Indeed, about the only skeleton not to fall out of this family's closet is Pearl's itself—it, at least, is securely entombed in a casket stage left. . . .

[***So Long on Lonely Street*** is] a professional, sincere attempt to merge the vulgarized Chekhovian theme-mongering of a Lillian Hellman melodrama with the off-center Southern humor of a Eudora Welty or Beth Henley. But, like that other recent Atlanta export, new Coke, this play is not the real thing. Much as Miss Deer gratuitously tells us exactly which stereotype each of her characters is meant to be, so most of her lines and plot twists are laborious replications of theatrical clichés rather than, as intended, loving representations of real life.

It's unusual to encounter a Southern writer with little discernible literature voice, but such, sadly, is the case here. Take away the actors' accents and the Dixie parlor setting, and Honeysuckle Hill could almost be situated in Keokuk. Miss Deer repetitively makes her plot points in prosaic dialogue such as "All my plans depend on getting this property free and clear by Sept. 1" or (spoken incredulously) "That's what you want the land for—a shopping center?" To pinpoint the message, the characters solemnly ask "What happened to the hopes we had then?" or declare that "We haven't exactly fulfilled our youthful promise." Even Raymond's network soap opera has the thematically utilitarian title of "All My Yesterdays."

The force-fed literary allusions (mainly to Poe) can't dress up the obvious, and the theatrical flourishes, including an outbreak of unconvincing labor contractions to bring down the Act I curtain, are as predictable as they are creaky. About the only real surprise (and entertainment) occurs when two family members consider indulging in a form of heterosexual love that dare not speak its name but nonetheless beats around the bush for a good 20 minutes in Act II. Miss Deer's one freshly observed character is the household's beloved and aged black retainer—a woman who recognizes the distinction between being treated "like" a member of the family and actually being a member of a white family.

Frank Rich, in a review of "So Long on Lonely Street," in The New York Times, *April 4, 1986, p. C5.*

RON COHEN

[***So Long on Lonely Street***] is a quirky piece of playwriting that might be described as Happy Southern Gothic. Sandra Deer has stuffed her script with all the familiar gothic elements. There's incest, a bastard child of mixed blood, suicide, a will to be read, squabbling over the family manse and a coffin in the living room. Deer bathes all these dark doings in the bright hues of a cheery family comedy, spinning out her story with jokey characters and situations. It's an uneasy mix, and Deer's writing, despite a few effective passages in a naturalistic vein, doesn't have the energy or wit to pull it off.

Ron Cohen, in a review of "So Long on Lonely Street," in Women's Wear Daily, *April 4, 1986. Reprinted in* New York Theatre Critics' Reviews, *Vol. XXXXVII, No. 5, 1986, p. 337.*

JOHN BEAUFORT

In certain ways ***So Long on Lonely Street*** recalls the melodramatics of a Lillian Hellman and the bizarre humor of a Beth Henley. But Miss Deer has yet to find her own voice. Her old-fashioned play relies too heavily on cliché and caricature. Among the theatrical Dixie stereotypes are greedy, conniving cousin King Vaughnum III . . . , his pregnant, nitwit wife Clarice . . . , and Bobby Stack . . . , the local lawyer engaged to unsnarl the legal problems inherent in "Big Jack" Vaughnum's will. . . .

While ***So Long on Lonely Street*** may not advance the claim that regional playmaking offers the present best hope of the American theater, the first-night audience found Miss Deer's comedy irresistible.

John Beaufort, in a review of "So Long on Lonely Street," in The Christian Science Monitor, *April 9, 1986, p. 24.*

BRENDAN GILL

Broadway has gone so woefully awry this season that one is tempted to snatch at any straw, but ***So Long on Lonely Street*** . . . is nothing like as strong as a straw, and I found it easy to resist snatching at it. Characteristically, the fatuous title bears almost no relation to the play; it comes from a song that the two leading figures sing at the opening of the second act. They are twins—a sister and brother who experienced their first sexual attraction to each other when as infants they were given a daily bath together. They have been fighting this attraction for decades. . . . Having failed to consummate their fatal passion, they seek surcease in idle sexual promiscuity. Now their ancient maiden aunt has died, and the twins meet in the ancestral home for her funeral and the reading of her will. To complicate matters, a black woman who has been the lifelong companion of the aunt is present to claim her due, which she believes will turn out to be the house and grounds; also present is the twins' first cousin, a boisterous businessman with a pregnant wife and a nasty plan to take over the property, throw down the house, and build a shopping center on the grounds. This précis of the plot so far might itself be a précis of a TV soap, and is surely sufficient to indicate that ***So Long on Lonely Street*** is trash, and trash of a particularly old-fashioned and repellent sort, grossly caricaturing a hundred or more Southern plays and novels. The author, Sandra Deer, reveals not a spark of literary talent; it is her idea of effective drama to have a coffin onstage throughout the play, to have the coffin lid raised from time to time in order that humorously inappropriate remarks may be made to the corpse ("Lie still!"), and to have the corpse itself—a crudely fashioned mannequin with a white wig—finally put in an appearance, in order to frighten the pregnant wife. It has been reported that the play was well received in Atlanta, where Miss Deer lives and works; I am at a loss to know why. (pp. 84-5)

Brendan Gill, "Airborne and Earthbound," in The New Yorker, *Vol. LXII, No. 8, April 14, 1986, pp. 84-5.*

WILLIAM A. HENRY III

A coarse, grasping Southerner, bellowing his frustration at not being able to seize his family homestead, halts in his tirade long enough to realize that he is talking to an empty room—empty, that is, except for the coffin containing his recently deceased aunt, to whom he kowtowed for years in hopes of getting his way. He turns to go and shouts, "You hateful old woman! I never liked you!"

It is not giving away much to reveal this gothic moment as the curtain line of ***So Long on Lonely Street,*** a zesty, poignant and fiercely funny comedy. Far more shocking revelations have already emerged along the way, on matters ranging from race to motherhood to incest. Playwright Sandra Deer has created a clan of faded gentry who mingle the greed of the family in Lillian Hellman's *The Little Foxes* with the lubricious dementia of Beth Henley's *Crimes of the Heart*. Yet Deer has a kinder heart toward her characters than either author. The result, while likely to strike some playgoers as scandalous, is the most impressive playwriting debut of the New York season. . . .

Deer's real interest lies in exploring the unexamined assumptions that families live by. Each of the Vaughnums has been suppressing some secret; each ends by realizing that some seeming impossibility has come to pass. While all this adroit plotting is going on, the characters are interacting so naturally, with rowdy humor so integral to their personalities, that ***Lonely Street*** seems more a slice of life than a "well-made play." Even in the two most finely honed scenes—when Ruth and Raymond discuss why, despite their affection, they have always avoided each other, and when Miss Anna learns the truth about her parentage—Deer never allows the audience enough emotional distance to perceive what is happening as mere craftsmanship.

William A. Henry III, "A Poignant, Fiercely Funny Debut," in Time, *New York, Vol. 127, No. 15, April 14, 1986, p. 103.*

J(ames) P(atrick) Donleavy

1926-

American-born Irish novelist, dramatist, short story writer, and nonfiction writer.

Donleavy is best known for his first novel, *The Ginger Man* (1955), which is regarded by many critics as his greatest work and a comic tour de force. *The Ginger Man* established Donleavy's rhapsodic, staccato narrative style, which vividly reflects the disordered state of his protagonist's mind. Donleavy creates a schizophrenic effect by shifting from a third-person description of his characters' actions to a first-person, stream-of-consciousness rendering of their thoughts. The attitudes of his protagonists have been strongly influenced by Donleavy's expatriate status. Born in Brooklyn, New York, Donleavy chose to attend Trinity College in Dublin, Ireland, after a stint in the United States Navy. He lived for several years in England and Ireland before becoming an Irish citizen in 1967. Donleavy has assimilated the distinctively Irish comic strain often found in the works of James Joyce and Samuel Beckett, although he cites Henry Miller and Franz Kafka as his main literary influences.

Sebastian Dangerfield, the protagonist of *The Ginger Man,* embodies the archetypal Donleavy protagonist. A solitary outsider in a hostile society who is motivated by greed, prurience, and envy, Dangerfield is preoccupied with death and desperate for love, stability, and meaning in his life. He spends most of his time pursuing women and alcohol while neglecting his wife, child, and law studies, and he aspires to upper-class status but is unwilling to compromise his nonconformist nature to attain financial success. *The Ginger Man* establishes several characteristics which became fixtures in Donleavy's later novels: a sense of despondency beneath a surface hilarity; a picaresque narrative structure; an elegiac tone; the conception of the United States as nightmare; and an emphasis on emotions over ideas.

Many critics consider Donleavy's subsequent works to be weak imitations of *The Ginger Man,* with repetitious subject matter and arbitrary endings. Others, however, view some of these novels as more thorough explorations of the human condition. *A Singular Man* (1963) centers on George Smith, a Howard Hughes-like figure who becomes enthralled with the idea of death and dedicates his life to building a huge mausoleum. Smith suffers a number of personal misfortunes which contribute to his reclusive behavior. Some reviewers conjectured that Smith's lifestyle reflects the way Sebastian Dangerfield would have behaved if he had achieved the success he desired, and several have seen Smith's paranoia as a microcosm of humanity's lot in contemporary American society. In *The Saddest Summer of Samuel S* (1966), Donleavy retains his usual stylistic techniques but shuns the picaresque mode for a more subdued setting in Vienna. After years spent roaming Europe as a libertine, Samuel decides to undergo psychoanalysis to help adjust to conventional society. He desperately wants a wife and children but becomes involved only with women who are uninterested in marriage. Samuel eventually realizes that he is mired in despair with neither the faith nor the ardor to change.

The Beastly Beatitudes of Balthazar B (1968) follows the loss of innocence of a young French nobleman. The book examines

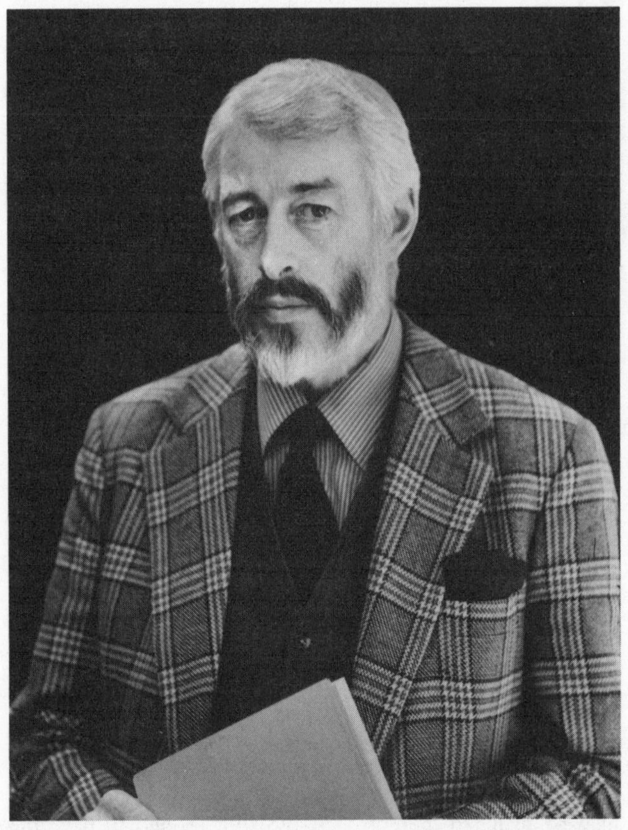

a theme integral to most of Donleavy's fiction—the loss of loved ones and the resulting emotional and psychological changes. Although the plot of this novel is melodramatic, Donleavy avoids bathos by infusing the story with ribald episodes and ludicrously comic scenes. Critics generally rank this book second only to *The Ginger Man* in Donleavy's canon. Donleavy's next novel, *The Onion Eaters* (1971), proved to be one of his least successful works. The plot concerns a young man who inherits an Irish manor. He confronts an unlikely array of guests who create bedlam and leave the estate and the protagonist in ruins. L. J. Davis wrote that "the tone of the book is somewhere between unsuccessful comic surrealism and unsuccessful pornographic comedy. . . . There is a lot of apparent symbolism, but none of it amounts to much." *A Fairy Tale of New York* (1973) focuses on the brutality and spiritual emptiness of New York City. The pervasive atmosphere of the city has made the protagonist, Cornelius Christian, feel powerless and depressed. He sees emigration as his only way to liberation, but he lacks the funds to move.

The Destinies of Darcy Dancer, Gentleman (1977) bears many of the traits of the eighteenth-century picaresque novel but is set in modern Europe on a country estate and features Donleavy's characteristic roving point of view and disjointed prose. The book chronicles the humorous and unlucky vicissitudes of Darcy Dancer, a Gatsby-like character whose destiny is to miss his only opportunity at love because he was born too late. A sequel, *Leila* (1983), continues the misadventures of Dancer and his confrontations with creditors, freeloading houseguests, and odd neighbors. The title character, one of Dancer's servants, is his ideal but unattainable woman. *Schultz* (1979) is virtually devoid of Donleavy's usual stylistic practices and is regarded as his most orthodox novel. This work centers on the capers of a Jewish-American theatrical impresario who tries to produce a vulgar farce in London. Critics generally faulted *Schultz* for gratuitously lewd language and for Donleavy's dependence upon slapstick sexual escapades. *De Alfonce Tennis* (1985) outlines the history and regulations of a variation of tennis invented by a club of fourteen young bachelors, all but one of whom apparently drowned after their yacht was sunk on the eve of the attack on Pearl Harbor.

Donleavy has also written two nonfiction works. *The Unexpurgated Code: A Complete Manual of Survival and Manners* (1975) is a send-up of etiquette books for the parvenu. *J. P. Donleavy's Ireland: In All Her Sins and Some of Her Graces* (1986) is an autobiography covering his childhood in New York, his Trinity College days, his literary friends, and the writing of and reaction to *The Ginger Man*. In addition, Donleavy has written a collection of short stories, *Meet My Maker the Mad Molecule* (1964), and has adapted several of his novels for the stage.

(See also *CLC,* Vols. 1, 4, 6, 10; *Contemporary Authors,* Vols. 9-12, rev. ed.; and *Dictionary of Literary Biography,* Vol. 6.)

ROBIE MACAULEY

In ***Schultz,*** the manic strain that is kept under some control in earlier J. P. Donleavy novels takes over the whole story, and the difficulty about reviewing an endless Minsky burlesque instead of a real piece of fiction is obvious. One can say that ***The Ginger Man,*** the author's best book, had a kind of banana peel humor that more or less equalled Laurel and Hardy, whereas ***Schultz***—with the same skits slightly refurbished—falls somewhat below the best level of the Three Stooges. It would be tempting to leave the observation at that.

Our hero is Donleavy's favorite madman-protagonist, this time introduced as a Jewish-American show producer in London. Despite many previous flops, Schultz is encouraged and backed by Lord Nectarine and Binky, two rich Englishmen who own Sperm Productions. Their main object, however, seems to be the playing of morbid practical jokes on their incredible client.

Still, even though he spends most of his time either in bed with a succession of girls or running around London crashing into things, Schultz manages to produce at last a barely successful musical. This unlikely happening is followed at the end by an even unlikelier visit to Prague, where he seeks out his family roots.

Despite the tedious sequence of pow-boom-whomp-splat in the story, it would be unfair to suggest that there is absolutely no intent of any kind. There is, though it is something that could hardly be called a thought, much less an idea. A kind of reflex, perhaps. In any case, it takes the form of a train of joking insults against women, blacks and Jews. I assume that this is intended to be a sort of daring, anti-fashionable humor.

Some women, according to the logic of events in the story, are good in bed—but all women are disasters. They have sharp teeth and nails, carry venereal disease, entrap men by cunning, possess violent husbands—from Greta the au pair girl to the aristocratic Lady Lullabyebaby. African blacks—witness a character such as King Buggybooiamcheesetoo of Boohooland—are fat, lecherous apes who dress in preposterous uniforms while trying to impress London.

Then, there is Schultz himself, who, as described by Donleavy, seems an example appropriate to the notions of the late Dr. Joseph Goebbels. Aristocratic Englishmen come off a bit better: Though they may be snobbish, amoral and at times fairly silly, they do have a kind of grand style that excuses these flaws.

In search of the Big Joke, I read on to the very end of the book. And I think that I finally identified the real straight man, the ultimate fall guy. Presumably, he is the one who sits in his chair, laughing like an idiot over the empty pages of ***Schultz.***

Robie Macauley, "The Slapping of Sticks," in The New York Times Book Review, *October 7, 1979, p. 14.*

JAMES JORDAN

Donleavy's caricatures of mankind are seemingly endless. Their common feature is extremism, their pathos is their humanity, their high comedy a burlesque of us all. This time around it's Sigmund Franz "Isadorable" Schultz, an oversexed, hypochondriacal American theatrical entrepreneur with more chutzpah than cash, more libido than brains. . . . The pace [in ***Schultz***] is breakneck, the language scatological, the prose pure and brilliant Donleavy.

The bedroom farce pales a bit in the book's repetitious sex scenes, yet all the individual incidents blur together into an exhausting, but convincing, impression of the high adrenalin world of stage hucksterism. Donleavy is one of the finest prose stylists of our time and, while ***Schultz*** is less rich in its characterizations than, say, ***The Destinies of Darcy Dancer, Gentleman,*** it is still Donleavy at the height of his inventive power. (pp. 122-23)

James Jordan, in a review of "Schultz," in The Antioch Review, *Vol. 38, No. 1, Winter, 1980, pp. 122-23.*

NICHOLAS SHRIMPTON

Give satire half a chance and the beast will end up eating its own tail. J. P. Donleavy's new novel, ***Schultz,*** is a melancholy demonstration of this subtly self-destructive tendency. The formula is the one he started with, in ***The Ginger Man.*** A rip-roaring, hard-drinking and sexually rapacious hero successfully passes himself off in respectable society, thereby debunking its ideals. 'Modern comedy,' in Saul Bellow's words, 'has to do with the disintegrating outline of the worthy and humane Self, the bourgeois hero of an earlier age.' But the trick only works in certain conditions. We need to believe in the picture of society which the comedian presents. And we have to feel that there is a gap between conventional social standards and the tastes and drives of the iconoclastic hero.

Neither of these demands is met by ***Schultz,*** a novel both sloppily written and far too long. It is set in the world of the West End Theatre, where Sigmund Schultz, a Jewish producer from New York, is attempting to find backers for a musical.

His two colleagues are called, with leaden humour, Lord Nectarine of Walham Green and Binky Sunningdale. Their firm is known as Sperm Productions. All three partners spend their lives on the casting couch with an endless stream of willing starlets. But Donleavy is not writing satire, either of the English Theatre or of the English Aristocracy. . . . No standards are defied by such behaviour, for there is now nobody in the novel who holds any attitude other than the greedy hedonism of the eponymous hero. And if the point is to suggest that English society is greedy and hedonistic then the retort must be made that this erotic fairyland is not English society. The truth is that a world which Donleavy once mocked he now enjoys. Satire has shifted, by gradual stages, into celebration.

The bohemian alternative to bourgeois respectability has, in the process, been debased. Schultz gives no sense of an untamed libido on the rampage. Instead, his guzzling and swilling come straight from the pages of a second-rate restaurant guide, his sex from a glossy manual. . . . The worst failure of all is the humour. At one point a feeble practical joke is dragged out for more than 50 pages and the author is reduced to telling us that its (easily amused) perpetrator is 'wracked by his choked up guffaws'. Wracked I wasn't. ***Schultz*** sets out to be a life-enhancing romp, and ends up as a very tedious piece of soft-core porn.

Nicholas Shrimpton, "Bourgeois v. Bohemian," in New Statesman, *Vol. 99, No. 2558, March 28, 1980, p. 483.*

RICHARD BROWN

To feminists the presentation of sexuality in ***Schultz*** will be a good hunting-ground for examples of male-dominated ideology. Women are described almost exclusively in terms of their legs, bottoms and breasts and their sketchy personal details resemble nothing so much as the captions to nude photographs in men's magazines or the popular press. Marriage is a trap and resistance to the hero's advances merely a way of baiting that trap. Throughout the word "cunt" is used as an insult and Sigmund Schultz, whose name suggests one of those American Jewish slang words for the penis and recalls the nineteenth-century explosives inventor Eduard Schultze, is an embodiment of phallocentricity. With these characteristic likes and (notably homosexual) dislikes, Donleavy sets up, under the guise of liberality, an institutionalized notion of sexual normality which is barely less tyrannical than the Victorian.

The sexual fantasy also directs the presentation of wider social realities. "If only screwing women did not result later in my getting fucked in so many other disastrous ways", Schultz at one point complains. If Wordsworth would have us born "trailing clouds of glory", Donleavy characters seem to arrive with unlimited supplies of money, which they proceed (with the full suggestion of the Victorian pun) to spend. Perhaps this is why Donleavy is so interested in a fantasy version of an urbane English aristocracy of which Lord Nectarine of Walham Green and Binky are the representatives in this novel.

His geographical locations are, as usual, touristique. Here fashionable West London is the scene, which, though it appears in some detail, is populated by such clichés as the taxi driver who says "Hey Gov". The mild apostasy from the rules of prose composition that we have come to expect in Donleavy is also present in ***Schultz.*** The truncated sentences which lack a finite verb or which have it replaced by a participle, do allow for some quite varied lyric, comic and erotic effects. The internal rhymes can also be quite amusing, but those quaint lineations of the last sentence in each chapter where prose is set as poetry, seem little more than a gimmick. . . .

The hero's struggle to finance a West End show, which provides (besides the sexual encounters) the plot of the novel, is ultimately greeted with a precarious success and he waits with anticipation for the reviews. These "stink". "Every one but two. One written by an imbecile. And the other by a guy thought he was writing about some other show." Through some enterprising editing, Schultz succeeds in making the hostile criticism read like praise.

In this comic moment, though, the recognition is forced upon us that Schultz, with all his comic vulgarity and stereotypical American brashness, is meant to stand in some self-parodic way for the author, or even for all authors. Significantly Donleavy does not make the more immediately obvious choice of playwright or theatrical director for his artist figure: Schultz is a producer. . . . It would be almost the opposite of the truth and not a little perverse to suggest some connection here with Walter Benjamin's Marxist notion of "The Author as Producer" but at least we can say in Donleavy's favour that his self-portrait as impresario does something to deflate aesthetic literary cant.

Richard Brown, "Phallocentricity," in The Times Literary Supplement, *No. 4019, April 4, 1980, p. 382.*

RONALD CURRAN

Schultz is an expatriate attempt to transform the Jewish schlemiel into a meretricious Don Juan. What materializes, to borrow from Fitzgerald, is a rag doll leaking sawdust from every pore. Donleavy tries [in ***Schultz***] a variation on ***The Ginger Man,*** but he creates a comically sultry picaresque tale which gets close, at times, to graffiti. Pricilla, Schultz's Eve, might have turned on an army of men, but she is rotten to the corps. Plot here becomes an excuse for Donleavy to conjure sexual clichés for Schultz to embody. Throughout, we have a welter of peep shows in which to display Schultz's olympic-proportioned appetites and endowments. This is the story of an innocent sexual rogue run amok and often aground.

Two wealthy English aristocrats provide the amusing decadence and social class required to counterpoint Schultz's crass American innocence. Far more engaging and witty than the main character, they sometimes threaten to steal the show. Donleavy's lower-middle-class Jew from New England postures among them like a crude Yankee cameo carved from a lump of anthracite coal. . . .

While Donleavy seduces his plot and the boys seduce all the girls, marriage wears the black moustache of the villain in this rather stock situation comedy. Not without difficulty, everyone gets hitched in the end. And Schultz, to no one's surprise, winds up with a saber-toothed mother-in-law and a wife who would make Hemingway's Brett Ashley look like Florence Nightingale.

There is something dated and predictable about this novel, a feeling that this would be a good story in a locker room of yesteryear. The humor shades uneasily toward that of a non-native speaker cursing in English: slightly embarassing and not quite appropriate or on the mark. Schultz belongs among the extended adolescents who have changed the complexion of modern American fiction. But meeting him is very much like revisiting an intriguing emotional landscape only to find it full of dandelions in seed. The book works in the ironic mode on the theme of the American innocent abroad—or, bachelors in danger. Not corrupted by European decadence, Schultz provides the English gentry with guerrilla theatre American style. He plays a boy tripping over his shoestrings in the service of a man's work.

Schultz cannot help himself because boys will be boys. He is not without principles because of an evil innocence. He is without them because he lacks character in the most elementary sense. No charm provides a saving grace, either. And it is the sense of hollowness at Schultz's center which causes most of what he does to have an aluminum resonance. This portrait of the hayseed American Jewish boy undone in London attempts to wring humor out of forms of male wish-fulfillment and fear of women which had more power in the 1950s and before. ***Schultz*** seems an attempt to develop an American hybrid rogue and to transplant him to England. But what turns out is more like a clone. The role requires an actor to embody it, perhaps even a change of genre (film) to transfuse Schultz in spite of his rioting hormones. Reading this novel will make readers recall Barth's essay on the literature of exhaustion.

Ronald Curran, in a review of "Schultz," in World Literature Today, *Vol. 54, No. 3, Summer, 1980, p. 431.*

DAVID PROFUMO

"More. I tell you I want more. More of the same, Whee!" Thus, the cackling Dangerfield to O'Keefe in Donleavy's stage version of ***The Ginger Man*** (1959); and it might, sadly, have served as an appropriate motto for much of his subsequent work which, since the early 1970s, has often seemed like a series of repeat performances. This sense of *déjà vu* is particularly strong in ***Leila,*** partly because it is a sequel to ***Darcy Dancer*** (1977), a book which in spirit belonged anyway to the earlier phase, characterized by the alliterative titles and evocative Irish settings. Throughout this sequel there is an unmistakable impression of straining for effect, a slightly desperate attempt to revive his earlier, more lyrical style of writing that was clubbed to death by the coarseness of the singularly disappointing ***Schultz*** (1980), the point where comic exuberance finally gave way to crudity.

As its full title—***The Destinies of Darcy Dancer, Gentleman***—suggested, the original was designed to follow the fortunes of an opportunistic hero in a sort of eighteenth-century fashion, a precocious young "imperialist member of the squirearchy" who, by the end of the novel, had come to some wisdom about the vagaries of the world. Leaving his collapsing ancestral pile, Andromeda Park, Dancer takes to the road, enjoys a variety of colourful experiences in Dublin, goes broke, and is saved by good fortune at the races. Such in effect is the shape of ***Leila*** too, though he is now a year older, and correspondingly more tough. . . . The prospect is Donleavy's perennial one of the upper classes on their uppers.

Dancer himself, extravagant as ever, is the focus of both the novel's narrative voices; first and third person. With arrogance and style he inspires the loyalty of his beleagured retainers as he struggles to maintain Andromeda Park against the depredations of creditors, sponging houseguests and bizarre neighbours. Dispirited by such a life and nearly skint, he goes to Dublin and gets embroiled in a seedy bohemian underworld, and he looks up a number of old acquaintances; living off credit all the while. Saved by another windfall, he returns home, presumably to start the process all over again.

For the most part, the cast is a familiar one. There's Sexton the gardener, a pottering polymath; Rashers Ronald, the irrepressible conman; lustful Lois, that portraitist of pudenda; the Mental Marquis, of gargantuan appetites; and alcoholic Crooks, a butler in the fine Donleavian tradition of Bitters, Boats, and Smears. Amongst such a gaggle of *poseurs* and parasites one character stands alone—Leila, the raven-haired new serving girl, a mysterious orphan, almost spectral in her presence, an alluring beauty instantly idolized by Dancer though, uniquely, eluding his grasp. Both modest and refined, she is however an entirely improbable creation in a world where most of the other figures are possessed of the morals of a blowfly. It is a *milieu* upholstered with snobbery and selfishness, a pack of characters all jostling together for the pursuit of foxes, fortunes and, of course, sex. . . .

J. P. Donleavy has published at least two novels that are very good, but ***Leila*** is not one of them. To be fair, there are places where the old fire flashes, but these serve rather as reminders of what has gone—that air of comic improvisation, and the interweaving of zaniness with pathos. At certain things he is still incomparably good: the dialogue often retains its poise, specialities being invective and the retort indignant, as readers of ***The Unexpurgated Code*** (1975) will remember. The quality of insults remains abysmally high. But the one-liners are crammed into scenes that are frequently no better than laborious slapstick, and the farce is often overblown. . . .

In the past, Donleavy's descriptive ability has also operated in a gentler, less clamorous direction; he was especially good at nostalgic reflection, on childhood, a family's past, the history of place. His dismembered sentences can be effective units of recollection, achieving (as in ***Balthazar B***) a real poignancy that nicely balances the humour. In ***Leila,*** such instances are rare. The sentimental focus is on the girl herself, Dancer's guiding light, but so remote and insubstantial a character is she that this can only be managed at the expense of a certain unpalatable mawkishness. . . .

As did ***Darcy Dancer,*** this novel ends on a deliberately unresolved note, and one feels that we haven't yet heard the last of it; that the author could go on spinning this material out almost indefinitely, shearing it off every few years or so in similar arbitrary lengths. That would be a shame, because however enjoyable it may be in places ***Leila*** is not an ambitious book, and its subject-matter has by now demonstrably exhausted itself. Even Donleavy can conjure only so much candyfloss from a mere handful of crystals.

David Profumo, "Continuing Destinies, Upholstered Uppers," in The Times Literary Supplement, *No. 4204, October 28, 1983, p. 1185.*

AUDREY S. EYLER

[In ***Leila***] Reginald Darcy Thormond Dancer Kildare of Andromeda Park grows more annoying than up, except for his penis, which both stays up and grows very annoying. For 782 pages Kildare follows his Shandyian nose, or in the predominant metaphor of the two books J. P. Donleavy has now written about him, he hunts the fox.

Through ***The Destinies of Darcy Dancer, Gentleman*** . . . Kildare holds our sympathy. After all, maturing is difficult for everyone. Moreover, this child has no mother alive and his father is a neglectful, sadistic thief. The adolescent instrument is tightly-strung, and experience will produce, we are promised, sweetened music. A picaresque, Tom Jones-lovability makes us forgive the youth and applaud his chancing. Kildare unsentimentally helps the down-trodden and fights the bullies. We celebrate his resolute escape from the burning public school and his determination at menial work. He seems to gain an empathy with the hunted when the hounds are suddenly after him, and the reimbursement of Stupid Kelly's stolen fudge suggests again that there is a kind nature in this temporarily misguided body. This beneficent spirit is slowly, surely directing the adult that Darcy will become.

In ***Leila,*** however, the resolution weakens, his body obeys a law of its own, and we realize that his kindness is limited. He loves the land and the house, he says, but the estate is disintegrating like the class it represents, and its management is beyond his control. The horsey hangers-on are all posers and imposters of some variety, and Darcy is spiritually overwhelmed. He gradually gathers around him a collection of reciprocally exploitive friends, who, we are sure, will help him spend the redemption for the estate finally discovered in his mother's hidden jewels.

The situation is sad, yes. Tolerant of the adolescent in it, however, we lose patience with the young man. We realize that Darcy acts generously only toward men. . . . We appreciate this generosity. But toward women Darcy behaves and thinks quite differently:

> Ah Miss von B. Removes her clothes so elegantly. Folding each garment. Laying them neatly upon the chair. Stepping out of her furry boots. She is really quite youthful. What pleasure to see such strappingly robust reliable thighs. What long dependable work one could get out of her.

When she takes him to task about those thoughts, he responds

> ". . . I think that women are capable of giving gentlemen damn shabby treatment, like pushing them into ponds, abandoning them on trains, conducting affairs behind their backs, taking their money, and even trying to kill them off. And then writing it all down in a book. Perhaps to gloat over the profits from publication or at least to amuse themselves with in their old age."
>
> "This is now, bog trotter, your opinion of women, eh."
>
> "It is quite."
>
> "And so what do you want or expect me to say. To such Irish idiocy."

Hard-working and hard-loving Miss von B. offers a clear voice of judgment upon this Darcy Dancer, and experience continues to chastise him, but we cannot see that he learns. The introduction of Darcy's ideal woman, the ultimately elusive Leila, makes him sadder, not wiser, sweeter, or less self-obsessed. By the time we are finished with 150 pages of ***Leila*** we begin to feel that if this blindness of his character is Donleavy's point, he has made it, and the continuing carousel of scenes where Darcy degrades women in fact and fantasy is gratuitous.

Donleavy is, nevertheless, a very skilled writer. The narrative is Darcy's interior monologue, and the mind portrayed through a powerful language fascinates while, for another reason, it angers us. We notice, for example of Donleavy's technique, his adroit use of the progressive verb form, leaving its precise identity—participle or incomplete regular—ambiguous, but letting its pure and fragmentary action convey the immediacy of our narrator's stream of consciousness. . . .

Darcy's references to himself in this modified third-person permit a drama, an objectivity, and a dancing lightness (often humor) to the characterization, which both endear him to us and contribute to our annoyance with him. The first person narrative enjoys a traditional proximity to confession, contrition, and humility, which we do not find in Darcy Dancer. He experiences regret, but not reform. There is reflection, but without restitution. In ***Leila*** he decides not to settle his fudge account with Stupid Kelly.

One might expect the heavily fragmented style to be rhythmically halting and therefore irritating. Not so. Donleavy's Darcy is poetic, lyrical, hypnotizing. . . . Darcy, without presuming artistry, is presented as a highly literary diarist, and his language holds us after sympathy for him wanes.

Audrey S. Eyler, "A Skilled but Sexist Artist," in Irish Literary Supplement, *Vol. 3, No. 2, Fall, 1984, p. 7.*

JOHN MELMOTH

De Alfonce Tennis is one of the very few novels to be prefaced by both a claim to intergalactic merchandizing rights and a timely health warning about the perils of keeping fit. It is a poignant novella, in the manner of ***The Saddest Summer of Samuel S,*** hedged around by the rules of the game and the interminable naming of sports-related parts. The setting is a transatlantic cruise to New York. PJ, through whom the author is engagingly present, falls for the fabulous Laura, peerless beyond the fatuity of her locutions: "Oh what a very sweet gentleman he is to make us poor ladies feel so esteemed." In the company of Lord Charles, a titled lush, and an enigmatic French professor, and under the all-seeing eye of Lieutenant Alias of the NYPD, they drift through a series of sub-Wodehousian jokes about KGB officials stuffing their faces with venison and caviar, wacky heiresses and English public schools. The ambience, customary in much of Donleavy's recent work, is distinctly *haute:* "not unamusing" White Russian counts, mummified, engemmed dowagers and drunken, impoverished lords rub shoulders in complete disregard of the way of the rest of the world.

Most disappointing is the language—a simpering, etiolated *schmaltz* which fails to exorcize excesses of the "smooth firmness of her balletic alabaster limbs" kind. Unblushingly, Donleavy permits himself to report "she let roll several big blue eyed tears down her rose-tinted cheeks to plummet on her bejewelled bosoms". All this is a long and not entirely satisfactory way from the cheery humpings, linguistic innovations and plonking *joie de vivre* of ***Schultz.***

All the protagonists are more or less inexplicably enmeshed in a legend. They are the spiritual heirs of the fabled "Bangokok Boys", experts in their esoteric sport, who disappeared at sea on the day that the Japanese attacked Pearl Harbor. Their ill-fated motor cruiser Hiyathere was last seen steaming northwards from Long Island. The memory of these alumni is kept fresh by the only one of their number not on board at the time—Horatio De Alfonce Adams IV, filthy rich, known to his friends as The Fourteenth. PJ inherits from him the responsibility for enshrining all that they stood for in the rules of De Alfonce tennis which, for all the cachet that its mastery confers, is not remarkable for its restrained use of colour: it is played on a green court with a purple and crimson net and a primrose ball. To the uninitiated or downright imperceptive it looks remarkably like badminton with a low net. Given that "a bible of philosophical discussion" would be required to explain the tactical niceties, PJ contents himself with detailed accounts of "the nurt service", "zekes" and "el floppo" (a glossary is appended.)

This simulated pedantry does little to animate conspicuous bad taste and a woeful fetishism. Because De Alfonce tennis can be played by the infirm as well as the firm the rules include advice on the advisability of wearing a prosthesis on court, suggesting that it should be examined for "stress factors, loose screws, springs, swivels and metal fatigue". Similarly, trusses should be double-checked. Large tits (ho ho) are a further hazard: the bra should therefore be of "a seamless cotton which can provide a reliable skid free cradle for the bosoms". To describe this as comic invention might be stretching a point rather.

John Melmoth, "Nurts and Caviar," in The Times Literary Supplement, *No. 4259, November 16, 1984, p. 1302.*

ANDREW BROWN

The great attraction of gentlemanliness, or chivalry, is that it offers a set of rules to make you a *glamorous* shit. It is all right to behave badly, but only to the wrong people. Perhaps this is why so many male American writers think of themselves as gentlemen. Consider the Mailer hero—tough to others, yet withal tender to himself, and much given to hungover existential broodings on this mysterious dichotomy. Much the same could have been said of the Ginger Man, except that Donleavy was then a funnier and more disciplined writer than Mailer has been for years, and he understood how to make his characters intentionally funny.

This was not a trick of language. It was the carefully observed gentility and decency of the Ginger Man's wife and mistresses that provided a frame of expectations for him to betray at every chance he got. The glamour of his life was funny and believable because it was so wholly imaginary, and could not be reconciled with the squalid frame of the book. But this tension disappeared in Donleavy's later works. The glamour remained an important, and imaginary, idea, but the real, oppressive rules of life and conduct disappeared. [Can people] bring themselves to care about a hero whose problem is that he has three balls and who is pursued throughout the book by randy nursemaids, countesses, serving wenches (there is no other word) and a wolfhound? (p. 33)

With [***De Alfonce Tennis***], the process has been carried to its logical extreme. It consists almost entirely of imaginary rules for an imaginary game; but there is nothing in the whole great slimy pudding of English literature that can prepare the reader for the result. Only a writer of some talent and much application could have produced anything so very difficult to read. . . .

[Practically] every sentence is stuffed like a supermarket sausage with as many unappetising ingredients as possible. A complete, and fairly typical sentence, goes like this: 'The brass name plate is upside down when carried so as to force an awkward inclination of the head upon anyone attempting to read a name they are not sophisticated enough already to know.' Short words do occur, but are surprisingly often misused towards the end of the book: there is 'curb' for 'kerb'. Perhaps even the editor's attention flagged. (p. 34)

It is pointless to speculate on the reasons this book was written as it was, or published at all. But why should anyone read it? Even if few people reach the end, plenty will make the effort; and the whole question of why some readers actively prefer bad books to good is well worth going into. I have in mind a special sort of badness. It is not shallow characterisation; nor cliché-ridden writing; these things do form a recognisable code through which some meaning can be transmitted. Nor is it bad plotting or any similar technical fault. No, it is a deliberate attack on language with intent to maim, to remove even the possibility of meaning. It is the literary equivalent of heavy metal music, or of the collected works of Enver Hoxha; and this, I think, suggests an answer to the question. What such books offer is oblivion. (pp. 34-5)

Andrew Brown, "Oblivion Books," in The Spectator, *Vol. 253, No. 8161, December 8, 1984, pp. 33-5.*

MARTIN TUCKER

Most of the action [in ***De Alfonce Tennis***] takes place on board a luxury liner the likes of which haven't been seen since Evelyn Waugh's steamier passages in *Brideshead Revisited;* the rest of the narrative runs aground in a mythologized New York studded with real names like Columbus Avenue and Armonk. Lurking behind this novel-as-road-guide is the disappearance of a yacht with 13 extraordinarily rich young American bachelors aboard. Quite possibly there was a 14th, a shadowy figure of a survivor who is seen fleeting in and out of this slim volume. On page 91 the fiction stops for all impractical purposes, and the author proceeds to offer 132 pages of practical rules for the alternative tennis game he turns into his eponymous title. Some funny passages score, and occasional flashes of allusive wit rank with earlier, vintage Donleavy. But while this outrageous idea has amusing possibilities, it remains a thin excuse for a book. There was an integrity to Mr. Donleavy's mad arrogance in earlier works. In this illustrated mockery of the novel and tennis, which he coyly calls a legend, his racket gets ensnared in its own strings of self-defeating ploys.

Martin Tucker, in a review of "De Alfonce Tennis," in The New York Times Book Review, *April 28, 1985, p. 24.*

PETER ACKROYD

J. P. Donleavy was born in Brooklyn but, as the result of some strange atavistic leap, he writes like an Irishman—the melodic cadences, the plangent vowels, the slight air of fustian, are all here. It is English set to music (to be heard as much in Wilde as in Yeats), a potent form of subversion that takes all the oppressive "sense" out of an oppressor's language. In Donleavy's case that style rarely errs on the side of precision and, like many novelists, when he is not in the company of his characters he is happy to slide into a dazed, circuitous, hypnotic monologue. And so it is that ***J. P. Donleavy's Ireland*** is part autobiography and part cultural travelogue, an account of his own growth as a writer, which might also pass as a Baedeker for some of the wilder aspects of Irish life. . . .

His first sight of the country itself . . . came in the cinema, when he saw Liam O'Flaherty's *The Informer*. So Donleavy's

Ireland was an Ireland of the spirit and of the imagination, something only heard of, "something which exists, untouchable and unknown." For most Irish Americans, of course, this is precisely what it remains; hence their lachrymose and ultimately repellent *nostalgie de la boue*. But Donleavy wanted the real thing. And where most of his "creative" contemporaries migrated to Paris or to London, hoping to rival Fitzgerald or Eliot with their exilic imaginations, in 1946 Donleavy flew across the Atlantic, only to arrive at Shannon and enrol as a student at Trinity College, Dublin. . . .

If nothing else, ***J. P. Donleavy's Ireland*** marks the sources for some of the more outrageous stories and incidents in his first novel, ***The Ginger Man***—although, given the innate Irishness of his imagination, it is conceivable that the fictional events have simply been given a new lease of life by being at last assigned to the real world.

The distinction is not an important one, however; Donleavy's writing is all of a piece. There is nobody quite like him for creating a mood of unforced gaiety and blithe insouciance: his ***A Fairy Tale of New York*** is one of the funniest novels of recent times; and for the purposes of this apparently more factual book he has reapplied his ear for comic dialogue and his eye for significant detail. It would be hard to find another narrative that so evokes the look and the feel of Ireland, with

> the first browny green sight of those small meandering fields clustered about some white tiny cottage with turf smoke rising from its chimney of this windswept land that reached to the edge of the great heaving Atlantic Ocean.

But the gaiety and the genial chaos that he found here have their less picturesque aspects, also. And, as so often, Dublin must bear the sins of Ireland: despite its ritual obeisances to the saints and scholars, you would come away from ***Donleavy's Ireland*** with the impression of a city where the reigning household gods are Mars and Bacchus rather than some more polite deities.

The young Donleavy seems to have spent his time largely in drinking and fighting along with everyone else; but if in his case these activities sprang from high spirits, for his Irish contemporaries they were only the most obvious manifestations of their frustration and despair. But, in the process of describing this, Donleavy has hit upon a curious truth of Irish life: this most witty and civilized of races can also become one of the most savage and the most erotic. In the shadow of the Church, they are seen to couple furtively, blindly, like animals. But of this comes guilt as well as sadness; and Dublin can be a treacherous, rancorous city: "Alleyways whispering out their sad sorrows of cold embraces. Pub walls repeating all their tales. The calumny, backbiting, and lies that begrudgers spoke".

And this is the other side of Ireland itself, expressed in ***The Ginger Man*** through Sebastian Dangerfield's desire to "get out of this god damn country which I hate with all my blood and which has ruined me." This is the Ireland that has been reared out of poverty and misery—precisely the Ireland which Donleavy's parents fled, but which he had to discover for himself. As a young man he had travelled to an imaginary country, but his vague myths were soon impaled upon the "narrow-minded, bigoted and bitterly resentful ways" of its real people.

It is a tribute to his imaginative honesty that this anger is embedded in a narrative that could so easily have turned into a self-indulgent fantasy. But . . . this is a book designed to evoke the "sins" as well as the "graces" of the country—just as, in Donleavy's novels, the gaiety consorts with the savagery, the poverty and meanness are to be seen within the broad ambience of a cheerful and almost visionary humour. He is an important writer because he can act out the fantasy at the same time as he sees the truth—and because he realizes that they need each other.

Peter Ackroyd, "On Wilder Shores of Irish Letters," in The Times, *London, July 17, 1986, p. 15.*

JEREMY LEWIS

Re-reading the books of one's youth—like ***The Ginger Man***—is a hazardous and sometimes melancholy business, for once the myth has been undone it can never regain its ancient power; rewriting the books of one's youth is, it seems, an even more dangerous exercise, still more so if the comical gusto has been replaced by the tedious ramblings of middle age. ***J. P. Donleavy's Ireland*** sets out to recreate in autobiographical form the world of his famous novel, and the wild student life of post-war Ireland: but although Mr Donleavy tells us of fellow-Americans tapping him on the shoulder in Dublin to ask 'Are you J. P. Donleavy who wrote ***The Ginger Man***? That's why I came here all the way from the U.S.A.', it's hard to imagine an earnest mid-Westerner in search of the boozy bohemian life booking a seat on the Dublin plane after struggling his way through these leaden-footed, semi-literate pages. (pp. 29-30)

Of Irish parentage, Donleavy came to Trinity in 1946 after a spell with the US Navy. Ever anxious to portray himself as the hard-drinking, hard-hitting colonial boy, giving as good as he gets and trading punches before reeling off to the nearest pub arm-in-arm with his erstwhile opponent, we find our hero 'squaring up' to Brendan Behan within several pages of his arrival. This, he intimates, was a meeting of giants and equals: certainly Behan comes across throughout the book as an almost entirely repellent figure, while his first appearance gives the author an opportunity to produce one of those ungrammatical and virtually meaningless sentences—consisting of a dash of ill-digested Joyce, a touch of Synge, several spoonfuls of bogus Irishry and a large dose of whimsical ineptitude—with which this shapeless and, at times, almost unreadable book abounds ('Behan, then recently released from prison, and I, were that afternoon's joke being played upon us when we were introduced to each other as writers').

Not long after, Donleavy finds himself at the kind of debauch that enables him to indulge in his apparent taste for snobbery with violence, for intimations of Anglo-Irish grandeur of a suitably seedy kind with the wearisome rain of stout bottles on the back of the head, lead pipes 'thudding on craniums' and 'the battering of a bottle in the ribcage'. At this particularly tiresome party we learn—and what follows is an all too typical example of the Donleavy school of prose—of a 'famed Dublin chastisement' whereby

> the aggrieved gent knocking the treacherous chap to the ground and grabbing him by both his port and starboard ears and engripped also with a goodly handful of hair, then pounding his skull repeatedly on tiles, while removing the hirsute plumage around his hearing appendage and shaking the living daylights out of his neurons. . . .

The book ends—not a page too soon—with Donleavy returning from Fulham to live in Ireland, earlier described 'to many of its native born winter non shivering inhabitants'—whatever that may mean—as 'a shrunken teat on the chest of the cold Atlantic'. (In Fulham, he informs us—with his curious sense of the spoken word—a 'young British elitist' had told him 'I'm awfully sorry, my dear chap, but I cannot proceed farther, you see we are about to enter the borough of Fulham and I never walk there.') Stranded amongst all this turgid windbaggery are some surprising regrets (for the loss of Trinity's 'elegance and tradition' over the past few years, and for the passing of the Anglo-Irish Horse Protestants who once held court at the Shelbourne but have been 'washed away by the more plebeian waves breaking with philistine inelegance upon this island nation') and the occasional spasm of vitality (Behan guarding the fort for a magazine editor, feeding the fire with typescripts and cooking sausages on the end of a fountain pen, or Donleavy's country neighbour who reported Hitler as being alive and well and living in County Wicklow and spotted 'more than once in the pub without his moustache'). Sad to say, such flashes are few and far between: for the most part, it's hard not to agree with Patrick Kavanagh's initial reaction to our hero's venturing into the life of a smallholder—'Phoney, phoney, phoney. Utterly phoney. The whole thing is phoney. Nothing but phoniness.' According to Donleavy, Kavanagh later retracted these harsh sentiments: but, as is so often the case, he may well have been right the first time round. (p. 30)

Jeremy Lewis, "The Dismal Doings of Debauched D." in The Spectator, *Vol. 257, No. 8245, July 19, 1986, pp. 29-30.*

JOHN KELLY

"Ireland is a state of mind", as J. P. Donleavy discovered during a disconsolate return to his native America, and ***Ireland: In all her sins and in some of her graces,*** largely an account of his first exposure to his adopted land, attempts a description of that state of mind. Such an enterprise depends as much on the beholder as the thing beheld, and this is a highly personal view. It is also partial: Donleavy writes less about Ireland than about Dublin, or, more precisely, the central square mile of Dublin; less about the native Irish than about the Anglo-Irish, who appeal to a strain of lace-curtain snobbery in him; and less about the contemporary nation than about a Romantic Ireland, dead and gone, that existed between 1946 and 1953, the seven years in which he was a student at Trinity College and picking up the experiences that were to issue in ***The Ginger Man.***

Although of Irish extraction, Donleavy might never have made his way from New York had he not discovered that Dublin boasted the widest street in Europe, the largest municipal park and the biggest brewery. These three apparently random superlatives touched something deep in an imagination which yearns perpetually for the epic but is shrewd enough to settle for the mock-heroic. And post-war Dublin could not disappoint so willing a mythologizer: displaced exotics from all over Europe, their tastes as dubious as their pedigrees, cavorted with demobbed warriors from America and Britain to enliven the indigenous ranks of eccentric Anglo-Irish and charmingly guileful natives. . . .

Dublin provided the raw material, Donleavy's myth-making imagination did the rest. His tale bristles with names that have the tang of folklore: Daniel the Dangerous, Molly of the Apes, Madame Splitcrocht, and the Awful Three. Never a man to pass up a superlative where a comparative might do, even a sordid cellar club is gothicized as "The Charnel-chambers", and "never in the modern or ancient history of the Irish state was there anywhere at anytime anything like it".

In those Gargantuan days no evening's drinking, whether in a bar, country house, or city flat, was complete without at least one pitched battle, and each closing-time scuffle is faithfully recorded. This, potentially as tedious as B-movie Hemingway, is transformed by Donleavy's unflagging enthusiasm for fisticuffs and exaggeration into the narrative equivalent of a Tom and Jerry cartoon.

But the emphasis on violence is symptomatic of something deeper—not in Ireland's state of mind, but in Donleavy's. For, through the rumbustious accounts of boozing, pugilism and would-be fornication seeps a profound loneliness. The pronoun he most favours is "one", and this seems less an acquired Anglo-Irish speech mannerism than a grammatical expression of an egotism and solitude that pervade the book.

John Kelly, "Days in the Womb," in The Times Literary Supplement, *No. 4368, December 19, 1986, p. 1433.*

E(dward) M(organ) Forster

1879-1970

English novelist, short story writer, essayist, critic, travel writer, biographer, dramatist, librettist, and nonfiction writer.

World Wide Photos, Inc.

Forster is the author of *Howards End* (1910) and *A Passage to India* (1924), two novels generally considered among the finest achievements in twentieth-century fiction. His novels of manners depicting Edwardian society and British morality are similar in style to those of Jane Austen and focus on three major themes: salvation through love, the deficiency of traditional Christianity, and the repressiveness of English culture. These themes are underscored by numerous allusions to paganism and mythology and are infused with Forster's liberal humanism and subtle wit. Forster's works are admired for their believable characterizations that simultaneously serve as representations of abstract ideas. Frederick P. W. McDowell noted: "A fascination exerted by characters who grip our minds; a wit and beauty present in an always limpid style; a passionate involvement with life in all its variety; a view of existence alive to its comic incongruities and to its tragic implications; and a steady adherence to humanistic values which compel admiration . . . such are the leading aspects of Forster's work that continually lure us to it." Recent film adaptations of *A Passage to India* and *A Room with a View* (1908), as well as the posthumous publication of his letters, unfinished writings, and homoerotic fiction, have helped further Forster's reputation as a major literary figure.

Forster attended Cambridge University, where he was a member, along with such noted intellectuals as Lytton Strachey and John Maynard Keynes, of the Cambridge Apostles. This society evolved into the Bloomsbury Group, which was informally led by Virginia Woolf and adhered to the philosophical tenets expressed by G. E. Moore in his *Principia Ethica*. Moore's work expounded the value of social interaction and cultural stimuli, two crucial elements of Forster's ideology which, according to Claude J. Summers, also included "Forster's belief in individualism and the sanctity of personal relationships, his scorn for conventionality and religion, his passion for truth and friendship, his unaffected love for art, and his intellectual romanticism." These factors abound throughout Forster's writings.

Forster's early novels derive from his experiences in the Cambridge and Bloomsbury coteries and examine the upper middle class of the Edwardian era. Both *Where Angels Fear to Tread* (1905) and *A Room with a View* are informed by Forster's travels to Italy and contrast European liberalism with more conservative English values. In these novels, the Italian characters are archetypes of instinct, spirituality, and imagination, whereas the British characters represent Victorian conventionalism and rational thought. Similarly, the protagonists of *The Longest Journey* (1907) personify opposite philosophies. Rickie Elliot, a Cambridge intellectual, and his half-brother, Stephen Wonham, respectively embody romantic and pagan ideals. *Howards End,* one of Forster's most acclaimed works, reveals his vision of a unified humanity and balances thematically upon the poignant phrase "only connect." In *Howards End,* Forster depicts the dichotomous aspects of English society and human nature as reconcilable through the application of Bloomsbury precepts and certain British traditions.

In the years immediately following the publication of *Howards End,* Forster became increasingly aware of Indian culture. In *A Passage to India,* which was awarded the James Tait Black Memorial Prize and is widely regarded as his masterpiece, Forster drew from his visits to India in 1912 and 1921 and from his friendship with Syed Ross Masood, who taught Forster much about Indian society. This novel's acclaim derives from its portrayal of widely diverse cultures—Muslim, Hindu, and Christian—and the difficulties inherent in their coexistence. Forster imbues *A Passage to India* with the Hindu principle of total acceptance, employing this philosophy to suggest an integrating force for which, as events in the novel suggest, the world is unprepared. The differences between Western and Eastern perceptions are exemplified by an episode in the Marabar Caves, where Mrs. Moore, an elderly British matron, presumably experiences nihilistic despair upon hearing an echo suggesting to her that "nothing has value." According to most interpretations, Mrs. Moore, unlike the Hindus, is unable to assimilate this despair into the totality of her religious sensibility, and she succumbs to spiritual passivity.

Forster published no more novels during his lifetime, concentrating instead on critical pieces, letters, biographies, and travel books. *Aspects of the Novel* (1927), Forster's seminal critical work, is his most highly regarded nonfiction volume. *Abinger Harvest* (1936) and *Two Cheers for Democracy* (1951) contain critical treatises as well as biographical portraits of other writers and essays outlining Forster's political beliefs. *Alexandria: A History and a Guide* (1922) and *Pharos and Pharillon* (1923) evidence Forster's knowledge of Egyptian locales, while *The Hill of Devi* (1953; republished as *The Hill of Devi and Other Writings*) collects his letters from India. Forster also published four collections of short stories: *The Celestial Omnibus and Other Stories* (1911), *The Story of the Siren* (1920), *The Eternal Moment and Other Stories* (1928), and *The Collected Short Stories of E. M. Forster* (1947). Forster's stories thematically resemble his novels but rely more heavily on supernatural and metaphysical elements.

Forster's posthumous reputation has been enhanced by the publication of *The Selected Letters of E. M. Forster: Volume I, 1879-1920* (1984) and *The Selected Letters of E. M. Forster: Volume II, 1921-1970* (1985), as well as by the appearance of *Maurice* (1971), a previously suppressed novel centering upon homosexual topics. Begun before *A Passage to India, Maurice* recounts a young man's growing awareness of his homosexuality and is generally considered to be autobiographical. *The Life to Come and Other Stories* (1972) and *The New Collected Short Stories of E. M. Forster* (1985) have been lauded by many critics for the inclusion of such esteemed works as "Dr. Woolacott" and "The Road from Colonus." *Arctic Summer and Other Fiction* (1980) includes many unfinished pieces, including the title novel, which predates *A Passage to India* and anticipates its themes.

(See also *CLC,* Vols. 1, 2, 3, 4, 9, 10, 13, 15, 22; *Contemporary Authors,* Vols. 13-14, Vols. 25-28, rev. ed. [obituary]; *Contemporary Authors Permanent Series,* Vol. 1; and *Dictionary of Literary Biography,* Vol. 34.)

ELIZABETH HEINE

[In ***Arctic Summer and Other Fiction***] are gathered all those extant works of fiction which Forster began but left unfinished: a substantial early attempt at a novel, here titled ***Nottingham Lace;*** a welter of draft material for a novel Forster called ***Arctic Summer;*** four novellas or stories in various stages of completion; and a handful of shorter sketches and fragments. Three of the stories and one of the shorter pieces—editorially entitled **"Simply the Human Form"**—are so nearly complete that they might not unreasonably have been included in ***The Life to Come and Other Stories,*** published in 1972 as volume 8 of the Abinger Edition. Like this predecessor, ***Arctic Summer and Other Fiction*** spans Forster's entire career as a writer—from his early twenties to his eighties—and includes an overtly homosexual ingredient, although this is here confined to a single story, **"Little Imber",** and to one or two of the shorter fragments.

The publication of such a volume may be thought—by certain critics the publication of its predecessor was thought—to require some apology. But Forster is a major writer whose reputation will not, in the long run, be damaged by work that falls below his own highest standards, and the more distinguished can often be illuminated by the less. . . . ***Nottingham Lace*** and ***Ralph and Tony*** are not without insight, nor **"The Tomb of Pletone"** and **"Little Imber"** without irony, however bizarre. Moreover, the works presented in this volume are those which survived Forster's repeated culling of his unpublished fiction; only a few of the shortest fragments appear to have escaped destruction merely by chance. Incomplete, imperfect, often untitled, still some gleam of imagination or humour or self-reflection keeps these unfinished narratives alive.

The two earliest of the longer pieces, ***Nottingham Lace*** and ***Ralph and Tony,*** are perhaps most interesting for the ways in which the central figure of each resembles the young Forster, though his uncertain control of the conventions of narrative, particularly the shaping of a plot, is also evident in both. . . . ***Nottingham Lace,*** the earlier, is the more substantial; Rose Macaulay, who had Forster's help in writing her perceptive study of his works, tells us that it was "written at about twenty years of age". (pp. vii-viii)

In subject, ***Nottingham Lace*** is the first of Forster's many stories about suburban class-consciousness, public-school insensitivity, and the awakening of a passive, inhibited youth by the example and encouragement of a more vigorous young man of different class and culture. Edgar Carruthers and Sidney Trent most closely prefigure Rickie Elliot and Stewart Ansell of ***The Longest Journey,*** where the town of Sawston and its public school also reappear. In structure, the three-fold plot of ***The Longest Journey*** is also vaguely foreshadowed in ***Nottingham Lace*** when Edgar, cut off from Trent, is first linked with a young Irish woman, Kathleen Logan, and then joins with his athletic cousin, Jack Manchett, in protest against the injustice of parental and school authorities. Unfortunately ***Nottingham Lace*** breaks off just at the point where the plot, weakly and episodically linear as it is, demands that the hero take action. Despite the awkwardness of the plotting, however, Forster even at this early stage uses the voice of the narrator for wise and ironical comment. Of Mr Manchett, away in Dublin, he remarks, "His personality, like himself, did not travel well." On Edgar's decision to live as "two persons", splitting his everyday life with the Manchett family from his ideal life of the mind, the narrator comments, "He did not realize that it was easy because at the moment the two persons coincided."

Forster was also experimenting in ***Nottingham Lace*** with the precept that actions speak louder than words. He allows the reader to learn from Mrs Manchett's outcry that Edgar in anger has knocked over his lemonade; he deletes interpretations which the reader ought to be able to make alone. If Trent continues his conversation, obviously ignoring Edgar's protests, then "quite ignoring Edgar's statements" is a bit of narrative description that can be cut. So can the remark that Mrs Manchett's efforts to break up Edgar's friendship with Trent "evinced more skill than was expected". A theory of fiction, if still embryonic, is clearly at work. Nonetheless, Forster's later opinion of this undergraduate novel, expressed in an unpublished memoir in which he credits his Cambridge tutor, Nathaniel Wedd, with calling his attention to his possession of the "special and unusual apparatus" of the novelist, is severely just: "that novel about a boy named Edgar . . . wasn't writing, though. The apparatus was working, not inaccurately, but feebly and dreamily, because I wasn't sure it was there."

At first reading, ***Ralph and Tony*** may also seem to break off at a crucial point. However, though the manuscript has been catalogued and bound as an unfinished novel, it can also be read as a complete story, ending with a kiss meant to signify the newly approved marriage of Margaret and Ralph. As Jane Austen's novels appear to provide the models for the shopping excursion and the picnic of ***Nottingham Lace,*** so the influence of Henry James's later fiction, in which much that is unspoken transpires in a gesture, seems to lie behind the story of Ralph's love for Tony and his sister Margaret. The writing of this manuscript can be dated and placed exactly, by a coincidence of paper and pencil, to the summer of 1903 and Forster's second stay at the Hotel Stella d'Oro, Cortina d'Ampezzo. A year earlier, he and his mother had retreated from the Italian plains to the then-Austrian Tyrol partly because of his health. It was then that he walked through a thunderstorm in the mountains, defying the elements in the name of "Justice", as he wrote to his friend E. J. Dent on 10 August 1902. But if some of the substance of the narrative dates to 1902, the foolscap paper and uncharacteristic pencil of the manuscript match exactly another letter to Dent, dated 30 July 1903; pencil was necessary because the hotel pens were "vile".

In his Introduction to his ***Collected Short Stories*** (1948), Forster tells us that one of his earliest published stories, **"The Eternal Moment"** (1905), is both a "meditation on Cortina D'Ampezzo" and "almost an honest-to-God yarn". ***Ralph and Tony*** is a much more personal celebration of the romantic possibilities of love, death, and "Justice" in the mountains, perhaps too personal. No story resembling it is mentioned in Forster's diaries or letters, and it seems never to have been submitted for publication. The author may have judged even in 1903 that the characterizations of Ralph and his mother came too close to home for publication. Moreover, Margaret functions as an entirely transparent medium for Ralph's love for Tony, a love indirectly requited when Tony rescues Ralph from what appears to be a suicide attempt, and then, despite or because of his weakened heart, is ready to allow Ralph to marry Margaret—or so the story, uncomfortably vague, seems to suggest.

The third piece transcribed here [is] **"The Tomb of Pletone"**. . . . Based on the fact that Sigismondo Malatesta brought the remains of Gemistus Pletho to Rimini from Mistra, near Sparta, the story developed in part from Forster's tour of Greece in the spring of 1903. . . . The story was nearly finished by the end of April 1904, when Forster wrote to Dent that he was "engaged on the impossible—a short historical story", and in need of information about fifteenth-century Italian boats. . . . [The essay **"Gemistus Pletho"** also] represents Forster's careful reading of Italian history. **"The Tomb of Pletone"** preserves his unsatisfactory efforts to fuse the history with imagined scenes of nightmarish violence, as well as with his characteristic themes of brotherly friendship and sacrifice.

The manuscripts of these . . . early works are relatively free of corrections, suggesting that Forster wrote out the stories with ease and then chose to abandon them rather than struggle with their unsatisfactory structures, though he might use the same material again in a different form. But the much revised manuscripts of ***Arctic Summer*** graphically preserve his unsuccessful efforts to complete the novel, begun later in 1911. Nor was ***Arctic Summer*** ever entirely abandoned, for Forster returned to it nearly forty years later, when he revised the first five chapters once again and read them at the Aldeburgh Festival on 10 June 1951. He explained then, in the note he wrote to accompany his reading: "I had got my antithesis all right, the antithesis between the civilized man, who hopes for an Arctic Summer, and the heroic man who rides into the sea. But I had not settled what was going to happen, and that is why the novel remains a fragment." Clesant March, athletic, unintellectual, military and conservative in both background and training, is the heroic figure; Martin Whitby, born of a Quaker family, a Fellow of his Cambridge college, conscientiously socialist, aesthetically sensitive, and unexpectedly attracted to young March's virtues, is the civilized man. As in ***Howards End*** (1910), the problem is to connect "the prose and the passion", but the idealistic passions for personal freedom and social reform expressed by the Schlegel sisters in ***Howards End*** have in ***Arctic Summer*** been modified into the day-to-day prose of Martin Whitby's civilized marriage and his work at the Treasury. In ***Arctic Summer*** the passion belongs to the heroic warrior, and the problem is to join the physical courage of the thoughtlessly chivalric hero with the moral tolerance of the civilized man, to re-educate the one and revitalize the other. Something of the same opposition underlies the friendship of Aziz and Fielding in ***A Passage to India,*** begun in 1913 under much the same pressures as ***Arctic Summer*** in 1911, but in the earlier novel Forster never worked out a suitable central test of the different ethical values and their accompanying codes of behaviour. The breadth of the perspective in the later novel perhaps begins in part from the failure of the earlier; in ***Abinger Harvest*** Forster dates **"Hymn Before Action",** his essay on the *Bhagavad Gita,* to 1912, and his diary entries show that he was studying Krishna's advice to the warrior Arjuna in July of that year, when he was trying to salvage ***Arctic Summer*** by beginning it again.

The genesis of ***Arctic Summer*** in 1910 and 1911 was as complex as the process of its decay in 1912. Definitions of heroism and the relations of codes of honour to "masculine" and "feminine" ideals were much on everyone's minds in these years of increasingly mechanized armies and growing agitation for women's suffrage; Forster's recorded reactions were at first focused exclusively on literature. A month or so after the manuscript of ***Howards End*** had gone to his publishers, Forster noted with asperity his reaction to a novel written by a friend of a friend:

> Am reading the novel of Lady Morison's friend with hostility. Blatantly feminine. Women have no self-respect. How *can* they quote *das ewig Weibliche?* Is there a corresponding complacency in men? I think not. Men have too much literary sense. (Diary, 31 August 1910).

The ideas engendered in part at least by this unusual reading experience were expressed some weeks later in an essay entitled **"The Feminine Note in Literature"**. . . . In the essay Forster defines the feminine note as a "preoccupation with personal worthiness", arguing that women writers measure "worthiness" only in relation to some other person. Men, on the other hand, "have an unembodied ideal". He uses Conrad's *Lord Jim* to illustrate the masculine values. . . . [Forster] seems at this point to have no doubt about the worth of the code itself, what Conrad calls that "shadowy ideal" of the English gentleman for which Jim in his "exalted egoism" sacrifices himself.

In the various drafts of ***Arctic Summer,*** however, the worth of the gentlemanly code is very much in doubt. It is nonetheless far from easy to tell how Forster wants us to judge either Martin Whitby's cowardice when he flees from a cinema fire, very much as Jim fled from his supposedly sinking ship, or the common-sensical response of Martin's wife Venetia. Her view seems wholly "civilized", closely resembling Forster's later support, in ***What I Believe*** (1939), of the values of "tolerance, good temper, and sympathy". Yet at the same time Venetia seems a caricature of the "new woman", somehow emasculating men by her refusal to be treated chivalrously, as "unworthy" of respect as the thrill-hungry adolescent girls Forster provides for contrast. In ***A Passage to India*** it is, oddly enough, Adela Quested who plays the role approximating Lord Jim's. Miss Quested faces up to her deeply personal fault in the midst of a trial much corrupted by an outdated code of chivalry, becoming both hero and outcaste as she does so. She and Fielding are the ones who have the courage—almost a kind of humility—to stand against the unjust demands of their communities, showing the kind of heroism Forster came to value most. Still, Adela Quested and Cyril Fielding are also emotionally limited, inhibited by their rational tolerance even though they are half-aware that they have little sense of absurdity or capacity for joy. In the ***Arctic Summer*** manuscripts, although their unfinished state must be taken into account, there seems much less emphasis on the development of a new, ''civilized'' heroic code, much more on the vigours to be admired in the old. (pp. ix-xiv)

If ***Arctic Summer*** is identified by its major public themes, it becomes little more than a thin period piece in the manner of Wells and Galsworthy, remarkably dependent on public events for its substance. But the continued saga of young March allows the unfinished novel to be identified as well with Forster's private doubts and desires, and read in this light ***Arctic Summer*** becomes an extraordinarily revealing work, intricately illustrative of what P. N. Furbank suggests in his biography of Forster was a ''fear of success'' of the kind described by Freud. That is, Forster's difficulties with ***Arctic Summer*** seem to some extent wilful, a half-conscious proof of the necessity of his refusal to continue to write novels about orthodox love and marriage, proof of the worth of his decision to write the homosexual stories whose influence on the portraits of the March brothers becomes more and more obvious. Years later, when Forster burnt his ''indecent writings'' to free himself for his work on ***A Passage to India,*** he remembered that when he began to write these stories, ''I had a feeling that I was doing something positively dangerous to my career as a novelist'' (Diary, 8 April 1922). None of these early erotic writings survive, but the manuscripts of ***Arctic Summer*** reflect deep sexual ambivalences which can be linked to a desire to refuse an achieved success, particularly a hard-won success—a desire to endanger a career just reaching a new height. (pp. xxiii-xxiv)

Of the two remaining longer pieces in this volume the earlier, as Forster noted on the manuscript, is ''not bad''. Both this note and the title, **''Unfinished Short Story'',** are in Forster's late hand, evidently inscribed at the same time. Nor is the title a bad one, for by preventing the suspicion that the three brief episodes might lead to a novel it gives a potential shape to the course of Gregory Dale's excursion to Alexandria from Cairo. The title also matches the strong impression that Gregory, like the story, has little sense of purpose, that the incidents, however varied, have at their centre a disenchanted middle-aged observer who is content to move from one episode to another as opportunity offers. The story may as well be ''unfinished'', embodying in its form this lack of determination. (p. xxv)

Forster wrote the last of the longer pieces, **''Little Imber'',** in 1961, as he was approaching his eighty-third birthday. In its fantastic dissolution of the obstacles to fatherhood ordinarily raised by homosexuality it echoes back to the ambivalences of ***Arctic Summer.*** Set in the future after a period of devastating warfare, the story once again tests ideas of sexual morality, gentlemanliness and heroism as the civilized Warham, virile but no longer young, is attracted despite his prejudices to Imber, both young and virile. There is even a faint verbal echo of ***Arctic Summer,*** for the notebook of Martin Whitby's sister-in-law, a collector of folksongs, records a meeting with ''Mr Lodge, Imber in the Down. Only when drunk.'' The tiny village of Imber can still be found on the map, ''derelict'' in the midst of the area of the Salisbury Plain now set off for military exercises. Forster may have learned the rhyme he gives to the Abbess in the short story, ''Little Imber in the Down,/Nine miles from any town'', on his early walking tours through Wiltshire; traditionally the miles are ''Four''. As the Abbess says, recalling that in Latin ''imber'' means a ''fertilizing shower'', the name of the young man is indeed apt. Her rhyme provokes the pun of the title, for young Imber won't be called ''little'', or ''gentle'' either.

This last of Forster's short stories, remarkably free from death and violence and guilt, deals in comedy and hope rather than tragedy. Some readers may find it grotesque, but it seems to me oddly moving in the simplicity of its desire for progeny. An allusion to the mythical twin founders of Rome, Romulus and Remus, and faint verbal echoes of Yeats's ''The Second Coming'', in Imber's slouching roughness, deepen the hope for a new civilization implicit in the story. (pp. xxvi-xxvii)

The collection of shorter pieces that rounds out the volume recapitulates Forster's writing career with nearly statistical accuracy. All can be roughly dated by subject or handwriting or both; the first five of the eight . . . belong to Forster's prolific Edwardian years. Of these the first three are concerned with conflicting perceptions of truth and beauty, whether culturally predetermined or consciously chosen. The earliest, **''Simply the Human Form'',** lacks a strong sense of conclusion but is essentially complete; at a superficial glance only an essay, it is on closer inspection a story, the first-person report of a visitor from outer space, of non-human form, who is intrigued by human reactions to nudity in art and life. The second item, **''Arthur at Ampelos'',** draws on Forster's tour of Greece in 1903, when he visited Crete as well, viewing Sir Arthur Evans's work at Knossos, still in process, and some of the newly excavated sites of Minoan and pre-Minoan pottery finds in East Crete. The story would have been extremely up-to-date; the fragment which survives retains a bit of beauty, like the piece of the red-figured Greek vase which Arthur, with his archeological interest in the more distant past, wishes to discount. The third of these early pieces, **''At the National Gallery'',** shares with Forster's Italian novels its cheerful mockery of a philistine immunity to the glories of Sienese paintings; Forster's handwriting, which changed rapidly in these years of steady writing, supports a date of about 1906. The fourth piece, **''Hassan in England'',** appears to have been written only a year or two later. It offers surprisingly early evidence of Forster's interest in Indian and English differences. . . . (p. xxviii)

The last of the earlier fragments, **''Votes and Boys'',** has on its verso in Forster's hand simply ***Howards End,*** written in a large script lengthwise on the page, as though the leaf served first as a cover sheet for the manuscript of the novel. The boys seem to be sitting somewhere beside the Kennet and Avon canal, perhaps as far west as the stepped locks near Devizes; in any case the description of the change from chalk to alluvial earth, Wiltshire to Berkshire, echoes the concern for the shape of England and its central chalk expressed in ***Howards End.*** The issue of suffrage and the focus on a boy's romantic ''personal loyalty'' to a candidate, ''an enthusiasm that the sophisticated can only let out into literature'', also confirm a date of 1910 or perhaps 1911, for they suggest the elements of conflict in ***Arctic Summer.*** They hint too at the reasons for the fifteen-year gap between **''Votes and Boys'',** and the next fragment, **"Stonebreaking"**, reasons confirmed by the indubitably homosexual nature of the later piece. . . . Considering that Forster culled his homosexual writings rather carefully, destroying many, **"Stonebreaking"** may have survived because it is an unusual exercise in dramatic monologue, not without narrative power.

"From a Forthcoming Blue Book" is the brief satiric prophecy Forster labelled "Nice Nonsense" in his late hand. He wrote it most probably in the late thirties, for the mimeographed sheets whose blank versos were used to draft the story refer with distress to Mr Chamberlain's government, an oncoming "hour of peril", and Nazi concentration camps. But the forerunner of Forster's spoof of governmental efforts to control both broadcasting and listening appears in his diary entry of 22 January 1935:

> All England convulsed since Saturday night because an improper joke was made over the wireless. . . .
> And Bernard Shaw in a Sunday surprise talk mentioned sex.
> A moral clean-up is at hand.

Forster's glimpse into the future began as a one-page sketch which was quickly expanded to three by the addition of an ignorant muse of history—named Thorach, apparently—but with this burst of liveliness, and without any definite conclusion, and in some illegibility, the story rests.

The last fragment, written with the careful, shaky clarity of Forster's late years, suggests some of the dream-conversations he recorded in his ***Commonplace Book.*** The narrator grows more and more angry with the officious, drunken, bullying little customs-inspector and at last, fluent with rage, turns the tables. Brow-beaten into submission as the arc lamp fades into dawn, the inspector at last answers his own question, "Have you anything to declare?" In the manuscript there is once again an illuminating slip, an uncorrected "her" where "him" would be expected. Even without such an obvious clue, the anger in **"Anything to Declare?"** could be matched to that expressed in a very late entry in Forster's diary, a comment he added to a paragraph he had written thirty years before on the relation of his homosexuality to his writing. There are two afterthoughts, the first unemotional, bracketed: "re-read without much interest when I am almost 80". The second speaks to his unwritten as well as to his unfinished fiction:

> adding when I am almost 85 how *annoyed* I am with Society for wasting my time by making homosexuality criminal. The subterfuges, the self-consciousness that might have been avoided.
>
> (pp. xxix-xxx)

Elizabeth Heine, in an introduction to Arctic Summer and Other Fiction *by E. M. Forster, Holmes and Meier Publishers, Inc., 1981, pp. vii-xxxv.*

ALAN HOLLINGHURST

[***Alexandria: A History and a Guide***] is ideal: History in the first half, Guide in the second, the two keyed together with cross-referring notes which precisely mime the connections the visitor must make between physical and imaginative tourism. . . . The History takes the typically Bloomsburian form of a pageant or procession, though in this case it perhaps has a precedent in the ancient List of Kings in the Temple of Seti I at Abydos, an important carved depiction of the pharaonic succession from an earlier period; Forster achieves clear and animated distinctions of one Ptolemy from another, and intersperses succinct essays on Greco-Egyptian and Islamic thought, theology and art. Then comes what was the first ever translation of a poem of Forster's friend Cavafy, "The God Abandons Antony", which intimates the elegiac and memory-laden experience which the city represents both historically and, to many, personally, forming a link to the methodical and eminently useful Guide. . . .

[This new edition] adds to the book a literary dimension which takes the hint of Forster's inclusion of the Cavafy poem, with a vengeance. Lawrence Durrell contributes an introduction and the publisher a postlude which explains his own debt to Durrell in coming to know the city. The notes are full of quotations from *The Alexandria Quartet* which parallel the real history with a fictional one which is thereby given a surely questionable dignity. Those who find Durrell unreadable can, of course, skip these extracts, but their presence is indicative of a different tradition of topographical writing from that of Forster in the text. Forster's fastidious manner is juxtaposed with one which posits the subjective experience of the writer as in itself a kind of travel-guide, a standard not simply of observation but of sensibility, which the reader must aspire to live up to. . . . Such writing, and the quoted fictions of Durrell and Neguib Mahfouz, illustrate a tendency to read a place through a book, as one might read Dublin through Joyce or Illiers through Proust; but beyond that the innately literary nature of these experiences of Alexandria emphasizes that it is a city of ghosts, where the writer counteracts the lack of present interest not only with history but with an orchestration of feeling.

Nothing of this happens in Forster's part of the book, needless to say. Forster's personal reticence is a perfect complement to that civic inexpressiveness beneath which he detects the shapes of the past. His own enigma, however, is never disclosed, though Lawrence Durrell, alerted perhaps by the knowledge that this was the case, suggests that Forster "must (one feels it) have been deeply happy, perhaps deeply in love" in Alexandria. As is now well known from P. N. Furbank's life of Forster. . . , Forster's time there—as a volunteer with the Red Cross—was crucial in his development as man and writer. There he had what appears to have been his first consummated love-affair, with a tram-conductor called Mohammed el Adl, who died in the year of the publication of the Guide. In a scrupulously secret way the book constitutes a tribute to and an elegy for this relationship, substituting for a personal explanation an external and factual account of a place which in itself Forster did not much care for.

The affair was part of a general deepening of understanding which promoted his increasing geographical movement, Alexandria being half-way to the India to which he would return after the War. Even when he was most naive as a person, his early novels had hinted at the inevitable relationship between travel and sexual knowledge and had carried within themselves a concealed prophecy of what would happen to Forster himself. After Alexandria he saw that he should have written ***Maurice*** better than he had (he would doubtless have lessened its dependence on fantasy); but by his love-affair he had also unconsciously reduced the actual therapeutic need to write, at the same time as both history and geography, the dual dimensions of the ***History and Guide,*** took him away from his primary Edwardian subject.

D. H. Lawrence had already recognized that all Forster's "thinking and his passion for humanity amounts to no more than trying to soothe with poetry a man raging with pain which can be cured"—and cured by just such means as sexual reciprocation and self-confidence. Forster was not a professional novelist of the kind whose technique guarantees productivity: his fiction-writing was intimately connected to his lack of experience, and his Alexandrian period is intimately connected to his ceasing to write fiction after ***Passage to India,*** a novel which anyway draws on his life in Egypt but moves towards a new and speculative remoteness from social concerns. First, however, came this lucid and concise guide-book, Forster's earliest work of non-fiction, and an indication of the move he would make towards history and biography and towards a tactful impersonality which yet always bore his stamp.

Alan Hollinghurst, "A Reticent City," in The Times Literary Supplement, *No. 4124, April 16, 1982, p. 429.*

FREDERICK P. W. McDOWELL

Critics have often censured Forster for the plots of his novels, for an excess of contrivance, an overuse of surprise, and a resort to melodrama. Others have felt that the direction of the action is arbitrary and that the characters are not free to develop normally. Such judgments stem from standards ordinarily applied to realistic fiction, standards that are appropriate in part to Forster's, since social comedy and moral speculation are some of its major components. But these standards are ultimately misleading, as we have seen, since Forster's fiction is romance as well as realism, comprising symbolic drama as well as social observation. Forster was a Moorean realist, but he also desired to reach the inner essence of his experiences. He used plot, therefore, to achieve effects other than the establishing of verisimilitude. He defined his own method best perhaps in defining Virginia Woolf's: "Required like most writers to choose between the surface and the depths as the basis of her operations, she chooses the surface and then burrows in as far as she can." . . . (p. 141)

Ultimately, he wished to communicate his subjective and ecstatic vision of reality, the result in large part of his intense Romanticism of temper. The emotional and transcendent impact of what he created was for him more arresting than its analytic implications. Thus, the facts of perception and the motives underlying action pale before his compulsion to relate them to his intuitive and mystical insights. This realm of the extrasensory overlies the rendition of the social milieu that Forster knew as insider and is intricately intertwined with it; but as it reflects an eternal order of value, this extrasensory realm is independent of such a milieu. The well-known critic, F. R. Leavis, who was unsympathetic to this side of Forster, nevertheless perceived why he rejected the realistic as basis for any final truth. Forster, Leavis said, was preoccupied with vitality to the extent that he inevitably was carried beyond social comedy.

In the tradition of romance with its archetypal figures Forster's books contain major characters that are often more arresting as felt presences than for the social relationships they exemplify. These figures become heightened or foreshortened as they help articulate Forster's vision; and they become symbols as they dramatize his intuitive realizations. On occasion, Forster designedly sacrificed probability of motive in the interests of ulterior truth. Characters like Gino Carella, Stephen Wonham, and Ruth Wilcox lack sufficient substance as real people to be entirely convincing, yet as presences they are not the aesthetic failures that some critics have declared them to be. What each lacks for our complete suspension of disbelief is not added consistency in motivation, but a completer conception on Forster's part of each personage and his role in the given book.

As fabulist, romancer, and prophet, Forster evolved complex plots which are, nevertheless, consistent within themselves and which communicate his intuitions more forcibly than would actions of greater moment and probability. The alternation of the idyllic and the violent, for example, establishes more vividly Forster's sense of the disjunctions in experience than would a more customary recounting of events. Such disjunctions achieve, moreover, some resolutions in a timeless entity extending beyond our ordinary lives in time, since Forster, as we have seen, was a mediator of extremes and something of a mystic as well.

Forster once declared . . . that theme in part determined the incidents. These are truly important, then, as they relate to theme; as they illustrate the inner tensions of the characters, their relationships to each other, and their aspirations; and as they embody the symbolic implications of the fable. Characters, insofar as they embody theme, must in some part have also antedated story line as Forster shaped his fiction; and, like the incidents of the plot, they readily attain general, symbolic dimensions.

Forster's characters, then, are often less significant in themselves than for what they suggest as we review the narratives. Except for the "flat" characters—such as most of the Indians and Anglo-Indians in ***A Passage to India,*** Mrs. Lewin in ***The Longest Journey,*** and Mrs. Munt and Frieda Mosebach in ***Howards End***—the characters have an allegorical aspect which varies in complexity from the crass philistinism of Paul Wilcox in ***Howards End*** to the complicated humanism and transcendental sensitivity of Margaret Schlegel. His best creations . . . are not only significant as recognizable human beings facing recognizable human difficulties but as participants in panoramic dramas of total human concern. They are all actors in spiritual crises and must choose between good and evil, the human and the inhuman, though the act of choice is often perilous for them and disastrous if they choose wrongly. They achieve illumination through risk and even through active suffering; and sometimes the path to transcendence or to salvation is difficult for them to discern or to follow unfalteringly.

More than the characters, some of the incidents—and even the objects—of Forster's fiction gather a symbolic, often a supernal, aura as they bring to focus the ineffable truths that Forster wished to communicate. Incidents and objects become more compelling for what they imply in the full design of the work than for what they literally signify. The dynamic quality of Forster's symbolism depends more on the fact that his characters and actions simultaneously face toward the actual and the ineffable than on the repetition of images and the heightening of style. Forster does not always achieve the fusion of social reality and transcendental value for which he strives, but the fusion is more adroit and the symbolism more organic to total structure than critics like F. R. Leavis and Virginia Woolf admitted. (pp. 141-44)

But, if artistry is not solely a function of Forster's use of rhythm (in the sense of repeated phrases and images) and the presence of a luminous and evocative style, these elements are still integral to his achievement. In ***A Passage to India,*** for example, such images as the "fists and fingers" of the Marabar Hills, the receding arches in mosque and sky, and the natural phenomena such as stone, fire, rain, and the parched earth all help generate the book's density. The world out there never ceases to be minimally real, however intense the drama within may become or however piercing the moment of visionary ecstasy. And it is the style that gives Forster's fiction—and his nonfiction—its freshness, individuality, and resonance. Almost any page illustrates the beauty and orginality of the style. . . . (p. 144)

Sensitivity to light and shadow accounts in part for Forster's luminous prose. The reactions to physical impressions are so heightened that he conveys through their means an impression that the physical and spiritual are parts of each other, that the streaming lights of nature and the visionary gleams in the soul share reality as parts of a divine entity which we can only intermittently apprehend. . . . [Exact] observation, supple sensibility, imaginative power, and spiritual exaltation blend to create an authentic poetry in prose. (p. 145)

Through statement, style, sensibility, and an active imagination, Forster's own personality and values suffuse his fiction. He approximated, in short, his own conception, expressed in ***Aspects of the Novel,*** of the perfect novelist as one "who touches all his material directly, who seems to pass the creative finger down every sentence and into every word." . . . Such a novelist's work becomes then a manifestation of his own geniality and passion, a reflection of his own lucid intelligence and his visionary intensity. (p. 146)

In his novels and miscellaneous books alike, Forster's aim was to shape refractory experience to the requirements of order and pattern, but not at the expense of its vitality or the intensity of his vision. He achieved harmony and shapeliness in his fiction, qualities he suspected, however, in writers like Henry James and André Gide who sought too avidly for satisfaction in technique and structure. Still, his own work emanated from that residual sensitivity to aesthetic forms and impressions that the truly creative novelist, according to Forster, must possess. In a general discussion in ***Aspects of the Novel*** he asserted that such sensitivity results in a beauty which we as readers find amply revealed in Forster's own works, that "beauty at which a novelist should never aim, though he fails if he does not achieve it." . . . He had, moreover, the faith, possessed by the Romantics, in the transforming aspects of the imagination, "the immortal God which should assume flesh for the redemption of mortal passion." . . . The creative imagination breathes through all his work and gives it incandescence, whatever its flaws may be.

If Forster lacks breadth, he is always fresh, personal, and original—often profound and deeply moving. A fascination exerted by characters who grip our minds; a wit and beauty present in an always limpid style; a passionate involvement with life in all its variety; a view of existence alive to its comic incongruities and to its tragic implications; and a steady adherence to humanistic values which compel admiration even if their entire relevance may sometimes be in question—such are the leading aspects of Forster's work that continually lure us to it.

As the recent interest in his work signifies, modern readers have affirmed their conviction of Forster's absolute worth as critical intelligence and creative artist. The sense of something uniquely human that is too precious to be lost and that, against all odds, must be preserved—the conveying of this conviction in his fiction and nonfiction is the secret of his ongoing appeal to the intellectual and the general reader alike. It is the steel in Forster's temperament, not the charm, that finally counts. (pp. 149-50)

Frederick P. W. McDowell, in his E. M. Forster, *revised edition, Twayne Publishers, 1982, 174 p.*

CLAUDE J. SUMMERS

There is no other writer quite like E. M. Forster. He expresses in a voice unmistakably his own a vision that uniquely combines passion and intelligence, romanticism and skepticism. A curiously old-fashioned modernist, linked both with the novelistic traditions of Jane Austen and Henry James and with the modernism associated with D. H. Lawrence and Virginia Woolf, he deftly combines social comedy in the manner of Austen and prophecy in the vein of Lawrence. At once a symbolist and a realist, a fantasist and a satirist, he is always the humanist in search of wholeness.

Forster ranks among the finest novelists of the century. His six novels—each of them quite individual—maintain an extraordinary level of quality. ***Where Angels Fear to Tread*** is a minor masterpiece, a perfectly controlled homage to the complexity of life, while ***The Longest Journey*** is a powerful and passionate if not completely successful expression of the mythopoeic imagination. A bold hybrid of domestic comedy and sexual celebration, ***A Room with a View*** assimilates into a heterosexual plot the ideology of homosexual comradeship, while ***Howards End***—among the finest works produced in Edwardian England—presents a comprehensive social vision, one that includes metaphysical as well as political dimensions. ***Maurice,*** Forster's most undervalued novel, beautifully articulates the pain and joy of personal growth in a repressive society. Finally, ***A Passage to India***—the novelist's supreme achievement—is both the classic study of imperialism in English literature and a brooding and unflinching exploration of the twentieth-century spiritual wasteland.

Forster is less impressive as a writer of short fiction than as a novelist. But his short stories include some distinguished achievements—as, for example, **"The Celestial Omnibus"** and **"The Road from Colonus"** and **"The Other Boat"** and **"The Life to Come"**—and they are especially valuable for their help in revealing the complexity of Forster's art and the richness of his imagination. The fantasies, parables, and prophecies make obvious the romantic base of his vision.

Forster's special place in literary history depends not merely on his achievement in fiction but also on a career spent in defense of humane values. His political and historical and critical essays and books are never narrow or parochial, solemn or dogmatic. They are always informed by a large and urbane perspective, by a quality that can best be defined as wisdom.

Forster faced the dangers and difficulties of his time with uncommon courage and sensitivity. Hence, he continues to function as a moral presence, and his liberal humanism, expressed with such disarming honesty and touching conviction, remains a viable faith. (pp. 357-58)

Claude J. Summers, in his E. M. Forster, *Frederick Ungar Publishing Co., 1983, 406 p.*

STEPHEN SPENDER

Members of my literary generation first met E. M. Forster in the early 1930s. Before this, while we were undergraduates, he was a legend to us. ***Howards End*** seemed one of those books that make each reader a unique discoverer of its partly realistic, partly symbolic world. It was a novel of scrupulous prose realism about poetic reality, and contained hidden clues to the meaning of life. Although about human tragedy, it also seemed a guide to values that led to happiness. It was a key.

It was difficult to believe that Forster's first novels were published between 1905 and 1910. When each of us, independently of the others, met Forster, it seemed even more difficult to associate the man with the work that we admired and yet felt was as remote from him as from us. He seemed to stand in the foreground at the edge of the plain of his whole life, which stretched back beyond the mountain range of the world war. In the furthest distance was a little compact four-peaked cluster of four novels, the highest peak of which was ***Howards End*** (1910)—a book that met with such resounding success when it appeared that, disconcertingly, Forster felt almost finished as a novelist by it. He thought he would never write another novel, and indeed did not do so until he wrote ***A Passage to India*** (1924), which everyone seemed to think would be his last.

A sign of being received into the inner circle of friends whom he trusted was when Forster sent one the typescript of his then unpublishable novel ***Maurice.*** This had the significance for him of having the subject—homosexuality—which concerned him greatly in his own life and about which he most wanted to write. It seemed to me strangely thin and one-dimensional, more like an extended version of one of his idyllic, wishful-dreaming short stories than like any other of his novels. . . .

If his fiction seemed to belong to its time, Forster himself seemed to belong to ours. His novels were in the past tense, he was wholly in the present. This was partly so because he was unassuming, unself-important—not that he did not realize that he was Forster, the man (first), author of the *oeuvre* (a remote second). . . .

Reading P. N. Furbank's introduction to [***Selected Letters of E. M. Forster, Volume I: 1879-1920***] I found myself a bit puzzled by his remark that reading them "we must not expect . . . to trace the creator to his lair, or to find 'explanations' of his novels." If this is taken to mean that the letters throw no light on the novels or their creator at the time of creating, this seems exaggerated, to say the least. To take an obvious example, the letters from India (which are really journals sent home to be read by the circle of family and friends) set down the impressions of India and Indians that form the background to ***A Passage to India.***

The letters do, however, leave the impression of there being a gulf between the novelist and the letter writer, not as though they were different beings but as though they were not synchronized, on different but parallel timetables. . . . Between 1910 and 1912, when the "novelist" Forster had already written his four early novels, which could be the complete body of work by a mature writer, the "man" seems almost a boy undergoing an extensive period of self-education. . . .

After leaving Cambridge University in 1901, he settled down to sharing a house with his mother, with whom he also traveled in Italy. In 1905 he went to Nassenheide in Germany to become tutor to the daughters of the Countess von Arnim-Schlagentin, the Australian-born author of a famous book, *Elizabeth and Her German Garden*. He wrote amusing letters to his mother and to Cambridge friends describing his life in provincial Germany. The letters in fact contain many scenes of the socially observing kind that make his novels high entertainment. It is exceptional for the young Forster to offer at any length literary opinions. . . . (p. 31)

There are marvelous passages in Forster's letters but, on the evidence of those contained in this volume, he cannot be ranked as one of the "great" letter writers. One reason for this may be that he does not like the idea of "greatness" anyway (except in the work of Dante, Shakespeare, Michelangelo, and Beethoven). His letters are not like those, say, of Keats, who runs in pursuit of his own poetic genius more than he keeps within the measure of comprehension of his set of friends in Hampstead. Forster is an egalitarian correspondent—always mindful of the limitations of his recipients' concerns and interests—never putting across on them the fact that he is a genius.

Forster is, indeed, so conscious of the person to whom he is writing that often his letters absorb something of that person's character. Letters to his mother seem to swim in vast reservoirs of intelligent but discreet intimacy. He is always worrying about her ailments. He keeps up the role of the very amusing only son in a household without a father. With the poet and scholar R. C. Trevelyan he writes as a colleague and fellow writer. But surely underneath this is an awareness that Trevelyan is a bit obtuse, though Forster accepts his criticism of his novels with grace.

Forster the novelist appears in very few of these letters. Forster the son, nephew, friend is an assiduous correspondent. Forster the man pursuing his own psychological and sexual salvation is a shy but very determined creature who puts in intermittent appearances—with increasing desperation as he grows older. . . .

The tone of the letters alters entirely as soon as Forster sets foot in India in September 1912. This is partly no doubt because his letters from India form a journal for his mother and were intended to be circulated among various other relations ("a haze of aunts"). They were too, to be kept for him to read on his return. They are essentially background notes of a most lyrical kind for ***A Passage to India,*** which he could not bring himself to write until twelve years later and which is above all a hymn to "personal relations" between himself and Indians, and a lament at their destruction by power, empire, officialdom, police—in a word the British Raj. It corresponds in Forster's work perhaps to another passionate, loving, and lamenting paean—Rilke's *Duino Elegies*. (pp. 31-2)

Perhaps the letter most revealing of Forster's tragic sense during the First World War that all that was innocent, sensual, beautiful in the life of personal relations would be destroyed by the impersonal forces of the war is one to Lowes Dickinson, dated July 28, 1916, when Forster was unhappily working in Egypt as a member of the Red Cross. . . . What strikes Forster more and more as the war goes on is the contrast between the public obsession with power and conquest and the private values of human personality which ought to be but are not capable of overcoming the public world. . . . The peculiar kind of persistence, carried on with the force of genius of Forster, is constantly to measure the powerlessness of the people and values that he cares for—and that he carries around as his own private and personal self meeting the selves of others—against the destructive forces of the world of nationhood and power politics. In these letters we read his own struggle, as a man and not as the novelist, to achieve fulfillment. The letters take us up to the point where at the age of thirty-eight he had sex, under slightly squalid circumstances, with a soldier. And later there was the worker on an Egyptian tram with whom he was in love. The reader may think such fulfillment a slightly comic anticlimax. But the anticlimax, one might suggest, was of the very essence of Forster's climax.

At any rate that could be true of the man, as distinct from the novelist. And perhaps the story of the man was only a distorted shadow cast on a wall, in Cambridge or Alexandria, of the novelist who was the genius. (pp. 32-3)

Stephen Spender, "Forster's Shadow," in The New York Review of Books, *Vol. XXXI, No. 8, May 10, 1984, pp. 31-3.*

LOUIS MENAND

E. M. Forster had two careers, one as the author of ***Where Angels Fear to Tread*** (1905), ***The Longest Journey*** (1907), ***A Room with a View*** (1908), ***Howards End*** (1910), and ***A Passage to India*** (1924), and a second, rather longer one, as the man who had written those books. If we consider the standards by which character is measured in the novels—of tolerance without insincerity, principle without program, sentimentality without nonsense—we can appreciate a little the size of the job Forster faced in living up to them. [The letters in ***Selected Letters of E. M. Forster, Volume One: 1879-1920*** and ***Volume Two: 1921-1970***] are part of the record of his success.

Forster was a case of arrested development. The phrase has a patronizing and pejorative sound, and it is certainly reductive, but of course if the development has been arrested at the right point, it describes a kind of virtue, and not an easy one. When Forster emerged around the time of the Second World War as an exemplary figure for such younger writers as Auden and Isherwood and Lionel Trilling, he did so as an unreconstructed champion of values the First World War was supposed to have made obsolete. Nor is the phrase unfair to Forster's view of himself. "Development" was one of the modern slogans he distrusted most. He declined requests, in interviews about his own work, to discuss his "development as a writer," and he began his lectures on ***Aspects of the Novel*** (published in 1927) by advising his listeners to ignore bothersome questions about the evolution of the genre, or the influence of one writer on another, by imagining all novelists to be seated in one circular room, writing their novels simultaneously—a conceit the audience of Cambridge dons and their spouses apparently found delightful, and which other commentators have usually found perverse.

But perversity of this sort was a hallmark of Forster's brand of liberal humanism. The liberalism asks that behavior not be judged without a sympathetic understanding of its circumstances, but the humanism assures that in the end circumstances are never an excuse, for in what is most important people are the same. In the case of Forster's criticism, what was most important were the requirements of art; in the case of everything else in his life, it was the requirements of friendship. Those were things, in his view, that did not "develop." (p. 30)

The editors of these volumes have had the job of choosing from some 15,000 letters, and their selection has naturally involved sacrifices. The edition is valuable for increasing the number of Forster's letters that can be seen without trips to the libraries and private collections where they are stored. Whether this makes the volumes valuable to other, less scholarly sorts of readers—whom they are certainly aimed to attract—is another matter.

There are some delightful moments, such as Forster's letter to the D. H. Lawrences after a particularly harrowing visit, during which he had been subjected to a session of double-barreled Lawrentian est-training. . . .

And there are the anecdotes of his visits to the ancient Thomas Hardy. . . .

But there is something lacking, due in part to the nature of the project, and in part, I think, to its execution. Forster conceived of letters as a mode of conversation. He usually has his correspondent's latest letter before him as he writes, so that we often feel, reading the letters now, that in hearing only Forster's half of the conversation we are missing what made it precious to his original auditor. And having this sense of obligation to his correspondent, he is usually concerned to present the experiences he is describing in a way that will amuse, and not alarm, his reader. This is especially true of the letters home from India, and many of them are consequently bemusing (not, usually, amusing); but one feels that there is a dimension missing. (p. 31)

It is on the literary side that I think a real chance has been missed, and some of the editorial choices do not, from what I know of Forster, make sense to me. Forster's friendship with Virginia Woolf is something that will interest most casual readers of these letters. One of its rockier—and from the perspective of literary history, more important—moments concerned Woolf's review of ***Aspects of the Novel.*** (His letter to her began: "Your article inspires me to the happiest repartee"; hers to him began: "I'm not particularly inspired to repartee by your letter.") But Forster's letter is not included. The other Lawrence—T. E.—was a man much admired by Forster, who wrote him a long letter, the best of his on a literary subject I have seen, about *The Seven Pillars of Wisdom,* in which he points out what the book's pathos owes to Walter Pater, and cautions Lawrence not to be so severe on his style. . . . The letter, though it is mentioned in a note, is not included.

I assume a decision was made not to consider letters to the editor, but some are among Forster's best. One misses particularly the exchange in *The Nation* and *Athenaeum* with T. S. Eliot at the time of D. H. Lawrence's death. . . . Readers of ***A Passage to India*** who want to know about Forster's experiences at the court of that fantastic character the Maharajah of Dewas will need to get Forster's ***The Hill of Devi,*** where his letters from that year are printed. Considerations of space, it is explained, have kept them out of this edition. This is reasonable, but it makes the volumes more like a warehouse and less like a display of treasures. And finally: Forster's first sexual relationship, and in many ways his most touching and remarkable, was with a young Egyptian tram conductor named Mohammed el Adl, whom he met while working in Alexandria during the First World War. Mohammed died, of tuberculosis, in May 1922; a few months later, Forster began a long letter to his dead friend, which he continued for a number of years. I suppose that such a "letter" is really a diary, and it may be that there are bars to its publication I am unaware of. But it seems a shame that in the case of a writer for whom human contacts were the staff of life some portion of such a tribute should not appear among the record of his friendships. (p. 32)

Louis Menand, "Aspects of the Man," in The New Republic, *Vol. 192, No. 12, March 25, 1985, pp. 30-2.*

JOHN DRUMMOND

There is a splendid irony in the appearance of the second volume of Forster's ***Selected Letters*** in the same month as the film of ***A Passage to India,*** for we can now read the much-quoted letter to Santha Ramu Rau, author of the stage adaptation, which begins: 'I didn't and don't want ***A Passage*** filmed.' There is to me no contradiction in Forster accepting an adaptation for the stage but not for the cinema, since the necessary limitations of the theatre prevented the play from pretending to solve the mystery at the heart of the book. . . . He rightly believed that a film version would find it impossible to be so unspecific, and that what the book was trying to achieve, on a larger scale, would be diminished. As letter after letter shows, he was sharply critical of his own writings; but in 1937 he wrote to Christopher Isherwood that ***A Passage to India*** was not only 'my best book' but, a crucial addition, 'the one most likely to do good'. Few would disagree, except perhaps those millions who will now see a film that, even with the best intentions, somehow manages to miss the point.

Today, 15 years after his death, Forster ought to be at the bottom of the critical trough that always follows the disappearance of a highly praised writer. Indeed, I suspect that he is less often read these days than invoked. But for someone of my generation who was hugely influenced by his attitudes, before knowing anything about the man or his life, his importance remains incontestable. Recent years have, through P. N. Furbank's biography and the accounts of Forster in the memoirs or biographies of a hundred others, revealed the whole man, in a way that leaves him fully exposed but quite unsullied by exposure.

In many ways, the personal revelations have deepened the mystery of the novels. Their poise and control seem the more remarkable, given the now public evidence of his own emotional immaturity and uncertainty. Of course, his style has dated—he knew it himself. . . . However, his moral or, rather, ethical stance, even if unfashionable in our abrasive times, seems to me as secure as ever and as necessary.

A new reader today, coming on Forster for the first time, possessing not only the novels, short stories and essays, but also the biography and the letters, could, in the current mood of amateur psychiatric interpretation, ask whether his hatred of prejudice and snobbery did not perhaps have its roots in the familiar aspect of so many upper-middle-class English homosexuals, who find people of other classes or colour more stimulating than their peers. The cynic has been heard to ask whether Forster loved mankind—or only working-class men. Did he understand India, or merely seek to comprehend the society of Indians he loved? After all, how could so clear-eyed a moralist put up with the rackety lives of so many of his close friends? The answers to these objections and the proof of their irrelevance is to be found in the letters. (p. 19)

One is sometimes daunted by the sense of perfect manners. There is never a trace of grandeur, let alone vulgarity. No writing for effect, but many telling phrases, much humour and, inevitably, a hint of prissiness. But so contemporary are Forster's preoccupations that it is hard to remember that the firm hand still writing in the 1960s was educated in the 1880s and 1890s. It is hardly surprising, then, that he retained some of the social conventions of his turn-of-the-century milieu, however shocking to them his subject-matter would have appeared.

What I find so memorable is the sense of his actively striving through his perception of people and places to understand attitudes or ideas that the majority of his contemporaries rejected as worthless or irrelevant. For him, the foreign was fascinating; the difference demanded study and understanding; Perhaps his own sense of differentness as a homosexual encouraged his sympathy for other outsiders; but the interest came first, and went far beyond the purely personal. Did he really understand India? It isn't a real question. His approach allowed him to write about India with all its mysteries, without patronage or pompousness, without imperial echoes or Christian hang-ups, but with a deeply humanistic belief in the value of otherness. This is surely, also, what makes the portraits of women in his fiction so memorable. (pp. 19-20)

So here is Forster revealed. There can't now be much left to know or discover. While I greatly admire the thorough and meticulous editing of the letters, I am still glad to have read the novels before I knew so much about the man. Not because knowing has in any way diminished the writer, but because a great writer remains in some unfathomable way so much more than the sum of his acts. In the last analysis, what Forster did is merely interesting; but what he stood for matters, and matters as much today as when he first found words to describe it. (p. 20)

John Drummond, "What Forster Stood for Matters, and Matters as Much Today," in The Listener, *Vol. 113, No. 2906, April 25, 1985, pp. 19-20.*

JOHN BEER

Would Forster have enjoyed seeing ***A Passage to India*** as a film? He wrote more than once to Santha Rama Rau refusing permission, but he had allowed her to produce a truncated version for the stage, so that his opposition cannot have been absolute. He seems rather to have feared what would happen to any script he approved, what kind of parody might be produced for a mass audience. He might have jibbed at the beauty of the current film version (he did not remember India as particularly beautiful) and he would certainly have objected to the ending, which is more like the "bridging" conclusion he hoped for when he first drafted the novel; he went on thinking about his characters, however, and would no doubt have enjoyed the opportunity to see actors who made some of them appear more intelligent than he had done.

The letters in [***Selected Letters of E. M. Forster, Volume Two: 1921-1970***] show him continually seeing his novel from different points of view, both during the composition and afterwards. He soon becomes aware that his old view of fiction is under strain. Until the First World War he thought that the novelist could achieve a controlling vision, worked for throughout the fiction and ending in a harmonic close. Now he has come to see that relativism is triumphing, in literature as in life. If writing fiction comes to him less easily than it used to, that is partly because he now questions some of its conventions—for example "that one must view the action through the mind of one of the characters; and say of the others 'perhaps they thought', or at all events adopt their view-point for a moment only". More than that, he thinks that novelists must recapture their interest in death—an interest which is preoccupying him because he finds his own emotions so often out of proportion with what he would have expected to feel. In letters and journals he returns to this question repeatedly, aggrieved that the difference death makes is always unpredictable in advance. . . .

Once the novel was completed he thought it rather good and the sales were reassuring, but he could not help noticing that its success was primarily political. Perhaps he had been at fault in his decision "to show that India is an unexplainable muddle by introducing an unexplained muddle—Miss Quested's experience in the cave''—which he now thought involved ''some confusion between the dish and the dinner''. (p. 569)

After such an extraordinary achievement of alternating discourses, where was he to turn? Not to total scepticism, certainly. Even in the caves, it will be noticed, Forster still restricts the possibilities to three. And that kind of ordered uncertainty is a key to everything that follows. His letters, too, pursue different modes, according to the correspondent. One, the homosexual, has the added barriers of a secrecy imposed by society. Otherwise he is sometimes the dutiful and affectionate son and nephew, sometimes the protesting liberal moralist, sometimes (most disconcertingly of all) a totally candid reporter of intimate feelings as demanded by the Bloomsbury Memoir Club. He could easily have rested in the first and second positions, tearing up his journals and erotic fictions, retaining the status that his public writings gave him, leaving no more than rumours of his private life. It was important to him, however, that those who were interested should be left with all the facts. When T. E. Lawrence was reading his work he sent him the proofs of ***Aspects of the Novel,*** the unpublished ***Maurice*** and **"Doctor Woolacott"**, commenting, "these are items which you must have in your mind if you wish to sum me up''. He was delighted when Lawrence liked the latter short story, where he felt that he had come as close as he would ever do to joining up his fragments and achieving—however momentarily—a unified voice.

The editors' method in this collection involves choosing the letters which say the best things, while omitting a number that have already been published. This brings out Forster's diversity of interests. . . . He is at his best when his position is askance and slightly damping, as when he tries to convince his friends that the best way of getting through the Second World War is to remember the trials of one's school-days, or when he speculates that the ''meek'' who are blessed in the New Testament might simply be those who realize their own smallness in the universe. Sometimes the voice obtrudes more awkwardly, as when he resigns from the PEN Club following their association with a cruise to the grave of Rupert Brooke, or, more importantly, objects to the manner in which the wartime BBC is becoming a department of the Ministry of Information (a protest which helped the struggle to establish their independence at that time).

It is safer for a writer to present his or her public and published statements and leave posterity to judge. Once more vulnerable writings are known some critics will be swift to pounce. But as far as Forster was concerned this did not matter—all the more so because he would not be there to see. Just as in India he was dealing with a country which could not be held in the mind as a unity . . . so with his own experience—and with his writings as a whole. . . . There is a ruefulness here, but also, round the corner, a touch of mischief, answering to that spirit of comic irony in the world to which he was more responsive than most—the kind of comic irony that gave him, the most anti-authoritarian of writers, an erotic taste for uniforms, or, when he returned to India to find how it all was twenty years later, oppressed him with crowds who thought him important and sent him in a car for two hundred miles at the side of a very kind Englishman who never stopped humming Schubert. . . .

Forster does not rank with letter-writers such as Keats or D. H. Lawrence: not quite enough of him comes out at a time. This selection gives us isolated perceptions—which are also a range of sidelights on an unusually turbulent period in British culture. Read with Forster's other work they join up more than they do here; in this collection what emerges above all is Forster's extraordinary resilience, his ''alertness to what has not yet been experienced''—even in extreme old age. (p. 570)

John Beer, ''An Orderly Uncertainty,'' in The Times Literary Supplement, *No. 4286, May 24, 1985, pp. 569-70.*

RONALD BLYTHE

[***Selected Letters of E. M. Forster, Volume Two: 1921-1970***] throws many a beam upon the short stories.

There are 15 of these [in ***E. M. Forster: The New Collected Short Stories***]. Although Forster once saw the first novel, ***Howards End,*** as a movement away from his interest in the short story, he continued to write them, though never prolifically, into his seventies. Furbank rightly sees them as an important part of his *oeuvre* and **"The Road from Colonus"** as a major achievement. The repressive climate which held back publication of the later stories is, viewed in retrospect, more baffling than indignation-making. What disturbs us now is not the homosexuality but the class and racial feelings which are so essential to its excitement. When Forster is writing as a young Edwardian these feelings are sufficiently distanced for them not to set up too much of an anxiety in the late 20th century breast. The fact too that the natives in these early stories are Greeks or Italians makes us smile rather than smart. But the P. and O. cabin romp of golden Captain March and dusky Cocoa in **"The Other Boat"** is quite another matter. It isn't the lovemaking which makes one blush here, but the normal talk of his English *en route* to administer the Empire. Painfully, one recognises the vocabulary, the tone, the power, the reasonableness of death rather than a moral collision with such people. The stories, as Furbank says, are strewn with deaths. Forster is the master of sudden death and there is no hanging around. **"The Road from Colonus"**, his masterpiece here, is about unspiritual youngsters physically forcing an old man away from a spot where death would have taken him, swiftly and in the right company.

The first story (1904), **"The Story of a Panic"**, is chiefly interesting as Forster's contribution to the pantheistic fantasies of the time. Victorian poets having stocked the countryside with forsaken nature deities, it was up to early 20th century writers to send out their, usually, amoral, epigrammatic youths to encounter them. While there is more than a hint of Saki in Forster's tale, plus a pointer to Forrest Reid, the actual moment of fright is a brilliant description of the kind of fear which can send one running from a lonely, wild place. Something like this effect occurs in **"Other Kingdom"**, a story set in Forster's childhood Hertfordshire, when ''the rain hissed and rose up from the meadows like incense smoke, and smote the quivering leaves to applause''. Conservationist principles have to be extended in this account of a saved wood when Evelyn Beaumont turns into a tree. (pp. 8-9)

Forster likes to see the ground cut away by sexual passion between unequals, the Italian porter and the English lady, the handsome missionary and the native chieftain, the invalid squire and the young farmworker (the latter is a First World War ghost story which refuses to fudge the sexual issues which are so large a part of the genre), and this tale, **"Dr Woolacott"**, will no doubt represent him in many an anthology to come. Its economy and the emotions and ideas it sets up sharp paragraph by paragraph, are strangely compelling. A bad doctor does for two young friends, enabling them to possess each other for ever more. Forster's agnosticism allows him much play with the external, which for him is a state of human, not Christian love, if it exists at all. Apart from such high matters, he is, almost unconsciously, the great authority on English middle-class fuss. His characters are for ever demanding and requiring, and using themselves as yardsticks for the rest of mankind, no matter what his inclinations or culture. (p. 9)

Ronald Blythe, "Master of Sudden Death," in Books and Bookmen, *No. 356, June, 1985, pp. 8-9.*

JOSEPH EPSTEIN

How did E. M. Forster manage to elude the Nobel Prize in Literature? He published his last novel, ***A Passage to India,*** at the age of forty-five in 1924 and died at the age of ninety-two in 1970. He must have been passed over, then, no fewer than thirty or forty times. Not winning the Nobel Prize put him in a select little club, Tolstoy, Henry James, Chekhov, and Proust being among its most distinguished members—rather a more select club, when one thinks about it, than that comprised by the winners. Still, one wonders, did Forster think much about it? . . .

True, Forster's work is relatively unmarked by the rather strenuous thinking on the cosmic level that Nobel Prize committees seem traditionally to favor. Yet E. M. Forster has long held a special place in the hearts of English-speaking readers. He is the novelist par excellence of modern liberalism, and during a period when the liberal point of view has been ascendant. If he had won the Nobel Prize, it would scarcely have been a surprise. On the contrary, it is rather surprising in retrospect that he did not.

The complicated truth is that E. M. Forster was probably better off without the Nobel Prize. It would have been unseemly, even slightly unbecoming to him, a man who made something of a specialty of claiming so little for himself in the way of literary aspirations. But aspirations are one thing, reputation another. Forster's reputation has never been other than high. Even today it sails in the literary stratosphere. The most consistent note in the often strident criticism of David Lean's recent film version of ***A Passage to India,*** for example, has been that Lean betrayed the richness and subtlety of Forster's novel. What has been almost universally judged to be a poor film has thus redounded to Forster's posthumous standing.

Not that this standing required much in the way of reinforcement. Apart from his attempt to write a homosexual idyll in the posthumously published novel ***Maurice,*** Forster's work has received no serious attacks, and his reputation has remained oddly inviolate. During his lifetime it appeared that the less he wrote, the higher his reputation rose. (p. 48)

I have called E. M. Forster the novelist par excellence of modern liberalism, but I am not the first to have done so. Lionel Trilling did it as early as 1943 in a critical study that over the years has immensely aided E. M. Forster's reputation [see *CLC*, Vol. 1]. As Trilling allowed in a preface to the second edition of this book, his study had "benefited by the special energies that attend a polemical purpose." Trilling had been attacking American writing for what he deemed its "dullness and its pious social simplicities," and against this he now posed Forster's "vivacity, complexity, and irony." Like many of those writers Trilling had attacked, Forster was a liberal, but a liberal with a difference—he was a liberal, in Trilling's view, "at war with the liberal imagination." Forster was of the liberal tradition yet at the same time would have nothing to do with its simple solutions, its crudities, its sentimentality, and its earnest belief in rationalism. In other words, without losing his idealism neither did Forster lose his head; never for a moment did Forster settle for received opinions and indeed, according to Trilling, he even "refuses to be conclusive." Forster possessed—a crucial element, this, for Lionel Trilling—"moral realism," which Trilling defined as not only "the awareness of morality itself but of the contradictions, paradoxes, and dangers of living the moral life." (p. 49)

E. M. Forster's intellectual ability was not of the ordinary kind. He never felt he had any commanding power of abstract thought. . . . His were the powers of serene observation, often oblique but usually telling. He had quiet wit and a lyrical streak and imaginative sympathy. He had a lucid mind and had early acquired a prose style of unobtrusive elegance that permitted him to state profound things with simplicity. In Forster, intellect united with sensibility, and their tethering in tandem produced the artist that, at Cambridge, he knew he would become. (p. 51)

Evelyn Waugh once remarked that most writers, even quite good ones, have only one or two stories to tell. The exceptions are the truly major figures; Balzac, Dickens, George Eliot, Tolstoy, James, Conrad. But E. M. Forster, I don't think many would wish to dispute, is not among their number. He was a one-story man. His is the story of the undeveloped heart. He told it four different times, then set it in India and told it again. In this story a character—an English man or woman of the middle class—is placed in a crucial situation, crucible of the spirit as it turns out, where his or her heart either develops or permanently stultifies. This crucible invariably entails a confrontation with the primitive, or the pre-literate, or the *déclassé*. In all Forster's novels culture is pitted against spirit, mind against feeling. It takes no deep reader to recognize that the author, though himself a habitué of the concert hall and of suburban teas upon English lawns, is on the side of spirit and feeling.

A paradigmatic E. M. Forster story is **"The Road from Colonus,"** a tale written when he was in his twenties. In it a group of English travelers are touring by mule in Greece. Mr. Lucas, the oldest member of the group, comes upon an enormous plane tree near a rather squalid Greek house. The center of the tree is hollowed out, and from it water flows, which irrigates and makes fertile the land below. The tree is a shrine from which little votive offerings hang. The sight of the tree stirs Mr. Lucas, who climbs into its hollow, the water flowing about him. In it he feels overpoweringly the urge to live. . . . He feels himself utterly at peace—"the feeling of the swimmer, who, after long struggle with chopping seas, finds that after all the tide will sweep him to his goal."

At which moment his daughter and the remainder of the party of English travelers arrive. They exclaim over the beauty of the tree, the crude little Greek dwelling, the entire scene. But Mr. Lucas "found them intolerable. Their enthusiasm was superficial, commonplace, and spasmodic." When Mr. Lucas announces that he plans to remain there, to stay as a guest in the house of the Greeks, his daughter and the members of the party humor him. . . . But of course he cannot be permitted to stay in any such place. In the end he is dragged off, brusquely set upon his mule by their guide. It is not to be.

In the second part of the story Mr. Lucas and his daughter are back in England. He is complaining about the disorderly behavior of their neighbor's children. She has just received a parcel from Athens containing asphodel bulbs, wrapped up in an old Greek newspaper. It happens that the newspaper carries a story about a small tragedy that occurred in the province of Messenia, where a large tree blew down in the night and crushed to death the occupants of a nearby house. It is of course the same tree and the same house from which Mr. Lucas had been forcibly removed. Now, in England, he is not much interested in the story. His daughter remarks upon what a near miss they have had. Had he stayed in the house as he wished, he might well have been killed, too. But Mr. Lucas is scarcely listening. Instead he rambles on about his neighbors and composes a letter of complaint to their landlord. "Such a marvelous deliverance," says his daughter, "does make one believe in Providence." But in fact Mr. Lucas had to all intents and purposes died the moment he had been dragged away; his heart had shriveled from that very moment and from that very moment, too, he had been consigned to live out his days in middle-class English suburban sterility.

To dwell on **"The Road from Colonus"** a bit longer, one grants Forster his concluding point: yes, it would have been better to have died happy, even that very night, in the rough-hewn Greek house, feeling oneself in touch with the spirit of the world, than to live out one's days a grumbly, grousing old man. That is conceded. What is less easy to concede is the validity of Mr. Lucas's mystical experience in the tree and the wisdom of the Greek family, who, however squalid the conditions of their lives, had never lost the gift of living in nature and hence had retained the secret of the art of life. Clearly, Forster hated middle-class life, the sterility of its culture, the aridity of its relationships, but all he could pose against it was the superiority of those who, through whatever accidents of geography or social class, eluded it.

For an otherwise remarkably subtle novelist, E. M. Forster could be remarkably crude in his division of characters into those who either were or were not in touch with life. In the middle were those characters whose personal drama—supplying the drama of his novels—revolved around the question of on which side they would fall. Like many another artist and intellectual of his day, Forster suffered the condition known as horror victorianus; in his novels villains and villainesses are, not very far under the skin, uneminent Victorians: people who believe in progress, empire, the virtues of their social class. As he presents them they are not so much cardboard as metallic; they continually give off sharp pings of their author's disapproval.

Nor did Forster have great powers of invention. All his novels are marred by unbelievable touches. Rickie Elliot in ***The Longest Journey*** falls in love with his wife-to-be when he sees her being passionately kissed by her fiancé; a bookcase topples onto the pathetic culture-hungry Leonard Bast in the crucial scene in ***Howards End;*** Lucy Honeychurch is kissed by George Emerson in a field of spring flowers in Italy, which is noted by a female novelist who later publishes a novel reproducing the scene, which causes a scandal that in turn forces the action in ***A Room With a View;*** a carriage crashes, killing a kidnapped infant in ***Where Angels Fear to Tread;*** characters regularly die on the instant ("Gerald died that afternoon," is an inspissated but not anomalous sentence in a Forster novel). I do not mean that such things don't happen in life, which provides the trickiest plots of all, but in Forster's novels there is a herky-jerky quality to his plots. If one of the things masterful novelists do is to make the unpredictable seem inevitable, in Forster the unpredictable tends to be expected, which is not at all the same thing. (pp. 54-5)

[If] E. M. Forster had few cards in his hand, he could nonetheless shuffle them brilliantly. He was an astute judge of character and a potent moralist, in the French sense of the word. Of Mr. Wilcox in ***Howards End,*** for example, he writes: "But true insight began just where his intelligence ended, and one gathered that this was the case with most millionaires." Adela Quested in ***A Passage to India*** fails to realize "that it is only hypocrites who cannot forgive hypocrisy." Forster's novels are studded with such small gems. Quite as much as for their action—perhaps rather more than for their action—one anticipates Forster's aphoristic commentary upon his characters.

In his book on Forster Lionel Trilling remarks that "in Forster there is a deep and important irresolution of whether the world is one of good and evil, sheep and goats, or one of good-and-evil, of sheep who are somehow goats and goats who are somehow sheep." Trilling refers here to Forster's propensity in his novels to allow good actions occasionally to derive from characters of whom he otherwise disapproves, and, going the other way 'round, to impute qualities of which he clearly disapproves to characters he clearly wishes us to admire. (p. 55)

Such curious turnings in character can lend Forster's novels verisimilitude, though sometimes, as in Charlotte Bartlett's radical turning to the side of good in ***A Room With a View,*** it can be quite unconvincing. But Trilling is at least partially correct in averring that E. M. Forster did not resolve the question of good and evil in his novels. I say partially because, with the exception of ***A Passage to India,*** I do not believe it loomed as a large problem for him. Forster seemed not to be greatly perplexed by questions of good and evil and of the meaning of life. He thought, within his own set limits, he knew life's meaning. As Mr. Emerson, one of Forster's guru characters in ***A Room With a View*** says, "Passion is sanity"; and it is he who shows Lucy Honeychurch, the heroine of the novel, "the holiness of direct desire."

The only novel of Forster's in which obeisance to the instinctual life is not central is his most famous novel, ***A Passage to India.*** It is, interestingly enough, the novel Lionel Trilling liked least. . . . Certainly, as Forster himself felt, ***A Passage to India*** is the best-made of his novels: the most elegantly written, in some ways the most filled with wise comment—it is the only one of his novels written when he was in his forties—and the most solidly organized. At the center of the novel is that grand old favorite of symbol-hunting English professors, the scene at the Marabar Caves which Forster, it transpires, allowed that he had fuddled. Of this scene he wrote to William Plomer: "I tried to show that India is an unexplainable muddle by introducing an unexplained muddle—Miss Quested's experience in the cave. When asked what happened there, *I don't know*." Still, muddle and fuddle, the novel is an impressive piece of work. . . .

So long has ***A Passage to India*** held the status of a modern classic that writing about it today one feels almost as if called to comment upon *The Rite of Spring* or *Sunday Afternoon on the Grande Jatte*. Rereading it after more than a quarter of a century, one is struck by how interesting a portrait it provides of the Indian character as viewed by Western eyes. One is also struck by its streak of unfairness. At various points in the novel it is difficult to determine which Forster felt more strongly: his love of India or his hatred of England's presence there. He gives the Anglo-Indians very short shrift, so short that there can be no doubt about his having taken sides. . . .

Books are created in history, and through the events of history is our reading of them influenced. Here it must be noted that history has dissipated much of the glory of ***A Passage to India,*** by revealing that the treatment of the Indians by the British had been nowhere nearly so cruel, indeed murderous, as the treatment of the Indians by one another, beginning with the massacres following upon independence and continuing even today with the bloody dispute between the Indian government and the Sikhs.

E. M. Forster probably never thought himself a very political writer. He tended, in fact, to think himself rather above politics. . . . To be above politics, to be seeking only truth, is ever the plaint of the emancipatory liberal. E. M. Forster, it is well to remember, was the author of a novel (***Maurice***) he could not publish and for the better part of his life was enmeshed in homosexual relationships he could not openly declare. The truth he sought was of a particular kind; it presupposed freedom. For him, indeed, without freedom, again of a particular kind, there could be no truth. And the particular kinds, both of truth and of freedom, were at their base political. (p. 56)

[The] novels upon which E. M. Forster's reputation rests now seem chiefly screens for their author's yearning for freedom for his own trapped instinctual life. He wrote about men and women, often commenting upon them brilliantly, yet other things must all the while have been at the forefront of his mind.

What these other things were are revealed less in the sadly sentimental novel ***Maurice*** than in a collection of posthumously published stories entitled ***The Life to Come.*** These are stories about the suppression of homosexuality and about giving way to it, about its costs so long as society disapproves of it and its pleasures nonetheless. One of them, **"Dr. Woolacott,"** T. E. Lawrence, to whom Forster showed it, thought the best thing he had ever written. Another, **"The Obelisk,"** has a touch of nastiness one would not have expected from the great proponent of personal relations. In it a husband and wife on holiday meet up with two sailors also on holiday. To make a short story even shorter, one sailor goes off into the bushes with the wife while, though we do not know this until the end, the other sailor has gone off into other bushes with the husband. It is arch and cruel, a stereotypical homosexual mocking of marriage, which is no prettier than heterosexual mocking of homosexuality. "Only connect," Forster famously wrote in an epigraph to ***Howards End.*** Indeed.

What ***The Life to Come*** along with the ***Selected Letters*** and P. N. Furbank's biography all conduce to make plain is that in E. M. Forster the emancipatory liberal appears to have hidden a homosexual utopian. Ironically, the victories of emancipatory liberalism, issuing in the breakdown of censorship and with it the freedom to know and publish hitherto private facts of writers' lives, have resulted in our having to reassess E. M. Forster's novels radically. It is no longer possible to think of Forster as a writer who happened to have been a homosexual; now he must be considered a writer for whom homosexuality was the central, the dominant, fact in his life. Given this centrality, this dominance, it hardly seems wild to suggest that the chief impulse behind Forster's novels, with their paeans and pleas for the life of the instincts, was itself homosexual. Given, again, all that we now know about his private life, it is difficult to read them otherwise.

In a curious way the effect of this is to render E. M. Forster's novels obsolete, and in a way that art of the first magnitude never becomes. Filled with wisdom though all of his novels are at their peripheries, ornamented though all of them are by his lucid and seductive style, at their center each conducts an argument. E. M. Forster was essentially a polemical and didactic novelist. He argued against the sterility of middle-class English life, he attempted to teach the beauty of the passionate instinctive life. In the first instance, he wrote out of his personal antipathies; in the second, out of his personal yearnings.

Viewed from the present, it can be said that in large part Forster won his argument. An English and vastly more sophisticated Sinclair Lewis (a writer whom Forster himself admired), with a sexual and spiritual twist added, he has, in his quiet way, been one of the most successful of those who in our time have written *pour épater les bourgeois*. As for his teaching about the instinctual life—the sanity of passion, the holiness of desire, and the rest of it—here, too, his side, that of emancipatory liberalism, has known no shortage of victories. If, then, his writing today seems so thin, so hollow, and finally so empty, can it be in part because we have now all had an opportunity to view the progress of emancipationism in our lifetimes, the liberation that was the name of Forster's own most ardent desire, and know it to be itself thin, hollow, and finally empty? (p. 57)

Joseph Epstein, "One Cheer for E. M. Forster," in Commentary, *Vol. 80, No. 3, September, 1985, pp. 48-57.*

STEPHEN SPENDER

In 1924 E. M. Forster found in the house in Surrey that he had inherited from an aunt, and where he was himself to live for over 20 years, a very large leather-bound notebook. This turned out to be a present from John Jebb, Bishop of Limerick—who had bought it in 1804—to his chaplain, Forster's grandfather. John Jebb intended to use it as a commonplace book but had only made entries (mostly in Latin and Greek) filling 18 of its 400 pages.

Forster, then 46, wrote in the flyleaf, "Continued it at Abinger Hammer, Wednesday October 21, 1925, E. M. Forster." . . .

Following Jebb's example, Forster starts off [***Commonplace Book***] by arranging it under headings of topics; but after discussing "isolation" and "resentment" he abandons this plan (though he does, intermittently, discuss various topics later on), deciding simply to put down "whatever I like." What he in fact puts down for the next 20 pages is his thoughts about the novel, in preparation for the Clark Lectures he would give at Cambridge in 1927, later published under the title ***Aspects of the Novel.*** He comments on, and quotes extensively from, *Tristram Shandy* and *Moll Flanders,* among other novels, and discusses their authors. Interestingly, he hates Jonathan Swift. Much of this book is taken up with similar notes and quotes dealing with novels, poems and plays and their authors: Dryden, Pope, Corneille, Samuel Johnson, Coleridge, Kipling, the church fathers (St. Augustine and St. Jerome). All these, and several others, are analyzed and discussed with the intelligence and style of a writer who throughout his adult life was a superlatively perceptive student and a professional writer learning from other professionals, never self-consciously a "critic."

The quotations are very revealing and the comments often pearls. . . .

Adoring literature, Forster is nevertheless extremely suspicious of people who are "literary" and has great reserves of admiration for the more or less unlettered who just live their lives. Things that people say in the street, on buses, at tables next to his in restaurants, are quoted side by side with paragraphs from the great masters. He judges his own life by standards of nonliterary living, as he also judges other people. This is admirable, yet in interpreting behavior he sometimes gives the impression that he is the one-man member of a club for which he has invented all the rules. Although he is affectionate toward literary and academic colleagues, the only people for whom he has unqualified admiration are an Egyptian tram driver and a London policeman, with both of whom he was in love.

Forster praises excellence in the literary work, but at the same time he keeps separate his judgments of the work and the writer. He casts terrible doubts on writers who console themselves by thinking that they will attain salvation as human beings for the anguish of their lives through the life-transforming achievement of their literature. He rejects such consolation also for himself. . . .

[***Commonplace Book***] is perhaps primarily about his inability during the whole 40 years it covers to create any important work of fiction. (***A Passage to India*** was published in 1924.) Inseparable from this is the theme of getting older and older.

Soon after he is 50 he is beginning to detect in his minding about the death of trees the symptoms of old age; and as the book goes on he becomes ever more aware of decrepitude, leading up to a coldly objective, almost scientific description of his physical appearance when seen naked in a mirror in old age.

Worse for him, though, than his own decline is his conviction that everything he most cares for in civilization, in individuals and in personal relationships is doomed by the ever-growing forces of power politics and by the destruction of the past and of nature. Already in the early 1930's he is beginning to feel that, although he supports the antifascist intellectuals against Hitler, the canalization of the energies of those who care about creation, individualism and personal relations into politics is a defeat for civilization; and he is certain that the world he cherishes will be lost if politics lead to war. . . .

As the book continues, Forster is more and more immersed in what Joseph Conrad in *Lord Jim* calls the "destructive element." But Conrad, it should be remembered, recommends such immersion as necessary to fortifying the human spirit, if it is capable of being fortified. And Forster, with his reading, his observing, his recording of incidents of friendship and sharp moments of hatred, his love for his friend Bob Buckingham, his humor, does gather together his resources, meeting the end he foresees from almost the first of his commonplaces. This is the record of the last 40 years of a very long life, one with an exceptionally long perspective—for Forster's world extends backward to 1905 at Cambridge University, and four of the novels on which his reputation is based were written before World War I.

His cry is that he is ineffective to prevent destruction—of a Europe of values that he cares for—of an England that is a network of green lanes. In the mouth of a more self-interested writer this might seem to express only petulance or impotence. But with him the sense of inadequacy has the kind of moral force it might have in the mouth of a Simone Weil or a George Orwell, because the integrity of the life of the human being—his behavior as such—remains separate and distinct from the importance he attaches to his achievement as an artist. Forster is speaking here for his own humanity, which he sees as identical with that of other human beings—even if these are only the chosen few—and not treating himself as a special case, that of the artist.

Stephen Spender, "Goodbye to Green Lanes," in The New York Times Book Review, *February 23, 1986, p. 11.*

CHAMAN L. SAHNI

Commonplace Book is a valuable record of Forster's intellectual, ethical, political, aesthetic, and personal concerns during the second half of his long career. As Philip Gardner points out in the introduction, "Parts of the first three-quarters of the ***Commonplace Book*** may be fruitfully set beside ***Aspects of the Novel*** and the polished essays collected in ***Abinger Harvest*** and ***Two Cheers for Democracy;*** its final quarter, a literary, aesthetic and spiritual diary, presents a picture of Forster available nowhere else." . . . (p. 100)

The picture of Forster, as it emerges here from his self-analysis, dreams, doubts, and comments on life and letters, reveals an intimate side of his mind and personality, in ironic contrast to his long-established public image of the humanist sage—liberal, serene, self-confident, gentle, kind, tolerant, demure, and idealistic. We discover a man antipathetic toward women, torn by doubts about his creative powers, haunted by the feelings of ineffectuality, displaced by war and industrialism, conscious of being drawn into lust and trivialities, preoccupied with physical decay and death, and sometimes uncharitable and malicious in his remarks on other writers.

Though Forster's career after ***A Passage to India*** took a notable turn toward the writing of non-fictional prose and criticism, the awareness of the decline in his creative powers runs like a leitmotif in the ***Commonplace Book.*** A 1927 entry reveals his interest in writing a "*middle-aged* novel," based on first-hand experiences of his life, but the thought of "How again [to] render this readable?" makes him abort the idea. . . . (pp. 100-01)

The book contains several pages of germinal notes for the Clark Lectures, published as ***Aspects of the Novel,*** and for another series of lectures Forster delivered at Cambridge in 1931. It is also filled with jokes, epigrams, poems, and letters by Forster and others. But above all, it is a rich compendium of quotations from a wide range of writers. Sometimes Forster copied out these quotations from other writers simply because "it is the best device known to me for taking one out of oneself." . . . His comments on these writers, interspersed with his reflections on literature, display a first-rate critical mind at work with sensitivity, penetration, and undiminished powers of perception and communication. There is hardly a page which is not animated by his brilliant wit, enduring insights, and the articulate beauty of his prose. This revealing and enlightening book is essential for all serious readers of Forster. (p. 101)

Chaman L. Sahni, in a review of "Commonplace Book," in Rocky Mountain Review of Language and Literature, *Vol. 40, Nos. 1-2, 1986, pp. 100-01.*

David (Emery) Gascoyne

1916-

English poet, translator, critic, memoirist, dramatist, novelist, short story writer, and editor.

Gascoyne is acknowledged as one of the leading English exponents of surrealism. Much of his best poetry, written during the 1930s and early 1940s, displays such affinities with the European Surrealist movement as the rejection of literary traditions, an emphasis on imagination over reason, and verbal automatism. With poet and sociologist Charles Madge and poet and documentary filmmaker Humphrey Jennings, Gascoyne later became associated with the technique of ''Mass-Observation.'' Eschewing the subjective approach characteristic of surrealism, the proponents of ''Mass-Observation'' made use of sociological and anthropological theories and employed images culled from the collective cultural subconscious. Gascoyne's subsequent verse is of a more visionary nature and has been likened to the mystical writings of Sören Kierkegaard and William Blake.

Gascoyne published a collection of poems, a novel, and a respected critical study before he was twenty years old. The pieces in his first book, *Roman Balcony and Other Poems* (1932), exhibit the influence of nineteenth-century aestheticism and often make use of imagist techniques. *Opening Day* (1933) is an autobiographical novel derived from Gascoyne's adolescent experiences. Perhaps the most impressive of Gascoyne's works from this period is *A Short Survey of Surrealism* (1935), which remains a standard source on the tenets of surrealism. This book, which includes translations of French imagist, dadaist, and surrealist poems, informs his second collection of verse, *Man's Life Is This Meat* (1936), considered by many critics to contain the best examples of surrealist poems written in English.

In the late 1930s, Gascoyne was briefly affiliated with Marxism and ''Mass-Observation.'' While living in Paris, he became friends with Pierre-Jean Jouve, a French poet and translator of the German romantic verse of Friedrich Hölderlin. *Hölderlin's Madness* (1938) is Gascoyne's reworking into English of Jouve's translations and also contains original poems by Gascoyne that connect the Hölderlin material. This digressive approach to translation was lauded by critics and inspired many to classify *Hölderlin's Madness* as an original work. The religious nature of Jouve's own writing enlightens Gascoyne's *Poems, 1937-1942* (1943), which contains several of Gascoyne's translations of Jouve's verse. This book also includes ''Miserere,'' a sequence comprising overtly Christian images and allusions that emphasize both the humane and prophetic natures of Jesus Christ, whom Gascoyne refers to as the ''Christ of Revolution and of Poetry.'' *A Vagrant and Other Poems* (1950), in similar fashion, features the sequence ''Fragments of a Religio Poetae,'' the aphoristic qualities of which resemble those in the visionary works of William Blake. Other poems in *A Vagrant* are noted for their stark representations of isolation and loneliness. *Night Thoughts* (1955), a verse play written for radio which is similar to Dylan Thomas's *Under Milk Wood* in form, depicts the quandaries confronted by contemporary civilization. *Collected Poems* (1956) serves to represent the various phases of Gascoyne's career as a poet. While some critics have faulted Gascoyne's poetry for its heavy reliance on external devices and its pervasive, somber tone, Derek Stanford noted that his verse displays ''the mark of a strong imagination, a fine verbal talent, stylistic impasto, and the constant impression of a deep feeling mind.''

Photograph by Frank Taylor. Courtesy of David Gascoyne.

While Gascoyne has produced little new poetry since his *Collected Poems,* the publication of *Paris Journal, 1937-1939* (1978) and *Journal, 1936-1937* (1980) has stimulated renewed interest in his career. Both volumes are respected for their insights into the poetic inspiration of a literary prodigy and for Gascoyne's impressions of the seminal figures of surrealism, ''Mass-Observation,'' and the ''Oxford Group'' of poets.

(See also *Contemporary Authors,* Vols. 65-68; *Contemporary Authors New Revision Series,* Vol. 10; and *Dictionary of Literary Biography,* Vol. 20.)

DEREK STANFORD

Unlike Walt Whitman and D. H. Lawrence—positive fundamentalists, poetic seekers who looked and found—Gascoyne stands out as a figure of negation, a poetic witness to the void within us all. This sense he possesses in a high degree; and his foremost contribution to our time is the feeling he has for those things we lack; the torturing knowledge of our insufficiency; the attrition of our spirit for want of grace in this universe where a god seems singularly absent.

While the Left Wing poets of the 'thirties were trying to preach Marx in verse to the people (but little interested in Marx and modern verse); while Laura Riding continued to publish her "strictly private" hieroglyphic ruminations; while William Empson and Ronald Bottrall were explaining their psychoses in terms of erudition, David Gascoyne was writing in a style whose syntax dispensed with the need for analysis; a style, for the most part, as sensuous and immediate as that of the great English Romantics.

It is true that for a while he immersed his expression in the bottomless well of Surrealism, and that he acquired from Rimbaud and Jouve a set of dark symbols and a lowering atmosphere which appear now as constant features in his work. This is not to say, though, that his attitude was false. What he has acquired has always been his; and sympathetic contact with the writing of others has merely served to precipitate delivery, to ignite the fuse already laid down.

Neither has his language fallen a prey to that obscurity which overtakes so many of Rimbaud's followers. He has not got lost in this subterranean land; and his meaning—even when darkest—is clearly expressed. Counterbalancing these passages of gloom are sudden occasional bursts of light, moments of magnesium intensity, day-spring visions in the crystal of words.

If Gascoyne never used the method and approach of the Left Wing poets of the 'thirties, it must not be thought that he stayed indifferent to the course of history between the two wars. In his verse we can read the symptoms of individual and communal uneasiness. We sense the uncertainty of living in a culture that has had its presentiments of doom; the frightful attraction and vertigo of those who dwell on the precipice of history.

In much of his later verse the reference to these events is direct; in his earlier verse it is allegoric; but always, inescapably, it is there. Thus the poetry of Gascoyne creates a world that is no escape from or substitute for the world we already know. All the problems reality makes us face, we face again in this poetry; and meeting them here for a second time we find them no longer modified by the small distractions of daily life, or the comic relief which existence offers. In this verse we are made to experience the total impact of wickedness—evil itself assumes an image. So, without mercy or mitigation, we are forced to look on this picture of our guilt and inhabit a sphere that seems to be sealed against the possible entry of hope. (pp. 41-2)

[Gascoyne's] work has reflected our gravest current problems—a poetry of question- and exclamation-marks. Along with such books as Djuna Barnes's *Nightwood,* the work of this poet may be viewed as a commentary and extension of *The Wasteland*—the subjective "Wasteland" of a conscript generation.

If the sentiment and thought of this poetry appears as specially adapted to the age, its language, at least, seems little determined by the latest contemporary fashions. Neither the styles of Thomas nor Auden have left the smallest mark upon it. Influenced, as far as imagery goes, by the example of Baudelaire and Rimbaud, by Eliot, Hölderlin, and Gérard de Nerval, the syntax is nearer to the English Romantics; to Wordsworth, Keats, and the Elizabethans. Especially does the language of Gascoyne belong to that of the great Romantic lineage in its use and combination of free and blank-verse. (p. 71)

A word must be said about the defects of this poet: namely, those of too often forcing the note. There is, for example, in many of his verses a somewhat melodramatic approach; the trace of a heavy underlining pencil; a powerful arc-light and saturnine pose. This urge leads Gascoyne, on occasions, to agonize his imagery; to attenuate and elongate his vision, as it were; producing a kind of willed El Greco verse. One of the symptoms of this hyperbole is the poet's fondness for what one may call the superlative mystery epithet: eg. "unfathomable", "insatiable", "impenetrable", "irreparable". "In the whole gamut of emotions there is no moment less advantageous than its topmost note . . . Beyond the top there is nothing more and nothing is left to arouse the imagination." So observed the critic Lessing: a remark whose relevance we often feel here.

To harp on this aspect, however, would be foolish. It is possible that certain artists can only attain to a full expression of their personality by such means. Their very excesses cleanse and free the imagination from which they draw. Perhaps, for example, in the sphere of music Tchaikovsky and Berlioz are cases in point. Without their emotional rhodomontade they would, no doubt, have been better musicians. They would, in addition, have been different men. Without applauding their faults, we must take them. Their merits are the compensation we receive. So it may be with David Gascoyne.

To conclude this account, let us recall the positive aspect of his gifts; everywhere the mark of a strong imagination, a fine verbal talent, stylistic impasto, and the constant impression of a deep feeling mind. (pp. 72-3)

Derek Stanford, "David Gascoyne," in his The Freedom of Poetry: Studies in Contemporary Verse, *The Falcon Press Limited, 1947, pp. 40-73.*

ELIZABETH JENNINGS

[David Gascoyne is the] only living English poet in the true tradition of visionary or mystical poetry. If David Gascoyne's work is not directly influenced by it, it does undoubtedly lead back to seventeenth-century religious verse such as that of Vaughan, Herbert, and Traherne. Yet his poetry is emphatically of this time and this place—concrete, rooted, exact; it takes the symbols and traditions of its own time and then transcends them.

David Gascoyne started publishing verse as a very young man. Much of his early work was surrealist in form and expression and greatly influenced by French writers of the time. . . . He has also written in French himself; I do not think, however, that he really found his own voice or his own individual means of expression until he started writing the poems which appeared in the volume entitled ***Poems 1937-42***. . . . (p. 567)

The prevailing themes in this book are war, suffering and the loneliness of modern man. These are the overt themes; beneath them, however, is the private voice seeking to express the poet's own struggle for meaning and for unity. The poems are profoundly Christian but, as Rouault, in modern times, has done with his paintings, David Gascoyne has revived and transformed the old symbols which bad 'religious art' so often renders lifeless, and displayed them, alive, in an entirely contemporary setting.

In the magnificent sequence of poems called **"Miserere"** which opens the book, the poet, in lines of extreme lucidity, examines the depths of man's guilt and the terror of life without God. The traditional 'dark night of the soul' is transferred to Christ himself—Christ who is both the victim and the conqueror. . . . The poet sees himself as a part of Christ, prepared to endure intolerable suffering and even to touch the edge of despair, but never finally to become hopeless.

In the second poem of the sequence, **"Pieta,"** the tough, lithe quality of David Gascoyne's language and imagery begins to display itself. The tenebral cry of anguish turns to a vision of the crucifixion: . . .

> The Mother, whose dead Son's dear head
> Weighs like a precious blood-incrusted stone
> On her unfathomable breast:
>
> Holds Him God has forsaken, Word made flesh
> Made ransom, to the slow smoulder of her heart
> Till the catharsis of the race shall be complete.

The last line of this poem shows the skill (except that 'skill' is too superficial a word) with which Gascoyne has involved the whole of mankind in the act of redemption and, in an entirely concrete way, has tethered past and future to the present moment. (pp. 567-69)

[The poem **"Sanctus"**] is the heart of the sequence. It shows more completely than any of the other poems that it is the poet's vision itself which sanctifies and radiates. The vision is the end not the means and, once it has been achieved, however fleetingly, it illuminates all things outside it while itself remaining locked in its own lyrical form and music.

"Ecce Homo" is a kind of coda to the whole sequence. It brings the passion and crucifixion down to human and contemporary terms; it refuses to ignore disgust and horror:

> Whose is this horrifying face,
> This putrid flesh, discoloured, flayed,
> Fed on by flies, scorched by the sun?
>
> Behold the Man: He is Man's Son.

(p. 570)

Terrifying as the subject of this sequence is, Gascoyne has handled it with a dexterity that never deteriorates into mere smoothness, and with an unremitting candour and clarity. His subject is confusion and despair, but his verse is easy and confident. The words embody the vision and the fact of being able to speak is itself a kind of small redemption.

The poems which follow **"Miserere"** in this volume deal with many subjects—light, landscape, music, the death of a friend—but even where Gascoyne is, on the one hand, most objective, or, on the other, most involved and personal, the mystical, visionary element is always present; if not in the lines, then between them. These poems are like brilliant chips splintered off a dazzling stone; they all come from, and belong to, the same thing, the same overriding preoccupation. In a poem which examines the idea of thought having 'a subtle odour', the poet moves, without any apparent straining, to a much deeper level of meaning:

> Nostalgic breezes: And it's then we sense
> Remote presentiment of some intensely bright
> Impending spiritual dawn, of which the pure
> Immense illumination seems about to pour
> In upon our existence from beyond
> The edge of Knowing.

These are large words and would be vague in the hands of a poet of less intensity, honesty and concern for language. With Gascoyne they convince because he only uses them when all other words have failed, when abstractions must overrule concrete images. It was the same with Dante when he was trying to describe Paradise. For the truth is that we have more precise words and images for horror and disgust than we have for ecstasy and vision.

The apotheosis of this volume of poems is reached not in the last poem, but in the penultimate one, **"The Gravel-pit Field."** Here, in beautifully controlled rhymed stanzas, Gascoyne conveys his own mystical experience. . . . The experience is entirely subjective but the poet's treatment of it renders it objective, as something we too can share. (pp. 571-72)

In his next book, entitled ***The Vagrant and Other Poems*** . . . , David Gascoyne made a more personal application of the symbols which he had restored and revivified in ***Poems 1937-42.*** He is a poet who, while never repeating himself, continually returns to the same themes and subjects. He finds them inexhaustible and indeed they are since they are concerned with the most fundamental problems of a man's life. In a very beautiful poem in ***The Vagrant,*** called **"The Sacred Hearth,"** he makes an affirmation of human, earthly love. . . . And again, in **"Eros Absconditus"** he speaks of a human love which, though never completely attainable in this life, is nevertheless valid and capable of fulfilment elsewhere. . . . The poem is a gesture of relinquishment, of assigning to others what one cannot possess oneself. . . . But in his sense of 'aloneness' Gascoyne is not inhabiting the kind of isolated world which Rilke created for himself; his loneliness is more akin to that of Hopkins—an acknowledgement of the existence of divine and human love even when both appear to be withdrawn temporarily from oneself. **"Eros Absconditus"** ends on a note of hope, a defiant recognition of the loveliness and transcendent power of friendship. . . . (pp. 573-74)

One of Gascoyne's most glittering and splendid poems appears in ***The Vagrant;*** it is **"September Sun 1947,"** a lyric in praise of light. Light has always been a favourite image with mystical poets. With a poet like Vaughan, for example, it penetrates his entire work. After a triumphant tribute to the sun,

> Magnificent strong sun! in these last days
> So prodigally generous of pristine light. . . .

Gascoyne moves on to a vision of the sun as an image of God himself:

> . . . with an angrier sun may He
> Who first with His gold seed the sightless field
> Of Chaos planted, all our trash to cinders bring.

As always the language is precise and concrete, the music controlled and assured. Yet control does not preclude a rising pulse of excitement and the formal design of the poem stresses this excitement. Passion held in check is always more potent than passion at liberty.

In a sequence of poems called **"Fragments towards a Religio Poetae,"** Gascoyne returns to a consideration of the themes he handled in **"Miserere"**; only here, as the title indicates, the approach is more personal, the setting more immediately contemporary. The two sequences might usefully be compared with St Augustine's conception of the Two Cities—the timeless City of God and the time-bound City of Man. (p. 574)

The penultimate section of the sequence is a return to a meditation on the crucifixion and the two thieves who died with Christ. The tone, however, is more bitterly ironic than that of **"Ecce Homo."** . . . In **"Ecce Homo"** Gascoyne emphasized the terror and compassion of Christ's suffering and the way in which mankind was redeemed through it. In this poem he stresses our own guilt in killing Christ and this guilt includes not only our individual acts of evil, but also the fact that we have tried to tame and reduce religion to small human terms. . . . But the sequence terminates on a note of pure hope, of hope achieved through suffering and acceptance:

> . . . the attic window-boxes above the market
> Offer tribute of happy beauty to the omniscient
> Heavenly Eye.

Few writers could get away with a phrase like 'happy beauty' and it is an indication of Gascoyne's power and perceptiveness that we accept it so willingly. It is because, in all his work, he never gives the easy answer or the facile half-truth, never stands outside either the struggle to live or the struggle to communicate, that he is such an important poet. Like all true visionary writers, he wishes to *share* (Aquinas said that 'the fruits of contemplation were to be handed on to others'); like Blake or Vaughan or, to move further back in time, like Walter Hilton or Dame Julian of Norwich, Gascoyne is in the direct line of English religious literature. He conveys a private vision in public terms; his view of life is his own world, but it is also rooted in ours. The 'rain-gorged Thames,' the gravel-pit field, the suburbs, the horse-butcher—in things like these he finds his images, his 'objective correlatives,' and then transforms them.

In his most recently published work, ***Night Thoughts,*** a dramatic piece written for broadcasting, David Gascoyne continued his theme of man's loneliness in a world where he is rooted yet, paradoxically, not at home. Part of this work is written in verse, part in prose. Strangely, however, the dramatic device of using various speaking voices is not entirely successful. Perhaps the reason for this is that the necessary *overt* objectivity of creating voices and characters causes a dilution of the poet's own intensity, a slight dimming of his vision. It is the final passages of ***Night Thoughts,*** where Gascoyne resorts to prose to speak of prayer and silence and loneliness, that are most successful. For the truth is that his lyric gift is an entirely personal not a dramatic one. His subjects are always dramatic but his treatment is meditative; he moves by monologue not by dialogue, he is more interested in the fears and aspirations which men share than in those emotions where they show themselves to be most diverse.

Night Thoughts should, I think, be regarded as an experiment, as a marginal occupation. It would be something more than a cause for mere regret if Gascoyne were to give us no more verse comparable with the best in ***Poems 1937-42*** and ***The Vagrant.*** For he is a figure outside literary movements yet perfectly within the English tradition. His influences from French writers have been completely assimilated into his own native English verse. His achievement is already formidable. . . . The radiance and honesty of his poetry are matched by an integrity that will not permit him to force anything. (pp. 575-77)

Elizabeth Jennings, "The Restoration of Symbols," in The Twentieth Century, *Vol. 165, No. 988, June, 1959, pp. 567-77.*

ROBIN SKELTON

David Gascoyne's first book appeared in 1932 when he was sixteen years old. Although he has since regretted having begun to publish so early in his career, ***Roman Balcony*** is an astonishing performance for an adolescent and some poems clearly foreshadow the work that was to come. Already in this book there is that interest in hallucinatory obsessive symbolism which gave so many of his poems of the later thirties their individual and disturbing quality. (p. ix)

Much surrealist poetry does not survive a second reading, for it so often depends simply upon shock-tactics and bizarre juxtapositions for its effectiveness that once the surprise is gone the poetry is gone also. [In ***Man's Life Is This Meat***], Gascoyne employed surrealist techniques to good effect, however. Though, at first, some poems look like products of a free-association game, a second glance shows them to be full of profound implications. Moreover, they show an astonishing range of attitudes. Compare the opening section of **"Antennae"** with a stanza from **"The Rites of Hysteria,"** for example. The first passage has an imagist, and almost oriental, precision.

> A river of perfumed silk
> A final glimpse of content
> The girls are alone on the highroad

The second passage uses a rhetorical tone, and, by means of bizarre and near-nonsensical imagery, produces a powerful expression of social and moral dislocation. It is as much a poem about the state of society as many of the more explicitly didactic poems of Auden.

> A cluster of insane massacres turns green upon the
> highroad
> Green as the nadir of a mystery in the closet of a dream
> And a wild growth of lascivious pamphlets became a
> beehive
> The afternoon scrambles like an asylum out of its hovel
> The afternoon swallows a bucketful of chemical sorrows
> And the owners of rubber pitchforks bake all their
> illusions
> In an oven of dirty globes and weedgrown stupors

The dislocation of sensibility of Gascoyne's early poems is usually expressive of a deeply moral perception. He expresses the *angst* of the period in richer imagery than that used by most of his contemporaries. (pp. xi-xii)

Hölderlin's Madness consists of an essay on Hölderlin, followed by a free translation or adaptation of some of his poems linked together by four of Gascoyne's own. These four (**"Figure in a Landscape", "Orpheus in the Underworld", "Tenebrae",** and **"Epilogue"**) develop the theme of the poet as seer, and as victim. He is representative of the whole of mankind, however. He sees farther than the majority and suffers more than the majority, but his vision and his pain are those of the human race. This is a simplified interpretation, but it makes it easy to see how Gascoyne's romanticism, left-wing sympathies, surrealist tendencies, and concern to explore deep into the world of dream, obsession, and suffering, could lead him towards a fundamentally religious poetry. His early work is filled with sympathy for the human predicament, but it is in his later work that the figure of the solitary sufferer and visionary takes on the lineaments of Christ. (p. xiii)

It was with the publication of ***Poems 1937-1942*** . . . that Gascoyne's stature became fully apparent. In this book, with its disturbing drawings by Graham Sutherland, he achieved a religious poetry which combines powerful symbolism with contemporary relevance. In **"Ecce Homo"** Christ upon the Cross is watched by centurions who

> wear riding-boots,
> Black shirts and badges and peaked caps . . .

"Kyrie" is as much a cry of guilt and anguish from war-torn Europe as from the individual soul. The appeal is not to a God outside politics but to a 'Christ of Revolution and of Poetry' that he may 'Redeem our sterile misery', which is the history of the whole world. . . . [The more personal poems show] Gascoyne's new economy of language and rigour. The symbolism that before was splendidly justified by its expressiveness is now handled with an intellectual subtlety reminiscent of the Metaphysicals. The poetry has not, however, forgotten its beginnings in the sociology-conscious thirties, and, however metaphysical or prophetic the poems become, they never lose sight of the actualities of the world in which they are written. . . . [Many] poems also fuse the shrewd portrayal of particular situations, places, and people, with a profound sense of all that is universal about them.

The theme which emerges most clearly from ***Poems 1937-1942*** is that of man's despair at his mortality, and his confusion; but often it seems that some illumination of the darkness is imminent. Knowledge and Intuition are forever reaching out, however unsuccessfully, towards a greater knowledge, a stronger intuition, and finding hope in the experience of love and in 'The startling miracle of human song'.

It was seven years before David Gascoyne's next book appeared. This was ***A Vagrant and other poems*** which was published in 1950. Now the tone is generally more quiet. The same beliefs are expressed, but with greater delicacy, and often with humour. Christ is again presented as the key to the human riddle in **"Fragments Towards a Religio Poetae"**, but the presentation is wry rather than rhetorical. (pp. xiv-xv)

The long colloquial lines, and the subtle cadences in this collection revealed that Gascoyne had taken a further step forward, and, as usual, perfected new modes of exploration. These new techniques were first fully employed in the long poem ***Night Thoughts***. . . . (pp. xv-xvi)

Night Thoughts is David Gascoyne's most ambitious work to date, and his greatest single achievement. In it he moves easily from Dantesque nightmare to social satire, from free-flowing prose to classically neat verse, and throughout the whole drama retains absolute control over his various themes and symbols. It is a study of our urban civilization and also of the universal condition of man. It sums up, in its exploration of solitude and despair, many of his earlier perceptions, and places him alongside Yeats, Eliot, Auden, and MacNeice as one of the select company of British poets who have attempted, and achieved, the construction of a major new form.

David Gascoyne has only completed two poems since the publication of ***Night Thoughts,*** although he has added considerably to the number of translations. ***Night Thoughts,*** therefore, must be regarded as the summit of his achievement so far. It is certainly a magnificent climax to the first thirty years of his poetry. . . . (p. xvi)

Robin Skelton, in an introduction to Collected Poems *by David Gascoyne, edited by Robin Skelton, Oxford University Press, London, 1965, pp. ix-xviii.*

THE TIMES LITERARY SUPPLEMENT

It is a long time since the Orphic voice has been heard in English poetry; but with the reissuing, in a single volume, of the collected poems of David Gascoyne, a generation to whom his work is unfamiliar will hear an unmistakable eloquence—yet a contemporary voice, too, speaking to, and from, our modern predicament.

[Robin Skelton, the editor of ***Collected Poems***], speaks of a new generation of poets "not so much influenced by the 'New Country' school as reacting away from it". . . . George Barker was of that generation, as well as Dylan Thomas and Vernon Watkins; but although all these (and Edwin Muir also) repudiated or disregarded the doctrine of the New Country school each did so in different terms. Even though Mr. Gascoyne and Mr. Barker were friends their formative influences were as different as their work.

None of these poets was, of course, reacting "against" anything or anyone; rather they were formed by different influences; and Mr. Gascoyne's poetry is different in kind from that of any other English poet of his generation. . . .

If from the *Surréalistes* Mr. Gascoyne learnt to find everywhere the reflection, in objective reality, of subjective intuitions, it was not only or principally his own subjectivity which he so discovered. From the first . . . we find a remarkable imaginative objectivity. . . . One of the most consistently imaginative of modern poets, he writes with an equal objectivity of the world's visible and its interior aspects.

For what makes Mr. Gascoyne's poetry so remarkable is its oracular quality. If this passed almost unnoticed at the time it was because no one was listening for the prophetic voice. Yet his imagination was from the first responsive, with a kind and degree of sensitivity unmatched since Blake, to the subtle indications of the spiritual condition of wartime and just postwar France and England; and especially London. The lonely poet (***A Vagrant,*** title of his last book of poems, describes the *persona* under which he has explored the human condition) speaks from an objective spiritual awareness in which each reader will discover not the poet's subliminal intuitions but his own. For this integrity of vision the poet has paid a high price: he has experienced the subliminal collective suffering as his own. . . .

Because inner and outer are continually so discovered and revealed in one another that the visible world becomes as if a region of the mind, Mr. Gascoyne's poetry is, like Shelley's, supremely of man rather than of "nature"; and the beauty of nature is an imparted, reflected human beauty. Yet he discovers continually in nature a principle at work which heals the rents man tears in her texture; as in man he finds a divine spark inextinguishable in those hells whose depths he knows as well as Mr. Francis Bacon, but sees differently. Like Blake he sees the holy spirit accompanying man into whatever depths he may travel; he is the poet of the world-long crucifixion to which mankind subjects that indwelling presence. His sustained eloquence, elegiac rather than lyrical, is appropriate to themes essentially (and often explicitly) religious. In these poems it is impossible not to recognize Blake's "one thing alone" which makes a poet, "imagination, the divine vision". Where the modern Accuser can so confidently point to ridicule and deformity, the poet is able to discern the holy, the tender, the tragically sublime. Mr. Gascoyne can accuse too; but the judgment of imagination falls, as always, on the judges, the "harsh souls and law-encumbered spirits" whose judgments are not those of love.

These he calls the "bourgeoisie", but his politics, if revolutionary, are not the politics of this world. For him there is only one struggle, waged in man himself and in his tragic cities and societies: of the spirit of love against all kinds of separative egoism. He is in the tradition of those Protestant mystics, Blake and Boehme, Kierkegaard and Buber, to whose works, after his *surréaliste* apprenticeship, he increasingly turned.

"The Orphic Voice," in The Times Literary Supplement, *No. 3311, August 12, 1965, p. 696.*

DEREK STANFORD

To page through David Gascoyne's ***Collected Poems*** must prove for numerous readers an autobiographical occasion. . . . To the post-war generation who grew up without experience of the holocaust or the heady cult of revolution, Gascoyne's poetry may seem histrionically intense, both as to its hope and despair; its sense of possibility and tragic limitation. Those of us, however, who share this era will recognise the author's past as their own. . . .

For me no single book summarises that period better than ***Poems 1937-42,*** Gascoyne's fourth collection of verse. No doubt, the poet was fortunate here in having Graham Sutherland's apocalyptic drawings, with their smouldering reds and sinister blacks, to illustrate the text and provide the reader with a visual image representing the whole. (p. 238)

But the intellectual ingredient which gave ***Poems 1937-42*** its distinctive quality was the influence of Kierkegaard. Here were the poetic equivalents of such notions as 'pleasure-perdition', 'the leap in the dark', and 'knights of faith'. Here, too, were the imaginative counter-parts of the Danish philosopher's dialectic of possibility and necessity—the systole and diastole of the human spirit. A Dostoievskian note of extremity marked most of these fervid pages. . . .

Poems 1937-42 represent the high-water-mark of Gascoyne's career; and it is the reprinting of them in his ***Collected Poems*** which gives this book its permanent interest. Unfortunately, they are not represented *in toto;* four translations from Pierre Jean Jouve, one from Jules Supervielle, and the author's poem in French **"Strophes Elégiaques: A la Memoire d'Alban Berg"** being omitted. Robin Skelton, the editor of these poems, tells us that 'to include translations in this volume could only result in blurring the image of his [Gascoyne's] own original compositions'. On the same principle, he has left out the translations from three other books included in ***Collected Poems.*** Since Gascoyne's translations are essentially *personae,* the editor's argument would seem to be doubtful. To imagine Gascoyne without the influence of Eluard, Jouve, and Jouve's versions of Holderlin is to imagine a quite other person. (p. 239)

Apart from this, there are other defections of a more serious nature. Gascoyne's first book ***Roman Balcony*** (1932) is completely omitted, though Mr Skelton's quotations from it in his Introduction [see excerpt above] show how verbally mature the poems are. Then, too, they are not mere exercises, preliminary doodles in verse-writing, but pieces unmistakably belonging to Gascoyne's characteristic inner-world. (pp. 239-40)

Mr Skelton's Introduction is more consistent than his plan of selection. He brings out the unity of Gascoyne's work and traces its development. He is particularly good on seeing the relevance of the surrealist pieces, remarking of one of them that 'it is as much a poem about the state of society as many of the more explicitly didactic poems of Auden'. He notes, too, that 'the dislocation of sensibility in Gascoyne's early poems is usually expressive of a deeply moral perception'. . . . (p. 240)

Where we might part company with Mr Skelton is in his evaluation. ***Night Thoughts*** he takes to be Gascoyne's 'greatest single achievement'. The thinking-processes in this poem are certainly of a most interesting order, and take us nearer to a resolution of doubt and despair than Gascoyne has attained to before. But what are we to say to writing of this order?

The Tyrant Negativity has usurped power and thrown
Men's captive souls into the silent pit
Of self-confounded Subjectivity.

Mr Skelton's assessment of the poet's language here—'he moves easily from Dantesque nightmare to social satire, from free-flowing prose to classically neat verse'—makes no mention of this sort of jargon. The fact is that Mr Skelton is too kind a critic; and equates appropriation of fresh subject matter automatically with poetic achievement. Of the pieces in ***A Vagrant and Other Poems*** he writes that 'the long colloquial lines, and the subtle cadences in this collection revealed that Gascoyne had taken a further step forward, and, as usual, perfected new modes of exploration'. Now while this holds good for **"A Vagrant"** and for some dozen other pieces, it takes no account of the pedestrian effect of most of the purely didactic poems. . . . (pp. 240-41)

Mr Skelton is dealing with a poet who has a certain permanency of appeal; who possesses, in short, a certain classic status; and it is the mark of a classic poet that he calls for the most severe and rigorous application of verbal standards. Time and again, when subjected to such a draconian scrutiny, Gascoyne can put our doubts to flight; and it is no service to the highest of which he is capable, not to be aware of his defections.

A few numbers ago, in these pages, Mr Frederick Grubb was remarking on the prevalent substitution of sociological interpretation in criticism. He suggested that a critic who 'places' his author in the social culture of the times feels exonerated from the necessity of making an artistic judgment. This just about defines Mr Skelton's procedure. He *does* place Gascoyne in the context of the era, and he does see the unity and continuity of the poet's work.

Generalising in this way, he pays scant attention to the poet's imagery. This, from Gascoyne's earliest days, had been expressively concrete and specific. In ***Roman Balcony,*** we find him writing of

a Chinese mask
That glares down upon me
From one high corner [of an old cupboard]

while in his surrealist period, amid all the heady riot, a sense of the specific is curiously preserved when, for example, we read of a woman 'burning the eyes of snails in a candle'. These two examples have a quality in common. In each one, the concrete element cannot be equated with the factual. The image is sensuous and material, but that to which it refers is fancy—to things in the world of the imagination. Another shared property these images possess is a power to convey the sinister. Gascoyne once described his creative condition of mind as one of 'continual expectancy which may at times become a state of hyperaesthesia'. Responding to these images, the reader understands this and registers the singular menace which all of them emanate. This is to say that Gascoyne's most characteristic imagery is both concrete and symbolic; and in his most mature poetry he puts such imagery to individual use.

'At the bottom of everything', Boussuet once wrote, 'one finds inanity and a void'; and it is this recognition of the psychological abyss in man which has most marked Gascoyne's awareness. (pp. 242-43)

The sense of nothingness, which Gascoyne calls the Void, is more easily felt than represented—the obvious features of a vacuum being absence and silence. Such, then, is the predicament of an art which quite deliberately sets out to create an idiom of the abyss, that psychological zone of negation. The problem for Gascoyne was to find a form for formlessness; in other words, by transforming it, to triumph. 'The Void itself', wrote the poet, 'cannot be apprehended except by means of symbolic expression. . . . By realising such a term of reference we can free ourselves from the terrible non-existence implicit in the negation of the Spirit.'

Following from this, we find in Gascoyne's verse a number of attempts to make *plastic* that which is the essential enemy of the concrete—of 'the holy fact', as Charles Williams called it. Some of these are more successful than others; the complex or oblique being generally the best, while the obvious ones tend towards a too crude sensationalism. (p. 243)

Most of Gascoyne's imagery from ***Poems 1937-42*** belongs to [the] field of *negative revelation,* to an intimation of our own age which Heidegger terms one of 'God's withdrawing'.

Nor is it only by images of emptiness that the poet expresses 'the constant imminence of the aimless Void which is concomitant with the denial of the Spirit'. Mr G. W. Stonier has remarked Gascoyne's predilection for a sepulchral palette and his obsession with the shade of black:

> Here I am now cast down
> Beneath the black glare of a netherworld's
> Dead suns, dust in my mouth, among
> Dun tiers no tears refresh.

In this passage he obtains his effect by means of a paradox: black being the negation of colour and light, a 'black glare' is factually impossible. In the same way, 'dead suns' could give no illumination, but are here taken to be the source of the contradictory 'black glare'. It is by means of such poetic chromatics that Gascoyne paints his inner landscapes of despair.

These images, which are like tightly coded messages, were perfected by Gascoyne in ***Poems 1937-42.*** Certainly, in no single poem in [***The Vagrant and Other Poems***] did he improve upon this method, the best of them hardly equalling what he achieved before. (p. 245)

Only in certain passages of ***Night Thoughts*** does Gascoyne elaborate upon his patented device of paradox; and it is significant that he requires the more extensive medium of prose for his purpose here (the verse in this volume being by far the less distinguished part of it). Indeed, Mr Skelton is right, in a way, in describing ***Night Thoughts*** as 'the poet's greatest single achievement'. What needs stressing here, however, is that this triumph belongs to the realm of religious thinking rather than to aesthetic achievement.

The section of ***Night Thoughts*** in which Gascoyne achieves his breakthrough is called **"Encounter with Silence"** and is one of the most subtle expositions of man as a spiritually communicative animal to be found in contemporary literature. The voice we hear speaking is that of the Solitary, who slowly realises that silence is the music not of the Void but of the Spirit. But first there is the question of language, the difficulty over forms and formulae. . . . It is this problem of language—this desire to make and keep it new—which has, with other factors, shut Gascoyne out from the world of traditional prayer and worship. (p. 246)

Gascoyne's difficult resolution of his 'aloneness' [in ***Night Thoughts***] seems, in part, to have removed the tension which is the root of his poetry. One recalls how Kierkegaard defines the poet as a man unhappily in love with God. Make the relationship a happy one, a positive one, a reciprocal one, and the protesting lyricism ceases.

For many of us Gascoyne will remain as the poet of the anguish of preconversion, recorder of a state of continual inner crisis, cartographer of negativity and the void. (p. 247)

Derek Stanford, "Gascoyne in Retrospect," in Poetry Review, *Vol. LVI, 1965, pp. 238-47.*

RICHARD HOWARD

David Gascoyne's career, which began with ***Roman Balcony***—not reprinted in these ***Collected Poems*** but published in 1932 when the poet was 16—concluded, according to the poet and his editor Robin Skelton, in 1956, when Gascoyne was 40. The courage to acknowledge oneself spent at an age when most have merely mustered their forces is matched in Gascoyne's case by an equal cowardice—the refusal to face the responsibilities of poetry unpropped by some convulsive external energy: the surrealist protest against the past of words in favor of their present force; the agonies of the Second World War, its antecedents and aftermath; a visionary Christianity that has nothing to do with the Sacraments but a lot of truck with the Symbols; and an invited, indeed an indulged madness which revels so masochistically in the identification of the Seer as Victim that it soon reaches the point where any victim, provided his suffering is sufficiently picturesque, can become a seer. None of the poems in this book does its own work, but appeals to a centrifugal violence—a violence done to the expectations of association, whether among words, ideas, or images—to drag out of utterance some recognition of the poet's personal style, which is characteristically the style of *resentment*. . . . I do not locate in these 150 pages . . . "a single poem" that chooses to solve by the means available to poetry—even the most conventional sort: meter, music, phrasing, and consecution of imagery—the problems Gascoyne insists he is confronting. . . . The poet's characteristic behavior toward his verse is to combine an impatience with texture and rhythm amounting to hysteria with an extreme license in matters of local imagery:

> The sewing machine on the pillar condenses the
> windmill's halo
> Which poisoned the last infanta by placing a tooth in
> her ear
> When the creeping groans of the cellar's anemone
> vanished
> The nightmare spun on the roof a chain armor of
> handcuffs
> And the ashtray balanced a ribbon upon a syringe.

That is some of the penultimate stanza of a five-stanza poem, **"The Rites of Hysteria"**; it is only one of Gascoyne's manners, but one extensively deployed. The extremity of these confrontations almost dictates a grossness in the texture: "the rocks relax, as the pallid phallus sinks . . ." Gascoyne's other chief mode is one of acute shrillness in self-abasement and torment (one of his collections is called ***Hölderlin's Madness***), and if I find it preferable in its self-exposure to the image-mongering of the dated surrealist pieces, there is something of the charlatan still in all this capitalized self-excruciation. . . . I spoke of Gascoyne's being *spent* at forty, but that was the wrong word, implying as it does some exhaustion of internal energies, some movement from within. The apposite participle is obviously *consumed,* for Gascoyne's poems have somehow devoured his energies without once feeding on themselves. That is why he insists so, I think, on the poet as ritual scapegoat, knowing himself "outside the barricades". (pp. 404-05)

Richard Howard, "British Chronicle," in Poetry, *Vol. CVIII, No. 6, September, 1966, pp. 399-407.*

KATHLEEN RAINE

The publication in 1965 of the ***Collected Poems*** of David Gascoyne brought to the notice of a generation to whom his name is unfamiliar (for his latest work, ***Night Thoughts,*** was published in 1956) the work of an outstanding poet. (p. 193)

From an extremely early age [Gascoyne] "trained himself consciously to annotate and classify for future contemplation the passing sights, sensations and sounds of each moment of existence". Yet far from becoming therefore a "realist", a camera-eye, David Gascoyne discerned always the qualitative essence; not for him the too-prevalent obscuring of all distinctions between the vile and the sublime, the beautiful and the ugly, upon which a pseudo-scientific "detachment" prides itself: these distinctions, on the contrary, become apparent only to the qualitative discernment of imagination; and if they often lie otherwise than as the world sees, that is nothing new. . . . The greater part of his novel [***Opening Day***] is in fact a meticulous qualitative record of all the poet's eye saw from the windows of bus and train on a journey from Cambridge Park to Waterloo Station. Commenting upon the obscuring of such observation which happens when we are preoccupied with our own concerns, he writes that trees, houses, people "appear to us individually to be comparatively not worth our attention because the universal law of appearance decrees it so, because otherwise all life would be tuned up to one high level of supreme importance, the strain of which no human mind could stand". That intense degree of experience of the real world has nevertheless been David Gascoyne's especial gift. (pp. 197-98)

[The technique of "Mass-Observation"] made possible a kind of poetic (or pictorial) imagery at once irrational and objective; and it was David Gascoyne who finally realized and perfected a kind of poetry (written also by Charles Madge and Humphrey Jennings) in which an imagery of precise and objective realism, gathered from the daily human (and therefore especially urban) scene, from the habitat of the common man, is informed with a content not only supremely imaginative, but infused with the imagination of the collective mind of which it is an eloquent, if unconscious, expression; a listening to the dreaming . . . of a nation or a world, itself unaware of the purport of its own fantasies. Thus the poet reassumes the ancient role at once of national prophet, and reader of the auguries; not from entrails or yarrow-stalks, but from (literally) the "writings on walls", the seemingly fortuitous recurring images in the daily records. Anything and everything speaks to the augur attuned to its meaning. The two apparently irreconcilable opposites are in such poetry brought together: imaginative inspiration, and a realistic objectivity. (p. 208)

So in his latest work, ***Night Thoughts,*** Mr. Gascoyne returns to a realization which characterized surrealism and, during its brief moment, "Mass-Observation"—an enchanted dream-like consciousness which imagination created for itself, by a confusion and interfusion of inner and outer worlds, in which the waking world was experienced symbolically, fraught with meanings and messages of the soul. We create the world continually in the image of our dreams; and see reflected in the outer, images of inner realities and preoccupations.

For if from the surrealists Mr. Gascoyne learned to find, everywhere mirrored in objective reality, subjective states, it was not only or principally his own subjectivity he so discovered; the rebel against the world of the common man returned to articulate that world's unspoken dreams. If the oracular quality which is characteristic of his finest poetry passed almost unnoticed at the time, it was because no one was listening for the prophetic voice. (pp. 208-09)

Night Thoughts is the final expression of a theme the poet had already attempted in two long poems, **"Phantasmagoria"** (before 1935, in his surrealist period) and **"Noctambules"** (1938). In **"Phantasmagoria"** the poet first begins to speak with his own voice; and along with the fusion of "the flagrant contradictions that exist between dream and waking life, the 'unreal' and the 'real', the unconscious and the conscious" we recognize the characteristic scope of the later poem. **"Phantasmagoria"** is a townscape; a seaside town, and, as always, at night, as befits the world between dream and waking. Already the poet has found his characteristic, nervous, rapid, long, flexible line. . . . (p. 214)

In **"Noctambules"** (dedicated to Djuna Barnes) he returned some ten years later to the city-scape; Paris, this time. By now he has shed his surrealist trappings; we see yet another manner being attempted by the poet, who was at all times so sensitive to the style of contemporaries. . . . A period-piece in the expatriate style of Eliot's early poetry—the voice is not quite his own, but, as with surrealism, with the objective "reports" of Jennings, and as later with Hölderlin, the style is not the merely superficial imitation of a manner, but the adoption of an imaginative attitude; it is acquired from within.

The grounds David Gascoyne gave for his break with surrealism were political; influenced, perhaps, by the climate of literary thought in England in the 'thirties, he thought that he was about to move in the direction of a more explicit Marxism; but what had surely begun to dissatisfy him in surrealism was the inadequacy of a theory of inspiration which did not go beyond psychic autonomy.

Hölderlin's Madness was published in 1938; and in Hölderlin he found a doctrine of poetic inspiration which was to transform at once his theory and his style. Indeed from this time traces of the surrealist manner and imagery almost entirely disappear from his work, to be superseded by a lyricism whose exaltation is reminiscent of Hölderlin; with whom, it seems (as formerly with Rimbaud), the poet now began for a time almost to identify himself, so close an affinity did he discover. This work is a series of "free adaptations" from Hölderlin, linked by original poems and prefaced by an introduction which is in the nature of a new declaration of prophetic faith. The bridge by which he was able to pass so easily from surrealism to Hölderlin was the theme of "madness". (pp. 215-17)

The group of **"Metaphysical Poems"** in the volume of ***Poems 1937-1942*** . . . bear the evident mark of Hölderlin's influence; whose imaginative flights David Gascoyne from this time dared, finding in his own wings an eagle-strength upon which he outsoared, in sublimity, all his contemporaries.

There was one more step to be taken by the poet who was to write the religious (and specifically Christian) poems which are his enduring gift to the world. Already before the second World War it was clear to imaginative people that catastrophe was inevitable. Hitler's persecution of the Jews had already begun. Among the multitudes to be put to death in the concentration camps, one was a close friend of the poet, who himself passionately embraced the Jewish cause. The crisis that brought the French surrealists who were most serious to political maturity, and swept away the rest, brought to David Gascoyne the spiritual maturity whose evidence is first seen in ***Poems 1937-1942***. Kierkegaard, Dostoevsky, Chekhov, Berdiaiev superseded the "sacred books" of his surrealist and romantic phases. . . . The eight poems of [the **"Miserere"**] series are in praise of the "Eternal Christ"; the poet speaks from those depths into which the divine Presence has descended in order to redeem our fallen world, in a voice of sustained eloquence, as if at last the angel spoke. . . . Not one of these poems falls below the level of that oracular speech which from this time possessed him. He often spoke of Joachim of Flora, first prophet of the "age of the Holy Spirit" which, so he foretold, was to follow the "age of the Son". In that age, so David Gascoyne believed, we live; or are about to live, for he is, supremely, the poet of the Entombment which must precede the Resurrection. The darkness in which Hölderlin and the romantics awaited the dawn had become for him that uttermost descent in which the *deus absconditus* (he used also the alchemical language, and spoke much of Jakob Boehme) redeems the souls from their darkest prisons. He prefaced the series of **"Metaphysical Poems"** with a quotation from the Egyptian *Book of the Dead:* "Without cease and for ever is celebrated the Mystery of the Open Tomb, the Resurrection of Osiris-Ra, the Increated Light." (pp. 220-22)

Such, in bare outline, has been the background against which David Gascoyne's poetry has developed, from small beginnings to an achieved, if briefly held, greatness. There are only five volumes of verse, two of them juvenilia. . . . His second volume, ***Man's Life Is This Meat,*** covers his surrealist period. Dedications to Ernst, Dali, and Magritte are no less revealing of his tastes at that time than the poems themselves. (p. 225)

Soon he was, in such poems as **"Lowland"**, **"Mountains"**, **"World Without End"**, assimilating (with a quality only to be attained by an interior identification with an underlying vision) the style of Hölderlin, his pure inhuman landscapes, the Orphic voice. A stylist: so much one might have deduced with certainty from these early exercises, experiments not only in the use of language and image, but in the assumption of imaginative attitudes, points of view. His vocabulary was, even at seventeen, remarkably large, expressive, and at the same time used with the ease and naturalness of speech. (pp. 225-26)

From the moment the poet first spoke with his own voice, his style is unmistakable; and in his fourth volume, ***A Vagrant*** (1943-50), though it contains nothing finer than the **"Miserere"** or **"The Gravel-Pit Field"**, the high level of pure poetry, the perfect command of language, never falters; whatever earlier "influences" formed the poet have been assimilated so completely that they cannot be detected. He is no longer searching or experimenting; no longer speaks "in the voice of another". Of the imagery of surrealism, the landscape of Hölderlin, the colloquial idiom of the 'thirties, the Churchillian rhetoric of Jennings, no trace is now discernible; the voice, sublime, grave, and beautiful, could be that of no other poet. His images are at the same time as objective as Jennings's, as true to the dreaming as to the waking mind as surrealism. . . . (p. 226)

Every image is here experienced, not with the intensity of mere sense-perception, of the "detached" camera-eye of the realist "mirror dawdling down a lane"; imaginative vision receives the qualitative mystery communicated by the ever-present signs written in the sky—the light of the sun, at once the light of the world and the ominous threat of the destroying fires. . . . [Gascoyne's] symbolic resonances seem re-created from his unusual insight into the intrinsic qualities of things both human and cosmic. There are no "surrealist objects", no search for "images", since all is raised to the same high degree of imaginative intensity, just as his long, elegiac lines sustain continuously the exalted speech of prophecy. With such apparent ease are his poems composed that only after repeated re-reading does it become apparent that their lucidity is not that of glass but of diamond. Such poetry achieves splendour without for a moment being pretentious. (p. 227)

[Gascoyne's] poems need no learned notes: for his culture has been more deeply absorbed than that of Pound. Steeped in the great currents of consciousness as imagination has revealed and discovered itself in works of art and in ways of life, in cities, in all expressions of civilization, David Gascoyne's culture is not (like that of so much merely academic education) extraneous to himself; its enrichment is not of memory but of imaginative consciousness—qualitative, and therefore perceptible only qualitatively. His style is, so to say, seamless, and apparently (and really) original, unique. Yet no poet has so fully exposed himself to, or so fully absorbed, all the important currents of the thought of his time, whether in the arts, in politics, or in philosophy.

David Gascoyne, under that "strain which no human mind can stand", has, like Hölderlin, endured for many years the "quasi-dereliction" of the oracle deserted by the gods who at times possessed him. He has been silent for a decade; but, not yet fifty, he may perhaps write again. Yet what he has attempted (and achieved) is what only the greatest poets (who are, in attempting what is beyond unaided human skill, also the most humble) set themselves as a goal: absolute imaginative truth. "Man [so he wrote in ***Night Thoughts***] has become above all the most indefatigable mimic of all the ways of being man that have ever been thought striking." But the poet's truth is never to be found where others have found it. (pp. 228-29)

Whatever the significance of the silence of this poet, the poems he has written are among the few of our times that bear such eloquent witness to that Truth for which they speak. (p. 229)

Kathleen Raine, "David Gascoyne and the Prophetic Role," in The Sewanee Review, *Vol. LXXV, No. 2, Spring, 1967, pp. 193-229.*

THE TIMES LITERARY SUPPLEMENT

David Gascoyne's ***Collected Verse Translations*** is a substantial though incomplete gathering of his work in this field. It contains principally his versions of French Surrealists, the whole of ***Hölderlin's Madness,*** and some poems of his own in French. . . .

[***Hölderlin's Madness***] is not only a quite different kind of "translation"; but its quality is startlingly superior. It consists of twenty versions from Hölderlin interspersed with four poems by Mr Gascoyne himself. The latter pieces also figure in the ***Collected Poems*** of 1965, but the whole sequence may be found only here and in the original edition of 1938. And one needs the whole. Mr Gascoyne rewrote Hölderlin for his own purposes, creating a moving, mature, and surprisingly non-hectic meditation on the modern poet. . . .

Hölderlin's Madness, which Mr Gascoyne called a "free adaptation", is close to Robert Lowell's imitations, and to Roubaud. Like their work, it differs from neo-classical imitation in that the foreign writer who is being used in the new poetry is explicitly present. But the inclusion of Mr Gascoyne's own poems makes the sequence something different again: a special kind of dialogue, a seminal new poetic mode, which has not yet been exploited. It has its weaknesses, which are basically those of the rest of this volume, but its strengths predominate. It is deeply imagined and intellectually alive. Its sounds are full and precise, though at times rather lush. When successful, its rhythms are creative and various, the stresses in the longer lines held and unerringly placed. Five poems in the series have a broken, catastrophic beauty, which is inwardly modern and which also calls up a whole region of the Romantic experience, in Hölderlin himself and in, say, the last quartets of Beethoven. The subtle introduction of Romantic verbal gestures, the shifts of mood and the tuning of the powerful images confirm the poetic intelligence of the writing. . . .

Hölderlin's Madness is unaccountably undervalued, one might even say forgotten. Though not a major poem, it remains an admirable work to which one ought to return. It was published when Mr Gascoyne was only twenty-two, a singular achievement; he has arguably written nothing better. It could be useful to contemporary poetry. Its republication is an event of some importance.

The first, short poem in ***The Sun at Midnight*** hints at a recovery of that accomplishment. A genuinely tragic statement, it imposes itself by the potent shaping of its feeling and by the precision of its developing cadences. But the rest of the book lacks both urgency and control. It is a series of aphorisms—as the subtitle puts it: "Notes on the Story of Civilization Seen as the History of the Great Experimental Work of the Supreme Scientist". The exploration of Christianity in terms of alchemy rarely leads to insight: the vision is quirky rather than eccentrically wise. The prose-poems miss the density and intensity which Mr Gascoyne himself defines as necessary to the "ideal aphorism". The whole, rather self-indulgent enterprise has a faded 1890s air: the properties of the vision—alchemy, bisexuality, Satan, Lucifer, Lilith, a relishing of the forces of darkness—suggest a footnote to the Romantic agony. Mr Gascoyne is capable of much better.

"A Special Kind of Dialogue," in The Times Literary Supplement, *No. 3631, October 1, 1971, p. 1168.*

GEOFFREY THURLEY

Perhaps as a result of his Surrealist apprenticeship, Gascoyne emerged, when he did emerge, as a far more archaic poet than many who had never been as significant exponents of the international *avant garde* style as he had. Rhythm and metre in the latter poetry are regular and almost bookish, the diction is sprinkled with 'e'en' and 'O'er'. Moreover, he never attained a facility which might have compromised the strange originality of conception which marks not only the surrealist pieces, but the later poems of relationship. He remains a slightly stiff poet, which is remarkable in someone who wrote something as mature as ***Roman Balcony*** in his seventeenth year. His poetry is at once the most archaic and the least conventional of its time, and the antique ungainliness of much of his work really does seem essential to its effect. **"Spring MCMXL",** for instance, celebrates the vernal goddess with an unabashed Botticellian paganism. Yet the goddess is seen, and the ancient celebration was never less stale:

> And through the smoke men gaze with bloodshot eyes
> At the translucent apparition clad in nascent trembling green
> Of one they still can recognize, though scarcely understand.

The sober tread of the rhythm in these lines reminds one, again, of what has really all along been a dominant characteristic of Gascoyne's verse—an incapacity for inner release, abandon, the Dionysiac frenzy. Gascoyne is the man of will, dominated by the ego, who perhaps for this very reason chose Surrealism, the idiom of 'the unconscious', which only to the uninitiated appears to offer freedom and release, but in fact demands a total denial of the self. The sober, forthright rhythm of Gascoyne's later poetry never becomes academic, yet it never gets its feet off the ground. It moves forward with a uniform tread, earnest yet exploratory. . . . In contrast to the Pylon poets, who all went into relatively early decline, Gascoyne persisted and persevered to produce his finest poetry late in life. It needs luck to be born a poet; courage and strength to stay one. For the time being, Gascoyne laboured: many of the poems he produced at this time are descriptive in the pejorative sense of the term. Poems like **"Walking at Whitsun", "The Gravel-pit Field",** and **"The Sacred Hearth"** are called upon to carry an enormous burden of observation, the whole being held together only by a remorselessly earnest effort of the will. This will is not rhythmic like that of Yeats—Gascoyne's rhythms are fairly uniform—it is rather strength of moral determination. The strange thing perhaps is that so many of his apparently ungainly descriptive assemblages do in fact hold the attention. So that although there is not often the felicitousness of observation that stamps the poetry of Day Lewis, for example, the painstaking closeness repays our attention by so patently not being mere orchestration: heavily though these poems are scored, their observations hardly ever provide mere background or fodder for 'meaning' to breed upon. Thus, while it is hardly possible, without ingeniousness, to provide satisfactory explication in thematic or structural terms for the series of facts narrated in a poem like **"A Wartime Dawn",** the significance of the poem is still curiously inseparable from the dense descriptive clutter:

> Nearest within the window's sight, ash-pale
> Against a cinder-coloured wall, the white
> Pear-blossom hovers like a stare; rain-wet
> The further housetops weakly shine; and there
> Beyond hangs flaccidly a lone barrage-balloon.

For succinctness and wit the poem as a whole cannot match Edwin Muir's excellent "A Wayside Station". Muir's poem ends, like Gascoyne's with the day waking to war; but it is achieved with greater deftness. . . . Yet the lines quoted earlier demonstrate the subtlety of feeling that informs the *un*subtle concentration of his poetry: the strange memorability testifies to the presence of something much more fundamental and valuable than the 'quality of the reporting' noted by Kenneth Allott. . . . More than fine reporting is in evidence here: the capacity for feeling in the presence of rare affinities displayed in the passage springs from the same sensibility as created the Surrealist poems, tutored by the Surrealist discipline.

But the Surrealist who emerges is likely to find himself lost, especially if he returns to England. The return to England and the coming of the War left Gascoyne stranded, high and dry on the mud-flats of a dubious reality. Much of the best poetry he wrote over the next ten years was about war. . . . Gascoyne is decidedly *un*decided about the events: the War is seen as an ignorant disaster, in which neither side can claim the moral right. Perhaps it was precisely his total estrangement—as Paris-oriented ex-Surrealist from culture, as pacifist from the War effort, as night-walking poet from social 'responsibility'—that gave Gascoyne in one way a more real appreciation of his position than partial integration in the corpus of society could have. For the poet is always alienated. Gascoyne's alienation was unusually complete. There could be no better symbol of the essential alienation of the poet than this Francophile ex-Surrealist pacifist wandering through a utility England. (pp. 109-12)

In much of the poetry he wrote after the war . . . Gascoyne seems lost—lost in a world of friends now married, lost in the demotic, egalitarian England of Attlee and Cripps, lost in the cultural turmoil in which the Surrealists in France were also confessing bankruptcy. The poetry is correspondingly heavy-hearted, plated with observations that only occasionally raise themselves above a disenchanted accuracy. Yet the proof and reward of a lifetime's dedication to poetry and the life of a poet (in a more serious sense than that of the saloon-bar parasite, the part-time publisher or the don) was only to come much later, when Gascoyne wrote the work that seems likely to be his greatest achievement, the ***Night Thoughts*** of 1955.

What **"Noctambules"** is to the world of sexual embroilment, ***Night Thoughts*** is to the wider-reaching world of meditation—a cry of and for sympathy. It begins in the world of the Surrealist poems, of **"Noctambules"** and *Nightwood*—the ocean of night in which isolated souls founder. It is the world, in fact, of *avant garde* art since Baudelaire and Rimbaud. Yet what is perhaps most impressive about a poem whose seriousness anyway puts to shame the socialized decline of most of the poet's contemporaries, is that what begins in *avant garde* isolation ends in the generalized human condition. (pp. 115-16)

While ***Night Thoughts*** is in one sense the culminating poem in the European *avant garde* movement, in another it annuls the *raison d'être* of the *avant garde*. Its confessed aim is

> to break through the silence and the noise in the great night
> Of all that is unknown to us, that weighs down in between
> One lonely human being and another. . . .

The will of the whole poem is to break through to those other islands of humanity, to reach the drifting rafts of those who, being alone, are also ready to make contact. Gascoyne's *avant gardisme* at this point joins him on to the rest of the human race in the most surprising way: by cultivating in the extreme degree the isolationist anti-conformism of the traditional *avant garde* poet, he discovers in himself the need which can actually succeed in bringing people together, where all the injunctions and exhortations of humanism and religion have failed. (p. 117)

David Gascoyne's poetry is especially interesting because its tone and seriousness are so English: paradoxically, Gascoyne's Surrealism, his choice of the European rather than the Anglo-Saxon tradition, helped him preserve that very quality for which the great poetry of the existential tradition is so precious. The almost morbid earnestness of Gascoyne's verse places it alongside that of Edward Thomas and Thomas Hardy, rather than that of Eluard and Char. (pp. 119-20)

Geoffrey Thurley, "David Gascoyne: Phenomena of Zero," in his The Ironic Harvest: English Poetry in the Twentieth Century, *Edward Arnold, 1974, pp. 98-120.*

RONALD BLYTHE

When David Gascoyne completed his [***Paris Journal, 1937-1939***] on his 23rd birthday, and in the sixth week of the last war, it was with the instruction that it was to be published should he be killed. He had put a match to nearly all his other papers, and the ***Journal*** was to be his last word and apologia. Emerging nearly 40 years later, its excitements are all to do with first words, with beginnings and promises. Many young writers draw up private manifestos and make statements of intention; but few at 20, which was Gascoyne's age when he began his, could have known themselves so fully or have had the literary maturity for such a self-portrait. It shows him as a penniless young man in Paris and amid scenes which are like the pages from some rare novel which it tantalises one not to possess the whole of.

Like most poets of the period, Gascoyne is immersed in individualism and symbolism, in Hölderlin, Rilke, Jarve and Rimbaud. He sides with Europe against England, and at such events as the International Association of Writers for the Defence of Culture against Fascism, he dissociates himself from the British delegation of Day Lewis, Rex Warner and Spender. Spender, it might be added, is busy dodging *him,* having just damned him in a review as a 'charming talent'.

The ***Journal*** certainly charms, but with something more than talent—perhaps by its ability to describe, with neither conceit nor tedium, all the initial *longueur* of a writer's existence. Lawrence Durrell tells him 'You are an expert on English Death', but Gascoyne attributes 'our obscure perpetual frustration' to a longing to live our lives 'like a story' when the demands of mere existence 'continually thwart our desire for clarity and significance'. He interprets his own life as one which is dominated by voracious imagination, for which he must suffer the consequences. Just as 'a kind of invisible darkness hangs in the sunlight' of the Munich summer, so it must within himself. . . .

He marks out where he stands in existentialism, Marxism, Christianity and homosexual love. In poetry he wants 'emotion, a raised voice, but a clear and coherent speech'. Beautiful writing but never just fine writing. (p. 316)

Ronald Blythe, "Writers and War," in The Listener, *Vol. 100, No. 2576, September 7, 1978, pp. 315-16.*

STEPHEN SPENDER

David Gascoyne's [***Paris Journal 1937-1939***], begun when he was twenty, covers two years when he was for most of the time in Paris, though sometimes travelling elsewhere on the Continent and sometimes, most unwillingly, returning to his parents' home at Twickenham. The young poet had already published a novel, poems, and ***A Short Survey of Surrealism,*** a delightful book conveying, almost for the first time in English, the fascination of this movement. Despite his early fame, Gascoyne was quite unable to support himself by his writing. As this journal shows, in Paris he often did not know where the next meal was coming from nor whether he would be able to pay the rent. The impoverished young poet is of course a stereotype. What seems exceptional in Gascoyne is the depth of the depressions into which he sometimes fell. The mood in the journal is often of an oppressive seriousness which made difficulties for him in his relations with other people. At the same time he can be gay and entertaining, and so funny in his descriptions of meetings with people that one feels a satiric poet or novelist is somewhere buried in him.

In many ways this book fits into a category of twentieth-century journals which includes those by Katherine Mansfield, Virginia Woolf, Evelyn Waugh, Lawrence Durrell, Anaïs Nin, Henry Miller and others. . . .

On several levels, Gascoyne's journal is a classic example of this genre. The young author is conscious not only of Lawrence Durrell and Henry Miller, but also of predecessors such as the Baudelaire of *Mon coeur mis à nu* and—if only by report—of Rilke's *Malte Laurids Brigge*. He describes meeting that most non-stop of self-unveilers Anaïs Nin (and is marvellously catty about her). He sends pages (not here published) to Lawrence Durrell (in a letter printed as an entry in this journal) expressing almost gushing admiration for Durrell's achievements. . . .

His book contains many of the ingredients of Durrell, Nin, Miller and the rest. There are sharply focused portraits of famous people—Tristan Tzara, Gertrude Stein, Anaïs Nin, Auden, Stravinsky (conducting "L'Histoire du Soldat") and of people met in cafés or at parties or, very occasionally, in bed (at one such point, describing a transitory and very happy relationship with a male lover who was a young Danish artist, the journal breaks into French). There is a very disgusted account of a meeting of the International Association of Writers for the Defence of Freedom against Fascism, which Gascoyne attended. Here he writes resentfully of Rex Warner, Cecil Day-Lewis and myself, who were among the English delegates. There are some beautiful passages of prose poetry evoking Paris street scenes and the French countryside—and also some very sombre ones. The young Gascoyne is a marvellously truthful and exact recorder of impressions made on him at concerts and art exhibitions. . . .

Yet despite its fitting so very agreeably into the conventions of the private confession which a public will be heir to, Gascoyne's journal seems different from the others. What makes it so is the quality of the writer's preoccupation with himself. The underlying theme of the book is the struggle going on in his mind between two kinds of self-involvement, the selfish and the heroic. The selfish, of which he himself is penetratingly critical, is pure self-absorption, what he calls "being sunk in my own depths, inescapably locked up in my own egoism", "my miserable small misery". He contrasts this self-indulgence with the misery of the world outside him. . . .

The heroic aspect of his self-involvement arises from his deep conviction that he can only get away from selfish self-regard by experiencing, and realizing through language, the objective historic world as his own and most intense subjective experience. . . .

Gascoyne does not write much in his journal about his childhood, but I suspect that he is one of those poet-mystics, like George Herbert, Vaughan, Wordsworth, Proust (whom I consider in this regard a poet), who seems to have had an original vision when he was very young in which the self and the not-self (nature) seemed completely interfused. With these poets the effect of this is to make their art a ritualistic act whereby they return in the imagination to the original experience. For Gascoyne this experience came perhaps later, in early adolescence, and was one in which, through empathy, he experienced the suffering of others as his own.

Gascoyne is critical of the English poets of the 1930s because he feels that they stand outside the historical events which form the subject-matter of much of their poetry and make them take part in activities such as those of the Front Populaire international anti-Fascist meetings. He deplores what he considers "the surrender of English poetry to rationalism", and observes: "The tradition of modern English poetry is something quite different from the traditions of Hoelderlin, Rimbaud, Rilke, Lorca, Jouve—I belong to Europe before I belong to England. The values I believe in are European values and not English ones.". . .

In a project for an essay on Lautréamont, Gascoyne asserts "the necessity for the poet today to create a super-rationalist faith *ex nihilo*". He reiterates the idea that the practice of magic (in poetry) involves "damnation" (Hölderlin goes mad, Rimbaud abandons writing) i e the poet's destiny is to risk madness, despair and death for the sake of the possibility of redeeming existence by means of the secret power of the word.

This view of poetry is certainly little shared in England, and one has to go back to Blake for an example of it. This may explain the peculiar position of Gascoyne here; his poetry seems elusive without exactly being obscure. It is to be hoped that the publication of this journal will encourage readers to study the poetry again, particularly the marvellous ***Poems 1937-1942*** . . . which has illustrations by Graham Sutherland exactly suited to the apocalyptic mood of the poems. Like Edith Sitwell in poems such as "Still Falls the Rain", Gascoyne employs the Christian theme of the Miserere to express and transform the agony of war. . . . The poems which Gascoyne wrote early in the war have the immediacy of terrifying events which, acting upon the poet's sensibility like a hand upon an instrument, produce music and images that become part of the larger religious history of mankind. Gascoyne's immediate reactions to these events, as recorded in his journal, are those of the poet struck into prophecy. . . .

Stephen Spender, "Out of the Depths," in The Times Literary Supplement, *No. 3995, October 27, 1978, p. 1249.*

MICHAEL SCHMIDT

No one would accuse [Gascoyne] of writing perfect or even finished poems. Like D. H. Lawrence, he would say that this is not his purpose, for how can a true poem be finished? But he would suggest—and this is indicated in his careful ordering and reordering of poems in sequences and groups—that the poems exist to signify in their relatedness to one another, that there is unity, or a progression, in the work which is nonetheless open-ended. The unity is not imposed but seems to rise out of the poems. They cohere as aspects of a developing vision.

Gascoyne moved away from doctrinaire surrealism as he recognized that English literature, and the English language itself, contain a powerful irrational element. Hence surrealism was not wholly novel nor particularly relevant to the language, as it seemed to be to French. Symbolism, surrealism, and Imagism (as Pound pointed out) were inherent in the English tradition, but English poets had not felt a compulsion until the early part of this century to tease out one thread to the exclusion of the others.

Gascoyne, in his mature work, adapted elements of surrealist technique to an English tradition, tending towards the Lawrentian (he celebrates Lawrence in an elegy). His recurrent religious imagery is often reminiscent of Lawrence's. In the **"Miserere"** sequence, however, his vision is unrelated to Lawrence's: he evokes the terror of being without God. Where George Barker internalizes his material, swallows the landscape, Gascoyne is swallowed by Christ, becomes Him. He psychologizes, but not in a clinical way—psychology is one of several tools in his search for truth.

He also discovered in English, through the prose of Henry James and others, the subtle variety of English syntax. He developed skill in writing long, penetrating sentences, full of suspensions, hesitations, and dramatic involutions in his prose poems as well as his verse poems. Often the sentence leads him astray. Equally often it brings him nearer to the dark opponent from whom he tries to wrest some meaning. **"The Gravel-Pit Field"** shows his syntactical subtlety at its best. What had marred the early surreal poems was the syntactical monotony—subject, verb, object—coming as regularly as heartbeats.

In the later poems the surreal elements serve to intensify a mental drama which is powerful for being rooted in the real. In **"An Elegy: R. R. 1916-41"** he balances real and surreal evocatively. The tension is between what he can say and what a language, wrenched and disrupted, can only hope to imply. . . . The main lesson he learned from surrealism was rhythmical. Throughout his work, his sense of line and rhythm units is subtle. In the surreal poems, it is rhythm alone that renders the distorted imagery effective, that fuses disparate elements into an apparent whole. Since the genuinely surreal pieces lack punctuation, the rhythmic unit must be the line; the lines work together to create certain rhythmic expectations, while content remains unpredictable. The poem's form is a function of its rhythmic arrangements. Rhythm conveys a sense of meaning, sometimes of humour, to the conscious mind while the images attempt their alchemy on the unconscious. . . . In the poems that are more intellectually organized, less overtly surreal, the sense flows from line to line, but the rhythmic unit remains the line. Stress falls on first and last words; Gascoyne becomes a master of enjambment.

In **"Unspoken"**, he writes of 'Following certain routes to uncertain lands'. The rhythm in all the poems, even the organized chaos of ***Night Thoughts,*** is the reader's 'certain route'. It is not a prosodic but a colloquial rhythm. In it, with few exceptions, we hear Gascoyne's compelling gentleness. He is firmly persuasive but not cajoling. He is not interested in personal power in any facile sense. His hallmark is the humanity of his tone. (pp. 286-88)

Gascoyne fuses religion and politics in poems such as **"Ecce Homo"**, where he invokes the 'Christ of Revolution and of Poetry'; in **"De Profundis"**, one of his best poems; in **"The Vagrant"**, where by inaction he retains spiritual integrity within a social context; and in ***Night Thoughts,*** which Michael Hamburger described as 'the most Baudelairean exploration of an urban inferno written since the war'. Gascoyne, even at his most anguished, is celebrating what might be. A poem of vivid insight such as **"The Sacred Hearth"** shows his power as a celebrant. He is interested, not in the image, but in what happens to it. This in particular is his postsurrealist originality. The surreal extends vision, renews words and objects. In his much anthologized elegy to Paul Eluard he speaks of: 'The youth who's rejected all words that could ever be spoken / To conceal and corrupt where they ought to reveal what they name.'

Desire and fear are the forces that pull at Gascoyne, one from the future, the other from the past. In their conflict in the early poems they produce frustration. The titles—**"The Renunciatory Beauty"**, **"The Unattained"**, **"No Solution"**, **"The Last Head"**, and **"Unspoken"**, with a strongly sexual element in their anguish—provide a key. From this frustration Gascoyne moved gradually through religious half-belief to conviction and celebration. His religion is always social *and* personal. He is a poet of immanence, working through the given world, representing it in ways which, when he is successful, reveal its moral and aesthetic qualities lucidly. Gascoyne is a far more original and accomplished poet than he is normally given credit for being. Dedication and integrity such as his are rare qualities. (pp. 289-90)

Michael Schmidt, "David Gascoyne," in his A Reader's Guide to Fifty Modern British Poets, *Heinemann Educational Books Ltd., 1979, pp. 285-90.*

PHILIP GARDNER

Even more than Dylan Thomas, David Gascoyne was the literary prodigy of the 1930s. At sixteen he published his first book of poems, at seventeen a novel, and at just turned nineteen his still very useful ***Short Survey of Surrealism,*** most of whose French examples were translated by himself. His own volume of surrealist poems, ***Man's Life is This Meat,*** appeared before he was twenty. . . .

Nevertheless, Gascoyne's first entry in his ***Journal 1936-1937,*** made on September 22, dismisses this early work: "*Nothing* I have written so far is of the least value." The rejection is balanced by his feeling that "a new period in my life is about to begin" (he had joined the Communist Party the day before, and had recently met stimulating new people like Humphrey Jennings and the novelist Antonia White); but not until the outbreak of war and his twenty-third birthday was he able to say with persuasive confidence that "the ploughing and the sowing have borne harvest. My life has passed on to another plane".

That statement comes at the end of his ***Paris Journal,*** begun in June 1937 and published in 1978. Shortly after its publication, Gascoyne rediscovered its predecessor, which covers the previous nine months—a period of alternating struggle and inertia, exaltation and self-contempt, concluded by a Freudian dream which illustrates the precarious co-existence in his nature of hetero- and homosexual elements and anticipates the wish expressed in his poem **"Venus Androgyne"** for a force which would "weld twin contradictions in a single fire". Taken together, the two journals offer admirers of Gascoyne's work an engrossing record of his self-realization and artistic growth, and they may well deepen . . . the literary historian's sense of the late 1930s not as a chasm dividing "social" poets from neo-romantic "poets of the 40s" but as a complex and rewarding period of transition.

Certainly Gascoyne himself is the finest poet on that bridge linking the 1930s and 1940s. In March 1937 he transcribed into his Journal part of a letter to George Barker, who earlier in the month had apprised him of doubts as to whether he would fulfil his early promise; in it Gascoyne spoke of wanting his work to be "propaganda for being . . . self-aware and socially aware both at once". That aim he most triumphantly achieved in ***Poems 1937-1942:*** in such pieces, particularly, as **"Ecce Homo", "A Wartime Dawn", "Walking at Whitsun"**, the elegy for his friend Roger Roughton, and most of all in his visionary poem **"The Gravel-Pit Field"** (1941), the modest prefiguring of which in April 1937 gave me my most excited moment in reading this Journal. . . . In his best poems one sees the answer to a question which, gradually emerging from Surrealism, Mass-Observation and Communism, Gascoyne asks himself later in this Journal: "Am I really a religious?" What he was eventually able to convey is summed up at the end of his poem of October 1939, **"An Autumn Park"**: "The true / And immanent glory breaking through Man's circumstance".

During the period covered by this Journal, however, Gascoyne was writing almost no poetry; only one poem is mentioned, his French **"Elegiac Stanzas for Alban Berg"**, in October 1936. Instead he was struggling much of the time with a novella called ***April,*** the first of a projected trio which was to deal with that insular shrinking from raw experience to which his friend Lawrence Durrell gave the name "The English Death". The subsequent disappearance of the finished novella may have been little loss, to judge from **"Death of an Explorer"** (1937), Gascoyne's only published short story. This is printed after the Journal to help increase the size of the present book (the Journal itself runs to only 70 pages), but despite the soupçon of Kafka dissolved in its semi-fantasy, its central character is too determinedly ingenuous to involve the reader's feelings in his final fall down a bottomless well.

More valuable is the book's other makeweight: Gascoyne's essay on the Russian emigré thinker Léon Chestov, originally published in *Horizon* in 1949, ten years after Chestov's death. In describing Chestov's philosophy, which distrusted the substitution of human reason and fixed ideas for a truly existential response to the "inevitably mysterious" nature of reality, Gascoyne is also describing his own process of self-discovery—a process which his Journal presents in the more halting terms of a young man; and in offering Chestov as the extension of a line which runs from Pascal through Kierkegaard and Nietzsche to Dostoievsky, he is only recapitulating his own ambition expressed in his Journal in July 1937: "to achieve significance and coherence. . . . to be worthy of Pascal, Kierkegaard, Dostoievsky, Baudelaire, Rimbaud, Nietzsche. . . ."

If all this seems unduly high-flown and high-minded (lacking, that is, the sense of humour which Gascoyne sees in his Journal as a typically English technique of avoidance), it should be said that the Journal reveals not only the dynamics but the drifting of a young writer's life. . . .

Although, on balance, Gascoyne treats other people rather less fully than he treats his own internal wrestlings, he is notably shrewd (and unflattering) in his descriptions of William Empson, fleetingly encountered in the London Library, and of Caitlin Macnamara, run into with Dylan Thomas in Piccadilly Circus shortly before their marriage. Occasionally, too, he turns an unintentionally humorous searchlight on his youthful seriousness, recording the almost visible shrug of the Belgian surrealist E.L.T. Mesens in response to his dramatic description (in French) of a world about to burst into "red flames"; and, resolved to win a "moral victory" over his weaker nature, plunging into the bathetic example of conquering his fear of the dentist.

But if he does not quite manage the wished-for "cross between Pascal and Jean Cocteau" which he proposes at the beginning of his Journal, Gascoyne succeeds very well in fulfilling the ambition he describes in his entry for March 19, 1937: "to make a record of what I am so that someone . . .may know me as I was, may feel some sort of contact with a sensibility, a passion, an imagination, a restlessness. . .". Gascoyne's Journal transmits his developing responses with an inwardness, and an immediacy, which can hardly fail to involve any reader who remembers what it is like to be young. His candid self-portrait will be even more fascinating to anyone admiring Gascoyne as a poet whose brief but intense moment was so soon to come.

The ***Journal 1936-1937*** differs from the ***Paris Journal*** in presenting itself not as a fragment of the past, but as something to be framed by an introduction, annotation and a postscript, all of which are provided by the David Gascoyne of the present. For this additional material the scholar is properly grateful; but its cooler and more rambling manner of presentation throws into relief the lack of powerful poetry from Gascoyne for fifteen years and more, and may well leave him sadly wondering "Where's the lost young man?"

Philip Gardner, "Propaganda for Being," in The Times Literary Supplement, *No. 4062, February 6, 1981, p. 132.*

ALAN ROSS

More precocious even than Gavin Ewart, David Gascoyne had published a novel, ***Opening Day,*** by the time he was seventeen, a book on Surrealism at the age of nineteen, by when he had written the first of the poems later collected into ***Poems 1937-42***. . . . Two further volumes of lesser poems appeared in the 1950s, but then nothing except some translations over the next 25 years. Depression and breakdown seemed to have shut him off and the writing days looked to be over. (p. 8)

[***Paris Journal, 1937-1939*** and ***Journal, 1936-1937***] reveal, over and above the morbidity and philosophical preoccupations one would have expected from his poetry, an acute feeling for period and place, an unexpected relish for gossip and anecdote, and an uncompromising view of physical shortcomings in the appearance of acquaintances. Beneath the gentle demeanour of the metaphysical poet, an autobiographer of some asperity has been lurking.

The earlier, though second to be published, journal I find the more rewarding. Less tortured and unprofitably introspective, it offers, as well as revealing glimpses of various literary figures—Grigson, Empson, Charles Madge, Humphrey Jennings, Esmond Romilly, Dylan Thomas among others—a detached, insider's view of Mass-Observation, surrealist activities, Mosley marches, the Spanish Civil War and the Communist Party. However mild and ineffectual Gascoyne may have presented himself as being, there were no flies on him. Frequently self-scolding, 'most of this journal seems unreadable. Pages and pages of turgid unreadable nonsense' etc, he manages to create in vivid and sympathetic terms the alternating euphoria and despair, excitement and disillusion, most writers feel before they quite know what they are doing. Immensely knowledgeable on certain subjects as Gascoyne already was, the poems on which his reputation rests had still to be written. When, shortly after the journal ends, he began publishing them, they were not really the poems one would have expected from an ex-surrealist and translator of Hölderlin. Rather, the purity and formality of their diction, their metaphysical intensity, reverts to an altogether earlier manner than that of Auden and the other main 1930's poets. The vision behind the grey, subdued landscapes of Gascoyne's poetry is a fragmented, threatened one. There is little variety of tone or obvious technical display. But in his best poems, like **"Noctambules"**, **"Jardin du Palais Royal"**, **"A Wartime Dawn"** and **"The Gravel-Pit Field"**, one becomes aware of a style and a note that is Gascoyne's alone. . . . What is encouraging about the journals is that they suggest a shrewd and amusing observer of contemporary foibles, to the extent that one could envisage a late period in the poetry that might be more anecdotal and idiomatic as well as lighter in mood. Gascoyne's literary career, after so long and distressing an interruption, deserves a happy ending. There are few writers from whom one would more welcome poems out of the blue. (pp.8-9)

Alan Ross, in a review of "Paris Journals, 1937-1939" and "Journal, 1936-1937," in London Magazine, *n. s. Vol. 21, No. 3, June, 1981, pp. 8-9.*

Robert (von Ranke) Graves

1895-1985

(Also wrote with Laura Riding under joint pseudonym of Barbara Rich) English poet, novelist, critic, nonfiction writer, short story writer, translator, dramatist, librettist, editor, and author of children's books.

© Rollie McKenna

Graves is considered one of the twentieth century's most versatile and talented authors and is acknowledged as one of the era's finest love poets. His poetry is admired for its adherence to romantic tenets within classical structures, its syntactical clarity, and its examination of a wide range of esoteric subjects. Graves's verse was influenced by three major factors: his World War I experiences, which inform his early verse; his personal and professional association with American poet Laura Riding, who helped refine his verse technique during the 1930s, when he composed some of his most memorable love poems; and his mythology of the Feminine Muses—the White Goddess and the Black Goddess—which are explained in detail in the prose studies *The White Goddess: A Historical Grammar of Poetic Myth* (1948) and *Mammon and The Black Goddess* (1965), both of which played an important role in the mysticism of his later poetry. Graves is also widely respected for his prose works, including the novel *I, Claudius* (1934), winner of the Hawthornden Prize and the James Tait Black Memorial Prize; a sequel, *Claudius the God and His Wife Messalina* (1934); and an admired autobiography, *Good-Bye to All That* (1929).

Graves began writing poetry while a student at Charterhouse, an English parochial school, before enlisting in the Royal Welch Fusiliers and serving in World War I. During the war, Graves published his first two major collections, *Over the Brazier* (1916) and *Fairies and Fusiliers* (1917). The verse in these volumes, unlike the humanistic war poems of Wilfred Owen and Siegfried Sassoon, confront the war digressively through the use of nursery rhymes, supernatural elements, and detached humor. In other poems, Graves avoids the war completely in favor of pastoral love ballads. In 1916, Graves was seriously injured during the Somme offensive, and his injuries eventually rendered him unfit for service. Following the war, he attempted to write poetry to relieve his emotionally crippling battle fatigue, a process recommended by W. H. R. Rivers, a psychologist whose writings also influenced much of Graves's criticism of the early 1920s. Graves published several volumes of poetry during this period, including *Country Sentiment* (1920), *The Pier-Glass* (1921), *Whipperginny* (1923), *Welchman's Hose* (1925), and *Poems, 1914-1926* (1927). Many of these poems, among them the popular "Rocky Acres" and "The Pier-Glass," contain desolate landscapes and ghosts which serve as metaphorical representations of Graves's neurasthenic psyche.

Graves's alliance with Laura Riding profoundly affected his poetry of the 1930s. According to Douglas Day, "The influence of Laura Riding is quite possibly the most important single element in [Graves's] poetic career: she persuaded him to curb his digressiveness and his rambling philosophizing and to concentrate instead on terse, ironic poems written on personal themes." While it is argued by some critics that Graves's verse was already progressing in this direction, Riding is most often credited with expediting his development. Unlike the pervasive sentimentality of his earlier work, Graves's poetry of this period is dispassionate and dialectic, exploring the division between human mental and physical processes. In such collections as *Poems, 1926-1930* (1931), *Poems, 1930-1933* (1933), and *Collected Poems* (1938), Graves eschews topical themes, focusing instead on love and morality.

Graves's personal and professional relationship with Riding ended in 1939, after which he formulated his personal mythology centering on the White Goddess. Described by Martin Seymour-Smith as "a threefold process of Birth, Copulation, and Death, or of Creation, Fulfillment, and Destruction," the White Goddess derives from *The Golden Bough,* Sir James Frazier's anthropological study of primitive matriarchal cultures and classical mythology, as well as from Celtic legend and Graves's reading of the English Romantic poets. In what is perhaps his most famous poem, "To Juan at the Winter Solstice," Graves states: "There is one story and one story only / That will prove worth your telling"; this singular tale is the adoration of the Goddess as Muse, who controls both life and death. Graves's poetry of this period, represented in *Poems, 1938-1945* (1946), *Poems and Satires* (1951), and *Collected Poems* (1959), is noted for its structural adeptness and lyrical qualities. Michael Kirkham noted: "In this poetry the romantic images of a few early poems, and the emotional involvement with his subject characteristic of his first period, combined with the technical discipline, intellectual control, moral insight and self-knowledge acquired during the Laura Riding years to produce a romantic poetry laced with toughness and scepticism.'' Graves's study of Sufism and other aspects of mysticism eventually led him to incorporate the Black Goddess of Wisdom into his poetic lexicon. The poems in *More Poems* (1961), *New Poems* (1962), *Man Does, Woman Is* (1964), and *Love Respelt* (1965) express a transcendent love that, predicated on pain and despair, culminates in elevated awareness. These volumes consist of short, epigrammatic pieces which display Graves's experimentation with assonance, rhyme, and *cynghannedd,* a traditional Welsh form of multiple alliteration. While critics acknowledge Graves's masterful handling of these devices, many maintain that they are utilized as substitutes for meaningful subject matter. Graves's later poems are amply represented in his last anthology, *New Collected Poems* (1977).

Graves claimed that he wrote novels only to earn money. Nevertheless, his prose is admired for the lucid qualities it shares with his verse. His most memorable works of fiction are the popular historical novels *I, Claudius* and *Claudius the God and His Wife Messalina*. These works document the political intrigue and moral dereliction of the Roman Empire's waning years in terms that suggest parallels with twentieth-century civilization. *I, Claudius* was adapted into an acclaimed British television series. In *Count Belisarius* (1938), Graves displays his knowledge of the Byzantine era, while in *Sergeant Lamb of the Ninth* (1940; published in the United States as *Sergeant Lamb in America*) and *Proceed, Sergeant Lamb* (1941) he demonstrates his understanding of military tactics through his depiction of a British soldier in the Royal Welch Fusiliers at the time of the American Revolution. In *The Story of Marie Powell: Wife to Mr. Milton* (1943), Graves attempts to debunk John Milton's reputation as a great poet by viewing him through the eyes of his first wife, who is depicted as Milton's intellectual equal. *The Golden Fleece* (1944; published in the United States as *Hercules, My Shipmate*) is a retelling of the legend of Jason and the Argonauts and is notable for its inclusion of poems and mythology informed by the White Goddess. *King Jesus* (1946) is a controversial novel in which Graves postulates that Jesus Christ survived the crucifixion. In *Watch the North Wind Rise* (1949), Graves presents a futuristic utopia that worships a feminine god and adheres to customary rituals. Graves's supernatural novella, *The Shout* (1929), was adapted for film.

Graves is also regarded as an insightful critic, although many of his judgments reveal his personal idiosyncrasies and have generated controversy. Graves's early criticism, including *On English Poetry: Being an Irregular Approach to the Psychology of This Art, from Evidence Mainly Subjective* (1922) and *Poetic Unreason and Other Studies* (1925), displays his understanding of the psychological theories of W. H. R. Rivers. These studies are viewed as precursors of modern literary analysis as practiced by such critics as William Empson and I. A. Richards. With Laura Riding, Graves wrote two acclaimed volumes, *A Survey of Modernist Poetry* (1927) and *A Pamphlet against Anthologies* (1928; published in the United States as *Against Anthologies*). Graves's later criticism, however, has been faulted for lacking systematic judgments of authors and literary movements. For example, *The Crowning Privilege: The Clark Lectures, 1954-1955, Also Various Essays on Poetry and Sixteen New Poems* (1955; revised as *The Crowning Privilege: Collected Essays on Poetry*) is remembered for Graves's hyperbolic attacks on such poets as Dante, William Wordsworth, William Butler Yeats, and W. H. Auden. *The White Goddess,* while providing valuable insight into Graves's own poetry, is a partially conjectural essay on mythology and literature. In *Good-Bye to All That,* possibly his most enduring nonfiction prose work, Graves relates events from his early life, including his World War I experiences and his tumultuous first marriage.

(See also *CLC,* Vols. 1, 2, 6, 11, 39, 44; *Contemporary Authors,* Vols. 5-8, rev. ed., Vol. 117 [obituary]; *Contemporary Authors New Revision Series,* Vol. 5; *Something about the Author,* Vol. 45; *Dictionary of Literary Biography,* Vol. 20; and *Dictionary of Literary Biography Yearbook: 1985*.)

GEORGE FRASER

[*The essay excerpted below was originally published in 1947 in* The Changing World.]

If we wanted to introduce Robert Graves's poetry to some receptive and intelligent person who did not know much about it—and there are many such people, for Graves as a poet is merely a fine artist preoccupied with a rather strange personal theme, what he says has sometimes a good deal of philosophic interest, but he has neither a warning nor a consoling message for his age—where would we start? We would wish to illustrate the solid excellence of style in much of his poetry, its occasional intense lyricism, a certain defiant toughness of mood which it expresses; and we would also wish to hint at that strange personal theme. **"Ulysses"** might be as good a poem to start with as another. . . . Graves set out, like Ovid, to comment, from an unheroic point of view, on a well-known heroic story; but his comments are more searching than Ovid's, and though this poem can stand by itself, it also fits into the general body of his work as a variation on his favourite theme, which is the relationship particularly between love and sexuality, more generally between the spirit and the body, more generally still between the mind and nature. That relationship Graves sees as sometimes a comic, sometimes a tragic, but always essentially an *awkward* relationship; it is never happy and harmonious.

Graves is peculiar among poets in that (though unlike Leopardi, for instance, who had something of the same attitude, he is a man of robust physical energy) he has a sense of awkward and unwilling attachment to his own body; and that awkwardness and unwillingness are, again and again, the main *theme* of his poems. He can treat the topic in a thoroughly amusing fashion, as in the comic and rather indecent little poem [**"Down, Wanton, Down!"**] . . . But his more common attitude to the body, to its lusts, to its energies, to its mortality, to the clogging foreign weight that it hangs about him, is a far more sombre one. . . . Graves is concerned not so much with the body's mortality as with what he regards as the bearable, just bearable nastiness of ordinary physical life. . . . As a love poet, Graves is essentially a romantic, along the same lines as (though probably not consciously influenced by) the troubadours and the poets of the *dolce stil nuovo:* a critic like Denis de Rougemont would connect his hatred of the body with their alleged Catharism, and it is true that Graves, in his latest novel, shows a great interest in the Gnostics, for whom the real fall was the creation of the world. But I think Graves's philosophy, in so far as he has one, springs from a fact about his personal nature: the fact does not spring from a philosophy. This sense of awkward and unwilling attachment to his body is, as it were, a *given* factor for him. A critic, too, must take it as a given factor.

Much of Graves's poetry, then, will be concerned with the dissatisfaction of the lover with sex, of the spirit with the body, of the mind with nature; and yet with facing the fact that love is bound to sex, spirit to body, and mind to nature. It is revealing to read, in this connection, some of his abundant and on the whole unsatisfactory early verses. Graves's early work does not show much promise of his present strikingly individual and distinguished style. He became known first as a war poet. After the war he relapsed for a little into very weak writing in the Georgian bucolic style, and in the preface to ***Whipperginny*** (1923) he describes some of these rustic pieces as 'bankrupt stock', and this whole manner as the result of a mood of 1918, 'the desire to escape from a painful war neurosis into an Arcadia of amatory fancy'. These escapist pieces have most of the qualities that we dislike today in the Georgians, the bucolic-hearty strain, . . . the manly beer-drinking note, . . . and what Belloc, in 'Caliban's Guide to Letters', calls the prattling style. . . . And today when we come upon this self-conscious rusticity, these awkward assumptions of innocence in verse, we remember the advice of Patrice de la Tour du Pin: 'Do not play, like children, with the parts of yourself that are no longer childish.' But if these escapist pieces are mostly rather mawkish, the war neurosis did not itself produce very memorable poetry. . . . Yet we may well suppose that the ardours and horrors of the 1914-18 war, and his retreat into 'an Arcadia of amatory fancy' afterwards, provided Graves with his main poetic material; in his later work he has, we may say, been largely concerned with refining, controlling, and generalizing the practical attitudes that were forced upon him in these exacting years. He had a facile success as a war poet and a writer of bucolics; it is very much to his credit that he should have struggled through from that sort of success to one more lonely but very much more worth having.

Examples of his early style at its least satisfactory can be found in ***Poems, 1914-1926.*** Graves's second volume of collected poems, ***Poems, 1926-1930,*** has an epigraph from Laura Riding:

> It is a conversation between angels now
> Or between who remain when all are gone.

and his style in this volume has suffered the astonishing purgation that this epigraph suggests. The Arcadianism has gone. Nature and a self-conscious bucolic childishness are no longer considered as cures for a poetic, or a metaphysical unease that has become a far deeper and wider thing than any war-neurosis. (pp. 125-31)

Graves, in his volume of 1930, anticipates Auden's early manner so often and so startlingly . . . that we may wonder why he did not enjoy a revival of prestige in the 1930s, on the tail, as it were, of Auden's sumptuous early renown. The chief reason was probably that, unlike Auden (who has had a succession of messages), Graves has no obvious message for the age. He is probably most moving and most beautiful as a poet in these love poems which are concerned entirely with themes from his personal life. . . . About politics, as about war, as about life in general, his feeling seems to be that people are to do their duty and not to expect things to turn out well. His Belisarius hates the corrupt, cowardly Justinian, rather admires the straightforward virtues of the barbarians he is fighting against, but never thinks of ousting Justinian from his place, or going over to the other side; and Belisarius is a hero very much to Graves's taste. He has a poem about that period, **"The Cuirassiers of the Frontier":** the soldiers who speak in it say

> We, not the city, are the Empire's soul:
> A rotten tree lives only in its rind.

Does Graves feel about the British Empire, or about western European civilization generally, more or less what he feels about Byzantium? He gives no hint about that. But whereas when he fought it was the horrors of war that came most closely home to him, in his later poetry he thinks more of the honour and nobility of a soldier's life, of the good fortune of an early death. . . . Yet if he has managed, in retrospect, to purge war of its horror, horror of another kind has gathered in his later poetry around the love in which he sought an escape from war. His love poems are nearly all, though wonderfully touching, almost unbearably sad. . . . Even in a love poem Graves cannot repress his faint grimace of disgust at the body; and in the saddest of all his love poems, **"A Love Story",** he describes how love had dispersed the winter whose horror besieged him, transformed it, how his loved one, 'warped in the weather, turned beldamish', how the horror came back again, and how he realized that it had been a mistake 'to serenade Queen Famine'. His advice, in fact, about love, as about other things, seems to be to make the most of the good in the evil, of the good moment which heralds the bad change. But his final note is always sad:

> And now warm earth was Arctic sea,
>   Each breath came dagger-keen;
> Two bergs of glinting ice were we,
>   The broad moon sailed between;
> There swam the mermaids, tailed and finned,
> And love went by upon the wind
>   As though it had not been.

Only the lucid wintry fantasy there, and the compelling canorous voice, only the romantic trappings of which Graves had never entirely divested himself, console us for the cruel thing said.

It would be wrong to think of Graves as an entirely pessimistic poet. He is pessimistic about the world that exists. He has no message for the age, in that he does not think that things will turn out well (as, in their different ways, Auden and Eliot do). Some writers, like Orwell, who expect things to turn out badly, are at least very much concerned about this: and that also gives them, in a sense, a message; it is their part 'to foretell visible calamity—'. Graves seems, on the whole, to think that it is in the nature of things to turn out badly, and only a fool would make a fuss about it. But there is some realm or other of subsisting value (in a recent poem, he calls it 'excellence') which the change, which is the badness, cannot touch. . . . And in his last volume there is also a religious poem (largely translated from ancient Greek texts), **"Instructions to the Orphic Adept",** in which it is suggested that complete self-recollection is a way of escape from change. The regenerate soul is admonished:

> . . . Man, remember
> What you have suffered here in Samothrace,
> What you have suffered.
> Avoid this spring, which is Forgetfulness;
> Though all the common rout rush down to drink,
> Avoid this spring.

In his poetry, Graves has obeyed these instructions; he has remembered what he has suffered, and, in remembering, has transformed pain into the excellence of art. He is a very fine poet, and a poet whose vision of some things, of love, of suffering, of pain, of honour, is much deeper, stronger, and calmer than the vision that most of us can claim. His temperament may estrange intimacy; his chief preoccupations may be irrelevant to our most urgent contemporary problems: And when he deals with the theme of the body in a prison he may be dealing with a theme rather excessively private (in the sense that readers, like myself, who have not a parallel feeling about their own bodies, have to make a rather conscious effort of sympathy). Nevertheless, in his later work in verse—as, indeed, in his better work in prose—he is a model for young writers of a strong and pure style. His journeys may lie rather aside from what we think of as our main roads; but his is a very pure and individual talent, which, if we do care at all for good and honest writing, we ought not to ignore or decry. (pp. 132-35)

George Fraser, "The Poetry of Robert Graves," in his Essays on Twentieth-Century Poets, *Rowman and Littlefield, 1977, pp. 125-35.*

MICHAEL KIRKHAM

While Graves's poetic progress cannot be described as a steady advance—there have been cul-de-sacs and digressions—yet a sequence can be discerned in it. His career falls naturally into four periods, the end of each coinciding with the publication of four out of five of his ***Collected Poems;*** but it has been my aim in this survey to draw attention as much to the continuity between them as to the differences in approach that separate them.

The first period, stretching from 1916 to 1926, was one of confusion. After a false start its two main themes, war—with its aftermath of neurasthenia—and romantic love, came to the fore in his third volume, ***Country Sentiment*** (1920), and dominated his poetry until the end of the period. It was a time of restless experiment in ways of absorbing, psychologically and technically, the impact of the two experiences. On the whole, during these years, they rarely received the full, honest, impersonal realization for which he strove; he was too much at the mercy, as he records in his preface to ***Whipperginny*** (1923), of 'unceasing emotional stress'. At first he contrived in his poems merely to escape from conflict into a literary or folk world of pastoral and simplified emotion; in the second half of this period, however, he sought relief in a more sophisticated self-deception: turning from the inner drama, which has always been his true subject, he applied himself to the exposition in a studiously flat, discursive style of certain theories centering on the abstract *idea* of conflict. The informing intention was antiromantic and self-disciplinary, and the most memorable poems in ***Poems 1914-1926*** are generally the later ones; but a very large proportion of them were external and pedestrian; some, again, were irresponsibly cynical, others—though these are altogether more attractive—practised an irony that was too elegantly detached.

The next twelve years, concluding with the publication of ***Collected Poems 1938,*** were the period of Laura Riding's influence. Her example and personal criticism were largely responsible for the compression, rhythmic tautness and rigorously intellectual approach characteristic of Graves's verse now. His poems achieved impersonality and intellectual control, not through the avoidance of personal involvement, but, at first, by a savagely self-critical, often self-mortifying attitude towards his emotions and by restricting themselves to the expression of such negative responses as scorn, aggression, scepticism and bitterness. During the 'thirties he relaxed this posture, and poems celebrating a new kind of love (romantic without being sentimental), a theme treated once or twice at the very end of his first period, became more frequent. His writing answered to a new conception of poetry and the proper subject-matter of poetry that had taken shape during his discussions with Laura Riding. A basic premise of her thought was that the poets were left with but a single task—'the determination of values'. Poetry was for him now not psychotherapy, as it had been, but the most direct means of apprehending reality. His new themes were his own earlier romanticism and present moral shortcomings, the falsity of social values, truth to self, and the evaluation of contemporary civilization. He came to see himself as having two poetic roles—that of moralist on the one hand and of love poet on the other, the two roles brought into close relationship by Graves's view of love as the source of the highest values. At the same time this period saw the stabilizing of a previous tendency to use emblem, allegory, fable and symbol rather than direct statement and comment aided by metaphor. Elements of the bizarre, humour, wit and irony were added to complete the impersonalizing process.

The third period, extending from 1938 to 1959, was dominated by the mythology of the White Goddess. Except in a few satires Graves's sole theme was the man-woman relationship. The Goddess symbolizes the feminine principle, woman in all her attributes, and the myths tell the story of the inevitable suffering that the poets who choose to serve her must undergo. Yet in that service Graves discovered the spiritual values on which until recently he has based his view of life. In this poetry the romantic images of a few early poems, and the emotional involvement with his subject characteristic of his first period, combined with the technical discipline, intellectual control, moral insight and self-knowledge acquired during the Laura Riding years to produce a romantic poetry laced with toughness and scepticism. It was during these two decades that Graves first succeeded in maintaining a *general* balance—achieved previously in only the exceptional poem—between a romantic desire for the impossible and miraculous, a state beyond conflict, and a realistic awareness of its impossibility.

The period ended with the publication in 1959 of his fourth ***Collected Poems.*** Since then four more volumes of poetry and another collection have appeared. This remarkable productivity signifies the beginning of yet another phase. Graves now celebrates the Black Goddess of Wisdom, who in early Jewish, Orphic and Sufi mystery cults brought to the few who, having suffered continuous death and recreation at the White Goddess's hand, had fully served their apprenticeship to her, knowledge of a final certitude in love. Incertitude had been hitherto the essential fact in Graves's experience of the relationship with woman; here is a new reality of love, that transcends the needs of physical expression, the *accomplishment* of the impossible and the miraculous. Behind the experience rendered in these poems and the imagery in which it is embodied there are the teachings and traditional stories of Sufism, a Wisdom-cult of uncertain origin which is known to have attracted adherents from all religions, especially from among poets (much of its literature is in poetic form), since the time of Mohammed; Graves has evidently discovered in Sufism a way of thought closely resembling his own.

This summary of Graves's career necessarily leaves out much that is important in his development. Interpreted in one way, for example, his first two periods tell the story of his search for a theme. The postwar neurasthenia which for a time psychologically crippled Graves was responsible for deflecting him, after a brief, unsuccessful spell as a war poet, from public to personal themes: he turned his attention to the problems of realizing poetically the violent emotional disturbances that afflicted him. At the same time his neurasthenia was partly responsible for the urgency with which he also turned, at first as an escape, to romantic love as a theme. The neurosis was an accident of circumstance but one that has had a long-standing effect on Graves's work. It not only accounts for the desperate quality of his early love poetry, but it has made a permanent impression on his personality and therefore on the nature of his love poetry ever since: his emotional life, as he records it, swings violently between the extremes of ecstasy and anguish. At every stage in his development this unbalance has been the focal point of much of his writing. The longing for some stabilizing certainty has been, perhaps, the chief moral compulsion behind his poetry, the basis of his kind of romanticism, as an undeluded awareness of the actual prevailing uncertainty has provided the counterbalancing scepticism and moral realism also characteristic of his mature work. In his second period Graves extended his range by expressing through his verse a complete system of values—attacking the falsities and hollowness of an exclusively social reality and declaring a personal reality based on truth to self and mental vigilance; but the love theme was still central. Supporting this position was a conception of love as a moral testing, of woman as man's judge, and specifically an idealization of Laura Riding's moral and intellectual qualities. The White Goddess mythology of the next period gave rise to a love poetry of a peculiar kind, in which the personal reality was celebrated as a *creation* solely of the man-woman relationship, and the phases of love were represented as a cyclic religious experience.

Of course Graves's development was also a growth in technical discipline—from the early prettiness, sentimentality and prolixity through the spare, taut, intellectual style of his second period to the more relaxed, emotionally more complex but strictly controlled verse of the early mythological poems, and so on. This growth roughly paralleled the poet's progress towards a viable moral and intellectual position. His experiences as a soldier had destroyed the simple Christian faith of his very earliest poems, and in the years immediately following the war he made no attempt to put anything in its place. But as early as 1921 the results of his studies in psychology, anthropology and the history of religion were being felt in his writing; in the phase that ensued he set himself to work out in his verse an attitude of (then fashionable) ethical relativism, while in his criticism he outlined a parallel scheme of extreme aesthetic relativism. This attitude ran counter to his deepest instincts and was poetically unfruitful. It lingered as a flavour in the early volumes of his second period, but the bitterness of these poems was in marked contrast with the studied neutrality of those that had preceded them and was a sign, rather, of his discontent with life lived in a moral vacuum. His work during this period showed a steady advance towards the acceptance, and a progressively more assured expression, of a consistent world-view and absolute moral standards. The White Goddess Myth made possible a different kind of poetry but the world-view and the standards embodied in it were essentially the same.

In yet another interpretation the history of Graves's changing style is the history of his various, more or less successful attempts to find an impersonal medium for personal, often distressing themes. The early, abortive experiments with the forms of ballad and nursery rhyme can be understood as part of this sustained effort. With a few exceptions his folk poems failed in their purpose because they were simplifications rather than impersonalizations of his conflicts. They were followed, in turn, by cynical, 'philosophical' and classically restrained poems, most of which were more successful in suppressing than expressing the poet's emotions. But, as I have already noted, the most satisfying strategy—the externalizing of the inner drama through allegory and symbol—Graves had discovered early in his career. During his second period he wrote almost entirely in this mode, enlarging the element of impersonation (the assumption of personae) and, by the practice of an austere, mocking, ironic, off-hand manner, the degree of detachment between the poet and his material. To accommodate the more positive emotions that began to appear again in his poetry during the late 'thirties and early 'forties he revived the earlier romantic symbolism, which now found its place in a rich mythology devised to express a broader range of experience and a more highly organized scheme of more complex attitudes. The mythology, considered retrospectively, was a natural if an unexpected conclusion to Graves's search for an impersonalizing medium. (pp. 4-9)

There are several ways of defining the unique character of his best poetry. No single definition, of course, will encompass all its qualities, but perhaps the most nearly adequate is that it is an individual blend of romantic and realistic impulses—the balancing of an aspiration towards a perfect, timeless state of being where contradictions are resolved against an acute sense of the limits set by actuality. His most impressive poems, it could be argued, are those in which the contrary pulls of romantic aspiration and realistic awareness are so strong and so equal that the effect is less one of poise than of a finely maintained tension. (p. 10)

• • • • •

Critics who differ over the nature of Graves's poetic achievement seem to agree about its limitations. A common judgement is that in some way Graves has evaded the problems of the twentieth century, forsaking the arena of general concern, where, for example, Pound, Eliot, Empson, Bottrall and Auden have honourably fought, for the less demanding labours, albeit performed with incomparable skill, of the private garden. It is true that his themes are not public and rarely topical, that his imagery, though exact, vivid and richly evocative, is uncomplicated, rural, and traditional and makes very little allusion to the realities of an urban, technologically sophisticated society or, except indirectly, to modern scientific and philosophic thought; he has, in fact, deliberately excluded from his collections those poems in which it does. But his poetry is no less fully engaged with the modern world for having these characteristics. We have a right to expect a contemporary poet to be in some sense 'modern'—that his work should bear the impression of the age in which it is written—even if he is profoundly at variance with the tendencies of that age; it is a question not of themes and images, however, but of sensibility. The quality of a poet's modernity can be gauged less from the amount of direct reference to contemporary history or direct indebtedness to contemporary thought than from the degree of (implicit or explicit) *awareness* embodied in his work of contemporary ideas and events, and the quality of his response to them. By this definition Graves's poetry is modern. He lives in spiritual exile from our civilization, but he rejects its values neither ignorantly nor irresponsibly.

The First World War, which for many societies marked the end of the old stabilities and the beginning of a new era, served also as Graves's initiation into our modern world. His direct experience of the war was the crucial factor both in his personal and poetic development. But, whether they were actively involved or not, it was a test that few writers passed. Graves was one of the few—Blunden and Sassoon, for example, psychologically did not survive—who in the end was toughened and enlarged by it. Slowly his poetry absorbed the impact of violence but, more importantly, between 1923 and 1938 he worked hard at coming to terms with the war's aftermath, the final collapse of the old religious values and social traditions. During the 'twenties he looked for an explanation of himself and his society, ultimately for a new order and new certainties, in contemporary psychology and anthropology, and his later studies with Laura Riding of ancient religion, mythology, philosophy, scientific and political thought were directed towards the same goal. The poetry of these years was written out of an honest, intimate awareness of the 'botched civilization' lamented by Pound and the spiritual wasteland depicted by Eliot. In the Foreword to ***Collected Poems 1938,*** noting the high proportion of his poems which are close and energetic studies of 'the disgusting, the contemptible and the evil', he interprets this as 'the blurted confession of a naturally sanguine temperament: that the age into which I was born . . . has been intellectually and morally in perfect confusion.' . . . At this time he considered it part of the poet's task—or fate—to be exposed to, but not to be destroyed by, such confusion. He comments, in an introductory letter to Ronald Bottrall's *The Turning Path* (1939), on 'the personal and immediate hell of living unfulfilment' reflected in Bottrall's poems, that it is 'a shameful hell, not to be satirized even, and hardly worth the harrowing—yet a hell through which we must all pass with greater or lesser laboriousness according to our sins of vanity'. Both passages refer in the main to the poems of moral criticism, such as **"Hell"** and **"Ship Master",** directed against either a worthless society or the poet's implication with the motives of that society. He believed, however, that the poet must go beyond negation to affirm a contrary reality. He took seriously the poet's duty to bring order into this intellectual and moral chaos. In **"A Private Correspondence on Reality"** between himself and Laura Riding, published in ***Epilogue III*** (1937), he recalls: 'It was as a poet in search of an integration of reality that you first knew me. The problem for me was at that time the same technical one that faced all my fellow-poets: what to do when the world of thought had grown unmanageable.' . . . The 'destructive' poems of Graves's second period were complemented, then, by poems of a 'creative', liberating purpose, which were no less responsive to the contemporary predicament. For they aimed at erecting a structure of values—mental clarity, hard work, commonsense, love—to replace the rotten edifice of Western, Christian civilization.

Graves was more immediately engaged with the problems of modern society during his second period than at any other time. This does not mean that he ceased to be a *modern* poet after that. One of the achievements of that period, I have proposed, was the creation of a style to answer the challenge of twentieth-century experience. It is unrhetorical, direct, taut, emotionally controlled, ironic, expressing intellectual stringency and a tough, sceptical sensibility. When his theme was no longer the haunted house and the 'fallen tower' (weak in the west wall and in the underpinning at the south-eastern angle) of modern civilization, when he turned, in the White Goddess poetry, to a reality not describable in a language of contemporary reference, then this style and manner of response brought with it evidence of previous confrontations with the contemporary world. I tried to demonstrate in my comments on **"End of Play"** the close relationship between the moral commonsense informing the destructive part of that poem and the creative affirmation of the concluding stanza: the latter asserts a new, unreasonable faith in the same fierce, strict tone that Graves uses in the earlier stanzas to dismiss the sentimentalities of the old faith. And **"End of Play"** points forward in theme and imagery to **"The White Goddess"** and other poems of the 'forties.

Graves's achievement is that, although, as he says in the Foreword to ***Collected Poems 1938,*** educated in 'the anodynic tradition of poetry' and owning a 'naturally sanguine temperament,'' . . . he survived through sheer emotional stamina the trauma of his war experiences and by scrupulous, unremitting hard work remade himself and his poetry; between 1923, when he left the Georgian fold, and 1926 he thereby turned himself into a *modern* poet. The language of desire in Graves has always been in the romantic tradition, but since 1926 his romanticism has been resilient, a moral protest rather than a retreat; and the tough, intellectual vein in his poetry shows the influence not only of Laura Riding but of the Elizabethans, Ben Jonson, the Metaphysicals and the Cavalier poets. As I have argued, Graves's peculiar fusion of romantic emotion, moral realism and a frequently classical elegance and urbanity makes for a more complex effect, a wider range of mood and tone, than is generally granted. His poetry shows that allusiveness, juxtaposition of parts rather than logical sequence, and dislocated syntax, the techniques of Pound and Eliot, did not in the 'twenties constitute the only way of solving the poet's problem 'when the world of thought had grown unmanageable'. In this he resembles Yeats; like Yeats, too, Graves sought meaning and consistency in a personal synthesis of knowledge.

The White Goddess Myth, of course, objectifies a personal drama, but one that takes place within a wider context, contemporary and timeless. It is necessary to insist that the aims of the mythological poetry are continuous with those of his previous work: the synthesis embodied in the Myth originated in the *full* emotional content of his earlier poetry, and is only the culmination of that search for an intellectual and ethical system which had animated his work since about 1923. The mythological poetry, therefore, as much as the poetry of his second period, arose from his intense concern with the spiritual dilemmas of the twentieth century: providing one answer to the radical problems of thought and belief—intellectual confusion, the collapse of absolute values, and religious apathy—that have marked out an age characterized by unprecedented social change and the waning power of the Christian tradition. He has compressed into the one symbol his total response to this situation. The Goddess is the principal of flux itself. She is also, however, a spiritual grace, a changeless certainty, on which the poet can call to defeat flux.

Graves has achieved consistency, despite appearances to the contrary, without sacrificing breadth of interest or variety of mood. The Goddess is at the centre of a complex of meanings. She represents, separately or together, the poet's inspiration, his aesthetic and moral conscience, the spiritual reality in the man-woman relationship (both the ordeal and the ideal of love), fate or providence in the poet's life, a force in history governing human destiny, an alternative to the Christian God, a goal of mystical perfection. Far from narrowing Graves's scope, as is frequently alleged, the White Goddess Theme is no less than 'the single poetic theme of life and death'; which takes in also the question of immortality, 'of what survives of the beloved'. The chief events in her story—love, death and rebirth—are in any religious conception the central experiences of human life. Her relevance extends beyond the particular chaos of modern history: she is the Mother of All Living, the necessary condition of existence, combining good and evil.

However, the mythic pattern does exclude from most of the White Goddess poems certain emotional possibilities. The seasonal, ritual and lunar symbolisms were designed to express the poet's subjection to a recurring cycle of experience, ending in the inescapable defeat of love. In ***The White Goddess*** Graves states that the main problem of pagan religion—and it is his own—is contained in the meaning of the Druidic letter-name of R, 'I flow away'; it implies the question: 'Must all things swing round for ever? or how can we escape from the Wheel?' . . . As Mr Hoffman says, in *Barbarous Knowledge,* the "expansion of feeling and intellectual joy which other poets from Shakespeare to Donne and Yeats have known," . . . though not absent from Graves's poetry, are in the White Goddess poems usually presented as transitory states, a tenuous hope created out of despair. But there are exceptions. Early in his third period, in his **"Instructions to the Orphic Adept"**, Graves described at least one solution to the problem of paganism, a kind of liberation. It was: not to forget past sufferings, to remember at each stage the whole cycle, and thus to transcend them. There were other poems—like **"Theseus and Ariadne"**, **"The Turn of the Moon"**, and **"Ruby and Amethyst"**—which, in celebrating without reservation the perfection of the female principle, freed the poet's psyche from the prison of a deterministic pattern. To his latest poems, written in honour of the Black Goddess of Wisdom, Mr Hoffman's words no longer apply at all. They proclaim Graves's final release from the wheel of suffering. Without any doubt such poems as **"Ambience"**, **"Whole Love"**, **"Iron Palace"**, and **"Deliverance"**—indeed, most of **"Love Respelt"**—manifest precisely an 'expansion of feeling and intellectual joy'. (pp. 269-74)

[There] should be no question of Graves's standing. I have avoided classifying his work as either 'major' or 'minor', vague categories usually implying standards extrinsic to literary judgement. One can say, however, that his best poems offer what in any one age only a few poems offer: they exemplify, with the accents of an alert mind and a passionate nature, possible moral stances in the face of contemporary experience—responses of such completeness, sureness and complexity as to satisfy the modern reader's need for a coherent, authoritative attitude to the world in which both he and the writer live. (p. 274)

Michael Kirkham, in his The Poetry of Robert Graves, *Oxford University Press, 1969, 284 p.*

D. NARAYANSWAMY

Robert Graves's poetry of the first period of his poetic career must be of interest to his readers from the viewpoint of the manner in which his early experiences of life were transformed into materials of his poetry and rendered a set of poetic aims inevitable and organically connected with his later mythological poetry. Taking to the composition of poetry as far back as 1909, "he had already begun a series of difficult technical experiments in prosody and phrasing," he turned it into an aesthetically rewarding means of refuge from the menacing privations of charterhouse. "I never sat chewing a poem. My poetry writing has always been a painful process of continual corrections, corrections on top of corrections, and persistent dissatisfaction"—this confession coming as it does from the author himself throws light on the extraordinarily painstaking efforts made by the poet to perfect his medium. This habit of rewriting—thirty-five revisions being the maximum—and selection has resulted in the radical modification or total loss of such poems as failed to satisfy his exacting critical standards. That only one poem survives from his first two volumes, ***Over the Brazier*** and ***Fairies and Fusiliers*** of 1916 and 1917 respectively, probably indicates the severity of the "weeding-out". (p. 126)

Graves exhibited his independence not only by the positions he took regarding two widely popular literary fashions: the theme of war and Georgianism, but also by the deft way in which he freed himself from the strait-jacket of the iambic metre and built up his own literary ancestor, Skelton, at a time when "Donne was the literary ancestor of the hour".

The impact of the First World War was so great on Graves's personality and his poetry that he became a neurasthenic as a result of his acute familiarity with trench warfare; and the theme of war, that made its appearance in the first two volumes, continued to engage his attention throughout the first period 1914-1926. . . . Simplicity of language was a favourite literary tenet he shared with the other Georgians and the way he evolved this—"the language of plain feeling"—indicates Graves's independence. He did not seek it because it was fashionable to do so; but it was "being true to his poetic instincts"; and, therefore, its need. Thus Graves stood out from the rest of his fellow-poets by his attitude to war and Georgianism even when they were adopted to serve his poetic needs.

The story of Graves's poetic career may be described as an attempt to restrain the force of his romanticism by various means of impersonality. Accordingly he turned to the traditional sources of folklore quite early in his career in order to fashion the method and style of his poems. Impersonality, the failure of which could be fatal to a poem, is the principle that Graves strove to hold fast to from the very start of his career—though the emotion he had to express [according to Michael Kirkham] was "deeply personal": "There is this paradox that the source of his emotion was more deeply personal than was the case with any of his contemporaries and yet from the very start he was busy perfecting various masks or techniques for remaining detached from his experience. His use of themes, tones and formal conventions of folk-poetry may be considered as part of the same endeavour."

Over The Brazier and ***Fairies and Fusiliers***, Graves's first two volumes of poems contain poems relevant to our study, but none of them merit inclusion in ***The Collected Poems 1965***—the latest of its kind. **"To Lucasta on Going to The Wars"; "To Any Dead Officer"; "A Dead Boche"; "Juan"; "Goliath and David"** and **"A Boy in Church"** throw light on the poet's attitude to his themes and the technique adopted by him in the treatment of such themes in his early poetry. Poetry was regarded as "anodynic". He composed poems in order to exorcise the trauma of War. Nursery rhymes, "externalising the inner drama through allegory and symbol"; the assumption of a personal tone and the use of irony provided the poet with the means of controlling his experience.

The next volume of poems, ***Country Sentiment*** (1920), "Written while serving with a cadet battalion in 1917", originated in the desire to escape from a painful war neurosis into an Arcadia of amatory fancy", and a personal theme which ***Over the Brazier*** and ***Fairies and Fusiliers*** lacked was supplied by the ***Country Sentiment:*** "romantic love in a country setting" became the principal theme of the volume. **"Apples and Water"; "Vain and Careless"; "Allie"; "One Hard Look"; "A Frosty Night"; "Rocky Acres"; "Haunted House"**, and **"Outlaws"** contained in this volume are a testimony to the degree of technical mastery acquired by the poet in the use of ballad, folk-song and nursery rhyme and the expression of a concept of love and fear theme that links this period with that of the mythological poetry.

"Apples and Water", adopting the ballad-form and **"Vain and Careless"**, combining the ballad and the nursery rhyme represent the present manner of Graves. The theme of **"Apples and Water"** is the suffering that recurring wars invariably cause in the lives of women and soldiers, generation after generation. (pp. 126-28)

The theme of **"Vain and Careless"** appears to be the incompatibility of "pride and carelessness". This theme is set forth in the poem by means of anecdotes pertaining to representative characters, the impressions of the neighbours concerning such behaviour, and the poet's final moral indictment of them. (p. 129)

A poem dating from this period and deservedly praised by Kirkham for its kinship with the later White Goddess poems by its expression of the ambivalence of love ("My health as a poet lies in my mistrust of the comfortable point of rest in law") is **"A Frosty Night"**, which presents this view of love in the form of a dialogue between an anxious mother and her daughter, who is "Dazed and lost and shaken" on a cold and frosty night after receiving the confession of love for her from her lover. (p. 130)

Aiming at the symbolic representation of the inner drama in the treatment of an ambivalent love-theme, the poem exemplifies Graves's method and attitude to love so coherently that Kirkham was prompted to observe, "out of this seed eventually grew the whole of the White Goddess mythology."

The importance of **"Rocky Acres"; "Outlaws"**; and **"Haunted House"** in relation to the mythological poetry lies in the nature of experience they seek to represent and also in the way in which the poet has tried to objectify his experiences. In giving vent to his neurasthenia, the poet relies on a technique that is similar to the enactment of individual love under the archetypal framework provided by the White Goddess myth. **"Rocky Acres"** exemplifies the method of adopting landscapes—"equivalent of a certain moral landscape" to "relate them to states of mind." Graves chooses a landscape, wild, craggy—"moor ample and bare" and overlorded by the buzzard that floats in the sky under whose rule meeker creatures such as "mice and song-birds" are struck dumb, immobilised and held in a state of unmitigated terror—to objectify his condition. The landscape, rugged and austere in its outlook defies identity with any aspect of time: "Time has never journeyed to this lost land." The "lost land" is singularly lacking in sympathy so that life has turned into "A hardy adventure, full of fear and shock." Such an unhospitable country is "beloved" by the poet "best" since it is "trampled by no shod hooves, bought with no blood" and symbolises not only his personal neurasthenia but also the condition of society in post-war Britain. (p. 131)

Judged by the themes, the method of composition and the relationship with the latter poetry, the poetry of this period 1914-1923, described as "the Anodynic Phase"—for poetry was now considered to be therapeutic in view of the kinship of the poet with the "Witch doctor"—appears to be important, despite its failure to establish Robert Graves as a popular poet in the minds of his readers. Even the publication of the **"Pier-Glass"** in 1921 proving ineffective in this regard, the poet ceased to expect it before becoming almost antisocial as indicated by **"Reader Over My Shoulder"**:

> Know me, have done; I am a proud spirit
> And you for over clay. Have done.

The poems of this period, as suggested by their themes (of **"Rocky Acres"; "Haunted House"; "Outlaws"; "Pier-Glass"** and **"Down"**) seek to represent a world, neurotic and terror struck, God-less and brutal—that is, spiritually dead. It is passing through a "blind December" that has driven away "songs and butterflies". Therefore, the possibility of love of "a happy sort"—of a Patmore, for instance—seems to have been ruled out; for it is accompanied by perpetual fear: "with the love theme went the old fear theme". Accordingly, **"A Frosty Night"** "important as being the first to frame a conception of love that has been fundamental to his poetic thought ever since", represents this ambivalent view of love, even as **"Reproach"** and **"One Hard Look"** stress:

> And one hard look
> Can close the book
> That lovers love to see.

The method of composition chosen by the poet—"for whom unusual things have happened" . . .—is proved right, in view of our knowledge of his future development as a poet. As observed already, the "bare impersonality" of the communal ballad appealed to him, and he became like Yeats, before him, a ballad poet—thus demonstrating his faith in the ancient and native elements of poetry in the urgent resuscitation of poetry; and was on guard against the "experiments", then fashionable. (**"Apples and Water"** and **"Vain and Careless"** are examples.) Robert Graves was writing, in his own words, "under unceasing emotional stress", as a consequence of which he "was putting a lot more of himself than he should into his poems." This realisation marked the beginning of a conflict in him between emotion and restraint, romanticism and classicism and he now yielded to the demands of restraint in the practice of poetry which resulted in a bout of "poetry of restraint". (pp. 136-37)

D. Narayanswamy, "The Early Poetry of Robert Graves," in Journal of the Karnatak University (Humanities), *Vol. VIII, 1974, pp. 126-37.*

ROBIN SKELTON

[There seems] to be a consensus among critics and reviewers that Robert Graves is a master craftsman, and yet there has been very little serious examination of his craft.

A thorough exploration of Graves' craftsmanship would occupy many years of study, for it would not only involve a close examination of his worksheets and of his many revisions of published poems, but also demand from the critic an intimate and practical knowledge of Latin and Greek prosody as well as English, Welsh, and Irish, for Graves has learned his skills from many and diverse traditions. In this essay therefore I can do no more than offer one or two observations upon one aspect of Graves' craftsmanship which interests me particularly, and which Graves himself seems always to have considered important. (pp. 37-8)

[It] was Welsh prosody that enabled him to create the greater part of that individual harmony which distinguishes his verse. Whether this was an altogether consciously planned manoeuvre or the result of intuition and accidents of circumstance need not concern us. What should concern us, however, is the way in which Graves, by use of the *cynghanedd* and allied techniques contrived to enrich and vary the conventional verse tunes of the Anglo-Classical tradition to such a degree, and with such subtlety, that he created a new mode for English lyric verse.

It is easy to see that the Welsh elements in Graves' poetry are most carefully and meticulously organized. (p. 41)

It is not Graves' practice to imitate the Welsh devices slavishly, but to utilize the principles behind the practice of creating harmony by means of clearly organized patterns of rhyme, consonance, and alliteration. . . . Many of Graves' revisions of already published poems reveal a desire to improve the verbal music of the lines which is quite as intense as the desire to clarify their message. . . . Some of these revisions may not seem as important as others which appear to have been made for different reasons. They are, nevertheless, significant, and an examination of . . . Graves' revisions of published texts reveals that they are typical. One might even state, quite emphatically, that Graves' revisions of his published poems invariably involve a deliberate 'celticization' of the harmonies. Indeed, the point of all this is not merely to show that Graves is a master manipulator of assonance, consonance, rhyme and near-rhyme, but also to suggest that this mastery is based firmly upon a profound understanding of the nature and utility of the Welsh tradition of versecraft, and that it is this Welsh element in his work which gives his cadences their peculiar authority and subtlety. These prosodic devices are not simply decorative elements; they are integral to the structure of the poetry, and the greater part of Graves' poetry of the last twenty-five years can only be properly understood, as craft, if it is examined with these techniques in mind.

Another characteristic of Graves' later work is the preponderance of poetry that is apparently ametrical. While some of the songs and occasional verses are constructed in orthodox Anglo-Classical metrics, the majority of them are written in Sprung Rhythm. The problem with Sprung Rhythm is that by itself, without rhyming devices, it tends to approximate so closely to the rhythms of conversational speech that all intensity is lost. Hopkins, who invented the term, forced intensity upon his poetry in Sprung Rhythm by means of compound words, wrenched syntax, and idiosyncratic diction, as well as some of the devices of *cynghanedd*. Graves has almost always written in a bare direct manner, with close attention to syntactical proprieties, and a lexicographer's distaste for the distortion of commonly received meanings. Consequently, he has had to find a way to provide an apparently unmetrical piece of conversational speech with a sound pattern strong enough to "hypnotize" (his own word) the reader without making the speech itself appear forced or tricksy. He has achieved this by means of sound patterns that alert the inner subliminal ear of the poetic receptor without alarming the outer ear of commonsense. (pp. 44-6)

It is this 'art concealing art' of which Robert Graves is the poetic master. Sometimes, it must be admitted, he succeeds so well in his concealment that only other poets as concerned with the craft as he are likely to recognize what is happening, and some of the more cloth-eared critics have dismissed many of his later love poems as trivial, which is rather like dismissing Monet's paintings of water lilies as trivial.

I use this parallel deliberately, for it is not in the actual content of the poem that we must always seek for greatness; it is in its implications, both particular and general. There is implied by Robert Graves' practice, a view of the profession of poetry, of the scope and range of the medium, and of the morality of craftsmanship that is of extreme importance. In his preface to ***Poems 1970-1972*** . . . he says

> Prosody is now generally underrated by English and American writers, who fail to recognize it as a necessary means of hypnotizing the reader into the same dream-like mood—the top level of sleep—which the true poet himself must enter.

In this "dream-like mood", in this "poetic trance" (to use Graves' own expression) both poet and reader are able to sense a pattern in experience that is at once more multifaceted and more profound than that which they perceive when fully awake. It is not only the state of mind in which all true poems (and all works of art) are created but also that in which many scientific discoveries are made. It is, indeed, the place where the boundary between conscious and unconscious knowledge, between reason and intuition is crossed; it is, perhaps, the place where ego and anima meet, the wedding chapel for that union of complements which creates the total self.

There is a poem by John Peale Bishop which puts the nature of Graves' strategy into clear perspective. The poem, *Speaking of Poetry,* opens

> The ceremony must be found
> that will wed Desdemona to the huge Moor

The ceremony 'found' by Robert Graves is all the more effective because it is so often secret; the union happens before the participants are aware of its immanence. John Peale Bishop's poem ends:

> The ceremony must be found
>
> Traditional with all its symbols
> ancient as the metaphors in dreams;
> strange, with never before heard music; continuous
> until the torches deaden at the bedroom door.

It is from this viewpoint that Robert Graves' craftsmanship, his fusing together of Welsh and Anglo-Classical prosody, must be seen. He provides us with the ceremonies we need to achieve wholeness, and proves to all who have ears to hear that the craft of verse is more than cleverness, but a skill and a mystery which must be practised with incessant labour and vigilance if poetry and vision are not to vanish from the face of the earth. (pp. 47-8)

Robin Skelton, "Craft and Ceremony: 'Some Notes on the Versecraft of Robert Graves'," in The Malahat Review, *No. 35, July, 1975, pp. 37-48.*

HELEN VENDLER

Graves remains unchanged, a poet who found his styles long ago, still moving familiarly in his world of dragons, goddesses, planetary influences, and ogres. He is archaic when it pleases him, and his poems are always construable and rhymed. It is intellectual poetry (for all Graves's preoccupation with love), and structured by its point more than by any gusts of feeling. His more complacent love poems . . . [in ***New Collected Poems***] are less moving than the poems written in abandonment. . . . In both sorts, peaceful and dismayed, Graves finds satisfying, if old-fashioned, last lines:

> It was impossible you could love me less,
> It was impossible I could love you more
> (**"Deliverance"**).

> It was not my fault, love, nor was it your fault
> (**"The Sentence"**).

On the other hand, the love poems, hundreds of them, come to seem almost like finger-exercises in a void, and the interruption of Graves's ironic and satiric tones is felt as a relief. . . . Accomplished though he is, Graves is not a compelling poet, whether in voice or attentiveness. His style is generic rather than shaped by each poem, and he believes too strongly that there is one story and one story only. The preordained plot precludes entirely any possibility of the erratic vagary, the unforeseen counterinstance. His poems are finished before they are begun, and proceed imperturbably to their destined point, discursive and magisterial. Confusion, bafflement, and surprise play less of a part in Graves than they do in life. Or perhaps it is truer to say that he is more a man of letters, a man who writes things in any form handy to him, than a poet. (pp. 80-1)

Helen Vendler, in a review of "New Collected Poems," in The Yale Review, *Vol. XLVII, No. 1, Autumn, 1977, pp. 79-81.*

JAMES K. ROBINSON

Robert Graves's ***New Collected Poems*** is described on the book jacket "as the capstone to a lifework of unparalleled creativity and beauty." "Unparalleled" is a fighting word. What ever happened to the *Collected Poems* of Hardy and of Yeats? A quarter century ago Jarrell remarked of Graves that he was "one of the few poets alive who can write a first-rate poem, and one of the very few who are getting better as they get older." Graves would appear to feel that he has fulfilled Jarrell's prophecy. In the "Foreword" to ***New Collected Poems*** he writes: "During each of the last ten years I have written more poems and discarded fewer than at any other time, with the exception of 1974 when I wrote only five." It is certainly true that the last decade has been marked by increased productivity. It is also true that while Graves has written more poems, he has also written briefer ones: of the fifty-eight poems published since his last collection, ***Poems 1970-1972,*** only half a dozen are longer than twenty lines. Ezra Pound grew silent as he aged. Graves becomes increasingly terse, and increasingly hard on his own early work. The *Collected Poems* of William Butler Yeats includes such magnificent last poems as "Lapis Lazuli," "News for the Delphic Oracle," and "Long-Legged Fly," but the early work (*Crossways, The Rose, The Wind Among the Reeds*) is, for all its inferiority, amply represented. Hardy, even less self-conscious than Yeats, put together 800 pages of verse—a collection twice as long as Graves's—though Hardy did most of his work in the last thirty years of his long life and Graves has been going for over sixty. Like Auden, Graves has worried his poems perennially, and has kept trimming his canon. One misses **"Recalling War"** from this collection—surely one of the better war poems in English.

And yet what remains is precious. Yeats sang an eloquent farewell to romantic love in "Adam's Curse" (1904); for Graves romantic love is the abiding subject. The difficulty and the power of that love are conveyed in the last poem in ***New Collected Poems:*** **"The Green Woods of Unrest":**

Let the weeks end as well they must
Not with clouds of scattered dust
But in pure certainty of sun—
And with gentle winds outrun
By the love that we contest
In these green woods of unrest.
You, love, are beauty's self indeed,
Never the harsh pride of need.

Here indeed is the last romantic, but classic too. Like Landor he writes with lapidary grace and precision. There is absolute rightness of diction, rhythm, voice. The difficulties of mortal love are not denied; they persist with the ideal.

Graves in his eighties is still a poet, a strong poet. (pp. 354-55)

James K. Robinson, "'Sassenachs, Palefaces, and a Redskin: Graves, Auden, MacLeish, Hollander, Wagoner, and Others'," in The Southern Review, *(Louisiana State University), Vol. XIV, No. 2, April, 1978, pp. 348-58.*

JAMES FINN COTTER

Each time Robert Graves collects his poetry (there have been six collections in 50 years), he discards as much as he includes. As a result, readers miss familiar poems or old favorites they might expect to find in a poet's complete collection. Happily, ***New Collected Poems*** offers a more generous sampling than any of its predecessors, especially of the poems written in the last 15 years. But if you are looking for the witty **"Traveller's Curse after Misdirection"** or **"Recalling War"** and most of the early war and mythological poetry, you will have to turn to the earlier volumes. Count your blessings anyway: There is enough Graves here for a lifetime's reading.

"In the Wilderness," "The Pier-Glass," "The Cool Web," "The Legs," "The Christmas Robin," "To Juan at the Winter Solstice," "The Portrait" and **"Call It a Good Marriage"** are a few of the mature works that reward constant rereading. They embody the variety of subject matter, the surprise in words and the intelligent manner that mark the best of Graves's poetry. He is a Casals of verbal performances, bringing new life to old myths and images, making us hear our language sing with resonance and love. . . . (pp. 331-32)

Graves's prolific late period has often won praise, especially for its love poetry. Many of the poems possess an almost Elizabethan eloquence and simplicity; they are more direct and have greater audience appeal than most of his earlier verse. Take **"Beatrice and Dante,"** for example, beginning: "He, a grave poet, fell in love with her. / She a mere child, fell deep in love with love / And, being a child, illumined his whole heart." Both the idealized lovers and the poet's own experience join here in a perfect marriage of myth and reality. . . .

Not all the love poems, however, sustain this high note of lyrical truth. Some descend to self-centeredness and (surprising in a poet so concerned with his craft) loose writing and word choice. . . .

If Graves had wielded the critical blade that cut out many of the earlier poems, much of the weakness of the last half of this book could have been avoided. The irreverent humor of **"Down, Wanton, Down!"** might have salted some of the bland seriousness and repetition. Variety has always been the spice of Graves's poetry, from **"Rocky Acres,"** through **"The Naked and the Nude,"** to **"Cliff and Wave."** In **"My Name and I," "The Second-Fated"** and **"The Face in the Mirror,"** he has etched the stern, quizzical, comic-ironic face posterity will remember from his poems. It is as fine a mask as any author has shaped in our century, a classical persona for both comedy and tragedy, by the wooer and courtier of his muse, the White Goddess. (p. 332)

James Finn Cotter, in a review of "New Collected Poems," in America, *Vol. 138, No. 15, April 22, 1978, pp. 331-32.*

ANTHONY THWAITE

In his autobiography, ***Goodbye to All That,*** written when he was thirty-three, Robert Graves presented himself as someone who had crammed into a brief space more extremes and oddities of experience than most people undergo in a long lifetime. He made a vow at the age of fifteen never to compromise himself in his vocation as a poet; and, though he has been a prolific writer in many different directions since the 1920s, his chief reputation has been as a poet. It is a reputation that stands on the subtly individual flavour of his work, and on its remarkable unbroken continuity, not on innovation. Though one can find traces of Graves's influence in many poets (and poets of disparate sorts), he has always been too quirky and isolated, too much his own man, to have had a keen following of dogmatic disciples.

He published his early poems during the First World War (in which he fought as an infantry officer, and indeed was reported officially dead of wounds on his twenty-first birthday), and in his successive volumes of collected poems he has continued to republish some of them—for example, **"In the Wilderness",** concerned with Christ's fasting in the desert and written in a short-lined, irregularly rhymed style influenced by an early Graves master, John Skelton, the late medieval poet. . . . Other early poems—and later ones too—have the air of being sophisticated folk-poetry or even nursery rhymes, or work on the level of childhood or child-like myth, as in **"Warning to Children"** and **"Lollocks".** The complex diversity of the physical world is reduced, in the first poem, to a kind of game, beyond which lie unspoken terrors. . . . In the same way, the Lollocks are inexplicable, malevolent presences; all we can do is blame them for their daily horrors, and attempt to keep them at bay by being neat and orderly. Whether we are rational or irrational, they exist and we cannot ignore them. . . . (pp. 93-4)

Such whimsical flirtations with horror are not cosily neutralized by being put in such terms; they employ that 'cool web of language' which (in his poem **"The Cool Web"**) is seen as a way of coping with experience:

> Children are dumb to say how hot the day is,
> How hot the scent is of the summer rose,
> How dreadful the black wastes of evening sky,
> How dreadful the tall soldiers drumming by.
>
> But we have speech, to chill the angry day,
> And speech, to dull the rose's cruel scent.
> We spell away the overhanging night,
> We spell away the soldiers and the fright . . .

This delicate, troubled poise is typical of Graves: stylish, subdued, deeply romantic in feeling but usually laconic in expression. His scrupulous, terse decorum is most apparent in his love poems, many of which exquisitely celebrate transience, chance, inevitability. . . . (p. 95)

Increasingly, Graves has come to see poetry as telling 'one story', of which there is only one theme and inspired by only one impulse—that of the Muse, the 'immanent Goddess'. Many of his poems during the past thirty years have been addresses to this figure, often an amalgam of an inspiring deity, a young woman adored by a much older man, and a character or characters (always female) out of distant but still passionate memory. The 'magic' element in all this, and Graves's abstruse, scholarly, but also eccentric and polemical delvings into mythology, history and religion, may have something in common in their need for a framework, necessary to the poet if not to the reader) with Yeats's categorizing in *A Vision;* though Graves has made it clear that he despises that side, and indeed most sides, of Yeats. (Graves's Clark Lectures, incidentally, delivered at Cambridge in 1954-5, made hilariously unfair attacks on a whole range of poets, from Pope and Wordsworth to Yeats, Pound, Eliot, Auden and Dylan Thomas.) The difference lies partly in Graves's reasonable and courtly unreason, his fastidiously classic tone as he celebrates the irrational. . . . (pp. 95-6)

Often he is arrogant, quizzical and sardonic, enjoying a talent for light verse though he has affected to belittle Auden for such things. In a short squib, he quotes (or pretends to quote—one isn't always convinced about the accuracy of Graves's sources) from a New York review:

> Robert Graves, the British veteran, is no longer in the poetic swim. He still resorts to traditional metres and rhyme, and to such outdated words as *tilth;* witholding his 100% approbation also from contemporary poems that favour sexual freedom.

The poem **"Tilth"** to which this is the epigraph runs:

> Gone are the drab monosyllabic days
> When 'agricultural labour' still was *tilth;*
> And '100% approbation', *praise;*
> And 'pornographic modernism', *filth*—
> Yet still I stand by *tilth* and *filth* and *praise.*

The wry sense of survival, mock embattled but perfectly sure of itself, is part of the bitter-sweet taste of Graves's poetry, consistent with the man who revealed himself in ***Goodbye to All That*** in 1929. (p. 96)

Anthony Thwaite, "Robert Graves, William Empson and Edwin Muir," in his Twentieth-Century English Poetry: An Introduction, *Heinemann Educational Books, 1978, pp. 91-103.*

KATHERINE SNIPES

The career of Robert Graves almost defies analysis—a fact that no doubt pleases him well. He has always resisted the "eyes that fix you in a formulated phrase," and the academic impulse that pins the neatly classified specimen on the wall. This butterfly has made an art of flying crooked, and to observe him impaled upon a pin is necessarily misleading.

Perhaps the only suitable approach to so eccentric a personality is one developed for the interpretation of myth by one of the most recent innovators in that field. According to the structural analysis of Claude Lévi-Strauss, the elements of myth are factors that mediate contradictories in a dialectic fashion. One must work with all known variations of a related set of myths. Thus Lévi-Strauss tabulates South American Indian myths that involve complicated relationships between polar opposites: origin of fire and origin of antifire (wind and rain), incestuous kinship relations and murderous kinship relations, raw food (perceived as natural) and cooked food (perceived as cultural). The process seems to call for an exquisitely programmed computer, which would provide algebraic formulae corresponding to the web of meaning peculiar to a particular society.

Obviously such a process was not designed to analyze the web of meaning peculiar to a particular person. Yet, if structural analysis shows there is a logic (non-Aristotelian, I presume) beyond seemingly nonrational, capricious, even outright contradictory ideas and emotions, then perhaps someday some combined literary critic-mythologist-psycho-historian with a computer will explain Robert Graves. The logic of the primitive set of myths operates unconsciously, however. How many dimensions must be added for the possibility of consciously assumed pose—the suspicion that Graves is often only half-serious, laughing into his sleeve?

Even so, Graves's career seems to be an oscillation between contradictory positions, which may (like Lévi-Strauss's sets of contrapuntal myths) make sense in a cultural context. How ironic it would be if future "social scientists" would regard Graves as their favorite case history, dramatizing a basic conflict between rationalistic, technological, modern society and an older poetic, religious, romantic sensibility! Nor will Graves emerge wholly in the second of these camps, but rather wandering in some uncertain no-man's-land between. He is, after all, a coolly calculating exploder of myths as well as a promoter of his own favorite monomyth.

In his personal dialectic of belief he has begun in a thoroughly conventional, fundamentalist Christianity, swung to an equally conventional liberal, socialistic atheism, to arrive ultimately at a nonpolitical, aesthetic doctrine (only quasireligious) as expressed in the mythology of the white goddess. This archaic set of symbols has not only fed his poetic creativity, but also seems to mirror his own stormy relationships with strong-minded women.

This personal application is no doubt beyond the scope of a mere reader untrained in psychoanalysis. Yet, the admitted autobiographical elements in such troubled works as ***The Shout*** and **"But It Still Goes On,"** the weird, unhealthy glow of ***No Decency Left*** and ***The Antigua Stamp,*** the dreamlike ***Watch the North Wind Rise,*** the cool revelations of ***Goodbye to All That,*** all invite personal observations about the man as well as his work.

Moreover, Graves launched his serious career in poetry under the influence of the Freudian psychologist, Rivers. Graves was convinced then, at least, of the relevance of dreams to poetic creativity and the psychologically therapeutic function of poetry in working out emotional conflicts. Not only did he later reject his former psychological views, he vehemently repudiated all psychological explanations of myth. Yet, the strength of his denial of Freudian and Jungian contributions to myth theory appears to be directly correlated to their relevance to himself. (pp. 189-91)

Graves actually has an impressive store of knowledge about the past. Moreover, he is honest about the fusion of his own intuition with the available evidence. But what he brings forth from the grave is his own image.

That, in itself, does not necessarily invalidate his worldview either of the present or of the past. After all, one of the tenets of his personal philosophy is that the true poet is essentially the same in function and motivation, whether he lived then or now or in the future. Ideally he acts as oracle and prophet, speaking the truths of the human spirit and interpreting the demands of a personified nature upon it. (p. 192)

[Graves] sang of the "one story only," which repeats itself endlessly in a round of birth, love, and death, in the sometimes nurturing, sometimes threatening shadow of the Eternal Female. . . . In spite of his seemingly radical shifts of orientation, there is that "persistent rearrangement of elements which are present from the start"—or at least from World War I and the shattering of his naive, conventional view of life.

The ambivalent character of the White Goddess haunted his poetry and prose long before he realized her place in history. And the personal, psychological element in his vision of the Goddess persisted even as he protested "She is not *my* White Goddess," pointing to the long ago and far away.

This is not to suggest that the White Goddess is "merely" a projection of Graves's imagination. Modern archeological scholarship supports his claims for the widespread goddess cults of Neolithic times. And the evidence for the preeminence of women in the social-religious life of that time, while not conclusive, is certainly impressive.

These observations about women are timely and provide a needed corrective to the exclusively masculine bias of western history. If nothing else, Graves's somewhat eccentric impulse to rewrite history reminds us that what is perpetuated as historical fact is often quite arbitrary. Graves may be at least partly responsible, along with other factors such as the emergence from obscurity of minority races, for a new sophistication about what has been accepted unquestioningly about the past. Historians, historical novelists, mythologists, anthropologists are all engaged in an imaginative reconstruction of the past, with personal bias inevitably coloring interpretation.

What is even more fascinating is that an ancient set of religious symbols still resonates in a modern mind, directing the imagination of one of our more impressive users of language. His absorption of these archaic thought patterns must indicate that they are emotionally and intellectually viable in some as yet unexplained way. (pp. 192-93)

Much of the animosity directed toward Graves is not really attributable to his scholarship, good or bad, however, but to his value judgments. Unlike the nineteenth century Bachofen, who claimed that civilization *advanced* from matriarchy to patriarchy, Graves presents the change as unmitigated disaster, from which spring all the evils of capitalism, technology, and war. He has also had the temerity to apply comparative methods to Christian mythology, still widely tabooed for some kinds of intellectual inquiry. Thus, for some hypersensitives, he is a trespasser on private intellectual domains, a traitor to his own sex, and a pernicious misleader of youth.

Though his elevation of the Female to godhead is convenient in feminist terms and entertaining for those simply annoyed with orthodox, unthinking sexism, it is nevertheless a mixed blessing. It attacks some stereotypes (for which women may be grateful) but reinforces others. It says far more, I suspect, about a male mythopoeic view of women than it does about female nature. Is it really flattering that the man can be in love with a woman only if she conforms to an archetype already dear to his heart?

Though he has written many good love lyrics, the beloved woman never emerges with any individual characteristics. Nor can he achieve, at least in poetry, the gentle mockery of his own literary convention, such as Shakespeare did when he wrote: "My mistress' eyes are nothing like the sun, / Coral is far more red than her lips' red, / If snow be white, why then her breasts are dun, / If hairs be wires, black wires grow on her head.'' ***Watch the North Wind Rise*** is, to be sure, a light-hearted, ironic treatment of his own myth—and charming for that very reason.

His historical novels, though remarkably diverse in plot and setting, also exhibit stylized women. Some of them are fascinating creatures, but they usually conform to the White Goddess character and temperament, even before Graves had written her gospel. Livia, in ***I, Claudius,*** displays all the power, worldly wisdom, and ruthlessness of the Triple Goddess as Crone. Messalina and Agrippina are sirens and witches on a smaller scale. They generally prevail over Claudius, as Livia controls the god-emperor Augustus.

Antonina and the Empress Theodora in ***Count Belisarius,*** for all their token Christianity, are thoroughly pagan. They are indomitable in protecting those they love, ruthless in avenging slights, eminently intelligent and sensible even when men are foolish or pretentious. In ***The Islands of Unwisdom,*** Doña Isabel, though seductive, has not an ounce of gentleness about her. She destroys men who oppose her and cancels out the ineffectual altruism of both her husband and her lover. Even Kate Harlowe is more at home in the American wilderness than stuffy Sergeant Lamb will ever be. She knows no sense of duty except to her own nature. Mary the Hairdresser of ***King Jesus,*** of course, is the embodiment of the Goddess on earth, the Crone who is both Queen of the Harlots and the Layer-Out who officiates at the death of the Sacred King.

The young virgin Nausicaa of ***Homer's Daughter*** is perhaps the most benevolent of the heroines, though the wholesale slaughter of her suitors belies that description. Mary Powell Milton is the most feeble—the goddess ignominiously dethroned by the male usurper. The Puritans destroy her queendom, the half-pagan countryside of Merry England with its rich tradition of festivals in celebration of nature.

Where honor, duty, patriotism, or Christian morality may motivate men, they have little relevance to women, who seem to represent the more elemental cycles of nature. These are ultimately triumphant over the sometimes civilizing, but largely futile, efforts of mankind to mold nature to their own desires. As one of Graves's poems points out, **"Man Does, Woman Is."** Jesus, who makes war upon the Female, nevertheless replays the ancient role of the sacrificed Sacred King.

Though men are the doers, their achievements are seldom permanent. How much did the exploits of a Belisarius or a Sergeant Lamb or a Don Alvaro or a Claudius change the structure or destiny of their world? It was as though they had never been. Belisarius, for all his brilliance, could not preserve the Byzantine Empire for long, nor could Claudius reactivate the Roman Republic. Sergeant Lamb fought on the losing side of the American Revolution, and the Solomon Islands were lost to Europeans for almost two hundred years after Don Alvaro's abortive attempt at colonization.

Human greed and folly, balanced by the persistent human need for love and propagation, bring so-called advancements back to nature's norm. There is an unfailing fountainhead of energy in the nonrational—and women know this better than men. That is why, at least in Graves's stereotyped view of gender differences, Fate is appropriately female and, like Mother Night, the Goddess behind all gods.

One might object that the strange case of Jesus, called the Christ, has reversed the trend. In spite of his reenactment of the ancient ritual of the Sacred King, who is the Goddess's consort, he established once and for all the dominance of the male principle. Yet the novels about the post-Christian world suggest that Christianity has made but little impact on human character and destiny. Milton brought paradise no closer, for all his immortalizing the Garden as God's domain, where the Mother of All Living, its former owner, had no right to pick the apples. (pp. 195-98)

Katherine Snipes, in her Robert Graves, *Frederick Ungar Publishing Co., 1979, 222 p.*

ROBERT H. CANARY

Graves has been an inveterate maker of lists of true poets and true poems, and he has always hoped to be included on such lists, as kept by the sovereign Muse; but he has generally resisted seeing poetry as a competitive enterprise or speculating on whether his poems will endure. . . . For Graves, poetry is a test of character, and his first demand on his poetry is that it be honest, true to himself and to the Muse. The judgment of either his present-day public or his posterity should, in Graves's view, matter less to the poet. The public, in any case, is likely to prefer poems which do not meet Graves's moral demands: "Those are the ones that usually the public likes best: ones that are not wholly jewels."

Critics, however, are allowed to think about posterity, though past experience should discourage them from too confidently predicting its judgments. A critic may legitimately use posterity as a way of asking what portion of a writer's present reputation is due to transient fashions and what portion is based on more enduring qualities. This is particularly important in assessing Graves because he has chosen to be an outsider, taking little or no part in the literary "movements" of our time since he left the Georgian fold. One says "movement" advisedly, for contemporary criticism tends to confuse movements with literary friendships and coteries. In the immediate perspective, writers seem inextricably linked to their friends and imitators, so that the name of Auden almost automatically conjures up the names of Stephen Spender and Cecil Day-Lewis, friends who wrote very different poems, and of a host of American academic poets who learned their craft from Auden. Posterity is unlikely to make such fine distinctions. Graves's most obvious affinity is with Robert Frost, another outsider, but it seems likely that his links with poets like Eliot and Auden will seem more striking once the memory of literary quarrels has died away. Graves's concern for integrity, his respect for courage, his underlying romanticism and surface restraint also link him to prose figures like Ernest Hemingway. Although Graves has played no large part in twentieth-century literary politics, he has participated in the evolution of the modern sensibility, and it seems likely that he will seem less of an outsider when later centuries write the literary history of our time.

How large a place Graves will assume in such literary histories depends on how much of his work survives—in his ***Watch the North Wind Rise,*** the biographies of poets have become hopelessly confused, but the poems survive on gold plates. We cannot, of course, predict the taste of future times with any great hope of accuracy, but we may ask ourselves what portion of Graves's work deserves to be inscribed on gold.

It is somewhat easier to decide the fate of Graves's prose. Among his works of nonfiction, ***Good-bye to All That*** (in the 1957 revision) should survive for some time. Mankind has a seemingly permanent appetite for works which succeed, as it does, in conveying the realities of war. Out of various epic cycles, the Greeks preserved Homer; Thucydides and Caesar have survived and still give pleasure, while many of their contemporaries survive only in fragments studied by classicists. World War I seems to have somewhat less intrinsic fascination than the American Civil War or the Napoleonic Wars, but we may feel fairly sure that ***Good-bye to All That*** will continue to be read so long as men love war. It does not and will not rank as a literary work with the confessions of Rousseau or St. Augustine, but men will keep it on plates of gold or, more likely, in paperback editions.

No such case can be made for the rest of Graves's nonfiction. Works like ***The White Goddess*** and ***The Nazarene Gospel Restored*** are curiosities of literature but possess no lasting literary merit in themselves, though some might claim more for ***The White Goddess*** and poets may continue to consult it. Graves's early psychological criticism will retain historical interest as early efforts of that kind, and ***A Survey of Modernist Poetry*** may retain a place in the footnotes to histories of criticism; but survival as food for scholars is a half-life at best. In any case, the assertion that criticism is or should be a branch of literature is a half-truth overvalued in the present period, which suffers from a surplus of critics. Graves's more recent criticism says little that is not implicit in ***The White Goddess;*** if one wants to read about the Muse, one should read the latter.

Graves's translations are a special case. His versions of Suetonius and Apuleius are the best now available, and some critics have a higher opinion than I can muster of Graves's rendering of the *Iliad*. But new times will require new translations, in language that suits an altered sensibility. We may still occasionally glance at Pope's *Iliad,* even though more modern and accurate translations are available, but it is unlikely that any of Graves's translations have such independent literary interest. Fine though some of them may be, it is unlikely that posterity will find them so.

Graves's novels are somewhat more serious candidates for preservation in gold. Their reputation may well increase, for most have been historical novels, a genre underrated at present and overdue for reevaluation. The test of a historical novel is its ability to remain a completely persuasive evocation of the past after its own period has passed and our perceptions of the period with which it deals have changed. The touchstone here, one must confess, is Sir Walter Scott. There seems to be a general consensus that ***I, Claudius*** meets this test, in which case ***Claudius the God*** should surely accompany it on plates of gold. There is considerably less consensus about the rest of Graves's novels, partly because many have received little critical scrutiny. My own choices would be ***King Jesus*** and, perhaps, ***Watch the North Wind Rise,*** but it is only fair to note that many other Graves critics would disagree, especially with the second choice. Graves himself refers to ***Wife to Mr. Milton*** [published in Great Britain as ***The Story of Marie Powell: Wife to Mr. Milton***] as "my best novel." Of Graves's shorter fiction, ***The Shout*** is clearly worth preserving and clearly alone in possessing this merit.

The conventional judgment on Graves's poetry is that he is a very fine craftsman, a poet of genuine integrity, but not quite a great poet. Critics have generally based this judgment on a feeling that Graves is a poet of rather limited range: "The highest intensities, the outermost splendors of language and emotion seem to be beyond" him. This may seem to be a critic's version of Graves's own views on the proper subjects of poetry, for it implies that certain subjects and effects are inherently superior; carried to this extreme, however, this is not an acceptable critical position. That Graves's poems deal with a relatively restricted emotional range is probably true, but this says nothing about the quality of the poems themselves, which is surely what matters.

Which and how many of Graves's poems deserve to be engraved on gold are questions to which different readers will give different answers, even if all should use the appropriately Gravesian test of asking whether the poems affect one like a stab in the heart. Of the poems included in the 1977 ***New Collected Poems,*** one might feel relatively sure of **"Rocky Acres," "The Cool Web," "Sick Love," "Ulysses," "No More Ghosts," "A Love Story," "Theseus and Ariadne," "To Juan at the Winter Solstice," "The Portrait,"** and **"Nothing Now Astonishes."** And one would want to find some place for such left-handed satires as **"The Laureate"** and such light pieces as **"A Slice of Wedding Cake."** The test suggested here is a hard one, and to have even a dozen poems survive it is a good life's work. If one applies a less stringent test, asking whether the poem is honest, necessary, and spoken wholly in the poet's own voice, the list would be much longer, for Graves is a remarkably consistent poet. One moves with pleasure from the poems of gold to the many poems of silver.

If we total up our list, we find that Graves has produced an autobiography which is likely to be read for many years to come, a novel (and perhaps more) which ranks high among the historical novels written in our time, and, most important, a handful of intensely memorable poems and a much larger body of distinguished verse. It is quite a bit for a single man to leave behind him. What he has been as a man, we may not know, nor should we claim to know when at last all the diaries and letters are opened, all the memoirs and recollections written down. What matters is that he has done his best to stay faithful to the Muse, and by that we know that he has been a true poet. (pp. 131-35)

Robert H. Canary, in his Robert Graves, *Twayne Publishers, 1980, 167 p.*

PATRICK J. KEANE

Graves has done almost all those things major poets do. He has written a great deal of poetry and, through revision and winnowing (judicious until recent years), has established a canon. An occasionalist in many modes and tones, he eventually sought a central, focusing theme. He found it, for both his mythological studies and his practice of poetry, in love. Love is the main theme and origin of true poems, he believes, and the true poet writes *with* love, treating poetry with a single-minded "devotion" that may be called "religious." Graves's religion is his myth of the White Goddess and, since 1959, her Black sister. The neolithic and Bronze Age religious faith in the Triple Goddess has survived among what are called the Romantic poets, and Graves is convinced that his studies have shown that the imagery of the authentic Romantics was drawn, either consciously or unconsciously, from the cult of the Goddess and that the "magic" their poems exert largely depends on an intimacy with her mysteries. . . . (p. 90)

What for Graves is a central theme will seem to others merely eccentric; what to him is the persistent survival of a timeless motif is for others an atavistic aberration. And yet, despite his obsession with the ancient world—with love magic and poetic magic, with dragons and dreams and rites of blood, with ancient Welsh prosody, Sufi mysticism, and Celtic romance—Graves is a man of the modern world. He fought in that war which has itself come to seem a zigzag trench cutting through this century, dividing the old from the "modern" consciousness; and he has lived long enough to see both his island retreat and his most esoteric speculations domesticated by cultural tourists. He may find little to admire in the modern world, but he is certainly aware of what it is he spits from his mouth.

There is, then, a considerable body of work—much, though by no means all, of it now conveniently available in ***New Collected Poems.*** There is a central theme: that "one story and one story only / That will prove worth your telling." There is an elaborate mythography and a vital poetic tradition to buttress the theme, to provide a larger sustaining context for the hundreds of skillfully crafted lyrics that make up Graves's poetic corpus. And there is Graves himself: soldier, scholar, craftsman he; a figure larger than life, yet a man whose sophisticated primitivism, whose characteristically modern double-mindedness, makes him our contemporary.

But Graves remains an anomaly. We seldom think of him as a "major" poet, certainly not as a major *modern* poet. A case can be made (and has, by Kirkham) for his modernity on the basis of sensibility and awareness rather than of themes, images, and advanced techniques; and certainly the author of ***Good-Bye to All That*** is aware of twentieth-century chaos and brutality and of the modern patriarchy and mechanarchy he repudiates. He also repudiates "Franco-American modernism" with its "major poems of truly contemporary malaise" written for "an aggregate public." While he denies opposing innovations in poetic technique, he is clearly wary of them and of the often extreme explorations of sensibility we associate with Eliot, Pound, and the later Yeats. The problems of sensibility and awareness in Graves have to do, not with his experience of the modern world, but with his failure to consistently translate that experience into poetry.

There is something at once heroic and perverse in Graves's stance. Yeats, a poetic traditionalist too, felt himself to be a man "flung upon this filthy modern tide" ("The Statues"); but he entered, however quirkily, the waters of poetic modernism and so was reborn after midlife. Graves has never ceased regarding the "foul tidal basin of modernism" . . . as a stagnant deviation from the mainstream of tradition. For him, the genuine poet, independent of fashion and of public service, is a servant only of the true Muse, committed on her behalf to "continuous personal variations on a single prehistoric, or post-historic, poetic theme." Writing in 1949 (in the introduction to ***The Common Asphodel***), and by then persuaded that he was himself such a Muse-poet, he tells us, in a most revealing metaphor, that he has "ceased to feel the frantic strain of swimming against the stream of time."

Actually, Graves had largely reconciled himself to swimming in his own way, against the modern mainstream, by the early thirties. And, with characteristic pride and cunning, he had turned his "limitations" into a claimed advantage. **"Flying Crooked"** is perhaps the best of his anecdotes on the theme, a poem in which he chooses an image emblematic for Yeats as well: the butterfly. (pp. 90-2)

In **"Flying Crooked,"** Graves typically celebrates his chosen crookedness in a craftsmanlike way—here, in impeccably metrical couplets (iambic tetrameters rather than pentameters . . .). As usual, too, the Romantic-intuitive is in balance with the Classical-rational aspect of double-minded Graves. (p. 93)

In a thematically related poem of the same period, **"In Broken Images,"** Graves contrasts the quick, confident, linear rationalist who thinks in clear images with himself, "slow, thinking in broken images." But in mistrusting his images and questioning their relevance, he becomes "sharp" as the clear-thinker grows "dull." And whereas when "fact fails" the logician he can only "question" his physical senses and instincts, Graves can "approve" his. So both continue, "He in a new confusion of his understanding; / I in a new understanding of my confusion." No images, clear or broken, appear in the poem. Yet even so abstract an exercise in verbal gymnastics demonstrates Graves's skill, the poem's construction (propositions in couplets) parodying as it does the discourse of Apollonian logicians. It also demonstrates, and exemplifies, Graves's ability to turn acknowledged limitations into an occasion for triumph: another instance of Goliath being toppled by underdog, "minor" David.

One way to pull off such triumphs is to claim to be part of the "true" mainstream. If modernist poetry was bogus, complex, ambiguous, stylistically idiosyncratic, dislocated, and pretentiously "major," then true poetry, consisting of personal variations on a single timeless theme, must be lucid, ecstatic, traditionalist, and—deliberately, aggressively—"minor." Graves, who has been called "the most prideful poet writing in the world today," has dismissed not only Auden and Thomas, but Yeats, Eliot, Pound, and Wallace Stevens as well: it has been observed that "if it is true Graves won't suffer fools gladly, it is even truer he suffers his betters not at all." At the same time, he himself eschews all claim to being a major poet. "Minor poetry, so called to differentiate it from major poetry, is the real stuff," he insists, pride characteristically mingling with that sense of limitation. . . . (pp. 93-4)

The transfer of allegiance from the White Goddess to Apollo, from ecstatic Muse poetry to nonecstatic, architectural, "major" Apollonian poetry, is the Gravesian sin against the spirit. "Nothing," he has said in a lecture on the legitimate criticism of poetry, "is better than the truly good, not even the truly great. . . . Good poets are exceedingly rare; 'great poets' are all too common. The poet who accepts his limitations but works to the point of exhaustion on getting every word of a poem into place, may yet fail, for one reason or another, to be as good as he intends." . . . (p. 95)

Even if we grant (I do) the partial validity of Graves's distinction, we yet pull up short of full assent—both to the general proposition and to its application to Graves himself: an idiosyncratic but perhaps major mythographer and a dedicated craftsman who, to alter his own distinction, stands firmly among the Good, but *beneath* the Great how far.

The Great I have had in mind throughout much of the present study are the Great Romantics, Graves's precursors both in devotion to the Muse and as mythmakers. While there is truth in Harold Bloom's observation that, unlike the "First Romantics," the "Last Romantics" (Yeats, Lawrence, and Graves) have succumbed to "shamanism" and "phantasmagoria," with the darkest phantasmagoria Graves's masochistic insistence on "the mutual rendings of poet and Muse as being true love," it is equally true that Gravesian wildness is tempered by stoicism and a stress on limitation. For Graves, true poetry is by definition minor poetry. The chief popular impact of the Great Romantics, too, has been achieved with short lyrics rather than with their attempted or accomplished epics. But even if those precursor-poems for Graves—"The Mental Traveller," "The Ancient Mariner," and the most condensed of these epical ballads, "La Belle Dame sans Merci"—were to be considered minor, the fact remains that the ambition of Blake, Coleridge, and Keats (one shared by Wordsworth and Shelley) was to create major poetry, specifically to out-Milton Milton. In contrast to these titanic overreachers and failed questers, Graves is teleological. His reach seldom if ever exceeds his grasp. Though surprise was a notable element in his earlier poems, the later ones seem sometimes so predictable that their end is in their beginning. And his vision, for all his abandonment to the vagaries of the Goddess, remains stoic rather than apocalyptic.

I am not arguing with Graves's dualistic temperament, a double-mindedness that has provided one of my main themes. But if we are reminded of Hardy and Frost, stoic traditional poets whom Graves admires, we must also remember not only that they are "major" poets compared to him, but also that they share little of his mythopoeic extravagance, his phantasmagoria. And yet, for all his attunement to archetypal mysteries, Graves is even more obsessed than they with the minutiae of craftsmanship and the need for poems to make "good sense." It is not necessary to endorse shoddy craftsmanship or perverse obscurity to observe the inherent dangers in such a program as Graves's. As he himself admitted in a preface to a reading, some of his later poems are so "cunning" that they lack exuberance. . . . (pp. 95-7)

To adapt T. E. Hulme's celebrated distinction between the Romantic and the Classic, Graves seems a poet who, while fully conscious of the vast ocean around him, prefers to dip his bucket in a limited well. And this Romantic-Classic distinction may be applied to that between major and minor poetry. In one unreprinted poem that clarifies the poet-Muse relationship, the ephebe is advised:

Never sing a song clean through,
You might disenchant her,
Venture on a verse or two
(Indisposed to sing it through),
Let that seem as much as you
Care, or dare, to grant her.

The jaunty rhythms of light verse embody the problem. For it seems less a fear of the Muse that inhibits Graves than his own sense of limitation and the precariousness of that bond with her that provides enchanted inspiration. One "dare" not press too far: to be disposed to "sing a song clean through" is to be willing both to penetrate to the experiential sources of creativity and to take the ambitious risks that separate major poetry from a modest verse or two. "Indisposed," "seem," and "care" slyly suggest that the effort is actually being made under a defensive show of laconic wit and nonchalance. But in fact Graves is rarely willing to "venture" into either length of conceptual depth. It may be true, as he says, that "all Muse poetry is minor poetry, if length be the criterion," . . . but it seems suspiciously convenient that his Muse should prefer brief finger exercises to ambitious odes.

This is an uncharitable way to put it, and unfair to Graves, who has after all produced an impressive and well-wrought body of work. His poetry—characterized by a lucid, tempered awe in face of the phantasmagoria he himself evokes—is poetry of the British middle ground, its climate of thought generally located in the temperate zone, content to be native and traditional in both technique and theme. "*Vers libre* could come to nothing in England," Thomas Hardy assured an admiring Graves in the twenties. "All we can do is to write on the old themes in the old styles, but try to do it a little better than those who went before us." . . . Graves has from the beginning maintained a traditionalist belief that certain principles cannot be violated without poetry turning into something else, and though his distillation of Hardy's "old themes" into the "one story" of his monomyth may seem idiosyncratic, that theme is, in Graves's eyes, even more traditional than his conservative poetic technique.

And he is proud of his old-fashioned virtues. An American critic recently complained in the *New York Times Book Review:* "Robert Graves, the British veteran, is no longer in the poetic swim. He still resorts to traditional metres and rhyme, and to such out-dated words as *tilth;* withholding his 100% approbation also from contemporary poems that favor sexual freedom." It is hard not to be won over by the veteran's response:

Gone are the drab monosyllabic days
When "agricultural labour" still was *tilth;*
And "100% approbation," *praise;*
And "pornographic modernism," filth—
Yet still I stand by *tilth* and *filth* and *praise.*

Here as elsewhere, craft triumphs over crankiness. This little poem, which might have been no more than a bit of reactionary grumbling, is manipulated so that the last line not only scoops up the three operative terms but concludes resonantly, its final word, "praise," elevating the poem well above its germinal anger. Reading **"Tilth,"** one feels no inclination to take issue with an arrogance that on other occasions can be monstrous. The stubborness of "Yet still I stand" here seems admirable. Like Swift and Yeats, Graves feels himself a man appointed to guard a position. (pp. 97-9)

Graves's stubborn "stand" is also the final position of an old man (**"Tilth"** was written in the seventies). At the end of the story as at its beginning, Graves's soldierly stance is both perverse and heroic, poignant and admirable. "The pride of 'bearing it out even to the edge of doom' that sustains a soldier in the field," he has written in a characteristic fusion of Shakespeare, war, and poetry, "governs a poet's service to the Muse." (p. 99)

If pride, determination, length of dedicated service, and courage in the field were the only criteria, Robert Graves would be second to no poet of this century, not even to Yeats. But they are not the only criteria; and Graves, for all his indisputable achievement and valiant refusal to give in to dead forces, remains a poet whose story ends honorably rather than gloriously.

Above all, it ends, Graves insists, with poetic integrity and commitment to that truthfulness he denied in Yeats. Yet as Pindar, Nietzsche's Zarathustra, and Zarathustrian Yeats have acknowledged, a poet's very skill can make him a liar. Auden once called Graves's natural facility for writing verse a valuable but dangerous gift, for the poet who possesses it "can all to easily forsake the truth for verbal display." . . . The source is as significant as the substance of the criticism. What has been said of Auden's employment of Skaldic meters and of the verbal tricks of late Norse poetry (that it can produce a verse that, in Goethe's phrase, "does the poet's thinking for him," and so can become a "substitute for any deeper movement and expansion of the poet's mind") might be said of Graves's employment of Welsh and Anglo-classical prosodic "tricks," particularly his use of *cynghanedd* and allied techniques of alliteration, assonance, and internal rhyming. There is, after all, no guarantee that an intricately "crafted" poem will not be trivial. (pp. 99-100)

Despite the lesser, thinner work of recent years, much of which sacrifices passionate intensity to a love-"magic" and "togetherness" more tedious than serene, Graves is a craftsman rather than a mere technician. His poems may be said to succeed or fail insofar as they fulfill the implications of the marvelous concluding line of his most celebrated lyric: "But nothing promised that is not performed." Beyond the bittersweet fruit of the votary's pact with his Goddess—ecstasy shadowed by the inevitable ax—the line implies that the poet puts on *something* of the power and knowledge of the Muse: that nothing is numinously conceived that is not executed by the devotee as man and craftsman. Though there are exceptions (of which **"To Juan at the Winter Solstice"** is among the most obvious), Graves's most ambitious work falls short of its promise when it fails, in performance, to memorably and dramatically embody the myth. Even in poems with few if any mythopoeic pretensions, failure results when Graves is too rationally reined in or when he succumbs to abstraction. Too often he tells rather than shows—and despite his deserved reputation as a love poet, the later lyrics only sporadically make us feel the passion Graves asserts.

But then there are the poems in which Graves succeeds. There are many of these; and the qualities that make them admirable—clarity, flexibility of tone and diction, syntactical and verbal precision, ironic wit and a genuine balance between wildness and civility—ought to recommend them to a wider audience. This is especially true at a time when the "common reader" of poetry, who still hankers after sense and meaning, has virtually nowhere to turn; when poetry itself has dwindled to a province largely restricted to practitioners and academicians. In Graves's tradition—though he sometimes grandly announces that he writes poems only for poets—the poet is still a man speaking to others. (pp. 100-01)

He may not be a "major" poet, and he is certainly not in the modernist swim, but Robert Graves's accomplishment—reflected, at its best, in his ability to start from mystery and yet render the choreography plain and the theme plain—makes him too good a poet to be politely dismissed, and considerably more than an archaic torso washed up at Majorca and out of the swing of the sea. (p. 102)

Patrick J. Keane, in his A Wild Civility: Interactions in the Poetry and Thought of Robert Graves, *University of Missouri Press, 1980, 110 p.*

Geoffrey (William) Hill

1932-

English poet, critic, and essayist.

Considered one of the most important English poets to have emerged since World War II, Hill creates densely complex poems in which he examines themes related to history, religion, and myth. While working within traditional poetic forms, Hill experiments with meter and rhyme to produce language that ranges from simple to opulent. His frequent use of paradox, irony, pun, and allusion contributes to the various layers of meaning evidenced in his verse. Hill's work is informed with a mythic and religious sensibility, through which he explores such themes as the relationships between sacrifice and salvation, ritual and violence, doubt and faith, and the discrepancies between artifice and experience. By blending historic and personal references and often using natural imagery, Hill constructs a vision, according to Seamus Heaney, that "makes contemporary landscapes and experience live in the rich shadows of a tradition."

Fay Godwin's Photo Files

Hill's first book, *For the Unfallen: Poems, 1952-1958* (1959), which includes three poems from an earlier pamphlet, *Poems* (1952), elicited mixed critical response. Some reviewers were troubled by the obliquity and the detached tone of the poems, while others were impressed with the coherence and maturity of Hill's vision and his skillful use of various techniques. A frequently discussed example of Hill's early verse is "Genesis," the opening poem of the collection. Using biblical imagery and language to describe a world of struggle, predation, violence, and myth, Hill introduces his concern with ritual, religion, and the paradoxical nature of life, which he explores throughout his poetry. Hill derived the title of his second collection, *King Log* (1968), from a fable by Aesop in which a group of frogs were given a log as their king. When the frogs complained that the log was unresponsive to their needs, they were delivered a stork, who began eating them. In the central sequence of the volume, "Funeral Music," Hill is concerned with the corrupting influence of power. Through frequent allusions to the medieval Wars of the Roses, the sequence portrays the brutality of war and the cruel paradoxes of human behavior. Andrew Waterman observed that in this sequence "Hill highlights the discrepancies, glaring in fifteenth-century life but by inference perennial, between the bloody and the formal." *King Log* also contains the widely anthologized poem "Ovid in the Third Reich," in which Hill places the Roman poet Ovid in Hitler's Germany. The striking combination of ancient and modern history and the speaker's apologetic tone helps dramatize the essential ambiguity of human existence and allows Hill to examine the social responsibilities of poets and the value of poetry. In the final sequence of the volume, "The Songbook of Sebastian Arrurruz," Hill uses the persona of a nineteenth-century Spanish poet to lament unrequited love. Displaying the simplicity and clarity of classical Spanish verse, the sequence is an example of Hill's ability to render personal experience by combining passion and formal detachment.

Hill's third collection, *Mercian Hymns* (1971), is a sequence of prose poems based on the legends of King Offa, a powerful eighth-century ruler of the area in west central England known as Mercia. In the sequence, Hill blends events from his own childhood in Worcestershire County with tales of the King to create what Grevel Lindop called "a revivifying marriage of past and present." Like much of Hill's verse, the poetry in *Mercian Hymns* is descriptive, relying on visual imagery and evocative landscapes to convey its meaning. Hill uses satire, irony, and anachronisms to examine the effect of social power on human behavior. Many critics consider *Mercian Hymns* to be Hill's most satisfying volume, praising his use of personal and historical allusions to suggest the relationship between the present and the past. In *Tenebrae* (1978), his next volume, Hill employs traditional rhymed forms, particularly the sonnet, to explore his concern with martyrdom and religion. The title of the book refers to an office of the Catholic ritual that commemorates the suffering and death of Christ, and the poems emote a dark, brooding tone. The seven-poem sequence "Lachrimae" focuses upon Robert Southwell, the austere Elizabethan Catholic poet and martyr, to examine the complex relationships between guilt, self-sacrifice, and salvation. In other poems, Hill explores the difficulties of maintaining faith in the presence of doubt and the value of imposing ritual and structure on human existence. Some critics found *Tenebrae* self-consciously devotional and abstruse, while others, noting particularly the sequence "An Apology for the Revival of Christian Architecture in England," praised the passionate lyricism of much of the verse and Hill's subtle use of irony.

Hill's fifth volume, *The Mystery of the Charity of Charles Péguy* (1983), is a sequence of poems in ten sections that functions as a meditation on the life of the French poet and social critic Charles Péguy, whose life was politically and spiritually complex. A devout Catholic who estranged himself from the Church and a socialist who later repudiated his Marxist sympathies, Péguy is a turbulent figure who shares with Hill a personal struggle with the forces of doubt and faith. The murder of a French politician following Péguy's impassioned cry for his blood reflects Hill's concern with the responsibility of poets for the effects of their words. Many critics have noted a fluency in *The Mystery of the Charity of Charles Péguy* not present in much of Hill's earlier work, as he moves easily from elegiac to casual language. Commenting on the similarities between Péguy and Hill, John Mole observed: "The more one reads this poem, the more one feels that it may well be the closest Hill has come to giving us an oblique autobiography of the spirit."

Hill has also published *Brand: A Version for the Stage* (1978), an adaptation in verse of Henrik Ibsen's *Brand.* Several critics cite this experience as an important influence on the style of Hill's later verse. His collection of critical essays, *The Lords of Limit: Essays on Literature and Ideas* (1984), provides important insight into Hill's artistic methods and poetic principles. Hill has also published two editions of his collected poetry. *Somewhere Is Such a Kingdom: Poems, 1952-1971* (1975) contains his first three volumes, and *Collected Poems* (1985) gathers all of his poetry through *The Mystery of the Charity of Charles Péguy* and includes the previously unpublished sequence "Hymns to Our Lady of Chartres."

(See also *CLC,* Vols. 5, 8, 18; *Contemporary Authors,* Vols. 81-84; *Contemporary Authors New Revision Series,* Vol. 21; and *Dictionary of Literary Biography,* Vol. 40.)

ANDREW WATERMAN

[It] is reassuring that over the twenty years since ***For the Unfallen,*** 1959, and still imperfectly, the exceptional excellence of Geoffrey Hill's poetry has come to receive acknowledgement. . . . No poetry, as Wordsworth put it, should 'level down/ For the sake of being generally understood,' or wrongly conscious of audience court fashionable expectations and so perish with them; but Hill's is extraordinarily uncompromising, has a wholly self-preoccupied air; the reader may wander among its compelling splendours, but hardly feels invited or directly addressed. It is poetry intense with feeling, but not the accessible kinds arising directly from everyday experiences and relationships central in much of at least most poets' writing. (p. 85)

Altogether, the poet Hill insistently recalls is Eliot, whose own poetry magnificently passes what he defined as the 'test that genuine poetry can communicate before it is understood'. Hill's has comparable memorability: poems, lines, phrases, incise themselves on the imagination. . . . In ***King Log,*** Hill's **"Funeral Music"** on the Wars of the Roses consummately realizes what his notes tell us he desiderated, 'a florid grim music broken by grunts and shrieks'; while **"'Domaine Public'"** has this image characteristically precise in its sensuous signification. . . . One can dip almost at random to find ***Tenebrae*** sustaining this ability to write poetry that stamps itself on the mind because definitively perfected. . . . Whenever poetry has such power, pervasive through Hill's, almost by imaginative sleight to make the reader feel he has known always lines just read, this arises not only from vivid precision of denotation and image, but also from the poet commanding the movement of his verse in a subtle distinctive music. Hill's frequent poem-titles with musical reference are as wittingly chosen as Eliot's "Four Quartets".

That his poetry *is* difficult has, inevitably yet surely shamefully, slowed and in some quarters apparently precluded its proper recognition. (pp. 86-7)

Yet, if very occasionally impenetrable, if sometimes as I think reading for example the striking **"Annunciations"** in ***King Log*** excessive ellipsis grindingly short-circuits his lines as poetry, Hill's work everywhere convinces of its authenticity, and his difficulty need not be exaggerated. So much comes to mind as touchstones of a sensuous intellection healing that 'dissociation of sensibility' Eliot talked about, lucid enough even when at its highest pitch. (p. 87)

Hill is impressively enough intensively himself to stand the comparison with Eliot. Both poets share historical awareness and perspective, and the poetic practice of bringing past and present into fruitful juxtaposition; though here, I shall argue, Hill's motives and effects generally differ from Eliot's. Hill also has an Eliotian predilection for poetic strategies calculated to achieve a seeming 'impersonality'. . . . Like *The Waste Land,* Hill's **"Funeral Music"** and ***Mercian Hymns*** assume at least some air of being objective statements on the human condition delivered dispassionately from God's right hand. Or, like Eliot with Prufrock, Gerontion, Tiresias, Hill masks utterance with personae discrete from the authorial identity: King Offa, or in that oblique fiction **"The Songbook of Sebastian Arrurruz"** what Hill's notes tell us is 'an apocryphal Spanish poet.' Thus much of Hill's poetry, like early Eliot, becomes essentially dramatic. In ***Tenebrae,*** **"The Pentecost Castle"** sequence deploys seemingly various voices. Even where, in his early work, in a thread woven through ***Mercian Hymns,*** here and there in ***Tenebrae*** more intensely than ever, Hill modulates into a personal 'I', the reader as with Eliot's use of the pronoun in "Ash Wednesday" or "Four Quartets" feels its terms are sharply delimited by the poet, offer no admission-key to his personality or autobiography. In Hill's **"Lachrimae"** sonnets the 'I' is keenly insistent, yet never naked of artifice, and incorporates voices, consciousnesses, other than Hill's. (pp. 89-90)

Again like Eliot, as well as masks of stance or personae Hill appropriates to his purposes and makes distinguishingly his own a range of poetic forms and manners, from the sonnet sequence, through verse with a Metaphysical ground-bass, to the prose-poems of ***Mercian Hymns*** and his recurrent Spanish derivations. C. H. Sisson has noted (*Agenda,* 13:3, 1975) Hill's 'singularly direct mind which, none the less, seems impelled to such indirect utterance.' Like Crashaw's, Sisson suggests, 'a mind in search of artifices to protect itself against its own passions.' No more than Eliot is Hill prone to offer personal experience with open straight-forwardness in the old-Romantic or new-Confessional I-fall-upon-the-thorns-of-life-I-bleed / My-mind's-not-right ways. His means are devious and oblique. His titles alone can be provocatively indirect: in ***Tenebrae*** the over-all entitling of thirteen superb sonnets only loosely related and on the evidence of Hill's notes not homogeneous in conception, as **"An Apology for the Revival of Christian Architecture in England",** seems less than inevitable. And yet, attentive reading shows any apparent 'impersonality' about Hill's poetry to be only his necessary guise or framework for a vision, a coherent array of attitudes and imaginative response, intensely subjective almost to idiosyncrasy.

If ***For the Unfallen*** was a first collection startling in the consummate finish of its writing and the amplitude of its aims, this sparing poet's next book, ***King Log,*** published nine years later in 1968, surpassed it in scope, penetration and mature poetic accomplishment. While in **"Ovid in the Third Reich"** extreme compression superbly justifies itself, I would allow that occasionally elsewhere in ***King Log*** Hill's power-pack becomes a logjam. In **"Annunciations,"** although such phrasing as 'the soul / Purples itself; each eye squats full and mild' stamps itself indelibly, and each line is in principle construable, the whole congestedly loses momentum. In **"The Stone Man",** language like 'Words clawed my mind as though they had smelt / Revelation's flesh. . . . The sun bellows over its parched swarms,' seems overpumped, even ludicrous. Intensity of feeling is pervasive through ***King Log,*** and the repelled notation in **"Annunciations"** of 'the steam of beasts, / The loathly neckings and the fat shook spawn', expresses a disgust for the flesh and its appetites recurrent in Hill, though coolly enough revolved through different perspectives. . . . The eleven Arrurruz poems intensify sexual passion precisely by stripping it of circumstantial documentation, an effect similar to Eliot's with sexual disgust in the three Thames-daughter songs in "The Waste Land", where the nature of his achievement appears clearly from comparing the finished poem's 'Trams and dusty trees' quatrain with the eleven-line equivalent in Eliot's earlier draft, full of background information about the girl and her family. If Hill follows a similar instinct to forfeit a documentary kind of intelligibility to bare finally more illuminating intensities, his results equally justify themselves. Thus, when in an unsympathetic review of ***Tenebrae*** [see *CLC,* Vol. 18] . . . Craig Raine takes a sideswipe at the woman lamented in **"The Songbook of Sebastian Arrurruz"** as 'shadowy', he seems wrongheadedly beside the point of Hill's psychologically subtle realizations of incandescent emotion. And within the sequence's cryptic framework and strategy, the writing is incisively fluent. (pp. 90-2)

But it is the **"Funeral Music"** sequence of eight unrhymed sonnets in ***King Log*** that marked a high point in Hill's poetic career. Here, the Wars of the Roses provide a gravitational field within which Hill can coherently cluster, explore, articulate, some of his huger themes and obsessions. The poems bear what Hill's notes term 'an oblique dedication' to three peers, variously representative of their time and encompassing humane and spiritual as well as ruthlessly worldly allegiances, all executed within the period. A central awareness in **"Funeral Music"** is that medieval life was at once nasty, brutish and short, and highly ritualized, ceremonious; fraught with spiritual aspirations liable to be broken with stark vividness on harsh and cruel actualities. . . . Everywhere, not through comment but by precise realization in the texture of his writing, Hill highlights the discrepancies, glaring in fifteenth-century life but by inference perennial, between the bloody and the formal, so that with two-way irony each becomes a criticism upon the other. His command of resonant ambiguity functions brilliantly to illumine the dichotomy. . . . A poetic style and tone Hill notes as 'ornate and heartless' is crucially instrumental to the total meaning of **"Funeral Music",** implying, and through interrupting grunts and shrieks endorsing, a critique of its own limitations; and so effectively transcending these. Rarely is artifice so artfully significant; this is poetry of a formal magnificence that, in its own words, 'whines through the empyrean' aware, as that verb's connotations suggest, of its own ambivalence.

Beyond which, through the lives and times it articulates, **"Funeral Music"** searingly meditates life's fundamental questions. . . . (pp. 92-3)

Mercian Hymns, in 1971, surprised superficially by being a sequence of thirty prose-poems; thematically however it is consonant with **"Funeral Music":** less intensively wrought, wider ranging, more sportive. It is no disadvantage to Hill's purposes that, Anglo-Saxon records belonging overwhelmingly to the later period of Wessex hegemony, and even archaeology having unearthed little, the powerful Mercian king Offa who controlled by conquest most of England and functioned as a European potentate, 'friend of Charlemagne', remains so sparsely documented, his testimony little more than his impressive money and the dyke he built against the Welsh:

> And it seemed, while we watched, he began to walk
> towards us he vanished
> he left behind coins, for his lodging, and traces of
> red mud.

Thus hymn **XXX.** That the grandest worldly show is passing, is an awareness ***Mercian Hymns*** utters incisively as Shelley's "Ozymandias". Earth, the struggle to master it, and that all returns to it, is 'invested in mother earth' (**IV**), features crucially through the sequence, its details delicately observed; Offa *Rex Totius Anglorum Patriae* is as transient as a snail that 'sugared its new stone' (**XIV**). Yet also Offa is something perennial, the 'creature of legend' Hill's notes tell us might 'in this sequence be regarded as the presiding genius of the West Midlands, his dominion enduring from the middle of the eighth century until the middle of the twentieth (and possibly beyond).' The final hymn's 'traces of red mud' intimate more than the historical Offa's grandiose dyke; **Hymn I,** listing his worldly attributes, has him also 'overlord of the M5 . . . contractor to the desirable new estates,' and gives clear guidance to Hill's framing strategy for the sequence, which is comprehensible enough. One should note though that if occasionally Hill collocates ancient and modern with the Eliotian motive of ironic contrast, as when suburban dwellings are named 'Ethandune', 'Catraeth', 'Maldon', 'Pengwern', generally his intention is the reverse, akin in its historical vision to that of David Jones in *In Parenthesis:* to suggest parallels, continuities. This allows him, through a book refreshingly humorous for Hill, to enjoy concocting anachronisms such as 'Merovingian car-dealers'; but the purpose is serious, and the vision coherent.

But the energies of ***Mercian Hymns*** flow not only along this axis between past and present, but concurrently along another vitally linking public and private worlds, those of temporal power and of a childhood evidently the poet's. Hill thus establishes a four-way system of metaphor of considerable resonance. . . . Concerned with power and self-aggrandizement, Hill is interested not in their means and instruments, but the underlying subtle private impulses which will and energize them. Richly fruitful here is his use of childhood, which has its fantasies of power and command, whim, wanton cruelty, grievances, terrors, egotistic desires, but confined to expression objectively trivial. But if in adulthood such impulses obtain the means of power, there ensues inordinate enactment, most extremely exemplified in a Hitler, Stalin or Amin, perhaps bridled generally only insofar as given political systems check it. Hill clearly believes that power corrupts and absolute power corrupts absolutely; and Offa, whose early-medieval society desiderated military autocracy, becomes the type of a human phenomenon perennial if modulating its guises in the modern England of motorways, commerce and political democracy. Yet by implicating his own boyhood as a single child who 'fostered a strangeness; gave myself to unattainable toys' (**VI**) in his unsparing creation of this figure, Hill enables us to understand compassionately his common human nature. (pp. 94-5)

Obviously Hill's strategy in ***Mercian Hymns*** allows enormous scope to his talent for verbal punning, refined and applied as felicitously as ever: the protagonist is a 'staggeringly-gifted child'; on his coins Offa appears 'cushioned on a legend', with a play on both 'cushioned' and the numismatic and larger meanings of 'legend'. Three of the hymns are about 'Offa's Coins': an arbitrary ruler's mark-making equivalent to the boy carving his name on desks. So, 'the masterful head emerges, kempt and jutting, out of England's well' (**XIII**), his name a 'best-selling brand, curt graffito. A laugh; a cough. . . . A specious gift. . . . The starting cry of a race. A name to conjure with.' (**II**). 'Hymns' implies, whatever else, celebration; yet Offa's legacy may be no more than—for the whole work's closing 'traces of red earth' bear another connotation—money and blood. Imagist epic seems an appropriate term for ***Mercian Hymns,*** where intensely worked and polished fragments cohere within a grand structure to intimate a vision of huge scope.

Tenebrae, the 1978 collection of Hill's subsequent work, shows some of his most purely beautiful writing in a return to traditional, rhymed forms, particularly the sonnet, by this poet always exceptionally intent on disciplining emotion. Much of the emotion in ***Tenebrae*** is religious, a desire trustingly to believe agonized by doubt; Hill's has always seemed perhaps a style learnt from a despair, and ***Tenebrae*** more than ever recalls Donne's observation, 'Grief brought to numbers cannot be so fierce, / For he tames it, that fetters it in verse.' But not only 'tames': also clarifyingly explores and articulates it as undisciplined utterance could not. And in any case, as **"Funeral Music"** particularly, but his work pervasively, has shown, for Hill the tension between artifice of expression and immediacies of experience, which his poetic forms enact, is itself a central troubling theme in his engagement with the human condition. . . . Sharp as ever in ***Tenebrae*** is Hill's fearful awareness that in 'composing', conferring articulate order, whether in life or upon the materials of a poem, we abstract, petrify, real feelings, cries, within a realm inaccessible and unsuccouring to the actual contingent world we thus invade. (pp. 96-7)

These considerations are especially relevant to the seven **"Lachrimae"** sonnets, which take their epigraph—'Passions I allow, and loves I approve, onely I would wish that men would alter their object and better their intent'—and more, from Robert Southwell the Elizabethan Catholic poet who despising all things worldly composed his life towards martyrdom and in suffering torture and death achieved the consummation he devoutly wished. . . . A 'self-seeking hunter of forms', the martyr makes his real agony the focal point of a contrived artifice in which even his torturers are his collaborators, material for his composition; within which design, as Hill's earlier **"Ovid in the Third Reich"** had it, 'They, in their sphere, / Harmonize strangely with the divine / Love. (p. 97)

To express his sense of a resonance irrefutable and formally perfect found paradoxically through extinction at the worldly level **"Pavana Dolorosa"** uses music and dance as analogy, a dimension of metaphor framing the whole **"Lachrimae"** sequence, subtitled "Seven tears figured in seven passionate Pavans" in allusion to the music of Southwell's Catholic contemporary John Dowland. Of course the relation between the violent human content and the poetry's formal qualities and tones of elaborate stately melancholy enacts the paradox at the heart of Hill's preoccupations. . . . (pp. 97-8)

That in **"Lachrimae"** Hill's poetic manner adaptively assumes some characteristics of the Elizabethan Southwell about whom the preoccupations of the sequence gather, is of course an effect knowingly managed and part of the poetry's point; and given that it works, preempts Craig Raine's complaint [see *CLC,* Vol. 18] . . . that 'the traditional diction makes for glum reading,' and his pejorative designation of Hill, a poet preoccupied with perennial man in temporal history, as 'archaeological'. The kind of languorous wordplay illustrated in . . . **"Lachrimae"**, typified by the close of **"Pavana Dolorosa"**,

> I founder in desire for things unfound.
> I stay amid the things that will not stay,

recurs in the book's title-sequence **"Tenebrae"**, where the second section is a tissue of it and the brief fourth has lines like 'Light of light, supreme delight; / Grace at our lips to our disgrace.' Distinct from the concentrated ambiguity within a single word or phrase by which Hill has always clarifyingly focused his understanding of life's paradoxes, this is less a 'metaphysical' than, consciously, a conventional Elizabethan kind of wordplay, a more decorative slow juggling of words to revolve their varieties of signification or merely achieve symmetries. . . . Of course this, in collaboration with traditional verse forms, procures a fluency Hill occasionally forfeited in earlier books when compressing meaning as ruthlessly as those machines which crush scrapped cars to cubic inches. The euphuistic manner might lend itself to formulations superficially neat and reductive, but Hill employs it to purpose in specific poems, not self-indulgently; and if ***Tenebrae*** is throughout his most fluent collection, this is certainly not at the expense of the intensities which are this poet's hallmark, nor of that meticulously expressive articulation of syntax characterizing all his writing.

I do nevertheless find the **"Tenebrae"** sequence a weak area in this collection, for overall it reads too much like Hill just letting his machinery tick over. And although in a way more enterprising, I cannot say that **"The Pentecost Castle"** interests me greatly. Fluency, an exceptional openness of style for Hill, its short-lined stanzas certainly have. The notes to ***Tenebrae*** tell us that **"The Pentecost Castle"** is 'particularly indebted' to Hill's reading of the *Penguin Book of Spanish Verse,* and browsing around that, with particular indebtedness in my case to the prose translations, I can see what Hill owes texturally, what has stimulated his poetry's tone, ballad musicality, temper, occasional piercing bitter-sweetness and glitter. These qualities acknowledged, there seems little more to say about **"The Pentecost Castle":** although each section is tellingly charged with implication, I do not feel that as a whole the sequence shapes sufficiently into gathered articulation of the themes adumbrated in its epigraphs, from Simone Weil about love's egotism, and Yeats's 'It is terrible to desire and not possess, and terrible to possess and not desire.'

But generally ***Tenebrae*** sustains magnificently the development within continuity Hill's poetry has always achieved. Among several excellent individual poems are **"A Pre-Raphaelite Notebook"**, **"Te Lucis Ante Terminum"** . . . , **"Ave Regina Coelorum"** brilliantly starting 'There is a land called Lost/at peace inside our heads', and **"Terribilis Est Locus Iste"**, dedicated to 'Gauguin and the Pont-Aven School'. . . . (pp. 99-100)

Particularly, the thirteen sonnets, less intensively interrelated than those of **"Lachrimae"**, gathered under the devious title **"An Apology for the Revival of Christian Architecture in England"**, gravitating meditatively around Coleridge's hankering for 'the spiritual, Platonic old England,' mediate its personal, geographical and historical intimations in poetry as impressive as any Hill has written. (p. 100)

Hill's poetry here loses nothing in intensity for being more than usually at peace with the world. If an excitement of following it has been that its development from collection to collection is at once surprising and recognizably harmonious, in ***Tenebrae***, his craftsmanship more adequate than ever to the intensity of his vision, and avoiding the occasional lockjaw hesitation of some of his earlier work, he has achieved his most eloquent poetry yet.

Generally, Hill's work, never condescending for the sake of yielding instant meaning, keeping aloof from superficialities of fashion and true to its imaginative temper and purposes, has through decades of much sloppy self-indulgent and makeshift writing, a certain literary chaos, conferred intellectual and emotional dignity on poetry. That in our place and time it exists, is an unqualified good for poetry and readers. Intricately exploring and enacting through diverse ramifications the central human tension between imaginative order and life's anarchy, employing a consummate technique commensurate with his ambitiousness, Hill like an old-timer panning for gold sifts life and language, prospecting among their silt for glinting richnesses. To borrow one of his own immaculately apt images, his poetry 'grows upon the mind / as lichen glimmers on the wood.' (pp. 101-02)

Andrew Waterman, "The Poetry of Geoffrey Hill," in British Poetry Since 1970: A Critical Survey, *edited by Peter Jones and Michael Schmidt, Carcanet Press, 1980, pp. 85-102.*

CALVIN BEDIENT

[Hill has] been savaged by 'the realization of . . . disappointment' and has been savage about it. His early poetry is sick with it, stymied. In ***Mercian Hymns*** [1974] he fared better, roused like a cornered animal despite his trembling. The volume has the scary control and exhilaration of Marlowe on the trail of Kurtz. Hill's moral rage magnanimously allowed human and natural life a barbarous glamour; his language prickled not only with irony but with ambivalence, a begrudging excitement. Then in the best parts of ***Tenebrae*** [1978] he tried a different tact, not unsuccessful—a disarming tolerance Christ-touched but also like that of time, time that survives its every mistake.

King Log (1968) and even more ***For the Unfallen*** (1959) now look like apprentice work spangled by greatness. To take to disappointment as to a cross is to court excess, and the early volumes show as much weakness as strength, as much sickness as health—as well as a good deal of derivativeness.

In the self-torturing state Hill was in then he could write brilliantly but not well. If a poet is only so good as his relation to his material Hill neglected his even as in one sense he made too much of it—he wanted history to confess the worst, the courtroom of conscience to cry 'Atrocity!' But really it was himself he had on trial; he was secretly self-absorbed. He could not get the tone right because he wanted to excoriate himself for being human, if not for being Hill; he was not humane to himself and tone, the crux of every poem, is the humane aspect of language.

For Hill, history effectively ended with the aftermath of the Second World War, the catastrophe of his own young postwar conscience. Always he writes back from there, his sensibility spreading back like a stain. (Where Larkin is chockful of contemporary England, Hill might never have left his wartime wireless.) Hill illustrates—tending as he does toward the exemplary—what Stephen Spender called the European position, that 'to be alive is to be an outpost' of the past.

Yet Hill was relating history less than inventing nightmares, and it showed in his febrile language, self-conscious silences, lurching ironies. The poems argued a staggering need to be blinded in 'renunciation's glare'. Moral sorrow lodged in Hill's breast like an arrow it would be death to remove. His humaneness harrowed him and *that* was what one noticed. His own guilt upstaged history's. (pp. 18-19)

Sicklied o'er with guilt, all too decent, Hill was incapacitated to write about brutal power with the fearless simplicity (witness Nazim Hikmet or Yannis Ritsos) that goes straight like a stake for the Cyclops's eye. He bit his own tongue, was too tragic-gestured. His compassion lacked warmth and directness. The two 'formal' elegies 'for the Jews in Europe' proved all too formal-bookish. They minced with obscurity, with overplayed fastidiousness. Nor was his despair clear and universal, like Beckett's. It retained something murky, private. (p. 19)

But as notable in the early volumes as the shadow-shows of guilt was a monstrous gift of expression. To be so sly of conscience is to be able to turn words queasy, discover soft places in them, make them burn; to be so anguished is to want an answering sonority. Hill's great if perfidious intelligence, his brilliantly unforgiving sensibility, was matched by an ear schooled in grand styles. (pp. 19-20)

What Hill had yet to gain was enough distance from his material (or himself) to be direct and just through an entire poem. In ***Mercian Hymns*** he was able to accomplish precisely that, and for an entire volume.

Here, though moral irony holds court, matters more nearly speak for themselves. . . . Although little of the little actually known about King Offa is used, the biographical idea of the work straitens it. Offa, part of Hill's childhood, is not overbad—he's just human, just bad. Human nature in its pride, caprice, treachery, guilt, Offa is brought onto the page in a tone that avoids both mercy and excess, a tone we cannot get around.

Poet and protagonist circle one another in mutual need and distrust. Offa needs Hill ('Exile or pilgrim') to set him 'once more upon that ground: my rich and desolate childhood'. The poet obliges, for, a Narcissus looking dizzily into the horror-pool of time, his own nature, is it not Offa that he would drown in?

He is saved by his irony—his askesis in the sensuality of time. Poet and king are close as conspirators, as ego and alter ego, crime and conscience—but Hill's irony, the thin end of a blade that never fully reveals itself, cuts him off from history, placing him at the juncture of Christian judgement.

Yet the end of the work is not judgement. This is its revolutionary change from the earlier books. Balanced between condemnation and celebration, it evades eschatological ideology, just as it evades the Modernist ideology of despair. (p. 20)

But not only Hill's moral antagonisms, his vital powers abjure despair. No matter that 'denial of history' seems implicit in the peculiarly disjointed structure, the anachronisms and the rejection of narrative. No matter, even, that the poem ends by annihilating the mythical imagination ('. . . he entered into the last dream of Offa the King'), an imagination that had already borne nothing-ward the paralyzed historical sense. The work none the less rests in confidence in its own construction, confidence in language, eloquence, arresting beauty, intimated splendor—in these as much as in tell-tale irony. Exquisitely crafted, with never a word too many or few, a word not mesmerizingly right, it is its own best testimony to the human power to manage recalcitrant material—a concern introduced at the juridical level by the epigraph from the Christian monarchist C. H. Sisson.

Hill's imagination enjoys what his judgment deplores. It creates the reality that justice must confront. And it thus does justice to worldly energies. As truculently splendid as they are ferociously economical, the hymns get at things—'bellow of whalebone and dung', 'peppermint and confetti'—with honest relish. Hill's imagination is brought over at last to the concreteness, more the atavism to which dreams are faithful. (p. 21)

By fending off neither the mind nor the senses, Hill opens his language to everything. To moral nuance in physical description: 'In dawn-light the troughed water floated a damson bloom of dust' (from a hymn on a nail factory, where neither beauty nor tragedy steps back for the other but together draw out a torn, uncompromised response). To drama, internalising pop-ups: 'Where best to stand? Easter sunrays catch the oblique face of Adam scrumping through leaves . . .' To surprises of voice: 'Tell everything to Mother, darling, and God bless.' To wit; rapture; rue. He creates a poetry at once crisp, sensual, and grand.

Everything in the hymns argues strength. Above all its refusal to smother things by wrapping them up. For the individual really is solitary, and not; time deniable, and not; the past a father—demonic, pathetic—who perhaps should, and perhaps cannot, be exorcised. A choice would be ideological. Art challenges ideology.

A work of rare inspiration, ***Mercian Hymns*** provided what was long overdue: a modern English poetic masterpiece of real magnitude (and at the same time, with the qualifications noted, a modernist masterpiece, disturbingly complex, tauntingly disjunctive). No surprise that Hill's subsequent volume proved a lesser achievement—but ***Tenebrae*** is disappointing, none the less. Reflecting a failure of nerve, it reacts against the strengths of ***Mercian Hymns.*** Structure is rounded up, style strapped, conscience sent to church, if only to other people's churches. And history, that cauldron of the hymns, is here a cold pot. If ***Mercian Hymns*** is the crime, ***Tenebrae*** is the penitence.

In the three devotional sequences Hill packs in his formidable powers and docilely copies sixteenth-century Spanish *a lo divino* lyrics (**"Pentecost Castle"**), sonnets by Lope de Vega and Quevedo (**"Lachrimae"**), and T. S. Eliot's type of variable long poem (***Tenebrae***). The writing is all ceremony and poorly lit, tenebrae indeed. What is Hill screening behind these imitations? What is the actual status of his faith?

The devotional sequences are cop-outs, dismaying to anyone who wants Hill to write at his best—to be honest. . . . The sonnets are still more mawkish:

> Crucified Lord, you swim upon your cross
> and never move. Sometimes in dreams of hell
> the body moves to no avail
> and is at one with that eternal loss.
>
> You are the castaway of drowned remorse,
> you are the world's atonement on the hill.
> This is your body twisted by our skill
> into a patience proper for redress . . .

Lackadaisical, sentimental, pompous. 'To no avail', 'that eternal loss', 'the castaway of drowned remorse', 'the world's atonement on the hill', 'proper for redress'—the writing is a curiously bored impersonation of devotion. Or take the title poem: 'This is the ash-pit of the lily-fire, / this is the questioning at the long tables, / this is . . .'—this is T. S. Eliot. 'The best societies of hell / acknowledge this, aroused by what they know' is simply bombast. 'O light of light, supreme delight'—you long to say it is all in fun.

Perhaps Hill is after all too proud and feral for the posture of penitence. It speaks to and of only a certain crushed part of him. So in his kneelings he mimics others, to get it 'right'. But the beanstalk was for Jack, not the giant, whose mistake lay in trying to go down.

That Hill is in retreat not only from his own powers but once again from worldly power in general—'Anything', he wrote in his early poem **"Solomon's mines"**, 'to get up and go / (let the hewn gates clash to) / Without looking round / Out of that strong land'—is apparent in his fine historical sequence, **"An apology for the revival of Christian architecture in England"**. Its thirteen sonnets unite in the theme of an England whose historical fires are so banked that it is ready for a religious revival: the other life. With its sweet trembling hope the theme almost goes underground in embarrassment and the oblique title is more wince than wink. (pp. 22-4)

Yet one or two short poems aside, the sequence contains Hill's best writing next to ***Mercian Hymns.*** Whatever his eschatological bias the poet does not confuse himself with his material. And tenderness, even tolerance acknowledges the world's body, giving substance to the line. (p. 25)

In ***King Log*** Hill reeled from carnality; in ***Mercian Hymns,*** teased it like a boy prodding a scorpion with a stick; in ***Tenebrae,*** interred it. Is the drama over? . . .

Perhaps his greatest liability is one other poets might envy: fear of his own powers. All the more remarkable then that he wrote ***Mercian Hymns.*** He thus illuminated a bold and difficult excellence, creating a standard of truth and structural genius to which we may feel disposed to hold him. Conspicuous elevation, evidence of upheaval, ups and downs—in this case there is something in a name. (p. 26)

Calvin Bedient, "On Geoffrey Hill," in Critical Quarterly, *Vol. 23, No. 2, Summer, 1981, pp. 17-26.*

HENRY HART

That Geoffrey Hill should choose to write a poem of one hundred quatrains about the life and death of Charles Péguy [***The Mystery of the Charity of Charles Péguy***], and find a title in Péguy's little-known verse-drama, *Le Mystère de la Charité de Jeanne*

D'Arc, must seem extraordinary to most readers. In Péguy's life, which began among peasants in La Beauce, the region surrounding Orleans, and ended in 1914 after years of financial and domestic hardship at the Battle of the Marne, Hill finds a moving example of a man comically and tragically at odds with both his age and his own ideals. 'A man of the most exact and exacting probity, accurate practicality, in personal and business relations', Péguy was also implicated in the assassination of the great socialist leader, Jean Jaurès, and was prepared to murder an officer in the French army because he suspected, on completely unfounded evidence, that the man had mistreated (and thereby killed) his friend, Marcel Baudoin. Péguy's otherworldliness, and the chivalric values engendered by it, made for heroic crimes. He was a saintly felon and felonous saint, whose vices were entangled in his virtues. A 'great soul', he was capable of the atrocities 'great souls' commit. In his ***Mystery*** Hill succeeds brilliantly in resurrecting from the past a hero whose charitable acts and gross misdeeds offer directives to the present.

In earlier poems, such as **"The Songbook of Sebastian Arrurruz"** and ***Mercian Hymns,*** Hill conferred upon fictitious characters the motives and actions of real men; in ***The Mystery*** he does the opposite. A historical figure, whose life is well-documented, is made mythical. Although Hill takes details, phrases, and even whole lines from Péguy's biographers, they become part of a new pattern. But why choose Péguy, whose life and art are so different from Hill's? The most obvious reason is that Hill, fascinated by a tortuous stance towards Catholicism and political conservatism, finds in Péguy, an instructive ally and enemy. Hill has described his poetry as 'a heretic's dream of salvation expressed in the images of the orthodoxy from which he is excommunicate', and Péguy's life bears an obvious resemblance. . . . Péguy joins Hill's army of martyrs, whose devotions are noble as well as vicious, and whose acts of faith are as condemnable as they are commendable. But if Jeanne D'Arc provides Péguy with a paradigm of self-sacrifice and charity, Péguy provides Hill with a model that remains, after much communing, deliberately elusive. Although Hill longs to talk with Péguy's ghost, he never gets beyond dramatic monologue, interspersed with salutations, denunciations, and repeated qualifications. As mystic and martyr, Péguy offers Hill symptoms to diagnose as well as heroic acts to enthrone.

Le mystère and *la charité* for Péguy, as for Hill, have specific rather than vague connotations. For Péguy *le mystère* is the secret impulse behind a moral act. The goal to which *le mystère* is directed is *la mystique*. In his life Péguy identified *la mystique* with Dreyfusism, Republicanism, Socialism, and Catholicism. 'The essence of mysticism', Péguy declared, 'is . . . an invincible anxiety'; for Hill, 'an anxiety about *faux pas,* the perpetration of "howlers", grammatical solecisms, mis-statements of fact, mis-quotations, improper attributions' is the generative impulse of poetry. for Péguy *la charité* was 'the spiritual, temporal and constant communion with the poor, the weak and the oppressed'. Socialism, based on charity, was 'a mystic socialism . . . profoundly related to Christianity' and 'no less than a religion of temporal salvation'—the socialism of St. Francis rather than Marx.

Hill's poem meditates on the mystery of Péguy's Christian charity but only offers momentary glimpses of requital. Charity is continually a possibility envisaged, like utopia, rather than concretely accomplished. Sublime fulfilment is tantalizingly out of reach. In "The Modern World", the essay from which Hill takes his epigraph, Péguy declares, 'Everything begins in mysticism and ends in politics'. Hill's poem maps *la mystique* and *la politique* as one is betrayed or corrupted by the other, and as they shift back and forth dialectically between sublimity and banality. 'The charge and counter-charge', as Hill calls it, is a structural principle of his poem as well as a rhythm inherent in the world outside it. Its origins may be mysterious; its path, as his poem demonstrates with great finesse, is eminently traceable.

Behind Hill's examples of charity, or 'the divine love', as he calls it in **"Ovid in the Third Reich",** the presence of Christ repeatedly asserts itself. For Hill Christ embodies perfect selfless devotion, but while He invites imitation He judges and damns whoever tries to abide by His example. In **"Lachrimae"** Hill summarized the situation in which Christ was imminent but always beyond the communicant—a conscience divided against itself. Péguy, as Hill portrays him, is similarly divided. 'We are one with the eternally damned', Péguy said in his early days. Hill places him among 'the damned in the brazen Invalides of Heaven' with good reason.

In pursuit of salvation, Péguy sinks his roots into the 'terre charnelle', which for Hill is the mystery of sin, anxiety, and death. The object is to re-incorporate the energies of earth, to free her natural abundance from unnatural constraint, to imitate her will to give—her charity. As in the Eleusinian mystery cult of ancient Greece, Hill's ***Mystery*** re-enacts the descent of a vegetation god, a Christ-like Demeter, through wintry death towards the centre of the earth (Jules Verne is mentioned in section 6) and a subsequent efflorescence in spring. We must 'turn away and contemplate the working / of the radical soul', Hill says in his fifth section, emphasizing the 'rootedness' of 'radical'. Although numerous mediating presences appear in ***The Mystery*** (Jeanne D'Arc, Dreyfus, Bergson, Foch, Charles George Gordon, Emile Zola, Jules Verne, Christ), Péguy predominates, and guides the meditation, not towards transcendental paradise, but towards a recognition and articulation of 'the "specific gravity of human nature"'. 'It is at the heart of this "heaviness"', Hill has said, 'that poetry must do its atoning work'. At 'the heart/of the mystère' the poet, like Lucifer fallen into hell, gathers together his powers and builds his palace.

Three years after translating Ibsen's *Brand,* Hill told an interviewer that working on it had widened the scope of his 'art in a quite unexpected way' and that it had given him 'self-confidence and the means to write fluently'. What is immediately noticeable in ***The Mystery*** is a new fluency; the poem moves from the casual to the elegiac, the fiercely declarative to the interrogative, and from ecstatic revelation to sarcastic gloom with an ease unattained in many of the earlier poems. The liability of this style is prosiness, but Hill guards against it by tightening his lines into loosely-metred iambic pentameters and half-rhymed quatrains. He divides his poem into ten sections, whose movements and counter-movements, as in section four and five, overlap. Hill's style is 'antiphonal', as he explains that term in **"Redeeming the Time".** It enacts 'the drama of reason'; it considers many positions from different angles and struggles towards decision and action: 'Its structure is a recognition and a resistance; it is parenthetical, antiphonal, it turns upon itself'. Rather than follow the traditional linear plot of a dramatic story, Hill's poem traces the mind's brilliant leaps, rapid associations, and spiralling moods. What is lost in narrative sweep is gained in lyrical intensity. Its discursive meditation is an impassioned argument, broken up by attacks and graced with eloquent praise. (pp. 312-15)

Although Hill's poem shows rituals of devotion continually breaking down beneath private misfortune and public disaster, and charity turning into bitterness and hatred, it also shows the strength of rituals to combat and order the darker side of experience. Memory and imagination, in the end, triumph over misfortune and death. Hill resurrects Péguy's virtues, along with his sins, and shapes them into an act of love and devotion, which is the marvellous poem itself. Hill's ***Mystery*** is a song to charity, not always mellifluous, which praises and warns against charity's zealous devotees. It is a powerful testament to a mind, both practical and principled, politically cognizant and mystically tensed, which is able to transform recalcitrant material into brilliant verse. Although Péguy's infelicities are never condoned or excused, his mystical ideal of charity, in the very care of Hill's craftsmanship, is faithfully served. (pp. 336-37)

Henry Hart, "Geoffrey Hill's 'The Mystery of the Charity of Charles Péguy': A Commentary," in Essays in Criticism, *Vol. XXXIII, No. 4, October, 1983, pp. 312-38.*

JOHN MOLE

The Mystery of the Charity of Charles Péguy is in ten sections, and is as intricate and allusive a pavan of violence and ambiguous redemption as Hill has yet written, an accumulation of beautiful and demanding lines, each in itself a facet for contemplation. It is also, though, remote in its sonority and its making of *ex cathedra* statements, as if it were being delivered to a particularly erudite congregation from the other end of the cathedral. When Hill meditates on suffering and action, doubt and faith, reputation and redemption, he often comes dangerously close to sounding like a parody of Eliot's priests addressing the Women of Canterbury:

Drawn on the past
these presences endure; they have not ceased
to act, suffer, crouching into the hail
like labourers of their own memorial. . . .

He's a brilliant phrase-maker, though, and each phrase is witness to a complex passion—an intense marriage of doubt and faith—which seems a match for Péguy's. The simplest combination of words, for Hill, is a feast of associations: "The guilt belongs to time", "Death does you proud" etc. Like the blood that, emblematically, dribbles from Péguy's skull on the battlefield it is "a simple lesion of the complex brain." In fact, the whole poem could be viewed as a succession of moments at which Hill's theme and method coincide in a celebration of his art and Péguy's example. It is as self-conscious as it is selflessly admiring. . . . Above all it is that "strange Christian hope" which reverberates throughout the poem, from the opening lines where Jaurès dies in the "wine puddle" of his own blood to the final stanza where Péguy offers up his "body's prayer." The power is that of a poem which hopes where it cannot prove, and which very elegantly founders, as did Hill's **"Lachrimae"** sequence, "in desire for things unfound." As he writes of Péguy in the postscript, "he had . . . rediscovered the solitary ardours of faith but not the consolations of religious practice. He remained self-excommunicate but adoring." Who, really, is this describing? *Solitary ardours, self-excommunicate, adoring?* The more one reads this poem, the more one feels that it may well be the closest Hill has come to giving us an oblique autobiography of the spirit. And grandiose as that may sound, it is appropriate to the whole tone of the poem. (pp. 64-5)

John Mole, "Expanding Elements: Recent Poetry," in Encounter, *Vol. LXI, No. 4, December, 1983, pp. 60-7.*

GREVEL LINDOP

As Geoffrey Hill proclaimed in **"Genesis"**, the first poem of his first volume, ***For the Unfallen***, 'There is no bloodless myth will hold'. His work since has been an investigation of the perplexing relationship between myth and blood: the sacrifices, worthy and worthless, exacted by political, historical and religious myths, and the way the shed blood germinates into new myths, blood-thirsty in their turn. In ***The Mystery of the Charity of Charles Péguy***. . . . Hill concerns himself with a figure upon whom a whole battery of myths is trained: myths not only diverse in their 'matter'—patriotic, theological, literary—but of varied status, from the world-myth of Christ crucified to the distilled (or oversimplified) versions of modern history promulgated by the newsreel and the political speech. Such a theme makes it natural that ***The Mystery of the Charity of Charles Péguy*** should have close affinities with Hill's earlier work, and that it should bring into question the nature and value of that work to date. A poem which recalls in so many ways the devices and concerns of earlier work may be, depending on how far it unfolds the latent implications of its predecessors, a consummation, or a rehash, or something between the two. (p. 147)

Hill is fully aware that his own poem is but a new contribution to Péguy's myth, though it is Péguy as enigma rather than Péguy as hero whom he elevates. As if to emphasise this, Hill ends several of his poem's ten sections on notes of bathos. (p. 148)

Such emphatic signals should warn us against reading the poem as hagiography, or from judgements which are fiercely for or against the poem (as some reviews have been) in response to Hill's supposed endorsement of the martial values that led Péguy to his death. Rather, it seems that Hill admires Péguy *as* an enigma, perhaps one whose commitment to the passionate contradictions of his nature is the only heroism possible in our fractured culture. Without a universally-accepted decorum, how can any fervent endeavour fail to look ludicrous from one point of view or another?

Péguy should perhaps be seen as a modern (and hence especially disturbing) instance of the spiritual enigmas Hill has often presented. His vision of human existence as a state of unresolveable ambiguity seems to have been expressed for the first time in ***King Log*** (1968), which opens with **"Ovid in the Third Reich"**, a poem depicting a state of mind not so much balanced as paralysed by a perception of total ambiguity. Where every phrase is capable of multiple interpretation it is hard to quote selectively, but to take one instance, the speaker of that poem tells us that 'Too near the ancient troughs of blood / Innocence is no earthly weapon', which at once asks whether innocence is, then, a heavenly weapon, or no earthly use, or both, and also whether failing to intervene, or participate, in evil can be 'innocent', or indeed possible. Words are placed against each other like mirrors, creating unlimited vistas of mutual qualification. In **"Annunciations"** 2, a voice exhorts religiously, 'O Love, . . . be vigilant; strive / To recognise the damned among your friends', which could equally well be an incitement to unlimited compassion or to obscene self-righteousness. In more recent poems, this ambivalence has become almost a mannerism; one suspects that in ***Tenebrae*** (1978) the Renaissance framework of **"Lachrimae or Seven tears figured in seven passionate Pavans"** was chosen partly to give a period sanction to a delight in paradox-for-its-own-sake:

> Ash-Wednesday feasts, ascetic opulence,
> the wincing lute, so real in its pretence,
> itself a passion amorous of love.

The intricately-wrought web of mannered rhetoric is still managing beautifully to define an important relation between religion and ritual, art and passion, each feeding the other, each valued for itself, each dangerously courting confusion with its partner. Yet the delight in stylised oppositions is threatening to clog the verse, to turn into a frigid patterning where meaning is only an accidental byproduct. Despite its picturesqueness, memorability and frequent lightness of touch, something of the kind does seem to happen in parts of **"The Pentecost castle"**, ***Tenebrae***'s opening sequence:

> And you my spent heart's treasure
> my yet unspent desire
> measurer past all measure
> cold paradox of fire . . .

Implicitly admitting the 'coldness' does not excuse it: the rhetoric is tired, the paradoxes perfunctory rather than revealing.

It is possible that the turn to greater expansiveness of form and to traces of narrative in ***Péguy*** represent a determination on Hill's part to break out of the constrictions of such a mode of writing and thinking. Paradox has not been abandoned, but it has enlarged. No longer confined within the phrase or sentence, it now governs the subject of the poem, the functioning of extended similes. The ambiguity of Péguy and of Hill's attitude to him is displayed first of all in the poem's title: adapted from that of Péguy's long poem *Le Mystère de la charité de Jeanne d'Arc,* it implicitly puts Péguy in the role of Joan of Arc. There is surely a deliberate touch of farce about this. Apart from the reversals of age and sex it involves, it somehow highlights the less charismatic aspects of Péguy's physical presence—the crooked pince-nez, the punctilious fussiness over proof-reading and parcel-tying. The same ambivalence is expressed in the poem's imagery. The references to childhood are especially prominent in this respect: Péguy's self-righteousness is conceded when he is addressed as 'Truth's pedagogue, braving an entrenched class / of fools and scoundrels, children of the world'; but 'still Péguy said that Hope is a little child'. Accordingly, as part of his vision, 'On the hard-won / high places the old soldiers of old France / crowd like good children wrapped in obedience / and sleep, and ready to be taken home', and that vision itself is categorised as 'not a child's . . . [but] what a child's vision can become'. (pp. 148-50)

At other points in the poem, references to childhood offer something far more positive, but for that reason less directly concerned with Péguy. (p. 150)

In Section 5 of ***Péguy,*** as much as in ***Mercian Hymns,*** Hill is merging himself with his hero. Perhaps this implies a confession that we view history through our own preoccupations; perhaps it goes further, to suggest that we can only understand the meaning of other people's myths by gathering to them some of the emotion that interpenetrates our own. Certainly, when such emotion involves nostalgia, as it often does, Hill is good at evoking it, and ***Péguy*** contains some formidably accomplished writing in a sensuous pastoral vein. . . . The problem for the reader is that such passages do not open any perceptible flaw in the texture of what they describe. One feels that Hill is in love with the vistas he pretends to repudiate, and that his sentiment infects the reader. Instead of exorcising the myths he renders them more powerful, and seems not to admit or cope with that power.

The root of this subtly dissatisfying quality in Hill's work has perhaps been identified by John Bayley when he writes that Hill's many distancing devices are 'a way of giving to pure aesthetics an air of the moral'. Hill is concerned, one feels, with composing structures from the materials of moral problems. But his structures do not engage with those problems. Rather they compose their elements in a manner that is static and so essentially pictorial. It may be significant in this context that one of Hill's central stylistic devices is the accumulation of noun-phrases without active verbs. This device first makes itself felt in ***King Log,*** at the opening of **"Funeral music"**: 'Processionals in the exemplary cave, / Benediction of shadows. Pomphret. London.' It becomes more insistent in **"History as poetry"**:

> Poetry as salutation; taste
> Of Pentecost's ashen feast. Blue wounds.
> The tongue's atrocities.

It is prominent in ***Mercian Hymns:***

> Tracks of ancient occupation. Frail ironworks
> rusting in the thorn-thicket. Hearthstones;
> charred lullabies.

Tenebrae too has its share. In ***Péguy,*** whose verse has a more fluid, discursive movement, strings of such sentence-fragments are rare, but still it is evident that Hill is happiest, gets most into his stride, when he can begin to pile up a heap of noun-phrases:

> It is Domrémy
> restored; the mystic strategy of Foch
> and Bergson with its time-scent, dour panâche
> deserving of martyrdom. It is an army
>
> of poets, converts, vine-dressers, men skilled
> in wood or metal, peasants from the Beauce,
> terse teachers of Latin . . .

It seems possible, even, that the verse of ***Péguy*** is shaped partly by a desire to provide space for such accumulations. The loose quatrains, linked by consonantal rhyme but varying their rhyme-scheme apparently at random, provide not so much a formal control as an evenness of tone which imposes minimal constraint upon the poet's language. They provide a form into which anything can be fitted without jolting an overall regularity that comes near to monotony. As with a drystone wall, the materials to hand can be fitted in, whatever their size or shape, with a little skilled juggling. And it seems essential to Hill's approach to his subject that he should be able to slot in a great deal of contingent historical material. The result is a quality of stasis manifest especially in Hill's reliance on pictorial imagery. The pivotal moments of ***Péguy*** are presented as tableaux, the poet enumerating a series of graphic details to build up an evocative picture. Jaurès' murder, the idealised French landscapes of Péguy's aspirations, the disgrace of Dreyfus, Péguy's death in battle are presented variously in visual terms which recall documentary photograph, landscape-painting, book-illustration and newsreel film. What is not really evoked is an unmediated vision. We find ourselves thinking not 'this is how it might have been' but 'this is how a contemporary painter/photographer/engraver might have portrayed it'.

Certainly the historical research which must underlie the poem is used for more than 'local colour'. Some important structuring devices emerge quite naturally from the descriptive imagery and they are full of significance. (pp. 151-52)

None the less, it is hard not to feel that there is an element of pastiche about the poem. This is a danger Hill has courted repeatedly, and is perhaps the besetting risk for any poet who combines great technical skill with a reticence that makes him unwilling to apply his resources to direct statement of his personal concerns. Hill's ***Tenebrae*** was surely, in the texture of its styles, the most determinedly archaic volume of genuinely modern verse since Pound's *Ripostes,* its immediate points of reference almost entirely medieval, Renaissance or Victorian. Already there seemed a tendency to work at the catching of period atmospheres rather than at that revivifying marriage of past and present which had occurred in ***Mercian Hymns.*** The ***Hymns*** challenged comparison with *The Anathemata* of David Jones in their dreamlike decipherment of archaic forms still shaping the pattern of contemporary life; in ***Tenebrae*** the sense of the contemporary had almost evaporated in a nostalgic, unfocused timelessness.

As a single experiment in such a mode, a work of Symboliste evocation, ***Tenebrae*** was entirely acceptable. But ***Péguy*** shows Hill taking further steps down the same road, more than ever seduced by his ability to create historical costume-drama. It seems likely that this bias is the outcome of a laudable wish to discipline painful pressures of emotion. The poems of ***For the Unfallen*** seemed intensely and bitterly personal, and it is startling to realise that the earliest poems **"Genesis", "Holy Thursday"**) are not far in diction from the work of the New Apocalyptics, or even of Dylan Thomas. . . . Hill has avoided the kinds of self-indulgence which a too-prophetic tone risked, but sheer fastidiousness may have led him to a point where his work is losing some of its authority and failing to take up the challenges it cannot help encountering. What, after all, does Charles Péguy mean to him? Is it sufficient for Hill to hold him up to us as a bundle of brave paradoxes? . . . There is something question-begging about Hill's closing line: '"in memory of those things these words were born"'. Adequate, perhaps, for a tomb or a monument, but a poem requires an engagement one shade closer.

If Geoffrey Hill were to stop writing now, his achievement to date would still put him among the most important English poets of our time. But if he is to extend that achievement, it may be necessary for him to chance his arm, reveal more of himself and turn away from the historical preoccupations and personae, the paradoxes and ambiguities that have so far refracted his concerns. As he has himself written, 'The nature of the world is such as we are constrained to recognise, the ineluctable fact, but to be content with the rich discrepancies which this offers is none the less dangerous and is sometimes treacherous'. There are signs in ***Péguy*** of too much satisfaction with such 'rich discrepancies'; and of the dangers that follow. (pp. 152-54)

Grevel Lindop, "Myth and Blood: The Poetry of Geoffrey Hill," in Critical Quarterly, *Vol. 26, Nos. 1 & 2, Spring & Summer, 1984, pp. 147-54.*

MARK RUDMAN

There used to be the sense that poetry issued from another consciousness, somewhere deep in the mind—"far back," as Roethke put it. Hill's poetry is of this order: bracing and difficult, turbulent and complex. There is pressure on every word to *mean,* and in [***The Mystery of the Charity of Charles Péguy***], the language bears the same stress as Péguy's life, as if, imbued with the desire to mate, each word were propelling itself toward the next. . . .

Hill's art is vastly more demanding than Péguy's; his courage and daring are esthetic and linguistic. But both poets reach out for something central to the human condition. Hill relies heavily on the traditional language of English poetry, from Shakespeare to Auden: "The world is different, belongs to them— / the lords of limit and contumely." From the key placement of the word "contumely" and the phrase "the lords of limit" and his use of the latter as the title of his new book of essays, ***The Lords of Limit,*** Hill seems to be saying that things have not changed as much as we may think. His words have a gravity that is more powerful than sound effects or particular images. In **"Redeeming the Time,"** he refers to "the inertial drag of speech," which must be accounted for by any "enquiry into the nature of rhythm."

Without being visual, his poetry makes you imagine a backdrop of the Renaissance—paintings and tapestries with battle scenes—a thicket of world in a thickness of words. . . . (p. 149)

Hill's early work is sharp and direct. It consists mainly of short poems, each one a whole: "true sequences of pain." His affinities are clear through his fine homages to Celan in ***Tenebrae*** and to Mandelstam in ***King Log.*** And there is no mistaking the ferocity in his work. Ted Hughes's *Crow,* to make the inevitable comparison, is playful set beside Hill's darkest passages. In **"Funeral Music,"** an essay at the end of [***King Log***], he tells of "attempting a florid grim music broken by grunts and shrieks" and, in an image that is emblematic of his own project, cites "the chronicler of Croyland Abbey" as "writing that the blood of the slain lay caked with the snow which covered the ground and that, when the snow melted, the blood flowed along the furrows and ditches for a distance of two or three miles." And, one might add, from there into the body of his next decade's work.

In ***The Mystery of the Charity of Charles Péguy,*** Hill's violence has found release through the use of the third person. He interweaves his own voice with Péguy's; he filters his concerns through Péguy and, in the process, gains a levity absent from his earlier work, though the tone is one of "dour panache" (to borrow a phrase from the poem), a cross between low tragedy and high farce. . . . (pp. 149-50)

Hill has always been at home with the sublime. He applauds Péguy's willingness to sacrifice, as long as his moral code is constant, in a style that is dense, not ornate. But he also sees human suffering as a consequence of history's mischievousness—except that the joke is at our expense. "History commands the stage wielding a toy gun, / rehearsing another scene"; it is perverse, at once "supreme clown" and "dire tragedian." Péguy allows Hill to introduce an element missing from his previous books: humor, albeit a kind of black humor, closer in essence to Webster and Ford than to Heller or Pynchon. . . .

Hill is precise, careful to show how tenuously meaning cleaves to a comma, a line break: "To dispense, with justice; or, to dispense / with justice." His harsh, crabbed style, with its rugged diction, does not lend itself to length. The quatrain is his primary medium in all his books, and he has few, if any, contemporary rivals in his ability to handle it. . . . (p. 150)

His variable rhyme schemes, alternating *a a b b* and *a b b a* with the more conventional *a b a b,* argue against monotony. And he writes as though the solution were locked in the quatrain itself. Péguy also used the quatrain frequently, but his formal impulse was almost the opposite of Hill's: where Péguy expands, Hill contracts. The only time the sections in ***The Mystery of the Charity of Charles Péguy*** run on is in the poem's most significant stanza, when Péguy meets the death he has so assiduously sought, his own:

So, you have risen
above all that and fallen flat on your face

5

among the beetroots, where we are constrained
to leave you sleeping and to step aside
from the fleshed bayonets . . .

It is through such density that a poem of only 400 lines can make a book.

There are some false moves in the poem tonally, a certain archness, as when Hill refers to Rimbaud's "Je est un autre" as "that fatal telegram," and reminds me that I prefer him where he's more cryptic and elliptical. His strange brand of academic formality (which mars the essays in ***The Lords of Limit***) is also off-putting in his otherwise concise and informative afterword. Citing T. S. Eliot's interest in Péguy—clearly to establish Péguy's undeniable importance to his audience—he writes that "T. Stearns Eliot, M.A. (Harvard), who made reference to Péguy's life and work in a series of university extension lectures in 1916, noted that he 'illustrates nationalism and neo-Catholicism as well as socialism.'" It is hard to tell whether he is trying to parody the academic or embody it.

Hill is one of the few contemporary poets whose work must be reread in order to be understood. He forces the reader to sound out the meaning: work of this density can only be grasped through the ear. He is not merely one of the best English poets but one of the best poets writing in English. Although I think ***Mercian Hymns*** is Hill's best work, ***The Mystery of the Charity of Charles Péguy*** shows him stretching in new directions, rescuing himself from direness, becoming more attuned to dramatic possibilities and enlarging his range. (pp. 150-51)

Mark Rudman, "Dour Panache," in The Nation, *New York, Vol. 240, No. 5, February 9, 1985, pp. 149-51.*

DAVID BROMWICH

Three decades ago, in the first poem of his first book, Geoffrey Hill made this beginning: "Against the burly air I strode, / Where the tight ocean heaves its load, / Crying the miracles of God." The poem, **"Genesis,"** recounted the first days of the world, in the language of the last days. With creation itself represented as a fall, the poem seemed to embody an apocalyptic conception that was far from Christian. But its ending was different: "And by Christ's blood are men made free / Though in close shrouds their bodies lie / Under the rough pelt of the sea." The opposition, in **"Genesis,"** between the poem's mood and its resolution could be discerned elsewhere in ***For the Unfallen*** (1959). In his later volumes, ***King Log*** (1968), ***Mercian Hymns*** (1971), and ***Tenebrae*** (1978), Hill continued to write a poetry of strife, with a wish to end in conciliatory prayer. Because he is the most powerful living poet, it has been natural for readers to suppose that his chief aim was power. Hill does not understand himself so. What seems to his admirers a vigilant self-command, he would prefer to regard as an expiatory self-denial. This restriction was noticeable in a recent sonnet sequence, **"Lachrimae."** It comes out more subtly and more insistently in his critical essays, with results that will be discussed below.

Hill's earlier books are out of print here, and his work is not yet familiar to American readers. Invidious comparison may therefore be helpful. He stands out now as the British poet who can be read beside the masters of the high style. He is, to suggest more precisely the traits in question, the poet of exemplary conscience that Robert Lowell aspired to become. Hill's writing, however, is unfamiliar in another sense as well. It has none of the unction of geniality; does not weaken itself with whimsies, or otherwise truckle for patronage; never says, brightly, "These oysters remind me of starlight!" or, gravely, "Forgive me this weak trespass." He does not want to be loved for his poems, or search out ways of being likable in his poems.

This distinct negative appeal—a charmless personal integrity—is a source of Hill's endurance thus far. And it has encouraged him to try for an uncommon success, and write a long poem about another poet. Like no other poem of the age, ***The Mystery of the Charity of Charles Péguy*** sustains its meditation with continuous intensity. Its motive may be described as an attempt to hold poetry and history in a single thought. Yet its eloquence is straightforward, chaste, and declarative, checked only by the thought that all eloquence terminates in action. In theme, it recalls earlier poems by Hill: **"Ovid in the Third Reich," "Annunciations"** and **"Funeral Music."** In style it is original, and widens the range of modern poetry. (pp. 43-4)

Tout commence en mystique, wrote Péguy, *et tout finit en politique:* everything begins in mysticism and ends in politics. Yet this was not less true of himself than of those whom he condemned.

Hill's poem turns upon the event in which the logic of Péguy's epigram came to include its author:

So much for Jaurès murdered in cold pique
by some vexed shadow of the belle époque,
some guignol strutting at the window-frame.
But what of you, Péguy, who came to "exult,"
to be called "wolfish" by your friends? The guilt
belongs to time; and you must leave on time.

This, then, is a poem about the complicity of words with their foreseen and unforeseen consequences, in the world of action that exists for the writer like a fate. That world, Hill says (borrowing a phrase from Auden), "is different, belongs to them— / the lords of limit and of contumely." Though limiting, they have their proper claim, for (to borrow another phrase that Hill has pondered), "The words of a dead man / Are modified in the guts of the living."

The Mystery of the Charity of Charles Péguy is written from the perspective of the lords of limit, who sometimes do speak on behalf of the living.

Did Péguy kill Jaurès? Did he incite
the assassin? Must men stand by what they write
as by their camp-beds or their weaponry
or shell-shocked comrades while they sag and cry?

Evidently there are two answers to these questions. *En mystique,* no: words are not binding on their author, they are germs of thoughts that he cannot know. But, *en politique,* yes: and not only bonds, they are shackles or grappling irons, that connect his name forever with the things he has described and changed. In short, the implications of words may be utterly distinct from the conscious motives that produced them; and yet, once they have issued in action, words may rightly be charged with having the force of such motives. The saying acquits as mere word, the doing convicts as absolute deed. What defense then remains for Péguy?

A usual exemption for writers who happen to be poets is that "poetry makes nothing happen," but Hill does not believe this. His purpose is indeed to explain Péguy's fate as that of all who use language powerfully. Poet and soldier at once, Péguy stands as a figure for the contest from which eloquence arises: his valor and cunning were at home in both vocations; and his apology belongs to all writers, whose words are liable to persuade. (pp. 44-5)

Large tracts of the poem, especially toward the end, are given over to an allusive sketch of Péguy's "dream of France, militant-pastoral." These passages are essential to the view of Péguy's character that Hill proposes, and also to the scheme of cinematic montage on which the poem depends throughout. Yet they seem more uncertain in tone than the rest of the poem, and they prompt the question of how far such a pastoral can be adopted by a poet whose national mystique, if he has one at all, cannot be the same as Péguy's. The descriptions are carefully poised, and never reflect a borrowed nostalgia. But their insistent presence implies a less suspicious understanding of historical myth than appeared in Hill's earlier long poem ***Mercian Hymns.*** There the archaic details were relished for their anachronism, and often touched by a grotesque humor. Here, with a foreign rather than a native subject, the landscape becomes very nearly a retreat, secure against the hostilities of the cenacle or the battlefield. . . . (p. 45)

All of the essays in ***The Lords of Limit*** ponder the same question of atonement that led Hill to write about Péguy. Yet they do so with less command than the poem, and now and then with a teasing fastidiousness:

> I cannot disguise from myself the awareness that I have been drawn towards my present theme by way of the technical and metaphysical problems which I have encountered as a practitioner of verse. To what extent I should disguise this awareness from my audience is a question that causes me some perplexity.

Not much of Hill's prose deviates into this style. Still, two such sentences are too much; and he ought to have scorned them as not his own. T. S. Eliot wrote them, or something like them, at the beginning of half his lectures. But Hill also shares certain interests with Eliot: a fascination, for example, with two periods above all others, the age of Shakespeare and Jonson, and the latter part of the Victorian age.

At this point the resemblance begins to fade. For though Hill's reading includes all sorts of literature, metaphysics, moral philosophy, and sermons, as well as poems and novels, he has no patience for intellectual argument, in any common understanding of the term. He makes his paragraphs of a tissue of quotations—sometimes striking, sometimes rather dull—from critics, philosophers, and historians. These he then weaves together with the texts of his subject, and contemporary observers of his subject, pestering some of his authorities and praising others with brief comments and judicial summaries. It is a style that sets up, and puts up with, a great many earnests of conscientious awkwardness, but that is perhaps a generous way of stating the case. It is a style well-designed to conceal from the author himself whatever distinction may exist between that which he knows deeply and that which he knows less deeply. It lacks or, perhaps, eschews the available graces of prose. Yet it provides a serious setting for some thoughtful aphorisms, and may be said to exhibit all the strictly privative virtues of Hill's temperament. It is never facile, careless, or merely ingratiating, and it is free of cant.

These essays present themselves as interrogations of the moral life of literature. The evidence that they judge comes from the use of language—what others would simply call, but Hill does not consent to call simply, style. In different ways they analyze betrayals (that is, treasons) of the moral intelligence, which leave their mark in the betrayals (that is, disclosures) of language. The heroes of the book, as much as its antagonists, are looked at in the light of such failures. (pp. 45-6)

Readers to whom books have mattered will generally admit that language and moral life are involved with each other. Sometimes they will admit more: that language, to a sensitive observer, may always be a revealing index of moral life. But granted that language is involved in moral conduct, it does not follow that a verbal choice is an adequate correlative of a moral choice, as Hill supposes it must be. The belief that it is, reliably, such an adequate correlative licenses him in many capricious surmises, and a few unhappy presumptions (p. 46)

[Throughout] ***The Lords of Limit,*** Hill seems balked in the attempt to formulate a relation between language, moral responsibility, and the power of poetic invention. Yet it is just such a relation that his poems do convey naturally, as part of their wisdom, and with a less baffled show of scruple.

A criticism of Hill's prose is thus suggested by his poetry. Often Hill argues against a narrow definition of poetry that would assign it to a special domain of aesthetic beauty, or against an equally narrow definition that would confine its significance to that of any other persuasive assertion. What he wants instead, he says, is "an atonement of aesthetics with rectitude of judgment." Notice, first, that the profession of such a need is itself non-aesthetic. But recall, second, that when Hill comes to assess the miscarriage of poetic power in a writer like Pound, he falls back on something very like the aesthetic view: "poets are not legislators."

If this meant that their assertions ought not to be liable to persuade wrongly, one might endorse the sentiment, and not only as applied to poetry. But Hill seems to mean, on the contrary, that their assertions, if rightly made, will not be liable to persuade at all: that poetry makes nothing happen. Having scrutinized Pound's statement, "All values come from our judicial sentences," Hill ends by preferring a revised version of the statement: "All values go into our judicial sentences." The inversion warrants some attention. Pound's original statement was Shelleyan in its stilted way, for it implied that poets were "unacknowledged legislators" of the conduct in which words may issue. The revision that Hill adopts is Coleridgean, for it identifies the poem itself as the repository of a moral knowledge that holds no commerce with the world of action. But to be satisfied with this latter view, as Hill sometimes wishes to be, is to ask at once too much and too little of words. They cannot offer the resistant place of repose that Hill looks for them to supply—not for Hopkins or Coleridge, any more than they could for Péguy or Pound. And the reason is that language is always subject to abuse, just as it is always subject to use. Its being turned around, or converted, or interpreted, is one remote but definite consequence of its having been created at all. (pp. 46-7)

Finally, one may be troubled by Hill's employment of the Christian implications of certain words, without, so far as the essays themselves allow, any firmly Christian intent. "Redeems the word" is an apt instance because it calls to mind the essay **"Redeeming the Time."** Both of these phrases compromise between two senses of two words: a compromise, and not an atonement. By contrast, when T. S. Eliot spoke of redeeming the time at the end of "Thoughts After Lambeth," there could be no doubt what sense he had in mind.

Nor does it help to think of Hill's foreshortened explanations as a "searching" of contexts. Judged by his own uncompromising standards, his essays, original and speculative as they often feel, are confused half-arguments for the moral act that his poems exist to perform. They would be better if their interrogations had more charity; if they beleaguered others less for the small vices they themselves occasionally display; if, for example, they did not condemn Iris Murdoch for once speaking unguardedly of a century as if it were a character ("the nineteenth century . . . could think itself a single world"), and then commit the same fault without apologizing ("The nineteenth century preferred a half-remorseful majesty in its great apostates"). Above all, the essays would be more enlightening if they addressed the reader in a tone of decision that matched their readiness to decide. And yet, one is sure at any rate that what Hill says of Ben Jonson's Catiline can never be said of himself: "We know that he takes himself too seriously and humanity too lightly." It is the opposite with the author of ***The Lords of Limit*** and ***The Mystery of the Charity of Charles Péguy.*** We know that he takes himself seriously, but this seems the condition of his always taking humanity seriously enough. (pp. 47-8)

David Bromwich, "A Poet and Power," in The New Republic, *Vol. 193, Nos. 12 & 13, September 16 & 23, 1985, pp. 43-8.*

JONATHAN BARKER

[It] is the qualities of "imaginative feeling", passionate plainness and vivid immediacy which most strike the reader who chronologically experiences the five individual books gathered in the ***Collected Poems.*** The cumulative effect is quite overwhelming. The range is wider than we had somehow supposed, the fusion of emotion and intellect finer, the evocations of particular times and places and their spirit richer, more sensuous, the command of rhythm and attack in the verse greater. The reader rediscovers how intellectually demanding the poems are, how they reward a sensitive close reading and how their intellectual breadth grasps a shared history and culture with formidable poise and learning. But this aside it is fundamentally that "movement of energy", that intellectual and emotional "imaginative feeling", which makes the poems so compellingly memorable, so intense and so unique.

Just as Hill employs a variety of literary devices—dramatic monologues, soliloquies, meditations in a variety of voices by individuals other than himself to communicate this feeling—his language modulates over a wide area too. From a tense and formal elegance which at times becomes opulent in the manner named by Gerard Manley Hopkins "Parnassian", to the opposite extreme of a pared down lyric passionate plainness of style. The literary resonances and ambiguities which register succeeding layers of meaning are critically well documented, but I am uncertain that the opposite pole of passionate plainness has been properly understood and valued. Not that the passion is restricted to that of the more direct emotions, or that the language is ever truly simple. Even at its most apparently artless the language of Hill's poems is always thoughtful: a carefully wrought formal artifice, expressing intelligence just as much as emotion. Hill is our most conscious poet, thinking through the language selected in the making of the poem.

These wide ranges of "imaginative feeling" and modulations of tone and language come out in an examination of one of Hill's main themes: the individuals and events in our history which are remade anew in the now of the poem. That sense of history ranges from specific happenings, such as the Wars of the Roses, the Anglo-Saxon Kingdom of Mercia, the Passion of Christ, Pentecost, the fates of poets, to the myth of King Arthur, the history of modern France and "the spiritual, Platonic old England". They share in common the dramatic empathy with which Hill brings them vividly to life, while also remaining scrupulously true to the facts of their place and time. Although **"Genesis"**, the first poem in the book, displays a certain poetic license in dealing with biblical history (a poem, incidentally, which along with others here, incorporates a number of amendments including the loss of its entire original second line), it does tell us that the work to come is that of a man who understands and accepts the complexity of our past on earth. . . . Even as early as this, Hill's imagination has a dramatic intensity which creates in the reader "primal human forces" of feeling; such as the tugs of moral conscience, the contrasting demands of private and public integrity, and more visibly perhaps, the horrors of the routine slaughter of men in armed combat. The sequence of sonnets, **"Funeral Music"**, here cinematographically record the scene after the Battle of Towton:

> Reddish ice tinged the reeds; dislodged, a few
> Feathers drifted across; carrion birds
> Strutted upon the armour of the dead.

Elsewhere the cross is present as both the actual object of the crucifixion in **"Canticle for Good Friday"**—another poem incidentally employing cinematographic images ("While the dulled wood / Spat on the stones each drop / Of deliberate blood")—and, in the sonnet sequence homage to John Dowland **"Lachrimae"**, a subject for meditation on the passion. . . . The language manages an energy and vividness which contrast with the usual tone of a meditative poem, and surely it is this dramatic attack which enlivens and compels the verse to the imagination through the medium of an immaculate and formal prosodic skill. The unshowy authority of that literary skill is the voice of the tradition, whose resonances make even more impersonal the already removed material of history through which the poet communicates and evokes "imaginative feeling" and sensation in the reader. Objectivity of form and phrase are at the heart of the remarkable counterpointing between form and content which time and again add a further edge and tension to the writing. To this quality we owe much of the sheer rhythmic memorability of the poems as in **"Ovid in the Third Reich"** where the classical author soliloquizes on private art and public evil:

> I love my work and my children. God
> Is distant, difficult. Things happen.

(pp. 5-7)

The history is not all political or religious. A personal family history can be seen in the **XXV**th Mercian Hymn which alludes to an obviously loved grandmother and John Ruskin's letters addressed to the working men of England. . . . The recent long poem ***The Mystery of the Charity of Charles Péguy*** presents a continuous portrait of the minutiae of the French landscape, from the wine-puddle at the beginning, to the beetroot field in the middle and the dust-motes that "jig to war" at the end. . . . Another place altogether is pictured in the sequence referring to Pugin's writings, **"An Apology for the Revival of Christian Architecture in England"**; that place is "the spiritual, Platonic old England" quoted from the notebooks of Samuel Taylor Coleridge. Sonnet 9 **"The Laurel Axe"** I take to be one of the most beautiful examples of Hill's "Parnassian" style, and a truly great poem of our times:

> Autumn resumes the land, ruffles the woods
> with smoky wings, entangles them. Trees shine
> out from their leaves, rocks mildew to moss-green;
> the avenues are spread with brittle floods.

The place "beset by dynasties of moods and clouds" so precisely painted for us is an England of the imagination, a metaphor for the inner life, an atmosphere, and a vision. The poem ends leading the reader indoors to:

> the rooms of cedar and soft-thudding baize,
> tremulous boudoirs where the crystals kissed
> in cabinets of amethyst and frost.

That benevolent, opulent and powerfully evoked spiritual landscape is another thing which takes centre stage in the poem in place of the "personality" or self of the poet just as successfully as the sense of history, or the dramatic voices of individuals. This aspect of Hill's writings has been well documented and seems to place the impersonal forces in his work firmly in descent from the "depersonalization" of T. S. Eliot's "Tradition and the Individual Talent". And certainly, on one level at least, such is the state of post-modernist lost innocence with which the informed modern reader approaches the work, a sequence like **"The Songbook of Sebastian Arrurruz"**, does put us in mind of the so called "impersonality" of "The Love Song of J. Alfred Prufrock".

And yet, if we can manage for a moment to forget the title of Hill's sequence and the concept of modernism and just examine the poem as itself, we find that the voice he exploits can be very personal and very passionate indeed. It is Hill's use of passionate plainness, a quality vigorously at odds with the intellectual argufying of all our textual literary criticism:

> i
>
> "One cannot lose what one has not possessed."
> So much for that abrasive gem.
> I can lose what I want. I want you.
>
> ii
>
> Oh my dear one, I shall grieve for you
> For the rest of my life with slightly
> Varying cadence, oh my dear one.

(pp. 8-10)

A conscious transparent plainness of language is also found in the sequence **"The Pentecost Castle"** which is prefixed by two quotations, one from W. B. Yeats: "It is terrible to desire and not possess, and terrible to possess and not desire." These unpunctuated song-like poems are spare, impersonally personal, and contain a near explosive passion, both secular and divine, which vibrates off the page as single-mindedly as the best of A. E. Housman:

> though I may never
> see you again
> touch me I will shiver
> at the unseen
>
> the night is so dark
> the way so short
> why do you not break
> o my heart

A metaphor for the sequence may be found in a verse which comments on the essentially emblematic nature of literary art:

> bread we shall never break
> love-runes we cannot speak
> scrolled effigy of a cry
> our passion its display

Again this poem is at one remove from the emotion. It is expressed in language (the "scrolled effigy of a cry") which remains formal artifice even at its most moving. The form is a device through which the poem is mouthpiece for Hill's "imaginative feeling", the power of which is maintained through counterpointing a shape or trope which restricts and focuses an intensity by the narrowness of the conduit through which it reaches expression. In this way language itself becomes an "objective correlative" which makes impersonal the emotion or thought it contains. Here we again sail into the waters of post-modernist impersonality and neo-classicism, and, while the link is an attractive and convenient one, I prefer to see Hill as belonging to an altogether more intuitive, and fierily imaginative line. His transcendence, intelligence and, yes, passion are far removed from T. E. Hulme's restrictive taste for the "dry hardness which you get in the classics" or his statement that "accurate description is a legitimate object of verse". Hill, in fact, is nearer in essence to, say, the intensity of the paintings of Paul Gauguin, a detail from whose painting "The Vision after the Sermon" is reproduced on the cover of the ***Collected Poems*** as a link with the poem **"Terribilis Est Locus Iste: Gauguin and the Pont-Aven School"**. . . . The luminous richness of Gauguin's colours is matched here by a linguistic intensity which elsewhere makes images as compelling as Hill's "the rood blazing upon the green"; or the golden light of the line from Ezra Pound, "In the gloom, the gold gathers the light against it", which is an epigraph to this book; the "hammered gold and gold enamelling" of W. B. Yeats's "Sailing to Byzantium", P. B. Shelley's faith in "thy light, / Imagination!" from "Epipsychidion" or the "uncertain light" playing on faded tapestries in an old house one overcast afternoon in R. M. Rilke's "Before Summer Rain". That I have to look to these names for equivalents to [the] . . . "imaginative feeling" of emotion and thought found everywhere in this ***Collected Poems*** surely demonstrates just how unique Geoffrey Hill is amongst our contemporary poets, and just how grateful we should be for him too. (pp. 10-12)

Jonathan Barker, "Imaginative Feeling," in Agenda, *Vol. 23, Nos. 3 & 4, Autumn, 1985 & Winter, 1986, pp. 5-12.*

PETER LEVI

When one read the first poems of Geoffrey Hill, what seemed amazing was simply their texture, a strong sound like tearing canvas. In the fifties, for various reasons mostly outside literature, softness, weakness and wetness were what we most despised in one another and in ourselves. Geoffrey Hill was so strong as to be beyond that kind of criticism, both intellectually and verbally. He was an extreme of style (and possibly of stylism) that we admired extravagantly. But it is now easy to see that what really drew us and gave a depth and power of growth to our admiration was something that underlay his surface texture; it was precisely an immediate heat, an interfusion of thought and feeling. It also had something to do with a religious element that somehow existed in suspension in both, and was treated by Geoffrey Hill with serious awe.

The genuineness of this underlying character can now be confirmed by Geoffrey Hill's development as a poet. His style and texture have remained in some ways the same until now, except for the extraordinary outbreak of the ***Mercian Hymns***. That suggested an influence of David Jones, though like everything he writes it was a very considered technical experiment; he is always a poet's poet. But he returned to his original style. Yet when all this is said, ***The Mystery of the Charity of Charles Péguy*** shows an enormous advance, an extension of range and an increase of suppleness, over the style of his early poetry. His development in fact has not been a superficial stylistic tinkering, admirable as that might be, but a genuine growth of thought and of feeling. I cannot but believe this growth has been nourished by the presence in his poetry of a religious element. The idea of a living God, like the prospect of being hanged, can sharpen one's wits and hone one's seriousness, whether one believes like Eliot or disbelieves like Empson and perhaps Milton.

The other great break-through of style in Geoffrey Hill's poetry was in his translation of [Henrik Ibsen's *Brand*]. . . . Everything about the Ibsen seems wonderfully strong except the ridiculous solution of the closing few lines. But for us its greatest interest lies in Geoffrey Hill's wingbeats of dramatic verse. I think they are the seed of the future, and the most convincing dramatic verse style we have seen in this century or the last in English. . . . One can see technical devices developed in it which recur in ***Charles Péguy***. Between the two, one can feel the increase of a confident lucidity of tone. With that comes a new freedom of irony. (pp. 13-14)

Peter Levi, "Geoffrey Hill," in Agenda, *Vol. 23, Nos. 3 & 4, Autumn, 1985 & Winter 1986, pp. 13-14.*

William Humphrey

1924-

American novelist, short story writer, nonfiction writer, memoirist, and critic.

In his works, Humphrey examines the ways in which individual identity is influenced by social, familial, and physical environments. Most of his fiction takes place in and around Clarksville, Texas, where Humphrey lived as a youth. Humphrey uses this setting to focus on Southern social and cultural traditions and to explore such topics as love and family relationships. This blend of regional concerns and universal themes has led several critics to compare his works to those of William Faulkner. Humphrey is praised for his technical craftsmanship, particularly his skillful use of flashback and his poignant mixture of tragic and farcical events.

© Jerry Bauer

Humphrey's first novel, *Home from the Hill* (1958), depicts a boy who is deeply affected by the volatile relationship between his parents. The book begins with the mother's funeral and then recounts in extended flashback the tragic events surrounding the father's murder and the son's subsequent attempts at revenge. Critics were especially impressed with Humphrey's depiction of the boy's chivalric initiation into the rituals of love and hunting. Humphrey's second novel, *The Ordways* (1965), is a picaresque saga spanning from the Civil War to the 1920s that details the westward movement of the Ordway family from Tennessee to Texas. Their history is traced by a fourth-generation family member in the early part of this work, while the narrative later focuses upon the melodramatic and farcical adventures of an earlier Ordway, who traveled around Texas in search of his kidnapped son. Family tensions again dominate Humphrey's next novel, *Proud Flesh* (1973), in which the children of the Renshaw clan gather at their mother's deathbed. Unlike Humphrey's earlier works, this novel offers little comic relief from the mystery and evil that plague the family, and critics generally faulted this work for stereotyped characterizations and for failing to engage reader sympathy. In *Hostages to Fortune* (1984), Humphrey departs from the setting, focus, and structures of his previous novels. This work centers on the thoughts of Ben Curtis, whose serene domestic life has been shattered by the dissolution of his marriage and his son's suicide. Ben travels to a resort in upstate New York, where he had previously gone for relaxation, to contemplate his ill fortune. In a review of *Hostages to Fortune,* David Profumo maintained that "[Humphrey's] strength is still the evocation of place and the influence that a particular environment can exert on people."

Humphrey's short stories are similar in theme and setting to his novels, as he typically draws upon the local color of small town and rural life and focuses on representative concerns and conflicts among the inhabitants. *The Last Husband and Other Stories* (1953), his first collection, was hailed by Pearl Kazin as demonstrating "the kind of skilled and persuasive originality which only the most respected practitioners of the short-story art can claim." The stories in Humphrey's second collection, *A Time and a Place* (1968), are set in Texas and Oklahoma during the Depression and chronicle the various ways people coped with dwindling prospects. The contents of these two volumes and several previously unpublished pieces are contained in *The Collected Stories of William Humphrey* (1985).

In his acclaimed memoir, *Farther Off from Heaven* (1977), Humphrey reminisces about his early years in the Clarksville area, where he lived until his father's death from injuries sustained in an automobile accident. Humphrey juxtaposes events from the four days between the accident and his father's funeral with memories of his childhood, including his parents' stormy relationship, the family's effort to improve their lives, and the devastating effects of the Depression. Humphrey has also published several humorous and informative essays on fishing and hunting. These pieces are collected in *The Spawning Run* (1970), *My Moby Dick* (1978), and *Open Season: Sporting Adventures* (1986). In *Ah Wilderness! The Frontier in American Literature* (1977), Humphrey critiques American frontier literature and objects to the lack of strong-willed heroines in this genre.

(See also *Contemporary Authors,* Vols. 77-80 and *Dictionary of Literary Biography,* Vol. 6.)

PEARL KAZIN

In Mr. Humphrey's first book he demonstrates through ten remarkably fine stories that he has the kind of skilled and persuasive originality which only the most respected practitioners of the short-story art can claim. To anyone familiar with the usual fiction harvest it is particularly delightful to find not one story in ***The Last Husband,*** though they all vary greatly in subject, length, method and temper, which makes one feel with the usual yawn of recognition that it was conceived in banality or written in tame obedience to the unending formulas of this or that magazine, big or little. . . .

Mr. Humphrey has left all the easy attitudinizing far behind perhaps because he is a writer, first of all, who can control the form he chooses as he, rather than its conventions, sees fit. Rejecting the familiar sin of sentimentality (of mind and heart, both) patched together with elaborate, elegant and hollow prose, Mr. Humphrey's subject itself is, often, sentimentality. . . .

All of his characters have the plain and richly complex dimensions of life which are more often expected—if not often found—in the wider room of a novel. He can deal with crabbed age and frantic youth—those two overeasy, overused subjects—and with unique freshness never forcing anything or anyone into a specious symbolic relief. And though he has a great comic, satirical talent, used with especial perception in **"The Fauve"** and **"In Sickness and Health,"** Mr. Humphrey brings as certain a method and meaning to the tragedy of **"Man With a Family,"** an almost unbearably poignant account of a freakishly unlucky farmer who moves inexorably from accident to accident to the one that makes his death.

Communicating the common without ever becoming commonplace, Mr. Humphrey can bring to his people, skillfully defined and brilliantly judged, a directness and openness of language, a precise, controlled ease of episode and image, which are altogether different from the all-powerful rituals of "technique" which so many short-story writers worship. Whether he is writing about an embittered, fraudulently bohemian painter or a sad adolescent who gives to her regiment of unweaned cats the love and attention she never gets from her egotist parents, they never seem trivial; detail, gesture and incident are manipulated with such deftness that the stories leave the deep, sure mark of mature comment and craftsmanship.

Pearl Kazin, "Casanova," in The New York Times, *April 12, 1953, p. 27.*

DAVID M. CULHANE

[The ten stories in ***The Last Husband***] make up a very uneven book. In thinking of it as a whole the flaws are emphasized, since they are pervasive; the relatively clear vein is found only in separate stories. In three or four of these Mr. Humphrey successfully brings off the usually awkward match of satire with sympathy. . . .

But even in the best stories there is a looseness of construction which tends to dissipate the final effect. **"The Fauve,"** an unhooded, free-flying assault on a small town artist's colony, for all its quick-touching humor, takes much too long to reach the kill. The same is true of the wholly different **"Man With a Family,"** perhaps the best story in the collection. This diffuseness is perhaps due to a desire for meticulous characterization, but this sort of string-saving has untidy results.

The other difficulty is stylistic—again a kind of privation. A prose writer's style depends largely on his ability to flesh a story with his finger-print reaction to movement, color and sound. Mr. Humphrey's description of a man with a cut hand stands out: ". . . carrying one of his hands in the other as if he were afraid of spilling it." Simple, and neatly captured. But the perceptions in these stories are generally more abstracted than this, less vivid and figured.

However, it is the characters that give point to the best stories here. The range of theme and locale is deceptive, for we are recurrently confronted with people's poses, or, more accurately, their images of themselves. Mr. Humphrey is not moving with the short story in any of its several directions. I do not suggest that he is necessarily wrong in this—only that his precise and objective discoveries of character might be more effective in a larger form. The people need more room. The milieus lightly sketched, for example, in **"The Fauve"** or **"Report Cards"** demand a more spacious existence. These are characters in search of a novel.

David M. Culhane, "Too Small a World," in Commonweal, *Vol. LVIII, No. 5, May 8, 1953, p. 127.*

WILLIAM PEDEN

[***The Last Husband and Other Stories***] is Mr. Humphrey's first book. His debut, if not spectacular, is highly promising. Mr. Humphrey's work is intelligent, disciplined, and talented, displaying admirable sincerity and variety.

Mr. Humphrey depicts a wide range of characters and character types from small idealistic boys to vicious aging women; his settings, similarly, include the farmlands of Texas and the suburbia of New York. He tends to be more successful with his adolescents than with his adults, more convincing when writing of rural than of urban life. I liked best his stories concerned with the problems of boys or youths in the alien territory of the adult world. I was particularly impressed with **"The Shell,"** a moving and convincing story of a boy trying to emulate the hunting exploits of his dead father; [and] with **"Quail for Mr. Forester"** (which I think the best story in the collection), a wonderful tale of a ruined artistocrat in a small Southern town, seen through the eyes of a boy who thinks that Mr. Forester "lowered himself for the sake of his appetite to have dinner at our house." . . . These are memorable characters, sympathetically and compassionately realized in their vague, inchoate efforts to adjust themselves to the standards of the adult world they are about to enter, a world whose values they apprehend but which they cannot at the time either accept or reject.

Throughout his work Mr. Humphrey makes effective use of the detail or symbol which either illuminates a scene or serves to center a story: the customer who averts her eyes in deference to his past greatness as Mr. Forester wraps her package, the shotgun shell which holds the boy rooted to the past. . . . (pp. 33-4)

These are the stories of a very good young writer. (p. 34)

William Peden, "From Farmlands to Suburbia," in The Saturday Review, *New York, Vol. XXXVI, No. 30, July 25, 1953, pp. 33-4.*

WALTER HAVIGHURST

It is morning in an east Texas town, when William Humphrey's smoldering novel ***Home From the Hill*** begins, and the loafers look up to see a dusty hearse stop in the long shadows of the village square. Back home, after a dozen years in a Dallas asylum, has come Mrs. Hannah Hunnicutt, and in a richly graphic scene we see her buried between the tombs of her husband and her son in the town graveyard. This is the final episode in a local legend, which with a vivid urgency the novel proceeds to unfold.

The title is from Robert Louis Stevenson, but the tale is from William Faulkner. For a hundred pages the reader is in Yoknapatawpha County with its summer somnolence and its winter chill, with pigeons scratching horse dung under the Confederate soldier in the square and back roads leading to deep woods where the wild game run. The legend-like story is approached from years after the final violence. We hear first the reverberations, and not for 300 pages do we know who fired the shotgun that ended the life of Captain Wade Hunnicutt and sent his son into the depths of Sulphur Bottom.

Like Faulkner's Ike McCaslin, young Theron Hunnicutt becomes apprenticed to the woods and learns the chivalry of the hunting camp. The test comes to him in a crucial encounter, not with a primordial bear but with an equally tremendous boar. . . . And for him, as for Ike McCaslin, the object of the chase was not the meat you brought home for the table. "It was to learn to be a man, the only kind of man. . . ."

Faulkner is not an easy school to go to, and Mr. Humphrey has gone with his own passions and prepossessions. His novel is his own, and it contains authentic tensions of character, inheritance, and relationship. Yet it does not sustain its original intensity.

In his youth Theron was pulled in two directions, toward his brooding mother and his wayward father. Then came a new involvement, with pretty Libby Halstead and so with her outraged father. In the middle chapters, where it least suggests the Yoknapatawpha saga, the novel loses its dark spell and its resonance, becoming a kind of tragi-comedy of misunderstanding. But in the final episode, when the action sends fatherless Theron Hunnicutt on a vengeful errand into Sulphur Bottom, the tale recovers the somber force with which it began. This uneven book will insure Mr. Humphrey of an expectant audience for his next fiction.

Walter Havighurst, "Prelude to Violence," in The Saturday Review, *New York, Vol. XLI, No. 2, January 11, 1958, p. 15.*

WILLIAM GOYEN

Though [***Home from the Hill***] almost writes away its power, it is brilliantly planned, wrapped all around with an envelope of epic grandeur. Despite its roundabout analyses of its characters' motivations, its Dreiser-like heaviness, its lapses into stereotypes of Southern romantico-tragic melodrama, ***Home From the Hill*** is without doubt a work of size and merit. . . .

The locale is East Texas, the people southern aristocrats of the old order. Conceived in the largest scope of the novel's tradition, the characters are not so much regional people as chorus-like mouthpieces for Mr. Humphrey's consideration of their tragic doom. When the major characters (Hannah Hunnicutt, Captain Hunnicutt and their young son, Theron) speak about everyday matters, the result seems trivial, especially when measured against the over-all narrative, the long passages that have delineated the characters' inner reasoning. His tragic conception of his tale exceeds sometimes the working details of it. This disproportion is the flaw of the novel; it is a question of control, not so much of craft as of esthetic.

Yet ***Home From the Hill*** is compelling reading—and serious writers should inform themselves of it. This is a novelist's novel, born within the genre, and no eccentric offshoot. It displays the painstaking consideration of an artist for his tradition; it is also a story of fatal contretemps, macabre color and theatrical ingenuity. Despite its faults of over-projection, this novel, it seems to this reader, is one of the most distinguished firsts by a young writer . . . to appear in some years.

The tale of young Theron Hunnicutt's innocent self-destruction in the image of his father, of his mother's cunning outrage that led to her own madness and end, and of the girl who was the victim of this fated triad, is a shattering one. Mr. Humphrey has rendered it for us as allegory, as fable, as melodramatic tale, and it remains a work of stature.

William Goyen, "Tragedy Awaited," in The New York Times Book Review, *January 12, 1958, p. 4.*

JEAN HOLZHAUER

Mr. William Humphrey in his first novel, ***Home from the Hill,*** indicates that domestic tragedy can transcend the limits of the Southern parish. Uneven and devious as the story certainly is, it demonstrates that a good writer is not dependent upon melodrama or tricks, even when they are his own.

The jacket blurb for ***Home from the Hill,*** in the way of all such literature, asserts that the novel is "magnificently readable and absorbing." It is, in fact, neither, often wearying the reader past the point of attention with its wandering, its eccentricities, and its early air of promising considerably more than it can deliver. In the home stretch, however, it proves better than "readable and absorbing." Unexpectedly and admirably, it proves to be moving, even in two or three scenes gripping.

"Miz Hannah" Hunnicutt, who appears in the first chapter dead and outlandishly dressed for her burial, creates a brief stir as the presumable residue of horror. When, in subsequent flashbacks, she and her family find their own level as deeply troubled human beings, their interest flowers. Only when Mr. Humphrey remembers his bizarre introduction and tries to recreate its mood does his story languish.

Just so, "Miz Hannah's" husband, Captain Wade, attains, so to speak, fictional manhood not in the legend of his masculinity but in his revelation as a loving, if inept, father. Just so, their son Theron stands best not in his final, crazed action, but in the preceding gradual resolution of his relationships to his parents and to his love.

Mr. Humphrey is quite at his own best in his understanding of men and their peculiar enjoyments: hunting, the outdoors, the company of their peers, their continuity of being as sons and fathers. His grasp of women is less profound, and even Miz Hannah, intended as a central figure, is conventionalized. In one painful scene, for example, he offers as explanation for her tenuous hold on her husband her memory of being one of the less attractive girls in her high school class picture.

Mr. Humphrey's virtues, then, are a sense of the masculine character, of family estrangements and family love, and the ability to dramatically develop these in a recognizable social framework. His local specifics (one of recurring reference to the inbred chivalry of the Southern boy) could, on a comparable social level, be true anywhere. The rest of his novel is sketched in, often luridly. But Mr. Humphrey is a serious writer, and he is young. Among the haphazard garden of Southern talents, he seems eminently worth watching.

Jean Holzhauer, "Transcending the Limits of a Southern Locale," in Commonweal, *Vol. LXVII, No. 22, February 28, 1958, p. 571.*

JAMES R. FRAKES

Few literary events provide so much healthy delight as the squelching of certain apparent truisms about American writers. This new novel [*The Ordways*] by William Humphrey invalidates quite a few such theories, and is thus a source of both primary and secondary joy.

An American writer who makes it with his first novel is supposed to invite disaster with its sequel. Humphrey had published a collection of stories in 1953 (***The Last Husband and Other Stories***), but ***Home From the Hill*** (1958) was his first published novel, and its critical and popular success had all the characteristics of the embrace of death. With that "major American novelist" label stuck to him, the slaughterhouse seemed the inevitable next stop. ***The Ordways,*** however, featuring the same East Texas setting and even some identical devices and episodes, emerges not as a cynical or uncertain carbon-copy but as a strongly independent work evincing growth and sureness.

American writers are also inviting the fickle finger by attempting anything that looks like a "saga" sweeping over four generations of one family, since evidently only Icelanders and Galsworthy possess the kneadable past and the staying power for such a project. Again, Humphrey takes the risk . . . , complete with a stereoscopic view of the shambles at Shiloh and discursive chats on Southerners living in the past. . . . And again he avoids the trap—mainly by artful shifts of emphasis, relevant selection of details, and an extremely precarious balance between ironic deflation and sentimentality.

Perhaps most threatening of all for a chronicler of the American South is the shadow of masters like Warren, Lytle, Styron, and—above all—Faulkner. Here Humphrey tries a different tactic: he admits the inescapable influence of these men, uses techniques established by them, and neither squirms nor hedges. A lot of readers will be forcibly reminded of such works as *The Unvanquished* and *Sartoris;* perhaps Humphrey sheds too much armor here, leaving himself too vulnerable to the ravages of parallel-tracers. But tone and attitude are not Faulknerian except in spots, and certainly the tranquil prose of ***The Ordways*** bears little resemblance to Faulkner's agonized rhetoric. . . . (p. 5)

Actually, one of Humphrey's major points is that Clarksville, Texas, is the point where the South stops and the West almost (but not quite) begins, that the West provided America with an escape from the memory of the Civil War. And so, after Shiloh, blind Thomas Ordway and his family moved from Tennessee to Texas, obsessively hauling with them the marble tombstones and—packed in nail- and sourmash-kegs—the disinterred remains of ancestors and kin. This trek alone, desperate and ghoulishly funny, would have supplied enough substance for a novel, but the author keeps it tightly under control, teases us with several more trim family anecdotes, and then launches into the central Ordway memory: Sam Ordway's legend-rich scouring of the vast world of Texas for his 3-year-old son, Ned, stolen by his down-the-road neighbor in 1898. Using the annual Texas rite of graveyard working day (also a vital element in ***Home From the Hill***) as pivot-point, Humphrey casts this novel in the form of a first-person narrator's shaded and sensitive recalling of his grandfather's self-critical account of this search 30 years later. (pp. 5, 19)

We follow Sam's trail with urgency and learn painlessly about the shaping forces of environment, and heredity, and—the distinguishing feature of the book for this reviewer—the subtle, intricate logistics of family affection. . . .

This is the way William Humphrey works, never shouting or surprising, never afraid of a cliche if it works for him, never sidestepping a complexity or a tempting digression. With his authentic feeling for ritual and custom, for the genesis of traditions, and for the trembling network of blood and marital relationships, he builds to the tenderly comic return of Little Ned and the ensuing family reunion deliberately and convincingly. All characters—especially the women—breathe and grow in a world made familiar through solid talent and love. (p. 19)

James R. Frakes, "An Abundance of Life in the Graveyard," in Book Week—The Sunday Herald Tribune, *January 31, 1965, pp. 5, 19.*

ELIZABETH JANEWAY

Great writers leave us not just their works, but a way of looking at things. Perhaps this crystallizes out of tendencies that were there already; it's impossible to say. We can't tell now just how we would look at the South if Faulkner had never written. All we can know is that when we do look, a bit of Faulkner's vision colors our own.

I don't mean to detract from William Humphrey's [novel ***The Ordways***] when I say that it asks his readers to place him with the help of the compass that Faulkner taught us to read. Humphrey's Clarksville is a real town in northeast Texas, almost due west across Arkansas from Oxford, Miss. It's in that part of the state which Texans call "Old South," cotton country, settled by Alabamans and Tennesseans moving west. More important, it's the fully created scene of moving fictional events, as Humphrey's first novel, ***Home From the Hill,*** attested. And yet part of what we know about it, part of the way we recognize where we are, is due to a debt owed by both Humphrey and the reader to Faulkner.

This isn't a debt that should irritate anybody, either the reader or Faulkner. Humphrey has written two fine novels; this one, I think, better than the first. He's too good a writer to copy Faulkner, any more than he's copying Chekhov or Mark Twain, both of whom are recalled by various pages in ***The Ordways.*** What Humphrey does is accept the vision that Faulkner and others have bequeathed to their heirs, and build on it. I suppose this means that he is not a primary writer. His books are less original than those of his masters', smaller and more constructed, and with a touch of conscious synthesis about them. Just the same, he stands up to the impossible comparison well.

The Ordways is a much better book than many of the lesser works of Faulkner, and of Mark Twain, too. No one has written as Humphrey does about Texas and its geography—which has got into the thinking and feeling of Texans, and is part of the social structure of that huge and consciously individual area. Only Chekhov, in "The Steppe," has recorded a more vivid journey through barren prairie country. And to forget its literary grandfathers, ***The Ordways*** is compellingly readable.

Home From the Hill was tragedy with trimmings of melodrama. This second novel is a comedy, a real one, which I suspect is harder to do. Humphrey still has a taste for melodrama, like Mark Twain before him. In comedy, this comes out as farce; and like Mark Twain, Humphrey is guilty of changes in tone. . . . The odd thing is that this doesn't matter, any more than it matters in *Huckleberry Finn*. One simply moves from one section of the book to another and finds oneself in a different milieu. Each section is exhilaratingly successful at what it sets out to do.

For Humphrey is a writer who can interest us in anything. He seizes the reader by the shoulder like the Ancient Mariner, but I can't imagine anyone wanting to get away. The plot of the book is the story of the Ordway family, centering on Sam Ordway, the narrator's grandfather, but the fabric is woven on a warp made up of geography, history, family traditions, the myth of the Civil War and the special character of the South. All this gives it a shimmer and depth. (p. 1)

The Ordways who first moved West were a blinded hero, wounded at Shiloh, and his still more heroic wife. They ventured out onto the prairie, but it was too late for them or too early for history. They could not bear the loneliness and turned back to settle in Red River County. There the family took root, there later generations returned for the annual Rite of the Dead on "graveyard working day" when the living met to tidy the plots where the ancestors rested. From there, the boy who is our narrator begins his journey into the past, back east to meet his great-grandparents, and west with them through the war-torn land. Then, with the tales of his grandfather, we move on a great sweep through Texas.

This section, Humphrey, with a wink at melodrama, has called "Sam Ordway's Revenge." Like the hero of every Western, Sam Ordway is in pursuit of a villain who has done him a grievous wrong: Will Vinson, his erstwhile neighbor. What Will's crime was, I will leave the author to tell. Sam Ordway, following his trail, is buffeted by absurdities but never overthrown. Here Humphrey slides from comedy into farce, time and time again. As he does, Ordway hardens toward a grotesque. Always, he is saved in time by a touch of true feeling. When he is confronted with the need to study his fellow humans, to learn how to ask the questions that will keep him on Will Vinson's trail, to think his way into the mind of the man he is after, he grows solid and real again.

And the episodes of farce are, in themselves, hilarious. . . . But meanwhile, under the farce, life rumbles along its track. Ordway never catches up with Vinson. Yet on a deeper level he finds a proper resolution to his search, the strength to break it off and go back home.

The Ordways is not only a comedy, it's one with an ending as aboundingly cheerful as any since Dickens. . . . There's no strain to the humor. It bubbles naturally out of Humphrey's characters and is constantly enlivened by his quick observations of the exact details which recreate the reality of a moment. Emotions are pinned down to making crops and milking cows. Without nostalgia and sentimentality, here is time past, childhoods spent in the solid bulwark of a family and the building of such families.

The Ordways isn't a perfect book, it's just a terribly good one, expansive, exploratory, with breathing space for its characters and their humors. Other people's writing is built into it, but they are the best people and the echoes are worthy of them. What's more, the way Humphrey handles the language is astonishing and individual. Funny, vivid and moving, this is a fine piece of work and a delight to read. (pp. 1, 40)

Elizabeth Janeway, "Journey through Time," in The New York Times Book Review, *January 31, 1965, pp. 1, 40.*

GRANVILLE HICKS

William Humphrey's ***Home from the Hill*** was the kind of first novel that makes reviewers sit up and pay attention, for the author had a story to tell, and he told it with great power. . . .

Now, after seven years, we have ***The Ordways*** . . . , which is not merely about but is in effect a love letter to the State of Texas. Although the action begins in the eastern part of the state, it moves west and south, giving Humphrey a chance to display both his affection and his descriptive powers.

A family novel, it introduces the Ordways on a "graveyard working day" in Mabry, a suburb of Clarksville. The narrator, who was a boy at the time, presents his relatives, alive and dead, and at once we have a sense of the character of the family. . . .

Sam's wanderings, which occupy more than half the book, take him over a good part of Texas. At first the account of the search is pathetic, as Sam is time after time disappointed; but as the journey lengthens the pathos diminishes, until Humphrey seems to be chiefly interested in telling a series of stories, in the manner of the picaresque novelists. We have Sam at a political rally, speeches and all; Sam robbed by a notorious con man; Sam as the caretaker of a circus elephant; Sam on trial for intended murder. Some of the episodes are tall stories in the tradition of frontier humor, and others, such as the trial, are pure farce. At last, having reached the valley of the Rio Grande, Sam gives up.

After these prolonged divagations, Humphrey is ready to wind up his novel, and he does so ardroitly and pleasantly. . . .

Since this is intended to be the story of a family, much of the material in the long account of Sam Ordway's search is irrelevant, so much so that the novel is curiously deformed. Why Humphrey, who knows as much about form as the next one, permitted this deformation is hard to explain except on the ground of his love affair with Texas. Some of the extraneous material is so good in itself, and he writes about it with such obvious pleasure, that one is tempted to forgive him, but the fact remains that the impact of the novel is seriously weakened.

On the other hand, there is Humphrey's feeling for Texas, which he manages to communicate even to one who has never set foot in the Lone Star State. More important, there is his feeling for the family as, so to speak, both a vertical and a horizontal institution. . . . (p. 25)

Whether Humphrey's generalizations hold true or not, his own feeling for what must be in large degree his own family permeates the book. It is significant that the novel begins and ends with family gatherings, the one a pious duty, the other a gay celebration. In between lie the struggles that Humphrey describes so intensely. Although I believe that the novel goes off the track, it will be read and deserves to be, for it contains a great amount of felt experience, of experience that has been acted upon by the imagination. Flannery O'Connor often said that one of the advantages of the Southern writer was the Southern habit of telling stories. There is surely a strong oral tradition behind this book, and if this tradition misled the author at various points, it must be recognized as one of the sources of the book's vitality. (p. 26)

Granville Hicks, "Texas Bound, Bones and All," in Saturday Review, *Vol. XLVIII, No. 6, February 6, 1965, pp. 25-6.*

LOUIS D. RUBIN, JR.

William Humphrey published his first novel, ***Home from the Hill,*** back in 1958. I have been thinking of it ever since as an example of what can happen when a younger Southern writer attempts to carry the Faulknerian primitivistic style—field and stream, the mighty hunter, etc.—into modern urban experience; halfway through, the characterization collapses as disastrously as that of Flem Snopes does in Faulkner's *The Mansion*. Humphrey's second and most recent novel, ***The Ordways,*** is in many respects much better than that first try; it isn't nearly as derivative, and it isn't pseudo-tragic. The writer's craft has improved considerably; no doubt of that. But, a serious attempt to give fictional order and meaning to experience? ***The Ordways*** starts off in true Southern style: a long scene involving the Ordway family's annual grave-tending day in East Texas, with everybody come home to take part. Various ancestral yarns, mostly humorous, are recalled by the narrator, who is the fourth-generation Ordway in the town of Clarksville. Next we get into the story of how the Ordways got there, involving a tale not at all humorous. . . . Much of this is very moving: an archetypal fictional journey, at times worthy of William Faulkner himself (and sometimes suggesting *Absalom, Absalom!* and *As I Lay Dying*). The best part of the book comes next: how Sam Ordway, born the day that the family forded the river and staggered into Texas, marries, loses his wife, marries again, and has a child stolen by neighbors. This section is first-rate writing, notable for the author's sympathetic insight into the situation of the second wife, and into how Sam Ordway handles it; when at length Sam starts out after his missing son, he has our keen attention.

But at this point, or not long afterward, the novel simply seems to disintegrate. The search, at first very moving, soon becomes funny; and then the humor gets really slapstick, with Sam Ordway joining a circus and then spending a term in jail along with a phony preacher, and any importance or dignity to the search for the lost child is dissolved in vaudeville comedy. Ultimately Sam goes back home, everyone grows old, and soon we are back in modern times again, with the long missing son Ned showing up at the end for several days of joyous reunion, followed by a wild mass automobile trip to his angora goat ranch in western Texas, whereupon the story ends.

What does it all mean? It comes to mean almost nothing. As in the first novel, there is the curious grafting of the traditional Southern storytelling milieu, with its primitives who are strong and feeling human beings, onto a modern mode, this time of slapstick humor and sentimentality (Truman Capote could have composed the final sequences). Any relationship between the two parts would have to reside in the meaning it has, or implies, for the narrator. But the narrator, after the opening section, becomes merely an "I" doing the telling and can embody or present no meaning. It will not do to say that the theme of the novel is that the narrator can *discover* no meaning between the historical past and the present, as with Faulkner's Quentin Compson or Allen Tate's observer at the cemetery wall; even that realization would be a way of giving meaning to what has been told. Humphrey doesn't achieve that; there is really no connection at all, other than the facts of the family history. It winds up as no more and no less than a nostalgic stroll along memory lane and so forth, amusing, quaint, but adding up to no more than the fact that it has happened. What might have been the pathos and the drama of a family come down to a new day and forced to assume a new identity is absent, and one is led to think that it is absent because for the author there simply isn't any discernible meaning to the family's survival; the novel divides into two stories, the olden day events and the modern, with an unbridgeable artistic gulf between them. The two can't be made into one, because the historical events haven't any meaning for the narrator, who is a modern Southerner, nor does it occur to him that they should have. Gavin Stevens, in Faulkner's *Requiem for a Nun,* declares to Temple Drake that "the past is never dead. It's not even past." Not so in ***The Ordways.*** The past is quite dead. (pp. 263-65)

Louis D. Rubin, Jr., "The Experience of Difference: Southerners and Jews," in his The Curious Death of the Novel: Essays in American Literature, *Louisiana State University Press, 1967, pp. 262-81.*

LARRY L. KING

William Humprey's fourth book [***A Time and a Place***] is perfectly titled. The time is the 1930's, those hard-scrabble Depression days of rootless wanderers and a nation stymied. The place alternates between dust-bowl Oklahoma and vest-pocket hamlets of East Texas's piney woods; and while there are differences of topography, the two locales are more identical than not in cultures, habits and attitudes. . . .

Though these are 10 "unrelated" stories . . . , they are held together by common and interlocking themes; for all their varied treatments, the reader must remind himself he is not reading a novel.

The Southwest of the 1930's was mean and hard; Mr. Humphrey adroitly captures its casual violence, frustrations, quick vengeances and rude country humor. In that time and place a sullen poverty not only of the land but of the soul often registered itself in routine inhumanities. Earnest, hard-working sons of a foot-dragging civilization saw in the nation's economic crumbling a mockery of all their frugalities and teachings and sure-handed Gods. . . .

The feel of that time and place leaps everywhere from Mr. Humphrey's book in an artful mixture of ancient poverty, new riches, constant cruelties. (p. 5)

William Humphrey is more than an accomplished raconteur. He has a grand ear; his descriptions of the land's brooding presence, and how it works its moods on its people, is at once reminiscent of Faulkner and William Styron. His cadence is his own as are marvelous subtleties of tone reflecting his awareness of the unending little contests and struggles comprising life. And certainly William Humphrey is more than the "regional writer" some have named him . . . because he so skillfully explores themes that are universal in their ironies and degradations. (p. 47)

Larry L. King, "A Setting Mean and Hard," in The New York Times Book Review, *November 3, 1968, pp. 5, 47.*

BRUCE COOK

[The ten stories in ***A Time and a Place***] simply do not work as a collection: They are too much alike. Many of them have not only setting in common but events as well. No fewer than five turn on the discovery of oil on the property of some poor farmer. Characters recur; themes are restated, then stated again; and by book's end a sense of weary familiarity covers all like so much red grit left over from an Oklahoma dust storm. Could it be that Mr. Humphrey, whose novels ***Home From the Hill*** and ***The Ordways*** have been quite well received, set out to write another novel here, only to have it fall apart into so many separate stories? Something, anyhow, surely went wrong.

Bruce Cook, "Corrington and Humphrey Offer New Collections," in The National Observer, *January 20, 1969, p. 21.*

PAUL BAILEY

The time is the early thirties and the place the Red River country, the borderland between Texas and Oklahoma—the ten stories in William Humphrey's fine collection [***A Time and a Place***] re-create a period and a way of life already familiar from the novels of Faulkner. Poor whites are Mr. Humphrey's concern, too—particularly those who suddenly find themselves rich after oil has been struck on their otherwise barren land.

He extracts mordant comedy from this situation, and walks an unnervingly thin tightrope between tragedy and farce, coming perilously close at times to the routine humour of that appalling television series, "The Beverly Hillbillies," with its grizzled, lumbering freaks. That he doesn't topple over is an indication of the quality of his writing: the joke-figures (the ancient illiterates utterly at a loss in stately mansions after years on the farm; the plain girls taking extensive beauty treatment in order to make better 'catches'; the rejected suitor who decides to emulate Clyde Barrow and is captured before even firing a shot) become objects of pity, with complex, untidy feelings and enormous, unsatisfied ambitions—Mr. Humphrey, in a word, makes them real.

But the main character in ***A Time and a Place*** is the Depression itself, and its implied presence adds weight to each of these seemingly light and easy-going stories—the longer one reads, the more one feels its terrible grip, its manacle-like hold on those humble, stunted lives. Apart from one excursion into parody (of the Old Testament, which he brings off) Mr. Humphrey writes an even, unrhetorical prose, making his effects in bold, swift strokes; when the drama hots up, which is often, he retains his calm. Not once does Social Realism rear its ugly, middle-brow head: history comes to life in these pages without recourse to mere 'facts.' An occasional nudging cuteness in the narrative is the only flaw I can discern in this remarkable book.

Paul Bailey, "Miniature Masterpieces," in The Observer, *March 2, 1969, p. 30.*

THE TIMES LITERARY SUPPLEMENT

When King James I was asked why he proposed to re-visit, after a prolonged absence, the land of his birth, he replied "the salmon-instinct". Three centuries later we know little more about the habits of this mysterious fish than did he, though in the meantime much research has been devoted to the subject, and some discoveries made. For those who would know all, and equally for those who as yet know nothing, no better guide could be found than ***The Spawning Run.*** Its author came to England to fish, assuming for the occasion the engaging disguise of an American backwoodsman. Thus apparelled, a not-so-innocent abroad, he set out to explore both the mystique of English fishing and the habits of its most notable victim. In neither quest was he disappointed: "Nowhere", he found.

> is the class division more sharply drawn than in the national pastime. "Fishing in Britain", says the pamphlet sent me by the British Travel and Holiday Association, "falls into three classes: game, sea and coarse." Read: upper, middle and lower.

With commendable discrimination, Mr. Humphrey opted for the first. . . .

Paradoxically, some of the best books about animals have been written by sportsmen, and to this class ***The Spawning Run*** belongs. As a fishing diary it contains all the excitement, the frustration of the chase, and can be commended not only to the proud possessors of ten-feet Farlow rods but also to almost anyone who has ever faced a salmon across a fishmonger's slab.

"Angling Saxons," in The Times Literary Supplement, *No. 3589, December 11, 1970, p. 1470.*

CHRISTOPHER LEHMANN-HAUPT

[***Proud Flesh***] is hands down the worst piece of fiction I've read so far this year. It's so dreadful that I'd like to begin a review of it with a few sneering-descriptive lines—something like "Psychology by Rose Franzblau tricked up as a parody of William Faulkner," or "The Southern gothic imagination gone rococo"—except that I see that among its many other ill effects, it has absolutely anesthetized my mind. I am dumbfounded. I simply can't believe that the author of ***Home From the Hill, The Ordways,*** and ***The Spawning Run,*** which was a charming little book about the sex lives of salmon and fishermen—could have produced such an awful mess as this. Even the title stinks a little, as I'll explain by and by. Well, at least Mr. Humphrey doesn't toy with us. Right from the start, one can see he is in trouble. It's not the cheap sight-and-sound effects in his opening segment I'm referring to. . . .

No, what arouses our suspicions from the very start is the prose that Mr. Humphrey lays on to persuade us that the Renshaws are the proudest, most clannish Texas family that ever remembered the Alamo, and that their matriarch, Edwina Renshaw—now a-lying a-dying up there in her bedroom in the old family homestead—is the most arrogant, domineering woman that ever bred a Texas brood. . . .

But, the reader is already wondering, if that's so, then why is the author telling us instead of showing us? And it's a good question, because, as we find out all too soon, it isn't so. Not only are the Renshaws not so clannish or "pharisaical"; not only is Edwina not such a tough, demanding old lady: the Renshaws, especially Edwina, don't even exist, except as a kind of half-hearted premise at the top of Mr. Humphrey's plot outline. They never even made it into his imagination, to be shown to us instead of thrust at us. And Mr. Humphrey knows it very well.

But instead of throwing in the towel on the Renshaws and writing about something that does exist in his imagination, Mr.

Humphrey keeps plowing ahead, keeps sewing inventions, keeps exaggerating their growth, keeps writing up a dust storm. . . .

Do I make it all sound awful? It's worse. The only hopeful comment I can think of to make is that Mr. Humphrey has now gotten out of his system a problem that he neither understood nor cared about to begin with—or maybe he did care a little about it to begin with, for what else but some obscure obsession could have kept him writing such balderdash?

And the title, ***Proud Flesh***? Well, you've got the main idea already—proud Texas flesh and all that. But there's also old Edwina's flesh: even after she does finally die for good, her devoted clan keeps her rugged old corpse around for days and days—even stashes it in the town's ice-house. Proud flesh, you see? But, after a while, it too begins to stink.

Christopher Lehmann-Haupt, "More Meat for the Boycott," in The New York Times Book Review, *April 4, 1973, p. 41.*

ROBERT LASSON

Proud Flesh has passages of magnetic description, detours of absorbing story, glints of original characterization, and a close knowledge of Texas rural life. But it smacks, as its title does, of the novel-like more than it reads like a singular novel. The author of ***Home From the Hill*** and ***The Ordways*** is not at his best this time out.

The novel's central problem is the central story of the novel. The matriarch of the huge, cotton-rich Renshaw family, Edwina, collapses one morning with a heart ailment and is taken to bed in grave condition. A vast number of relatives, including all her 10 children but one, is summoned to keep vigil at the house. The absent Renshaw is Edwina's last-born, Kyle, and he is profoundly resented by his siblings—for whom loyalty is so grim a religion it reads here like a curse—because he, a traitor to Texas and the family, has gone off to live somewhere in New York City. He is also, not surprisingly in a novel-like novel, Edwina's favorite. And the family has to get him home so his mother can see him once again. The search for Kyle is one of several stories surrounding the indomitable Edwina's prolonged dying. (pp. 26-7)

Humphrey's use of Edwina's suspended death as a narrative convenience—as what clearly becomes a narrative convenience—contributes to one's sense that Humphrey doesn't take the event as seriously as he would like us to, that he manipulates it, as if improvising. And thus we can't take it seriously. The reader is not permitted into Edwina's bedroom until late in the book: one's distance from the bedroom equals one's distance from the dying woman. The trick does not create curiosity, it increases detachment.

Our emotions are exhorted but never persuaded. Edwina's authority over her family is declared and described over and over. But in fact her authority works only because the novel has dubbed the family loyal. The connection between the loyalty and the authority is never palpable.

In fact, the Renshaws are a bunch of maniacs; and in fact Humphrey finally says this himself, but not until long after we've given up hoping Humphrey knew it too. For most of the book he treats his Renshaws misleadingly as "larger than life." You know, Texans. (p. 27)

Robert Lasson, in a review of "Proud Flesh," in The New York Times Book Review, *April 29, 1973, pp. 26-7.*

THE TIMES LITERARY SUPPLEMENT

In Texas, as we all know, everything is much bigger than it is; and when the American novelist wants to strive after the heroic, this large, proud region—where men *stride* rather than just walk—provides the obvious backcloth. But the heroic is a precarious idiom: the point of toppling over is never far away, the point at which the wrath of Achilles becomes only the petulant sulking of a delinquent, the point at which Milton's Satan loses the defiant grandeur which the romantics saw in him, turning out (as in the sharp analysis by C. S. Lewis) to be only a *diminuendo* of querulous self-pity.

In [***Proud Flesh***], the author of ***The Ordways*** sets before us the Renshaws, a vast and heroic clan if ever there was one, lavish, proud, passionate, wilful, splendid, absurd: in the last analysis, a shower of boring twits. It's the ambiguity, it's that point of toppling which fascinates Mr Humphrey: he plays with it scrappily and inconclusively but with delight. . . .

Mr Humphrey is working on the ambiguity of pride. The splendour, yes; the sin, perhaps; the boring narrowness, all the time. There is a precarious moral about the dangers of family mindedness in one version, and a sounder but corny moral about the matriarchal nature of American society and the young male's consequent need to prove his maleness at every point. Sardonic, extremely amusing in places, this is a collection of episodes and comments rather than an integrated novel: Mr Humphrey sets his stage magnificently, then handles his puppets rather uncertainly. It makes good, preposterous reading, and suggests lines along which certain still-prevailing notions of heroism and greatness might usefully be reconsidered, and not only in Texas.

"Gee Whiz!" in The Times Literary Supplement, *No. 3726, August 3, 1973, p. 893.*

REYNOLDS PRICE

A reader of William Humphrey's three novels will know that their central fascination is with family—the oddly ramified and riven but intensely close families of his homecountry, east Texas—and that Humphrey's own experience of family, while apparently mixed, was not so gorgonian as to have frozen him into vengeance nor so caustic as to have sent him chattering down the compulsive verbal and structural escape-routes of non-realistic experimentation. He has stood his ground; and in ***Home From the Hill, The Ordways*** and ***Proud Flesh,*** he has provided elaborately imagined, honorable and useful description of the institution which is not only the chief and inexhaustible object of the human creature's narrative curiosity (from Genesis to soap opera) but also the sole means by which a vast majority of the race has been able to imagine existence itself. Now in this memoir of childhood and adolescence [***Farther Off from Heaven***], Humphrey offers the story of his own home and family, the matrix of his work.

The story as he tells it is purposely arranged against calendar-time. He begins with the night in July 1937—he had just turned 13—when his father was injured in an automobile wreck and he and his mother were called to the crushed unconscious body. Their long vigil beside him becomes the barely glimpsed spine of the story, from which long and short nerves of memory and knowledge probe into past and future action. Rearranged chronologically, the shape is simple enough—a young man and woman (both the children of unloving cotton farmers from Red River County, Texas) marry and move to Clarksville, the county seat. Clarence becomes an uncannily good auto-mechanic; Nell excels as wife and homemaker. Soon a son is born. Young William arrives with a deformed foot; and though the foot is eventually straightened, Nell will not consider other children. . . . The boy grows up in the shade of his gypsy parents' love and delight—with the sense of being a full member to their laughing union, not a junior appendage. . . . The only sounds audible above the steady murmur of mutual gratitude are Clarence's high spirits, William's pair of mishaps (a near-drowning and a knee accident) and, in time, the rising friction between his parents as William's growth produces in Nell a craving for "improvement" and respectability—a change unimaginable for the roaring Clarence, who begins to seek his own diet elsewhere: willing women. Then the wreck, the vigil, Clarence's death at 38, Nell's and William's exit to Dallas as destitute guests of more fortunate relations.

The story told thus is not exceptional; but as I said, it is not told thus. The happy primeval past is constantly forced to communicate with the appalling present of tragic waste and the death of affection; and we come to see that those disarrangements of time, which at first seem willful and annoying, are the only technical means of transmitting to us something like the full resonance of a finding which Humphrey first states baldly—"We retreat from unhappiness as far as our experience, or our imagination, allows us to go." And the slow counterpointing of agonized death with mostly happy memory (his mother's fevered gaiety, two genuinely epic hunts of his father's), the accumulation of intricately detailed portraits of two sizable and patently lovable people, does finally succeed—for me, at least. I believe in the truth of his final sum.

What Humphrey has worked out is in fact a sum, an equation. The hardscrabble Humphreys and Varleys combined to equal Clarence and Nell, who combined to equal William, who has in turn combined with their lives and memories to equal this book and the other books behind it. His childhood, happy as it was, ended early in a bloody disaster. The eternal-seeming warmth of parental care ended in death and expulsion. That the apparent end was only a pause is the door which opens in the book's potential final blankness. As Auden said of Rimbaud, "the cold had made a poet."

The son of Clarence and Nell Humphrey reflects before Clarence's funeral, "The lesson of [my father's] life was: live, don't learn. For tomorrow you die—if you last that long; today is not over yet. Then the living they can't take from you, and the learning you can't take with you." What the son doesn't say, though all his work does, is better—more hopeful, truer. If you burn high enough—warmly not fiercely, with care not hunger—then someone will watch and carry the sight and feel of fire to his own quiet grave. And if that watcher has a voice of his own and is old enough and fair enough to pay his first debts, then you may well have lived for longer than you planned and more than you knew.

With his sinewy story, William Humphrey has fathered new lives for his parents—lovely again and lasting now. That is surely the highest duty of a child, if his parents have earned it. These parents did. From their strong new youth, may they send him the gifts he has plainly earned—long life in his homeland, his hard work honored. (pp. 7, 31)

Reynolds Price, "Homecountry, East Texas," in The New York Times Book Review, *May 22, 1977, pp. 7, 31.*

BERT ALMON

Clarksville, a small town at the northeastern corner of Texas, has always been William Humphrey's postage stamp of earth, though the soil is transformed by imagination. Clarksville is located in a region where South begins to blur into West, and it has a rich history and folklore. (p. 84)

Humphrey's fictional Clarksville is so vivid that his readers may be surprised to learn through the autobiography that he left the town at thirteen and vowed never to return. He kept the vow for thirty-two years. In ***Farther Off from Heaven*** he explains why Clarksville became an inexhaustible well of fictional possibilities. Family misfortune disrupted his childhood, making those early years indelible. The trauma was the death of his father from injuries after a car crash. The book begins with Humphrey's mother waking him at three o'clock in the morning on July 5, 1937, to tell him that his father had been hurt, then moves slowly toward the father's death in a Paris, Texas, hospital three days later. The slowness is created by Humphrey's exploration of his boyhood memories and his probings into the relationship between his parents. Here and there the reader may find sources for characters and situations in Humphrey's fiction, but that kind of interest is incidental: the value of the book lies in the evocation of Clarksville and the people in it, especially the parents, Clarence and Nell Humphrey. The integrity of the narrator is remarkable. He loved his parents, and he demonstrates the intensity of that love by his careful inquiry into their backgrounds and even their courtship; but he is honest about their shortcomings and the decline of their relationship. The book is an act of sympathetic and searching understanding. (pp. 84-5)

One of the finest scenes in the book comes in the last chapter, as Humphrey recalls one dispute between his parents. Sunday dinner was a rite of respectability, more hallowed than any church service, and one Sunday the father showed up late. In the course of an angry squabble, he broke his wife's string of pearls, then stormed out of the room. Determined to keep up the pretense of a respectable family dinner, the mother insisted that young Humphrey eat his soup. He forced a spoonful into his mouth and found a pearl in it. He had to run from the room.

The craft of the book lies in such scenes, and in their careful arrangement into chapters of reminiscence that Humphrey correlates with his father's descent into death at the hospital. Each chapter takes shape around a theme or a segment of family history: the father's skill as a hunter dominates the third chapter, the parents' courtship unites the fourth. The organization appears casual, but the chapters cohere even when they ramble on like a familiar essay. The prose is restrained, a real contrast with the stylistic virtuosity of a novel like ***The Ordways,*** and the simplicity of diction and sentence structure seems appropriate for recollections of childhood.

The reader is always aware that the memories are being arranged by a mature mind. The images are sharp, and the ease of style does not hinder the creation of powerful scenes like the Sunday dinner episode or the superb, harrowing rendition of an alligator hunt in the wilderness of Sulphur Bottom. And the clarity of the scenes, along with their dramatic power, establishes just how indelible Humphrey's interrupted childhood became. Foreshadowing serves the author well: full information is withheld about certain key events, such as his "death" in childhood, and the full anecdote is always told where it will have the most impact. Certain thematic images—mutilation and physical handicaps—recur as leitmotifs. Such narrative strategies give richness to a book marked by stylistic austerity.

William Humphrey gives the story of his family wider meanings by showing the influence of the Depression in damaging the marriage. The American dream was failing: the Humphreys were squeezed between bills they couldn't pay and bills they couldn't collect. . . . Humphrey presents his parents as a couple who shared real affinities (high spirits and ambition) along with their incompatibilities, and he shows the malign influences of growing poverty in heightening their tensions.

Yet Clarksville was a colorful place in which to grow up, with its courthouse clock ("Old Red") and its aromas of cottonseed meal and fresh bread. The town was small and friendly, and the countryside was always there when the boy wanted to explore or could go hunting with his father. Humphrey vowed never to return to Clarksville because he didn't want to reopen his wounds, not because the town was a miserable place in which to live. And like a salmon he inevitably returned, to make some surprising discoveries that no reviewer should reveal.

The parents and town dominate the book. The decision to become a writer came after Humphrey left Clarksville with his mother, so he has not given us a *bildungsroman*. He possesses, however, the prerequisite that Henry James proposed for the artist: he is the sort of person on whom nothing is lost. The autobiography reveals that very little was ever lost on Humphrey, for what he could not understand as a child, adult reflection and imaginative sympathy would clarify. The epigraph from Thomas Hood might suggest that the work will be a sentimental one: Hood's verse claims that the loss of a child's point of view makes one "farther off from heaven." But Humphrey has retained the child's sharp perceptiveness, while adding the intelligence and wisdom of a mature artist to this account of life in Clarksville, his flawed heaven. (pp. 85-6)

Bert Almon, "William Humphrey's Blue Heaven," in Southwest Review, *Vol. 63, No. 1, Winter, 1978, pp. 84-6.*

PETER S. PRESCOTT

Only a fool believes a fish story; certainly this one [***My Moby Dick***] offers ample cause for incredulity. But when a fish story is as entertaining as William Humphrey's is, I'll go along with the old Carthaginian who said that a thing is certain just because it *is* impossible. When not writing fiction, Humphrey fishes for trout, enjoying the silence and solitude as much as whatever luck he may have wresting speckled creatures from the water. . . .

One summer Humphrey discovered in a Massachusetts stream a 30-pound trout—very likely the biggest trout there ever was. Its great size suggested great age, and its great age suggested great wisdom. "A fish that big cannot be caught," Humphrey concluded, but he decided to try. . . . "I had not lost a leg to him," Humphrey observes, "but he had certainly taken a big bite of my brain."

I mustn't reveal the outcome, but any browser will notice that the book contains no photographs. Suiting his style to his subject, Humphrey makes a mock epic of his story: "Call me Bill," he begins, and his first paragraph continues as a witty parallel of Melville's. Like all good essayists, he darts off at tangents, discoursing on the technical problems of casting a line and on the social distinctions imposed upon anglers by their choice of bait. It's a brief story, and altogether charming; the reader who avoids it because he doesn't fish will be as misguided as the reader who avoids *Madame Bovary* because he doesn't commit adultery.

Peter S. Prescott, "Go Fish," in Newsweek, *Vol. XCII, No. 18, October 30, 1978, p. 96.*

ROBERT WILSON

Angling combines contemplation and action, Izaak Walton wrote; in this tale of a trout [***My Moby Dick***] there is too little of either. Perhaps it is unfair to expect more of a book that is modest and good-natured, but Humphrey is more than a fisherman: He is the author of ***Home From the Hill*** and other honorable works of fiction.

The trout weighs 30 pounds, and you can judge for yourself whether that makes this a work of fiction, too; Humphrey urges us to take it as fact. He discovers the trout in a Berkshire Mountain stream, and spends the better part of a fishing season on his stomach, studying it from the bank. So noble a creature must be caught in the most sporting way possible, he decides, and he studies the arcane art of dry-fly fishing as well. On the last day of the season, Humphrey manages to hook the trout. . . .

His fish gets away, but it is one of the book's best moments, because it is one of the few moments Humphrey bothers to dramatize. Instead of using his novelist's skills, Humphrey more often tells, in his genial, literate voice, in the lazy way a story might be told over a campfire, a tale that is unremarkable except for the titanic trout.

My Moby Dick serves best as a reminder to turn, or return, to the novels and short stories for which its author is known.

Robert Wilson, in a review of "My Moby Dick," in Book World—The Washington Post, *December 17, 1978, p. E7.*

JONATHAN YARDLEY

This powerful if rather lugubrious novel [***Hostages to Fortune***] is about a man who has been dealt a devastating series of personal blows and is trying to put the pieces of his life back together. Ben Curtis, 50 years old, has in two years lost his only child, his goddaughter and his best friend, all to suicide; his wife has walked out of the house in grief and fury, and their marriage seems beyond repair. Now he has gone to a fishing club in upstate New York, the site of many of his happiest hours as husband, friend and father. At every turn he is assaulted by "too many memories of a life now lost," and by terrible misgivings. . . .

The novel is told primarily in flashbacks, and William Humphrey's use of them is artful. Everything Curtis sees inside the clubhouse and along its trout-fishing stream reminds him of a moment in his past, invariably a happy one, and with the reawakening of memories comes the hard, unanswerable question: *Why?* "In every sound he heard that question asked." Why is his life in pieces? Why has his wife, the only woman in the world for him, walked away? Above all, why did his son kill himself?

This really is the central subject of ***Hostages to Fortune.*** More than a novel about one man's attempt to find something worth holding onto in a shattered existence, it is a novel about parents whose children kill themselves. . . . Unsparingly, Humphrey takes the reader through the "total confusion of feelings" caused by "unnatural death"—the grief, to be sure, but also the bitterness, the anger, the humiliation, the uncertainty. . . .

Humphrey has managed the considerable feat of writing a novel that manages to be intensely emotional and at the same time almost clinical in its examination of the aftershocks caused by suicide; he writes with particular force about what may be the most painful subject of all, the necessity to acknowledge the cruelty to others, whether deliberate or not, that suicide causes. But ***Hostages to Fortune*** is more successful as a work of reflection and introspection than as a work of fiction. Whether Ben Curtis will decide that life is indeed worth living is not a sufficiently strong thread on which to hang a plot, and the vitality of the characters is smothered by the remorselessly bleak tone of the book; Humphrey really seems more interested in pondering the psychological undertones of his subject than in creating strong characters and situations through which to explore it.

It remains, though, that William Humphrey is a marvellously accomplished writer, one of the best we have, and that any book of his commands the most serious attention. That is no less true of ***Hostages to Fortune*** than it is of his finest work, ***Farther Off From Heaven.*** The voice in these books is intelligent, compassionate, civilized; we could hardly ask for more.

Jonathan Yardley, "A Death in the Family," in Book World—The Washington Post, *September 16, 1984, p. 3.*

SEYMOUR EPSTEIN

William Humphrey is a novelist who likes to work from effect to cause. . . . [In ***Hostages to Fortune***] he begins with two fishing licenses issued to the same man two years apart and reveals to the reader that Ben Curtis, the tormented protagonist, has lost 25 pounds and his hair has gone from black to white. Naturally one wonders why and suspects tragedy. And indeed there is tragedy, a harrowing amount of it. In this respect, the author remains true to his early Faulknerian theme of dark, hounding destinies.

Mr. Humphey has cast his novelist-hero in the Hemingway mold, a man who loves to fish and hunt and is most at ease among trees and rivers and in the company of hard-drinking, like-minded fellows. The outdoor life is clearly a source of Mr. Humphrey's best writing. A boar hunt in ***Home From the Hill*** prompted some of his most deeply felt and lyrical passages. Similarly, the fishing and hunting scenes in the new book are described in language that is both rough and rhapsodic in its paean to nature.

Hostages to Fortune, however, is not primarily about nature or hunting. It is about suicide—and the most poignant kind—the suicide of the young. For no apparent immediate reason or past presage, Ben Curtis's son, Anthony, a student, hangs himself at Princeton. A gruesome event at any time, but one of particular contemporary significance as newspapers carry almost daily stories of suicides by the young.

Why did the boy hang himself? The question becomes his father's anguish and obsession. The mother, a shadowy figure at best, believes—or pretends to believe—that the suicide was not a suicide, but some kind of ghastly accident. Shaky even before the suicide, the Curtis' marriage is finished off by the death of the son. Ben is left to bear his agony alone. . . .

What Ben is seeking . . . is relief from the horrible rejection implicit in his son's suicide. To gain this, he goes deeper and deeper into himself, until he reaches the very core of a negation that ends all reason and explication, that is the terminus of *why.*

There is seriousness and dedication in almost every line of ***Hostages to Fortune.*** It is faithful to its purpose of examining an agonizing question. One hesitates to say that it is not wholly successful in its execution in the face of so much honesty of purpose, but one must quickly add that the flaw is inevitable and perhaps a guarantee of the novel's integrity.

Because of Ben's isolation, the examination he is conducting becomes increasingly more clinical than narrative. The result is a falling off in dramatic involvement. One doesn't lose interest in the vital question, but one does lose sight of its victim. Anthony, the proposed center of our curiosity and sympathy, fades into the background. But this is almost compensated for in the fierce reality of Ben's Gethsemane.

Seymour Epstein, "Gone, Inexplicably," in The New York Times Book Review, *October 14, 1984, p. 38.*

DAVID PROFUMO

In terms of setting, at least, William Humphrey breaks new ground with his latest novel [***Hostages to Fortune***]; the action occurs in the countryside of New York and New Jersey, rather than the Red River county which his previous work has staked out as his own, microscopically-observed terrain. His strength is still the evocation of place and the influence that a particular environment can exert on people, and some of the best episodes in ***Hostages to Fortune*** are to be found in his vignettes of the outdoor pursuits—falconry, hunting (ie shooting) and fishing—with which his characters occupy themselves. . . .

There are some powerful moments (especially in Humphrey's handling of the son's death), but while the agony is sincere enough, the agonizing is badly overdone. Relentless self-questioning can make for monotonous reading, and there is in the representation of Ben's melancholy a distinct tendency towards the histrionic. Humphrey seems incapable of suggestive understatement; there are more serious stylistic lapses, into novelettish pap and psychodrivel. Saxophones sob, rivers purl, a rose expires.

A writer by profession, Ben has a mind that mutters like a dictionary of quotations: he recites Browning in the duck-blind, Dante on the river-bank, and *Hamlet* at his reflection in a barroom mirror. None of this helps our perception of a mind under stress, which is a shame, because the novel's concerns are serious, and there are moments of real poignancy.

David Profumo, "Casting Around," in The Times Literary Supplement, *No. 4276, March 15, 1985, p. 284.*

MICHIKO KAKUTANI

With the publication of his first two novels—***Home From the Hill*** (1958) and ***The Ordways*** (1965)—William Humphrey was hailed as one of the South's brightest new literary voices. His novels, set in Texas where "the woods joined the prairie," where the legends of the old South collided with the new myth of the frontier, earned considerable acclaim for their assiduous delineation of a time and place, and Mr. Humphrey won comparisons with Faulkner and Mark Twain.

Reading [***The Collected Stories of William Humphrey***], however, one is more inclined to compare Mr. Humphrey's work with that of O. Henry or the worst of John Steinbeck. There is an unearned sentimentality to many of these stories, a tendency to heap more symbolic weight on ordinary people—impoverished farmers and small town folks—than they can reasonably bear. Even in his finest novels, Mr. Humphrey evinced a somewhat overripe taste for ironies, and when compressed to the smaller canvas of the short story, his gift for tragedy, for evoking an inexorable sense of doom, results in tricked-up plots, filled with contrivances and symmetries that seem too obvious and too pat. . . .

Such neatly packaged stories feel synthetic because they attempt to manipulate the reader's emotions in the same plodding, self-conscious way that they try to orchestrate people and events. It is as though Mr. Humphrey set out, each time, with a specific message or theme in mind—the disruptive effect of new money on the Southwest, the vain nostalgia Southerners harbor for the Civil War, the Job-like struggles of an accident-prone farmer—and then chained his characters to one-way tracks within a schematic framework designed to illustrate those concerns.

Some of those characters—most notably the aging couple in **"The Hardys,"** the boy in search of his past in **"The Last of the Caddoes,"**—have the lineaments of real individuals, with hints of hidden complexities; and others, like the self-deluded painter in **"The Fauve"** or the philanderer in **"The Last Husband,"** help underline Mr. Humphrey's instinctive feel for satire. Unfortunately, Mr. Humphrey has a way of continually interceding in his characters' lives, and even his most vital creations, stripped of free will and inner conflict, become chess pieces, mechanically moved about to serve the author's strategic ends.

To make matters worse, Mr. Humphrey often elects to explain to the reader what everyone is feeling—and what those feelings are supposed to mean—rather than dramatizing his characters' difficulties or relying upon his ear for dialogue and inflection. . . .

The better stories in this volume are the ones in which Mr. Humphrey relaxes, restrains his impulse to moralize, and simply concentrates on chronicling, through the slow accretion of details, a vanishing, vanished way of life. The place is usually Texas or Oklahoma of the 30's, places where the old belief in the pastoral American dream—"a place of his own and land which a strong young fellow not afraid of a little work could make out on"—is yielding to the more hectic fantasies of quick money and easy living, brought west by businessmen and oil barons.

The disparity, here, between people's wishes and the meagerness of their actual lives, between the sunny axioms they were raised on and the dull reality of their daily routines, often erupts into violence or death—or just eats away, bit by bit, at the structure of their families and their faith. Houses are sold, possessions are auctioned, children move north to the cities, and Mr. Humphrey's heroes realize, in a sudden glimpse of recognition, that they are either too old to start over or too weary to begin again. Such too infrequent moments, lucid and unfettered, make the author's straining after effects seem all the more awkward—and unnecessary.

Michiko Kakutani, "Tales of Lost Ways," in The New York Times Book Review, *June 22, 1985, p. 16.*

JONATHAN YARDLEY

William Humphrey is a writer of considerable, and considerably varied, accomplishment. His books include . . . two collections of short stories, the contents of which are republished in [***The Collected Stories of William Humphrey***].

Although Humphrey's prose is unfailingly graceful and interesting, the short story is not the form in which he seems most comfortable. While brevity is his style in nonfiction, he apparently wants space in which to stretch when he is writing fiction; in many of these stories he seems cramped, as though he had denied himself the breathing room he really needs and is paying the price as a consequence. The intensity of feeling that he generates in his longer work—I think in particular of ***Farther Off From Heaven***—is never fully achieved in the stories; they are etudes, and Humphrey's specialty is the symphony.

The best of them are quite fine, though, and in the best ones Humphrey's admirers will find him working familiar territory with his accustomed skill. The physical territory is Texas and Oklahoma during the Depression; the psychological territory embraces such matters as the relationship between father and son, the bonds of marriage and family, the life of small towns. As in his longer works, Humphrey is concerned in the stories with the gift and denial of love, the decay of the Old South, the shaping effects of hard times; his sympathy for his characters is firm, but so too is his refusal to permit them easy answers or to overlook their innate flaws.

Perhaps the best of all 22 stories, and thematically the most characteristic, is **"The Ballad of Jesse Neighbours."** Its title character is a 20-year-old Oklahoman, a poor but honorable and hard-working fellow, who aims to marry the beautiful Naomi Childress. He slaves away to provide a dwelling for them—a condition of her father's consent to the marriage—and is right on the verge of doing so when oil is struck on the Childress farm. Bull Childress takes his wife and family off to Dallas, and when they return Naomi will having nothing to do with the broken-hearted Jesse. . . .

Humphrey gets a lot done in the 20 pages of this story. He describes the brutal, suffocating poverty of hardscrabble Oklahoma in mid-Depression; he quickly, expertly creates a memorable character, a decent young man fated to be cheated in love and life; he depicts the corrupting effects of sudden, unearned wealth; he writes a surprisingly affecting elegy to the bygone days of "storied outlaws past and present, of Baby Face Nelson and Dillinger, of Sam Bass and Billy the Kid, and always, here among Jesse's crowd in particular, the word *poreboy, a poreboy,* sounded, like the bass string which the hand must always strum no matter what the chord, on a guitar." That brief passage is typical of the prose in the story, prose that is almost dreamily evocative yet specific in detail and, where required, humorous. (p. 3)

[When] Humphrey shifts his locale to the North, as in **"The Last Husband,"** he seems less sure of himself—of local customs and characters—even though his eye for human foible remains clear as ever. These stories you can skip at no great loss; but you owe it to yourself to find half an hour for Jesse Neighbours. (p. 7)

Jonathan Yardley, "William Humphrey's Hardscrabble Stories," in Book World—The Washington Post, *July 14, 1985, pp. 3, 7.*

ISA KAPP

Of the many curious aspects of Mr. Humphrey's career, most curious perhaps is the fact that only his first 13 years were spent in Clarksville, Tex.—so that the time and place of his fiction are remote both from him and from us. Yet in their very plainness, in their old-fashioned moral assumptions and their very contrast to the urban sophistication that has preempted our fiction, these stories from decades ago [contained in ***The Collected Stories of William Humphrey***] come closer to our sense of reality than many more recently published works.

In the earliest stories, the author, not yet 30, observes his fellow men with all the wariness of a hunter stalking his prey, alert for trickery or unfair advantage, his mind constantly poised for danger. **"Quail for Mr. Forester"** starts with a benign recollection: a 12-year-old boy and his father have brought home nine plump quails, and his mother, fancying association with a man of property, seizes the opportunity to invite the owner of the hardware store, once the richest man in town, to dinner. Mr. Forester, an elderly widower, relishes the good food and company, and the boy and his father enjoy the festivity. But the mother, egged on by envy, irritates them all by directing the conversation to the decline of the South and, more embarrassingly, the decline in her guest's fortunes. Even in so unlikely a context for psychological distress, Mr. Humphrey has introduced a notion that reappears to dampen many of his stories—if there is any option, the least wholesome impulses are bound to prevail: "I felt that there was no hope for me in these mean times I had been born into," the boy muses.

This sample of Mr. Humphrey's lighter dolefulness is a reliable harbinger of things to come. Marriage and parenthood are always losing propositions, with husband and wife, even mother and son, as disattuned as if one were on a rising, the other on a descending escalator. . . .

In **"The Last Husband,"** Mr. Humphrey gets uncannily close to Henry James in his episodic method and use of an omniscient yet uninvolved narrator. On a commuter train, the narrator meets a neighbor whose bland smile and furtive connivances hint at promiscuous liaisons and a jealous wife. Many train rides later, both narrator and reader divine that the presumed bounder is actually an old-fashioned, conventional husband, perhaps the last of the species. There is something Jamesian in all this. But the lesson is not clear, the narrator's omniscience not quite justified—mainly, it misses the patient Jamesian pursuit of changes in feeling.

While Mr. Humphrey's raw-nerved susceptibility to psychological dissonance constricts and depresses his outlook (though not his verbal resourcefulness), his spirit and style expand in the presence of natural forces. Droughts, oil booms, dust storms—nature, however violent or resistant, turns down his querulous notes, gives power to the acceptant, life-affirming part of his imagination. In the later stories, when Mr. Humphrey comes into his Twain legacy, the timbre of his language turns from high-strung tenor to rich bass. **"The Ballad of Jesse Neighbours"** radiates Mr. Humphrey's special empathy for those who are at the mercy of nature's whims. When Bull Childress's oil well suddenly turns into a gusher and he becomes a millionaire, he lets "the slimy, thick, foul-smelling black rain spatter in his face and into his open mouth like sweet California wine." The family blots out years of backbreaking work and hightails it to Dallas and Neiman-Marcus. As you can tell by the title, things end sadly.

It is astonishing, in view of Mr. Humphrey's predilection for disaster, to find him giving vent to a wicked comic streak. . . . [The title character of **"The Rainmaker"**] is a most unlucky confidence man who produces either dust storms or devastating tempests, and in the opening sequence is found escaping via ferryboat, tarred and feathered: "Basically he was white Leghorn, but there was an intersprinkling of barred rock, Rhode Island red, some gray goose, some guinea hen, and even some bright bantam rooster."

That a writer so diverse and so gifted should seem minor and lacking in force has less to do with his skill than with his outlook. We expect in the authors who profoundly affect us a sound, persuasive philosophy. An ornery pessimism prevents Mr. Humphrey from giving us that. But even without it, his stories are fascinating and, in contrast to much contemporary fiction, unspoiled.

Isa Kapp, "Irascible Heroes and Innocent Blockheads," in The New York Times Book Review, *August 18, 1985, p. 3.*

JANET LINDQUIST BLACK

William Humphrey is a mythopoetic artist who loves his characters even while Fate commits them to doom. In [***The Collected Stories***], personal isolation takes multitudinous forms, deriving from the endless combination of environments and human conditions. The author compassionately takes his characters between loneliness and the difficulty of involvement with others. What tugs one into these uncomfortable lives is the vivacity and immediacy of Humphrey's rendition. The voice is full of splendid imagery, graphic, tactile, poetic, and honest—plain and educating in its universal implications. Life teems with vivid detail in a wide range of settings, often in and around depression-era Texas and Oklahoma. The author penetrates layers of pride, failure, humiliation, selfishness, small-mindedness, and even the backhanded kind of love that can arise among the abject.

The first two stories in this collection, both from the forties, show little of Humphrey's later deftness. Style and plot have not yet gained elegance and subtlety. . . .

But quickly—by the fourth story in the collection—Humphrey's mastery emerges like one of his unforgettable oil wells exploding out of the red Oklahoma dust. His riveting depression tales capture the unrefined impulses of people with bent wills who have repressed their dreams. Life is basic and they live in fear of stepping out of line. But when they do, it is with American frontier fire. A woman stands in awe of the new washing machine she will forfeit all too soon, relishing the gumption with which she pledged to pay for it. Inside Jesse Neighbours, grievances accumulate like a gathering storm; but it is upon himself he brings the cyclone of ill fortune. Each fate is founded in the same epic vision of uncontrollable economic forces, of naive attempts to wrest better from life.

What makes these characters enduring is their affirmation of life in the face of tragedy that could inspire cynicism. Within a form that often seems folkloric, William Humphrey evokes a world painfully and hilariously real.

Janet Lindquist Black, in a review of "The Collected Stories," in Wilson Library Bulletin, *Vol. 60, No. 3, November, 1985, p. 71.*

KIRKUS REVIEWS

The first seven essays [in ***Open Season: Sporting Adventures***] are devoted to varieties of fishing, mostly dry-flyfishing, which Humphrey deems the aristocrat of sports. And perhaps it is, to judge from the graceful writing and zest for the chase displayed in the lead-off **"Moby Dick,"** a hilarious yet poignant account of a summer spent trying to land One-Eye, a 30-pound monster trout. The quarry finally eludes Humphrey, but insight into fishing and himself do not; self-revelations swathed in humor pervade this delightful piece, as they do the sparkling pieces that follow, most notably **"Cast and Cast Again,"** about the quixotic life of France's premier fly-fisherman, and **"The Fishermen of the Seine,"** the startling story of the men who successfully fish Paris's supposedly barren river. In mid-stream the collection changes course, churning into the more sentimental waters of Humphrey's youth spent hunting in the wild Texas landscape. . . . The standout piece here is **"Guardian Dragon,"** an exciting recreation of Dad's hand-to-hand combat with an alligator.

Humphrey's reflective essays are as much about the inner workings of those who fish and hunt as the chase itself; although their primary appeal is to those familiar with rod or gun, their wealth of insight swathed in gentle humor can delight a general readership as well. (pp. 1347-48)

A review of "Open Season: Sporting Adventures," in Kirkus Reviews, *Vol. LIV, No. 17, September 1, 1986, pp. 1347-48.*

ROBERT F. JONES

Humphrey is to minimalists of the Raymond Carver school what an old silk-wrapped, split-cane fly rod is to a shiny new graphite lunker stick. The proof lies in these 13 glowing tales gathered [in ***Open Season***]. . . .

"The Fishermen of the Seine" evokes, in a style as spare as Maupassant or Simenon, the *ponts* and *îles* of Paris at dawn, when rough-clad men hunker in the fog to hook Gallic mysteries like *goujon, brème* and *chevaine*. Two hunting pieces extracted from Humphrey's poignant 1977 memoir ***Farther Off from Heaven*** call back the hot dust and snaky swamps of his Depression-era boyhood in east Texas, along with the ghost of his hard-drinking, bar-fighting, trick-shot artist of a father.

The loveliest, most self-revealing story appears near the end. **"Birds of a Feather"** is an ode to the woodcock, that plucky, reclusive little game bird of the uplands. Preparatory to a hunt in upstate New York, Humphrey reads up on the bird. "He gets curiouser and curiouser. His brain is upside down. His ears are in front of his nose . . . Like the woodcock, I too am an odd bird; I know I am, and I would change if I could, because being odd is uncomfortable, but, no more than the woodcock can, I can't, not anymore—it's too late even to try. My brain, I often think, must surely be upside down, so out of step with the world am I."

No, not out of step. Merely another rare bird: the best damned boot-in-the-mud nature essayist—piscine, avian or human—in the business.

Robert F. Jones, "Rare Bird," in Time, *New York, Vol. 128, No. 23, December 8, 1986, p. 94.*

Joseph (Otto) Kesselring

1902-1967

American dramatist and scriptwriter.

An author of light comedy for thirty years on Broadway, Kesselring is best remembered for his madcap farce *Arsenic and Old Lace* (1941). Centering on a Brooklyn family whose members suffer from hereditary insanity, this drama relates the attempts of adopted nephew Mortimer Brewster to shield and institutionalize his two charming aunts, whose well-intended, charitable acts include poisoning lonely, homeless old men, whom they bury in their cellar. They are aided by a relative who believes he is Theodore Roosevelt burying yellow fever victims in the Panama Canal Zone. This situation is further compounded by the arrival of another nephew, Jonathan, an escaped homicidal maniac who jealously discovers that his aunts have poisoned a dozen men and seeks to outdo them by adding Mortimer to his own list of victims. The play, which ran for over three years and remains one of Broadway's longest-running productions, received largely favorable reviews during its initial performances for Kesselring's ingenious plot and effective use of black humor. Although faulted by some critics during its 1985 revival for dated humor and an overlong first act, *Arsenic and Old Lace* was generally greeted with enthusiasm by audiences.

Kesselring's earliest play, *Aggie Appleby, Maker of Men* (1933), a light domestic comedy, and his succeeding plays are considered less accomplished than *Arsenic and Old Lace*. *There's Wisdom in Women* (1935), Kesselring's first play to attract significant attention, depicts an adulterous artist and his forgiving wife. Although some critics acknowledged comic potential in *Four Twelves Are 48* (1951), this comedy about a family of American Indian women living in New York elicited largely negative response. Kesselring's last play, *Mother of That Wisdom,* was produced in 1963. Kesselring also wrote several film scripts, including that for Frank Capra's popular adaptation of *Arsenic and Old Lace*.

Courtesy of Exposition Press

GRENVILLE VERNON

[***There's Wisdom in Women***] is a play that has been written a thousand times—the story of a great musician whose wife understands and forgives his philandering. Sometimes, as in *The Concert,* a brilliant comedy is produced, but more often we get just what Mr. Kesselring gave us. Such a play must be brilliantly conceived and clothed in witty dialog, or it is nothing. Mr. Kesselring has written some amusing lines and has concocted some amusing situations, but the play as a whole, and especially the first act and three-quarters of the second act, is repetitious and forced. I will not go into its morality, for though the pianist's wife is strictly virtuous and though this virtue is at the end rewarded, the moral confusion which is so evident in the modern theatre is certainly not absent either from dialog or situation.

Grenville Vernon, in a review of "There's Wisdom in Women," in Commonweal, *Vol. XXIII, No. 3, November 15, 1935, p. 76.*

BROOKS ATKINSON

Although the characters of ***There's Wisdom in Women*** are children of the music world they fit cozily into the theatre's ageless scheme of things. Two women, one man and a faithful friend loitering hopefully around the corner, a few smashing bars of concerto music, some reasonably bawdy conversation, and there you have the pattern of a comedy by Joseph O. Kesselring. . . . You have, also, a formula for routine playwrighting that needs the breeziest lines . . . to keep it on the bright side of entertainment. . . . But is Mr. Kesselring's wisdom of women old hat or comedy con brio? The question is difficult to answer simply, but there is too much old hat in it for the comfort of this play reviewer.

Now, they are mad folk, these myrmidons of music, and Leo Nordoff, the celebrated pianist, is a terrific egotist. He has absorbed his wife and his faithful agent and he takes whatever he wants, including women. When he tries to take a dissembling little baggage who artfully refuses him, he loses his head and asks his wife for a divorce. The wisdom of women, according to Mr. Kesselring, consists in snaring their rivals. The wife manoeuvres until the trollop has submitted. After that there are a few more misunderstandings to keep the curtain up until 11, but devotion to music affects the final reconciliation. When the pianist has had what he wants he sees just how to finish that troublesome concerto. Cause and effect keep the music world rosy.

All this Mr. Kesselring has related in alternate cynicisms of the comedy of manners and purple patches of the great artistic passion; some of his lines are affably audacious and some of his situations are viable theatre.

Brooks Atkinson, in a review of "There's Wisdom in Women: A Comedy in Three Acts," in The New York Times, *October 31, 1935, p. 17.*

BROOKS ATKINSON

Let's not exaggerate. At some time there may have been a funnier murder charade than ***Arsenic and Old Lace***. . . . But the supposition is purely academic. For Joseph Kesselring has written one so funny that none of us will ever forget it. . . .

It may not seem hilarious to report that thirteen men succumb to one of the blandest murder games ever played in Brooklyn. But Mr. Kesselring has a light style, an original approach to an old subject, and he manages to dispense with all the hocus-pocus of the crime trade. Swift, dry, satirical and exciting, ***Arsenic and Old Lace*** kept the first-night audience roaring with laughter. Although there have been some other good plays recently, this is the freshest invention. It is full of chuckles even when the scene is gruesome by nature.

As a matter of fact, the Brewsters of Brooklyn are homicidal maniacs. But Aunt Abby and Aunt Martha are, on the surface, two of the nicest maiden ladies who ever baked biscuits, rushed hot soup to ailing neighbors and invited the minister to tea. Part of their charitable work consists in poisoning homeless old men who have no families to look after them. Their lunatic brother, who, for no apparent reason, imagines that he is Theodore Roosevelt, buries the bodies in the cellar with military and presidential flourishes.

If their brightest nephew who, of course, is a drama critic, had not discovered a body under the window seat, the murder game might have continued indefinitely. But he is normal, although naturally more brilliant than ordinary people and he is so upset that he can only stay one act at the play he is supposed to review that evening. The riotous amusement of ***Arsenic and Old Lace*** consists in his attempt to keep the murders a secret and, at the same time, to commit his dear aunts to an institution where their foible will be stopped.

Nothing in Mr. Kesselring's record has prepared us for the humor and ingenuity of ***Arsenic and Old Lace.*** He wrote ***There's Wisdom in Women*** in 1935 and ***Cross Town*** in 1937. But his murder drama is compact with plot and comic situation. In addition to the homey aunts it includes a sinister maniac who looks enough like Boris Karloff to be Boris Karloff. . . . The lines are bright. The story is mad and unhackneyed. Although the scene is always on the verge of the macabre and the atmosphere is horribly ominous, Mr. Kesselring does not have to stoop to clutching hands, pistol shots or lethal screams to get his effects. He has written a murder play as legitimate as farce-comedy.

Brooks Atkinson, "Joseph Kesselring's 'Arsenic and Old Lace' Turns Murder into Fantastic Comedy," in The New York Times, *January 11, 1941, p. 13.*

JOSEPH WOOD KRUTCH

Future students of the Spirit of the Age during the first half of the twentieth century will probably find no literary phenomenon more puzzling than the farce-melodrama. I can foresee them earnestly pointing out that while the comic relief of Elizabethan tragedy comes immediately to mind as a possible parallel, it is not really the same thing. Thus though Shakespeare and his contemporaries shocked classical taste they at least did not usually confuse the comic and the tragic, since the comic characters and the tragic ones were kept separate and we were supposed to stop laughing when the porter went off and Macbeth came on. During the early twentieth century, on the other hand, and at least as early as *Officer 666* and some of George M. Cohan's later works, it appears that the audience was expected to laugh when the corpse fell out of the closet and to regard the more extreme forms of violence as comic *per se*. (p. 108)

[All] previous assaults upon mixed emotions were surpassed by a gruesome extravaganza called ***Arsenic and Old Lace*** which was . . . reviewed in terms which indicated unmistakably that the majority of contemporary critics regarded it as perhaps the supreme masterpiece of the generation. The text makes strange reading. It is concerned primarily with two apparently harmless old ladies living in Brooklyn—a notoriously bourgeois section of New York City—who, because of a hereditary taint of insanity, have fallen into the habit of poisoning homeless old men who come seeking a lodging. They are assisted in disposing of the bodies by a nephew who believes that he is Colonel Theodore Roosevelt, and the action of the play begins when an adopted nephew discovers what has been going on just at the moment when the household is further recruited by the appearance of a third nephew—a homicidal sadist escaped from an asylum in the company of a mad surgeon who carries a set of instruments with which he tortures victims for the entertainment of his companion.

The action can be imagined, or rather it probably cannot. In a moment of extraordinary insight one of the characters describes the events in progress as "what you would expect if Strindberg had written *Hellzapoppin*"—the latter being a currently popular piece of clownage notorious for its irrational violence. But perhaps students of more familiar literary fields are more likely to find such scenes as that in which the mad doctor prepares to operate upon the helpless hero reminiscent of some of the outrageous scenes in the decadent tragedies of John Webster or of Cyril Tourneur; and, in fact, the final scene, which is reserved for a curtain call and which consists of a parade of the twelve corpses supposed to have been buried in the cellar before the play begins, is strikingly reminiscent of the dance of cadavers in *The Duchess of Malfi*—except of course that our later Webster expected his audience to be amused. Yet [Brooks Atkinson (see excerpt above)] . . . described the performance as "so funny none of us will ever forget it," while the *Herald Tribune* called it "the most riotously hilarious comedy of the season," and the *Sun*'s critic protested, "you wouldn't believe homicidal mania could be so funny." . . . In fact, there seems to have been no dissent unless one wishes to count as such the remarks of the reviewer for *The Nation*, . . . who admitted that he had been considerably amused but suspected that the importance of the play had been overestimated. . . . [He] added that whereas the possibility of considering murder as a fine art was as old as De Quincey, his own age was the first to regard it as frankly hilarious. (p. 109)

Joseph Wood Krutch, "Homicide as Fun," in The Nation, *New York, Vol. 152, No. 4, January 25, 1941, pp. 108-09.*

ROSAMOND GILDER

[Kesselring has written] the ultimate in the [murder] genre. ***Arsenic and Old Lace*** lives up to its beguiling title and succeeds in turning homicide into side-splitting farce. The playwright concocts his own capsule review when he has one of his characters remark something to the effect that the goings-on in the sedate Brooklyn home of the Brewster sisters might be taken from a Strindberg play written by the authors of *Hellzapoppin*. Like characters in Restoration comedy, the charming, charitable ladies who dispense hot soup and death-dealing elderberry wine with equal kindness and solicitude live in a world of their own where 'no cold moral reigns'. Or rather, they transpose their normal and highly conventional morality into the plane of their particular obsession, and live there happily, sweetly, harming no one, perhaps not even the succession of lonely and homeless old men whom they polish off with arsenic and bury, with appropriate religious ceremonies, in the cellar.

It is not until a prying nephew discovers what is going on and brings standards of everyday life to bear on the situation that complications arise. At the same time another nephew, who shares their little idiosyncrasy about murder but not their refined taste in technique, comes home, creating havoc by importing a strange corpse and injecting a Boris-Karloffian atmosphere into the amiable late-Victorian home. . . . The utter innocence and child-like secrecy with which [the old ladies] surround their macabre doings make for continuous hilarity. When their [normal] nephew catches them up to their tricks and stops them as they are about to do away with the latest recruit, their attitude is one of mild irritation; they sulk when he scolds them and find it both silly and annoying that he should get so excited about so small a matter. . . . By way of contrast, the homicidal nephew goes in for all the horrors. His pet phobia, however, is that he is constantly taken for Boris Karloff whom he strikingly resembles. . . . [The normal nephew] grapples with the problem of being the only sane member of a family whose ultimate destination is the asylum. His discovery that he is a bastard is one of the high points of an idiotic evening, only capped by the final curtain when we see the dear ladies, having learned to their annoyance that their [homicidal] nephew has as many 'gentlemen' to his credit as they have—a round dozen each—turn their eyes on the elderly head of the asylum for which they are bound. They exchange a glance which speaks volumes, approach him with kindly solicitude and pour him out one last, hospitable glass, as the curtain descends on their thirteenth victim. (pp. 185-86, 189)

Rosamond Gilder, in a review of "Arsenic and Old Lace," in Theatre Arts, *Vol. XXV, No. 3, March, 1941, pp. 185-86, 189.*

BROOKS ATKINSON

Joseph Kesselring, author of ***Four Twelves Are 48,*** . . . was lucky enough to be author of ***Arsenic and Old Lace*** a decade ago. At the time malicious people suggested that . . . [the play's producers] had a keener sense of humor than the author.

After taking a glimpse at ***Four Twelves Are 48,*** even a skeptical theatregoer might be inclined to think that the malicious gossips of a decade ago had their heads screwed on right. For Mr. Kesselring's current comedy is one of the sorriest episodes of the season. . . .

Nearly anything can be funny if it is written with skill by an original author and if it is staged with gusto and drollery, as ***Arsenic and Old Lace*** was. That is to say, Mr. Kesselring's plot might conceivably be hilarious in other hands. The "four twelves" of the title refer to three generations of Indian girls who have become unmarried mothers at the age of 12 and a fourth who innocently imagines that she is going to be.

Mark Twain and Billy Nye, working in shifts, might get something out of this that would not be both dull and distasteful. But Mr. Kesselring never has strayed very far from stupefying dullness, and his sense of taste appears to be seriously impaired. Apart from the plot, he seems to have tried to imagine a household of amiable individualists like those who made history in *You Can't Take It With You*. But it took George S. Kaufman and Moss Hart to do that job, working in shifts, relays and pairs.

No, Mr. Kesselring has no talent for fabulous skylarking, if we are to judge by ***Four Twelves Are 48.***

Brooks Atkinson, "Joseph Kesselring's 'Four Twelves Are 48' Put On under Otto Preminger's Direction," in The New York Times, *January 18, 1951, p. 30.*

WALTER KERR

[In ***Four Twelves Are 48,*** Mr. Kesselring has] conceived a comic situation which takes precisely four minutes' acting time to exploit. Toward the end of the first act, the twelve-year-old ingenue sits down with the other distaff members of the household to be informed that the woman she regards as her mother is really her great-grandmother and that the female relatives nearer her own age are in turn her grandmother and her mother. Each, it develops, has given birth illegitimately at the age of twelve, and it is now to the family interest to see that she *doesn't*. This sequence, unlikely as it seems, is mildly amusing, more or less in the manner of those old jokes about nephews being their own great-uncles. The effort of making this little mathematical joke, however, exhausts Mr. Kesselring, and he thereafter is able to supply the ingenue with nothing more than some half-hearted scenes out of *Kiss and Tell* and the rest of the company with a lot of idle profanity. I believe Mr. Kesselring once wrote plays for what is known as the amateur market, and if so he has come down with an occupational complaint. A writer for the amateur market is under injunction to avoid, as the plague, Sex and Swearing. After some years of feeling unduly bound by these limitations, and prostrate from the effort to think up new twists on the junior prom, he fondly begins to imagine that all he has to do to make his work professional is to add the missing ingredients. Whereupon he adds them in the lavish manner of a little boy who is determined to show that he has grown up, his play quickly closes, and he is right back at the junior prom. Whether or not this may be fairly said of Mr. Kesselring, ***Four Twelves Are 48*** had a strong air of the junior prom packed up with illegitimacy. . . .

Walter Kerr, in a review of "Four Twelves Are 48," in Commonweal, *Vol. LIII, February 9, 1951, p. 447.*

THEATRE ARTS

[In ***Four Twelves are 48,*** opera] star Nellie Bawke, an Osage Indian, shares her luxurious New York home with three young ladies whom the world believes to be her daughters, but who are, in fact, her daughter, granddaughter, and great-granddaughter, all three illegitimate. Nellie begat Mary, Mary begat Philippa, Philippa begat Dorothy. This obstetric chain reaction was set off by a lunatic Indian named Joe Hungry Horse who raped Nellie when she was twelve; the subsequent births also took place at the same tender age. On *her* twelfth birthday little Dorothy, who has been kept ignorant not only of her heritage but of even the most rudimentary facts of life, is kissed by a young carpenter. She believes that the kiss has made her pregnant. Enter Uncle Snake Tooth, a millionaire from the Oklahoma oil fields, come to give Nellie money for her pet charity, a Home for women in trouble. Enter Philip Dupre and his Aunt Jane, owners of a Long Island estate which Nellie wants to buy for her Home. Philip reveals himself as the father of Philippa; Aunt Jane leaves in disgust. Joe Hungry Horse enters, threatening blackmail; he is scalped (mercifully offstage) by another Bawke relative, Cousin Cutfinger. As the play careens into the home stretch, Dorothy is declared not pregnant and the other Bawke women find husbands.

Four Twelves are 48 offers several nearly comic situations, particularly those involving Uncle Snake Tooth and the socialite Dupres. Unfortunately the humor is neutralized by the tasteless treatment of bastardy, to which references occur with the maddening persistence of the Chinese water torture. It is difficult to laugh at the plight of a sheltered child who thinks herself pregnant. Had Mr. Kesselring been less infatuated with this aspect of his play he might have approached the standard set by his earlier comedy, ***Arsenic and Old Lace.***

A review of "Four Twelves Are 48," in Theatre Arts, *Vol. XXXV, No. 3, March, 1951, p. 20.*

CLIVE BARNES

In a sense, ***Arsenic and Old Lace*** was always an improbable hit and on its revival . . . , its probable and deserved success will doubtless seem as improbable as ever. . . .

[The] play itself is a delight. It actually gives life and credence to that old critical cliche, "screamingly funny."

Its concept is odd, because it is a murder mystery with no mystery—we know from the outset that these two sweet old ladies in lace and Brooklyn are bent on putting lonely old gentlemen out of their misery with merciful doses of lethal elderberry wine—and the murders themselves are hilarious rather than chilling.

Broadway legend has it that the author, a former music teacher and actor, Joseph Kesselring, originally wrote this as a straightforward melodrama, *The Bodies in Our Cellar*.

However the producers, Howard Lindsay and Russell Crouse, it has been said, came to the cellar's rescue, and helped rewrite the present script, which—whether the legend is true or not—became Kesselring's solitary Broadway hit.

What is lovely about the play is its matter-of-fact tone. It makes murder into a pleasant, genteel fantasy, with its nutty Brewster sisters amiably competing for laughs with their equally nutty nephews.

One, Teddy, imagines he is Teddy Roosevelt forever charging San Juan Hill, and the other, Jonathan, a less refined killer than his aunts, is a pathological brute who has had his face mistakenly turned into Boris Karloff's by his sidekick, Dr. Einstein, an uncertified plastic surgeon and maniac.

The only touch of sanity—as so often on Broadway—is brought by a beleaguered and blase drama critic—another nephew, Mortimer, who upon discovering his aunts' homicidal peccadillos, tries valiantly to cover them up.

It is the seeming normality of madness added to the effortless confusion of sanity which gives the play its special off-center charm. But the work is also extremely well-constructed; the disclosures are delivered express, and the farcical doors open on time.

The characterizations—especially the dear old ladies addicted to their mercy slayings—are pure delight, and the play is bountifully supplied with one-liners that are well enough aimed to penetrate beyond their one line. . . .

Arsenic and Old Lace is not a potion for over-sophisticated palates—it never has been—but for audiences wanting a splendid, uncomplicated belly-laugh, this is just the ticket.

Clive Barnes, "'Arsenic': Laugh 'til You Die," in New York Post, *June 27, 1986. Reprinted in* New York Theatre Critics' Reviews, *Vol. XXXXVII, No. 9, Week of July 7, 1986, p. 261.*

FRANK RICH

Those who haven't recently encountered ***Arsenic and Old Lace*** . . . may be surprised to discover that its hero is a drama critic for a New York newspaper. His name is Mortimer, he's the nephew of the murderous Brewster sisters, and he is, of course, the most likable character on stage. . . . [Early in the play he] can be heard muttering about the "stinker" he has to cover at the theater that night. But Mortimer is such a nice guy that he's willing to revise his judgments according to his mood. . . .

Times have certainly changed. In 1986, it might take a visit to an orgy to make Mortimer smile benignly on ***Arsenic and Old Lace***—and even then, he'd be within his rights to insist that the orgy run as long as the play's first act, which seems to go on for about three weeks. The years haven't been kind to Mr. Kesselring's farce, which once provided escapist entertainment for theatergoers who had a real reason to seek escape (World War II) and who had not yet been presented with television, the invention that now permits audiences to watch situation comedies in the privacy of their own homes. Seeing the play now . . . is to understand why high schools have been more inclined than Broadway managements to revive it over the past four decades.

To be sure, Mr. Kesselring had a good idea in ***Arsenic.*** He imagined that two pious spinster sisters in Brooklyn . . . would be models of propriety in every way except one—they insisted on murdering (for mercy's sake) the lonely old men who came to their Victorian mansion for lodging. The trouble is that the author, having established this once-daring premise early on, is left with no energy or ideas for developing it. ***Arsenic*** quickly devolves into a flat imitation of the eccentric-household comedies of Kaufman and Hart. The sisters' ghoulish hobby is regularly upstaged by Mortimer's dreary romantic travails and by the machinations of his two nutty brothers, one a vicious insane-asylum escapee. . . . Although there's a rudimentary farcical structure . . . the plot takes forever to crank up and is less than ingeniously resolved. "Things are going to start popping around here any minute!" says Mortimer once the machinery finally starts to click—but by then it's already 10:15, and "any minute" is still almost a quarter-hour away.

About all that remains funny in the script are the gags about critics and the theater. . . . There are cheering references to Nora Bayes, Brooks Atkinson, *Hellzapoppin* and, in the evening's one sure-fire sight gag, Judith Anderson. One must also admire the exchange in which Mortimer's fiancée demands that he "be fair" to the plays he reviews. With just the correct note of righteous indignation, . . . [he] snaps back, "Are these plays fair to *me*?"

It could be argued, perhaps, that this staging is not entirely fair to Mr. Kesselring. . . . While we wait in Act I for the Brewsters' latest corpse to be let out of the bag (or window seat), there are gaping pauses—they might as well be accompanied by winks—around any line that all too ironically hints of the forthcoming revelation of the sisters' dirty secret. Later, the corpse-switching slapstick takes roughly 10 times as long as the equivalent business in *Loot* (in which Joe Orton, a quarter-century later, took Kesselring's repressed themes and gave them a full and nasty airing).

Frank Rich, "'Arsenic and Old Lace' Revival," in The New York Times, *June 27, 1986, p. C3.*

ALLAN WALLACH

For a comedy about killing innocent people and disposing of their bodies, ***Arsenic and Old Lace*** has been remarkably popular. . . .

Only now, though, is Broadway getting its first taste of ***Arsenic*** since the four-year run of the original 1941 production. The audience at the critics' preview I attended laughed as though all the carrying on about two innocently murderous old ladies were fresh out of the word processor. But to me this ***Arsenic*** seems laced with lemonade.

It may just be that familiarity breeds ennui; my memories of the movie and earlier productions kept getting in the way of the laughs. This time around, the fun seems a little . . . well, stiff. . . .

The production arrives on the heels of another revival of a comedy in which a body keeps getting switched from one hiding place to another—Joe Orton's *Loot*. A big difference is that Orton, in 1966, used the grisly framework to make malicious comments about society, while Kesselring was just fooling around. And Orton's dialogue is devastatingly funny; Kesselring relied chiefly on the situation. (p. 258)

The play's original producers, playwrights Howard Lindsay and Russel Crouse, did some extensive rewriting, including some knowing (and previously excised) lines about Mortimer's occupation as drama critic. At one point he observes that the dark doings in his aunts' house are "what you'd expect if Strindberg had written *Hellzapoppin*." That could serve as his review of ***Arsenic,*** but I think Strindberg would have given it more bite. (p. 259)

Allan Wallach, "Revival of 'Arsenic' on Broadway," in Newsday, *June 27, 1986. Reprinted in* New York Theatre Critics' Reviews, *Vol. XXXXVII, No. 9, Week of July 7, 1986, pp. 258-59.*

Ursula K(roeber) Le Guin

1929-

American novelist, short story writer, poet, author of children's books, editor, and scriptwriter.

A highly respected award-winning author of fantasy and science fiction, Le Guin is praised for combining traditional literary techniques with science fiction elements and for her speculations on alternative societies and philosophies. Le Guin writes from a subjective humanist perspective, usually avoiding such technical sciences as physics and chemistry in favor of cultural anthropology, political science, and psychology. Her fiction makes use of psychic phenomena, including telepathy, clairvoyance, and precognition, and commonly incorporates the philosophies of Taoism and Zen, resulting in themes of reciprocity, unity, and holism. By presenting complex, often paradoxical symbols, images, and allusions, Le Guin stresses the need for individuals and societies to balance such dualities as order with chaos and harmony with rebellion to achieve wholeness.

Le Guin's first novel, *Rocannon's World* (1966), is the first in her series of works commonly referred to as the Hainish Cycle. These novels and short stories depict the descendants of the first race of humanity, which arose on the planet Hain and colonized other planets until war isolated the various settlements. The Hainish Cycle spans 2,500 years, in the course of which most of the colonies have forgotten their common origin and humanity. *Rocannon's World* is a conventional "space opera" featuring Le Guin's typical hero, whose mythic quest to discover his purpose and identity results in the integration of the conflicting parts of his personality and his discovery of "mindspeech," or telepathy. An ethnologist specializing in the study of alien cultures, Rocannon must warn his home planet of the location of a dangerous anarchist military base. Mindspeech is in common use in *Planet of Exile* (1966), in which two equally hostile human cultures must cooperate in mutual defense against barbarian invaders. Major themes in this novel include the importance of technological responsibility, the ill effects of xenophobia, and the benefits of establishing ties which transcend racial and cultural barriers. *City of Illusions* (1967) details an amnesiac's quest to unite his past and present selves in order to recognize the Shing, a conqueror race of aliens who dominate humanity through their unprecedented ability to "mindlie."

The Left Hand of Darkness (1969), for which Le Guin received Hugo and Nebula Awards, is widely considered among her best novels. In this work, which continues the Hainish Cycle, an envoy attempts to persuade members of an alien world to join a federation of allied planets known as the Ekumen of Known Worlds. Interwoven with the protagonist's narrative are ethnological reports, accounts of native legends and myths, descriptions of religious ceremonies, and entries from the diaries of the envoy's closest ally. *The Left Hand of Darkness* is particularly noted for its creation of an androgynous alien culture, through which Le Guin explores the ramifications of a society in which individual identities and social status are divorced from stereotypes of gender. Through this approach, Le Guin emphasizes a favorite theme: the idea that unity is achieved through the vital interaction and tension of such opposites as likeness and unlikeness, native and alien, and male and female. In *The Dispossessed: An Ambiguous Utopia* (1974), another highly regarded novel in the Hainish Cycle, Le Guin details the visit of an inhabitant from an anarchist moon colony to its mother planet. A novel of political analysis, this Hugo and Nebula Award-winning work depicts two planets as polar opposites: Anarres, a barely habitable desert where people share simple joys by living according to a code of personal responsibility; and Urras, a luxurious, capitalistic planet where property arrangements and class distinctions are less than ideal. *The Dispossessed* won praise for its complex characterizations and well-integrated social and political ideas.

Le Guin is also the creator of the Earthsea trilogy, a series based on magic which appeals to both adult and young adult readers in the manner of J. R. R. Tolkien's *The Lord of the Rings. A Wizard of Earthsea* (1968) depicts the adolescence of a future magus under the tutelage of wizards and his Jungian struggle with the evil within him. *The Tombs of Atuan* (1971) is a love story relating the coming of age of high priestess Arha, who is rescued from the evil of the underworld by the protagonist of *A Wizard of Earthsea. The Farthest Shore* (1972), for which Le Guin received a National Book Award for children's literature, is about the acceptance of mortality, or what Le Guin called "a coming of age again, but in a larger context." Critics praised the trilogy for its evocation of a fantasy world and for its development of themes relating to commonplace human conflicts.

Several of Le Guin's other works deal with political ideology. *The Lathe of Heaven* (1971) is a satirical novel about a man who can alter the physical world through his dreams and a psychiatrist who manipulates this power for his own benefit. This novel emphasizes the Taoist ideal of inaction and highlights weaknesses of Western civilization by exaggerating such modern-day problems as pollution, overpopulation, and bureaucracy. In the story "The Ones Who Walk Away from Omelas," for which Le Guin received a Hugo Award in 1974, a group of revolutionaries protest the prosperity of their city because it is dependent upon the suffering of a child. Le Guin also received a Nebula Award in 1974 for "The Day before the Revolution," a story which details events preceding the revolution which caused the break between Urras and Anarres in *The Dispossessed*. Le Guin won another Hugo Award for *The Word for World Is Forest* (1972), a dialectical novella about colonization and imperialism set in the Hainish universe which some critics interpreted as a protest of the Vietnam War. *The Eye of the Heron* (1978) depicts a group of pacifistic peasants defying a brutal network of "Bosses," who seek to establish themselves as feudal lords.

Always Coming Home (1985) is a work which defies categorization. Presented as an archaeological report, the text is accompanied by drawings, notes, maps, a glossary, and a music cassette. Through the stories, novellas, legends, plays, and poems of characters and fictional personages, the book loosely depicts a tribal society called the Kesh, who live a native American existence in a post-catastrophic far West. Although some critics noted occasional didacticism and contrivance in the work, many were impressed by Le Guin's ambition, broad imagination, and intelligence. Carol McGuirk commented: "By turns utopian and realistic, didactic and descriptive, sheer 'message' and sheer 'story,' this new novel marks a fresh and welcome recommitment by Le Guin to her two most remarkable gifts: world-building and character-study."

In addition to her novels, Le Guin has written stories throughout her career which have appeared in numerous science fiction and literary publications. Many of these stories are collected in *The Wind's Twelve Quarters* (1975), *Orsinian Tales* (1976), and *The Compass Rose* (1982). Le Guin has also written two volumes of poetry, *Wild Angels* (1975) and *Hard Words and Other Poems* (1981). Critical essays, lectures, reviews, and introductions by Le Guin are collected in *The Language of the Night: Essays on Fantasy and Science Fiction* (1979). Le Guin has also edited several science fiction anthologies and has written a children's book, *Leese Webster* (1979).

(See also *CLC,* Vols. 8, 13, 22; *Children's Literature Review,* Vol. 3; *Contemporary Authors,* Vols. 21-24, rev. ed.; *Contemporary Authors New Revision Series,* Vol. 9; *Something about the Author,* Vol. 4; and *Dictionary of Literary Biography,* Vols. 8, 52.)

SARAH HAYES

[***A Very Long Way from Anywhere Else*** (published in the United States as ***Very Far Away from Anywhere Else***)] is a curiosity. [The novel] has all the trappings of a teenage magazine story. Divided into tantalizing chunks ideal for serialization, its plot is a familiar one: boy meets girl on bus; boy and girl are smitten; sex rears its ugly head (not a little reluctantly it must be admitted); girl retreats; boy smashes car up; boy observes girl from afar; reconciliation; girl departs for college. . . .

Mrs Le Guin has done a brave thing: not only has she confronted the stereotype and transmogrified it; she has also made a firm stand for intellectual elitism. Her lovers are highly precocious misfits, not at all fashionable creatures these days: Natalie intends to be a composer and Owen, against his mother's quiet but indomitable will, has his sights set on MIT and research psychology. Both boy and girl have had to find ways of coping with their gifts and their oddity. Natalie has withdrawn from her peer group into a too adult life of music and teaching: the world is earnest and ambition is all. Owen has established an unsatisfactory jokey relationship with two other boys that exists only on a funny-voice level. With Natalie he can talk unselfconsciously about ideas and about Thorn, the Gondal-type country he escapes to; and he can delight her with his puns and acts.

These are recognizable teenagers; Owen's voice, as he describes his reactions and his fluctuating emotions, is a familiar and compelling one. But this is, nevertheless, a novella. A long short story perhaps: whatever the description, the words have a slighting tone, and this is a slight work. Beautifully and intelligently written with wit and sensitivity, it still remains a very small slice of life.

Sarah Hayes, "Untypical Teenagers," in The Times Literary Supplement, *No. 3890, October 1, 1976, p. 1238.*

NAOMI LEWIS

Ursula Le Guin has, improbably, stepped out of Earthsea, one of the great fantasy regions of the century, into this no-man's-land of the modern teenager. In ***A Very Long Way from Anywhere Else,*** the American boy and girl—he's 17, she's a year older—are not in the average stream, though; she because she is a dedicated musician, he because, however much he tries to conform to the commonplace, the rest of the class or gang see through him straightaway. And who else would *hate* the gift of a car from his loving father, preferring to walk a couple of miles to school? But Owen and Natalie are in tune, and the friendship reaches a height, then goes awry on the age-old grounds, the when, the why, the how. One of Browning's themes, when you think of it. But read to the hopeful end. You can be sure with Le Guin, of point and style, and a rightness in the plot. (p. 623)

Naomi Lewis, "No More Nannies," in The Listener, *Vol. 96, No. 2483, November 11, 1976, pp. 623-24.*

MARY KINZIE

The problem with writing [poetry] in form is that when you risk little, or fail, everyone knows. Furthermore, the sense of disappointment is greater when a formal poem is flat than when a free-verse poem is flat, because there is so much native music to hand, waiting to be embodied in the accentual-syllabic line. Le Guin has a number of formal poems [in ***Hard Words and Other Poems***] that are still amateur work, either because she is not *thinking* about her subject but merely toying with its fringe (**"Danae"**), or because the rhymes and meters deflect her attention from the idea or mood she started out to express (**"The Mind Is Still"**). The following is a poem that, treating *word* as dense matter, fails for both reasons, formal seduction away from content, and a prior refusal to consider the heart of the idea.

"The Marrow"

There was a word inside a stone.
I tried to pry it clear,
mallet and chisel, pick and gad,
until the stone was dropping blood,
but still I could not hear
the word the stone had said.

I threw it down beside the road
among a thousand stones
and as I turned away it cried
the word aloud within my ear,
and the marrow of my bones
heard, and replied.

The Orphic delirium of the stones and the speaker's justified annoyance fall just short of making a coherent composition: we cannot guess what the word could have been. What this poem lacks and a poem like George Herbert's "The Collar" embodies is a continuous sense of what the speaker's desires and aggravations entail, thus what the reunion might mean. Herbert's poem begins and ends in the same relationship. Not so **"The Marrow,"** which, for all its stone-cry and -blood, may be less a Christian exercise than another surrealist allegory for making (or being) poetry: "the marrow of the bones / heard, and replied." Odd, that if words and poems were at issue, they should not only have no content, but be bestowed on the first comer to achieve indifference to them.

Le Guin's light air **"Vita Amicae"** has a stunning first stanza whose momentum is lost in the second. . . . It is not formal constraint that mars the poem, but neglect of idea. What begins as tribute to a friend's gravity, endurance, and shock wave of grace, ends in irrelevant riddle. If Le Guin has one persistent problem, it is that she does not know how to prevent her poems from being deflected in the wrong places. Her three long descriptive poems about walking in Cornwall are shapeless. They share with her "hard word" poems a spondaic tendency. . . . I hear in [**"Chun"**] (although the lineation is deceptive) some of the same bright rhythms, syncopated by rhyme, that Julia Randall uses so well. . . . But the remainder of Le Guin's Cornwall poem is poor company; she does not yet know how to sustain her insight that these cromlechs once framed devotional rites. When she returns to the present, nothing is readable, and her lines, rhythms, and level of attentiveness betray that loss of literacy. The poet grows fulsome in describing what is left after heather, earth, and bones have been blown away:

Sun's gold on the old stones.
Lichen is lovely, grey-green, violet, gold.
Clouds drift and pile up, grey, grey-blue, and white.
They pass on southward on the wind
over the high place, over the old place,
the rock-wall rings, the grave, the shallow well.

All very pretty, but tiresome and diffuse. Are we supposed to feel regret? pleasure in the moment? the word to which the marrow replies? The poet has to keep tacking on further lines and verse paragraphs to get herself out of the poem, and even then we are not sure just how the elegiac mood is being modified. . . . (pp. 18-19)

Hard Words contains one superior free-verse poem, **"Landscape, Figure, Cavern,"** and a tiny suite of Arthurian fantasies called **"The Well of Baln,"** three poems that come nearest to feeling to the Ursula Le Guin who writes fiction. These, together with [a] passage from the Cornwall poem [**"Chun"**] and the handful of short lyrics quoted and cited above, sum to nine pages of moderately graceful writing. I am disappointed that a writer who can produce these nine pages cannot be more judicious about selecting, or more patient about accumulating, material for a book. (p. 19)

Mary Kinzie, "A Generation of Silver," in The American Poetry Review, *Vol. 10, No. 4, July-August, 1981, pp. 13-20.*

BARBARA J. BUCKNALL

"The Diary of the Rose" is only one of several short stories that Le Guin published between 1974 and 1978. Three stories that appeared before ***The Dispossessed*** are **"The Author of the Acacia Seeds and Other Extracts from the *Journal of the Association of Therolinguistics*,"** **"Intracom,"** and **"Schrödinger's Cat"** (all 1974). They are comic and highly entertaining. The first speculates about the possibility of studying the art forms of animals and plants. The second describes through the metaphor of the crew of a spaceship the thoughts of a young woman who has just realized she is pregnant. And the third is a takeoff on a famous "thought experiment" by the physicist Erwin Schrödinger. Suppose a cat is put in a box with a gun attached to the inside of the box. Depending on the behavior of a photon emitted inside the box, the gun may shoot the cat or it may not. Le Guin turns this demonstration of uncertainty into a lively narrative, full of unexpected twists.

The short stories she has written since ***The Dispossessed*** are on the whole much less exuberant. **"Mazes"** (1975), a horrifying little story, describes the last living moments of an alien whose culture attaches great importance to performing dances in mazes of increasing complexity. A human scientist is testing its intelligence by putting it through mazes, without in the least understanding what the alien is doing in them. He is also starving it to death by feeding it the wrong kind of food. **"SQ"** (1978), a grimly humorous story, tells how a psychologist with great political influence invents a test to measure levels of sanity and forces everyone in the world to take the test. More and more people are committed to mental hospitals as a result, including the psychologist himself. His secretary, who is imperturbably sane, is left to run the world, since the psychologist is no longer capable of doing it.

"SQ" is reminiscent of ***The Lathe of Heaven,*** while **"The Eye Altering"** (1976), which describes the adjustment of a colonist's vision to a new world, is reminiscent of the idea of genetic adaptation in ***Planet of Exile.*** **"No Use to Talk to Me"** (1976) depicts a conversation in a space ship that is about to crash, while **"Gwilan's Harp"** tells the story of a woman's life, from famous musician to wife and mother to widow. Both these stories depend much more on emotional tone than invention.

Two other stories represent a mingling of fantasy and realism. **"The First Report of the Shipwrecked Foreigner to the Kadanh of Derb"** (1978) is a deeply personal description of Venice in terms that make it seem at first like a fantasy. It is not unlike the descriptions of imaginary cities in Italo Calvino's *Le Città invisibili*. . . . In contrast, a very sad short story, ***The Water Is Wide*** (1976), which was published as an entire book, starts realistically and then turns into complete fantasy. . . .

The Water Is Wide seems to mark a new direction in Le Guin's writing, continuing the trend begun in ***The New Atlantis***. . . . (pp. 129-30)

Another new departure has been in the direction of complete realism, with the only fantasy element being the private fantasies of the characters. This is the case with ***Very Far Away from Anywhere Else. The Eye of the Heron,*** in contrast, continues the tradition of ***The Dispossessed*** in being a science-fiction story with a political subject, although it is much slighter and also less successful than ***The Dispossessed.*** (pp. 130-31)

Wild Angels is a short collection of lyrical poems that expresses the author's feelings with dignity and reserve. Between the expression and the reserve there is a conflict that is resolved by the use of symbolic landscapes, expressing feelings in visual terms, as in the works of W. H. Auden and Rainer Maria Rilke. But Le Guin is not a great poet, as she would readily admit, and the symbolic landscapes she likes to use become more effective when they are presented as real landscapes with people in them, in her more poetic prose works, such as the Earthsea trilogy and ***The Left Hand of Darkness.*** When she is writing about invented characters, she is much more powerful than when she is writing about herself. This seems to be because the lyrical passages in her novels and stories are set in a pattern of allusions that link up with each other to create a great richness of texture. This texture is lacking in the poems, which are not strong enough to carry the same kind of weight by themselves.

Orsinian Tales and ***Malafrena*** concern Orsinia, which does not exist in the real world, but which is described as if it were real, with references to real places, such as Prague, and real historical personages, institutions, and events, such as Napoleon, Metternich, and Hitler, the Austro-Hungarian Empire, and the 1956 Hungarian uprising. Some reviewers have supposed that Orsinia is actually a real country, such as Hungary or Romania, in disguise, but in fact it cannot be identified as any particular Central European country.

For those who have acquired a taste for the marvelous and want all Le Guin's books to satisfy it, there is something a little thin about Orsinia, a little lacking in richness and density. However, this is more the case with ***Orsinian Tales*** than with ***Malafrena,*** which reads like an historical romance. ***Orsinian Tales,*** moving about in time, covers the history of Orsinia from 1150 to 1960. ***Malafrena*** is about Europe between 1820 and 1830, when reactionary governments tried to impose order and young liberals dreamed of revolution. In both books, as in so many of Le Guin's works, love, friendship, integrity and fidelity play an important role.

Very Far Away from Anywhere Else is a very short book, but a moving one. It is written for young people, about young people, and concerns the attempt of a young man of seventeen and a young woman of eighteen to achieve excellence in their chosen fields, science and music, and integrity and respect in their relationship with each other. To do this, they have to resist pressure from society, which would like them to abandon excellence, for the sake of normality, and spoil their beautiful friendship for the sake of premature sex.

Because of their very intelligence and talent and the ways in which they plan to use that intelligence and talent, they are not yet ready for a full sexual relationship. But they share each other's thoughts and feelings. The young man, Owen Griffiths, tells his friend, Natalie Field, about an imaginary country he has invented, called Thorn, where he can be free and himself. She sympathizes with this fantasy and writes some music for Thorn. She also gets him interested in the Brontës, and he finds that they too had imaginary countries. So his private fantasy, which he had come to feel too old for, is accepted by his dearest friend instead of being dismissed as immature. This is the only fantasy element in ***Very Far Away from Anywhere Else,*** which is a wise, tender, and loving book, written with understanding and concern. (pp. 131-32)

The Eye of the Heron (1978) is a science-fiction novel that, like so many of Le Guin's works, uses shifting points of view. It tells the story of Luz Marina Falco Cooper, the daughter of Boss Luis Falco, who lives in Victoria City, on the planet Victoria, some time in the future. Luz has been brought up to recognize the power of men and expect an arranged marriage and motherhood. But she is much stronger than she thinks she is, and, from the first time we see her, she defies her father, in small ways at first and then in open rebellion. Through Luz, Le Guin continues to explore the feminist point of view, which she had started to examine in ***The Left Hand of Darkness*** and taken farther in ***The Dispossessed.***

But, as in ***The Dispossessed,*** the theme of feminism is secondary to that of politics. Victoria is largely unexplored, and there are only two settlements on it, Victoria City and the town of Shantih (which means "peace" in Hindi and Sanskrit). Victoria City was founded a hundred years previously by criminals exiled from South America, although the citizens prefer to say that they are descended from men who were too strong and brave to be tolerated by the womanish people of Earth. The men of Victoria City have a cult of violence and domination, and despise the people of Shantih, which they call Shanty-Town. For them, the farmers of Shantih are peasants, made to serve them by producing the food they need.

The people of Shantih arrived on Victoria fifty-five years previously, having been exiled from Earth for being demonstrators for peace. They cherish the memory of the Long March that their parents had led, starting out in Moscow and walking across Europe to Lisbon, where they had taken ship to North America. There, in the north, they had been promised land to build a new community. Two thousand people were expected in Montreal, but so many people joined the Long March, in protest against war, that ten thousand arrived. There was not enough land for all of them, and they were put in prison camps. Finally, two thousand of them were sent to Victoria.

The people of Shantih have kept the memory of the techniques of nonviolent resistance worked out by Mahatma Gandhi and Martin Luther King. So when a difference of opinion arises between them and the Bosses of Victoria City, they know exactly what to do. First they have to try negotiation by existing means and institutions. Then they have to go on to noncooperation. After that, they have to issue an ultimatum, and if the ultimatum is not accepted, they have to move on to civil disobedience. But at no point must they use violence.

Since their arrival on Victoria, the people of Shantih have not had occasion to use these techniques. But by the time of this story, there are too many people in Shantih and Victoria City for the farmers to feed, and the people of Shantih want to start a new settlement in the north. But the Bosses do not want to let them go. Instead, the Bosses plan to establish large estates, with the Shantih people working on them and the Bosses living like little kings.

The people of Shantih, led by an older woman, Vera Adelson, and a young man, Lev Shults, organize resistance to the Bosses' plans, using the techniques of nonviolence. The Bosses, led by Luis Falco, plan to use violence against them in order to outrage them into using violence back, so that they can punish them as rebels by using them on the new estates. Luis Falco is assisted in this plan by Herman Macmilan, the young man whom he sees as his prospective son-in-law, and Herman Macmilan gets a little brigade together.

But Luz discovers the plan and goes off to warn Lev Shults, with whom, without realizing it, she is in love. Once in Shantih, she decides to stay. Luis Falco is in despair at losing her, and when a confrontation takes place between the people of Shantih and Herman Macmilan's soldiers, and Herman Macmilan starts shooting, Luis Falco kills him. But Lev is also dead, killed by Herman Macmilan, and Luz has lost her love. However, she still refuses to go back to her father; and, at her instigation, groups of people leave Shantih in secret and set out to found new settlements. Out in the wilderness they find a "beginning place."

This is a sad story, for the nonviolent techniques of the people of peace are shown to be inadequate to resist effectively the violent techniques of the Bosses. After Lev's death, there had been a physical struggle between the people of Shantih and Herman Macmilan's brigade, and the principles of nonviolence were abandoned. After that, there was nothing to do but go back to negotiation and accept compromise, or else run away. Running away is Luz's solution, and it is accepted by many of the people of Shantih. But it is a very discouraging solution for someone who has taken part in the peace movement, and ***The Eye of the Heron*** is far less optimistic than ***The Dispossessed.***

There is another rather disconcerting aspect to ***The Eye of the Heron,*** for those who are accustomed to the way strange fauna and flora blend in with familiar species in the places Le Guin invents. The fauna and flora of Victoria are very different from those we know on Earth, and there is no way in which the animals can be tamed. The people of Victoria have given familiar names, such as "heron" and "coney," to the animals, but the animals called by these names have very little in common with real herons or rabbits.

The Eye of the Heron owes its title to a passage in which Lev is returning the gaze of a "heron." . . . That gaze puts the human being in his place and points out how ephemeral and ineffective his activity must be. Lev dies young and to no avail. The animal, which is concerned with being, not doing, outlives him. And Luz has to go on without Lev, adding one exile to another, with no hope except that of beginning again.

There is something about ***The Eye of the Heron*** that is reminiscent of ***Planet of Exile.*** Like Rolery, Luz leaves her home and family for a despised stranger. And although she is more aggressive than Rolery and Lev is more idealistic than Jakob Agat, the choices Luz has to make, like Rolery's, are both limited and important. Like Rolery, Luz fights no war. She does not even fight the war of nonviolence, although she brings help, but has to stand by while the man she loves risks his life and dies. And if Jakob Agat had died and the Gaal had conquered, Rolery too might well have run away. It may even be a Taoist solution, since the early Taoists frequently lived in obscurity or even committed suicide to escape being obliged to take office, which they considered a disaster. (pp. 142-45)

Unlike ***The Eye of the Heron, The Beginning Place*** is set in the present, in an American town that is depressing in its ugliness and artificiality. The first chapter tells how Hugh Rogers, a young checker in a supermarket, finds a marvelous place in the woods, a place where it is always twilight and time runs much more slowly than it does outside. . . . He explores the woods, rejoicing in the absence of people and cars and litter. But then he comes across a sign that reads, "Keep Out—No Trespassing." It has been put there by Irene, the girl we meet in the second chapter. She has been going to the twilight land for years, and resents anyone else coming to what she calls "the beginning place"—the place on the very outskirts of the enchanted land, where Hugh Rogers had been content to stay. From then on, the story is told from their alternating points of view, for eight chapters. The ninth chapter shows Hugh and Irena, as she is called by those who love her, united and back in the United States. This chapter is told from both points of view. (pp. 145-46)

[Told] that there is danger menacing the twilight land, . . . Hugh and Irena go forth to face it, with a sword presented to them by the Lord of the Manor. The danger takes the shape of a thoroughly disgusting kind of dragon, white, ice-cold, and sobbing in hunger and pain, quite different from the fiery, wise, and beautiful dragons of Earthsea. When Hugh and Irena first see it, the shock is too much for them, and they run away and hide. But then they go on to the dragon's cave, where Irena challenges it to come out, and Hugh kills it. However, Hugh does not escape uninjured. The dragon falls on him in its death throes, breaking one of his ribs and cracking another. . . . [Upon Hugh and Irena's return to the United States], Hugh's mother says that she does not want him back, and the two young people prepare to share an apartment. (pp. 146-47)

But the union in which they end was not there at the beginning. It takes them some time to trust and love one another to the point where Hugh can say that they are married, even though no official ceremony has been performed. (p. 147)

This account invites a psychological interpretation. One possible interpretation might go as follows. Two adolescents are having a very difficult time with their families. They are held down and prevented from branching out by their mothers' need for them. To make up for this, they live more and more in a world of fantasy. This has its dangers. . . . But the two young people are basically healthy and sane, and so their fantasy is basically healthy, too. (pp. 147-48)

When the dragon appears, it is like the mother, calling out for pity and ready to devour her children in the name of that pity. Hugh takes the sword and kills the dragon. And, in the real world, it is the fact that Hugh breaks with his mother that gives the two young people their freedom. (p. 148)

This is only one interpretation, and other interpretations are possible. For instance, John Updike, who reads ***The Beginning Place*** in a much more sexual way [see *CLC,* Vol. 22], sees the dragon as representing "our sorry carnality," which menaces Hugh and Irena in their passage from solitary masturbation to a true sexual encounter. But what makes any interpretation of this novel very difficult is that Le Guin herself has said, in a personal letter, that she has "very little idea what it 'means.'"

The idea that Le Guin did not write this novel with a definite message in mind is disconcerting, for her faithful readers are used to her presenting a message or pointing a moral in most of what she writes. But it seems that there is no message in ***The Beginning Place*** except the familiar one of the importance of love. It is true that this does come through clearly, but in much of this novel Le Guin is playing with the contrast between the fantasy world and the real world for the sheer joy of it.

The Beginning Place is rather reminiscent of magic realism. That is a genre in which realism and fantasy are interwoven, so that the real world becomes magical. This fantastic version of reality is cultivated for its own sake, without any didacticism. It is widely used in South America, particularly by Jorge Luis Borges, a quotation from whose poem ''Heráclito'' is included as an epigraph to ***The Beginning Place.*** The poem, which is strange and beautiful, is about the river of time, with night and day, waking and dreaming. It seems that ***The Beginning Place*** is also about waking and dreaming, as well as about love and the lack of it. But the dreams are intended to speak directly to the unconscious of the reader, as dreams do.

In this way, this novel marks a new departure. The references to the ''beginning place'' that we have noticed in the last three works discussed indicate that Le Guin has been trying to reach beyond the point she has previously reached and begin again. This makes waiting for her next novel even more interesting than it usually is, and also makes any conclusion only temporary—as is always the case with a living writer. But it is noticeable that, however much Le Guin may strike out on new paths, nothing can make her abandon her affirmation of the importance of love or her longing for a place where things are fair and seemly, where nature is not spoiled. (pp. 148-49)

Barbara J. Bucknall, in her Ursula K. Le Guin, *Frederick Ungar Publishing Co., 1981, 175 p.*

J. D. McCLATCHY

[Is ***Hard Words and Other Poems***] meant to capitalize on Mrs. Le Guin's popularity as a science fiction writer? She is no poet. Her phrase, ''the action of writing / short lines,'' describes the extent of her technique: chopped-up prose. Banalities (''I am not I / but eye'') and jingles (''As I went over Simple Hill / I saw a woman dancing: / Give it away, away, away, / Give it away to the west wind.'') and other embarrassments proliferate. This collection includes a diaristic group about a trip through Cornwall, sketches of Hindu gods, a few parables (one begins ''I am nobleman of vast estate . . .''), bread-and-butter verses to friends, some rueful thoughts about aging. It may be a book for Le Guin's fans, but it is not for the serious reader of poetry.

J. D. McClatchy, in a review of ''Hard Words,'' in Poetry, *Vol. CXL, No. 6, September, 1982, p. 348.*

CAROLYN WENDELL

Le Guin's third volume of short stories [***The Compass Rose***] shows her range as a writer. The twenty stories, (18 previously published, two originals), are widely varied enough that each reader will find something to like. The title suggests the extremes contained. And to the basic four directions, Le Guin has added **''Nadir''** and **''Zenith.''** . . . (p. 37)

Some stories are satiric: **''The Author of the Acacia Seeds,'' ''Some Approaches to the Problem of the Shortage of Time,''** and **''Schrodinger's Cat''** poke fun at scholarly pomposity. **''Intracom''** takes dramatic form and mainly tackles clichés of the spaceship crew, particularly the *Enterprise*'s. While it is awfully silly, my heart does warm to a female Captain who complains that every time she's on the verge of something great, she has to ''turn around and decide whether it's to be macaroni and cheese or rice pilaf. Why can't somebody else do the cooking?'' The answer, of course, is that she's the only one who knows how. . . .

Other stories are fantasy: **''The White Donkey,'' ''Gwilan's Harp,''** and **''The Wife's Story''** (new in this volume), the lament of a wolf whose mate has been horribly transformed into a man intent on the death of her and their children.

Several stories show survivors coping with the deaths of people they love (Le Guin's own extraordinary and much-loved mother died in 1979). My favorite is **''Malheur County,''** in which a widowed mother-in-law, a strong-willed woman who is well aware of her own losses, gives support and a firm push to her son-in-law who has become too dependent on her after the death of his wife. Harriet Avanti has enough verve to her to be a character in a much longer work.

A handful of stories deal with Le Guin's perennial theme of political rebellion and freedom: ***The New Atlantis,*** **''The Diary of the Rose,''** and **''The Phoenix.''** . . .

But it is probably **''Sur''** . . . that will attract most attention. This report of an Antarctic expedition, written by its Peruvian leader, tells of nine women who reached the South Pole two years before Amundsen or Scott. They wanted only to see, not to accomplish, and were glad they had left no sign of their presence, for ''some man longing to be first might come some day, and find it, and know then what a fool he had been, and break his heart.'' The narrator tucks her report in an attic trunk, thinking it would be ''nice'' if a grandchild read it someday. As a comment on women in history, the story is heart-wrenching. . . .

The Compass Rose demonstrates again why Le Guin is regarded so highly: the spectrum she writes in is broad, and her fiction is both entertaining and provocative. (pp. 37-8)

Carolyn Wendell, in a review of ''The Compass Rose,'' in Science Fiction & Fantasy Book Review, *No. 7, September, 1982, pp. 37-8.*

NOEL PERRIN

For about 15 years I've dreamed of reviewing a book by Ursula Le Guin. The reason is simple. I love science fiction. She is either the best or one of the two best science fiction writers in America, and it would have been pleasure to praise ***The Left Hand of Darkness*** or some new novel about the star system Gamma Draconis. . . .

Now that I finally have the chance, I seem to be a few years too late. It's not that Le Guin's powers have declined. If anything, they're still growing. It's two quite different problems. One is that her interests have clearly shifted. Two of her recent books are collections of poems. Two others are ordinary mainstream fiction. Well, not ordinary—both the novel ***Malafrena*** and most of the short stories in the collection called ***Orsinian Tales*** are superbly told—but their subject is ordinary life on the planet Earth. . . . Le Guin swims well in the mainstream, but her glory has come in leaping the cataracts of science fiction.

The other problem is that insofar as she has kept her interest in science fiction—and the stories in the book I am getting to review are roughly half sf—she has fallen victim to the common fate of very successful practitioners in the field, a fate sometimes called asimovitis. The symptoms are clearly visible in ***The Compass Rose.***

Asimovitis, like the much older disease *cacoethes scribendi*, leads to overproduction and underrevision. It has a curious origin. Up until about a generation ago, science fiction was a notoriously low-paid and low-prestige genre. Those who wrote it had to work at high speed to make any sort of living at all. . . .

Respect was even scarcer than money. Science fiction ordinarily didn't get reviewed at all, except in sf magazines. It virtually never got picked up in the year's best this or that, virtually never appeared in hardcover, virtually never won prizes. The results were just what you'd expect: a closed society. Science fiction writers huddled together for protection. . . .

Now that science fiction is wealthy and successful, these patterns persist. To this day, almost any sf writer will write something to order for almost any other sf writer or editor who asks. Even Ursula Le Guin will. There's a pleasing modesty and lack of pomp involved; there is also a lot of hasty writing appearing on acid-free paper at high prices.

Take, for example, the longest story in Le Guin's new book. It originally appeared in an anthology called *The New Atlantis and Other Novellas of Science Fiction,* edited by Robert Silverberg, a man with a bad case of asimovitis. In his preface, Silverberg stresses the fact that the novella form permits a "richness of detail and narrative development" that the ordinary sf story does not. So it does. And for two of the three works he has assembled, the point is relevant. . . .

The New Atlantis, 27 pages, is not a novella, not rich in detail or narrative development. It's a competent story on her familiar theme of an oppressive society that proves just a little too strong for the free men and women who defy it. To read it, knowing Le Guin at her best, is something like watching a Porsche being driven entirely in second gear.

Sometimes she doesn't even get into second. Several of the science fiction "stories" are not stories at all; they are conceits, ideas for stories. **"Ms. Found in an Anthill"** is in fact three linked conceits, one of them breathtakingly successful, two of them dull mechanical variants. **"The Wife's Story"** is a mere trick. **"Intracom"** is another trick, but one performed so deftly as to make one cheer for the magician's skill, while still lamenting the absence of much substance.

There is, happily, far better work in the book. There is **"The Diary of the Rose,"** for example. It has a similar theme to ***The New Atlantis,*** and it was written for a similar kind of instant anthology. But because Le Guin found a way of telling the story that obviously challenged her, it does not come out perfunctory at all; it comes out almost unbearably powerful.

And best of all, in the non-science fiction half of the book, there are some stories that go far toward reconciling me to her new interests. **"Malheur County"** is an apparently simple story of a strong Oregon woman in her sixties named Harriet, her son-in-law Edward (the daughter is dead), her 2-year-old grandson Andrew. What perception is here! It's as fine a study of how strength deals with age as I have ever seen. If the whole book were on the level of **"Malheur,"** its publication would be a major event.

As it is, publication of ***The Compass Rose*** is a minor event in the career of a major author.

Noel Perrin, "Ursula Le Guin: Striking Out in a New Direction," in Book World—The Washington Post, *September 5, 1982, p. 9.*

HOWARD WALDROP

[The novella ***The Eye of the Heron*** is] not one of Le Guin's best. There are some wonderful patches of description, a few good characterizations, and Le Guin reminds you what it's like to live in a society where everyone (but a select few) has to walk everywhere.

The setting (especially the background, how the people got there) doesn't make much sense. Essentially, her space colony of Victoria was settled by two groups: a) prisoners, who have turned into the Bosses and b) pacifists, who have turned into peasants. The straw-man Boss society is set up to fail, the peasant society to undergo a lot of grief in the name of noncooperative, nonviolent protest. (It would have been much more logical for the governments of Earth that didn't want either the criminals or pacifists to set them down in Antarctica, or the middle of a desert, or anywhere in the solar system. This is a prison planet, which is fine if you've got a galaxy-spanning civilization, but all these people came from *Earth,* on *one-way* rockets. This is real pulp thinking, something Le Guin has never done before.) I hate to give it the oldest of genre criticism, but here it is: except for a few alien bugs and some giant rabbit-like beasts, there's no reason this couldn't have taken place somewhere on Earth, just post-gunpowder, perhaps during the Thirty Years' War.

The main character, Luz, is a Boss' daughter. ***The Eye of the Heron*** is the old science fiction standby, the tale of conversion-to-the-rebels, with an overlain consciousness-raising, and some few hard truths about what it takes to be a real pacifist and how far short people always fall of the ideal.

If you're a Le Guin collector, you'll get this anyway. If not, my advice is to wait for the next novel or story collection.

Howard Waldrop, "Lem, Le Guin and Spinrad: Other Worlds, Other Times," in Book World—The Washington Post, *February 27, 1983, p. 10.*

GERALD JONAS

As a novelist of ideas, Ursula K. Le Guin has no peer in science fiction and few rivals outside the genre. In ***The Left Hand of Darkness*** . . . , she explored the question, what would human society be like if gender distinctions were erased? In ***The Dispossessed*** . . .—which she classed as an "ambiguous utopia"—she contrasted a social system based on anarchistic communal principles with an acquisitive, competitive society. While Mrs. Le Guin's sympathies clearly lay with the anarchists, she scrupulously considered the weaker points in their system, especially the lack of privacy and a certain leveling of human passions. One problem she did not confront directly was how such an "undisciplined" society could resist a would-be conqueror. In ***The Eye of the Heron***—first published in 1978 as part of a collection entitled *Millennial Women*—Mrs. Le Guin draws the lines even more clearly, by positing a conflict between two groups of human colonists, one pacifists and the other bullies, who have been dumped side by side on the same planet.

The scale is pleasingly human, and Mrs. Le Guin exercises considerable art in setting the stage. But the telling is marred by a didacticism that was masked in the earlier novels by richly detailed accounts of character and background. Precisely because the scale is so small and the style so economical in ***The Eye of the Heron,*** the bare bones of the argument keep poking through. In the end the drama is reduced to an either-or proposition: When bullies attack, can a dedicated, well-trained band of pacifists survive with their principles and lives intact? It's a good question, and Mrs. Le Guin's answer is far from simplistic. But because it has neither the rigor of a philosophical essay nor the immediacy of strong fiction, ***The Eye of the Heron*** ultimately fails to engage the reader on either level. (pp. 15, 37)

Gerald Jonas, "Inside Elsewhere," in The New York Times Book Review, *May 22, 1983, pp. 15, 37.*

PHILIPPA MADDERN

In the 1960s and 1970s science fiction underwent a regeneration, largely at the hands of women writers. I shall offer a very sketchy selection of the undoubtedly complex causes below; but the one writer who did most to bring it about was undoubtedly Ursula Le Guin, with her ***Rocannon's World*** (1966), ***Planet of Exile*** (1966), ***City of Illusions*** (1967) and ***The Left Hand of Darkness*** (1969). These swung science fiction away from adventure stories and the cerebral solutions of physical problems towards the contemplation of anthropological, ethnological and psychological truths.

The full weight of the change was not, I think, immediately perceived. Writers creating intergalactic scenarios had always, perforce, to construct with more or less painstaking sensitivity alien life-forms and societies. At first it seemed that Le Guin simply did it better. Her aliens, even when humanoid, were completely alien, their language, arts, religions, ways of thinking, family structures, body language and histories irrevocably foreign to middle-class America. Nor were the comprehension gaps between them and the human characters glossed over by the introduction of magic intergalactic translating machines. Instead, the hard truth that it is difficult, a death to the ego, to meet and understand someone truly other, was squarely faced.

This consciousness sustains the whole of ***Planet of Exile.*** The setting is a planet with an immensely long orbit—so long that each season lasts approximately fifteen Earth years. On it, some six hundred Earth years before the story opens, a small colony of Terrans was stranded. Their chemistry being slightly different from that of the rest of the planet, they could not eat the food untreated, be infected by the local bacteria, nor interbreed with the indigenous nomads. Two important viewpoint characters in the story are Wold, a nomad chieftain, and Rolery, a nomad girl; this fact in itself emphasises the alienness of the humans. But Rolery herself is alien in her own society; where most children are spring or autumn born, she was born in summer, and is literally the only one of her generation. Both cultures are rigid and unchanging—the nomadic keeping up ancient orally-transmitted traditions, the Terran maintaining a dwindling and sterile purity. The novel is about many things—the coming of winter, a siege with Terrans and nomads pitted together against a third tribe, and a love-relationship between Rolery and one of the Terrans. But it is always about the breaking of familiarities in the meeting between mutual aliens. Rolery deliberately forsakes her tribal custom to marry Jakob Agat. Yet he is truly foreign to her. . . . Terrans wounded in the siege begin to show signs of developing infections and gangrene. This deadly evidence of life-supporting adaptation is at first passionately denied by those devoted to the notion of their group's purity, the more so since it implies the possibility of interbreeding with the nomads. The metaphor of meeting, change and growth is completed in ***City of Illusions.*** This work, set some six hundred years later again, shows the combined race grown together away from both unchanging traditions. Clearly, these books can be read on several levels. Their immediate lesson, that real aliens are more interesting than white Anglo-Saxon protestants in fancy-dress, was quickly learned. Younger writers, such as George R. R. Martin and Lisa Tuttle produced work in which technological interest tended to give way to sociological and ethnological issues.

Yet though this opened up an area of fictionalised truth which science fiction, despite its unique qualifications for the enterprise, had hesitated to explore, it was only part of Le Guin's shattering influence. For she saw beyond the inevitably mind-broadening value of ethnological science fiction to further uses, as her retrospective introduction to ***The Left Hand of Darkness*** shows. This novel is set on a planet whose inhabitants differ most strikingly from humans in that they have, instead of continuous sexuality, an oestrus period ('kemmer'), in which either of the partners may assume male or female sexuality indifferently. In between kemmer they are completely androgynous (except during pregnancy and lactation), and are not predisposed to either sexual role ('the mother of several children may be the father of several more' notes one human scientist in the book). Le Guin writes:

> In the mid-1960s the women's movement was just beginning to move again, after a fifty-year halt . . . I considered myself a feminist; . . . but I had never taken a step beyond the ground gained for us by Emmeline Pankhurst and Virginia Woolf . . .
>
> I began . . . to want to define and understand the meaning of sexuality and the meaning of gender, in my life and in our society . . . But I was not a theoretician, a political thinker or activist, or a sociologist. I was and am a fiction writer. The way I did my thinking was to write a novel . . . ***The Left Hand of Darkness*** is the record of my consciousness, the process of my thinking . . .
>
> Why did I invent these peculiar people? Not just so that the book could contain, halfway through it, the sentence, 'The king was pregnant'—though I admit that I am fond of that sentence. Not . . . to propose Gethen as a model for humanity . . . I was not recommending the Gethenian sexual setup: I was using it. It was a heuristic device, a thought-experiment . . .
>
> (pp. 114-16)

The thought-experiment itself has its limitations, which Le Guin freely points out. Gethenian psychology is left rather vague, and family life even vaguer. And the principal Gethenian character appears inappropriately masculine, because he (the pronoun used) is hardly shown in any role which we would consider traditionally female. Despite this, the experiment is a great and exciting one, and its readers could hardly avoid reconsideration of the significance of gender roles. It demonstrated unequivocally what I have called the quintessence of fiction; to organise the imagination in search of truth. No less importantly, Le Guin wrote elegant, cogent, subtly-structured English, thus helping to make science fiction aesthetically respectable to those who would not willingly be seen dead holding a copy of *Analog*. (p. 117)

Philippa Maddern, "True Stories: Women's Writing in Science Fiction," in Meanjin, *Vol. 44, No. 1, March, 1985, pp. 110-23.*

SAMUEL R. DELANY

With high invention and deep intelligence, ***Always Coming Home*** presents, in alternating narratives, poems and expositions, Ursula K. Le Guin's most consistently lyric and luminous book in a career adorned with some of the most precise and passionate prose in the service of a major imaginative vision.

Mrs. Le Guin has created an entire ethnography of the far future in her new book. It's called a novel. But even to glance at it is to suspect it's more than, or other than, that: the oversize trade paperback is boxed with a tape cassette of delicate songs, poems and haunting dance pieces, purportedly recorded on site. Liner notes are included. Are they by the composer, Todd Barton, or by Ursula Le Guin? It's not indicated. I would like to know, since each entry, with its song or poem, is a small story in itself. Margaret Chodos's fine line drawings portray animals, birds, sacred implements and symbols, tools, mountains and houses (but no people); and we have charts, maps, alphabets and a glossary. The book contains a short novel, ***Stone Telling,*** spaced out in three parts, narrated by a woman called Stone Telling; and "Chapter Two" from another novel, *Dangerous People,* [narrated by the author] Wordriver. Along with Marsh, Cowardly Dog and Mote, Wordriver is among the great novelists of the Kesh, the people of the Valley, the subjects of Mrs. Le Guin's pastoral vision. In addition there are poems, children's stories, adult folk tales, verse dramas, recipes, essays and a host of Kesh documents. Though the word "Indian" does not appear from one end of the book to the other, the reader is likely to feel after only a few pages that much Native American culture has become a part of this dark, wise, stocky people's way of life. Mrs. Le Guin has given us the imaginary companion volume of "Readings" that might accompany a formal anthropological study.

When did the Kesh live? They haven't, yet.

The Kesh have access to a daunting computer system. But they live 500 years or more in our future, on the northwestern coast of what's left of a United States gone low-tech and depopulated by toxic wastes and radioactive contamination. The Kesh are an attractive people. One noun serves them for both gift and wealth. To be rich and to give are, for them, one verb. They do not share the West's present passion for origins and outcomes: their pivotal cultural concept is the hinge, the connecting principle that allows things both to hold together and to move in relation to each other. Their year is marked off by elaborate seasonal dances. Their lives and work are organized in a complicated system of Houses, Lodges, Arts, and Societies. (pp. 31, 56)

The emotional high point, for me, was the transcription of a Kesh play, *Chandi,* a retelling of the biblical tale of Job. A society in which such a tale is important cannot be a simple utopian construct: a Job, (or a Chandi)—that most antiutopian of myths—reminds us too strongly that as long as culture is fitted against nature, along whatever complex curve, the best of us may slip into the crack to be crushed by unhappy chance. . . .

Mrs. Le Guin has put some expository pieces in a 100-plus-page section called "The Back of the Book." These are among the most interesting, the most beautiful. I suggest going straight to them and reading **"What They Wore," "What They Ate,"** and **"The World Dance"** before beginning the book proper. They will enhance Stone Telling's tale of her childhood considerably. (By the same token, don't read **"The Train"**—or you will spoil a pleasant narrative surprise earlier on.)

Grouped between the prose pieces, the 70-odd poems slow up a straight-through reading. Not particularly difficult or particularly bad. But a contemporary reader, for whom poetry is still a high art, and for whom the poet is at once on the margins of society while oriented toward the center of culture, simply finds it hard going through the Kesh's overwhelming poetic saturation. And while we understand the poems as simple surface utterances, at a deeper level, where we expect poems to be meaningful, they don't make much sense. I only wish Mrs. Le Guin had written more prose *about* the practice of poetry in the Valley with, say, the same energy and vividness she employed to write about the cosmogenic Dance of the World or the Saturnalian Dance of the Moon—two of the book's most spectacular set pieces.

Mrs. Le Guin is among the half-dozen most respected American writers who regularly set their narrative in the future to force a dialogue with the here and now, a dialogue generally called science fiction. She is also a much loved writer. And ***Always Coming Home*** is a slow, rich read, full of what one loves most in her work: a liberal utopian vision, rendered far more complex than the term "utopian" usually allows for by a sense of human suffering. This is her most satisfying text among a set of texts that have provided much imaginative pleasure in her 23 years as an author. (p. 56)

Samuel R. Delany, "The Kesh in Song and Story," in The New York Times Book Review, *September 29, 1985, pp. 31, 56.*

BRIAN ALDISS

The endeavor [in ***Always Coming Home***] is to create not a novel but a world. A fashionable exercise. The world to which that contorted conditional leads lies in Northern California in the far future, after a destructive nuclear war. All that we know has gone, or has been changed. The Indians have their country back.

There are diseases caused by long-term genetic damage wrought by radioactivity. Otherwise, this is a harsh, ascetic pastoral, set in a land where poverty is wealth and animals are also people. Dances are danced for every season, songs sung for every insect. Humans are not just close to nature. They are again part of nature, and that they see visions is taken for granted.

Le Guin's book . . . is stuffed with poems, songs, patterns, maps, dried flowers, feathers, stones and drums. Her folk, the Kesh, scuttle into the shadows as one turns the page. . . .

Among this vernal bric-a-brac are set stories, legends, and tales. The longest story, ***Stone Telling,*** is divided into three parts in order to give some kind of narrative backbone to the book. . . . It is unsensational, its explicit anti-military note giving it a bite which some of the short stories lack.

Among the lesser stories, glimpses of the alien in **"At the Springs of Orlu,"** and the visions of **"The Bright Void of the Wind"** are particularly strong. ***The Visionary,*** too, has true power, rendering the remarkable banal and the banal remarkable.

Such marvelous transformations do not take place as frequently as hoped. Pretentiousness is no substitute. ("Owl hears itself: that makes sound be; sound comes into time then, four times . . .")

Occasionally one hears the dry rasp of the anthropologist's voice. The tone of the superior teacher, present in earlier Le Guin, still echoes here and there. But by and large, this is a deeply worked-for attempt at another world than ours, an insight into what—with luck—might be our true natures.

Mutants, dragons, telepathy, and the ghouls in which earlier writers delighted, find no place here. Even the Condors, the baddies, die out. We find the Kesh boring at times—the fate of quietists. They have no gods, no faith. "What they appear to have had is a working metaphor." That's a bit of a dry crust for people who name themselves after pumas.

It comes as a considerable shock, about a third of the way through the book, to encounter a piece of inventiveness which is new—or newish—to the not particularly distinguished genre of post-catastrophe novels.

Mankind's materialist culture has long gone, but communities of computers and cyborgs survive. Eleven thousand such communities across the planet form an intercommunicating entity, the City of Mind. This is explained in a section entitled **"Time and the City."** Human beings can tap into this City via exchanges, if they so wish.

The city has no ambitions to take over mankind and enslave it; it has its own affairs, and is proceeding with the exploration of space. Information-gathering is its main function. As far as humanity is concerned, it is neutral. This sort of neutrality, a passionlessness, pervades Le Guin's thought. Here it is effectively embodied. . . .

On the whole, [Le Guin] sails with flying colors across the tenebrous world of dreams with which science fiction has always flirted. Swallowing the message is another matter. Whether one cares to think of the Stone Age as utopia is a question of personal preference. My preferences are strongly against.

Reading this gallimaufrous book is like tickling for trout. You wait a long time on the bank, patiently. Your hand grows cold in the water. Suddenly, the mysterious creature is there beneath your touch. You pull it out of the stream. You rejoice. You have a feast. But not everyone can acquire the knack.

Brian Aldiss, "Ursula Le Guin's Field Guide to the Kesh," in Book World—The Washington Post, *October 6, 1985, p. 11.*

BRIAN D. JOHNSON

Ursula K. Le Guin, the queen of American fantasy writers, has based her new novel on an audacious premise. She introduces it as an "archeological dig" into the distant future—a search for "shards of the broken pot at the end of the rainbow"—and extends the metaphor to extraordinary lengths. ***Always Coming Home*** is partly a compendium of stories, poems, plays and songs from the Kesh, a peaceful people living in a northern Californian valley. Accompanying those literary artifacts are anthropological essays that explain the lifestyle and language of the Kesh in minute detail. . . . Le Guin "reconstructs" the future with such thoroughness that it becomes as tangible as the past. . . .

For the Kesh, time is an open landscape rather than a straight line, and Le Guin's writing obeys the same perspective. Woven through the text, the only substantial narrative is an autobiographical story by a woman named Stone Telling. . . .

Stone Telling's childlike account lacks some of the basic elements of character and intrigue that have made Le Guin's previous novels so gripping. But ***Always Coming Home*** is not designed as a conventional novel with a beginning, middle and end. Instead, its narrative fragments form a polemical jigsaw held together by ideas rather than events. The Condor people, with their military technology and avaricious God, are throwbacks to the current industrial age. And the author uses them as a foil to highlight the communal qualities of the Kesh. . . . Keyed to the rhythms of nature, Kesh culture echoes the traditional beliefs of native societies. Although the Kesh have no gods, everything from their dance rituals to their town planning is patterned after the sacred *heyiya*—the spiral or helix that serves as "an inexhaustible metaphor" for the sense of mystical unity pervading their culture.

Le Guin is most compelling when she plays with the links between existing society and her distant future. According to Kesh creation myths, life on earth has ended numerous times with meteor showers, ice ages, floods, volcanoes and finally with a holocaust that caused "fires and smoke and bad air and then ice and cloud and cold." Eventually, life returned to the earth, but for a long time "even the rocks were sick." The actual history is vague because the Kesh have little interest in any chronology more complex than the cycles of the moon. And they have developed a whimsical attitude toward technology: their railway has trains with leather couplings and wooden wheels that ride on oak tracks. Although they have free access to a planet-wide network of cybernetic computers called the City of Mind—a system with a bottomless memory, belonging to no one—they rarely bother to use it. Explains one Kesh archivist: "It keeps the dead. When we need what's dead, we go to the Memory."

Part social satire and part utopian blueprint, ***Always Coming Home*** strikes an uneasy balance between contrivance and enchantment. At a time when such novelists as Doris Lessing and Margaret Atwood have turned to science fiction to express their feminist visions, Le Guin, who pioneered that connection, is destroying and rebuilding science fiction from the ground up. . . . With the arcane lexicon that she has invented for ***Always Coming Home,*** she may have taken her own wizardry too far. The result is not a novel so much as a cult-in-a-box, and readers might well expect a board game and a rock video to be next on the Kesh agenda. But despite the cloying gimmickry of Le Guin's approach, she has created a *heyiya* that works—a spiral staircase that offers the reader a breathtaking view at the expense of a tedious climb.

Brian D. Johnson, "Artifacts from the End of the Rainbow," in Maclean's Magazine, *Vol. 98, No. 44, November 4, 1985, p. 72.*

JACQUELINE AUSTIN

Many of Ursula Le Guin's followers will be ecstatic about ***Always Coming Home.*** Written in a brave new style, about a brave new world, it's as intelligent and passionate as ***The Dispossessed.*** Le Guin combines the social scientism of her early work with her recent romanticism to make an ambitious and intermittently beautiful statement. She's gambled on something risky in this book. The problem is not that she's lost, exactly, but that she hasn't yet won.

First, the physics. . . . ***Always Coming Home*** is a baby blue cardboard Creamsicle. A sculpted niche cradles a cassette containing Todd Barton's rampantly lovely music (a combo of Steve Reich, the 15th century, and Sioux lullaby), plus a full page of accompanying textual notes on heavy paper. The exquisite pen-and-ink illustrations, hand-drawn maps, and calligraphy are equally elegant—perhaps too elegant. Usually I enjoy such embarrassments of riches. But here the production, craft- and quality-conscious as it may be, seems to choke an instinctive, exploring sensibility. It's as though Julia Child had pulled out her lemon zest graters and pastry weights to assemble her 1010th roast beef. In Le Guin's recent works—poems, ***Malafrena, The Beginning Place***—she has denied such enormousness, concentrating instead on intimate, almost antimaterial, motivations. ***Home,*** in letting loose physical restraint, contradicts those basic tendencies even as it attempts to assert them.

Home's content suffers from similar confusions. In an attempt to synthesize Native American, Taoist, classical, and contemporary concerns, Le Guin has overaggrandized some cultural traits (spirituality), romanticized others (connection to the land), and diminished the rest (science, technology). A Caucasian writer may of course attempt to assimilate Native American symbology—anything's permitted in fiction—but then there will be questions to be answered, connections to be made. What predominantly white culture would derive its words, its mores, its mythological figures from Native American ones, while excluding WASP, Black, Hispanic patterns? Does the future practice conceptual genocide?

Though Le Guin has earned the right to her version of the collective unconscious . . . , she fails to mortar the bricks in ***Home***'s four walls. Even the cassette, which practically screams "I'm real," doesn't pull together all its ethnographic sources. Yet Le Guin's alternative would have been to generate an earthly, American, nature-motivated culture completely from scratch—an endeavor which probably would not have had half of this project's historical resonance.

Home is ostensibly a series of about a hundred "anthropological" fragments. Its fictive impulse seems to have been to confront death—wholesale and individual. This is a *Foxfire* book that not only records "true" voices but urgently asks: What comes after the nuclear holocaust? Why create, when everything is about to be destroyed? The Kesh themselves are an answer. A spiritual people, they have learned from our mistakes: they've chucked much of "civilization" on the philosophical garbage heap where it belongs, and kept what matters—that old California style. The Kesh are wonderfully centered, but they suffer from conceptual flaws. Their language could not etymologically derive from English; their customs and symbology—Native American, proto-Taoist—have similarly arisen, it seems, from air. I suppose anything can develop from anything else, given enough time. . . .

Le Guin writes to give us hope that after the ultimate destruction will come creation. Her responses to holocaust—other than denial of the technology which fomented it—are, on the surface, modest. On a deeper level, they assert that nothing human is ever lost. With her folk tales and descriptions of sacred ritual as well as oral histories, Le Guin has attempted a realism deeper than that of her "traditional" fiction. As she observes and describes Kesh customs, musical instruments, and attire, Le Guin is, for the most part, refreshingly unintrusive. She permits the Kesh a wide range of expression, a sense of humor: sexual taunts, slapstick, gentle chiding, even formal exchanges of insult. . . .

Le Guin's most immediate, journal-like voice is linked to an image of Pandora, opening her treasure-chest to loose the world's woes and find the hope beneath. It's an appropriate, though somewhat hysterical, image. . . .

Pandora, intended as a mediating voice linking past to present to future, should have unified science fiction with myth, today's Americans with the Kesh. But there's something jarring and undigested about Le Guin's mythological eclecticism, and it's exacerbated by setting the isolationist Kesh on earth, where the writer who fudges culture is far more vulnerable than, say, in the Hainish Empire. ***The Lathe of Heaven***'s projected future was similarly disturbing, jumbling Norse, Greek, and Christian figures with scientific tropes. Le Guin's alien utopias and dystopias—***The Dispossessed,*** the Earthsea trilogy, ***The Left Hand of Darkness,*** even her story **"Vaster Than Empires and More Slow"** (about an astronaut's assimilation into the alien forest he explores)—all ran on similarly potent cultural fuel, but got more miles per gallon.

Home turns Le Guin's old ambitions inside out. Moralism—once subordinate to the dream shared by writer and reader—is on the surface here, and it has become exhortation. Though at times the narrator steps back to become an anthropologist, often, because of the form, the cuts, the hesitations, she's too present. Trying not to tell the reader what to see, she *shows* how to see, and with what emotions. In her "scientific" utopian novels, Le Guin's narrative voice had a wide range, but it never intruded. Here, in search of a wide range of expression—hortatory, poetic, and dispassionate all at once—her voice intrudes again and again.

The old Le Guin would have filled all the holes in the system. The new Le Guin recognizes how distracting these holes are, but insists that her readers stumble. She's to be congratulated for taking such a risk. In refusing the tidiness of plot, the scientism, of her previous work, in changing her reader from seduced page-turner to meditative, questioning browser, she has set herself the task of being original in structure as well as concept, embracing as well as overturning her own writerly past. What a thing to try to do in a single revolutionary novel. What a shame that the wrapping job, so gorgeous, so overdetermined, forces one to judge the rest of ***Home*** against its formidable cover.

Jacqueline Austin, "Kesh Flow: Ursula Le Guin Sees the World," in The Village Voice, *Vol. XXXI, No. 8, February 25, 1986, p. 49.*

KEITH N. HULL

Science fiction has undertaken the theme of defining humanity with vigor, ingenuity, and depth, yet the basic device for introducing it is common in popular literature—the alien, the other. Here is the science fiction buff's familiar ground; we all know the forms that aliens can take: extraterrestrials, monsters, machines with human personalities, animals evolved into telepathically speaking companions, human beings who acquire sub- or superhuman capabilities. Frequently, the alien figure raises the question of defining humanity, a phenomenon that stretches to modern science fiction's origins. (pp. 66-7)

One of today's most praised and read science fiction authors has incorporated wholesale the question of defining humanity as a dominant theme in her work. Ursula K. Le Guin, in her several major novels, brings into conflict beings that by appearances and behavior could be human, though there is some factor present that creates doubt or, on the other hand, misguided certainty. Earlier, when I used the term "other," I was borrowing from Le Guin, who defines "other" as "the being who is different from yourself." . . . When she uses the term regarding her own work, however, Le Guin means something apart from the usual robot-alien-telepath-superhuman. Her others tend to be less different from us than those of most writers and deliberately suggest conventional humanity. Generally, in LeGuin's work important other-human differences give way to important similarities.

Rocannon's World presents a whole range of types termed "humanoid." On the novel's first two pages we find listed three distinct races, one composed of two "pseudoraces" that appear to contain at least cousins to Rocannon, the novel's one more or less certified human being. In ***Planet of Exile*** Terran settlers live next to the Hilf, primitive nomads who appear to be human and who become the Terrans' allies in a fight for mutual survival against the Gaal, another possibly human race. An obvious parable about real-world conservationist, racial, and colonial politics, ***The Word for World Is Forest*** pits human beings against a smaller, primitive race, the Athsheans, whom they regard as nonhumans subject to exploitation as animals. ***City of Illusions*** starts with Falk on Terra; except for his cat's eyes he is apparently human and has been raised by a human family to possess the full range of human emotions. As the novel pits him against obviously alien invaders, Falk finds out the truth about his alien origins while his own sense of humanness deepens. In these instances, the theme of defining what is human takes shape in the alliance that human beings form with possible humans; physical and cultural differences prove relatively superficial in the face of mutual concerns; respect, affection, and love cross lines drawn between apparent species. The inevitable result is to broaden the definition of human in the characters' and the readers' minds.

Two Le Guin novels of unquestionably high standing, even among readers who generally do not care for science fiction, are ***The Left Hand of Darkness*** and ***The Dispossessed.*** In these novels Le Guin continues the practice she describes in her Introduction to ***Rocannon's World,*** where she describes herself as writing science fiction based on "social science, psychology, anthropology [and] history," presumably instead of on mathematics, the physical and biological sciences, or engineering. . . . The result, too infrequent in science fiction, is an emphasis on culture, with barely enough hard science to justify the alien circumstances in which Le Guin's characters find themselves. Perhaps because of this cultural emphasis Le Guin's questions about humanness are as profound as any in science fiction.

In Le Guin's universe humanity—if it is humanity—was scattered in a past too remote for most races to remember. Instead, people have mostly rumors, speculations, and legends. One race, the Hainish, claims to be the source of all mankind, though the other races often doubt the claim and Hainish history itself is incomplete. In much of Le Guin's work then the question is literally universal, "are all these beings truly one race?"

Sometimes the differences between races are completely social and not biological. Interbreeding is possible, and outward appearances are identical. Rolery, a Hilf woman, and Jakob, a Terran, in ***Planet of Exile*** are from races that have lived side by side for six hundred years, neither convinced that the other is human; only when they must fight together do Hilf and Terran learn enough mutual respect that Rolery and Jakob can cross cultural barriers, love, and eventually bear children.

In other Le Guin novels, however, the differences are not so superficial. Falk, a descendant of Jakob and Rolery in ***City of Illusions,*** appears human in all respects but his eyes, which are like a cat's. In ***Rocannon's World*** and ***The Word for World Is Forest*** massive cultural differences and size call into question the humanity of the various humanoid races. The greatest differences between humans and possible humans, however, are found in ***The Left Hand of Darkness.*** On the planet Gethen the inhabitants are androgynous; individuals possess male and female sexual organs and can impregnate or become pregnant. Unlike our branch of humanity, they are not constantly capable of sexual activity; rather, like animals, they become sexually active periodically. Clearly such people can be defined as nonhuman on the basis of sexual characteristics; after all, among humans as we know them—and as the Hainish in the novel know them—distinct sexes and nonstop sexual capability constitute powerfully definitive characteristics. In our world we are alone among mammals in our sexual readiness, and among the Gethenians the Hainish—by Le Guin's witty twist—appear perverted.

Is sexuality a fair test of humanness? Are the Gethenians indeed human? After all, their appearances are not quite human either; their faces' softness belies their "ambisexuality." If we relegate sexuality to being only one test of humanness and introduce sociological evidence, the Gethenians fare better; in fact, they ironically excel us in fulfilling some of our own Western humanitarian ideals. Because every Gethenian is a potential mother, the great disparity between male and female roles that we know so well does not occur to Gethen. This means that "anyone can turn his hand to anything," as a Hainish observer notes; gender-related limitations on careers or status do not exist. Furthermore, the sexual urge is so powerful that the Gethenians make special provisions for those in "kemmer"—estrus—to be together to give free expression to their drives. This means in turn, as the Investigator Ong Tot Oppong says, "There is no unconsenting sex, no rape." . . . (pp. 68-70)

This social situation adds up to a telling comment on being human. Here is a race whose estrus cycle and sex drive are like those of animals yet whose alien androgyny—a true androgyny—means that they have surpassed us in achieving a society free of sex-related crimes and stigma. Surely, if complex social behavior and altruism are definitive human characteristics, the Gethenians have a fair claim to being human.

Then where do they stand? Are they human? Le Guin's greatness as a novelist partially hinges on the fact that she often poses fundamental questions, then does not offer easy answers; in fact she may not answer at all. As to whether Gethenians are human, there are answers of sorts, but they give little satisfaction in terms of a simple yes or no. Ong Tot Oppong theorizes that the Gethenians are the result of ancient Hainish experiments that attempted to raise a Terran colony to nobler status by eliminating individual debasement because of gender. This means that the Gethenians may be another species of genus *Homo,* but like the Eloi and the Morlocks they might not be quite human in other terms.

One aspect of their social lives is superior to ours, although other aspects are backward; so engaged are they in a struggle for survival that their technology and social structures are primitive and static. One could say such a thing about chimpanzees, and not so long ago our own ancestors had doubts about the fully human status of people they considered socially, technologically, and physically primitive; some people still have such doubts. Genly Ai and Estraven, Le Guin's Hainish and Gethenian protagonists in ***The Left Hand of Darkness,*** settle the issue of Gethenian humanness in a way when they disregard all cultural and biological barriers to become firm, mutually respecting friends. . . . [Humanness] in this case seems to be a function of what characters emotionally accept as human. Certainly one of the most important lessons in Le Guin's novels is that humanity is a broader, deeper entity than we ordinarily think and that the definition of humanity requires constant expansion as our experience broadens.

Because of this theme, Le Guin's work risks being polemical and sentimental, but her best work exploits it beautifully. ***The Word for World is Forest*** is obvious and righteous, but ***The Left Hand of Darkness*** integrates its lesson so thoroughly with Gethenian culture, biology, and geography that, like *Dune,* the main theme is too rich to be sentimental, no matter how uplifting it may sound when abstracted. ***The Dispossessed*** completely avoids the dangers of sentimentality and righteousness; rather than demonstrating that humanity is a broader concept than we realize, it approaches mainstream work by inverting the question of what is human.

This excellent novel takes the position that all its characters, Terrans, Hainish, and Cetians—the people of Urras and Anarres—are human, and doubts to the contrary seem small-minded. Conventional science fiction devices, interstellar travel and earthlike planets, here put human beings in a situation in which they encounter what are clearly other humans. Though the three main human cultures are strikingly different in some ways, they are strikingly similar in others, and, by appearance as well as major aspects of behavior, Terrans, Hainish, and Cetians are human, living pretty much within the standards of twentieth-century Western culture. (pp. 70-1)

Within this subtle situation Le Guin delineates a profound theme. The people of Anarres, anarchists who have migrated from Urras to establish their own utopian, thoroughly communistic society, call the Urrasti "profiteers," a scornful term for capitalists and private propertarians. Though the Anarresti know that the Urrasti are human, they fall victim to the propensity we know too well of assigning a derogatory, dehumanizing name to those they dislike. Shevek, Le Guin's Anarresti protagonist and one of modern fiction's great characters, transcends Anarresti bias by doing the unthinkable—living among the profiteers.

The Urrasti by our lights are human, so they have the full range of strengths and weaknesses we would expect, and their basic human nature does not seem different from that of the Anarresti. But Urras' geography allows wealth and privileges Anarres could never support; consequently, Urrasti culture is so different from Anarres' that Shevek, the first Anarresti visitor in the 170 years since the anarchist emigration, is regarded on Urras as the "moon man." Hence the novel moves from dehumanizing someone by assigning a derogatory name to a situation in which a human literally becomes a being from an alien planet, a true alien in most Urrasti eyes.

Among Shevek's Urrasti acquaintances, however, he is regarded as an educated, scientifically accomplished human being, though a bit loutish socially—he is a bright but human hick. Ironically, this same class of educated people who scorn the distorted views of the masses is quick to relegate the Hainish to nonhuman status though they are virtually indistinguishable physically from the Cetians and Terrans. Here lies one of the great ironies of ***The Dispossessed.*** Whereas the masses of both planets dehumanize each other with terms such as "profiteer" and "moon man," Shevek and his friends, Annaresti and Urrasti, attempt to transcend such narrow views, but Shevek discovers that biased thinking can exist on a different scale.

Between neighboring planets the charge of being nonhuman is for the prejudiced, the unenlightened, against whom Shevek struggles so movingly, and he pins his hopes for a broader view of humanity on the more varied, complex Urrasti society with its privileged scientific caste. Among them, however, he merely finds the ante raised. Although they accept Anarresti as fully human, he nevertheless finds bigotry raised to an interstellar level and, worse, associated with dangerous, chauvinistic politics. Talking to his Urrasti friend Atro, a great scientist and an influential figure on Urras who has hitherto shown himself a great humanist about Urrasti-Anarresti differences, Shevek discovers yet another misguided human-human conflict. Atro says:

> I mean by "Cetians" precisely what the daily paper writes and their lip-moving readers understand by the term. Urras and Anarres. . . . A hundred years ago we didn't need the word. "Mankind" would do. But sixty-some years ago that changed. . . . My elder sister called out the window, "They're talking to somebody from Outer Space on the radio! . . ." But it was only the Hainish, quacking about peace and brotherhood. Well, nowadays "mankind" is a bit over-inclusive. What defines brotherhood but nonbrotherhood? Definition by exclusion, my dear! You and I are kinsmen. . . . To know it, one only has to meet—to hear of—an alien. A being from another solar system. A man, so-called, who has nothing in common with us except the practical arrangement of two legs, two arms, and a head with some kind of brain in it!
>
> (pp. 71-3)

Shevek initially passes over this speech's illogical narrow-mindedness, thinking it one of Atro's humorous spells, but is then surprised to find that Atro is serious. Though Shevek is tolerant and affectionate toward the old man, he recognizes a horrifying distortion of what made them friends. Atro's ready acceptance of Shevek as fully human is born of the same attitude that excludes Terrans and Hainish. Basically he defines humanity as Cetians, those inhabitants of his own solar system. The very basis of tolerance on one hand becomes the basis for bigotry on the other. Illogically, he excludes some races, though we must remember that there really is no acceptable proof for anyone in the novel that Cetians, Terrans, and Hainish are mutually human. Thus neither we nor Shevek should feel too righteous about Atro's narrow views; there is room for doubt.

Furthermore, Atro's motivation is completely recognizable. What could be more human than what he next tells Shevek:

> I don't want those damned aliens getting at you through your notions about brotherhood and mutualism and all that. They'll spout you whole rivers about "common humanity" and "leagues

> of all the worlds'' and so on, and I'd hate to see you swallow it. The law of existence is struggle—competition—elimination of the weak—a ruthless war for survival. And I want to see the best survive. The kind of humanity I know. The Cetians. You and I: Urras and Anarres. We're ahead of them now, all those Hainish and Terrans and whatever else they call themselves, and we've got to stay ahead of them.
>
> (p. 73)

Though Shevek takes these ironies with good graces, he withholds from Atro further news of his work, a scientific theory with boundless political impact. Instead, he arranges for it to be broadcast everywhere as his gift for ''the common good,'' a commonality based on the mutual humanity of three great cultures. At the novel's end he returns to Anarres, a failure in his effort to bridge the gap between his world and that of the propertarians; in both places virtually nothing has changed, but Shevek has made his gift to mankind, and in the final pages he achieves an ambiguous triumph that contains the potential for building among human cultures a sense of common humanity.

The ship that takes Shevek from Urras to Anarres is crewed by Terrans and Hainish. One Hainishman, Ketho, is a minor character in the novel's action but a major character thematically. In defiance of Anarresti laws Ketho wants to visit the anarchist planet, partly because it is his duty as a ship's officer to explore, but more, he hints, because he is personally interested in Anarresti culture. He has learned the language and read the works of Odo, Anarres' principal ideologue, and may even want to stay. In any event he will be the first outsider allowed on Anarres since the settlement and must accept, Shevek tells him, the risks of being free. . . . (pp. 73-4)

By consenting to Ketho's accompanying him Shevek assaults the wall—the book's opening image—that keeps apart not just Anarresti and Urrasti but Cetians on the one hand and Terrans and Hainish on the other. The last two have long since accepted each other. What remains is for Ketho and Shevek to lead the Cetians through a wall that finally exists only in their own minds. They may or may not succeed, but their effort redefines humanity nobly. (p. 74)

Keith N. Hull, ''What Is Human? Ursula Le Guin and Science Fiction's Great Theme,'' in Modern Fiction Studies, *Vol. 32, No. 1, Spring, 1986, pp. 65-74.*

Gordon (Jay) Lish

1934-

American novelist, short story writer, and editor.

Lish has established himself as an advocate of innovative literature through his work as fiction editor of *Esquire* magazine, his editorial positions with several publishers, including Alfred A. Knopf and McGraw-Hill, and his writing workshops. In these roles, he has promoted the works of such unconventional contemporary authors as T. Coraghessan Boyle and Mary Robison. Lish's own fiction is similarly idiosyncratic. Most of his work features obsessive first-person narration and eschews plot, characterization, and linear progression. This technique is evident in Lish's first novel, *Dear Mr. Capote* (1983). The book's narrator, Yours Truly, professes to have murdered twenty-three women and plans to kill a total of forty-seven. His claims, however, are wholly subjective and, therefore, highly dubious. The book is written as a rambling letter to Truman Capote, whom the narrator tries to persuade to chronicle his crimes in a book. Yours Truly devises an arrangement whereby half of the resulting royalties would be split with his son, whose future he hopes to secure. While some critics complained about the novel's formlessness and Yours Truly's ill-defined motives for murder, many commended Lish for his compelling and original style and his ability to transform clichés and mixed metaphors into a fresh idiom. Stanley Ellin called *Dear Mr. Capote* "a subtle and profound, dreadful and wonderful addition to the literature of mass murder."

Lish's second novel, *Peru* (1986), explores in detail the workings of childhood memory and its effect in shaping adult personality. The narrator, Gordon Lish, recalls a murder he committed when he was six years old. Although Gordon is now fifty, his language has the repetitive verbosity of a child unleashing a long-suppressed confession. The novel's rapid shifts in time and space and its recurring details emerge like fragments of a puzzle, structured in a circular manner which blurs the boundaries between reality and illusion, fiction and autobiography. Through Gordon's compulsive monologue, Lish presents a resolute psychological study of guilt, jealousy, and narcissism. Stephen Dobyns called *Peru* "an amazing book—not attractive or likable but amazingly built, almost like a corkscrew."

Lish's short story collection, *What I Know So Far* (1984), was less acclaimed than his novels. Most of the volume's stories are brief and, according to Alan Friedman, "read like riddles and satires or like sketches and blackouts." The distinctive voices of first-person narrators are again manifest, this time recalling the dialects and inflections of Jewish-American comedians. Among the book's longest and best regarded stories is "For Jeromé—With Love and Kisses," a parody of J. D. Salinger's "For Esmé—With Love and Squalor." Lish's story consists of a long letter from Mr. Salinger to J.D., his reclusive son. The fictional Mr. Salinger, who lives in a Florida retirement home with the parents of such Jewish-American authors as Philip Roth and Joseph Heller, pleads with his son to reveal to him his new, unlisted telephone number and urges him to appear on television talk shows.

(See also *Contemporary Authors,* Vols. 113, 117.)

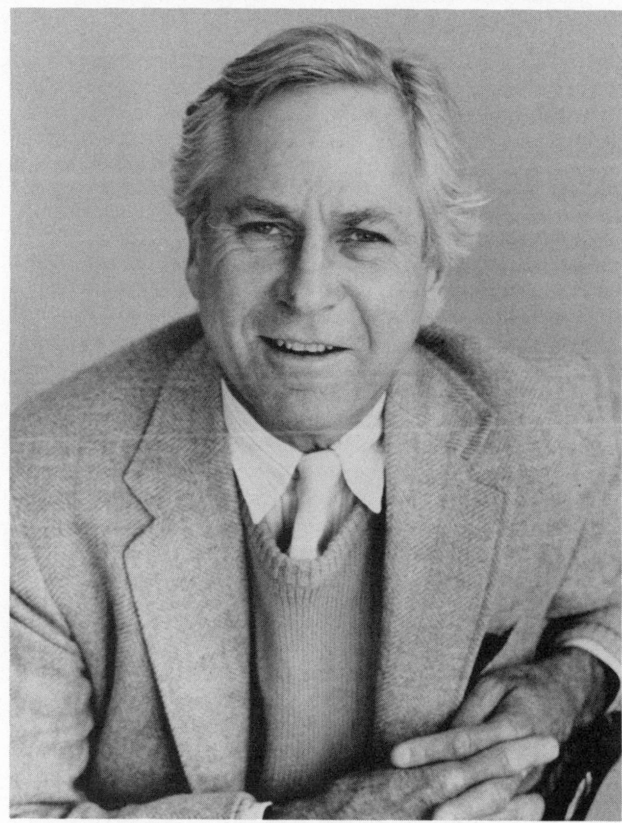

ELIOT FREMONT-SMITH

James Dickey pronounces [***Dear Mr. Capote***'s] effect "radium-rare." Cynthia Ozick asks, "Who else has shaped the shapelessness of madness with such horrific artistry?" This is fine; I have nothing against endorsements; and Ozick's, if you study it, is not inaccurate. Artistry is discernible, not to mention horrificness. And shaping too—so much it's a bore. But there's also an ultimate shapelessness. One has to read ***Dear Mr. Capote*** all the way through to appreciate fully the hard place it leaves one in. Anyway, I did (so maybe you don't have to). The novel progresses from confusions it promises to make coherent to apparent lucidity and then back into confusion. Even givens on the flap are in the end suspect—that the letter writer is a husband or a father or works in a bank or has the name David or is even (or yet) "a killer on the loose," which is kind of crucial.

Dear Mr. Capote starts with lurid panache:

> Dear Mr. Capote, Effectuate a good grip on your socks! Get ready to shake, rattle, and roll! Is this your lucky day or is this your lucky day? . . . This is the person who can make a

> certain writer millions! All he has to do is play his cards right, which I do not have to tell you is not what a certain Mr. Norman Mailer did!
>
> Dear Mr. Capote, with your permission, I will go ahead and introduce myself. Hint: I am the one who is killing the people. Correction: Just the ones which when Nature calls sit down to you-know-what. (p. 54)

And so on. The whole thing is a letter in this vein, supposedly written overnight, by a 47-year-old New Yorker (and neighbor, practically, of Capote's) who has killed 23 women so far by stabbing them in the eye socket and plans to kill 24 more, all at random, one for each year of his existence, unless he and Truman can come to terms on a book-and-movie deal that will set his son up for life. *Well!*

And oy. Right away one knows what one is in for—and a single-spaced saga from a crazy obsessive is only the half of it. One is to keep in mind that this is a fiction and therefore it's not David "Son of Sam" Berkowitz who's writing it, but a character made up by Gordon Lish, whose technical challenge one must be witness to. Epistolary novels are extremely difficult to bring off, especially when they're monologues; they demand from the reader an extra degree of trust, patience, and attentiveness. The payoff will be—else why bother?—ultimate clarity plus shivers that are so integral to understanding that one can call the experience something more than ghoulish. That's the compact. In the end, satisfaction is expected: what terrible things the letter writer has actually done and why.

At about the quarter mark I began to suspect there would be no satisfaction. The rhetoric was great—a hopelessly dated striving for a familiar, hipsterlike tease that could also be grim. But the book wasn't getting anywhere. The same phrases were being repeated: "Am I right or am I right?"; "It's ridick"; "End of discussion, period." I was even ethnically destabilized; I grew up with ridick, and there's just no way to align it with a shrug. But mainly, things were becoming more muddled, not less. I peeked at the end, which was no help. So, Big Decision, I continued on—to check things out as a dutiful reviewer should. Am I right or am I right?

Here's what I found: the letter writer was crazy from the beginning and his mother didn't like that fact. He was a picture-pretty child and thought inanimate objects, like the sky, would eat him up. He maybe killed a neighborhood youngster. He maybe caused the death-by-drowning of his dancer-swimmer brother, Davie. He thought radios had little people inside them. His father was in the liquor business and then left home. As a teenager he had a hot fellatio affair with a girl who became an object of an "endless love" and with whom several bouts of mirror and telephone sex are described. He doesn't like his wife, whose initials are the same as Truman Capote's. He studied vocabulary and mouthed a new word each time he stabbed a girl in the eye. He gloats, he gets flustered, he also gets "boners" while he writes his letter. He was twice in a mental institution. He has a two-way radio with his son, for whom he bought a three-speed bike when 10-speeds were all the rage. He visits his father, who refuses to recognize him and calls the police. He works as a messenger at a radio station, but thinks he played the lead in *Young Doctor Malone*.

And so on—hints galore. But nothing is pinned down. His brother may be himself (though I would never have thought so without the jacket assertion). Mailer may be a father figure. The two T.C.s (wife and Capote) may be aspects of his mother. His stabbing knife, he almost realizes (but only through Lish's metaphorical manipulation), is ye olde symbol. Indeed, his entire sexual identity is up for grabs; like his anonymous victims, he urinates sitting down. One has to ask, what else is new?

But mostly I asked, when is ***Dear Mr. Capote*** going to make coherent sense out of all these maybes?—because another "maybe" may be that he hasn't done any killings at all and is just fantasizing everything. As far as I can make out, whacko turns out to be whacko, and the reader ends up with no clues at all as to what isn't. (pp. 54-5)

Eliot Fremont-Smith, "Three Ways to Sunday," in The Village Voice, *May 31, 1983, pp. 54-5.*

STANLEY ELLIN

[In ***Dear Mr. Capote,*** Gordon Lish] has made a subtle and profound, dreadful and wonderful addition to the literature of mass murder.

There is also one small Catch-23-and-a-half I must deal with before getting down to the bloody meat of the matter. Midway through the book I found myself troubled by its epistolary form. Ironically, its language so perfectly captures the whole complex nature of [the protagonist, Yours Truly], that he could not really have written it. It is oral history, transmuted into living prose by a superb talent. It makes me wonder why You-know-who, a great one for cute little electronic gadgets anyhow, was not at his kitchen table that night, talking his heart and mind and guts out into a tape recorder.

Beyond that, however—and it costs very little suspension of disbelief to read it Gordon Lish's way—there can only be awe at the creation of this terrifyingly real [Yours Truly].

In his *Murder for Profit,* William Bolitho, grandmaster of this literature, wrote: "The Mass-murderer lies to himself. Also, he is often a good family man." And, indeed, in his tormented, self-evasive, often diffuse and rambling narrative, [Yours Truly] lies to himself, the bitter truths only accidentally bubbling to the surface. And he is a very good family man. He is hard-working—a faithful employee of a bank, one of the top-ten banks as he vigorously points out—and while he and his wife have their differences, he is passionately devoted to their 9-year-old son, a nice kid who, hell or high water, shortage of money being both hell and high water, is going to be brought up to have some class. As for example, that big daily calendar laid out on the desk beside his bed, so that first thing each morning the boy will see its "Word for the Day"—*effectuate, capstone, impediment,* whatever—and early get a grip on a high-class vocabulary. [Yours Truly] tears off that page each morning and gets a handle on the word himself, so has come to mark his murders, not by number, but by that word of the day. He may seem the grayest of gray mediocrities when you pass him by on the street, but he has his own touch of class.

Because even the murders are no mere clumsy butcheries. The victims are always female, always dispatched by one deft blow of a needle-sharp knife through the left eyeball, the instant results of the blow sometimes disconcerting [Yours Truly] and leading him to scientific considerations of the job done. And he is not only a thinking man but a feeling one, certain deliciously steamy—though highly relevant—memories of his past leading to quick tumescence, probably slowing down his writing a bit here and there.

"As for the contemplation of the ways and walks of these monsters," wrote William Bolitho,"—only imaginative curiosity is necessary, and as unsqueamish nerves as possible."

No one could have put it better.

Stanley Ellin, "Maniac Writes to Capote, Tells All," in Book World—The Washington Post, *June 5, 1983, p. 4.*

GEORGE STADE

Dear Mr. Capote may well turn out to be one of the best first novels of the year, in spite of its title. Although it is written in the form of a letter to Truman Capote, it is by no means an exercise in camp. And there are other surprises: It is original in style and detail, even though its given is a staple of formula fiction, even though its narrator, "Yours Truly," expresses himself almost entirely through stock phrases, through dead or mixed metaphors. It is also a real grabber, well able to stir your deepest wells of pity and horror, even though its central character is a creep, a nerd, a pipsqueak, a henpecked and penny-pinching bank clerk, a madman who has murdered 23 women.

His plan, so he writes Mr. Capote, is to murder a total of 47 women, one for each year of his life, and then turn himself in. His purpose, so he believes, is to provide for his 9-year-old son, whom he loves with a desperate and displaced narcissism. An account of his doings, after all, ought to be worth a lot of money. . . . His immediate problem is that he is not himself very good with words. . . . What he needs is one of "your top wordsmiths" to write his story up. He has already sent a letter to Norman Mailer, who (this time) didn't bite. Therefore he is writing this letter to Truman Capote . . . who, in return for an exclusive, is to write another immortal masterpiece and split the proceeds with "a certain someone's" son.

Such are the narrator's reasons, so far as he has thought them out. . . . But there are reasons behind his reasons, among them guilt, fear and thwarted love. His mother was stupid, selfish and apt to play mean tricks. She mocked her 7-year-old son when he asked whether dust motes were little animals, when he heard his name in the whine of a vacuum cleaner, when he assumed that tiny people lived in the radio. She compared him unfavorably to the boy next door, whom Yours Truly half-accidentally killed. Out of unbearable guilt he then invented a brother, blamed him for the crime and imagined that he half-accidentally drowned his imaginary brother: "God paid him back." "You can see the child I was. But in my personal opinion, every child is." All this Mr. Lish has to reveal to us obliquely, for Yours Truly can't bear to know what he knows. (p. 9)

His wife of 17 years is as stupid and selfish as his mother. Money troubles and the violent streets of "Gotham" put him in an acute state of perpetual anxiety. . . . But none of these reasons are good enough [to explain his actions]. Behind the reasons are still others, of which we get glimmers, as though a nimbus of madness hung over all human thought and action. The circumstances of Yours Truly's life do not explain why he went mad, but they do explain why his madness expresses itself precisely as it does.

Through scattered clues, we learn, for instance, why he fears the number three; what he has against the word "camisole" and the name "Simon"; why he hates cameras; why he loves feet; what bothers him about ice; why he sits down to urinate; what ritual meanings adhere to his *modus operandi* (which will make you wince). To be mad, we gather, is to live in a world that is totally symbolic; nothing is random or simply itself; everything you see is looking at you. "There's no window, no world. There's a mirror." The faces you see and the voices you hear are your own, but your own faces and voices (and emotions) are put on and derivative: Well into the novel we learn—with a definite shock—that the narrator's speech habits duplicate his mother's.

The narrator's pet phrases may be derivative, but not Mr. Lish's use of them, which is strikingly original. In this novel, the awful detritus of vulgate Americanese (phrases like "from the word go," "enough said," "over my dead body," "what the doctor ordered," "am I right or am I right?," "one for the books," "as the day is long," "who's kidding who?," "take it from me") is transformed into a kind of weird and haunted poetry. As they recur, combine, recombine and undermine each other, these empty phrases one by one fill up with new meanings. Yours Truly wheedles, threatens, bargains, flatters, insults, flies into a rage, falls into despair, forgets what he is saying and then remembers something very much else, all in rapid succession and without transition. But behind his disconnections we gradually make out the iron laws of psychological determinism, which, in Mr. Lish's hands, soon begin to look like the associative laws of poetic imagery. Yours Truly cowers behind his ready-made phrases as behind a borrowed suit of armor, the exoskeletal remains of dead tropes; when, near the end, interior pressures blast them apart, he goes with them.

There are, of course, other representations of distracted utterance in literature—in Renaissance tragedy, in Poe's obsessed narrators, in Browning's monologues, in Dostoyevsky's Underground Man, in Faulkner's Quentin and Jason Compson, in Nabokov's Humbert and Kinbote. But the distraction of such characters is revealed more by *what* they say, than by *how* they say it. The distracted *how* of Mr. Lish's narrator is like nothing else I have read. It is all the more convincing because Mr. Lish has no sneaking admiration for his narrator's murderousness. He does not excuse, justify or condone anything; he doesn't pretend that madmen have achieved a higher sanity or that society is to blame. How Mr. Lish manages to make us feel for and with his lamentable monster is a mystery. But it is sure that he wrings from his monster's suffering the special exhilaration that is hard to get from anything but the most exacting art. (p. 41)

George Stade, "Missives from a Murderer," in The New York Times Book Review, *June 12, 1983, pp. 9, 41.*

EMILY BENEDEK

[In ***Dear Mr. Capote***], Lish's Yours Truly is ingenuous, repulsive, lonely, capable of compelling imaginative flights. His letters flow from accounts of crucial events to non sequiturs, from philosophical comment to news. The tempo increases as he works himself into the core of his story and afterward disintegrates rapidly, forced to acknowledge the facts of his life. . . .

The symbols that help his world cohere are the eye and the word: the eye that cannot see, the camera eye that catches you, and words that reveal, or have no meaning. His language is a cacophony of clichés that allows him to avoid the truth. . . . Yet out of the useless phrases he parrots from his wife, his mother and the radio he manages to wring a stark eloquence. . . .

His carefully wrought speech breaks down and signals a swift end when the final pressure comes—after he has told us about the straitjackets (they are not soft except for the laces); the victim whose death revolted him ("the mush, the brain, the whole business"). . . . Unfortunately, the novel wears the scent of a private joke. Yours Truly's constant jibes at Mailer and nasty familiarity with Capote approach the exploitive. The novel, though brilliantly crafted, its form and texture bound into Yours Truly's resolute march to madness, leads nowhere. . . .

[Cynthia Ozick has contended that the] best stories "touch on the redemptive," that is, "the sense that we act for ourselves rather than are acted upon . . . above all, that we can surprise ourselves." Lish's book plays mercilessly, albeit with great style, with psychological determinism, leaving no room for redemptive surprises. (p. 20)

Emily Benedek, "In Search of Celebrity," in The New Leader, *Vol. LXVI, No. 14, July 11-25, 1983, pp. 19-20.*

ALAN FRIEDMAN

When you read a writer as terribly clever as Gordon Lish, an inescapable question comes up—is he only clever? I doubt it. I think he's earnest and reckless besides. Mr. Lish, who made his mark first as the fiction editor of Esquire and then as a publisher's editor, has lately chosen to join the madding crowd of authors he has edited. I say this because, to judge from the two books he has written recently, he seems obsessed with writers—with their magical power as tricksters and big shots, with their vanities and inanities, with their techniques of deception, including self-deception.

Dear Mr. Capote was an eccentric first novel that earned justified high marks when it appeared last year. Sensational, it is difficult to read because it is written in the form of a long disjointed letter from a homicidal maniac to the famous author. . . . Among Mr. Lish's terrifying perceptions was one that particularly appealed to me—the discovery by the letter writer, your ordinary subliterate madman, that fancy words can serve as agents of death. Fancy words, uncomprehended, could confuse unwary victims (readers too? one wonders), conveniently turning them toward the killer's knife. The killer's line of attack, begun with a word, was through the eye and into the brain.

Now we have ***What I Know So Far,*** a collection of Mr. Lish's short stories. Short they certainly are—two to four pages long, for the most part—and edgy and subtle. To call them stories, however, is mere force of habit. Some of them do tell a tale of sorts, but even these read like riddles and satires or like sketches and blackouts. Some of them resemble narrative essays, bearing titles like **"Fear: Four Examples"** and **"How to Write a Novel"** (which is really about several kinds of suffering other than writing a novel). But virtually every story, whatever else it may be, is a monologue delivered by a first-person narrator who characterizes himself as he speaks his piece. His voice is everything; other characters have walk-on roles, but they hardly count. Never mind. It turns out that the author of these 18 stories is a cunning ventriloquist who can throw his voice with lethal accuracy. His narrators do not merely characterize themselves, they skewer themselves.

The first story, for example, is narrated by a man who is very likely sane in a clinical sense. Yet he is so detached, deaf to tones and uninterested in other people that he can commit an act of violent insanity without so much as noticing it. His wife, he tells us, cries at night. He wonders why, but only vaguely. In his repellent voice, he manages to narrate the story of another man's downfall without once realizing that what he has in fact recorded is his own catastrophe.

The longest story is the one most likely to command the attention of readers. A longwinded Jewish joke, it's also a literary "in" joke, perhaps even a cruel one. No one is likely to forget how often Philip Roth has been accused of fostering anti-Semitism (among other things) for allowing his mordant wit to bite the hand of the mother who fed him. Mr. Lish now bravely sinks his teeth into the Jewish father. He does so through a comical letter from father to son. But its jokiness is deceptive. Under the story's winking and whining, beneath its smiles of compassion, lies a satire that snarls.

It's called **"For Jeromé—With Love and Kisses,"** a kitschy echo of the title of J. D. Salinger's heart-rending story "For Esmé—With Love and Squalor." . . .

The premise of this sunny piece of savagery is that the retired or widowed parents of the most famous Jewish writers in America now live in Florida, all of them together at the Seavue Spa Oceanfront Garden Arms and Apartments. They play cards, they one-up each other, they compare their children's triumphs in the literature business. Murray Mailer and Burt Bellow live there, as do Gus Krantz, Dora Robbins, Mort Segal, Charlie Heller, a certain Mrs. Roth, the victorious Allen family (temporarily located in the penthouse) and "the Malamuds on 6, a one-bedroom facing front." The honor rolls on. And among all these literary Moms and Pops, only J.D.'s father—and a mysterious Mrs. Pinkowitz—have trouble getting in touch with their famous kids.

Can't J.D.'s father simply pick up the phone? No, because these days his "hermit" sonny boy has a *new* unlisted phone number. . . . By turns furious, cajoling, abject, hectoring, breast-beating, unctuous, crude and crafty, [J.D.'s father is] especially ticked off because his "boychikel" has abbreviated those two gorgeous names, Jerome David. With a quip, he swears he'll stop lecturing. "If I ever utter one more word in this department, may I inherit the Waldorf-Astoria and drop dead in every room." But he's unable to stop.

And I can't, without ruining the suspense on which Mr. Lish's fable turns, reveal its ending—its punch line. It's a haymaker, all right. Thrown at the jaw of Mrs. Pinkowitz's son, Tommy, who turns out to be quite as real a writer as J.D., this literary sideswipe strikes me as exploitative. Yet I suppose that Jews and gentiles alike will read **"For Jeromé—With Love and Kisses"** as a work of broad humor and high hilarity.

Alan Friedman, "Writers as Tricksters," in The New York Times Book Review, *April 22, 1984, p. 13.*

DENNIS DRABELLE

In his introduction to a recent anthology, *Great Esquire Fiction,* L. Rust Hills, the magazine's fiction editor, credits his predecessor Gordon Lish with founding the New Fiction. Since Hills doesn't define this category beyond singling out two exemplars reprinted in the anthology—William Kotzwinkle's hilarious "Horse Badorties Goes Out" and T. Coraghessan Boyle's wicked "Heart of a Champion"—let me try my hand. In a time of egregious turmoil (1969-77), these and dozens more stories published under Lish's imprimatur offered rude, gab-drunk, disorienting, fearful alternatives to mainstream magazine fiction. (p. 3)

Many of the New fictions rely heavily on outlandish suppositions, some of these not far removed from the "What If" segments of the original *Saturday Night Live*. In "Heart of a Champion," for instance, the premise is that Lassie has a sex life. The trick (by which I mean art) is to extend such potent *données* full length without sacrificing spontaneity to design.

"For Jeromé—with Love and Kisses," the longest story in Lish's collection [***What I Know So Far***], belongs to the "What If" school, and it's a lulu. As the title indicates—by punning on J. D. Salinger's "For Esmé—with Love and Squalor"—the story is a send-up of America's second most elusive literary hermit. (You might try to identify numero uno as we move along.) The premise is that Mr.Ess, J.D.'s widowed father, a resident of Miami's Seavue Spa Oceanfront Garden Arms and Apartments, has some bones to pick with his famous son and sits down to write a kvetching letter.

For one thing, Jerome has just changed from one unlisted phone number to another without notifying guess whom. Has the son's obsession with privacy gone so far as to freeze out his sole surviving parent? If it's reached that stage, Mr. Ess might as well do himself in. "One miniwink," he writes, "and your father will be only too happy and glad to make you a present of his own dead body." (pp. 3, 13)

[What crowns **"For Jeromé—with Love and Kisses"**] with glory is Mr. Ess' acrid, self-lacerating, guilt-dispensing tone. He's the most spellbinding Jewish complainant since Stanley Elkin's "Bailbondsman" raised his voice in outrage, and the story is a classic screed. . . .

Among the 17 other stories, I marked half-a-dozen for rereading some rainy day—not a bad percentage as story collections go. One of these, **"For Rupert—with No Promises,"** augments Lish's debt to Salinger by purporting to extend the Glass family saga. **"Guilt"** is an affecting story of an emotion that needs no foundation in fact. **"Frank Sinatra or Carleton Carpenter"** memorably depicts the bogies that plague earnest parents. **"Fear: Four Examples"** is notable if only for a wonderful phrase: the narrator suffers from a "rogue cramp."

Other stories in the collection are irritatingly obscure. Owing to the excessive archness of their narrative voices, they manage to fall on their faces and make the reader feel clumsy. No matter. **"For Jeromé—with Love and Kisses"** alone is reason enough for you to buy Lish's book—and for J.D. to mend his ways. (p. 13)

Dennis Drabelle, "Playing the Game of 'What If . . .'," in Book World—The Washington Post, *May 20, 1984, pp. 3, 13.*

ANNE TYLER

Mention Gordon Lish and most readers will think of short stories, logically enough. Gordon Lish was fiction editor at *Esquire* for a number of years. . . . This is what makes it so odd that of the two books he has written—a novel published last year and a collection of stories published this month—it's the novel that's the stunner.

Dear Mr. Capote is a letter of proposal: Would Truman Capote, the "famous celebrity," consider writing the authorized biography of the man who is randomly murdering young women on the streets of New York? Norman Mailer has already turned the offer down. Our letter-writer—who is, of course, the murderer himself—cannot forget this, and refers to it repeatedly throughout the book. "Norman muffed it," he tells us, and, "Let's face it, the nervy s.o.b. played himself right out of the picture!" and finally, "Face facts. Norman could see how this was over his head!"

Crazy, right? Well, naturally. We assume that much from the start, when we're dealing with a mass murderer. But we assume it in a summary, remote, dismissing way, cataloguing him: one more case in a textbook. Then all at once we're face to face with the actual man, very close up—with his scary single-mindedness, with the brilliant glitter in his eye. He pushes in upon us. The room in which we're reading becomes uncomfortably close.

And he talks. Does he ever talk! He has a speech pattern that's both comical and dreadful; it grates on the nerves; it's so distressingly familiar that we almost turn to look for the madman behind our armchairs. . . . He is insufferable, and the miracle is that by the end of the book we honestly do feel for him.

And what brings this about? Well, Gordon Lish's superb control, for the most part—an inspired sense of exactly when to unreel which thread of the story. When the letter-writer reveals his past, he first alludes to a moment so cryptically that we're baffled; then he passes on to other moments; then he returns to the first and enlarges upon it like a theme in a piece of music. A street fight he once witnessed; his mother's preference for a neighbor child long ago; the goriest of his murders; his adolescent interludes with a 13-year-old girl to whom sex meant power. . . . And finally, when all of these elements have begun to swirl together indistinguishably, we discover that we're caught in the swirl ourselves. We're no longer outsiders.

By contrast, the characters in the short story collection, ***What I Know So Far,*** remain peculiarly distant. The single exception is the narrator of **"Guilt,"** which is a strong and affecting study of a boy grown just past the curls-and-dimples stage whose mother finds a neighbor child more beautiful. (Yes, just like the mother in ***Dear Mr. Capote.***) But the other stories—seventeen of them—seem less stories than "turns," in the theatrical sense. The author steps forward, presents a little piece, and retreats. Next, please.

"For Rupert—with No Promises" is his J. D. Salinger turn. ("Wall-to-wall cigars and three packs of Raleighs a day for almost twenty-five years, and I get cancer of the goddamn *spleen,*" a character says. (pp. 33-4)

And speaking of J. D. Salinger, we also have **"For Jeromé—with Love and Kisses,"** which is a letter to "Jaydeezie darling, dear cutie fellow, sweetheart, cutie guy" from the man who keeps calling himself "I your father." . . . This is entertaining for a while, but when you come right down to it it's just a very long dialect joke—albeit one with a powerful punch line.

Then there are the more serious pieces. **"Fear: Four Examples"** describes in three pages the various kinds of anguish, both grand and trivial, that the father of a daughter can experience. **"How to Write a Poem,"** while it dumps us with a thud at the end, has at its core an ingenious, mad, deceptively reasonable idea. The narrator is a poem-stealer; he's good at detecting the moment in a poem when the poet has suddenly "seen it coming at him—an ordinary universe, the itemless clutter of an unraveling world." . . .

On occasion, a story's briefness is its only drawback: **"How to Write a Novel"** has much of the eerie, sad quality of ***Dear Mr. Capote,*** except that it's over and done with so quickly we can't fully experience it. **"Two Families"** reads like a writer's preliminary notes for a plot—and only the very sketchiest of notes, scrawled on the back of a matchbook. In fact, several of these stories are so skeletal, so elliptical, so connect-the-dots that readers feel overworked. Wait a minute, we want to say, who's getting paid for telling this?

"This is my first major rule," says the hero of ***Dear Mr. Capote.*** "Think a thing all the way through. I say you have not thought it through enough when you come out on the same side you started on." For Gordon Lish, ironically, the novel seems to be the form in which he does his best thinking-through. ***What I Know So Far*** is a hit-and-run book. ***Dear Mr. Capote*** hits and stays. (p. 34)

Anne Tyler, "Uncommon Characters," in The New Republic, *Vol. 190, No. 21, May 28, 1984, pp. 33-4.*

KEVIN J. GALLIVAN

Like captive Israel sitting by the waters of Babylon and mourning Zion, West Coast Manhattanites sit in their redwood hot tubs pining for the "real life" of Broadway, the Village, Soho, the Bronx and Staten Island, too. . . . [***What I Know So Far***] will remind them of the darker side of what they've left behind.

These are actually short works, rather than stories. Most of them have no linear progression, plot or character (other than a first person narrator). They are more like fictive ruminations. Consequently, depending upon the reader's mood at the time, the works can be either provocative and amusing, or pretentious and irritating. More often the former. . . .

The dominant theme throughout most of the book is fear. The modern terror of people intruding into our lives and disrupting the complacency and worse—the fear of being forced to become involved. Stories such as **"Frank Sinatra or Carleton Carpenter"; "Three";** and **"Fear: Four Examples"** are Lish at his best. Anyone who has walked through a city can respond to the sentiments he evokes. **"What Is Left To Link Us"** is a disturbing tale of complacency masking a will to self-destruction. . . .

"I'm Wide" is a genuinely funny four pages about the idiot inside us all taking control when we're left unattended. However, **"For Jeromé—With Love And Kisses"** is Lish with a case of the cutes. . . .

When Lish gets esoteric, he's at his worst. **"How to Write A Poem"** and **"How To Write A Novel"** were probably good for a laugh with the gang 'round the water cooler at *Esquire* but they ring hollow west of the Hudson. **"Entitled Story"** reads like something a college English major with dreams of greatness would submit to *Esquire*—with a much needed self-addressed stamped envelope.

Kevin J. Gallivan, in a review of "What I Know So Far," in West Coast Review of Books, *Vol. 10, No. 5, September-October, 1984, p. 43.*

RICHARD MARIUS

What makes fiction immediately perceptible as fiction? We cannot precisely say. . . . We may not be able to define fiction; but we know it when we see it. Or do we?

In Gordon Lish's new novel ***Peru*** we are sometimes not quite sure. The title page tells us that it is a novel. But it reads like the real thing—whatever that is. A narrator named "Gordon" recalls a trauma of his infancy when as a six-year-old he murdered another six-year-old. That child's name was Steven Adinoff. The two of them quarreled in Andy Lieblich's sandbox in 1940.

Andy was Gordon's rich and delicate little neighbor. Andy's father owned a Buick, and the Lieblich house had a big grassy back yard. Gordon's family rented a house next door—without a back yard. Sometimes Gordon was permitted to play with Andy. Then one day Steven turned up to play, too. Steven hit Gordon with a rake; Gordon hit him back with a toy hoe—and kept on hitting him until Steven fell over with bloody trenches cut in his face, and died.

The thing stays with Gordon—stays with him until he is fifty years old and has a child of his own and sees somebody stabbed to death in a TV news story and bumps his own head and bleeds; and Steven Adinoff's death pours out of him to drown him in blood. The book is his account of his recollections, a sort of exorcism. Gordon Lish is around fifty years old. "Gordon" or Gordon must tell the story to get rid of it. Or to put us on.

The book is a triumph in its evocation of how we remember things from childhood. Freud long ago showed us that our conscious memories of childhood are broken fragments held together by an unconscious sense of the self that creates an illusion of continuity. But the unconscious and the subconscious are always with us, repressed horrors lurking like demons in the dark, haunting us, tormenting us until we can dredge down into that dark and bring those demons to the day where they die and can harm us no more.

Lish wants us to suspend disbelief and accept the seemingly chaotic and repetitious collection of memories in ***Peru*** as the account of a man harrowed by horror to throw light on his darkness. Among those to whom the slender book is dedicated is "Steven Michael Adinoff, b. 1934, d. 1940."

"Gordon" tells the story in the fragmentary way of adults trying hard to piece all those disconnected parts together. Most of us have little chronological sense of childhood. We remember the vivid details, but we cannot recall something as abstract as the flow of time, of things happening in an orderly way one after another. We recall instead the pieces. . . .

In our own memories, the pieces end in darkness. We recall something vivid that happened in the afternoon. But what happened that night is eternally lost. We recall the furniture of our lives. But we do not remember what happened to it. We leap from fragment to fragment, ending with the consciousness of this moment, knowing that our present identity is a weaving of mysterious connections, a pattern invisible.

Out of the pieces that he gives us, Lish makes us reconstruct "Gordon's" life with our own fragments. He demands that we bring to his tale not only "reality" but also our bloodiest childhood fantasies, so that if we have not actually murdered a playmate in a sandbox, we still must recover gory reveries of aggression, especially that peculiar sort of nightmare where we are not the hunted but the hunter doing some terrible thing. In making that demand, Lish is not only spinning a yarn about "Gordon," but he is also making some assumptions about us.

Is this real? Did Gordon Lish actually murder Steven Adinoff with a toy hoe? Is the actor who comes up out of the audience to share the stage in the new theater "real"? No, except as our fantasies are real, and for this novel, our worst fantasies are reality enough. Lish writes in the tradition of Henry James, William Golding, John Calvin, St. Augustine, and all those others who have found wickedness in children seemingly too young for evil. More important, he writes in the tradition of those who seek to break down the wall between something we call "art" and something we call "life." No one finally succeeds in that effort, but Lish comes as close as anyone I have read recently. In doing so he creates a special sort of art that is vivid, disturbing, and profound.

Richard Marius, in a review of "Peru," in Boston Review, *Vol. XI, No. 1, February, 1986, p. 28.*

STEPHEN DOBYNS

The process of memory can be compared to pulling a bit of string to find a longer piece of string or peeling layers of an onion or seeing a picture take shape like a Polaroid shot. In ***Peru*** by Gordon Lish . . . memory is like a round, a piece of music circling and circling, picking up new details with each return.

Peru is about memory. A man engaged in packing his son for camp sees a snippet on television in which two men on the roof of a Peruvian prison stab each other repeatedly while being machine-gunned by police. The sound is off, it is late at night and there is only this visual image. The next day, while rushing to get his son to the bus, the man is accidentally struck on the head by the trunk lid of a taxi. These two events rouse in him the memory of killing little Steven Adinoff when both boys were 6 years old. . . .

We learn that the narrator, Gordon, lived next door to Andy Lieblich, who was also 6, but delicate and under the constant supervision of a nanny. Playing in Andy Lieblich's sandbox was the most important thing in the world to Gordon. One day he found a new boy there. He had a cleft palate and talked funny; he tried to interest Gordon in his Johnny Mize baseball card but Gordon has never been interested in baseball. Even now, at age 50, he has no interest in baseball. The new boy, Steven Adinoff, spilled sand on the ground, thereby breaking one of the nanny's cardinal rules. Shortly afterward, Gordon started hitting him with the hoe.

We learn these details in the first quarter of the book, then go back over them again and again. . . .

No guilt is expressed for killing Steven Adinoff, nor is the story told in expiation. The boy was a stranger, a trespasser who broke the rules and didn't seem to mind being killed. Even the boy's mother was relieved, thinks the narrator, and secretly thanked Gordon for killing him. It was exciting, almost fun, any other 6-year-old might have done the same. Besides that, it was very hot and he wasn't really responsible. As for punishment, Gordon's family had to move to another part of town. He had to go to another school and couldn't play in Andy Lieblich's sandbox anymore.

Well, what is one to make of this? At first it seemed the book might have an allegorical level: the killings in Peru, the dictatorial nanny, the wealth of the Lieblichs as opposed to the lower-middle-class status of the narrator. But while this is suggested, the connections are never drawn.

Then there is the fiction of the fiction itself. The narrator's name is Gordon. He dedicates the book to his parents, Regina and Philip Lish, which are the first names of the narrator's parents. The book is also dedicated to Steven Michael Adinoff "*(b.* 1934, *d.* 1940)," and the critic Denis Donoghue, which, considering the mixture of apparent fact and fiction, is perhaps a clue. The illusion is that this isn't fiction but autobiography.

As the repetitions and details accumulate, the paragraphs grow shorter, the transitions more abrupt and the book increases speed to a kind of frenzy. It is an amazing book—not attractive or likable but amazingly built, almost like a corkscrew.

One's final question might well be, Why? Is the book's purpose simply the retelling of this childhood murder that the author tries to show truly took place? And what is the connection with Peru, other than the fact that it was something on television that brought the murder to mind? One has to conclude that the book isn't about the murder or the quirky personality of young Gordon but just memory, how it works, what is dredged up, how we become the creatures we become, how through memory we keep our past contemporary with our present, draw strength from it and maintain our identity into an uncertain future. The result is not a pleasant book, but it's obsessive and obsessions remain fascinating.

Stephen Dobyns, "The Blood in Andy's Sandbox," in The New York Times Book Review, *February 2, 1986, p. 7.*

WALTER BODE

At a time when COBOL's logic is our most stylistically avant-garde writing, and the pornographies of sex, violence, money, fashion, or nihilism are common coin, it is a signal accomplishment for literature to disturb us deeply, to offend our deliberately cultivated sophistication. Few writers have done so with more elegance, care, and gravity than Gordon Lish, first in ***Dear Mr. Capote,*** and now in ***Peru.***

In "The Cellar," the central section of Lish's new novel, the narrator meticulously recalls the day in 1940 when he chopped up six-year-old Steven Adinoff with a toy hoe in Andy Lieblich's sandbox. Murder, vicious bloody murder, is the subject of all Lish's books, but that is not what disgusts those who run screaming from them. He sandpapers the nerve ends with a finer gauge. In ***Peru,*** for instance, the narrator chills us with his Nietzschean lack of remorse. . . . Add to that the sensuous, almost loving description of the murder and everything his six-year-old mind associated with it, and you'll begin to understand why ***Peru*** cuts so close to the bone.

The bone here is consciousness, and the narrator makes it clear that the murder of Steven Adinoff was in some sense the beginning of his conscious life. . . . But of that day, and of the people connected with that day, the narrator remembers everything in almost obscene detail. . . . "Here's the best way to say it," he tells us, "on the inside I was listening to myself, listening to the words—whereas on the outside I was all ears, I didn't miss a peep.

"Not words, but like words."

On the inside, the things like words plunge us back to the mind of a six-year-old filled with frighteningly circumscribed, authoritarian limitations, with suffocating *do*s and *don't*s, unrealized fears and unfulfilled hopes. Although he was the boy who followed all the rules, who was the best at sandbox and sat in the front seat at school, he was caught in the trap of adult language. Andy Lieblich's nanny, for instance, "probably thought to herself how could boys like this ever hurt each other? On the other hand, it was she herself who said that boys will be boys and that you could never tell a book by its cover.'' Judged by platitudes, condemned to second-class citizenship but suffused with the need for love and praise, he is trapped into violence.

The narrator's psychology is drawn with such finesse and precision that the reader is tempted to put ***Peru*** on the couch, especially given the tripartite, metaphorically Freudian division of the book: ''The Cellar'' is preceded by ''The Property,'' set 50 years after the murder. The narrator frantically calls a television station about some newsreel footage showing white-pajamaed South Americans being shot and stabbed on a rooftop. Despite his entreaties, all he can learn is that the footage was shot in Peru. In the third section, ''The Roof,'' as the narrator is packing up the taxi to take his son to camp, the cabdriver smashes the trunk lid on his forehead and fingers, unleashing cascades of blood, and more, of memories. The narrator's id, ego, and superego are transmogrified in the suburbs into the cellar, the property, and the roof. . . .

This might trap us into thinking that the narrator's erotic development was consummated by murder, but Freudian schematics detumesce in the face of the more subtle personal textures of the prose. (Indeed, Lish's writing is such a tour de force that it nearly distracts us from its substance.) One telling linguistic gesture after another recreates the shabby world of clichés and codes that confronts a hamstrung six-year-old. As the story erupts from him in thwarted confessions and unbidden details, it becomes clear that from the day he killed Steven Adinoff, he was arrested not by the authorities, but by the authority of the language he knew then. Trite evasions of phrase and linguistic hypocrisies left only the events clear, and turned guilt and remorse into mah-jongg tiles played for the neighbors' benefit.

Peru's redeeming social value lies in its picture of a mind seeking precision with only the crudest tools, and what saves the language from self-parody and self-trivialization is Lish's resolute effort to put everyday idioms to work. This aggressively task-oriented telling forces the narrator to describe completely, to exhaust himself in these events, to squeeze everything out of himself in them—''There's nothing I will not tell you if I can think of it.'' Plotless ***Peru***'s rich story is the result of a narrative strategy that eschews narration and focuses on the thing itself. ''Believe you me,'' the narrator pleads,''the words are never the point.''

And despite the shimmering surface of ***Peru,*** words are not the point, words are beside the point, which is the idea of the thing, the idea of the intensity of the feeling that creates a murderous impulse out of the ordinary, the everyday, the worlds within the words.

Walter Bode, ''Child's Play,'' in The Village Voice, *April 29, 1986, p. 50.*

MARTHA BAYLES

Let's be honest, novel readers. We expect a distinguished teacher and editor of avant-garde fiction to come up with a novel that is structured like a corkscrew, that uses deliberately banal and repetitive language, and that is about—if it can be said to be ''about'' anything—the convoluted processes of memory. Yet deep in our hearts, when we see all the reviews describing Gordon Lish's ***Peru*** in such terms, do we really want to read the damn thing? Despite our best reconstructed-highbrow efforts to appreciate innovative fiction for its ingenious tricks of structure, language, and memory, don't we still sneakingly hope that a novel will be about society and the individual, reason and passion, good and evil? Allow me to report, as most reviewers haven't, that ***Peru*** is very much about these human themes—thanks to, not in spite of, its innovations.

First, the structure. A narrator named Gordon begins in the present as a middle-aged family man, catching a bit of horrifying footage on TV. . . . Gordon's memory is jolted into an obsessive quest for the truth about a crime he committed in childhood: the murder of another small boy in a sandbox. Spiraling round and round past the same details, the narrative bores a deep hole into the buried strata of Gordon's mind. Summarily sketched as an adult, Gordon the child is, by contrast, a fully realized character—for a child. We must accept that he is a child.

Which brings us to language. Most reviewers have found Gordon's motivation obscure, and have concluded that the novel has nothing to say about morality. Certainly it is befuddling to read a fiction completely lacking in the language of feeling, to say nothing of right and wrong. From the details he relates, we are able to deduce that Gordon is neglected, perhaps even abused by his parents, . . . and that he is frighteningly lonely, inventing company and meaning out of the measliest scraps of attention. Yet none of these characterizations appears in the text. (p. 40)

That's exactly the point. Gordon is reaching back to the mental state of a six-year-old starved for love and adult guidance. In this era of Spielbergian fantasies about the purity and wisdom of childhood, we forget that it is we who socialize our young, not vice versa. For most six-year-olds, there's a trusted adult around to help sort, classify, and above all, name the mixed-up chaos of emotion, impulse, and half-formed ideas. It's a brilliant stroke to omit the vocabulary and concepts of emotion, morality, and psychology from this narrative of murder, because they are missing from the little murderer's consciousness. In young Gordon we see a child turning into a monster because he's trying to socialize himself.

Surprisingly, the little murderer grows up to be a normal adult, who neither represses the memory of the crime nor possesses any rationalization about how and why such a thing could have occurred. Instead of a convincing link between our (and Gordon the adult's) present and that past, we get innovative-fiction touches: the characters are named after Lish and his family, and the dedication includes the name of the (presumably) fictional dead boy.

At first I thought it diminished the effect of the novel to have Gordon start out with the same voice he ends up with. If there's no difference between his adult mind and his mental condition on the day of the murder, then how has he avoided committing a slew of other crimes over the years? But then I realized that Mr. Lish was toying with me. He resorts to fictional trickery to distract us from the more obvious meanings and resonances of his story. Take the setting, for example: an American suburb in 1940, where Jewish children are told not to cross the street to the ''Christian'' side. Like the vocabulary of feeling, the vocabulary of war, Jewishness, and the Holocaust are scrupulously omitted. Gordon talks about ''the Christians,'' but never mentions the word ''Jews.'' No parallel is drawn between this portrait of a resentful self-aggrandizing little boy, distracted by half-baked paranoid notions and expecting to win approval for killing, and grown men in the same world at the same time with the same problem.

But it's there. Very likely Mr. Lish means to prevent us from making his tale into an allegory. Certainly it reduces the horrific impact of the murder to consciously read it as a stand-in for something larger. As it is, the event is so imperfectly tied into the present, and into normal consciousness, that the hour of the murder stands quite alone with a compelling, continuous reality seemingly outside ordinary space and time.

The link with larger horrors is made plain when Gordon identifies what he sees on TV with that hour which, for him, has never stopped occurring. ***Peru*** is simply the name Lish gives to that endlessly prolonged moment during which we human beings keep on staggering around, bleeding from the wounds we inflict on each other, understanding nothing of what is happening to us, thinking only of how to deliver the next blow. (pp. 40-1)

Martha Bayles, "What Gordon Knew," in The New Republic, *Vol. 194, No. 3720, May 5, 1986, pp. 40-1.*

IRVING MALIN

Peru is an impressive, disturbing novel about construction and destruction. It begins with an epigraph from Mother Goose: "One, two, buckle my shoe," and the rest. The epigraph, if we look at it closely, suggests that there is order in the universe—situations can be *counted, arranged, patterned*—but it is also frightening because the order contains quirky, mysterious elements: "my plate's empty." The epigraph is an attempt to put things in the right place, but it has a dreamlike (nightmarish), odd quality.

When we start to read the novel we are suddenly introduced to a disorderly world. The narrator sees a violent prison rebellion on his television screen. He is unsure, frantic, mad; he wants to understand the pattern. What is the scene? What frames it? Why is it being shown? Thus, the narrator recognizes that he doesn't really have the whole pattern, only a *momentary picture*. The prison scene—in Peru?—is in conflict with the Mother Goose rhyme; it symbolizes a fragmented, distorted reality.

The heart of the novel is about the murder of a child by the narrator. The narrator is suddenly a six-year-old—there are quick shifts of time and space in the entire novel—and he kills a boy he doesn't really know. The murder occurs in a sandbox, another frame if you will. Again, we have disorder within order (or vice versa). Our terror is clear: How and why can destruction occur in the midst of *rules, patterns*? The murder is apparently approved of—or unnoticed—by the nanny whose favorite saying is: "A place for everything and everything in its place." She echoes the nursery rhyme; she believes in clear shapes, demarcations, places. But the murder shouldn't occur; it is unnatural. Or is murder *natural* and the rule *unnatural*? Consider the reflections: the murder, the epigraph, the television scene—all are fusions of construction and deconstruction. (pp. 153-54)

[***Peru***] moves in a circular, reflexive pattern. It is the imaginative creation of destruction and the marriage of opposites which, like the epigraph, are at the heart of ordinary and extraordinary adventures. And because the novel is narcissistic—it is a reflection on reflection—it makes us uneasy. It underlines the profound underground, "the cellar"—to quote one of the section titles—of routine existence. (p. 154)

Irving Malin, in a review of "Peru," in The Review of Contemporary Fiction, *Vol. 6, No. 2, Summer, 1986, pp. 153-54.*

Roland (Glyn) Mathias

1915-

Welsh poet, editor, critic, biographer, short story writer, and nonfiction writer.

Mathias is considered among the most significant contemporary Welsh poets writing in English. His poetry reflects the history and geography of Wales and displays Mathias's concern with the preservation of Welsh identity. Mathias also details his conflicting personal experiences and feelings as a Welshman who writes only in English. Often employing alliteration, complex syntax, and concrete images, Mathias creates densely concentrated verse that is sometimes faulted for sacrificing clarity and passion in favor of technical perfection. However, most critics concur with Glyn Jones's assessment: "[Mathias's] poetry, full of striking lines and startling imagery, is strenuous, gnarled, thoughtful, highly individual and original."

In his first major collections, *Break in Harvest and Other Poems* (1946), *The Roses of Tretower* (1952), and *The Flooded Valley* (1960), Mathias explores relationships between humanity and environment and between past and present through vivid descriptions of Welsh landscapes. Mathias's themes become more personal in *Absalom in the Tree and Other Poems* (1971) and *Snipe's Castle* (1979). Documenting Mathias's alienation in his homeland as a result of his inability to speak the native language and his education in England at Oxford University, these volumes also lament the cultural decline of Wales. *Burning Brambles: Selected Poems, 1944-1979* (1983) was described by Michael Collins as "an important and welcome book, not only because it brings together the major work of a distinguished poet who deserves wider recognition than he has yet received, but because its skillful, resonant poems transcend the particulars of place and history to illuminate our lives and speak with unusual honesty to them." In addition to his poetry, Mathias has published a collection of short stories, *The Eleven Men of Eppynt and Other Stories* (1956), a biography of the Welsh poet Vernon Watkins, and a critical study of John Cowper Powys. He has also served as editor of the *Anglo-Welsh Review*.

(See also *Contemporary Authors,* Vols. 97-100; *Contemporary Authors New Revision Series,* Vol. 19; and *Dictionary of Literary Biography,* Vol. 27.)

© *Welsh Arts Council*

THE TIMES LITERARY SUPPLEMENT

The immediate attraction of Mr. Roland Mathias's ***The Flooded Valley*** is the exact imagist portrayal of Welsh town and country scenes that its poems offer.

> There are four kestrels in this single field,
> Tweedy hangers-about that the wild
> Sun misses.

However the use of such clear descriptive power is not an end in itself in the best of Mr. Mathias's poems. There, the few taciturn, rather stoically unhappy references to himself give another point to the details of the scene around him. They are not simply symbols for his mood, they are real things; but one sees that he is driven to this hard appreciative looking at them because he feels that their slight beauty is all that there is.

> I watch the muster of grasses between the stones
> The wind pitching dead in the porch
> As the afternoon passes,
> And I feel my free soul bounden, all of a sudden
> lodged, its habit bones.

Mr. Mathias's sound-play is bare and equally fine for his purpose—rather a clashing together of pebbles, a stonechat's call on one of his own hillsides. These are uneven verses, but in them a defined personality is revealed by an undoubted poet.

"Sensuous and Bare," in The Times Literary Supplement, *No. 3057, September 30, 1960, p. 630.*

GLYN JONES

A poet who has never seemed to me to have had anything like his true measure of consideration is Roland Mathias, historian and critic, now editor of the *Anglo-Welsh Review*. Roland's poetry, full of striking lines and startling imagery, is strenuous, gnarled, thoughtful, highly individual and original. What has excluded it from a wider audience than it now enjoys, I think, may be its author's unremitting concern for truth, which seems to play its part in producing in some of his poems an impression of opacity or impenetrability. Although not a didactic poet Roland gives the impression of a man who would reject out of hand anything which did not conform to or point up his profoundly experienced vision of reality. Life is an agonizingly serious matter, and so is poetry. So much honesty of thought and feeling packed into his poems give them, in spite of their marvellous diction and imagery, something of that rather compressed and baffling solidness one gets from time to time in Hopkins, although I am sure Roland owes nothing to the Hopkins technique. One would not wish Roland's poetry to be different. Its wholesome brilliance, its contempt for what comes easily, seem to me ineradicable elements in its make-up. I hesitate to use a shabby word like 'integrity' in speaking about work as genuine as Roland's, and yet it is the only one that really conveys the impression created by the poems in the volumes ***Break in Harvest*** and ***The Roses of Tretower.*** (pp. 138-39)

Glyn Jones, "Introduction to Poetry," in his The Dragon Has Two Tongues: Essays on Anglo-Welsh Writers and Writing, *J. M. Dent & Sons Ltd., 1968, pp. 124-39.*

JEREMY HOOKER

Both place and period are of particular importance to Roland Mathias, a great deal of the poet's significant personal experience being associated with the geographical areas that are the focus of his historical research. . . . Above all, his imagination returns again and again to the places in Wales that were deeply involved in the seventeenth century's great disturbances over the rights of conscience. The figure of Henry Vaughan moves questioningly through several poems.

Thus Roland Mathias's Welsh landscape is an historical one; but it is not the historical landscape most familiar to us in modern Anglo-Welsh verse, which seems, rather too often, to be oblivious to anything between the Age of the Princes and the Age of the Chapels. Deeply interested as he is in those who fought for questions of conscience, his own poetry enacts the hesitancies and complexities of a conscientious mind. And in this too Roland Mathias's voice is highly individual among modern Anglo-Welsh poets: it is totally without the strain of rhetoric that is both a strength and a weakness in poets as diverse as R. S. Thomas, John Tripp, and Harri Webb. If he is not hard-hitting with the quality of anger that can become poetry, he is also without self-righteousness.

But one outcome of these virtues is the difficulty of his poetry. Among the poems in Roland Mathias's three important collections there are some that can be understood only with a degree of concentration exceeding even that which Shakespeare in the language of *Troilus and Cressida* demands. Thus when uncomplicated poems, which are also very good, such as **"The Flooded Valley"** and **"Argyle Street"** give release to one's mental tension, it is impossible not to get irritated with lesser poems that are much more difficult. Of course, the difficulties are by no means invariably defects: they can derive from compression organic to the poem's meaning, or from subtle nuances of meaning, or from mysteries the understanding can only hint at. But they can also derive from a failure of communication in the poet.

In *The Dragon Has Two Tongues* Glyn Jones includes a generous and sympathetic account of Roland Mathias's poetry in which he describes 'an impression of opacity or impenetrability' in some of the poems to their author's 'unremitting concern for truth' [see excerpt above]. While I believe this account to be just, full critical justice perhaps requires the less generous observation that this opacity can be infuriating. For instance ***Break in Harvest,*** 1946, the poet's first important book is in parts almost as maddening to read as the period apocalyptics that for a time claimed even Vernon Watkins. Yet the book reveals a considerable individual talent, especially in the title poem, and in **"Pastoral"** and **"Balloon over the Rhondda".** Verbal inventiveness of a high order is everywhere apparent, not least in the witty description of the balloon in the latter poem:

> A silver elephant with wings
> Came curvetting and lolloping
> With a one-sided smile.
> He turned and chortled, lay down on his back
> And laughed, helpless and rolling.

But in these fine personal poems the same syntactic and imagistic originality that sustains them also overreaches itself, becoming tortuously compressed and oblique to the point of incomprehensibility, especially in the poems' endings. In a sense the poet's very inventiveness becomes an embarrassment; it is as if he, like Mercutio in creating his vision of Queen Mab, becomes almost hysterically imaginative in pursuit of his individual apprehension of reality. More prosaically, one's grasp on the dramatic situation in the poem is rendered extremely tenuous. As in some poems in which Roland Mathias's knowledge of history far exceeds the reader's, one isn't always sure what is being done, where, and by whom. But perhaps there is another reason for the difficulty of certain poems. It is worth asking whether in them the historian has such control of the poet's urge to self-expression that he can speak of himself and of his own emotions only obliquely and with extensive qualifications. It is significant surely, that personae play a large part in the best of Roland Mathias's later work just as, in ***Break in Harvest,*** **"London Welshman"** and **"Drover's Song"** are among the most successful poems.

The poet's most recent book, ***The Flooded Valley,*** 1960, is by far the best so far. It includes the best poems in ***The Roses of Tretower,*** 1952. . . . He has achieved haunting speech rhythms before, notably in the beautiful **"Coed Anghred"**, but this gift has all too often been sacrificed to a verbal density that, even though it serves a conscientious concern for the truth still deserves to be called over-writing. But what looks like density in other poems such as **"Freshwater West"** is an extremely subtle, and very Welsh, word-music of assonance and alliteration. (pp. 8-11)

The landscape Roland Mathias experiences in the present is charged with his awareness of the past. His poetry is filled with imagery of walls, bounds, bourns; with metaphors for the limits of the known. Beyond the known the unknown attracts, and is a source of fear. . . . Nowhere is Roland Mathias's ability to evoke the past more vividly realized than in **"Orielton Empty"** and **"Cascob".** In each poem vital physical impressions of place serve to establish a strong sense of the period associated with it:

> Blank wall facing west, belfry of weather-board
> Raised on a druids' mound, none of it
> Reassuring. Within, a brass of familiars, habit
> Of clergy, pater pater pater noster noster noster
> Three times for Saturn, O save our sister
> Elizabeth Lloyd from spirits, amen. Behind
> My back a thin mediaeval tongue, the wind
> Carrying it woodward, tang and tone.

("Cascob")

Each poem uses the image of a circle:

> The lake is reedy, indistinct with flies:
> Durgi and Soda, gundogs of the Rosebery age,
> In this red evening whimper, the cortege
> Halting again at their graverails. Rhododendrons drink
> Gapingly like mangrove roots from the nearer bank.
> Of the whole circle there is no one left to thank
> For the windbreak, for the island hopes
> Of the heart, for the sickle that blunts and stops.
> (**"Orielton Empty"**)

The recurrent image, with its different meanings, defines one of Roland Mathias's leading themes. The past has created circles of life, enclosures of reality, within which it lives on. Its powerful but disturbing personality is a magnetic force by which the poet is at once attracted and repelled. But to where can he escape from it? 'Outside the circle the sea winds scut and kill.'

Originality, strong feeling and an extremely subtle mind are all features of Roland Mathias's poetry. Each poem is an unique occasion, and yet there is a strength—if not a singleness—of purpose revealed by certain preoccupations, as well as by the gestures and tone, which recur in a number of them. Surprisingly, despite these qualities and the verbal inventiveness which riots through ***Break in Harvest,*** assertion of self is what the poet finds most difficult. In order to speak directly as a man to men he has to become another. (But in making this observation it is worth stressing how well he succeeds with the voice of intimate experience when he does achieve it and how infrequently it is to be heard in any form except in outstanding poets.) Sometimes, when speaking in his own person, the poem becomes convoluted with reservations and qualifications. Admittedly, the result is often an attractive knottiness of texture. But it is not only modesty and honesty that produce this effect, though these are important qualities of his voice. It is also the sense of history, the ability to render palpable the thick rotundity of an historical landscape; to bring alive his apprehension of time in depth. He cannot and probably does not wish to cast off the burden of history in order to make room in his poetry for more expansive self-expressiveness. This poetry can be self-expressive only modestly in relation to the presences he moves among. Roland Mathias celebrates others, and discovers himself among them in a landscape in which the bounds of existence tend to be measured by the past. No single feeling is inclusive of the many stimulated by the Welsh landscape—reverence, comfort and dread, sadness and the sense of limitation are all currents within his work. Perhaps it is this very truth to complexity that has caused him to receive less attention as a poet than some noisier but far less gifted talents in England as well as in Wales. He will neither simplify nor popularize an emotion. Nor will he exploit the isolated self. As his poetry shows, the landscape with a single figure can be a richly crowded place. (pp. 11-13)

Jeremy Hooker, "The Poetry of Roland Mathias," in Poetry Wales, *Vol. 7, No. 1, Summer, 1971, pp. 6-13.*

EDMOND LEO WRIGHT

The poems of Roland Mathias [in ***Snipe's Castle***] draw the reader repeatedly to a serious concern. He is a man aware of the fading of a supportive myth. Across a variety of forms, rhymed and unrhymed, dramatic and meditative, the theme recurs. One speaker of his stands above a Welsh valley, looking about for signs of that support, and of the redemption it might bring. His impartial eye will not let him miss a plume of smoke from a rubbish-dump, which he sees as the town's "Burning its pages from the Domesday Book". Mathias suggests here as elsewhere that an answer to the problem of loss of myth is to be found in the persistence of history and that there is therefore an increasing danger in the carelessness with which we throw out our traditions. In another poem of four brief and gnomic verses, **"After Christmas"**, he reflects on the worth of the Christian message. We are left in doubt, a doubt which both shocks and invigorates, about who are the wise and who are the fools with regard to that message, and whether there might be some interpretation of it other than those of sincere believer and sincere atheist. There is the same healthy indecision between outright acceptance and outright rejection as in Hardy's "The Oxen".

> All humours and all wills
> Consult the dark: except fools
> Trading a whisper that the Child
> Is back from Egypt.

The myth has shrunk to a whisper, but Mathias has a keen ear that can pick out what matters. Such perceptiveness alone would not make a fine poet, but Mathias also has the power to create a text that can go on growing in meaning. One of his personae who seems to have lost his "nation" looks down at a broken fragment of tombstone and asks it for help:

> I who would quickly refashion
> My stony fathers, had I learned
> But how, call you to speak,
> Speak.

In that unforced use of self-reference—a text of someone speaking to a text and calling upon it for self-renewal—it is plain that Mathias has "learned how". To quote from something he himself has written about David Jones, here is "tradition working in the present". There is great variety of drama in ***Snipe's Castle:*** we overhear personae in many voices and rhythms, and forget the interposing of prints. As a Big-Englander, and in spite of aid from a reliable Welsh annotator, I must confess myself outside a myth like the dramatic sequence **"Madoc"**, but within some of the less allusive sections of **"Tide-Reach"**.

Edmond Leo Wright, "Myths and Elegies," in The Times Literary Supplement, *No. 4035, July 25, 1980, p. 851.*

G. B. H. WIGHTMAN

[***Burning Brambles: Selected Poems 1944-1979***] contains a selection of poems from five books of poetry published between 1946 and 1979. Mathias's work echoes his peregrinations: it constantly returns to his Welsh roots. His poetry is soaked in Welsh culture. Even the complex metrics he employs reflect his understanding of the twenty-four measures permitted to official Welsh poets. These measures were regularized in the fourteenth century but go back to at least the sixth century. The reader does not have to be familiar with Welsh poetics to enjoy these poems. Nevertheless, many of the Welsh references are obscure and explanatory notes would have helped.

Mathias is not a famous poet (his fellow countryman R. S. Thomas is much better known). Yet his poems are beautifully devised; he captures sensations, and thoughts, in highly original images. The way he shapes a poem, the intelligence of his language and the clear purpose of his themes have a deeply satisfying effect. However, the level tone he maintains signifies not only his mastery of the subject in hand, but also the fact that he remains outside his observations. His control betrays an absence of emotion. Notwithstanding this aspect of his work, Mathias is an underestimated artist. ***Burning Brambles*** is a valuable collection and I recommend it.

G. B. H. Wightman, in a review of "Burning Brambles: Selected Poems 1944-1979," in British Book News, *May, 1984, p. 309.*

MICHAEL COLLINS

For almost forty years now, Roland Mathias has played a major role in the recognition and preservation of an Anglo-Welsh literary tradition. . . . As a serious and accomplished poet, he has himself made a major contribution to Anglo-Welsh literature and is generally recognized as one of the finest English-language poets writing in Wales today. . . .

While the history and heritage, the people and places of Wales appear prominently in [***Burning Brambles***], the poems grow for the most part out of the poet's personal encounters with them. In **"They Have Not Survived,"** for example, a poem from ***Absalom in the Tree*** that recounts the migration of poor country farmers to the mining valleys of Wales, the speaker ends by suggesting that his own success in the Anglicized world may be in some sense a betrayal of his nation and people. In one of the finest and most resonant poems in the collection, **"Brechfa Chapel"** from ***Snipe's Castle,*** the speaker's visit to the old chapel reveals his own deeply felt isolation in the fragmented world of contemporary Wales and his sadness at the passing of a shared faith and heritage. While the poems in ***Burning Brambles*** offer a wide range of subject and manner, they characteristically seek to understand the speaker's relationship to the larger world in which he lives his life.

Burning Brambles is an important and welcome book, not only because it brings together the major work of a distinguished poet who deserves wider recognition than he has yet received, but because its skillful, resonant poems transcend the particulars of place and history to illuminate our lives and speak with unusual honesty to them. While one looks forward to a collection of new poems from Roland Mathias, ***Burning Brambles*** is a remarkable achievement and a fitting tribute to a man who has, for so many years, served his nation and its writers with skill, generosity and love.

Michael Collins, in a review of "Burning Brambles: Selected Poems 1944-1979," in World Literature Today, *Vol. 58, No. 3, Summer, 1984, p. 417.*

JEREMY HOOKER

[Roland Mathias's ***Burning Brambles: Selected Poems 1944-1979***] reveals an inheritor who is uneasy in his inheritance, which, as a result of his rather complicated family history, . . . embraces both Welsh-speaking Wales, in the Rhondda as well as rural Carmarthenshire, and the tensions between languages, cultures, and nationalities of a border people. Yet, taking into account two or more generations, there are few of us who do not have complicated family histories, and Roland Mathias's special unease as an inheritor has an additional cause in his feeling that he is unworthy of the inheritance. This feeling, in turn, reflects the Puritan tradition of which he is, among writers in modern Wales, one of the most faithful sons. The paradox of one who is faithful to his inheritance, especially in his feeling of unworthiness, is central to his poetry.

In a sense, Roland Mathias has remained a borderer, first reclaiming a foothold in Wales through historical research and poems set in Gwent and Powys, then moving deeper into the country, both geographically in his movement west, and in his involvement with Welsh history and culture, but remaining one who, in the words of **"Porth Cwyfan",** feels that 'I can call nothing my own'. Consequently, it is from deep within the tensions and complexities of the Anglo-Welsh situation that he writes, not from some ideal resolution in the achievement of 'real' Welshness. In his autobiographical essay in *Artists in Wales,* he has described himself as standing outside 'the house' of Wales, 'sorry in my heart to be shut out', and as going on knocking at the door, with 'memory and guilt'. Certainly, memory and guilt are the main springs of his poetry, but the metaphor is characteristic of his humility toward what he would undoubtedly regard as the primary language and culture of Wales, and it belies his achievement. Here, however, another qualification has to be entered; for achievement is not a word to be used easily of Roland Mathias, not because his poetry does not merit it, but because the Puritan conscience engendering his conviction of personal inadequacy also involves the most radical questioning of all man's actions, works and motives. (pp. 94-5)

The natural flight of time and the visionary moment that transcends or transfigures it are a recurring theme of Roland Mathias . . . , but to claim that he often realises the theme with directness and clarity would be to substitute another half truth for the allegation that he is usually opaque. It is more useful, I feel, to demonstrate the relationship between the strengths of his poetry and the demands it makes upon the reader.

Anne Stevenson, in a perceptive review, has described Roland Mathias's style as 'that of a poet bruised by those experiences he most loves, and the density of his syntax mirrors the complexity of his emotion'. Syntax and verbal texture are conspicuous features of his style, and both serve meaning. At the outset, in many of his poems published in the 1940's, there is a troubled and partly occluded poetry, in which a strong emotional impulse is impeded by its means of expression, and the very eloquence is inarticulate. This is probably due in some degree to his extreme consciousness of the poem as an artifact, and his preoccupation with the madeness of verbal texture. . . . Later, increasing skill has made verbal texture one of the main sources of pleasure in his poetry, but when combined with his essentially qualifying voice, which is bent on being truthful at all costs, in a largely non-colloquial language, it can also make considerable demands on the reader. . . . Roland Mathias's concern with verbal texture leads him to sculpt each phrase, while his concern with truth nourishes a wealth of implications. In addition, he develops an intricate metaphor, and uses words—'trug', 'summary', 'gentling'—that are either dialectal, or unusual or ambiguous in context—and phrases, such as 'tricking the human aberration', that require an extra effort of thought. And where is the effort to come from, when the mind is already at full stretch? The question is how to grasp all the meanings of a sentence that is longer than a sonnet and employs the capacity of an imagist poem in every line. . . . At times, he can madden the patient reader (the impatient having turned back at the first subsidiary clause, knotty piece of syntax or dense cluster of words), but there is something heroic about a poet who is so intent on the poem as a made thing, instead of pretending that he is just talking much like anyone else, and on telling his truth, that he makes no concessions to frailty of ear or attentiveness, or to lack of knowledge.

When occlusion occurs in work of his poetic maturity, which he achieved in the 1950's, it results from his struggle to dramatise the difficult relationship between himself and his subject, and is often a necessary part of the poem. But my dwelling on the demands of his poetry must not be allowed to obscure either his splendidly vigorous dramatic monologues, whether in his own person or that of an historical figure, such as Henry Vaughan, Absalom, and Sir Gelli Meyrick, or the emotional directness and force of many poems, such as **"The Flooded Valley"**, **"A Letter"**, and **"Departure in Middle Age"**. . . . (pp. 96-8)

In the first verse of **"Departure in Middle Age"**, the poet has described himself as 'cold / And strange to myself'; this is the 'sickness' of the second verse, and it is a characteristic state of the poet. The primary cause of this is stated in **"God Is"**:

> God is who questions me
> Of my tranquillity

Accordingly, there is little tranquillity in Roland Mathias's poetry, and his Christianity manifests itself principally as a conviction of sin. While R. S. Thomas in his later poems is a mystic concerned with the ways in which God hides or manifests himself, Mathias is a moralist concerned with what God asks of him personally and of man in general. There are more difficult poets who have found a wide readership, and I believe that it is the radically disquieting focus of his attention, together with its mediation by Welsh history and places, that is the main cause of his relative neglect. There has probably never been another time when a preoccupation with sin was less likely to attract readers. The seriousness makes embarrassing demands, even though Roland Mathias, in common with most important modern religious poets, uses the metaphors and images of Christianity—fountain, dust, light, fall, and so on—instead of its dogmatic or technical terms; his use of 'convenant' and 'justification' does however indicate the specific religious provenance of his concerns. (pp. 98-9)

[In **"Channels of Grace: A View of the Earlier Novels of Emyr Humphreys"**] Roland Mathias has written that Emyr Humphreys's 'writing and its preoccupation are the result of Wales's heritage of the last three centuries: they begin in that Puritan seriousness about the purpose of living, about the need for tradition and the understanding of it, about the future of the community as well as the individual, that has almost no place in the writing of contemporary English novelists'. These words apply almost equally to his own poetry, and help to explain, incidentally, why neither poet or novelist has had anything like his due outside Wales.

Roland Mathias writes well about people, especially those who could not write or speak for themselves. . . . [Mathias] is not only concerned with memory and loss. His consciousness of time colours much of his poetry with an elegiac mood, and his settings and metaphors taken from an eroding coastline, as in **"For an Unmarked Grave"** and **"A Letter from Gwyther Street"**, produce some of his most evocative and haunting lines.But he is not primarily an elegist in the sense that Hardy was: for Mathias memory that brings back the pain of loss also demands that justice be done. While visiting historical places invariably provokes a self-questioning which finds himself wanting in comparison with the dead, justice requires that he questions the dead, too, even the craftsmen he greatly admires, like Charlie Stones, or John Abel, the King's Carpenter, in **"Sarnesfield"**. But the most remorseless questioning is reserved for himself, and his celebrations or commemorations of others are likely to include a self-condemnation. . . . The Puritan conscience is reinforced by his sense of isolation in a country where he can call nothing his own; indeed, it is relevant to ask whether, in a situation in which tradition has been largely eroded and the future of the community is in doubt, the 'puritan seriousness about the purpose of living' does not focus too narrowly on the self, with morbid results for a poet whose strongest words are kept for castigating himself.

This point is worth pursuing if the peculiar demands of Roland Mathias's poetry are to be understood. His conviction of sin is acute, leading to self-dislike: 'the smell of a life ill lived' of **"Burning Brambles"** is typical, and throughout his poetry the temptations of the flesh are felt and bitterly regretted. He asks in **"The Mountain"**, 'Give me the punishment that saves', and in a much later poem, **"The Green Chapel"**, he writes that, 'the fear within / Is the worst, the horror of separation / From meaning', so that physical and spiritual torment, in a condition of penitence, is at the heart of his poetry. . . . [In] many poems a state of mind approaching hysteria is held in tension with the life-enhancing qualities of his verbal energy and spirited imagination. At the farthest extreme, verbal pyrotechnics and a sense of complete personal inadequacy cause a particularly uncomfortable tension. (pp. 99-100)

To expect from Roland Mathias anything other than an art that questions himself and implicitly questions the reader is as impertinent as to expect R. S. Thomas to chat about his poems at the end of a reading: what he has to give, he has given; now, with the poems in our minds, we should go away and submit to their questioning. In both cases, the art is Puritan, but Roland Mathias's is far more grudging with the consolations of nature or affirmative vision, and is morally the more demanding. His is a poetry that is suspicious of everything that is natural and everything that is human, including itself. (pp. 100-01)

I share the frustration expressed by some reviewers at Roland Mathias's refusal to annotate his historical poems. Yet it also seems to me that this is a positive reflection of his regard for the integrity of the poem, which appears negatively in **"Not Worth the Record"**, and of one of his most attractive qualities—his stubborn insistence on the importance of people, places and events outside areas of conventional reference, which in Britain reflects the extreme selectivity of a particular version of English history. Thus, Roland Mathias, like the Irish poet Patrick Kavanagh, affirms the epic scale of his 'parish', and therefore, by implication, of every other parish in the world, by assuming its human centrality. Many poets of his generation have looked to London; he has remained true to the Romantic rediscovery of an original Christian value: that life here and now, or there and then, in the individual soul and in the particular community, is as important as life anywhere at any time. The only part of his thought that threatens to belie this truth is his tendency to see a more 'real' Wales from which he is excluded, but in practice he has been loyal to the people and places that have made him. He is not a poet to make concessions to those who, whether in Wales or outside, patronise Wales with Anglocentric ideas of 'Welshness'. The consequence of his loyalty is that he has taken his Anglo-Welsh situation far more seriously than all but a few writers with whom he shares it, and he has done so partly out of his humble sense of himself as an outsider who cannot claim to be fully Welsh, and who must earn his place in Wales by the quality of his effort and understanding. This, indeed, accounts for the passion informing the meticulous care of his historical sense, and evident equally in his poems, criticism, and historical writings. Care of this order is both an emotional need and a moral obligation, and justice is its object. As I have already argued, the discomfort at not belonging which reinforces his Puritan conscience thereby helps to ensure that he is much more of an insider than he would ever claim to be, and in his representation and exploration of the Puritan tradition he is one of the small group of modern writers in English who reveal Wales from the inside. Indeed, there comes a point when to speak of a poet's 'situation' is as external as it is to speak of sin or love as a 'theme': Roland Mathias writes from his life in Wales, concerned not with his 'achievement' in the public eye, but with the truth and integrity of the action. (pp. 101-02)

[A] good poet is known not by the 'correctness' of his answers according to any dogma, but by the intensity with which he lives the questions, and the integrity of his response to the tensions and complexities to which, as a man living at a certain time, he is subject. In any case, it would also be to ignore the force with which the decay of the Puritan tradition of individual and communal responsibility is dramatised. . . . And the fact that in his fidelity to that tradition throughout his writing, Roland Mathias has earned the right to his anger and pessimism and embattled resolution. 'The strong remembered words' have been the basis of his poetry for some forty years. They are the words he has lived by, words of the tradition from which he derives no false comfort and has none to offer; no comfort at all, in fact, except the comfort of poetry which, in its concern to tell the truth and to embody it, treats the reader as an equally serious person. (p. 103)

Jeremy Hooker, "Roland Mathias: 'The Strong Remembered Words'," in Poetry Wales, *Vol. 21, No. 1, 1985, pp. 94-103.*

Greg Matthews

1949-

Australian novelist.

© Jerry Bauer

In his first novel, *The Further Adventures of Huckleberry Finn* (1983), Matthews evidences his interest in American culture. A continuation of Mark Twain's masterpiece, the book begins with the murder of Judge Thatcher. Although this crime was committed by Pap, who Matthews resurrects in the novel, Huck is wrongly accused and jailed. The slave Jim frees Huck, however, and the two flee to California. Like its predecessor, *The Further Adventures of Huckleberry Finn* unfolds episodically and contains narrow escapes, heroic deeds, identity changes, and numerous deaths. Although some reviewers contended that Matthews's examination of social issues failed to match Twain's standards, others praised him for capturing Twain's sound, style, and humor. David Kirby declared that it was "hard not to prefer the pure adventure of Matthews' book to the weighty themes of the original."

Matthews moved to the United States to research and write his second novel, *Heart of the Country* (1986). Set in nineteenth-century Kansas, the book chronicles the frontier adventures of Joe Cobden, an illegitimate half-breed. In *Heart of the Country,* Matthews abandons the homespun dialect of his first novel and adopts what Gene Lyons called "a tone-perfect rendering of the omniscient, moralizing voice of Victorian fiction at its best." Matthews also examines grander themes, including the randomness of fate and the destructiveness of the human will. Although some critics found passages of the book gruesome and risqué, Donovan Fitzpatrick commented that Matthews "glosses his descriptions of sexual adventures in a euphemistic prose of almost Proustian delicacy."

FREDERICK BUSCH

"All modern American literature comes from one book by Mark Twain called *Huckleberry Finn,*" Ernest Hemingway wrote in *Green Hills of Africa*. He wrote at least two clear expressions of that sentiment—the sexually ambivalent story, "The Last Good Place," and *A Farewell to Arms*. In each, a couple flees the States, and in each they are fugitive not only from laws but from constraint on their love; in each, a young woman cuts her hair short and appears mannish; in each, the flight becomes a quest for the state of nature, the New Eden—an America of the mind.

Greg Matthews, an Australian, in his first novel [***The Further Adventures of Huckleberry Finn***], writes a sequel to Twain's great *Adventures of Huckleberry Finn*. Matthews has read Twain ardently and no doubt he has read Hemingway too. But he overlooks the implications of "modern" in Hemingway's famous statement. Hemingway wrote about the American fiction he was helping to make in response to Twain and to the spirit of America. But he also wrote, and wrote about, a fiction that Twain helped to define for Hemingway. It had to do with a young man's loss of his father, his attraction to and flights from figures of the mother; and that young man's utterly American journey to the dark frontier (a psychic as well as physical one) in the absence of women, but in the presence of the other-colored companion and guide. . . . Hemingway's comprehension of, and love for, Huck Finn's adventures was intense, American, both personal and literary, and was made palpable in his fiction.

While I intend no disrespect for Matthews—he has labored long and hard, and he has mastered much of the apparent sound of Twain—his sequel echoes none of the personal or cultural resonances to which I allude. It strikes me that nearly any intelligent reader or writer can digest some Twain and emerge with such lines as, "Dirt on its own's a mighty good thing . . . and water on its own is mighty good too, but when you mix 'em together you get mud." This is what Matthews does: he mixes a lot of events and conversations and remembered Twain together, and he emerges muddied. He ventriloquizes for 500 pages. After the Widow Douglas' house burns down—the fire gets rid of the burden of Jim's family, freeing Jim and Huck to journey on—our lads make their way with Forty-Niners to the California gold rush. We find once more that Huck is in drag, that religion's a sham—there is a Whorehouse of Christ the Lamb—and there are traveling theatricians, hundreds of lies, and some amusing though not inspired doggerel. Jim is in and out of danger because of American bigotry; sex is alluded to; Huck on and off sees signs, and then the person, of his "dead" father. (p. 9)

Pap, in Matthews' book, is a shallow, cunning wastrel. As such, he loses the force he had in the original. A ghost is of course less frightening if it is subsequently seen as natural; in Twain's book, Pap was, alive or presumably dead, a nightmare figure out of childhood's deepest terrors. Now, in Matthews' book, he is only a second-rate crook. . . .

Twain once considered writing a sequel to his *Adventures,* in which Huck would be a mad old man. Twain's Huck is more likely to have been a persuasive Ahab than Matthews' Jim would be a Queequeg or Huck an Ishmael—and Matthews does threaten a sequel to *Moby-Dick* on his final page, To him, apparently, all American fiction is susceptible of endless visits and revisits, a kind of literary Disney World.

Why not, then, a sequel to *A Farewell to Arms?* And then a sequel to Papa's African writings, with a sequel Papa saying to a sequel Kandisky that all modern American sequels begin with a sequel to *Huckleberry Finn?* A novel must feel necessary to live and work. I am wondering, then, without wanting to be as cruel as Matthews is to Jim, why his novel came to pass, and then survived its author's fiery gaze. (p. 10)

Frederick Busch, "New 'Huck Finn': Never the Twain Shall Meet," in Book World—The Washington Post, *September 4, 1983, pp. 9-10.*

TOM LeCLAIR

Greg Matthews substitutes audacity for ambition in ***The Further Adventures of Huckleberry Finn,*** a sequel to Mark Twain's novel that reruns Twain's characters, comedy and sentiment in Huck Finn dialect. Mr. Matthews fails to equal Twain's art, which may be expected, but he also fails to try to do more than copy him, which is unexpected a hundred years after the original. To rewrite *Huckleberry Finn,* as John Seelye did in *The True Adventures of Huckleberry Finn,* is an act of respect and interpretation. To create a new Huck as, say, a banker in Omaha or a retiree in Miami might be an act of understanding and invention. Mr. Matthews's continuation of the teenage Huck is merely exploitation. Not even Twain, who was known to re-use material, kept Huck going. . . .

Coincidences, "harebreath" escapes (at least nine of them), heroic deeds, accidents and convenient deaths give the plot a manic motion and reduce everyone but Huck and Jim to the clichés of old Western movies. Huck witnesses greed, chauvinism (the women are mostly good, again) and racism against Indians, Mexicans and Chinese, as well as blacks, in incidents that provide obvious sentiment. His malapropisms, tall tales and minstrel-like discussions with Jim often strain to repeat Twain's comedy.

The world Mr. Matthews's Huck sees in 1849 is darker than Twain's Mississippi world: cholera, mass murder, prostitution, adultery, madness, political corruption. In response, this Huck is more philosophical, frequently vulgar and increasingly assertive about injustice. These situations and Huck's maturing are predictable extrapolations from Twain's time and novel but without Twain's texture of place and observation of minor characters. Mr. Matthews skillfully mimics Huck's voice and wittily deflates some American pomposities with Huck's innocent eye. Moving west, Huck seems to be moving toward the 20th century. But ***The Further Adventures of Huckleberry Finn,*** like the fraudulent perpetual motion machines exposed in the 19th century, runs on borrowed energy. (p. 28)

Tom LeClair, "A Reconstruction and a Sequel," in The New York Times Book Review, *September 25, 1983, pp. 14, 28.*

ZACHARY LEADER

Huck Finn and *Tom Sawyer* are old and proven favourites of the young, but they also, especially *Huck,* express feelings and needs which are fundamentally adult. As juvenile books, they're "all mixed up and splendid", to quote Huck. Greg Matthews's ***The Further Adventures of Huckleberry Finn,*** though also splendid, seems to me to be much more exclusively in tune with childlike feelings, despite being issued for grown-ups. Though many of Twain's adult themes are retained, and sometimes cleverly developed (as when Jim is driven almost mad by prejudice), there's something self-consciously "worked up" about them. They are part of this novel's *homage,* of a piece with its skilful handling of dialects. ***The Further Adventures,*** though, is more than parody or tribute; it has a life and energy of its own, and its adult pleasures and interests (the cleverness and tact of its allusions, for instance, or the astuteness of its treatment of the relations between Huck and Pap) are overwhelmed by essentially childlike ones, in particular those taken in heroic adventures and adventurers. (p. 1045)

The dangers Huck and Jim encounter on the frontier involve Indians, outraged citizens, cholera, starvation, trigger-happy gunmen, madmen, and drunks. Though these adventures unfold episodically, as in Twain's novels, there's little sense of drift or aimlessness—of the arbitrary or the picaresque—about the narrative. In part, this is a product of Matthews's care with geography; we always know where we are and how much progress has been made in the journey West.

The novel is less satisfying, as one would expect, in its treatment of the relation between Huck and Jim. The sweetness and intimacy of that relation in *Huck Finn* is central to its achievement (as are comparable moments of intimacy in the relation between Tom and the Widow Douglas in *Tom Sawyer*). In ***The Further Adventures*** Jim is a more distant if dignified figure (Matthews provides reasons for this), and the tenderness of his and Huck's feelings towards each other are often assumed rather than expressed; Huck is no longer "chile" or "honey", for instance. Twain deeply valued such openness of expression, and resented its absence in his own childhood. "I was born *reserved* as to endearments of speech and caresses", he wrote of his upbringing in the *Autobiography*. In a truly free childhood, his fiction implies, one lived outside civilization ("the root of all evil"), such openness, though vulnerable, is possible.

Matthews may well share this conviction or hope, but it is not a major concern of his novel. His creative energies are focused elsewhere, principally on a host of memorably eccentric minor characters. These include the proselytizing harlot daughters (or Seven Graces) of McSweeney the Evangelist; the wild-eyed Reverend Mordecai, a pederast; Mrs Ambrose, who has a hand "like a chicken foot, hard and thin and cold"; Andrew Collins, the feebly heroic "poet of the plains"; Frank/Obadiah, a schizophrenic; Randolph, the ice-cold gambler; and the Amazonian Lydia Beckwith, with whom both Andrew and Randolph fall in love. "That Mrs Beckwith", says Huck, "she's sure some kinder woman. Sergeant Hollander says she's one of them Amazons that cut their right titty off so's they can aim their bows better. He says one of these nights he aims to find out for sure if she's got the full pair or not. I'd sure like to see that myself." This is one of several "indelicate" passages in ***The Further Adventures,*** and it's by no means the most daring. The grounds for defending such passages are their invariable appropriateness to character and setting, and the manner in which Huck reacts to and relates them. Huck's response to sexual matters is a disarming indifference or incomprehension—or in the case of dirty jokes, innocent glee. There's nothing prurient about "I'd sure like to see that myself", nor about the pleasure Huck takes earlier in a joke—the novel's broadest—about a suspicious husband and the dubious virginity of his mail-order bride. Though these moments of sexual explicitness are startling, they are told in a way that contributes, paradoxically, to the novel's childlikeness. (pp. 1045-46)

Zachary Leader, "Celebrating the Virtues of Childhood," in The Times Literary Supplement, *No. 4200, September 30, 1983, pp. 1045-46.*

DAVID KIRBY

Following the success of *The Adventures of Huckleberry Finn,* Mark Twain tried to revive the novel's main characters a decade later in *Tom Sawyer Abroad,* and *Tom Sawyer, Detective,* but both books were failures. Now the true sequel to Twain's masterpiece has appeared almost 100 years later in the form of a first novel by, amazingly, a young Australian-born writer named Greg Matthews. . . .

[***The Further Adventures of Huckleberry Finn***] begins when Huck is wrongly accused of the murder of Judge Thatcher. Along with the faithful Jim, Huck lights out for the territory, joining the 1849 Gold Rush and encountering on the trail a cast of characters as wily, scabrous, and entertaining as those in Twain's original.

In this sequel Huck and Jim are a little older and a good deal wiser than they were originally. It is refreshing to see them holding their own in a world of grown-up nonsense and bullying, and it is especially gratifying to follow Jim as he slowly and painfully creates a newer, freer self.

In his genius, Twain used a trick which has been the downfall of lesser authors: He showed us everything through the eyes of a child. The same device works here. Even as he matures, Matthews' Huck retains an innocence that blinds him to much of the world's rascality yet which reveals marvels not to be seen by a more jaundiced eye. . . .

Matthews' novel is not the only recent attempt to revive Huck and Jim. In 1970 John Seelye came out with *The True Adventures of Huckleberry Finn,* a literal rewrite of the original which attempts to satisfy Twain's critics, especially the ones who objected to the ending of the novel. (Seelye substitutes a despairing, "realistic" ending for Twain's high comic one.) Though the story Matthews tells is totally new, he, like Seelye, appropriates Twain's style so skillfully that it is often necessary to remind oneself that one is reading a work of the late 20th century, not the late 19th.

Indeed, from time to time I found it hard not to prefer the pure adventure of Matthews' book to the weighty themes of the original. With sympathy and penetration, Twain examined the greatest social problem this country has experienced, and it goes without saying that an honest novel about slavery isn't always a pretty novel. In ***The Further Adventures,*** the social issues are smaller, and consequently there is more of a focus on pure adventure.

This book makes terrific reading, but it is something more as well: it reintroduces the original to old friends and perhaps to a new audience, as no purely scholarly book could. *The Adventures of Huckleberry Finn* is the closest thing we have to a Great American Novel, and Mr. Matthews' faithful, energetic continuation of the tale is an important reminder of that.

David Kirby, "Energetic Sequel to 'Huckleberry Finn' Is Faithful to Original," in The Christian Science Monitor, *October 11, 1983, p. 39.*

MARY ANN LOWRY

Greg Matthews has guts. How else can a first-novel author who dares to write a sequel to *The Adventures of Huckleberry Finn* (*Adventures,* hereafter) be described? He dares, and, what's more, he does it well. ***The Further Adventures of Huckleberry Finn*** (***Further***) is a tour-de-force of 36 chapters, with the bulk of them covering the trek westward. (p. 233)

Echoes of *Adventures,* such as "You ain't playin' no joke on ol' Jim is you, Huck?" and Jim's father-sermonizing to the boy, permeate the story. Also, allusions to other Twain works, especially *Roughing It,* a sub-title in Chapter 31, crop up frequently. Huck is called a "puddin-head," a town is named Hedleyville, signs and hexes, the "It don' pay to mess wid kings" philosophy, several references to Tom Sawyer's envy at the friends' adventures, and more, are present.

Differences appear in ***Further,*** too. Perhaps because mores are different in 1984, the humor in Matthews' novel is sometimes more risque, but humor it is and just as basic as Twain's. Although Twain might have thought of depicting the practical method of checking the virginity of a mail order bride, Matthews wrote it. Prejudice also appears in ***Further*** but rather than applying only to "niggers" it embraces "Greasers" and "Chinky Chinky Chinee" as well, depicting clearly the ugliness and brutality of prejudice anywhere. And Jim comes into his own when he says, "I ain't steppin' down no mo'."

Matthews seems comfortable when writing about women. As Twain did in *Roughing It,* he shows how men outnumbered women in the Old West. He, too, depicts the usual low-class whores who followed the gold strikes and the just-as-usual higher-class whores who plied their trade in the burgeoning cities on the Coast. Mrs. McSween, the ex-whore who forces her five daughters into her old trade to insure the success of her preacher husband's camp meetings, seems a part of the Twain burlesque tradition, as is Mrs. Ambrose, widowed and embittered on the trail, but mellowed by remarriage. It is with Lydia Beckwith, the married woman who runs off with the doggerel-scribbling poet, that Matthews delineates a woman of depth. She chooses to nurse the dying-of-cholera poet, contracts the disease, instructs Huck to burn their wagon, then shoots herself, so Huck and Jim will leave the desert death spot and have a better chance for survival. Thereafter, she is Huck's measure of what a woman should be. Her death also brings Huck, who turns 15 in the novel, the revelation that he is no longer a child. (pp. 233-34)

Matthews' novel suggests that there might be more adventures of Huck and Jim. Huck favors "them South Sea islands and howling adventures among the cannibals," while Jim says "he wants to go to Africa and see for himself if it's true there's nigger kings there." If the future does, in fact, bring with it more such Matthews-supplied adventures, they should be on the reading list of every Twain fan. Only in the first few chapters of ***The Further Adventures of Huckleberry Finn*** does Matthews seem straining at times to make connections with Twain's novel. Thereafter, he's on his own, and his writing makes mighty fine reading. (p. 234)

Mary Ann Lowry, in a review of "The Further Adventures of Huckleberry Finn," in Western American Literature, *Vol. XIX, No. 3, November, 1984, pp. 233-34.*

PUBLISHERS WEEKLY

If the vast buffalo herds that still roamed Kansas in the mid-19th century were in some sense the heart of the country, then the white pioneers committed some kind of spiritual suicide by wiping them out. So suggests [***Heart of the Country,*** a] sprawling and doggedly fanciful tale by the Australian author of ***The Further Adventures of Huckleberry Finn***. . . . The story includes incest, murder, whoring, drunkenness, opium taking, ghoulish burial and shovelfuls of insanity, as well as a spectral white buffalo, among other echoes of *Moby-Dick*. Dickens (with whom Matthews has been capriciously compared) could treat reality in a fanciful manner, Matthews treats fancy as though it were reality. His story is enjoyable by dint of its vitality, but also exasperating because of its lack of clarity and substance.

A review of "Heart of the Country," in Publishers Weekly, *Vol. 229, No. 10, March 7, 1986, p. 83.*

DONOVAN FITZPATRICK

Think of the Marquis de Sade writing a history of the West and you have an approximation of ***Heart of the Country,*** a big book about goings-on in the village of Valley Forge, Kan., in the last half of the 19th century. One of the few good guys is Joe Cobden, offspring of an Indian woman and a white ne'er-do-well. Blessed with a quick mind, Joe is a kind of prairie intellectual and iconoclast. He is also bitter because fate dealt him a low blow—he is deformed and ugly, and thus most people recoil from him. Unhappy, longing for affection, he becomes variously a bouncer in a bordello, a buffalo hunter, a wood chopper, a carver of cigar-store wooden Indians.

Another decent fellow is Sheriff Ned Bowdre, who commits suicide when he learns that his brother, a farmer, is fond of sexual relations with his pigs. You'll meet Phoebe Pike, an intelligent young woman who runs away from her domineering father and tyrannical grandmother in a household where never is heard an encouraging word.

The rest of the cast consists largely of a prime collection of petty, ignorant, Bible-thumping hypocrites, so superstitious and vicious as to make Erskine Caldwell's Georgia crackers seem like the most upright of citizens. . . . All in all, the characters live in unrelieved misery, their existence, in the words of Thomas Hobbes, "nasty, brutish and short."

Mr. Matthews's dialogue is right on the mark, and he's done his research. The reader gets a thorough introduction to the agony of unattended childbirth and a fascinating report on the wholesale slaughter of the buffalo that once roamed the Kansas plains by the millions, as well as a graphic course in the art of embalming. The book is a page-turner that may be too grisly for some; but fortunately for the faint of heart, the author glosses his descriptions of sexual adventures in a euphemistic prose of almost Proustian delicacy.

Donovan Fitzpatrick, "Bleeding Kansas," in The New York Times Book Review, *May 4, 1986, p. 52.*

GENE LYONS

Imagine, if you can, a Thomas Hardy novel set not on the heaths of Wessex but the bare plains of western Kansas. That's the best way to get a fix on Greg Matthews's remarkable historical novel ***Heart of the Country***. . . . Like many a 19th-century novel, ***Heart of the Country*** tells us the episodic, eventful tale of a foundling—in this case Joe Cobden, a half-breed who grows up to be a "hunch-backed" buffalo hunter—and his adventures on the frontier.

But what's memorable about the book is less the story than the way it's told. Without any of the winking and nudging that often accompanies such efforts, Matthews manages a tone-perfect rendering of the omniscient, moralizing voice of Victorian fiction at its best. His themes are the grand ones: the blindness of fate, the persistence of madness and folly and the destructiveness of the human will. Like Hardy, Matthews drives his themes home somewhat repetitiously, but the flaw is more than made up for by the richness and amplitude of his prose. . . . It's a stunning, mesmerizing performance.

Gene Lyons, "The Crude Joy of the West," in Newsweek, *Vol. CVII, No. 19, May 12, 1986, p. 78.*

SAM CORNISH

Heart of the Country is a novel about Joe Cobden, the illegitimate son of a farmer who is the self-proclaimed mayor and builder of a Kansas town settlement called Valley Forge. Joe's mother, Millie, is a Native American who is rejected by Joe's father (who is unaware that she is pregnant) because she is considered, in the eyes of the town bigots, a "squaw." But this is Kansas in 1854, and Millie brings Joe into the world at the cost of her own life. . . .

Greg Matthews, author of ***The Further Adventures of Huckleberry Finn,*** has created a hero that Dickens and Fielding would admire, and has written a novel containing harsh, vivid depictions of children and parents which may remind some readers of the opening chapters of John Irving's *The World According to Garp*. It is also, however, a bittersweet portrait of long-suffering relationships between generations of men and women and children and their parents. Matthews has an understanding of how 19th-century America was shaped in a way which nearly destroyed ethnic society and the nuclear family. . . .

Matthews presents all his people and landscapes so as to extend the conventions of historical fiction, and ***Heart of the Country*** succeeds in a way in which few novels of the American West have done.

Sam Cornish, "Novel of the 19th-Century American West," in The Christian Science Monitor, *June 9, 1986, p. 30.*

JOHN BRYNE COOKE

It is a daring thing for a writer to travel to a strange land halfway around the world and tackle its most enduring myths, but Greg Matthews, an Australian, has done just that, not once but twice. In his first novel, ***The Further Adventures of Huckleberry Finn,*** he tried with mixed success to give new life to one of America's best-known literary characters. In ***Heart of the Country,*** his second, he tackles the Old West, and he poses himself a further challenge by choosing for his protagonist an illegitimate halfbreed hunchback named Joe Cobden, surely one of the most unlikely figures ever to ride the frontier. . . .

Matthews moved to Kansas to write the story and his love for the West is plain. He writes with confidence and skill. In ***The Further Adventures of Huckleberry Finn,*** he copied Twain's dialect-narrative; here he adopts a far more literate, indeed a literary, style. (It should be said that his fondness for graphic descriptions of the sordid and gruesome may be distasteful to some.) He has done the extensive research necessary to familiarize himself with a land and century not his own, and except for the flagrant misspelling "Sharpe's" for Sharps rifle, and a few lesser historical errors, he presents the facts of life on the frontier credibly. However, the use of British spellings and conventions throughout the book is jarring to American eyes. (p. 8)

But although Matthews has the facts at his fingertips, something essential about the feeling of the Old West eludes him. The picture he paints remains flat and lifeless, and in the end he fails to offer us a fresh view of the West or to make for the unlikely figure of Joe Cobden a place in the pantheon of engaging literary heroes.

The story is populated with familiar stereotypes: the pious preacher whose private life is anything but admirable, the sheriff too impressed with his own authority, the creepy undertaker, the gossiping townsfolk. It would seem that Matthews, like Joe, is best at creating wooden figures. Those he offers here are of a particularly mean-spirited sort, and they show no trace of the qualities that enabled real 19th-century Americans to settle the western vastness. Many have little to do with Joe, except in passing. The few characters with an original twist are allowed to drift out of the story too soon. There is a hint of misogyny as well. The women have scarcely two dimensions, more like one and a half, and they suffer some appalling indignities at the author's hands.

Matthews fails most seriously in the way he handles Joe. Here he has created an original character, yet he treats him as he does the rest, like a puppet on a string, and what Joe truly wants is difficult to grasp. His feelings are described, never evoked. He has no clear goal or ambition; except for his early desire to become a buffalo hunter, he is aimless most of the time. . . . (pp. 8-9)

And yet once I had finished the book and set it aside for a day or two, I found, somewhat to my surprise, that I missed Joe Cobden. Rather, I missed what Joe might have become if only Greg Matthews had cut his strings and let him grow to full size in spirit, if not in body. For I saw in Joe the potential to be what I think he wanted to be more than anything else: a true Man of the West. (p. 9)

John Bryne Cooke, "Where the Buffalo Roam," in Book World—The Washington Post, *June 22, 1986, pp. 8-9.*

James (Phillip) McAuley

1917-1976

(Also wrote with Harold Stewart under joint pseudonym of Ern Malley) Australian poet and critic.

An important figure in Australian literature, McAuley valued classical poetic forms and techniques as means for achieving clarity and precise meaning. He is often compared to such neoclassical writers as John Dryden, Alexander Pope, and Jonathan Swift for having stressed the importance of the intellect in ordering poetic inspiration. After having concentrated on writing satirical lyrics early in his career, McAuley composed meditative verse following his conversion to Roman Catholicism in 1952. He frequently employed symbols from Christian and Greek myth to explore universal social and spiritual values.

McAuley first gained international attention for collaborating with Harold Stewart in a literary hoax that resulted in the publication of *The Darkening Ecliptic* (1944). This collection of randomly constructed and purposely obscure lyrics was credited to Ern Malley, who was supposedly a deceased, untutored, working-class poet. The poems were hailed by an avant-garde literary group, the "Angry Penguins," fulfilling the collaborators' intention of revealing the need for stronger aesthetic criteria than those evidenced by their contemporaries.

McAuley's first collection, *Under Aldebaran* (1946), contains emotive lyrics fueled by his intensely satirical wit. While McAuley was praised for his skillful use of unusual symbols to depict social chaos, several critics contended that his self-conscious examination of the creative process detracted from his poignant observations. Following his conversion to Catholicism, McAuley published *A Vision of Ceremony* (1956). The poems in this volume are more restrained than his previous work, as McAuley attempts to achieve order through clarity and simplicity. McAuley employs Greek myth in a sequence of poems entitled "The Hero and the Hydra" to develop what he termed an "adequate symbolism" to express his appreciation for the presence of God.

In his book-length poem *Captain Quiros* (1964), considered his most ambitious and successful work, McAuley abandoned his use of the lyric in favor of the long narrative form. Written for oral presentation, *Captain Quiros* relates the story of a Portuguese explorer who searched for the "Great South Land" in hopes of founding New Jerusalem. Through extensive use of symbolism and metaphor, McAuley presents parallel physical and spiritual journeys in which the good intentions of his characters are threatened by inherent human weaknesses. McAuley's next volume, *Surprises of the Sun* (1969), contains autobiographical poems which focus on his childhood. In this and subsequent volumes, including *Music Late at Night: Poems, 1970-1973* (1976) and *A World of Its Own* (1977), McAuley returns to the meditative lyrical style of his early work and achieves a more relaxed and personable manner of presentation. *Collected Poems, 1936-1970* (1971) contains his most important early work.

In addition to his poetry, McAuley published several nonfiction works. In *The End of Modernity: Essays on Literature, Art, and Culture* (1959) and *The Grammar of the Real: Selected Prose, 1959-1974* (1976), he stresses the importance of classical poetic values while discussing the works of a wide range of poets. McAuley authored studies of such writers as Edmund Spenser, George Eliot, and Christopher Brennan, and he compiled *A Map of Australian Verse: The Twentieth Century* (1975), which introduces and reprints the work of a number of contemporary Australian poets. McAuley was also a founding editor of *Quadrant,* a leading Australian literary journal.

Promotion Australia

(See also *Contemporary Authors,* Vols. 97-100.)

VINCENT BUCKLEY

McAuley has (and without intending it) forced controversy about himself. He has done this first by the comparatively simple device of publishing a book [***Under Aldebaran***]—a book which contains some very good poetry indeed; secondly, by the relatively more complicated business of engaging in a literary hoax which shattered some dearly-held reputations; and, last of all, by remaining a 'Classicist' and becoming a Catholic. And he has managed all this despite the fact that very few of the people who consider him most controversial have ever seen him. . . .

When, in an age like this, one calls a poet a Classicist, one ought to consider it just as important to avoid question-begging as to eschew glib definition. McAuley was educated in the University of Sydney; and I have recently scanned certain issues of the magazine *Hermes* to see what kind of poetry he published there as an undergraduate. . . . And I found that what had most exercised McAuley the undergraduate was a romantic rebellion, seemingly against the dour necessities of life itself. It was a rebellion compounded equally of fierceness and irony, of realistic analysis and romantic yearning, of an urge to self-expression and an urge to self-laceration in the very act of expression. McAuley, in fact, was the very type of the Joycean intellectual; in some moods, I think it is sufficient to say, of the modern intellectual. His poem **"In Honour of Chris. Brennan"** may go some distance towards proving the point. . . . One of the interesting things about this early piece is the fact that it establishes a strain which seems to be constant in McAuley's poetry—at least until its most recent development. That is the strain of the rhetorical gesture, a gesture striving always to be not vague and self-defeating, but rather general and graceful at once, sensuous perception striving to become either mime or music. . . . It establishes beyond the slightest doubt that the later position to which McAuley came was earned by struggle, made firm by a process of self-purification rather than by any easy assumption of its rightness. It establishes, too, that his classicism (for so we must no doubt continue to call it) is a matter not of cold formalism and of withdrawal from life, but of a realism at once personal, social, and philosophical. (pp. 177-79)

[***Under Aldebaran***] is an uneven book, both in the quality of the poetry and in the positions or attitudes which it states. Some of the poems in it seem to me comparatively worthless, and it is not necessary to devote marked attention to them; what is more disturbing is that certain of them are in danger of undermining the completeness and maturity of the position, the cast and quality of life, which he adopts in the really fine poems. . . . The two groups seem to belong to two different and mutually exclusive worlds of imagination. (p. 179)

One half of McAuley's poetic sensibility reaches out towards the general, to treat in symbolic terms the movements of society or the values which concern all men; the other half reaches deeper into itself in order to find out the meanings of its own experience. In both operations, he is engaged in kinds of discovery, and in neither kind does the process itself reach any definitive resolution within the scope of ***Under Aldebaran.***

In the more general poems, he makes an affirmation and an attack—an affirmation of the values which give real life and real stability to society, and an attack on the factors, whether they be institutions or human attitudes, which thwart those values, and which, moreover, set up false images of life and a false stability. . . . (p. 180)

McAuley does not work only through direct statement and through images common to a minority group, as so many of the Left-Wing or the *Bulletin* poets do; he takes symbols which are unusual yet capable of being recognized by the educated reader, and invests them with a personal feeling, puts them into a context of images always personal, and sometimes bordering on the private or cryptic. (pp. 181-82)

Something remains to be said of the other great preoccupation in ***Under Aldebaran***—the attempt to discover the meaning of his own inner states, and in particular of the inner processes which beget poetry. We must notice that the way in which McAuley poses this question to himself is very far from the impressionistic excitement and self-congratulation of the Romantic. He really is trying, by a sort of personal depth-analysis, to see what are the archetypal meanings of the poetic process. The poetic spirit is represented by the sun, which can irradiate consciousness only at the cost of recurrent withdrawal into the subconscious. Self-discovery must precede contemplation of the external world. . . . (pp. 183-84)

Such a universe is not the poet's alone, it belongs to all men; and by engaging in the labour of self-discovery necessary to reveal it, the poet is working as a representative of all mankind. That is his peculiar glory, as the effort of self-discovery needed to achieve it is his risk, his occupational hazard. . . . (p. 184)

The poet is entitled to his exultation, as he is irrevocably committed to his risk. And the exultation . . . is one achieved momentarily, almost fortuitously, and certainly only at the expense of great effort on the part of its author. . . . [In many of the poems in ***Under Aldebaran,*** wherever] exultation appears, it is an exultation hardly won and mixed with intimations of the possibility of despair. Wherever we find rage and scorn, we find them directed at himself and his own precarious vocation as much as at human folly; rage is often, in McAuley's poetry, an index to a hidden fear; and it cannot be vented in the impersonal tone of commentary which so much poetry demands. Despite the persistent care for control, for precision of statement and clarity of image, the poet seems to be fighting a continual rearguard action—against the menace of history and the frightening demands of his own nature. Wherever anything is gained, it has had to be fought for; and the battleground was the personality itself of the poet.

I do not know if McAuley would still be prepared to advance this conception of poetry as a sort of edifying adventure. Certainly, if his rather shoddy satirical poem, **"A Letter to John Dryden"**, may be adduced in evidence, he would now completely reject that view, derived from Blake and Jung, of the relationship between the imagination and the subconscious which gives point to such poems as **"Chorale"**. And certainly, his later poetry shows a marked change in emphasis, a new feeling of subjective freedom. We may see this if we look at any of the lyrics written since his conversion to Catholicism. . . . The exultation here is one of release—a liberation not so much of one precarious and menaced impulse as of a whole personality. . . . We might say that, since it is a released poetry, it is also to some extent a disembodied poetry.

Yet it is true that McAuley has found a new use for poetry—a use of which he had scarcely been aware previously. Poetry may now be used to praise; it is seldom used to propagandize. Since he has become a Catholic, he has sought to make his poetry perform the double function of helping him to place the movement of his past life into a new perspective, and to give a new lyrical context to traditional images in which, during the years of Christendom, the traditional truths had been expressed and embodied. Indeed, all the poetry which he has written since the publication of his first book seems to me to be an attempt, on two different levels, to objectify and make new sense of the problems which so exercised him in his earlier development. This attempt, of course, takes in both 'context' and 'form', and it is precisely in its inclusiveness, I should suggest, that the danger of this kind of poetry lies.

First, we have the series of Greek poems called **"The Hero and the Hydra"**—a series of which the best-known example is **"Prometheus"**. . . . In these poems, McAuley seems to be trying to 'distance' himself from his own poetic experience, to give that experience both a general application to the affairs of man and a stability derived from its roots in Greek myth. The myths of Prometheus, of Chiron, and of Heracles are revived in order to provide a framework within which the dilemma of modern man can become intelligible. . . . Myths for the modern age are effective only if the images of human action which they present are readily seen by a modern audience to be images of *their own* state. This is the big problem of the modern poet who is a 'classicist' in sympathies and in form. And in McAuley's case, one gets the impression that the mythological poems represent a sort of spiritual experiment which was left quickly behind him.

For he has outlived this phase of his development, and has passed into another phase—a phase in which the dominating impulse behind the images is not Greek, but medieval or perhaps Baroque. He is even more interested than before in the presentation of life as a ceremony; what has changed is the nature of the ceremony, and the dominant images in which it is re-enacted. (pp. 184-87)

The new strain in McAuley's poetry seems to take on two slightly different forms. The first is the simple (and often lovely) giving of praise and thanks that the poet has been permitted to discover the meaning of his life. . . . (p. 187)

Some of this later poetry tends towards the hymn or canticle, and some towards a narrative structure. . . . This poetry seems to me inadequate to McAuley's fine intelligence and great lyrical grasp of the factual. The point is that a wedding of the sacred and the secular depends on the secular's being there to be married; ritual feeds not only on its own tradition but on the common life of the people as the poet experiences it and makes it his. And I cannot help feeling that his work at the moment is not sufficiently rooted in the actual; it is not quite earthy enough; there is too little flesh to afford incarnation to the word. (pp. 187-89)

His main virtue is his magnificent intellectual and artistic sanity. He seems never to embark on a poem unless its symbolic relationships, and the way in which those relationships express an idea, are alike clear to him. (p. 190)

This is a poetry of statement, of a statement general, graceful and exalted; consequently, it is largely out of the main stream of modern poetry, which tends to play down statement in favour of imagery, or imagings. Yet it is more even than that; for the statement is accomplished largely by means of a symbolism derived from external nature, which has been submitted to the process of a Blakean vision, caught, stylized, and as it were converted into the figures of a verbal dance. It is not only the statement, but the imagery itself, which strives to be luminous and exact. What is to be understood, to be made clear, is the poem itself; the concepts and statements simply provide its core.

If we are to call such poetry intellectual, we had better be quite sure what we intend by the word. It is certainly not abstruse poetry, and it is philosophical in its materials rather than in its method. (pp. 190-91)

It is not a passive poetry, as so much intellectual poetry is. On the contrary, it is forceful and active. Within a tight framework of images and ideas, the poet gives his line a flexible, swaying quality in which the impression of directed force is provided by the unusual yet precise use of verbs and adjectives, and by their careful placing. . . . (p. 192)

The grace and accuracy of the diction cannot be faulted. When it is the instrument for effecting a marriage of clear ideas and sensuous realism in a poetic line which approaches the condition of dance, it gives us some of the best poetry ever written in this country. Its danger (and it is one to which McAuley sometimes succumbs) is of a paradoxical kind: it is the danger of using poetry to make intellectual points instead of enacting living ideas. (pp. 192-93)

The second reservation which I have about some of the poetry in ***Under Aldebaran*** is one concerned not so much with weaknesses in the completed works themselves, as with a factor which inclines to cramp the future development of their author. . . . McAuley's earlier poetry feeds a little too greedily for its subject-matter upon its own processes, upon the processes of poetry. (p. 193)

Where his later poetry tends to arouse reservations, it is not for the same reason. Now, McAuley is tending not to the overspecialized, but to the over-simplified. The best of his most recent poetry has either a lyric beauty or a calm and authoritative eloquence which do not appear in the same way or to the same extent in his earlier. But it reads as though it had been freed of all tensions, all complexities of mire and blood. . . . And he seems content to let his militant and rather exclusive Catholicism remain curiously remote from the human preoccupations, the intense distresses of the world, which it is so wonderfully fitted to vivify and integrate. Despite its fervour and occasional vibrancy, this is not a fully incarnational poetry; for it seeks not to be warm in inclusion, but precise in exclusion. . . .

However McAuley's work may develop in the future, he has given to poetry a mind and sensibility passionate, graceful, and intelligent. (p. 194)

Vincent Buckley, "Classicism and Grace: James McAuley," in his Essays in Poetry: Mainly Australian, *Melbourne University Press, 1957, pp. 177-95.*

NORMAN TALBOT

It seems as though very few critics are sure how to treat McAuley's poetry. Vincent Buckley follows one of the most useful lines in his title 'Classicism and Grace' [see excerpt above]. : . .

I don't think the term 'classicist' means that his style and subject-matter—or attitudes—are like those of the great Greek and Roman writers. Nor do I think it is simply the opposite of 'romantic', whatever that means. Perhaps it should be 'neo-classicist'. . . . Certainly it must have something to do with those great neo-classic concerns, Reason and Decorum, and therefore with McAuley's conviction that modern poetry, like modern society, is engaged with what is unreasonable (what oughtn't to be done) and indecorous (what is not done). . . .

His regard for Decorum is related to his conviction that the traditional verse-forms provide the richest and best vehicles for poetry, while Reason persuades him to keep 'poetic imagination' within 'the frame of rational order'. In this second attitude, though not the first, he is in line with most modern poets, but his 'Reason' is different from Pope's.

A more challenging aspect of this 'classicism', though one far less classical, is shown in McAuley's constant search for a valid, adequate and accessible symbolism for the present day. He points out that what remnants we have of the traditional symbolisms—such as the Cross or the Crown—are dying quickly in the human mind. Since his conversion to Catholicism, one might have expected a firm reliance on the furniture of Church ritual, but McAuley sensibly continues with his older material too. (p. 69)

In much of McAuley's early poetry there is violent apocalypse imagery—especially striking in **"The Incarnation of Sirius"**—which is obscure until we equate the apocalypse with the final contest of either Chaos and Order or Energy and Curb, according to our point of view. . . . Indeed, in a way the early McAuley is the Romantic revolutionary, denouncing a sterile, false society. In spite of the strikingly 'modern' mode of expression there is a recognizable similarity to Shelley. Both poets are technically assured, intensely intellectual, even more intensely visionary, passionately subjective yet grappling all of human concerns to them. Of course they are different too, especially in their faults: Shelley becomes formless and muzzy through over-conceptualizing, while McAuley tends towards earnestly clamped stanzas and hermetic symbols, possibly through too ready an acceptance of dogmatic and formal corsets. At their worst, both ecstasists find themselves incapable of communicating their vision. . . .

McAuley has claimed that the major characters or implied figures in his poetry are '. . . the lover, the saint, the artist, the ruler, the hero'. I don't think this list is accurate, however, though a combined figure of artist and saint (or rather visionary) is certainly of great importance. I would suggest that the Chris Brennan (or Shelley) figure of the Wanderer is the central character of most of McAuley's important poetry. In Brennan, the Romantic soul-voyager becomes more Symboliste, but still recognizable. In McAuley he is likely to put on the favourite Australian fancy-dress of the Explorer, but even then he is recognizable. The physical journey is symbolic of the journey of the individual soul, and the Wanderer himself is a metaphysical universe. . . .

Admittedly, McAuley renounces the subjective, but he is too much of a poet to ignore the romantic effort to discover himself which appears so consistently. Buckley cites some dubious evidence: the sun under the sea in the opening of **"Chorale"** is beautiful, but surely not as obviously a soul-journey as is implied in all those navigators, discoveries and maps that extend from before **"Henry the Navigator"** and **"Terra Australis"** (*Voyage within you, on the fabled ocean*) to their culmination in [his new volume] ***Captain Quiros.*** (p. 70)

The selection of Quiros as hero is not unimportant. Even without the evidence of the reference in **"Terra Australis"** or the claim in **"The Inception of the Poem"** that the 'theme' had come to him in youth, we could see how suitable the partnership was. Quiros is, especially in McAuley's interpretation, a Catholic visionary, rigidly righteous even when exhausted, rejecting the cruelty, self-indulgence and cupidity of his contemporaries. The story of his attempt to find the South Land and claim it for Christ scarcely needs to be altered in one detail for McAuley's purposes. Partly, I admit, the discovery does not take place because of chance, time and weather, but the main reasons are the spite and greed, cruelty and dishonesty, meanspiritedness and spiritual blindness of his superiors, followers and collaborators. The lack of greatness of purpose is the most important point, of course, and this is seen as springing from narrow, futile self-interest.

Like Quiros, McAuley feels the world's degeneracy very keenly, and perhaps it would have been better had he acted as his own narrator (since Quiros cannot well do so) rather than inventing the poet-secretary Belmonte. He is kept out of things much of the time, but when present he ruins things. . . . It seems as though, quite untypically, McAuley has used Belmonte as a stalking-horse, an ironic cover for his own poetic personality; certainly the worst sort of persona.

The intense faith and purpose of Quiros's life, frustrated by events but also, and mainly, by corrupt men in a false, decaying society, presents a resolution of the contradiction posed above. In this situation one may have a firm faith yet resent and despise the human world; certain of the truth but isolated in it, one may fight a rearguard action against past and future history, against contemporary civilization, against the folly and vice of man.

This, however, is an attitude that seems to have a debilitating effect on ***Captain Quiros.*** Thinking back to **"The True Discovery of Australia"**, we may be excused for feeling that it is as well the explorer did not find Australia, since any spiritual paradise, like any Eden, might be defiled and destroyed by man:

> Land of the inmost heart, searching for which
> Men roam the earth, and on the way create
> Their kingdoms in the Indies and grow rich
> With noble arts and cities; only to learn
> They bear the old selves with them that could turn
> The streams of Eden to a standing ditch.

This passage leads to the difficulty which is implied in the account of Malope and the other inhabitants of Santa Cruz, and again in the second voyage with reference to Gente Hermosa, while the vision contains both the references to Bougainville at Tahiti and the mention of the aborigines in Australia. These passages not only conflict with each other about the concept of the Noble Savage and the religious questions of sin and innocence, but also leave us wondering whether McAuley's attitude to them is not made ambiguous by his dislike of 'civilized' corruption. (pp. 70-1)

The Santa Cruz passage is one of great impressiveness, describing from the islanders' point of view, the religious ritual associated with the volcano. It not only creates difficulty in understanding the necessity of Quiros's faith for the islanders, but it also provides a splendid symbolic enactment of McAuley's concept of religion (possibly because the doctrinal tension has eased temporarily). The ritual is described, employing the elements of chant, music, mime, and especially dance, with a full realization of their power and an authority quite in McAuley's best manner. In his early poetry it had seemed that his best use of narrative was for the mythic accompaniment of ritual, and so it is here. The dance merges into the connected symbol of the maze, figure of man's comprehension of the relationship between himself and eternity. . . .

The character of Quiros is not complex, but the great purpose would perforce overwhelm it if the poem were somewhat more successful—as it is, the purpose depends on Quiros for its credentials. This seems to happen in McAuley's earlier work, too, when the subject's 'distancing' has a flattening and mechanizing effect, and the sense of the presence of the poet alone can rescue it. (p. 72)

Clearly, McAuley has several very astringent things to say about modern society, but it is not often clear *why* he says them. It is to be hoped that ***Captain Quiros*** will make this clearer (if not more acceptable), but there is one major reason why I am not sure that the poem succeeds in doing this. The last book has as its climax a tripartite vision by the dying Captain, showing Australia's actual discovery, settlement and fate up to the Second Coming. This part of the poem gives the historical perspective and the relationship with the present which we require, but unfortunately it does not seem to work properly. (pp. 72, 74)

The last four stanzas recapture the authority that has been intermittently detected throughout the poem, and this ending may be the only passage of great poetry that McAuley has so far written. These stanzas make sense of the vision of the South Land in a way the description itself did not, and they also make sense of both Quiros and McAuley, though they are supposedly about Belmonte's feelings after Quiros's death. . . . McAuley's reputation has been somewhat inflated in Australia, but episodes of ***Captain Quiros*** may come close to justifying it. It is not in the passages of religious assertion and spiritual definition that the poem is most triumphant, but in the recording of one man's firmness of purpose in unfavourable surroundings, and even in final failure. (pp. 74-5)

This is by far the most important poem McAuley has written, and it is striking that his odd blend of neo-classic, symbolist, and romantic traits should excel in that most Australian of modern poetry modes, the meditative narrative, in spite of his largely lyric work in earlier poetry. This is also the first poem where that Yeatsian gift for symbolic extrapolation so clearly valued by McAuley has been used by him in a way that is moving as well as merely intelligent and dignified. (p. 75)

Norman Talbot, "Reasonable, Decorous, and Epic," in Quadrant, *Vol. VIII, No. 4, October-November, 1964, pp. 69-72; 74-5.*

CHRIS WALLACE-CRABBE

James McAuley's poetry has created strong contradictory impressions ever since his first book, ***Under Aldebaran,*** was published in 1946. Sometimes, indeed, it is very good, but even when it is not good the poetry raises teasing issues or displays interesting symptoms. Much, even in his thinnest or most uneven poems, testifies to the activity of an alert intelligence trying to make sense of the life which faces it; many unresolved poems bear witness to recurrent conflicts in the poet's sensibility. Because so much of his work makes explicit reference to its own procedures or makes overt statements about personal attitudes and values, we are frequently forced back from individual poems to evidence of a life in art, forced back from local resolutions to our larger sense of an intellectual history in process. Problems, themes, arguments lead us on from poem to poem and from volume to volume. (p. 323)

By the time we come to McAuley's most recent poems the emphasis on simple clarity of discourse, transparent verse forms and open syntax is dominant, even in a group of poems with declared autobiographical content. Early in his career, the case was far more complicated. (pp. 323-24)

James McAuley, I suggest, set out with a lyric talent which was fragile, sensitive, highly subjective, poignantly romantic, and bent towards a symbolist evocation of moods rather than to dramatic re-creation of a solid external world: onto this talent he has steadily but increasingly tried to graft a view of poetry and of the poet's rôle, a view which inclines to classic simplicity, transparency of language, the availability of basic common truths and plain traditional symbols. There has been a running war between McAuley's lyric impulse to inward exploration and the enforced clarity of his more public muse, and the latter seems to have triumphed. . . .

To set out with a few placing shots, I would like to glance at the little group of early lyrics which McAuley has explicitly dated 1936-1938. (p. 324)

In this earlier section of ***Under Aldebaran*** I see two related impulses at work. On the one hand there is a lyrical movement which is freely emotional, aspiring, yearning for a fullness which the consciousness cannot reach. . . .

The other of the two impulses I mentioned is the dispassionate intelligence's insistence on revealing the limits of feeling, the limits of romanticism, the limits of human love. (p. 325)

These themes and divisions continue at the centre of that larger sequence (or group) of poems dated 1939-1942 in ***Under Aldebaran.*** Separation, loss, the gap between lust and love, narcissism, erotic fantasy and cynical reduction, compete, jostle into articulacy and develop until they are dismissed in the last poem of the group, **"Revenant".** (p. 326)

More recently McAuley has returned to this painful world again, or rather he has pressed back past adolescence and its baffled emotions: two avowedly autobiographical poems in his latest book ***Surprises of the Sun*** (1970), look back on a time when the poet as a small boy struggled to make some contact with his parents, all three feeling themselves separated, 'locked apart'. . . . Throughout his career I find in individual poems, stanzas, passages, a falling back into strange deadness: a sense that the will continues to prompt, and the mind continues to produce the forms of verse when the heart has withdrawn from it all. There seems to run zig-zag through McAuley's poetry a strong distrust of the emotions. (pp. 326-27)

I take the poems listed as belonging to the period 1939-1942 to be a composed group in which individual poems state or suggest tentative or partial positions in a larger quest for the true self. The self, as a noisy satirical sequence called **"The Family of Love"** indicates, is felt to be fragmented, a battleground of conflicting forces and inadequate personae, all of which are struggling for supremacy as the whole man struggles to find stability. Here the three main antagonists are felt to be the sceptical but moralizing modern intellect, 'the backward-looking emotional spirit' and a more basic under-self of continuing biological urges—all three and their captain, the would-be orderly ego, held awkwardly together. (p. 327)

The two poems we may take as pointers into the world of McAuley's later work are **"The Tomb of Heracles",** which stands as the last part of a longish poem on mythological themes, and **"Invocation",** the first poem in ***A Vision of Ceremony.*** . . .

"Invocation" . . . is the poem in which McAuley comes explicitly into the world of classic clarity which he spoke of in his essay **"The Perennial Poetry".** His aspirations towards such a timeless simplicity of diction have seldom met with much success: too often the search for a classic order has entailed a loss of response to the language as a *living* thing, with the result that McAuley has produced a species of deadened English—he has 'writ no language', but has instead laid down stunned words side by side. (The third stanza of **"To Any Poet"** is a salutary example of this.) But **"Invocation"** is a striking success, not modern, not colloquial, not even local and specific: constructed of highly general and traditional terms, the poem is nonetheless instinct with a real inner life. Here impersonal diction is made to testify to a vital movement of feeling, and we can feel the confidence of phrasing to be earned, not merely imposed. The imaginative life of **"Invocation"** plainly springs from its subtle and assured rhythms, which carry through a continuous dramatic play of mind and emotion. (p. 329)

Lastly, I cite **"Canticle"** briefly to suggest that McAuley has found this lucid confidence very difficult to sustain. There is considerable delicacy of cadence and lyrical poignancy in this celebration of love. . . . Nonetheless, McAuley's high celebrant manner permits extraordinary lapses. . . . We are reminded that universality can not be won easily: it can certainly not be won by elevating poetry above the world of common experience, even if that world contains so many of one's fears and so many ghosts of a troubled past. That classical clarity to which James McAuley is intellectually driven continues to require intrusions of the personal, the flawed, the vulnerable sources of lyric energy. The operations of the will are not, of themselves, creative. (p. 330)

Chris Wallace-Crabbe, "'Beware of the Past': James McAuley's Early Poetry," in Meanjin, *Vol. 30, No. 3, September, 1971, pp. 323-30.*

R. F. BRISSENDEN

At the centre of James McAuley's ***Collected Poems*** stands his longest and most ambitious work, ***Captain Quiros.*** Although not completely successful this minor epic of physical and spiritual exploration is undeniably impressive: its most effective passages are among the best and the most distinctively individual things McAuley has done. And its limitations, which are to a degree inherent in the story the poem tells, are in a curious way not finally damaging—and this is so, I suspect, mainly because human limitation, man's ineradicable capacity for evil and stupidity, the inevitability of failure, is one of its central concerns. In this, as in so much of his work, McAuley is preoccupied with the ironic contrast between man's vision of an ideal order and beauty and his inability even to realize it fully. The theme is announced in the concluding stanza of the **"Proem"** to Part One of the whole work:

> *Terra Australis* you must celebrate,
> Land of the inmost heart, searching for which
> Men roam the earth, and on the way create
> Their kingdoms in the Indies and grow rich,
> With noble arts and cities; only to learn
> They bear the old selves with them that could turn
> The streams of Eden to a standing ditch.

The corrupting stink of man's "old self" and the despair which it generates permeate the world of McAuley's poetry. "Despair", indeed, is a word which recurs at key points throughout his work. (p. 267)

The atmosphere of McAuley's poetic universe is not, of course, one of all-pervading and unrelieved gloom. "Living is thirst for joy; / That is what art rehearses," is the assertion he makes "to any poet"; and it is the note of strong and simple joyfulness which distinguishes some of his most successful and individual pieces. His love poems in particular, especially the later ones, are remarkable both for their eloquence and for the sense they convey of assured, uncomplicated fulfilment and happiness. But in the context of his work as a whole this happiness appears all the more precious because it so clearly occurs in, has been won from, an imperfect and at its worst inimical environment. There are occasions when love, or domestic tranquillity, or merely a feeling of personal well-being coincide with and are reinforced by our sense of some deep and pervasive natural order; and McAuley can render such occasions with a rare tact and authenticity. (pp. 268-69)

Running throughout McAuley's poetry there is a persistent note of radical disquiet and uneasiness, of dissatisfaction not only with the nature of man but with the nature of the world in which he finds himself or has been placed. It is much deeper and more disturbing than the conventional modern lament for the fact that we live in an age in which the traditional bases of faith have been eroded. . . . [In] his collection of essays, ***The End of Modernity,*** he has given a very clear account of his own responses, as a poet and a Christian, to the crisis of contemporary civilization. But basically I would suggest his despair has nothing to do with the specific problems of the twentieth century. The muted horror, outrage and bewilderment which find their expression in his rendering of **"A Leaf of Sage",** a tale from the *Decameron,* for instance, are intensely personal; at the same time one feels that they have been evoked through the forced contemplation of a problem which the poet reluctantly acknowledges as perennial, as inherent in the inscrutable order of the universe. And it is this same complex of feelings which permeates the structure and to some extent determines the tone of ***Captain Quiros*** and a number of smaller pieces; and which is quite directly expressed and contemplated in an unusually interesting group of poems from an earlier period, **"Philoctetes"** and **"The Hero and the Hydra".**

"A Leaf of Sage" tells an unbearably sad story of pointless suffering and death. Two lovers meet in a garden where a sage plant, "like a small tree of knowledge", is growing. The girl plucks a leaf from the bush and offers it to the boy with the words, "Rub this / Against your teeth, and it will give your kiss / Its aromatic virtue". He does as she suggests, and shortly after dies in agony. The girl is accused of poisoning him—and to show what has happened and prove her innocence rubs a leaf from the bush against her own teeth. She dies too. The sage bush is then cut down, and a poisonous toad "the Satan of the bower", is found squatting at the root. Throughout the tragedy a hidden bird sings nearby.

Two stanzas from the poem give us some idea why the story has fascinated the poet. In the first place he obviously finds it extremely hard to reconcile such needless suffering with the notion of a benevolent creator (and the analogies he draws between this situation and the original scene of temptation in the Garden of Eden imply that he finds it equally difficult to reconcile the fallen condition of humanity with the presumed intentions of a good and loving God). . . . This is a familiar theological problem. But the way in which the poem images it, and the emphasis on the "terrible" nature of the Divine purpose in the lines I have quoted, suggest that the problem has more than a theoretical interest for the poet. (pp. 269-71)

The most horrifying aspect of Boccaccio's tale is that the girl brings about the suffering and death of her lover *through an action which is intended to help him.* This ironically tragic reversal or transformation of good intentions is clearly a situation by which McAuley is at once appalled and fascinated, a situation, moreover, which he sees as archetypal in a very profound sense, one that is inextricably woven into the fabric of reality. Moreover the irony of the situation is compounded and accentuated when the good intentions are not simply benevolent, but are seen to be in accord with or to be part of some underlying and presumably divine purpose. To have some inkling of what this purpose is and to attempt to bring it about can be extraordinarily dangerous: the man who attempts to carry out the divine will, or who is charged by the gods with doing so, can in this always possible and worst of all situations bring pain and suffering both on those he wishes to help and on himself.

This, at any rate, appears to be the insistent message of the group of myths with which McAuley is concerned in **"Philoctetes"** and **"The Hero and the Hydra".** The main figures in these myths—Prometheus, Heracles, Chiron and Philoctetes—are all heroic, strong and benevolent. Moreover the courses of action towards which their divinely given courage or wisdom, their sense of justice and loyalty, their basic good nature and philanthropy, impel them are seen ultimately both as having a beneficent result and as being part of some total process which is not without significance. Yet at the same time what they do also involves them and sometimes those whom they most wish to help in a degree of injury and pain which seems calamitously disproportionate. (p. 271)

[It is] interesting that when A. D. Hope dedicated his first volume *The Wandering Islands* (a title which now perhaps acquires an added resonance) to James McAuley he chose as an epigraph the three lines beginning "Men must either bear their guilt and weakness"—an affirmation of lonely stoicism which was certainly in keeping with his own view of man, but which was to become increasingly inappropriate as an account of McAuley's.

The most extensive poetic statement and exploration of his Christian beliefs is given by McAuley in ***Captain Quiros;*** and it is instructive to set this work in the context of the ideas and feelings expressed and embodied in these earlier poems. In ***Captain Quiros*** he tells the story of two Spanish expeditions of exploration and colonization in the Pacific—the first by Alvaro de Mendaña de Neyra in 1567-68 which resulted in an abortive attempt to discover gold and establish a settlement in the Solomons, the second by Pedro Fernández de Quiros (who had been a pilot on the first expedition) in 1605-6. Quiros, driven by the dream of discovering the great south land and establishing there the New Jerusalem, made landfall on the eastern coast of the New Hebrides, and believing it to be the continent he was seeking, formally took possession of it and named it Austrialia del Espiritu Santo. His associate Luis Vaez de Torres went on to sail through the strait that now bears his name; Quiros returned to Peru and eventually to Spain. After some years of penury he received royal approval for another expedition, but died in Panama on the way to organize it.

In ***Captain Quiros*** McAuley is concerned with a number of things—with the impact not merely of Christianity but of western civilization with all its corruptions and complexities on the native peoples of the Pacific; with the catastrophic inability of ordinary human beings to realize their potentialities; with the way in which the character of a visionary and dreamer like Quiros can be developed, and the role he can play in history; and with the multiple ironies of such a hero's apparent failure as an individual and as a representative of Christendom.

To my mind the first part of the poem, **"Where Solomon was Wanting",** which gives an account of the Mendaña expedition, is the most impressive. McAuley's manner of narration, cool, detached, compassionate and seriously witty, is beautifully suited to the presentation of this story of weakness, folly, brutality and greed. (pp. 273-74)

In his essay, **"Tradition, Society and the Arts"** [included in ***The End of Modernity***], McAuley has given an account of what he envisages a society to be in its normal condition:

> Human societies commonly acknowledge a realm of the sacred, which they regard as the ultimate source of being and order and value in the physical universe and the world of man. It is by standing in right relation with this spiritual order that man and his culture become *authentic*. Not only is the sacred tradition accorded a primacy over culture by those who receive it: it actually does possess that primacy; it does in fact preside over culture, giving form and meaning to men's experience, serving as a principle of coherence and order.

The most convincing rendering given by McAuley in his poetry of this condition of normality occurs in his account of the society of the Santa Cruz islanders on the eve of the arrival of Mendaña. Led by their chieftain Malope, "a man instinct with power, authentic, whole", their lives follow a ritual pattern which perfectly reflects and unites them with the natural world in which they live. (p. 275)

This account of the Santa Cruz community is balanced by the section, **"New Jerusalem",** in Part Two, **"The Quest for the South Land",** which deals with the Corpus Christi feast held by Quiros and his men to celebrate the discovery of Austrialia del Espiritu Santo and the foundation of New Jerusalem. Again the order of the poetry is high: the passage is a bravura performance, tropically brilliant with colour, musically sonorous, and moving with all the ritual pageantry of the church. But the occasion specifically lacks the authenticity which so clearly characterizes the celebrations of Malope and his people. Quiros, unlike the chieftain, is sick and weak, the streets of the New Jerusalem are "temporary", the settlement is ringed about by hostile natives, one of whom had been shot and killed on the day the first members of the expedition landed, the religious ceremony stands in no obviously relevant relationship to the environment, and it is not even taking place in the Great South Land.

McAuley, of course, is patently aware of the ironies implicit in the situation: indeed they are very much what the poem is about, and in the concluding sections he attempts to resolve them at the level of theological argument. The attempt is an admirable and an honest one, but ultimately unsuccessful. It is in the nature of the case—and in the nature of the poet—that it should be. No matter how sincere McAuley may be in his belief that "all shall be made perfect at the last", he is compelled here, as in the earlier poems I have discussed, to acknowledge the tragedy of the situation. The problem which the poem raises but understandably fails to solve is not that God should move in a mysterious way his wonders to perform, but that his way should so often appear to be so terrible and in simple human terms so destructive. (p. 276)

I have dealt at such length with these longer poems not because I necessarily think they are the best things McAuley has done, but because I believe that an examination of them may provide us with an insight into one of basic intellectual and spiritual dimensions of his poetic world. He is a religious poet in a time of doubt and scepticism; and in his work he "[plays] a match against the age's mind". But his quarrel is as much with the nature of things as it is with the twentieth century; and the great strength of his poetry is the honesty with which he faces up to this. Looked at in one way his poetry can be seen as a strenuous attempt to reconcile his tough empirical sense of the realities of our immediate everyday world with his conviction that man is a spiritual being. . . . Although it may not have been easy, the effort to come to terms with himself and his faith has been of inestimable value to McAuley as a poet—indeed it has been an essential element in the developing life of his poetry. And it is particularly valuable to have some sense of this when we read some of his more recent poems. In isolation many of these seem slight and merely charming. In the context of his total achievement, however, they take on unsupected depth and meaning. Even a piece such as **"Pietà"**, a dignified and moving elegy which can stand completely on its own, acquires an added resonance and authority:

Once only, with one hand,
Your mother in farewell
Touched you. I cannot tell,
I cannot understand

A thing so dark and deep,
So physical a loss:
One touch, and that was all
She had of you to keep,
Clean wounds, but terrible,
Are those made with the Cross.

In a full-scale review of McAuley's poetry some note should, I've no doubt, be taken of his limitations as well as his virtues. And it cannot be denied that his is in some ways a limited achievement: to assume an orthodox religious position can be both a crippling and a liberating business for a poet; and perhaps the ultimate irony, in terms of the argument I have been developing, is that the poet who proposes, as McAuley has done, to wield the sacred bow of Heracles, runs the risk of dropping an occasional arrow on his foot. But it is not my purpose here to present an audited account of debits and credits: James McAuley's ***Collected Poems*** is an impressive testament of a very gifted poet's attempt to come to terms with himself and the world. And the attempt bears throughout, particularly in his finest pieces, the undeniable mark of authenticity. (pp. 277-78)

R. F. Brissenden, "The Wounded Hero: James McAuley's Collected Poems, 1936-1970," in Southerly, *Vol. 32, No. 4, December, 1972, pp. 267-78.*

CHOICE

McAuley's taste, his technique, and his scale of concerns [as evidenced in ***Collected Poems, 1936-1970***] seems to have shipwrecked in the 19th century, and not, unfortunately, in a lively part of that century. Is there any other contemporary poet writing in English whose metaphorical faculty turns invariably to classical examples? Many of the poems, especially the shorter lyrics, are intelligent, compassionate, and prosodically flawless; but they seem to have escaped both the contamination and the inspiration of the raging issues, social and esthetic, of the 20th century.

A review of "Collected Poems, 1936-1970," in Choice, *Vol. 10, No. 1, March, 1973, p. 95.*

JAMES McAULEY

The earliest phase from which I have retained any poems, 1936-39, was influenced by some aspects of the work of Stefan George and R. M. Rilke. What I most wanted to do was to write short poems with a delicacy of texture, lyrical, intimate, based on personal experience. . . . In the years that followed, another impulse emerged strongly: an interest in cultural and historical crisis and a search for means to express its meaning poetically. . . . Later poems, up to and including the narrative ***Captain Quiros*** which was written 1958-59, were concerned with seeing the world in the light of a recovered acceptance of Christian tradition and orthodoxy.

My first volume of poems, ***Under Aldebaran*** (1946), had a favorable critical reception. Its elements of tension, wryness, serious comedy, the vivacity of unusual imagery, as well as the lyricism and personal feeling, made it acceptably modern, though traditional in verse-form. But some poems in fact were symptoms of a dissatisfaction with the precariousness inherent in my method or lack of method. (pp. 201-02)

My second volume, ***A Vision of Ceremony*** (1956), did not chime so well with prevailing preferences. It was felt to have sacrificed too much of the qualities offered by the first volume. The emergence of a Christian basis was not in itself a hindrance; but some felt disappointment with the way it emerged. On the one hand it was acknowledged that there were some beautiful lyrics in the volume, but they were felt to be serene rather than tense and unresolved, too clarified of the messy substance of life. On the other hand the discursive poem **"A Letter to John Dryden"** displeased some by its aggressive polemic.

The subsequent decade was a difficult one in my poetical development. I had an inner necessity—the word is not too strong—to move still further away from contemporary critical preferences in order to grow in my own way. I felt the need to reabsorb some residues of nineteenth-century poetry which were part of my experience: Byron's lyrics, Tennyson, William Morris; Eichendorff, Heine, Mörike. In the midst of dryness and uncertainty I suddenly took up again an almost forgotten project of writing a long narrative poem about Quiros. . . . ***Captain Quiros,*** which was not published until 1964, was written for reading aloud. It takes about two hours, and by repeated test holds its audience very effectively. But in silent reading on the page the deliberately flatter parts are more noticeable; and in any case long narratives are not particularly welcome nowadays, nor does the language they require meet the taste of those who look for the intensities of short poems. Chris Wallace-Crabbe, in regard to some of the writing of this period, has spoken of 'a species of deadened language' [see excerpt above]. It was at any rate clear that I had moved to a position as opposite as possible to prevailing expectations—not by a wilful intransigence but by the need to follow a path intuitively sensed and dimly descried. In spite of the difficulties, in the late fifties and early sixties I produced a number of poems which I still consider among my best, including **"Pietà".** (pp. 202-03)

An unexpected turn in development came late in 1966 when I suddenly began to write some autobiographical poems about childhood and youth, which in the volume ***Surprises of the Sun*** (1969) were grouped under the title 'On the Western Line'. These poems caused some surprise when they appeared, but were well received. Inevitably they were compared with the kind of 'confessional' poetry Robert Lowell had been writing. I had no sense of influence from that quarter. Oddly enough, a vivid stimulus, rather than influence or model, was provided during those months by constantly reading in English translation the late poems of Pasternak.

In 1970 I had a serious illness and emerged with that exquisitely keen sense of life and its fragility which such experiences give. The result was a number of short poems which use a language of sense-impressions to render aspects of a world. . . . An influence of the poems of Georg Trakl is evident, stronger and more identifiable than any other poet has exercised on my work since the attraction of Rilke faded; yet the effect has been to liberate, not to deflect, my native impulse. (pp. 203-04)

James McAuley, "James McAuley," in his A Map of Australian Verse: The Twentieth Century, *Oxford University Press, Melbourne, 1975, pp. 201-18.*

SYED AMANUDDIN

According to James McAuley, "the intellectual is he whose delight it is to *know,*" and the prose works of this eminent Australian poet [collected in ***The Grammar of the Real: Selected Prose, 1959-1974***] are proof of the delight he takes in exploring and knowing various literary works, theories and themes. . . . He writes with the perspective of a comparatist who has devoted his life to the study of world literature. British, Russian and German literatures enkindle his enthusiasm the same way Australian poetry does. His search everywhere seems to be for what he calls in his poem **"Credo"** "The grammar of existence, / The syntax of the real."

As a poet and critic of poetry, however, McAuley is hung up on the problems of traditional technique and wastes too much space on metrical ambiguities and stress profiles, although he does realize the significance of interrelations between the phonic system of a poem and the syntactical and semantic elements. Perhaps his best critical essay is one on Judith Wright, where he is less preoccupied with the physical features of Wright's poetry than with its total experience. . . .

Reading these essays one gets the feeling that the author is attempting to define his own poetic practices and that his insights into the poetry of other poets are but the indirect interpretations of his own poetry. This is probably true of most poet-critics, and it is certainly true of Coleridge, Keats and Eliot. If McAuley's attempt is to define the traditions he belongs to by discussing poets of varied periods and backgrounds, it is a successful attempt. He seeks only what is vital in all literatures, "for it belongs to a full human culture to extend our awareness of the past, as well as to have regard to the future." McAuley both as poet and critic does not seem to be bound by regional, linguistic or national values. He is a part of the human family, and his contribution is to human culture.

Syed Amanuddin, in a review of "The Grammar of the Real: Selected Prose, 1959-1974," in World Literature Today, *Vol. 51, No. 1, Winter, 1977, p. 158.*

C. L. INNES

Reading through [***The Grammar of the Real: Selected Prose, 1959-1974***] published just before the untimely death this year of Australian poet and critic James McAuley, one is at first impressed by the range of his interests. There are careful evaluations of Australian poets; there are attempts to define the principles of metre and diction in verse; there are comparative studies of Spenser and Eliot, of Milton and Dryden, of Wordsworth and Crabbe; there are essays on politics, sex and love in English and Russian literature, autobiographical accounts of the author's encounter with natives and missionaries in New Guinea (the latter contributing to his conversion to Catholicism), and, finally, there is new poetic work in the form of translations of the German poets Albrecht Haushofer and Georg Trakl.

Of these essays, the four on Australian poets (Shaw Neilson, Judith Wright, Kenneth Slessor and Rosemary Dobson) are the finest. . . .

When McAuley moves away from home ground, however, on to subjects which might have greater immediate interest to readers in England, he often gives the impression of a mind which is not at home, a speaker who feels alienated, above all, from his audience. As a result, the tone of these essays sometimes seems strident and unnecessarily combative, the focus blurred or inappropriate. This stridency affects most seriously the essay **"On Being An Intellectual"** (originally published in *Quadrant* in 1959). Having castigated those intellectuals who depart from the ideal proposed by Jakob Burkhardt ("to contemplate the truth . . . not as a partisan, or as enslaved by passions and fears, but in a free and disinterested way"), McAuley proceeds to write the most prejudiced of polemics against modern intellectuals, whom he labels indiscriminately with all the debased labels which were common in the cold-war fifties: positivist, liberal, Communist, progressivist, agnostics "who would fain settle for peace, comfort, co-existence and neutralism". McAuley's "voice crying in the wilderness" moves more distinctly into the Old Testament prophetic mode as in the last paragraphs he foresees "a resurgence of genuine realist intellectuality, determined to break the delusional grip of a pseudo-rational secular gnosis", and asserts that "the heart of culture is the divine *culius,* and until this ceases to be thought of as a private and peripheral irrelevance or intrusion, and becomes central, the new springtime of history will be postponed."

I have cited this particular essay at some length not only because it reveals the implacability of McAuley's commitment to stand firm against "this filthy modern tide", but also because it is symptomatic of the felt alienation from his audience that commitment has generated. It is an alienation reflected in a use of language and rhetoric which undermines the very values which McAuley seeks to restore and which noticeably mars the essays on Milton and on New Guinea. In other essays, however, McAuley's conservative moral, political and literary stance yields more interestingly provocative judgments.

C. L. Innes, "Against the Modern Tide," in The Times Higher Education Supplement, *No. 283, March 25, 1977, p. 21.*

PETER KIRKPATRICK

In spite of the consolations of the Catholic Church, not the least of which is the far-reaching spectacle of that long civilized presence, maintained against forces of disruption, both from without and within, there seems to be a strongly agnostic strain in the later poetry of James McAuley—the poetry of ***The Hazard and the Gift*** (in ***Collected Poems***) and ***Music Late at Night***—as there is to be seen in the earlier verse of ***Under Aldebaran.*** I do not mean to suggest that the poet somehow lost his faith towards the end; far from it: the very last collection, ***Time Given,*** qualifies the growing tendency to despair and partly reverses it. What I wish to do here is to indicate some of the ways in which the ceremonial vision becomes impaired by a conscious poetic reacquaintance with the harsh, unconsecrated spaces of the real world. The "sad alternate fire" of Aldebaran, as it is described in the famous **"Incarnation of Sirius",** can in fact stand as a symbol of what becomes a deeply personal spiritual ambiguity. Certainly not enough has been said about the pessimism that activates so much of McAuley's writing.

The power which Vivian Smith so justly praised in the **"Black Swans"** lyrics of ***A Vision of Ceremony*** comes, he said, "from the fact that they apprehend and affirm order in front of a deeply experienced sense of the constant threat and possibility of disorder". It is McAuley's sense of such disorder that I wish to examine, and the manner in which he finally, perhaps, comes to terms with it. In the later poems the poet is testing, imaginatively, his hard-won vision of cosmic order in an often untransfigured, mundane context—that of the suburbs and a corrupt natural world, which the creative soul struggles in vain to harmoniously render. The images reflect longing and desperation, however, and by looking at the local environment it seems he is looking fixedly within himself. One could point to the number of poems about childhood, as well, to show how thorough McAuley's need for re-examination really was. It is only by again breaking through the Romantic solipsism that dogged his work that he eventually reaches a peace of mind. (pp. 191-92)

Consistently throughout McAuley's poetry after **"The Hero and the Hydra,"** the only presence that gives meaning to experience is that of God. His appreciation of the presence of God has been a factor of his search for an adequate Christian symbolism to both express and (ceremonially) enact it. With ***Captain Quiros*** the cycle of celebration reached its climax: in the verses he went on to write the symbols he chose began to challenge cosmic order, even to the point of doubting faith itself. (pp. 194-95)

In a poem actually entitled **"Absence"** from ***Under Aldebaran*** he makes use of the Eden myth, treating it romantically. . . . The lovers' joy in each other creates the innocent Edenic vision that "revives" the mythic landscape: as in Brennan's poetry, Eden is a Romantic symbol for an ideal state of mind. The "absence" of the title is consequently the loss of that vision which, as it renders the spirit in harmony with another, may be said to liberate it from the prison of selfhood. (p. 195)

In **"Absence"** the harmonizing vision is achieved through the transfiguring delights of sexual love; elsewhere, as it becomes the ***Vision of Ceremony,*** it is seen to come about through the love of God—for McAuley, the supreme manifestation of the not-self. **"Nuptial Hymn"** from that volume uses the Eden theme again, this time in a ritualized context where the lovers are subsumed by the greater mystery which the ceremony serves to symbolize. . . . (pp. 195-96)

These two poems, **"Absence"** and **"Nuptial Hymn",** help to illustrate the development of McAuley's vision of a liberating order, from a secular paradise compromised by the demands of the waking world—a typically Romantic view—to a ceremonial marriage in which the physical act of consummation symbolizes that profounder union between the soul and its creator, thus renewing the promise of Eden. The landscape of paradise here is purely symbolic—a metaphysical abstraction—but it seems fair to suggest that the earthly, often dismal landscapes of the later poems are similarly representative of the state of the poet's spirit in its relationship to God. (p. 196)

To feel that God is not present in the world or in one's life is, for McAuley, to despair of meaning, for the reason that God creates whatever meaning is manifested in the natural world. . . . Yet in despairing of meaning, may not the truant soul be wilfully isolating itself from the harmonious pattern by indulging in a solipsism? Is despair simply a response to and acknowledgement of corruption and disorder, or is it in fact the inherent corrupting agency? Undoubtedly the problem is an ancient epistemological and theological one; but for McAuley as a poet an understanding of the presence of God has continually been a factor of his search for a suitable Christian symbolism to express it. (pp. 196-97)

[In] his verse very often we find the symbolism carries the faith. There is a feeling in the later poetry, however, that he has fallen out of grace with his images; certainly they fail to express an awareness of the presence of God in a way that the grander, more rarefied symbolism of ***A Vision of Ceremony*** and ***Captain Quiros*** did. Those symbols, in fact, created that presence. . . . [Throughout] his poetry there is an associated awareness of the limitations of the real things which give rise to the symbols; that in some measure they do not satisfy the creatively religious urge which selects them, and which, as it were, transubstantiates them into the language of the heart—hence the "struggle for an adequate symbolism". (pp. 203-04)

Music Late at Night demonstrates a lonely, obsessive need to find the facts of faith in the world around, but that longing merely doubles back upon the lying soul which contradicts them. McAuley's poetic temperament is natively pessimistic; his hope is contained in the never-ending search for symbols. Between his reality and the ideal religious emblem is a great visionary gap, and it seems that he found it continually harder to make the necessary imaginative leap. (p. 204)

The very last group of lyrics which McAuley collected as ***Time Given*** display a mood of qualified thanksgiving, which grows out of the later few poems of ***Music Late at Night*** and is bound up with the meaning of the title-poem of that volume. . . .

In the later poetry generally, it is fair to say that there has been a return to a personal mood comparable to the prevailing scepticism of ***Under Aldebaran*** and **"The Hero and the Hydra"** (Aldebaran, interestingly, appears again in **"At Assissi"** from ***Time Given***). Hope there sometimes is, thinly glimpsed in a moment of ecstatic stillness, or in the movement of birds—especially black swans—and occasionally, at last, it is faintly acknowledged in the whole of the changing pageant through a rediscovered innocence, a fitful calm of mind: "The day was there for everything we chose" (**"At Jeanneret's Beach"**). The nuances of despair, however, form the major theme and variations of these often poignantly beautiful lyrics. . . . Where the art of James McAuley conceals or even overcomes his pessimism it is nonetheless shaped by it. Indeed, the art itself is the overcoming. (p. 205)

Peter Kirkpatrick, "Patience and Despair: James McAuley's Pessimism," in Southerly, *Vol. 44, No. 2, 1984, pp. 191-205.*

NOEL MACAINSH

In 1975, a year before his death, [McAuley] wrote: "It seems that in the last decade I have come full circle back to the kind of poem I began with, but with a greater depth of experience which has brought me closer to fulfilling the persistent desire to write poems that are lucid and mysterious, gracefully simple but full of secrets, faithful to the little one knows and the much one has to feel." The dichotomies expressed here, of the lucid and mysterious, the simple and repletely secret, of little knowledge and much feeling, are a guide to understanding the particular form of McAuley's late poetry. That is, the poet's "persistent desire" has been for a form of expression duly proportionate to knowledge and feeling, to little of one and much of the other. The implication is that for the poet knowledge and feeling are not commensurate, that the latter far exceeds the former. (p. 331)

The structure of McAuley's late poems is essentially paratactic. That is, the individual sentences and parts of sentences are frequently lacking logical connection; they are simply presented in sequence. (p. 332)

The relatively passive, non-directing and only occasional presence of the "I" is not only accompanied by marked parataxis but also by a mosaic-like arrangement of individual images, themselves briefly presented and isolated. There does not appear to be an argument or anecdote to which they are subordinated. Nevertheless, the diminution of syntactic relationship of the mosaic elements is compensated for by other relationships of language, associative and paradigmatic. These other relationships, whatever we may think of their contribution to a whole, do not contribute to an overall statement of knowledge, in which individual images are retrospectively illuminated and seen to be justified in their nature and sequence by their contributions to overall meaning. In the late poems, a contrary process occurs: the individual images are clear, even coloured and luminous, but as they succeed each other in juxtaposition the overall statement becomes blurred. (p. 333)

Thus the poet's desire "to write poems that are lucid" is met by his presentation of images in brief sentences or clauses one line long; while his desire to write poems that are "mysterious" is met by paratactic juxtaposition of these images, so that they lack logical coherence. In turn, the lack of coherence at the logical level is met by a lexical coherence which suggests a meaning that is mysterious. (p. 334)

In **"Another Day, Another Night"**, two opposing modes of awareness are seen to operate, as is the case in McAuley's late poems generally, namely the modes of knowing and feeling. "Knowing", as opposed to feeling, is characterized by objectivity; in the process of knowing one strives to distinguish clearly the object of thought both from oneself and from other objects. In contrast, feeling transcends definition and passes on into the indefinite. Since the indefinite does not offer a clear goal or resistance, the feeling subject is prone to lose self-reflection, his sense of separate self implicit in thought. . . .

In the late poems, the distinction between the reflective ego and its objects appears in a characteristic way: the poet, knowing that he is distinct from the particular object of his thought, knows also that he is distinct from all things and persons, even those closest to him. . . . In presenting life to himself as an object of reflection, the poet at the same time distances himself from it, passively noting its process.

This reflective mode and concomitant estrangement appears to structure not only these poems in the first person but also those more numerous poems, in which the first person is not overtly present. (p. 335)

There is a further consideration: not only is the poet's oversight of processes external to him gained at the cost of his direct participation in them, but these two modalities of participation in life, that is reflection and naive engagement, are seen by him as irreconcilable and hence as the ground of his awareness that life is withdrawing from him. The irreconcilability acutely points up for him the process of decay. Quite apart from his actual age or his reflection on a specific earlier stage of his life, the poet stands under a general sense of being changed, past, beyond what has been, of leaving reality. The role of the reflecting ego is itself grasped. Compared to the distinction between the ego and its objects, this self-reflection, or introspection, represents a further intensification: the ego is confronted not with this or that object but with itself as its object of reflection. . . . (pp. 336-37)

[So] too does reflection on himself lead to self-alienation, a division of the self, which he can no longer bring into a unity. The sense of decay of the world, attendant on recognition of the irreconcilability of the ego and its objects, now extends into the ego itself. Dread of utter dissolution appears. Self-reflection in which the ego schizophrenically becomes its own object, is attended by acute distress, by an imagery of division and despair. . . . (p. 337)

Typically, in these expressions of a shift of reflective focus from the world to the self, "the world sinks out of sight" or dies, or at the very least becomes "hazy", "blurred", problematical. This turning from a world which Peter Coleman has characterized as "a world of gashed trees, tossed sheets, drooping flowers, rifted sky, dead leaves, and circling ravens but also of tremulous reeds, soundless music, blue sky, white birds, new sprigs and cut firewood", implies also a turning from the traditional conception of Nature as in some way a meaningful unity and emanation of God. . . . (p. 338)

Peter Coleman has remarked of McAuley's late poems that they have almost nothing of the direct statement of his earlier poems: "Now almost everything is evoked in symbols". . . . Nevertheless, it also becomes evident that the "symbols" of this poetry cannot be seen as traditional metaphors. No longer is metaphor employed in the late poems simply as one literary device among others; rather, it signifies the basic method of the poetry, the way in which the poet's imagination actualizes the transition from reflection to immediacy of feeling. . . . Because the metaphors here have the utmost simplicity, generality, and unity, they cannot be referred back to other features; they are self-contained. . . . Nevertheless, as already indicated, the images of this poetry are linked to each other by lexical features, suggesting coherence. . . . Thus the transitions from metaphor to metaphor can be seen in both objective and subjective terms. Various recurrent metaphoric features can be distinguished, particularly colour. (p. 339)

The simplicity, generality and directness of McAuley's imagery . . . naturally appeals to the cultural reserves of the reader, allowing him considerable freedom to bring his own associations. The poetry stands between concretion and abstraction. It avoids the normally binding, hypotactic features of language but nevertheless freights its imagery with a significance based on coherence of an alogical kind. . . . The structure tends to empty any potential symbol, such as an object of Nature, of any clear conceptual content, so bringing the poem to a point where reflection, the conceptual process, fails. Thus symbolism in the normal sense, as denoting representation of a particular group of ideas, cannot be said to apply to the empirical particulars of the poems; these particulars are not symbolic but literal. Their literal character is assured by their "blurred", "hazy", "absurd" aspect, that is by their lack of meaning.

Necessarily, the structure of the poem itself becomes a symbol, a kind of icon, because it appeals to the kind of experience that is bound to its language, to a coded system in which the paradigmatic or substitution axis is the bearer of uncertainty, decay, disorientation, alienation, division, loss. It is this axis that is the real signifier of McAuley's late poems; and if its signification appears limited in range then that is the consequence of a reflective subject that progressively withdraws from its objects, up to a point where it loses all distinguishing distance and is eclipsed by feeling. The quality of this feeling is indicated by the paradigmatic axis each time; in general: decline, meaninglessness, loss. (pp. 341-42)

Noel Macainsh, "The Late Poems of James McAuley," in Southerly, *Vol. 45, No. 3, 1985, pp. 330-42.*

Thomas (Francis) McGuane (III)

1939-

American novelist, scriptwriter, short story writer, essayist, and journalist.

Best known for his first three novels, *The Sporting Club* (1969), *The Bushwhacked Piano* (1971), and *Ninety-Two in the Shade* (1973), McGuane writes irreverently comic fiction that often satirizes the vulgarity and materialism of what he has termed America's "declining snivelization." McGuane's novels generally focus upon young male protagonists who have rejected the stability of their privileged social positions for more adventurous and stimulating lifestyles. Through recurring motifs, including practical jokes, sporting events, and restless travel, McGuane explores such themes as the nature of male rivalry and competition, the relationship between actions and their consequences, the search for meaning in contemporary life, and the degenerative state of American society. McGuane's respect for the beauty and power of the natural world sharply contrasts with the depravity that he believes is undermining American culture.

The Sporting Club is set amid the splendor of Michigan's north woods and centers on the follies of masculine pride and virility. Concerning a group of wealthy weekend sportsmen whose inane outdoor games degenerate into violence and chaos, this novel has been viewed as an allegory of the corruption of American society. In *The Bushwhacked Piano,* McGuane relates the picaresque story of Nicholas Payne, an eccentric youth whose travels through Michigan, Montana, and Florida, ostensibly in pursuit of his wealthy girlfriend, reveal his restless aspirations for change and his feelings of alienation. *Ninety-Two in the Shade* is a black comedy focusing upon Thomas Skelton, a marine biology student who quits college and escapes what he perceives to be the decadence of American civilization by guiding fishing expeditions in Key West, Florida. However, Skelton's ideal existence is challenged by Nichol Dance, a brutish Key West guide inclined to playing practical jokes. Dance's antagonistic behavior leads to a climactic confrontation between the two men in which Skelton is killed.

Following years of personal and career crises which profoundly affected his fiction, *Panama* (1978) represents a reorientation of the concerns McGuane explored in his earlier novels. A hallucinatory and macabre story set amid a squalid world of drugs, insanity, moral indifference, escapism, and despair, *Panama* is the tragic tale of Chester Hunnicutt Pomeroy, a fallen celebrity who has returned to his home in Key West in hopes of reestablishing a relationship with his estranged wife. Often considered McGuane's most openly autobiographical work, *Panama,* according to Donald R. Katz, "is a sadly bitter book about what became of the alternative American dream." In McGuane's next book, *Nobody's Angel* (1982), Patrick Fitzpatrick, a former army captain, takes over his family's Montana ranch in an effort to bring stability to his life. His attempt is unsuccessful, however, and after an affair with a wealthy oil heiress whose husband commits suicide because of his wife's infidelities, Patrick rejoins the army in Europe. Charles G. Masinton commented that *Nobody's Angel* "is full of reminders that the real West, the contemporary actuality, is but a pale imitation of the traditional image of the West that Americans carry in their heads." *Something to Be Desired* (1984) revolves around the experiences of Lucien Taylor, a government employee who discards his life with his wife and son to fulfill a restless urge to lead a passionate existence with an attractive, mysterious girlfriend from his high school years. Lucien's inability to reconcile his dreams with reality leads not to despair, however, but to contentment in his domestic life.

Photograph by Paul Dix. Courtesy of Thomas McGuane.

In addition to his novels, McGuane has written screenplays for the films *Rancho Deluxe, Ninety-Two in the Shade, The Missouri Breaks,* and *Tom Horn*. His collection of nonfiction prose pieces, *An Outside Chance: Essays on Sport* (1980), gathers assorted articles originally published in various sporting periodicals. McGuane has also published a collection of short stories, *To Skin a Cat* (1986).

(See also *CLC,* Vols. 3, 7, 18; *Contemporary Authors,* Vols. 49-52; *Contemporary Authors New Revision Series,* Vol. 5; *Dictionary of Literary Biography,* Vol. 2; and *Dictionary of Literary Biography Yearbook: 1980.)*

VANCE BOURJAILY

By the time one has read the 18 pieces in ***An Outside Chance,*** one has a comfortable sense of acquaintance with Thomas

McGuane; and since he is one of the better, funnier and less pretentious novelists around—best known for ***The Sporting Club*** and ***Ninety-Two in the Shade***—and turns out to be the sort of man you'd expect from that, it's a pleasure to meet him.

He is a man whose outdoor interests have some range to them, so we get to know him in a number of vividly rendered locations, where he's doing a number of interesting and sometimes even dangerous things like riding a big motorcycle and roping steers from horseback. In three pieces he is fly-fishing shallow, salt-water flats in the Florida Keys for bonefish, tarpon and mutton snapper. From the standpoint of information, these pieces seemed especially fresh, and it is characteristic of the easygoing self-deprecation with which Mr. McGuane writes that though he catches a 15-pound mutton snapper that is a world record for his fishing method, he almost apologizes for having kept it to be weighed and eaten. Most of Mr. McGuane's fish are released alive as soon as he has brought them in.

One can release a fish, but there's no way of putting a bird back in the air or a dead antelope onto its range. "Nobody who loves to hunt," Mr. McGuane says, "feels absolutely hunky-dory when the quarry goes down. The remorse spins out. . . ." Perhaps because of this, and assuming that Mr. McGuane distributes his sporting hours in the same proportion as his reports on them, there are ten fishing pieces, but only three about hunting, and one of the three is really about a dog called Molly. She is one of those lovable, enthusiastic dogs whose company in the field comes close to guaranteeing that her master will get no shots, let alone actual game. (p. 11)

Among the pieces that seem most memorable is one on roping. Mr. McGuane has moved from his boyhood country, Michigan, to the Florida Keys with their fly-fishing flats, and to a ranch in Montana. It's a workaday ranch, and he learns workaday roping; he also learns competitive team roping for rodeo prize money. The focus in this piece is on the hand: "There came a day when I couldn't find the saddle horn and broke my thumb in a few places, tearing off the end of it. When I went to the emergency room, the nurse said: 'Miss your dally?' " The dally is that turn of the rope that allows the weight of the plunging steer to be countered by the weight of the horse. The nurse understands perfectly what happens when the roper is trying to hold 600 to 800 pounds of going-away muscle one-handed with a thin rope. So does Mr. McGuane's 10-year-old son, to whom the book is dedicated, and who rejects the sport for himself: " 'I like my fingers, Dad. Look at your hand.' I looked at my hand, crooked thumb, rope burns, enlarged knuckles. . . ."

The piece ends with candor and a certain sadness. Like many of us, Thomas McGuane has found that love for any sport, to sentimentalists a lifetime affair, can fade. This year's pleasure and excitement may be next year's pain and aggravation. He and his partner have won a roping event, and are off to the Two Bit Saloon, where

> . . . everyone was getting warped and the kids were playing pinball. . . . I felt for the first time in a decade that I could do without the ranch. The Midwest wasn't a bad place to grow up; and maybe pinball was as interesting as my boy thought it was. After all, things keep moving on.
>
> (p. 23)

Vance Bourjaily, "Doings of a Sporting Man," in The New York Times Book Review, *February 8, 1981, pp. 11, 23.*

THE VIRGINIA QUARTERLY REVIEW

McGuane's essays, written over a ten-year period [and collected in ***An Outside Chance: Essays on Sport***], celebrate the sports of the rugged individualist—fishing, hunting, motorcycling, and the rodeo. These essays, smirking at spectator sports, glory in the meaningless, Zenlike experience of "ecstatic resignation to the moment." McGuane, "who wants to be a rugged guy in the West and not some horrid nancy with pink palms," affects the accents and manners of pokes from Montana and conches from Key West. In these essays, he prefers comedy to morality, recalling other centerless writers like Brautigan and Tom Robbins. Whereas Hemingway's masculine posture reflected his inner conflicts, McGuane's machismo is just for the hell of it.

A review of "An Outside Chance: Essays on Sport," in The Virginia Quarterly Review, *Vol. 57, No. 2, Spring, 1981, p. 67.*

JONATHAN YARDLEY

Nobody's Angel brings Thomas McGuane, abruptly and prematurely, to the end of the line. Only a few years ago he seemed to have as bright a future as any young American writer. His first novel, ***The Sporting Club,*** had been published in 1969 to general and justifiable applause. His second, ***The Bushwhacked Piano,*** won the 1972 Rosenthal Award for fiction. His third, ***Ninety-Two in the Shade,*** was a nominee and a serious contender for a National Book Award.

All three of these novels were the work of a writer with a vivid, idiosyncratic style and outlook. The central character in each of them was a young man who had been raised in privileged surroundings but had rejected materialism in favor of a closer relationship with the natural world, especially as expressed in sport. All three novels voiced sharp contempt toward what McGuane saw as America's "declining snivelization." All three had a rich, bawdy humor and a strong undercurrent of anger. . . .

I described [***The Bushwhacked Piano***] in a review as the work of a writer possessing "a talent of Faulknerian potential," one whose "sheer writing skill is nothing short of amazing." Two years later I wrote of ***Ninety-Two in the Shade:*** "The satire is still there, and the mordant view of American vulgarity, and the fierce anger over despoliation of the land and water, but here McGuane is far more compassionate and understanding toward his characters." I called his prose "vivid, ironic, filled with surprising and revealing insights."

I quote from these reviews not out of any pride of authorship—quite to the contrary—but to recall the high praise with which McGuane's work was greeted in his salad days. To younger reviewers and readers, he was one of the most prominent and promising of a new generation of writers: one willing to cast a cold and critical eye at American excesses and follies, one with a piercing unsentimental appreciation of American vulgarity. Either we did not notice, or were willing to overlook, a strong strain of condescension, snobbery and self-aggrandizement in his work.

Then McGuane went to the movies. He took over direction of the film of ***Ninety-Two in the Shade,*** a movie that quickly turned sour. His personal life took several flamboyant and melodramatic turns, all of them reported in the gossip columns. If he wrote any fiction in the mid-'70s, I am unaware of it. The film of ***Ninety-Two in the Shade*** was a complete disaster, as were virtually all of his subsequent ventures in the medium. He became more noted as a celebrity, even if a third-string one, than as a writer.

None of which should be pertinent to a book review except that McGuane, like his hero Hemingway, had by this point made himself of as much consequence as his books. That was made embarrassingly clear in ***Panama,*** a short *apologia pro vita sua* in the form of a novel that was published in 1978. It was a drearily self-indulgent little book, a contemplation of the price of celebrity that was, in point of fact, merely an exploitation of the author's new notoriety.

Nobody's Angel is more of the same: a book that can be of no conceivable interest to anyone except those who still, for whatever reason, remain his admirers. Its publication has been preceded by a small barrage of magazine articles and publicity, the effect of which apparently is supposed to be that McGuane has, at his ranch in Montana, found a new peace and his old skills. If he has indeed discovered the former, more power to him; but there is no evidence in ***Nobody's Angel*** that he has retrieved the latter.

It is the story of Patrick Fitzpatrick, 36 years old, "a fourth-generation cowboy outsider, an educated man, a whiskey addict and until recently a professional soldier." He has left the service and returned to the family ranch on the outskirts of the small Montana settlement of Deadlock. . . .

In fairly rapid order, Patrick gets into a contretemps with the editor of the local newspaper, which gives McGuane a chance to take a shot at his critics in the press by noting that people are "not out there just as cannon fodder for boys with newspapers." Then he becomes involved with a wealthy couple, Tio and Claire; when he and Claire begin an affair, he is forced to confront questions about love and emotional commitment, and to risk the vengeance of the quietly berserk Tio.

The action is interrupted over and again by windy philosophizing and pontificating. ***Nobody's Angel*** is a talky, self-important novel in which much is made of very little. (p. 3)

The strutting, swaggering man about saloons has been displaced by a rueful, edgy, death-haunted man of tender emotions—macho's answer to the whore with a heart of gold. A decade ago McGuane wanted us to see how tough and sarcastic and knowing he was; now he wants us to see his soft and vulnerable side. But in either case, in the world according to Thomas McGuane, the beginning and the end are—you guessed it—Thomas McGuane. (pp. 3, 14)

This is adolescent self-absorption, pure and simple. For whatever reason, McGuane's view does not extend beyond the range of his own experience and fantasies. When he does reach past himself, his view of the rest of the world is arrogant and condescending. His prose has lost his precision and his sense of humor has vanished. Literature is the loser, I suppose, but I have no further interest in the case. (p. 14)

Jonathan Yardley, "Thomas McGuane Reaches for the Big Sky," in Book World—The Washington Post, February 28, 1982, pp. 3, 14.

VANCE BOURJAILY

When Patrick Fitzpatrick uses the word superfluous about himself four pages before the end of Thomas McGuane's new novel, ***Nobody's Angel,*** it may or may not be an accurate self-assessment, but he has been placed by his author in a clear line of literary descent. His ancestry is German, British and romantic; but the first of these romantic idlers were Russians, beginning with Pushkin's *Eugene Onegin* and the central figure in Lermontov's *A Hero of Our Time* and reappearing in many other books as the 19th century went on.

These men were young, gifted and alienated. They were socially accepted, but bored with the society that admired them. Their friendship was destructive to men, their love destructive to women, and they were self-destructive as well. Seeing no place for themselves and no meaning in life, they were equally contemptuous of death. If, as readers, we are put off by their carelessness and cruelty, we are won back by their casual acts of courage.

This is not to suggest that ***Nobody's Angel*** is some sort of ersatz Russian romantic novel. Thomas McGuane has not set out to write "Onegin in Montana." There does, though, seem to be an interesting subtext, subtle allusion rather than open parallel. For example, Patrick Fitzpatrick is a name derived in the manner of a Russian patronymic. Like Lermontov's Pechorin, McGuane's Fitzpatrick has been a military officer, though with no great sense of vocation; he loves hunting, he has a sense of family honor and he has led a wild and risky young life. Like Onegin, he has returned home to try to manage his family's place (in this case a Montana horse ranch); and like both literary predecessors, he will gain and lose love, leave a dead adversary behind and travel on.

Patrick Fitzpatrick is, on the other hand, an older and less foolish man than Onegin and Lermontov, more emotional, more vulnerable. He cares for and takes care of his grandfather and his sister. He likes to cook and he loves horses. The young Russians were far more cynical, elegant and aloof. The subtext of allusions is there only as a point of departure. Thomas McGuane is, after all, a thoroughly American writer of his time.

What stamps this as a McGuane novel are the bizarre episodes he invents for his character and the wit with which he reports them; what is new in ***Nobody's Angel,*** his sixth book, is a depth of feeling. Thus we are made to share the rage Patrick feels when he visits the local newspaper office and canes the editor for what he considers a violation of his privacy. We feel pathos as well as the comedy of the situation when the grandfather is told he has a good chance of being cast in a western movie because the scars and deformities he has accumulated during his hard cowboy lifetime make him look authentic. And we feel the despair of Patrick's sister, Mary, who worked as a prostitute for the local madam, left the brothel to live with an Indian ranch hand, disappeared for a while and then came home pregnant. Mary is the most appealing character in the book, but like Patrick she is a victim of the family melancholy that McGuane calls "sadness-for-no-reason." One day, when their mother is visiting the ranch with her second husband (the first is dead), Patrick goes to Mary's room and finds it empty: "the sheet on the bed was drawn taut, and Mary had outlined herself in ink, life-size, carefully sketching even the fingers. Across the abdomen she had traced the shape of an infant; and she was gone."

With Mary gone, the book's main concern is Patrick's love for a woman named Claire, and the strange verbal and emotional duel between Patrick and Claire's husband, a magnetic, complicated man named Tio. . . . (p. 9)

Except when the subject is horses, McGuane is an elliptical and sometimes oblique writer, which some readers may find troubling. Events that we have been led to anticipate are then only briefly referred to after they have taken place offstage; characters say things to one another which they seem to understand, though the reader may not. But the play of wit is constant and redeeming. . . .

If ***Nobody's Angel*** presents difficulties, they are worth bearing. It's Thomas McGuane's best book so far, and he is a very good writer indeed. (p. 30)

Vance Bourjaily, "The Story of a Superfluous Man," in The New York Times Book Review, *March 7, 1982, pp. 9, 30.*

GEOFFREY STOKES

It's been fourteen years since ***The Sporting Club,*** and a number of folks are ready by now to accuse Thomas McGuane of breach of promise; though I'm not yet among them, I understand the temptation. First of all, McGuane still seems unable to resist making a joke. A lot of these are funny (his characters tend to talk like Oscar Wilde on Maui Wowee), but many are out of place (I mean, *all* his characters tend . . .).

And another thing. Despite their flashy stylistic changes, McGuane's first four novels had but one subject: Formerly Catholic young man of responsible age and good though eccentric family attempts to live fully moral life while moseying to a different drummer and enjoying guilt-free—and ultimately, perhaps, *committed*—sex with a woman in a relationship that seems, from the giddyup, doomed.

Comes now the much-ballyhooed ***Nobody's Angel***. . . . [The] book is about a formerly Catholic young man of good but eccentric family attempting to live a fully moral life *on a ranch in Montana* while moseying to a different etc. . . . What does make ***Nobody's Angel*** different from McGuane's Key West novels is its protagonist's drug of choice. After exploring the outer limits of cocaine—so convincingly in ***Panama*** I suspected he'd never write again—McGuane has returned to the drug that animated his very first novel: alcohol. "Patrick Fitzpatrick lived on a ranch thirty-one miles outside of town. He was a fourth-generation cowboy outsider, an educated man, a whiskey addict and until recently a professional soldier." Each of these attributes is important to the 36-year-old Fitzpatrick, but only whiskey is central to the book; ***Nobody's Angel*** is about hangovers.

Mornings after aren't new for McGuane (in ***Panama,*** Chet Pomeroy found himself "beginning to sense that the night had written a check that daylight couldn't cover," but he never acted as though he might believe it), but here, there is no illusion they can be easily cured. Not with a line of coke, not with an early whiskey. The hangovers in ***Nobody's Angel*** aren't mere inconveniences that yield to aspirin or sleep; they are the cripplers you can only earn by taking a continent from its inhabitants—or one spouse from another. Such short-term pleasures guarantee long-term pain. (p. 341)

In this novel's harsh world, the only sure-fire way to avoid life's pain is to kill yourself. And even that has consequences for the people you leave behind. For such a genuinely funny book, ***Nobody's Angel*** is pretty grim. . . .

Now the notion that actions have consequences—that the means not only justify but determine the ends—is not among the great intellectual breakthroughs of the late twentieth century. And McGuane's apparent belief that hangovers are good for us—that without such cruel feedback mechanisms we would all be at one another's throats and genitals—offers only bleak, Hobbesian comfort. Still, it is an *idea*. Not a large one, maybe even a dumb one, but an idea. ***Nobody's Angel*** is not just pyrotechnics.

And that's a problem. As *writing,* the novel is a flat-out success; I often caught myself laughing aloud, and even once or twice imagined how nice it would be to commute on my horse—or even in my battered pickup—instead of the D train. But it's pretty fragile stuff. I mean, what is all that rigmarole in the beginning with Grandpa and the film company? Does McGuane have some Hollywood scores to settle? And why does Claire disappear for almost fifty pages in the heart of the book? If McGuane means to argue that she's really unimportant, he's wrong; we miss her. And maybe it's slack season in the ranch biz, but it occurs to me that Patrick doesn't *work* very much, which he probably ought to if his return to the ranch is to have any meaning at all. . . .

But except for Claire's vanishing act, one notices ***Nobody's Angel***'s problems only after the book is closed. Mostly, there is so much *interesting* going on that, like Wile E. Coyote, we don't realize the road has turned until we're already strolling in midair. Real falls hurt. As Patrick, training a horse, observes, "By your late thirties, the ground has begun to grow hard. It grows harder and harder until the day it admits you." And McGuane stays true to this vision. Patrick finally winds up, without Claire, back in Europe with the Army. And with, when he's drinking heavy, his longtime imaginary girlfriend, Marion Easterly. Who has, given the cowboy context, an interesting name.

Patrick does not come back; McGuane has. (p. 342)

Geoffrey Stokes, "Hung Over in Montana," in The Nation, *New York, Vol. 234, No. 11, March 20, 1982, pp. 341-42.*

DAVID W. MADDEN

"You would have to care about the country. Nobody had been there long enough and the Indians had been very thoroughly kicked out. It would take a shovel to find they'd ever been there." Thus begins Thomas McGuane's fifth and perhaps best novel [***Nobody's Angel***]. It is, as the quote suggests, another alternative Western, a term which, if it has meaning any longer, certainly defines this work. Returning to this setting is thirty-six-year-old Patrick Fitzpatrick, "a fourth-generation cowboy outsider, an educated man, a whiskey addict and until recently a professional soldier."

Like other McGuane heroes before him—Tom Skelton (***Ninety-Two in the Shade***) and Chet Pomeroy (***Panama***)—Fitzpatrick is an emotional casualty who hopes to find in Deadrock, Montana (a pun on McGuane's home in Livingston, Montana), the enduring values of love and family that will give some meaning to his exhausted condition. Like Skelton and Pomeroy, Fitzpatrick is an existential hero, a figure whose angst stems from "the jaggedness-of-the-everyday . . . [which was composed of] edges and no middle" and which afflicts him with "sadness-for-no-reason." But unlike those heroes from McGuane's earlier novels, Fitzpatrick has a better claim on his sorrow, for he has actually suffered. (pp. 376-77)

Although Fitzpatrick takes himself very seriously, McGuane does not, and by means of an extremely subtle irony, he reveals his protagonist's weakness and often self-conscious absorption in his deserved sorrow. In these ways, Fitzpatrick is, in fact, the complete antithesis of the traditional western hero; he lives in fantasies that rarely give meaning to his life, and deals in bad faith with himself and those about him. For instance, when Tio asks if he is sleeping with his wife, Fitzpatrick can offer no answer except to hang up the phone. Similarly, after he rushes Tio off to the hospital after a devastating nervous seizure, Fitzpatrick lies that he hasn't seen the man in order to spend more time with his wife.

Operating almost as a mirror of the hero, the West that McGuane presents is a landscape that "lack[s] the detailed human regimen he imagined he could find in his Castilian walk-up," a place "less and less appropriate to epic poetry and murals." Nevertheless, McGuane does rely upon a classic western situation—the settlers under siege; however, the siege in this case comes not from those native to the West, but from the marauders of self-pity, frustration, rootless anxiety, and a past that no longer provides meaning and cohesion. When he moves away from Fitzpatrick's condition to the details of the frontier itself, McGuane is capable of writing passages which evoke a compelling and almost lyrical beauty. (p. 377)

In ***Nobody's Angel*** Thomas McGuane has given readers a work that is rich in wit and humor and that offers a vision of a distinctly American ideal gone to seed. With his remorseless irony and probing questioning, McGuane demonstrates once again why he is considered one of America's most accomplished novelists. (p. 378)

David W. Madden, in a review of "Nobody's Angel," in Western American Literature, *Vol. XVII, No. 4, Winter, 1983, pp. 376-78.*

CHARLES G. MASINTON

Thomas McGuane is an intellectual cowboy, a writer and social critic who feels as much at ease in a saddle as he does in a study. He raises cattle and trains cutting horses on his ranch in Livingston, Montana, and he excels at team roping, a rodeo event that requires excellent horsemanship and a certain athletic ability as well. McGuane has also written five novels, a superb book of essays on outdoor sports, and several screenplays. He is well known for the comic flair in his writing—the wry, off-center view of American life that comes across in his prose style as a kind of hip, ironic detachment. But he also has developed a reputation as an acute social observer: with each succeeding novel or screenplay, McGuane's preoccupation with the loss of sustaining values in American life has grown more evident.

In three of his screenplays—***Rancho Deluxe, The Missouri Breaks,*** and ***Tom Horn***—and in his most recent novel, ***Nobody's Angel,*** McGuane's social criticism focuses specifically on the American West. In a fairly recent issue of *The New York Times Magazine* dealing with contemporary writers of the American West, McGuane is quoted as having said, "The West is a wreck. I'd like to document that without getting totally depressing about it." His documentation of the "wreck" that the West now represents is clear to see in ***Rancho Deluxe*** and ***Nobody's Angel,*** both of which have contemporary settings. McGuane easily avoids "getting totally depressing about it" in the movie by balancing his depiction of the decline of the West with his humorous sense of the absurd, which is reflected both in dialogue and in action.

The novel, however, conveys a considerably more dark and pessimistic vision of the American West than the movie does. ***Rancho Deluxe*** . . . is full of high jinks and a kind of throw-away humor that does not take itself altogether seriously. But although the story in ***Rancho Deluxe*** differs greatly from the ill-fated ranch romance in ***Nobody's Angel,*** the 1975 film can be seen as a sort of pop version of the corruption of the American West that McGuane later returns to with more seriousness in the novel. . . . (pp. 49-50)

Nobody's Angel tells the story of Patrick Fitzpatrick, thirty-six years of age, an ex-tank captain in the U.S. Army who patrolled the borders of East Germany. He has left the Army and returned home to Montana to find stability and meaning in his life by taking over the family ranch. While in the Army he had thought of going home as a return to "bright ceremonies" . . . and of life on the ranch as a series of "rituals" . . . that would bring stability and order to his existence. These terms suggest that he seeks something approaching a sacramental order, something more than the mere comfort of daily habit. But Patrick is a self-confessed "whiskey addict" . . . who suffers from what he calls "sadness-for-no-reason". . .—a deep melancholy that is an expression of the insanity that runs in his family. In addition, the ranch does not offer the possibilities for contentment that he had imagined in the Army.

At home lives his grandfather, an old cowboy whose limp and facial scars are the result of his vigorous life outdoors, a man who remembers authentic gunmen of the West in their fading years. Grandpa Fitzpatrick, however, has a new interest: he wants to be in the movies. One of McGuane's most stinging (and genuinely humorous) criticisms of the broken-down West of today comes when Patrick learns, shortly after his homecoming, that his grandfather has won a tryout for a movie called *Hondo's Last Move,* a patent abomination that, luckily, will probably never be made. There is a huge irony in the fact that the old cowboy's scars and limp make him appear authentic to a slick and probably phony producer who wants to make a Western movie. This situation contains an implicit commentary on what the West has become: the revered picture of the lone cowpoke, the proud hero of countless novels and movies who sits tall in the saddle and brings dignity to the endless, beautiful landscape of the open West, is replaced by the seedy reality of a crochety old man who wants to hire himself out as an image for mass entertainment. Grandpa Fitzpatrick's movie aspirations represent the West's unintentional self-parody. (p. 50)

[The] contrast between the myth of the Old West and the unsavory actualities of the New West underlies much of the comic effect in ***Rancho Deluxe,*** and it runs throughout ***Nobody's Angel*** as well. ***Nobody's Angel*** is indeed a "Western," but the West that we see in it is played off ironically against our inherited picture of a pristine land where the cowboy, like a knight in shining armor, defends truth, justice, and goodness and where a man's character can grow to fit the great outdoors. In McGuane's modern West there are too many tourists and outsiders in cowboy outfits and not enough of the genuine article. Moreover, the landscape has been defaced by billboards. . . . These billboards trivialize the heroic image of the Old West and desecrate the glories of the mountains and rivers that McGuane so ably evokes in his loving descriptions of the setting in this novel.

In ***Nobody's Angel*** Patrick's antagonist is an outsider, a gone-in-the-head Oklahoma oilman named Tio who has bought a ranch in Montana largely as a plaything and who is the husband of the woman Patrick falls in love with. Tio is an interesting and even sympathetic character, but he clearly represents the ethical and psychological rot that McGuane associates with the ruination of the West. (p. 51)

Tio, however, is not a villain, despite his grotesque behavior. In fact, he is more of a victim than Patrick. A poor boy who married into his wife Claire's very rich oil family, he has been driven to his own special kind of insanity by trying to live up to the demands placed on him to grow rich and enter the social class of oil barons. He has, in a sense, lost his soul: the pleasant young man that he used to be has been completely absorbed into the role-playing that he has obsessively thrown himself into, the role of the swaggering good old boy that he apparently thought he needed to play in order to keep Claire. The pathetic element in their relationship is that this beautiful young woman cheats on her husband. When she cheats on him with Patrick (and it is their adulterous romance that dominates the novel), Tio becomes more and more irrational and finally kills himself.

In his desire to become rich and powerful as a way of deserving what Patrick thinks of as "a former Oklahoma golden girl," . . . Tio resembles the Great Gatsby, who also seeks wealth and social position to possess Daisy Buchanan, F. Scott Fitzgerald's archetypal "golden girl." Daisy is less admirable than Claire, in the end not fit at all to be the incarnation of Jay Gatsby's dream of splendor. But she is no more destructive to him than Claire is to Tio. Since Fitzgerald's *The Great Gatsby* is a commentary on the corruption of the American Dream, the connection between Jay and Tio is not inappropriate. Although Tio is not the protagonist of ***Nobody's Angel,*** the waste of Tio's character and energy in quest of the good life with a woman who is not quite worth it all repeats the narrative pattern of *The Great Gatsby*—only this time the setting is the West, not the East. It is instructive to recall that F. Scott Fitzgerald has his narrator Nick Carraway call the novel "a story of the West, after all" when Nick looks back in disillusionment to consider what forces have defeated him and the other transplanted Midwesterners who had (in a reversal of Horace Greeley's dictum) "gone East" to fulfill their dreams. It becomes clear in *The Great Gatsby* that Fitzgerald wants his readers to connect Gatsby's downfall and death with the failure of the sense of endless possibilities associated with the American West—and in extension, as the last scene of that novel shows, with the failure of the promise of the New World, which was reached by sailing west. McGuane's vision of the erosion of life's possibilities is not constructed on such an imaginative scale, but ***Nobody's Angel*** at points reflects the literary tradition so brilliantly illuminated by Fitzgerald's elegant lament of the failure of the American Dream. (p. 52)

After Tio's death Claire and Patrick split up. Tio's suicide leaves them guilt-ridden, and their relationship cannot survive the knowledge of what they have done to him. Claire goes back home to Oklahoma, the grandfather moves to town, and Patrick leases the ranch and returns to the Army in Europe. On the last page of the novel McGuane communicates indirectly and almost casually the harrowing information that Patrick has succumbed to the madness that runs in his family. He has purchased a flat in Madrid and is reportedly seeing an American woman named Marion Easterley. Earlier in the novel Patrick has imagined that in Spain he might achieve the life of order, small daily rituals, and carefully planned hours that "the remorseless West," . . . as he calls it, makes impossible. If his inability to lead a sane and ordered life in Montana is any basis for judging, however, it has to be said that his dream of finding in the Old World what the New World lacks is probably another illusion. But if it is an illusion, it at least does not demonstrate his madness. The figure of Marion Easterley does. Marion does not exist: she is an imaginary young woman, someone Patrick made up as a teenager when he needed an excuse to tell his parents when he stayed out late drinking in town. Although he actually thinks of this figment of his imagination during the course of the novel, and somewhat embellishes his mental picture of her, he knows that she is not real. Apparently he now no longer does. He has retreated into the world of dreams.

His return to the West, to his home on the range, has led to his defeat. In an ironic reversal of the motif in American literature that shows the unhappy or defeated protagonist running away from civilization into the woods or relatively unsettled landscape, which is often the Western frontier, McGuane takes Patrick back to the Old World after his frustrated attempt to settle down happily in the New World, in the American West of soaring peaks, wide vistas, and clear, clean air. (pp. 53-4)

Charles G. Masinton, "'Nobody's Angel': Thomas McGuane's Vision of the Contemporary American West," in New Mexico Humanities Review, *Vol. 6, No. 3, Fall, 1983, pp. 49-55.*

R. T. SMITH

Thomas McGuane's new novel, ***Nobody's Angel,*** doesn't work, and it's a damn shame. McGuane, who is perhaps as well known for his screenplays (***Rancho Deluxe, The Missouri Breaks, Tom Horn***) as for his novels (***The Sporting Club, The Bushwhacked Piano, Ninety-two in the Shade, Panama***), is a writer capable of amphetamine-paced, acetylene-bright prose, a writer capable of creating characters who live in the curl of an emotional wave always on the verge of breaking. He is one of that breed of writers—John Sayles, Jim Harrison, Barry Hannah, Harry Crews, James Welch—who might at any moment write the book that will scramble the tepid landscape of American fiction. It is no accident that all these authors are men. There is a kind of story that men are still more likely to write well because it involves the outdoors and activities and attitudes that men have been encouraged to explore throughout the course of American history and literature. But now an element of sass joins the force that has traditionally characterized these stories. Of all the books by all the above authors, most of Harrison's *Farmer,* the first half of Hannah's *Geronimo Rex* and the first half of ***Nobody's Angel*** involve the most gripping and moving writing, but half a book is not enough. (p. 20)

What [***Nobody's Angel***] lacks might have been the easiest thing to give it, a well-structured plot line in which something of significance is discovered. McGuane told us earlier that, when Nichol Dance shot Tom Skelton through the heart [in ***Ninety-two in the Shade***], "It was the discovery of his life." A meaningfully resonant phrase. But what Fitzpatrick discovers when Tio, Claire's ominous husband, refuses to shoot him is not so clear. Events come to a climax, then the characters broadcast like so many windblown seeds. Patrick drifts back into the Army, rents a flat in his dream-Madrid and is rumored to be living there with his dreamed-up adolescent sweetheart. He has saved no one from the "sadness-without-reason" up there in "the high lonesome"; he has become nobody's angel.

What McGuane did have all along was an interesting, believable, vital character who has a series of one-to-one encounters. . . . But these encounters, every one a fine scene, never connect, never adhere. All the beads are there, but no necklace.

Two other things demand to be mentioned. McGuane's zany humor is still present in his writing, but reserved more, perhaps timed better. One is not likely to forget the urbane savages who engage in verbal "lawn war" with Bloody Marys in their fists. McGuane's satire of money-cum-arrogance is right on target and funnier for being true. . . . It is going to be easy for the critics who prefer their literature more "cooked" to call this a cowboy novel about "characters" instead of people. They could hardly find an easier way to be wrong. Granted, McGuane gives us people living in something like a last frontier, a place where helicopters land and old men find mummified Indians in caves and refuse to tell anyone where. But it was this tangle of past and future that Faulkner often found crucial, and if Thomas Hardy were writing today, he might be more than tempted to create, or discover, such people. I began by saying that the novel does not work, but McGuane has worked on this novel. If it is a failure, it is so because McGuane has kept his gaze too steadily ahead, has refused to unlock his word-hoard and write wildly and glibly, as he can certainly do. The epigraph of the novel is from Malcolm Lowry, who wrote, "I love hell. I can't wait to get back." I can't wait for McGuane to try again. (p. 21)

R. T. Smith, in a review of "Nobody's Angel," in The American Book Review, *Vol. 5, No. 4, May-June, 1983, pp. 20-1.*

GARRETT EPPS

Something To Be Desired . . . is a painful and oddly indeterminate book. After bedding Emily in college, Lucien finds that nothing else seems worth concentrating on. When Emily murders her husband years later, he dumps his diplomatic career, his beautiful wife Suzanne and their son James and hastens home to get her out of jail. When Emily jumps bail, Lucien is left with title to her ranch, an unappeasable thirst and degenerate personal habits. He turns the ranch into a ritzy hot-spring spa, drinks virtually anything in bottles and sets a new depth level for Montana low life.

McGuane is, as always, witty and confident as he evokes the squalor of too much sex and too little feeling, and Lucien has a kind of seedy charm. . . .

Lucien's not a bad guy, he just has a short attention span. . . . But because Lucien can't focus, the reader doesn't learn much about Suzanne or James or for that matter, even the seductive, murderous Emily, who's the kind of woman I'd like to observe intensely from a safe distance.

And I had a problem—which I didn't have with his earlier books—with McGuane's elliptical, epigrammatic narrative style. He can vault across a decade in a paragraph, or sum up a character in an impromptu proverb. Sometimes this effect strikes home ("if dismounting were given the same importance in sex as it is in horsemanship, this would be a happier world.") and sometimes it misses. . . .

McGuane certainly deserves credit for trying—against the trend of fictional fashion—to write about the problems of men, and men who aren't writers or artists at that. But perhaps the problem is just what Emily suggested: We're all getting older, and the habits that served us in youth are getting a little grimy as the years wear on. In books like ***Ninety-two in the Shade,*** McGuane was describing the inarticulate, almost offhand passions of young men. But as they age, his heroes need to pick up some wisdom, some kindness and something to say for themselves. That means bidding farewell to the insouciance and the obsessions of youth. Lucien can't. "Is it all that terrible that I've gone on having these feelings?" He asks Emily. "Not everyone has such a happy view of his own past."

We all know men like Lucien; but to be frank, I think their problems are getting a little old, at least in novelistic terms. Characters like Lucien—inarticulate, charming, inwardly decent, outwardly passive—have become clichés. I wanted Lucien to surprise me—to show some reserve of courage or gumption or even wickedness that would set him off from the dozens of other men like him I have read about. He didn't come through for Suzanne or me.

Garrett Epps, "The Big Sky's the Limit," in Book World—The Washington Post, *December 16, 1984, p. 10.*

ROBERT ROPER

[***Something to Be Desired***] is Thomas McGuane's seventh book and also, I think, his best, a remarkable work of honest colors and fresh phrasings that deliver strong, earned emotional effects. In the world of this novel, which is a physical world brought into high, astonishing relief in almost every sentence, Lucien Taylor, a native son of Montana, embarks on a half-witted, half-unwilling voyage of self-discovery. Eschewing The Good (his wife and son) and gravitating, temporarily, toward The Bad (in the person of Emily, a passionate old flame who happens also to be a murderess), he stumbles and gropes and seems often on the verge of complete collapse.

What saves Lucien, in the end, is nothing very dramatic: just common sense, that slight increase of it that sometimes comes with age. The something to be desired of the book's title—that feeling that led him astray in the first place—turns out to be his own family, and as Lucien reorients, blessings naturally start to rain down on him. . . .

What we have in Thomas McGuane is a writer whose comic gifts, like Nabokov's, cause him to write a prose too inherently lively, too highly colored for the tragic effects that he—as a literary son of Hemingway—feels belong in serious books. As a result, some of his earlier novels, such as ***Ninety-Two in the Shade,*** are marred by a grafting on of violent, *mano a mano* incidents, as if Mr. McGuane had lost faith in his own technique—his dead-on, wonderfully comic writing—to carry a weight of darker meanings. But in ***Something to Be Desired,*** he overcomes this tendency. The clarity of heart and mind that Lucien, like other of Mr. McGuane's heroes, is seeking emerges on its own and more convincingly. . . .

[Lucien] acquires an aura of general high-focus, of mental and perceptual precision. But there is clarity of mind, and then there's the other kind. Clarity of heart can elude him totally. He can have not the vaguest idea how to save himself (and his family), how to work his muddled, disaster-intoxicated will into some sort of responsible shape.

Lucien, like other of Mr. McGuane's central characters, is a little like a peacetime soldier, a finely tuned, avid physical specimen who senses within himself the capacity for acts of heroic derring-do, who, however, finds himself condemned by inexplicable historical accident to live life mainly on the domestic plane, in that mucky realm of feelings, evanescent moods and fluctuating attachments for which he feels constitutionally unsuited. That part of him that partakes of the primordial male, of the freedom-loving, clean-sensation-seeking Old Adam, in

D. H. Lawrence's parlance, turns out to be just that, just a part (and even a faintly absurd one); and, as nobody ever bothered to tell him, certainly not his own father, he must now make it through a long maturity on exactly those softer qualities that he never much wanted to have.

He discovers a few of these, already, in secret, rather exquisitely developed in him, and this is the drama of his story.

Robert Roper, "Lucien Alone in Deadrock," in The New York Times Book Review, *December 16, 1984, p. 11.*

RONALD VARNEY

Something to Be Desired . . . begins in Montana, where Lucien Taylor, the hero, is raised by his embittered mother, "a daylong tippler" who gets by on alimony and handouts from relatives. Lucien's father has abandoned his family to head for adventure in the mountains of Peru. ("Adventure" turns out to mean using sheep dung for cooking fuel, drinking too much and mailing "deranged letters" to his son.)

Lucien reacts by flunking his courses and getting kicked off the baseball team. When he decides to attend the state university, his mother goes haywire. She accuses him of being "the leading killjoy of my life."

At the state university Lucien dates two girls from his hometown, Emily and Suzanne. . . .

Lucien desperately wants Emily, imagining that, under her inspiration, he could become "a rancher and a painter of sporting subjects." But Emily dumps him for her beloved doctor, whom she marries and Lucien is left with Suzanne as his consolation.

Lucien marries Suzanne, and takes up a career with the U.S. Information Agency in Latin America, "spraying leaflets on the mestizo millions." They have a son. The years pass and Lucien grows increasingly irritable and distracted, still unable to get Emily out of his mind. He decides to leave his family and go back to Montana to look up his old flame. . . .

Back home Emily is facing charges that she has murdered her husband. Lucien posts bail, moves in with her on her ranch, and once again becomes her lover. When she jumps bail and flees the country, he's left owning the ranch. He turns it into a hot-springs resort. He lures his wife and son back. Then Emily shows up.

The somewhat bizarre plot twists of Mr. McGuane's story occasionally seem implausible. Lucien's transformation, for example, into a canny, tough-talking entrepreneur seems hard to believe, given his zonked-out, whimsical nature. And yet Mr. McGuane manages to pull this story off rather well, giving it, as in his other novels, such a compressed dramatic style that the reader is constantly entertained and diverted. Much of this entertainment is provided by Lucien, whose hip, throwaway manner helps us overlook some of the plot's oddities.

Lucien, who wants "more than anything . . . to grow up," is so deeply absorbed in self-analysis, so fixated on understanding what makes himself tick, that his girl-chasing and outdoor-adventuring come as nicely balancing character traits. Gradually, Lucien is able to cope with his self-doubts and crazy behavior and, as it were, grow up. (It is a sly McGuane touch here that growing up is equated with making scads of money.)

The cowboy-cool atmosphere of the novel is effective in the way it takes people rolling with emotional tension and gives them a laid-back, contemplative, almost dazed quality. The great open spaces of Montana seem to haunt the characters, leaving them subdued, their minds plunged into deep, solitary thought. Lucien's frequent outings to hunt, ride and drift down the river thus become meditative interludes where time is suspended. . . .

In the end, what makes ***Something to Be Desired*** remarkable is its setting, the mountains and flatlands of Montana that Mr. McGuane so lovingly describes. In showing how this land shapes and defines the characters who for all their modern anxieties and illusions seem to have much in common with their forebears, those early settlers, wild and solitary, who "had hidden whiskey bottles under the porch or made the dog graves by the creek."

Ronald Varney, "Even Cowboys Get the Blues," in The Wall Street Journal, *December 24, 1984, p. 5.*

JILL NEVILLE

In Thomas McGuane's restless odyssey [***Something to Be Desired***], Lucien holds on forever to a moment of wholeness in his otherwise fragmented boyhood, when his self-dramatizing, juvenile father for once pulled himself together and took his son on a trek into the American wilderness.

As the air gets purer, phrases shine like pebbles in a mountain stream before anyone ever heard of acid snow. Underneath is the all-American yearning of a son for a father, one who will not refuse to grow up, who is honourable and knows about men's things like horses and tents and fishing.

They come across a remarkable hot spring and for a brief time forget their troubles and float in "thermal blue". The spring is the central symbol of the book. It is the stillness inside the chaos, the ecstasy. Having seen it, Lucien must own it. The way he achieves this is barely credible. Not only is Lucien's father always arriving and departing, red-eyed and shouting, looking for kicks and reconciliations; his mother is a monster in hair-rollers. Then he has the misfortune to meet at the same time those twin stereotypes of Western movies, the good girl (Suzanne) and the bad girl (Emily). Emily is so bad, in fact, that she shoots her husbands, but she is the one who wears, psychologically at least, the black fishnet stockings, and brings out the sexual volcano in Lucien. It is with her that he makes love in the very waters of that thermal blue spring. Emily's ex-husband owns a ranch on the land where Lucien and his father once trod, and she leaves it to him as a sort of consolation prize when she runs off with the ranch hand. By this time Lucien is married to Suzanne and they have a son, James. The marriage has been good, but there is too much of his father in Lucien to tolerate contentment. One day the devil speaks to him in the form of a "deep realization" that his life is without high adventure, so he decides to leave.

The process of what he calls "stain" has begun; it sinks deeper inside him and causes turbulence, damage and shame. But on Emily's ranch he can look out through the tall prairie grasses on the stream bank and "start to lose his sense of irony"—then maybe Emily will love him. But Emily is irredeemable. There follows a period of chaos; the action is a little hard to follow, but the sense of debauch is clearly conveyed. . . . Eventually, though, he is ready to put away childish things. He can even put away Emily when she next comes to tempt him. He has sloughed off his self-destructiveness and his father. He might even be rewarded with his wife and son, if they can ever trust him again.

All this is written in high sharp style, with humour and a touch of vulgarity. The lawyer, Wick, who wearily watches Lucien's capers, has one-liners worthy of Woody Allen. But there is no escaping the painful and deep wish for health, emotional stability and Nature which is the crux of it all. McGuane is at his best when he conveys the sense of the psycho-physical stirring of the cells in the midst of untramelled landscape, the oxygen entering the soul.

Jill Neville, "Getting Away from It All," in The Times Literary Supplement, *No. 4286, May 24, 1985, p. 573.*

KIRKUS REVIEWS

McGuane fans—who love his act-up and act-out, post-fraternity, much-too-rich and far-too-bored heroes—surely will eat up the title story [of his short story collection, ***To Skin a Cat: Stories***]: a prime example of the species, named Bobby, buys hawks and goes jetting from London to New York to San Francisco, in the patient pursuit of his fantasy of becoming a pimp for his beautiful but not-amused girlfriend Marianne. The Robert-Stone-like violence at the end and the generously amusing dialogue throughout finally don't counterweight the essential callowness, though. No better—as glitzo—are shorter stories from the same mold: **"Little Extras," "The Road Atlas," "Partners."**

But McGuane (***Something to be Desired, Nobody's Angel,*** etc.), when he isn't pressed to be inventive—it's then, it seems, that the callowness always sneaks in—can also be quite good here. Two memoirs of boyhood—**"Sportsmen"** and **"A Skirmish"**—are very precisely fine; and the opening story, **"A Millionaire"**—which has to do with a man in effect selling his unmarried daughter's baby for adoption—has a special obliquity and assurance that's concentrated and impressive. The same goes for **"Like a Leaf"**—a man clearly undergoing a breakdown, given to touching eccentricity; here the McGuane hero has no swagger, only vulnerability and poetry.

If you can overlook the gloss and smirks, there are nuggets for the finding here.

A review of "To Skin a Cat: Stories," in Kirkus Reviews, *Vol. LIV, No. 16, August 15, 1986, p. 1237.*

PUBLISHERS WEEKLY

[***To Skin a Cat: Stories***] seems to prove once more that McGuane is a writer who lacks consistency. When he is good, he is very good; at other times he can be underpowering. Some of these tales are highly interesting, imbued with power and the ability to startle; in others, McGuane seems to be coasting, failing to deliver the bite that makes the difference between a good and a great story. [**"To Skin a Cat"**] the last [story] in the collection, has that bite. The tale of a jaded young man who aspires to become a pimp, it teeters on the edge of the bizarre until it finally crosses over. Another story, **"The Millionaire,"** exhibits a delicious tension as the parents of a pregnant teenager await the arrival of the child whose adoption has already been arranged as a sort of birth of convenience. Taken as a whole, the collection is entertaining, sometimes memorable.

A review of "To Skin a Cat," in Publishers Weekly, *Vol. 230, No. 9, August 29, 1986, p. 385.*

ELIZABETH TALLENT

The stories in ***To Skin a Cat*** have in common with Mr. McGuane's longer work their heroes' restlessness, their lapses into anomie and their skepticism, sometimes slow to dawn, about the virtues of being in business. In fact, acquisition of that skepticism constitutes a plot with echoes in several of the stories. In **"Partners,"** Dean is taken under the wing of an older lawyer, Edward. Dean's half resentful, half admiring relation with his mentor is conjured with authority:

> Friday evening, Edward caught Dean in the elevator. . . . One side of the elevator was glass, affording a view of the edge of the city and the prairie beyond. Dean could imagine the aboriginal hunters out there and, in fact, he could almost picture Edward among them, avuncular, restrained, and armed. Grooved concrete shot past as they descended in the glass elevator. The door opened on a foyer almost a story and a half high with immense trees growing out of holes in the lobby floor.
>
> 'Here's the deal,' said Edward, turning in the foyer to genially stop Dean's progress. He had a way of fingering the edge of Dean's coat as he thought.

As a writer, Mr. McGuane is keenly alert to any trace of the oppressive in male/male interactions, and the play of detail suggests that what is at stake is Dean's independence—that while Edward is already deep in the life of the tribe, Dean himself has just been fingered for membership. From here on out, what is expected of Dean is the sort of canny, dignified behavior Edward exemplifies. But Dean can't bring himself to be diffident, not even with one of the law firm's richest clients; defiantly, Dean attempts an affair with the client's wife, who happens to be an old girlfriend of his. This ends in a brawl with the client. (p. 13)

During a meeting with his brothers, who are more absorbed in the family business than he is, Bill in **"The Road Atlas"** "felt a gust of power in the room, a brief touch of the thing that held these men's interest, and he did not necessarily despise it any more than he would despise weather." Unlike weather, though, businessmen closely observed yield unwitting comedy: "'What we have long understood,' said Walter, 'is that you feel a mandate for greater meaning, and we don't oppose that. John and me are just two little old MBAs. We want more of what we've got, and we're too old to change. When we get this thing right, we—or one of us—might run for office. That's where significance as we see it kicks in.'"

In his novels, Mr. McGuane has often relied on this kind of dialogue, in which the absurdities speed by with the slipstream beauty of utter unselfconsciousness. His odd corners of parlance have ranged from prostitutes arguing back and forth in front of a TV to little brooding duets between mechanic and owner over a boat engine; the vocabulary was apt, the introspection nil. The novels were enlivened by that pure, oblivious note of self-parody, but if too many characters in a short story are flattened by self-parody, there's little left to generate tension. Bill can't seem to scrape up meaning anywhere, though he recites a stylized, almost Hemingwayesque incantation: "'As against apathy,' he told himself, 'I have the change of seasons, the flowing waters, the possible divestiture of my brothers.''' His thinking remains so detached and so addled that he never has a real chance at the one woman who interests him. When his aimlessness kills their plans for traveling together, she takes off alone. Her parting line to him has a nice righteousness: ''Something's got to give.''

When it's not at work on human beings, Mr. McGuane's eye is frequently gentler, and if there are in his fiction few well-ordered human psyches, there do exist bird dogs whose behavior is exemplary, and honest cutting horses. From his general mistrust of surfaces, Mr. McGuane exempts woods, mountains, trout streams and high stubble fields where quail might be startled out. When an epiphany occurs in these stories, it occurs outdoors. **"Flight"** deals with the suicide of a mortally ill hunter whose bequest of a pair of pointers to his friend, the story's narrator, is significant as much because of the beauty and smartness of the dogs as because of the bond between the men. In **"Two Hours to Kill,"** Jack is informed his mother has died, but he can't bear to go up to the house where she still lies, so he passes the two hours before the ambulance arrives by hunting, working a pair of dogs who make a haunting mistake, pointing to distant white shapes that prove to be gravestones.

In **"A Man in Louisiana,"** the ''future was an unbroken sheen to Barry, requiring only irreversible solvency,'' yet he's 30, and ''a backward move could be a menace to his whole life. . . . He wanted to stay long enough to learn oil lease trading so that he could get out on his own. Once he was free he could do the rest of the things he wanted: have a family, tropical fish, remote-control model airplanes.'' This list casts the killing shade of authorial irony over that future. Barry is sent by his boss to fetch a dog in Mississippi as a bribe for a crooked oil dealer in Louisiana, and the story's first hint of ''meaning'' lies in Barry's observing the dog. ''He looked at fidelity writ large in the peaceful bird dog's anciently carved head and was entirely unable to picture the kind of fool he'd run off on.'' Barry proves himself to be that kind of fool, of course, but the chase is instructive, through Mississippi landscapes that lie with great stillness on the page. . . . (pp. 13-14)

Two stories in the collection are particularly bleak. **"Like a Leaf"** and [**"To Skin a Cat"**] suffer from an odd tension: rickety construction and yet a hermetic airlessness which is, maybe, only the exclusivity of fantasy—where it doesn't enthrall, it repels. In **"Like a Leaf,"** the woman the elderly narrator fears he's in love with proves to be a nymphomaniac who takes on the convicts in a prison yard; the narrator shoots her, and her body ''becomes a ghost of the river trailing beautiful smoky cotton from a hole in her silly head.'' In **"To Skin a Cat,"** prickly with changes of setting, non-sequitur discourse among its many characters and bits of black comedy, Bobby attempts to cajole, seduce and bully his girlfriend, Marianne, into becoming a prostitute. ''Three in the morning. . . . Marianne is bound, gagged, and naked, eerily delineated by a small amount of light that is sufficient, nonetheless, to reveal her tangled hair, stained face, and sense of all-consuming defeat and pollution.''

It may be that the broad strokes of the fantastic at which Thomas McGuane is so adroit require the larger canvas of a novel; even **"To Skin a Cat,"** which runs nearly 50 pages, seems straining to contain its proliferation of events. These stories are stronger and less prolix when they deal with emotions smaller than all-consuming defeat, when they touch, as **"The Millionaire"** does, on the confusions of a pregnant 15-year-old whose father has made a business deal to give away her baby, or turn, as in **"The Rescue,"** to the strangely guileless good cheer of a CPR instructor's speech: ''Partial obstruction. Our boy sounds like a crow. Say to him, 'Can you speak?' And say it like this: 'Can you *speeeeak?*' Victim clutches neck. There's your answer. And now my dear rescuer, you are on your own. You don't have any of the goodies! You don't have the resuscitator, the inhalators, the oxygen. Rescuer, you are alone.''

These partly surreal, partly artful stories leave their reader no alternative except to confront the extent and intensity of that aloneness. (p. 14)

Elizabeth Tallent, ''The Sign of Life Is Mayhem,'' in The New York Times Book Review, *October 19, 1986, pp. 13-14.*

W(illiam) S(tanley) Merwin

1927-

American poet, short story writer, autobiographer, dramatist, translator, essayist, and editor.

An important and prolific American poet, Merwin writes stylistically diverse poetry that frequently displays a moral concern for the state of contemporary society. In much of his writing, he presents a despairing view of civilization that is only occasionally tempered by expressions of hope. Merwin has been consistently praised as a technically accomplished writer and has won several prestigious awards for his work.

The poems collected in Merwin's first three volumes—*A Mask for Janus* (1952), *The Dancing Bears* (1954), and *Green with Beasts* (1956)—are characterized by his use of traditional prosodic forms, symbolic imagery, mythical and legendary motifs, and anachronistic language. In these poems, Merwin explores such themes as the universal cycle of birth, death, and rebirth; the loss of order and the search for identity in contemporary society; and the tensions between spiritual and temporal existence and between art and experience. While faulted by some reviewers for indulging in overly intellectual themes and techniques, Merwin was often praised for successfully revitalizing conventional forms in these works.

In his poetry of the 1960s, Merwin began to explore experimental techniques. Although the poems in *The Drunk in the Furnace* (1960) share many themes with his earlier work, including his obsession with death and his concern with the erosion of social and spiritual order, Merwin's subjects become more personal, and his methods incorporate colloquial language and metrical irregularities. In his next book, *The Moving Target* (1963), Merwin advances the stylistic transitions he initiated in *The Drunk in the Furnace*. Many of the poems in this volume, which feature discordant rhythms, a lack of punctuation, and informal diction, explore Merwin's recurring concerns with self-alienation, human pain, and social disorder. Although some critics regarded Merwin's evolving style as obscure, many viewed his new approach as subtle and rewarding. In *The Lice* (1967), Merwin continues to focus upon humanity's irresponsible relationship with the natural world, its delusions of self-importance, and its abuse of power. In these poems, however, Merwin often displays a tone of resignation toward the plight of civilization, while occasionally finding hope in the sensitivity of individuals.

The Carrier of Ladders (1970), for which Merwin received the Pulitzer Prize in poetry, is commonly regarded as one of his most successful volumes. Displaying in these poems what many reviewers considered greater maturity, Merwin combines the classical detachment of his early work with personal elements from his verse of the 1960s. While still decrying the shortcomings of society, Merwin also celebrates the unity of humanity in both honor and disgrace. In his next volume, *Writings to an Unfinished Accompaniment* (1973), Merwin emphasizes symbolism and imagery to examine such themes as humanity's relationship with time and the dangers of habit.

Merwin's verse during the late 1970s and the early 1980s is often considered slight in comparison to his earlier work. *The Compass Flower* (1977), *Feathers from a Hill* (1978), and

Finding the Islands (1982) display the influence of classical Chinese poetry in their direct, seemingly simple portrayals of the beauty and sanctity of life, love, and nature. Often written in haiku tercets, the poems in these volumes are generally introspective and personal. In the first part of *Opening the Hand* (1983), Merwin interweaves elements of myth with memories of his childhood, while in the final two sections he contemplates natural phenomena and urban landscapes. Through these poems, Merwin examines the intimate relationship between past and present and discovers parallels between the natural world and human civilization.

Merwin has also published two books of short fiction, *The Miner's Pale Children* (1970) and *Houses and Travellers* (1977), in which he combines mythic, fabulous, and legendary elements and employs dense, poetic prose. *Unframed Originals: Recollections* (1982) is a collection of autobiographical sketches focusing upon Merwin's family and early life. *Selected Translations, 1948-1968* (1968) and *Selected Translations, 1968-1978* (1978) gather many of his highly respected English renderings of such authors as Jean Follain, Antonio Porchia, Osip Mandelstam, and Pablo Neruda. Merwin has also written several plays, including *Darkling Child* (1956), *Favor Island* (1957), and *The Gilded West* (1961).

(See also *CLC*, Vols. 1, 2, 3, 5, 8, 13, 18; *Contemporary Authors*, Vols. 13-16, rev. ed.; *Contemporary Authors New*

Revision Series, Vol. 15; and *Dictionary of Literary Biography,* Vol. 5.)

MARK CHRISTHILF

In his first four volumes W.(illiam) S.(tanley) Merwin (1927-) . . . harkened to the voices of the literary past. This habit, demonstrated in ***A Mask for Janus*** (1952), ***The Dancing Bears*** (1954), ***Green with Beasts*** (1956), and ***The Drunk in the Furnace*** (1960), earned him critical repute as a traditional poet. Often, however, the term has been applied in a manner that does not do justice to Merwin's early work. Awareness of the past was a cardinal virtue in the poetic milieu into which he was born. Especially in its dominant current, established by T. S. Eliot and Ezra Pound, literary modernism stressed the use of the past as poetic material. Impersonality of statement, literary allusiveness, and the formal qualities of ambiguity and complexity were its aesthetic tenets. But in the 1960's critical reaction began. The new demand was for direct, personal statement and a vivid portrayal of the poetic emotion. From the viewpoint of this existentially oriented criticism, Merwin's early work suffered. It was too loosely associated only with Eliot; and more often, only with the practices of the New Criticism that Eliot popularized. This identification obscured Merwin's actual debt to Eliot. At the same time it minimized the wide variety of influences that have furnished Merwin's talent with richness and depth. At mid-career the poet's work was found lacking in emotional intensity. In critical terms, Merwin needed to "suffer a little at the hands of his subjects." His early volumes belonged to a "museum world." His early poems were "perfect stone statues."

In fact Merwin's relation to the modernist tradition is both conservative and innovative. Like any representative poet, in any era, he recognized that an individual idiom must be fashioned out of respect for past achievement. He also realized where the ossifications of tradition made improvisation necessary. In the late 1940's, in his formative years at Princeton University, Merwin absorbed the modernist aesthetic apparently through the agency of R. P. Blackmur, an eminent New Critic. But his desire to amalgamate the whole range of literary modernism led him outside its main current. He assimilated its peripheral voices, among them those of William Butler Yeats and Robert Graves. The early Merwin plumbed modernism's tributary streams; he explored their preoccupation with pagan mythology. Ultimately his work discloses that poetic attitude which distinguishes all major poets; that search for permanent value and poetic truth in a world that does not credit either. It is a work that appears stylistically diversified rather than intimidated by the strictures of any one current of tradition. As one critic discerningly noted, Merwin's uniqueness among contemporary poets consists of the fact that his work represents "a microcosm of the history of modern verse." (p. 167)

In his comments on near-contemporary British writers, Merwin demonstrates an awareness of the whole scope of modernism, including the source of its reaction to nineteenth-century verse and its developments in the 1930's and 1940's. He laments lingering Romantic tendencies toward "diffuseness" and emotional vagueness in the work of Kathleen Raine and Edwin Muir. . . . Merwin's notation of the "Cambridge group," which influenced Raine, and of the politically motivated "thirties poetry," from which the work of Louis MacNeice derived, indicated a keen appreciation of poetic developments subsequent to the modernist revolution. Having placed Muir within this "current of English poetry," as a practitioner who contributes little in the way of innovation, Merwin goes on to state this view of literary tradition:

> For a tradition proceeds, it would seem, both by the continuities and by the variations which it can contain alive; as long as it is alive itself it manages to make a continuum out of the necessary departures from itself. The work of the imagists, say, of Ezra Pound, of Mr. Eliot himself, enlivened the tradition by departing from it—it had to change in order to include them. . . .

This insight raises uninvestigated issues with respect to Merwin's early career. Exactly how should his own work be placed in this pattern of a tradition's "continuities" and "variations?" Here Merwin implies that Eliot's influence has been exerted. Yet the precise rôle that Eliot played in the formation of Merwin's poetic self-image has never been fully explicated. Especially in the permanent qualities of mind they shared, their relationship transcends that initial closeness indicated by Merwin's first published poem, **"On John Donne"** (1946). Donne, of course, was the Metaphysical poet championed by Eliot early in his own career. But the point is that the crucial directions Eliot indicated help to define the whole conservative tendency of Merwin's attitude toward tradition. Rather obviously, Merwin's statement about tradition echoes Eliot's seminal essay, "Tradition and the Individual Talent." Eliot defined tradition as a living organism whose life was altered by the birth of an authentic, individual work: "what happens when a new work of art is created is something that happens simultaneously to all the works of art which proceeded it." This process would occur by virtue of the artist's "historical sense," which Eliot maintained as "a perception, not only of the pastness of the past, but of its presence." The poet, Eliot noted, would be aware that he "must inevitably be judged by the standards of the past." In Merwin's poem, **"The Master,"** in ***Green with Beasts,*** this historical sense surfaces explicitly. The poet appears meditating the presence of a deceased literary figure, whose identity cannot be fully ascertained. There is a touch of irony in Merwin's portrait of this figure. . . . Yet in the poet's literary relationship with this mentor, there is a serious and vital respect. Unmistakably a consciousness of the presence of the past is heard. (p. 168)

For Merwin, as for Eliot, literary tradition would serve as creative restraint. It would provide not only a past standard of judgment, but also a hierarchy of aesthetic forms. Furthermore, tradition would comprise the means for transcending one's limitations of cultural perspective. Explicitly and implicitly, Merwin's first published essay, **"The Neo-Classic Drama"** (1949), embodies these views. In it he professes interest in a "live contemporary poetic drama," an interest born from "our responsibilities to the past." The same concern with drama and with dramatic modes preoccupied Eliot throughout his career. In the first decade of Merwin's career, through ***The Drunk in the Furnace,*** dramatic presentation is a dominant feature of the poetic idiom. In this essay, however, the exemplars on whom Merwin concentrates are the French neo-classicists, Corneille, Molière, and Racine. In that these figures are foreign or continental ones, the essay presages the fifteen volumes of translation that would accompany Merwin's own original work.

The whole storehouse of European literature would be the poet's home; for as Eliot claimed, a tradition would include all of European literataure from Homer to the present.

Merwin's early interest in the neo-classic period extended to its Spanish representative, Lope de Vega. As a translator, he apparently moved backward in time, through the minor traditions of Portuguese and Provencal poetry, and toward the Latinic source of the Romance languages. Although his ***Satires of Persius*** did not appear until 1961, Merwin must have been at work learning Latin at the time of ***Green with Beasts.*** It is in this volume that his poem, **"Learning a Dead Language,"** fully captures his view that even in its disused branches tradition serves the artist as a source for self-discipline. Of itself, for a poet, translation is an act of self-effacement. But in the subject of rendering a dead language, Merwin espouses a more general attitude toward learning: one dependent upon the human virtue of humility. . . . As Merwin develops the poem, it becomes apparent that the "Dead Language" represents not just Latin but the language of the past as a whole. The attitude of humility makes possible the discipline of memory. In this process, crucial to the preservation of culture, an individual attains full human stature. . . . From humility and the self-discipline that memory requires, an harmonious dialectic of past with living present occurs. The "dead" past comes alive as a vital and instructive force:

> What you remember saves you. To remember
> Is not to rehearse, but to hear what never
> Has fallen silent. So your learning is,
> From the dead, order, and what sense of yourself
> Is memorable, what passion may be heard
> When there is nothing for you to say. . . .

With its dichotomy between man's "order" and his "passion," this poem points to yet another quality of mind that Merwin and Eliot share. In **"The Neo-Classic Drama,"** Merwin used as an organizing principle T. E. Hulme's statement: "man is the chaos lightly organized, but liable to revert to chaos at any moment." It was Hulme who helped Eliot formulate his awareness of Original Sin; both stressed the centrality of human limitations in their view of man's social destiny. Their classical point-of-view—one resigned and without illusions—was to be set against the unfounded optimism of nineteenth-century liberal doctrine. A classical mind looks skeptically on liberal hopes for social progress and human perfection. In his essay Merwin demonstrates this realistic awareness, an unflinching attitude toward the moral paradoxes of human experience. In tragedy, he maintains, the crucial conflict is always based upon the struggle between society's laws and an individual's rights. In the dramas of Racine, a disintegration toward social chaos is likely to occur just when the social order is most nearly complete. It is in this sense that tragedy often reveals "evidence of human helplessness to control the human process." This qualified assessment of man's social possibilities is what leads Merwin to stress the need for order and self-discipline. False hopes and great expectations, an emphasis only on humanity's goodness, obscure an awareness of the reality of sin, cited by Eliot as the virtue of a mature artist. In ***A Mask for Janus.*** Merwin speaks out repeatedly against illusory hope. In the dramatic poem **"Rime of the Palmers,"** for instance, the palmers advise the narrator that hope is a sentiment which leads one on a false road. (pp. 169-70)

Merwin's classicist temperament indicates that another of his "continuities" with the modernist tradition is ideological. His early work continues that criticism of liberal social trends initiated by Eliot. Unlike Eliot, Merwin has never focused on the pitfalls of liberal doctrine *per se*. But in his socio-political comments, as in his poetry, Merwin opposes the same social maladies which Eliot associated more specifically with liberalism. For Eliot, liberal thought with its premise of cultural change led directly to the pagan or religiously neutral attitudes so apparent in modern societies. As it was promulgated in twentieth-century America by John Dewey, liberalism accepts "what is modern in human organization, in the 'law' of progress, in the planned human will." Because it is founded upon a scientific image of man, liberalism places all of its stock in the collective human intelligence to control and to shape human nature and destiny. In this sense liberalism is melioristic: It advances the belief that through the human agency the world will become increasingly better. Through the application of technology and the scientific method to nature and to the human social order, liberalism would fashion a world ordered solely by human consciousness. From these perspectives, humanistic and anthropocentric in essence, the world was created for man's disposal.

Merwin indicts this feature of the liberal ethos in a review-article of four books about man as a species. This essay, **"On the Bestial Floor,"** concerns man's relation to the environment and to his own self-image. Though written at mid-career, it sets forth directly those principles which are latent in Merwin's early work. Here Merwin castigates modern man for according to human intelligence "a spontaneous moral splendor." As a result of this tendency man has severed his connection not only with God, the author of creation in the "myth of genesis," but also with the earth he inhabits. Holding out "his intelligence . . . as the great exoneration," modern man has desacralized his world, assuming "superiority to the rest of creation" and the "right to hold over it the powers of life and death." According to Merwin, man has arrogated to himself the absolute rights and privileges of a creator in a world he did not create. Moreover, for Merwin, man's intelligence itself is suspect. Not only has man been irresponsible with regard to the rest of nature, but he is also far from the self-contained and autonomous status that he presumes for himself. The poet goes on to lament that

> . . . as man's power over other living things has become if not more perfect at least more persuasive, his dominion over himself, however conceived, seems here and there to be escaping him despite analyses and institutions . . . . . .

In its desacralizing and profane emphases, liberalism challenges Merwin's view of man. Liberalism, like all secular philosophies, refuses to account for the way that man exists on two levels of being. . . . For Merwin, as for Eliot, man possesses innately a transcendent awareness, an intuition of such "other-wordly" realities. For Eliot in fact it was just this religious awareness that liberalism ignored. By its affirmation of cultural change liberalism severed man from the historical past, in which spiritual authority ordered human societies. For Eliot this process left man alienated and uprooted. Merwin has never gone so far as Eliot; he has never declared that the collapse of Western cultural values is the result of Christianity's decline. Yet Merwin's opposition to the modern liberal ethos springs from the same type of religious sensibility. . . . In his poem **"Her Wisdom,"** in ***Green with Beasts,*** Merwin maintains that spiritual understanding—as both the source and the end of poetry—transcends the physical senses and so arrives at mystery. (pp. 170-71)

For Merwin this mystery also ascribes the limitations of man's intelligence. Human hopes for progress and for social perfection must always be referred to it. In his poem **"White Goat, White Ram."** also in ***Green with Beasts,*** Merwin subverts the "spontaneous moral splendor" of man's intelligence. Implicitly, this poem also questions the extent to which man may be innocent. In doing so, it debates the critical premise of liberal thought; for from the standpoint of liberal thought, man is innocent by nature. As the poet ruminates on the meaning of two goats that graze on a mountainous hillside, he makes successive discoveries about man's need for innocence—rather than his actual possession of it. . . .

Thus Merwin posits the limitation of all human purpose, since he has recognized the distortions of human need. Even in its symbolizing processes the human intellect will err.

> . . . For our uses
> Also are a dumbness, a mystery,
> Which like a habit stretches ahead of us
> And was here before us . . .

From the humility apparent in this statement, and from his awareness that man cannot ultimately penetrate the world's mystery, the poet comes to understand its true potentialities. (p. 171)

The focus on human limitation rather than on human capacities is constant in Merwin's early work. It is the surest index of his antipathy against liberal expectations for social progress. (pp. 171-72)

For Merwin man's incapacity is what most limits his historical future. In ***The Drunk in the Furnace,*** in revealingly lifelike and satiric portraits, the poet depicts humanity as recalcitrant to improvement or change. In **"Pool Room in the Lion's Club,"** for example, after his initial assertion—"I'm sure it must be still the same"—Merwin portrays from memory the characterless and indolent pool players. In them he captures that lack of moral fiber which Eliot foresaw as the outcome of liberal ideology. . . .

In liberal ideology the need for personal effort and internal restraint is removed. This occurs because the task of human discipline is placed on the collective social whole. All that is necessary to attain the full flower of man's natural goodness is the right arrangement of individual desires within the society at large. Hence liberalism nullifies the necessity for personal moral conflict; it neutralizes the individual's potential to realize moral values. What results is the blank and vacuous human condition that Merwin imagines in his poem **"No One."** In fact this poem can be read as an ironic address to liberal ideologues. For by abdicating the need for personal morality, and by gazing upon the future with optimism, liberals are bound to experience the betrayal that this poem registers. . . .

A Mask for Janus, Merwin's earliest work, initiates his commitment against two specific instances of the liberal ethos. His early indictment of liberalism is focused upon its egoism and its materialism. Liberals, of course, advocate materialism as the primary means to accomplish social perfection. But for Merwin, as for Eliot, no genuine social progress, no improvement of man's spiritual state, could result merely from the satisfaction of his physical needs. Much later in his career Merwin was to declare unequivocably: ". . . I put no faith in material utopias . . . they . . . seem to me to be projections of a poverty that is not in itself material." Behind his early poetry there lies a keen awareness that liberal designs for social progress have resulted in society's enslavement to materialism. This awareness is sounded in the two poems which begin ***A Mask for Janus,*** **"Anabasis I"** and **"Anabasis II."** Taken as one whole poem, Merwin's **"Anabasis"** again discloses his need to provide literary traditon with its vital "continuities." The original *Anabase* by the Greek poet, Xenophon, described the conquest and the foundation of cities in Asiatic territories of the Ancient East. This work was given a free translation by the French Nobel Prize winner, St.-John Perse; it was then brought to the attention of English readers by Eliot, who translated the French poet's version in 1938. . . . In Merwin's **"Anabasis,"** as in the French poet's, the speaker, or persona, is an explorer, a veteran of many voyages. In the images of the poem, in the persona's recollection of encounters in far-away countries, Merwin renders the threat posed by society to man's spiritual needs. The physical and the social landscapes are blended together to make one feel the dangers inherent in modern liberal civilization. In their sea journey, the explorers have passed

> Straits whose rocks lean to the sound,
> Monstrous, of their declivities,
> As lovers on their private ground
> See no distance, but face and face;
>
> We have passed in a warm light
> Islands whose charmed habitants
> Doze on the shores to dissipate
> The seasons of their indolence.

The twin threats of egoism and materialism are caught here in successive stanzas. The lovers "see no distance, but face and face"; in other words, because of their privacy of feeling and their self-absorption, they miss their connection to the whole human family. The islanders are simply "charmed" into sloth in an image suggestive of pure material surfeit. This social condition, soporific and static, is linked more clearly to liberal ideology in **"Anabasis II,"** in the speaker's claim

> . . . we suffered music that declares
> The monstrous fixities of innocence. . . .

These "fixities of innocence" necessitate the perpetual resistance, the cycle of voyage, encounter, and renewed setting forth, upon which the poem depends. And in the phrase itself, Merwin captures the characteristic indulgence and the dissipation of human potential that Eliot saw as the informing spirit of liberalism. There is no necessity for moral resistance in a society fixated on innocence. In such a society the individual's potential for creative achievement will be blunted or stultified. For this reason, as St.-John Perse maintained, the poet will understand that "Inertia is the only mortal danger." In **"Anabasis II"** Merwin communicates his own awareness of this threat. His speaker asserts that the "sick repose" of his "saeculum," or era, calls for continual exploration.. (pp. 172-73)

Mark Christhilf, "W. S. Merwin: The Poet as Creative Conservator," in Modern Age, *Vol. 23, No. 2, Spring, 1979, pp. 167-77.*

RAINER SCHULTE

Merwin stands in a long line of modern international poets. He belongs to a tradition that was started with the French poet Baudelaire over a hundred years ago. When Baudelaire wrote at the end of his long poem "The Voyage," "to plunge into the unknown to find something new," he is very close to Merwin's words "An hour comes / to close a door behind me /

the whole of night opens before me.'' It is not the obvious that Merwin searches for in his poetry, not the object that can be reproduced with a photographic camera lens, not the landscape that is fixed in time and space. His mind opens up at the moment between light and darkness beyond the realm of logical comprehensibility, to portray an inscape that lives on silence and paradox.

Merwin achieves Rilke's lucidity, Stevens' philosophical perspective and Paz' rhythmic and conceptual intensity. His poems begin on the page and end on the page without having a definite point of beginning or a definite point of arrival. He needs no punctuation in the flow of the mind that detects the life-generating power behind each object: the eternal paradox born in moments of silence.

Merwin does not want to punctuate his poems; even though he breaks words into lines and lines into poems on the page, each poem carries beyond itself into the next. . . . Merwin's poems never stop, they create energy for both the reader and the poet himself, an energy that finds release and form in the next poem. (pp. 12-13)

Fortunately, Merwin has been exposed not only to the American literary tradition, but to the contemporary international literary scene. He has translated a book of poems by the French poet Jean Follain, he has transposed poems by Pablo Neruda, Nicanor Parra, Guillaume Apollinaire, García Lorca, Gottfried Ben and others. That he translates is not amazing: many other poets have done translations. But it is revealing which poets he has chosen to translate. Almost all of them share with his own poetry a conceptual intensity that reaches far beyond the instability of poetic fashion and makes them, in the true sense of the word, international in scope and meaning.

There is a vast silence in Merwin's poetry, and words lie only on the topmost surface. Voices from below beckon their submergence and the poet's ear is bent toward these voices. Still, this silence cannot remain silent; it has to find expression and form through words and the new meaning they create in the unique juxtaposition the poet has invented for them. Each time the poet touches a word, he must rely not on its fixed meaning but on the threads of its magnetic field that make new meaning possible. It must be a language comfortable in the realm of paradox, removed from the restricting barriers of visual representation and reproduction. . . . And then there are those moments when he desperately and nervously pushes us deeper and deeper into the zone of silent intensity: ''dream after dream after dream walking away through it / Invisible invisible invisible.'' Like isolated notes, simple and insistent, the words fall on the reader's mind, force him into the rhythm of his inner landscape where his words create new colors on the horizon. Once the rhythmic ritual has happened, he must fill the distances of the mind both in time and space. Natural to his vision, time and space lose their linear existence and become multiple in their simultaneous existence. (p. 13)

His poetry represents the fierce attempt at recreating or perhaps even at inventing the moment in the present that makes us not aware of what was there before and what might come thereafter, but involves us in the life of the present. To populate the inner distance with the energy of life through the invention of words is the poet's commitment and goal. The distance never ceases to exist since it always goes beyond itself into some other distance. ''Beyond'' is the key word that embraces Merwin's poetic vision. The paradox of words carries us beyond the meaning of words, the paradox invents new meaning between the words, and it is this sense of the paradox put into a rhythm of words that always flows without punctuation from one poem to the next. The struggle and the illumination of the inner distance celebrated through the color of words generate Merwin's poetic energy and make his poems universal, not just as an American poet but as an international poet. (p. 14)

Rainer Schulte, ''W. S. Merwin: A Portrait, Introduction and Poems,'' in Mundus Artium, *Vols. XII-XIII, 1980 & 1981, pp. 12-14.*

JOYCE CAROL OATES

W. S. Merwin's third book of prose [***Unframed Originals: Recollections***] might have as its subtitle ''What to Make of a Diminished Thing,'' for this collection of six related essays on the poet's family refuses to present its modest subject in anything but understated and relentlessly un-self-conscious prose. Merwin, the author of nine books of poetry and 12 books of translation, creates by way of the uncompromising plainness of his language a haunting and frequently disturbing portrait of Americans who seem, in this convincing account at least, to have had no language—no interest in literature, very few books in their houses, a minimum even of curiosity about one another's sometimes tragic lives. . . .

In ***Unframed Originals*** the poet-narrator, sometimes called Billy, inhabits his childhood life as we have all inhabited ours—from the inside, invisibly, seeing and listening keenly but rarely experiencing himself. The son of a Presbyterian minister in Union City, N.J., the grandson and nephew of exceptionally dour and closemouthed Methodists who lived in small settlements along the Allegheny River in Pennsylvania, Merwin endured what seems to have been a particularly joyless—and remorselessly bookless—childhood. ''At home our lives were surrounded by injunctions. On visits there were more of them'': Hence the refrain *Don't touch* runs through the earliest recollections with a dull, comic insistence. Why is Mr. Merwin so ''harsh'' and ''peculiar'' in his behavior toward his son, people inquire, and the answer is typically ambiguous, the sort of thing one recalls as an adult with a stabbing sensation in the region of the heart: ''He always answered that he treated us, and me, that way, only because of love, and that he was afraid I might get hurt.'' Having been encouraged to believe himself superior by his own mother and confirmed in this ''superiority'' by the parishioners of his various churches, Merwin's father seems to have inhabited a private world so insular and so crudely in sympathy with others as to verge upon pathology. One of the memorable scenes in ***Unframed Originals*** is a comically despairing account of an attempt on Mr. Merwin's part to be more of a ''pal'' with his son. (pp. 7, 29)

The narrative strategy of ***Unframed Originals*** is one beloved of poets. Each essay is a brooding, speculative, interior piece arising from and circling about an image (a picket fence in Grandfather Merwin's tomato garden, for instance, the New York skyline as it was seen from Mr. Merwin's yellow-brick church in New Jersey). As a much honored man of letters, W. S. Merwin is cautious about presenting himself, even inadvertently, as ''superior'' to his subject, hence the monochromatic tone, the pages of straight family history—catalogues of names, dates, places, summary careers and fates. These ''originals'' are deliberately ''unframed'': Merwin's book is no autobiography along the lines of *The Education of Henry Adams* with its covert claim for singularity, nor is it a memoir in the service of an ongoing polemic, as in Lillian Hellman's autobiographical writing. Indeed, the manner is improvisational, the tone self-effacing. In a typical aside the author says of a long-dead relative: "I cannot be sure now how much of her I remember and how much I have dreamed."

Nevertheless, there are memorably eccentric characters here. Though rarely presented directly and allowed their own voices, certain of Merwin's relatives declare themselves as marvelously idiosyncratic. There is cousin Mary ("Some meaning of the word 'naphtha' was inexplicably hers, and echoed the smell of her damp apron that reached below her knees, and of the duster on her head, and of her hands, long shapeless and rough, running from gray to orange. . . . Whatever she touched was the wrong size"). . . . There is Mr. Merwin himself, who never spoke of his father (that is, Billy's grandfather) and allowed the grandson to meet him only once, on the day the old man was being committed to an institution for the elderly and infirm.

Only as the narrator matures and detaches himself from childhood scenes does the book lose its quirky, obsessive quality and become, by its end, a nostalgic reverie of a more conventional sort. But Merwin's prose is never less than graceful and his effort—to understand, to record, perhaps even to celebrate inarticulate lives—is ambitious and laudable. (p. 29)

Joyce Carol Oates, "Family Portrait," in New York Times Book Review, *August 1, 1982, pp. 7, 29.*

SANDRA PREWITT EDELMAN

I wish I could say that ***Unframed Originals*** is one of those evocative, lyrical, endlessly haunting autobiographical works to which we know we shall return again and again as the years pass. I wish I could say with Pascal, "We are delighted and astonished; for we expected to see an author, and we find a man." I cannot. Here we expected to see a man and, regretfully, find only an author—an author, granted, of sometime brilliance, but who seems to have pushed his language facility beyond poetry into a new technology of the spirit.

We have, I think properly so, certain expectations when a poet of Merwin's stature chooses to publish recollections of his early life: if not wisdom, at least a special vision; if not revelation, insight; if not evocation, at least access to how the man feels about things and people and experiences. And above all, we expect to share something of a unique and irreproducible self. Poets, after all, are the great mentors of the soul. None of these qualities—whether through the conscious choice or the unconscious defensiveness of the poet who has been hailed as a prophet of solitude—inform this rather peculiar collection.

In another genre, the failure (or withholding) of the Eros function—the capacity for relatedness—might not be at issue. In autobiography, Eros should pulsate at the core; when it does not, the reader has been cheated, perhaps even betrayed. Some unnamed person at the *Kirkus Review* commented, according to the dust jacket promo, that in Merwin's "best poetry—but especially in his prose pieces . . . there is often a patch of vacancy, a whitened space or interval that seems to core mysteriously with a suggestion of odd, undefined depths." Here the patch of vacancy is the very space that ought to be occupied by Merwin the man, and the mystery lies in how and why he can at once write so meticulously of his background and remain essentially disengaged from it. If these essays are photographs, they are both unframed and underdeveloped, left vague, rather colorless, ghostly. (Merwin's father, for example, occupies a prominent place in the collection, but he is spoken of as though he were an activity instead of a person, a verb instead of a noun; he leaves scarcely a footprint.) If this is life, it's life in a hospital ward: there's activity, movement, population, but the colors are muted, the palpability obscured, scrimmed over by the nictitating membrane of defensive retention. It's as though nostalgia had been programmed by a computer. (p. 92)

Sandra Prewitt Edelman, "A Patch of Vacancy," in Southwest Review, *Vol. 68, No. 1, Winter, 1983, pp. 92-3.*

EDMUND FULLER

W. S. Merwin, acknowledged as one of this country's most gifted and prolific poets, also is an accomplished writer of prose, seen again in the "Recollections" he captures in a splendid book, ***Unframed Originals*** . . . Though it is a mesh of memories, it is not a straight autobiographical chronicle. It is impressionistic, a collage of portraits intricately overlapped, giving rise to remembrances and reflections, many poignant.

They are of his family, both immediate and ramified, ranging in scene from Union City, New Jersey, where he grew up, son of the pastor of the First Presbyterian Church, in a manse with a view of the skyline of New York. Other locales are various cities and towns of central and western Pennsylvania, between Scranton and Pittsburgh, mining and industrial regions. Rivers and railroad tracks figure largely. Though that is the geography of the principal scenes, the assimilation of these recollections into his adult perceptions takes us also to the French provinces and to Greece.

Even as seen through the eyes of a young child, this seems a family of more than usual eccentricity. All childhood is full of mystery and puzzles, but among some of these Merwin and Jaynes (the mother's side) connections the perplexities were exceptional. There are eight chapters, written over a considerable span of time. "The one memory in which all those lives still appear is what now unites them."

In **"Tomatoes,"** 9-year-old Billy gets his one fleeting glimpse of an 81-year-old paternal grandfather, by which we were led into intricate family webs, approached in other pieces from different angles. **"Laurie,"** the most bizarre, traces almost frighteningly the long decline of two of his father's sisters, Alma and Edna, into a subdued, contained, accepted but outright insanity, side by side.

The chapters gather emotional force, culminating in the two last, most brilliantly woven, **"Hotel"** and **"La Pia."** In the former, he traces the unlikely ways by which his mother's older first cousin, Margie Cubbage, whom he knew only at second hand, came to leave all her sparse worldly effects "unto my cousin, Billy S. Merwin." In lovely linkages we see how that small sum later acquired for him an old, dilapidated, small farmhouse in the Dordogne region of France—an acquisition not without ambivalence.

Both this chapter and **"La Pia,"** the latter especially, deal with the deaths of his father, and then his mother. His last times with her are poignantly portrayed. Her death occurred while he was on Mount Athos, in Greece, visiting the monasteries. The image of **"La Pia"** is from Dante's "Purgatorio." In the short span between his father's death and his mother's he learned more about her than he had ever known. ". . . I am gradually fitting the new glimpses into what I remember . . . during my childhood and later."

The book is superbly written, offering deep glimpses into the complexities and mysteries of family bonds, with just that distancing from people and events necessary for artistic control.

Edmund Fuller, "Autobiographies of a Satirist in Line and a Gifted Poet," in The Wall Street Journal, *January 3, 1983, p. 22.*

KENNETH FUNSTEN

W. S. Merwin's ***Finding the Islands*** . . . is a radical departure from what might have been expected of him.

The entire book is composed of haikulike triplets. The familiar Merwinesque figure of poet as grail-questing, cave-dwelling *vates* has been de-glamorized. By the book's second section, Merwin—his head through the clouds—is no longer dark, alone or even obscure. He has climbed his mountain, he announces, and now worships the muse he found there, his companion, Dana. But Merwin's style remains skillful with beautifully pure diction. Merwinesque, all fit for your grandmother, except perhaps some later pieces with their vague eroticism. . . .

Kenneth Funsten, in a review of "Finding the Islands," in Los Angeles Times Book Review, *January 23, 1983, p. 3.*

JAMES FINN COTTER

With stunning sense for detail, setting, character and situation, Merwin employs flashback and story-within-story [in ***Unframed Originals: Recollections***] to recreate his parents, aunts, uncles and cousins in rural Pennsylvania. His father was a Presbyterian minister in Union City and in Scranton, a loving extrovert with everyone but his only son. Withholding love in order not to spoil the boy, he surrounded him with a myriad of don'ts so that one marvels how little Billy did not break into smithereens. He looks back without anger at this man on the go, so typically American and yet so strangely alone.

Merwin's mother emerges in the last of the six family studies as a woman prepared to die with the developed concentration with which she lived. She is a warm, unselfish person who also finds it difficult to express her love. The poet is walking to Athos, in the midst of the monks' praise of the Virgin Mary, unaware that his mother is about to die far away. He prays for her, remembers lines from Dante's *Purgatorio,* and brings his book to a peaceful closing, reconciled to his own limitations and to the unfulfilled lives from which he has come.

Merwin is a staring eye that misses no gesture or sign; each word and motion points to the whole. What appears on the surface to be a list of trivial observations or a mere digression, helps illuminate the final portrait with a Flemish painter's light. He is master of color and line, and ***Unframed Originals*** belongs in the gallery of great word-portraits. (p. 76)

James Finn Cotter, "Poets Then and Now," in America, *Vol. 148, No. 4, January 29, 1983, pp. 75-6.*

THE VIRGINIA QUARTERLY REVIEW

In [***Finding the Islands***], Merwin pares down his style into bare, unpunctuated, three-line stanzas. Part 1, **"Feathers from the Hill,"** presents a series of highly impressionistic landscape poems, held together by an interplay of alliteration and off-rhyme. Part 2, **"Turning to You,"** transforms landscape into idyll in a sequence of more discursive and personal love poems, evoking a land where "The fish swim by our feet / as we eat from the same hand / and drink from the same mouth." The poet's mastery of a new form produces poems alive with conviction and, perhaps more importantly, word music; indeed, Merwin's ear seems almost infallible in this collection of delicate and graceful lyrics.

A review of "Finding the Islands," in The Virginia Quarterly Review, *Vol. 59, No. 2, Spring, 1983, p. 62.*

JOHN MARTONE

[***Finding the Islands***] is as startling and sustained a celebration of loved life as his earlier volumes were cries of anguish. It gives us a new poet. This isn't to say, of course, that ***Finding the Islands*** doesn't look back to and build upon Merwin's earlier work. Made up of unpunctuated haiku-like moments (I think Merwin is pretty clearly using Japanese linked verse as a model), his twenty-three new poems look back formally to his sequences of ***Asian Figures*** and to **"Signs"** from ***The Carrier of Ladders.*** The poems are constellations (archipelagos?) of insight; they invite us to participate in the perceptual process.

The collection's two parts (**"Feathers from the Hill"** and **"Turning to You"**) take the world and the lover, respectively, as their subjects, and they complement each other with a wonderful simplicity. In the poems of the first part, the speaker loses himself in natural phenomena, as in this moment from **"Summer Canyon":** "Sunlight after rain / reflections of ruffled water / cross the ceiling." And in the poems of the second part, an equally simple and compelling erotic vision predominates: "I hold your toes and ankles / kiss the backs of your knees / draw them apart."

Merwin—whose vision in earlier books has rightly been called "postapocalyptic"—has come full circle. We stand with him now at the *beginning* of a world. There's an almost vulnerable simplicity about this collection, and in these terms it is a daring book. Having taught us about the last light, Merwin has moved on to teach us about the first.

John Martone, in a review of "Finding the Islands," in World Literature Today, *Vol. 58, No. 1, Winter, 1984, p. 105.*

HOWARD McCORD

[***Opening the Hand***] is divided into three parts. Eight of the poems in the first part are constructed with a medial caesura indicated by a quarter-inch gap in each line. This serves no discernible purpose except to irritate me. It is a visual affectation, probably arrived at in idleness and boredom. The lines are not alexandrines (most are closer to rude fourteeners) and need no such signature; and though on occasion the hemistiches reflect the pattern of Old English alliteration and draw attention to it in such lines as

they that were shaken at the sink   and stripped of water

I still cannot see the usefulness of the gap.

Beyond typography, the poems are the shaped memories of a father, a family, of a time past but still treasured. We all have such memories, even the whey-faced adolescents who swagger like Rimbaud. I am not averse to sharing such memories offered by a fine poet, and I anticipate an intimacy, the warmth of being called to a neighboring family's gathering with acceptance and friendship. But what I find in these poems is just the semblance of that intimacy. There is flatness and distance where there should be heightened awareness. I think there are times where Merwin feels that too, as though the passion he hoped and intended the memory to release has been blunted and dulled; that perhaps the very reality it supposedly revealed was itself only partially formed, and the life remembered with such forcefulness had been no more than a series of hesitations. Now to communicate that subtlety may be worth a poet's time, but not in such rough-carpentered lines as

> Now it happens in these years at unguarded intervals
> with a frequency never to be numbered
> a motif surfacing in some scarcely known music of
> my own
> each time the beginning and then broken off. . . .

Section Two continues the hemistichery, and the poems bring the reader in contact with the poet's more recent past, especially his sojourn in Hawaii. But the vision is not much more than a tourist's. We see children swimming in the lagoon, natives, hippie farmers klutzing through life, and some sharp and totally conventional contrasts with the rat race back on the Mainland. In a respite from this banality comes a wonderfully exuberant **"Questions to Tourists Stopped by a Pineapple Field"** which would have made Gertrude Stein laugh with delicious laughter until her fat belly shook and Alice had to pour her a brandy. Unfortunately, more representative is the metaphysical oatmeal of this meditation on roaches which notes

> it is true that they do not know any thing about me
> nor where we are from we can have
> little knowledge—we look at each other and wait
> whatever we may do afterwards.

The third section contains a story about Berryman good enough to repeat at a party, and a few sweet quiet lyrics not as marred by the numb and stodgy language which clogs the first two sections. A poem such as **"Hearing"** has something of the sonority, rich imagery, and magic that I remember from Merwin's earlier books, as does the haunting narrative, **"The House,"** in the first section. But what are we to do with the bathetic **"Ali"**? Here is a poem about the attempted rescue of a sick, starving pup. When the pup dies, it is *Bambi, Beautiful Joe, Black Beauty,* and *Old Yeller* ascending on high like a squadron of silk handkerchiefs. . . .

I was disappointed by the book, for I had hopes of memorable poems. Merwin has written such in the past, and, given the abysmal state of our literature, has a moral and social obligation to do so again. His best work coincided with his many volumes of translations, and it is possible that he needs the influence of that necessarily disciplined work to keep his own poems from floating away.

Howard McCord, "Bill, Get Back to Work!" in Exquisite Corpse, *Vol. 2, Nos. 5-7, May-July, 1984, p. 16.*

DAVID ST. JOHN

What a pleasure it is to read W. S. Merwin's new collection, ***Opening the Hand***. . . . It is perhaps his strongest collection since ***The Carrier of Ladders,*** and the supple, muscular lines of these new poems exhibit the quiet authority we've come to associate with Merwin's finest work. The first section of ***Opening the Hand*** is concerned with family portraits, most specifically of the poet's father. This section is in some ways a poetic correlative to Merwin's superb prose recollections of his family, ***Unframed Originals,*** and it is equally powerful. One of Merwin's finest poems *ever,* **"Apparitions,"** seems to me to be the gravitational center of his poems of the family. A dazzling meditation upon his parents' hands, **"Apparitions"** is as fine an interweaving of mystery, personal myth, and family intimacy as appears anywhere in Merwin's work.

In the book's other two sections, Merwin writes often of his two homes—Hawaii and New York City. The poems of Hawaii are delicate and lovely, full of Merwin's great sympathy for the natural world. But it is his new poems about New York City—**"Coming Back in Spring," "Sheridan,"** and **"The Fields"**—that show that Merwin is also one of our most powerful poets of urban experience (as earlier witnessed by his poems **"St. Vincent's"** and **"Numbered Apartment"** from ***The Compass Flower***). (pp. 364-65)

David St. John, "Raised Voices in the Choir: A Review of 1983 Poetry Selections," in The Antioch Review, *Vol. 42, No. 3, Summer, 1984, pp. 363-74.*

PAUL BRESLIN

Of the many poets who turned inward early in the 1960s, W. S. Merwin developed the most purely oneiric style; his unpunctuated, vatically declarative lines called up images—of hands, boats, water, stone—floating in a psychological space wherein could be found no other people, no places, no memory of any event. But beginning with some of the poems in ***The Compass Flower*** (1977), Merwin has been turning outward once more, situating his poems in recognizable contexts, "opening the hand" of his hermetically closed style. . . . [***Opening the Hand*** begins] with a series of poems about the death of the poet's father; it includes landscapes recognizably belonging to New York, Hawaii, Los Angeles, and elsewhere.

Merwin is still recognizably Merwin, of course. His autobiographical poems are in large part visionary: they describe the son's ominous dreams at the time of the father's death, or the recurring apparition, afterwards, of the father's hands. In **"The House,"** the son, out camping with his father, believes he sees a house (described in considerable detail) near the campsite; the father says that there is no house. There is a similar incident a few years later, after which "the boy stops telling what he has seen."

So even the literal is visionary; nonetheless, the Merwin of ***The Lice*** or ***The Carrier of Ladders*** would not have bothered to describe his father crumpling "newspaper from the luggage compartment / of the polished black Plymouth parked under the young leaves / a few feet away in the overgrown wagon track." There has been a significant change, and Merwin's style has not entirely adapted to the new intentions. The flat, declarative syntax and lack of punctuation that were appropriate for the trance-like poems of fifteen years ago become tiresome in narrative. Sometimes the lack of punctuation creates pointless ambiguity, as in **"Yesterday":**

> My friend says I was not a good son
> you understand
> I say yes I understand

It takes a while for the reader to determine that the friend is talking about himself, not about the speaker. Although the speaker implicitly makes the same judgment on himself, confusion at the literal level coarsens the irony rather than enhances it. Nonetheless, there are some attractive poems here, and two exceptional ones. **"The Black Jewel"** is a meditation close to the older Merwinian style, in which the cricket becomes a talisman of mystery:

> the cricket never sleeps
> the whole cricket is the pupil of one eye
> it can run it can leap it can fly
> in its back the moon
> crosses the night

The grounding of the mysterious in the natural (the observation that the cricket's shiny back is like a convex mirror or an eyeball) gives the poem a sharpness often lacking in the earlier poems it otherwise resembles. And in **"Sheridan,"** Merwin's style does adapt to the new demands placed on it; the poem recounts the Civil War cavalry commander's ride into battle at Cedar Creek, but also attempts to reconstruct Sheridan's consciousness at that moment. . . . Here, Merwin evokes both the turbulence of the battle and the turbulence within Sheridan. This is, I think, the best poem in the book, certainly the most surprising. (pp. 167-69)

Paul Breslin, in a review of "Opening the Hand," in Poetry, *Vol. CXLV, No. 3, December, 1984, pp. 167-69.*

STEVEN GOULD AXELROD

The first section of W. S. Merwin's new book of poetry, ***Opening the Hand,*** contains numerous poems in which a son remembers his dead father with mingled feelings of bitterness and regret. Poems concerning the tension between a father and his child have, of course, been a staple of the American poetic tradition. . . . The central figure in this tradition, surely, is Robert Lowell, who made the terrain his own in such poems as "Commander Lowell," "Terminal Days at Beverly Farms," "Middle Age," "Mother and Father" (1 and 2), "Father in a Dream," and "Robert T. S. Lowell." Plath and Bidart, both students of Lowell, escaped his shadow by strongly revising his texts. Merwin, half a generation younger than Lowell and never his student, does not escape.

Merwin's poems are meditative and somber where Lowell's are satiric or impassioned, but they echo Lowell's at every turn in their stance, phrasing, and tropes. Merwin's **"Apparitions,"** for example, considers the relationship between the speaker's hands and his father's, finding that what first seemed differences were actually similarities. The father's hands

> evoked no music ever   had no comeliness
> that I could recognize   when I yet supposed
> that they were his alone   and were whole
> what time they were younger   than mine are

This poem, effective and affecting as it is, almost inevitably evokes Lowell's "Middle Age," in which the speaker similarly finds that "At every corner / I meet my Father, / my age, still alive." In the work of both poets, the dead father haunts the son as if he were still living, or as if the son had become, most unwillingly, the father's double, as if the father, estranged and disliked in life, had somehow absorbed the son's identity and even body in death. . . .

Merwin's poems are poignant and moving, but we may feel that we have been here before, and the visit was more vivid, more elaborated the previous time. Merwin holds back something in these poems, as he seems to throughout ***Opening the Hand.*** The poems contain innuendos where we want the richness of a Russian novel. Much is held in reserve—narrative, detail, feeling. Merwin attempts to escape the shadow by giving less, by reducing the arc to an essential point, as if all the truth of the poem could be implied by a few words and a grand silence. Still, what Merwin says is often too attenuated and self-humbled to evoke a sufficiently powerful silence. It is as though the poems shrivel in the presence—in the memory—of an anxiety-provoking rival.

Merwin is generally most compelling when he defeats Lowell's influence and overcomes his own emotional and esthetic reticence. At their worst, Merwin's poems exhibit some of the same traits they impute to the father: remoteness, an introspection that verges on hostility, a refusal to show oneself or be known. They are like tips of an iceberg—visible tokens of all that is submerged. At their best, conversely, they take the risk of revealing themselves more fully. The strongest selections include **"Two Houses," "Ali"** (on what must seem the most umpromising of topics, the death of a pet dog), and **"The Black Jewel,"** which ends the volume strongly. Although the poem may make us think momentarily of Dickinson or Eliot or Ted Hughes, we essentially hear Merwin's own sweet, grave voice emerging self-confidently here. In its mixture of sadness and mystical acceptance, and in its sense of connection, we hear nothing at all of Lowell. The "sound of the cricket" at night swerves to become the pulse of that which transcends life and death: "the death of the cricket / is still the cricket / in the bare room the luck of the cricket / echoes."

Steven Gould Axelrod, in a review of "Opening the Hand," in World Literature Today, *Vol. 59, No. 1, Winter, 1985, p. 94.*

FREDERICK GARBER

Opening the Hand moves immediately into a series of poems on family. It closes with a series on changing seasons, others on his departure and exile and finally a few on specifics of nature, that last group lovingly Wordsworthian in their texture and sensibility. Yet these last belie the changes; or rather, place them in careful perspective. The final poem, **"The Black Jewel,"** explores the sound of the cricket, of whom there is only one, which is there when mice and lightning are born blind and die; the cricket which is "neither alive nor dead" but beyond time, just as nature is. Still, this putting of change into perspective had actually been with the book from the beginning, the ending therefore not a surprise. The unchanging is found in certain events we perform as well as the places where we perform them. Merwin eases the book in cannily with **"The Waters,"** a rich and distant vision as though seen through layers of gauze, then moves in the following poems into further and further specifics with three more on the sea. As they move they tie that grand and general sea more closely to our lives, his father's life and his own, especially the father's death. The speaker boats to the shore and goes inland or, alternately, comes down from a mountain toward the sea. We enter the book at the archetypal and, wherever else it takes us on the surfaces of things, it never loses touch with the level at which it begins. The speaker walks on mountains, stares at them while shaving, knows how they bulk on permanent horizons. The cricket holds no surprises because we have been with the eternal all along, through all the changes. Image and theme are different ways of making the same statement.

What Merwin does with that archetypal grounding reaches deep into the way he wants his poems to work. They often end with whispers or simple statements, gestures so unassertive that they cannot, as they are, be taken as conclusions. **"The New Season"** takes him out in an autumn night with his dog to scare off rats. He hears black blossoms falling and knows that bees are not there but that worms and beetles and leaves are awake. At the end: "I stand with a flashlight / in a smell of fruit / and we wait." Events so simply put do not, at their best, stay put but continue with the resonance on which Merwin depends for the poems' fullest working. . . . [The] archetypal gestures on which this book is built open out other dimensions of meaning, spaces within which resonance can sound and continue, even when the events are simple, perhaps most when they are so. Merwin cherishes the enigmatic, the mysterious and unexplained. He can do so because what happens in these poems finally resounds in the largest, deepest caves of our experience, at levels beyond enigma. When this works, as it usually does, detail, feeling and import go wonderfully together, calling to each other in full and mutual support. It works in **"The New Season"** and the quite different **"Green Water Tower."** When the latter ends ("white sun emerges / the green tower swells in rings of shadow / day comes we drink and stand listening") we continue to listen to all that the tower has come to mean, the context of these waters. When it fails, as it does in **"The Sea Cliffs at Kailua in December,"** the ending is merely portentous, touching on affectation, the resonance dead in the water. Though that happens very rarely it happens often enough to keep the reader uneasy, alert to the possibility.

Merwin seems always to have been attuned to the intricate intertwining of the immediate and the elemental—even in **"Leviathan,"** even in **"The Drunk in the Furnace,"** even in the series of city poems in ***Opening the Hand.*** See, in that series, **"Sheridan,"** a tour-de-force of movement and texture, and also **"The Fields,"** showing as many others do what he can do with the facts of a scene. The voice in this book is always intense but never raised, its modulations subtle, its words middle-level, its dignity compromised only in moments of affectation. If not always of its own best quality . . . , ***Opening the Hand*** adds generously to a significant body of work. (pp. 20-1)

Frederick Garber, "Frederick Garber: Geographies and Languages and Selves and What They Do," in The American Poetry Review, *Vol. 14, No. 5, September-October, 1985, pp. 14-21.*

MARK CHRISTHILF

An interest in painting informs the career of the American poet, W. S. Merwin. In a poem in ***Green with Beasts*** (1956) Merwin takes inspiration from two seascapes by the English artist, Alfred Wallis; more recently he indicates knowledge of the French postimpressionist, Paul Cézanne [***Selected Translations, 1968-1978*** . . .], and the Austrian expressionist, Oskar Kokoschka [***Unframed Originals: Recollections***]. Like William Carlos Williams, who studied Cézanne and wrote poems based on Breughel's paintings, Merwin explores potential relationships between an art made of language and one in which experience is actually visual. This interest surfaces in his poetry as a facility with imagery—with that aspect of composition in which poetry and painting are related. (p. 277)

In poems of ***Green with Beasts*** and ***The Drunk in the Furnace*** (1960), Merwin's imagery is relatively representational. Influenced early by such writers as Eliot, Joyce, and Auden, he writes in a dramatic mode, and from an aesthetic distance seeks to endue with vivacity human character and natural forms. Compiling the details of scene and background, he creates the illusion of life through which the reader participates, so that early poems have a quality decidedly picturesque. Around 1960 Merwin concludes that such art is too abstract: it is merely a copy instigating a secondary order of experience. Merwin begins to write a poetry that dramatizes the way in which knowledge of the world occurs, a poetry based upon preconscious apprehension of natural forms and creatures. In this later intuitive mode, this imagery reveals the fusion of the poet with the world. Poetic imagination grasps the inward essence of forms, purifies them of associations, and strips them of variety of detail.

In painting these are the creative techniques of a tradition of continental expressionism, of which one line is represented by the French painters, Paul Gauguin and Henri Matisse. Unlike the Cubists who analyzed forms intellectually, these artists simplified them on the basis of an emotive identification which penetrated appearances and grasped an essential aspect. It was Matisse especially who realized the expressionist aesthetic, and it is to his work that Merwin's has been briefly compared. Reviewing Merwin's ***Writings to an Unfinished Accompaniment*** (1973), Laurence Lieberman notices that his style resembles "a Matisse-like notation" in which objects are represented with a "few irreducible lines and images". . . . Another reason for approaching Merwin through the example of Matisse is that, painting until the 1950s, Matisse resisted the trend toward non-objective or purely abstract art. Between pure abstraction which is "all-too-human" and realism which is not human enough, his art adheres to the reality of the world-image even as it projects human vision. Similarly, Merwin opposes pure abstraction, remaining committed to the world. In his avoidance of an ego-centered art, he would agree with the dictum of fellow-poet, Wendell Berry, who declares that for the poet the poem should be "a point of clarification or connection between himself and the world on the one hand and between himself and the reader on the other . . .". . . .

Comparison of early and of later poems reveals Merwin's development of an expressionist imagery. **"Two Horses,"** in ***Green with Beasts,*** and **"In the Time of the Blossoms,"** in ***The Carrier of Ladders*** (1970), are interesting examples because both are centered exclusively upon natural forms. In the early poem Merwin would create a sense of awe at the strength and vitality of the horses, for they unconsciously endure impervious to human conflicts—and to human history. Thematically similar to Edwin Muir's poem "The Horses," Merwin's is more evidently focused upon actual creatures: as it begins they graze before an objective observer who communicates what he sees to the reader. . . . Comprised of the details of scene and circumstance, this imagery is designed to suggest that the horses are particular creatures—existing in an actual place. They are "tethered improbably," for instance, with "neither saddle nor bridle," and Merwin sharpens their image visually by employing a highly specific diction. Nouns name actual parts of the horses' bodies; adjectives describe these; and verbs vivify, so that the horses will appear on the eye of one's imagination.

As Merwin develops **"Two Horses"** to nearly fifty lines, the . . . [immediate scene] becomes the foreground of a more inclusive setting. Adding image after image, and placing each with exact spatial reference to the next, he creates the sense of an actual background unfolding behind the forms. As the speaker looks at the horses, he observes that it is morning: that beyond them to the east the sun is rising; and that to the west the sky is dark. With the poem's final image he suggests further depth, noticing that behind the horses the land drops away toward the sea—"and northward / Beyond the terraces the misted sea / Swirls endless." As though painting a horizon in an actual picture, Merwin precisely reduplicates the action of organized vision perceiving a scene's dimension of depth.

"In the Time of the Blossoms," centered upon an ash tree in early spring, illustrates Merwin's simplification of forms. Like **"Two Horses"** the poem would create a sense of the world's existence, yet it has only ten lines and almost no detail. No longer preoccupied with a descriptive imagery, Merwin disregards the ash tree's height and width, trunk and branches, and actual background. . . . [The] tree is sketched briefly "on white heaven" in an image that may refer to a colorless sky. Yet it also suggests a blank space, perhaps a white piece of paper or a neutrally colored canvas, against which the form of the tree is flattened. In his later work Matisse rendered a number of such trees, presenting them as line drawings—outlined forms without color, detail, or volume. (pp. 277-81)

For the expressionist artist the appearance of forms is primarily a point of departure. In Matisse's words the creative challenge is to penetrate surface appearances: "Underlying this succession of moments which constitute the superficial existence of beings and things . . . one can search for a truer, more essential character, which the artist will seize so that he may give to reality a more lasting interpretation." . . . These words reveal that creative activity is apprehension through intuition: the artist "seizes" the subject in an act of spontaneous insight in which both are caught up together. In doing so he or she projects into the work the emotions elicited by the form, thereby giving to it a human "interpretation." Merwin's **"In the Time of the Blossoms"** indicates this penetration of appearances, for the speaker identifies with the blossoming ash tree, that is, with its essential character of reaching out—of aspiring. This identification inheres in the form of the poem which, as direct address, signifies communication. It also inheres in the final image in which the speaker aspires to be renewed like the tree, to be part of the world's rhythmic life unfolding within it. Begging to hear the music that will play in its branches, he utters, "Sing to me."

Merwin's penetration of appearances is evident in **"The Plumbing,"** a poem published with **"In the Time of the Blossoms"** in ***The Carrier of Ladders.*** Here he imagines a visible scene dissolving until only its essential lines appear. In fact, **"The Plumbing"** dramatizes the way in which creative vision occurs. As the poet walks out late at night in the city, he begins to intuit its essential character. In the stillness and the darkness he recognizes that millions of people crowd into the city in the hope of material success, and he understands that its vertical organization into high-rise buildings expresses their desire to climb above one another. In this overcrowded place he feels the lack of air and water—of the life-supporting elements. Grasping the city's essence as its sterility—as its absence of vitality—he describes its visible presence as it fades before him. He characterizes the city with "the buildings vanished," with "the windows extinct," and with "the names wiped away." Finally, the only things appearing are the pipes of the plumbing: only "the plumbing / that is all that is left / of the great city." (pp. 281-82)

The pipes of the plumbing typify the expressive image, for they are not unrelated to the city's appearance. In fact hundreds of pipes do rise into the sky to support the city's life-style in which millions live in high-rise apartment buildings. These pipes are not visible, but are present within the buildings; and they conform to the city's predominantly vertical structure. Although Merwin's image of the pipes distorts the city's visual character, the appearances are not avoided as they would be in abstract art. Further, the image allows Merwin to express his values—to incorporate his conviction that the city is barren. In his art expressionist images have two reference points: the natural form or scene and the artist's reaction to it.

Merwin's realization of an expressionist imagery is also evident in poems focused upon human forms. In early poems Merwin portrays human personalities who are complex characters with variety of traits. In fact, the emphasis in poems of ***The Drunk in the Furnace*** is nearly novelistic: characters are described in social contexts seeming actual and vivid. In later poems human characters are anonymous—sketched according to one general feature, as Merwin eliminates all social background and reference for their identity. He expresses in later human figures a universal posture, for he would communicate a need or experience common to humanity. Two poems illustrating these differences are **"Grandmother Dying,"** from ***The Drunk in the Furnace,*** and **"The Helmsmen,"** from ***The Compass Flower*** (1977).

In **"Grandmother Dying"** the human form is Merwin's own grandmother, Arvilla Denton, and his ultimate purpose is to expose the Puritanism the old woman represented. Yet his aproach is through a concrete and immediate portrait, and therefore the poem's imagery is specific. To make the old woman seem lifelike, Merwin compiles images in the sixty-eight lines of the poem, relating the details of her existence: ninety-five years old, she has several daughters; a devout Christian, she lives in a house, "smelling of coal-gas and petunias." As the poem begins Merwin pictures the old woman in the final days of her life, after a fall that has crippled her by breaking her back so that she must be tied down in her rocking chair. He enhances this effect of the old woman's particular condition by creating a social background in which others speak about her and in which the old woman herself speaks. After her fall she endures for eighteen months with surprising strength, and pesters her daughters as though she were much younger. That her mind is alert is revealed in Merwin's image of her suspicion of her daughters for helping themselves to her candy. (pp. 283-84)

As the poem develops, the depth of the old woman's personality emerges, for Merwin captures human complexity by adding imagery. . . . In a final extended image near the conclusion of **"Grandmother Dying,"** Merwin embodies the old woman's defining character trait—her strength of hatred for those aspects of life which are vital and natural. This part of life is represented by the image of a "crooked river" that "flowed easy" just beyond the old woman's house. As Merwin intimates in the autobiographical prose of ***Unframed Originals,*** the old woman hated the river because her husband, a riverboat pilot, escaped upon it leaving her to raise their children. . . . In the poem, as she dies, she shakes her fist at the river, expressing Puritanical resentment for its easeful flow. . . . (p. 285)

Like **"Grandmother Dying,"** Merwin's **"The Helmsmen"** has satiric intent, but he depicts two anonymous characters. Concerned with a general conception of human life, he presents life as a voyage: it is a journey on which events require negotiation—or navigation. This metaphor controls the poems's imagery, as Merwin uses it to simplify the human forms. (pp. 285-86)

As the poem unfolds Merwin's full meaning emerges. Each helmsman is looking for the other, believing that the significance of life inheres in the other. In the poem both leave messages for the other concerning their voyage through life, and "year after year they / try to meet." Yet Merwin reveals that neither helmsman will ever meet the other and that both are doomed to a life of yearning and frustration. Describing the manner of their calculation, he indicates that both are too single-minded: both operate on only one level of reality. The first helmsman plots his way by the stars but never sees them except as calculations "on white paper." Through such an image Merwin suggests a dedicated realist—perhaps the modern statistician who can account only for facts and figures. The second helmsman is less clearly errant, but like the first, appears to be limited by a single-minded approach. Perhaps an idealist, he names for "the visions of day," yet Merwin denigrates his procedure by depicting him as a headstrong dreamer who also names for "what he will never see / and he never sees / the other." The principles of both helmsmen are obviously in inverse relationship: one moves by day; the other, by night. Blind to conditions under which the other lives, both helmsmen seem to lack imaginative sympathy—the faculty most necessary for social relationships.

The effect of the generalized imagery in Merwin's **"The Helmsmen"** is two flattened human forms. In the image that the poem as a whole makes, the helmsmen might appear as silhouettes against a background of space and stars. Their postures would be identical, as both are engaged in a search, yet they would be in some reciprocal relationship to one another, perhaps facing one another across an unbridgable gulf. Finally, the Helmsmen are two images of the same person—like a picture and its negative. In the poem's concluding lines they appear bewildered: beset by "rumors of resemblances between them," and "thinking of each other constantly." (pp. 286-87)

In **"The Helmsmen"** Merwin communicates the poverty of lives lived without imaginative sympathy, and by concentrating imagery upon this human flaw, he renders it more forcefully. The generalized sketch is designed to convey human qualities with impact, and it is for this reason the expressionist artist eliminates detail. Speaking of capturing the charm of a woman's body in one of his paintings Matisse declares: "I will condense the meaning of this body by seeking its essential lines. The charm will be less apparent at first glance, but it must eventually emerge from the new image which will have a broader meaning, one more fully human." . . . When the artist brings out only "essential lines," he facilitates access to the artistic product—by enabling one to locate personal experience within the general lines. Because attention is not diverted by variety of detail, one draws upon private associations: the absence of elements encourages use of imagination to complete the aesthetic event.

Merwin brings the reader fully into the poem **"Come Back,"** published in ***The Lice*** (1967). In this poem he generalizes both character and event in order to intensify a single experience. **"Come Back"** is thematically similar to **"The Helmsmen,"** depicting two anonymous characters who are unable to communicate. Yet in **"Come Back"** there is more differentiation of character: one is a man; the other, a woman; and in the past a relationship has existed between them. In addition, the imagery is more dramatic, for the poem is a direct address in which Merwin speaks in the first person. (pp. 288-89)

"Come Back" indicates a recurring tendency in Merwin's poetry. He generalizes his personal character in poems in which he speaks in the first person, removing factual references for the speaking voice. For this reason he has gained a reputation as a mythicizing poet whose concerns are universal actions and events. Richard Messer, one of Merwin's commentators, claims that with respect to poetic voice: ". . . he achieves an oracular tone by avoiding strictly descriptive or personal references to the occasion of the poem." . . . In his latest work, however, Merwin experiments. In ***The Compass Flower*** and in ***Finding the Islands*** (1982), division of the poetry into separate sections reveals that Merwin is reconsidering his method of rendering poetic experience. In these volumes there are at least two kinds of poetry, of which neither could be termed expressionist because there is no penetration of appearances. The first kind is love poetry, involving direct address; in it Merwin is quite candid and personal. In fact he moves closer than ever in his career toward the occasional poem that reveals personal circumstances—a movement that may be his response to "the personalization of poetry" occurring in America in the 1970s. . . . (pp. 291-92)

A second kind of poetry continues Merwin's preoccupation with the forms of the world. In it he returns to a view of the images as a representational and descriptive device, yet there is little stylistic similarity between his early and latest poetry. In ***Finding the Islands*** poems have little pictorial emphasis; Merwin does not organize descriptive imagery to render a particular scene. Instead he represents the world at random, leaving the images of the poem unfocused. **"In the Red Mountains,"** in ***Finding the Islands,*** transmits the sights and sounds of the world in unrelated images separated in the poem by horizontal dividing lines. In an attempt to re-create the way in which the world is experienced in unconjoined impressions, Merwin effaces himself as human subject so that the world's sights and sounds come through directly to the reader. He would place the reader at the center of the poem and at the center of the world at once. This stylistic direction derives from Merwin's career-long concern to lead the reader to an appreciation of the natural environment. (p. 292)

Mark Christhilf, "Expressionist Imagery in the Poetry of W. S. Merwin," in The Midwest Quarterly, *Vol. XXVII, No. 3, Spring, 1986, pp. 277-93.*

Lorrie Moore

1957-

© Jerry Bauer

(Born Marie Lorena Moore) American short story writer, novelist, essayist, and critic.

Moore won critical acclaim for her first book of short stories, *Self-Help* (1985). Six of the nine stories in this collection parody the form of "self-help" manuals, as Moore subverts this popular type of book through her satirical and ironic approach to solving personal problems. Moore's characters cope with such difficulties as a senile and dying mother, a neurotic daughter, divorced parents, and failing relationships and marriages, often using poignant humor to offset the seriousness of the situations. Although some critics faulted the "how-to" device of the book and found the emotional scope of Moore's protagonists to be limited, most extolled her precise social observations and keen sense of absurdity.

In her experimental novel *Anagrams* (1986), Moore repeatedly shifts the point of view from first to third person, alternates between past and present tense, and abruptly changes the occupations and relationships of her characters. *Anagrams* is divided into five sections, all featuring Benna and Gerard, who are friends and occasional lovers. Benna, a junior college English instructor in the novel's concluding chapter, is beleaguered by unsuccessful love affairs, unsatisfying jobs, and her inability to bear a child. Critics have suggested that the first four chapters of the novel comprise Benna's alternate renderings of reality that ease the pain of her actual life, which is depicted in the final chapter. To protect herself from life's disappointments, Benna engages in constant wordplay, invents an imaginary daughter, and confides in a female friend who might be real or imagined. Some critics contended that Moore's narrative experiments caused confusion, and Benna's incessant comic bantering led April Bernard to claim that "Moore's message seems to be that all tragedies are alike, and they all merit the same jokes." However, several reviewers admired Moore's lyrical prose and her willingness to take risks in her approach to fiction.

(See also *CLC,* Vol. 39 and *Contemporary Authors,* Vol. 116.)

MICHIKO KAKUTANI

To avoid getting hurt—that is what all the characters in ***Self-Help*** want, and to insure their safety, they run away from commitments and relationships, they do magic tricks, watch television, buy clothes, quote Shakespeare—anything to escape entanglements that might prove emotionally damaging. Most of all, they like to tell terrible jokes and play little words games: "I long for you, I short for you, I wear shorts for you." It's like a nervous tic, this impulse to blurt out something silly—a way for Miss Moore's characters to short-circuit possible connections.

When her people do make an attempt to talk to one another, their conversations sputter out in gasps of non sequiturs or clichés, or their sentences simply hang there, in the air, dangling and incomplete. In **"Amahl and the Night Visitors: A Guide to the Tenor of Love,"** a couple, on the brink of breaking up, continually mishear one another. . . . In **"The Kid's Guide to Divorce,"** a girl and her recently divorced mother sit in front of the television, watching late-night horror movies and pointedly *not* speaking about the dissolution of their family. And in **"Go Like This,"** a woman dying of cancer announces that she intends to kill herself, and her smart, self-conscious friends can only respond with remarks like "suicide can be, often is, the most definitive statement one can make about one's life."

Like her characters, Miss Moore possesses a wry, crackly voice, an askew sense of humor and a certain reticence about emotions—qualities that lend her fiction a dry, almost alkaline flavor. In keeping with the title of this collection, several of her stories (**"How to Be an Other Woman," "The Kid's Guide to Divorce," "How," "How to Talk to Your Mother (Notes)," "Amahl and the Night Visitors," "How to Become a Writer"**) take the form of a "how-to" manual, told in the second person; and some also employ a diary-like structure—narrative strategies that keep the reader at a distance, while at the same time allowing the author to eschew more traditional story-telling conventions.

This approach results in some fine, funny and very moving pictures of contemporary life among the yuppies that help establish Miss Moore as a writer of enormous talent. Given her gifts—her sharp eye for absurdity, her keen prose—one can only wish that she would release her lyrical gifts more often from her straitjacket of cool decorum, that she would play around a bit more with other narrative forms. There is a sameness of tone to many of the stories in ***Self-Help,*** and the weaker ones resemble those amateur works of sculpture, made of found objects, welded together into an interesting, but jumbled, assemblage—though individual anecdotes and observations are amusing and well-crafted enough, they fail to come together to form a coherent work of art.

While the heroines or narrators of each of the stories in ***Self-Help*** have different names, they might well be the same woman—a smart, fairly hip young woman, so bland in looks that she is always being mistaken by others for their sister or, maybe, Tricia Nixon. At once insecure and terminally self-absorbed, she is someone who must filter everything through the lens of her own ego—"Reagan is elected President, though you distributed donuts and brochures for Carter"—and she consequently spends a lot of time looking at her reflection in shop windows, trying to recognize herself.

She's something of a masochist, this woman—always falling out of love with the right man or falling in love with the wrong one. . . .

In ***Self-Help,*** the curve of a love affair is almost always downward—when things appear to be impossibly bad. Miss Moore seems to believe they can only get worse. . . . In fact, as far as Miss Moore's characters are concerned, enduring, unconditional love doesn't exist between men and women—everyone is too busy hedging their bets ("make room in his closet, but don't rearrange the furniture"), waiting for something better or thinking up new defenses.

Often, in these stories, emotional hurts and bruised psyches are things inherited along with the family silver—many of Miss Moore's heroines trace their difficulties with men back to difficulties with a cold, unfeeling father; their sense of disconnection, of being "incorrect," to a mother's instability. Yet if pain can be handed down, generation to generation, so too can more tender feelings—and Miss Moore's women, who feel so alone, not only try to understand their mothers and their children, but some of them actually succeed in forging tentative connections. In such moments, both they and the reader of ***Self-Help*** experience a glimpse of redemption.

Michiko Kakutani, in a review of "Self-Help," in The New York Times, *March 6, 1985, p. 21.*

MARCIA TAGER

When the dust settles and the smoke clears from Lorrie Moore's dazzling performance on the high wire, the reader [of ***Self-Help***] perceives enormous talent. Moore's humor is manic, her wit sardonic. Some of her funniest stories, written in the style of the self-help manuals that presently inundate us, tell us **"How To Become A Writer," "How To Talk to Your Mother (Notes),"** and **"How To Be an Other Woman."** . . . Behind the bright bromides Moore is parodying, behind her satire on all the advice to the lovelorn columns ever written, Moore is dealing with genuine emotion. In many of her stories, life doesn't work. Moore's sophisticated wit cannot change the heartbreak of longing for what one cannot have and she knows it.

In the quieter stories, as in **"What is Seized,"** a daughter is dealing with her mother's last illness. She remembers the woman her mother was when she was eight, she sees the woman her mother is now, and she wonders about the woman her mother was before she herself was born. She is probing, investigating, remembering, coming to terms with both parents, with her father who was a cold man and with her mother who was destroyed by his coldness. . . .

Moore is preoccupied with loss, death, divorce, and suicide. Behind the humor . . . there is a great deal of pain.

Marcia Tager, "Witty Stories Mask Pain," in New Directions for Women, *Vol. 14, No. 4, July-August, 1985, p. 16.*

DAVID MONTROSE

Samuel Smiles, author of the original *Self-Help* (1859), idealized the great entrepreneurs of the Industrial Revolution: they provided "illustrations of character and conduct" from which his readers might learn how to get ahead in the world. Ostensibly, Lorrie Moore's début collection of stories [***Self-Help***] comprises something similar: a woman's guide to various (mainly emotional) aspects of modern life. Six of its nine stories, indeed, are written in the form of instructions, albeit unconventional ones: "Meet in expensive beige raincoats, on a pea-soupy night", runs the opening sentence of **"How to Be an Other Woman".** Also among the contents are **"The Kid's Guide to Divorce"** and **"How to Talk to Your Mother (Notes)".** On this occasion, though, ***Self-Help*** is a tongue-in-cheek title. Following the examples set by Moore's "instructors" (who are actually retailing their own, by no means enviable, experiences) and the heroines of her less unorthodox stories would lead to disappointment, regret, even premature death. Unlike Smiles's paragons, they have problems controlling their destinies: events overwhelm them, things fall apart. . . .

Moore's women fare badly in matters of the heart. **"What Is Seized"** tells of a wife "destroyed" by her husband's coldness; the protagonist of **"Amahl and the Night Visitors: A Guide to the Tenor of Love"** sees the man she adores gradually drift away from her. Admittedly, a measure of self-reliance does occur in **"How to Be an Other Woman"** and in **"How",** stories which cast a knowledgable eye on the stratagems of romance. Both end with the heroine discontinuing an unsatisfactory affair. In each case, though, the decisive step is taken only after much vacillation and finishes a relationship that had been a mistake from the outset.

Written differently—all tangled prose and anguish, say—Moore's stories would make bleak reading. Her prose, however, is clean and sharp, if marred slightly by a penchant for Richard Brautigan-style similes (eg "The moon rummages in the alleyway like somebody's forgotten aunt"); she also deploys a deadpan wit to admirable black-comic effect: her characters joke even as they hurt, *because* they hurt.

David Montrose, "Stratagems for Hurt," in The Times Literary Supplement, *No. 4310, November 8, 1985, p. 1267.*

LAURA FURMAN

In her first novel [***Anagrams***], Moore ventures an anagrammatic experiment in storytelling. She takes four characters—Benna Carpenter; Gerard Maines, the love interest in various guises;

Benna's perfect, wise daughter Georgianne Michelle; and Benna's wisecracking best friend, Eleanor—and changes their relation and circumstance in each chapter. Benna teaches aerobics to senior citizens, teaches creative writing at a community college, and is a nightclub singer in the Midwestern town of Fitchville, where the novel is set. Gerard teaches aerobics to pre-schoolers, sings in local nightclubs, is devoted, distant, a friend, a successful lover and a failed one.

Moore makes her novel even more of a game by letting us know early on that Eleanor and Georgianne are not real—as the fictional Benna and Gerard are—but are imagined by Benna. (Benna and Gerard sometimes indulge in such cute dialogue that one concludes that the difference between imaginary fictional characters and plain old fictional characters is that the imaginary ones get the better lines, at least in Eleanor's case.)

This device, perhaps meant to show levels of imagination and perception, best serves the slow revelation of Benna's childhood in Upstate New York and her relationship with her parents. But it is hard to care for the real imaginary and fictional imaginary characters when the writing makes little distinction between them.

Because of its form, the novel is episodic, often seeming like a series of one-liners or illustrations of contemporary middle-class social problems, a kind of novelized "Hers" column. I missed the sense of a continuing, dramatic present.

What Benna wants (at least in one incarnation) is a traditional family life. . . . But she seems thwarted in her desire by something that the novel never quite communicates. Is it her wit? A fear of intimacy? She has a lover whom she can't accept because, as he puts it, he wants to be an orthodontist, and she wants him to be a tragic Vietnam vet.

Perhaps the puns and anagrams are to blame for Benna's loneliness and sadness. Nothing is accepted for itself. Every small piece of action sparks another game rather than a direct reaction. Benna as a teacher demands passion from her students, demands that their work look like pictures of their souls that she asks them to draw at the beginning of the term. I wonder what she'd think of this novel. If ***Anagrams*** is about writing, about the slipperiness of imagination, then the form might have been pushed further, to make this clearer to the reader.

There are passages in ***Anagrams*** where Moore shows feeling for language and for her characters all at once, and it is on such passages that I base my hope for Moore's future work.

Laura Furman, in a review of "Anagrams," in Los Angeles Times Book Review, *September 14, 1986, p. 8.*

MICHIKO KAKUTANI

One of the best things about Lorrie Moore's new novel is its title—***Anagrams.*** It's a reference, of course, to her heroine Benna's habit of "trying to make anagrams out of words that weren't anagrams" (moonscape and menopause; gutless and guilts; lovesick and evil louse), her tendency to mis-hear and jumble sentences spoken by friends ("I never want to see you again" becomes "I want to see again"). At the same time, it's also an allusion to Benna's efforts to reinvent herself, to become someone else through fantasy and imagination—and in that sense, it's an allusion as well to the fiction-making process as practiced by Ms. Moore.

Cleverly assembled as a sequence of five overlapping stories, ***Anagrams*** appears at first to give us a series of variations on the characters of Benna and her pal and sometime lover, Gerard. . . .

It's a clever narrative strategy, designed to give us a variety of takes on Benna; and Ms. Moore uses the form to achieve a hefty emotional payoff at the end. The realization that Eleanor and Georgianne are totally imaginary, that Benna has made them up (the same way she's given us fictional versions of herself and Gerard) to alleviate her own loneliness, comes as something of a shock. We've already been told, point-blank, what Benna's up to, but her relationships with these people—especially with Georgianne—have come to seem so vivid and necessary to her emotional survival that their exposure seems a terrible loss. We are moved by the ending of ***Anagrams*** and we are also left with an appreciation of Ms. Moore's ability to go beyond the cool detachment that characterized her short stories (collected in the recent volume ***Self-Help***), her capacity for tenderness and felt emotion.

Unfortunately, these qualities are in short supply in the rest of the novel; the bulk of ***Anagrams*** is so glib and self-consciously witty that the reader is kept at arm's length from Benna and her problems. No doubt the tone is supposed to reflect Benna's own wary, cynical turn of mind, but even so, it grows tiresome, and the constant stream of one-liners has the added effect of making Benna sound more like a wind-up comedian than an English teacher—or a sympathetic woman.

Although Benna has moments of introspection—devoted to the pondering of overly general questions like "what is the essential difference between men and women?"—she makes so many terrible jokes and puns that the reader begins to suspect she's afflicted with a variation of the mental disorder that causes people to utter obscenities all the time. . . .

Given the fact that they're Benna's creations, it's not all that surprising that Eleanor ("you know, I just hate it when I lose my composer") and even 6-year-old Georgianne ("these cobs sure do make webs") are compulsive joke-tellers as well, but when it becomes evident that Gerard and his friends also share this sense of humor, the reader wonders whether Ms. Moore is simply incapable of creating independent characters and voices.

In Benna's case, the joking serves as a kind of coping mechanism, for her life seems irretrievably lonely and depressing. Having been deserted by a husband who later committed suicide, she is now teaching poetry at some rinky-dink community college. . . . Benna spends her own free time worrying about ants and cracks in the wall (signs, the author portentously hints, that all is not well in her life), and talking to her imaginary daughter.

Even with Gerard, Benna rarely engages in anything approaching a real conversation—instead, she dispenses witticisms, quotations and world-weary apercus. In fact she fears that Gerard will turn to her and say:

> That's it with you, isn't it? You don't really want to talk about anything, do you? You know invention and indignation and slamming car doors, but what about serious conversation, Benna. People have lives. As difficult as your own has been, there are others whose lives have been even more so.

Although Gerard doesn't really say this, the reader can't help but agree: Benna's relentless joking has turned into a defense strategy that precludes the very intimacy she thinks she wants. And in the case of Ms. Moore, a similar defensiveness keeps ***Anagrams*** from being the fully gratifying novel it might have been.

Michiko Kakutani, "Jokers Wild," in The New York Times, *October 18, 1986, p. 13.*

CAROL HILL

In Lorrie Moore's ***Anagrams,*** there's a fierce, hot eye that makes you wonder whether you're going to be stranded in the familiar desert of the modern imagination. But the book has a saving grace: Benna Carpenter—who is either a poet, teacher, nightclub singer, aerobics instructor or all of these—is appealing as the heroine of this extraordinary and often hilarious first novel. . . .

Benna's closest real friend is a musician, Gerard Maines. Their apartments share a thin wall, and Gerard sits one night, dopey with love, fully dressed in his dry bathtub, waiting for Benna to return, yearning only for the sound of her toilet flushing. Gerard loves Benna, and she kind of likes him. . . .

Benna and Gerard eventually . . . become lovers, and she sits in a rinky-dink cocktail lounge where he sings and plays piano and dreams of becoming an opera star. Then Benna gets pregnant, the imaginary Eleanor sleeps with Gerard, and Benna has an abortion. Miraculously, the relationship between Benna and Gerard not only survives these events but becomes a deep, close friendship. Throughout all of this we are treated to Benna's reflections, which often take the form of quirky, fond musings on words. . . .

Words roll around in Benna's mind like Life Savers on a tongue. Beneath the sweet pleasure of play, however, we sense her need for something else, some deeper articulation that will exorcise distance, bring her love and keep her from death. Watching a flock of birds, she muses: "From four blocks away I could see that the flock had a kind of group-life, a recognizable intelligence; no doubt in its random flutters there were patterns, but alone any one of those black birds would not have known what was up. Alone, as people live, they would crash their heads against walls."

To avoid hitting the wall, Benna falls in love with Darrel, a black Vietnam veteran who is taking her poetry class. Race is something Benna tries to avoid through her almost magical belief that whatever separates us can be overcome if we find the right words. She assigns sestinas to her poetry class, writing on the blackboard the end words "race, white, erotic, lost, need, love, leave." Darrel raises his hand and says that's seven words, not six. Benna erases "love," then changes her mind and erases "white."

It is a loss in the novel that this particular relationship is not developed further. It's unfortunate too that the changes of place and point of view in the beginning chapters interrupt and confuse us, so that we move away from the story. Some of the early chapters read almost as if they were independent entities, and it may be that Ms. Moore's talents as a short-story writer, revealed in her collection, ***Self-Help,*** tempted her in that direction. These opening chapters are like a magnificent engine alone on its track. We watch, waiting for the hookup, which we get only in the last section of the book.

Here we meet a wondrous 6-year-old, Georgianne Michelle Carpenter, who is Benna's imaginary daughter. And it is here that so much of the power and impact of the novel begin to make themselves felt. George and Benna have a very good time: a sweet happiness flows between them as they watch the news, take showers together on Saturday mornings to the tunes of Broadway shows, dust the living room and revel in the intimacy of sickroom caresses and goodnight kisses.

Benna loves Georgianne intensely, and in this love, which is sustained only by words, we discover how much this novel is about language, about the power of sounds to slice through the darkness, and through meaning to join us. It is a tribute to Lorrie Moore's talent that the reader believes in Georgianne.

Unexpectedly, Gerard dies, a brutal blow to Benna, who makes one last, painful effort to connect by visiting her lost, hapless brother, Louis. When she and Louis wind up watching a sitcom about a dog on Christmas day in a dreary Queens apartment, Benna's humor erupts in a swift, savage swipe: "Her mind wandered. She thought of pets growing tired and committing suicide, what notes they would leave: 'Dear Benna: It's all a crazy game. Farewell, Max, Your Schnauzer.'"

We think Benna may now have lost her real connections in the world. But we're wrong. There are stronger ties still. There are Benna's gifts, imagination and language—and there is the child, Georgianne. Benna's love for this child—like ***Anagrams*** itself—is a powerful example of how imagination can save us with temporary pleasures.

Carol Hill, "Sestinas and Wisecracks," in The New York Times Book Review, *November 2, 1986, p. 15.*

APRIL BERNARD

Lorrie Moore is a highly evolved specimen of the wisecracking yuckster. In her new book, ***Anagrams,*** a classroom of freshmen in a community college is "Twenty faces with the personalities of cheeses and dial tones." . . .

That Moore is a serious writer who deserves to be taken seriously may not readily be apparent. So seemingly endless are her one-liners, whether they emanate from a (sometimes) invisible narrator or from the characters themselves, that reviews of her first book, ***Self-Help,*** misled the likes of me by referring to those stories as comedies, and to the writer as a humorist. A reading of that book reveals something quite different. . . . [The stories are] grotesque tragedies, ten-handkerchief dramas. In which everybody cracks jokes. The biggest joke of all, though I am not sure Moore intends it, is the utter uselessness of all advice, the impossibility of applying the specifics of one person's pain to another.

Self-Help was tremendously popular, and Moore, now teaching at the University of Wisconsin, has come out with ***Anagrams: A Novel.*** That this is actually only sort of a novel is not surprising; Moore had already shown a Church of the Latter Day Modernists interest in form. This is the novel's "experiment": two young people, Gerard and Benna, live in Fitchville, U.S.A., and they have a relationship. That's the given. But in each of the five chapters, the relationship is a different beast. (p. 525)

Yet, by the final story—chapter, whatever—of the book, we are presented with an entirely different way to read it. "The Nun of That" takes up at least two-thirds of ***Anagrams,*** but more than length qualifies it as the "true" account of Gerard and Benna. Here, Benna is teaching a course at a college and has a close, non-sexual relationship with Gerard, who works as a lounge singer. Benna has an affair with one of her students, Darrel; he eventually leaves her. Gerard then has a freak accident and dies. Various other complications—an "imaginary" daughter, Georgianne, with whom Benna has long, intimate conversations at home; Benna's late ex-husband, oft-discussed; a holiday visit to her brother that ends miserably; and the constant switching from first to third person, and from past to present tense—all add to the reader's troubles. (There's nothing wrong with giving the reader a hard time, as long as there's a payoff). When Benna confesses to Gerard, who's in his hospital bed, that she has an imaginary daughter (which we already knew) and that she also has an imaginary friend, Eleanor (whom we had thought real)—we realize that the first four stories may well have been Benna's own revisions, alternate versions of this final, "real" story, futile devices to kill its pain.

There's a crucial moment in the second chapter when the reader is clued in to the higher purpose of this exercise in plot. "I kept trying," says Benna, "to make anagrams out of words that weren't anagrams: *moonscape* and *menopause; gutless* and *guilts; lovesick* and *evil louse*." Thus, these five stories are bad anagrams—which is to say, not anagrams at all—of one another. What are we to make of this? Unfortunately, I think, Moore, like her fictional counterpart, has not yet accepted that an anagram isn't an anagram if the letters don't match exactly. But even more important, even if there is a correspondence of letter for letter in each word, and character for character in each plot, "live" and "evil" are only the same in certain theologies. . . . Contemporary clichés such as Moore strews before us are not the final judgments that can be made about our lives. These equivalencies are insidious. . . .

Even as Moore explicates the central flaw in her use of equivalencies, she uses the humor of the error to undercut her point, to deflect from the emotional agony at hand. The overall effect of ***Anagrams*** is one great, tedious sameness, one enormous sigh of "Oh, rats" about the way we live and love today. Benna and Gerard are the same couple no matter who's got the career in aerobics, who leaves whom, or who hurts more. Moore reveals herself to be a writer who does believe that "close is good enough." And it isn't.

Moore's confusion is a shame, since she is, in spots, an exceptional writer, capable of much more than just very good jokes. There are soft, lyrical passages unimpeded by wisecracks: between a mother and child, between a sister and a brother, between lovers. Moore also writes well about how friendships mutate, she does the sex scenes without titillating or nauseating the reader (very tricky, that) and she has a commendable, if slightly drunken, love of the language. But just as the jokes deflect attention from the tragedies, so the machinery of this novel impedes an otherwise unselfconscious narrative gift. It would be interesting to see what Moore could do with the final story of this book if the daughter and the friend were real, if there were no fussing about with point of view, if she had more room to stretch out and if she ditched the anagrams.

False equivalence is the basis for puns as well as anagrams, after all, and Moore has an almost clinical weakness for puns. "The ants are my friends / They're blowing in the wind," sings the imaginary daughter. The line is incanted once or twice thereafter. It's funny, it's endearing, but what does it mean here? That the original line, and the original sense, of "Blowing in the Wind" means the same as this? Or what? (p. 526)

Moore's whistling past the graveyard gets pretty shrill. Somehow, her message seems to be that all tragedies are alike, and they all merit the same jokes. This is, no doubt, perfectly tenable from the point of view of stand-up comedy. That popular genre informs Moore's sensibility quite markedly; her characters perpetually tell jokes to one another, self-consciously trying out lines in preparation for a routine in the classroom or at a party. It's as if they were all lined up in the greenroom at Dangerfield's.

No matter how funny Moore is, she isn't on the stage, and cannot use the potentially redemptive personal link of performer to audience to offset her pessimism and avoidance. Her jokes represent an effort to assert control over a frightening, chaotic world, and Moore typically tries to get over by evening things out, making everything the same. As surely as the asphalt spreaders are paving over the fields and streams of America, this kind of writing paves over the culture. This is not social commentary; it is capitulation to the very things it purports to despise: sloppiness, easy outs, heartlessness. (pp. 526-27)

April Bernard, "The Whiny White Whine," in The Nation, *New York, Vol. 243, No. 16, November 15, 1986, pp. 525-27.*

MATTHEW GILBERT

[***Anagrams***] is witty, witty, witty. Lorrie Moore, author of last year's winning collection of stories, ***Self-Help,*** never forgets to wiggle her reader's ears with puns and one-liners and repartee. Her characters teeter on the edge, and comedy—absurdist or stand-up depending on the degree of pain—is their safety rope, their sanity-giver. As Benna, the hyperimaginative heroine of ***Anagrams,*** says, "Sometimes anything but cartoons is too real."

The danger is that the fiction itself will seem finally to be as unsatisfying as its characters' dependency on their own jokes. ***Self-Help*** worked because when Moore exhausted the comedic tension in one setting she could begin again elsewhere. Like the poignant and humorous characterizations of Lily Tomlin, those stories were just long enough. And many of them were compelling in their use of the second person—the reader believed that he was actually overhearing internal conversations between a character and her self-berating conscience. ***Anagrams*** falters once the jokes become predictable. How often can we chuckle at Benna's word play and her high-powered banter with her friend Eleanor? . . . It's as if any let-up would cause us to doubt that this book is really tragic, that its humor is meant ironically.

Perhaps to combat monotony, Moore has given her first novel an intriguing and changeable structure. There are four short sections at the start, then an extended fifth that is the focus of the book. All of the sections involve the same characters, but circumstances are radically different in each one. . . . The method quickly becomes clear: the stories *are* anagrams—rearrangements of the same set of themes. Unrequited love, unsuccessful careers, and childlessness, as well as other minimalist matter, repeatedly appear wearing different costumes. With the fifth section, "The Nun of That," it's as though rehearsals are over and the real play is going to start.

"The Nun of That," which is itself broken up by a regular leaping from first to third person, is the story of Benna as writing teacher at a community college, Gerard as Holiday Inn piano man and friend, and Darell, a new character, as hard-to-get student / paramour. Two other prominent characters, friend Eleanor and daughter Georgianne, turn out to be vivid creations of Benna's imagination. As this truth dawns on us, as we wonder if the first four sections were similarly "imagined" by Benna, her troubled mental state becomes frighteningly obvious. And herein lies the unity and the punchline of the novel: Benna is a broken woman for whom fiction and humor are preferable realities, solutions to the emptiness and mediocrity of her life. Benna is having a breakdown.

That so much cleverness has been used only in order to illustrate Benna's insanity is like waking to find it was all a dream, that it didn't matter anyway. The denouement of the novel seems too convenient, a blanket that holds disparate elements together and hides their randomness. And we never discover exactly why Benna is cracking up, only that she is a victim of the modern world who, it turns out, needs a vacation.

What makes ***Anagrams*** a promising first novel is the inventiveness of its author. Lorrie Moore is a writer teeming with conceits and willing to try them. This is an experimental novel, after all, one that risks failure in fighting The Good Fight—and that's always an exhilarating, and these days rare, sight. While reading ***Anagrams*** you often realize that *anything* could happen. . . . And Moore is a nimble craftsman. When she is not indulging her limerick tendencies, she is often pithy, even moving. Unfortunately here her complex talent is not in the service of anything genuinely complex. Perhaps next time Moore will take her jokes more seriously.

Matthew Gilbert, in a review of "Anagrams," in Boston Review, *Vol. XI, No. 6, December, 1986, p. 30.*

Howard Moss

1922-

American poet, critic, editor, dramatist, and author of children's books.

A distinguished poet, critic, and editor, Moss writes formal poems in iambic meter and traditional structures. Critics describe him as an insightful poet who writes with wit and compassion about ordinary objects, people, and events. Moss commonly addresses such topics as change, love, death, and human relationships, and he employs images and metaphors drawn from both the urban and natural worlds. An honored poet, Moss received the National Book Award for *Selected Poems* (1972) and the Lenore Marshall/Nation Poetry Prize for *New Selected Poems* (1984).

Most of the poems in Moss's first three volumes, *The Wound and the Weather* (1946), *The Toy Fair* (1954), and *A Swimmer in the Air* (1957), are formal lyrics that focus on personal concerns. Selected pieces from these books are collected with several new works in *A Winter Come, A Summer Gone: Poems, 1946-1960* (1960). Although Moss's early verse drew mixed reviews, critics praised such individual poems as "Elegy for My Father," in which Moss evokes a melancholy tone while meditating on death, and "Horror Movie," which features wit and evocative imagery. *Finding Them Lost and Other Poems* (1965) and *Second Nature* (1968) firmly established Moss as an important contemporary poet. Several of the poems in *Finding Them Lost* concern the effects of time and evidence Moss's talent for creating emotive lyrics that blend wordplay and urbane wit with formal control. The narrative tone and musical rhythms of many of the pieces in *Second Nature* are the result of Moss's attraction to the theater. In several of these poems, Moss examines the relationship between art and reality. Moss's varied interests are reflected in three of his volumes of verse published during the 1970s: *Buried City* (1975) focuses upon New York, *A Swim off the Rocks* (1976) consists of light verse, and *Tigers and Other Lilies* (1977) is a book of verse for children which examines sundry aspects of nature.

Notes from the Castle (1979) is considered by several critics to be Moss's finest volume of poetry. Moss was praised for his relaxed yet learned tone, his mastery of technique, particularly internal rhythm, and his disciplined use of rhyme. In such poems as "A Fall" and "Gravel," Moss presents metaphorical connections between natural phenomena and the human condition. He commented: "What my poems are really about, I think, is the experience hovering between the forms of nature and the forms of art. My work is the response of someone who is equally *moved* by nature and art." In *Rules of Sleep* (1984), Moss continues to focus on such themes as death, loss, and the passage of time, evidencing a more pronounced awareness of mortality.

Moss is also respected for his nonfiction works. These volumes include two studies of individual authors, *The Magic Lantern of Marcel Proust* (1962) and *Chekhov* (1972). Moss's essays and reviews collected in *Whatever Is Moving* (1981) and *Minor Monuments* (1986) include discussions of such poets as W. H. Auden and Elizabeth Bowen as well as general pieces. Critics praise Moss's accessible prose, in which he blends an informal, conversational tone with wit and poignant epigrams. Moss has also served as poetry editor of the *New Yorker*.

Photograph by Layle Silbert

(See also *CLC*, Vols. 7, 14; *Contemporary Authors*, Vols. 1-4, rev. ed.; *Contemporary Authors New Revision Series*, Vol. 1; and *Dictionary of Literary Biography*, Vol. 5.)

ROBERT B. SHAW

Notes From the Castle is at once technically smooth and curiously uncompelling. . . . It could be said that as *New Yorker* poems Mr. Moss's hold their own. It is a poetry of dimmed lights and muted sounds, in which the dominant feeling is one of ennui. There is a bland urbanity to the style, a refusal to exhibit anything as vulgar as personality. It may seem churlish to censure verse that sure-footedly avoids any lapses in taste, but the sameness of tone in these poems, their pose of stereotypical middle-aged melancholy gradually benumbs the reader. . . . [One] of Mr. Moss's repeated obsessions is to find in landscape emblems of the passage of time. His sense of nature is so inextricable from his sense of a self-suffering gradual diminishment as to shadow all his vistas. His metaphors project an apprehension of unreality onto the visible scene, as if the world were a stage set soon to be struck. "Tensed against the wine-soaked washrag / Of the sky the trees erect themselves / In the last small oblivion of lights . . ."

There is ingenuity to this sort of writing, and a kind of charm in Mr. Moss's frequent recourse to the pathetic fallacy, as in these lines from **"Standards"**: "The seeds with their little valises fly / Over the scene and look for a landing." Such stratagems, however, wear thin with repetition, and seem at last (if they didn't at first) to be selling nature short. A quirky piece of fantasy, **"The Night Express,"** is different and interesting enough to make one wish that this impeccable stylist would venture more frequently beyond the sort of poem he writes most often and altogether too well. (p. 24)

Robert B. Shaw, "Mixed Report," in The New York Times Book Review, *February 3, 1980, pp. 9, 24.*

PETER STITT

The light which illuminates ***Notes from the Castle*** . . . is filtered through autumn leaves; beautiful, rich, enticing, it is yet nostalgic, seeming to say that most of life is in the past tense now. This is a time more for reflection than passion, though the possibilities of passion do quietly linger on. Many of the best poems in the volume are written in the mode of loss—one thinks first of the long and moving **"Elegy for My Sister."** Others present memory in a more gentle way, accentuating the passions of autumn. . . . Moss has rarely used quite the personal voice we find . . . throughout ***Notes from the Castle***. The work benefits from this change; it seems the right time for a new tone.

The real sense of life expressed in the volume is carried by its images, its metaphors, its figures of speech. Moss is at his best when operating in the realm of those twin devices, animation and personification. There is a passage in **"The Research of Dancers"** which can be read as a metaphorical expression of the function of the poet, a poet such as Howard Moss:

> As the dancer places a tentative foot
> On the floor of the stage, it rises to meet it,
> The inanimate everywhere shudders awake,
> The library stacks have just been struck
> With their first good idea for a book in years;
> Outside, the straw is dreaming of bricks,
> As if it, too, had been activated
> By beautiful, personal, spontaneous forms.

This is the sort of thing that happens when Howard Moss sets pen to paper—dumb objects come alive and begin doing things undreamed of. (pp. 436-37)

Grandiosity is not beyond Moss's reach, and he has the delicacy and precision to make it work. In a comment he once made on Proust, Moss defined one of his own most salient qualities: "He works by expansion. . . . A lot of people who imitate Proust are just slobs. They don't understand the precision of his mind. It allows for any kind of elaboration. Because everything he says really is true." Howard Moss himself has this power, the power of precision, of elaboration, of truth. He has demonstrated this many times in his career, but nowhere better than in a long poem in this volume, **"Gravel."** I leave the experience of this remarkable work to you, but note that Moss operates on every level imaginable to cover his topic completely; after six pages of beautiful verse, much of it presenting the world from the point of view of the gravel itself, we suspect there really is nothing more to be said. Such are the riches to be found in ***Notes from the Castle.*** Howard Moss is a master of his craft and handles with ease topics and artistic problems others can't even think about. (pp. 437-38)

Peter Stitt, "Resemblances and Transformation," in The Georgia Review, *Vol. XXXIV, No. 2, Summer, 1980, pp. 428-40.*

DAVE SMITH

Howard Moss is a multi-talented man, an anthologist and influential editor, a writer of criticism, plays, light verse, and now a tenth volume of poetry. Of him one critic was inspired to write that he has "that distance between upper lip and nose that betokens a generosity of spirit." Although one searches ***Notes from the Castle*** in vain for that curious measure of poetic quality, there is a yeoman's plenty of delight and wisdom in the poems. Moss is a superior poet whose constant occupation is to observe, and turn to fine musical compositions, the cause-effect play between nature and the intellect. If one takes the castle of [**"Notes from the Castle"**] to be, roughly, both the speaker's house (a man's house being his castle) and the house of the ruminating intellect, one comes at once to the special quality of Howard Moss. His vision begins at home and is therefore personal but sweeps inclusively outward toward an impersonal sifting of what is true and what is merely apparent. However reductive an American "castle" may be, it is where the spirit or intellect begins and where "each childish wish / Grows hopeless finding this is what the world is." The world, Moss tells us, is a wind with "too much / Of motivation" and birds "boring themselves to death / Or, drunk on instinct, doing their thing . . . ," or a kind of pained, indifferent, intractable population. . . . Importantly, Moss views the world not as a place defined by, say, trees or bodies of water but by people and their actions. He is, as poet, a social man who reminds me of Conrad's way of glimpsing the ineffable through the ordinary. It might be said that, for Moss, life consists in the despair caused by the ideal *much* betrayed by the actual *little*. But Moss is less a poet of despair than of wry and considered hope, for he knows there is always another "hoped-for-redeemer" to set the heart banging with desire, be it the loved one, an object, or obsessive pursuit, whose appearance shows "you had merely stumbled on / Another temporary battlefield / As never-lasting as the shine of water."

Because his poetry is reticent, careful, characterized by a linchpin precision with words, Moss qualifies that ordinary simile wherein life is like a war and surprises us with "never-lasting." Life, it seems, is never clearly enough or permanently enough a war, but rather is a shifting brightness one cannot seize or look directly at for very long. In consequence, Howard Moss has turned through his last three books of poems insistently toward a poetry of ellipsis and image, in increments and sequence, more than traditional metrics. Even so his poems are intensely musical individually as well as in the orchestration of long poems and short lyrics which comprise sections. ***Notes from the Castle,*** in fact, is organized as an extension of the compositional arrangement of ***Buried City*** (1975) and should be read as a refinement of Moss's shift toward potentials of music in the open or sonically variable contemporary poem. Moss's earliest work is that of a poet faithful to and mastering traditional and conventional lyric verse, a poet who was nevertheless restless enough and skilled enough to stretch conventions to accommodate a surprisingly personal, sometimes jarring, engagement with the world. Certainly those poems seem now a little constrained by a bookish language and a determination to be everywhere symmetrical, but they remain among the most readable work of Moss's generation. And the more one reads Moss the less one feels he is really like anyone else, which is to say that his evolution of style is in fact a continuing and, I think, successful effort to render the house of the mind and the house of the world as they really are. Conrad named this as the task of disclosing "the stress and passion within the core of each convincing moment."

If there is, however, a changing style in the poetry of Howard Moss, there are also constants. ***Notes from the Castle*** shows the blatant delight in pun, irony, and outright joke that has been one of the ingredients of what Helen Vendler called a conversational style of "light and feeling" [see *CLC*, Vol. 7]. Poetry has always been for Moss a most civilized and synthetic discourse, one whose formalities have been designed to examine and even to celebrate the shades of human experience. He is a determined poet of the modern city (who could imagine his poems in Orange County?) and yet the city, like the castle, seems increasingly more the beginning of perspective than the subject.

Indeed, in ***Notes from the Castle*** Moss is more than ever attentive, perhaps even reverential, toward the natural world which he regards both as a mirror and a window. The elements and forms of nature have become almost a dramatic script from which it is his task to tease out human meaning. Moss repeatedly portrays the poet as translator of nature by rendering through simile and metaphor the natural particular in a literary, artistic, or craft term. In **"Gravel"** he describes a leaf-vein on a stone as "the smallest / Lithograph." In **"The Sleeper"** a storm theatrically "Rattles its foil for the last time." He causes shoreline and ocean to become halves of one parenthesis; hills in Mexico City are "rolltop" desks. In **"Aspects of Lilacs"** the moon has "the goldleaf halos / One sees in the early Italian masters" and in **"A Fall"** Moss says "I wander among the distributed notes / Of the leaves." The point, however, is not that Moss is a nature poet, a leaf-looker, but that he means to bridge the known life of the castled self and the unknown life hidden within nature's other houses; he seeks solidarity. "Poetry," Stevens wrote, "is a satisfying of the desire for resemblance." And added, "Reality is not the thing but the aspect of the thing." Moss seeks to compose fragments, aspects, nuances in linkages that result in "beautiful, personal, spontaneous forms" as he says in **"The Research of Dancers."** All of these forms may have the effect of revealing, hence creating, a wholeness of self in the world. . . . Moss's wonderfully formidable and emblematic poem **"Gravel,"** which has almost to be experienced spatially—considers at once the relationship of the one and the many in ten essentially imagistic parts. The stones are seen as exiles, lovers, the dead, countries, soldiers, and more. They are, perhaps, the many castles of the world. . . . This sense of unredeemable division is reflected, as is the thinker-translator perspective, in the language of Moss's titles, in *notes, news, research, senses, aspects,* and *incomplete sonatas,* but—far from incomplete—his poems are themselves wholes, unities, moments in which we see and feel not only the natural surface but also that stress and passion behind all.

The power to create the illusion of permanence, to draw us into consciousness through the creation of symbols, and yet to impress us with the mutability of all things that somehow bears an aura of beauty is rare enough. And often one finds this power in poets of main force, though inconsistently. It seems to me an attribute of that character on whom the least is lost. Art's finest effects arrive only in the poet whose language aspires to and rises to the condition of poetic music. That is the poet's final responsibility and it is, I think, the most remarkable aspect of ***Notes from the Castle.*** Moss is, at bottom, a tragic poet, but never mawkish or ragged. His book has sweet grief, but also anger, wit, gentility, understanding, and wisdom. **"Gravel," "Many Senses: Mexico City,"** and **"Stars"** are long poems of sustained vision and will bear happy returns. Among the shorter poems perhaps the most memorable are **"At the Cafe," "The Long Island Night," "What the Heart Wants,"** though on the whole I find Moss's shorter lyrics less continuously exciting than his mid-length and long poems. I think this is because in those poems he allows himself the fuller and more musical resources of line, image, and rhetorical variation. (pp. 37-8)

It is, I think, Howard Moss's power, and his poetic signature, to continue fitting the world's fragments into the order of formal beauty, to find yet that "music still to be heard." If his poems constantly push through the literal to the signified, if what is signified seems all too often the ruination of our best hopes, we might expect with increasing age an increasing anger and terror. There is enough of both in ***Notes from the Castle*** to give the poems the human edge of passion. But there is more dominantly a courage, an embrace of what is, and a willingness to know what a man is and why. The result is a vigorous and sustained will to joy, a poetry of grace. (p. 38)

Dave Smith, "Castles, Elephants, Buddhas: Some Recent American Poetry," in The American Poetry Review, *Vol. 10, No. 3, May-June, 1981, pp. 37-42.*

MICHAEL DIRDA

[Moss' essays, collected in ***Whatever Is Moving,***] reveal a man who loves his subjects—not by accident are the best pieces memoirs of Auden, Elizabeth Bowen, and Jean Stafford. That affection Moss duly supports with precise thinking, telling example, and a prose that is lucid, musical and confident. Among men of letters perhaps only V. S. Pritchett writes a better plain style.

As a reviewer, Moss does several things well. A much admired poet himself, he brings a practitioner's understanding to the evaluation of poetry. Auden and Elizabeth Bishop recur throughout ***Whatever Is Moving*** as his touchstones, both masters of their craft from an early age, ever themselves. (p. 11)

Not content with merely describing a book—"What pleasure is there in writing criticism that reveals what everyone can see for himself?"—Moss also knows how to *use* the review form: he slides from Cavafy's appealing blend of the historical and erotic into shrewd observations on why homosexuals chronicle urban life so well; he gives lilt to a close reading of Chekhov's *The Three Sisters* by interlacing suggestive musical analogies. And in both essays, he drops in sentences that might be aphorisms from La Rochefoucauld: "The truth is that what is interesting about love is how it doesn't work out."

In the more general essay, Moss proves equally good, as in **"The First Line,"** a fugue-like meditation on the importance of a poem's opening, of the weight of seeming inevitability to such lines as "April is the cruellest month". "One would," he says, "no more think of revising a rock." Similarly, the concluding appreciation, **"One Hundred Years of Proust,"** sharply defends Proust against charges of being frivolous and effete, then defines his true achievement concisely and beautifully.

But that is ever Moss' aim: to bring a writer's work into such sharp definition that we discover qualities otherwise overlooked or underappreciated. He accomplishes this, deftly, stylishly, for Eudora Welty, Christopher Isherwood, Jean Rhys and a dozen others, making criticism look as easy as conversation. It isn't. (pp. 11, 13)

Michael Dirda, in a review of "Whatever Is Moving," in Book World—The Washington Post, *December 20, 1981, pp. 11, 13.*

WILLIAM PRITCHARD

Unlike most writers who collect their back reviews and essays, Howard Moss doesn't preface his by announcing a unified theme which runs through and justifies the collection; just as well, since such attempts aren't often convincing. All that holds together these pieces [in ***Whatever Is Moving***] on poetry, on poets, on novelists is a manner: polite but firm, coolly urbane, never at a loss for words and almost always treating the writer under consideration with admiration. Like Mr. Moss's own expert if somewhat too unruffled verse, his prose manner is unaggressive and in the main uncontroversial. No one is going to object to his sympathetic praise—in the book's first five essays—of Whitman, Cavafy, Auden, Elizabeth Bishop and James Schuyler. In the case of Bishop—Mr. Moss's favorite contemporary poet—one welcomes such just analysis of her art as is represented by the following discussion of the verbal magnetic field set up by her "odd couplings of words": "A deep division—reserve at war with the congenial—undercuts the authority of the poems. . . . A New England iron in the manner—or, I should say, in the *lack* of manner—in conflict with an easygoing willingness to accept life as it is, its perkiness and variety, is everywhere present." The whole essay backs up its high estimation of Bishop's work, by resourcefully dealing with the couplings of words through which it lives.

But Howard Moss is not mainly, certainly not exclusively, a verbal critic. In three of the first five essays homosexuality is a concern: for Whitman as it informed his "most intense emotional affairs"; for Cavafy as it provided him with "built-in advantages as a spokesman for the city," since the homosexual explores "byways of the city" and gets to know it "in ways most people don't—strange places at strange hours." And for James Schuyler, in whose 60-page "The Morning of the Poem" the sexual motif weaves in and out as it holds together the "men Schuyler has been attracted to, described lovingly." Mr. Moss likes Schuyler's sexual frankness ("He is in touch with parts of himself not usually available for examination and not often handled by most writers") for the way it gives us "the straight stuff." But at one or two points the critic draws back, characterizing one of Mr. Schuyler's particularly frank lines as a "no-holds-barred journal entry" and "a question hardly worth asking." Exactly so (and the ghost of Yvor Winters is temporarily assuaged), but if one is going to welcome, as Mr. Moss does with Whitman, the "poem of pure feeling," then that feeling a century later may have turned into the campily permissive kind of thing we encounter in Schuyler or John Ashbery (they wrote together the cutely titled *A Nest of Ninnies*). And attempts to draw the line here rather than there, to decide which questions are worth asking and which are not, will surely be ineffective.

The one poet whom Mr. Moss is severe with is Robert Frost, finding (in the course of reviewing Richard Poirier's book on Frost) that he lacks emotional range—"a refusal to be either naked or gorgeous." But why shouldn't it be highly desirable for a poet to be neither naked nor gorgeous? Frost, we are told, doesn't have "the city" in his poems, which "narrows his field of vision." Yes, if you like, but to find "little sense of the street side of life, little true humor" in the poems seems to me a travestied account of this century's most humorous poet. . . . To refer, as Mr. Moss does at one point, to the poet as a "mean-spirited megalomaniac" who manifested "one of the more hideous personal lives on record" is to fall from urbanity into a sensationalism that is gullible besides. Auden, who has lots of The City in his poems, has therefore a wider emotional range, and his views about politics are treated as heroic ones ("he waged a long battle against hokum") no matter how often he changed his mind (often). Frost's politics, on the other hand, are just "embarrassing," as if the liberal critic must avert his eyes from the sad spectacle. Is there not here a too automatic assumption of an enlightened "we" who understand oh so well which politics are embarrassing and which will pass muster?

The most original essay about poetry in the collection is one called **"The First Line,"** which talks inventively about different ways first lines by Eliot, Donne, Auden, Jarrell, Bishop and others launch the poem. . . . In one instance the critic gets carried away to the extent of substituting "courageous" in a Williams first line quoted as "On the way to the contagious hospital"; but the line as Williams wrote it reads "By the road to the contagious hospital." (Memory slips in a couple of other instances; Auden did not say, as Mr. Moss says he did, "Poems do not make anything happen.") But he is altogether plausible in concluding that "the writing of poetry seesaws . . . between the desire to attain the first line and the desire to evade it," and in pointing out that a main habit of contemporary poets is to be "against" the grand first line.

The book's second half contains good writing about Chekhov, including an extended, large-minded reading of "Three Sisters." But I found myself most taken by the section dealing with women writers—with Eudora Welty, Jean Rhys, Elizabeth Bowen, Katherine Mansfield, Jean Stafford and Sylvia Plath. The two pieces on Elizabeth Bowen are particularly attractive, the first of which capably and succinctly argues for her importance as a novelist, identifies her true subject as "manipulation—emotional, social, sexual," pays discriminating tribute to her powers as a stylist and daringly terms her "a true wit, in the Restoration sense," with a "flair for comedy that eluded Virginia Woolf"—that last observation a convincing one. (pp. 6, 25)

William Pritchard, "On Poets, Poetry and the Writing of Fiction," in The New York Times Book Review, *December 20, 1981, pp. 6, 25.*

HARRY THOMAS

Now that we have ***Notes from the Castle,*** Howard Moss's tenth and best book of poems, it ought to be delightfully obvious to everyone that Moss is one of the most accomplished and original poets in this country. That he is "accomplished" even his detractors have admitted. That he is "original" may take some showing. I call him "original" because he has not only striven to discover less canonical images by which to express his sense of life, and to devise the structures in which those images will unfold most richly, but he has perfected a metrical system. That system is both old and new, as I will show in a minute. Its presence and Moss's skill in keeping it from appearing systematic give his poems a lushness, a musical wit, and a rhetorical authority few poets (Wilbur, Bell, Walcott, Hill, the late James Wright and Robert Hayden, and who else?) possess. Listen to the opening lines of **"The Night Express"**:

> That moment we neared the reservoir
> Dry wit dried up aware that water
> Was no longer there for the taking. Hazel
> And birch, those secret, solitary drinkers,
> Were suddenly duplicated everywhere,
> Even the ground consuming its potion.

The recurrent "r"s here, registering like a bass chord through the first five lines, and the medial and slant rhymes, remind me of Roethke (see "A Light Breather" and "Elegy for Jane"). And the resolution in the metallic "n"s of the sixth line is masterful. As for the meter: it's decasyllabic, mostly in iambs. What distinguishes the meter from, say, Wilbur's pentameter verse, is Moss's strategy of evading the fifth stress. He has several ways of doing this. He can employ two anapests in a single line; he can cut a line to nine syllables; he can reverse the last foot; he can place polysyllabic words so as to disrupt the stress pattern. This may strike you as sterile in summary. In the poems Moss's achievement is marvelous.

Moss splits his seventy-three pages into eight sections. Sections one and three consist of single poems in several parts. Neither poem quite comes off and both can be dispensed with. Section four contains six negligible lyrics of the kind Moss has been turning out for forty years. They are exercises in style; they appear to have been written to *charm*. Section eight is made up of translations of two poems by Joseph Brodsky. . . . The translations are particularly good. We are left, then, with half a book: two sections of magisterial lyrics, the long and very poignant **"Elegy for My Sister"** (a poem that rivals **"Long Island Springs,"** the masterpiece of Moss's ***Selected Poems***), and **"Stars,"** the book's show-piece and, in my judgment, one of the permanent things written in the last decade.

So far I have noted the book's design and stylistic triumphs. Do I have something to say of its matter? I do. People who dislike Moss's work sometimes say that it's matterless. They are wrong. ***Notes from the Castle*** distills the experiences—New York, Long Island vacations, music, loneliness, friendship—of Moss's previous books, and it deepens those experiences with an awareness of death. This awareness extends beyond the personal, as in **"The Night Express,"** in which Moss imagines a planet without water. . . . An "abyss underlies even the most Arcadian of Moss's landscapes," Helen Vendler writes on the jacket. "Arcadian" seems to me just the right word, though it is not one destined to win converts to Moss. If there has been a long-standing complaint against Moss's work, it is that he sidesteps the indecorous, the threatening, the destructive. Richard Howard phrased it most succinctly in *Alone With America:* "We long for some single thing to happen that will not always bypass the self, the person, in a cosmic undulation." This was valid criticism in 1969. And even now Moss is not ashamed to begin a poem with: "After the plagues and the dispossessions, / Survival's one idea gives way / To ideas of civility." Which is Arcadian surely. But elsewhere in ***Notes from the Castle,*** in **"Have You Forgotten,"** in **"Elegy for My Sister,"** in **"Stars,"** and in [**"Notes from the Castle"**], Moss brings the self's abyss up close to the verbal surface. The suffering, refrangible self is no longer erased by art's decorum; it is presented openly and made resonant.

There is no point in my trying to defend Moss. His excellence is there for anyone who isn't stigmatized to see. I suspect, after all, that Moss is objected to in some quarters because he is, as Roethke said of himself, a poet of joy. (pp. 200-02)

Harry Thomas, "Poets and Peddlers: New Poetry by Hopwood Winners," in Michigan Quarterly Review, *Vol. XXI, No. 1, Winter, 1982, pp. 200-17.*

PHOEBE PETTINGELL

Howard Moss loves to evoke the atmosphere of places. His eleventh collection of poems, ***Rules of Sleep*** . . . , conjures up vivid, sensual impressions of Manhattan, Miami Beach, Rome, Umbria, and diverse New England landscapes. He perceives us all as artists *manqué* who improve on what we see or cut it down to our size. . . .

Moss is a skilled miniaturist. . . . In fact, one of the most charming aspects of his work is its many tiny "slices": A swimming pool becomes "this Mediterranean in a match-box"; an expanse of **"Rooftop"** provokes the question, "Rain, will there ever be enough / For the black-tarred roof / Desiring to become a mirror?" . . .

Another poem develops a homely gesture—the trick of making your own bed while still in it, useful for invalids—into an *unheimlich* conclusion: "Though death, I think, has more than clever / Household hints in mind and wants / The bed made once, and for good."

That Moss' sense of mortality seems sharper here than in the past is no doubt a result of his recent heart attack. Several poems describe the humiliation and terror of an intensive care ward. Others dwell on the acute loneliness experienced by the critically ill, who learn that pain and death cannot be shared. . . .

Moss' more expansive pieces are equally impressive. **"Einstein's Bathrobe,"** the most ambitious, seeks to capture the essence of the century's absent-minded genius. The speaker is the titular dressing gown, a favorite garment of the subject.

> From signs Phoenicians scratched into the sand
> With sticks he drew the contraries of space:
> Whirlwind Nothing and Volume in its rage
> Of matter racing to undermine itself,
> And when the planets sang, why, he sang back
> The lieder black holes secretly adore.

The ear slides over the polished musical surface of these lines almost too quickly at first to grasp their meaning. For his poem about science Moss has transmuted into imagery an astounding amount of physics. In the end, he summons a vision of the universal death by nuclear destruction that our age collectively fears:

> I felt the dawn's black augurs gather force
> As if I knew in the New Jersey night
> The downcast sky that was to clamp on Europe,
> That Asia had its future in my pocket.

The heroic style needs large themes not to sound windy. In **"Einstein's Bathrobe,"** it seems appropriate, even understated, considering the horror the poem encompasses.

Howard Moss can toss off a villanelle with grace and relishes traditional poetic forms. Yet his sense of the world is more truly of the times than that of many younger writers. It is also very much his own. The intricately crafted ***Rules of Sleep*** surprises us again and again. (p. 18)

Phoebe Pettingell, "Through Memory and Miniatures," in The New Leader, *Vol. LXVII, No. 15, August 20, 1984, pp. 17-18.*

JOHN MARTONE

The speaker of Moss's **"Gallery Walk: Art and Nature"** defines the scope of [***Rules of Sleep***] when he tells us, "I am only trying to teach you / What pleasure is, and also about / The end of things, / And how the two of them go hand in hand." Moss's notions of pleasure and the end are carefully cultivated; there is little recklessness to his universe, little of the unrestraint of lust and death. For all its craft, in fact *because* of its craft (rich with New York School irony), I found myself responding to the book with impatience.

Predictably, Moss's most common strategy involves a kind of contemporary *ut pictura poesis*. He relies on elegant ecphrasis (in poems like **"In Umbria"** and **"The Summer Thunder"**) and on an iconography drawn from the old and recent masters and recognizable objets d'art. The effect is usually one of delicate anxiety. All these features are signifiers of literariness, of high culture, but all of them have been so for a long time. More important, they attempt to place the poem within the context of postsymbolist and postmodern writing while sparing poem and reader alike the difficulties of postsymbolist and postmodern language. Throughout this collection, I felt Moss rehearse his very substantial skills, but I failed to hear him test those skills, much less push them to a breaking point, the point at which the conventional language of New York might tell us yet something more about our experience. Poems like **"The Light Put Out"** and the title poem, **"Rules of Sleep,"** come closest. . . .

I hope I am not being unfair, but I am looking for poets whose visions integrate all of experience; and a world that includes "Florence's serene Annunciations," the Vatican Museum, a clavichord cover, the ginkgo, a cello concerto, Ravel, Schubert, Bartók, and Einstein's bathrobe does not include enough.

John Martone, in a review of "Rules of Sleep," in World Literature Today, *Vol. 59, No. 2, Spring, 1985, p. 270.*

PETER STITT

Howard Moss's ***New Selected Poems*** illustrates beautifully the suppleness that can be attained by a poet working within the restrictions of a tight formalism. Mr. Moss published his first book, ***The Wound and the Weather,*** in 1946, the same year Robert Lowell's *Lord Weary's Castle* appeared. Later, when Lowell set the world of poetry on its ear by converting to free verse and patently personal subject matter, Mr. Moss made only a slight alteration in his style. He tried his hand at drama, as he has said, to reinvigorate his verse with a greater sense of directness and immediacy. He did then loosen his forms, it is true, but never abandoned his firm grounding in the essential iambic pentameter line.

In **"Piano Practice,"** published in 1968, Mr. Moss explains what he has always been seeking in his work:

> Grammar becoming poetry is what
> You're after—say, a rational derangement
> Requiring that you forget technique
> And concentrate on what is harder.

The harder thing is that supple, almost spontaneous artistry achieved by performers who have truly mastered the rudiments of their craft. Not that Mr. Moss's earlier, less free efforts should be neglected. It would be hard to imagine a better formal poem than **"Elegy for My Father."** . . .

But there are other places in his early work where a too rigid formalism leads to a kind of woodenness, a lack of flexibility. That is why it is so satisfying to find in more recent work so great a liveliness in both content and form. Grammar turned to poetry is indeed what Mr. Moss seeks, in life as in art. . . .

Mr. Moss works his miracles with a quiet subtlety. Perhaps it is that quietness that has made him so relatively neglected as a poet, when reputation is measured against talent.

Peter Stitt, "Poets Witty and Elegiac," in The New York Times Book Review, *September 1, 1985, p. 11.*

FREDERICK GARBER

[***Rules of Sleep*** begins] with a loving look at Assisi and the region of Umbria, a place transformed by light and passion, lucent with something more than itself. It ends with **"Morning Glory,"** a poem to Lee Krasner that works with supple sensuousness on the facets of the flower and ends with a glance (no more than that) at transcendance. These are not only the poles of the book but of the best work within it. In an interview in *The American Poetry Review* in 1984 Moss speaks of his verse as mainly light, a point that critics have made, and of course the point is correct; but the best can be that and more, transforming light verse in the way that light transforms Umbria. Consider the title of the book . . . and also **"Umbria"** with which it begins (*umbra* is Latin for "shade" or "shadow"). Much of ***Rules of Sleep*** images a world aglow, Moss seeking out the light from a restaurant window or in upstate New York or New Hampshire, watching it woo the world into elaborate transformations. Such metamorphoses are always sensuous yet at their most intricate they hint (never more than that) at something else. "How calm the sensuous is! How saintly!"; so he puts it in **"The Summer Thunder,"** and in that touch of saintliness we see not only the metaphorical potency of the poem that speaks of Assisi but also the way Moss lets such potency work with only the slightest suggestion. It works in [**"Rules of Sleep"**] and other spots of suggestion, hinting at the undoing of all that changes and glows. **"The Restaurant Window"** moves its meditations on the sounds and incandescence of oncoming evening toward more ominous changes ("in the white capsule of a hospital room / After the warm visitors have left, / The chill of what is about to happen / Settles between you and a stranger / Walking into the room politely") and ends with a look at "the sunset, already settling for less." It is then that an earlier line ("gradually night sponges up vision") comes back to haunt and qualify the context in which it appeared. . . . Moss described himself in the *APR* interview as, however urbane, finally "a creature of feeling," and his passions extend not only to the sensuous play of light and color—sun and streetlamp, the morning glory's blue, the lavish delight in what he can see in art and nature—but also to the absence of these—the decline of seeing, the hunter hurrying home, finally the remark in **"The Swimming Pool"** that "you will be a shade of nature soon," an *umbra* within the world. Light and darkness fall alike on place and self. Self openly pursues the pleasures of art and seeing not only for the sake of sheer delight but because light will slip into sunset and universal shade, shade within and without, ourselves as shade.

In this book of transformations, metamorphoses linked with pleasure but never only that, there is not a single misstep. Moss shares with [Marvin] Bell the love of sensuous surface. . . . He shares that loving look at the world's changes with Levertov but shows no trace of the bathos that sometimes defies her passion for purity. He is like Merwin in a certain penchant for empathy but he takes it into odd places, becoming, alternately, a rooftop and Einstein's bathrobe. Such oddness, the kooky or slightly strange, comes in at occasional moments to show how self and its language can do what light and color do, transform the world. . . . The poems go through their changes with always the finest elegance, eloquent and matured, light verse, of course, but sometimes somewhat more, suggesting through the lightness the shades where self and place and text are ultimately held, beholden. (p. 19)

Frederick Garber, "Geographies and Languages and Selves and What They Do," in The American Poetry Review, *Vol. 14, No. 5, September-October, 1985, pp. 14-21.*

ASHLEY BROWN

As poetry editor of the *New Yorker* for many years, [Moss] has been remarkably generous to certain other poets, and it would not be an exaggeration to say that he has sponsored several careers. There is a kind of generosity about his own poetry too in his response to nature and the arts, above all to certain literary artists such as Chekhov and Elizabeth Bishop. . . .

It may be that there is a limitation in such generosity, for the great poets usually have strong feelings which we may not share but which we can certainly understand. . . . [In his verse represented in ***New Selected Poems***] Moss is never bland or simplistic, though, and on occasion he can generate a real power from trivial, almost journalistic material. In **"The Wars,"** for instance, he takes us from a "botched affair" in a Chinese restaurant in New York to the war in Southeast Asia, which in 1968 was a component of almost everyone's imagination, thanks to television; the metaphor of the "wars of love" thus describes the situation precisely.

More characteristic, however, are such pieces as **"Going to Sleep in the Country,"** which Moss once described as "effortless" in its composition, or **"Water Island,"** a beautiful elegy to the memory of a friend who drowned. Moss has the gift of friendship too, and this comes through frequently, sometimes indirectly, in many of his poems. The level of technical accomplishment is very high and a delight in itself. Altogether, ***New Selected Poems*** is one of the most civilized and satisfying collections of poetry in our generation.

Ashley Brown, in a review of "New Selected Poems," in World Literature Today, *Vol. 60, No. 1, Winter, 1986, p. 109.*

VERNON SHETLEY

Howard Moss has devoted a lifetime of work to the great theme of art and nature, and devoted himself to it with as thoroughgoing an artistry as any American poet. Of the generation that, generously defined, included Richard Wilbur, Anthony Hecht, Howard Nemerov, James Merrill, and many another like-minded poet, he began in the Forties and Fifties school of metaphysicality. His decorous virtuosity resembled Wilbur's, but avoided the ostentation of wit so recognizable a part of Wilbur's style, while from the first Moss sounded the note of minor-key plangency he has gone on to develop and refine. . . . Like his peers, he soon grew anxious about the manifest artifice of the period style; when his King Midas prays to be given back "Ten fingertips that leave the world alone," one sees in that prayer Moss's own fear lest his bejewelled style render lifeless the material it would transmute into art. Moss has responded to that anxiety, not by abrupt transformations, but rather by a progressive movement toward rhetorical openness and metrical relaxation. Reading through the four decades or so of work represented in [***New Selected Poems***], one sees a steady growth in maturity and power from the brittle brilliance of the early work to the rich, fluid meditations of his most recent volumes.

Just as Moss sought though, in his highly self-conscious early mode, the perfectly framed and chosen colloquialism, so in the plainer style toward which he has evolved, his performance is never less than perfectly artful. Paradox remains his favored form of statement, his goal a balancing or suspension of contraries in a poised structure of fruitful ambiguity. In keeping with his preoccupation with the theme of art and nature, Moss treats most readily the experience of art or the aestheticization of experience; water is his chosen element, as it turns nature into art through the power of reflection (**"Sea Change"**), but also threatens all aesthetic fictions by its elemental violence (**"The Sea to Hart Crane," "Miami Beach"**). Moss wants to prefer the aesthetic, to find the realm of art unimpaired by its necessary exclusions. . . . But nature will not be so answered; death and mutability impinge. . . . Perfection appears, and it is indeed perfection, but does not last, and there lingers a note of sadness behind every *carpe diem*.

Throughout his career Moss has had the happy skill of knowing the scope of his talents. It is no shame to realize one's limitations, and Moss has lived within his lyric gift fully, without any irritable reaching after ultimate pronouncements. In an age in which the poet has been variously presented as analysand, as shaman, as cultural conscience, Moss has held fast to the definition of poet as maker, and his reward is this volume, representing a lifetime of exquisitely made work. (pp. 299-301)

Vernon Shetley, in a review of "New Selected Poems," in Poetry, *Vol. CXLVII, No. 5, February, 1986, pp. 299-301.*

J. D. McCLATCHY

New Selected Poems is not just a collection of superb work. It is a long look at a career that has unfolded in surprising ways, and without the kind of critical recognition that has sustained others. The urbane but astringent lyricism of Moss's first book, ***The Wound and the Weather*** (1946), heralded a distinctive voice. Over the next forty years and in ten subsequent books, culminating in this definitive selection from them all, Moss has refined and darkened that voice. Without sacrificing the wit and rhythmic finesse that characterized his poems from the start, he has come to write with a more startling simplicity as his subject demands, and everywhere his poems speak eloquently of the wounds of experience, the weather of the spirit.

In his essay **"The Poet's Voice,"** Moss once identified the problem of establishing a human voice for itself as a central theme in the poetry of the last half-century. Art is a civilized, not a natural phenomenon, and there will always be a "pull between speech and eloquence . . . how to speak in the name of something real without being merely commonplace." To solve this problem, Moss himself has never sought—as so many others have—a temporarily striking fashion. He is not ornate or homely, journalistic or swaggering or surreal. He never preens: his poetry is neither a public platform nor a private salvation. Instead, he has cultivated the gift of a true style, a manner of heightened but human speaking that is as unique as a voiceprint.

We recognize a Howard Moss poem at once. It never fakes a pleasure or an insight. It does not pretend to emotions it does not feel. Though he can make phrases with the best, as when he calls Venetian palazzi "spun-stone" or Jackson Pollock's paintings "wounded linoleums," his rhetoric is calculated not to impress but to confide and suggest, ponder and console. And especially in his later books, it is charged with a poignant wisdom and rare feeling.

Moss speaks in a quiet tone of voice, and sometimes an elusive one. One must listen attentively—too great a demand on many readers today. He knows "how much restraint / Enhances skill," and how the poet can "sometimes sound the depth / With the lightest touch." His is the style of the reflective intelligence: a sea surface, as he writes in **"Bay Days,"** "Currents, always running, gauged to light / And wind, the depths varying the colors." He is not a discursive poet, but one for whom thinking and sensibility command the same impulses. . . .

Alert to the nuances of happenstance and meaning, he is also open to the underside, the dreamlife of art and memory and the unconscious. The architecture of ideas yields easily in Moss's work to what in one of his best poems he calls the "buried city" we set out each night to explore in ourselves. "To be a diver and a scholar both" is his ambition.

In this ambition he has linked himself to—and learned from—some of this century's major figures. If Moss's early work declares its allegiance to Auden and Yeats, his more mature poems owe something to James Merrill's heartfelt wit, and to Elizabeth Bishop's passionate detachment, her meticulous descriptions, her "sane imagination." Moss has made these qualities entirely his own, and added to them the narrative aplomb of those writers—like Chekhov and Proust, Eudora Welty and Elizabeth Bowen—his prose pays homage to. (p. 412)

Even in his early books there was a sharp satirical edge to some of his poems. **"Drinks with X," "A Dead Leaf," "Ménage à Trois"** and **"Fern Dying"** have an uncommon ability to make the reader laugh and wince at the same time. But the more compelling side to his work is the elegiac. Beginning with **"Elegy for My Father"** in ***The Toy Fair*** (1954), on to **"Water Island"** and **"September Elegy"** in ***Finding Them Lost*** (1965) and on through **"Elegy for My Sister"** in ***Notes From the Castle*** (1980), he has written haunting formal examples of this genre. Beyond that, there is a melancholy that pervades all his poems. Unlike the pruned tree which speaks in the poem of that title, Moss cannot say "Shorn, I rejoice in what was taken from me." Resigned and diminished, he turns back to what Freud called the ordinary unhappiness of life. The enduring cycles of nature—the seeds and seasons of growth and decay—are his standard, and he searches for his mysteries in the everyday.

These two sides to his temperament are not contradictory; it was Auden who said that an unimaginative or a cowardly or a happy person is seldom very amusing. Nowhere are satire and melancholy more appropriate, nowhere are isolation and diminishment more telling than in the city. Moss is the cosmopolitan genius of that infernal, exhilarating place. . . . Even more than of the boulevard, he is a poet of the shoreline, of the margin between elements. The distance between mind and dream, or between survivor and ghost, the longing of settled habit for unsettling doubts, or of love for dissolution—these are the precarious in-between states he has charted with an uncanny accuracy. It has been exciting for his readers to follow that expedition, to listen to that human voice. . . . (pp. 412-13)

J. D. McClatchy, "The Lenore Marshall Prize," in The Nation, *New York, Vol. 243, No. 13, October 25, 1986, pp. 412-13.*

WARREN WOESSNER

For Mr. Moss, [the writing of Anton Chekhov and Elizabeth Bishop] exemplifies accurate observation and truthful characterization. His own gift for hitting a target after taking careful aim keeps the critical blood pumping in even the briefest reviews [collected in ***Minor Monuments***]. His image of Dylan Thomas as "a wildly gifted and brilliant child, not only stumbling and bumbling his way to the grave, but digging it for himself," is precise and chilling. Pronouncements like "the nature poet is usually religious and seeks a god, the city poet mythological and seeks a hero" and "detective stories can never become literature" are provocative. He presents vivid portraits of W. H. Auden, the poet James Schuyler and Jean Stafford, which are drawn with personal details without seeming to pry. In **"The Poet's Voice"** he deftly differentiates "nature," or unshaped expression, from style (or literary "voice") and from fashion, which must change in order to exist. It is his preference for writers with style as opposed to stylish writers that unifies this collection.

Warren Woessner, in a review of "Minor Monuments: Selected Essays," in The New York Times Book Review, *November 2, 1986, p. 27.*

HELEN VENDLER

Moss's essays [in ***Minor Monuments: Selected Essays***]—most of them on prose or plays—possess, in addition to wit, an incomparable deftness in their economical sketches of what a Chekhov play or a Welty novel are like in the reading. They are unobtrusively aesthetic in their discreet play of light and shade, balancing facts and impressions. . . .

Looking at Moss's choices as a critic, it is apparent that he prefers, on the whole, writers who exhibit delicacy as well as strength—Chekhov, Proust, Flaubert, James, Auden, Bishop, Mansfield. He understands writing by women—Bishop, Welty, Bowen, Porter, Rhys. He writes often about homosexuals—Proust, Whitman, Cavafy, Auden, Bishop, James Schuyler. He seems as much at home in plays and novels as in the world of poetry, where he has made his own secure reputation. Unlike most poets, he extends his psychological acuteness beyond the bounds of the private psyche into the conflicts of the social world; a shrewd and tolerant knowledge of men and women lies behind the *pensées* that illuminate his pages.

Moss's great gift as a critic is his temperament, at once intense and dispassionate. It is no accident that his deepest affinities seem to lie with Chekhov, in whom sympathy and irony combine to attain a rare equilibrium between generosity and clarity. Of one of Rhys's works, Moss writes, "(It is) the most harrowing of the novels"; but even as he has been harrowed, he has been able to watch ironically as well, and he remarks coolly about Rhys's heroines, "When the lovers run out, the one night stand takes their place." Moving from the justice of sympathy to the justice of observation, Moss is a critic to be trusted—limpid, accurate, tempered. Poets will want to read his essay **"The First Line,"** a meditation of great charm on what the first lines of poems intimate, promise, and deliver. (p. 32)

Helen Vendler, "What the Poet Had for Breakfast," in The New Republic, *Vol. 196, No. 3767, March 30, 1987, pp. 30-3.*

Lewis Nkosi

1936-

South African novelist, critic, dramatist, scriptwriter, and short story writer.

Known in England for his scholarly studies of contemporary African literature, Nkosi has elicited critical attention in the United States for his first novel, *Mating Birds* (1986). In this work, Nkosi explores the ramifications of miscegenation under apartheid through the ordeal of Ndi Sibiya, a young Zulu student who is about to be hanged for allegedly raping a white woman. As Sibiya awaits his execution in a South African prison, he vividly details the events which led to his arrest and death sentence. Some reviewers faulted Nkosi's use of interracial sexual relationships as a means of defying the South African regime. Henry Louis Gates, Jr. commented: "The treatment of miscegenation as a political indictment of a racist South Africa is not without its literary dangers and risks . . . and Mr. Nkosi's novel does not entirely escape them." Nevertheless, critics enthusiastically praised Nkosi's prose style and narrative structure, and several compared the mysterious and surreal atmosphere surrounding the crime to that evoked by Albert Camus in his novel *The Stranger*.

Among Nkosi's other works is *The Rhythm of Violence* (1963), a drama focusing upon a group of revolutionaries who conspire to blow up the Johannesburg City Hall during a pro-apartheid rally. His nonfiction books include *Home and Exile* (1965), a collection of literary, political, and autobiographical essays, and ***Tasks and Masks: Themes and Styles of African Literature*** **(1981).**

(See also *Contemporary Authors,* Vols. 65-68.)

© Lütfi Özkök

THE TIMES LITERARY SUPPLEMENT

[Lewis Nkosi's] ***The Rhythm of Violence*** is frankly programmatic and rather thin in texture, but it has the same kind of effectiveness that *Waiting for Lefty* had thirty years ago. In dramatic technique the play owes a good deal to Genet; here too the characters act out and identify with their own most hated fantasies, though without achieving the black poetry which Genet strikes from such scenes. Nevertheless, the simple plot is an acceptable projection of some of the dilemmas facing every kind of political activity in South Africa. A racially and ideologically mixed group of revolutionaries decide to blow up the Johannesburg City Hall during a Nationalist Party Rally. Can one declare war and yet retain the right to discriminate between "good" whites (or blacks) and bad? Can one accept the help of whites who may prove unreliable in the end because they have too many hostages to the other side? and yet, who but a Fascist, of whatever colour, can relish the prospect of an all-out clash pitched along the colour line? England has for too long accepted the shibboleth that propaganda cannot be art, thereby impairing the potentialities of both. Mr. Nkosi offers us the salutary shock we often get when abstractions suddenly turn into people with the same right to life as ourselves.

"Africa into England," in The Times Literary Supplement, *No. 3259, August 13, 1964, p. 723.*

ROGER OWEN

Most of [Mr. Nkosi's] limitations as a writer can be related to the facts of his experience—to his being an African, writing about the problems of being an African, and to his doing this for a small, white metropolitan audience in Britain and America, and for a smaller African élite in his own country. One of the many indignities of this situation is that it forces him away from whatever disposition his private feelings might have taken him to, into the role of 'African writer', a role which necessarily has a good deal about it which is 'public', representative and even histrionic. His subject-matter [in ***Home and Exile***] is less of his own choosing than it would be were he British. There is a sense in which it is out there already, lying around in all its forbidding significance, waiting to be written about—the African Personality, the Problem of Identity, the Clash of Cultures. These subjects have been exhaustively discussed and it is hard now to approach them without the wrong kind of self-consciousness.

This, I think, is present in many of the pieces in this collection of essays and reminiscences. The very uneven quality of the writing shows how easy it is for private feeling and public attitudinising to blur into each other. There are frequent fallings-off into platform eloquence. We read of books which are 'powerful pleas'; of treatment which is nearly always 'shabby'; of 'subconscious desires', 'desperate longings' and the earning of 'undying respect'. Another kind of public pressure is also at work, one to which some African writers are, perhaps forgivably, vulnerable. It leads to a sometimes strained display of sophistication and wide reading, to name-dropping and cultural lifemanship. (pp. 434-35)

The best parts of the book are the narrative parts—the bizarre apartheid yarns and the gay times on *Drum* [magazine]. By now, though, the *Drum* era is beginning, in the thin history of South African culture, white or black, to take on the quality of a literary Golden Age or Heroic Period, a status to which it has little claim. Mr. Nkosi reminds us again that they were 'an exciting bunch of young writers' who turned out 'cool, sober prose' and possessed a 'unique intellectual style, urbane, ironic, and morally tough'. The essential fact is that they were extraordinarily brave in getting material for their reports. (p. 435)

Roger Owen, "An African Writer," in New Statesman, *Vol. 71, No. 1828, March 25, 1966, pp. 434-35.*

CHARLOTTE H. BRUNER

Tasks and Masks is an incisive and comprehensive critique of contemporary black African literature by Lewis Nkosi, one of its most astute and uncompromising critics. He posits the African writer's goal as twofold: his commitment to affect social change; and his task, as respectful heir, to continue what is worthy in the African tradition, as symbolized by the mask. In eight essays Nkosi defines this dichotomy. Treating the concomitant problems of language, history, Négritude and modernism, Nkosi relates these to the genres of the novel, poetry and drama.

Nkosi has long insisted that the African writer must not exploit exoticism but must compete on equal terms with writers of international stature. Himself an impeccable stylist and a dispassionate logician, he is severe, incisive, profound. For example, he locates Négritude in the context of the twentieth century, among the Marxists and socialists, in the absurdist movements of the 1920s and 30s: "Négritude is really a bastard child whose family tree includes, apart from the living African heritage, Freudianism, Marxism, Surrealism and Romanticism." (pp. 336-37)

Nkosi's own virtuosity is evident. Whenever available translation is inadequate, he provides his own for the Francophone poets. His study is thorough: he includes many writers and treats the work of each comprehensively. His fluent prose and admittedly personal judgments make his book interesting to the specialist and to the lay reader alike. ***Tasks and Masks*** is a landmark in African literary criticism, a must for any student in the field. (p. 337)

Charlotte H. Bruner, in a review of "Tasks and Masks: Themes and Styles of African Literature," in World Literature Today, *Vol. 57, No. 2, Spring, 1983, pp. 336-37.*

HENRY LOUIS GATES, JR.

Mating Birds, [Lewis Nkosi's] first novel, confronts boldly and imaginatively the strange interplay of bondage, desire and torture inherent in interracial sexual relationships within the South African prison house of apartheid. His play ***The Rhythm of Violence*** and his short story **"The Prisoner"** explored related themes. The treatment of miscegenation as a political indictment of a racist South Africa is not without its literary dangers and risks, however, and Mr. Nkosi's novel does not entirely escape them.

Black and white miscegenation has a long and curious history in literature, ranging in extremes from Shakespeare's representation of self-destructive jealousy in the figure of the noble blackamoor Othello to the pseudonymous American novelist Oliver Bolokitten's bizzare and perverse 1835 novel, *A Sojourn in the City of Amalgamation, in the Year of Our Lord 19—*. In Bolokitten's novel, white male and black female "amalgamation" is made possible only by the invention of an "ingenious" machine that protects "the husbands from those disagreeable evaporations exhaling from the odoriferous spouse . . . by fanning off the offensive air, and at the same time dispensing, by means of the vials, a delightful perfume." Perhaps Bolokitten was an Afrikaner.

We have come a long way from Bolokitten's racism to civil rights romance films starring Sidney Poitier *(A Patch of Blue, Guess Who's Coming to Dinner?)* and the cross-racial sexual encounters on prime-time television, from "Dynasty" and "Falcon Crest" to "The Jeffersons" and even "Kate and Allie." Miscegenation in these instances is a metaphor for social harmony and individual possibility.

More often than not, black authors write of interracial sex as a metaphor for self-destruction or in terms of the penalties exacted for violating a taboo. LeRoi Jones's allegorical play *The Dutchman* (1964) is a prime example of this genre. Clay, a middle-class black man, is stabbed to death by Lula, a white prostitute, after he flirts outrageously with her during a subway ride. Even where the sexual taboo is only implied, as in Richard Wright's *Native Son* (1940), the results are the same: Bigger Thomas, discovered alone with a drunken white girl in her bedroom, panics, smothers her while trying to stifle her drowsy voice and is sentenced to death. The white woman, in black literature, is bad news.

Mr. Nkosi's novel leaves this pattern undisturbed. Indeed, ***Mating Birds*** recalls in several ways both *The Dutchman* and *Native Son,* as well as Camus's *Stranger, Othello* and Hegel's well-known essay "Of Lordship and Bondage," with a dash of Freud thrown in for flavor. It also brings to mind the persona of Eldridge Cleaver's *Soul on Ice,* obsessed with white women. These echoes seem intentional; indeed, this novel often reads as if Bigger Thomas had raped Mary Dalton before he killed her, then written a prison memoir from his cell on death row, discussing the social forces that made him do it and using Camus, Cleaver and Hegel as sources.

The novel, indeed, takes the form of a prison memoir, which 25-year-old Ndi Sibiya writes as he awaits execution by hanging, convicted of raping a white woman, Veronica Slater. Sibiya, expelled from his university for his political activities, is a sensitive, articulate and lyrical narrator. He tells of his irresistible and manic obsession with a woman he chances to see sunbathing on a beach in Durban—he on the nonwhite side and she in the border area between the two sides. Meeting on the beach almost daily, the two—according to Sibiya's not untroubled account—enter a dreamlike ritual replete with the subtle gestures of wordless flirtation and the silent exchanges of cues of desire. . . . This encounter unfolds under a stifling, "blazing" South African sunlight as blinding to reason as Camus's Algerian sunlight was in *The Stranger*.

Mr. Nkosi intentionally echoes the existential leap into the abyss of Camus's narrator with the one Sibiya is bound to make. First there is an explicit and erotic pantomime of sexual intercourse on the beach. . . . Then Sibiya follows Veronica home. With her door left ajar, she undresses and lies on her bed. Sibiya enters the bungalow and consummates his passion, only to be discovered, beaten, arrested and sentenced to death for rape.

This plot outline does not capture the book's lyrical intensity or its compelling narrative power. Mr. Nkosi has managed to re-create for his readers all the tortures of an illicit obsession, especially the ambiguities and indeterminacy of motivation and responsibility. While by the novel's end our sympathies are drawn to the black narrator, we are never certain who did what to whom or why: "But how could I make the judges or anyone else believe me when I no longer knew what to believe myself? . . . Had I raped the girl or not?" We cannot say. Accordingly, this novel's great literary achievement—its vivid depiction of obsession—leads inevitably to its great flaw.

Lewis Nkosi has created an allegory of the master and slave relationship that frequently echoes the language of Hegel's "Of Lordship and Bondage" in its description of the curious reversal of roles that occurs between them. Phrases such as "the ultimate mirror in which she saw reflected the power of her sex and her race," "a horrible kind of duality within me" and "in the movement of the merest shadow she saw a subtler kind of power she could not yet acquire for herself" tip us off. (Sibiya's recollection of a racist university professor's lecture on African history even contains a reference to Hegel's *Philosophy of History.)* But Mr. Nkosi's novel never achieves Hegel's reversal of roles.

At the novel's end, the master remains the master, and the slave remains a slave and is doomed to die; never does Sibiya, the slave to his obsession, become the master even of his will. The ambiguities created by his own troubled story prevent the liberation that he and the reader eagerly seek from the novel's beginning. Unlike Bigger Thomas, then, who accepts that he is guilty of murder and walks eagerly to his fate, Sibiya in this tale leaves us far more perplexed and worried about the origin and nature of his obsession. As in *Native Son,* we are expected to identify an evil social environment as the ultimate cause of the protagonist's aberrant behavior. But by depicting Sibiya's obsession (rather than apartheid itself) so powerfully, perhaps Mr. Nkosi has created more ambivalence of motive than he wished or than is politically comfortable for blacks in a segregated South Africa.

The novel's very strength, perhaps, will make it a subject of heated debate, especially in a South Africa desperate to remain the last outpost of the West's fantasy of colonial subjugation.

Henry Louis Gates, Jr., "The Power of Her Sex, the Power of Her Race," in The New York Times Book Review, *May 18, 1986, p. 3.*

ALAN RYAN

The self-inflicted wounds of South Africa are so raw that both observers and participants often fall to shouting. Much of the literature dealing with the country's problems is shrill, intense, insistent. Perhaps, for many reasons, it should be; certainly we understand why it is so. But the problems spawned by apartheid—indeed, the nature of apartheid itself—touch the innermost areas of human life: feelings, attitudes, stances so unconsidered that their inhumanity cannot be felt.

Lewis Nkosi's ***Mating Birds*** addresses these very areas, in a quiet, poetic voice, set down in prose of glowing simplicity. Nkosi, a Zulu, was exiled by his country's government more than 20 years ago. . . . What a shame that his own country can no longer claim him, because ***Mating Birds*** is very possibly the finest novel by a South African, black or white, about the terrible distortion of love in South Africa since Alan Paton's *Too Late the Phalarope*.

"In a few days I am to die," writes a young Zulu student named Sibiya. He is in a prison cell awaiting execution by hanging. He has—it is alleged and the court has found—raped a white woman. From the cell, he recounts the bizarre events leading up to his destruction, his early life in a Zulu community, the conditions of his life as a student at the University of Natal in Durban, and as a young man in a country where whites are "accustomed to regarding the blacks as nothing but pegs on which to hang their hats."

Beneath an ominous warning sign ("Bathing Area—For Whites Only") he first sees the white woman sunbathing on the beach. For reasons he barely understands—such thoughts should be impossible for him—he is drawn to her. Although neither utters a word or approaches the other, it is obvious that Veronica Slater responds to him and, with carefully measured glimpses of her body, courts his interest and keeps it alive. They "meet" every day. On days when she fails to appear, he misses her. When they come into accidental contact in a shop, they are both embarrassed and uncomfortable.

Denied all contact by the world in which they live, they are, Sibiya says, "lovers in everything but name." In fact, they are "locked in a sickening but unloving embrace," which leads, first, to a terrible (because distorted) pantomime of love-making on the beach and, later, to the violence of physical contact. And, because this is South Africa, the contact means death for Sibiya. . . .

Yet the great irony is that it is not even for the sake of love that he is going to die: "For love, I repeat, anything can be forgiven. But love is not what I felt for this girl. To such a cheap, worthless emotion only the name of lust can be given. For mere servile desire is what I will hang for, that impossible dream of all disconsolate, dissatisfied young men, which is the attainment of the forbidden fruit, a hunger and thirst enjoyed more in its contemplation than in its satisfaction." Thus is he reduced. And the glowing object of his desire, the woman, who easily lies in court and turns out to be a stripper in a Durban nightclub, has no grace other than the color of her skin.

Nkosi writes vividly of Sibiya's Zulu childhood, and of the conflicts among the native people, both desiring and fearing to approach the white world and then being corrupted by its touch. He writes movingly of Sibiya's mother, a vibrant young Zulu beauty degraded first by the slums of Durban and then destroyed by the fate of her son. And most memorably he writes, in language that is both passionate and perfectly controlled, of the sad fate that South Africa has inflicted on itself. It is a world that, like Sibiya (and like Stephen Kumalo in Paton's *Cry the Beloved Country),* is awaiting death, but Nkosi's quiet voice is likely to linger in the ear long after the shouts and cries have faded away.

Alan Ryan, "Passion in Black and White," in Book World—The Washington Post, *June 8, 1986, p. 14.*

ROB NIXON

With ***Mating Birds,*** the exiled black South African Lewis Nkosi provides a rare perspective on miscegenation in a tale recounted entirely from the vantage point of a young black man charged with raping a white woman. In the ensuing court case, Sibiya, the novel's narrator and heroic victim, comes to feel the full weight of white paranoia, as he is abstracted from his humanity and tried as a cipher of "black brutality." The result is a book of bold psychological insight, but one marred by vexing sexual politics.

At its best, Nkosi's prose moves between an ascetic sensuality reminiscent of Camus and of Lawrence Durrell's more luxuriant eroticism. The novel turns on the relation of sensuality to violence—that is, of desire to the anger that prohibition stirs. However, Nkosi's handling of the sexual themes complicates the distribution of our sympathies, which he means to be unequivocally with the accused man. For in rebutting the prevalent white South African fantasy of the black male as sex-crazed rapist, Nkosi edges unnecessarily close to reinforcing the myth of the raped woman as someone who deep down was asking for it.

Although set in South Africa, ***Mating Birds*** bears the melancholy mark of Nkosi's 25 years of exile. The sun, the sea, the sand of the Durban beach where Sibiya first encounters the white girl who becomes his obsession are described with a sensuality sharpened by nostalgia. Yet it is a very *literary* sensuality; it seems more indebted to Camus's writings about North Africa than to a full, deep memory of South Africa.

Camus is doubly to the point, since Nkosi models ***Mating Birds*** so closely on *L'Etranger*. The hero of each is defiantly indifferent to his imminent execution—Meursault for the unprovoked murder of an Arab, Sibiya for the alleged rape of a white stranger. Each disdains the charade of the court proceedings and refuses to kowtow to the moral pressures of his society. And each man's account of the fateful incident is blurred by amnesia.

Yet Sibiya's claim on our moral sympathies should be the more clear-cut of the two. Meursault is a French colonial, a *pied noir,* who randomly murders a member of a subject race; Sibiya belongs to a subject race. His trial is thick with racial slander, with "ethnopsychology" emitting an "odor of racial conspiracy," with the noxious rhetoric of a prosecutor intent on making "an example of him as a deterrent for other misguided natives." Quite clearly, he is to hang not only for rape but also for the "crime" of daring to sleep with a white woman.

But there are problems. By turning the whole narrative over to the accused man, Nkosi screens out the woman's perspective entirely. This would matter less were Nkosi's tale of miscegenation not impeded by an undertow of misogyny. Veronica, set apart on her whites-only beach, is a "monstrous provocation." She is "seductive bait," dismissed as "a high-class tart" replete with "sexual taunts," a "serene temptress" and "tormentor"; in short, says Sibiya, "the girl became a kind of sickness for me." His detailing how he came to commit an act that he himself sees as straddling rape and seduction is, from one perspective, the novel's source of strength. For we certainly gain insight into the power of one pathology to breed another: Veronica's extravagant, legislated remoteness unsexes and almost unhinges Sibiya. It is scarcely surprising, therefore, that when Sibiya determines to "smash the facade of propriety" he has in mind the white woman as (to misappropriate Reagan) the white man's window of vulnerability.

There is a redeeming honesty to Nkosi's portrait of a society so steeped in violence that it has throttled more innocent desires. But his preoccupation with the political corruption of sex also makes his sometimes unthinking treatment of sexuality all the more jarring: "I seized her then, seized her roughly with a long stoked-up violence that was a halfway house of love, murder, and rape. I even enjoyed the swift mobile look of fear that shot across her face, but there was also in the depths of her eyes a perverse excitement. She groaned, she moaned softly." If he hopes to capture our sympathies fully, surely Nkosi is obliged to create a character who would at least recognize a rape if he were perpetrating one?

Veronica's orgasm transforms her into an "abject animal," "a crushed animal." In another sexual episode, a woman becomes "a dumb suffering beast . . . still haughty but humbled by a seemingly seething lust." When Nkosi has exhausted his menagerie, he reaches for the military motif. Female flesh "surrenders" all over the place; Veronica's nylon stockings and lace panties hang "like a conqueror's flags on the rail above the shower tap."

Nkosi, like Sibiya, has evidently been afflicted with the Helen of Troy Syndrome, the perception of women primarily as loot for male wars. He has been taken to task in the past for ill-considered remarks like "the image of the white female beauty is the one that rings most frequently the cash register of the Negro psyche. In any case, we all know how notoriously alluring women of the ruling class have always proved to be for aspiring revolutionaries, black or white." This comment, among other offenses, wipes from the record the leading role of black women in striking back against the violence of apartheid.

Mating Birds leaves me with a strong, sad sense of Nkosi writing out of the frozen time of exile. Nkosi is a rare literary survivor of the late '50s, a time in South Africa that brought forth an extraordinary flurry of talented black writers. Their ability so alarmed the regime that it determined to silence them. Their options closed down rapidly and the majority fled abroad. . . .

In the wake of that ravaged generation, the tenor of black South African writing has altered radically. The obsessions of ***Mating Birds,*** in this context, appear somewhat anachronistic. Other writers have moved well beyond stories about the isolated anger of single victims of racism and have forged, instead, a formidable literature of retaliation deeply textured with the life of the black communities. I have in mind works like Alex La Guma's *In the Fog of the Season's End,* his *Time of the Butcherbird,* and above all Mongane Serote's *To Every Birth Its Blood,* one of the most astute and affecting novels ever to come out of South Africa. . . .

In the past 70 years, over 150 black South Africans have been hanged for raping or allegedly raping women, most of them white; no white man has *ever* been executed for raping a black woman, although, given the white man's political and economic supremacy, his is by far the commoner crime. ***Mating Birds*** provides a view from below of a baroque system of legal procedure in which justice isn't even an option, far less the probable outcome. For Nkosi is at his most convincing when he intuits the power of morally tone-deaf legislation to mangle both sexual fantasy and act.

Rob Nixon, "Race Case," in The Village Voice, *Vol. XXXI, No. 30, July 29, 1986, p. 46.*

ADEWALE MAJA-PEARCE

The relationship between the black man and the white woman is a well-worn theme in African fiction. Such novels are interesting less for their literary quality than for what they tell us about the African's response to the colonial encounter. This is evident in the treatment of the women, who are made to carry a symbolic weight that has nothing to do with them as individual human beings and everything to do with them as representatives of a former colonial power. The levels of brutality inflicted on them can only be a compensatory act for the humiliations of imperialism.

It is also an outdated theme. African writers over the past decade or so have turned their attention to the more urgent issues confronting their continent. All, that is, except the South Africans; it is in South Africa, after all, that the demands of history are being resisted by the forces of the old order, with predictably violent results.

On a segregated beach in Durban a black man, on one side of the fence, catches sight of a white woman sunbathing on the other. A relationship of sorts develops between them as he becomes increasingly obsessed with her and she, in turn, flirts outrageously with him. They never speak. . . . That they can have anything approaching a normal relationship is impossible under apartheid.

One day something extraordinary happens. As they lie facing each other, the fence as always between them, the woman begins to move as though she were making love. He responds, and they both climax at the same time. The next day he follows her to her bungalow and stands outside watching her. She, noticing him, undresses in front of the open door and lies down on the bed. He enters and they make love—or perhaps it is better to say that they have sex—during which they are discovered and she accuses him of rape.

All this is recounted by the man as he sits in his prison cell awaiting execution. The ambiguity, for him, is whether or not he did in fact rape her; and if so, whether or not she invited the attack. Either way he does not blame her. . . .

The woman, then, about whom we know nothing and who is perceived only through the man himself, is a symbol of the sickness of the society. This seems to me the central problem of what [*Mating Birds*] is, as one would expect from Lewis Nkosi, a well-written novel. It means that the woman remains one-dimensional and the story itself wooden and unconvincing. There is no drama or conflict, no suggestion of the ambiguity which the author would have us believe to be at the heart of the book. The woman's extraordinary act on the beach, hardly ambiguous, is an extraordinary scene in itself, and raises the question as to whether there is more going on than even the writer is aware of. That the issue of rape even arises leads one to suspect that a fantasy is being acted out in compensation for humiliations endured, and acted out on the body of a white woman. Simply to rape her is not enough; she must be seen to collude in order for the rape to be given a justification it should never have had.

Adewale Maja-Pearce, "Compensatory Acts," in The Times Literary Supplement, *No. 4349, August 8, 1986, p. 863.*

SARA MAITLAND

I found [***Mating Birds***] a troubling and difficult novel—as I suspect Nkosi intended, though perhaps not in the way that he intended. The difficulty here is not a formal one: ***Mating Birds*** is a classic first-person account with a narrator assessing his life at its climax and end, written in moving, lucid prose with controlled flashbacks and a firmly located present. The problem is one of content. Nkosi's narrator is a South African awaiting execution at dawn for the rape of a white woman; the hero—coming from a rural childhood destroyed by apartheid land policy, a promising academic youth ruined by the racism of the university system and his own political involvement—faces up to his own sexual obsession with the woman, and indeed with white women more generally. He further acknowledges his sudden and impersonal sexual assault of her: his 'defence' is that she 'asked for it', that she was already promiscuous, cavorting naked at pornographic parties, that she blatantly 'led him on', 'wanted him to really'. And so forth: the classic defences of all rapists of all races under all regimes.

Nkosi is superficially ambiguous about his character's degree of guilt but the first person denies the woman her reality and experience, she remains pure fantasy object: the narrator says she lied. And this is an overtly political book: at the very end the political prisoners in the gaol are singing freedom songs in the dawn as he goes out to die. Surely there must be another way for Nkosi's commitment, passion and beautiful writing to describe the violence and injustice of how things are rather than this stock image of the pale evil seductress, the eternally corrupting female? The polarisation of the choice between sexism and racism cannot be part of Nkosi's political or literary intention. (p. 25)

Sara Maitland, "Small Worlds," in New Statesman, *Vol. 112, No. 2892, August 29, 1986, pp. 25-6.*

GEORGE PACKER

Mating Birds feels like the work of a superb critic. Heavy with symbolism, analytical rather than dramatic, it attempts nothing less than an allegory of colonialism and apartheid, one that dares to linger in complexity. Dr. Dufré, the Swiss criminal psychologist who pries Sibiya's story out of him "for the augmentation of scientific knowledge," wants to hear the Freudian family saga, the psychopathology of this one man. But Sibiya's tale eludes the doctor's formula; at heart this case history is political. "What in the end can we say to each other, this white man and I," thinks Sibiya, "that can break the shell of history and liberate us from the time capsule in which we are both enclosed?" For Sibiya, the crucial moment came after a fairly happy village childhood when his mother pushed him into the Lutheran seminary school: "The truth of the matter is, I am lost. To be more precise, I'm doubly lost. Unlike my father, I believe in nothing, neither in Christian immortality nor in the ultimate fellowship with the ancestral spirits."

His own experience appropriated, he turns to the temptation of his oppressors; when he is rejected intellectually, what remains is a terrible lust. The urge to "discover the sexual reasons for the white man's singular protectiveness toward his womenfolk" drains his autonomy and self-worth. The sexuality that feeds on a rotting soul is infected with oppression: it can consist only of voyeurism, the sense that life is elsewhere.

Until very near the end, Nkosi's story succeeds in powerful passages: the sudden disruption of village life that comes with [Sibiya's] father's death and the family's forced removal; the portrayal of his uneducated but ambitious mother, who slowly succumbs to the degradation of shebeen life in Durban; the desperate mood of young blacks "with a great deal of time on their hands and no idea of what to do with it.'' But the last pages can't meet the task that Nkosi has set himself.

The final scenes—the trial and the rape—present an almost insoluble problem. Nkosi has poignantly rendered a black's loss of self; but faced now with the harder task of finding a language for the white girl, the Other, he falls back on literary and political convention. Veronica turns out to be a stripper, a treacherous temptress—the ''bait'' Sibiya's old father had warned him about. Under the pressure of realism allegory turns into caricature, and Sibiya is just another victim. The language becomes stylized. At the bungalow doorway the narrator sounds like a highbrow pornographer. . . . And at the end of the book he resorts to the language of the pamphleteer. . . . (pp. 571-72)

The novel sets out to chart the hidden terrain of the oppressed, the link with the oppressor. But apartheid, dehumanizing oppressor and oppressed, is hardly available to the language of human complexity. Nearing its white-hot center, ***Mating Birds*** retreats. (p. 572)

George Packer, ''Reports from the Inside,'' in The Nation, *New York, Vol. 243, No. 17, November 22, 1986, pp. 570-74.*

Simon J. Ortiz

1941-

American poet, short story writer, essayist, and editor.

Photograph by M. Foster; reproduced by permission of Simon J. Ortiz

In his poems and short stories, Ortiz, an Acoma Pueblo Indian, develops universal significance from the experiences of Native Americans. His work is infused with Indian history, mythology, philosophy, and contemporary social concerns. Best known for his poetry, Ortiz uses simple, direct, smoothly flowing language that reflects the oral storytelling tradition of his heritage. He usually writes from the standpoint of observer, contrasting Indian and contemporary American lifestyles while interweaving sociopolitical analyses and emphasizing compassion and humanity over racial, ideological, and material concerns. Although he frequently employs an ironic and sorrowful tone, Ortiz tempers his writings with humor and optimism.

The poems in Ortiz's first full-length collection, *Going for the Rain* (1976), are structured as a journey that begins in the Indian world, goes through contemporary America, and returns to its origin. In these pieces, which are conversational in tone and contain spiritual and mythic elements, Ortiz expresses concern for his people, but his vision encompasses American society as a whole. Coyote, the traditional cultural hero of several Indian tribes, appears as a recurring narrator or subject of these and subsequent poems. A humorous, powerful, and versatile figure, Coyote functions for Ortiz as an embodiment and lover of the natural world and as a symbol of survival. *A Good Journey* (1977) continues the structure and conversational narrative of *Going for the Rain*. In this work, Ortiz writes extensively of his tribe's history and current circumstances while also addressing environmental and social issues. In some poems, Ortiz relates the effects of the modern American lifestyle upon the Indian consciousness.

Most of the poems in *From Sand Creek: Rising in This Heart Which Is Our America* (1981) depict Ortiz's experiences as a patient in a Colorado Veterans Administration hospital. He combines personal reminiscences with meditations on an Indian massacre which occurred near the site of the hospital in 1864. The main theme of this work concerns violated sacred relationships, which Ortiz conveys by focusing on the striving of his people for reconnection with the land and their heritage. Although powerful in his depiction of pain and sadness, Ortiz is optimistic for the return of human respect toward the environment. *Fight Back: For the Sake of the People, For the Sake of the Land* (1980) collects poems which detail the lives of uranium mine workers in New Mexico. "No More Sacrifices," the unifying poem in this collection, concerns an alienated narrator who envisions the Acoma people before the encroachment of white settlers. Ortiz details the effects on natives of railroads and uranium mines and the transitions these people were forced to make in their working relationship with the land. As with his other works, Ortiz concludes this volume by confidently predicting that a balance between human and environmental necessities will be successfully achieved.

Ortiz's stories are collected in *Howbah Indians* (1978) and *Fightin': New and Collected Stories* (1983). The former volume comprises poignant anecdotes about ordinary Indian experiences, through which Ortiz intimates that all events provide valuable lessons. *Fightin'* contains tales about the people of the region where Ortiz lived as a youth. The underlying theme of this work—the connection between the survival of Indians and that of the American nation as a whole—is revealed through stories depicting the struggle among his people for a higher quality of life. Ortiz suggests the mutuality between Indians and America's poor and working classes; he asserts that each has been exploited for national and economic goals. Included in this collection is the story "To Change in a Good Way," which depicts how Indian wisdom helps non-Indians endure a time of despair. Ortiz has also edited *Earth Power Coming* (1983), an anthology of Native American short fiction.

CHOICE

Ortiz, an Acoma, is one of several good Native American poets—Scott Momaday, James Welch, and Leslie Silko are others—who combine ideas, images, and ways of seeing from the Indian tradition with subjects from contemporary life. ***Going for the rain,*** his first collection, has four sections, beginning in the Acoma world, leaving this world for travels throughout the country, and then returning to home and family. The poems that consist of brief character sketches are particularly good.

A review of "Going for the Rain: Poems," in Choice, *Vol. 14, No. 2, April, 1977, p. 202.*

BRIAN SWANN

In one of [the poems in ***A Good Journey***], Ortiz tells us how to make good chili stew. Chili, beef, herbs go into it, sure. But also Rex the dog gets into the act and "the earth, clouds, sounds, the wind." The totality of life goes into the art of nourishing. The poem might be an image for the whole book. A way of life, of living, is presented to the full. . . . These are poems in the Native American oral tradition; the culture hero is Coyote, a kind of American Odysseus, surviving on his wits. The book . . . is an odyssey of America. An authentic voice is heard, poignant, tough. Ortiz is no poet of antics and gestures. There is real emotion, the genuine earth; fresh air blows through this book.

Brian Swann, in a review of "A Good Journey," in Library Journal, *Vol. 103, No. 10, May 15, 1978, p. 1065.*

KARL KROEBER

Like all the best American Indian writers, Simon Ortiz achieves originality by transforming a traditional heritage of song and story-telling. Formalistic experimentation *per se,* therefore, is of little interest to him. Modernistic verbal ingenuities are alien to his art, which, like so much traditional Indian story-telling, unpretentiously reveals the significance in ordinary experiences. The stories [in ***Howbah Indians***] show, this is to say, that there is no such thing as ordinary experience: all portions of all our life are important. But the teller so reveals not to gratify his ego, not to dazzle us with his insight, but so that we, too, may see. The Native American teller is self-effacing, because he shares, and his stories are objective, so his "ethnicity" is uniquely unrestrictive, accessible. Indian writers tend not to argue, even surreptitiously, for their ways of life. Rather, their absolute assurance about their ways of life is the condition which gives rise to story-telling. (p. 280)

The two brief opening stories, of a veteran who raises an enormous sign over a gas station he may or may not own, and the monologue of a young girl, widowed by war, leaving her home village to take a job with the Indian agency, are slight but poignantly elegant. Both unselfconsciously affiliate with traditional oral narratives in their directness, especially in ignoring analysis of motive, and in their unostentatious revelation of how personality is defined through human relationships. The last story, **"Something's Going On,"** the most ambitious and complex, is slightly flawed. I feel the central narrative within the interior of the story is still in process, and that Ortiz will improve it as he "retells" it. But **"Something's Going On"** compellingly dramatizes the trials and courage of the family of a veteran who has lost a leg in combat. Events are seen through the eyes of his young son, a device not always handled smoothly: one is aware at times of viewpoint exploited for expository purposes. But the evolution of the youngster's feelings effectively develops our perception of his father's dilemma, and the scene of the boy discovering his father's way (in all senses) is both emotionally evocative and spiritually serene.

Four cheers for Simon Ortiz. (p. 281)

Karl Kroeber, in a review of "Howbah Indians," in Western American Literature, *Vol. XIII, No. 3, November, 1978, pp. 280-81.*

WILLARD GINGERICH

Some seventy miles west of Albuquerque, south of the main highway into Gallup and Arizona, a small mesa rises three hundred feet or so in a vast landscape of low brown mountains, cliffs, and a shallow valley which rests green with centuries of nurture and carefully guarded fertility. On top of this mesa sit the irregular adobe houses of Acoma Pueblo, the Sky City, of a color with the cliffs below and invisible from a distance. This is the matrix of the Acoma people, first built, they say, sometime before history when Masaweh, one of the Divine Twins created by Earth herself, led the people up the cliffs. This is the context of Simon Ortiz's origins, and his first complete poetry collection, ***Going for the Rain,*** . . . is a vast extension, radical in its implications both socially and poetically of his knowledge of that precarious but infinitely secure American context.

The growth of writing out of indigenous sources among us shows signs of becoming our "Encyclopedia of Tlon," that complete study of another reality which Borges, in his story "Tlon Uqbar," describes slowly but inexorably dissolving the reality of common four-square occidental rationality. With this collection Ortiz shows himself one of the acutest edges of that indigenous penetration into the rotund body of Anglo-American reality, all the more acute for the apparent innocuousness, even transparency, of his voice. In a poem not in this book Ortiz describes how an Anglo couple fishing by a lake in Navajo country turn toward the narrator in alarm as their little dog bursts into frenzy, only to assure one another, "Oh, it's only an Indian." The opposite deception surfaces in **"I Told You I Like Indians"** when the narrator, driven to exasperation by the skin-level curiosity of the sight-seeing mentality ("You're Indian aren't you?"), defends himself with "Yeah, jeesus christ almighty, I'm one of them." But Ortiz is not deceived or deterred by either of these illusions; he knows the spirit of the land moves, with increasing fluency, to a new dance, in which the old voices of Acoma are as natural as the lasers of Bell Systems Labs. (pp. 18-19)

The "American sensibility" is not a commodity bought and sold like turquoise but an awareness of life and geography that finds outlet in voices as diverse as Henry James and Stick Dice Gambler, legendary practitioner of the Navajo Blessingway Chant. An Indian writer has no franchise on such consciousness, nor has he any guarantee of being more apt at its expression; it is a tradition like any other but more elusive and ill-defined than most, acquired like any other, in Eliot's painful terms, "at great labor," by Anglo, Black, Chicano, and Indian alike. If the Indian, Black, or Chicano writer has any advantage in the struggle to achieve such sensibility, it is in that his labor is greater, though not necessarily as painful, as the labor of an Anglo-American writer. This is the source of such vitality as now grows out of the "minority" literatures in vogue: not that these authors are poor, or sons of depressed and oppressed parents, or speak Spanish, or ride buses, or have no air conditioning, but that the felt distance they travel to arrive at full sensibility of themselves and their contexts is greater and generates therefore a finer tension of meaning, phrase, and allusion in their writing. Their active literary traditions, simply put, are not less but greater, and it is always the bearer of greatest tradition who eventually directs the central flow of literature in his culture.

The weight of tradition which sustains Ortiz through the poems of ***Going for the Rain*** is truly glacial. Moreover, the book is indigenist in Vallejo's terms, a work of both artistic and political inevitability and innocence—not folkloric innocence, but clairvoyant sophistication that sees the continual rebirth of spirit in all materialism. It is a diverse collection, the work of years whose unity Ortiz has called together according to the ancient formula of Pueblo rain ritual: Preparation; Leaving; Returning; The Rain Falls. This structure is also the sacred enactment of the quincunx, touching the four directions and centered about the self. As Ortiz explains in the Prologue, there is a song which says,

> Let us make our prayer songs.
> We will go now. Now we are going.
> We will bring back the shiwana.
> They are coming now. Now, they are coming.
> It is flowing. The plants are growing.

The reference to the *shiwana* is one of the very few specific uses of Pueblo mythology Ortiz makes in the entire ninety poems, and this song tells us all we need to know about them. The *shiwana* are kachina spirits who are or control the rain and all its spiritual meaning. They live somewhere west of Acoma in the mountains and inhabit rain clouds. One assumes them as one assumes the Los Alamos atomic testing grounds to the northeast. (pp. 19-21)

The voices of Ortiz's indigenism are diverse, and they begin with Coyote, the ubiquitous storyteller, at creation itself. " 'First of all, it's all true,' " he assures us, and at once we are on guard, aware we are on a voyage of playful irony where wit and laughter will be our only defenses. (p. 22)

The quality of . . . belief in Coyote's voice(s) is a current that rises and falls through the collection, through scenes as diverse as Pacific beaches, Florida bars, Kennedy airport, and of course the Pueblo and Navajo Nations, where moments of diaphanous beauty occur. Nor is Coyote any respector of persons. . . . In another time, as a boy following Coyote's tracks along the stream near Acoma, the narrator tells how he was startled by the blast of a shotgun, and suddenly Coyote was in him. "The animal in me crouches, poised immobile, eyes trained on the distance." This instinctual response to visceral fear left the knowledge that

> Coyote's preference is for silence
> broken only by the subtle wind,
> uncanny bird sounds, saltcedar scraping,
>
> and the desire to let that man free,
> to listen for the motion of sound.

It is in that desire "to listen for the motion of sound" that Ortiz's indigenism passes over into the broader dimensions of his tradition, into that language common to a whole American sensibility. These are listening and speaking poems, and the grace of interplay in voices is such that one can say poetry occurs, and its occurrence is often the leap between mythic being and casual conversation with a child's easy complexity. . . . Listening for "the motion of sound" gives Ortiz a true mythic attention to objects, an attention of the sort W. S. Merwin does not achieve in spite of his assertions in "Mythic Thinking." In a prose meditation appended to a poem called "Buzzard" Ortiz touches the current of mythic thinking that reaches back to the poet-creators of Pueblo religion, and is, at once, a comment on that thinking.

> I've heard an older man say, "They take the eyes first." I wonder why? I think it must have to do with ritual, some distinct memory consistent with the history of its preceding generations. And the buzzard pays ritual homage to the memory of its line, the tradition that insures that things will continue. Yes, that must be what it is. Eyes have a quality of regenerating visions which must continue first and last of all.

This is a truly ancient American voice, the acute natural observation combined with profound anthropomorphic awareness which characterizes the best of native North American myth, yet cast in English rhythms with the authentic contemporaneity of Robert Creeley. This is mythic thinking profoundly indigenous, but accessible in its implications to us all.

The measure of any poet's voice must finally rest in the quality of the tension he sustains between the widest common speech of his time and the pure rhythms of human sound he is able to extract from that speech. It is an ideal rather more complex than Eliot's "common speech of cultivated men"; more to the point is Zukofsky's eminently useful definition of poetry as a mathematical integral between the two infinite terms, common speech and music, never resting in the former but never purely achieving the latter. My quotations have already demonstrated the direct feeding of speech into Ortiz's verse, immediately obvious in the most casual reading; but has he found in that speech a music of sufficient grace and subtlety to mark it off as poetry? There is a markedly smooth and readable surface quality to Ortiz's work which might be misread at first as prosaic and not, as I believe it is, a remarkable transparency of language whose range and freshness is worth serious attention, combining the irony of Coyote with the conversational rhythms of Ezra Pound.

There are first the language and tones of his own background. "I try to listen to the voices of the people back home," Ortiz has said, "and use their sounds to direct my composition." These voices are a new rhythm for English poetry, and "a new rhythm is a new idea." There is first his father; "His voice, the slight catch / the depth from his thin chest." And there is the private song of that voice, recalling the father's father, and by implication the infinity of fathers before, always held just that one generation away. . . . The father who says the things of a thousand generations, things accessible only through that voice. We touch here the sacred core of what oral tradition means to those who carry it, not only in the grand affairs of religion and culture, but in the small, everyday acts of family life. Some degree of the conviction in Ortiz's rhythms must surely come from this glacial memory of voices that is oral tradition. Its depth is almost incomprehensible, yet its voice is always near, its tone continuous in the poet's memory, and its artistic implications complex. . . . The voice of the glacier itself is there, in living memory. . . . Then there is the voice of singing, apt to break in at any moment. . . . And there is a further, private voice, not singing, but prepared and directed by the songs. (pp. 22-5)

The diversity of these rhythms, easy and accessible in their attachment to contemporary American English as it plays in our mouths and yet arranged with the smooth grace of endurance in the play of syllable against syllable and image against image, argues a poetic range of major proportion. It is linguistic intelligence and sensitivity that makes a poet, nothing more or less, and Ortiz demonstrates such sensitivity with a force that is seductive and compelling. Just how compelling became apparent to me in comparing two of his pieces with two poems by Frost. **"How Close"** brought to mind Frost's "For Once, Then, Something." . . . The rhythms [in **"How Close"**] are not as complex as Frost's, but word for word it carries more variation, more music. And Coyote, whose intricacy I have hinted at, adds a dimension to the narrative self totally inaccessible to Frost. The "mica stratum," in context with the mother, her pottery clay, and Coyote's curiosity, is an image at least as intellectually muscular as Frost's "a something white, uncertain" in its context of poetic mimesis and spiritual typology in nature—or lack of it.

More impressive is the reflection of **"A Story of How a Wall Stands"** against Frost's "Mending Wall." . . . Here, in a shorter space, I find both rhythm and thought equal to Frost in subtlety and suggestiveness, though more limited in music for the lesser word-notes to play on. In comparison with Ortiz's power of allusion within succinct statement and observation, his refusal to moralize, Frost's first lines . . . almost seem padded and rhetorical. The interwovenness of bones, stone, and mud in Ortiz's wall is a complex image of foundations, implying a specific vision of human society, and with political overtones as clear as those in Frost's unnecessary wall.

Though consistently refusing to moralize over or around his images, Ortiz permeates the image itself with moral sense, with a social vision that touches even the most personal functions and experiences. The ritual format of the book itself—going out and returning—is an image of action taken not for personal aggrandizement but for benefit of the community. It is an anthropological cliché that Pueblo culture encourages the suppression of individualism to the prior demands of communal life; Ortiz has not suppressed but expanded his concern for community to us all. His theme is survival. . . . While he is often preoccupied with the continuity of Indian culture, "how we have been able / to survive insignificance," Ortiz is too astute not to see the intimate interconnections between Indian survival and the sickness in the larger American community. His politics are as radical as they are simple and direct. . . . (pp. 26-8)

The concern translates often to attention for children, and there are many passages addressed to them with proportionate simplicity, sometimes as straightforward poetry of statement, extracting essential wisdom from the complex problems of survival. . . . At his most lucid points this moral vision blends into the poetics and even the physical sight of the narrator. Pound once said we all live in certain landscapes, and through the movement of the eye rhythms are imparted to or through the physical movement of the body. In a passage which is key to his entire collection, and unique, I believe, in contemporary writing for its combination of clear expression, unifying vision, and vital utility, Ortiz develops the full implications of that idea.

> On Friday, Joy and I talked
> about sense of presence.
> What is it? How does it come about?
> I think it has to do
> with a sense of worth, dignity,
> and how you fit with occasion, place,
> people, and time.
> It's also a physical thing,
> carriage of body,
> hand and head movements,
> eyes fixed upon specific points.
> And then it is an ability
> which is instinctive and spiritual
> to convey what you see
> to those around you.
> Essentially, it is how you fit
> into that space which is yourself,
> how well and appropriately.

I can find little in current writing that offers me, personally and poetically, as much.

Ortiz is an "Indian" poet as Gerard Manley Hopkins is "Catholic." The values they embody and pursue move with the spirit of the language itself, and are at once beyond and inseparable from the images in which those values are given life. I too, with Ortiz, believe Coyote, as with Hopkins I believe Duns Scotus.

There is a ceremony of initiation for village leaders at Acoma in which the initiates go to distant springs in the four directions, leaving prayer sticks at each spring and bringing water back from each to the pueblo. With this book Ortiz performs such an investiture, becoming "War Chief" (as these leaders were called) of a larger Acoma. He will not, I think, succumb to the commercial pressures the "ethnic" industry will bring upon him. The political pressures are more subtle and perhaps pressing. The most flawed poem I find in this collection, one called **"Relocation,"** is an attempt to speak the bitterness of Any Lost Indian in the urban wilderness, but goes empty for lack of an emphatic and specific image. Occasionally other lines suffer the same disjunction between political and poetic obligations, apparently written in the pressure of those moments when the sense of an entire culture's suffering is intense but before its image comes clear. **"Relocation"** is canceled out, however, by **"Blues Song for the Phoenix Bus Depot Derelict"**; the image is luminous, the voice is clear.

Nor will Ortiz go academic; his simplicity is already too profound to fall prey to illusory complexities. Telling how he camped one cold night by the road in the Navajo Nation, he brings all those complexities down to one sustaining point, one desire:

> In the morning,
> I woke up to find
> a puppy, you, yapping
> like the original life,
> a whole mystery crying
> for sustenance.
>
> We prayed.
>
> What I want is a full life
> for my son,
> for myself,
> for my Mother,
> the Earth.

(pp. 28-30)

Willard Gingerich, "'The Old Voices of Acoma': Simon Ortiz's Mythic Indigenism," in Southwest Review, *Vol. 64, No. 1, Winter, 1979, pp. 18-30.*

PATRICIA CLARK SMITH

[*The essay excerpted below was originally published in* Minority Voices, *Spring, 1979*.]

Coyote's been showing his face these last ten years and more in a lot of [poetical works]. . . . There's a whole debate going on about the legitimacy of these sightings, about whether Anglo poets have the reason and the right to appropriate Coyote as their own. That they do so, of course, is not surprising; for better or worse, Coyote has always been as he is in the traditional Pueblo and Navajo oral tales, too striking a presence not to attract attention, whether envious or scornful. (p. 193)

Of all contemporary poets' Coyotes, Ortiz' is the most natural, the least self-conscious, the least tamed and trained to do vaudeville turns, the least given to emitting offstage howls just to provide atmosphere. Perhaps this is true because Ortiz is an American Indian; in any case, Ortiz writes out of a deep familiarity with Coyote and coyotes and is, quite simply, a fine poet. To be sure, Ortiz' Coyote also lusts and flimflams and brags, but Ortiz' art reaches beneath this popular Coyote surface to reveal depths and nuances of Coyote's character that underlie or are implied in the traditional tales of his fortunes. This Coyote is no mere con man, no stubborn self-preserver, although he knows that con games and self-preservation are important. Simon Ortiz' Coyote was present at the creation, and Ortiz reveals Coyote's profound connection with the natural world; he shows us the complex spirit that lies beneath the comic hide. If comparing Coyote to Buddha makes some of us uneasy, maybe we would come closer to the truth by saying that Coyote's antisocial and outrageous behavior, like that of Pueblo clowns, springs not merely from foolishness and conceit, but from a vision of creation so deep and true that it can make human rules for proper behavior and discreet action seem ripe for mocking. (p. 194)

In any event, the Ortiz Coyote is no one-dimensional comic; his comedy embraces tragedy and touches on high truth. Yellowman, the Navajo storyteller, told Barre Toelken that Coyote stories "are not funny stories. . . . Listeners are laughing at the way Ma'ii [the Navajo name for Coyote] does things, and at the way the story is told. Many things about the story are funny, but the story is not funny." And Yellowman also said, in explanation of Coyote's wildly inconsistent behavior, "If he did not do all those things, then those things would not be possible in the world." In his myriad-mindedness, his actions silly and shrewd, Coyote establishes the range of human possibility. He is what we are and what we could be.

From one poem to another, Ortiz' Coyote reveals that range of possibilities. Sometimes he appears in his most popular incarnation—Old Man Coyote, southwestern Trickster, scruffy charmer, and chump. A number of Ortiz' poems are retellings—in which he deftly creates a sense of both storyteller and responding audience—of tales in which Coyote figures as a sort of negative behavior model, a creature delightfully uncontented to be modest, careful, chaste, and incurious. In **"Telling about Coyote,"** from ***Going for the Rain,*** Coyote gambles away for all eternity his luxuriant fur coat; in **"And there is always one more story,"** from the same book, Coyote—a female this time—suspended over a cliff from helpful Grandmother Spider's anchor skein, falls to her death because she can't resist peeking up Grandmother's dress.

Ortiz' Coyote, then, in the most popular tradition, is often self-destructive and foolish. But throughout the body of Ortiz' work, even more so than in the traditional oral tales, the emphasis is unremittingly on Coyote's survival. The old stories Ortiz chooses to retell and the new situations he records or invents all make Coyote's continuance far more prominent than his foolhardiness. Even though, as Ortiz says, there is of course "always one more story," many of the traditional tales Ortiz *could* choose from do end momentarily in indignity, injury, or death, with Coyote's restoration understood and remarked, occurring somehow in the silence between the completion of one tale and the beginning of the next. For example, in one much-recorded story, "Coyote and Horned Toad," told at Acoma and elsewhere, a story that Ortiz does *not* use, Coyote—or Tsuushki, as he calls himself in Keresan—is enraptured by Horned Toad's singing and asks to be taught his song. Horned Toad obliges, and Tsuushki trots off singing, only to forget the song when he is startled by a flight of ducks noisily taking off. He returns to Horned Toad, who has anticipated Coyote's scatterbrained forgetfulness and has casually slipped out of his skin and wrapped it around a sharp flint. When the skin doesn't respond to Coyote's four ritual requests for a reprise of the song, Coyote grows angry, snaps the skin up, and swallows it, and "the sharp flint within cut his stomach and throat, and he died." (pp. 194-95)

Significantly, Ortiz' Coyote stories never end in this way; Coyote always gets up and brushes himself off and trots away *within* the narrative itself, perhaps not quite as good as new, but alive, in motion, surviving. In the gambling tale, for example, mice take pity on Coyote's naked body and patch together a substitute pelt out of old fur scraps and pitch; after Grandmother Spider has indignantly let Coyote Lady plunge to her death, Skeleton Fixer happens upon her dried remains at the foot of a mesa and by his magic makes the dry bones live. In the sequence from ***A Good Journey*** that begins, "Like myself, the source of these stories is my home . . . ," an Acoma man, an in-law invited along on a rabbit hunt, kills Coyote even though the Laguna field chief has already warned him to avoid shooting Coyote at all costs for the sake of the Laguna Coyote clan people. The Coyote clansmen, of course, chase the culprit, hollering what Ortiz translates as "you confounded no-good dirty Acoma," but "Coyote suddenly jumped up and he ran away," and the Acoma gets a reprieve. . . . In Ortiz' stories, you never need to worry; Coyote will indeed be back, and you don't have to wait around long for his resurrection.

Even in one teller's stories, Coyote is never quite the same, even in stories that turn on the same theme. Movingly, Ortiz assumes a gentler tone in his short story **"Men on the Moon,"** as he tells of a far less jaunty Coyote, also threatened, also surviving. Faustin, an old Acoma man, watches with concern a film of a moon rocket blasting off on the new tv his daughter has given him, and then he falls asleep to dream of a terrible *mahkina,* an apocalyptic engine that reminds Faustin of drilling rigs he has seen, moving inexorably across the landscape on metal legs, crushing trees and causing streams to boil. In the dream, as Flintwing Boy watches its terrible progress, Tsushki the Coyote runs to his side, breathless and trembling with fear. Flintwing Boy soothes him, calms him, and together the two perform a ceremony, facing the east and praying for protection and guidance: "that is all we ask," says Flintwing Boy. Then he sends Coyote off to warn the people that they must come together and decide what to do, while he remains to observe: "Coyote turned and began to run. He stopped several yards away. Hahtrudzaimah, he called. Like a man of courage, Anawah, like a man."

The dream gives Faustin reassurance; like the drillers around Acoma, the misguided scientists may give up if they do not find what they are looking for, in this case, "knowledge useful in finding out where everything began and how everything was made"—knowledge, of course, in which the puzzled old man at Acoma, watching the expensive and complex rocket on tv, is already secure. (pp. 195-96)

The significance of Ortiz' special feeling for Coyote as resister and survivor is made explicit in this story. As an American Indian and as a lover of the natural world, Ortiz finds no fact of history more moving than any creature's survival; while whole species and whole groups of human beings have been assisted into oblivion, others have managed to persist. At a poetry reading in Albuquerque several years ago, Ortiz spoke with delight of the native flocks of crows and ravens that scrounge the yards and parks of suburban Albuquerque, unloved by indignant householders, yet still thriving and vocal. And likewise, for all the official and unofficial policies of genocide, for all the *mahkinas,* "Indians are everywhere": this is Simon Ortiz' proudest and most repeated theme. A park ranger in Florida may tell him that "This place is noted for the Indians / That don't live here any more," and yet a "big Sioux" walks unexpectedly into a bar in Flagler Beach ("Christ's sake, how's relocation, Brother?"). The owner of a hot dog stand in Pensacola can direct him to the home of big Chief Alvin McGee in Almore, Alabama, whose face reminds the poet of the face of his grandfather, of the mountains of home, of the old Creek faces "when they bothered to put them in the history books," Chief Alvin McGee, who, out of his large vitality, will smile and bless the poet. "You meet Indians everywhere," and Coyote, another American Indian who has also insisted on staying around "like a man," to the annoyance of many, is a natural embodiment of that proud Indian survival.

But Coyote is important in Ortiz' works as more than an emblem of blessed Indian chutzpah and sheer cussed Indian continuance. Ortiz' narrative strategies are interesting. Sometimes he tells *about* Coyote, as an observer, a third-person voice, most often in the poems that retell the old stories, that deal with Coyote the comic shill, the Coyote who manages to survive his own cleverness. But in other poems Ortiz draws into a closer narrative relationship with Coyote, taking on the persona himself, and he does so most often in those poems in which Coyote is something like a seer. Consider **"How Close,"** in ***Going for the Rain:***

> I wonder if I have ever come close
> to seeing the first seed, the origin,
> and where?
> I've thought about it, says Coyote.
>
> Once I thought I saw it in the glint
> of a mica stratum a hairbreadth deep.
> I was a child then,
> cradled in my mother's arms.
> We were digging for the gray clay
> to make pottery with.
>
> That was south of Acoma years back;
> that was the closest I've gotten yet.
>
> I've thought about it, says Coyote.
>
> (pp. 196-97)

Coyote here remembers a moment of pure childhood vision when, like one of Blake's innocent augurs, he comes close to glimpsing the world, not in a grain of sand, but in a mica hairline in a bank of clay, a crack that seems to hold the possibility of opening out and permitting him to glance into the heart of creation.

The poet's deepest self lives in touch with that creation, and Ortiz' name for that self is Coyote. In the poems, Coyote is often a voice speaking straight out of the genes, out of both tribal and personal memory. In **"Albuquerque Back Again, 12/6/74,"** Ortiz again takes on Coyote's voice as he recalls an act of communion with the mountains before a return to urban life, to

> the traffic
> and ordinary insanity
> of people going places
> they might not actually know
> the destinations of . . .

Coyote touches the mountains as some bless themselves with holy water before leaving a church, in hope that touch will sustain them in the world beyond the doors of the sanctuary. . . . (pp. 197-98)

Coyote, then, draws strength from touching the earth, the natural world of which he is at once a part and a worshiper. But Ortiz sees Coyote's survival as tenuous, constantly threatened not alone by Coyote's propensity to do himself in, the main threat in the traditional Coyote stories, but also by a *mahkina* world, a world grown noisy, heedless, and hostile to coyotes and to the Coyote in the Indian, in the poet. In **"The Boy and the Coyote,"** the speaker is confined to a veterans' hospital, a circumstance hinted at in the dedication of the poem and chronicled more fully in the hospital poems of ***A Good Journey.*** As he walks the saltcedar thickets beside the Arkansas River, he remembers his childhood self. If in **"How Close"** he remembers being the Coyote-child drawing near to seeing the infinite in a mica hairline, here he remembers and feels "lonesome" for that same child's auditory sense, a hearing so acute as to bring him into a mystic's union with the life around him. Here, he so clearly remembers the listening boy he once was that memory slides out of the past and into the present tense: "He listens to the river / The slightest nuance of sound."

Fittingly, at this moment when through memory he is united with the child in him, he comes across the prints of the animal who is the natural emblem of what lies deepest in him, a self that somehow endures despite the indignities and distractions of hospitals and exile, a self that is always there, awaiting rediscovery, and leaving signs of its continuing presence. . . . (p. 198)

This moment of discovery and integration is shattered by the reports of a shotgun. The moment widens out as the speaker, now fully one with Coyote, freezes, encroached upon and threatened, but with his senses honed once more to that childhood Coyote acuity. . . .

This is a world where shotgun blasts reverberate through Coyote's thicket, where men are confined in hospitals. And yet the speaker, for all his fear, is able to affirm his deepest Coyote-loves, his continuing desire to be the one who listens for the mystery, for the pulse of the blood's country, for what lies at the heart of things. . . .

But the most beautiful and moving transformation Ortiz works on the Coyote of oral tradition is to make Coyote himself into the loremaster, the preserver and teller of the stories, as well as the chief and most multifarious character in them. (p. 199)

Although I know of no Acoma tradition in which Coyote himself is the teller of the tales and the one most aware of their importance, the role Ortiz gives him is a logical imaginative extension of Coyote's personality both in nature—his is the most striking natural voice of the Southwest—and in the old tales. For one thing, the Coyote of these tales, while he may not be a storyteller in the sense of a keeper and passer-on of lore vital to his people, is highly verbal, to put it mildly, a storyteller in the sense that he is consummately skilled at pulling the wool over people's eyes and talking them into doing things. In the crudest sense, like any con man, he survives, he "continues," by telling stories. On the surface, at least, his credibility is low among the creatures (including human beings) who have been hanging out with him for millennia. (pp. 199-200)

Still, for someone widely known as a braggart and a trickster, Coyote's batting average is not zero. In the **"Like Myself"** sequence from ***A Good Journey,*** Pehrru—Coyote in his Old Man form—with a few well-chosen laconic words convinces a troop of white soldiers that a kettle that happens to be resting on hot ashes is really a magic kettle that boils all by itself without fire, and he sells the kettle to them after much well-acted reluctance. . . . (p. 200)

In the kettle story, the soldiers are gullible, and the trick is both easy and sweet. But even with a tougher audience, where Coyote's survival depends not on gulling people but rather on winning them over, Coyote can sometimes succeed, as in **"And Another One,"** when Coyote comes across four people eating supper. They are not pleased to see him:

> One of them said
> "There comes Pehrru.
> Don't anyone invite him to sit down and eat.
> He's much of a liar."

Gradually, however, Pehrru-Coyote works the conversation around to a tale about a cow that has given birth to five calves:

> One of them, beloved, was just standing around,
> looking hungry, not feeding because
> as you know, cows usually have only four nipples. . . .

At that, the four invite Coyote to sit down and eat, not because Coyote has tricked them into it, but because the tale shrewdly suggests the sorrow and the pity of his own hunger and, more especially, the unnaturalness of hunger unappeased.

In a number of poems, Ortiz confronts the issue of Coyote's credibility and, for the most part, concludes that one must know when to trust him and have the faith to do so at those times. In **"The Creation, According to Coyote,"** the fine poem that opens ***Going for the Rain,*** Ortiz begins with a reference to the problem of credibility. . . . Coyote goes on to recount the Acoma creation story, the tale of the emergence of the first people in their soft larvaelike form out of the First World. . . . (pp. 200-01)

In this poem, although the speaker will ultimately believe Coyote, Ortiz, until the last line, deliberately maintains a tension between the stereotype—the Coyote we wouldn't trust as far as we could throw him—and certain facts that argue strongly for Coyote's trustworthiness on this particular matter. In the first place, Ortiz gives Coyote a story to tell that the imagined Acoma audience already knows and accepts as true, since it is the orthodox Keresan creation story. The People really *do* emerge from the lower world; hero twins really *are* born to lead them. In the second place, Ortiz here puts Coyote in impeccable company, because the story is told not only by Coyote but also by the speaker's uncle, the male relative who is his proper teacher, the child's natural external source of true stories about his own people. The story is generally accepted to be true; uncles are trustworthy in such matters; both Coyote and the uncle tell the story. The audience, then, knows that Coyote is a truthteller even before the last line certifies him as one.

Ortiz plays throughout with the shiftiness of the stereotypical Coyote—"You know how he is"—but the way he is, really, is the way good poets are: he is to be believed on the matters that count the most, to be believed from the gods' perspective, to be believed in a realm of meaning that lies beyond surface manipulative foolery. For instance, Ortiz states that Coyote "was b.s.-ing probably" when he lay claim to Uyuyayeh and Masaweh as his brothers, but probably it is a Coyote lie on only the most literal level. From the gods' point of view, the world is intended to be a place of reciprocity and mutual alliance, a world of brothers. Incredible things like creations do happen, have happened, and one loses out on something precious and life-restoring by narrowly mistrusting Coyote just because of his surface trickiness, his propensity to sell you a wormy sack of flour or to speak in metaphor and hyperbole. On the important matters, he knows. He was there. And so are the stylistic signals; Ortiz hems and haws parenthetically in the lines where he is discussing Coyote's credibility, but when he switches to retelling the story that the supposed charlatan told him, the pace alters radically. Ortiz' narrative of the creation itself, derived from both uncle and Coyote, is firm, rapid, authoritative, carrying with it all the emotional energy of conviction. The questioning of credibility is almost ritual; the speaker *knows* that Coyote knows, when it comes to important things. (p. 202)

One can say of Coyote's stories what one says of all good poetry: even if it didn't really happen, it's true. The simple facts, in this case, are as much to be marveled at as any embellishment that a storyteller might give them: a blonde girl and a ginger cake materialize out of the night, reminding us of the man—perhaps a mountain kachina or perhaps just a Navajo—who appears to the narrator in Leslie Silko's "Yellow Woman." In any event, we can trust Coyote about the heart of the matter: something strange and wonderful has happened.

Coyote, then, gets to be the storyteller and the poet in Ortiz' works for a number of reasons: because of his traditional verbal skills and his ultimate reliability and because "you know, Coyote / is in the origin and all the way / through," as Ortiz remarks in **"Telling about Coyote,"** the opening poem of ***A Good Journey***. . . . In mythic time, throughout historical time, in personal present-day experience, Coyote has been there and seen it all, and he is one of the best witnesses to the multiplicity, to the "many exciting and colorful and tragic things of adventure."

We should take note of one remaining affinity between Coyote and poet that Ortiz seems especially drawn to: the particular way in which both manage to continue. The central Coyote poem that sets forth this shared method of survival is **"And there is always one more story,"** the tale of Coyote Lady and Skeleton Fixer that I referred to earlier. . . . Ortiz is unusually concerned to establish this particular tale as ancient and well shared, as one of the stories Indians always tell in order to continue. Furthermore, of all the poems, this is the one on which he lavishes the most care in trying to create a sense of the storytelling occasion, with interjections from children's voices and familiar asides from the speaker ("I don't know why she wasn't grinding corn too—that's just in the story''), asides that break into the formal pattern of the narrative.

The images in Ortiz' tale of Coyote and Skeleton Fixer underlie a number of his poems about the survival of the American Indian coyote-poet. Even where they do not specifically invoke Coyote, the poems say that the poet, like Coyote, can be renewed from fragments. In the poet's case, they are fragments of his culture, not of his physical body, and the renewal comes about not through Skeleton Fixer's magic but from the miracle of his own will to remember and cherish, and so to survive.

Two poems in particular—**''Fragment''** and **''The Poems I Have Lost,''** both from ***Going for the Rain***—embody most explicitly this theme of the poet re-creating himself from fragments. In **''Fragment,''** the renewal is possible, not because of bones, but rather through a small stone. . . . (p. 206)

The speaker tells us he is on his way ''to be judged again,'' implying but not detailing the actions and events that have eroded his sense of himself. Easter is approaching, the Christian festival of redemption and the time of seasonal renewal for the whole natural world. It is a time to wish for a new beginning, to wish ''that I had never / been in jail / that first time.'' The speaker knows that his wish is ''vain,'' but the hope of finding himself again is not. The stone is the fragment that recalls for the speaker the origins, the heart of things, that which endures despite his present circumstances. It embodies what Ortiz, in the preface of ***A Good Journey,*** says is necessary for people to survive; it tells him something about himself that he needs to know, just as children need to know ''how they were born, how they came to this certain place, how they continued.'' The little stone is a fragment of the earth's center, just as the mica hairline can be ''the first seed, the origin''; it is a fragment from which all other things that matter may be inferred. It enables him to transcend the present circumstances of loss and self-destruction, and the story of finding it becomes, in itself, a story of how he continues. The stone is indeed a **''Fragment,''** but it is enough.

''The Poems I Have Lost'' presents a tale that is almost a contemporary analogue to the story of Coyote and Skeleton Fixer. . . . (p. 207)

As in the tale of Coyote and Skeleton Fixer, Ortiz seems careful here to present the situation as not entirely the result of either a hostile world or a personal weakness. To be sure, he begins the poem by evoking a vision of an impersonal urban America, where subways bewilder, where apartments need five locks, where neither letters nor poets can be certain of finding their destination. Nonetheless, it *is* a world containing friends to whom one is moved to write, where there are still sunsets, where one meets openhearted people, where even strangers ask to hear poems, and where, sometimes, the impersonal postal service *does* function, but the poet does not. Ortiz is too honest, too good a poet, to indulge in mere angry militancy, unilaterally denouncing Amerika-spelled-with-a-k. As the speaker straightforwardly admits, human fallings-off into alcohol and forgetfulness and despair do occur, and Anglo *mahkina* America and the speaker himself both seem reciprocally involved in the falls that occur here. The falls are not, in this case, from mesa tops, but from horseback, from the gangways of planes, and they are falls that are outward signs of deeper fallings away, forgetting one's origins, where one is going on the journey. Still, the important thing seems not to assign blame but to get the scattered self back together, to flesh out the bones. And, as in the old Coyote tale, there *are* bones. The speaker may fall, poems may be lost in some indefinite space, but something even more important than the poems remains, and that is the source of the poems: the bare skeletons, the old things.

Memory, then, and a sense of continuity. If the speaker can retain the old stories and traditions, nothing is really lost. Ortiz here is talking about more than the possibility of reconstructing lost manuscripts from memory. The surface of the world has altered desperately and a person can feel overwhelmed by the loss of a vital culture, of the native Coyote-self. But despite appearances, Ortiz in his poetry, like Leslie Silko in *Ceremony,* is saying that the old stories are more than cultural artifacts and childhood memories. They hold true and remain relevant as a way of understanding the world; indeed, the old stories are still going on, continuing to happen. In **''The Poems I Have Lost,''** the ''new visages pass many many times,'' again and again, because beneath those new visages lie old bones. In remembering what is old, one can deal with what is new. Coyote is not dead; his bones are continually being refleshed. Nor is the poet's self lost as long as he can hang on to the truth of that continuance, as long as he can remember and pass on the stories.

Flintwing Boy, then, is not just a cardboard figure in an old man's tale. He is alive in a new form and confronting old enemies. Coyote is not to be met with only in quaint stories that happened, if they ever did happen, back in ''myth time.'' He walks Albuquerque's Central Avenue, shows up at the Laguna fiesta, hangs out around a campus in Tulsa. These days, he is even writing some pretty fine poems about himself, poems about his continuing presence that in themselves are powerful restoratives. Ask him his name, and he'll probably grin and give you some long story about how he's this and that and his name is legion. But one of his right names, surely, is Simon Ortiz. (pp. 208-09)

Patricia Clark Smith, ''Coyote Ortiz: 'Canis Latrans Latrans' in the Poetry of Simon Ortiz,'' in Studies in American Indian Literature: Critical Essays and Course Designs, *edited by Paula Gunn Allen, The Modern Language Association of America, 1983, pp. 192-210.*

GEARY HOBSON

A Good Journey is the second collection of poems by Simon J. Ortiz, not including two slim chapbooks that appeared with little notice several years ago. Partly because of the chapbooks, but largely because his poetic voice is unique, Ortiz has been recognized for the past ten years, especially in Indian circles all across the nation, as possibly the best contemporary Native American poet. . . . [His first collection, ***Going for the Rain***], received enthusiastic response from readers and critics alike. Now ***A Good Journey*** is out . . . and at 165 pages, it is a remarkably substantial book of poems, both in size and content, and one that should do much in establishing Ortiz as not only the major contemporary Indian poet but as a major American poet as well.

While Ortiz is certainly concerned with his particular Acoma Pueblo Indian heritage, and mirrors his tribe's history and present-day circumstances in almost every line of his work, it would be a disservice to overlook his contribution as a remarkably incisive critic of contemporary society, both in the Indian as well as the non-Indian world. For instance, few poets writing today are more deeply concerned with environmental issues. In **''For Our Brothers: Blue Jay, Gold Finch, Flicker, Squir-**

rel," the poet presents a series of elegies for each of these birds and animals, killed by passing motorists and seen lying dead at the side of the highway. The poem contains a subtitle, or explanatory note, which reads: "Who perished lately in this most unnecessary war, saw them lying off the side of a state road in southwest Colorado," and the poet tells us in the first line "they all loved life / And suddenly, / it just stopped for them."

As modern American life presses irrevocably upon the Indian world, the poet in **"Long House Valley Poem"** observes the contrasts:

The Yei
and hogans and the People
and roadside flowers
and cornfields and the sage
and the valley peace,
They are almost gone.

Lately, quite a few non-Indian poets are writing "Coyote" poems, using the quintessential trickster figure of Western Indian tribes as the principal symbolic character. It is refreshing to read Ortiz's poems about Coyote, in which the persona of Coyote is seen in the most authentic way possible and not merely as a convenient literary symbol culled from textbooks and other second-rate poems. (pp. 87-8)

Geary Hobson, in a review of "A Good Journey," in Western American Literature, *Vol. XIV, No. 1, May, 1979, pp. 87-9.*

THE SMALL PRESS REVIEW

This new book of poems by Native American Simon Ortiz [***From Sand Creek***] is named for the site of the unspeakable massacre of the peaceful Cheyenne and Arapaho in 1864. The poems are in some measure inspired by the fact and consequences of this horror of history. But they do not stop there; they move to present understandings and future hopes. The poems tell of both crying and singing, of "Dreams / thinned / and split," of "October songs" in the glory of Autumn, and they are populated with farmers, magpies, Salvation Army clerks, Texans, and always, always the spirit of Indians, children, old ones, young men who dream of California, those dead and those waiting.

Ortiz says in his preface:

> A Poet never knows how successful he is sharing his words—or how unsuccessful. . . .

In this gracefully designed and carefully crafted book, Ortiz is certainly "successful". The poems are a rare gift.

A review of "From Sand Creek," in The Small Press Review, *Vol. 13, No. 11, November, 1981, p. 8.*

CHOICE

[***From Sand Creek: Rising in This Heart Which Is Our America***] is a collection of poems in which Ortiz focuses on experiences he had in a Veterans Administration Hospital in eastern Colorado and contrasts those experiences with meditations on the Sand Creek massacre, which occurred near the hospital. . . . The poems come to the reader as the observations of a traveler, as in Ortiz's other collections, ***Going for the Rain*** . . . and ***A Good Journey***. . . . No one has traveled the paths Ortiz has and returned to tell the stories of his travel. This is a painful journey reported in sharp, exact language that is written for the voice. No other Indian poet presently writing can equal Ortiz in evoking such a range of experience and emotion.

A review of "From Sand Creek: Rising in This Heart Which Is Our America," in Choice," *Vol. 19, No. 5, January, 1982, p. 628.*

HAROLD JAFFE

American Indians have always known a good deal about relationships, communion; more than others, their relationships have been forcibly severed. Ortiz's fundamental theme concerns these sacred relationships—and their violations. Although his poems are usually about American Indians, the audience addressed in his work includes the poor, the dispossessed *and* the untranquilized middle class of various hues.

Both new volumes of poetry are testimonials: ***Fight Back*** to the revolt of the Pueblos (along with mestizos, mulattoes, Navahos and Apaches) against the Spanish colonialists in 1680; ***From Sand Creek*** marks the 1864 massacre of 133 Arapahoes and Cheyennes, nearly all women and children, in southeastern Colorado.

From Sand Creek is the more cohesive volume of the two. It contains forty-two poems on consecutive recto pages, with the same number of brief prose passages on the facing versos. The prose often introduces a theme or an image that is taken up in the corresponding poem or elsewhere in the volume. Most of the poems contain details about a Veterans Administration hospital in Fort Lyons, Colorado, where their narrator is a patient in 1974 and 1975. . . .

The words and images with which Ortiz repeatedly characterizes the hospitalized Indians are *blood, dream, breath, shadow, compassion, memory, love, ghost*. Combined, these words have the impact of a mountain or tree rooted in the natural cycle, which, when unimpeded, is perpetual. Only there is impediment everywhere in Ortiz's poems, and his people are reduced to shadows striving, usually fruitlessly, to reconnect with their bodies, their earth, their birthright. . . . (p. 406)

Almost seamlessly, Ortiz imbues his sad, spare hospital scenes not only with the dreadful echo of the Sand Creek massacre but with a selective history of Native American faith, oppression and resistance. Yet the cumulative impression is, admirably, not of gloom and despair but of a renewed faith in the prospect of relationship with the land and solidarity among the dispossessed.

The single non-Indian literary precedent for these poems who comes to mind is Whitman during the Civil War, especially in his "Wound Dresser" letters from the veterans hospitals in Washington, D.C. Ortiz is himself a wound dresser, but unlike Whitman, whose rhapsodic brotherhood was often celebrated without identifiable basis, Ortiz's final affirmative, mined as it is from the grieving poems, glows with the luster of someone who has come through.

Ortiz owes much to the great body of invocation, song and prayer that is central to the Native American oral tradition. Aside from a modest number of books, such as Paul Radin's *The Autobiography of a Winnebago Indian* (1920) and Ruth Underhill's *Singing for Power* (1938), this "literature" has been largely unrecorded until recently. But contemporary American Indians have begun to draw on this tradition and to create an impressive canon of imaginative prose and poetry.

Because the strongest of these writers (Ortiz, N. Scott Momaday, Vine Deloria, Leslie Marmon Silko, James Welch, Luther Standing Bear and others) have succeeded in fusing fractured present to coherent past, their writings are frequently more problematic than those of their forebears. In Ortiz, for example, the apparently simple, yet elusive, syntax sometimes seems fractionally off, as if the English were adapted from another language.

> They should have eaten
> whole buffalo.
> They should have,
> like the people wanted for them.

Fight Back seems a simpler volume than it is. Except for the 27-page **"No More Sacrifices,"** the poems are usually brief narratives about the Pueblos and Navahos and whites who live in the "Uranium Belt" west of Albuquerque, New Mexico. Ortiz shows us these people working in the uranium mines or the mills, riding in car pools, planting in a clayey soil, bathing in the sacred hot springs. We observe their distress, their joys and the persistent faith in the natural order that sustains them.

"No More Sacrifices" is the linchpin of the volume and one of the strongest poems in recent memory. Strictly speaking it is more prose then verse, part meditation, part sociopolitical analysis. The poet has climbed a volcanic mountain called Srhakaiya, west of the village that the white people named McCartys in which he was raised. Descending the mountain and walking home,

> I was sick
> feeling a sense of "otherness."
> How can I describe it?
> An electric current
> coursing in waves through me?
> "Otherness."

It becomes clear that his disconnection was produced by his vision on the mountain. Not so much what he physically saw (though pollution and industrialization were visible) as what he saw through to: the history of the Acoma people from the days before the Spanish conquest to the Pueblo revolt. He saw the invasion of the "Mericanos" with their railroads and cavalry and uranium mines. And he saw the people's painful transition from productive land-laborers to wage slaves.

His vision sickens the poet, but then, while resting under a juniper on his walk home, the "otherness" recedes, and he sees something else. . . . (pp. 406-08)

The sight of . . . horses enforces his relationship with the land, even as it underscores his realization of what must be done for the future he envisions:

> The future will not be mad with loss and waste though
> the memory will be there; eyes will become kind
> and deep, and the bones of this nation will mend. . . .
> (p. 408)

Harold Jaffe, "Speaking Memory," in The Nation, *New York, Vol. 234, No. 13, April 3, 1982, pp. 406-08.*

WILLARD GINGERICH

Ortiz is one element of a renaissance about to occur in the American Southwest, a region that may well become one of the most agitated and lively districts of culture-making activity in the country. This dry territory, from Colorado Springs to El Paso and west to the Colorado River, is of course long famous for its photogenic sunsets, its Hopi snake dancers, its Navajo sheepherders posed against abrupt and blunt mesas, and the seemingly endless displays of cacti and mountains filling page after page of *Arizona Highways*. The richness has obscured the riches of an apparently barren and empty region. (p. 208)

[Ortiz] knows the spiritual geography and the secret histories of power, struggle, exploitation, deceit, promise and survival which cycles of conquest and desert have taught the peoples of this region. No region in the U.S. is so rich in narratives of myth, history, and anecdote, and no people is quite so fond of spinning them as the Pueblo. The nineteen stories of ***Fightin'***—less stories than tales, some only a few pages long—retrace but also move beyond his previous work. In **"No More Sacrifices,"** a long autobiographical essay closing his 1980 book ***Fight Back: For the Sake of the People, For the Sake of the Land*** (issued in commemoration of the successful 1680 Pueblo revolt against the Spanish) he makes a statement which summarizes the thematics of nearly all his work:

> The Southwestern U.S. is caught in the throes of economic ventures and political manipulation which are ultimately destructive if the U.S. government and the multinational corporations do not have people and the land and their continuance as their foremost concern. . . . It is the survival of not only the Aacqumeh hanoh or the Dineh or other Southwestern native peoples, but it is all people of this nation. If the survival and quality of the life of Indian peoples is not assured, then no one else's life is, because those same economic, social, and political forces which destroy them will surely destroy others. It is not only a matter of preserving and protecting Indian lands as some kind of natural wilderness or cultural parks; rather it is a matter of how those lands can be productive in terms which are Indian people's to make instead of being forced to serve a U.S. national interest which has never adequately served them. Those lands can be productive to serve humanity, just like the oral tradition of the Aacqumeh hanoh says, and the people can be productive and serve the land so that it is not wasted and destroyed.

None of the pieces in ***Fightin'*** is as overtly political as this statement suggests, but the struggle for survival and quality to which Ortiz here directly refers is a steady but muted theme through them all. We are not just dealing with local or regionalist issues, he insists; as one aware of the symbolic role the Indian has always played in the historical imagination of Anglo-America, he believes in a link of destinies. The more overtly "Indian" stories in the collection—**"Man on the Moon," "Woman Singing," "The Panther Waits," "Kaiser and the War," "Pennstuwehniyaahtsi: Quuti's Story,"** and **"What Indians Do"**—are all clear fables of this linkage, often cast from a perspective which throws unexpected light on events and relationships.

"Man on the Moon" is the account of a Pueblo family simultaneously watching one of the Apollo moon missions on a new TV and explaining it to Grandfather. "Are those men looking for something on the moon?" Grandfather asks. "The men are looking for knowledge," his grandson responds. "They brought back some rocks." Grandfather dreams that night of

Flintwing boy and coyote who are frightened by an invincible machine that marches slowly across the landscape crushing everything in its path. Flintwing boy calms coyote, shows him a corn flour ritual and prays for humility, fits a flintheaded arrow to his bow, and sends coyote off to reassure the people. "Tell them I am here to meet it. I will give them my report when I find out." The juxtaposition of myth and science vivid for Ortiz, and the old man's dream raises a question not about the economics of our space program but about the knowledge it engenders.

In another story the same grandfather watches the astronauts collecting rocks on the moon then goes outside and returns with a small rock hidden in his hand. "'Okay then, Grandpa, what is it?' the boys said. And their Nana opened his hand and the boys said, "Ah, that's just a rock, Grandpa, you tricked us again.' 'No,' their grandpa said with a chuckle, casting a glance at the TV, 'that's knowledge.'" Seen through the knowledge of his dream, the scepticism of the grandfather becomes more than quaint stubbornness; it is a value and a question. (pp. 208-09)

Then there is another sort of story in ***Fightin'*** which represents a new power in Ortiz's fiction: tales of an intimately domestic nature in which the characters are Indian only by implication. These generate some of the finest moments in the book, though some, like **"Loose,"** a one-scene encounter with a street bum in an Albuquerque coffee shop, are scarcely more than vignettes. But **"Feeling Old," "3 Women,"** and **"Feathers"** are powerful tributes to the unresolvable pain and desperate, silent dignity of age, beaten wives, and broken families. **"Feathers"** in particular overwhelms with its unstated struggles of love, anger, disappointment, yearning and despair around a brief moment when a separated father brings his five-year-old son home to mother's apartment, along with a stray kitten they have found. The emotional tone is filtered through such a fine stylistic cloth that all obvious, easy pathos is purged away and the story gleams like a dark jewel of pain.

Another thematic group of stories in this collection is a type unique, as far as I am aware, to Ortiz, and the foremost reason why I believe him profoundly significant. In these stories the central action is the passage of non-Indian characters across that brief yet vast and persistent mythic gap in American history between Indian and non-Indian, to "become themselves, Indianlike," in William Carlos Williams' phrase.

I remember clearly my fascination with **"To Change in a Good Way"** when it was first published as a narrative poem in *Shantih* in 1979. It reappeared, as a poem, in ***Fight Back*** and now as the lead story of ***Fightin'***, and with one minimal but very significant revision. **"To Change in a Good Way"** is the third person narration of the relationship between Bill and Ida and Pete and Mary. Bill and Pete are miners at one of the Kerr-McGee uranium mines near Milan. Bill and Ida are displaced, landless Okies; Pete and Mary are Laguna Indians with a small garden. The couples become familiar friends and come to depend on each other for sheep fertilizer, working the garden, and company when the men work graveyard shifts. Bill's younger brother, Slick, comes to visit on his leave between hitches in the army, meets Pete's family, and then is off to Viet Nam. When word comes back to Bill that Slick has been killed by an American mine, Pete is the first to find him and learn of it. The next day Pete and Mary bring corn, a corn husk medicine bundle, and prayer sticks to Bill and Ida: "This is just a corn, Bill," Pete explains, "Indian corn. The people call it Kasheshi. Just a dried ear of corn. You can take it with you, or you can keep it here. You can plant it. It's to know that life will keep on. . . ." Then he offers Bill the husk bundle. ["You] take these sticks and feathers and you put them somewhere you think you should, someplace important that you think might be good, maybe to change life in a good way, that you think Slick would be helping us with." Bill is puzzled, thoughtful, confused. After the funeral, he knows suddenly what to do with the husk bundle. He takes it to work in the mine and lays it far down an abandoned shaft and then prays this stumbling, visionary prayer:

> Slick . . . I got this here Indian thing, feathers and sticks, and at home, at home we got the corn by your picture, and Pete and Mary said to do this because it's important even if we're Okies and not Indians who do this. It's for your travel they said and to help us with our life here from where you are now and they said to maybe change things in a good way for a good life and God knows us Okies always wanted that. Well, I'm gonna leave this here by the rock. Pete said he didn't know exactly all the right Indian things to do anymore but somehow I believe they're more righter than we've ever been led to believe. And now I'm trying too.

The words "led to believe" are absent in both earlier poetic versions of this story; the difference is of course highly suggestive and with those three additional words the passage moves from an insight to an inspiration.

Ortiz is certainly aware of Leslie Silko's attacks on "the unmitigated egotism of the white man, and the belief that he could 'in some sense become an Indian'" through the intellectual agency of poetry. But Ortiz's vision is of a different order; his "Indian" is not a symbol of anything but is a man or woman like the rest of us. To admit, to feel this simple reality requires a leap across centuries of conditioning, myth, "science," and faith. It requires us to, in effect, un-discover America, an enormous imaginative effort, in which, I believe, Ortiz leads us. He has insisted throughout his work that Indians in the social economies of the mining, railroading and farming industries of the Southwest have a common cause with Okies, Mexicans, blacks, displaced Appalachian whites that is stronger than race. In the fight for a mutually productive relationship to the water, mineral, timber, and grazing resources of the land Ortiz would have us seek the requisite change "in a good way." "The American poor and the workers and the white middle-class, who are probably the most ignorant of all U.S. citizens, must understand how they, like Indian people, are forced to serve a national interest, controlled by capitalist vested interests in collusion with U.S. policy makers, which does not serve them," he wrote in ***Fight Back.***

Here also is the root of the hostility to the figure of the anthropologist which surfaces strongly in the last piece of ***Fightin'***, **"What Indians Do."** The anthropologist's deficiency is not so much his insistent, analytical curiosity as his alienation from the real struggle of living Indians for the elements of basic human dignity, for work, water rights, land tenure, and autonomy. His insistent fascination with the dead and the strange, the "otherness" of Indians in relation to white civilization, makes him the prime agent of the continuing myth of the Mysterious Indian. This is unfair, of course, to many serious and committed anthropologists who do also work with compassion and diligence for the interests of the living, but Ortiz wishes to emphatically assert the priority of humanity and compassion over knowledge, race, and religion.

The vision and desire of ***Fightin'*** for non-Indian people finds its best image, I think, in this little scene on the final page of the book:

> Before I speak, I go to the men's room. There were two little white kids in there. While I am washing my hands, the older one, who is about five years old, keeps lingering and then he asks, "You're a Indian aren't you?" I say, "Yep, I sure am." "I thought so," he says, "you know how I know?" The younger boy, about three, kept tugging at his brother's hand. I smile and ask how he knows. He says, proudly, "Because you're wearing red and black. That's a Indian's colors." I look at my checkered shirt and then at them and say, "Yessir, you're perfectly right about that." And then they smile and leave.

The child, always a powerful figure in Ortiz's work, sees the Indian for what he is, a man with a red and black shirt. His eyes, unconditioned to "myth," see the "Indian's colors" not in his skin, nor in his bone structure nor in his genes, all aspects of an unfamiliar otherness, but in his removable, symbolic shirt. Would that the priorities of culture were so clear to us all. (pp. 210-12)

Willard Gingerich, "Simon Ortiz," in fiction international, *Vol. 15, No. 1, 1984, pp. 208-12.*

DIANA COLE

In ***Fightin',*** Simon J. Ortiz's new collection of short stories, he celebrates the myths and mourns the plight of the American Indian. Most of the stories are set in an area that is now the State of New Mexico, but Mr. Ortiz makes us vividly aware that this land once belonged to an ancient people who, despite being broken, are still proud. The spirit of defiance endures in such characters as Kaiser, a fierce fighter who, in the collection's best story, **"Kaiser and the War,"** refuses to learn the "Mericano" language of English, or be inducted into the United States Army to serve as a target for foreign bullets. Nothing much happens in most of these stories. The characters work, drink, eat, talk and dream of the old stories, the old customs and traditions, from the old days. Yet Mr. Ortiz manages to infuse his simple plots with mythological elements. In **"To Change in a Good Way,"** an Indian worker helps a colleague mourn by giving him a simple corn husk and a sack of sticks and feathers—objects not to mourn or bury but to plant, symbolically, in order to insure the continuation of life. . . . At times Mr. Ortiz bemoans his role as a professional "Native American" spokesman, yet most readers of ***Fightin'*** will be grateful to him for playing that role. . . . While the stories are uneven, and Mr. Ortiz's flat, dispassionate tone at times risks becoming monotonous, we have much to learn from these tales.

Diana Cole, in a review of "Fightin': New and Collected Stories," in The New York Times Book Review, *April 29, 1984, p. 32.*

ROBERT BERNER

The position of Simon Ortiz as one of our most important American Indian poets is assured, but most of his stories have been scattered in publications which have not always been easy to find. ***Fightin'*** brings together nineteen, about half of them previously unpublished. The book's title may suggest a political militancy which the stories do not deny, but this is hardly their real value. As in his poetry, Ortiz has set for himself the essential task of relating traditional Indian material both to Indian readers to whom it is vital and to non-Indian readers who will find in the stories the universal qualities that characterize the only writing we can value beyond its own moment.

The stories are a mixed lot. A couple of apparently autobiographical pieces seem incomplete and rather disjointed, and some stories are less successful than others. Several are distinguished, however, and all show the author's desire to discover "the words that are sacred because they come from a community of people and all life." . . .

For me, Ortiz's best efforts are those which relate an Indian tradition to contemporary Indian circumstances and those which make clear the value of Indian culture to non-Indians. An example of the former is **"The Panther Waits,"** which illuminates contemporary Indian experience by combining the history of Tecumseh and his brother The Prophet with the archetype of the twin culture heroes. An example of the latter is **"To Change in a Good Way,"** which tells the story of a white couple who find strength in the traditional wisdom of their Indian friends when their son is killed in Vietnam. This seems to me the best story in the collection, and future anthologists are hereby advised to pay attention to it.

Robert Berner, in a review of "Fightin': New and Collected Stories," in World Literature Today, *Vol. 58, No. 4, Autumn, 1984, p. 647.*

ROBERT L. BERNER

In his preface [to the reprinted editions of ***A Good Journey***] Ortiz maintains that his poems are meant to be heard rather than read. This is a crucial point, because his role is that of a storyteller, creating narratives of his own Acoma and the other pueblos. In a fragment of an interview which prefaces the book, Ortiz makes his point that storytelling is a matter of life and death: "The only way to continue is to tell a story." The poems, therefore, often tell stories—of Coyote in his modern form ("existential man / Dostoevsky Coyote"); of frightening journeys into the labyrinths of Cleveland, Los Angeles, Gallup, and a VA hospital; of the birth of a daughter, of three birds and a squirrel killed by cars on a fast highway; of his children coming to consciousness; even of making chili stew.

Ortiz seems to me to be most successful (and most moving) when he adapts the traditional poetic utterances of Indian people to poems of his own which are simultaneously personal and traditional: for example, in Coyote stories learned from his own parents; or **"Apache Love,"** which is structured according to the traditional chanting repetition of four elements. . . .

Ortiz believes that the experiences he captures in his poems are only at their first level those of Native Americans, that finally they have to do with the true nature of all of us. He is right. American Indian culture is among our most precious national treasures; the final significance of a poet like Ortiz is that he and the other gifted Indian writers of his generation are the locus of relationship between that culture and the American culture of which it is a vital part.

Robert L. Berner, in a review of "A Good Journey," in World Literature Today, *Vol. 59, No. 3, Summer, 1985, p. 474.*

John (James) Osborne

1929-

English dramatist, scriptwriter, and autobiographer.

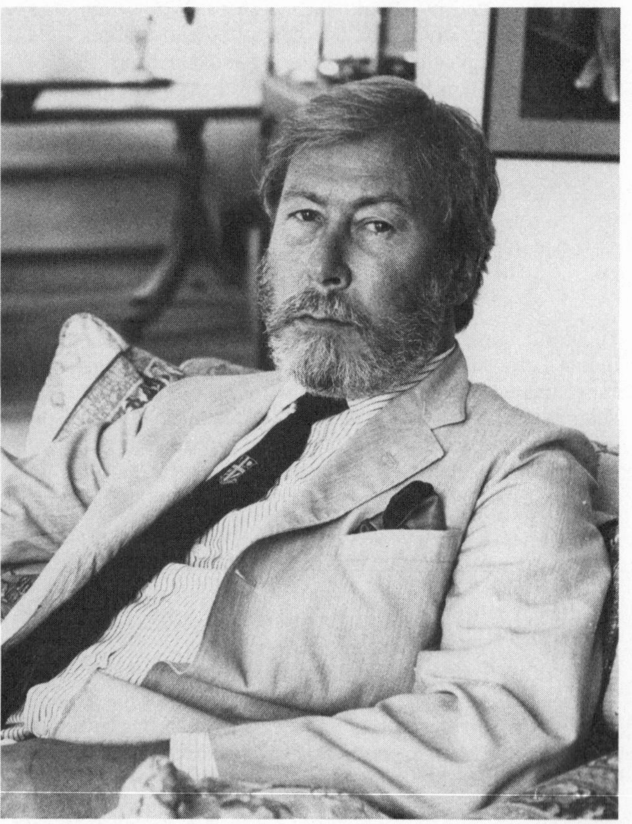

Photograph by Mark Gerson

Osborne's landmark play, *Look Back in Anger* (1956), established him as a leading young English dramatist and helped initiate a new era in British theater in which aggressive social criticism, authentic portrayals of working-class life, and antiheroic characters became important elements. Osborne is commonly linked with the "Angry Young Men," a loosely categorized group of English writers, including John Wain, Kingsley Amis, and John Braine, whose literary output during the 1950s and 1960s reflected and contributed to the heightened social and political awareness that was developing in England. Osborne's plays are often dominated by strong, articulate protagonists whose violent outbursts of abusive language express disgust with bourgeois complacency and materialistic social values. The rebellious attitudes of his characters added to the popularity of his early dramas among postwar British youth. Osborne's most accomplished works, *Look Back in Anger* and *Inadmissible Evidence* (1964), are credited with helping to liberate British theater from the prevailing genteel style of his contemporaries and immediate predecessors. He has received numerous awards and honors for his work.

Look Back in Anger, Osborne's first major work, focuses on Jimmy Porter, a twenty-five-year-old university-educated sweetshop owner who shares a cramped attic apartment with his wife, Alison, and his co-worker and friend, Cliff. Embittered and alienated by his inability to advance socially and angered by the apathy he encounters in others, Jimmy strikes back at the world with explosive verbal intensity. Often directed at Alison, whose upper middle-class background Jimmy resents, his diatribes range in subject from the failings of his marriage to the inequalities of English society. Many critics who reviewed the play's original productions considered *Look Back in Anger* to be an insightful commentary on England's social and political situation during the 1950s. Subsequent interpretations of the play have emphasized the personal nature of Jimmy's vituperation. James Gindin observed: "Jimmy Porter does rant against bishops and 'posh' Sunday papers, against any form of aristocratic gentility or pretense, but his invective is part of a plea for human honesty and vitality, for people to live emotionally as fully and deeply as they can." *Look Back in Anger* won the New York Drama Critics Circle Award for best foreign play. Osborne's next work, *The Entertainer* (1957), is the story of Archie Rice, an irascible vaudeville comedian whose emotional instability is mirrored in the deteriorating music-hall tradition to which he is closely allied. The failing state of the music hall has been viewed as a metaphor for England's decline in world power and loss of national identity following World War II. *The Entertainer* is noted for Osborne's inventive adaptation of vaudeville techniques; he uses short sketches, or "turns," as structural devices, and his characters directly address the audience.

The World of Paul Slickey (1959) is often considered to be Osborne's angriest and most uncompromising work. A biting musical satire of the London press and an attack on the individuals who allow themselves to be influenced and manipulated by mass media, the play received predominantly negative reviews, although critics acknowledged Osborne's attempts to expand the scope of the musical and to challenge the conventions of British drama. *Luther* (1961), a critical and popular success, is a historical and psychological portrait of the leader of the Protestant Reformation beginning with his years as an Augustinian monk and including his confrontations with royal and papal authority as well as his later role as husband and father. Osborne emphasizes Luther's private life and centers on his troubled relationship with his father. Many critics noted the influence of Bertolt Brecht in Osborne's use of a narrator to supply background information and his reliance upon epic costumes, set designs, and other theatrical devices. *Luther* won both a New York Drama Critics Circle Award and an Antoinette Perry (Tony) Award. Osborne's next major work, *Inadmissible Evidence,* is regarded by many critics as his finest dramatic achievement and a culmination of the themes developed in his earlier plays. An examination of one man's descent into alienation and despair, the play concentrates on Bill Maitland, an unscrupulous London lawyer who is haunted by feelings of guilt and self-doubt that eventually lead to his disengagement from society and his nervous breakdown.

Osborne's subsequent plays, while considered to contain some of his best writing, have been less successful than his earlier works. In *A Patriot for Me* (1965), a vast historical drama set against the decline and fall of the Hapsburg empire in Austro-

Hungary during the early twentieth century, Osborne examines the tragic military career of Captain Alfred Redl, a double spy who is blackmailed because of his homosexuality. The play's production was hampered by British theater censors, who demanded large deletions due to Osborne's treatment of unconventional sexuality. *The Hotel in Amsterdam* (1968) is an ensemble play—an uncharacteristic form for Osborne—in which three English couples escape the unwelcome presence of their boss for a weekend of rest and revealing conversation. In *West of Suez* (1971), which also features several central characters, Osborne examines the decline of England's colonial tradition through the experiences of an expatriate family on a former British colony in the Caribbean that is undergoing political upheaval. *Watch It Come Down* (1976), Osborne's most recent full-length play, concerns an emotional crisis in the lives of a film director and his wife, who share a renovated railway station in the country with several other people. Their attempts to reconcile their marital problems eventually involve the other characters.

Osborne has written several plays for British television, including *A Matter of Scandal and Concern* (1960) and *You're Not Watching Me, Mummy* (1980). He has also contributed to the scripts for the film adaptations of his stage dramas, including *Look Back in Anger, The Entertainer,* and *Inadmissible Evidence,* and in 1963 Osborne won an Academy Award for his screenplay of Henry Fielding's novel *Tom Jones*. He has adapted plays by Lope de Vega, Henrik Ibsen, and Shakespeare. The first installment of Osborne's autobiography, *A Better Class of Person* (1981), has received wide critical attention for its insights into Osborne's early artistic development.

(See also *CLC,* Vols. 1, 2, 5, 11; *Contemporary Authors,* Vols. 13-16, rev. ed.; *Contemporary Authors New Revision Series,* Vol. 21; and *Dictionary of Literary Biography,* Vol. 13.)

SIMON TRUSSLER

Osborne's major plays have never ceased to be the "lessons in feeling" he first proclaimed them: and those few which have had an ulterior purpose have deservedly been the least successful. ***The World of Paul Slickey*** and ***The Blood of the Bambergs*** were excursions into musical and political extravaganza: and they failed not only in their chosen comic styles, but in contorting themselves into formal shapes which were too orthodox for intended onslaughts upon orthodoxy. ***A Subject of Scandal and Concern,*** on the other hand, in contradiction of its own narrator's claims, demanded a cerebral judgement from its audience—which it ostensibly discouraged, and for which it failed to assemble adequate evidence. And ***Under Plain Cover*** lost its theatrical way as soon as its own lesson in a certain kind of sexual feeling got sidetracked into a personal lesson Osborne was trying to teach the press.

These several kinds of failure suggest, albeit negatively, that Osborne is a dramatist who works best within certain limitations: but that his failures have been infrequent, and belong mainly to the earlier years of his dramatic career. This hopefully confirms that he is learning either to transcend or to work within those limitations—which probably have to do with temperament rather than technique. For as a craftsman Osborne has grown out of several immaturities which flawed—though in these cases not fatally—his other early plays. (p. 213)

Osborne has never entirely broken the habit of over-structuring his plays. That he can work the necessary business of exposition well enough into a naturalistic sequence of events is amply demonstrated by ***The Entertainer,*** by ***The Hotel in Amsterdam,*** and by the first act of ***Look Back in Anger.*** That he is equally liable to let it sore-thumb its way into his action ***Epitaph for George Dillon, Time Present,*** and the *middle* act of ***Look Back in Anger*** bear all too eloquent witness. These expository successes and failures make no chronological sense: so it can only be assumed that Osborne reverts to being a well-made dramatist in the worst sense when he is unable—or can't be bothered—to set up a situation which *requires* a mood of retrospection, or to fashion a form, such as that of ***A Subject of Scandal and Concern,*** which interpolates its narrative element straightforwardly into its text.

Overplotting can also mar Osborne's work. . . . [A] compulsion to inject action into a naturally static situation has haunted him from ***Epitaph for George Dillon***—in which George's tuberculosis and his first wife tied for top marks in irrelevance—to ***The Hotel in Amsterdam,*** in which the arrival of Gillian proceeds to beg all the questions it might have helpfully raised. But the drag ball in ***A Patriot for Me,*** redeemed though it is by its supreme theatricality, is the grossest blunder of them all, for it is not only disproportionately interruptive to the plot, but a violation of the character of Alfred Redl—who is introduced almost apologetically into the transvestite proceedings.

But Redl, in any case, jumps from stage to stage of his sexual development like a pederastic grasshopper. And in almost all of his plays Osborne has shown a similar disinclination to *develop* a sexual relationship in front of his audience. Thus, at the openings of the first and third acts of ***Look Back in Anger*** he is willing enough to explore fully-matured stages in the development of Jimmy's marital and extra-marital relationships: but he prefers to let each stage *consolidate* itself during an audience's ice-creams and scotch-and-sodas. It, too, then becomes a "given" situation, ready for its dramatic definition. In consequence, the *least* "developed" plays are usually the best. ***Epitaph for George Dillon*** and ***Look Back in Anger*** both have emotional hiatuses, while George and Josie and Jimmy and Helena get into their sexual strides. And ***Luther*** and ***A Patriot for Me*** jerk as erratically between psychological states as they do between their historical settings. But ***The Entertainer*** and ***The Hotel in Amsterdam*** do not have to "develop" in any such senses, either in time or in the temperaments of their characters: whilst ***Inadmissible Evidence*** and ***Time Present*** work their changes retrospectively, exploring backwards in time as their central characters move forward towards self-destruction. It should be noted that Osborne has never mastered the episodic style—or at least, adapted it to his own purposes, of conceiving a fuller social context for a single character. In consequence, he delineates the environments of ***Luther*** and of ***A Patriot for Me*** far more fully, and with more justifiable self-containment, than the men those environments should be helping to shape—and his ***Bond Honoured*** works most arbitrarily of all, revealing neither periods, places nor persons in any depth, but developing each along its own parallel line, which has been tortuously separated out from the inexorable, single-track movement of Lope's original.

No less arbitrary, though somehow more forgivable, are those authorial sports which recur with predictable regularity at every opportunity: notably the stabs of derision at the monarchy and the press in the earlier plays, and an increasing love-hatred towards the young in the later. Osborne's antipathy towards dramatic critics has, however, been recently the hardest ridden hobby-horse of all. But it must be added in all fairness that none of Osborne's marginal quarrels has taken over a whole play since ***The Blood of the Bambergs***: and if his journalistic broadsides against the critical confraternity have purged him of an incipient *World of Milton Hobson,* then they are minor wounds eminently worth the bearing.

Maybe Osborne's hatred of his reviewers has something to do with his reluctance to remedy the defects in his own craftsmanship—which are mostly slight, measured against the assurance of his total dramatic structures. His earlier press notices in particular—before his commercial success began to be accorded its invariable respect—tended to sneer at the hypostasised anger of his heroes, and to treat each successive play like a symptom of some lurking threat to the British way of life. But rebutting such non-criticism need not have left Osborne so anxious to defend rather than learn from his real mistakes—the fracas over ***A Bond Honoured*** is the classic case of such over-reaction to adverse criticism—and to pay a mite more attention to the details of his craft. (pp. 215-17)

I have been straying into incidental criticisms of particular productions and thus beyond my self-imposed terms of reference. But this has been in order to suggest what is probably Osborne's only major dramatic defect according to *his own* terms of reference—for within this defect are compounded so many of his minor weaknesses. And this is the kind of instantaneous, take-it-or-leave-it attitude towards his craftsmanship which tempts him to ignore informed or at least well-intentioned advice—and which incidentally diminishes his triumphs by forcing him into over-strenuous defences of his artistic failures.

But whatever the advantages or disadvantages of Osborne's instinctive approach to the manner of his playwriting, an increasingly cerebral orientation in its *matter* has recently been evident. And so has a sense of *social* complexity, such as too seldom counterpointed the personal complexities of the earlier plays. Osborne still writes mainly about "exceptional" people—those whose character traits are writ large, as he once put it, and who are thus, in conventional terms, "neurotic". His single attempt to set such a neurotic person within a "normal" environment, in ***Epitaph for George Dillon,*** was least convincing at its cosiest, and least acceptable as an acting-vehicle for those cast in its unexceptional roles. Thus, the unspeakably ordinary Pauline in ***Time Present*** is in a tradition established by the vacuous Norah in ***George Dillon,*** and continued by Graham Dodd in ***The Entertainer,*** and by Jones in ***Inadmissible Evidence.***

Until ***The Hotel in Amsterdam,*** even those few "normals" who were conceived as sympathetic rather than self-satisfied—Jean Rice in ***The Entertainer,*** for example—lacked much dramatic interest. They were not exceptional, but neither were they "interesting"—that is, normal according to standards more engaging than those of the fifties and sixties, as were the long line of leftovers from previous generations from Colonel Redfern to the unseen Gideon Orme. It has thus been the *middle* generation, neither old enough to cling to the certainties of an imperial past nor young enough to retain much hope for their futures, from whose ranks the "exceptional" heroes have generally been recruited. And it has been the upper and the lower classes who have filled in a sufficiently "interesting" background—so that the bourgeoisie have come in for the severest treatment, both at Osborne's hands and from the mouths of his central characters. Except in ***George Dillon,*** however, they have been least well represented in the cast-lists. Even Osborne's early antimonarchism, it is pertinent to recall, was directed *in his plays* more against royalty-worshipping middle-class mums than against royalty itself—which was embodied by Princess Melanie in ***The Blood of the Bambergs*** with as much sympathy as was the journalistic profession by Stanley in ***Under Plain Cover*** and by the ambiguous Oakham in ***Slickey.*** It is, indeed, true to say that once Osborne's figures of furious fun have been so dramatised as to become "interesting", they have generally been humanised in the process—and accorded a sympathy such as the uninspiring Elliots could never hope to win.

Thus, only in ***The Hotel in Amsterdam***—and with unexpected abruptness after the archetypicality of ***Time Present***—was Osborne able at last to render a balanced, mutually-adjusted group of characters. Simultaneously, he was also able to strip away most of the overlay of plot with which he had previously felt impelled to fill out—and sometimes to overburden—his plays. I think that ***The Hotel in Amsterdam,*** in these senses, marks the end of a phase in Osborne's creative development. His early preoccupation with the atrophying effects of rationalised nostalgia—with which Jimmy Porter and Archie Rice were both stricken—had persisted even in ***Time Present.*** But by this time Osborne's interest had already shifted to alienation of another sort—the existential alienation of the loss of one's sense of objective identity. This was Bill Maitland's estrangement, and the theme of ***Inadmissible Evidence***—a theme expressed in a more appropriate *form* than in any of Osborne's previous plays. This same theme was latent, though buried beneath a debris of renaissance leftovers, in ***A Bond Honoured.*** And then, in ***A Patriot for Me,*** it was as if Osborne were trying to make out with a telescope what he had put beneath a microscope in ***Inadmissible Evidence***: for instead of compressing a world into Bill Maitland's mind, he set Alfred Redl against a broader social tapestry than he had ever before tried to weave—reassembling its military, social and sexual patterns into all kinds of permutations, but permitting Redl himself to pick up threads in none. In that play, however, it was the society rather than the stranger lost in its midst which came to life: but in ***Time Present*** Osborne again chose to depict a solitary figure in an almost suspended environment, so that Pamela found herself alone against a hazily hostile background of family and friends, and of actors and affluent agents.

Such was the mainstream of Osborne's development until ***The Hotel in Amsterdam.*** In ***Slickey, Luther*** and the ***Plays for England*** he had been temporarily diverted into other courses—but only to return to surveying the struggle for an honourable reconciliation with self and with society. At last, in ***The Hotel in Amsterdam,*** that reconciliation seems to have been achieved. The curvature of its action follows neither the well-made semicircle of ***Look Back in Anger***—from exposition to development to resolution—nor the vicious-spiral of a modern tragedy, such as catches up Bill Maitland in ***Inadmissible Evidence,*** returning the play's action not to its *status quo* but to the beginning of another action in another dimension: the drawing-out of an endgame into a perpetual stalemate. But in ***The Hotel in Amsterdam*** that tragic action is taking place in the wings, to a life that touches those of the characters very closely, but whose traumatic climax offers them a choice—the choice between asserting a new freedom, or of accepting disintegration, deprived of the common object of hatred which has previously been binding them together.

Thus, ***The Hotel in Amsterdam*** ends neither on a note of hope, such as is briefly sensed in ***Look Back in Anger,*** nor in that resignation which is the best ***The Entertainer*** can offer—nor in the self-destruction with which ***Inadmissible Evidence, A Patriot for Me*** and ***Time Present*** alike conclude. Although the circle in ***The Hotel in Amsterdam*** may not be vicious, however, it is, undeniably, closed—both physically, within the four walls of its hotel-suite, and temperamentally, in the exclusiveness shared by its in-group of occupants. But this in-group is not, in Osborne's usual sense, exceptional: it is not cut off from society, nor yet is it slavishly absorbed into it. And perhaps most important, it can exist, talk and act on a common level of assumptions, each member adjusting to the individualities of his fellows.

This adjustment depends, too, on a development in Osborne's use of dialogue—from its more-or-less conventional to-and-froing in ***George Dillon*** to the rhetorical fillibustering of ***Look Back in Anger,*** and from the more genuine but limited reciprocity of ***The Entertainer*** to the solipsistic, subjective realism of Bill Maitland's stream-of-consciousness in ***Inadmissible Evidence.*** Again, ***The Hotel in Amsterdam*** marks a kind of culmination: for here speech-patterns are neither conventionalised out of recognition, deployed like defensive strategies, nor transmuted into the processes of thought. Language becomes, at last, a mode of communication between characters who mutually accommodate its use to each other's foibles and feelings, and who pick up and volley each other's verbal motifs and idiosyncrasies. This isn't to imply that ***The Hotel in Amsterdam*** is necessarily a better play, or that it uses language better, than its predecessors: rather, it is a *different* play, and uses language differently—as a medium for understanding, not as a weapon of class or sexual war.

Osborne himself has, thematically, now come full circle as a dramatist. The dubiously talented George Dillon settled down to the mediocre comforts offered by the Elliots and by Josie's animal warmth. The members of the in-group in ***Amsterdam*** are resigned to their own kind of intellectual affluence, and bask self-sufficiently in each other's glow. They are perhaps kinder and certainly more articulate than the Elliots: and their play closes not on the full stop of an epitaph for themselves, but on the question-mark inscribed on someone else's.

That question-mark hangs, too, over Osborne's future development as a dramatist. That his best works of the past will survive seems to me beyond doubt, especially after the evidence offered by the revival of ***Look Back in Anger,*** which opened just as this book was nearing completion and which has confirmed my own feelings about the universality of the play's implications—firmly pinned-down though the production was by the fashions of the mid-fifties. Personally, I would nominate ***The Entertainer, Inadmissible Evidence*** and ***The Hotel in Amsterdam*** as additional candidates for permanent survival, and would offer ***Luther*** as a respectable set-text until a new fashion in historical drama catches up with examiners. Of the rest, ***Epitaph for George Dillon*** and ***Time Present*** will probably be good for rep revivals for no more than a decade or two. But four plays out of Osborne's first twelve will surely secure themselves permanent places in the international repertoire: and such a proportion is one in which any dramatist can take pride. (pp. 219-24)

Simon Trussler, in his The Plays of John Osborne: An Assessment, *Victor Gollancz Ltd, 1969, 252 p.*

JOHN ELSOM

In many respects . . . , ***Look Back in Anger*** is just a conventional, wordy and rather clumsy play, and twenty years after, we might well wonder what was so significant about it. It has been both over- and under-estimated. 1956 was a year of theatrical changes, as well as of political disillusion. *Waiting for Godot* transferred to the West End, the Berliner Ensemble visited London for the first time, and while regional theatres were closing around the country in the face of commercial television, there were . . . hopeful signs for the theatrical future. (p. 74)

In a year of changes, ***Look Back in Anger*** came to symbolise the urgent demand for change, and if we require a useful illustration as to what we were changing from, the leading H. M. Tennent production of the year was Enid Bagnold's *The Chalk Garden* . . . , which concerned a widow living with an old retainer in a country house on the South Downs. It was a comedy with sinister undertones whose dialogue (according to Kenneth Tynan) provided speech of 'exquisite candour, building ornamental bridges of metaphor, tiptoeing across frail causeways of simile, and vaulting over gorges impassable to the rational soul'. The key word, indeed, was exquisite.

The Chalk Garden was the high point in a West End season dominated (as before) by middle-brow, middle-class, middle-aged tastes. Terence Rattigan's invention, 'Aunt Edna', represented the audiences for whom he was supposed to write; genteel, tea-sipping matinée fodder. She would have hated ***Look Back in Anger,*** just as the young audiences who supposedly liked Osborne's play would have hated to be associated with Aunt Edna. Kenneth Tynan wrote in the *Observer*: 'I agree that ***Look Back in Anger*** is a minority taste. What matters, however, is the size of the minority. I estimate it at roughly 6,733,000, which is the number of people in this country between twenty and thirty.' Did ***Look Back in Anger*** represent a class and age rebellion? Was that its true significance?

Perhaps so, but on this level it is easy to exaggerate its claims. Class may have been a barrier to widespread appreciation of the theatre, particularly in the West End, but ***Look Back in Anger*** was scarcely the chief battering ram against it. Jimmy is snobbish in his tastes, more of an Aunt Edna than Alison. The only character who emerges with his solid good sense intact is Alison's father, the Colonel. Nor was Jimmy a typical proletarian example: he was a minor spiv. Nor could Osborne claim to be a 'working-class writer', like Arnold Wesker or Bernard Kops. ***Look Back in Anger*** expressed, above all, middle-class discontent, and its class significance (if we want to consider the play in such terms) was not that it was a proletarian play but that it presented such a gloomy picture of a dispossessed ex-graduate that the truly working-class plays at the Theatre Workshop seemed cheerful by comparison.

Was it then a play of Oedipal rebellion? Osborne quickly became associated with a group of writers, including Colin Wilson and John Braine, who were known as angry young men. Osborne, through Jimmy Porter, was voicing the natural uncertainties of the young, their frustrations at being denied power, their eventual expectations of power and their fears of abusing it, either in running a country or a family. The familiar features of Oedipalism are there, staring through Jimmy's malignant-innocent eyes, his desire to shock, his loquaciousness, his sexual longings and his dread of responsibility, his curious ambivalence towards the Colonel, who is both noble and an *éminence grise*. Did this play acquire its prestige because it was staged in an 'old' country, with firm traditions, relentlessly upheld? Was Jimmy a youth knocking at the door of a stately country mansion, threatening to knock it down if it is not opened. In a sense, it is opened to him, through his marriage to Alison. He has one foot in the mansion's hall, and this is what confuses him. He has wandered into a world which looks more impressive from without than within. He has lost his main enemy, but not the habit of fighting. (pp. 75-6)

But the Oedipal argument also has its flaws, for the effect of ***Look Back in Anger*** was not to glorify the young rebel, but rather the reverse. Although there were many films and plays in the late 1950s which presented the angry young man as a hero, uncertain or otherwise, they came from different territories, from the United States (with James Dean and Marlon Brando) and from British universities, with their satirical revues. Jimmy was neither an *East of Eden* rebel, nor a *Beyond the Fringe* one. Osborne made no attempt to glamorise the anger. Jimmy was not just the critic of his society, he was also the object for criticism. He was the chief example of the social malaise which he was attacking. Through Jimmy Porter, Osborne had opened up a much wider subject than rebelliousness or youthful anger, that of social alienation, the feeling of being trapped in a world of meaningless codes and customs. Osborne's ambivalence towards Jimmy is apparent even from his descriptions of him in the script: Jimmy is 'a disconcerting mixture of sincerity and cheerful malice, of tenderness and freebooting cruelty'. The significance of these divided feelings was that it represented as well the tension between the longing for security and the desire for change: alienation, in short, in action, where we feel dissatisfied whatever we do. (p. 77)

In his subsequent plays, Osborne also developed two themes expressed in ***Look Back in Anger,*** the rottenness of the State (usually, but not invariably, Britain) and the problems of being an alienated man. This is not to suggest that his plays do not have a wide range of historical situations and techniques, but rather that, at some point and particularly in his early plays, this variety combs and folds around these central preoccupations.

These themes also suggest the limits of his work, for at worst Osborne can become a confused and predictable writer. He can hit out clumsily at easy targets, as in his satire on royal weddings in ***The Blood of the Bambergs*** (1963), and diffuse his 'State of the Nation' attacks until they include everyone and everything, as in ***A Sense of Detachment*** (1972). He botched up an adaptation of a difficult play, ***A Bond Honoured*** (from Lope de Vega's *La Fianza Satisfecha*), by not appreciating the difference between an existentialist rebel, living in a world where 'good and evil are men's opinions of themselves', with the God-defying hero of de Vega's play, whose sacrilege is the reverse side of his god-centredness and who experiences a miraculous conversion.

At best, however, Osborne managed to combine these themes within precise and direct statements. His capacity to write strong central characters and vivid, passionate dialogue fired the imagination of other writers, who without his rhetorical gifts caught something of his inner urgency. In ***The Entertainer*** (1957), Osborne considered the decline of Britain through the dead eyes of a stand-up comic, Archie Rice, who works within the tatty variety shows (with nudes), the remaining fragments of a once-great music-hall tradition. . . . The loss of ordinary dignity, in private and in public life, leads to a personal despair. In ***Luther*** (1961), Osborne was concerned with a man who is frightened of his own rebelliousness. It is partly a historical account of Martin Luther's life, although the second act, which condenses history, is less successful than the first, where Luther grapples with the conflicts caused by his intellectual belief in the justice of his cause, his doubts that his rebelliousness may derive from more personal, less honourable reasons and where he finally forces himself to defy the Papacy at the Diet of Worms: 'Here I stand. God help me, I can do no more.'

With such characters as Jimmy Porter, Archie Rice and Martin Luther, Osborne proved his capacity to write magnificent single roles, a talent which no actor or manager could ignore. . . . [***Inadmissible Evidence***] was a play about a guilty, middle-aged solicitor, Maitland, whose sexual fantasies merged into (and derived from) the realities of his daily life, his different relationships with his wife, mistresses and daughter. In ***Inadmissible Evidence,*** Osborne extended his attacks on society to include the way in which social codes can deform the sexual instinct, a theme which was also part of ***Under Plain Cover*** (1963) and ***A Patriot for Me*** (1966). In ***Under Plain Cover,*** a quiet young couple, brother and sister, play sexual games together, mainly sado-masochistic, until their secrets are exposed to the world of a meddling reporter; while in ***A Patriot for Me,*** based on the career of the master spy Redl in the Austro-Hungarian Empire before the First World War, he showed how a prevailing social atmosphere, encouraging homosexuality, might still not prevent, may indeed assist, the blackmail of a homosexual—with international, as well as personal, repercussions.

The year 1966 appears to have been a turning point in Osborne's career. He had formed a particularly close association with the Royal Court Theatre whose artistic director, George Devine, discovered ***Look Back in Anger*** and appeared briefly in ***A Patriot for Me.*** Devine had the insight to encourage Osborne and the authority to give him advice: but in 1966, he died, which was a great personal loss to Osborne. The impact of this loss can perhaps be seen in ***A Bond Honoured,*** written at Kenneth Tynan's instigation for the National Theatre: the conversion episodes at the end of this play give the impression of being absent-mindedly written, very clumsy and brief. But after 1966, there was also a change in direction in Osborne's plays: they were no longer so heavily dependent on strong central characters. In the quiet ***Hotel in Amsterdam*** (1968) . . . , the main character is off-stage, the domineering father-figure of a film crew for whose instructions the others wait. ***Hotel in Amsterdam,*** like ***West of Suez*** (1971) and ***A Sense of Detachment*** (1972), is an 'ensemble' play. ***Time Present*** (1968) was a return to the theme expressed in ***The Entertainer*** in that a dead Edwardian actor-manager is remembered as having belonged to a golden age of Britain (and the theatre): the nostalgia attached to the music hall in ***The Entertainer*** now spreads to the whole Edwardian period, and it was this mixture of nostalgia and self-loathing which characterised ***West of Suez,*** about the decaying colonial heritage of Britain. Osborne's later plays, however, lack that telling ambivalence towards the alienated man, so notable a feature of his early plays. The attacks against society are all-out slaughter; the nostalgia becomes sentimental. Sometimes both emotions are present, cheek by jowl, in the same play. (pp. 77-80)

Osborne's contribution to the theatre cannot be seen simply in terms of his plays. His influence particularly during the late 1950s and early 1960s was pervasive, but largely indirect. Few dramatists tried to mimic the Osborne style in the way in which Pinter was imitated. The success of ***Look Back in Anger,*** however, destroyed several inhibiting myths about plays: that the theatre had to be genteel, that heroes were stoical and lofty creatures, that audiences needed nice people with whom to identify. Even the recognised clumsiness of Osborne's plays were indirectly encouraging to other dramatists, for it seemed to prove that passion and dramatic substance mattered more than obedience to the rules. Other writers of the time were not likely to be so overawed by the complexity of writing plays, nor, with the example of Osborne's success, were they so likely to be deterred by the hopeless impracticability of finding managements to produce their works. Osborne also demonstrated that it was possible to write vivid and powerful speeches without making them sound verbally narcissistic. His background as an actor gave him an instinctive knowledge as to what lines would work in the theatre and which would not. He had also given the first telling expression in modern British theatre to the theme of social alienation. (pp. 80-1)

John Elsom, "Breaking Out: The Angry Plays," in his Post-War British Theatre, *Routledge & Kegan Paul, 1976, pp. 72-87.*

PETER KEMP

More hit list than autobiography, ***A Better Class of Person*** finds Osborne heading down Memory Lane like a vengeful mugger. Its paragraphs are littered with the remains of gutted kith-and-kin: Grandma and Grandad Osborne ('terminally lazy'), Cousin Jill ('looked like a slightly indecent ice-cream salesgirl'), Cousin Tony ('an ingenious and malevolent schemer . . . flagrant lying . . . dwarfish bullying'). With surly zest, the book reconstructs, then pulverises, the lino-cold homes, all peevish whine and sub-genteel sadism, of Osborne's relatives.

Not that its fury is confined to them. Snorting onslaughts fling themselves at all and sundry—from Australians to the *Daily Telegraph,* the National Theatre to the catering trade ('largely given over to neurotic self-servers'). Sometimes, there are puzzling passages of mysteriously unfocused vehemence, not unlike the mutterings of someone you decide it's better not to sit near on the Tube. Those which refer to 'dog shit and fag ends' eventually turn out to have much to do with Lynne Reid Banks, whose campaign against such detritus has left an unfavourable impression on Osborne's mind. Dark but ferocious mention of her 'unspeakable' behaviour keeps returning. . . .

The book also chortles reminiscently over the discomfiting of an actress—irritatingly prone to ignore Osborne when he worked as a call-boy in rep—'by knocking on the door and entering immediately as she was inserting a Tampax. She never tried the trick again.' Press-ganged into Osborne's retrospect, a monstrous regiment of women get bitterly reviewed. At school, he is terrorised by an Amazon called Daphne, given to spreadeagling some boy-victim in the playground, 'lifting up her skirt and placing her navy blue gusset firmly on his head'. Christmases are blighted by Grandma Osborne's withering remarks. Joan, an early sweetheart, is 'spitefully snobbish'. Stella, his first mistress, jilts him. Pamela, his first wife, prefers the attentions of the local dentist.

Overshadowing all these, however, is Osborne's greatest female monster: his mother, usually referred to as 'Nellie Beatrice' or 'The Black Look'. Remorselessly, his book heaps up an indictment of this luckless lady—still around, he notes glumly, and apparently 'hell bent' on surviving to a ripe old age. Her appearance is loathingly itemised: face, a 'floury dark mask'; lips, 'covered in some sticky slime'; perfume, 'fleurs des dustbins'. Her behaviour generally alternates between 'snarling, raw-nailed boredom' and 'gibbering with irritability'—though at times of particularly gratifying disaster for others, 'The Black Look flaked its powdery surface and broke into a yellow grin.'

Only once does she succeed in giving her son unrestrained pleasure. This is during the war when a bomb narrowly misses the house and she stumbles in terror from the lavatory, knickers round her ankles: 'the funniest, most enjoyable sight I had ever seen,' laughs Osborne, remembering happily how his mother had been 'blasted into a blob of stupidity and fear'. (p. 441)

What seems especially churlish about Osborne's response is that it's his mother who appears to have done so much towards fostering his career. Besides funding him for years, she regularly took him to the music-hall. And the music-hall, this book makes very clear, is the big influence on his dramatic techniques. His plays function in terms of 'solo spots', 'turns', 'feeds' and 'double acts'. They replace the standup performer with the knock-down one.

The book halts at 1956, so it covers the writing of only two of Osborne's published works: the co-authored ***Epitaph for George Dillon,*** and ***Look Back in Anger.*** While not having much to say about the plays themselves, it is extremely revealing about the atmosphere they came out of. Jimmy Porter's diatribes can be seen as variants on Osborne's late-adolescent-sounding fulminations against those he was dependent on. ***Epitaph for George Dillon*** strikes even closer home. Like the hero of that play—a sneering parasite on a vulgar family he exploits and derides—the Osborne of ***A Better Class of Person*** often seems a sponger soaked in vinegar. (pp. 441-42)

Peter Kemp, "'This Is a Talent Not to Amuse, but to Abuse'," in The Listener, *Vol. 106, No. 2731, October 15, 1981, pp. 441-42.*

DAVID HARE

The first half [of ***A Better Class of Person***], more detailed, more careful, tells of a painfully repressed childhood in the dank air of the English lower middle class, while the second describes his escape, the flight into the theatre, and above all, the discovery of the pleasures of Being Rude. No moment in the book is more heady than when as a young Fleet Street reporter he finally meets an employer who addresses him as he has always dreamed of being addressed: 'Quit your laughing, you fucking little shithead.'

For Osborne's youth had been a mealy-mouthed torture with a mother whose awfulness acquires grandeur by anecdote. My favourite scene has her sitting in the next-door room to where her newly-dead husband is lying in an open coffin. She is flicking through the *News of the World* and complaining of how much work will be involved in fumigating the room. 'For the first time,' writes Osborne, 'I felt the fatality of hatred.' (Her revenge, not mentioned in the book, appears to have been the warmth with which she congratulated him on writing *A Taste of Honey*.) Each branch of the family—from Grandma Grove to Auntie Queenie—reveals fresh horror, yet strangely in this, the larger part of the book, his writing is never unkind, for he loves what he calls the 'anomaly and eccentricity' of English class. He understands better than any modern writer that emotion repressed in the bricked-up lives of the suburb-dweller does not disappear, but that instead it leaks, distorted, through every pore of the life: in whining, in meanness, in stubbornness, in secrecy. . . .

The achievement of this part of the autobiography is to make the ordinary extraordinary, to show by the meticulous accumulation of detail just how strange and complicated human beings become when they cannot Blast Off. The young Osborne is held under, friendless, in a tyranny of Black Looks and social convention, so that even fried food ('an easeful fry-up') at someone else's house becomes a symbol of pleasure, of style. (p. 23)

As he grows up, food and sex become conspicuously mixed up together. When he loses his virginity, it seems inevitable that his friend, waiting for him on the bed, should first have to put aside her bag of chips, though not, admittedly, before finishing them. 'The pyjamas peeled away like clothing cut through before surgery. I had never known anything like it.'

All Osborne's theatrical judgments are shrewd. Eliot is put in his place, rightly, in my view, as the man who 'beckoned audiences to watch the Greek Furies enter from French windows, in tweed skirts, gardening gloves, and brandishing trugs and secateurs . . .', and Shaw does no better: 'Shaw avoided passion almost as prudently as Coward. Frigidity and caution demand an evasive style, and they both perfected one.' The theatrical historian will be happy in this book, for although Osborne stops short before the moment when ***Look Back in Anger*** was produced, he does give the most pungent account of the work of everyday theatres after the war. There will be no better nor more hilarious source of research into the Saga Repertory Company, Ilfracombe, nor the Victoria Theatre, Hayling Island, where Osborne interpreted the part of Hamlet as 'a leering milk roundsman from Denmark Hill'. Throughout also, Osborne makes clear just how close his life and his plays have been, so an unhappy marriage to Pamela Lane is unashamedly offered as the model for Jimmy and Alison Porter.

Overall, you come to feel Osborne cared little for the theatre as such. The company of queens and fools and friendly women is what attracted him there. When the seediness died, so, it seems, did his love of the theatre itself. And his prose is so supple, so enviably clear that you realise how many choices he has always had as a writer. The theatre, if anything, was singled out for the lavish opportunities it will always provide for Giving Offence.

It saddens me, I suppose, that a childhood about which he has so much reason to be bitter produces such affectionate writing, whereas his adult life seems streaked with cruelty. If Blasting Off comes to be the very purpose of his adulthood, then here at least, vividly recollected, is the explanation. His rudeness as he grows older is indeed shocking, though no more shocking than he intends it to be. Once he gets the hang of it, nobody can make quite such a dirty wound. (pp. 23-4)

David Hare, "Opportunities for Blasting Off," in New Statesman, *Vol. 102, No. 2639, October 16, 1981, pp. 23-4.*

JOHN LAHR

A Better Class of Person, Osborne's superb account of his early, unfamous years, is haunted by [Noel] Coward. As a dissection of English life and the origins of his own volatile temperament, the book surpasses Coward's *Present Indicative* as the most vivid chronicle of the making of an English playwright. "That voice that cries out in the wilderness doesn't have to be a weakling's does it?" says Jimmy Porter, the hectoring hero of ***Look Back in Anger.*** Jimmy Porter's disgust isolates him from the world he wants to purify with his rage. Osborne, like his hero, was hell on a short fuse. His loathing of mediocrity and his loneliness were the byproducts of a lifetime of lower-middle-class making do. He reacted to the lace-curtain gentility on both sides of his family with a hatred of quiet resignation, of routine, priggishness and the ambitions of the herd. To Osborne, peace was something for the dead; and the suburbs were a cemetery for the living: "women pushing prams along the clean pavements with their grass verges, fresh as last week's graves." He grew up boxed in by class inferiority, a terror built into the pretensions of language as well as personality. (pp. 1, 30)

Although Osborne claims "no adult ever addressed a question to me," he remembers the adults with photographic clarity. "Disappointment was oxygen to them," he writes of the bitter, quarreling family whose Christmas rows were the only action in their fixed lives. They had no hope, no dream, no energy. And Osborne saw no courage in their winded lives. "The grudge that was their birthright they pursued with passionate despondency to the grave."

Osborne's fierce determination to live intensely came from an early immersion in death. His sister died at 2 of tuberculosis; and Osborne's father, absent for long convalescent periods throughout his childhood, finally succumbed to the same disease when Osborne was 11. Osborne himself was a sickly child, often kept home from school so his mother would have company and later because of rheumatic fever. Relentlessly scrubbed and cleaned by his mother, Osborne's home was a joyless place, barren of ornaments or books, with "hardly any evidence of life lived or being lived."

Osborne's mother, to whom "hospitality was as unknown as friendship," is wickedly referred to throughout the memoir as Nellie Beatrice, a name which captures both her commonness and her pretension. Describing wartime treat luncheons with his mother at the Trocodero, a restaurant in Kensington whose French menu confounded them and where they invariably settled for fish and chips, Osborne writes; "Her technique with waiters, as in life, was to either bully or fawn upon them. 'Oh, you really are very kind,' 'Oh, yes, we *did* enjoy that.' If this ladylike charm got no response from the waiter she would resort to her usual bad temper, giving both the waiter and myself Black Looks." Osborne's depiction of her blackmailing Black Looks, her "flare-ups," her constant moving from house to house and her mania for a germ-free home, with the vacuum cleaner "bellowing and bullying a filthy uncomprehending world," is brilliant. (p. 30)

Expelled from his minor public school for punching the headmaster, who'd slapped him, Osborne fell into theater as an escape from the drudgery of daily routine and the responsibilities of being both son and, at 18, fiancé. The theater became at once his family and the repository for his vague, untested passion for excellence. Osborne's account of his lackluster career as a bungling stage manager, leching actor, gouging company manager and occasional playwright is wonderful.

Few famous names grace the regional backwaters and town halls where Osborne got his training. The desperation and delight of those days are stylishly re-created. "We committed our lines," he writes of being imprisoned in yet another dreary, dispirited rep company, "as if we were sewing mailbags." Already the young Osborne, who as a student had formed a secret society of spleen called "The Viper Gang" with his only high-school chum, was exhibiting the arrogance and talent for invective of the playwright-to-be. In his outspoken hatred of toadies, timeservers, prigs, form-serving bullies of postwar

Britain, he was frequently fired from jobs. "The sack," he writes, "was becoming my only foreseeable work satisfaction."

Osborne's initiation into sex and writing plays came at the hands of a 30-year-old rep leading lady, Stella Linden, with a pelvic arch like the skull of an ox. Stella, whose husband was a small-fry impresario, schooled Osborne in the plays of Pinero and in all the boulevard folderol that Osborne would turn upside down in 1956. Osborne in love is as swaggering and exhilarating as Osborne in anger. His account of his passion for Stella and for his first wife, the actress Pamela Lane (the model for Alison in ***Look Back in Anger***), is full of bittersweet nostalgia. Of his separation from Pamela he writes, "I was absorbed in loss, unmistakable loss, inescapable loss, unacceptable to all but gamblers."

A Better Class of Person is the best piece of writing Osborne has done since ***Inadmissible Evidence*** (1965). After that, his verbal barrages became grapeshot instead of sharpshooting. He neither revised his scripts nor moderated his cranky outbursts. His plays, like his pronouncements about an England he could no longer fathom, became second-rate and self-indulgent. But ***A Better Class of Person*** takes its energy from looking backward to the source of his pain before fame softened him. In this first installment of his autobiography, Osborne rediscovers the daring and cheek which distinguished his early, good work. With ***A Better Class of Person*** John Osborne once again is making a gorgeous fuss. (pp. 30, 32)

John Lahr, in a review of "A Better Class of Person," in The New York Times Book Review, *November 8, 1981, pp. 1, 30, 32.*

JOHN RUSSELL TAYLOR

Osborne seems for the moment to have forsaken drama for autobiography; or perhaps he has simply recognised that autobiography was his true vocation all along, and that ***A Better Class of Person*** is a longer and less interrupted monologue than he could ever hope to get away with in the theatre. Certainly, though in it he deals only with his childhood and youth, stopping short in 1956 on the threshold of ***Look Back in Anger,*** success and fame, he does not seem to be very interested in exploring or understanding the roots of his young (or middle-aged) anger. The book is in fact hardly reflective at all, let alone analytical: like the great tirades of Jimmy Porter in ***Look Back in Anger*** or of Bill Maitland in ***Inadmissible Evidence,*** it is a cry of fury and frustration, if not quite despair. Again he is looking back in anger on his mother, his background, his life, and what affects us is not the sense of what he is saying, but the sheer force with which he says it.

This is why it is impossible to believe that he is through with the theatre, or that he could be really at home as a writer anywhere else. There is something so naturally histrionic about everything he does. Perhaps all he needs is a new subject (for scandal and concern, of course). Back in the old days, when people said he did not seem to sympathise with anything, it was not quite true: his sympathetic characters were there for everyone to see, but they seemed so wrong for an angry young man that no one could quite believe their eyes and ears. The only ones let off lightly were the old, the established, the upper-class—that better class of person he always wanted so desperately to join. Now that he has joined it, and bids fair to become the Evelyn Waugh of the Eighties, fulminating at the dreadfulness of foreigners and the stylelessness of life from the comfort and seclusion of a semi-stately home, it must be hard to whip up the old outrageous indignation—as ***The End of Me Old Cigar*** rather clearly indicated—and make it seem urgent or important or even shockingly funny. But once a dramatist, always a dramatist, and surely Osborne, the only one of the Royal Court's new dramatists with a real common touch, will not be content to memorialize for ever—not, at least, without a real live audience reacting, somewhere out there in the dark. (p. 23)

John Russell Taylor, "After Anger and After," in Plays & Players, *Vol. 29, No. 339, December, 1981, pp. 22-3.*

BENEDICT NIGHTINGALE

John Arden has said that ***Look Back in Anger*** supplied the theatre with "passion and contemporary relevance" at a time when their absence was no longer even noticed; and Tom Stoppard has doubted whether he would have become a playwright at all, had it not been for the excitement Osborne's play generated, the feeling it created that the drama was "the place to be at." It did much to resuscitate a comatose British theatre, increasing the sweep of its subject-matter and, hence, of its audience appeal; and, in spite of ups and downs, the patient's heart, brain and lungs have been firing more or less satisfactorily ever since. Yet what has happened to the man responsible for that feat? . . . Off the stage, and to a large extent on it, the battling dramatist has transformed himself into a puny blimp—and the obvious question is, why? Have his brains been turned by the strain of living up to his own legend? Or is there something more deeply lacking in his character? Perhaps the first episode of his autobiography [***A Better Class of Person***] may have a clue or two to offer.

Since it comes to an end immediately before George Devine accepted ***Anger*** for performance at the Royal Court, the book does not contain a great deal of obvious and overt interest to the dramatic historian. (p. 64)

The real interest of Osborne's autobiography is what it tells us about his formative years, or, rather, what it tells us he felt about them. (p. 66)

[The] picture we're given is of a young man of strong likes and (and more often) dislikes, capable of passion but also, as he himself wryly recognises, of a disconcerting pettiness; a dedicated rebel, though mainly in the sense of not hesitating to make himself objectionable to the dull, drab or conventional. Interestingly, he seems to be without social or political convictions.

It is always presumptuous to put a writer on the psychiatrist's couch on the basis of his work, even if that work includes an autobiography; but, in so far as it is possible in Osborne's case, we may, I think, conclude that his family, and especially his mother, did much to define him both positively and negatively. His upbringing presumably helps explain his work's insistence on the primacy of emotion, the idea that we must keep caring, keep responding, or die. He once said that his aim as a writer was to give "lessons in feeling", meaning in love, friendship, outrage, hate and, perhaps, despair; and from the time of Jimmy Porter, who incessantly makes it plain that a sentient war is to be preferred to a moribund peace, to that of Ben and Sally Prosser, the acrimonious yet loving couple at the heart of ***Watch It Come Down,*** he has attempted to do precisely that. And, at least in the early days, the public enthusiasm for his work suggests he substantially succeeded, too.

But from the start, or at least from the time of his first failure, ***The World of Paul Slickey,*** it was apparent that his strength was also his limitation; and the passing years have made his weaknesses the clearer. Bluntly, he lacks mind, meaning both the organising and the appraising intellect. He has always tended to allow a single character, one in conflict with apathy, triviality, stupidity, cupidity, or some other manifestation of an uncaring society, to dominate the proceedings and shape what, for want of a better word, we'll call the plot. In recent years, however, both character and plot have become thinly camouflaged excuses for Osborne to propagate his feelings about and to the world.

This might not matter if those feelings were arresting in themselves, or were at least the result of sharp observation and analysis. But even those who were his warmest admirers of yore find it difficult to make any such claim. . . . Increasingly, his "drama" has consisted of using thinly realised characters to offer unsubstantiated opinions about the state of Britain from a stance that one can call nostalgic, reactionary or blimpish, depending on one's own convictions and charity.

Take Pamela, the actress-heroine of ***Time Present.*** She admittedly has a generosity that counteracts what would otherwise be unrelieved bitchiness, and gives her some solidity as a character; but her identity is mainly rhetorical, her function to be a blend of sentimental obituary and searing editorial. For her father, a thespian of the old school dying offstage, she has the respect Osborne's people all seem to share when they look back towards the Edwardian era; for those around her, little but distaste. Her verbal hit-list becomes positively encyclopaedic: hippies, drugs, boutiques, trendy clothes, swinging London, underground papers and bookshops, Viet Nam protesters, women novelists and biographers, women politicians, the Labour Party, the nation's technological pretensions, committed actresses, "faggots" and "pooves", Americans, American drama, modern poetry, and, of course, the critics, with their "frigid little minds."

This list is expanded by subsequent plays, perhaps most contentiously by ***A Sense of Detachment,*** at once a desultory satire on avant-garde theatre and an exploitation of its techniques. What, after all, is proved by juxtaposing snippets from Shakespeare, Yeats and other poets with extracts from modern pornography? That our generation uniquely lacks the capacity to love? This idea comes to the surface when a character goes on to denounce technological innovation, industrial progress and economic union: "People don't fall in love: that idea is no longer effective in the context of modern techniques." The interesting questions, of course, are why people need porn and whether the Common Market will alter the British way of life for the better or worse; but Osborne's puppets are not there to explore and argue, rather to buttonhole and pronounce on his behalf.

What makes this still more maddening is his fondness for dividing the world into Us, who for all our faults safeguard honest feeling and decent values, and Them, the enemies of such things. This is so in ***West of Suez,*** at the end of which an eminent writer, centre of a group of expatriate English, is first harangued by an American yippie who conveniently incarnates much that Osborne finds mindless in the young, and is then killed by rampaging blacks. "They've shot the fox", incants someone over his body, implying, with scant justification, that all that is cultivated and honourable has been desecrated. The tendency is still more marked in ***Watch It Come Down,*** at whose end a commune of writers and artists is assailed by country "yobbos." "We all, *the few of us,* need one another", wails Sally Prosser over the dying Ben. The italics are Osborne's; but nothing he has shown, as opposed to declared, proves that this is a cultural élite worth conserving or that those outside are as malevolently philistine as we're meant to believe.

This was in 1976, and Osborne has written no play since, which may be just as well. His most recent work represents the victory of vague feeling over hard thought, impression over observation, notion over idea, prejudice over conviction, paranoia over anger, clutter over art, and, just conceivably, his mother over himself. He has, one feels, reacted violently and often usefully against her. Yet something of her temperament continues to fester inside him, as he himself seems ruefully to recognise. At any rate, his autobiography contains suggestive extracts from his writer's notebooks, including this: "I am ashamed of her as part of myself that can't be cast out, my own conflict, the disease which I suffer and have inherited, what I *am* and never could be whole. My disease, an invitation to my sick room."

Something of that "disease" is surely there in his quick contempts, his instinctive and sometimes barely rational distastes, and the mean-mindedness with which he is capable of expressing them. . . . Indeed, there are many times in the biography when one's natural empathy with the author disappears, and one is left wondering who is the real villain, the "costive slug" (or whomever) he has just been gleefully evoking, or Osborne himself.

And so, of course, it is with many of the hate-objects in the plays themselves. Who wrote much of ***Time Present, A Sense of Detachment*** and ***West of Suez***? Was it the Osborne we once knew, the crusader (so it seemed) for a society at once more caring and more responsive to the oppressed individual? Or was it his dear old mum, casting Black Looks from above her knitting, and peevishly animadverting on the inexplicable failure of a bad world to accord her her infinite due? Both, no doubt. Both were probably there from the beginning. The trouble is that the second seems substantially to have taken control of the house.

When I say that both were there from the beginning, I have in mind not only ***Look Back in Anger,*** whose main character had his share of peevishness, self-pity, lack of charity and prejudice, but ***Inadmissible Evidence,*** whose main character suffered from all that and more. The difference is that in those days Osborne seemed to know it. Those traits were coolly perceived aspects of a variegated personality, and not items in a critique, attack or sermon we were supposed to applaud. This was particularly so in the case of ***Inadmissible Evidence,*** probably Osborne's masterpiece, and certainly the last play in which he turned his limitations into a positive advantage.

One character dominates the stage throughout. The supporting characters barely exist, and then only in relation to the solicitor, Bill Maitland. Indeed, the plot consists mainly of their mass exodus from his life. He has betrayed his wife, offended his friends, seduced the office girls and dropped them, insulted his daughter, bent his mistress's ear with a torrent of self-doubt, and given every indication to both his subordinates and clients that he's losing control of himself and his business; and consequently one after another rejects him, leaving him alone at the end in his empty office, awaiting the arrival of a representative of the Law Society, which has been investigating his dubious professional ethics.

Again, he spends long monologues railing, complaining or simply introspecting. The opening scene is actually one of his nightmares. He appears in a court accused of having published an obscenity, namely his life, and proceeds emotionally to expose himself in lurid detail. We gather he's a heavy drinker, a hypochondriac, forever dosing himself with pills; a self-made man, envious of those with more pukka backgrounds than his; self-disgusted, to the extent that he feels "irredeemably mediocre" and suspects he has never made a decision that wasn't shoddy or wrong; fearful of the rejection that, as we've seen, his behavior tends to court; friendless, and, though not loveless, inclined to think he's inflicted more pain than pleasure in love. And the litany of self-accusation rises to an anguished climax: "I can't escape it, I can't forget it, and I can't begin again."

It could all add up to self-pity and acrimony. Yet we don't feel, as we do so often with the later plays, that Maitland is just a cracked trumpet through which the baleful playwright is woozily blazoning his own manifold beefs. On the contrary, Maitland is a character he sees with complete clarity, in the round, from outside as well as inside. Indeed, ***Inadmissible Evidence*** may be seen as a scrupulously chronicled journey into the head of a man on the brink of mental, emotional and spiritual breakdown, an arena that naturally limits the reality of the supporting cast. It is an objective picture of a subjective experience, and, by the end, an archetypal—no, *the* archetypal—study of middle-aged ennui, despair and disintegration. Ronald Bryden did not vastly exaggerate when he called the play a modern tragedy—"Osborne has gathered our English terrors in Maitland's image, and purged them pitiably and terribly."

That was in 1964, an achievement worth recalling and celebrating when one has been goaded and exasperated by his later work to dismiss Osborne from serious consideration. If one can't in all honesty see him writing with the same scathing detachment in the future, one must surely remember that he produced one play of historical importance in ***Look Back in Anger,*** one of undoubted excellence in ***Inadmissible Evidence,*** and, in ***The Entertainer*** and ***A Patriot for Me,*** two plays that future generations may well think worth reviving. Very few modern playwrights may have made such abject fools of themselves as Osborne; but very few can claim as much as that. (pp. 66, 68-70)

Benedict Nightingale, "The Fatality of Hatred," in Encounter, *Vol. LVIII, No. 5, May, 1982, pp. 63-4, 66, 68-70.*

Francine Prose

1947-

American novelist and short story writer.

Prose has garnered recognition for her novels, in which she interweaves the real with the supernatural, the rational with the irrational, in a style reminiscent of traditional folktales. Her works often feature writers or actors who are involved in creating their own stories or characters. Employing a wide range of locations and time periods, Prose explores such themes as the importance of being true to one's beliefs, the role of faith in human life, and the nature of storytelling. Critics generally commend Prose for her ability to maintain a lucid, unaffected narrative style while often treating fantastical subject matter.

Prose's first novel, *Judah the Pious* (1973), was praised by Thomas Lask as "notably successful in tone and over-all finish, full of sudden delights and mocking humor." This work, which utilizes mystical and supernatural elements, follows the efforts of a Polish rabbi to have traditional Jewish burial rites reinstated as part of modern custom. Prose's next novel, *The Glorious Ones* (1974), is set in seventeenth-century Italy and focuses upon a group of *commedia dell'arte* actors who struggle to maintain identities apart from their dramatic roles. *Marie Laveau* (1977) is a fictionalized account of the life of Mary Laveau, who lived in New Orleans during the nineteenth century and who was believed to possess magical abilities. Prose demonstrates that while many of Laveau's powers emanated from simple common sense, they remain mysterious and largely inexplicable to the novel's other characters. *Animal Magnetism* (1978) examines the nineteenth-century practice of using hypnosis to cure physical ailments.

Prose's fiction of the 1980s centers on many of the same themes as her earlier work. *Household Saints* (1981) reveals the ways in which religious beliefs and chance happenings have shaped the lives of members of an Italian-American family. *Hungry Hearts* (1983) again focuses upon actors and their roles. The principal players, who comprise the Yiddish Art Theater in the early 1920s, learn a valuable lesson in separating their private and public lives when an actress becomes possessed by a dybbuk while onstage. Stephen Harvey noted: "Like [Isaac Bashevis Singer, Prose] recreates the momentum of a picaresque fable, in which any number of primal issues simmer beneath its anecdotal, folksy manner." In her recent novel, *Bigfoot Dreams* (1986), Prose combines humor and pathos in her portrayal of Vera, a writer for the sensationalistic fictional tabloid *This Week*. Through a series of misfortunes, Vera has lost her job and her lover by the book's end, but she finds comfort at a meeting of cryptologists, who seek the unusual in reality instead of in fiction. Prose has also published *Stories from Our Living Past* (1974), a collection of Jewish folktales, and her short stories have appeared in such periodicals as the *Atlantic*, the *Village Voice*, and *Commentary*.

(See also *Contemporary Authors*, Vols. 109, 112.)

Photograph by Howie Michels

THOMAS LASK

Francine Prose's first novel, ***Judah the Pious,*** reads like a folk tale, full of mysterious and improbable happenings, strange encounters and unpredictable turns of events. The hand of God can be felt hovering over all that occurs. . . .

Although the setting for ***Judah the Pious*** is Poland, the court of the king and the city of Cracow, with the types of Jews one has encountered innumerable times before, it is not a novel of the generation gap between the orthodox and the agnostics or a novel of the breaking up of society under pressure of war and pogrom. It is, in short, not a work similar to Robert Kotlowitz's recently published *Somewhere Else* or I. B. Singer's *The Manor*. It is rather in the tradition of the European tale, in spite of certain Hasidic trappings, similar to "The Pardoner's Tale" in Chaucer or to Isak Dinesen's *Seven Gothic Tales,* to cite a modern example. But whatever category it belongs to, it is an unusual and impressive effort, especially for a first novel, notably successful in tone and over-all finish, full of sudden delights and mocking humor. The author . . . navigates serenely between the real and the fantastic, between the rational and the supernatural. Puzzling occurrences turn out to have ordinary human causes. But other equally puzzling events simply "happen." They can't be explained through ordinary means. There are wild Gothic elements in the book and simple common-sense ones, and by alternating them, the author keeps the reader happily off balance. Part of her success is surely due to her tone, which suggests the narrative exposition of a Jewish sage—a tone that never falters and that is half the fun.

To the court of the King of Poland comes an old, nondescript rabbi, Eliezer of Rimanov, to ask the young monarch to rescind a ban on Jewish custom that has to do with the burial of the dead. In a few moments, the rabbi, without half trying, has the courtiers dismissed, and is himself seated on the throne, with the king at his feet listening to his rabbinic wisdom. King and sage make a formal wager. If the rabbi can convince the ruler that it is an error not to allow in one's philosophy for the unseen in improbable, then the king will allow the burial practice to be restored. Whereupon begins a long story, with digressions, interlardings and surprising twists that eventually convince the king.

But between that opening gambit and the final concession lies a wealth of inventive story-telling. The novel belongs to a genre better served, I think by being brief, and I must admit to a certain impatience as the story neared its end. Nevertheless, Miss Prose's fictional foray into this untraditional mode, still untraditional for an American writer, is a sure guarantee of interest in her future work.

Thomas Lask, "The Sage and the Gentleman," in The New York Times, *February 17, 1973, p. 29.*

D. KEITH MANO

Judah the Pious astounds. Not superficially at all. The novel reads as if it were some bad translation of itself: bald, literal, rather like the much overrated Jerusalem Bible, dry. Francine Prose . . . freeze-dries her writing, presumably so that stylistic and metaphorical pleasures will not distract. I'm disposed, as you notice, to make her the beneficiary of my doubt. Vocabulary is familiar; is, to be honest, quite banal. . . . Descriptions unfurl in series: predictably three sentences or a bracelet of three phrases linked by semi-colons, or three words. The author has staked a first novel reputation on the inherent, elemental force of her narrative. Not even that: on the force alone of its splendid conclusion.

For the narrative is provisioned with folk-legend staples. Story-telling inside story-telling: young ruler educated by a wise rabbi. Unknown paternities; the quest through suffering and disillusionment; a conception that seems immaculate, give or take a few maculae. . . . There are sufficient eerie happenings to maintain interest, but not an overabundance, as the genre goes.

Yet the conclusion fascinated me; fascinates me still. It is at once reversal and consummation. I cannot abstract it fairly here, but God and Judah the Pious (a great Jewish saint) are found to be mountebanks and finaglers of a kind: yet their fraudulence only serves somehow to confirm holiness. As a Christian novelist-reviewer I was reminded of matters that I have tended to forget. That the New Testament has over-simplified the Old, has bowdlerized it in a sense. That the Son—mediator and advocate—has also distanced the Father I share with the author. That "The Lord, thy God, is a jealous God"—not to mention angry, fickle, full of humor, and closer to an Old Testament people who have always better understood these mysterious words "made in His image." A God who is willing to let His grace, His revelation be made known by methods that a liberal priest or rabbi might condemn in . . . well, in *The New York Times*.

That's a lot to learn, or be reminded of, in just one novel. I don't think my reaction can be altogether due to a special sensitivity; this is available more or less to anyone who reads ***Judah the Pious***. At 25, Francine Prose appears to perceive more than a writer of that age decently should. I cannot, in good conscience, say that she is a novelist yet. But she may well be a prophet, no small thing. (pp. 2-3)

D. Keith Mano, in a review of "Judah the Pious," in The New York Times Book Review, *February 25, 1973, pp. 2-3.*

PATRICK CRUTTWELL AND FAITH WESTBURG

[***Judah the Pious***] appears to be a sophisticated pastiche of the tales of Jewish folklore. Its story, fantastic and picaresque, is supposed to be told by a wise old Jewish "mountebank" to a boy-king of Poland, at a time when the Jews are in some danger of a pogrom. The tone—*faux-naif,* more or less—is kept up very successfully through a prose of studied elegance: but we did feel that it was kept up too long for comfort. This is in the genre of the moral tale, the genre of *Candide* and *Rasselas,* and such moral tales should be brief. And we couldn't decide what the "moral" of this one was. That the "telling of stories," the exercise of fancy and imagination, is a way of, as it were, making sense out of pogroms? Maybe: in which case ***Judah the Pious*** has a certain remote kinship with *A Woman Named Solitude*. But the latter does have a quality of memorable evocativeness: ***Judah the Pious,*** against it, seems dim, self-conscious, contrived.

Patrick Cruttwell and Faith Westburg, in a review of "Judah the Pious," in The Hudson Review, *Vol. XXVI, No. 2, Summer, 1973, p. 421.*

PUBLISHERS WEEKLY

Francine Prose transports us in [***The Glorious Ones***]—with remarkably little sense of anachronism—to 16th century Italy, building her story around a group of Commedia dell'Arte actors. . . . There's a lot of individualized life in her characters, some of them adapted from history, and there's a magic to her tale, which is written with luminous simplicity and catches the humor, pathos and passion of Lover, Pantaloon, Doctor, Inamorata and so on, their roles in life and on stage subtly interfused. These people carry the story forward turn and turn about, but the chief protagonist is the swaggering troupe leader who poignantly fails in both his roles. Round and perfect as a water bead, what this enchanting world a little lacks is solid substance—as though Miss Prose hadn't given her imagination quite the necessary grist.

A review of "The Glorious Ones," in Publishers Weekly, *Vol. 205, No. 3, January 21, 1974, p. 78.*

PEARL K. BELL

Francine Prose's curious little novel, ***The Glorious Ones*** . . . , recounts the history and adventures of a troupe of commedia dell'arte actors traveling through 17th-century Italy. In seven powerfully written chapters—each told by a different typecast character such as the Clown, the Miser and the Lover—we learn about the company's triumphs and failures as it performs its repertory of farce and romance wherever it can find a paying audience. . . . Torrid love affairs and backbiting, jealous contempt and slavish devotion, camaraderie and black rage make up the climate of this gaudy little world, beyond the reach of normal society and ordinary emotion, where artists of improvisatory brilliance hang together by sheer bravura, though they fight like wildcats.

But in the end ***The Glorious Ones*** is disappointing, because Miss Prose isn't saying anything that matters. Unlike her fine first novel, ***Judah the Pious,*** a hypnotically resonant tale modeled on Hasidic parables, her latest work seems an exercise in esoterica. "All human life is . . . just a series of stories and plays, most of which are exactly the same," the author tells us. Maybe so, yet ***The Glorious Ones*** more strongly suggests something else—that perhaps Miss Prose, much as one admires her strenuous avoidance of the familiar autobiographical roads taken by most novelists under 30, has now gone too far in the other direction. Despite her cleverly executed somersaults and cartwheels through an obscure theatrical pocket of the past, she fails to convince us that a razzle-dazzle stunt is a solution to a young writer's pursuit of originality. (pp. 17-18).

Pearl K. Bell, "The Artist As Hero," in The New Leader, *Vol. LVII, No. 5, March 4, 1974, pp. 17-18.*

PATRICIA MEYER SPACKS

Francine Prose, in ***The Glorious Ones,*** makes her novelistic subject the novelist's difficulty of determining the proper balance between internal and external life. Her characters, who tell versions of a single story from varying points of view, belong to a troupe of traveling players in seventeenth-century Italy. Ms. Prose avoids the dreariness of the historical novel, making little attempt at external verisimilitude—the book contains no visual world, few objects, only the sketchiest reference to large happenings—and writing as directly and naively as if she were reporting events in a college dormitory. She tells of the impossibility of separating truth from fiction. The parts actors take on the stage and in real life merge, they don't know when they're acting. Initially, it seems that their director has an inspired eye for physiognomy, for finding faces and bodies appropriate to the roles he needs to fill. But it may be, rather, that the roles shape the men and women playing them. Their ambiguous situation penalizes them through their gradual separation from reality. . . . Their separation from the real also involves danger for spectators: "We made them believe that we loved them; at the very same time, we made them think our love was all in their minds, a fantasy of their own creation. . . . It wasn't our fault. For the truth of the matter was that *we* never knew what we really felt, and what was just in our imaginations." The slippery antithesis between *really* and *just* epitomizes the tensions of which the novel is made, beginning with the opening allusion to Dante, whose vision of hell existed "just" in his imagination. Reflecting back on that allusion, one understands more than any of the narrators realizes. Perhaps, in fact, one can "really feel" *only* what exists "just in the imagination," imagination being the single valid source of emotion. At any rate, ***The Glorious Ones*** provokes such speculation. Yet it's a book more satisfying to think about than to read: the actual narrative suffers from thinness, flimsiness of verbal texture; it's a one-gimmick book; you get bored with the gimmick; the different points of view don't tell enough. (pp. 293-94)

Patricia Meyer Spacks, in a review of "The Glorious Ones," in The Hudson Review, *Vol. XXVII, No. 2, Summer, 1974, pp. 293-94.*

PUBLISHERS WEEKLY

Marie Laveau is New Orleans' voodoo queen, a beauty, mysterious and fascinating. Eighteenth century Louisiana is the stage for this captivating, otherworldly, romantic tale [***Marie Laveau***]. The novel is Marie's life story: the strange circumstances of her birth, her Catholic upbringing, her education at the glittering cotillions where quadroons and octaroons flock to seek out rich men to make their lives secure. Marie finds herself in "business," a business that makes her privy to the secrets of the New Orleans élite and gives her power to go along with her magic. Her own search for love and the strange fulfillment of her prescient dreams leads to the birth of a child who will one day wear her crown. Ms. Prose creates an enchanting, spooky world and fills it with exotic happenings.

A review of "Marie Laveau," in Publishers Weekly, *Vol. 210, No. 23, December 6, 1976, p. 53.*

THOMAS LASK

Francine Prose's gothic imagination and exotic style, characteristics of her earlier books, serve her well in [***Marie Laveau,*** a] retelling in fictional form of the story of Mary Laveau. Part black, Mary Laveau was a well-known 19th-century New Orleans figure, who had second sight, performed various feats of magic, talked to spirits and healed those wounded in body and mind. She was also a power in local politics. She got things done in ways not always allowed by law. . . .

Miss Prose follows Mary Laveau's career from her birth (with a caul) to the end of her life, when she became a figure of legend. She conveys well that peculiar mixture of down-to-earth living and transcendental experience that marked New Orleans society of that time. And she shows that no matter how matter-of-fact the lives of her characters were or how easily their magic could be explained, there remained nevertheless a side to their existence not easily explicable in rational terms.

In spite of a number of dramatic incidents, the novel tends to be one-toned; the happenings repeat themselves, but the life the author recorded is an intriguing exploration of that area between dreaming and waking, when reality loses all its hard edges.

Thomas Lask, "Tale of a Noble Blackmailer," in The New York Times, *September 15, 1977, p. C22.*

KIRKUS REVIEWS

Animal Magnetism has all the ingredients for a pot of tripe, and yet the delivered dish is elegantly satisfying. The subject is no less than the life and death of the animal magnetism fad in early 19th-century New England, a lecture-circuit phenomenon later eclipsed by the moonburst of Spiritualism. Somehow, we are moved by the passing of this briefly flaring belief in "a universal fluid" that moves through and connects everything and can "do anything" required of it. And the reader agrees, because animal magnetism is essentially self-improvement through self-hypnosis. This is the real secret of the process (that you can do it alone), but it eludes the mesmerist hero here who thinks *he* is doing the healing. . . . Rooted in the pathos of fact, this is a psychic historical with persuasive social portraiture and considerable storytelling verve.

A review of "Animal Magnetism," in Kirkus Reviews, *Vol. XLVI, No. 12, June 15, 1978, p. 657.*

PUBLISHERS WEEKLY

[In ***Animal Magnetism***] Charles Jordan, a young Frenchman, is a practitioner of Animal Magnetism, a mysterious process in which the magnetist and his subject share one nervous system and experience each other's sensations and thoughts. When he arrives in Lowell, Mass., he becomes involved in experiments with a 24-year-old factory girl named Zinnia, who is suffering from assorted mental and physical ills. She becomes his perfect subject. He goes on the road to give lecture-demonstrations and is a huge success. Zinnia herself regains her health, but unfortunately, Charles cannot cure his own ills. In fact, he even contracts her personal "female complaints." A local dentist, desperate to use Animal Magnetism himself, begins a campaign of gossip about them. Then Spiritualism becomes the fad. . . . Prose has more than enough mesmerizing tricks up her sleeve to make this tale intriguing.

A review of "Animal Magnetism," in Publishers Weekly, *Vol. 213, No. 25, June 19, 1978, p. 95.*

PUBLISHERS WEEKLY

Funny, pathetic and touching ***Household Saints*** is a wildly inventive tale of what may be a modern miracle on Mulberry Street, the center of New York's Italian quarter. When Joseph Santangelo, the sausagemaker, wins his bride, Catherine, in a pinochle game, he sets in motion a patten of events laced with ancient Mediterranean customs, superstition and religion that affect the women in his life. . . . A skillful fabulist, Francine Prose, whose earlier novels have won praise, not only captures the domestic scenes and smells of Little Italy but allows her *naifs* to unfold in recognizable earthiness and warmth as they confront life's mysteries.

A review of "Household Saints," in Publishers Weekly, *Vol. 219, No. 19, May 8, 1981, p. 247.*

DONNA L. NERBOSO

[***Household Saints***] is the story of three generations of Italian-American women: Catherine, won by her husband in a pinochle game; her mother-in-law, who lives her life by signs and portents; and her daughter Theresa, born to be a saint. Their lives are devoted to housekeeping and sausage-making, but their tasks are transformed by an intensity of vision that perceives life's patterns as God's miracles. This is a simple but powerful tale, rich in the texture of a narration that juxtaposes the ordinary with the supernatural, elevating the lives of its characters from the commonplace to the mythic.

Donna L. Nerboso, in a review of "Household Saints," in Library Journal, *Vol. 106, No. 11, June 1, 1981, p. 1244.*

RANDOLPH HOGAN

From the very first sentence of Francine Prose's fifth novel [***Household Saints***], you know you're under the spell of a first-rate storyteller: "It happened by the grace of God that Joseph Santangelo won his wife in a card game."

The time is the late 1940's, the place is Manhattan's Little Italy and the storyteller paints it vividly. . . .

Joseph is a neighborhood butcher who weighs his thumb along with the sausage, tipping the scales. . . . Catherine Falconetti is the girl he wins at pinochle, a girl whose family has endured the withering gaze of the malocchio, or evil eye, for generations.

The heat is hellish enough to make men desperate: Catherine's father, three sheets to the wind and cursed with perennial bad luck, stakes his daughter against the chance for a blast from the North Pole—the meat locker in which Joseph keeps his sausage chilled.

After only a few pages, most of the elements of Miss Prose's modern-day legend are already in place: the grace of God, the feast day of a saint, the luck of the draw, the chance beginning of a marriage—and that sausage, which is strung through the entire novel. . . .

One element is still to come. After the Santangelos' chance marriage turns into love, deepens and becomes a real marriage, Catherine finds she is pregnant. Joseph's mother, whose mysticism eventually blossoms into madness, asks him, "How could you bring children into this world with that lousy Falconetti luck?" The evil eye prevails. Catherine suffers a miscarriage. After a long, depressed convalescence in which Catherine loses her faith in God, spring comes, and with it renewal. Joseph's mother dies, and a child is born. Theresa is the perfect child, everything a parent could hope for: obedient, helpful, devoted, almost . . . saintly. (p. 12)

Like all fine novels, ***Household Saints*** is an equation, everything held in delicate balance until the pieces fall into place with the certainty of algebra. And like all fine novelists, Miss Prose concerns herself with the elemental: randomness and predestination; good luck and bad; cheating and being cheated; God's will and man's will; sainthood and sin; madness; patterns weaving their way through generations. . . . It's hard to convey the richness and the engaging complexity of this deceptively simple novel, to provide some idea of its wisdom and humor, and to tell you that its appeal is by no means special—it deserves the widest possible audience. Francine Prose is a splendid writer. (p. 37)

Randolph Hogan, "The Butcher Won a Wife," in The New York Times Book Review, *July 12, 1981, pp. 12, 37.*

STEPHEN HARVEY

Hungry Hearts is a Yiddish tall tale whose plot would be most aptly described as cockamamie. Francine Prose's collective subject is a high-minded troupe known as the Yiddish Art Theater, determined circa 1922 to exalt the aesthetic tone of the Jewish stage by rendering out the schmaltz then peddled so successfully along Second Avenue. Its main dramatis personae are impresario Dalashinsky . . . and Benno Brownstein, the company juvenile, renowned for his Trigoristein in a certain bowdlerized Chekhov play and secretly wedded to ingenue Dinah Rappoport, whose memoir this novel is. The ensemble embarks on a turbulent tour through culture-hungry ghettos of South America, during the course of which Dinah, playing the possessed bride in *The Dybbuk,* is invaded by her own personal dybbuk, who makes her utter things like "inside the clouds, the air drips with diamonds," in the middle of a performance, in Spanish yet. This revenant turns out to be no less than Paco Engelhart, gangster/aviator and the late beloved of one Mamie Rifkin-Ramirez, an Argentine trollop who, underneath all the road-company *Carmen* finery, is a dead ringer for Dinah.

It's tempting to cull endless samples of Prose's subversive wit from her account of this transcontinental shlep—the bit actress in a Buenos Aires hotel room decorated with bedbugs and crucifixes, who is reduced to clasping her insect-bitten hands and supplicating, "Jesus, make me stop itching"; a Chassidic exorcist in Montevideo who likens Dinah's little dilemma to that of a wireless set that has picked up a bit of unwanted static (the solution, he says, is to turn off the radio). The confident terseness of Prose's prose is an unflagging pleasure. In a few handily distilled paragraphs, she manages to evoke the entire trajectory of the Yiddish-American stage, from its barnstorming heyday to its assimilationist twilight. Likewise, she can summon vast South American vistas with the pithiest of phrases. . . . Her language is true to the voices of her first-generation protagonists, without descending to the quaint—clear and colloquial and somehow never anachronistic.

This book's most authentic marvel is its least easily parsed element—a breadth of imagination that thoroughly succeeds in effacing the craft which propels it. ***Hungry Hearts*** gleefully abounds in the sort of symmetries and parallelisms that can seem arch or laborious in naturalistic novels. Prose's work bears a certain kinship to Singer's, though she's never cowed by her forebear. Like him, she recreates the momentum of a picaresque fable, in which any number of primal issues simmer beneath its anecdotal, folksy manner—the interplay between logic and the mystical, the pleasure of role-playing, the quest for our own singular identities. ***Hungry Hearts*** seeks to conclude on a note of joyous serenity, and it succeeds because the reader has long since surrendered without fear of disappointment to the skill of the writer: Francine Prose is possessed by a dybbuk called Talent.

Stephen Harvey, in a review of "Hungry Hearts," in VLS, *No. 15, March 1983, p. 3.*

BRINA CAPLAN

[In ***Hungry Hearts,*** the central character, Yiddish actress Dinah Rappoport, speculates that perhaps] "what happened happened because Leon Dalashinsky took us on tour to South America, to the other side of the world—where everything was upside down and a different gravity" prevailed. But truth to tell, gravity in a Francine Prose novel is always a little strange. ***Marie Laveau,*** her third book, dealt with spells, conjury and prophetic dreams in nineteenth-century New Orleans; ***The Glorious Ones,*** her second, was narrated in part by a dead Renaissance actor who leaves heaven to check up on his earthly fame. In fact, what gives her fiction its charm is just this ability to create worlds with dimensions more flexible and boundaries more fluid than our own—but which feel, nonetheless, comfortably familiar. It is no mischance that the demon that possessed Dinah was in life Pincus (Paco) Engelhart, son of the best dentist in Buenos Aires.

Even so, like Dinah, Prose is not entirely in control of her performances. At times, her exuberant storytelling could use more careful management. In ***Hungry Hearts,*** the conflict between high art and communal tradition presented at the outset is never resolved, and there are discrepancies in tone, as well: How does a rabbi in South America in 1921—even a wonder-working rabbi in rainbow knee socks—come to mouth a phrase like "modern technology"? But if such questions must be asked, they need not be pressed. Although Prose does not answer them, she does respond to one of our most enduring reasons for reading fiction, our wish to be delighted. Her sixth novel offers a story of "sweet-hearts reunited . . . prodigal children returned" and order restored. It's food for the hungry heart. (p. 519)

Brina Caplan, "The Jewish Stanislavsky," in The Nation, *New York, Vol. 236, No. 16, April 23, 1983, pp. 518-19.*

GARY DAVENPORT

Hungry Hearts deals with problems of appearance and reality, fiction and truth. Like many other novels . . . , [it] is a study of the conflicting claims of the ordinary and the extraordinary—in this case taking the form of a struggle between life and art. The book is the memoir of the protagonist, Dinah Rappoport, and centers on her days in the Yiddish Art Theater of the 1920s. She is the protégée of Leon Dalashinsky, "the Jewish Stanislavsky"—a man capable of referring to Stanislavsky as "the Russian Dalashinsky"—and she has the principal female role (Leah) in a long and successful run of Anski's famous play *The Dybbuk* (1920). In her intense devotion to her art she neglects her kindly but earthbound parents and cooperates with Dalashinsky in concealing from everyone, fellow players as well as general public, her real-life marriage to Benno Brownstein, the actor who plays Leah's star-crossed lover. (Dalashinsky fears that if the groundlings learn the truth, they will be unable to keep Art separate from Life.) Dinah's concealed marriage begins to deteriorate under the strain. Then, during an Argentine performance on the company's South American tour, she is possessed by a *real* dybbuk, and neither she nor the company can have any peace until it is finally exorcised. (p. 133)

Dinah learns her lesson all too well, and for the last third of the novel the reader is inclined to feel like the Ancient Mariner's wedding guest, buttonholed and sermonized. ("Where in all Stanislavsky was it written that an artist couldn't do something for her mama and papa? Whoever said art wasn't wide enough to accommodate the daily kindnesses, the favors of family life?") The author clearly wants the final position understood as a synthesis that benefits both life and art, but the net effect is that of a mere swing of the pendulum to the opposite extreme, an uncomplicated embracing of life at its most ordinary level. It is a disappointingly simple solution to an old and serious dilemma. And it is all the more disappointing because of the ingenious and interesting formulation the author gives that dilemma. Finally it is a betrayal of her lucid and engaging prose, which manages to be distinctive without a trace of gimmickry or affectation. (pp. 133-34)

Gary Davenport, "The Two Worlds of Contemporary American Fiction," in The Sewanee Review, *Vol. XCII, No. 1, January-March, 1984, pp. 128-36.*

JAN HOFFMAN

Bigfoot Dreams is a book about questers, with a heroine named Vera, and you have to believe in it because it was written by a woman whose name really is Prose and who was born on April Fools' Day.

In her seventh novel, Francine Prose celebrates caustic optimism—she doesn't exactly encourage you to dive into bed with your private monster, but at least she shows how the two of you can do lunch. ***Bigfoot Dreams*** follows what must be the worst week so far in the life of Vera Perl, and cheerfully concludes with the promise that she's bound to have more.

Thirty-seven-year-old Vera turns out stories on topics such as Bigfoot, astral rape, and miraculous births for *This Week,* a supermarket tabloid. Facts are as unwelcome as taxes at *This Week;* the nasty things only leave a newspaper vulnerable to libel suits. Reporters are required to stick closely to that legally defensible ''gray area—it *could be true,* it just *isn't* true.'' In other words, they purposely, gleefully . . . fabricate. Vera is highly qualified for the job. Her hyperactive imagination, overheated daydreams, and abundant neuroses have all been fanned by the complexities of her life. She's the only child of overprotective, lefty parents; the single mother of a precocious 10-year-old daughter; a sometime lover of *This Week*'s kindly, unexciting photographer/airbrusher; and a sort-of ex-wife of an unreconstructed hippie who signs his letters ''Big Youth.'' Moreover, she's recently quit smoking, and the novel opens with her planning a story called ''Bigfoot Lights Up,'' in which her favorite behemoth breaks into a southern town's Texaco station, just to get at its cigarettes.

Vera has no illusions about what she's writing; she knows articles should tap into *This Week*'s female readers' common fear, which is also their common hope: ''Fate can just pick you up and put you down somewhere else.'' Ten years ago she was an idealistic, fact-faithful journalist. Now, what ''saddens her is not just the time wasted, but that the passing years have turned her brain into a complicated trash compactor, shredding her inner life into Grade B drive-in Grand Guignol.'' . . .

Things are bad but they're about to get worse. One of Vera's weekly fictions happens to imitate reality, and a lawsuit hovers darkly in the air. Exactly as she had written, a cardiologist named Martin Green does live in Flatbush, with a lovely wife, Stephanie, and their two children, Joshua and Megan, who sell sidewalk lemonade. Since that much is true, the Greens' neighbors and hundreds of strangers believe the rest of *This Week*'s story must also be. As its headline says, ''Fountain of Youth Flows in Brooklyn Back Yard.''

Though elegantly constructed, ***Bigfoot Dreams*** reads like a neverending roller coaster ride, with Vera and her mad companions careening around the edges of possibility, diving into the unimaginable, soaring into the patently absurd. I won't give away how, but the tale loops again, as reality imitates fantasy. Vera is vindicated. Another loop. And then she's fired for writing the truth.

Much of this is funny as all get-out, quippy and chock-full of clevernesses. . . . The book is also richly comic. Though Prose's characters might easily be typecast, each one is drawn in full dimension, so that a cardiologist, an elevator operator, a hippie all have their grandly humorous moments. . . .

But the questing, the hungry fervor of the novel, is a reaction to hopelessness. The distance between *This Week*'s unhappy readers and smart, stable Vera Perl keeps shrinking, as Vera ever more tightly embraces her fear that ultimately she too is a born loser. The novel is flecked with images of despair. The Basenji, a breed of dog that can't bark, becomes a motif: for *This Week*'s soundlessly screaming readers, for lovers locked in lonely silence, for Vera herself, who so often keeps her intense responses mutely inside. Francine Prose can be excruciating. . . .

Having lost her job, her husband, her lover, her child, her best friend, and perhaps even the comfort of Bigfoot, Vera goes to a convention of cryptobiologists—professors and laypeople who believe in the unexpected, who trust that the Loch Ness monster and Bigfoot are just sitting around, waiting to be found. ''These people aren't looking for magic in the magazine racks by the supermarket check-out line. They're going out to seek it. Their myths are still vital to them, intact and so important they'll go almost anywhere to find out if they're true.'' And at the convention, set in a hotel perched on the edge of a canyon, some things happen.

Jan Hoffman, in a review of ''Bigfoot Dreams,'' in VLS, *No. 44, April, 1986, p. 3.*

MICHIKO KAKUTANI

Vera, the heroine of Francine Prose's seventh novel [***Bigfoot Dreams***], sees everything around her as a tabloid headline—it's kind of a nervous tic. . . .

Vera's headline-itis is partly the result of working too long at *This Week,* a sleazy, supermarket tabloid; and it's partly a reflection of her need to put her own problems—with her flaky, estranged husband and non-communicative daughter—in perspective. Indeed, as orchestrated by Miss Prose, the ridiculous stories that appear in *This Week* become a kind of metaphor for what Vera calls ''the profound and fantastic heart of daily life''—both the happy miracles that can surprise us when we least expect it, as well as the terrible disasters that can befall us, unawares. . . .

Miss Prose lays out a view of the world as a place peopled with unlikely characters and animated by improbable, even fantastic, events. This time, she delineates that view by combining precise, psychological descriptions with quirky humor and a kooky, slightly larger-than-life feel for New York City—its subways and its streets, its crazies and its weirdos, its noise and heat and distractions.

It's a likable, idiosyncratic combo, and, at her best, Miss Prose shifts gears mellifluously—moving from a very funny litany of a day's disappointments culminating in a spoiled chicken salad . . . , to a mother's lament for her daughter's vanishing youth, to a sad-awful description of an anonymous letter writer's plea for help, reminiscent of Nathanael West's *Miss Lonelyhearts.*

Kept off balance by these modulations, the reader is drawn into the story—goaded, one moment, to sympathize with the characters, teased, the next, to laugh at their incongruous predicaments. The effect, fittingly enough, is not unlike reading one of Vera's stories for *This Week.* A feeling of comic superiority is leavened by an insistent sense of kinship, just as the impulse toward sentimentality is undercut by an awareness of the absurd.

This approach, however, is not without its pitfalls—the same shifts of tone that give the novel its odd, nubbly texture also make it difficult to build and sustain a larger narrative arc of emotion—and Miss Prose occasionally veers dangerously close to cutesiness and caricature. Though Vera, herself, emerges as a fully drawn heroine—given to bad dreams, superstitious imaginings and soft, tender feelings for the people she loves but cannot protect—the supporting cast of characters (from her mercenary editors who are willing to sack her to win a libel case to her nice, rather dim boyfriend) are mechanically drawn figures, designed to either move the plot along or provide an easy, symbolic book. . . .

As for the plot of ***Bigfoot Dreams*** it, too, is a curious mixture of a sort of basic post-liberation woman finding herself in the

80's story line, with some rather more old-fashioned narrative contrivance. Not only do Vera's problems converge all at once . . . , but they're also overtly stage-managed to underscore the author's overall message: Vera loses her job when a story she's made up . . . turns out to involve real people, who are eager to sue.

Yet, the reader nods, coincidences are quite remarkable—and, yes, life can, in fact, be stranger than fiction. What Miss Prose seems to have been arguing all along is that stories, all stories—whether they are the nutty stories that Vera manufactures about U.F.O.'s and cancer cures, or the stories that she and her friends tell one another about lost loves and new jobs—provide narrative order. They give us hope and sustain our wonder, they give us a sense of who we were, and whom we are becoming. Miss Prose, herself, possesses the gifts to tell a fine story—one just wishes she wouldn't try quite so hard. We get the point, without having to read the moral of her story in italics.

Michiko Kakutani, "Stranger than Fiction," in The New York Times, *April 12, 1986, p. 12.*

SUSAN ALLEN TOTH

In the murky gloom of much contemporary fiction, one seems always to be following the fate of an aging, alcoholic writer, an unfulfilled Manhattan wife or a troubled survivor of the 1960's. Francine Prose offers lively alternatives. In six previous novels, she has set out exuberantly onto roads less taken, winding between myth and reality, exploring the legends with which people give meaning to their lives. (p. 8)

Her new novel, ***Bigfoot Dreams,*** begins . . . : "In the subway going to work, Vera decides to write about Bigfoot." Vera Perl, 37 years old, defiantly riding the front car and thinking about that ever popular strange creature, feels oddly akin to the other passengers, "every imaginable variety of halfway house resident, shopping-bag lady, and screamer." Since she works as a writer for *This Week,* a tabloid that emulates *The National Enquirer* but sticks to unprovable stories about untraceable people, she sees these riders as her audience. "On good days she likes to think of herself as a kind of screamer spokeswoman, bearing their messages to the world." . . .

Unfortunately, one of Vera's stories *does* turn out to be true. Inventing a legend about the fountain of youth to go with a photograph of a kids' lemonade stand, she somehow invents the real names of the people who live in the house. Because her story asserts that the water in their faucets restores youth and vitality, the family has been mobbed, and its lawyers have been contacted. Vera's job is on the line. All that may save her is the unexpected discovery that some of the neighbors *have* been cured. What is real, and what is not? What has Vera made up and what divined? Is she offering her readers hope or deception?

If ***Bigfoot Dreams*** tried only to resolve these twists and turnings, with varying glimpses of comedy and pathos, it would have the tidy structure of Miss Prose's earlier works. But ***Bigfoot Dreams*** seems to have escaped her usual control. Vera's life is focused not only on *This Week* but at various points on her aging-hippie husband, their precocious 10-year-old daughter, her retired, liberal parents and her best friend, who has spent a year in a mental institution. The plot gets very crowded. By the time it ends in a long report of a cryptobiologists' conference at the Grand Canyon, even Miss Prose's ingenuity can't entirely rescue it.

In deciding to center her plot not on legends and lies but on Vera's personal unhappiness, the author veers close to the fictional clichés she has always avoided before. Her wonderfully quirky imagination, however, still appears on almost every page. Miss Prose is sometimes at her best in throwaway anecdotes: "The reason she remembers is that the checkout clerk—a real teenage horror, his face the color and apparent consistency of cherry vanilla ice cream—picked up the package of diaphragm jelly and looked at her and said, 'Great stuff. I use it on my cat every night. Are you part Indian?'" To heck with Vera's love life, I thought; I wanted to find out more about the clerk. (p. 9)

Susan Allen Toth, "Psychic Sued for Telling Truth," in The New York Times Book Review, *May 25, 1986, pp. 8-9.*

Kathleen (Jessie) Raine

1908-

English poet, critic, autobiographer, translator, and editor.

© Jerry Bauer

In her verse, Raine employs symbols drawn from nature, Christianity, and mythology to represent spiritual and intellectual growth. Much of her poetry displays such Neoplatonic characteristics as an emphasis on the eternal over the temporal and a preoccupation with concepts of truth and beauty. These elements, combined with her concern for humanity's relationship with the universe, reveal Raine's affinities with the English Metaphysical and Romantic poets and invite comparisons with the visionary writings of William Blake and William Butler Yeats. While a strong pantheistic sense has been detected in Raine's work, many critics have also expressed admiration for her extensive scientific knowledge, as evidenced by her Aristotelian descriptions of nature. One critic noted that Raine's poetry is "the record of certain lucid perceptions of the timeless world by a mind religious in its first emotions and scientifically intellectual by training. It is Platonic poetry of a very fine order."

Raine's father, an English teacher, and her Scottish mother, who was well-versed in Hebridean folklore and ballads, both exerted strong influences on her poetry. Raine published her first poems while a student of natural sciences at Cambridge University during the 1920s. Her transcendental nature poetry is considered anachronistic in comparison with the empiricist temperament exemplified in the works of Cambridge philosophers A. J. Ayer and Bertrand Russell, as well as those of Raine's fellow students, poet and critic William Empson and scientist and critic Jacob Bronowski. The poems in her first two volumes, *Stone and Flower Poems, 1935-1943* (1943) and *Living in Time* (1946), which contain many objective, scientific descriptions of nature, are infused with Roman Catholic symbols, references to World War II, and Raine's personal dreams and love interests. While many critics attest to the lyrical beauty of these poems, Raine excluded most of them from *The Collected Poems of Kathleen Raine* (1956) and *Collected Poems, 1935-1980* (1981). She explained: "The ever-recurring forms of nature mirror eternal reality; the never-recurring productions of human history reflect only fallen man, and are therefore not suitable to become symbolic vocabulary for the kind of poetry I have attempted to write." Raine's next two volumes, *The Pythoness and Other Poems* (1949) and *The Year One* (1952), exhibit her transition towards a more mystical poetry reliant upon universal symbols that represent the development of the feminine psyche. Raine's poetry of this period, which blends natural and mythological archetypes, reveals her study of the psychological writings of Carl Jung, Robert Graves's mythological literary study *The White Goddess,* and the prophetic works of William Blake.

In her later poetry, Raine has continued to examine Platonic ideas in volumes that are often informed by personal experience. Poems in *The Hollow Hill and Other Poems, 1960-1964* (1965) and *The Lost Country* (1971) document Raine's fascination with dreams and display an amplified concern with the soul, developed through the passing with age of physical beauty. Both volumes also feature poems that begin as dedications to Raine's friends but become elevated, impersonal musings on philosophy and art. Similarly, *On a Deserted Shore: A Sequence of Poems* (1973), an elegiac sequence in honor of poet and filmmaker Gavin Maxwell, is also a prolonged consideration of the myriad aspects of love. In *The Oval Portrait and Other Poems* (1977) and *The Oracle in the Heart and Other Poems, 1975-1978* (1980), Raine examines her role as daughter, mother, grandmother, and poet in brief, epigrammatic poems resembling the Japanese *haiku*.

In addition to her poetry, Raine has also written three volumes of autobiography. *Farewell Happy Fields: Memories of Childhood* (1973), *The Land Unknown* (1975), and *The Lion's Mouth: Concluding Chapters of Autobiography* (1977) chronicle events in Raine's life that have affected her poetic vision. Raine's work as a critic has also drawn admiration. Her scholarly efforts include several works on Blake and books on Samuel Taylor Coleridge, Gerard Manley Hopkins, and Yeats.

(See also *CLC,* Vol. 7; *Contemporary Authors,* Vols. 85-88; and *Dictionary of Literary Biography,* Vol. 20.)

DEREK STANFORD

Poetic variations on a pantheistic theme—such are the verses of Kathleen Raine; a statement brusque and bold enough to require a certain elucidation. (p. 202)

[The pantheistic sense] can be described as the faculty by which we feel a closeness to nature, imagine that we share a common life along with the animals, fishes, and birds, plants, water, soil, and atmosphere. This is not merely a case of recognizing the varied phenomena of animate life as belonging to the category of our existence, but of admitting and celebrating our inclusive unity with the inanimate as well.

Sometimes the sense of a total union of all things is stronger in us than others. Something is needed to promote this sense; to awaken and stimulate this faculty into awareness. Sometimes this pantheistic lever is religious mysticism; at others it is love. In the work of Kathleen Raine both these stimuli are felt; the first, in part, produced by the second. (p. 203)

Living in Time [Raine's second volume] is distinguished from the earlier ***Stone and Flower*** by an increased metaphysical element; a poetic transcendence of the realm of sensuous matter. Given the passionate nature of the poet, it was just this earlier 'secular' living, this rejoicing in the region of the 'here and now', which made her first poetry pantheistic. Following upon a sudden deep awareness of death, the interest in the present has waned and passed; and the sunny pantheism of her former verse has yielded to a Christian mysticism. . . . (p. 213)

With this change from poetic pantheism to mysticism there goes a corresponding change in diction. The imagery ceases to represent the same amount of material things, and seeks increasingly to express remote concepts and abstract ideas. This loss of interest in a tactile idiom sometimes has unfortunate results. As Hulme remarked, with partisan exaggeration by no means devoid of a pertinent truth, "You might say if you wished that the whole of the romantic attitude seems to crystallize in verse round metaphors of flight. Hugo is always flying, flying up into the eternal gasses. The word infinite is in every line." ***Living in Time*** certainly contains its quantum of these vague-outlined terms, its adjectives beyond time and space, its far-flung epithets of Nirvana.

This pit-fall the best of these poems avoid; especially **"Ecce Homo"** and **"Sparrows in March"**. The first of these pieces succeeds in giving to a spiritually limitless theme precise, distinct, yet suggestive imagery—a triumph of mind over subject-matter (the emotional poet's most powerful foe). . . . (pp. 214-15)

Kathleen Raine has been praised for the tender and sensuous elements in her poetry. This award, though just, is not the product of any deep critical perception; yet, none the less in the last resort, these are the qualities her verse possesses which guarantee pleasure if not excitement. (p. 215)

More interesting (in the sense of more original) as the [pantheistic] verses are which set out to describe this pulsing connection with nature and God, the poems in which Kathleen Raine excels speak of the more understood relation between man and woman. It is not that in these love poems the mystic or pantheistic sense is absent, but that a more usual, more vital affinity generates the power of expression with a happier lyrical confidence. We can, in fact, say that Kathleen Raine, like most successful women verse-writers, is a poet of direct emotions, and that like Emily Brontë and Christina Rossetti, her most appealing poems are those that express a strictly human love. (pp. 215-16)

In her best love poems a sustained spate of feeling drives the verses along, assuming a clear and cogent expression, encompassing each image with a warm affective aura, rounding each separate figure of speech with an unhesitant sensuous gesture, varying the movement with the emotion. (p. 216)

In spite of Kathleen Raine's attempt to write in a concise, pointed way, her verses often lapse into the vague, with figures borrowed from past Romantic writers. Like many of the weaker Romantic poets, she often writes from the midst of her experience; from the still unformed core of feeling, with the contours of the poem still far away. This nervous oscillation without an outline is revealed in her verse **"Invocation"**:

> There is a poem on the way,
> there is a poem all round me,
> the poem is in the near future,
> the poem is in the upper air. . . .

It is this sense of the indefinite disposition of the poetic body that reduces the value of much of her work, and turns what is often an interesting inner incident into something violent, inarticulate and strained. (p. 220)

Another characteristic which Kathleen Raine seems to have inherited from the weaker Romantic writers is the excessive use of a code of vague lush images. These are sometimes employed as symbols whose meaning remains unstipulated, as in the poem **"The Hyacinth"**:

> It is the world unfolding into flower,
> the rose of life, the lily and the dove. . . .

From Kathleen Raine's inability to find a more modern poetic syntax a purple passage too often results. . . . Likewise a sort of uncritical trust in mere intensity of emotion produces such bathetic ejaculations and closes the poem **"To My Mountain"**:

> and oh, the sweet scent, and purple skies.

(p. 221)

The greater body of pantheistic poetry turns its back on one half of life. It ignores, for the greater part, all the reflections of the town upon the heart and mind of man. It presupposes a pastoral existence. Only the greatest pantheistic verse is able to assimilate shapes of decay, images of disintegration which the surface of life holds up today, even more so than in the age of Wordsworth, Shelley, and Lamartine. Only the greatest pantheistic verse is able to resolve these discordant forms within the magic retorts of art. This calibre the work of Kathleen Raine does not possess.

In a somewhat like fashion her mystical poems too often appear to lack that double discipline—that twin concentration—of thought and speech. Her subject occasionally swallows her up, and then her verse loses shape; is engulfed in waves of feeling. But now and again Kathleen Raine has her triumphs: poetic statements that seem to appeal as much by their poignant naturalness as by any earnestly laboured art.

To succeed as a poet, to succeed as a mystic—both of these are tremendous tasks. To combine these functions and succeed in them both demands a grace achieved or given to the rarest few upon earth. (pp. 222-23)

Derek Stanford, "Kathleen Raine," in his The Freedom of Poetry: Studies in Contemporary Verse, *The Falcon Press Limited, 1947, pp. 200-23.*

EVAN OWEN

Miss Raine's poetry, from ***Stone and Flower,*** through ***Living in Time,*** and up to ***The Pythoness,*** is a revelation of the poet's search for the faith and the love that will integrate; that will weld all the broken particles of modern life into the perfection of a rose, a tree. Her symbolism is of the mandala; that magical pattern that is at the heart of all life and of all death; that is at once the rose, the cross and the sun, the seed that is contained in the womb and the womb that is in the seed. The end of her search will come, in the words of T. S. Eliot,

> . . . When the tongues of flame are infolded
> Into the crowned knot of fire
> And the fire and the rose are one.

For Mr. Eliot, the rose is the symbol of natural beauty and natural love, while the fire is the divine love of God in Christ. His attitude is that of a devout observer who remains an observer even in the act of ritual participation. Kathleen Raine, on the other hand, identifies herself with the rose and with the fire. She is natural love and passion, lust and pain, the womb and the seed; she is in herself creation, in herself both the redeeming Christ and the devouring Pythoness. . . . (pp. 33-4)

The pantheism of Kathleen Raine's early poetry in all its mystic intensity, broadens out to cover the whole universe, and the object of her veneration is no longer the individual microcosm; it has become the Creator who is above and beyond the miracle of the finite. (p. 35)

It was particularly appropriate that her first book of poems, ***Stone and Flower,*** was decorated by the artist and sculptor, Barbara Hepworth, in whose work the fluidity, the crystalline nature, and the artless brilliance of the poetry is paralleled in line and in stone. There is a similar affinity between Kathleen Raine's poetry, the sculptures of Brancusi, and the paintings of Matta. In the work of these four artists—a poet, two sculptors and a painter—can be sensed the essential oneness of time and eternity, of the finite and the infinite, of illusion and reality.

''Poetry is the language,'' writes Christopher Fry, ''in which man explores his own amazement.'' The explorer cannot do better than take Kathleen Raine with him as a guide, though he should be warned that on the journey he may uncover more than he anticipates, for Kathleen Raine is no poet for the complacent, who had better stay at home, happy in his illusions. (p. 36)

Evan Owen, ''The Poetry of Kathleen Raine,'' in Poetry, *Vol. LXXX, No. 1, April, 1952, pp. 32-6.*

DUDLEY FITTS

It is the technical aspect of Miss Raine's poetry [in ***The Pythoness and Other Poems***] which strikes the reader first. As for form, her range is not great; but like Richard Wilbur in this country, and William Empson in her own, she demonstrates at every point a taut assurance of control which goes far to establish the quiet violence characteristic of her work at its best. She is, moreover, unusually sensitive to modulations of sound: the placing of rimes, the crisscross of internal assonances, the deftly constructed pattern-play of consonants—in short, whatever sonal devices can be contrived for establishing a mood or heightening a feeling. Which is to say that she is a craftsman of a very high order; and if she were no more than this, she would still be a refreshing phenomenon in an age of slick, mechanical technic. But she is much more than this. She is her own Pythoness: a seer. Her insight is deep, her mysticism real and sometimes troubling. . . .

The scope of this poetry is not large. Miss Raine has wisely chosen to limit herself—wisely, as though realizing that the lyric sweep, the sustained flight, are not for her—and the result is a contemplation of the great basic themes in miniature. Love, birth, death, renewal; the apprehension of the whole *in parvo;* a highly personalized and very lovely version of the Wordsworthian ''natural piety.'' There is a strangeness of perception here that can convert the matter-of-fact into a kind of mystical brutality:

> Through the hole in my body
> I bleed away
> Through a void as vast
> As the lack of love.

(Indeed, the whole of the poem **''Nativity''** from which these lines are quoted deserves study as an example of the imaginative transformation of unlikely material into something rich and complex.) (p. 27)

So tricky a manner of seeing and writing has its dangers, naturally, and Miss Raine does not always avoid them. I think it significant that her failures occur most often when she tries to exceed, whether in diction or in movement. In the last two stanzas of **''Winter Fire,''** for example, things have got out of hand (I quote the next to the last):

> Once Troy and Dido's Carthaginian pyre
> And Baldur's ship, and fabulous London burning,
> Robes, wooden walls and crystal palaces
> In their apotheosis were such flames as these . . .

Not merely are the syntax and punctuation annoyingly ambiguous: this is moving towards the epic, it is a putting on of the singing-robe; and Miss Raine can not sing in this way without appearing selfconscious. She fails for a different reason when she affects the vocabulary of science, of which she is fond. . . . Possibly I am more troubled by these lapses than I should be. Their very infrequency may enforce more attention to them than they deserve. And of course Bacon has his saw about there being no excellent beauty without some strangeness in the proportion. Let us admit the strangeness, then, for certainly there is much excellent beauty. (p. 28)

Dudley Fitts, ''In Minute Particulars,'' in The New Republic, *Vol. 127, No. 14, October 6, 1952, pp. 27-8.*

W. EMPSON

[***The Year One***] struck me as more exciting than Kathleen Raine's previous books, and on pulling myself into a calculating frame of mind I became puzzled to see how she had got so much breadth into a mystical theme which seems inherently narrow. Mr. Robert Graves and his White Goddess have had an important effect, I think; not because he invented this topic, which he would fervently deny, but because he would sometimes express such vomiting loathing of the goddess he revered and told us we so urgently needed to revere. In her previous book ***The Pythoness*** Kathleen Raine made some attempts to appear in person as this murderous bitch, sow and what not, patiently following out the formula; but though the formula gives a certain range to the gentleman poets it is hard to handle for a lady poet, in particular for a rather saintly character; and Kathleen Raine seems now to have absorbed it by keeping to the narrower form of presenting herself as a disgusting sinister old witch, muttering spells. This may seem a flippant view of her very sincere verse, but it is needed, I think, when you read **"Northumbrian Sequence IV,"** where the main dramatic force comes from the variety of orchestration. . . .

Such a poem has the direct hitting power on the page which is one of the crucial tests; you are forced to feel how it reads aloud. I am less fond of the "I am" form to which Mr. Robert Graves's researches gave prominence: "I am the shudder in the udder, I am the scramble in the bramble, I am the third lamp-post on your left." The English language is so fond of this game that it lies on its back, as soon you start, and asks to be tickled; one can't feel very solemn about that; and apparently the ancient riddles had very detailed pedantic answers. Kathleen Raine, as I understand, uses it to assert that each individual soul is at bottom identical with the Divine Ground (not that the prophet is here the mouthpiece of the god), and uses the surprise of her details only for incidental poetic pleasure; a different aim from her originals at both points. The effects are good, but it is a limited formula; whereas when she uses modern science she gets it right.

The technical merit of her free verse is something much harder to talk about, an exquisite ear. It is full of half rhymes which are much better for not being full rhymes, so much so that her occasional rhymes sometimes feel a mistake, a slight flatness rather than an emphasis. It comes off the page as a beautiful voice.

W. Empson, "Cauldron Bubble," in The New Statesman & Nation, *Vol. XLIV, No. 1130, November 1, 1952, p. 518.*

THE TIMES LITERARY SUPPLEMENT

In the years before the war, poets [in England] as elsewhere were too readily acclaimed for their first books. Professor W. H. Auden and Dylan Thomas acquired premature reputations which were heavily contested when, after a few years, their achievement seemed to fall short of their initial promise. In the last decade, on the other hand, few new reputations have been established, and such acceptance as there has been has followed on the publication not of a small volume but of a substantial collection. Miss Raine has now assembled in just such a collection [***The Collected Poems of Kathleen Raine***] all that she wishes to preserve of her four books, the first of which, ***Stone and Flower,*** appeared in 1943. Some decade and a half of scrupulous writing now comes up for judgment; it establishes her as a poet of singular purity with the clear vision of one who comes as a stranger to a too familiar world.

The trajectory of Miss Raine's poetry has been a singularly flat one. Her last poem has reached a place neither higher nor lower than the best pieces in her 1943 collection, and in the interval she has been comparatively unaffected by fortuitous experience and by fashion. Her sense of values has throughout been strong, and she has not allowed herself to be deflected into writing on subjects that did not deeply affect her. Such discarded pieces as **"The Silver Stag"** from her first book seem to have been sacrificed only because of some superfluous decoration; their purpose is the same as that of the work that she has retained.

If the trajectory of Miss Raine's poetry has been flat, the contrast between her point of departure and her present place of arrival is equally slight. Her viewpoint and perceptions remain the same; they were mature at the start. Only, in the course of the years a "metaphysical" poetry consciously influenced by Donne, and containing many deliberate Baroque features, has yielded to a visionary utterance perhaps less consciously modelled on the example of William Blake. Like her two masters, Miss Raine has all along been concerned with ultimates: with love, death, time, being, and with that modern topic which is but an old topic in pseudoscientific disguise, the relation of dream to reality, of reality to dream.

To these elementary subjects Miss Raine has brought a mind moulded by an early discipline in the sciences . . . and this has exercised as decisive an effect upon her choice of symbols and her manner of reasoning as similar scientific interests exerted in the Baroque age on Maurice Scève, on Donne, or on du Bartas. It has caused a poetry which sometimes set out to be theologically Christian to take a Platonic turn, and only secondarily to point a religious moral. Miss Raine herself remarks in her preface that when her vision has been most pure the ecclesiastical symbols have never come to her mind. What has moved her most has been the contemplation of Nature's processes and a deeply emotional apprehension that her life is a part of them. . . . She sees herself too as an insignificant sharer in vaster, cosmic processes of death and birth, of which the motive power is that same love that she has herself known, on a tiny scale, for Nature, for animals and for other human beings; and that this personal love—to quote her preface once more—"is important only in Plato's sense, in so far as it gives wings to the imagination." On an even vaster scale, she thinks of herself, too, as partaking of the life of the sun and planets, in the scale of whose existence a single being counts as nothing. This consciousness in the poet of her position in the Universe may, in the first place, have been the product of her scientific training. In her poetry, however, it appears as an immediate experience, deeply moving to her, which often dictates the form of the poem itself. Even when, in her first volume, she is writing of personal love, it is this self-identification with Nature that is her true subject. . . .

In Miss Raine's second volume, ***Living in Time,*** from which she has preserved fewer poems than from ***Stone and Flower,*** there continue to obtrude the themes of dream and doubt.

She comforts herself, however, with a thought which conforms to the fashion of the time that "dreams are also true"; and here some confusion seems to arise between moments of mystical awareness, which the poet in such a piece as **"The Moment"** finds to be escaping and eluding her, and confused dream-states, which come more freely and leave their deposit of haunted images. Yet, at her most clear-sighted, Miss Raine continues to proclaim that even in the sombre waters of the temporal world the Platonic *ideas* have their reflections which may be glimpsed at any moment of stillness. . . .

What may crudely be described as the impact of Jungian psychology on the poet resulted in a broader and more colourful use of myth in her third and finest volume, ***The Pythoness,*** of 1949, which contains the outstanding poem **"Isis Wanderer,"** in which two levels of meaning that in some of her earlier poems fail to coincide perfectly fall exactly together. As the poet journeys through the underworld in the person of Isis searching for the dismembered body of her consort, she walks among the débris of war, the memories of her own losses and the consciousness of her diminishing certainties. Yet she emerges in a mood of affirmation, with the strength to acknowledge that

This passing of reality itself is real.

From her descent into the underworld, the poet returned as a sibyl. Her allegiance has since been to the visionary Blake rather than to the emotionally reasoning Donne. Now her poetry is more uncompromising in its assertions; what was once wrapped in *conceit* now appears as bare statement. . . . The poems of Miss Raine's last book, ***The Year One,*** no longer draw on myth for their imagery. Instead they carry overtones of ballad, nursery-rhyme and jingle. At times the poet seems to be striving for a traditional anonymity, to construct poems as free from their author's signature as those *objets trouvés*—strange shapes in weathered wood or stone that were once the delight of the surrealists. . . . Now her eyes inevitably pass over the human foreground, pausing only momentarily to view the natural or man-made middle-ground, and come directly to rest on cosmic perspectives. Her moments of heightened apprehension are by now so vivid that even the most remote of spiritual distances take sharp outline:

I saw on a bare hillside an ash-tree stand
And all its intricate branches suddenly
Failed, as I gazed, to be a tree,
And road and hillside failed to make a world.
Hill, tree, sky, distance, only seemed to be
And I saw nothing I could give a name
Not any name known to the heart.

Such moments, familiar to us in the poetry of Vaughan, Traherne and Wordsworth, amply justify Miss Raine's assumption of the pythoness's robe. Even when, in such a poem as **"The Company,"** she invites comparison with Yeats, in his "All Souls' Night," her poem is no second-best, but the genuine distillation of a similar experience caught in the crystal vase of her own less colourful style. The moment of vision described in **"Seventh Day"** conveys its own authenticity, even though particularized experience rather quickly gives place to general statement:

Every natural form, living and moving
Delights those eyes that are no longer mine
That open upon earth and sky pure vision.
Nature sees, sees itself, is both seer and seen.

The poet places herself in the position of Nature; her eyes no longer convey messages to a personality which accepts and rejects, loves and despairs. Now in truth a stranger to the world of appearances, she allows image to succeed image with the apparent inevitability of natural objects passing a stationary observer. What she records is both in her mind and outside it; she is both the seer and the seen.

Who will take away
Carry away sorrow,
Bear away grief?

Stream wash away
Make away sorrow,
Bury the lark's bones
Under the turf
Bury my grief.

Such is the force of Miss Raine's self-identification with the grief which is implicit in all decay that it is not until halfway through the poem that she speaks of "*my* grief." This movement from the personal to the impersonal gathers momentum in the book's final poems. The poet finds in herself qualities that relate her to rock and to water, and explores each of these elemental substances as they live in herself. The first of these poems is deeply felt throughout, and the second leads by way of a curiously theoretical exposition to a close of great emotional purity.

Miss Raine's poetry has moved over a flat trajectory; its manner has changed, its experiences have been accepted and deepened; yet it remains essentially what it has been from the beginning: the record of certain lucid perceptions of the timeless world by a mind religious in its first emotions and scientifically intellectual by training. It is Platonic poetry of a very high order.

Miss Raine has succeeded in making her technique appear uncontrived; at its best it has the inevitability of a natural product, shaped by the wind of her inspiration and a faultless ear. Examined more closely, it reveals a sensitive use of irregular rhyme-schemes, of assonance, half-rhyme and repetition, and of the most subtle variations of rhythm. It fails only in certain ungainly passages, in which Miss Raine may feel herself justified by Blake's practice in the *Prophetic Books*. These passages are few, and occur, as with Blake, when emotion fails and intellectual argument gains the upper hand. Then scientific statement, which might not have been out of place in a footnote, finds its way into the lines of the poem. There may at the present day be no language that cannot be fused into poetry; there is however an unforgivably unpoetic tone, and into this Miss Raine's voice occasionally drops at such moments as the retort cools and the processes of the experiment are explained. But such lapses are few.

The total impression of these ***Collected Poems*** is of a rare and objective mind that has evolved a medium perfectly suited to express its apprehensions. In its reflected landscape it alternates only between the London of the blitz and the landscape of Cumbria or Northumberland, with its starkly contoured hills that follow the lines of the rock beneath as faithfully as Miss Raine's poetry conforms to her first perceptions. In its subjects it is equally narrow, and so does not challenge the greatest writing of our time: the poetry of Yeats or of Rilke. In its purity, however, it has its own great, and perhaps feminine, virtue. Miss Raine is one of the finest poets writing to-day and her talent is still in its prime.

"The Timeless World," in The Times Literary Supplement, *No. 2819, March 9, 1956, p. 148.*

ANTHONY HARTLEY

At first sight the last thing Kathleen Raine's poetry [in ***Collected Poems***] could be called is abstract. It abounds in images and in archetypal evocation which often produces beautiful and striking lines. The subject-matter of these poems is perhaps the most fundamental that a poet can take. They deal with the 'intimations of immortality' to be gathered on this earth. The poet contemplates a stone or a flower (to take images which have given a title to one of the volumes included in this collection) and endeavours to extract from them a common quintessence, which, however differently it may express itself, exists on the same dynamic level. Religious sentiment, after all, is not what you feel about the universe around you, but how you feel it. A poem like **"The Pythoness"** tries to focus in one nexus of symbolism all that we mean when we talk about a 'life force,' whether sexual or transcendent:

I am that serpent-haunted cave
Whose navel breeds the fates of men.
All wisdom issues from a hole in the earth:
The gods form in my darkness and dissolve again.

The method is the assertive use of archetypal symbols to evoke the appropriate responses in the reader, and, always risking a kind of empyrean sanctity, it produces poetry which must either succeed or fail completely, poems that are lyrical or nothing. For myself it is only occasionally that Miss Raine succeeds. In a deep sense I find her poems lacking in humanity or, at any rate, in sensuality, in that part of humanity that walks on the ground and frequently falls into a ditch. The trouble with statements like 'I am fire / Stilled to water, / A wave / Lifting from the abyss,' is that neither fire, water, wave nor abyss seems to have any tactile reality or inevitability within the poem. Too much is omitted from this poetry for me ever to regard it as having that relation to life which I believe to be essential. Some of these poems are mere collections of images strung together and left to fend for themselves. In her preface Miss Raine writes, 'The measure by which I have judged my own poems is . . . how nearly does the poem approximate to the imaginative vision of which I am, in my best moments, capable?', and I could hardly disagree more as to method. Poetry is criticism and shaping of vision as well as expression of it. It involves the reason as well as the imagination, and anyone who neglects this element in the creative process does so at the risk of failing in communication with their audience. Even at her best I personally find this failure in Miss Raine.

Anthony Hartley, in a review of "Collected Poems," in The Spectator, *Vol. 197, No. 6688, August 31, 1956, p. 296.*

W. S. MERWIN

Miss Raine, as well as being a poet, is a student of the natural sciences and a Blake scholar. Both of these interests have had effects on her writing. The importance of the former to her poetry is not easy to measure. The influence of Blake is more obvious. My own feeling that he is a dangerous master remains with me after reading Miss Raine's poems.

In her introduction [to ***The Collected Poems of Kathleen Raine***] Miss Raine restates the extreme romantic's traditional distrust of the formal element of poetry, quoting Blake to support her own formulation. I would not take space here to disagree with Miss Raine's opinions, if it were not that they seem related to the most common failure of her poetry. I cannot regard poetic form as "external," and a necessary betrayal of the poetic impulse, as she does, but rather as an integral control of all the rhythms—of the sounds, meanings, emotions and subject—of the poem. When Miss Raine's poems fail, it is usually because they lack form not only in her sense but in the one I have just suggested: they are shapeless, without development.

Her poetry is often rapt, reverential or invocatory. It courts a bleak mysticism in whose visionary distances Plato's Ideal and Jung's archetypes take turns at being conjured and descried. I confess to a prejudice against this sort of thing in poetry, especially when, as in much of Miss Raine's work, it is not embodied in articulate experience, but merely made explicit in more or less detailed and excited statement. It tends to vagueness: it can state that love is crucial to experience and poetry, and yet celebrate generalities rather than the minute particulars of the Creation.

Having said so much about her limitations, I must hasten to acclaim the genuine beauty and strength of Miss Raine's best poems. Some of her more recent work, in particular, has a spare assurance and precison, and a quality of transparence, that deserve every kind of welcome and admiration; such poems as **"The Holy Shroud"** and **"The Victims"** should be widely known.

W. S. Merwin, "Romantic Distrust," in The New York Times Book Review, *January 27, 1957, p. 14.*

HAZARD ADAMS

Kathleen Raine, an English poetess who has not been read as widely as she deserves in this country, has attempted to develop . . . a mature image of herself. This development may be seen in her recently published ***Collected Poems.*** Miss Raine's first book, ***Stone and Flower*** (1943) indicated by its title the direction her work was to take: in subsequent volumes she has consistently drawn her symbolic images from the elemental things of nature. She has linked the natural elements (things of air, earth, fire, and water) with other traditional mystical and occult symbols (mandala and rose, at the centers of which the paradoxes of time and eternity resolve themselves). The result is a system of poetic conventions based upon a fourfold scheme. In working within an occult tradition of symbolism, which she would undoubtedly assert is a systematization of the true poetic tradition, Miss Raine has rather naturally adopted a position similar to that which Graves prescribes for the poetess [in *The White Goddess*].

As early as 1946 in her second volume, ***Living in Time,*** Miss Raine took the nature of the goddess as her subject. . . . Here Miss Raine casts herself as a prophetess addressing man as lover and poet. In two subsequent volumes, ***The Pythoness*** (1949) and ***The Year One*** (1954), she acts the role of prophetess, priestess of the goddess, and even the goddess herself. "The pythoness" is one of the names given the fabulous prophetess of Apollo, the Delphic oracle. . . . [In **"The Pythoness"**] the poetess treats the various aspects of her powers. She is fate, the source of all wisdom, the created universe. She is the vehicle both of death and birth, the end toward which man strives, the end toward which inevitably he must come.

To project all of these functions in one symbolic image the poetess must treat of her own ambivalence and capriciousness. Miss Raine's poetry is a series of gestures toward and expressions of her various personae. Her best poems fall roughly into two groups, invoking the different female powers and expressing female attitudes toward those powers. In the first group are those poems in which the woman, aware of, and apparently comfortable in, her role of pythoness, priestess, and goddess, casts spells and makes invocations. In the second are poems in which the woman is a medium *for* rather than a source *of* magical powers. The different personae give rise to contrasting attitudes.

Miss Raine's invocations and spells are bids of occult propriety for control of a natural world which has been reduced imaginatively to the four elements—air, earth, fire, and water. Study of occult science reveals that the conventional symbolic systems of alchemy, astrology, magic, and Cabalism are rough analogies of each other, each having a different surface aim. Alchemy proposed transmutation of baser metals into gold and discovery of the elixir of life; astrology and Cabalistic study proposed divination; magic proposed the subjugation of spirits and nature. (pp. 114-16)

Throughout Miss Raine's poetry the elements are constantly invoked as forces: the apocalyptic conflagration which is fire, the fecundity and flux which is water, the tempest and breeze of destructive and creative thought which is air. All are unified in the greater symbol of which each is a microcosm, for the elements compose everything. Though the world can be seen in each of these aspects separately, the nearer they are held together by the mind in an ever-marrying system the more complete is man's imaginative perception and thus the more complete his world. Water grows, moves, and erodes life; fire consumes it even as it energizes and purifies it; air blows experience past the soul. . . . The fourth element, earth, is not invoked because to invoke it would be, for the poetess, to invoke herself. The pythoness is the earth mother, the archetype of woman. She is both the earth watered and fecund and the earth blown dry and burned to dust. She is the grave, the cave, and that which surrounds them. The four elements in harmony form the wheel of life.

Invocations suggest the spiritual or truly creative side of the poetess' power—the cave as womb. Spells suggest the profane—cave as enclosure, woman as demon. (p. 118)

Tradition shows that the goddess has been seen in two aspects—the true and the false, the spiritual and the delusory. Most encyclopaedic poems—*Paradise Lost* is perhaps the notable exception—present some female principle as the pure vision of spiritual perfection. More often than not, a delusory female vision must be overcome before the hero can attain to the perfection. Una and Duessa represent these two aspects of woman in the *Faerie Queene*. Dante shows us perfection in Beatrice, Milton delusion in Dalila. Blake's prophecies abound in both archetypes—the spiritual Jerusalem, a true emanation of the giant Albion, and Rahab, Vala, and other figures who stand for "female will" and delusory selfhood. Each female emanation in the prophecies has two forms—one true, one false.

The speaker of Miss Raine's poems sees herself from time to time in both ways. Sometimes she sees herself as the goddess in what Graves calls her "orgiastic" form. She accepts living sacrifices, destroys as well as creates. She is the earth as grave:

> We offer them bunches of buttercups and spring grass
> With all the inexpressible love of guilt:
> We strike, even as we look,
> The first wound of sacrifice.

Elsewhere she characterizes herself as a woman with a "Goneril heart" in whom the four elements blow up a tempest. She is starkly aware of the exaltation of selfhood which can result when her female powers are combined with certain human passions. She is still, after all, a human being, though she may be playing a traditional role. With spells she may be able to chain the lover, envelop him in the cave of her selfhood, and consume him. . . . The difficulty is that the woman may have a conscience and deplore her own deceitfulness. Then, too, there is always the danger that the spell will not endure. Circe could detain Odysseus only so long; the Bowre of Bliss was eventually destroyed. The most potent necromancy cannot always hold the lover, who may be a bit of a magician himself. . . . (pp. 119-20)

Awareness of these difficulties leads to the poems of the second group previously mentioned. Here the poetess often sees herself not as an enchantress but as a medium of forces she cannot always control. In **"Formulation,"** which can be read as a poem about poetic inspiration, the poetess knows that her own powers are capable of terrifying her. . . . In **"Nativity"** the poetess directly dramatizes the agony of creation—mental and physical. . . . In giving birth the poetess is as much a medium as a creator.

Although Miss Raine treats mediumship as prevalent in all ages, she suggests here and there in her poems that the proper role of the goddess as creator is more difficult to sustain now than in ancient times, that the point of view of mere mediumship is more prevalent than ever before. She feels her control dwindling.

The myth of Isis is peculiarly relevant to this situation. The goddess discovers her lover in pieces:

> The dismembered world that once was the whole god
> Whose broken fragments now lie dead.

The modern world is a world of multiplicity and fragmentation; the modern Isis resembles one of Eliot's old women gathering fuel aimlessly in vacant lots. Even the goddess herself is dissected:

> Chemistry dissolves the goddess in the alembic,
> Venus the white queen, the universal matrix,
> Down to molecular hexagons and carbon-chains.

Today the goddess must gather not only Osiris from the four corners of the world but also herself. That gathering must take the form dictated by ancient truths now hidden in esoteric lore and considered pointless archaisms by a science which according to the poetess "applies its insect lens to the human form divine." The tradition reaches back through Blake and Dante to the alchemists, the neo-Platonists, and the Hermetic philosophers—back, in fact, to the beginnings of life. The true incantations of the goddess are the radical obverse of those of science—creation and unification rather than dissection. The lens of science is a lid for the eye, not a window for the imagination. Following her mentor, Blake, Miss Raine argues that man's spiritual form, which is the form of the universe, must be restored. . . . What the human being really sees when he opens his spiritual windows is himself—"the human form divine" (Miss Raine takes the words from Blake). Too often, however, the windows become corporeal eyes and create forests of confusion. (pp. 120-22)

To close the spiritual eye generally expresses spiritual failure. Prophets or prophetesses must run the risk of such failure, for they must work in the world which they may even detest in order to gather up its fragments. The lidded eye leads to the false dreams of science in which "Swim strange monsters, amoeboid erythaeon spawn." But there are true windows or visionary dreams in which the beastly creatures of darkness become the vehicles of light, just as Blake's tiger becomes an apocalyptic creature of fire. (p. 122)

In perfect tension and harmony the four elements form the traditional mandala or circle, each assigned a cardinal point or quarter. This harmony is a symbol of cyclical temporal movement as well as spatial form: the "indifference" of the soul. For Miss Raine life is cyclical; her most ambitious work to date, **"Northumbrian Sequence,"** treats the life cycle from beginning back to end. The sequence is based upon a parable from Bede's account of the conversion of a Northumbrian king. In it the life of man is compared, according to Miss Raine, to a sparrow which "flies in at one door and turns for a moment in the light and heat of the hearth fire, then flies forth into the darkness whence it came." As a whole, the sequence not only presents Miss Raine's central myth but also illustrates several typical forms and moods in which she works. Poem I describes the speaker's life before birth and even before the creation: one major principle in Miss Raine's poetry is the traditional occult view that the single human life is a microcosm of the life of the cosmos, so that any poem on birth has overtones of Genesis. The images which describe this pre-existence have further symbolic force. . . . In the state of pre-existence the bird is songless; the dancer in complete movement circles on a materially nonexistent still center—lonely, aloof, perfected. Motion is married to an abstract motionless joy. . . . In the state of pre-natural perfection the circling of the axis of joy, the silent bird, and the dancer present the traditional image of eternity, the centerless and circumferenceless circle. This circling, which represents spiritual life, encompasses the universe, dips down into the mundane world, yet is a timeless whole. The passage through the room of life, described by Bede, is in Hermetic lore a "copy below," a part of that circumference which emanates from the motionless, whirling center. The journey through the room is a slice from this circle, a timeless archetypal moment which expands into days, nights, and years. In a sense, then, it is an illusion, gone as it comes, the beginning continually reasserting itself as an ending. God sees this movement from the timeless center. Man seeks the timeless center as he whirls on the circumference. The dipping down into life and the coming out are temporal expressions of the soul's own timeless and spaceless unity, expanded from that center into the temporal and spatial forms of human perception. The end is the beginning.

The cycle of life which the sequence celebrates appears microcosmically in each poem. The poems are also thematically organized through repetition of bird images. In poem II there is a celebration of physical and spiritual marriage, which is another temporal representation of the closing of a circumference to a center. . . . (pp. 123-24)

In poem III the bird image is thematically restated in a vision of masses of birds crossing the skies—the blind, irrational force of life. This constant flux, in which some birds are dashed against cliffs and others buffeted by storms, is another representation of the "continuum of self" described in another poem; yet here that continuum really transcends the self. It is the sheer flying which is important and which endures, a flying which is abstract like the abstract joy remaining after death and before birth. The bird is the vehicle of that great endless act analogous to the dance in poem I. . . . (p. 125)

Poem IV recapitulates a theme seen elsewhere in Miss Raine's work: it takes the form of an incantation interspersed with protests against what is being invoked—the lover and his child in the midst of storms of nature and passion. In poem V the pace changes. The subject is the nature of inner and outer experience and the dividing line between the two. Together, poems IV and V are poems of experience, written *from* the swim of life.

The Northumbrian sequence ends in a poem on death and remembrance in which the poetess, moving out of the world, identifies herself with the bird image and divests the heart finally even of that, having been gathered up again in the perfect emptiness of pure flight, the axis of joy with which the sequence begins.

> Dark into dark, spirit into spirit flies,
> Home, with not one dear image in the heart.

Traditionally the effect of the mundane journey is attainment of a purer, stark clarity of vision almost terrible to the reader.

Working in the symbolic tradition of the great religious mystics, of the occultists, of Dante and Blake, Miss Raine has chosen the personae of the Muse. The poet sees the Muse as capricious and irrational. Writing as the Muse, Miss Raine shows that although she may seem capricious, she is either the source or the medium of a higher rationality. This dramatic vacillation in her attitude toward her powers presents a critical commentary on modern life as well as an assimilation of it to the past—in truth, a timeless present—through an archetypal symbolism. If her art is severely limited by her choice of convention and point of view, her peculiar power arises at least in part from these limitations. In an age of philosophic relativism in which art is taken so seldom to offer more than private truths, Miss Raine strives to present a microcosm of reality rather than a fragment. She recreates a world where objects assert themselves as extensions of a communal mind, floating on its circumference like the symbolic birds of her poems. (p. 126)

Hazard Adams, "The Poetry of Kathleen Raine: Enchantress and Medium," in Texas Studies in English, *Vol. 37, 1958, pp. 114-26.*

H. FOLTINEK

The publication in 1955 of the ***Collected Poems*** of Kathleen Raine and the general praise accorded to her work by the reviewers make the need for a critical study of her poetry evident. In a period where the chief merit of a poet is usually sought in his ability to bring unity out of diversity emphasis has been put on the apparent simplicity and lucidity of Kathleen Raine's writing, but not on its truly complex quality. Now that the worth of her poetry seems generally recognised, it is time to examine the creative process behind it.

Although erudition is never a special effect but always an organic factor in Kathleen Raine's poetry, her work is, far more than is usually believed, based on knowledge. Its main sources are extensive reading in science and modern psychology, the study of mystic literature and the forms of religious experience throughout the ages—and within this subject in particular the myths and rites of primitive man, which anthropology has shown to be still part of our tradition. (p. 15)

An analysis of the poetry of Kathleen Raine must start with a discussion not of the themes of her poems but rather of the attitude of mind in which they were written. Her work is always extremely personal and yet at the same time universal; it is determined by her idea of the poet as prophet and visionary. In view of this high office she has excluded all occasional and conventional poems from her collection. It is noticeable that Kathleen Raine does not wish to have any verse preserved in which the traditional forms tend to become merely allegorical. Whenever old religious symbols are used they are filled with a new and rich meaning drawn from an experience that is always her own although its origins may be manifold. Her deeply religious outlook is essentially Christian but transcends in fact confessional boundaries. Her belief in the order of the cosmos is based as much on theological or scientific dogma as on emotional confidence. Thus the insight into the heart of creation which she is craving for, and which she feels joyfully granted now and then, is really hers. Truly personal, also, is the idea of man driven by love to the 'kindling fire' which she feels active throughout the universe, in every flower or leaf.

Kathleen Raine is deeply aware of the primitive roots of all belief, and this ancient tradition is often the essential element in her poems: It may be consciously employed, as for instance in her **"Spells"** in which the intensity rather than the form of magical poetry is re-created; it may be personally felt, as in the **"Transit of the Gods"** where the myths of old vegetation gods seem to reflect the different stages in the life of woman. The connection between primitive and modern perception is indeed revived here. (pp. 15-16)

Frequently the poet tries to envisage the universal law which is the cause of all change. Thus the poems of the **"Northumbrian Sequence"** contemplate various facets of the awe-inspiring and enigmatic alternations of creation and destruction. A less complex view is expressed in earlier works like **"The Fall"**, where the hidden law is conceived as an ever-recurrent flux, . . . or **"Desire,"** in which she sees a gradual decline towards stillness transform the earth. (pp. 16-17)

[The] office of the poet is to unite the fragments of belief, age-old or modern, discovered or revealed, and, if we may add, to inspire this coherent structure with fresh impetus, to recreate the image of god so essential to a harmonious world. Kathleen Raine has, in a way, taken up this task in her writing. Her intense desire to open new vistas for the human mind and a wisdom that has come from suffering and learning make her work truly prophetic. (p. 20)

H. Foltinek, "The Primitive Element in the Poetry of Kathleen Raine," in English Studies, *Netherlands, Vol. 42, No. 1, 1961, pp. 15-20.*

FREDERICK GRUBB

Kathleen Raine has the scientist's wariness before emotion and his impertinence before the unknown. She controls, from the centre, her unruly material where Muir disperses his powers by straddling his. Her use of scientific terms—'retina', 'alembic', 'chromosome', 'metabolism'—has more practical relevance than Auden's: where he is a bit of a playboy, Miss Raine is relating a scientific appreciation of nature to a moral enthusiasm about its meaning for the enhancement of personality. Her insights are produced as evidence in an often impassioned, always enunciated and sometimes original, poetic argument. Each poem is a felt experiment; as they accumulate we feel encouraged to accept them as truth, attuning ourselves to unfamiliar insights as if we had always known, not just in our emotional wits, but in our perceptive common sense that 'air filters through the lungs fine branches as through trees' etc. Even lines which appear less forensic, more poetical—'the baroque assumption of the clouds'—have a terse, authoritative correctness.

The virtue of the poem is: this scientist is feminine in a rare sense. Women poets too often run to ecstasy or gentility, the *Magna Mater* or Bride of Christ pose. Miss Raine has the wisdom, basis, and tact that one associates with Emily Dickinson and Frances Cornford. She is more cautious in the sense that she evades metaphor (Dickinson's strength) and the robust domesticity of Mrs Cornford. Her learning is fertilized by feminism. Her femininity consists in magnanimity—her readiness to entertain her experience; to her, science is not a *weltanschauung,* nor is nature a mine of symbols awaiting exploitation. Science is a means to sympathetic understanding and nature is to be invited, rather than forced, to enrich the personality. She considers what T. S. Eliot adopts as symbolism and Edwin Muir relegates into fable. She remains juridical: her poems are full of natural breaks, moments when she seems to stop or deflect the action when it threatens to run away into some emotional orgy or facile absolute. Admitting the maximum of emotion—and it is feminine emotion, taking more and staking more than masculine affection or feeling—she knows, by a sort of matriarchal good sense, how to accommodate it. (pp. 106-07)

Frederick Grubb, "War and Peace," in his A Vision of Reality: A Study of Liberalism in Twentieth-Century Verse, *Barnes & Noble, Inc., 1965, pp. 73-136.*

HARRIET ZINNES

What immediately impresses one upon reading the ***Collected Poems*** of Kathleen Raine, one of the finest English poets writing today, is her singleness of purpose and the constancy of her vision. (p. 289)

It will be rewarding, I think, to consider Miss Raine's poetry in the light of her preface. Essentially, she believes that a poem is a captured glimpse of the eternal mind. She argues that when a poet begins to write a poem, "there is no poem in the sense of a construction of words; and the concentration of the mind is upon something else, that precedes words, and by which the words, as they are written, must constantly be checked and rectified." The "something else" is the platonic idea. The poet's method by which she hopes to capture the timeless order is based upon what can be called an exclusion principle. She calls for a "pure" poetry, that is, poetry that excludes human history from its subject matter. "War, religion, and love all present themselves as serious and important matters, but no poet is to be forgiven who allows himself to be duped. Love is important only in Plato's sense, in so far as it gives wings to the imagination—whatever in love is personal and not imaginative, matters not at all." . . . This declared willingness on the part of a poet effectively to neglect for poetic purposes human emotions is a new twist to the contemporary belief in the uniqueness of the aesthetic experience and a return in a new and, unfortunately, sterile way to the prophetic methods of William Blake, Miss Raine's master. Blake, who also believed in a transcendental reality and in the power of the imagination to realize that eternal order, unlike his later disciple, did not limit but extended the range of human emotions fit for poetry. . . . One line from Miss Raine's poem the **"Crystal Skull,"** illustrates how characteristically she turns her vision away from the human present. She writes, "the perfection of light is the destruction of the world." The suggestion of despair, of hostility to man underlying the verse, would be antithetical, I should hazard, to Blake (and to his time, I may add). The vision is joyless, too suggestive of disgust for man (so typical of the writers of our own anxious times) even to approximate the Blakean joy in the union of the human and divine. It is this kind of orphic statement, a sterile prophecy, that I find so unsatisfactory in the poems of Miss Raine. Her symbolism is often, perhaps as a result of her essential joylessness (her concern with death and endings) fuzzy, not confused or over-rich as in Blake, but meaningless. She uses frequently without new illumination, the traditional mystic signs: the wind, rose, day, star, rocks, angels, bird, sun. What is lacking is not only Blake's turbulent and abundant imagery but his profound belief in contrarieties. (pp. 289-90)

[Miss Raine] is rather casual about form; and her purism, in her weakest poems, consists largely in attempting to evoke an isolated vision of eternal love and beauty with too few poetic means. She allows neither the varied materials which the use of mundane experiences (the personal suffering and place and event) offers nor the richness of metaphor, direct in analogy and diverse in possible interpretation. Blake once asked: "What is the price of Experience? Do men buy it for a song? / Or wisdom for a dance in the street?" It is true that all Platonists have to regard in some way as inconsequential or contingent human events and feelings. But if human experience must be transcendent before it matters for poetry, that is, must already be purified of the personal and defiled, then poetic art would have no function. The art transmutes through the imagination the shadow into the real, if you will. Any experience should have the possibility, therefore, of reawakening the imagination, of recollecting to a slumbering mass the perfections of eternity. It is up to the poet to make his words (based not on arbitrarily chosen or pure experiences, but on all possibles) become the instruments of Platonic music.

Miss Raine's beautiful **"Love Poem"** bears witness to the falsity and conceit of advocating the impossible, a virginal art, that is, an art reflecting the transcendent without the mirror of the mundane. I quote the following lines from it:

> Here, where I trace your body with my hand,

eternal in a way which makes even transcendent reality bend to the egocentricity of spirit.

> . . . I can close
> The eternal mind to all it knows,
>
> Deny
> The love that moves in me
> When the spirit blows.

Of course, the imagination worked the miracle that is the artifact, the poem, in the above instances, but it was not a chaste imagination. Humanity, impure, was the agent. The poet was not duped.

Certainly, the visionary poet must always work with the paradoxes of the pure and impure experiences (of innocence and experience, in Blake's terms), of reality and its shadows. He is always in exile—whether it be from the "lost garden," as Miss Raine puts it, or from lost innocence. To the mystic, consequently, man's productions are trivial and obstructionist, and he looks to a dream, to childhood, to the collective unconscious, even to the supposed pure, innocent life of birds and animals, who, through some uncanny, and, ironically enough, anthropomorphic fashion, seem imbued with the "eternal mind." But Miss Raine indeed often becomes quite maudlin as she contemplates the "sweet-eyed, unregarding beasts" who "waking and sleeping wear the natural grace." I must say that the mystical notion that animals can contain such unambiguous innocence and eternal love (wisdom) is rather hard to take today. . . . When the poet begins the poem with "Yours is the face that the earth turns to me," the reader knows that human love has mattered for poetry, and that the poet's art has transmuted it into some kind of intimation of immortality.

Another example of a memorable poem indicating concern with natural fact or human experience also stands as a contradiction to Miss Raine's professed theory of poetry. With what pathos the poet is able in a single stroke to describe the full but trapped human heart, which feels beyond its limitations: In the poem **"The Moment,"** she writes: "And I have only two hands and a heart to hold the desert and the sea." Again, in the simple and powerful ballad effect of **"The End of Love,"** there is more than the impersonal imagination in the lament over the dead lover. It is universal enough but it is nonsense to say that whatever was personal was removed from the imaginative experience behind the poem. . . . With great urgency of feeling, she writes poem after poem in which her transcendent vision captures for the reader that "something else," through a close association with an immediate object, with *Existenz*. (pp. 290-92)

In brief, the success of her finest poems (in addition to those already cited one ought to mention **"The Victims," "The Company,"** or **"Isis Wanderer"**) suggests that the writer of the preface as a practicing poet transcended her own wit. Miss Raine herself in a kind of afterthought seems to have modified her original simplistic (or unfortunately expressed) view of the relation of the most primitive human emotions to art. (p. 292)

Miss Raine, who admits somewhere that personal suffering made her a poet, has been too chaste in her conception of poetry. The lute has strings and fingers play upon it. Without Eurydice, would Plato have heard celestial music? (pp. 292-93)

Harriet Zinnes, "Kathleen Raine Collected," in Prairie Schooner, *Vol. XXXI, No. 4, Winter, 1967, pp. 289-93.*

JAMES OLNEY

[Kathleen Raine] has never been a very fashionable poet. In England, her poetry is known, certainly, and honored with an occasional award, but it is largely neglected by those who create trends and fashions; in this country, though her scholarly writing (her splendid work on Blake for example) is generally admired, her poetry remains very little known. Yet, Kathleen Raine obviously believes, and rightly, that it is her poetry that defines and justifies her being—she is possessed by the *daimon* of poetry, not any other; and, unacknowledged though it be, she has written half-a-dozen lyric poems as beautiful as any produced in our time. But that very fact is no doubt the explanation for the unfashionableness of her poetry: as a critical term, beauty is more of an anachronism than anything else and a simple embarrassment to us as readers devoted to "modernity." . . .

It is quite true, of course, that Kathleen Raine is not really up-to-date, and she refuses even to try to be modish. While she may in fact live just off the King's Road in London with its hysterical agitation and its shoddy "trendiness," in spirit and in her poetry she dwells somewhere near Beulah with such dusty ancients and celebrants of beauty as Orpheus, Pythagoras, Plato, Plotinus, Porphyry, and Iamblichus—not to mention the even more unusual company of Heraclitus, Thrice-Greatest (and Thrice-Oddest) Hermes, Macrobius on Cicero, Swedenborg, and Thomas Taylor, the Platonist. Moreover, she insists that she *is* Persephone (at least she is Persephone when she is not Demeter, the Virgin Mary, or Aphrodite); in other words, she insists on imagining her life and all life to be the stuff of myth rather than statistical matter for sociology. She would live a life, and celebrate it in her poetry, that has been lived countless times before and that only in recent days has been scorned as outmoded by people with a frenzy for the new and different. (pp. 29-30)

Kathleen Raine's poetry—her hymn to beauty—is nearly always elegiac in mood. Her song is a song of pathos and poignance, of sorrow and lament; indeed, she seems almost to cultivate and to caress what Hopkins called "Sorrow's springs." It is the condition of beauty in this world, existing in time and as a natural fact, that it must be transient. (pp. 30-1)

Behind the best of Kathleen Raine's poems one feels something that I can only call the form or the Platonic idea of the individual poem. Yeats had the notion that the form of a poem exists before it is ever captured and quite outside the consciousness of the poet; Eliot said that his poems first came to him as wordless rhythms without content. And this is what I feel about Kathleen Raine's finest form or idea—a sort of underlying, speechless rhythm, a delicate harmony of sound and emotion—and one feels that ghostly presence exerting its pressures in every line and every phrase, as if all had come right and all were right, nothing lacking, nothing left over, the finished poem completely at one with its preexistent model, a created beauty that, unlike natural beauty, will not—any more than the artifacts of Blake's Beulah or Yeats's Byzantium—change with time or be lost: "indescribable harmonies of knowledge and meaning." (p. 32)

James Olney, "Reconsideration: Kathleen Raine's Poetry," in The New Republic, *Vol. 175, No. 25, December 18, 1976, pp. 29-32.*

GEORGE BARKER

It would be invidious to remark that Miss Kathleen Raine has been writing poems for many years, and yet, in order to appreciate the achievement of her new collection, I think the remark pardonable. The poems in [***The Oval Portrait and Other Poems***] are truly simple where her earlier poems were unduly imponderable, they are lucid where the earlier poems were often profoundly trite, they are unpretentious where her earlier poems were on some occasions flatulent. For once upon a time she gave, to the present reviewer at least, the impression of a mature undergraduette in blue stockings walking abstractedly around a gallery full of Jungian plaster casts; her tone of voice tended to be at once condescending and obfuscatory; she wore, then, an ostentatious robe that not only sang, it positively harangued. Myself I much prefer her garbed in the modest smock of her present style: the simplicity of this style is in no way bathetic, nor is its bareness in any way embarrassing. I think that she is now writing the poems that the shibboleths of Jung and the Prophetic Books of Blake had in the past both inflated and diminished. To those readers who have been, for many years, admirers of her undeviating devotion to the art of poetry and sympathisers with her confusion in the labyrinths of mythological psychology, it will seem, I think, that she has at last found both peace and a place.

There was a time when her verse, like much of her theoretical prose, seemed determined to propel itself towards the intellectual altitudes simply by substituting abstract nouns for wings. Those poems seldom, if ever, left the ground. What purities and simplicities they possessed seemed always to exist in a condition of mystifying thaumaturgy. They wore sandwich boards on which was cabbalistically inscribed a sentence which, if we could have transcribed it, would have read something like: 'Beware of the god'. But the poems in her latest book do not carry sandwich boards: they carry wooden bowls containing the wisdom and the sensitivity of a woman who could never have been a man. I think that where her earlier poems elaborated upon a wholly unwholesome and literary self-consciousness, so that one read them without really believing they could have survived outside a library, in this sense these new poems can honestly and honourably be called both a bowl of goldfish and a bowl of cherries. . . . It would be, I think, frivolous not to refer, even incidentally, to the extraordinary fact that these poems are so indisputably feminine. This is extraordinary because feminine poems are, on the whole, quite rare birds. (pp. 38-9)

George Barker, "A True Simplicity," in Books and Bookmen, *Vol. 22, No. 10, July, 1977, pp. 38-9.*

ANNE STEVENSON

No poet (unless it were Eavan Boland) can provide a greater contrast to Patricia Beer than Kathleen Raine. The latest collection of this possibly great poet is called ***The Oracle in the Heart,*** and it is well named. For where Patricia Beer eschews emotions, Kathleen Raine plunges into them; where Miss Beer would withdraw so as to get a detailed view, Miss Raine stirs up tears and ecstasies in the valleys of memory. Anyone who has read Kathleen Raine's extraordinary three-volume autobiography will recognize the mixture of personal anguish and spiritual faith which distinguishes her work. Through particular recollections, regrets, places, dreams and memories, Miss Raine seeks not so much a view as an explanation of life. Like Blake's, her vision is archetypal; she attempts to reconcile the 'unendurable' with immortal longings. . . . There is hankering throughout this book for that other world which even this world's 'paradise' will not suppress. So although these are poems of reconciliation and apology, they are not without signs of strain.

A group of short poems at the end are strong when they touch on memory and a keen sense of place, but sometimes they break up in personal speculation which mars their Haiku-like purity. . . . Kathleen Raine's thoughts of fury serve her better than her guilt. In a magnificent poem called **"Medea"** she pits the madness of the wronged woman ('passionate love that slaughters her own children') against 'earth-bound Jason who rated calculation above the gods'. It is with Medea, 'to herself most cruel', departing on 'the dragon chariot of her desolation', that Kathleen Raine identifies. No woman writing today knows female anguish more intimately nor is more aware of its dangers and punishments. Her line of Platonic vision intersects somewhere with her line of personal anguish, and at that point Kathleen Raine builds her best poems. ***The Oracle in the Heart*** keeps its balance between the forces of creation, but it is an uneasy balance. The visionary is not quite in the ascendancy over the lover. But with **"Medea"** we plunge into an area of myth which has become in many ways female property. The poems of Kathleen Raine and Patricia Beer could be seen as the poles of women's writing. Miss Raine speaks for the inner, Miss Beer for the outer woman. In the one we have a prototype of a confessional sacred mythology, in the other, an example of sophisticated good sense and acceptance. (pp. 61-2)

Anne Stevenson, "Houses of Choice," in Poetry Review, *Vol. 70, No. 3, December, 1980, pp. 57-65.*

ALAN HOLLINGHURST

[***The Oracle in the Heart***] closes with a "remarkable sequence" of 60 short lyrics which is remarkable, frankly, only for its unmoderated banality. The small forms seem welcome in principle in a poet who has tended to be too repetitive and long-winded in the past, but the reduced compass has not in the event brought forth any new sharpness. . . . Raine is a neo-Platonist and associates her work with a frequently submerged stream of visionary writers of whom Blake and Yeats are the most prominent. She intensifies the intractability of her poetical subject by closing her eyes to the wealth of experienced life which Yeats incorporates in his work, and reiterating the same vocabulary (bird, tree, wind, water) without the resonance and transmitted passion of Yeats's symbolic repetitions. Almost all the poems fall into the same crooning, lilting and monotonous rhythms, and use a language which is frequently inert:

Do I return
To the presence in the garden
The same or not the same?

This way of ending a poem with a wondering question, as if the answer were obvious, is also typical and unsatisfactory because the poems make no equation between moral and linguistic discovery: they state rather than enacting or demonstrating their ''verities'', and carry on as removed from life as their language is. There are some attempts at coming further into life in a set of ''Occasional Poems'', but the difficulties of this kind of address are immense, as is witnessed even by Eliot's occasional work.

At a recent reading Raine spoke of being ''bitterly sickened by the Women's Movement'', and her poetical stance, like her political one, is so exclusive that it risks seeming arrogant and condescending. There is so much that she overlooks. (p. 84)

Alan Hollinghurst, ''Telling Tales,'' in Encounter, *Vol. LVI, Nos. 2 & 3, February & March, 1981, pp. 80-5.*

CATHERINE PETERS

Few poets are as sternly self-critical as Kathleen Raine. This [***Collected Poems, 1935-1980***] has been pruned of more than half the contents of her ***Collected Poems*** (1954), which now seem to her 'not the achievement of a young poet, but the juvenilia of an old one', yet the earlier collection was itself a selection from previous volumes. This attitude to her work is not a symptom of insecurity or overconscientiousness; it is integral to her view of poetry and the poet's calling.

For Kathleen Raine, as for Blake and Yeats, the poet is not so much the author as the medium of poetry, the channel through which ancient wisdom flows, and by which it is formed into a unique, but at the same time universal expression which speaks directly, without superficial cleverness, to the hearts of others. . . . For her, poetry must always be seen 'primarily as a way of experiencing and not as a craft, or an aptitude for conceptual acrostics.' (The Poetic Symbol). So the discarded poems are those in which the 'archetypal epiphanies' arising from the Collective Unconscious have not been properly attended to by the Self (two Jungian terms which, though not a thorough-going Jungian, Kathleen Raine accepts), but have been muddied and contaminated in their delivery by a poet who is temporarily untrue to the vision she has been granted.

It follows, then, that her imagery is not only taken from nature: 'The ever-recurring forms of nature mirror eternal reality; the never-recurring productions of human history reflect only fallen man, and are therefore not suitable to become a symbolic vocabulary for the kind of poetry I have attempted to write' but are often generalised rather than particular; rock, tree, water, wind, dance and dancer. This kind of poetry can sometimes seem flat (something of which she is no more afraid than Wordsworth was) or repetitive. I do not think such accusations would seem relevant to her. In a striking image such as 'The kitchen-midden of my dreams' for example, the echo of Yeats's 'foul rag-and-bone shop of the heart' is surely deliberately evoked; the linking traditions which bind poet to poet, generation to generation, are the important thing; rediscovery, rather than the shock of the new.

To read the autobiographical accounts which lie behind this kind of poetry, *A Vision,* or Kathleen Raine's ***The Lion's Mouth,*** is to enter an alternative world where curses are fulfilled, dreams come literally true, and a daimon accompanies the poet through the scenes of everyday life, the inner journey parallelling the outer one in a more than metaphorical sense. Whatever one's own feelings about this kind of visionary experience, there is no doubt that the poems gain an extraordinary power from it that cannot be accounted for in everyday terms. This power, and the pain to which Kathleen Raine has forced herself to remain open, come through strongly in the incantatory poems, which are like spells, or religious rituals.

More recently, Kathleen Raine has written many short poems, something like *haiku,* and some graceful but less substantial occasional poems. The sustained intensity of her earlier writing has perhaps diminished, but so has the sense of strain and anxiety to keep herself screwed to the highest pitch of poetic endeavour which sometimes worked against the poems' ability to communicate emotion. But her development over the long period—almost half a century—in which she has been writing is extraordinarily consistent, and adds up to a very considerable poetic achievement. (p. 21)

Catherine Peters, ''Visionary,'' in The Spectator, *Vol. 247, No. 7984, July 18, 1981, pp. 20-1.*

TOM DISCH

The most immediately appealing feature of [Kathleen Raine's ***Collected Poems, 1935-1980***], evident in even the earliest of her poems, is its sheer lyric loveliness. Loveliness does not stand high these days in the vocabulary of critical praise, but one need only stroll among spring flowers to be reminded that it does, verily, exist, and can't easily be called by any other name. Consider these lines from Raine's early collection, ***The Pythoness*** (1948):

> Primrose, anemone, bluebell, moss
> Grow in the kingdom of the cross
>
> And the ash-tree's purple bud
> Dresses the spear that sheds his blood
>
> **(''Lenten Flowers'')**

Or this mini-theory of lyrical evolution, from the first poem in the collection:

> Stone into man must grow, the human word
> carved by our whispers in the passing air
>
> is the authentic utterance of cloud,
> the speech of flowing water, blowing wind,
> of silver moon and stunted juniper.
>
> **(''Night in Martindale'')**

There is not a syllable in any of those lines that Christina Rossetti would not have coveted for her own Collected Poems. They have the impersonal, overdetermined, instantly memorable ring of one of Palgrave's redolent Golden Oldies, those poems that transcend mere prosody and issue directly into song. This is not the least of poetic ambitions, but in its nature it invites readerly much more than critical attention, since critics can do little more in such cases than to point out how the sounds are heaped up and sewn together, a process the ear has already perfectly assimilated.

This is not to say that Raine has no subject of greater moment than spring flowers or that one need not heed what ''the speech of flowing water'' is actually flowing on about. Raine has two grand themes, two bardic purposes, on which she discourses with a persistence that makes most other poets seem mere ramblers, motes in the breeze of any passing meaning. The first of these is the fusion, in the furnace of the *''Sophia Per-*

ennis'', of world and self into a transcendental unity. . . . The second theme is a corollary and precondition to the first:

> A Gaelic bard they raise who in fourteen adjectives
> Named the one indivisible soul of his glen . . .
> (**''Eileann Chanaidh''**)

One is grateful to that Gaelic bard for welcoming a rabble of adjectives to the one and indivisible, for without some spice of variety the loftiest wisdom will come to sound received rather than perennial. The chief occupational hazard of oracles is a tendency to stumble into hollows and to mumble riddles that can't be answered. . . . If this is the price a reader must pay for sublimity (and Raine is nothing if not sublime), so be it. Such spirit-trumpetings and wafting of the ectoplasm are rare, in any case, and the moments of Delphic authority vastly preponderate.

Whether, the oracle having been delivered, we are bound literally to believe it—there's the rub. Even Raine in a rare latitudinarian moment will allow that ''. . . the song makes the singer wise, / But only while he sings'' (**''Eileann Chanaidh''**). The point of prophetic utterance—at least for those who do not attend to it as catechumens—is not so much truth as a condition of inward authority (call it ''star quality'') that commands unquestioning respect. . . . Intellectually I am inclined to dismiss much of Raine's paraphrasable discourse as theosophy, a branch of the tree of the perennial wisdom only a little loftier than astrology and rhabdomancy. Those who share her predilections will take her to their hearts as the best things since Yeats, but it would be unfair to let her reputation be immolated in the Magicke Fyres of the Golden Dawn—even at her own vatic insistence.

For there is this redeeming paradox: Raine's authority as a prophet derives in good measure from a deeply integrated understanding of the very organon she professes to refute, modern materialistic science. Admittedly the science she knows best stops short of the latest wrinkles in cosmogony and particle physics. Quarks and black holes have no roles in the masques of her imagination, but the loss is theirs. One may more reasonably regret that plate tectonics and the caduceus of the DNA molecule came to be formulated too late to have been apotheosized in her meditations, for it is in the mid-range of apprehensible reality (neither too macro nor too microscopic) that her muse is most effective. In any case, the range of scientific knowledge she does command and transmute is quite wide enough to span the Two Cultures gap, with room to spare. Only Ammons, among her peers, can move back and forth with as easy grace between the mist-haunted woodlands of the Sublime and the crystalline cognitions of the chemist, the patient observations of the field naturalist. . . . [Raine] has no ambition to play Lucretius to the nuclear age. Rather, that when she reaches for one of the fourteen glen-defining adjectives what comes to hand is resonant with knowledge of (in her own phrase) ''the world and its unwinding.'' Unwinding in the sense both of its motions in space and of its entropic destiny. In another poet such a confluence of suggestion might be serendipitous; in one who was in her student years a friend and colleague of Empson and Bronowski there can be no such suspicion. . . .

Nothing so sustains a poet as an irresolvable dilemma. Throughout her career Raine's Aristotelian intellect has wrestled with the neo-Platonic angel of her soul (''My soul and I last night'', one poem begins), and if no clear victor emerges from the battle, nor ever can, the ringside view is terrific. Other irresolvable dilemmas of her life have not been so conducive to good poetry. In her long elegy for Gavin Maxwell, ***On a Deserted Shore*** (1973), sorrow and slight contest for primacy under the watchful eye of a merely theoretic serenity. Never does the poet allow herself to express what, despite her engrained reticence, becomes so clear in ***The Lion's Mouth,*** the third volume of her autobiography: that Raine, her love long unrequited, felt passionately injured by—and vindictive towards—the late Mr Maxwell. In such circumstances elegy is not the best revenge, and, indeed, may backfire. The poem manages to be both facile and strained in its lyricism; in its discourse it is tendentious, repetitive, and dull; as confession it is disingenuous and self-protective.

The question must be asked whether Raine is the best judge of her own work, whether she has not entrenched herself too determinedly in the role of prophet, forgetful or contemptuous of those poems she wrote when she was only human. From her first book, ***Stone and Flower*** (1943), she reprints in the ***Collected Poems*** only twelve poems; in her earlier ***Collected Poems*** of 1956 there were forty-seven. Some of the poems newly excluded were fustian, but others, such as **''Invocation''**, **''Cattle Dream''**, **''Tiger Dream''**, and **''Maternal Grief''**, have a kind of raging energy and extravagance of gesture that doesn't deserve oblivion. . . . One senses that the Pythoness (as her third book was titled), sedate upon her tripod, must wince to recall such outbursts of the old Delilah, but how much better a poem ***On a Deserted Shore*** would be with a small infusion of such honest, complex anger.

If only by right of seniority, Kathleen Raine deserves to edit her lifework by whatever principle of selection she chooses; nor would it be seemly to look forward yet to a *Complete Poems* (though poetic justice requires it in the fullness of time). After the lapse of ***On a Deserted Shore,*** her more recent collections offer work as magistral as anything in the three definitive books of her mid-career (represented here very fully). Poets of the sublime traditionally shine most brilliantly as twilight deepens about them. I look forward with something bordering on reverence to the *Collected Poems 1935-2000,* with whatever omissions its author chooses to indulge. Meanwhile no serious reader can afford to ignore the present volume.

Tom Disch, ''The Science of the Sublime,'' in The Times Literary Supplement, *No. 4089, August 14, 1981, p. 930.*

JEAN MacVEAN

[***Collected Poems, 1935-1980***] represents an austere pruning, particularly of Kathleen Raine's early work. In the introduction she sees herself as a late developer owing to the struggle to free herself from current values.

'For the one value to which I instinctively clung—. . . was the sense of the sacred. I hope that in a few poems this sense communicates itself.'

Kathleen Raine, therefore, set her sights high and in some of her work does achieve a breathtaking beauty. . . .

In the early poems the poet is feeling her way. She has naturally not developed to her full strength and her language lacks the richness and authority which was to come. This begins to show itself in the selection from ***The Year One***. . . . (p. 99)

Kathleen Raine's work on Blake first took her to that 'older wisdom' in Plato, Proclus and Plotinus. She has also drawn on Indian philosophy, Greek myth, Hebridean folk lore and varied metaphysical systems. There is little Christian symbolism in her work: 'I was, quite simply, unable to project into these outer forms my own inner life.' Her studies have meant that she is working a richer and deeper seam than most contemporary poets. (p. 101)

There are many poems in this collection in which natural scenes, flora and fauna become one with the poet. Kathleen Raine's scientific studies give them a precision of observation and an exact language, thus, allied to visionary intensity, creating some of the most important nature poems of our time. (p. 102)

Not every one will agree with all aspects of Kathleen Raine's philosophy. The language is sometimes awkward, especially when dealing with occult meanings. Occasionally, too, the music is not subtle enough.

These are, however, mere quibbles in the light of a remarkable achievement. Kathleen Raine is a poet of the spirit and has learnt to use its wings. (p. 104)

Jean MacVean, "Kathleen Raine," in Agenda, *Vols. 19-20, No. 1, Winter-Spring, 1982, pp. 99-104.*

Augusto Roa Bastos

1917-

Paraguayan novelist, short story writer, journalist, poet, critic, scriptwriter, and editor.

Roa Bastos is an important figure in contemporary Latin American literature whose novels and short stories are informed by Paraguay's turbulent history. Displaying a strong command of language, Roa Bastos blends myths, legends, and idioms of Paraguay's Guaraní Indians with social realism to evoke an intricate and surreal portrait of his homeland. *Yo, el supremo* (1974; *I, the Supreme*), the first of his books to be published in the United States, was praised by Carlos Fuentes as "one of the milestones of the Latin American novel" and prompted him to call Roa Bastos Paraguay's "most eminent writer." Roa Bastos has lived in exile since Paraguay's civil war in 1947.

Roa Bastos's short story collections, including *El trueno entre las hojas* (1953), chronicle the social upheavals of colonial tyranny, war, and revolution. These concerns are further developed in his first novel, *Hijo de hombre* (1960; *Son of Man*). Consisting of several stories linked by the narrator, Lieutenant Miguel Vera, *Son of Man* examines thirty years of Paraguay's history—including an ill-fated peasant revolt in 1912 and the Chaco War between Paraguay and Bolivia during the early 1930s—to detail the political emergence of Guairá, a rural section of the country. Irving Wardle noted that the novel's epic qualities "spring from careful design as well as from feeling: as in epic poetry, the narrative is timed to refer back to already distant events so as to establish a pattern of historical recurrence."

I, the Supreme is a dense, multilayered novel that depicts the evils of despotism. In this book, Roa Bastos assumes the identity of "The Compiler," whose task is to gather various government documents, pamphlets, and other writings to present a panoramic account of nineteenth-century Paraguay under the rule of Dr. José Gaspar Rodríquez de Francia. Known as "El Supremo" by the subjects who despised him, Francia was the country's first post-colonial leader to seize absolute power. Francia's own extravagant reminiscences of his life and his certainty of retaining power, even after his death, are interspersed throughout the novel, suggesting the stature of a supernatural being. Roa Bastos evokes a surreal atmosphere by employing such devices as shifting perspectives, bizarre imagery, and labyrinthine structure.

IRVING WARDLE

Augusto Roa Bastos is a patriotic writer of a type that has almost died out. His subject is Paraguay, or rather a small corner of it; and he covers 30 years of the country's luckless history in terms of martyred heroes and vile oppressors, projecting his story on the scale of tragic legend remote from the ironies and supra-national exchanges of the modern world. Bastos fought for his country in the war against Bolivia of the 1930s and now lives in political exile in Argentina; his book [*Son of Man*] reads like a dedicated act of commemoration towards the forgotten men of an unvisited land.

For all its emotional directness and black and white loyalties, ***Son of Man*** is no simple-minded piece of work. Its epic qualities spring from careful design as well as from feeling: as in epic poetry, the narrative is timed to refer back to already distant events so as to establish a pattern of historical recurrence. As, in fact, the most distant event in the book is Paraguay's War of the Triple Alliance in the 1860s, it is the sign of a remarkable technique that this and subsequent events seem to be bubbling up from the remote past. Bastos's method is to present a series of interlocked episodes so arranged that whatever happens in one episode is transmuted into folk-lore in the next: the novel creates its own mythology as it goes along.

The setting is the forest province of Guairá, which displays the usual characteristics of the Latin American hell on earth—a constant losing battle against destitution and leprosy, with the attendant tyrannies of the police and the Church. Bastos at one point remarks that in the Guarani language there are no sad words, and much the same is true of his book. However cruel and ugly its material, the spirit of the writing saves it from becoming intolerable. The excitement of its straight passages of heroic action is matched by the excitement of watching these being absorbed into legend—as in the story of a couple who escape from a terrible State Plantation and are later rumoured to have returned to Guairá in a mysterious coach with burning wheels. Such transformations, says Bastos, are typical "among a people whom misfortune had made a prey to superstition."

From a succession of such episodes, a larger pattern gradually takes shape: an endless cycle of rebellion and defeat, purity and corruption enacted by generation after generation of anonymous men. And if the actual time-span of the novel is brief, it has its roots in the pre-Christian sub-soil—revealed in the episode from which the book takes its title: a Good Friday ritual in which the figure of Christ is nailed up as an act of vengeance. [***Son of Man***] is a harsh and noble book.

Irving Wardle, "Instant Mythology," in The Observer, *August 8, 1965, p. 21.*

MALCOLM BRADBURY

Augusto Roa Bastos is a Paraguayan writer, and [***Son of Man***] first appeared in 1961. Its action covers a long historical sweep, and details the painful emergence of a backward section of the country, the Guairá, and the phases of oppression which accompanied it. It is a novel about human aspiration, then; but scarcely a political novel. The action, shifting from location to location and character to character is one which brings together a variety of similar stories, stories about a region and the men within that region who manifest its suffering—and also its possibilities. Here is a world in which men, time and time again, crucify one another, and where Christianity becomes the faith of suffering. Its characters are linked in a chain of experiences in which men of special power and merit assert their fragile influence, make their singular attempts to secure their permanence and humanity. The breadline peasant existence admits no frills; the tone is a kind of primitive lyrical assertion; and yet the impact of the book is immensely sophisticated.

Malcolm Bradbury, in a review of "Son of Man," in Punch, *Vol. CCXLIX, No. 6519, August 18, 1965, p. 252.*

JEAN FRANCO

Yo el supremo, by the Paraguayan writer, Augusto Roa Bastos, gives a new twist to one of the oldest devices of the novel, for he converts the materials ordinarily used in historical discourse—documents, records, travel accounts, decrees—into the infrastructure of fiction. Instead of an historical novel in the Lukácsian sense, however, we have the ramblings and lucubrations of the bizarre nineteenth-century dictator of Paraguay, Dr Francia.

A lawyer, educated in the writings of Rousseau, Diderot, Montesquieu and Voltaire, a furious hater of the Jesuits who once controlled his country, detesting the Spaniards whom he tried to force into *mestizaje* by forbidding them to marry white women, Dr Francia epitomized the problematic side of the Enlightenment and its equation of power with knowledge. The few travellers who penetrated the fortress into which he turned his country after Independence wrote of his striking appearance, his solitary nature, his celibacy, his habit of nocturnal prowling, the scarlet cloak he wore, his suspicion of every foreigner who entered the country, his penal colony at Tevego, the harsh treatment of conspirators and supposed conspirators, some of whom he kept in irons until they died. . . .

In 1840, just before his death, Dr Francia burned his papers, in strange anticipation of the paper shredders of more modern times and—one final, bizarre incident—vandals stole his body from his tomb and threw it into the river.

Roa Bastos's brilliant idea is to let the supreme dictator talk back. The author claims to be merely the compiler of the evidence, the copyist of what has already been said and written. Out of the fragments of the burned papers, the "perpetual circulars" and his conversations with the last secretary, Policarpo Patiño, he pieces together the other side of the history, which is not only that of a country's isolation but that of the dictator himself. The irony is that this "supreme I" who suppressed Paraguay's one secondary school, forbade newspapers and punished the supposed authors of lampoons with draconian severity is finally at the mercy of the words which have been written about him. . . .

The purgatory of the dictator is that he lives only in the language of others, so that even his self-justification is merely a response to accusations. The novel parades the ghosts of a past in which Dr Francia reads only his good intentions but which now comes to haunt him with monstrous truths. He boasts of having saved his country from the labyrinth of post-Independence politics by outwitting the Argentine General Belgrano and the Brazilian, Correia de Cámara; he relives his old quarrels with the Robertsons and with Rengger, justifies the isolation of his country and himself. After his death, his voice goes on, restlessly monitoring its tomb, classifying the flies that buzz around his decomposing body. Yet writing is the one area he has never been able to control, for even "dictated" texts are open to ambiguity. The text of his life is glossed by hostile readers, interrupted by dissenting footnotes and contradicted by legend.

Yet ***Yo el supremo*** is something more than the account of a case of paranoia sublimated into *raison d'état*. For the text shows us the devastating fate of that rational and rationalizing self invented by the Enlightenment. The title is an ironic pun which brings together both the historical dictator and the all-devouring ego, dedicated to domination and power, unable to tolerate the existence of anything outside its control. Dr Francia, who was, in fact, an astronomer and possessed of scientific curiosity, becomes a powerful symbol of the darker side of Enlightenment man. Roa Bastos's romantic assumption is that print, precisely because it lasts beyond the individual life span and because it can always indicate a negative side (what is not said), defies control and is, in consequence, the supreme form of subversion.

Jean Franco, "Paranoia in Paraguay," in The Times Literary Supplement, *No. 3831, August 15, 1975, p. 925.*

DAVID WILLIAM FOSTER

It is not infrequent that, although they may possess excellent qualities when viewed in isolation, the early literary efforts of a writer suffer to some degree from a comparison with what comes to be recognized as his "mature" production. Such is the case with the seventeen stories in [Augusto Roa Bastos'] first collection, ***El trueno entre las hojas*** (***Thunder Among the Leaves,*** 1953.) It is easy to assert that these stories, with their emphasis on violence, on social injustice, and on the particular circumstances of the Paraguayan experience, anticipate the themes, language, and techniques of Roa's first published novel, ***Son of Man***. . . . Seen in this fashion, the stories are noteworthy as foreshadowings of the novel and are examined accordingly. (p. 26)

Roa's unmistakable goal in ***Thunder*** is to provide a series of stories that represent a characterization of aspects of the Paraguayan experience. Toward this end he chooses topics that constitute focal points of his understanding of that experience. Yet Roa has also become aware of the emerging feeling among Latin American artists that documentary fiction, whether in the form of socialist realism or in the form of regionalism, is simply not an eloquent enough vehicle to represent the complex issues of the Latin American experience. Hence the interest in myth, in magical realism, in variants of European expressionism and, more recently, in structural and semiological experimentation. There is little doubt that Roa avails himself of the general principles of nonregionalist fiction. We realize this in his choice of a highly poetic language, the mixing of Spanish and Guaraní [the language spoken by rural Paraguayans of Spanish and Indian descent], the use of exceptional circumstances that imply a meaning far beyond the surface texture of sequential events, and the creation of individuals that are less typical in a folkloristic sense and more figurative in a mythic one.

Although many of the stories of ***Thunder*** have become standard anthology pieces—**"La excavación" ("The Excavation"), "El prisionero" ("The Prisoner"), "La tumba viva" ("The Living Tomb")**—the seventeen titles are on the whole overwritten, as though Roa had yet to find his own proper level of writing. Certainly it is not necessary to judge a writer's production in terms of a developmental trajectory: often the success of later works highlights the imperfections of early pieces, and it may be difficult to evaluate the latter on their own terms. (pp. 26-7)

"Los carpincheros" ("The Carpincho Hunters") is the lead story of ***Thunder;*** as such it sets the tone of the entire collection. In it Roa presents a number of basic themes of his work: the elusive mysterious quality of the life of the Indian, whose silence is a mask for violent and unexpected emotions; the contrast between the Indian, locked in the marginal existence imposed by the white power structure, and the foreigner, who exploits the land without understanding its people and their ways; the lack of concern for the indigenous population on the part of the majority of the Europeans (here represented by a group of German immigrants, twice-removed from a sense of the land) and the realization on the part of a few that there is an alternate human experience lived by the natives; the jealously guarded values of "civilization" held by the Europeans and those of tribes like the *carpincheros* who, despite their existence as pariahs of the dominant European society, manage to maintain an ancestral existence with their own forms of freedom and fulfillment. (p. 28)

The *carpincheros*—hunters of the South-American rodent, the *carpincho* or *capybara*—are a fierce, nomadic people who inhabit the area of the rivers. Roa refers to them as the only people who have not succumbed to the foreign exploitation described by the story. In his story Roa undertakes to describe a confrontation, a collision between the primitivism of these people and the encroaching civilization represented by the opening up of new lands to immigrant homesteaders. In this case, the homesteaders are a German family—a man, his wife, and their young daughter, Gretchen. They live on the bank of the river where the silent *carpincheros* pass by in their canoes. Roa provides ample pictorial detail of individuals and events, a characteristic of the stories in ***Thunder***. One could well insist that the author even dilutes his stories by an overabundance of "poetic" description that diverts the reader's attention away from the underlying human tensions being portrayed.

For example, we might cite the case of the story's basic perspective: Gretchen's interest in and fascination with the primitive *carpincheros*. The young girl, of course, barely speaks any Spanish, much less the indigenous language of the natives. Thus although she is the focal point of the story, she is unquestionably the outsider contemplating a reality from the immense distance imposed by an entire range of cultural differences. Gretchen, in turn, becomes the central actor in the event narrated. Unlike her parents, for whom the natives are presumably simply part of the unpleasant tropical setting to which they must become accustomed if they are to survive, Gretchen takes special note of the natives who travel the waters of the river in their canoes. She is intrigued by them and, ultimately, obsessed with their mysterious nature. Finally, . . . she throws herself into the river after them; she is hauled aboard one of the canoes and carried off into the jungle. Gretchen first becomes aware of the *carpincheros* on the Noche de San Juan, or midsummer's night (which, of course, falls at the beginning of winter in the Southern hemisphere). On this night the inhabitants of San Juan de Borja send burning rafts down the river in honor of their patron saint, St. John the Baptist. With the rafts come the canoes of the *carpincheros*. It is at this point that we can appreciate Roa's attempt to evoke with a highly poetic language a single image that can serve as the central narrative point of reference. . . . (pp. 28-9)

The story follows through on a series of contrasts . . . : the untamed primitivism of the river people versus the "solid" habits of the civilized German immigrants. Gretchen is shown as the pivotal point between these two poles: a part of the latter structure of values, but attracted, in ways that she cannot even realize much less understand, to the silent natives. To this scheme—natives-Gretchen-civilized outsider—is added a fourth constituent, a native with whom she changes places in life when she is carried off by the *carpincheros*. When Gretchen is carried off after throwing herself into the waters, one of the Indians is left behind for dead. In an exchange that seems a bit too schematic, he rises from his coma to take the place of the little girl: between the two opposing sets of values—one primitive and free, the other civilized and circumscribed—there has been a trade. But Gretchen is carried away in a state of semiconsciousness, still fascinated by the allure of the Indians, while the *carpinchero* left behind erupts in violent rage against the situation in which he has been abandoned. Thus, rather than simply an even exchange between the two opposing ways of life, Roa suggests the ultimate captivation of the civilized by the primitive and yet the impossibility of the primitive accepting the constraints of European civilization. The collision between these elements comes with the despair of the parents over their daughter's "escape" into the arms of the *carpincheros* and the fury of the native who is left behind, as he attempts to force his way out of the claustrophobic confines of the immigrants' cabin. . . . (pp. 30-1)

A number of the stories in ***Thunder*** deal with the topic of human will: the will to survive in the face of insurmountable odds, the will to overcome social injustice, the will to sacrifice oneself for the good of his people, the will to find a private meaning for existence. At the same time that Roa deals with these positive values associated with the free will that Catholic theology ascribes to man, the stories also portray manifestations of will that are part of a collective original sin: the will to control the destiny of others, the will to destroy fragile human existence gratuitously, the will for one to prevail at the expense of his brethren. **"Audiencia privada" ("Private Audience")** exemplifies the stories of human will. It concerns the role that this aspect of human nature plays in the shaping of the destiny of a people and the necessity for the individual to exercise control over his own frail nature. Although the plot is weak and the juxtaposition of opposites somewhat extreme, the story is interesting for Roa's structuring of the encounter between the strong will of the oppressor and the weak will of the visionary reformer, an event with unquestionably ethical and political implications.

The story involves the stark juxtaposition of the solidly entrenched, corrupt, and pompous minister and a young, eager, and dedicated reformer. The former is visited by the enterprising young engineer, who has drawn up plans for a public works project that will benefit thousands of suffering peasants. Of course, it must be carried out with the consent of the powerful minister, for without his approval there is no hope for its success. Roa sets up the opposition between the two men with considerable detail, providing a caricature of the government official and a sympathetic portrait of the engineer. The story is basically schematic and it is clear that the author has made use of hoary rhetoric in order to "guide" our perception of the fundamental conflict involved between the servant of the power structure and the would-be servant of the people. In this case, the story is one of facile position taking.

However, **"Private Audience"** becomes interesting in the subsequent modification of the portrait of the engineer. The young man is cursed by a major defect of character that detracts from his positive value from the point of view of the reader's sympathy and allows his positive value within the context of the story to be annulled by the negative value of the minister. The man is a kleptomaniac. The minister has on his desk a set for taking Paraguayan tea; the set includes a golf straw (the *bombilla* used to suck the tea from the *mate* gourd). During an interruption when the minister is out of the room, the man puts the straw into his pocket, it is missed, and he is discovered to be the thief. He is arrested and disposed of, along with the project that would have benefited so many of his impoverished countrymen. No one will miss the detail that the engineer is defeated by his uncontrollable desire to appropriate the valuable objects of the privileged power brokers: the gold straw is a pivotal sign in the narrative between the minus value of the minister and the plus value of the engineer. In stealing the straw the latter unconsciously affirms a desire to partake of the luxuries of the oppressors (luxuries that they can afford because of their exploitation of the masses). For this reason, he is destroyed by the powerful minister and eliminated as a positive symbol for the value system represented implicitly by the reader (who cannot accept the engineer's uncontrollable kleptomania for the artifacts of power). (pp. 31-3)

One of the key stories in ***Thunder*** is **"La excavación" ("The Excavation")**. It belongs to a group of stories that involve individuals who can be called Roa's figures of the true Paraguayan man. Roa is concerned with individuals who run the gamut from unconscious suffering to the initial stirrings of the sort of awareness of self that revolutionary commitment demands. Such a commitment may involve the open assumption by certain individuals of a sacrificial role that they fervently believe will contribute to the liberation of their people. This type of individual is to be found in the title story, **"Thunder Among the Leaves,"** where Solano Rojas is a prefiguration of the Christ figures in Roa's first novel, ***Son of Man***. The spirit of sacrificial responsibility of these figures is summed up by Solano in a charge to his fellow Paraguayans, who must be led out of their silent bondage through the sacrifice of men of redemptive commitment: "'Never forget, my sons, that we must always help each other, that we must always be united. The only brother that a poor man really can count on is another poor man. And together we all form the hand, the humble but powerful fist of the workers . . .'". . . . While this sounds like rather standard Marxist revolutionary rhetoric, Roa couches it in the same sort of quasi-mythic context to be found in the opening story of the collection. Rojas's death, which results from his leadership of the workers in a strike against the implacable owners of a sugar refinery, is given not only a "socialist" meaning, but a mythic one as well. . . . (p. 34)

In **"The Excavation"** we have less of a sense of revolutionary commitment on the part of the central figure and more the personal struggle for survival, born of an awareness of circumstances that leads to sacrificial commitments. The story is political in nature and relates the efforts of a group of political prisoners to escape from the cell in which they are being held. They die one by one in the attempt, the tunnel that they are excavating in the struggle to attain physical freedom is discovered, and the few who remain alive are summarily executed for their efforts. The story is metaphoric of man's spiritual imprisonment by social injustice and of his strivings for self-liberation; in the end, the simple fact is that those strivings are frustrated with his annihilation by the forces that oppress him. The metaphoric value of the story is carried through with the symbol of the tunnel—the arduous conduit of the individual's movement toward liberation—and the story is effective in portraying the enormous physical suffering of the prisoners in their incarceration and in the overwhelming obstacles presented by attempts to attain freedom through the laborious excavation of a subterranean tunnel.

The story, then, has several apparent levels of meanings; that is, it can be viewed as a composition that invites parallel readings. The most obvious level is political: the harsh, unrelenting portrayal of tyrannical oppression in all of its boundless cruelty. A secondary level, dependent on the political one, concerns the futility of endeavors at liberation in the face of certain failure and annihilation. The ethical basis of society is neutralized by the existence of forces—entrenched dictatorships, imperialistic exploitation, foreign domination—that thwart natural human aspirations (Roa's work throughout assumes, of course, that man is endowed with a range of natural aspirations that, once made conscious of their lack of fulfillment, he strives to attain). The intensity of the effort expended in the excavation is completely vitiated by the discovery by the authorities of the prisoners' escape attempt.

A third level of the story is more generalized in mythic terms: the prisoners are seen not simply in terms of their futile attempts to free themselves from an unjust imprisonment, but as engaged in liberating themselves from an all-encompassing oppression signified by the choking morass of mud through which they must make their escape. Here man's subconscious is evoked, and the prisoners are endowed with a level of mythic awareness that highlights the importance of their struggle to escape. . . . (pp. 34-5)

Continuing the flashback and the confusion of the levels of time and event in the feverish mind of the prisoner on the verge of both escape and suffocation, the story stresses how the individual effort is figurative of the struggle of an entire people:

> That tunnel in the Chaco and this tunnel that he had himself suggest they dig in the floor of the jail, that he personally had begun to dig and that, finally, had served him only as a mortal trap—this tunnel and that one were one and the same: a single hole that opened up straight and black and that, despite its straightness, had surrounded him from the time he was born like a subterranean circle, irrevocable and fatal. A tunnel that was now forty years old for him, but that in reality was much older, really immemorial. . . .

In this fashion, the tunnel is transformed into a static symbol. It is a symbol not only for the prisoner, for whom it represents a lifetime of endless, useless struggle against oppression, but it also represents the narrative's emphasis on the unceasing yet seemingly futile collective struggle of an entire people. Life is a black and bottomless pit (or endless tunnel) in which a sector of mankind is permanently trapped. The suffering individual's conscious perceptions—the unconscious witness of a circumstance raised to the level of myth—is the central, controlling force of the story. And when those making the escape attempt are discovered and executed, it is not only a group of unknown unfortunates who are liquidated. It is the annihilation of a group of figures of a suffering collective identity. Despite the tremendous effort expended and, ultimately, wasted by the prisoners, the journalists who are invited to examine the tunnel are indifferent to the desperation it bespeaks, and oblivion reigns as the incident is forgotten in the daily course of events.

"The Excavation" is a key story in ***Thunder*** because it joins the theme of the human struggle for liberation with a bleak realization of the little chance of success for that struggle. Unlike [**"Thunder Among the Leaves"**] **"The Excavation"** does not offer the image of facile revolutionary accomplishment, and as a consequence it is more satisfying for its sober judgment that oppression is likely to remain a way of life for the Paraguayan people for the foreseeable future. (This sober judgment also underlies the portrayal of revolutionary figures in Roa's novel ***Son of Man.***)

The stories of ***Thunder*** are variations on themes associated with Roa's perception of the Paraguayan experience, and the three that have been examined in detail in this chapter exemplify cardinal points in that perception. While a good number of the stories are technically and artistically defective because Roa had yet to find a balanced literary voice, they are valuable for the seriousness of the author's attempts to elaborate the themes and symbols with which he chooses to deal. (pp. 36-7)

David William Foster, in his Augusto Roa Bastos, *Twayne Publishers, 1978, 133 p.*

MICHIKO KAKUTANI

Having taken part in the Paraguayan revolution against Spain, José Gaspar Rodriguez de Francia declared himself dictator of the country in 1814 and exercised absolute power until his death in 1840. Known as "El Supremo," Francia tolerated little opposition: he suppressed the aristocracy, limited the power of the church, jailed and reportedly tortured his enemies, and effectively cut Paraguay off from the outside world. And it is his story that the exiled Paraguayan writer Augusto Roa Bastos attempts to reimagine and relate in [***I the Supreme,*** a] huge, Rabelaisian novel.

Originally published in Argentina in 1974 as ***Yo el Supremo,*** the book will doubtless remind the reader of Gabriel Garcia Márquez's masterful novel *The Autumn of the Patriarch.* Both provide extravagant, surreal renditions of Latin America's extravagant, surreal history. Both create portraits of paranoiac dictators, isolated—from their families, friends and colleagues—by the solitary vice of power. And both use shifting narrative points of view to convey, at once, the solipsistic mindset of their heroes, and the collective sensibility of the nations under their rule.

In the case of ***I the Supreme,*** Mr. Roa Bastos has cleverly adopted the pose of "compiler." The novel, he writes, "has been culled—it would be more honest to say coaxed—from some twenty thousand dossiers, published and unpublished, from an equal number of other volumes, pamphlets, periodicals, correspondences and all manner of testimony—gleaned, garnered, resurrected, inspected—in public and private libraries and archives." The bulk of the book, however, takes the form of Francia's own reminiscences . . . and for the most part, those reminiscences concern the dictator's attempts to answer the critics who accuse him of turning "the nation into a doghouse stricken with hydrophobia"; to rationalize his actions, in short, to explain his life.

When we meet him, he is on his death bed, ailing, bitter and vituperative, but his voice echoes back and forth in time—recalling his birth and his youth, only to jump ahead to the future, speaking to us from beyond the grave about the flies that disturb his corpse, the bandits who dare to disturb his sleep. . . . He gives an account of his rivalries with such fellow revolutionaries as Bolivar and San Martin; he brags about his populism ("I promulgated laws that were the same for the poor man, the rich man"), and he defends his anti-education policy ("I have preferred you to be loyal functionaries rather than cultivated men. Capable of carrying out my commands").

Between such discussions of politics, Francia plunges in and out of dreams, nightmares and weird imaginings. Though they lack the intense lyricism and strange magic found in Garcia Márquez's work, these passages reverberate with a fierce surrealism—peopled with dwarfs, women warriors and clairvoyant animals; studded with Borgesian images of mirrors and labyrinths, mystical eggs and blankets made of batskin, and embroidered with subsidiary tales about madness, death and humiliation.

Francia, it seems, wants to account for everything (his own history, as well as the history of his nation, which he personifies as its leader) and as he pours out his story, it becomes clear that he possesses an insatiable desire for power and control—he has even chained a huge meteorite to his desk, as punishment for being a cosmic runaway—and that he also sees himself as two separate beings: as a conniving, paranoiac "I," beset by the average ego's fears and doubts, and as the "Supreme," a monstrously powerful presence that even Francia himself must refer to in the third person.

A believer in the persuasive powers of logic, Francia does his best to manipulate the facts of his life and the facts of his regime. But how much of what he says is true? Does he mean what he says, and for that matter does he say what he means? . . . Even as Francia speaks, in fact, he has the sense that language is betraying him; he feels his words slipping into puns, strange neologisms and unintended metaphors, his thoughts curdling into bizarre formations. "Forms disappear, words remain, to signify the impossible," he declares at one point. "No story can be told. No story worth the telling. But true language hasn't yet been born. Animals communicate with each other, without words. Better than we, who are so proud of having invented words out of the raw material of the chimerical. Without foundation. No relation to life."

To make matters worse, Francia's words often seem to take on a life of their own that survives his own existence. Even after the dictator's death, his documents, his memories, endure—waiting to be annotated, amended, interpreted and footnoted by future historians as they are in the book at hand. Just as his own public statements serve, at best, as a response to the "outrageous falsehoods, wicked tricks and diabolical machinations" of his enemies, so his memoirs become fodder for the manipulations of successive generations. In fact, however cumbersome and rhetorical ***I the Supreme*** may often feel, the novel remains a prodigious meditation not only on history and power, but also on the nature of language itself.

Michiko Kakutani, in a review of "I the Supreme," in The New York Times, *April 2, 1986, p. 25.*

CARLOS FUENTES

The Paraguayan Augusto Roa Bastos has his hands full with one single life story—that of the Paraguayan despot, José Gaspar Rodríguez Francia, who ruled his country as "Perpetual Dictator" from 1816 to his death, at age 74, in 1840.

The result is a richly textured, brilliant book—an impressive portrait, not only of El Supremo, but of a whole colonial society in the throes of learning how to swim, or how best to drown, in the seas of national independence. Students of African and Asian decolonization will find much to reflect on in ***I the Supreme,*** one of the milestones of the Latin American novel. (p. 32)

[Mr. Roa Bastos] left Paraguay in 1947 and has been in exile ever since, as the present tyrant, Gen. Alfredo Stroessner, outreigns El Supremo. Mr. Roa Bastos will certainly outlive them both. He is his country's most eminent writer; his works are few, self-contained (very Paraguayan) and brilliantly written. Yet his masterpiece, ***I the Supreme*** . . ., is the kind of *summa* that absorbs everything that the writer has done before. This is Mr. Roa Bastos' dialogue with himself through history and through a monstrous historical figure whom he has to imagine and understand if he is ever to imagine and understand himself and his people.

The literary ploy used by Mr. Roa Bastos in the novel poses, by force, the relationship between self and other, between individual destiny and historical destiny. The ploy is writing: the writing of history and the writing of a novel, the writing of a life that can only be ours if we take it upon ourselves to understand the life of the other. ***I the Supreme*** is a voice addressed to you the reader, Francia the historical figure, El Supremo the fictional character and Mr. Roa Bastos the Paraguayan writer. It begins, literally, with the handwriting on the wall: an anonymous pamphleteer has nailed a piece of paper to the door of a cathedral (shades of Lutheran rebellion!) and forged El Supremo's signature. In the document, the Perpetual Dictator orders that "on the occasion of my death my corpse be decapitated; my head placed on a pike for three days." The people are to be summoned by church bells to see El Supremo's head, and all his civil and military servants are to be hanged at once.

This announcement of his own death by the Eternal Tyrant unleashes the protean writing of the novel. The dictator demands of his bumbling secretary that the author of the libel be found (he never is), the secretary writes down things El Supremo says, El Supremo corrects him, talks to the dog Sultan, writes down his own secrets in a private notebook that is really (this is a nice Dickensian touch) "an outsized ledger, of the sort that from the beginning of his government El Supremo uses to keep track of the treasury."

He now sets forth in these folios, "in a disjointed, incoherent fashion, events, ideas, reflections, minutely detailed and well-nigh maniacal observations on any number of entirely different subjects and themes: those which in his opinion were positive in the Credit column; negative, in the Debit column," says the Compiler who annotates the book throughout, creating a kind of second or ghostly text, parallel to, sometimes in opposition to, sometimes supportive of, El Supremo's own ruminations. Add to this official documents, a log book, snippets from memoirs by people who knew El Supremo, selections from biographies (including one by Thomas Carlyle), diplomatic dispatches, . . . and the chillingly naïve responses of schoolchildren to the Government's query: How do you see the Sacrosanct image of our Supreme National Government? (p. 33)

Mr. Roa Bastos is especially good at rendering, in a flash, the fascinating cultural gap of Latin America, where the elite worships modernity, progress and the law, and the people worship Guaraní jungle deities. The Roman legalistic tradition is one of the strongest components in Latin American culture: from Cortés to Zapata, we only believe in what is written down and codified. But next to this belief, another faith accepts the power of a cacique who can sneeze three times and become invisible. Poised between Voltaire and Pocahontas, the Eternal Dictator fills the desperate vacuum: reason or magic, law or practice. He does it through whim and repression . . . and reform . . ., but, above all, he does it through the feeling that he must do what he does, and do what he wants to do, because if he does not, no one else will: El Supremo unwittingly reveals that he is occupying the space of a weak or inexistent civil society. But instead of helping to nurture society, he draws the tragic conclusion of hubris: he is indispensable, therefore he is history: "I don't write history. I make it. I can remake it as I please, adjusting, stressing, enriching its meaning and truth."

Here lie both the servitude and the grandeur of El Supremo. He offers his people a sick utopia, where law and order are values unto themselves and, indeed, Paraguay under his rule was a peaceful place. But so are graveyards. His grandeur is that, finally, he has no way of approaching the making of history except by writing it: he cannot remake it, adjust it, stress or enrich it otherwise. He pretends that he can issue a "perpetual circular," a kind of bureaucratic metaphysical ukase for the ages. Yet he is painfully wise and even tragically aware of what awaits him. He is an illusion: "A chimaera has occupied the place of my person." He is incapable of controlling everything: "The thing is, no one ever manages to understand how our deeds survive us." He cannot say, along with Joseph Conrad's Kurtz, "The horror, the horror," because he has not been able to reign over nothing. The human interest of Mr. Roa Bastos' creation is that, far from inventing a stereotypical dictator, the novelist has given us a man at odds with himself, a monster blessed with a kind of baroque freedom who can judge himself irreplaceable while at the same time conceiving his dead body as a few remains in an old noodle box—which is, in effect, where he ends. (pp. 33-4)

I hope that this wonderful book, so late in coming to the English-speaking world, will find a wide readership here. (p. 34)

Carlos Fuentes, "A Despot, Now and Forever," in The New York Times Book Review, *April 6, 1986, pp. 1, 32-4.*

PAUL WEST

Augusto Roa Bastos is himself a supreme find, maybe the most complex and brilliant, the densest-textured Latin American novelist of all. And ***I the Supreme,*** his lavish novel . . . makes me wonder, not just about the familiar and seemingly endless fecundity of Latin American imagination (which shows up in many more than a few fashionable novelists) but about the givens of Latin American life over the past two centuries. What a political demonology these novelists inherit, of ready-made, eccentric, monstrous tyrants such as they might invent only if they didn't otherwise exist. The price of admission to this Satan's gallery, however, has often enough been the right to reside in one's own country. For the past 40 years, for example, Augusto Roa Bastos has been exiled from his native Paraguay and living in France, teaching at the University of Toulouse until 1985.

What is it that makes Latin American tyrants, more than others, so usable—for Latin Americans, of course, such as Alejo Carpentier (*Reasons of State*), Gabriel García Márquez (*The Autumn of the Patriarch*), and Roa Bastos? . . .

Perhaps the answer lies in something peculiar to Latin American imagination itself: unobligated to European and North American models, to logic, to what's verifiable, and perhaps the only continental imagination *capable of inventing* the weird things it finds on hand. Perhaps, in order to do such novels as ***I the Supreme,*** you have to be able to imagine what it *would* have been like to create that ostensibly "supreme" being yourself. Knowing that, you do a kind of reverse obeisance to the facts you then exploit, murmuring *I could have invented you all, all the time*. The confidence generated by that hypothetical triumph of literary creation carries over into the semi-documentary writing feat. Knowing you could have cooked up The Supreme, or Amin, you pillage his image with cogent vigor and so have energy to burn on minor matters, vesting them with unusual intensity. (p. 1)

As here. Put at its barest, ***I the Supreme*** imagines its way into the head and heart, the life and times, of Jose Gaspar Rodriguez de Francia (1766-1840), who in 1814 contrived to get himself declared Paraguay's "Supreme Dictator for Life." But that is like calling World War II an upset, an oak tree something invented to cast a shadow, a book a paper tile. Roa Bastos not only reconceives the life of tyrant Francia, but also makes Francia reconceive that reconception. At some point before beginning, Roa Bastos has all the "facts" in order; he knows what happened in history. Then he lets Francia, his own creation by now, play fast and loose with those facts expressionistically, at the same time that he plays fast and loose with Francia himself. Indeed, Roa Bastos tampers not just twice but three times, handing over the facts to Policarpo Patiño, the tyrant's longtime secretary, who notes down (and alters) Francia's deathbed ponderings about his childhood in a Spanish monastery, his fellow tyrants in other countries, the egotistical sublimity that denied him family, friends, intimates, and the massive meteorite chained to his desk for having turned its tail on its place in the cosmos. . . .

The book is littered with warnings: "I don't write history," Francia says, "I make it. I can remake it as I please, adjusting, stressing, enriching its meaning and truth . . . *the order of the facts does not alter the product of the factors* (my italics)." Roa Bastos writes with a cylindrical white-ivory pen containing a "memory lens" that turns everything into metaphor, which of course is what the five-page footnote describing the pen does to the pen itself. This footnote's author is someone called the Compiler, whose task is to join several modes of writing into a readable whole, from an outsized ledger called "the private notebook," some pages of which are burned, torn, illegible, crushed into a ball, worm-eaten, stuck together and petrified, or written in a hand other than Francia's, to a text that Patiño calls his "Perpetual Calendar," which at first sight seems more of an attempt at reliable, official narrative, but isn't. Rumination blurs both ledger and calendar just as incessant, engrossing footnotes blur them, not to mention ukases found nailed to the cathedral door, rough drafts of documents, excerpts from a logbook, bits scrawled at midnight or in "The Tutorial Voice," loose leaves, and a list of toys.

The effect of all such textual sea-changing, as you gradually get used to the Compiler's ways, is that of a familiar-looking constellation rising and setting in the wrong order, at the wrong time. Pieced together from a thousand disparate pieces, this *Supremiad* samples all the ways there are of revealing someone through his miscellaneous writings. Indeed, the Compiler doesn't always identify his sources, so there you are, a willing accomplice among the motions of a mind learnedly overheard, and you are obliged, like all the king's horses and all the king's men, to put Humpty Dumpty Francia together again.

What a glory of echoing voices this Paraguayan portmanteau is, more Joycean than Cortázar's *Hopscotch,* every bit as volcanic and visionary as Lezama Lima's *Paradiso* or Osman Lins' *Avalovara*. If the "Boom" of the Latin-American novel's world pre-eminence is over, then this novel begins the Boomerang, arriving 12 years after its publication in Spanish in Argentina. . . .

Demanding our time and indulgence, ***I the Supreme*** is a work of graceful, voluminous genius. . . . (p. 13)

Paul West, "From South America, an Epic Novel of Tyrants and Trickery," in Book World—The Washington Post, *May 11, 1986, pp. 1, 13.*

RONALD CHRIST

[***I the Supreme***] is a profoundly spoken novel that is impossible to imagine as being spoken, a sort of political *As I Lay Dying* by way of *Tristram Shandy*. Every textual fold is pleated by sumptuous wordplay; arcane, absurd, and (mostly) accurate annotation and quotation; as well as fact so much stranger than fiction that nobody knows for sure which evil lurks in the mind of what possible man—or even the correct date (1766 or 1776?) of [José Gaspar Rodriguez de Francia's] birth. Because whatever else ***I the Supreme*** may be—and it is many things, including biography, bibliography, anachronistic history, metafiction—it is a novel that attracts by repulsion all the vast archival material collated by Roa Bastos. (p. 314)

The collision of data and views, like the tension between spoken and written word, is the equivalent of the book's plot. The novel gets its start when a vilifying pasquinade is nailed to the cathedral door about this strange figure, a dictator who welcomed notable visitors to his country only to keep them captive for years, who developed his nation's resources and sealed them from external contact, who achieved fame from books reviling his reign of terror and inspired praising portraits from Sir Richard Burton and Thomas Carlyle. The latter extolled him as a "sovereign of iron energy and industry, of great and severe labor."

The strange mix in Francia, embodied in the novel's tiers of texts, conversations, notes, and commentaries, also reflects the truth of Roa Bastos's country, where the Guarani Indian language flourishes side by side with Spanish, and literature is as much oral as printed. A truly Paraguayan writer, then, must simultaneously write in two languages and, at the same time, appear not to be writing at all. Roa Bastos inventively triumphs over both challenges. (pp. 314-15)

But let the reader beware: this is no easy read, no page-thumping, quick-study course in Latin American history and politics, no *One Hundred Years of Solitude* fantastic circus for readers of all ages. ***I the Supreme*** demands concentration, a welcoming rhetorical palate, and, I suggest, a browse through an encyclopedia's entries under "Paraguay" and "Francia." On the other hand, this maximal novel delights with a learned playfulness, a sophisticated modernity, an incredible factuality (such as the many-ton meteor Francia chains to his desk for being a runaway in the cosmos), and a many-ended detective story about identity and control (including self-control). This Supreme—just like the rest of us—produces powerful, not absolute, solutions. We read wonderingly by sewing and unsewing this crazy quilt of mutilated documents. No more than the recording author can the supreme dictator answer directly the question of who he is. "One can only speak of another," he says. "The I manifests itself only through the *He*. *I* do not speak to myself. I listen to myself through *Him*." After all, Francia may well ponder, perhaps he wrote the pasquinade himself. He dictated most of this novel. (pp. 315-16)

Ronald Christ, "A Labor, Great and Severe," in Commonweal, *Vol. CXIII, No. 10, May 23, 1986, pp. 314-16.*

DANIEL BALDERSTON

I the Supreme differs from previous dictator novels of Latin America by reason of the intensity of its authoritarianism, which is transferred from the thematic sphere to the discursive one. Roa Bastos' dictator is nearly solipsistic in that he admits of no interlocutor. His amanuensis is expected to take dictation without reflecting on it, and his subjects are supposed to translate his words immediately to action. The dictator announces that his book is "read first and written afterwards," and this reversal of the usual order of things is intended to produce an unambiguous, authoritative reading of an authorial discourse which admits of no reply. . . .

The novelist's pretense of supreme authority—we may think of Faulkner or Juan Carlos Onetti—is contrasted to the truly supreme authority of the dictator. That authority consists in creating an other, a reality. Authority so conceived is absolute but solipsistic. The Supreme Author's creation—the republic—is mute, or perhaps asleep like the "son" in Borges' *Circular Ruins*. It is no interlocutor, since it exists only in function of the Dictator's will. The word *will* refers both to the Dictator's resolve and to his written legacy. The republic is heir to both that will to be and that last testament. It is a sort of Janus figure, with an eye to the future and an eye to the past. The prophetic streak is important throughout the novel, but particularly in regard to Paraguayan history for the period following Francia's rule; hence, the references to the future Paraguayan dictator Francisco Solano Lopez, who ruled from 1862 to 1869, to a general in the Chaco War, and the veiled references to Alfredo Stroessner, who is a more recent avatar of the authoritarian streak seen in Francia but without those redeeming social values—honesty, vision, intelligence—which Francia so abundantly possesses in the novel. . . .

Many readers will feel a kind of claustrophobia as they make their way through ***I the Supreme***. It is surely a mark of Roa Bastos' craft that we feel oppressed by a dictator who died almost 150 years ago (as Roa Bastos himself also suffered, as he testifies in one of his published letters). The novel is an airless prison fashioned of words.

The ultimate prisoner of the Dictator's web is he, himself. His Corpus is his corpse, and he is caught in the web of his own words. ***I the Supreme*** is fundamentally the story of a self-multiplication of that self-mutilation which is inherent in all solipsism. When he denies others he cuts himself off from dialogue. Ultimately, he dictates only to himself, in the grave. By violating the conventions of discourse, he does violence not only to his enemies but also, and especially, to himself. (p. 9)

Daniel Balderston, in a review of "I the Supreme: A Novel," in Los Angeles Times Book Review, *July 13, 1986, pp. 1, 9.*

JOHN UPDIKE

[***I the Supreme***] is a deliberately prodigious book, an elaborate and erudite opus saturated in the verbal bravura of classic modernism. (p. 106)

Many books have gone into the making of this book: contemporary and historical accounts of Francia's Paraguay, government documents and the eighteenth-century sources of the dictator's own extensive erudition, and the exemplary modern works of Joyce, Borges, and García Márquez, among others—there is even a sharp whiff of contemporary French interest in the elusiveness of texts and the multiplicity of signs.

In books as in dinosaurs, however, grandeur asks a strong spine, and ***I the Supreme*** holds no action as boldly intelligible as Napoleon's invasion of Russia or the hunt for the Great White Whale. The looming, and virtually only, human relationship exists between the dying Francia and his obsequious secretary Policarpo Patiño; their dialogues are given not only without quotation marks but without dashes or indentation, so that the secretary and the dictator (himself once a secretary) tend to merge, even while allusions to Don Quixote and Sancho Panza thicken around them. The central issue of suspense—the authorship of an anti-Francia pasquinade nailed to the door of the cathedral—is never, that this reader noticed, resolved. Nor does the author's attitude toward his polymorphous, logorrheic hero come into clear view. Repulsion and fascination, clearly, but to what end? A kind of long curse concludes the novel—an enthusiastic descriptive catalogue of the insects and worms that will devour El Supremo's corpse, and some condemnatory sentences in the author's (or Patiño's) voice. . . . (p.107)

One is led, by this learned book bristling with quaint particulars and amiable puns and verbal tumbles . . . , into a spiritual dungeon, a miasmal atmosphere of hate and bitter recalcitrance. The fictional Francia is most eloquent in his inveighing against the others—the devilish ecclesiastics, the "Porteños" of Buenos Aires—who threaten his power. He knows no positive connections; all is betrayal and potential assault. The inanimate objects that inspire and console and fortify him—a polished skull, a fallen meteorite, his ivory pen—supplant human faces and voices and whatever humane motives inspired, at the forging of a nation, his polity. The static, circling quality of many modernist masterworks is here overlaid with a political rigidity, an immobilizing rage that seizes both the tyrant and the exiled writer. ***I the Supreme*** differs from García Márquez's *Autumn of the Patriarch* in that the dictator-hero of the latter is a coarse ignoramus, whereas Francia, in Roa Bastos's reconstruction, suffers, amid the trappings of omnipotence, the well-known impotence and isolation of the modern intellectual. (p. 108)

John Updike, "The Great Paraguayan Novel and Other Hardships," in The New Yorker, *Vol. LXII, No. 31, September 22, 1986, pp. 104-08, 111-16.*

Delmore Schwartz

1913-1966

American poet, short story writer, critic, essayist, editor, dramatist, translator, and author of children's books.

A prominent figure in American literature, Schwartz created poems and stories that are deeply informed by his experiences as the son of Jewish immigrants. His work often focuses upon middle-class New York immigrant families whose children are alienated both from their parents and from American culture and society. Schwartz explored such themes as the importance of self-discovery, the necessity of maintaining hope in the presence of despair, free will versus determinism, and the machinations of the subconscious. His themes evidence the influences of Sigmund Freud, Karl Marx, and Plato, while his admiration for the work of such modernists as William Butler Yeats and T. S. Eliot is displayed in his inventive use of symbolism. Schwartz is usually associated with a group of writers and critics who were prominent during the 1940s and are often referred to as "the New York intellectuals." Comprising such literati as Lionel Trilling, Philip Rahv, Irving Howe, and Meyer Schapiro, many of whom were affiliated with the influential magazine *Partisan Review,* this group was linked by leftist political views, an endorsement of modernism, and the Jewish heritage of many of its members.

Photograph by Sam Chambliss. Courtesy of the Literary Estate.

Schwartz was born in Brooklyn to Jewish immigrants whose troubled marriage contributed to the turbulence of his childhood. Following his graduation from high school, Schwartz studied philosophy at several universities and received his degree in 1935. In 1937, his short story "In Dreams Begin Responsibilities" appeared in the inaugural issue of *Partisan Review.* This work was immediately hailed as a masterpiece and is widely considered Schwartz's finest achievement. An account of an evening spent in a darkened theater viewing a film about the narrator's parents, "In Dreams Begin Responsibilities" provided a voice to the disenfranchised of American society through its synthesis of the themes of alienation, self-discovery, and determinism. The story was subsequently included as the title piece of *In Dreams Begin Responsibilities* (1938), Schwartz's first collection of poetry and prose. This volume contains some of Schwartz's most highly praised and frequently anthologized verse, including "The Heavy Bear Who Goes with Me," a tragicomic lyric concerning the conflict between mind and flesh, and "In the Naked Bed, in Plato's Cave," based upon Plato's famous allegory in which human perception is declared to be limited. The volume also includes the long narrative poem "Coriolanus and His Mother," adapted from Shakespeare's drama, and the verse play "Dr. Bergen's Belief."

Schwartz's next major work, *Shenandoah; or, The Naming of the Child* (1941), is a surrealistic verse play in which the narrator, Shenandoah Fish, witnesses such past experiences as the acquisition of his unorthodox name and his circumcision. Through such events, Schwartz examines conflicts between Jewish immigrants and American culture. Schwartz's long autobiographical poem, *Genesis: Book One* (1943), the initial volume of a series that was never completed, depicts the first seven years of the hero's life and also investigates his family's history in Eastern Europe. Schwartz held great expectations for the success of this epic, but many critics faulted the work for obsessive self-absorption. Following several years spent teaching at Harvard University, Schwartz returned to New York and published his first collection of short stories, *The World Is a Wedding* (1948). The volume contains some of Schwartz's best-known pieces, including "In Dreams Begin Responsibilities," "America! America!," and "The Child Is the Meaning of This Life," all of which are concerned with the identity of the Jew in America. In "New Year's Eve" and "The World Is a Wedding," Schwartz satirizes many of his colleagues at Harvard and the *Partisan Review.* Irving Howe observed that these stories "capture the quality of New York life in the 1930s and 1940s with a fine comic intensity."

In *Vaudeville for a Princess and Other Poems* (1950), Schwartz mixes short, humorous prose pieces on a variety of topics with poems concerning the value of poetry and a sequence of forty sonnets entitled "The Early Morning Light." *Summer Knowledge: New and Selected Poems, 1938-1958* (1959) collects most of the poems from *In Dreams Begin Responsibilities,* an excerpt from *Genesis: Book One,* several pieces from *Vaudeville for a Princess,* and many of his poems from the 1950s. In his later verse, Schwartz displays his interest in the poetry of Walt Whitman by turning away from concerns with urban alienation and celebrating in loosely structured lines the transcendent qualities of the natural world and the innocence of childhood. The last book to be published in Schwartz's lifetime, *Successful Love and Other Stories* (1961), contains much of his fiction from the 1950s. Most of these works are regarded as unfocused and inconsequential in comparison to his earlier stories. Although the quality of his fiction and poetry is generally considered to have declined after the late 1940s, Schwartz continued to earn respect for his exceptionally insightful literary criticism, which he had been writing and contributing to periodicals since the mid-1930s. He has been particularly praised for his essays on R. P. Blackmur, Yvor Winters, John Dos Passos, and Ring Lardner.

A copious writer, Schwartz left many unfinished and uncollected manuscripts at his death. These works form the basis for several posthumous publications, including *Selected Essays of Delmore Schwartz* (1970), *In Dreams Begin Responsibilities and Other Stories* (1978), *Last and Lost Poems of Delmore Schwartz* (1979), *The Ego Is Always at the Wheel: Bagatelles* (1986), and *Portrait of Delmore: Journals and Notes of Delmore Schwartz, 1939-1959* (1986). A tragic and often mythologized figure whose later years were plagued with depression, paranoia, and personal and career crises, Schwartz was the model for the protagonist of Saul Bellow's novel *Humboldt's Gift,* and his life inspired poetry by such writers as Robert Lowell and John Berryman. In commenting on the relationship between Schwartz's personal life and his career as a poet, David Lehman observed: "It is hard not to see Schwartz as an emblematic figure, capable of stirring us in his ravings no less than in his brilliant and original literary creations, meant to reproach and admonish us with the purity and grandeur of his aspirations as well as with the unbanished image of his demise."

(See also *CLC,* Vols. 2, 4, 10; *Contemporary Authors,* Vols. 17-18, Vols. 25-28, rev. ed. [obituary]; *Contemporary Authors Permanent Series,* Vol. 2; and *Dictionary of Literary Biography,* Vols. 28, 48.)

IRVING HOWE

However we may regard the story of Delmore Schwartz's life—as pathos, melodrama, or an experience both terrible and resisting easy explanation—there is a real danger that his work will be brushed aside as he himself becomes the subject of a lurid cultural legend. I don't want to be righteous about this, since I find Schwartz's life as fascinating (though also frightening) as anyone else does. The image of the artist who follows a brilliant leap to success with a fall into misery and squalor, is deeply credited, even cherished in our culture; it is an image that, despite sentimental exploitation, has a costly share of reality behind it. Nevertheless, we ought to insist that what finally matters is the work that remains, far more so than the life that is gone. What matters is the stories, poems, essays Schwartz wrote, perhaps most of all his stories, five or six of which are lasting contributions to American literature. The rest is pain, gossip, regret, waste.

Schwartz's most famous story, **"In Dreams Begin Responsibilities,"** came out in 1937, as the leading piece of fiction in the first issue of the new *Partisan Review*. Those of us who read it at the time really did experience a shock of recognition. The intellectual heavyweights of the *PR* group had been mobilized for this opening issue, and they performed in high style. Young readers like myself who looked forward to the magazine as a spokesman for "our" views on culture and politics—that is, the views of the anti-Stalinist left—were probably more interested in the polemics than the fiction. Still, we did read Schwartz's story, if only because the editors had put it at the top of their table of contents; and we were stunned. Many people I know have remembered the story long after forgetting everything else in the first issue.

We were charmed by the story's invention, though this could hardly explain the intensity of our response, since you didn't have to be a New Yorker, you could as well live in London or Singapore, in order to admire Schwartz's technical bravura. Still, it was the invention—the sheer cleverness of it—that one noticed first. A movie theatre becomes the site of dreams; the screen, a reflector of old events we know will soon be turning sour. The narrator watches father propose to mother at a Coney Island restaurant. Already, during the delights of courtship, they become entangled in the vanities and deceptions that will embitter their later years. But what can the audience do about it? The past revived must obey its own unfolding, true to the law of mistakes. The reel must run its course: it cannot be cut; it cannot be edited. (pp. vii-viii)

The tone of **"In Dreams Begin Responsibilities"**—flat, gray, a little sluggish, but with sudden spinnings of eloquence and literary self-consciousness—is distinctively urban. It speaks of Brooklyn, Coney Island, and Jewish immigrants fumbling their way into the new world, but also of their son, proudly moving toward the culture of America and finding there a language for his parents' grief. (p. ix)

For a decade there followed story after story in which Schwartz wrote about his characteristic themes: the pathos and comic hopelessness of the conflict between immigrant Jewish families and their intellectual children, the occasional recognition by those children that they had left behind not only a ghetto parochialism but also a culture of value, and the quasi-bohemian life of New York intellectuals in the 1930s and 1940s, with its frantic mixture of idealism and ambition, high seriousness and mere sententiousness. These wry, depressed, and insidiously clever stories—**"America! America!," "The World Is a Wedding," "The Child Is the Meaning of This Life"**—were put together in a form that Schwartz was making his own: longer than the story but shorter than the novelette, with little visible plot but much entanglement of relationship among characters, stylized dialogue replacing action or drama, and a major dependence on passages of commentary, ironic tags, deflated epigrams, and skittish ventures into moral rhetoric.

The risks of this kind of story were very considerable. To an unsympathetic reader, Schwartz's stories could seem ill-fitted, self-conscious, excessively parochial in reference and scope. Some of the inferior ones are precisely that: manner becoming merely mannered, an adept mimicry of itself. But this hardly counts, since a writer must be judged by his strengths, not the necessary failures along the way.

One charge frequently made against Schwartz's work, however, merits a closer look. The "tougher" literary people of his time—and it was then very much the fashion to be "strict" and "severe" in judgment—often said that Schwartz's work suffered from self-pity. They were sometimes right, but in the main they lacked the patience to see that in stories about the kinds of people Schwartz was describing self-pity is a necessary theme—how else can you write about young intellectuals, at once lost in the coldness of the world and subsisting on dreams of later achievement and glory? Schwartz had the rare honesty to struggle with this out in the open, struggle with it not merely as a literary theme but a personal temptation, so that in his best work he could control or even transcend it. A good many other, less honest writers learn to mask their self-pity as comic heartiness or clipped stoicism. But no one reading **"America! America!"** or **"The Child Is the Meaning of This Life"** is likely, I think, to suppose that the self-pity which plagues some of the characters is unresistantly shared by the author.

The stories Schwartz wrote in the years between **"In Dreams Begin Responsibilities"** and the publication in 1948 of his collection ***The World Is a Wedding,*** capture the quality of New York life in the 1930s and 1940s with a fine comic intensity—not, of course, the whole of New York life but that interesting point where intellectual children of immigrant Jews are finding their way into the larger world while casting uneasy, rueful glances over their backs. . . . Sliding past the twin dangers of hate and sentimentalism, Schwartz's best work brought one to the very edge of the absurd, I mean to that comic extremity in which the characters of, say, **"New Year's Eve"** and **"The World Is a Wedding"** were wrenched almost to caricature even as it remained easy to identify their "originals." It was as if ironic distancing, even ironic disdain were a prerequisite for affection, and thereby one could gain through these stories a certain half-peace in contemplating the time of one's youth. The mockery Schwartz expended upon the New York intellectuals and would-be intellectuals can be caustic, even bitter and, to be honest, sometimes nasty; but it is not dismissive, it does not exclude, it does not relegate anyone to the limbo of the non-human. Finally, Schwartz's voice is sad and almost caressing, as if overcome by the waste of things.

What is more, this comedian of alienation also showed a gift for acceptance, a somewhat ambiguous reconcilement with the demands and depletions of common experience. Schwartz's work gained its fragile air of distinction partly from the fact that he avoided the pieties of both fathers and sons, established communities and floundering intellectuals. (pp. ix-xi)

In the early stories (more disturbingly in the later ones) there was also a strong awareness of the sheer foolishness of existence, the radical ineptitude of the human creature, such as reminds one a trifle of Dostoevsky's use of buffoonery in order to discharge aggressiveness against both readers and characters. The *persona* of buffoonery, which goes perfectly well with a sophisticated intelligence, brings with it some notable dangers, but at its occasional best it enabled Schwartz to catch his audience off guard, poking beneath the belt of its dignity, enforcing the shared ridiculousness of . . . I guess, everything.

By the time Schwartz published ***The World Is a Wedding,*** he had developed his own style. Some years ago I tried to describe this style, and since I can't now do any better, I beg the reader's pardon for quoting myself: "it seemed to be composed of several speech-layers: the sing-song, slightly pompous intonations of Jewish immigrants educated in night-schools, the self-conscious affectionate mockery of that speech by American-born sons, its abstraction into the jargon of city intellectuals, and finally the whole body of this language flattened into a prose of uneasiness, an anti-rhetoric."

An anti-rhetoric is of course a rhetoric. But more important: in his stories dealing with immigrant Jewish families Schwartz may have begun with an affectionate and deliberate mimicry of immigrant speech, but very soon, I think, he yields himself to it almost entirely. Yielding himself, *he simply writes that way*. It becomes his language. (pp. xi-xii)

Of dismay and disintegration, chaos and ugliness, waste and malaise there was more than enough in the life, sometimes also the work, of Delmore Schwartz. Yet there is something else in his poems and stories, so rare in our time and so vulnerable to misuse and ridicule I hesitate to name it. What complicates and enriches Schwartz's comedy is, I think, a reaching out toward nobility, a shy aspiring spirituality, a moment or two of achieved purity of feeling. (p. xiii)

Irving Howe, in a foreword to In Dreams Begin Responsibilities and Other Stories *by Delmore Schwartz, edited by James Atlas, A New Directions Book, 1978, pp. vii-xiii.*

DAVID LEHMAN

Last and Lost Poems of Delmore Schwartz [is] designed, its editor tells us, as "a rescue mission," a companion volume to ***Summer Knowledge,*** meant to save from oblivion unpublished poems found among the poet's papers as well as a sampling of published works previously uncollected. It is intended as "a rescue mission" in a polemical sense also. Robert Phillips would like the book to rescue Schwartz from his numerous detractors and from such of his admirers—the majority—who mourn . . . the great falling off there was in Delmore's career as a poet. In this latter aim, Phillips cannot be said to have fully succeeded. He offers, in his preface to the volume, few reasons beyond his native enthusiasm for his repeated contention that the last poems radiate "energy and delight," that they merit the praise that once came unsolicited from impressive quarters. While his enthusiasm is genuine and therefore affecting, it does not prevent Phillips from citing, with apparent disapproval, some slightly misquoted lines from Frank O'Hara's "Memorial Day, 1950," with its jubilant reversal of Schwartz's most famous title ("Our responsibilities did not begin / in dreams, though they began in bed"). Phillips holds up the O'Hara poem to throw into relief the "lyric talent" of Delmore's last period, the "refreshing" celebration of "the natural, the lovely, the beautiful, and the harmonious." Under the circumstances, however, it is a most unfortunate comparison, in which the older poet comes off a bad second best. . . . For all their euphony—the gift of melody never deserted their author—many of the ***Last and Lost Poems*** seem tired by contrast, written in a kind of forced ecstasy, a gush of words contrived to create an artificial happiness which Schwartz could only feel when transported out of himself.

Brought up on Eliot as he was, Delmore Schwartz had always managed to engender new ideas for his poetry out of the past's great examples, but as his end drew near his sounds grew less distinct than their echoes. . . . The instinct to paraphrase Shakespeare's Sonnet #116, retaining as structural elements certain key phrases, is a good one, but the poem produced thereby suffers from sheer verbosity. . . . (pp. 227-28)

On the other hand, one can see in **"Spiders,"** which is a kind of wry meditation on the subject of Robert Frost's "Design," the wit that Kenneth Koch found so enchanting in his Harvard mentor; the poem anticipates the jolly didacticism that Koch brings to perfection in *The Art of Love:*

Sometimes the male
Arrives with the gift of a freshly caught fly.
Sometimes he ties down the female, when she is frail,
With deft strokes and quick maneuvres and threads of silk:
But courtship and wooing, whatever their form, are informed
By extreme caution, prudence, and calculation,
For the female spider, lazier and fiercer than the male suitor,
May make a meal of him if she does not feel in the same mood, or if her appetite
Consumes her far more than the revelation of love's consummation.

In another late poem, the theme of Keats's "In a Drear-Nighted December" receives a treatment that is noble in its simplicity. . . . On the whole, however, it is to the poems dated 1937 and 1941 that we are likely to respond with pleasure, for the precocious intelligence and sharp prosodist's ear which they manifest. . . . (pp. 228-29)

A comparison of the two longer works with which the new volume closes spells out the difference between what might have been and what, sadly, there was to be. Labeling itself "An Entertainment," **"Paris and Helen"** (1941) begins with an epigraph from Pope's translation of *The Iliad* juxtaposed with the naming of an ideal cast—Robert Montgomery as Paris, Madeleine Carroll as Helen, Greta Garbo, Myrna Loy, Hedy Lamarr, and Dame May Whitty taking turns as Venus, in her various guises. It is a verse play in the Yeatsian manner, and its burlesque of Hollywood is an effective counterpoise to the weight of final reflections. . . . **"Kilroy's Carnival"** (1958) similarly wishes to conflate high culture and low, this time in the form of "A Poetic Prologue for TV." But here the voice turns shrill, the humor without sufficient subtlety. Much of "the show" is devoted to the reading of letters and queries sent in by viewers. "You are a nut: a complete nut: that's why your program keeps becoming more and more popular," one writes. Another asks, "Are you a conscientious objector to life like the inspired novelist Count Leo Tolstoy?" The answer conveys the full pathos of Delmore Schwartz. "The answer is that I am conducting an interminable filibuster against the death of the heart in the little death of each day."

In his poem "At the Grave of Henry James," Auden prays for the many writers "whose works / Are in better taste than their lives," and if we remember to trust the poet rather than the man, we will not fail to experience a pleasurable intellectual commotion upon reading the works of Delmore Schwartz. And in that spirit we will, when reviewing the sad facts of his life, look on him not as a failure or an object lesson on the perils of egotism but as the sleepless "veteran of childhood" who wanted his eyes to "burn like the street-light all night quietly, / So that whatever is present will be known to me," but who could not transcend the profound nervousness which gnawed "at the roots of the teeth of his being." (pp. 229-30)

David Lehman, "Delmore, Delmore: A Mournful Cheer," in Parnassus: Poetry in Review, *Vol. 7, No. 2, Spring-Summer, 1979, pp. 215-30.*

JEROME MAZZARO

In the "last" poems [contained in ***Last and Lost Poems of Delmore Schwartz***], unexpected collapses of response explain the souring of lyrics like **"This Is a Poem I Wrote at Night, Before the Dawn"** (1961). After proceeding derivatively but beautifully for thirteen lines, Schwartz moves into minstrel-show humor with "It is always darkness before delight" and effectively ends all interest in the work. Although equally indebted to Whitman, **"All Night, All Night"** carries through brilliantly. [Editor Robert Phillips] is right in attacking the view . . . that Schwartz "was bright, then burned out like a candle": "His poetry did not, in fact, 'improve.' It became different. . . . With their accumulations of details and syntactical repetitions, Schwartz's late poems seem to be modeled after Whitman rather than his early master, Yeats." They differ from his early work in that they are clearly not attempts "to mythologize himself, or to dramatize history, or to pay homage to the world of culture. Rather, [they] often accurately recreate a sensuous experience and do so in language that is musical, free-associative, and highly communicative." The style is one of "spontaneous effusion, characterized by energy and delight." Readers will be thankful to have available such good poems as **"Poem (Remember midsummer)," "The Choir and Music of Solitude and Silence," "Late Autumn in Venice (After Rilke)," "The Journey of a Poem Compared to All the Sad Variety of Travel,"** and the classic **"A Dream of Whitman Paraphrased, Recognized and Made More Vivid by Renoir."** They may enjoy reading anew early poems like **"At This Moment of Time"** and **"Poem (Old man in the crystal morning)"** and delight in the good moments of **"America, America!"** and **"The First Night of Fall and Falling Rain."** But Phillips' "rescue mission" indicates, too, that further literary yields from the twenty boxes of papers left after the poet's death may, indeed, be slim. (p. 714)

Jerome Mazzaro, "'Delmore, Delmore'," in The Georgia Review, *Vol. XXXIII, No. 3, Fall, 1979, pp. 712-16.*

THEODORE HALL

With the exception of **"The Track Meet,"** the stories [in ***In Dreams Begin Responsibilities and Other Stories***] illustrate Schwartz's achievement as voice and interpreter of the fate of Jewish immigrants and their children in the New World. Unfortunately, Schwartz's understanding of that fate is not clearly indicated by [editor James Atlas], who restricts himself to an appreciation of the author's close observation and skillful representation.

The lives of the immigrants were determined essentially, according to Schwartz, by the "deity America"—by the false, inevitably destructive hope of escape from the entanglements, frustrations, and failures of the past; by the presumption that happiness is a right and tremendous success not far away. Schwartz saw the immigrants blindly embracing the bitch-goddess Success—the vulgarized American Dream—and begetting endless miseries. There is no escape from the past, Schwartz declares time and again. The reality of American life is exile—deracination and alienation.

At least two stories in the collection are masterpieces. **"In Dreams Begin Responsibilities"** is primarily a complex demonstration of the immortality of the past. The narrator of this story dreams that he is in a theater viewing his parents' excursion to Coney Island on the day of his father's marriage proposal. He is increasingly distressed and at last loudly protests, "Don't do it! It's not too late to change your mind, both of you. Nothing good will come of it, only remorse, hatred, scandal, and two children whose characters are monstrous." . . . "The narrator's outcry," [Irving Howe suggests in his foreword], "is not so much a protest against mistakes as a protest against life itself, inconceivable without mistakes." . . . It may be argued that the narrator protests against neither "mistakes" nor "life itself," but rather, against frightful irresponsibility. His parents' marriage is contracted not in Heaven, but in Coney Island—the fantastic amusement park of the American Dream.

In **"The Track Meet,"** Schwartz employs again the device of the dream and an "escape" setting (a sporting event). His principal aim is to illustrate the crisis of modern Western man, who, having lost the governance of traditional institutions, is condemned to a chaotic and devastating "scrimmage of appetite" or to anguished, futile protest. The history of modern man, in Schwartz's view, is the history of his fall from the biblical order into a hell of egoistic ambition. God and his hosts of ideals have been deposed; the new reigning deity is "Mother," whose throne is the id, whose wisdom is science and cynicism, and whose will is success—at whatever cost.

Schwartz was a child of fantastic expectations, an American dreamer who, like many of his characters, came in the end to desolation. No matter how one judges his vision of the modern condition, one must respect the courage and intelligence with which he struggled to understand the modern ethos of egoistic ambition. (pp. 70-1)

Theodore Hall, in a review of "In Dreams Begin Responsibilities and Other Stories," in The International Fiction Review, *Vol. 7, No. 1, Winter, 1980, pp. 70-1.*

ROBERT DANA

Delmore Schwartz was an obsessive. Most poets, most artists probably are in certain ways. . . . [Poets] are obsessed with language, with particular bits of language, even with particular words. . . . [Poets] are obsessed with trying to render human experience, that "certain slant of light," through the exactly right word. A strange occupation at best. And nothing comes through more clearly and more sadly in reading Schwartz's ***Last and Lost Poems*** than the obsessive nature of the craft, and the tragic consequences of losing control of it. . . .

[***Last and Lost Poems of Delmore Schwartz***] is not, on the whole, an enjoyable book, unless you enjoy watching the slow but inexorable disintegration of a poet's mind and talent.

Troubled by my reaction to this book after I had finished it, I reread parts of ***Summer Knowledge,*** Schwartz's new and selected poems which had been published . . . in 1959. So many things came clear! So many things I had forgotten or taken for granted. It was from Schwartz and the poets of his generation that many of us now writing had first learned to formulate the casual details of day-to-day American life. "A fleet of trucks strained uphill, grinding / Their freights covered as usual." Or "Morning, softly / Melting the air, lifted the half-covered chair / From underseas, kindled the looking-glass . . . /" (**"In the Naked Bed, in Plato's Cave"**). And Schwartz, along with Robert Lowell, was one of the inheritors of that Yeatsian style of half-narrative poem constructed on a powerful lyric base. **"The Heavy Bear Who Goes With Me,"** for example. **"O Love, Sweet Animal,"** a poem I had forgotten or overlooked in earlier readings of Schwartz, shows how skillfully he could deploy what used to be called "the argument" of a love lyric, and how fine an ear he had for the use of feminine endings. . . .

Schwartz, in his precociousness, was one of those who taught us that knowledge and thought are the armatures of instinct, the muscle that controls the wings.

To be sure, there are flashes of that old control and brilliance in ***Last and Lost Poems.*** There is even a little of a new kind of precocity, and such fragments and poems are all the more heartrending for being set, as they are, amid the dregs of the poet's *oeuvre:*

> Remember midsummer: the fragrance of box, of white
> roses
> And of phlox. And upon honeysuckle branch
> Three snails hanging with infinite delicacy
> —Clinging like tendril, flake and thread, as self-
> tormented and self-delighted as any ballerina just as
> in the orchard,
> Near the apple trees, in the overgrown grasses
> Drunken wasps clung to over-ripe pears
> Which had fallen: swollen and disfigured. . . .

Passages like [this] . . . and a few whole poems such as **"Metro-Goldwyn-Mayer"** and **"Philology Recapitulates Ontology, Poetry is Ontology"** and its companion piece, exist side by side with such gaffers as

> Noel, Noel
> We live and die
> Between heaven and hell
> Between earth and sky . . .

and

> another form and fountain of falsehood's fecundity

and

> Knowledge is only the knowledge of love,
> and every story is the story of love,
> and every story is a lovelorn ghost!

The last two quotations are not untypical of the weak sections of **"The Studies of Narcissus"** which editor Robert Phillips announces "is published in its entirety here for the first time." That the poem is "clearly unfinished" could not be more evident. And here one must take issue with Dwight Macdonald's dust-jacket assertion that the publication of such scarred and raw work was in any sense "necessary." Necessary to whom, one asks. No reader will be much edified by reading such work. . . .

In a poem entitled **"All Night, All Night,"** one is aware that the poet's fascination with sound is barely under control:

> . . . a bird /
> Flew parallel with a singular will. In daydream's moods
> and attitudes
> The other passengers slumped, dozed, slept, read,
> Waiting, and waiting for place to be displaced
> On the exact track of safety or the rack of accident.

The balance between sound and sense here is precarious, disturbed. It is only the narrative structure that keeps the poem from flying off into the incomprehensible, "empty symphonies of sound" that James Atlas fears so much. Clearly the control of sound is not in the late poems what it is, say, in [**"The Heavy Bear Who Goes with Me"**]. . . . Instead, in these late and last poems, one sees the mind of the poet begin a fatal kind of circling, progressively helpless, drowning in the very medium he would control. . . . (pp. 118-19)

Last and Lost Poems is, finally, a sad, instructive book: a tragic documentary of a decaying imagination, of a great spirit in isolation, of a mind fraying toward exhaustion. As documentary it will certainly have solid value for scholars of the poet's life and work, for here we can observe, perhaps more closely than we could wish to, a once powerful talent dying into mode. (p. 119)

Robert Dana, "Differences of Opinion," in New Letters, *Vol. 48, No. 1, Fall, 1981, pp. 116-19.*

ELIZABETH HARDWICK

The letters [contained in ***Letters of Delmore Schwartz***] begin outside the family, since those to mother, father and brother, Kenneth, have not survived. It is 1931 and Delmore has gone to the University of Wisconsin, his first escape from Brooklyn and the Washington Heights section of Manhattan. He writes to Julian Sawyer, a high school friend. . . .

The youthful letters are more lyrical and more exposing than the best of the later years. They are rich in exalted ambition, the agitated, opinionated, tireless reading of a mind already concentrated upon the challenge of literature. Also, the spendthrift, self-dramatizing inclination is full-blown, the unsteadiness of a displaced son of the Jewish middle class. Delmore's father was somewhat flashily successful as a business man, but the parents were divorced, the mother hysterical and unforgiving: the promised legacy to come at the father's death did not arrive, but remained, nevertheless, a taunting, maddening birthright denied.

In the valuable letters to Sawyer, Schwartz enters the "whole provincial collegiate world," and because it is Wisconsin it is, to this son of the pavements, the surprising world of nature, "the woods full of fresh-water brooks, springs and creeks, deer, too, and rabbits, squirrels. And the long quiet streets, tree-lined (tall trees!), New England white houses." Such is the backdrop, although not long to be considered. Instead, Delmore is immediately recognized as a formidable intellectual and a group forms around him that looks to him for "authority."

The letters reveal the almost helpless fascination with his own character, and tenacious the absorption was to be. He is confident enough to see himself as the object of love and also confident enough to caution Julian against counting upon him too greatly. "I always cause those who are near to me more suffering than pleasure." He is gossipy about the great, insofar as he knows about them from hearsay and from books. He begins to drink alcohol in the collegiate manner, without ceasing to drink from the spring of Stendhal "whose taste is of a coolness." He is rebuked by the threat of a poor grade (C) for refusing to write a paper on Stephen Vincent Benét's long poem, "John Brown's Body"; but he floors them, so to speak, by the substitution of "an essay on Paul Valéry, making fifteen quotations in French." Feeling his awkwardness and bursts of aggression, he wishes to study gracefulness so that "life may be a poem." He is a success, he is somebody in the classrooms and yet, "'Tis bitter chill, and I am sick and hurt."

Thus, here is the man, Delmore Schwartz, a troubled prodigy who is to become, in Karl Shapiro's interesting and emotionally charged foreword, "the touchstone of his generation." We do not have any more communications with Julian Sawyer and the scene changes the following year to New York University, then to Harvard as a graduate student in philosophy, back to New York and beginning to publish, marriage, Harvard once more as a teacher, on and on in the literary and academic world.

The cast of the letters becomes then confined to the friendships and occasions of a career among the well known. There is correspondence with his first wife, Gertrude Buckman, and a few letters to his second wife, Elizabeth Pollet, and to four or five scattered others; for the rest, it is fellow-writers, editors, publishers, professors, almost all of them hyphenated beings, writer-editor, poet-professor, like Schwartz himself.

The most impressive of the letters concern poetry and the occasion is often the disputes or rebuttals arising out of Schwartz's brilliant critical essays on the most intimidating masters of his time—Hart Crane, R. P. Blackmur, Eliot, Auden, Allen Tate, Edmund Wilson, Wallace Stevens, Yvor Winters, and the masters of comedy, W. C. Fields and Ring Lardner. . . .

Philip Rahv, in a review of Schwartz's critical essays, suggests that their power and genuineness lay in the fact that, in this form, the author was not so nerve-wrung about "greatness" as he was as a poet and short-story writer. Two letters to Ezra Pound bear on this precocious and unpretentious critical discrimination. They also show a valiant and disinterested attention to important texts.

The first letter, from 1938, came about because of an essay on Pound Schwartz published in *Poetry* magazine. He was then only 25. The essay is a tribute to Pound as a tireless salesman and patron of the best writing of his day; it is also a careful tribute to the prodigious talent and originality of Pound's own poetry. . . .

A year later, 1939, Schwartz writes Pound once more. He has just read "Culture." "Here I find numerous remarks about the Semite or Jewish race, all of them damning. . . . A race cannot commit a moral act. Only an individual can be moral or immoral. No generalization from a sum of particulars is possible, which will render a moral judgment. . . . I should like you to consider this letter as a resignation: I want to resign as one of your most studious and faithful admirers." It is interesting to note another essay on Pound, written 22 years later. Schwartz examines with distaste the improbabilities in the echoing chambers of Pound's mind, but a book is an object in the world and not an exact equivalent of the whole person. The essay ends: "The first and most important thing to say about Pound's Cantos is that they ought to be read again and again by anyone interested in any form of literature." . . .

There is plenty of malice in the letters written by Delmore Schwartz, most of it amusing, except to the object.

Schwartz addresses himself to Tate, Berryman, Mark Van Doren and many others. The letters are always interesting, but perhaps only a colleague can decode the fever about reviews, what appeared here and what there. They show a powerful soul of a certain shape, but are not at all like the undisciplined, evocative, unexpected letters of, for instance, Hart Crane. For one thing, Delmore never went anywhere; and did not travel much in his Concord, downtown New York.

Amazingly for one of his generation, Schwartz added amphetamines and tranquilizers in great quantity to his lifelong heavy drinking. During his last years he was a heartbreaking puzzle. The physical deterioration might have been endured with pity and respect by his friends, but the development of his paranoid derangements of the most assaultive kind made many friends flee and others despair of offering help. These distresses are only skimpily represented by his surviving letters.

No doubt it is just as well since the final two are answers to creditors, one to a landlady and the other to a doctor. (p. 20)

Elizabeth Hardwick, "Son of the City's Pavements," in The New York Times Book Review, *December 30, 1984, pp. 1, 20.*

MARIA MARGARONIS

Schwartz was a compulsive writer. Words came to him in euphonious chains, and he often seems to have invented himself on paper, producing reams of unpublished autobiographical material. His copious correspondence was a part of that process, and also of his careful, dedicated work as a poet and literary critic. The letters [in ***Letters of Delmore Schwartz***] show a rich sense of the pleasures of language and of its many uses—for thought, polemic or play, and as a conduit for friendship and affection. The voice in them is easy and refined; the subjects are usually poetry and culture, anecdotes, jokes or gossip about friends. Although Schwartz's famous depressions are increasingly in evidence as the years go by, the wild and woolly literary lion is generally matched by his keeper: the serious, professional poet trying hard to live fully in his time.

In the late 1930s and 1940s, when most of these letters were written, Schwartz was a literary star, very much an insider. Much of his correspondence during those years is concerned with editorial politicking: "One owes it to literature to be virtually Machiavellian for the sake of good writers." Schwartz schemed endlessly about his own career, suggesting reviewers for his books and providing his publisher with enthusiastic jacket copy, but he schemed, too, on behalf of his friends. Some of the most touching letters describe his efforts to get John Berryman's poems published or to find him a job. His concern for the less well-known poet is almost motherly. . . . (p. 599)

Schwartz was an intelligent and uncompetitive reader of his friends' work and could express criticism so sympathetically that it reads like praise. In one of his many letters to R. P. Blackmur, he kindly diagnoses the critic's poetic difficulty: "I think maybe it is that helpless strength of yours, that overwhelming consciousness of the possibilities of meaning of single words, which if it continues will make you end up like Samson dragging the temple of the whole English language down on your head."

Of his own work, Schwartz writes sometimes with ecstatic conceit, sometimes with blocked despair, especially in the letters about his long, unsuccessful autobiographical poem, **"Genesis."** He was usually brimming with plans and projects ("I'd like very much to write ballet scenarios for [Lincoln] Kirstein, and have two ideas, one involving comic-strip motifs, the other a baseball game") and his energy seems to have been a constant threat to his self-discipline. But precision in writing and thought were very important to him, and he maintained an exacting commitment to craft. (pp. 599-600)

Schwartz was an agile polemicist and used his philosophical training as a sharp weapon (sometimes sharp enough to split hairs) in his many literary disputes. In mid-century New York, the intellectual elitism of Eliot and Pound operated alongside socialist politics; the cutting edge in literary criticism was the close textual analysis of the conservative Southern Agrarians, and the political avant-garde was represented by the Trotskyist sympathies of *Partisan Review*. Schwartz negotiated his own path among these tendencies, keeping up a vigorous correspondence with Tate as well as with Dwight Macdonald, whom he often chastised for making "a profession of against-ness." It is in reading the letters to Macdonald that one most regrets hearing only half the conversation. They sketch a passionate friendship riddled with quarrels that reach deep into the political culture, and it is especially frustrating not to have Macdonald's reply to Schwartz's irritation at his departure from *Partisan Review*, or his criticisms (apparently ruthless) of **"Genesis."**

If Schwartz complained about Macdonald's contrary moralism, he also took issue with the New Critics over their exclusive concern with style. In 1938 he wrote to Tate: "It seems to me that if you analyze what we mean by technique, craft, and style in the concrete . . . they are inseparable, in a certain way, from the beliefs and values of the poet." But in the case of Ezra Pound, Schwartz cleanly cut the knot between poetry and politics. . . . In 1945, when Pound was on trial for wartime treason and other literary figures rushed to his defense, Schwartz continued to distinguish between poetic talent and morality: "If he is attacked as a poet, then we will certainly defend him. . . . But . . . no one's actions can be defended on the ground that he is a great poet, as he is."

Schwartz criticizes his own actions in the letters, too, but in a characteristically ironic, evasive way, as in this rhyme, sent to Blackmur in 1943, about his own wife and Berryman's:

All poet's wives have rotten lives,
Their husbands look at them like knives
(Poor Gertrude! poor Eileen!)
Exactitude their livelihood
And rhyme their only gratitude,
Knife-throwers all, in vaudeville,
They use their wives to prove their will—

Both Gertrude and Schwartz's second wife, Elizabeth Pollet, suffered bitterly at his hands, and one could see callousness here. Yet the poem also shows Schwartz's capacity for making cruel fun of his faults: the humor does not imply indifference but guilt and pain. Schwartz seems to have lived with his driving superego and terrible depressions by trying to outsmart them or charm them away with words. The letters have an astonishing array of vivid phrases to describe misery. . . . The prose flashes with darkness until the more ominous silence of the 1960s sets in, broken by abjectly polite business letters and sheepish requests for loans or apologies for unpaid bills.

But just as often, or more so, the letters flash with humor—anecdotes about Schwartz's students at Harvard, his friends' children and his cat Oranges, jokes about writers (he liked to refer to Eliot's "East Coca Cola") and extempore digressions. Many of the best jokes are about himself: "I have decided not to be a bank clerk, since I would probably be paralyzed by the conflict between my desire to steal money and my fear of doing so." At the great American art of the one-liner, Schwartz was a master. It was he, after all, who said, "Even a paranoid has enemies."

The most personal and moving letters here are those Schwartz wrote to Gertrude in the months after she left him. They are simple, lonely, romantic and full of the domestic details of affection. . . . For all their virtuosity, reading these letters occasionally seems an intrusion. Schwartz's life has been thoroughly scrutinized, rehashed, packaged and promoted; although he lived out much of it in public, he was an intensely private person, protecting himself with elaborate verbal and emotional strategies. To his friend and publisher James Laughlin he once wrote, "My only desire, as you indicate, is to be a late Shakespearian fool.'' His letters, more than all the memoirs and biographies, show that he was exactly that: a man whose feeling revealed itself most fully in play, evasiveness and poetry. (pp. 600-01)

Maria Margaronis, ''The Heavy Bear,'' in The Nation, *New York, Vol. 240, No. 19, May 18, 1985, pp. 599-601.*

ROBERT LEITER

Reading [***The Letters of Delmore Schwartz***] is a dismally claustrophobic, wearying affair, and not simply because the life depicted in its pages is leaden with sorrows—insomnia, alcoholism, madness. The problem is a good deal more complex. As a young man, Schwartz wrote a certifiable masterpiece, the astonishing short story **''In Dreams Begin Responsibilities,''** which continues to speak to us today. There he explored his most important theme. According to the critic Harry Levin, Schwartz ''reversed the happy ending of the immigrant legend; instead of joining a transatlantic utopia, the eternal wanderers got lost in a deeper and darker wilderness . . .'' And then wreaked havoc upon their American children.

For the rest of his brief life—he died of a heart attack at the age of 53, alone and lonely in a fleabag Manhattan hotel, as much a victim of his paranoia as of ill health—Schwartz wrote variations on this one story, with less and less technical expertise each time out. Why he thought anyone would care to hear about his life again and again, especially in the case of his 200-page poem, ***Genesis,*** which manages to take its hero, Hershey Green, only as far as his seventh birthday, remains one of the mysteries of Schwartz's life. Still, he persisted in tilling the same forbiddingly narrow patch of literary ground, until everything he wrote sounded like a parody of his best work.

Not surprisingly, Schwartz's letters are as irritatingly self-absorbed as his poems and stories. The earliest ones collected here date from his college years at the University of Wisconsin, when his sole correspondent was his friend, Julian Sawyer, who also had literary aspirations. Schwartz played the campus genius to the hilt, spouting grand pronouncements about world literature with unflagging confidence. Yet the most important note sounded in these early letters is the tone of faint derision directed at Sawyer. One might smile at such a sophomoric display and move on, but the tone never moderates. In fact, it grows more vicious as Schwartz's fame increases. The poet made a habit of befriending people, then cutting them out of his life with a vehemence that is shocking. There is little evident wit, charm or high jinks in these letters. When Schwartz is feeling good, when he has boarded the manic depressive roller coaster, as he calls it, and is heading up, the mood is genuinely manic and its intensity far from pleasant. The only glee the poet expresses comes when he is gossiping—incessantly, meanly—but because his remarks are generally so unpleasant and he is so unremittingly ill-tempered, it is difficult for anyone to share in this mood.

Schwartz's much-touted devotion to literature was also narrowly conceived. Discussions of books and authors are plentiful in the early part of the correspondence, but often the letters are of interest not for their remarkable insights but as demonstrations of Schwartz's alarming precocity. In 1938, at the ripe old age of 25, with the success of his first book under his belt, he thought nothing of writing to Ezra Pound and lecturing him on how he had ''slowed up.'' But Schwartz's literary interests eventually fell prey to his narcissism. Even before his confidence as a writer had slipped and his paranoia had blossomed, there is talk only of *his* poetry, *his* career, *his* enemies.

What the letters make clear . . . is the extent of Schwartz's career as a literary politician. Part of the tragedy of his life, aside from his madness and slow dissolution, was that so much of his energy, energy that might have been invested in creative work, went instead into *plotting* his next triumph rather than actually writing it. (pp. 503-05)

Schwartz had the misfortune of being overpraised throughout his career—and long after. . . . But even at the start there were dissenting opinions. The myth is that Schwartz's first book ***In Dreams Begin Responsibilities*** met with unanimous praise. But as Atlas reports, critics like Babette Deutsch and Louis MacNeice, who were ''unrestrained by friendship,'' proved less charitable. (p. 505)

Schwartz's tragedy, as his friend William Barrett has said, had nothing to do with society's hostility to ''the Poet.'' ''Few persons of his age were ever given more opportunities to follow their calling,'' [Sidney] Hook wrote, ''or enjoyed more kindnesses, or received more praise and encouragement . . .'' Schwartz's failure was a human one; he and he alone was the culprit. The romantic myth of the poet who *suffers* his poetry seems firmly lodged in Western consciousness. We have little interest in writers who are steadily productive and lead tidy lives. But if any book could help dispel this fallacy, it would have to be ***The Letters of Delmore Schwartz.*** There is no mediating voice here—no memoirist or biographer shaping reality to suit his purposes. There is only a sad, wretchedly unhappy man raving on and on. (p. 506)

Robert Leiter, ''The Poetry Competition,'' in The Hudson Review, *Vol. XXXVIII, No. 3, Autumn, 1985, pp. 503-06.*

ROBERT PHILLIPS

Delmore Schwartz appended Jonathan Swift's phrase, *''Vive le bagatelle,''* to his most playful book of poetry and prose, ***Vaudeville for a Princess,*** and I think of the [essays included in ***The Ego Is Always at the Wheel***] as Schwartz's bagatelles—short pieces in a light style. They are distinctly different from those appearing in ***Selected Essays of Delmore Schwartz***. . . . Those pieces were Schwartz's serious and public pronouncements on literature of the twentieth century—on general questions of poetry and criticism, as well as on individual fiction writers and poets. [***The Ego Is Always at the Wheel***] represents Schwartz in a less serious mood. The pieces seem to have been written primarily for his own amusement. He did publish a handful, as prose interludes between the poems of ***Vaudeville for a Princess***. . . . He appended another to a selection of his poems in an anthology, and three others appeared in magazines. But the remainder were found among his uncatalogued papers now housed at Yale. Written in the 1940s and '50s, the most recent was dated 1958, fairly late in his writing career. . . .

Unlike his posthumous collection of poems, for which he made several tentative tables of contents, there is no evidence Schwartz planned to gather these prose pieces. Yet each had undergone numerous revisions, from handwritten drafts to corrected typescripts. . . . [The] pieces, as a little book, communicate much of the comic spirit and wisdom which endears Schwartz to readers. Like Thurber and Lardner, to whom he might in this instance be compared, Schwartz knew that the serious and the funny are one. For Schwartz, comedy was an escape—not from truth, but from despair. Time and again his comic sense constituted a leap into faith. (p. ix)

The personal essay seems a form especially congenial to Schwartz. It allowed his far-reaching imagination to play, even cavort. Witty, bright, full of satirical energy and verve, these amusing pieces at times may seem glib. But for the most part they are light-hearted and mocking views of the poet himself, of the literary world, and of the world-at-large. (p. x)

The reader will also find character sketches of Othello and Don Juan, as well as of the poet's twelve-year-old brother-in-law (here renamed Claude rather than Sylvester), and Marilyn Monroe. The poet had a bit of a fixation on the latter; he also wrote a poem, **"Love and Marilyn Monroe,"** posthumously published in *Partisan Review* in 1976. Other subjects are the mixed blessings of the telephone, corporate executive seminars, the discomforts of being interviewed and photographed, the paperback revolution, and the vicissitudes of being a New York Giants fan. All are written in Schwartz's highly idiomatic style which lends an incongruous air to his serious subjects and personal theories. . . . Throughout, high seriousness lies just beneath the brittle surface. And Schwartz's prose is admirable for its freshness, as when he posits the unexpected adjective in the phrase, "indigestible cocktail parties," or when he recalls a streetcar from his youth, looking in its jangling voyage like both a schooner and a butterfly.

These pieces reveal that Schwartz was passionate for personal glory as well as for poetry and the writing of poetry. (pp. x-xi)

Robert Phillips, in a foreword to The Ego Is Always at the Wheel *by Delmore Schwartz, edited by Robert Phillips, New Directions, 1986, pp. ix-xii.*

DAVID SOWD

Though Schwartz is best known as a poet, . . . [***The Ego Is Always at the Wheel***] reveals him to be a master of the humorous personal essay as well. In these 19 amusing pieces, most of which were only recently discovered among his papers at Yale, Schwartz considers such matters as the American passion for automobile ownership, the real meaning of existentialism, the telephone as a mixed blessing, and the fear of having one's picture taken. His delightful character sketches of subjects as diverse as the "manic-depressive" Hamlet, Marilyn Monroe, and his 12-year-old brother-in-law, Claude, are as entertaining—and frequently instructive—as anything by Thurber.

David Sowd, in a review of "The Ego Is Always at the Wheel," in Library Journal, *Vol. 111, No. 7, April 15, 1986, p. 82.*

THE NEW YORKER

[***The Ego Is Always at the Wheel*** is a] collection of what the poet called "bagatelles"—informal, brief prose pieces written for his and his friends' amusement. Most are done in a mock-solemn style that suggests a pedant making fun of himself. Schwartz discusses, deadpan, such matters as Hamlet's behavior, Iago's motivations in egging Othello on to throttle his wife, and the possibility that Don Giovanni was a lesbian, because he liked to sleep with women. There are reminiscent excursions into boyhood and the grandeurs and miseries of being a Giants fan, and there are airy and consciously irresponsible disquisitions on the art of poetry. A piece about Existentialism elicits this definition: "Existentialism means that no one else can take a bath for you."

A review of "The Ego Is Always at the Wheel," in The New Yorker, *Vol. LXII, No. 24, August 4, 1986, p. 87.*

MONROE K. SPEARS

[***Portrait of Delmore: Journals and Notes of Delmore Schwartz, 1939-1959***] is edited by Schwartz's second wife, Elizabeth Pollet, who divorced him in 1957. . . . The editing seems rather casual and minimal, though the labor of transcribing the difficult manuscripts must have been enormous. The trouble is that much of the journals consists of quick jottings—often only names of people or places—which Schwartz must have intended as aids to memory, to be expanded later. Many such passages become intelligible only with Atlas' biography [*Delmore Schwartz: The Life of an American Poet*] at hand, and many remain cryptic. These journals are hardly ever fully-developed renderings of experience, inner or outer, as good journals from Boswell's to Stephen Spender's have been.

They are, rather, a curious mish-mash of hasty and incomplete diary entries, memorable passages from and thoughts by and about other writers, and Schwartz's reflections on his own life and career. There is an exact and increasingly depressing daily account of his consumption of alcohol, drugs, and food; his sexual performance; his reading; and his position on the manic-depressive cycle, of which he is excruciatingly aware. . . .

Probably the largest component of the journals is poetry in all stages of composition from ideas or phrases or prose summaries that he hopes will develop into poems to extensive finished passages. The editor's justification for publishing all these fragments and notes—that they cast light on the creative process—does not seem tenable, since the process is in most cases never finished. But many of the fragments are certainly worth preserving. . . .

But, as one might sadly expect, most of the poetry is pretty bad, and getting worse, especially the passages intended for ***Kilroy's Carnival,*** the projected long poem which was to be (like Berryman's *Dream Songs* and Lowell's *Notebooks*) a loose and open-ended interweaving of the personal with social and philosophical commentary. Schwartz had a much greater comic gift than either Lowell or Berryman, and while in his manic phase often seemed funny to others, while the elation and hilarity of the other two did not. But unfortunately not much of that gift appears in these journals.

Why did Schwartz fail so conspicuously to grow and develop as a poet in the same way that Lowell and, to a lesser extent, Jarrell and Berryman did? On the evidence of these journals, he was far more self-absorbed, far less aware of other people and of the external world than they were. . . . It is the same psychological limitation that prevents these journals from being better than they are. But the considerable body of readers who are still fascinated by Delmore Schwartz or by the interplay of personalities among the American Bloomsburians will find much treasure in the roomy and cluttered attic of this book. (p. 13)

Monroe K. Spears, "Last Words of a Student of Joy," in Book World—The Washington Post, *September 28, 1986, pp. 3, 13.*

ROBERT PHILLIPS

[Much of ***Portrait of Delmore: Journals and Notes of Delmore Schwartz, 1939-1959***] is depressing—accounts of gas and lights being turned off for non-payment, insomnia, a heart attack in Bellevue (the result of abrupt withdrawal from all drugs and sedation), rejection by friends and publishers. Just as Henry James dutifully recorded the number of dinner engagements he accepted in London society, so Schwartz renders astonishing accounts of the number of pills and drinks he consumed. One day he took eight Dexedrines (which gave him a lift for only one hour). Another day after dinner he drank three glasses of sherry, three quarts of beer, and three shots of whiskey.

Yet there are reasons why anyone interested in Schwartz and the poetry of America's Middle Generation should read this book. For one, there is a surprising amount of new poetry. While none ranks with Schwartz's best—typically he would copy out the most promising poetic passages, type them, and begin revision for possible publication—some of the unpublished poetry is fine. . . . [Some] interesting poems include **"Old Letters"**; poems on his alter ego, Rinehart; and sections of a long work never finished, **"Dear Pope."** There also is uncollected light verse, including a seven-line invective against **"Bogan, Louise, a Poetess."** La Bogan never gave Schwartz a good or even fair review.

The journals also contain ideas and beginnings for essays. Subjects include Dostoevsky's later work, Ring Lardner, Heinrich Heine, and comparisons between Fitzgerald's Gatsby and James's Isabel Archer. There are beginnings of short stories, and he also posits notes toward symbology in his own work: snow, a central image for Schwartz, he calls "Newness, renewal, freedom, the space in which we walk."

More important are Schwartz's notes on prosody. There are instructive entries on form, diction, meter and rhythm, color and stress. . . . Much of this material is stated epigrammatically, and elsewhere in writing his journals he discovered witty phrases and puns he later would lard into his poems, stories, essays, and letters: "A horse divided against itself cannot stand"; "The wife you save may be your own"; "Gentlemen prefer bonds"; "You are all a tossed generation"; and the mathematician's song, "I love my wife, but oh, Euclid!"

Much of the black humor involves wives. ("She was frigid, he was rigid. What a marriage.") A psychoanalyst could have a field day. Schwartz seems to have had an Oedipal trauma early in life. His mother, the redoubtable Rose Schwartz, is however depicted in some hilarious moments, as when she exclaims, on hearing her sister has cancer, "Everything happens to me!" (p. 562)

One revelation of this book is that Schwartz did manage to write splendidly late in his career, a feat not commonly acknowledged. Poems such as **"All the Fruits Had Fallen," "The Innocent & Infinite Windows of Childhood," "The Fulfillment," "Vivaldi,"** and his luminous late **"Seurat's Sunday Afternoon Along the Seine,"** demonstrate, as editor Elizabeth Pollet states, that Schwartz was writing poems "in a key of transcendence and exaltation" even in the midst of disintegration and desperation. (pp. 562-63)

Ms. Pollet, a novelist who was also Schwartz's second wife, has devoted four years to transcribing and editing 2400 sheets of journal entries and notes, which became a 1400-page typescript eventually reduced to 900 pages. Her notes are scrupulously accurate and her observations fair. Clearly a labor of love, ***Portrait of Delmore*** is indeed a portrait of the writer's innermost thoughts. It is a valuable document. (p. 563)

Robert Phillips, "Punished, Unfinished, Untouched," in Commonweal*, Vol. CXIII, No. 18, October 24, 1986, pp. 562-63.*

Timothy (Reid) Steele

1948-

American poet and nonfiction writer.

In his two volumes of poetry, *Uncertainties and Rest* (1979) and *Sapphics against Anger and Other Poems* (1985), Steele uses traditional metrical structures and conventional forms. His reliance on formal techniques enables him to precisely express the complexities of contemporary life in poems that are witty and accessible. While some critics contend that Steele's use of classical forms results in monotonous rhythms and unoriginal themes, others admire his work for its adherence to the disciplined verse styles of Yvor Winters and W. H. Auden. According to Dana Gioia, "[Steele's] work announces no brave new ideology. It projects no compelling persona. What one notices instead is a carefully cultivated sensibility flawlessly translated into words. Steele believes he can command the reader's attention by writing well about ordinary things."

(See also *Contemporary Authors,* Vols. 93-96 and *Contemporary Authors New Revision Series,* Vol. 16.)

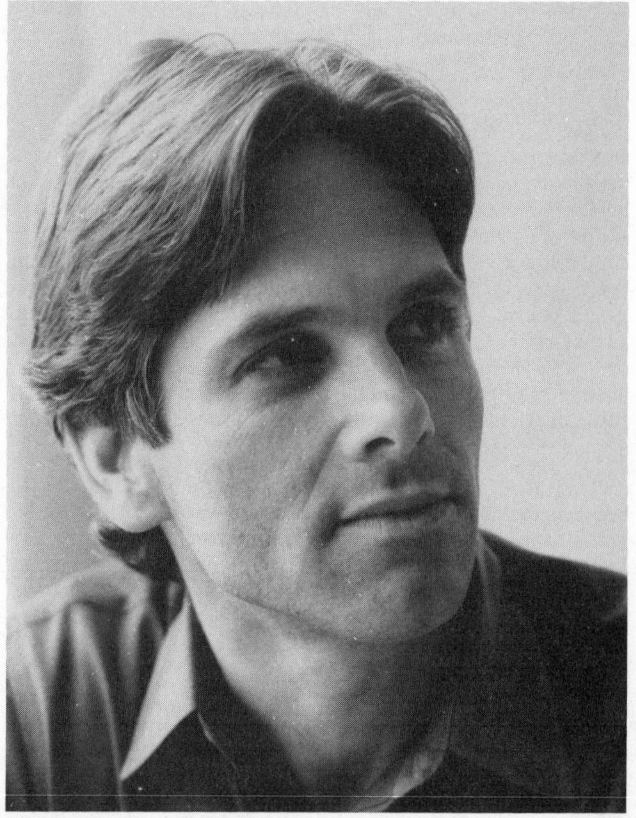

Photograph by Julie Kwan

JOHN N. MILLER

Tradition holds a consistent but precarious place in the poems of [***Uncertainties and Rest***], manifesting itself most firmly in the formal patterns, the careful rhyming and metrical order of Steele's versification. Poetic tradition, thus recalled and created, brings to mind our endangered traditions of civility, sociability, and human settlement. To give elegance, dignity, and almost ritual precision to the details of personal or interpersonal life: this is the task that Steele quietly but effectively accomplishes in his best poems. (p. 60)

Nostalgia is a keynote in these poems. Many of them celebrate what is tenuous, passing, or lost: an order that is aesthetic and personal as well as civil or social. This is evident in the dying fall of two poems which appear early in the collection. In **"Sunday Afternoon"** he writes, "So calm, so settled. Such peace is the best. / And sheltered in the remnants of the day, / I gather what I want, / and leave the rest / To the vague sounds of traffic, far away." And in **"Evening, After the Auction"** we hear "If there is no mark / Of better times, at least the air is cool / And the lawn empty as the sky grows dark." . . .

Steele's poetry is usually more traditionally patterned than is the work of Lowell's middle period, but not always. **"This Is"** and **"Even Then"** are written in carefully controlled free verse, while a larger handful of poems—**"Autobiography," "Cowboy," "Stargazing at Barton,"** and **"The Messenger"**—employs syllabic verse. The last two of these poems are among Steele's finest. (p. 61)

Despite the strengths of these poems, though, I also noticed two shortcomings. One is technical, and is perhaps a by-product of rhymed and metered verse. That is, the poet sometimes overemphasizes certain words, for the sake of rhyme or meter at the end of lines, or fails to achieve effective movement between one line or stanza and the next. . . . Almost in technical desperation, it seems, Steele also gives undo weight to prepositions and conjunctions at the ends of certain lines (e.g., *upon* rhyming with *on*) in the abovementioned poem, *while, and,* and *for* in **"Family Reunion,"** *to* in **"Wait,"** and *with* in **"Baker Street at Sunset."** More rarely, an unearned abstraction slips in ("As thought retreats from the oblivion / It took on trust" in **"Wait"**) or an entire poem (**"Incident on a Picnic"**) seems glib or patently artificial because of a disjunction between form and content.

The more pervasive shortcoming of Steele's poetry is its almost unrelieved privatism. Ultimately I find its stance toward experience limited and somewhat self-indulgent. Personal observations and sensibility, a studied delight in sensory particulars of its own milieu, a strictly individual order and clarity as his retreat from the chaotic, kaleidoscopic larger world—these are Steele's typical offerings. The larger public or social issues of our time exist only as a vague ambience, never seriously defined or confronted. Steele's world-weariness and genteel withdrawal into elegant, decorous sensations (as in **"Sunday Afternoon"**) threaten to become an habitual pose. One has only to read other contemporary formalists such as Edgar Bowers and Peter Scupham to miss their larger range of experience—both public and private—in Steele's verse. Though he mentions Plato, St. Augustine, Descartes, and

Whitehead in his poems, it is Epicurus who reigns almost unchallenged.

Yet the craftsmanship and controlled detail in ***Uncertainties and Rest*** admirably demonstrate that traditional poetry still lives in America. Serious readers can be thankful for that. (p. 62)

John N. Miller, "A Renewable Disguise," in The Chowder Review, *No. 14, Spring-Summer, 1980, pp. 60-2.*

J. D. McCLATCHY

Those poets who have persisted in Yvor Winters's discipline and prejudices have produced a poetry that seems to me pinched and crabbed, neither heartfelt nor mindful of the expressive and emotive extremes poetry can deftly accommodate. But Timothy Steele's first book ***Uncertainties and Rest*** should not pass by unnoticed merely because he resumes a Wintersian mode. True, his prosody is traditional and strict, but it is deployed in an entirely engaging, convincing manner. And yes, the kind of poetry he now writes is neither ambitious nor pretentious; it has its limitations, but its advantage lies in knowing what they are. His book fairly sparkles with its acknowledged predilections and its own bright promise. It has given me, in short, more pleasure than any other first book I have read this year. It comes equipped with all the modern conveniences—cocaine and Chardonnay, jeans and jogging, even a neighborhood deli—but they are in service to something more than its altogether smart surfaces, more even than its common nostalgias and uncommon ideas. Whether, in his guise of detached, lonely observer, he is writing thoughtful poems that contemplate the possible joys of abandoning thought (as he does in **"Rural Colloquy with a Painter"** and **"For My Mother"**), or drawing on deep reserves of sense and sensibility (as he does in his bravura **"Three Notes Toward Definitions"**), the emphasis throughout is on a clear-eyed estimate of the contemporary intelligence at odds now with itself, now with everything else. Steele's book also includes a waggish series of epigrams in the manner of J. V. Cunningham—a stinging manner one might have thought it impossible to emulate.

J. D. McClatchy, in a review of "Uncertainties and Rest ," in Partisan Review, *Vol. 47, No. 4, 1980, p. 642.*

WYATT PRUNTY

Throughout ***Uncertainties and Rest,*** Timothy Steele exercises technical mastery. Grounded in a quiet, conversational style, his poems have the effect that a series of well-crafted miniatures spaced along a wall might have. Each poem is both concentrated and complete in and of itself. At the same time, the isolated moments these poems create reveal a preoccupation with relationships, particularly with the contingencies that beset relationships. (p. 634)

Uncertainties and Rest is a strong book, but I have a quarrel with it, one which stems from Steele's perspective on his subject matter. Concerned with relationships, at times his poems have less significance for an outsider who reads them than they apparently have for Steele and the various people he addresses. An additional problem is caused by occasional slips into an overly detuned, conversational tone that reminds one of Philip Larkin. The opening lines of **"Homecoming in Late March"** will demonstrate what I mean:

> Things change, of course: the girl next door, just turned
> Twelve, now affects indifference and a bra.
> And in the backyard, the snow fence is down—
> Wind, I suppose.

And "suppose" is the right word. The poem continues with nominalistic observation ("leisurely shoots of skunk cabbages curl") and supposition to its conclusion, where the speaker's "mind can close" on a "tentative repose." But more about Steele's penchant for closure and repose later.

Another difficulty I have with ***Uncertainties and Rest*** is that despite there being a significant number of excellent poems in the volume, reading it straight through becomes monotonous. Repetitiveness results from the poems' similarity in length and movement. There are too many one-strophe poems that end with quiet turns in perception. Taken in isolation, however, several stand as objects worthy of our admiration. **"This Is"** enjoys a directness and specificity that other poems often lack, and at the same time it avoids the flatness (both stylistic and thematic) of **"Homecoming in Late March."** (p. 635)

[Too] often Steele's poetry amounts to the acceptance of solipsism, indeed its magnification. In his approach to relationships, Steele takes the gaps between people that result from various causes and makes dramatic predicaments of them. Things do not get better. Often the only movement that occurs is the poet's re-cognition of the stasis that was already present. . . . Steele's method may be "a resolution of sorts," but, as he says, it is also a "masquerade." "A life . . . In which there's space enough for us and for / Lies we no longer care to contradict" is a solipsistic life insofar as each person avoids the objective restraint that contradiction brings to bear upon opinion.

But, as I said before, in isolation many of the poems, in ***Uncertainties and Rest*** are admirable. I should add that I am giving particular emphasis to a volume's working as a series, and such emphasis tends to overlook Steele's special accomplishments. (p. 637)

Certainly Timothy Steele and [British poet] Peter Dale are not foreign to one another. They share a conversational tone, an affinity for understatement that leads to subtle turns in perception, a keen interest in and eye for relationships, and ears sharp enough to write formal poetry that is striking for its vitality. (p. 641)

Wyatt Prunty, "Reciprocals," in The Southern Review, *(Louisiana State University), Vol. 17, No. 3, Summer, 1981, pp. 634-41.*

MARY KINZIE

If it is true that not every passage of every poem can be white-hot with passion; if there's a place in many poems for the quieter approach, the undramatic exit, the bittersweet revolution of a thought; if poetry can concern itself with culture and shared trouble, with society and with family, with history and with ideals; then much of the poetry we are permitting, sanctioning, churning out, and shrugging off in America not only fails to satisfy technically by using language strongly and thoroughly: it also embraces very little of the area that used to be in poetry's domain.

Timothy Steele's ***Uncertainties and Rest*** is a splendid exception to such criticisms. Like the technicians one most admires, Steele cultivates restraint as a mechanism for the release both of wit and feeling. Indeed, many of his poems fall into one of two groups: those that adjust emotion to the demands of category, like the first stanza of his poem **"Of Friendship"**:

> Byron considered it *Love without wings*.
> Others associate it with long views
> Of hills and lakes. Still others tend to muse
> Upon the darker side of things:
> Stale beer, unanswered letters, or a pal
> All too Shakespearean. (Cross references:
> Iago, Enobarbus, Brutus, Hal.)

or those that admit category and hierarchy to the silences of the spirit:

> This is a child's forest: moss
> and stunted pine, the casual
> arbutus. In the pre-dawn dark,
> lichen grows on the tree trunks,
> and then, among the trees, smoky
> light, the ironwork of our breath
> on the cold air. No rider passes,
> no hooves recall the earth . . .
>
> (**"This Is"**)

Timothy Steele shares with poets like George Herbert and W. H. Auden yet another quality—the prose of ordinariness, the assumption that what he sees and feels is known to everybody, consequently that he is at most refreshing a familiar memory when he invokes our common humanity. "I've learned," he says in one poem, "what too much self-scrutiny / Does to the spirit." . . . [Frequently], the poet will wake from his brief delirium (of desire, of drugs, of exhaustion) to confront his essential limitations, only to find in them new and pleasurable truth. The book's final poem speaks of an epiphany that comes when the plain light of day brings into focus what heretofore had seemed aimless and disjoint. The revelation seems to speak to the will:

> One morning, rubbing clear the window pane,
> He grows coherent.
>
> . . .
>
> It is his time, whose coming even he
> Could never quite imagine—simple, clear,
> And endlessly complete. Right now. Right here.
>
> (**"One Morning"**)

But the return to the present time is not always welcome. Roughly a third of the poems in ***Uncertainties and Rest*** dramatize a speaker peculiarly crippled by some pain the poem itself cannot touch. (p. 16)

Uncertainties and Rest is by no means a perfect book: laconic, when every fibre in the poems strains toward tears, and over-enthusiastic in the assumption of poses one might call statesmanlike, it is nevertheless one of the most exciting first books of poems to appear in the past decade. It is brief, yet gives great breadth of tone and subject. Above all, it shows the writers who might follow after Steele the enormous potential of verse that is in some way bound, style that is answerable. (p. 17)

Mary Kinzie, "The Overdefinition of the Now," in The American Poetry Review, *Vol. 11, No. 2, March-April, 1982, pp. 13-17.*

DANA GIOIA

In his second collection, ***The Prudent Heart,*** Steele reveals himself a connoisseur of images and emotions. . . . [His] intelligence is directed toward personal concerns rather than pure ideas. His imagination characteristically returns to his own past trying to discover order in the detritus of experience. . . . (p. 101)

Steele's virtues are not ones that contemporary criticism is used to praising. One feels in his case . . . that the current critical vocabulary is strangely inadequate to describe exactly those qualities of style and perception that one most admires in his work. The words one reaches for first—traditional terms of approbation like *graceful, polished,* and *controlled*—have become so loaded with evaluative associations that they can no longer be used descriptively in any simple sense. They have become debased into code words that imply covert criticism of the very qualities they once described. One may say "graceful" or "controlled" about a particular poem, but what one will communicate to the educated reader are double-edged statements like "graceful but effeminate" or "controlled but stiff and passionless." This problem reveals the particular nature of Steele's achievement. He has revived precisely those traditional resources of the formal lyric that modernism convinced us were exhausted.

In the past decade most young poets have made claims on our attention through the forceful sincerity of their tone and the urgent topicality of their concerns. They have been less interested in the problematics and potentials of language and form than in the development of their particular thematics and ideologies. Language has been treated as the means to immediate communication rather than as an end in itself. This concentration has tended to produce poets whose total *oeuvres* are more interesting than any of their individual poems, writers whose personae are more fully developed than their sensibilities.

Steele stands in sharp contrast to this trend. His work announces no brave new ideology. It projects no compelling persona. What one notices instead is a carefully cultivated sensibility flawlessly translated into words. There is no urgently prophetic tone, just the voice one educated person might use in talking to another. Steele believes he can command the reader's attention by writing well about ordinary things. His ambition is the poet's traditional goal of writing a few perfect poems. Each poem stands as a carefully balanced, self-contained unit. It represents a complete poetic experience, not a flamboyant piece cut from some larger visionary cloth. These are—to use another old-fashioned phrase whose meaning has also been recently unjustly debased—well-made poems.

The poet whom Steele most resembles is Richard Wilbur, an elusive master whose genius is so natural and accessible that it seems inimitable. Like Wilbur, Steele has talent without eccentricity, a normal sensibility with an abnormal gift for expression. Like Wilbur, too, Steele differs from most of his contemporaries in that his vision of life is fundamentally positive. He writes about the beauties of the everyday world, the abiding love in marriage, the forgiveness and self-knowledge that can come from anger. In the book's longest poem, **"Near Olympic,"** Steele walks through the poor Japanese and Mexican neighborhoods off Los Angeles' Olympic Boulevard and sees the beauty and gentleness of the people's lives rather than the superficial squalor. Finally Steele resembles Wilbur in the great technical skill and ease he exhibits in every poem. Steele's metrics are conservative. Except for one powerful piece in long syllabic lines, all of the poems in ***The Prudent Heart*** are highly regular rhymed iambics, but within this register Steele experiments with line length and stanza patterns to achieve a great variety of effects. But while his metrics are skillful, it is Steele's command of rhyme that is most noteworthy. Unlike most young formal poets, he uses rhyme as part of his natural poetic language, not a learned accomplishment. (pp. 102-03)

Dana Gioia, in a review of "The Prudent Heart," in The Ontario Review, *No. 19, Fall-Winter, 1983-84, pp. 101-03.*

PUBLISHERS WEEKLY

[Timothy Steele's ***Sapphics against Anger and Other Poems***] should help establish him as one of the finest contemporary poets to write in meter and traditional forms. From sonnets and syllabics to classical Greek Sapphic stanzas—and a marvelous selection of biting and terse epigrams—Steele's work has a clarity of thought and a precise phrasing of language that is stunningly poised. While some poems recall the poet's rural Vermont childhood, as in **"The Skimming Stone"** and **"Shucking Corn,"** other longer pieces, such as **"Near Olympic,"** are set in Los Angeles, Steele's current home. Such figures as Martin Luther, King David and Dickens's David Copperfield and Dora Spenlow are subjects of other outstanding poems; reflective pieces like **"On the Eve of a Birthday"** and **"Old Letters"** are at once provocative, emotionally powerful and masterfully wrought.

A review of "Sapphics against Anger and Other Poems," in Publishers Weekly, *Vol. 230, No. 8, August 22, 1986, p. 91.*

R. S. GWYNN

Because Timothy Steele chooses to work almost exclusively in traditional forms and, thus, has little company among his peers, any discussion of his poetry must take into account his immense facility with meters and stanzas. Steele, I suppose, must get tired of being referred to as "that formalist poet," an irony I cannot let pass without noting that as little as thirty years ago the designation would have placed him among the majority. But even in poetry, fashions come and go; *Howl* is now approaching respectable middle age, and in a few years the Black Mountain College Alumni Association can join AARP en masse. . . . [For Steele] the commitment is almost total: only two poems in his new collection, ***Sapphics against Anger, and Other Poems,*** are plainsong, and they suffer by comparison with his other work. Yet, while Steele's emergence as a major poet may well signal a swing back to tidier stanzas and a less uncritical acceptance of the dictum that "form is only an extension of content," I would hate to see him tossed among that mysterious cabal occasionally labeled "The New Formalists," a soubriquet coined to describe a handful of younger poets who specialize in inflated *vers de société*. True, he is at his best when he writes in demanding formal patterns, but his technical skills should not overshadow the intense personal vision of his best poems.

Steele's first book, ***Uncertainties and Rest*** . . . , consisted, for the most part, of short lyrics that described a life apparently spent in uneasy transit from one coast to the other. . . . Often it seemed that Steele's personae sought rest only in escape and anonymity. (pp. 117-18)

Sapphics against Anger, as the title should indicate, is a book that praises self-control ("May I recall what Aristotle says of / The subject: to give vent to rage is not to / Release it but to be increasingly prone / To its incursions.") and urges a strategic retreat from the "paper-gusting plazas / Of the New World's shopping malls" to "quiet courtyards [where] friends sketch / The dust with theorems and proofs." Much of the calm light that suffuses the poetry seems to stem from friendship and marriage, which, as Steele indicates in **"Love Poem,"** do not have to exclude each other:

> If, like poor Pierrot, I've anxiously
>   Dwelt in my life, the spell is broken.
> Awakened to your touch and voice, I see
> That evil is the formless and unspoken,
> And that peace rests in form and nomenclature,
> Which render our two natures—formerly
> Discomfited, self-conscious—second nature.

Steele's ease in handling the personal poem should be evident. He is, however, much more versatile than the examples I have previously cited would indicate. With equal facility he writes epigrams ("He pours forth his fierce, quarrelsome twaddle; / If others speak, he's loath to hear. / Had men evolved along his model, / They'd have two mouths and but one ear."); a choral ode; a **"Chanson Philosophique"**; Johnsonian descriptive verse (**"Near Olympic"**) describing the "Fords and Oldsmobiles, / Lowslung and ancient; or—with raised rear wheels / And sides flame-painted—Mustangs and Chevelles" that, in the West Los Angeles barrio, must seem as natural to the environment as the jacarandas and banana trees; and a trio of poems (**"Last Tango," "In the King's Rooms,"** and **"Life Portrait"**) that take their subjects from film, the Bible, and literature, respectively. It is the last of these, subtitled "thinking of Dora Spenlow and David Copperfield," that I would like to examine in closing. **"Life Portrait"** is a poem which I came across in *Threepenny Review* several years ago. It was one of the first of Steele's poems that I had seen, and, even on the first reading, it struck me as, well, a masterpiece. Having since become more familiar with Steele's work, I can guess that his homage to Dickens's autobiographical novel is, in a very private way, yet another act of self-examination. . . . Though Steele's formal technique and literary subject would seemingly have a distancing effect, the opposite is true. I wonder what writer hasn't thought of himself (or *herself* either) in terms of Dickens's archetype, doubly haunted by the memory of an intolerable presence and the reality of an absence that is even worse. Like David, Timothy Steele should receive the acclaim that is his due, and I gather, from the assured tonalities of his sensible voice, that he has succeeded in putting time and distance between himself and his demons. (pp. 119-21)

R. S. Gwynn, "Second Gear," in New England Review and Bread Loaf Quarterly, *Vol. 9, No. 1, Autumn, 1986, pp. 111-21.*

MERLE RUBIN

Dedicated to Vikram Seth, who has received a good deal of notice for writing an entire novel in verse, [***Sapphics against Anger and Other Poems***] by Timothy Steele is marked by a similar fluency—and similar tendency toward glibness.

Steele, born in Vermont in 1948, lives in Los Angeles. The sights and sounds of Southern California figure prominently in this, his second collection. **"At Will Rogers Beach,"** we find surfers, skaters, gulls and a dog catching a Frisbee, and **"Near Olympic,"** a neighborhood "part Japanese and part/Chicago" of small stucco houses, ancient cars and burgeoning nursery gardens. Banana trees, pepper trees, jacarandas and many species of birds flourish.

Classical allusions mingle cosily with the contemporary. . . .

There is a felicity in this poet's facility. But often, in these poems, the irredeemably facile rears its head, and we find, to our disappointment, that there may be less here than meets the eye.

The title poem, **"Sapphics Against Anger,"** offers the prospect of the angered poet imagining himself in the Inferno, where Virgil tells Dante how he got there:

> That fellow, at the slightest provocation,
> Slammed phone receivers down, and waved his arms like
> A madman. What Attila did to Europe,
> What Genghis Khan did
>
> To Asia, that poor dope did to his marriage.

Following this excursion into the realms of mild wit, the poem concludes with a homiletic stanza that sounds a little too close to the advice a master gives a student in a Kung-Fu movie:

> For what is, after all, the good life save that
> Conducted thoughtfully, and what is passion
> If not the holiest of powers, sustaining
> Only if mastered.

The message is creditable, the poetic medium serviceable, but the concepts and verbal counters have been worn too smooth with use to yield any fresh value or insight.

Accessibility is clearly a cornerstone of Timothy Steele's poetic enterprise. Although written in traditional patterns of meter and rhyme, his poems sound very much like the spoken word in all its colloquial ease. Warm, light, conversational and witty, these are the sort of poems that ask to be read aloud to a friend. In an age when many poets remain more willfully abstruse than the genuine complexity of their thoughts may merit, accessibility must be welcomed. . . .

Simplicity has a strength of its own, and the use of ordinary, everyday language (first championed by Wordsworth nearly 200 years ago) rightly invites a wide audience. But simplicity without depth risks sentimentality, sententiousness and sheer obviousness. And the language of these poems, though admirably clear and precise, does not always reverberate.

One senses also a shying away from the very themes the poet has chosen to invoke. **"On the Eve of a Birthday"** finds him wishing to deny the fearful passage of time.

> At times I fear the future won't reward
> My failures with sufficient compensation,
> But dump me, aging, in a garret room
> Appointed with twilit, slant-ceilinged gloom
> And a lone bulb depending from a cord
> Suggestive of self-strangulation.

Foolhardy as it may be to generalize about a generation, especially one's own, I hear in those lines that increasingly familiar sound of protest against the unthinkable indignity that we, born in the Baby Boom and brought up to regard ourselves as embodiments of the boundless promise of Youth, should be faced not only with age, but with an age in which our chances have seemed to decline. Yet by dragging in the stock images of the garret roof and cord, the poet evades his own question with a weak joke.

If, indeed, these "light" and "natural" poems are a sign of the times, I am led to wonder for what, in the end, our generation will be remembered. Personally, I would have preferred something less easily digested.

Merle Rubin, in a review of "Sapphics against Anger and Other Poems," in Los Angeles Times Book Review, *September 21, 1986, p. 2.*

DAVID SHAPIRO

[In ***Sapphics Against Anger and Other Poems,*** Timothy Steele] attempts to wrestle with measure and a moderate, by now unconventional, metrical grid system and emerge with an urban realism like a vision: "It is as if dawn pliantly compels / The city to relax to sounds and shapes, / To its diagonals and parallels . . ." (**"From a Rooftop"**). He does not seem to want the ferocious cinematic sleight-of-hand of a Hart Crane, say, nor does he mind the relaxation into a "laundered sweetness." Those of us who have loved the so-called sins of rhyme will appreciate these exercises in style, but one must recognize the perils of what may look like an aesthetic neoconservatism. The bravery of Steele's strategy here is knowingly to provoke us by a Nabokovian parody of finesse. Elegance here is a kind of dream of stylish condensation, and the rhetoric is ruled by unspoken caveats of decorum.

The intransigence of this poetry is seen not only in the rhyming and rhythms of some "silver age" but in the dedication to a constant moralizing tone. . . . The small lives that fascinated Roethke with a dark sense of his own humiliation and self-doubt here fascinate with the seduction of what is not difficult. In "Mockingbird," the poet more self-consciously berates himself, in the light of his poetic inheritance, here most obviously of Frost: "For all his virtuosity of tone, / The singer has no note which is his own." This theme of an almost agonistic parody links Steele with the melancholies of the avant-garde in more ways than one. Both the pedant and the adventurer are linked by their reactions to the *traditio*. The archaistic has a quest about it for freshness, if only for the freshness that, as Stevens says, has been fresh a long time. Sometimes the sharp edges of this poetry reveal a taste for the photographic: "a brisk adaptive bath." The poet is not an antiquarian but uses the old forms as much as a defense system as a nostalgia.

Steele's **"Sapphics Against Anger,"** a good narrative moralizing music, shows that the poet believes aesthetically and ethically in "principles of restraint." In this poem, the defense against rage, however, more than teases the reader into thinking that the poet has loaded all dice in favor of Aristotelian moderation, while still a temptation to reveal, to sulk, even to revel in rage makes for an obscure undertow. . . . I find this again in the contortions of a poem about that odd nonsite, West Los Angeles, not a likely target for decorum. Here, something more like terror than moderation invigorates the poet's art: the Gothic of Robert Frost and not the bucolic. It is a world of "casual casualties," and the pathos of contingency lunges out at the reader in choppier cadences. These are rightly poems shocked by modernity and escaped into a species of Utopian pre-Modernism: **"Golden Age"** is the title of one piece. But Steele's own wise conclusion is for friendship and an art mixed with the grief of the shopping malls and tyrants. Some of the most charming notes of this poetry are in the comical and mottled epigrams for his sister. . . . (pp. 342-44)

Steele, perhaps too confidently, writes that "evil is the formless." A little more receptivity to the formless might help here. But the poet, with his thrifty sonnets and sapphics, would of course object moderately and move on. (p. 344)

David Shapiro, in a review of "Sapphics against Anger and Other Poems," in Poetry, *Vol. CXLIX, No. 6, March, 1987, pp. 342-44.*

John (Ernst) Steinbeck

1902-1968

American novelist, short story writer, nonfiction writer, scriptwriter, and poet.

UPI/Bettmann Newsphotos

Perhaps best known for his controversial Pulitzer Prize-winning novel, *The Grapes of Wrath* (1939), Steinbeck is considered among the most significant American novelists of the twentieth century. When he was honored in 1962 with the Nobel Prize in literature, the awards committee cited Steinbeck's "sympathetic humor and sociological perception" and his "instinct for what is genuinely American, be it good or bad." In his fiction, Steinbeck professed both sympathy and anger toward American society. An active opponent of social exploitation, puritanism, and materialistic values, Steinbeck is noted for his sharp, forceful writing style, his wry humor, and his profound compassion for the poor, the inarticulate, and the politically maligned. Early in his career, as a result of his study of biology at Stanford University during the 1920s, Steinbeck developed a "biological" view of humanity. He insisted that such evolutionary concepts as adaptation and natural selection apply to human society and that more profound observations could be gleaned from examining people in groups than as individuals. Steinbeck's characters usually live in harmony with nature until such malevolent political or natural forces as progress, scarcity, or drought upset that balance. Through mutual cooperation, the will to adapt, and a mystical religious faith in the power of the just individual, Steinbeck's characters are usually able to survive destructive circumstances.

Many of Steinbeck's novels and stories are set in and around the Salinas Valley in California, where he was born and where he held a variety of jobs prior to his writing career. Steinbeck achieved popular acclaim with his fourth novel, *Tortilla Flat* (1935), a colorful and sentimental treatment of the idle, antimaterialistic existence of a group of *paisanos*—California natives of mixed Spanish, Indian, and white descent—in Monterey, California. Writing in a modernized epic style and influenced by Thomas Malory's *Le morte d'Arthur,* Steinbeck characterizes the *paisanos* as "whores, pimps, gamblers, and sons of bitches" and also as "saints and angels and martyrs and holy men." The novel ends somberly, with Steinbeck's assertion that the *paisanos* lack the material selfishness necessary to modern survival. A grim clash of interests is again evident in his next novel, *In Dubious Battle* (1936), which depicts a strike of migrant fruit pickers and the conflict which results between union organizers and California apple growers. In this book, Steinbeck questions whether humanity is capable of postponing individual differences to work for the greater benefit of the group. Steinbeck's examination of political and social concerns throughout *In Dubious Battle* prompted critical reassessment of his reputation as an author of light social commentary.

Steinbeck achieved national recognition with *Of Mice and Men* (1937), a pastoral novel which addresses such themes as the conflict between idealism and reality and the loneliness which divides people of all classes. This work centers on two itinerant ranch hands—Lennie, a strong retarded man, and George, who looks after Lennie and dreams of owning a small farm. After Lennie accidentally kills the conniving wife of his employer's son, George mercifully kills Lennie to spare him a crueler death by a lynch mob. Steinbeck adapted the novel for the Broadway stage in 1937 to great popular and critical acclaim. The drama, for which Steinbeck received a New York Drama Critics Circle Award, was described by Stark Young as an "absorbing work of theater art," by Brooks Atkinson as "a masterpiece," and by John Mason Brown as "one of the finest, most pungent, and most poignant realistic productions."

From 1937 to 1939, Steinbeck studied the problems of a large group of migrant workers during their trek from Oklahoma to California. *The Grapes of Wrath* is his attempt to understand and authenticate this experience. Considered Steinbeck's masterpiece and a landmark in American literature, the novel presents both a biological and political view of the role played by economic conditions in upsetting the delicate balance between humanity and nature. The inability of farmers to seasonally rotate their crops due to market demands, together with drought and the depressed American economy, culminate in *The Grapes of Wrath* in the loss of once-productive farms and the displacement of many rural Oklahoma families. One such family, the Joads, is lured to California by promises of high-paying jobs from large landowners who seek to ensure cheap labor by creating a massive supply of jobless people competing for a limited number of employment opportunities. The Joads discover brutal, systematized migrant labor camps where low wages and the threat of starvation make the workers increasingly dependent upon their employers. *The Grapes of Wrath* is a work of contrasts, dramatized in alternately humorous and horrifying episodes: the hopeful westward migration of the Joads is ironically compared to that of the original Western settlers, and the family's dreams of a "land of milk and honey" contrast sharply with descriptions of California farm corporations which destroy crops to maintain high market prices. *The Grapes of Wrath* provoked heated controversy. Community, agricultural, and political interest groups charged Steinbeck with exaggerating conditions in Oklahoma and California, and according to Daniel Aaron, "spokesmen for the Association farmers . . . accused Steinbeck of writing a brief for Communism." However, the novel won international acclaim as a powerful depiction of the common person's vulnerability to social and natural forces. Peter Lisça summarized the novel's importance: "*The Grapes of Wrath* was a phenomenon on the scale of a national event. It was publicly banned and burned by citizens; it was debated on national radio hook-ups; but above all it was read."

Steinbeck's critical favor began to decline during the 1940s, and many of his later works received mixed reviews. *The Moon Is Down* (1942), a war novel set in an unspecified country which many critics assumed to be Norway during the German Occupation, was often interpreted as an antiwar statement. Although some reviewers praised Steinbeck for attempting an unsensationalized portrayal of both oppressors and oppressed, many charged that he failed to fully examine the evil of his Nazi characters. Steinbeck adapted the novel for the theater in 1942. *Cannery Row* (1945), his next novel, centers upon a group of indolent Monterey vagrants and their bumbling adventures with a sympathetic biologist. According to F. W. Watt, *Cannery Row* satirizes "contemporary American life with its commercialized values, its ruthless creed of property and status, and its relentlessly accelerated pace." Although highly popular, the book was generally regarded by critics as light entertainment. In *Sweet Thursday* (1954), a sequel to *Cannery Row* written as the basis for a musical comedy, Steinbeck bids farewell to the disappearing way of life of carefree American vagabonds.

Steinbeck regarded *East of Eden* (1952) as the culmination of his career. Written as a family epic ranging from the Civil War to World War I, this novel is a parable of the fall of man focusing primarily on the Trask family. Paralleling the biblical story of Cain and Abel, three generations of brothers must resolve disputes between one another; in each conflict, evil results from the inexplicable rejection of one child's gift to his father. Steinbeck maintained: "The greatest terror a child can have is that he is not loved. . . . And with rejection comes anger, and with anger, some kind of revenge for rejection, and with the crime, guilt—and there is the story of mankind." The novel centers on Adam, who attempts to create his Eden in the Salinas Valley with Cathy, his beautiful but remote wife. Cathy, who was sexually involved with Adam's brother, Charles, is a figure of evil and destruction reminiscent of the biblical serpent. She gives birth to the twins Caleb and Aron before deserting Adam to assume a new identity as Kate, a vicious and sadistic prostitute. Caleb, the son whose gift Adam rejects, believes his desire for revenge to be preordained, and he exposes Aron to the truth about their mother. Although Aron is eventually destroyed by this revelation, Caleb is offered the possibility of salvation through understanding the meaning of *timshel,* a Hebrew word indicating humanity's power to choose between good and evil. Although *East of Eden* initially drew positive reviews, its overt symbolism and allegorical structure has resulted in critical controversy, and the book has not attained the stature of *The Grapes of Wrath*.

Steinbeck's last novel, *The Winter of Our Discontent* (1961), concerns the disintegration of American moral values. Set in the fictional Long Island community of New Bay, the book depicts a member of a prestigious New England family who succumbs to materialism and the enticements of success. Steinbeck's last major work, *Travels with Charley in Search of America* (1962), describes his reflections on American values and society during a tour of forty states with Charley, his pet poodle. Steinbeck's other nonfiction works include *A Russian Journal* (1948), a heavily illustrated collection of pieces based on his travels in the Soviet Union, and *The Acts of King Arthur and His Noble Knights* (1976), a modern rendition of Arthurian legends. Many of Steinbeck's works have been adapted for television, film, and the theater.

In addition to his novels, Steinbeck produced several volumes of short fiction during his early career. Although his achievement in this genre is less highly regarded than that of such contemporaries as William Faulkner and F. Scott Fitzgerald, several of Steinbeck's novellas and short stories are considered significant accomplishments. *The Pastures of Heaven* (1932), one of Steinbeck's earliest works to use Eden as a symbol and metaphor, is a loosely related collection set in California's Corral de Tierra Valley. These stories concern a group of "unfinished children of nature" who fail in their attempt to establish an idyllic farming community free from restrictive urban pressures. The novella *The Red Pony* (1937; revised, 1945) showcases Steinbeck's descriptive talents by detailing a boy's maturation and his acceptance of death when he loses his colt to pneumonia. *The Long Valley* (1938), Steinbeck's first collection to achieve wide critical acclaim, contains *The Red Pony* and the light novella *St. Katy and the Virgin* (1936). The volume also includes the widely anthologized stories "The Chrysanthemums" and "Flight." "The Chrysanthemums" involves a woman who seeks love but is manipulated by a crafty vagrant, while "Flight" chronicles the destruction of a headstrong young Mexican who dies in the mountains after killing a man. *The Pearl* (1947), Steinbeck's last attempt at short fiction, is a lyrical parable about a poor Mexican fisherman's discovery of a giant pearl which brings evil to his household.

(See also *CLC,* Vols. 1, 5, 9, 13, 21, 34; *Contemporary Authors,* Vols. 1-4, rev. ed., Vols. 25-28, rev. ed. [obituary]; *Contemporary Authors New Revision Series,* Vol. 1; *Something about the Author,* Vol. 9; *Dictionary of Literary Biography,* Vols. 7, 9; and *Dictionary of Literary Biography Documentary Series,* Vol. 2.)

In this volume commentary on John Steinbeck is focused on his novel East of Eden.

HARVEY CURTIS WEBSTER

Perhaps ***East of Eden*** isn't a great novel according to the strict conventions of formal purity so widely accepted today, but it will take almost equal quantities of pride and stupidity to deny that it is one of the best novels of the past ten years and the best book John Steinbeck has written since ***The Grapes of Wrath.*** Most people will like it and many will buy it. They should, for it is to be doubted if any American novel has better chronicled our last hundred years, our trek from East to West to discover an Eden that always somehow escapes us and that we as a people yet continue to hope for and believe in.

East of Eden is not a compact novel like ***Of Mice and Men,*** not brilliant sociological fiction like ***The Grapes of Wrath*** and ***In Dubious Battle,*** not a temperately ironical tale of the disreputable who are more lovable than the respectable like ***Tortilla Flat.*** It belongs really in the tradition of the novels Fielding wrote and Thackeray tried to. It gangles, yet is full of vitality . . . as you are carried forward by a narrative flow that encompasses vulgarity, sensibility, hideousness, and beauty.

In another sense, ***East of Eden*** can be taken as a long parable expertly told. Mostly it centers about Adam Trask, appropriately and Biblically named. He is a fallible, gullible, intelligent man who thinks he has found his earthly paradise in the Salinas Valley, is seduced by his Eve, and comes out of the moral wilderness this sends him into to achieve belief in himself and in the world he must learn to live in.

But as its length of six hundred pages suggests, this parable is as full of incidents and people who deviate from the main line of narrative as *Tom Jones*. Some of the episodes, like the compact and highly interesting story of Cyrus Trask who never forgot the Civil War or learned gentleness, seem at first to be largely irrelevant. One feels that Steinbeck spends altogether too much time on the whores Adam's wife [Cathy] ultimately controls, too much loving description on the Salinas Valley, that he overcrowds his canvas with characters. Yet in the end the reader must conclude that there is little real irrelevance and that even the actual irrelevance is so full of vitality that he is glad Steinbeck did not do a sterner job of pruning.

The novel marks a definite advance in Steinbeck's thinking which has been defined by Edmund Wilson as too barely naturalistic. In his earlier novels, men approach the condition of animals with a uniformity that sometimes becomes monotonous. In ***East of Eden,*** the animality is still there but it is joined to a sense of human dignity and what it may achieve. There is none of the sentimentality about the outcast you find in ***Cannery Row,*** none of the unconvincing mysticism of ***The Wayward Bus.*** The main characters are good-and-bad, good, and bad; and one always has a sense that they are endowed with a freedom of choice that permits them to change their moral category.

The central core around which all the action convincingly moves and has its meaning is a long and profoundly interesting discussion of the story of Cain and Abel. Samuel Hamilton, Steinbeck's most convincingly lovable failure, Lee, a plausible learned Chinese who was raised a Presbyterian, and Adam are the talkers; but it is Lee, significantly, who makes Steinbeck's universally religious point: Every man is potentially Cain (including Abel). . . . [Every] human being has the power to choose, whatever his conditioning. (pp. 11-12)

No one more hatefully probable and understandable than Cathy, more humanly good and errant than Lee and Samuel Hamilton, more uncomfortably and representatively perplexed than Adam, has appeared in contemporary fiction. These focal characters who bring meaning and focus into what superficially seems a sprawling narrative full of unguided life are Steinbeck's artful instruments in a novel that convincingly demonstrates that he is still one of the most important writers of our time. (p. 12)

Harvey Curtis Webster, "Out of the New-born Sun," in The Saturday Review, *New York, Vol. XXXV, No. 38, September 20, 1952, pp. 11-12.*

JOSEPH WOOD KRUTCH

[The essay from which this excerpt is taken was originally published in The New York Herald Tribune Book Review, *September 21, 1952.]*

Mr. Steinbeck's [***East of Eden***] is described as his most ambitious effort since ***The Grapes of Wrath.*** That is inevitable, but it is also entirely inadequate because ***East of Eden*** is a novel planned on the grandest possible scale. . . . Here is one of those occasions when a writer has aimed high and then summoned every ounce of energy, talent, seriousness and passion of which he was capable. The most unfriendly critic could hardly fail to grant that ***East of Eden*** is the best as well as the most ambitious book Mr. Steinbeck could write at this moment.

The scene is mostly the Salinas valley in California; the action mostly events in the lives of three generations of two families. In each generation two brothers in one of the families play the leading roles and in each case there is some sort of Cain-Abel relationship between them. Obviously the action is intended to be significant on three levels. . . . Besides being individuals first and types second the characters are also something else—they are also symbols.

Here, so we are being told, is not only the story of certain families and the story of a frontier, but also the story of mankind. Mr. Steinbeck is not, either as man or writer, very much like Thomas Mann, but one thinks of *The Magic Mountain* as the most obvious example of another modern novel which operates upon the same three levels. And like Thomas Mann, Mr. Steinbeck employs almost the whole repertory of novelistic devices. Besides highly dramatized scenes there are panoramic descriptions, philosophic dialogues and interpolated disquisitions in which the author, speaking in his own person, discourses ironically upon such subjects as the whore house as a social institution or what goes on when women meet at the village dressmaker's.

Leaving aside for a moment the question of symbolic meaning, the first thing to be said is that the whole ramifying narrative holds the attention to an extraordinary degree throughout the six hundred long pages. Quiet, almost idyllic, passages alternate with scenes of extravagant violence. There are sadistic beatings, a rape, murders and even worse horrors almost too numerous to count. But considered at least as separate self-contained episodes they nearly always come off because Mr. Steinbeck's talents seem to be under that disciplined, self-critical control too often absent in his lesser works, which often degenerated into sentimental melodrama. The violent scenes are, moreover, thrown into high relief by the consequences of the fact that Mr. Steinbeck seems to know when, as narrator, to participate in the hysteria of the scene, when to withdraw into the detached, faintly ironical spectator. Never, I think, not even in ***The Grapes of Wrath,*** has he exhibited such a grip upon himself and upon his material. If one has sometimes been tempted to dismiss him as merely a routine manipulator of the more obvious tricks of the tough-tender, hardboiled-softboiled school, he cannot be so dismissed here. There is seriousness as well as violence; passion rather than sentimentality. He is also, when the occasion requires, master of a quietly and humorously deft little phrase of description or comment which strikes precisely that note of serenity necessary to highlight the violence. (pp. 302-03)

What is most likely to disturb a reader, at least during the first third of the book, is the tendency of the characters to turn suddenly at certain moments into obviously symbolic figures as abstract almost as the dramatis personae in a morality play. This awkwardness—and awkward it certainly is—becomes less and less noticeable as the story proceeds. Whether that is because Mr. Steinbeck learns better how to fuse the individual and the symbol or because the reader comes to accept his method I am not quite sure. But in any event it is not because the symbolic intention becomes any less clear or important. In each generation the Abel-Cain relationship is symbolized by a childish gift offered by each brother to the father and always in one case seemingly rejected. And in each generation one of the pair carries a scar on his forehead. Indeed, Mr. Steinbeck states explicitly as one of his theses: "The greatest terror a child can have is that he is not loved, and rejection is the hell he fears. I think everyone in the world to a large or small extent has felt rejection. And with rejection comes anger, and with anger some kind of revenge for rejection, and with the crime, guilt—and there is the story of mankind." (pp. 303-04)

Mr. Steinbeck does not stop with this attempt to embody a meaningful myth in the chronicle history of a modern family. He goes on to draw a further moral and to pronounce a further thesis. Stated in the barest and most abstract terms this thesis is, first, that Good and Evil are absolute not relative things and, second, that in making a choice between them man is a free agent, not the victim of his heredity, his environment, or of anything else.

This thesis is first announced parenthetically, casually, and without any hint of its importance on page twelve. . . . Nearly three hundred pages later it receives its most explicit discussion in a dialogue between two of the characters concerning the meaning of a phrase in the Cain-Abel story which refers, apparently, to "sin."

In the King James version the phrase reads "and thou shalt rule over him"; in the American Standard Bible it appears as "Do thou rule over him." But according at least to one of Mr. Steinbeck's characters, the crucial Hebrew word is *timshel* and it means "thou mayest." "Don't you see?" he cried. "The American Standard translation *orders* men to triumph over sin, and you can call sin ignorance. The King James translation makes a promise in 'Thou shalt,' meaning that men will surely triumph over sin. But the Hebrew word, the word *timshel*—'Thou mayest'—that gives a choice. It might be the most important word in the world." (p. 304)

Moral relativism and some sort of deterministic philosophy have commonly seemed to be implied in the writings of that school of hardboiled realists with which Mr. Steinbeck has sometimes been loosely associated. It is difficult to imagine how any novel could more explicitly reject both than they are rejected in ***East of Eden.*** The author, who was acclaimed as a social critic in ***The Grapes of Wrath*** and sometimes abused as a mere writer of sensational melodrama in some subsequent books, plainly announces here that it is as a moralist that he wants to be taken.

The merits of so ambitious and absorbing a book are sure to be widely and hotly debated. The final verdict will not, I think, depend upon the validity of the thesis which is part of a debate almost as old as human thought or upon any possible doubt concerning the vividness of Mr. Steinbeck's storytelling. On the highest level the question is this: Does the fable really carry the thesis; is the moral implicit in or merely imposed upon the story; has the author recreated a myth or merely moralized a tale? There is no question that Mr. Steinbeck has written an intensely interesting and impressive book. (p. 305)

Joseph Wood Krutch, "John Steinbeck's Dramatic Tale of Three Generations," in Steinbeck and His Critics: A Record of Twenty-Five Years, *The University of New Mexico Press, 1957, pp. 302-05.*

ROBERT R. BRUNN

[In ***East of Eden,*** a] rambling and ambitious novel spread out over more than half a century, John Steinbeck wrestles with a moral theme for the first time in his career, certainly a hopeful sign of the times. Yet his obsession with naked animality, brute violence, and the dark wickedness of the human mind remains so overriding that what there is of beauty and understanding is subordinated and almost extinguished.

This is true to such an extent that to read the book can be a punishing experience. His portrayal of Catherine Ames alone, "a monster" in his own words without a spark of humanity or sensibility, is so hopelessly evil as to make her incredible and the book a chamber of horrors. His excursions into the mellow light of normality with their wit and joy and poetry are clouded and often blotted out by the shadow of the revolting Ames theme.

Yet the book is worth considerable discussion, for Mr. Steinbeck, obviously, is trying to say something which reaches a higher level than the plane of bitter frustration and senseless brutality upon which such books as ***Of Mice and Men*** and ***The Grapes of Wrath*** moved. To do this, he has gone back to the story of Cain and Abel, to the ancient problem of good and evil. . . . [The] title of the novel is taken from the passage in Genesis which tells how Cain "dwelt in the land of Nod, on the east of Eden" after being "cursed from the earth." . . .

[Mr. Steinbeck's] characters are overjoyed at one point to discover a translation of the Hebrew which has this passage read "thou *mayest* rule over him," that is, thou *mayest* overcome evil or sin, not thou *shalt*." To Mr. Steinbeck, believing that man is enmeshed in a web of good and evil this latter translation offers boundless hope—for in it he sees man with a private mind or intelligence, free to choose between a real good and a real evil.

The "thou *mayest*" with its intimation of dignity for the human mind and the reality of evil is transcendent to him. It is the last thing said in the book. Yet the [new] Standard Revised Version of the Bible. . . . gives this translation of the passage: "If you do well, will you not be accepted? And if you do not well, sin is couching at the door; its desire is for you, but you *must* master it."

Now this is not a carping discussion. The implication of the word *must* denies man the choice between good and evil, affirms the King James translation, and implies the inescapable fact of man's perfection as "the image of God" as stated in Genesis. Can this perfect man know sin or have a private mind to know it?

And it is his belief in the gloomy philosophy of good *and* evil and of a human mind apart from God, the divine Mind, that seems to have caught Mr. Steinbeck in the net to which he refers, a mesmeric net from which he has not yet broken free—

free of its arguments of violence, bestiality, and compulsive wickedness.

Robert R. Brunn, "'You Must Master It'," in The Christian Science Monitor, *September 25, 1952, p. 15.*

ARTHUR MIZENER

After I had struggled through to the last of ***East of Eden***'s 602 pages, I began to think I must be wrong about the earlier Steinbeck, that it couldn't possibly be so good as I remembered it: one of the worst things about a bad book is the way it infects your recollection of the author's good work. So I went back and reread some of the stories in ***The Long Valley*** and it was a great comfort; they are every bit as good as they seemed originally, maybe better. The animals, the people, the places, the weather are all there (in about that order of importance), realized with a remarkable delicacy and humor. And out of this fully realized material there emerges imperceptibly Steinbeck's feeling for life, a feeling that only the continuity of life itself is sure, and that it is enough. This feeling allows him to face things like suffering and death and especially that part of growing up which consists in recognizing and accepting these things, with an odd but impressive dignity. They are part of the process of life and therefore, however painful, justified and fine. Steinbeck's sense of the process controls his sympathy for the individuals involved and keeps it genuine. (p. 22)

[Until ***East of Eden***'s] moral turns her into an illustration for a Salvation-Army speech, Cathy is, like the characters in good animal epics, a fine macabre fancy. Most of the characters are not that interesting. They are comic-strip illustrations of Steinbeck's moral, like Adam and Cal, or they are stock figures who act as mouthpieces for the moralizing—a philosophical Chinaman from some novel by Erle Stanley Gardner or a merry-and-sad Irish blacksmith who says things like, "In a bitter night, a mustard night that was last night, a good thought came and the dark was sweetened when the day sat down." . . . Steinbeck is always catching this old gentleman posed against the sky with "his white hair shining in the starlight;" and his manner keeps spilling over onto the other characters so that they begin to say things like, "In some strange way my eyes have cleared. A weight is off me."

The book's action is always getting lost in a swamp of solemn talk from these philosophers. The Chinaman even reads aloud from Marcus Aurelius and the Irishman from *Genesis*—the whole Cain and Abel story. It isn't enough that Steinbeck's title is from the passage in *Genesis* . . . or that his hero is named Adam, or that Adam's brother tries to kill him and has a scar on his forehead, or that Adam's sons are named Caleb and Aaron (Aaron likes hunting but Caleb is a gardener). Steinbeck is far more interested in bludgeoning us with his hopped-up commonplaces about abstract evil and abstract good than he is in making us see his people and their lives.

Luckily he cannot fill six hundred pages with Deep Thoughts from the Best Thinkers. ***East of Eden*** was apparently conceived as an epic about the Salinas Valley and Steinbeck seems to imagine that the basic principle of the epic is "plenty of everything." He doesn't even get the hero to the Valley for over a hundred pages. One of the fortunate results of this catch-all method is that he puts in a number of things which, though they are never effectively related to the action, are entertaining in themselves. There are amusing scenes like Olive Steinbeck's airplane ride and Dessie Hamilton's return to King City; there are a few spare, exciting episodes like Adam's escape from the chain gang or Cathy's murders of her parents and of Faye. Occasionally Steinbeck's old ant-hill-observer's feeling about humans and their institutions asserts itself and we get wryly sympathetic accounts of how difficult it is to run a good whorehouse and how Kate does it. And once in a long while his fine feeling for the animals and plants and weather of the Salinas Valley emerges. Most of the time the characters and events are forced into stagey postures and well-made-play situations by the moral, and sometimes they are forced off the stage altogether while Steinbeck himself lectures us about Life. (pp. 22-3)

There is evidence even in ***East of Eden*** of what is quite clear from Steinbeck's earlier work, that so long as he sticks to animals and children and to situations he can see to some purpose from the point of view of his almost biological feeling for the continuity of life he can release the considerable talent and sensitivity which are naturally his. As soon as he tries to see adult experience in the usual way and to find the familiar kind of moral in it, the insight and talent cease to work and he writes like the author of any third-rate best-seller. Let us hope that some day he will go back to the Long Valley he really knows. . . . (p. 23)

Arthur Mizener, "In the Land of Nod," in The New Republic, *Vol. 127, No. 14, October 6, 1952, pp. 22-3.*

PETER LISCA

Having asserted in ***The Wayward Bus*** his belief that despite the "weak and sick and ugly and quarrelsome" nature of man, this six-cylinder world does go on, and having made the point in ***Burning Bright*** that "so long as human beings exist anywhere every man is immortal," Steinbeck went on in ***East of Eden*** to insist at great length that every man has the power to choose between good and evil. (p. 261)

Although the story of Cain and Abel is [***East of Eden***'s] main theme, what it is intended to be essentially *about*, a great deal of the book is taken up with an accurate, factual account of Steinbeck's own maternal family, the Hamiltons, and the author himself appears sporadically in the novel as the narrator "I," as "me," and as "John." The explanation for this agglutination of materials, and the book's essential failure, lies in the history of the novel's composition.

Steinbeck's original plan for ***East of Eden*** was "to set down in story form for his two small sons the full record of their ancestors from the time they moved westward to Salinas Valley just after the Civil War." (p. 262)

Somewhere in the early stages of this family saga, however, Steinbeck introduced a fictional family, the Trasks, and he soon found himself at the mercy of his materials. The importance of the Trask family in the novel grew until the author realized that he had a far different book on his hands from what he had originally conceived, one which centered on the Trasks and not on the Hamiltons, Steinbeck's maternal family. By this time, however, the two families were inextricably entangled, and the author decided to keep them that way, but reduced the story of his own family to its vestigial elements. . . . (pp. 262-63)

Steinbeck's attempts to impose an order on his diverse materials proved unsuccessful, and many reviewers pointed out that because he tried to say too many things at once, Steinbeck failed to achieve fictional concentration. (p. 263)

The dissenting voices were few, but they included the French critic Claude-Edmonde Magny, Mark Schorer [see *CLC,* Vol. 21], and Joseph Wood Krutch [see excerpt above]. Mme. Magny found in the book a "special type of coherence, which is not in the least novelistic," and Mr. Krutch thought that never, "not even in ***The Grapes of Wrath***," had Steinbeck "exhibited such a grasp upon himself and upon his materials." Mark Schorer, like Mme. Magny, found a new kind of unity in ***East of Eden:*** ". . . yet the tone of this book, the bold ease with which the 'I' takes over at the outset and appears and disappears and reappears throughout, both holds it together and gives it its originality, the relaxations of its freedom."

It is instructive to examine the reviews of Mark Schorer and Joseph Wood Krutch in a little more detail, for they contain a certain ambivalence which is an accurate index to the peculiar effect of Steinbeck's novel, one of both greatness and failure. For example, although both critics praise the author's grasp on his materials, they also admit doubts about the book's structure. At the end of the review Mr. Krutch poses an unanswered question which might well have been the basis of his discussion: "On the highest level the question is this: Does the fable really carry the thesis; is the moral implicit in or merely imposed upon the story: has the author created a myth or merely moralized a tale?" Mr. Schorer not only remarks on "the gap between speculative statement and novelistic presentation," but points out elements of "sentimentalism" and "melodrama." At times this critic's remarks convey the impression that he is trying to talk himself into something: "This account of the book's style and themes may suggest a kind of eclectic irresolution of view which is, in fact, not at all the quality of the book. . . . I am trying to praise the audaciousness with which this novelist asserts his temperament. . . ." Comparing the novel with other Steinbeck works, Mr. Schorer admits that ***East of Eden*** is, "in a sense, more amorphous, less intent on singleness of theme and effect," while at the same time he asserts that it is "the best of John Steinbeck's novels." It is interesting that three years later Mr. Schorer refused to allow his review to be reprinted . . . , saying that, after rereading the novel, he found the review totally mistaken in judgment and regretted its publication. The paradox in this kind of criticism is a close approximation of what Steinbeck himself wrote to his editor while ***East of Eden*** was in progress: "It's a kind of sloppy sounding book, but it is not sloppy really." (pp. 264-65)

Even a casual reading, however, will reveal just how sloppy, or to use Mr. Schorer's terms, how "audacious" is Steinbeck's "eclectic irresolution of view." Of the Hamilton family, only Samuel and Will, Steinbeck's maternal grandfather and uncle, respectively, become in any way involved with the Trasks. . . . Will's only contacts with the Trasks consist of three short scenes. . . . Except for these contacts and a brief visit by Liza, Samuel's wife, the Trasks and the Hamiltons pursue separate courses, and nothing *results* from their juxtaposition. There is not the organic relationship between these parts of the novel that there is between the scenic and panoramic sections of ***The Grapes of Wrath,*** or even the parallels and contrasts which exist among the separate sections of ***Cannery Row, Tortilla Flat,*** and ***The Pastures of Heaven.*** Steinbeck simply shifts back and forth between the Trasks and the Hamiltons with no apparent purpose or method, and his efforts to keep the two stories abreast result in many awkward flashbacks and lacunae. (pp. 265-66)

The domestic problems of the Hamiltons and their eight children—George, Will, Tom, Joe, Una, Lizzie, Dessie, Mollie, Olive (Steinbeck's mother)—are given in detail. Some of these anecdotes, such as the death of Dessie, the suicide of Tom, and Olive's airplane ride, are interesting in themselves, but at no point do they contribute to some greater purpose, and they remain essentially distracting and unintegrated fragments.

In addition to this peripheral contact between the two families, as a device for pulling the book together, Steinbeck also makes use of the narrator "I" to interlard the objectively rendered details of plot with moral essays in the manner of Thackeray. What makes this device particularly unsuccessful is that whereas Thackeray wisely kept himself and his family out of the action, remaining a detached commentator on a moral tale, the narrator "I" in ***East of Eden*** is confused with the "me" and the "John" and the "my" and the "we" of the actual narrative. By far the greater part of the book is not told by the autobiographical "I" at all, since it concerns events which he not only could not have witnessed, but could not even have heard about. This "I" is plainly a vestigial element from the first draft of the book as a family saga addressed to his children, and is ill-mated to the "I" as narrator. Finally, this "I" (whether narrative or autobiographical) comes up so infrequently (about twenty times in six hundred pages) and so briefly that no permanent association with the story is created. Each time it appears it effects a momentary shock of intrusion. The novel is in no sense dominated or given form by its narrator, and the narrator is in no sense defined by the novel. He is merely the third major fragment.

The moral philosophy of the narrator is no more convincing than its structural function, and at times seems to be in direct variance with the action. While Samuel and the Chinese servant, Lee, explicate the Cain and Abel story, and thus the Trask story, as giving evidence of man's free will in choosing between good and evil, Lee later denies free will to Adam Trask: "He couldn't help it, Cal. That's his nature. It was the only way he knew. He didn't have any choice." The author himself denies free will to the novel's most wicked character—Cathy: "And just as there are physical monsters, can there not be mental or psychic monsters born? The face and body may be perfect, but if a twisted gene or a malformed egg can produce physical monsters, may not the same process produce a malformed soul?" (pp. 266-67)

That the author is truly confused on this question of free will is evident in other moral essays scattered throughout the book and in the fact that the reader learns, quite suddenly near the end of the novel, that the monster, Cathy, has become a religious penitent (Episcopal) and has committed suicide because of moral loneliness, leaving a great fortune to her "Abel" son, Aaron. (p. 267)

The Cain and Abel theme fares much better as it is worked out in [Cathy's son] Caleb, who inherits both good and evil and in whom a genuine moral struggle takes place. . . . Unfortunately, Caleb's story takes up only a small part of the book.

Furthermore, Steinbeck is so anxious to make his theme evident that he badgers it into an uninteresting obviousness. All the Cain characters in the novel are identified by names beginning with "C" (Cyrus, Charles, Cathy, Caleb) and the Abel characters by names beginning with "A" (Alice, Adam, Aaron, Abra). The weighty paraphernalia of the "C" and "A" initials is made still more ponderous by the fact that both Cathy and

Charles have livid scars on their foreheads. . . . There are possibly hundreds of such allusions to the details of those sixteen verses in Genesis which contain the story of Cain and Abel. (pp. 268-69)

To these faults of structure and theme must be added one other fault which, except for Steinbeck's first novel, had not been evident until ***Burning Bright***—the failure of language. . . . [Samuel Hamilton's] blarney may be excused as coming from an old Irishman, but it seems to be a contagious language which infects the other characters—especially the Chinese Lee, who has attended the university at Berkeley for several years, smokes opium, and drinks wormwood, as well as quoting from "*The Meditations of Marcus Aurelius* in English translation." Even the author speaks in a kind of blarney reminiscent of ***Burning Bright***. . . . The scrambled syntax and awkward expression are evident everywhere. (pp. 269-70)

There are few passages of pure description in the six hundred odd pages of ***East of Eden***, relatively fewer than in any other of his novels; but in these, too, which are usually among the best pieces of writing in Steinbeck's books, it is possible to see the failure of his language. . . . Even the few descriptions of animal life in ***East of Eden*** suffer from . . . artificiality. (pp. 271-72)

This affectation is the result of [Steinbeck's] attempt to exploit an aspect of prose style which, after his first novel, he had avoided until ***Burning Bright.*** Previous to this play-novelette, his mastery of prose styles could be attributed to his keen ear for the idioms and rhythms of speech (whether those of the *paisanos* of ***Tortilla Flat***, the laborers of ***In Dubious Battle***, or the folk of ***The Pastures of Heaven***) and a fine sense of appropriate narrative style (the cold prose of ***In Dubious Battle***, the poetic realism of the Jody stories and ***The Pearl***, or the elevated periods and American rhythms of the interchapters in ***The Grapes of Wrath.***) In ***East of Eden***, as in ***Burning Bright***, Steinbeck's exploration of language as technique concerns itself almost exclusively with figurative language, and the result is disastrous. . . . For the most part, the prose of ***East of Eden*** alternates between [a] kind of pseudo-poetry and an abandoned, unstudied carelessness incapable of organizing the sprawling materials, and, because the narrator himself is so ambiguously defined, incapable of emphasizing them.

As the failure of prose style is allied to the failure of structure, so both are allied to the new emphasis on character. In ***East of Eden***, for the first time since ***Cup of Gold***, Steinbeck is concerned with his characters primarily as individuals who exist and have importance apart from the materials of his novel, for it is through them rather than through structure and language that he tries to establish his theme. While lesser novelists have succeeded with this method, Steinbeck fails because his characters are neither credible as individuals nor effective as types but are an incongruous mixture of both. Samuel is too much like the Old Testament prophets for one of whom he was named to be effective as a human being, and too much of a human being to be convincing as an Old Testament prophet. . . . Cathy is too much like Satan to be a credible human being, and too much like a weak, pitiful human being to be properly Satanic. (pp. 272-73)

Where Steinbeck does succeed is with the portraits of minor characters and of his maternal family—excepting Samuel Hamilton, who is nevertheless more credible and effective than any of the other major characters. These are successful because they are drawn from memory, with no attempt to make them fit into a myth or illustrate a type. Unfortunately, these warm, credible human beings are in no way involved in the novel's narrative. The element of greatness which both Joseph Wood Krutch and Mark Schorer noted in their reviews might have been brought to fulfillment in a subtle fusion of ***East of Eden***'s imposing theme and its more credible human beings and events—a fusion which is not accomplished in the novel.

The generally favorable reception of ***East of Eden*** is an amazing phenomenon in Steinbeck criticism, because whereas commentators had gone to ridiculous extremes in finding highly technical faults with his earlier well-made novels, they now bent over backward to celebrate the excellence of his latest book by avoiding all technical considerations and exulting over its great moral theme. . . . "In this novel," wrote [Robert R. Brunn (see excerpt above)], "John Steinbeck wrestles with a moral theme for the first time in his career. . . ." [Harvey Curtis Webster (see excerpt above)] thought he observed in the novel "a definite advance in Steinbeck's thinking which has been defined by Edmund Wilson as too barely naturalistic." Joseph Henry Jackson believed that "***East of Eden*** reflects a Steinbeck who has now put past him something [his biological view of man] which once . . . threatened to close him in, to narrow him as a creative writer. . . . he has been thinking more deeply than ever before about life and the human beings who live it."

The only important dissenting voice in this chorus exalting moral theme over art was that of Arthur Mizener [see excerpt above] who, also perceiving the new departure in ***East of Eden***, went directly to the heart of the matter. Far from seeing hope in Steinbeck's overt concern with moral theme, Mizener advised that the author return again to the world of ***The Long Valley*** and ***The Red Pony***. . . . (pp. 273-74)

It is impossible to agree with the author when he says of ***East of Eden***, "I think everything else I have written has been, in a sense, practice for this. . . . If ***East of Eden*** isn't good, then I've been wasting my time." . . . Actually, there is very little in ***East of Eden*** which goes back further than ***Burning Bright.*** Mr. Mizener's suggestion that Steinbeck return to ***The Long Valley*** and ***The Red Pony*** may be extreme, but it is certain that the new direction of ***Burning Bright*** and ***East of Eden*** had disastrous consequences for his art. (p. 275)

Peter Lisca, in his The Wide World of John Steinbeck, *Rutgers University Press, 1958, 326 p.*

JOSEPH FONTENROSE

In the forties Steinbeck was clearly turning his principal interest from biology and sociology to individual ethics. He was one of several writers whom the Second World War and its aftermath made aware of the "problem of evil." . . . [In ***East of Eden***, Steinbeck] completed the transition; it is a lengthy treatment of man's capacity for both good and evil. In it Steinbeck "plainly announces . . . that it is as a moralist that he wants to be taken," as Joseph Wood Krutch expressed it [see excerpt above]. (p. 118)

[In 1947, Steinbeck] started work upon a book that he called "Salinas Valley," which would be the story of the Hamiltons, his mother's family. Early in the drafting he introduced a fictitious second family, the Trasks, whose role expanded to the point of taking over the novel; and in 1951 the title was changed to ***East of Eden.*** The finished novel is still two stories, the Trasks and the Hamiltons, or rather three: the story of Cathy Ames is really a separate strand that becomes entwined with the central Trask story in one phase only; thereafter it goes its own way, a parallel strand that comes occasionally into important contact with the Trask strand. The Hamilton story is a subordinate and independent strand that barely touches the other two: the Hamiltons have almost nothing to do with Cathy and little to do with the Trasks. The Trask story needs Cathy Ames, but not the Hamiltons, who can be dropped out without affecting the Trask story at all.

[***East of Eden***] has four Parts. In the first (1862-1900) the three stories are begun, and the Trask and Cathy stories are developed until Adam Trask marries Cathy. Part Two (1900-1902) brings the Trasks and Hamiltons together in the Salinas Valley, ending with the naming of Cathy's twins, after she has abandoned them and her husband and become a whore (called Kate) in Salinas; and her story is carried to the point where by devious means she acquired ownership of the brothel in which she worked. In Part Three (1911-12) the Hamilton story moves forward on its own from the last days of Samuel Hamilton to its conclusion in the deaths of Dessie and Tom Hamilton, while the Trask story marks time (Adam Trask becomes half alive after ten years of spiritual coma), and Cathy is all but absent. Part Four (1812-18) is the story of Adam Trask and his sons after they had moved from the Trask ranch to Salinas; the parallel Cathy-Kate story ends with her suicide; and the Hamilton story is touched upon only in Will Hamilton's role as Cal Trask's partner in a bean brokerage. The central narrative throughout is the fictional biography of Adam Trask from his birth in the second year of the Civil War until his death in the last year of World War I. . . . The design and magnitude of ***East of Eden,*** and Steinbeck's own remarks about it, indicate that it was meant to be a climactic work, his greatest achievement, for which every earlier book was practice. But few Steinbeck readers will place it higher than ***The Grapes of Wrath;*** the majority may see it as a second peak in his career, but not nearly so high as the first. (pp. 118-19)

After ten years in the army and more years wandering across the country, Adam was living with Charles on the Trask farm when Cathy Ames crawled to their door, terribly beaten by the whoremaster Edwards. Adam fell in love with her while nursing her, and married her, obstinately refusing to inquire into her past. Cathy was the sort of person who would put sleeping medicine in Adam's tea on her wedding night so that she could enter Charles's bed; and she appears to have been impregnated by both brothers, for she bore nonidentical twins, one of whom (Caleb) looked like Charles and was like Charles in nature. Contrary to the Biblical story, it was Adam (Abel), not Charles (Cain), who left the family land and went west to California, where the twins were born and Cathy deserted him. There he became the first Adam who lost his Eden (a happy life with Cathy and his children on excellent farm land in the Salinas Valley) and was father of Cain (Caleb) and Abel (Aaron). Adam preferred his son Aaron (later spelled Aron), who in boyhood raised Belgian hares (the herdsman role); the less likeable Caleb (Cal) wanted to be a farmer. When he was seventeen, Cal, in partnership with Will Hamilton, contracted for bean crops to sell to the British Purchasing Agency; he made $15,000 and gave it to his father, who had suffered severe losses in a business venture. Adam cruelly refused Cal's gift on the ground that the money was war profit, unfairly gained, and invidiously compared it to Aron's success in entering Stanford one year early. . . . Cal got revenge by taking Aron to watch the "circus" at Kate's whorehouse and revealing to him that Kate was their mother (Cal had discovered this some time before). Aron, a pure boy who had intended to enter the Episcopal ministry, was profoundly shocked, as Cal had expected, since the knowledge shattered Aron's unreal image of an angelic mother who had died in his infancy. The very next morning Aron enlisted in the army, soon was sent to France, and died in action. (p. 121)

Steinbeck, of course, puts more into the story than can be found in Genesis 4, which says nothing about either brother's attitude towards Adam. The irony of the father's partiality in ***East of Eden*** is that neither Adam nor Aron loved his father, whereas Charles loved [his father] Cyrus and Cal loved Adam, and each tried hard to please his father. Again, Steinbeck introduces rivalry over a woman into both generations of brothers, more obscurely in the first, since Charles disliked Cathy; but he did admit her to his bed and left her half his fortune when he died. In the next generation Abra, Aron's boyhood sweetheart, transferred her love to Cal after Aron's enlistment. Steinbeck read a good deal about Genesis while writing ***East of Eden*** and probably came upon a later Jewish legend (current before 300 A.D.) which elaborates the brief and bare scriptural narrative; both Cain and Abel had a twin sister, each intended to become her twin's wife and so ensure the survival of mankind. Abel's twin sister was so beautiful that Cain wanted her; therefore he picked a quarrel with Abel, killed him, and married Abel's twin, that mysterious wife of Cain who bore his son Enoch in the land of Nod (Genesis 4:17).

Furthermore, Steinbeck had to fuse Adam and Jehovah in one person, Cyrus Trask in the first generation, Adam Trask in the second. Cathy is a fusion of Eve, the Eden serpent, and Cain's wife—the beating which the whoremaster gave her had left a scar on her forehead. Steinbeck emphasizes her serpent nature by giving her a heartshaped face, an abnormally small mouth, a little pointed tongue that sometimes flicked around her lips, small sharp teeth with the canine teeth longer and more pointed than the others, tiny ears without lobes and pressed close to her head, unblinking eyes, narrow hips. (p. 122)

The story of Cain and Abel, Lee said to Adam and Sam, "is the symbol story of the human soul," "the best-known story in the world because it is everybody's story." The three men found the story perplexing when they first discussed it. Ten years later, when they had gathered for the last time, Lee had cleared up the difficulties with the help of four aged Chinese sages, who had studied Hebrew for just this purpose. They solved the problem of Genesis 4:7, as given in the King James version, "And unto thee shall be his desire, and thou shalt rule over him," by translating the verb form *timshol* (not *timshel* as Steinbeck has it) "thou mayest rule" instead of "thou shalt rule"; and they took "sin" as antecedent of the masculine pronouns. This, Lee said in triumph, "was the gold from our mining": the translation "thou shalt rule" implies predestination; "do thou rule," as in the American Standard version, orders a man to master sin; but "thou mayest rule" gives a man a choice: he can master sin if he wants to. " 'Thou mayest,' " Lee said, "might be the most important word in the world," for "that makes a man great, . . . for in his weakness and his filth and his murder of his brother he has still the great choice."

This, then, is the message of ***East of Eden,*** a message that many can accept, even though those who "love true things" must reject Lee's interpretation of Genesis 4:7. That verse has an obviously corrupt text, and the sentence at issue appears to be out of place. For one thing, the masculine pronouns cannot refer to "sin," which translates a Hebrew feminine noun. And *timshol* will not bear the meaning which Steinbeck puts upon it. He apparently read or was told that the Hebrew imperfect tense, which indicates incomplete action at any time, is used where English employs either the vivid future tense (*will, shall*) or the potential (*would, should, may, might*); in either case the action is unfulfilled. If a translation as potential suited this verse, it would be simply "you would rule"; it cannot be a permissive "may." Steinbeck, furthermore, constantly translates *timshol* "thou mayest," dropping "rule," as if the Hebrew form were simply an auxiliary. Many a sermon, however, has drawn a fine meaning from a faulty translation of a corrupt text.

According to Lee, the story of Cain and Abel is important because it is a story of rejection, from which all evil flows, since "with rejection comes anger, and with anger some kind of crime in revenge for the rejection, and with the crime guilt—and there is the story of mankind." Or as the author states it in a moralizing chapter . . . , "most of . . . [men's] vices are attempted short cuts to love." . . . As Krutch has pointed out, for Steinbeck as moralist good and evil are absolute and objective. We have come a long way, it seems, from Jim Casy's doctrine in ***The Grapes of Wrath*** that "There ain't no sin and there ain't no virtue. There's just stuff people do," and from Doc Burton's refusal in ***In Dubious Battle*** "to put on the blinders of 'good' and 'bad,'" because they would limit his vision and destroy his objectivity. And it seems to me that Steinbeck has limited his vision in ***East of Eden.***

The reader is never clear about the relation of good to evil in this novel, for it is presented in four inconsistent ways. (1) Good is opposed to evil. . . . Charles, Cathy, and Cal have bad traits opposed to the good traits of Adam and Aron. In the "thou mayest" doctrine, evil can be rejected and good chosen. (2) Good and evil are complementary. Lee thought that they might be so balanced that if a man went too far either way an automatic slide restored the balance. Good and evil are symbolized by the church and the whorehouse, which "arrived in the Far West simultaneously," and each "intended to accomplish the same thing: . . . [to take] a man out of his bleakness for a time." (3) Evil is the source of good and may even be necessary to good. The evil Cathy, quite without intending it, "set off the glory in Adam." The wealth which Cyrus Trask acquired dishonestly was inherited by Adam Trask, an honest man who used the money to rear and educate his sons. . . . (4) Good and evil are relative terms. Lee said to Adam in that same speech, "What your wife is doing is neither good nor bad," although she was operating the most perverted and depraved brothel in California. This seems to hark back to Casy's doctrine: Kate's activities were simply not nice.

Good is identified both with admirable individual qualities (philanthropy, kindness, generosity, self-respect, courage, creativity) and with conventional moral goodness (sexual purity, abstinence from carnal pleasures of any kind). Evil is identified with ignoble individual qualities (meanness, cruelty, violent temper, avarice, hatefulness, selfishness), with criminal acts (murder, arson, theft, embezzlement), and with carnal pleasures, particularly sex acts; and not only with prostitution and perversions, but with sexual satisfaction in general. That is, the author appears to accept Cal's label of "bad" for his adolescent desires and impulses, and of "good" for Aron's self-indulgent purity and abstinence, and to accept Abra's use of "good" and "bad" when she says that Aron is too good for her, that she herself is not good, and that she loves Cal because he isn't good. Of course, this is the way that young people talk. But Cal and Abra are never allowed to reach a more enlightened view of "good" and "bad"; Steinbeck is using them to illustrate his thesis: that there is good and bad in everyone, and that some bad is necessary (that is, it is good to be bad); and he is understanding good and bad in their terms.

We should notice that in contrast to Steinbeck's treatment of sex in earlier novels, there is no good or healthy or lusty sexual intercourse in ***East of Eden.*** It is always sordid, joyless, depraved, or mercenary. . . . This is not at all like the old Steinbeck who celebrated sexuality. It turns out that Steinbeck's view of good and evil is that of his mythical source: it is the Mosaic view, which is to say a legal view; particular acts are good or bad, regardless of circumstances. The earlier Steinbeck saw acts in context and evaluated them accordingly, if he evaluated them at all, dismissing the religious conception of "sin" entirely. For a novel on good and evil, ***East of Eden*** strangely lacks ethical insight. It is true, as I have pointed out, that its author evaluates qualities as well as acts, but they remain abstract. Adam is honest and kind, we are told; but these are negative virtues in him. In truth, virtue seems to be a function of lack of energy: pernicious anemia may account for George Hamilton's sinless life, and Adam Trask was passive, inert, non-resistant. The positive behavior of the "good" characters is at best unpleasant. Aron is selfish, inconsiderate, unloving. Adam neglects his boys for twelve years, never loves anybody except Cathy, and loves her blindly. His rejection of Cal's gift was brutal, unfeeling, and this after he had begun a cordial relationship with his son. Did Steinbeck, perhaps, intend to show that these "good" persons were not what others thought them to be? Hardly. Lee, his spokesman, said about Adam, "I think in him kindness and conscience are so large that they are almost faults. They trip him up and hinder him." Like Aron, he is too good; a man needs a little "bad" in him; you can be good if you don't have to be perfect, said Lee. We come back to moral confusion, since "good," "bad," and "perfect" are given conventional definitions, never questioned. If Steinbeck had delved into a father's ambivalent feelings for his sons, his awareness of favoring one son over the other, his fairness or unfairness to either son, and the moral and spiritual problems arising from his relation to his sons, then ***East of Eden*** might have been a great novel. As it is, we do not understand Adam's actions; in this novel we cannot resort to saying that they just happened. (pp. 123-26)

Joseph Wood Krutch's favorable review ended with the questions: "Does the fable really carry the thesis; is the moral implicit in or merely imposed upon the story; has the author recreated a myth or merely moralized a tale?" He did not answer the questions. Our answer must be, "No. The moral is imposed upon the story, which is not a recreated myth." A reader can enjoy ***East of Eden*** for its many fine passages of description and many pages of skillful narrative; but the myth invoked does not adequately interpret the narrated events. (pp. 126-27)

Joseph Fontenrose, in his John Steinbeck: An Introduction and Interpretation, *Barnes & Noble, Inc., 1963, 150 p.*

HOWARD LEVANT

[*In the book chapter on* East of Eden *excerpted below, Levant refers to a literary theory of Steinbeck's which he terms "'is' thinking." Levant defines this term as a theory which "implies that characters and events have an order and a rationale as they appear in the objective world; that art cannot improve on this order and rationale; that hence the only function of the artist is to report accurately whatever he sees in the natural world."*]

The culmination of five years of determined labor, ***East of Eden*** is clearly Steinbeck's earnest effort to attain major status as a novelist. . . . [Yet] ***East of Eden*** is a strangely unblended novel, an impressive, greatly flawed work, and a major summation of the various stresses between structure and materials which abound in Steinbeck's novels.

The real importance of ***East of Eden*** does not lie in Steinbeck's mistaken claim to greatness, revealing as it is, but in its testimony—much like a completed blueprint—to the author's enduring difficulty in fusing structure and materials into a harmonious whole. (p. 234)

New and old, different and the same, ***East of Eden*** relates suggestively, not bindingly, to Steinbeck's postwar fiction and to his earliest efforts to elevate materials into mythology within a functioning structural framework. He is a mature craftsman in ***East of Eden,*** but his grasp of the major aesthetic problem, the harmonious unity of structure and materials, remains as fumbling as ever.

As its title suggests, ***East of Eden*** draws on Steinbeck's moral insight into the biblical story of our most remote (and perhaps mythical) ancestors, Cain and Abel. . . . Steinbeck's insight develops from the fact that we are descended from the murderer, Cain, and only through him from the good brother, Abel. . . . [In] principle and in practice, God presents to Cain and to his heirs the free will to choose between good and evil. This insight is a mutation of Steinbeck's fairly constant interest in the nature of the good life, presented as a mythology in ***East of Eden.***

Steinbeck embodies this ambitious thematic insight in the histories of two families, the Trasks and the Hamiltons. (pp. 235-36)

The essential structural presumption is the necessity of a close, working parallel between the two families. Steinbeck does not provide any structure of this kind. Certain minor, inadequate, or strained parallels occur. Samuel Hamilton's life is happy and Adam Trask's is not; Liza Hamilton has many children, unlike Cathy–Kate Trask, and in old age Liza develops a taste for alcohol, of which only a little is poison to Cathy. . . . These limited, somewhat mechanical parallels are incapable of unifying a novel as massive as ***East of Eden.*** Finally, Steinbeck gives far more attention to Cathy's history outside the Trask family (as Kate) than proportion alone could warrant. (p. 237)

Steinbeck's disregard for structure is so thorough that it may be a "given," not a conscious choice. Certainly there is consistency in Steinbeck's narrative choice to have chronological association substitute for organic form within the two family histories. This consistency prevails in smaller details. Cathy represents evil as Adam represents good, but the pattern is broken at crucial points. . . . [Adam] exists to suffer, but his suffering is so passive that Steinbeck himself—through chiefly Samuel and Lee—must explain its nature. Conversely, as Adam becomes a universal father, given his name and the modern Eden he tries to establish, so Cathy might be expected to become a universal mother, but she does not. Cathy rejects her two sons when they are born, shoots Adam in order to get away from him, reenters whoredom (dyeing her hair black and changing her name to Kate); many years later, she attempts to corrupt Caleb and then Aron. Evidently Cathy–Kate got out of the author's control, thus destroying his minimal order of chronological association. . . . The sense of improvisation cannot be put down, and strongly manipulative devices are obviously required to assert a concluding optimism. The narrative effect is similar to the last third of ***The Grapes of Wrath.***

A lack of organic form is evident in particular aspects of the narrative. For example, Adam Trask's wanderings after his service in the Army relate but remotely to his later "good man" role, and an amusing episode like Olive Hamilton's plane ride has no relationship to plot or theme. Steinbeck's presence may be an intentional means of drawing together the diverse plot elements through explicitly moral essays; if so, the device is a failure. Steinbeck speaks in his own voice in ten interchapters and injects himself into events, often in the role of an interested bystander unaware of the outcome of events. The device recalls ***The Grapes of Wrath,*** but the familiar tone and the sense of personal involvement produce unusual strains on credibility. . . . The image of the working author involved in a direct authorial comment assumes the fiction of an inchoate "time present" in which Steinbeck discovers exactly what the reader sees at the moment. The point is not that Steinbeck is coy or disingenuous (although he is) but that he is willing to manipulate his own persona in the development of the novel. (pp. 238-40)

A similar disregard for a harmonious relationship between structure and materials is evident in the handling of quite minor characters, such as Lee, Abra Bacon, and Samuel Hamilton. . . . Samuel Hamilton is the most striking instance of the lack of organic form in ***East of Eden.*** Samuel is an impressive character, despite some unfortunate language that Steinbeck gives to him. But his roles are split somewhat at random. At first, as an allegorical figure, he exemplifies moral success through economic failure, since he can make all men rich but himself; his joyous and total understanding of good and evil is an end to itself. Later on, Samuel becomes mainly a mystic. . . . In the end, Samuel is transformed into a kind of human divinity or an expression of the divine in man; his last phrase recalls God's language in the Garden of Eden after the Fall ("Here am I"), and the visual imagery is consciously mystical, an identification of man and nature. . . . Unfortunately, the biblical impressiveness and even an appeal to "our Father who art in nature" cannot hide Samuel's ultimate lack of narrative function. Rather, the variety of his roles is evidence of Steinbeck's old fault of structuring a series of immediate, differing effects, not the creation of a unified character. The problem is embarrassing. Steinbeck takes the option of killing off Samuel, his most impressive character, before ***East of Eden*** is half finished.

The two family histories and the minor characters are handled less than lucidly. Just so with the moral philosophy—the *timshel* doctrine. Beyond question, that doctrine of the releasing power of free will is intended to unify ***East of Eden.*** At most it affects events to some extent. Lee's explanation of the doctrine motivates Samuel to tell Adam that Cathy is now Kate and the madam of a whorehouse in Salinas; Adam visits Kate and thus frees himself of her influence. Adam shares with Kate in Charles's estate, according to directions; this association confirms his freedom. (pp. 241-42)

These unities are the results of a literally associational unity—schematic rather than organic—not quite the same as a harmony between structure and materials; and the unity tends to collapse, once its particulars are examined in any detail. The collapse begins with the doctrine itself as Steinbeck presents it.

Steinbeck alters the Cain and Abel story to present the humanitarian notion that good and evil are intermixed in men in order to force individual choice between any specific good or evil. The original story is strained and distorted by the intrusion of an optimism that allows Steinbeck to juggle rather than explore the thematic elements of moral philosophy. A similar optimism is imposed at the conclusion of many of the earlier novels. The difference is that a juggled moral content appears sooner and is more thoroughly woven into the novel's texture in ***East of Eden*** than in any of the earlier novels except the immediately previous work, ***The Wayward Bus*** and ***Burning Bright***. Obviously, the materials must be manipulated in order to take the shape that optimism requires.

The effective means to this end is *timshel,* the controlling allegorical sign. . . . *Timshel* suggests a new reading of the Cain and Abel story, which may be summarized as follows: Cain murders Abel because he feels unloved and rejected by God; that is, he feels that he is evil by nature. Murder is Cain's twisted "good" effort to substitute himself for Abel and perhaps to force a punishment he is certain he deserves in any event. Abel does not murder because he feels loved and accepted by God. But his serenity precludes self-knowledge; he does not have to *find* good, as Cain may, so his dramatic interest is less. By an irony, in this reading, Cain's self-equated guilt and physical ugliness are the index of his real humanity. Abel is too pure to be believably human. (pp. 242-43)

[In] proposing the *timshel* doctrine as the essential key to a harmony between structure and materials, Steinbeck ignores its possibly inherent defects. The doctrine asserts that Cain and Abel symbolize man's eternally divided moral condition. Since this division tends to polarize good and evil, each quality becomes an allegorical absolute, with evil subject to humanitarian modification. A consequent logic produces good from evil: Since evil is man's birthright (we are children of Cain), no one is responsible for personal wrongdoing; thus, free will is negated. In the narrative, this twisted logic permits Caleb's elevation—not development—at the close. Free will is also negated in the sense that Cathy–Kate is born a monster. . . . She is presented from the beginning as an allegorical quality, a representation of pure evil; many of the good characters remark that she is not quite human. However, a brilliant, sustained exercise of "is" thinking images Cathy–Kate's personality and experience through a series of sharply realized details that are entirely convincing. Allegory and "is" thinking allow an enriched, two-level development of the narrative, and the drive of the narrative removes most of the strain of the storyless experiment, ***The Wayward Bus***. Of course, *timshel* does not apply to Cathy–Kate, to the advantage of the narrative. For example, there is little but an allegorical reason for such flatly reported events as Cathy's grim marriage to Adam and her ironic will in Aron's favor, but there is a wealth of precise detail in the presenting of such events as Cathy's murder of her parents, Kate's later murder of Faye, the complicated process that leads to Kate's own suicide, and the suicide itself. "Is" thinking has an organic function here, since the series of closely realized details tend to imply Cathy–Kate's limitation to the material world and her complete divorce from moral claims, humor, and imagination; the very style of "is" thinking corresponds to what Cathy–Kate is and is not. Through this happy use of technique, Steinbeck creates in Cathy–Kate a female character who ranks just below Ma Joad in intensity and conviction. . . . Nonetheless, there is considerable difficulty in defining her function in ***East of Eden***. She is so fully realized that she appears more credible than her structural opposite, Adam, supported though he is by Lee and Samuel. Hence, there is a diminished clarity in the allegorical structure; for so far as Cathy–Kate is proof, within the world of the novel, that a humanitarian solution to the problem of evil is not wholly possible, the novel simply does not work. At the very least, Cathy–Kate's brilliant autonomy is a serious assault on the integrity of the novel as a whole. . . . Death itself lends a comparative moral structure to Cathy–Kate at Adam's expense. She selects the time and manner of her death, gaining an ironic sense of free will; Adam blesses Caleb, but as directed by Lee. In short, the central statement of free will is so qualified in these paralleled events that it cannot have the intended effect of strengthening the triumph of good. Cathy–Kate gets away to that extreme degree, and *timshel* is somewhat muted in the process.

The device of the coincidence of initials, indicating moral divisions and types, is a Steinbeck favorite. Never convincing in itself, the device must be supported by a context to have any effect. Its immediacy can suggest a larger structure which is not there. Perhaps because of these dangers, Steinbeck uses the device sparingly in most of the earlier novels, but it is worked beyond the point of absurdity in ***East of Eden*** and in a context that is not entirely lucid. *C* and *A* alternate as initials throughout the generations of the Trask family to emphasize the permanence of the Cain and Abel story. . . . The device is too trivial to bear that much repetitive weight, especially given the twists of the *timshel* doctrine and the relative lack of control of Cathy–Kate. The device is much too broad to signify much particularized difference between the varying Cain and Abel figures, and its internal incoherence produces more confusion than clarity. (pp. 244-47)

Along with the *timshel* doctrine and the initial device, a third allegorical sign is used to juggle moral philosophy. The associational unity of the scar across the forehead (the mark of Cain which Charles and Cathy share) and the repetition of "Am I my brother's keeper" (which Charles and Caleb share) are merely plot mechanisms, in view of the real differences that separate Charles, Cathy, and Caleb. A gulf functionally divides Cathy–Kate's monstrous nature from the need for love which Charles and Caleb share. The purely mechanical surface is [again] evident. . . . (p. 249)

These devices and parallels preclude a direct exposition of differences in character. The substitution of mechanisms for an organic development constitutes one of the weakest aspects of ***East of Eden***. Character is flattened out; minute particulars conflict; an external determinism prevails.

Even the main allegorical assumptions that seem intended to control values are not always intellectually coherent in ***East of Eden***. For example, the allegorical meaning of Cathy–Kate's suicide and of Aron's willed death in war must be that pure evil and pure good cannot exist in the realized world where good and evil are intermixed. . . . [The] idea that evil results from a frustration of love is repeatedly stated and acted out: Charles's gift to Cyrus, Adam's offer of "Eden" to Cathy, and Caleb's gift to Adam. . . . The point is qualified when evil rises from several other unrelated sources: Cathy–Kate's inborn hatred and greed, the sexual frustration which results in the horrible murder of Lee's mother, and Tom's ignorance which causes Dessie's death. These qualifications cannot be dismissed as the inevitable looseness of a large work, because they cut at the heart of the allegorical structure, and they could be controlled with relative ease within that structure. Hence, they may not be accidents but intentional defects, possibly devised to broaden the scope of the narrative.

This lenient view of faulty structure is less than convincing in view of the fact that a broad thematic element, the function of money, is not given a coherent development. . . . [Moral] excellence is presented as the exact opposite of the possession of worldly wealth. This rather simple contrast is the sum of the morally accepted attitudes toward money. Good characters such as Samuel, Lee, and Adam are happy in relative poverty or are too rich to care about money. Cathy–Kate is the major exception which proves the rule; her lust for money is equated with her will to do evil. Quite flatly, money transactions connote guilt. (pp. 249-51)

The general identification of wealth with evil places the focus of attention on moral excellence, but there is no gain in narrative coherence. For example, Steinbeck manipulates the Cain and Abel theme. Caleb wishes to be a farmer in order to deny his role as Cain (the hunter), but he gains a moderate fortune in wartime speculation in beans (symbolically, from a successful economic hunt). . . . But in contrast, the Cain figure in the earlier generation, Charles, remains a successful farmer all his life. Finally, Adam contradicts his "good man" role by feeling in time that he is the Cain figure. Adam's feeling denies the evidence, but it paradoxically increases his "good" identification by adding humility to his virtues.

Because a Cain-and-Abel allegory requires a Lilith figure and a serpent in Eden, Cathy–Kate is described frequently "in terms of a serpent, from the shape of her features and her flickering tongue to her dislike of the light." . . . These details are coherent, but only in a mechanical sense; the substitution of mechanics for organic form is the primary technique of the play-novelette. What is not mechanical in ***East of Eden*** tends to be incoherent. (pp. 251-52)

The moral treatment of money connects with the moral treatment of knowledge, since all of these instances demonstrate that knowledge is good and creates moral excellence. In contrast, as with the allegorical structure, the separation of knowledge and poverty from ignorance and wealth tends to negate Steinbeck's basic assumption that good and evil are intermixed. Steinbeck lets virtue triumph all too easily, as in the typical instance of Adam Trask. At first Adam is a confused rich man, but Samuel and Lee are artificially "placed" to devote their best insights to fostering Adam's growth of moral sense. . . . Luck seems to govern the pattern. This factor forces the reader to notice that details are presented for the sake of a pattern which rejects them, for the allegory tends to float above the narrative because it has no consistent base, and the narrative tends to move at random because it, too, has no firmly credible base. The abstract theme, "the never-ending contest in ourselves of good and evil," is at odds with the realistic power of the narrative.

Therefore, in Cathy–Kate evil is equated with strength of will and mastery of the material world, while in Adam good is equated with moral weakness and an inability to master the material world. . . . Of course, good and evil are too complex to divide neatly into the extreme opposites of the allegorical pattern that Steinbeck imposes on the materials, evidently to solve the moral paradox that the evil are strong and even fascinating while the humility of the good appears to be a weak indecision. The difficulty is in part technical, since the realistic technique of "is" thinking erodes the moralistic allegory: the difficulty is also in the uncertainty of Steinbeck's hand. The structure and the materials are out of phase. The massive claims of the novel emphasize the massive seriousness of Steinbeck's defective view of harmony in longer fiction.

Still, a peculiar impressiveness survives the organizational failure of the manipulated, superficial devices and parallels. To understand this survival is to comprehend a crucial aspect of the art of fiction.

The *timshel* doctrine enables Steinbeck to broaden an autobiographical kernel into the spiritual autobiography of mankind, of life itself, since all ideas, characters, and events can suggest the vast confusion of life. This is the lasting impression of ***East of Eden.***

A fiction which is purposefully a grab bag of history, which extends the manipulation and simplification of the play-novelette form into the vast range of the prose epic, and which relies on a thematic development to the exclusion of a formal harmony of structure and materials, need not be an artistic failure by definition. Certainly ***East of Eden*** is not simply or merely [a] pandering, best-selling opus. . . . Steinbeck's materials resist a definite structure, but they are not frivolous. . . . The allegorical machinery of snake imagery, moral isolation, and personified evil is too overtly lurid or too qualified to account for Cathy–Kate's "power of blackness" as a fictive creation. Her ugliness is not structured. Instead, Steinbeck creates her in fragments, "moments," even in phrases. . . . [The result of such] "is" thinking is a sharp realization of detail, combined powerfully with structural elements, as in . . . the implicit, metaphorical association of Kate's moral nature with the broken-down house and the wild grounds. In the larger frame, moral darkness is there in the dim lighting; the house is there in terms of a distant, then a close view, then specific imagery ("crumple," "squealed") which suggests ugly age. Kate's depraved helpers and her personal ugliness flow out of this sympathetic context. This account of things seen, implicitly inviting a moral evaluation, does far more to realize what Cathy–Kate *is* than all of the ponderous, sometimes uncontrolled mechanics of the allegory.

Generally, then, what remains impressive in ***East of Eden*** is not the theme (ideas, content, allegory), but specific, detached "moments" of sharp realization—of "is" thinking. The language is observational and precise in those moments, but it is tortured by inversion and inflation in passages where the allegory is most visible. Similarly, the grab bag nature of the novel encourages Steinbeck's skillful concentration on the creation of the sharp particulars of the moment . . . within an allegorical frame which is so loose it does not interpose itself on the memorable images. In brief, ***East of Eden*** is a triumph of "is" thinking and a vehicle for incredible or forced allegorical elements which suggest to the reader that plot need not be taken seriously. It is clear that Steinbeck intended to produce a mythological–allegorical novel, not this interesting effect. The allegorical myth is absurdly reductive, but a number of episodic, sharply realized fragments are impressive in the selection of memory. At worst, the machinery can be accepted on faith, as a fictionally necessary footing for the flashes of image, the intense passages of thereness. This much is enough to maintain a flow of narrative, but not enough to ensure a finished masterpiece, a shapely work of art.

Steinbeck's most sympathetic critics have attempted to praise the structure of ***East of Eden*** or even to explain it away. . . . These critical reactions are not false, but they mark an increasingly strong movement away from novelistic considerations to something like a pure consideration of the value of Steinbeck's content. (pp. 253-57)

[Critical] views strike one balance, namely, that ***East of Eden*** really is the novel Steinbeck had been trying to write from the beginning—a novel that "has in it everything I have been able to learn about my art or craft or profession in all these years." But its limited aesthetic conviction, combined with its mature certainty, point a pronounced direction in Steinbeck's career, which is pursued at a further extreme in the succeeding three novels.

This conclusion alters the frequently stated assumption that versatility is evidence of Steinbeck's lack of direction. On the contrary, ***East of Eden*** really is the capstone, the mature summation of Steinbeck's great abilities and failings, and thus an illustration of the art of the novel as Steinbeck sees that art in the perspective of his long career. ***East of Eden*** has every element that is characteristic of Steinbeck's impressive but flawed art. . . . Not surprisingly, then, the impressive aspects of ***East of Eden*** are its narrative power and its strong characterizations, but its negative aspects are a deadening counterweight which qualifies all but the most blindly favorable critical judgment. Indeed, ***East of Eden*** is utterly characteristic: an admirably massive, essentially flawed narrative. Critical judgment has an easier time with the simple extremes of the good novel or the bad novel. Steinbeck's great effort lies between these poles, and there a critical judgment must take its abode if it is to be at all accurate. (pp. 257-58)

Howard Levant, in his The Novels of John Steinbeck: A Critical Study, *University of Missouri Press, 1974, 304 p.*

DANIEL BUERGER

My purpose here is to provide a brief history of the critical response to ***East of Eden,*** to outline the major patterns and trends in our perception of what Steinbeck thought was the most important work of his career. . . . But the conception of "history" involved in this undertaking is far more problematic than it appears on the surface, for it assumes that there are discernible, empirical "facts" which exist in an unchanging reality. It assumes that the critic/historian *finds* the truth revealed in these facts, and, as a scientific, objective historian, mirrors that inherent truth. What I wish to suggest is that in the late twentieth century this is impossible. Modern historiography has begun to recognize that even a list of historical events partakes of the narrative mode, and thereby becomes a literary artifact, a form of poem. An overview of ***East of Eden*** criticism is not a discovery of pre-existent patterns; it is rather the historian's subjective conception of critical responses which are in themselves subjective re-creations of the work and the man who wrote it. (p. 6)

I preface my remarks with these notions not because I wish to stress the relativism of modern criticism, but because it seems to me that the problem of the translation of fact into history, especially history conceived in narrative form and presented in a work of fiction, is at the core of our critical problems with ***East of Eden.*** Steinbeck criticism, for the most part, has failed to examine the man's works of art as art. It has attempted to discover the man behind the author, including his friends and family, to recover the socio-economic philosophy exhibited, and to uncover the world-view revealed in the writings. All of this is important in its own way for interpreting the literary material, and has produced numerous extremely valuable insights. Nevertheless, it is also incumbent upon us that we approach fiction as fiction, that we see the aesthetic artifact for what it is, before we turn it into pseudo-sociology or metaphilosophy. This may seem to be a statement of the obvious, but a survey of ***East of Eden*** criticism shows that art has rarely been the primary concern of Steinbeck scholars.

Ever since the novel first appeared in September 1952, critics have been puzzled by the book, usually concentrating on one or two of three major elements: (1) the moral theme of *timshel,* (2) the manifestation of the Cain and Abel types in the various characters, and (3) the juxtaposition of the Trask and Hamilton story lines. Most first reviewers were upset by what they read because it either didn't fit their preconceptions of a believable, realistic novel, or their preconceptions of Steinbeck as a social critic and regional humorist. From their perspective, the *timshel* concept was "a tissue of platitude and tinsel rhetoric." The Cain and Abel characters were melodramatic types, neither clear nor credible, especially Kate, who was the central focus in review after review. Clifton Fadiman called her "the book's center—perhaps the wickedest woman in the world's fiction." And the mingling of the "fictional" Trasks with the "factual" family history usually was seen as a confusing failure, even irrelevant: one reviewer wrote that the "family chronicle is as dull as anybody talking about his ancestors when their doings seem to have no relation to the story."

The general response was negative, though some praised the power of the purely dramatic sequences. There were exceptions to this general view: one was Mark Schorer's [see *CLC,* Vol. 21]. . . . Schorer understandably stressed the roles of the narrator and the Hamiltons in the artistry of the novel, and decided it was Steinbeck's best novel. Schorer's excellent but necessarily cursory insights generated by this approach to the novel were abandoned until the 1970s, primarily because of Peter Lisca's major critical study in 1958.

Students of Steinbeck owe a tremendous debt to Lisca's *The Wide World of John Steinbeck* [see excerpt above] . . . , for this book helped more than any other to establish a serious literary reputation for Steinbeck. However, it has been a disaster as far as ***East of Eden*** is concerned, for Lisca's unmitigated hatred of the novel has dominated almost all subsequent analyses of it, and indeed, of most of Steinbeck's later work. Lisca lambastes the moral theme as unconvincing, obvious, and uninteresting. More importantly, he insists that the structure of the book is seriously flawed, probably due to Steinbeck's method of composition. In his words, the Trasks and the Hamiltons "pursue separate courses, and nothing *results* from their juxtaposition" . . . ; the novel simply shifts back and forth between the two families with no apparent purpose or method, resulting in awkward flashbacks and distracting fragments. Lisca insists that the first person narrator is plainly a vestigial element from the first draft of the book and has no significant effect other than to interlard the objectively rendered Trask plot with moral essays and to disrupt the novel. Furthermore, Lisca proudly proclaims that Schorer had recanted his earlier praise of ***East of Eden*** . . . and singles out for analysis the favorable reviews of both Schorer [see *CLC,* Vol. 21] and Joseph Wood Krutch [see excerpt above] . . . as evidence of "a certain ambivalence which is an accurate index to the peculiar effect of Steinbeck's novel." (pp. 6-8)

Thus, within a few years after the novel appeared, the *gestalt* of ***East of Eden*** criticism was set, and R.W.B. Lewis could pronounce the novel "a literary disaster, and of such proportions that it sheds a very disturbing light on the career that has allegedly culminated in it." By the end of the 1950s, the book was perceived as a sloppy failure and a symbol of Steinbeck's decline after World War II; he was only an image and shadow of the divine writer he once was.

In the last two decades the critical debate over ***East of Eden*** has focused on the same elements singled out by the first reviews. In addition, most of the major critics have developed their arguments in the prescriptive framework of their own critical biases. Often these studies do inform us about particular aspects of the novel; yet the conclusions reached about the book as a work of art are usually repetitions or variations on Lisca's view. Joseph Fontenrose, for example [see excerpt above], clarifies Steinbeck's use of the Biblical myth, but, without fully examining the structural presentation of events, asserts that "the myth invoked doesn't adequately interpret the narrated events." Fontenrose analyzes the *timshel* theme as if it were part of a theological tract, and, of course, finds it wanting.

With Lisca and Fontenrose, Warren French has made invaluable contributions to the significant re-assessment of Steinbeck's overall reputation which took place between 1957 and 1963. And like them, French has found ***East of Eden*** lacking. In his first book on Steinbeck, published in 1961 [see *CLC*, Vol. 1], French called the novel a "patchwork leviathan" and compared it unfavorably to *Moby-Dick,* in which Steinbeck's Cathy became a pale echo of Melville's Ahab. French concluded his brief section on ***East of Eden*** by directing readers to Lisca's discussion of the novel in *The Wide World of John Steinbeck*. In his revised and rewritten version, published fourteen years later, French still accepts the standard theory that the post-war work reveals a dramatic decline, and uses the novel to prove his thesis that the shift from Realism to what he calls "Dramas of Consciousness" precipitated that decline. Despite his unique emphasis on ***East of Eden*** as a "cosmogony," and his realization of the fictive intentions of Steinbeck's art, French charges that the Trask-Hamilton stories clash because the self-conscious Hamiltons are believable, sympathetic, and familiar (though uninteresting), while the Trasks are incredible and thoroughly nasty and priggish. French maintains that "biography" and "fiction" in ***East of Eden*** cannot be distinguished, with the result that the control necessary to provide a philosophical framework is missing.

In 1974 Howard Levant published the first significant study of Steinbeck's aesthetic achievement, concentrating on the relationships between structure and material in the works [see excerpt above]. As valuable as Levant's criticism is in many instances, however, it does not fulfill our expectations when dealing with ***East of Eden.*** Levant's reductive thesis that there are only two types of structure in fiction, the panoramic and the dramatic, dominates his analysis and forces the conclusion that the novel is an impressive but greatly flawed work because it does not fuse structure and materials into a harmonious whole. The Trask and Hamilton stories are merely paralleled versions of a moral story and a factual story, the one imposed on the other to the utter destruction of organic form. Levant speculates that the presence of "Steinbeck" in the narrative may be an attempt to draw the diverse plot elements together, but, if so, it is a failure. Finally, he maintains that ***East of Eden*** is an example of "is" thinking upon which incredible or forced allegorical elements have been imposed. (pp. 8-10)

[Critics now] seem to be on the verge of a complete reevaluation of Steinbeck's early and late phases. This radical revision of Steinbeck's achievement, especially in ***East of Eden,*** was foreshadowed in Lester Marks' *Thematic Design in the Novels of John Steinbeck* . . . , in which Lisca's received notions are carefully examined and, for the first time, critical emphasis is placed on the work as fiction rather than autobiography. As a result, Marks finds coherence in the themes, artistic control of the structure, and no proof that the narrator is anything other than a part of the fictional construct.

In 1973 Lawrence William Jones broke even further from the phalanx order of Steinbeck scholars and, using the scholarship of contemporary American criticism . . . , made a case for Steinbeck as a fabulist. Jones argues that ***East of Eden*** is a romance, a form of "open parable," in which the reality presented is "primarily of the mind." Further, he insists that we recognize the experimental nature of Steinbeck's work in the light of post-modern critical theory, rather than as part of the older traditions of Naturalism and Realism. (p. 10)

This exciting shift in critical scrutiny of the early and late Steinbeck takes us back to my comments at the beginning of my discussion. The use of fable in post-modern American literature is a rebellion against the notions of fictional propriety derived from versions of realism which no longer suffice. . . . Just as nineteenth-century Realism grew out of positivism, fabulation, which sees that attempts to signify the truth are relative, does not turn away from reality, but attempts to find more subtle correspondences between the reality which is fiction and the fiction which is reality. One only has to recall the controversial passage in Chapter 17 of ***East of Eden,*** in which the narrator meditates upon the conception of Kate, in order to see the new perceptions available to us when we view Steinbeck in this light:

> When I said Cathy was a monster it seemed to me that it was so. Now I have bent close with a glass over the small print of her and reread the footnotes, and I wonder if it was true. The trouble is that since we cannot know what she wanted, we will never know whether or not she got it. If rather than running toward something, she ran away from something, we can't know whether she escaped. Who knows. . . .

This is not what Lisca calls an example of "the irresolute, arbitrarily changing function of the narrator and the nature of his voice," for Lisca assumes it is lack of craftsmanship which causes the irresolution, rather than a conscious aesthetic response within Steinbeck's developing post-modern world-view. Again and again the narrator of ***East of Eden*** qualifies his moralisms and assertions with "I do not know," or disclaimers which demonstrate that all knowing is tentative. . . .

When we consider ***East of Eden*** in terms of post-modern literary criticism, therefore, we can begin to understand that calling the narrator "intrusive" or the characters "incredible" is an inaccurate response to what Steinbeck was attempting to do. To split the novel into fiction (the Trasks) and fact (the Hamiltons) is to assume that what Franz Stanzel has called the "authorial narrator" is simply identical with the personality of the author. . . . This authorial narrator is Steinbeck's romantic alter ego, who, like so many post-modern narrators, is fundamentally concerned with the process of writing. The hero of ***East of Eden*** is the Romantic "I" narrator, not Adam, or Sam, or Cal, and it is through this persona that the author defines and recreates his history and, thereby, himself. The shape of such fiction, however, is imposed by the author upon the chaos of experience; he does not discover pre-existent *gestalten,* but creates a pattern where there was none before. (pp. 11-12)

The groundwork for a positive reinterpretation of Steinbeck's relationship to Modernism, and his role as a transitional figure in the shift from Modernism to post-Modernism was the subject of a long and provocative essay by Warren French, who admitted a broader scheme is necessary than the opposition between Naturalism and Drama of Consciousness he had presented in his revised *John Steinbeck*. But the place ***East of Eden*** occupies in French's new alignment is still minimal, and we have to look to several other recent critics for consideration of the abiding precepts behind Steinbeck's shaping imagination. . . . [It is now] appropriate that [Paul McCarthy's study (see *CLC*, Vol. 21)] treats the novel without condescension as a product of "the elusive and challenging forms of romance."

But even given the fact that a more tolerant and sympathetic awareness is operative in recent Steinbeck studies, there are numerous elements of his art which demand further investigation. If we are to take the full measure of ***East of Eden***'s worth, we need a thorough study of its fabular structure, including an analysis of the fictive narrative voice. Such a study would lead to re-evaluations of ***The Winter of Our Discontent,*** with its extremely self-reflexive mode; of ***Travels With Charley,*** with its transformation of "fact" into fable; and of ***Once There Was a War,*** with a preface which overtly recognizes (even if belatedly) the fabulation involved in the work: "Once upon a time." We need to know the extent and depth of possible Romantic influences like Byron's *Cain* and Melville's *Moby-Dick,* as well as contemporary influences. . . . A study of Steinbeck's use of the cyclical and past-oriented concept of history in Hellenic writings would balance the totally one-sided, linear view of Judeo-Christian time which we now use to scrutinize Steinbeck's work. We also need a more thorough understanding of Steinbeck's war experiences and the aesthetic use to which he put them, especially since ***East of Eden*** is framed by wars and ***Winter*** uses the metaphor of war in extremely significant ways. Finally, I think we need a critic who is competent in music theory (and perhaps Structuralism) to analyze precisely the way Steinbeck used musical counterpoint, tempo, and rhythm in constructing ***East of Eden.*** (pp. 12-13)

We should no longer be content to see Steinbeck as an unchanging artist caught in the slowly-evaporating tide pool of the realistic/naturalistic tradition. . . . As John Gardner has put it, "metaphysical systems do not, generally speaking, break down, shattered by later, keener insight; they are simply abandoned." (p. 14)

Daniel Buerger, "'History' and Fiction in 'East of Eden' Criticism" in Steinbeck Quarterly, *Vol. XIV, Nos. 1 & 2, Winter & Spring, 1981, pp. 6-14.*

JOHN H. TIMMERMAN

In public and critical perception, ***The Grapes of Wrath*** has always been Steinbeck's "big" novel; for Steinbeck it was ***East of Eden.*** While the former was a novel that nearly possessed him, and sucked him physically and emotionally dry in the fevered writing, the latter was a novel that he nurtured, in his own words, all of his life and that seemed to grow with him until the time of writing was at hand. (p. 210)

Of no other work had Steinbeck spoken with such persistent fondness, and several factors account for his feeling. Nearly all of Steinbeck's work arises out of his own peculiar experience, and the stories are of people and places Steinbeck knew. The further Steinbeck moved from this spring of personal experience that nourished his work, the less successful his work was. The strictly cerebral works such as ***The Short Reign of Pippin IV*** lack the compelling quality that fascinates a reader. ***East of Eden*** is unique among the works based on Steinbeck's life experience because it is, in part, the story closest to him—his own. And it is the only story in which he enters directly as a character. (p. 211)

Despite the careful structuring and labor Steinbeck gave [***East of Eden***], it has met with little critical respect. Critics have objected to the presence of the first-person narrator as an intrusion. They have condemned the sprawling nature of the narrative. Perhaps the most detailed such criticism is given by Peter Lisca [see excerpt above], who calls into question everything from the novel's structure to the author's confusion on the question of free will. But Lisca's deepest criticism is reserved for the rhetoric: "The scrambled syntax and awkward expression are evident everywhere," and "Steinbeck's prose is not so much casual or careless as affected." The redeeming quality of the novel for Lisca is the successful presentation of the

> minor characters and of his maternal family—excepting Samuel Hamilton, who is nevertheless more credible and effective than any of the other major characters. . . .

In the twenty years between the publication of his *The Wide World of John Steinbeck* and his later study *John Steinbeck: Nature and Myth,* Lisca moderated neither his views nor his tone toward ***East of Eden.*** The work remains for him a failure. (p. 215)

The negative comments about stylistic lapses and ethical confusion have been persistent and significant in any critical consideration of the novel. Yet aside from what the novel may fail to do, there is considerable value in what it does—its response to earlier themes, its grappling with the problem of good and evil, its profound insights into human nature and human aspirations, and its potent character portraits. (p. 217)

The question remains, then, in critical appraisal of ***East of Eden:*** Is there a structural and thematic core to the novel that roots the whole in the groundwork of the artist's technique and vision? The response lies in the very character whom critics fault as the most flawed, thematically ambiguous, and structurally unassembled in the novel, Cathy Ames. My first intention in this chapter is to examine Cathy Ames's role as thematic and structural center of the novel. The novel is also, however, Steinbeck's rendition of a contemporary *Paradise Lost,* one in which Cathy is the seducer east of Eden. My second intention is to examine the relationship of several other characters to Cathy on the issue of good and evil. The result, I believe, is to demonstrate that Steinbeck possessed a far clearer perception of structural unity and of moral theme in this novel than has been commonly assumed. (pp. 217-18)

Steinbeck often probed the violence that seemed poised just on the other side of love. Early examples may be Elisa of **"The Chrysanthemums,"** Peter Randall of **"The Harness,"** Tularecito of ***The Pastures of Heaven,*** and George and Lennie in ***Of Mice and Men.*** Cathy is a focus in the same way. From his earliest conception of her Cathy was a figure of evil to Steinbeck, but one in relation to whom other characters find their own good or evil. I believe this also explains the ambiguity of good and evil which Fontenrose finds in the novel [see excerpt above], for the fact is that everyone reacts to evil in a different way and with varying degrees of attraction or repulsion.

As Steinbeck describes her, Cathy is a monster, devoid of moral sensibility. . . . While it is questionable how and when Cathy's role developed in the novel, it is clear that from the earliest stages Steinbeck conceived of the novel as a moral statement, and Cathy came to serve as the pivot around which other characters discover their own "story of good and evil, of strength and weakness of love and hate, of beauty and ugliness." Cathy provides a kind of diabolical backdrop for all such discoveries, and if these discoveries are not clearly categorical, as Fontenrose suggests, it is simply because for Steinbeck there are few such clear categories in anyone's life. Yet he works from this fundamental premise: evil is an inward force that sucks all things into itself in order to feed and perpetuate itself, and therefore evil is essentially destructive; good, on the other hand, is always open to life, is outwardly directed and altruistic. (pp. 218-19)

[Cathy's evil is] the evil of lovelessness: instead of affirming life, she perverts and bends life to her darkness. Steinbeck introduces Cathy as a monster (chapter 8), a statement he partly retracts later in the novel (chapter 17). Yet she is and remains a monster for two reasons. First, she bends and twists life: "Some balance wheel was misweighted, some gear out of ratio." Second, she debases sexuality, and in Steinbeck's fiction human sexuality is always a sign of robust vigor and energetic life. . . . The sexual weapon that Cathy wields wounds everyone in the novel.

Cathy's moral monstrousness is enforced consistently in two important stylistic ways throughout the novel. In keeping with Steinbeck's biblical use of the Eden story, Cathy is consistently presented in the serpent imagery of Satan who lured Adam and Eve into the transgression that drove them out of Eden. She is attractive, and the lure of the serpent in Genesis is attractiveness—the fruit of the tree "was a delight to the eyes, and that the tree was to be desired." She is subtly described when she takes over Faye's whorehouse as knowing the secrets of men. The serpent is described as "more subtle than any other wild creature that the Lord God had made." Cathy is subtly adept, Adam Trask discovers, in using "all the sad, weak parts of a man." (pp. 219-20)

Complementary to the distinguishing snake imagery, Steinbeck develops a second pattern of light and dark imagery, employed often in his fiction with both psychological and spiritual significance. In the opening chapter of ***East of Eden*** the Salinas Valley is depicted as a place caught tensely between light and dark, life and death, good and evil. . . . It is in keeping with Cathy's character that she retreats to the dark. Her excursions into light become more infrequent. At Adam's ranch she already huddles in the deep shadows as if afraid of the light, and Adam, tragically, believes that all his labor is for her: "I'm going to make a garden so good, so beautiful, that it will be a proper place for her to live and a fitting place for her light to shine on." . . . Instead, Cathy brings darkness like a storm of night upon the ranch. (pp. 222-23)

Cathy's retreat into darkness accompanies her retreat into evil. This narrowing isolation is the curse of evil, a violation of every life-loving principle of Steinbeck's from the relational vision of ***Sea of Cortez,*** the "fambly of man" theme of ***The Grapes of Wrath,*** and the "song of the family" of ***The Pearl***. . . .

The pattern of isolation, darkness, and evil intensifies when Cathy takes over Faye's whorehouse. At first she incubates her evil from Faye's old room, and then, as if narrowing and hardening, or, perhaps, as if slinking into her serpent's den, she has a small, windowless lean-to attached to the room. The room is decorated in gray, as if a miasmal cloud hung there: "Indeed the gray walls seemed to suck up the light and destroy it." . . . She is a thing of abject and thorough darkness now, reduced to a predatory animal lurking in her den. . . . (p. 223)

In artistic terms Cathy Ames is a compellingly complex character who goes beyond the biblical Satan archetype and the respawning evil associated with light and dark imagery. She also clearly resembles the *belle dame sans merci*. Given Steinbeck's strong and lifelong attraction to medieval literature, it is not particularly surprising to find the *belle dame* here in relation to Cathy Ames, and also the Morgan Le Fay figure from Arthurian literature. But the Romantic counterpart of the Lamia figure, the dream goddess who destroys those who dare dream of her, also figures prominently in the character of Cathy Ames. One finds the clearest parallel in Keats's work, where the Lamia figure is depicted in snake imagery and functions symbolically as the dream goddess, the deluder, and the sexual tormentor. In each of Keats's three *belle dame* poems, "The Eve of St. Agnes," "Lamia," and "Isabella," the parallelism holds. It is interesting, furthermore, how Keats frames the figure in light-dark imagery as Steinbeck does Cathy's figure in ***East of Eden***. . . . Keats's "Lamia" focuses almost exclusively on the delusive dream in which the serpent is perceived as the lovely goddess. . . . As Keats's Lycius suddenly fears his master Apollonius, "my trusty guide / And good instructor; but to-night he seems / The ghost of folly haunting my sweet dreams," Adam Trask's dream is "haunted" by the clear realism of [his grandfather] Samuel Hamilton. Samuel points out to Adam that he has only worshiped a dream Cathy and has never seen the reality of the destroyer behind her fair appearance. . . . (pp. 224-25)

While it is the case that Cathy Ames's self-destructive and all-consuming evil is the negative pole in relation to which we understand the good and evil of other characters, Steinbeck provides a context for this understanding in the changes in modern civilization itself. This is the external backdrop that also structures the novel. Steinbeck believed that modern civilization was in a process of devolution fairly similar to the narrowing of Cathy Ames. It is impossible to say when civilization reached an apex for Steinbeck . . . , but it is clear that he saw modern civilization as threatening the spirit of man and the individual creative consciousness. The intercalary chapters of the novel evoke that threat as surely as they did in ***The Grapes of Wrath,*** with the exception that here they are general and wide-ranging, like a vast curtain of events against which the Trasks and Hamiltons work out their particular story, while in ***The Grapes of Wrath*** the intercalary chapters always focus sharply and urgently on the narration and the immediacy of the Okie migration. That external world of ***East of Eden*** is vast and fairly amorphous in its generalized threat, yet it parallels the narrower struggle captured in the narrative. In part two of the novel Steinbeck introduces the movement from the narrative world of the Salinas Valley to the world at large. . . . Like the press and urgency of the narrative struggle with good and evil, that larger external world explodes from a general moral malaise to the viciousness of world war. When Steinbeck introduces part four with his reflection that "humans are caught—in their lives, in their thoughts, in their hungers and ambitions, in their avarice and cruelty, and in their kindness and generosity too—in a net of good and evil," . . . the two stories, narrative and intercalary, have merged. The diabolical nature of Cathy is counterpart to the diabolism of world war. Aron flees one for the other but is destroyed by both, psychologically in the Salinas Valley and physically in combat. (pp. 227-28)

Within the narrative account Cathy is the pivot of the other characters' lives, for there is a part of Cathy—or her essentially evil nature—in every man, according to Steinbeck: "Nearly everyone in the world has appetites and impulses, trigger emotions, islands of selfishness, lusts just beneath the surface. . . . Everyone concealed that little hell in himself, while publicly pretending it did not exist." . . . The narrative plot is the process of characters discovering that nature and dealing with it. (pp. 228-29)

In many ways, surely more than the mere structural link of the twice-rejected offering, Caleb's character runs parallel to Charles's character. Both feel some inward alliance with Cathy. Both confront their own inward evil. But their responses to that confrontation differ. To appreciate fully Caleb's ability to achieve psychological balance in relation to Cathy, consider first the effort of Charles.

When Cathy crawls up to the Trask farm after her beating by Edwards, she immediately recognizes Adam as the one she can manipulate . . . but she is fearful of [his brother] Charles. Why? When Charles calls her a devil, Cathy says to him in sardonic rejoinder, "That makes two of us." But she is also frightened of Charles because, as she believes, "If he had recognized her, so had she recognized him. He was the only person she had ever met who played it her way." . . . Without exception, reactions of fear govern Cathy's actions; she is a predatory animal in that sense, always conniving and striking out when threatened. But this is not the case with Charles. Something of Cathy is indeed recognizable in him; but his violence is of a different nature and gains definition and clarity in relation to her.

Charles's violence is triggered by jealousy, evidenced most clearly in the gift his father rejects. In reaction Charles beats Adam and later returns with an ax to kill him. Charles is a violent person; he would have killed Adam had he found him. But he did not, and he does feel remorse for his act. . . . When Adam returns [from the army], Charles tries to establish some reconciliation. But it proves impossible; he is a man set apart by his own psychological horror, and the Cain scar that he receives sets him apart. The biblical mark of Cain, however, functions not so much as a mark of sin as a mark of protection. When Cain was filled with remorse upon slaying Abel (as Charles feels remorse at being rejected by his father and beating Adam), he is driven from the company of men, and the Lord lays the mark of protection upon him. . . . Charles also lives in isolation on his land of Nod, tilling the earth alone, protected by his alien status against his own violent nature.

Clearly, Charles's violent nature is qualitatively different from Cathy's. Charles feels remorse, while Cathy never does. Charles is able to control his violent nature by his separation, while Cathy deliberately inflicts her evil on the men she lures to her whorehouse. An ironic parallel prevails here: Charles regularly visits a whorehouse to "relieve" himself—but this Steinbeck accepts as a normal and even healthy thing. Cathy, on the other hand, runs a whorehouse that debases and perverts man's sexual urge. . . . [While] Cathy becomes the monstrous, conscienceless animal Kate, Charles sets himself apart from humanity because of the pain of his conscience. There is some of Kate in him, surely—as Steinbeck said, "She is a little piece of the monster in all of us," . . .—but what we do with the monster in all of us, whether we attempt to order it as Charles does, or whether we allow it to devour us as Kate does, is the essential tension of ***East of Eden.*** (pp. 232-34)

With [Cathy's son] Caleb it seems that the Edenic cycle is revisited, but Adam's ranch is a devastated Eden in which his Eve is in fact the destructive serpent. The lush land lies fallow as the sons [Aron and Caleb] grow nameless. Yet Steinbeck reminded himself while writing these passages that "although East of Eden is not Eden, it is not insuperably far away." . . . The story of Caleb is the story of this discovery, a story of reclamation by discovery both of what he is and what he is not. Caleb forms a new principle, a psychological and social ordering principle as opposed to Charles's isolation. . . . [Caleb must] achieve his own psychological order in relation to the novel's pivotal figure—Cathy.

Caleb's struggle to achieve psychological balance occurs in two phases: the first in his relation to Aron and Adam, the second in relation to his mother, Cathy, and his biological father, Charles. The first phase seems a near repetition of Charles's uncontrollable anger, as the boys grow up in a devastated and disordered Eden in which "laid-out vegetable gardens rioted with weeds." . . . When Caleb receives his first knowledge of Cathy, he wields it insinuatingly like thrusts of a weapon to hurt Aron, but always his cruelty is followed by remorse. . . . [When] Caleb discovers himself with a power to cause confusion and helplessness–the same power that Cathy so malevolently uses—Aron says to him: "I'd like to know *why* you do it." . . . Flayed by Aron's simple bewilderment, Cal intuitively feels sullied, and he loathes it: "A pain pierced Cal's heart. His planning suddenly seemed mean and dirty to him. He knew that his brother had found him out. And he felt a longing for Aron to love him." (pp. 234-35)

In discovering what to do, Caleb is granted the benefactor that Charles never had, the patient servant, Lee. Lee teaches him that the first step toward controlling evil is to confront it and control it within oneself. . . . [One] must also know oneself by openly and honestly confronting the truth. This belief, which Steinbeck held throughout his career, at once forms both the thematic foundation and also the psychological foundation of the novel. (pp. 235-36)

This belief in seeing the true thing as it is, and seeing it whole in its life environment also undergirds Lee's *timshel* doctrine, for there is no "thou mayest" unless the truth is first confronted. Guided by that premise, Samuel dares to tell Adam the truth about Cathy; and also by that premise, stumbled on in his own way, Caleb dares to confront the truth about his mother. Only at that point can he begin to dominate and order his own psychological nature. . . .

[Caleb says of Cathy], "I hate her because I know why she went away. I know—because I've got her in me." . . . But Caleb's claim thoroughly controverts Lee's *timshel* doctrine: each person is his own person; only the free, independent individual is also free to excercise choice. This, finally, Caleb also realizes when he confronts his mother. . . . (p. 236)

Having confronted the truth about Cathy, and thereby also having discovered the truth about himself, Caleb tries to order the devastated Eden about him. He speculates in the bean crop, is successful, and gives his father the offering that Adam so brutally rejects. For a time hatred descends in a blind rage; Caleb's world narrows. . . . In his lust to hurt, Caleb takes Aron to the source of hurt, his whore-mother Kate.

The violence remains in Caleb, as it always will and as it always did with Charles, standing side by side with bitter remorse. There is no purgation for that violence, but one may learn, as Horace Quinn learned to establish social equilibrium, to hold good and evil in social balance, to confront the truth of evil's presence and control it by choices. Caleb burns the $15,000 as testimony to his freedom to choose, a sacrifice that frees the power of his psychological control. This is not a desperate act but a controlled and freely chosen one granting him psychological serenity. In a sense, he has grown up. . . . Only the truth can set him free, and this truth, this recognition of his own capacity for evil, his confrontation with it, and his willingness to master it by free choices, does set Caleb free. (pp. 237-38)

[Samuel Hamilton] seems to represent a life that lies in direct opposition to Cathy. While her world devolves inward in a hideous cyclone, Samuel's life always radiates outward. If he has a fault—and Samuel himself would list many—it is that he thinks too seldom of himself. . . . Because he has steeped himself in humanity, Samuel ranks as one of Steinbeck's most eminent heroes. Although his narrative presence in ***East of Eden*** is relatively brief, that presence hovers like a benedictory spirit over all the action. He shows a way a person might go, and be the better for having gone that way. (pp. 242-43)

The first time Adam meets him, Samuel is described as a "patriarch," but perhaps it would be more accurate to call him a prophet. As a lover of light and goodness and natural urges, he divides the valley into the high, arid, sun-washed hills, and the verdant lushness below. But Samuel feels a darkness descending upon that valley. . . . The feeling is made specific and concrete when he first meets Cathy: as if they were antipodes of each other, each intuits the spiritual chasm between them. While in Cathy this intuition stirs a kind of predatory withdrawal, in Samuel it evokes a profound sadness.

Samuel functions thematically in the novel as a life bringer, an antithesis to Cathy, and one who immediately intuits her diabolical otherness. . . . Samuel is human—subject to fear when he enters Cathy's den to deliver her babies; subject to emotions when he tells her bluntly, "I don't like you"; subject to pain when he suffers the sting of her evil; subject to hard anger when he threatens Adam at the naming of the twins. . . . Yet somehow in his very humanity, full and overflowing, he represents a presence that gives guidance and direction. (pp. 243-44)

In the first portrait the reader sees of Samuel, he is pictured as the gray-bearded patriarch, full of humor, yet a leader of the people; in the final portrait he is imaged as the prophet. Lee sees "old Samuel against the sky, his white hair shining with starlight," while Doxology stumbles over the ridge of a hill. It is an overt but apt image and thoroughly consistent with Steinbeck's design for the character. If Cathy is the measure of man's capacity for evil, Samuel is the measure of man's spirit to endure and to work a good work. If Steinbeck saw a bit of Cathy in all human beings, it is clear that he also sees the possibility of Samuel in all humans. (pp. 245-46)

The heart of ***East of Eden,*** and it is a black and perverse heart, is Cathy Ames. She represents a dark force unleashed in the world, a dark principle in relation to which other characters must order their lives. There are many small stories—that of Olive Hamilton; that of Tom and Dessie, which Steinbeck described as a "dreadful and beautiful story"; those of Aron Trask, Will Hamilton, Joe Valery, Ethel, Abra Bacon. But none of these, finally, are separable from Cathy, and each attains thematic clarity when understood in relation to her. She is the pivot for Steinbeck's moral vision; the actions of the characters in relation to her represent his answers to her and the articulation of his moral vision. (p. 247)

John H. Timmerman, in his John Steinbeck's Fiction: The Aesthetics of the Road Taken, *University of Oklahoma Press, 1986, 314 p.*

Elizabeth (Ann) Tallent

1954-

© 1987 Allan Timuss

American short story writer, novelist, and critic.

Tallent writes technically refined, richly detailed fiction in which she examines the difficulties of maintaining human relationships. Her characters are usually young men and women employed in such esoteric professions as anthropology, art, archaeology, and astronomy who often feel alienated from others and attempt to reorder their disappointing lives. While some critics fault her fiction for lacking thematic depth and for the similarities of her characterizations, others praise her exacting eye for detail, her evocative descriptions, and the impeccable craftsmanship of her prose.

In the stories collected in her first book of fiction, *In Constant Flight* (1983), many of which originally appeared in the *New Yorker,* Tallent evokes poignant images rather than developing plot or analyzing behavior. Her use of precise visual details results in a series of related scenes through which she documents the emotional difficulties faced by her characters. Tallent's novel, *Museum Pieces* (1985), explores the effects of a couple's separation and their attempts to restructure their lives. Tallent also focuses upon the struggle of the couple's teenage daughter to establish her place amid her parents' new relationships. While some critics considered *Museum Pieces* lacking in complexity, others lauded Tallent's accurate description of her New Mexico setting and her authentic reproductions of southwestern adolescent and adult idioms, as well as her technical skill and the poetic quality of her writing. Tallent has also published a critical study, *Married Men and Magic Tricks: John Updike's Erotic Heroes* (1982).

(See also *Contemporary Authors,* Vol. 117.)

ANATOLE BROYARD

In some of the 11 stories in [***In Constant Flight***], Elizabeth Tallent tries one's patience. There's a woman lying on a rubber raft, for example, watching her lover skim stones across the water. "It is hard to tell," she muses, "how often a stone will touch the water before it sinks." Another woman says, "My knees are cold, and I have been drinking Pinot Noir."

I can't imagine a situation in which either of those sentences could do any good. Nor do I find it easy to warm up to a man who works as a mind reader, or to a used-car salesman who walks around on stilts inside a huge, authentic-looking iguanodon costume. I can't find much common ground with a young woman who is an ice skater in a traveling show, or another woman who goes to Peru to direct a provincial dance company. I feel instinctively that Miss Tallent is trying too hard to pry her characters away from the ordinary.

On the other hand, she can make you think with some of her effects. Her couples, for example, get along in what I can only call a contrapuntal way, and after a while I began to feel that this is perhaps how we are meant to be together—at cross purposes, instead of chiming in the way the manuals urge us to. . . .

Though they don't say much, Miss Tallent's characters often seem to be on the brink of epiphany. They hang there, like people standing, unmoving, at the top of a flight of stairs. And when they do achieve epiphany, it is one "without concrete associations," as Harold Rosenberg said of Barnett Newman's paintings. They are charged with unidentifiable emotions, and if everything else is neatly in place, it can be a pleasant game to try to put a name to these emotions.

Sometimes the nonhuman world takes over the stories of ***In Constant Flight,*** and people function rather like landscapes, or nature. One story is about swans, another about a bird of paradise, another about a dog. In one piece, a man calls his wife from a taxidermist's to tell her that he wants a divorce. A woman's mother says, "Roses have become my whole life." Miss Tallent is reminding us that we are only a small part of the forces in the world and that we mustn't take ourselves too seriously.

If you're after nice metaphors, you have to take chances. When a woman calls an undertaker to discuss the question of which perfume to put on her dead mother, this could come off either as cold punctiliousness or as a daughter's anxiety to love her mother accurately. When a child refuses to take off her Halloween mask for days after the event, it could mean everything or nothing. . . .

They tickle our consciousness with a feather, Miss Tallent's stories, and that's something. It's not what I would want if they were my stories—the correct response might be a sneeze of recognition—but they're hers. In one of these stories, a man talks about "bioluminescence," and I think it might be possible to say that, at their best, this is what Miss Tallent's characters have: a kind of bioluminescence.

Anatole Broyard, in a review of "In Constant Flight," in The New York Times, *April 29, 1983, p. C29.*

ANDREA BARNET

Elizabeth Tallent is an elegant miniaturist. Her quiet, elegiac stories [in ***In Constant Flight***] are shaped less by plot than by immaculately precise imagery. She is concerned with nuances of character and feeling, the fugitive, telling moments.

Tallent's people are artists and promising young academics in esoteric fields—astronomers, cellists, ornithologists, poets, choreographers, anthropologists—the kind of people who keep finches named after Henry James' characters, drink Perrier, collect Indonesian baskets, and eat macrobiotic food. The stories are about lovers who have parted, about refugees from mismatched marriages, and about people caught in the transition between husband and lover; all are paralyzed by failed expectations and the complications created by need. (pp. 56, 58)

What makes these eleven short stories unusual is Tallent's keen and original eye for detail; her characters' obsessions read as though grounded firmly in fact. The lab procedures of a naturalist documenting the migration of a rare breed of swans are described as scrupulously as the hallucinations of a charming, senile ornithologist who sees birds in his house and "ferns unfurling like seahorses from cracks in the floorboards." Even in the fragile moments when words fail her characters—the moments around which all of these stories pivot—her meanings surface with the liquid ease of daydreams. (p. 58)

Andrea Barnet, in a review of "In Constant Flight," in Saturday Review, *Vol. 9, No. 8, May-June, 1983, pp. 56, 58.*

BARBARA KOENIG QUART

A number of the stories in Elizabeth Tallent's ***In Constant Flight*** appeared first in *The New Yorker*—which is not surprising considering the high polish of their surfaces, their sureness of tone, their characters and imagery drawn heavily from prosperous WASP life. Set in Colorado, but really set nowhere special, Tallent's stories are full of exotic and precious characters: a mother obsessed with her rose-eating Abyssinian cat which keeps having spontaneous abortions; an astrophysicist, who discovers a new moon of Saturn, and his oboe-player ex-wife; an old ornithologist whose many years in the New Guinea rain forests have made him expert in the ways—especially the courting and mating ways—of birds of paradise. No paradise in sight for the humans, however, all their matings having gone awry—the old man's, his son's, just about everyone else's. . . . Though the stories are almost all written from a young woman's viewpoint, the male characters—mostly ex-husbands and lovers—are endearingly tender and vulnerable.

With their artfully wrought, often beautiful surfaces, Tallent's stories are pleasurable to read, and they can be moving too. But they're somewhat thin, airy, not quite embodied. Their moments of poignance—when achieved—are conveyed indirectly, through displaced images often drawn from the esoterica of natural history. Sometimes the stories strain for virtuosity at the expense of substance. But this is a fine young writer who one hopes time will deepen. (pp. 740-41)

Barbara Koenig Quart, "First, the Bad News," in The Nation, *Vol. 236, No. 23, June 11, 1983, pp. 738-41.*

EDITH MILTON

The 11 stories of ***In Constant Flight*** are all to one degree or another studies in modern alienation.

Technically they are close to perfect—not merely well-written but constructed with a subtle authority that develops the themes of each story with admirable precision and economy. Mrs. Tallent also has a remarkably good ear for spoken language and an excellent eye for gesture, and whether she is portraying a rebellious adolescent in **"Asteroids"** or a learned octogenarian in **"The Evolution of Birds of Paradise,"** her characters are authentic. Her control is sometimes awe-inspiring as she defines the minutiae of her characters' lives in terms of the universe at large and suggests the timeless quality of their ordinary actions. . . .

Though the theme of ***In Constant Flight*** is sexual love and each story centers upon a failed romantic relationship between a man and a woman, the inability of people to reach one another and speak with warmth and meaning is always projected against a larger and more consuming void.

And yet, despite the stories' high ambition and excellent execution, ***In Constant Flight*** is disappointing. Something about the stories brings to mind the sentence James Thurber suggested as one way not to start a story: "Mrs. Ponsonby had never put the dog in the oven before." Mrs. Tallent does in fact start **"Refugees"** this way: "The poet Zinbanti is tall and elegant and he was shot in the back eleven years ago." This may not be a match for Mrs. Ponsonby, but it demonstrates that earnest insistence on being surprising against which she is a warning. . . .

That reaching for constant surprise, constant incongruity, palls like overspiced food. In **"Ice,"** an ice-skating ballerina dances with a homosexual man in a bear costume. In **"Why I Love Country Music,"** a woman sleeps with a short, 200-pound miner, though she lusts mildly for a tall, svelte cowboy. In **"Comings and Goings,"** a girl is in love with a mind reader who teaches her to skip stones by a kind of Zen principle. Most of these stories are written in the first person in the voice of a young woman who is always somehow the same young woman—middle-class, educated, passive, rejected by her men. And the men who reject her or whom she rejects, though they are dressed in different roles for every story, are also oddly the same.

In the end, these stories seem like little more than 11 variations on a single theme. And each variation, tediously predictable, has its allotment of paradox and its helping of the unexpected. Even the metaphorical paraphernalia—the men in bear and bunny suits, the faces hidden under masks—is too obvious and too much used, and the ironies about self-conscious scientists studying spontaneous nature are a bid for profundity that is not in itself profound. (p. 26)

Edith Milton, "What Changes and What Doesn't," in The New York Times Book Review, *August 14, 1983, pp. 12, 26.*

CLARE SUMNOR

[Tallent's stories in ***In Constant Flight***] could be considered the founding creations of the Fashion Drawing School of Literature—more arty than art-full, meandering and weightless, but attractive and sometimes, indeed, very beautiful. Tallent has a striking descriptive gift. Each narrative moves through a sequence of images, a technique that places these stories on the borders of poetry, where the eloquence of the image-as-story has gradually acquired dominance. One of the major freedoms of prose—to get inside the chosen character and ask its questions, share its memories, as part of the narrative device—is rarely explored. Tallent's art, so far, is one of surfaces.

Sometimes she fails to take these much beyond fashionable urban myth. Details of what the characters (invariably slender, as photographic models should be) wear and eat, and how their attics and bathrooms are decorated (dear reader, all you need is Dulux and imagination), proliferate, colour supplement-style. In the lust for surfaces, nothing must be overlooked, for who knows what is significant, what peripheral; like the desires of the heart, the dictates of fashion are crooked as corkscrews, and mutable. . . .

This said, ***In Constant Flight*** is full of memorable passages, for example the description of the dissection of a leech-infested swan, or the fine pen-and-wash delineations of the rather more exotic birds nesting in the ornithologist's house in **"The Evolution of Birds of Paradise"**. The exactness and poise of such description sometimes recall Ian McEwan, but there is no suggestion of the macabre or squalid; even the dissection of the swan has nothing chilling about it. Tallent's characters are civilized, even tender-hearted, suffering low-key emotional disturbances, rarely raising their voices, wistfully displaying their courtship plumage. Like the participants in the high-fashion drama of the television commercial, their rôles are, fundamentally, intensely, traditional; the men have, and are shown to have, interesting jobs in astronomy or architecture, whereas the women are mostly displayed in a sexual light, their postures childlike, fey, provocative. An ambition towards greater psychological depth is hinted at in **"Bridges"**, and, at not yet thirty, Elizabeth Tallent has plenty of time in which to develop. But perhaps her *métier* is simply to be an elegant skater over the seductive surfaces of life, mirroring its narcissism without naming its tragedy.

Clare Sumnor, "After Her Fashion," in The Times Literary Supplement, *No. 4198, September 16, 1983, p. 1002.*

MICHIKO KAKUTANI

At first, Elizabeth Tallent's ***Museum Pieces*** may seem like just another trendy novel about trendy, fashionably artsy people. It isn't. Writing with a keen, quicksilver appreciation of her characters' inner lives and with a poet's eye for the luminous, skewed details of daily life, Miss Tallent has created a lyrical, resonant novel, a novel about the complicated geometry of emotions between men and women, parents and their children—the sad, surprising ways in which we engage and disengage our feelings, our difficulty connecting with those for whom we care and our labored mediations between time past, time present and the time to come.

Peter Barnes, who is trying to come to terms with his previous marriage so he can get on with his life, is, appropriately enough, an archeologist—a student of the past, engaged in piecing together fragments of potsherds and old bones, the broken remnants of a vanished order. Since his separation, he's been camped out in the basement of the museum where he works. . . .

His estranged wife, Clarissa, leads, on the surface at least, a more ordered, careful life—she keeps an immaculate house, maintains her psyche with regular visits to the therapist, sticks to a rigorous regimen of painting. Apparently, that's just the thing: she feels safer, more in control, manipulating light and color than dealing with messy emotions—"she doesn't trust human beings, she trusts the shapes of things"—and yet, she feels there's a kind of desiccation to her life, an incompleteness that she tries to fill by having transitory affairs.

The sense of drift and impermanence that haunts the grownups in this book is also handed down to their children. Clarissa and Peter's daughter, Tara, has had a fast, brief childhood, devoid of the old securities. She and her best friend Natalie hold intense gossip sessions about boys, divorce, a friend's mother's heroin addiction; and they speak in a curious, hybrid language, at once sophisticated and vulnerable, mixing up Valley Girlisms ("It's chaos," Nat says of a pair of brightly colored stockings. "Pure, pure vomitous chaos."), words like "paranoid" and "scabrous," and old-fashioned girlish giggles.

Miss Tallent's finely tuned ear, the reader quickly realizes, is keyed not only to the nuances of adolescent speech, but also to their elders' elliptical use of language, the circumlocutions, elisions and stammering invocation of psychobabble they employ to cover over their feelings of love and fear and hurt. Often, her characters don't talk to one another at all—they use going to the movies as "a sort of surrogate conversation," they read and misread signs in incompleted gestures (a glance averted, a car door unheld, a silly blurted remark), and cling to omens found in the inconsequential details of domestic life (a dead moth caught in the screen, the sign of a heart carved in a tree, a strand of hair caught on a button). Their emotions, they discover, can be irritatingly instransigent, illogical and ill-timed.

Like so many of the characters in Miss Tallent's collection of short stories (***In Constant Flight***), these people in ***Museum Pieces*** frequently seem poised on the brink of fleeing from one another or themselves, but in the course of the novel, Peter slowly begins to assemble a new, if thoroughly provisional, life for himself and Mia [his new girlfriend]. . . . [In] relating his efforts to sort things out, Miss Tallent demonstrates her ability to sustain a lengthy narrative, elegantly and with compassion.

The somewhat annoying tendency of her prose to constantly coagulate into self-consciously important metaphors is still here, especially in the first portion of the novel, where we're treated to a stream of "significant" images including an apple held magically intact within a Coke bottle, a hummingbird's nest containing a pearl and a silver thimble, a broken easter egg, a woman wearing a Halloween fright mask.

As the novel proceeds, however, these well-written but distracting showpieces diminish in frequency, and Miss Tallent instead begins to use her generous verbal gifts to delineate her characters' states of mind, their conflicted yearnings for safety and adventure, privacy and love, their precarious sense of the future. She has written a lovely novel.

Michiko Kakutani, "Geometry of Emotions," in The New York Times, *March 30, 1985, p. 13.*

LOUISE ERDRICH

There may be no one who writes as gracefully about debris as Elizabeth Tallent. Throughout her second work of fiction, ***Museum Pieces,*** which follows the story collection ***In Constant Flight,*** are complicated lists of rubbish. . . . In a glove compartment one finds "a broken sand dollar, a box of crayons, and Perrier bottle, nearly full." The remarkable thing is that the bottle is not filled with Perrier water but sacred Ganges River water. Elsewhere, bones appear—the bones of hummingbirds, horses' skulls, the ribs of deer.

The life's work of one principal character, Peter, an archeologist who lives in the basement of a museum, is the piecing together of potsherds and the serious consideration of ancient garbage. His work serves as a metaphor for the book.

Museum Pieces is the re-examination of the debris of a marriage, an attempt to describe a once-whole vessel by showing us the fragments.

The book concerns itself with the strange, tender and painful things that happen between children and their parents. Peter and his wife, Clarissa, a painter, have separated. Their one child, Tara, must now redefine herself and attempt to maintain her equilibrium among changing casts of her parents' lovers and friends. Unless she fights for a place in their new lives, Tara stands in danger of becoming the tragic detritus of her parents' marriage. . . .

Mrs. Tallent apparently knows a great deal about young girls and their friendships with one another. She understands not only how Tara and her best friend, Nat, behave in moments of crisis, but also the nuances of their ordinary conversations, what they do and how they act, how they fight and make up. In fact, the relationship between these two young girls often seems the most mature and sustained in the book.

Mrs. Tallent's characters live in a Santa Fe that is richly and lovingly described. Though the local Pueblo Indians appear merely as part of the landscape—picturesque formations who offer jewelry or food to the major characters—the city's resident artists, former dancers and members of community arts collectives are more fully realized. They live casually, among Ball jars of sprouting mung beans and toasters full of singed crumbs. They are self-absorbed, carelessly esthetic. In one woman's bathroom, among wrinkled tights and bottles of shampoo, there is "an abalone shell containing a single green marble." Kitchen tables come from monasteries, not Goodwill stores, and are decorated with such centerpieces as "a nest containing a pearl and a silver thimble." Their children eat croissants in French pastry shops, and drink either *cappuccino* or macrobiotic teas made of boiled twigs. Lovers leave one another because of the irritating sounds their appliances make in the night, or for no reason at all.

Peter and Clarissa have separated for inscrutable reasons, perhaps because of "their accumulated weariness with each other," or perhaps, as their daughter and her best friend speculate, "over nothing." They try to find a better explanation by sorting through their shared experiences in the period the book covers—a time when a husband and wife either go their separate ways or return to one another. During this interim, they find lovers, minor characters who are among the book's most vivid figures. . . .

Many of the book's truest moments take place in the past, in precisely detailed chunks of memory that the characters laboriously examine. . . .

The book's most economical scenes often leave an impression through carefully chosen images, such as a doctor's nervous tic or cherry blossom petals on a wet newspaper. Peter cleans the vertebrae of an antelope with a toothbrush "splayed from use on his own teeth, now burnishing ancient bone." Listening to Clarissa's voice on the phone he keeps his legs away from the wall "where scorpions and children of the earth scuttled up and down in the dark, making quick skeletal noises, like dice rattled in a cupped hand." Tara curls up with her father's tweed jacket, "her chin against cloth that is scratchy as an old tennis ball and has no color in the darkness." But like the best of writers, Mrs. Tallent's strength can also be her weakness. There is a tendency to overdescribe mundane gestures, such as the way a child sucks on a pen. And there is an occasional excess of minutiae.

Throughout ***Museum Pieces*** the writer, like archeologists described in the book who shattered pots to make them easier to transport in bags, has offered the reader fragments of people to be made whole. Through her loving attention they do become whole, understandable, human. But their marriages continue to be baffling shards, broken irretrievably, mysterious as bits of sky lost out of an interlocking jigsaw puzzle.

Although ***Museum Pieces*** is not a dramatic story but one that grows by the accretion of small discoveries toward a conclusion rather than a climax, it is nevertheless engrossing and beautifully expressed. As a novel, it is a sure-handed extension of Elizabeth Tallent's short stories. She has kept the humor and immediacy, the telling quirks, the odd and inventive bits of circumstance, while at the same time rendering her characters in deeper tones.

Louise Erdrich, "Life in Shards and Fragments," in The New York Times Book Review, *April 7, 1985, p. 10.*

ANN DERMANSKY

Elizabeth Tallent has written [in ***Museum Pieces***] a terrific first novel, a clear-eyed examination of the ways things go between men and women, at the way things work in families. . . .

Unusual in current fiction, Tallent has created a real man in Peter Wu-Barnes, a multi-faceted character with vulnerabilities, generosity and kindness. She has also created a strong sense of place, Santa Fe, NM. We explore the streets, the restaurants, the narrow, rutted dirt roads leading to outlying canyons. We taste the food and sample the weather.

Museum Pieces sparkles, an example of honed-to-the-bone prose. The dialogue is real, the clothes the characters wear are real, the problems they confront speak of contemporary dilemmas.

Ann Dermansky, "Santa Fe Trials Told," in New Directions for Women, *Vol. 14, No. 3, May-June, 1985, p. 16.*

WENDY LESSER

Tallent is an extremely skilled short-story writer, as her collection ***In Constant Flight*** and her more recent work in *The New Yorker* demonstrate. But ***Museum Pieces,*** in spreading that skill over the length of a book, has left behind the sharp pointedness of her stories without acquiring the necessary breadth of a novel. We can still find, in this book, the best qualities of Tallent's writing—notably her eye for visual detail, her perfect sense of gesture, and her ability to formulate the exact linguistic expression of a state of mind, whether through metaphor, through surrounding environment, or through direct speech. And ***Museum Pieces*** has its compelling moments, especially when its narration resides with Peter, the Santa Fe archaeologist whose profession provides the book's title. But as a story of a modern-day separation and divorce, seen from the viewpoints of teenage daughter Tara, wife Clarissa, husband Peter, and Peter's new girlfriend Mia, the novel lacks propulsion. It meanders, contemplates, and sidesteps, but it rarely progresses (except in a gratuitous car-accident scene thrown in, I suppose, as a "necessary" climax). There is nothing really wrong with Tallent's characters; they just don't seem animated enough to occupy 233 pages. They don't offend or irritate, but neither do they invite sympathy or curiosity. (pp. 468-69)

Wendy Lesser, "Bloated and Shrunken Worlds," in The Hudson Review, *Vol. XXXVIII, No. 3, Autumn, 1985, pp. 463-72.*

DAVID WELLENBROCK

[***Museum Pieces***] seems pretty superficial, even assuming the characters are fairly ordinary folks and not terribly complex. There are few ambivalent feelings being explored. No character seems to have a full life (maybe there is nothing to be said about Peter's work, which is reconstructing clay pots, but it taxes the imagination to believe it is no more than working a jigsaw puzzle to him). There is little tension throughout the book. Briefly, one wonders how (not if) Mia and Peter will get together. Later, one wonders if the relationship will terminate. But that is all.

Museum Pieces is a long short story, not a novel, because it lacks the complexity one expects. . . .

Ms. Tallent is stronger as a short story writer. Despite its lack of complexity the book is enjoyable and readable. It is interesting as a document of modern American relationships. (p. 164)

David Wellenbrock, in a review of "Museum Pieces," in Western American Literature, *Vol. XXI, No. 2, August, 1986, pp. 163-64.*

(Alfred) Charles Tomlinson

1927-

English poet, translator, editor, critic, and artist.

A respected English poet whose verse focuses on the philosophic implications of sensory experience, Tomlinson uses acute observation and detailed description to explore the relationship between the external world and the self. Tomlinson suggests that through sensitive perception of natural phenomena, human beings are able to gain an awareness "that teaches us not to try merely to reduce objects to our own image, but to respect their otherness and yet find our way into contact with that otherness." Tomlinson's admiration for the works of such American writers as Ezra Pound, William Carlos Williams, Wallace Stevens, and Marianne Moore is reflected in the clarity of his language, the musical cadences of his verse, his detached tone and objective point of view, and his reliance upon the inherent symbolism of natural objects. Although he has been faulted for his preoccupation with surfaces, Tomlinson is well regarded for the precision, restraint, and originality of his verse.

Tomlinson became attracted to modern American literature while a student at Cambridge University during the 1940s, and its influence on his writing contributed to the resistance his work originally encountered in England. His first major collection, *Seeing Is Believing* (1958), was rejected by numerous British publishers before being accepted in the United States, where it was widely praised. In these poems, Tomlinson's visual detail and his emphasis on disciplined and accurate observation in forming an understanding of reality results in avoidance of distortion and excess. Tomlinson's succeeding volumes, *A Peopled Landscape* (1963) and *American Scenes and Other Poems* (1966), reflect his exposure to American landscapes and his contacts with such American poets as George Oppen, Louis Zukofsky, and William Carlos Williams. In verse deeply influenced by these and other writers, Tomlinson eschews Romantic and Surrealist tenets and instead advocates objectivity in life and art.

Tomlinson's next two major collections, *The Way of a World* (1969) and *Written on Water* (1972), continue his explorations of the interaction between man and nature. In these poems, Tomlinson presents his themes through the recurring motifs of water and time. *The Way of a World* contains some of Tomlinson's best-known poems, including "Against Extremity" and the widely anthologized "Swimming Chenango Lake." In *The Way In and Other Poems* (1974), Tomlinson introduces personal elements into his poetry while continuing to probe the nature of perception and reality. His verse in this volume reflects the shifting balance of constancy and change as he returns to the landscapes of England, creating imaginative portraits of familiar scenes in such poems as "At Stoke" and "The Marl Pits." The poems in Tomlinson's next book, *The Shaft* (1978), pursue themes and employ techniques similar to those of his earlier volumes. Although often considered among Tomlinson's least successful collections, *The Shaft* contains the highly praised poem "Lines Written in the Euganean Hills," in which the poet denounces human imposition on the natural world.

Fay Godwin's Photo Files

Tomlinson's next book of poems, *The Flood* (1981), reflects his travels in England, North America, and Italy. The volume contains a variety of literary styles, including elegiac and narrative verse and prose passages. In *Notes from New York and Other Poems* (1984), Tomlinson imaginatively recreates various urban landscapes of New York City. These poems attest to Tomlinson's concern with the consequences of human interaction on the physical environment. Tomlinson has also published two retrospective volumes, *Selected Poems, 1951-1974* (1978) and *Collected Poems* (1985).

In addition to his poetry, Tomlinson has translated works by such poets as Fyodor Tyutchev, Antonio Machado, and Cesar Vallejo; he has edited collections of poems and essays by Marianne Moore, William Carlos Williams, and Octavio Paz; and he has collaborated with Paz and other poets on two books of verse, *Renga* (1971) and *Airborn/Hijos del aire* (1981). *Some Americans: A Personal Record* (1981) contains prose sketches of American poets and artists whom Tomlinson visited during his journeys to the United States. An accomplished graphic artist, Tomlinson has also published several volumes of his visual images, including *Eden: Graphics and Poetry* (1985), which combines poetry and artwork.

(See also *CLC*, Vols. 2, 4, 6, 13; *Contemporary Authors*, Vols. 5-8, rev. ed.; and *Dictionary of Literary Biography*, Vol. 40.)

JOHN CASSIDY

Selected Poems reveals more clearly than ever that Tomlinson's work is a continuing argument, dogged in tone and subtle in reference, that presses home his convictions. Employing allusions, actual and concealed quotation from many sources, embracing foreign cities, painters and other poets as his subjects, he has always been defiantly unfashionable. In despite of Kingsley Amis ("A Bookshop Idyll") his poems announce that he has travelled, he has thought, and he has read, and that these experiences are inextricably woven into his sensibility.

Tomlinson's earliest books established him as a poet of intense visual experience, a poet-painter, for whom accuracy of perception was vital. There has rarely been a more apt title for a collection than that for his first (in England), ***Seeing is Believing*** (1960). The exact recording of appearances, however, is charged with intent, becoming a moral preoccupation. It demands alertness to change, and any motion of finality is dismissed as "a static instance, therefore, untrue".... [The] sheer existence of things, their otherness, is celebrated throughout this book. Personality withdraws in the face of them, allowing them to assert themselves fully. Thus the word "I" is largely avoided, and the natural world is examined with determined objectivity; the world, in his sense, cannot be too much with us. The self is a grateful observer, most effective when withdrawn, but the eye is deceivable; these poems note counterfeit snow, conflicting comparisons for the sea, shivering reflections—so that the lines move in a cautious, insistent uncovering of reality.

The weight accorded to things, to landscape or architecture or clouds, demands from the poet a particularly fine technique in their presentation, or re-creation. Here Tomlinson's skill is apparent in almost every poem. (pp. 51-2)

The effect of the appearance of his lines on the page is something else that Tomlinson enlists, more especially as an element in his free verse poems, where the eye is induced to lead the inner voice through rapids and hesitations. The pace of his poems is always perfectly controlled. This technical adroitness has irritated some critics, seeming to lead nowhere beyond all this fiddle. Yet the leading nowhere beyond is its point: "I leave you," he says to a meticulously described fallen tree, " / To your one meaning, yourself alone." Objects are allowed to arrange themselves into "an observed music", and Cézanne is praised for painting the "unposed" mountain which simply "is". The point is made repeatedly though, obsessively, and one begins to sympathise with those who ask of Tomlinson some new perspective, some more humane engagement.

The poems which offer this are relatively few, but of great interest and power. **"Prometheus"**, relating Scriabin's apocalyptic music to the ferocity of political revolution, is a closely pressed complex argument against extremes, which moves with an assured rhythm towards "the cruel mercy of solidities". Apocalypse, in historical, political or personal terms, is coolly put down. Tomlinson believes in a sense of the continuing rather than the sense of an ending, in "the bond and list of sequential days" and in the cicadas which chafe on in the midst of decay (**"The Compact: At Volterra"**). **"Descartes And The Stove"** encapsulates his gifts and concerns in its twenty-eight confident lines. There is the perfectly realised account of the stove, its negroid belly thrusting for the philosopher's attention, of the particulars of the snowy landscape behind him, of a reality forming and re-forming its ineluctable shapes around the doubting mind. The whole piece enacts its meaning in a most subtle but decisive way.

The Shaft, Tomlinson's most recent collection, continues these preoccupations and strategies. (pp. 52-3)

There is much variety in this book, with a section of "bagatelles" and a boisterously amusing biography of Sir John Denham. Five poems in the section called **"Perfections"** insist yet again on the faculty of seeing: "Perfect is a word I can never hear / Without a sensation as of seeing".

Tomlinson's American reputation, his adherence to an aesthetic deriving from Williams and Stevens, and his published statements have all fuelled antipathies, and his refusal of extremism in any sense has run counter to some contemporary feeling. But his concern with civility is more than mere urbanity and polish. It is a strong and admirable concern with the perception of reality, with an art which is "An ordering, the darkness held / But not dismissed" (**"Civilities of Lamplight"**). (p. 53)

John Cassidy, "Seeing as a Faith," in Poetry Review, *Vol. 68, No. 4, January, 1979, pp. 51-3.*

ALAN GOULD

Selected Poems 1951-1974 contains a choice of Tomlinson's work from his eight published volumes, as well as some of his translations from Vallejo, Machado and Fyodor Tyutchev. The poems range widely in their settings from pastoral, coastal and industrial England to those prompted by travel in the USA, Mexico and Italy.

This poet is also a painter and it is the detached organization of visual details, and the restrained inferences that grow from their presentation, that give the best poems their exquisiteness. In such pieces as **"How Still the Hawk"**, **"Cezanne at Aix"** or the anthologized **"Paring the Apple"**, the tone is that of an intelligence fascinated and drawn wholly outwards by the object it contemplates, of an eye acutely alert to this object's vivid separateness from all that surrounds it *and* its ensconced part in a larger picture. The ambition, it seems, is to suggest an entire map of relationships without shifting focus from the object for one moment. . . . (p. 55)

On close inspection there is in many of these poems a rich deployment of sound-effects, full-rhyme, half rhyme, internal rhyme, assonantal agreement. I say 'on close inspection' because the cadences seem to have been deliberately randomized. For instance the end-rhymes are unaided by any metrical principle, therefore creating no expectation of sound-agreement in the reader's mind. The result is that the rhymes have on occasion a pleasingly unfamiliar echo-effect within a stanza; more often they are not noticed. For the voice in this selection never *sings,* it invariably talks, and although it talks with unswerving fidelity about the object or concept in view, the unrelief in its mode I find wearisome when reading large numbers of poems at a sitting. Take, for example, this extract from **"A Meditation on John Constable"**, a homage to that English painter, but also a description of Tomlinson's own ambitions in poetry, and I think his achievement:

> A descriptive painter? If delight
> Describes, which wrings from the brush
> The errors of a mind, so tempered,
> It can forgo all pathos; for what he saw

Discovered what he was, and the hand—unswayed
By the dictation of a single sense—
Bodied the accurate and total knowledge
In a calligraphy of present pleasure.

A fine discriminating intelligence at work? Certainly. But the poetry fails to intoxicate me. For one thing my delight is inhibited by the frequency here and elsewhere of abstract vocabulary. There are poems that are exceptions to this, that are vividly sensual, such as **"Winter Piece"** where the speaker wakes 'all windows blind—embattled sprays / grained on the medieval glass. / Gates snap like gunshot', but exhilarated and exhilarating descriptions are rare, and it appears deliberately so, for Tomlinson's intention is to inform rather than to intoxicate. The consequence of this is that he has suppressed the presence of the ego, be it his own or a projected persona. The advantage of this is that he avoids the distraction of egoism, be it the exuberant self-regard of a Dylan Thomas, or the morbid self-regard of a confessional poet. The disadvantage is that the voice of the poems, speaking in rhythms with little or no incantatory charm, using much conceptual vocabulary, and denied displays of excitement, fails to perform that magic of sedation and arousal by which all complete distractions are dispersed and my imagination is transported, not so much by *a poem,* but by *his,* Charles Tomlinson's poem.

But here the ground shifts from beneath my feet, for undeniably the mountain in **"Cezanne at Aix"** and the door in the poem of that title are the re-creations of this poet's ego, and no other, and the discipline with which this ego has projected the object to the exclusion of all distracting material including the 'self' is rigorous and coldly effective. (p. 56)

Alan Gould, "Control and Parsimony," in Poetry Australia, *No. 72, October, 1979, pp. 54-9.*

WILLIAM S. SAUNDERS

The Shaft is Tomlinson's least poetically vital book. The unclotted flow of feeling and the sharp self-awareness have disappeared. With two exceptions, we have, I'm afraid, mere artifacts, mere exercises in versification, characterized by discursiveness and formal fussiness. ***The Shaft*** is written "from the head" rather than the whole being, even more than ***Seeing Is Believing*** was, and its aestheticism matches that of ***The Necklace.*** Its poems are too often like fortune cookies: sweet, brittle shells with messages inside. And that is our serious loss. . . . ***The Shaft,*** except for two poems, is a lifeless book. (p. 36)

The first section, **"Histories,"** seems to have taken its cue from Donald Davie's book-based verse. Most of it is fundamentally scholarly: it presents interesting facts from a dispassionate point of view. The opening poem on Charlotte Corday's murder of Marat should be contrasted with **"Prometheus"** and **"Assassin"** in ***The Way of a World.*** Whereas in the earlier works Tomlinson empathizes with both the violent and their victims, and thus creates poems of stunning emotional complexity, here he keeps his distance. He simply forgives all parties. . . . Other of these history poems are similarly slack. A long **"Biography"** of Sir John Denham is chatty, witty and urbane in the manner of Davie's historical verse: it makes one feel pleasantly superior. There is one solid, unadorned poem (**"Casarola"**) on the shamefulness of abandoning an old house, but compare it to the early **"On the Hall at Stowey"** and you will find a dearth of personal engagement. Yet out of these **"Histories"** leaps **"Lines Written in the Euganean Hills,"** a masterpiece I will save for my final comments.

The next two sections, **"Perfections"** and **"Seasons,"** should be discussed together, for they are both not just lightweight, as the fourth section (aptly called **"Bagatelles"**) openly is, they are for the most part positively and disturbingly bad, morally so. Their preoccupation with form over feeling, sound patterns over poetic realizations, is decadent. And, although Tomlinson's poems have always had an element of verbal fussiness, Tomlinson at his best, as in **"Adam"** (in ***The Way of a World***), is aware of the moral dangers involved: **"Adam"** argues that if words are not devoted, transparent evocations of felt worlds, then their user is a 'mouther and unmaker, madman.' . . . The kinds of 'perfections' Tomlinson is concerned with in the section of that title are aesthetic, with "the finality and satisfaction / Of the achieved act of an artisan" (**"Prose Poem"**). He *speaks* of other perfections—those of rich, full experiences of nature—but his poems are an artisan's. A poet/artist synthesizes feeling and form, idea and body; a versifier/artisan tinkers with form and the body of his verse lacks spirit. In **"Prose Poem,"** Tomlinson uses the phrase "dialogue between air and ear." In content grotesque, it sounds good.

But the artisan, splitting form and spirit, can easily become the philosopher, who does not seek a sensuous embodiment for his ideas. In **"Prose Poem,"** Tomlinson listens to a jar and writes:

A low, crystalline roar that wholly
Possessed one's cavities, a note (as it were)
Of unfathomable distance—not emptiness,
For this dialogue between air and ear
Was so full of electric imponderables. . . .

Mere assertion: the "imponderable" and the "unfathomable distance" are not poetically suggested. In **"The Metamorphosis"** of the next section, Tomlinson has the idea of comparing wild flowers to water, but the poem is just the communication of this *idea,* without intuitive enactment in the lines. (pp. 36-7)

The more noticeable half of this artisan/philosopher is the artisan. With the content so much 'in the head,' the form seems to take off by itself and put on essentially trivial linguistic displays. One such display is alliteration serving no onomatopoetic function. We see this in **"The Metamorphosis"** ("bell on bell," "rope and rivulet") and in many other poems ("flint, fleck or feather," "stone or stain"). Tomlinson also plays excessively with internal and end rhymes. Contrary to the assertion in one of his favourite poems (**"The Chances of Rhyme"**), the coming to mind of a rhyming word does not have any deeply intuitive significance unless intuition is probing in more vital ways. The utter emptiness of this 'fine phrasing' can, I hope, be conclusively felt in this embarrassing spate from ***The Shaft:*** "into the sky / And air [What distinction is this?] of earliest day"; "word to dance with, dally, and outfly"; "a vertical unfathomed. / A vertigo that dropped" (Can a vertigo drop?); "in runes and hidden rhymes, in chords and keys"; "this / Raised torch, this touch" (Ouch!); "all its likes and links stay true" (Is "likes" different from "links"?); "wherever ripeness has not filled its brood / Of rinds and rounds"; "bell on bell"; "spray on spray"; "wing on wing"; "statue on statue"; "tree on tree"; "column on column"; "star on hairy star"; "gobbet on slithering gobbet"! I'm afraid I could go on. The "X on X" structure becomes a verbal tick, and, like the frequent echoing of first lines in last, gives one the sense of writing by rote. It is also significant that in line length, rhythm and spacing these poems are more uniform than those in other Tomlinson volumes.

I don't want to exaggerate. The middle sections of ***The Shaft*** have at least three poems (**"Departure," "... Or Traveller's Joy," "The Race"**) which are genuine, unpretentious and warm—one can hardly dislike them, although they do not need or reward rereading. The final section, **"In Arden,"** on the other hand, offers somewhat more dense material in its title poem. This poem seems intended to go with **"Adam"** and **"Eden,"** companion poems from ***The Way of a World*** which have an unusually strong inwardness resulting in the creation of abstract phantasmagoria. **"In Arden"** uses Adam and Eden as abstractions, but into this poem intrudes social commentary that disrupts and clashes with the generalizing:

Ownership will get what it can for Arden's trees:
No acreage of green-belt complacencies
Can keep Macadam out.

It is difficult to make an allegorical figure out of Macadam. The poem is ambitious, but it finally collapses in pretentious vagueness. Adam (modern fallen man) in Arden (the "less-than-Eden" natural world) is said to hear "voices / Of the [Eden] that rises through this place. . . . Where Adam, Eden, Arden run together / And time itself must beat to the cadence of this river." Like [**"The Shaft"**] . . . (in which we read "a vertical unfathomed, / A vertigo that dropped through centuries"), this claims a weightiness it lacks. The final poem of the book, an elegy echoing the powerful final section of **"Under the Moon's Reign"** with none of the earlier poem's intensity, clinches one's angry dismay.

There are, fortunately, two poems in ***The Shaft*** which have real artistic vitality. **"The Scream,"** which appears in the last section, is strong because much more experiential than the other poems. It tells of being awakened by and finding the source of a mysterious, terrifying cry. All abstractions are subsumed into the account of the lived event. . . . But the one real masterpiece is **"Lines Written in the Euganean Hills."** . . . With the fierceness characteristic of his great poems, Tomlinson condemns human impositions on the nonhuman, natural world, calling them stale stains on the "thrust of origin." Yet he does much more. Nature is by no means romanticized. In stanza two Tomlinson bemoans and fears the seemingly vengeful sterility of a long-exploited earth, turned to dust and merely glossed over by man's countermeasures (irrigation). In stanzas three and four Tomlinson decries the replacing of a sensitive humanism, represented by Palladio and Petrarch, by a crude, raucous humanism, represented by scrawled political slogans (and linked to the wine stains in the first stanza). Yet soft-headed nostalgia is resisted: one may empathize with the lugubrious custodian reciting Petrarch, but Tomlinson sees that Petrarch is consigned to the cellar, where his recitation is heard only by a mummified cat grotesquely and sentimentally (or mockingly?) named after Petrarch's loved one. The custodian is behind the times. As if all this were not richly significant enough, Tomlinson compounds his response in showing himself both horrified by D'Annunzio's vision of nature swallowing up the man-made world and critical of this vision for its naiveté.

Dominating nature, exploited nature, Renaissance humanism, modern humanism—none of these offers comfort. The poem resolves into the lack of resolution one finds in all great Tomlinson poems. The poet's ideal is clearly some sort of balance between man and nature, but he is strong enough to admit that he will not find it realized. Understanding and desire clash with astounding force. And the words, charged with these felt thoughts, are more than just words. . . . Nowhere in **"Euganean Hills"** is there trivial fussing with the medium. We need the help Tomlinson can give us, in poems like this, to be alive in our time. (pp. 37-40)

William S. Saunders, "Artifice and Ideas," in Delta, *No. 59, 1979, pp. 35-40.*

BEN HOWARD

As is now well known, Tomlinson's first mentor was Wallace Stevens; and his abiding concern has been with epistemology and the "fineness of relationships." Admirers of Tomlinson's work praise his density of thought and precision of observation. Detractors complain that his poems evade engagement in human conflicts and partake too much of the mind of winter. For many readers, Charles Tomlinson is primarily a visual or "painterly" poet, whose strength lies in the intelligent ordering of visual perceptions.

Tomlinson's ***Selected Poems,*** spanning twenty-three years of work, provides a corrective to narrow views of his achievement. To begin with, the poet's imagination is not exclusively visual. It is also auditory. . . . Throughout his career, in his prose statements as well as in his poems, Tomlinson has urged an alert receptivity, a willingness to be led into the "unpremeditated consonances" of language, the potentialities of randomness and chance, the daunting otherness of nature. . . . [Nature] is not so much an emblem for human emotion as an alien force, in the presence of which the human mind, unprejudiced and watchful, comes into an earned "relation / With all that is other."

That "earned relation" is visual, musical, and tactile. It inheres in the rhythm of the poetic line. In a statement for the British magazine *Agenda,* Tomlinson has explained his concept of rhythm:

> Rhythm, as it is felt in the act of writing, signifies the creation of a continuum, an imaginary space within which words and memories, the given and the possible can be felt as co-present, held over against each other, yet constantly crossing one another's paths. As the mind attends to the pulsation of the growing poem, it is as if it enters and shares this created space which, filled by the invitations of movement and sound, seems at once landscape and music, perhaps more music than landscape.

The adventurous receptivity of Tomlinson's stance, and his emphasis upon "the invitations of movement and sound," call to mind other endorsements of experimental form, most notably those of William Stafford. What distinguishes Tomlinson's view is his metaphor of landscape as music and music as landscape. The figure recurs throughout his work:

'Written on water', one might say
Of each day's flux and lapse,
But to speak of water is to entertain the image
Of its seamless momentum once again,

To hear in its wash and grip on stone
A music of constancy behind
The wide promiscuity of acquaintanceship,
Water-ways permeating the rock of time.

Beyond their intrinsic beauty, these lines do Tomlinson the service of dispelling any notion of his work as primarily visual, literal, and empirical. Tomlinson's compound metaphor transmutes duration into water and water into music, ringing these changes in a flexible four-stress line that Tomlinson has characterized as a "version of sprung rhythm": a fluent measure whose physical counterpart is water itself. The passage is both an act of empathy and a masterful cadenza.

Tomlinson's newest collection, ***The Shaft,*** appears concurrently with his ***Selected Poems.*** For the most part, the new poems pursue the themes and styles of the earlier volumes, but one marked change can be seen in a group of historical pieces, in which the poet broods on figures and scenes from the French Revolution, particularly Charlotte Corday. . . . [Tomlinson has remarked] that his historical poems have grown naturally from his earlier work, since he has always been concerned with the processes of change and with "a sense of time impinging on place." Perhaps that is true; but the historical-critical mode of the new poems and the rhymed pentameter stanzas in which they are written seem unnatural and even regressive in a poet whose best work has been rooted in the contingencies of the present moment, and whose poetic strengths are not so much critical as scrupulously contemplative. One can admire Tomlinson's venture without applauding the result. (pp. 110-12)

[It] is not too early to say that among post-War British poets Tomlinson is the one who has drawn on the broadest range of modernist traditions—British, Continental, and American—and brought them into the closest harmony, both with one another and with the descriptive-meditative tradition of English poetry. However he comes to be ranked, I should think that Tomlinson's distinction will rest not on his ambitious historical poems, much less on his "American scenes" in the manner of Williams, but on his concentrated meditations, brief but in no way slight, in which subtlety and intricacy of thought find their equal in originality of rhythm and texture. (p. 112)

Ben Howard, "Chords and Keys," in Poetry, *Vol. CXXXVII, No. 2, November, 1980, pp. 105-12.*

DONALD HALL

[***Some Americans***] gathers in its 134 pages a variety of pleasures. A British poet of the first rank, Mr. Tomlinson is more indebted to modern American poetry than are any of his peers. In ***Some Americans,*** he touches on his beginnings as a poet, describes his isolation in England, and records the process by which he educated himself in an alien literature.

A different pleasure is Mr. Tomlinson's sensitivity to landscape. When we read his descriptions of Brooklyn or New Jersey, New Mexico or Italy, we recall that the poet is also a painter. He evokes a drive in New Mexico: "Among the ghostly greys of the winter cottonwood trees, behind the tin-roofed adobes, along the banks of the snow-filled Rio Chama, everything rekindled, glittered, sending up mica showers, crossing blades of light."

But the best parts of this book are the character sketches of American poets. In the first essay the young Tomlinson visits the United States and meets his generous American elders. The portrait of Marianne Moore is especially vivid, showing forth her affection, her humor and her literary intelligence; no one has captured her as well as Mr. Tomlinson. And he writes engagingly about William Carlos Williams, energetic despite a series of strokes, welcoming, enthusiastic. As the author writes, "It is strange to have met the innovators of one's time only when age had overtaken them." ***Some Americans*** is about aging as well as about poets, poetry and landscape.

In Mr. Tomlinson's America there is room for a variety of poets, and he interprets them judiciously. Meeting Yvor Winters in California, Mr. Tomlinson praised another poet by using a word Winters was not fond of. "'Original?' said Winters; 'there is no particular virtue in orginality, you know.'" Mr. Tomlinson's understanding of Winters is exact: "One could imagine a tone in which that could have sounded crushing, yet it was offered not coldly but rather as advice." When Mr. Tomlinson describes George Oppen and Louis Zukofsky in the book's second essay, he embodies character as well as he judges it; two shadowy figures walk into light as the author relates with melancholy scrupulosity the quarrel that developed between them late in their careers.

The last two chapters of the books are less coherent as essays. A visit to Georgia O'Keeffe in New Mexico is brief and enigmatic; but Mr. Tomlinson's admiration for her work (and for the landscape of her paintings) makes the prose a pleasure. The last chapter, about his experiences in Italy, portrays the by-then silent Ezra Pound and praises the old Italy while lamenting its prosperous self-destruction. Mr. Tomlinson's feeling for Italy helps us to remember how English a figure he is—one who exists in Britain mostly at the edges of literary favor, still charged by some with the treason of modernism. (pp. 12, 16)

Donald Hall, "Poet's Progress," in The New York Times Book Review, *March 1, 1981, pp. 12, 16-17.*

PHOEBE PETTINGELL

[In ***Some Americans: A Personal Record***], the British poet and painter Charles Tomlinson charts his own "mental emigration" from "that suffocation which has affected so much English art ever since the death of Byron" to the fresh air of our land of poetic liberty.

A few lines from Ezra Pound, discovered in a Faber verse anthology, were what initially propelled Tomlinson in the direction of "that unknown quantity, American art." For a student at Cambridge in 1945, modern American poetry was unmapped territory; little of it had been published in Britain, and that was mostly uncharacteristic. "Pretty self-conscious, I should say," sniffed a roommate with whom Tomlinson tried to share his enthusiasm for Marianne Moore's "The Steeple-Jack." But Moore's austerity opened Tomlinson's eyes to "a kind of probity possible in verse for which seemliness would be no bad description." He missed this quality in the neometaphysical followers of Eliot and Auden, still favored by the British literary establishment. It was, he notes, "an unpropitious time to write the kind of verse that interested me, and England an unpropitious place in which to publish it. An heir of Pound, Moore, Stevens must inevitably appear an odd fish in English waters." Small wonder, then, that he seized every opportunity to visit the United States, to meet many of the poets he had admired from afar, and to see for himself the American scenery that had shaped their art.

The subjects of ***Some Americans*** are the artists who made Tomlinson feel, for the first time, "part of a small clan." In addition to Moore, the group included Ivor Winters, William Carlos Williams and two other original founders of the "objectivist" school, George Oppen and Louis Zukofsky. Tomlinson also pays tribute to the more remote presences of Georgia O'Keeffe, whose paintings altered modern ways of seeing, and to Pound—the patriarch of modernism.

In keeping with the objectivist credo, "No ideas but in things," Tomlinson conveys the essence of his experiences through details. He immediately recognized the house he was seeking in Abiquiu, New Mexico, when he spotted "a gateway adorned by an immense deer skull complete with branching antlers. It brought to mind O'Keeffe's painting, *From the Faraway Nearby,* where the sky is filled with a horned floating skull, behind it the empty blue, and bare desert hills beneath." No less tellingly, the silence of the aging Pound during a chance encounter at the Spoletto Festival in 1967 is an emblem of the enigma of that poet's last years. "He sat concentratedly engaged in removing every particle of ice cream from the bottom of his dish with a plastic spoon. Though once the conversation among the rest of us had taken fire and no one was looking at him, he began to examine each face with minute scrupulousness, losing not a word as he leaned forward, picking avidly at the skin on the palm of his left hand." Tomlinson is content to record Pound's behavior without guessing whether it is sagacity or senility. Perhaps that is why the image speaks louder than any description of the late poet I have read.

Eventually, Tomlinson became intimately involved in the circle of Oppen and Zukofsky, although the artistic fellowship that so encouraged the Englishman operated less powerfully between the two American poets. Tomlinson was a sorrowful spectator of their growing misunderstanding of each other's work, a situation all the more poignant to him because "from both their windows in Brooklyn they had shared the view of the same 'lighthouse'—the beam from the statue [of Liberty] shining back in the dusk toward the windows of Manhattan."

In the second half of ***Some Americans,*** Tomlinson tries to cast that beam on the origins and unifying sources of America's artistic strengths. This quest carries him to the "enfiladed mesas commanding their orange, juniper-stippled spaces" of Abiquiu, a place of Asian starkness and simplicity. He is reminded that O'Keeffe and Pound were inspired by the work of the American Orientalist, Ernest Fenellosa. A more important influence is that first magisterial transatlantic exile, Henry James: "Some of the urban poetry James catches out of the corner of his eye, as it were, often contains the kind of detail out of which Williams would construct an entire poem."

Despite his attraction to American poetry, Tomlinson decided not to make his home here. Having found his poetic voice, he has settled down at the quintessentially British address of Ozleworth Bottom, Wotton-under-Edge. He concludes his account of ***Some Americans*** with James and Pound in Italy, where they left "a ponderable impression in the literate Italian mind" and helped its modern writers rediscover the glories of their own past. Taking this as exemplary, Tomlinson sees the American poetic tradition less as a paragon for Europeans than a force liberating the old world's imagination toward its boundless spiritual vistas. (pp. 14-15)

Phoebe Pettingell, "America in 'Metres'," in The New Leader, *Vol. 64, No. 11, June 1, 1981, pp. 14-15.*

JONATHAN BARKER

The Flood is Charles Tomlinson's tenth book of poems, his first—***Relations and Contraries***—being published exactly thirty years ago. These ten books contain over four hundred poems. In addition to this output, Tomlinson has since the late 1960s produced paintings and graphic works in great profusion. . . .

Tomlinson's work as a poet has developed with a steady, meticulous, and startlingly consistent assurance. His first book contained only one poem which he felt worth preserving in his ***Selected Poems 1951-1974*** but that one is recognizably his. It describes a horse-driven float in terms of sound (the horse's hooves breaking "clean and frost-sharp on the unstopped ear") and sight ("The hooves describe an arabesque on space"). Tomlinson went on to produce memorable books at both ends of the 1960s. ***Seeing Is Believing*** (1960) contains his famous rejection of Symbolism in the poem **"Antecedents":** "the shut cell of that solitude" is seen as a view of life too subjective to allow accurate contemplation of the outside world. Tomlinson's personal poetic of thinking and feeling with the eye was an attempt to break free from what he saw as the neo-Romantic view of the poet: it was as if he needed to write a poetry which respected objects as things with their own independent life. ***The Way of a World*** (1969), surely Tomlinson's most impressive single book, combined his passion and respect for language as a means of precisely exploring the world with his equal passion and respect for objects outside ourselves. This produced a masterly title poem [**"The Way of a World"**]. . . .

The Way In (1974) introduced Tomlinson's personal history with **"At Stoke"**, an autobiographical piece that also provides insight into the poems and the graphic works: "I have lived in a single landscape. Every tone / And turn have had for their ground / These beginnings in grey-black". The printed poems had always naturally enough used black ink on white paper, but eventually this colour, or lack of colour, extended to the black gouache of Tomlinson's graphic works. These are executed in ascetic black, white and grey and create imaginary worlds and chance relationships between images. The fact that Tomlinson's visual education took place in the industrial landscape of Stoke ("This place the first to seize on my heart and eye, / Has been their hornbook and their history") may not be beside the point here. The sense of his urban roots is stressed in a poem called **"The Lesson"** (included in Tomlinson's new book, ***The Flood***) on the Gloucestershire countryside: "I still keep the eye of a newcomer, / a townsman's eye". Even though he has lived in the countryside for twenty years, his outsider's eye ensures that everything he sees is continually revalued.

Tomlinson's central themes have always been sensation and the mind examining sensations in relation to natural phenomena. Once we grasp this we can see that the chief poetic precursor of Tomlinson is not Wallace Stevens, William Carlos Williams or Giuseppe Ungaretti (although their techniques have influenced him considerably), but the William Wordsworth who talked of nature "feelingly watched" and who was able to watch a butterfly for half an hour so as to discover whether it slept or fed.

The Flood is different to the five books which have preceded it in one very noticeable way. Instead of arranging the poems by theme, the book moves apparently chronologically through the poet's travels. The sequence of places seems to be: Gloucestershire, North America, Italy and back to Gloucestershire again. The forms of the poems change with the locations. The Gloucestershire poems are generally longer, utilizing a meditative and fluid unrhymed run-on line. The poems set in New Mexico or other parts of the United States tend to be shorter travel snapshots (the titles are often place-names, as in a travel diary), and the topics touched on include the decline of power of tribal spirits in Jemez, the cries of the eagle dancers at Cochiti, divers at San Fruttuoso, and the noises of the frogs in Poolville, NY. The poems lead naturally from one to the next, the link being the almost invisible "I" of the poet as he moves from the snow of the first poem through the desert garden in New Mexico to the tributary of the River Severn which dominates the final poems.

These travel poems could possibly be used as evidence to support the traditional complaint (usually made by those who later admit to not having read much of his work) that Tomlinson does not write directly about what Robert Frost called "inner weather". But to Tomlinson whatever happens around him defines his inner nature: he discovers the world through his relationship to it. . . . Hence Tomlinson's need to record clearly what he sees and experiences without moving directly into the limelight.

The Flood contains a great variety of poems, among them the very personal elegy **"For Miriam"**; the unashamed prose passage **"The Near and the Far"**; the humorous **"Albuquerque"**, in which a cinema built in the same year as the birth of the poet is being restored—"I am antique already" the poem ends; **"Programme Note"**, on a musical concert (it is the latest in a series of poems by Tomlinson on music, "the wholly imaginary passion" as he calls it); a narrative poem for Charles Olson; and the strange little poem **"Parsnips"**, which sees parsnips as "this image of perfection". Cézanne commented similarly on carrots; and Cézanne and Tomlinson are alike in their ability to look at familiar things in a new way.

But the best and most essentially Tomlinsonian poems in ***The Flood*** are those gathered towards the end of the book and set "beside a stream in Gloucestershire", as home is described in a touchingly personal and public poem, **"Instead of an Essay"**, addressed to Donald Davie. Davie, the first and surely still with Michael Schmidt the best critic and champion of Tomlinson's poems, is called "Brother in a mystery you trace / To God, I to an awareness of delight / I cannot name". This delight in the act of sensually experiencing the world is an aspect of Tomlinson's poetry which has been curiously understressed by critics. . . .

[**"The Flood"**] is a personal meditation on the night the "stream in Gloucestershire" rose violently during rain and flooded the poet's home. (The cover of the book shows a detail of Leonardo's "The Deluge"). The almost symbolic water of the river, and the stone of the house once "perfectly reconciled" side by side with it, are incongruously mixed when the river floods. Stone, "the image of a constancy", becomes "as porous as a sponge", although "the walls held"; meanwhile the "we" of the poem sleep upstairs, hung "between a dream of fear and the very thing"—an idea to be returned to in the final poem in the book, **"The Epilogue"**. Characteristically **"The Flood"** ends with the poet's pleasure next morning when he sees his flooded rooms downstairs, where reflections of water and light dance "in whorls on every ceiling" and produce "this vertigo of sunbeams everywhere". Sight overcomes everything else as the poet pauses "to praise the shimmer". Seeing is believing indeed; and daylight enables the poet to hack down a bank so that water can return to the river.

"The Epilogue" is an extraordinary poem, a rare but not unique example of Tomlinson using the surreal or "so real", as he punningly and tellingly calls it elsewhere. The inner world of imagination is usually the domain of his graphic works, but here chance and dream enter a poem in which the possible death of "Myself and you" under an apocalyptic tidal wave is averted when the poet wakes from nightmare to the real world and its sounds. "Caught back from epilogue to epilogue" the poem ends—the first epilogue being the possible end of the world, the second and more immediate ending being that of the book. **"The Epilogue"** is also, of course, the epilogue to the poem **"The Flood":** in both it is the world of light, and the sight and sounds of morning, which dismiss fear felt at night.

In his best poems, and I am inclined to include [**"The Flood"**] among them, Tomlinson achieves the very thing that he once praised John Constable for doing: "for what he saw / Discovered what he was, and the hand—unswayed / by the dictation of a single sense— / Bodied the accurate and total knowledge / In a calligraphy of present pleasure". Pleasure is indeed the word to end on: if not his best book, ***The Flood*** is certainly one of Tomlinson's most varied and rewarding.

Jonathan Barker, "An Awareness of Delight," in The Times Literary Supplement, *No. 4085, July 17, 1981, p. 816.*

DENNIS O'DRISCOLL

No one, it would seem, has managed to write about Charles Tomlinson's poetry without invoking the names of his mentors, of Marianne Moore or William Carlos Williams, of Ungaretti or Wallace Stevens. Tomlinson's refreshing open-mindedness as reader, editor and critic has left his own work open to the influences of the very poets he has championed; and it is one of the curious features of his mature—even recent—poetry that derivative verse is to be found alongside brilliant original writing. (p. 79)

It would, nonetheless, be a mistake to dwell too long on the many influences to which Charles Tomlinson's poetry has proved susceptible, since at his best he is capable of more genuine individuality than the majority of his English contemporaries. . . . Tomlinson's books may be uneven—and ***The Flood*** is no exception—but his commitment to a catholic view of poetry has been consistent.

The Flood includes many lean, muscular poems of the kind which Tomlinson has mastered over the years but begins and ends with poems in the longer line which he has tended to favour in recent work. The leaner poems move in geography from New Mexico to Italy and in subject-matter from frogs to tribal spirits. . . . (pp. 79-80)

Although in Tomlinson's keenest verse the world is more than the sum of the parts observed, he mars an otherwise perfectly-observed poem, **"Parsnips"**, with didacticism. Other less successful poems include underdeveloped items like **"The Order of Saying"** and **"The Conspiracy"**, which should have remained in the poet's notebook, and meandering and overextended ones like **"Programme Note"** and **"For Miriam"**. However, many poems in ***The Flood*** prove Tomlinson's eye to be as sharply reflective as ever. (p. 80)

While indisputably prolix, the elegy **"For Miriam"** is interesting in its confrontation of religious matter. If Charles Tomlinson is in any sense a religious poet, it is because for him—as for Paul Celan—"attention is the natural prayer of the soul". In **"For Miriam"**, he casts himself as "a pagan", but wonders what form the resurrection of the "woman preacher" to whom the poem is addressed might take. Characteristically, it is in earthly terms that he imagines it, before the lines taper off into doubt. . . . In a poem for Donald Davie, entitled **"Instead of an Essay"**, Tomlinson asserts his fidelity to "an awareness of delight / I cannot name" rather than to a deity; but several poems in ***The Flood*** do adopt religious imagery and it is with an apocalyptic poem envisaging the end of the world that the collection concludes.

Of course, the very title of the book has Biblical connotations and the title-poem, **"The Flood"**, tells dramatically and in appropriately fluid lines of how the poet's Gloucestershire house, his "ark of stone", was surrounded, and its walls penetrated, by the flooding that followed thirty days of rain. This is the most packed and powerful poem in a book that glitters frequently with memorable descriptions of water. (pp. 80-1)

Dennis O'Driscoll, in a review of "The Flood," in Agenda, *Vol. 19, Nos. 2 & 3, Summer & Autumn, 1981, pp. 79-81.*

DANA GIOIA

The Flood marks no new breakthrough for Tomlinson. Rather it is a deepening of themes developed in his earlier books. Most of the poems describe the places one associates with the author—Italy, New Mexico, and Gloucestershire, where he now lives. Yet there is no sense of repetition. Though the places may by now be familiar, the inspiration behind the new poems is fresh and genuine. Tomlinson has often written about the coast of Italy, but **"San Fruttuoso: the divers"** is still a revelation. The author's eye for precise detail catches just those elements which made one day in that city unique.

Tomlinson is an artist as well as a poet, and his critics usually label him as a visual poet, one who uses close observation of the natural world as the basis of what one might literally call his artistic vision. Certainly Tomlinson has a sharp eye for images, but to consider him primarily a painter with words misses the most distinctive thing about his work—its sound. One can always recognize one of his poems (a hard claim to make for most English poets), whatever its subject, whether it is in free or formal verse. (p. 582)

Along with ***The Flood,*** Tomlinson has also published an unusual bilingual book written in collaboration with the Mexican poet, Octavio Paz. ***Airborn/Hijos del Aire*** consists of two short sequences of unrhymed sonnets each written around a central theme—**"House"** and **"Day."** The poets collaborated by writing alternate stanzas of each poem, Tomlinson in English, Paz in Spanish, which the other would then translate (thereby making the collaboration even more complex). Each sequence then ends with a poem written entirely by one poet (which, of course, is then immediately translated by the other). It all sounds like a lost novella by Nabokov, but the result is a remarkable little book.

Tomlinson and Paz are both fascinated with collaborative poetry, especially the linked verse of Japanese literature. (Their previous effort, ***Renga,*** in 1971, involved four poets working in four languages.) After reading ***Renga,*** I thought that such collaborations were doomed to be interesting curiosities. Yet ***Airborn*** comes so close to success that I now believe it may be possible to bring off these Japanese forms in a contemporary Western context. The best poem in the book is the one written entirely by Paz, but many of the others do work well in a curious way. The act of reading this poetry is very different from reading traditional texts. Here one is always conscious of the transitions from one poet to the next. Will Paz be able to follow the challenge of Tomlinson's stanza? Will Tomlinson be able to develop the images of Paz's opening lines? One cannot read these poems without continually judging whether one poet has built successfully on what came before. It is exciting, exhausting reading that challenges one's notion of what a poem (and a translation) really is.

For example, Paz begins one poem in the **"House"** section with a complex stanza that simultaneously recalls his own childhood home, which no longer exists except in memory, and also suggests that the poems he is now writing have become a kind of shared imaginary home for the two poets:

> *House that memory makes out of itself*
> *between the spaces of blank time—more thought*
> *than lived and yet more said than thought,*
> *house that lasts as long as its own sound takes.*

In Tomlinson's continuation one can't help noticing how the imagery becomes more concrete, the idea of the house less Platonic and more Proustian:

> house, you began in milk, in warmth, in eating:
> words must retongue your first solidities
> and thought keep fresh your fragrance of bread baking
> or drown in the stagnation of its memories . . .

One could ask whether this is a continuation of Paz's opening or an entirely new poem. Something in between, the authors would probably reply, and, whatever that something is, it's worth looking into. (pp. 583-84)

Dana Gioia, in a review of "The Flood" and "Airborn/Hijos del aire," in The Hudson Review, *Vol. XXXIV, No. 4, Winter, 1981-82, pp. 582-84.*

MICHAEL HENNESSY

Much recent interest in Charles Tomlinson's poetry has centered on his later work, particularly the long, meditative poems and sequences of poems from ***The Way of a World*** (1969), ***Written on Water*** (1972), and ***The Way In*** (1974). Although he has favored the meditative style less in the two volumes since ***The Way In,*** for many it has become the characteristic mode of his "major" poetry. As a result, his early work is now neglected, relegated more and more to secondary status and viewed largely in the shadow of the body of work which follows it. What I wish to do here is look in some detail at Tomlinson's early poetry, specifically his first two volumes, ***The Necklace*** (1955) and ***Seeing Is Believing*** (1958). In doing so, I aim to challenge the assumption that his early work is a preface to his real achievement, interesting mainly as the work of a poet whose talent—at least initially—was in rendering still lifes and in carefully and precisely recording the contours of the visible world.

I believe that even a cursory look at his earliest work shows that Tomlinson is far more than a recorder of surfaces. His first two volumes, it is true, offer a world dominated by the eye; everywhere we are brought into the sheer presence of mass, shape, and color, and our attention is directed continually—as by a painter—towards the subtle shifts of light and hue in the landscape before us. The early poems turn again and again toward the visible world, examining its surfaces and textures and excluding as much as possible the "subjective" interpretations of the poet in favor of a lucid objectivity.

But Tomlinson's insistence on "objectively" recording the world's surfaces is neither naive nor simplistic, for he is intent, even as he records, on recognizing the complexity of man's perceptual relationship with the world. In fact, the nature and limits of perception become an implicit theme in much of his early verse, and, although many poems strive simply for an accurate description of the phenomenal world, Tomlinson often questions the very basis for such description. . . . He is interested, then, not only in recording a world of objects, but in describing the process through which we know that world. (pp. 95-6)

Tomlinson's early poetry, while it acknowledges the capacity of the "I" to shape reality, focuses most intently on the way sense perception limits the self and defines our experiential relation with the world. Typical early poems like **"Venice"** . . . and **"Paring the Apple"** . . . , with their strong visual appeal, demonstrate this interest in sensation and show the direction in which that interest leads Tomlinson. His is an outer-directed, rather than an introspective poetry which—though it does not ignore thought and emotion—generally gives them second billing in favor of a more immediate apprehension of present things. Tomlinson is given over, he says, to "trusting sensation." Although he is obviously a careful and deliberate craftsman, he suggests that a number of his poems "have arisen by writing done very swiftly, before the object, before the actual scene, what was perceived, just as a painter might do a preliminary sketch from nature."

But if his poetry is grounded in sensation, Tomlinson insists that it is not limited thereby. Sensation for him is not merely "the naked impact of objects" on consciousness but rather, as he says, a "grasping for significance," a reaching out from the isolated self towards a relationship with the "other." It is not simply a matter of the "I" passively recording the presence of the "Other," and nowhere does Tomlinson suggest that poetry is merely a photographic enterprise in which the poet faithfully, and without comment, produces images of the world before him. Indeed, for Tomlinson, sensation implies an involvement with the world, a relationship in which we are continually "constructing ourselves." In his poetry the "Other" exists neither in an "isolate intensity" apart from the perceiver, nor as an extension of the perceiver's consciousness. Denis Donoghue describes the poems in terms of a "stillness, in which the self and the other are acknowledged for what they are, separate but not alien." And Tomlinson himself turns repeatedly to the idea of "relationship" in order to explain how sensation forms the basis of his poetry. . . . Rather than limiting the range of his poetry, Tomlinson sees sense perception as the basis for a broadening out, a movement away from the particular towards a larger concern with the human, towards an ethical awareness of man's relationship not only with things but with himself and others.

Even in ***The Necklace*** and ***Seeing Is Believing,*** where the focus on things is most intent, there is constant recognition of the complexities involved in every perception. The perceiver is no longer at the center; objects are brought into prominence or, as Tomlinson might say, into their rightful position as partners in the act of perception. The early poems strive for perspective, often delimiting the human by what surrounds it, placing man in a mutual relation with the world, with the things which surround him. In **"At Delft,"** for instance, the objects in a room are of interest as objects, but more importantly they serve to define human limits: "All that is human here stands clarified / By all that accompanies and bounds". . . . And in other poems man becomes the passive partner in his relation with the "Other." At one point in ***The Necklace,*** for example, "Objects regard us," thereby relegating us to the role of observed, chastening us to a forgetfulness of self and an acknowledgement instead of the "demands of a relationship."

The concept of perception that underlies Tomlinson's early poetry suggests, with its emphasis on the idea of relation, that the perceived world plays a central role in the formation of the self. Confronted by the world's surfaces, we are constantly molded, transformed, and renewed. "Surfaces," Tomlinson tells us, "are already leading one into depths." In **"Distinctions"** he bears this out, showing how even the simplest perception can lead to a shaping of the speaker's consciousness:

> A pine-branch
> Tugs at the eye: the eye
> Returns to grey-blue, blue-black or indigo
> Or it returns, simply,
> To blue-after-the-pine-branch. . . .

The "pine-branch" draws us into a relationship, it demands the attention of our eye and it leaves the mind not with some distorted image, but literally, with the after-image of a "pine-branch." "Here," the poem continues, "there is no question of aberrations / Into pinks, golds or mauves." At the precise moment of perception "Between the minutest interstices of time / Blue is blue." Tomlinson insists that the precision and simplicity of such a perception are significant; the self has given way to a recognition of actualities and thereby denied its potential for molding the world to its own image.

Another more complex statement of the way the world shapes the self is offered in **"The Atlantic,"** a poem in which the observation of waves upon a beach becomes the basis for describing how the "Other" defines, and in this case, "replenishes" the human. At the end of the poem the sun, reflected in a "lucid pane" of water on the sand, is "like an after-image / Released from the floor of a now different mind." The "Other" renews us, provides a fresh perspective, and assists in defining our own humanness. . . . (pp. 96-8)

When his early poetry moves away from observation, as it does in **"The Atlantic,"** it almost always does so in order to remind us of our proper place in the world. Tomlinson urges us to recognize human limits rather than striving to go beyond them. From observation of the world's surfaces, he moves quickly and surely into the depths of the self. And if we are unable, like some reviewers, to recognize the "human" in his early poetry, it is because we have failed to recognize our human dependence upon the world around us. He continually draws us towards this recognition, especially in ***Seeing Is Believing*** where his earlier concern with observation opens into a more overt interest in exploring the ethical implications of his epistemological stance. **"In Defense of Metaphysics"** typifies his capacity to draw a moral inference from a simple moment of observation. The poem—a meditation on stones—carefully defines our relation to the nonhuman world. It begins with a question: "What is the language of stones?" And it moves rapidly to insist that their significance is not merely a symbolic one. . . . The poem continues with a moral lesson, urging us, as Tomlinson writes elsewhere, "towards relation, towards grasp, towards awareness of all that which we are not, yet of relation with it." . . . Just as the pine branch acts by "tugging" at our eyes, so here the stones become the active partner in their perceptual relation with us. Our contact with them is the "melting of person and presence" that Tomlinson speaks of, and it is that contact that brings us to a realization of human limits and to a recognition of our place in the world. Poems urging the same recognition abound in both ***The Necklace*** and ***Seeing Is Believing.***

His insistence on defining man's place in the world makes Tomlinson far more than a detached observer of appearances. His poetry, it is true, grows out of an epistemology that places high regard on the world's surfaces as a source of knowledge. But his concern with surfaces transcends its obvious limitations and leads Tomlinson away from simple observation towards much larger issues; finally, even the simplest perception leads to the question of belief. Thus Tomlinson's early poetry is more than a mere affirmation of the senses. It is an expression of belief in the existence of a world outside the subjective consciousness, a world that serves as the basis for moral observations and actions—and, hence, the equation in the title of his second volume: ***Seeing Is*** (that is, equals) ***Believing.*** (pp. 99-100)

Tomlinson's poetry, as we have seen, consistently looks outward. Its ethic enjoins against the kind of self-serving egotism that allows us to impose our internal world upon the world around us. His poetry opposes what Denis Donoghue sees as "one of the dominant assumptions of modern literature, that nothing is real unless we have made it," that "the phenomena of earth are tokens of nothing but ourselves." Indeed, when our concept of reality loses its dependence on everything but the subjective self, there is, in Donoghue's words, a "temptation to be Master, to set up as God."

In ethical terms Tomlinson's poetry urges us away from this temptation, away from an egotism that makes man the sole master of his world. He sees such egotism, especially in the early poetry, as a problem of willfulness. In place of willfulness, he offers not a withdrawal of personality, but (in the terms of Taoist philosophy) a "containment of the will" and a recognition instead of the limitations of the individual. His ethic leads us towards a cleansing of the self, an acceptance of restraint rather than license, and hence his avowed differences with Yeats and Dylan Thomas, the two figures whose aesthetic and moral presences dominated the poetic climate when Tomlinson began his career: Yeats's ego stands at the center of his poetry, his god-like presence felt everywhere; Thomas takes us into a private and notably unrestrained communion with nature in which he discovers primarily a reflection of himself. Tomlinson, on the other hand—and this is at least partly the source of his striking originality—denies the expansive ego in favor of a containment of the self. . . . Tomlinson urges us in both ***The Necklace*** and ***Seeing Is Believing*** to take solace in the world's actualities, to accept them on their own terms with an openness to that which we are not. (pp. 101-02)

Michael Hennessy, "Perception and Self in Charles Tomlinson's Early Poetry," in Rocky Mountain Review of Language and Literature, *Vol. 36, No. 2, 1982, pp. 95-102.*

MICHAEL O'NEILL

[It] would be difficult to imagine a more fastidiously attenuated poetic landscape than the one portrayed in [***The Flood***]. All threads lead into the labyrinthine meditations on the nature of perception and the respective roles of subject and object at which Tomlinson is an adept. **"At the Edge"** distils the theme and displays the skill:

Edges are centres: once you have found
  Their lines of force, the least of gossamers
Leads and frees you, nets you a universe
  Whose iridescent weave shines true
Because you see it, but whose centre is not you:

The discovery which that last line formulates and the whole poem enacts—that freedom comes from accurate attention to one's true place in the universe—is the goal towards which most of the good poems in this book (**"Snow Signs"**, **"The Flood"** and **"The Recompense"** are all examples) take their individual routes. . . .

I find the poet's vocabulary less satisfactory, inducing a cerebral taming of life. This is opposed to the poetry's desire to remain open to the unpredictabilities of existence, but it emerges through the reliance on a series of elegant surrogates for acts of mind. . . . These terms are meant to stand in for the poet's modified objectivism, his search for austere epiphanies—but sometimes they stand in its way, instead. At his best Tomlinson has helped his reader to *see,* and to learn from the process of seeing a more purified form of feeling. In ***The Flood*** he seems to have relaxed his visualising ambitions. Though there are some fine short poems in the book—**"Cronkhite Beach"** is one—they lack the taut linguistic resourcefulness of which Tomlinson is capable. Nevertheless, the volume is always well-crafted and, if short on deep feelings for other people (despite the brave gestures of the elegy **"For Miriam"**), rewardingly intense in its concerns.

Michael O'Neill, "Charles Tomlinson," in Poetry Review, *Vol. 72, No. 1, April, 1982, p. 64.*

CLAUDE RAWSON

Charles Tomlinson and Octavio Paz collaborated in producing 'the first Western renga', a Japanese name for a poem by several poets writing alternating parts. That first experiment was quadrilingual, and ***Airborn*** is a bilingual variant 'in slow motion': alternating sections of sonnets were passed to and fro by correspondence. There were two linked sequences of four sonnets each, on the theme of **"House"** and of **"Day"**, translated where appropriate, so that the end-product exists entire in both Spanish and English. The passages originally written in Spanish are given in italics in both versions, those in English in roman.

"House" is a characteristic Tomlinson theme. He inaugurates the whole operation by contributing the first stanza of **"House"**, and closes it by writing the entire last sonnet of **"Day"**, itself composed around the idea of the house, his house. There is an easy sense of rootedness, contrasting oddly at times with Paz's contribution, which constantly tugs towards a greater abstraction, a separation of thought from thing. *'We are born in houses we did not make,'* says Paz, forcing Tomlinson back in the next poem to insist afresh on primary solidities of belonging. . . . 'Thought' is a reifying, not a rarefying, process. 'Letters are stones that fly,' he says in the first poem of **"Day"**, 'to settle in a wall.' Words, poems, are used for establishing or recovering contact, rather than defining a distance. Where visual definition is involved, there is a painterly, not a photographer's perspective, a stress on remaking rather than on viewing, posing, arranging; or on recapturing essential lines rather than reproducing the visible surface.

This is everywhere evident in his latest book, ***Flood,*** from the opening poem, **"Snow Signs",** onwards. It shows itself even in **"On a Pig's Head"**, a festive grotesquerie in which the very hacking and gore of the butcher's knife are submitted to the studious artist's sense of line and angle:

transforming the thing
to a still life, hacked
and halved, cross-cutting it
into angles with ears.

The transformation 'to a still life' is no aestheticising reduction. It shows the poet responding to the thrust of lines and angles, not watching them, as Richard Eberhart watched the bones of his Groundhog, 'like a geometer', but catching essential shape even as it resides in driving energy. Tomlinson's poem recalls Eberhart's, and also Ted Hughes's "View of a Pig", where the 'view' is neither the geometer's nor the painter's. This cut-up pig is not lines and angles but all energy and no 'shape', a bravura of disfigurement: 'The gash in its throat was shocking.' The cooking of the pig, in Hughes, is a large amorphous cleansing, a scalding and a scouring, while Tomlinson's pig will be confected with peppercorns, cloves of garlic, bay-leaves and wine, and kept down in boiling water by a great red rock from Macuilxochitl, an orderly event, disciplined, decorative and fraught with pleasurable solidities at once domestic and exotic. ***Flood*** is an attractive volume, with some good new poems in the vein of ***American Scenes,*** sharply observant, wry, affectionately ironic, and some characteristically delicate meditations on Italian themes and landscapes. (pp. 20-1)

Claude Rawson, "Kelpers," in London Review of Books, *June 17-30, 1982, pp. 20-1.*

MICHAEL HENNESSY

Tomlinson has gradually matured in the past fifteen years, forging his own meditative style out of the earlier American influences on his art. His most recent work—two new collections and a gathering of older writing—confirms my belief that he is one of the most important talents to emerge in Britain since the War. After nine collections, he has established a body of work impressive both for its intellectual and emotional depth, as well as its technical fineness. ***Selected Poems, The Shaft*** and ***The Flood*** offer an impressive confirmation of his talent.

There is much to see in Tomlinson. Here I can hope only to touch down in a few poems, to at least suggest something of the various pleasures I find in reading him. First among these is the sheer joy of seeing; underpinning all the poetry is Tomlinson's ability to record "otherness," to see and simply to describe an "objective" world of phenomena, and to find in the visible world a basis for belief. What Witter Bynner says of the great Chinese poets can be said also of Tomlinson: They "accept the world exactly as they find it . . . and with a profound simplicity find therein sufficient solace." . . . Tomlinson typically avoids the lush, the opulent; his doing so is a deliberate choice, a chastening of the excesses of the romantic ego, of the confessional extremes of much contemporary verse. The imagination need not "lie," need not distort or alter the world. Tomlinson insists, in fact, that its proper function is the opposite; it engages us firmly with the real. . . .

Besides the pleasures of seeing, of experiencing the world "out there" through the cleansing imagination, Tomlinson offers the bracing, unexpected pleasure of didacticism. He is willing to explore openly the ethical implications of his art, and he reaffirms, it seems to me, the teaching function of the poet, sharing Ben Jonson's view that a direct moral injunction, when presented convincingly, can be a source of delight. In a century which Aldous Huxley has dubbed "The Age of Noise," Tomlinson stands on the side of silence. He is openly and insistently "against extremity," against the apocalyptic temper of the times. . . . Tomlinson is sometimes accused of having little to say of the anguish and pain that are embodied convincingly in much contemporary verse. Though his stance "against extremity" may seem facile in a brief excerpt, it becomes credible, I think, when drawn out in the particulars of his best poems—as credible, surely, as the anguished extremes of many of his peers. To Larkin's "Life is first boredom, then fear," I imagine Tomlinson saying:

Well, if mourning
were all we had,
we could settle for a great simplicity,
mourn ourselves mad.

But that is only half
the question: blight
has its cures and hopes
come uninvited.

The gentle acceptance of such lines, in one sense, sets the tone for much of Tomlinson's recent work. ***The Shaft*** and ***The Flood*** by no means abandon the essential Tomlinson themes, and both books add important poems to his corpus, mostly in the lengthy, meditative mode in which he has written much of his major work—**"Charlotte Corday," "Marat Dead," "For Miriam,"** and **"The Flood."** But the more typical recent poems are lighter in tone, continuing a direction initiated in Tomlinson's 1974 volume, ***The Way In.*** In such poems he is increasingly present as a subjective "I," foregoing some of his earlier objectivity, making his writing more relaxed and conversational. His subjects are often commonplace, his approach anecdotal, as in **"Prose Poem,"** one of the best of the lighter pieces in ***The Shaft.*** . . .

I have said nothing here of the dense, meditative intellection of Tomlinson's later poetry (**"Swimming Chenango Lake"** and **"Prometheus"** are among his best); nothing of his technical innovation; nothing of his impressive sense of humor which has been largely ignored by reviewers; and nothing of the fine translations (several of which appear in ***Selected Poems***). That there *is* so much to say testifies amply to the many talents of this poet, to the numerous and varied pleasures he continues to offer his readers.

Michael Hennessy, in a review of "Selected Poems: 1951-1974," "The Shaft," and "The Flood," in The American Book Review, *Vol. 4, No. 6, September-October, 1982, p. 22.*

ALAN YOUNG

Two recently-published books by Charles Tomlinson—***Some Americans*** and ***The Flood***—enhance his already considerable status as a writer. The first, a readable, short yet richly-detailed prose account of the contributions made by some modern American poets and a painter to the growth of his art, is invaluable for several reasons. Not only does the book throw much light on Tomlinson's own debts to the legacy of Ezra Pound and other Americans influenced by *il miglior fabbro,* it gives readers over here fascinating vignettes of major figures in American art of this century. Wallace Stevens, William Carlos Williams, Yvor Winters, Marianne Moore, George Oppen, Louis Zukofsky, the painter Georgia O'Keeffe, and Ezra Pound himself—all these heroes and heroines of American modernism are vividly and variously portrayed at first hand. They are shown in spirited struggle against artistic isolation (even in the United States) and philistinism (everywhere), involved in all-too-human misunderstanding, as well as suffering from the ills which come with old age.

Tomlinson's record of encounters with American art and artists shows too how one English poet found that he could make use of their discoveries without any threat to his own identity or, indeed, his Englishness. Confirmation of this comes in the second book, ***The Flood,*** Tomlinson's latest volume of poems, which confidently achieves assimilation of some characteristics and qualities of American literary modernism to help shape a distinctively personal yet essentially English voice and vision.

The opening chapter of ***Some Americans*** tells how a boy from the North Midlands, going up to Cambridge in 1945 to read English, found gradually that a few poems, stanzas and lines from modern American verse carried haunting messages for him. . . . [Lines] from Ezra Pound in particular stayed in his mind, like Stephen Dedalus's 'messengers from the secret morning' or, as Tomlinson calls them, 'talismanic fragments'. One quality which drew him to Pound's work was 'a sense of cleanliness in the phrasing'. Nobody else he knew of could produce such *clean* writing as, for instance, the opening line of 'A garden': 'Like a skein of loose silk blown against a wall'. (pp. 67-8)

For several years after he had left Cambridge the American modernist presence was to remain a relatively fragmented, though increasingly formative, part of Tomlinson's experience. . . . In American writing he began to distinguish between two quite different positions. Crane, Whitman, Poe, and Emerson represented in various degrees an other-worldly, even suicidally self-negating approach to existence. In Pound, Moore, Stevens, and Williams, however, Tomlinson recognised a stance closer to his own 'basic theme': 'that one does not need to go beyond sense experience to some mythic union, that the "I" can only be responsible in relationship and not by dissolving itself away into ecstasy or the Oversoul'.

A belief in the individual's world of here and now is at the heart of Tomlinson's essentially moral vision. In the well-known poem **"Against extremity"**—published in ***The Way of a World*** (1969)—he says: '. . . extremity hates a given good / Or a good gained'. These lines and others from an earlier poem, **"Aesthetic"**—'Reality is to be sought, not in concrete / But in space made articulate . . .'—may help us understand both the celebratory and the selective nature of his poetic imagination.

In his poetry of the 1950s (***The Necklace*** and ***Seeing Is Believing***), besides Pound, Stevens, and Moore, there are also the tones of Coleridge's conversation poems and a confident aesthetic consciously derived in part from Coleridge (and Kant?), Ruskin, and T. S. Eliot. From the last-named, Tomlinson tells us, he absorbed the limitations on individualism: 'a suspicion of the romantic ego and of the notion that poetry can be carried through by the gust of personality and intensity'.

Towards the end of the 1950s Tomlinson had begun to correspond with Marianne Moore. At this time he was experimenting with William Carlos Williams's 'three-ply' poems and he exchanged letters with Williams too. His work—almost disregarded in [Great Britain]—was increasingly well-received in the United States. ***Seeing Is Believing*** came out in New York after many rejections from British publishers. It is little wonder, then, that he found himself estranged from the closed-in attitudes of English *Movement* poetry, even though the best writers in that critical cage, including Larkin as well as Davie, were always breaking through the bars.

In 1959 Tomlinson visited the USA for the first time. During this and later visits he met Marianne Moore, Yvor Winters, William Carlos Williams, and several younger writers. His descriptions of these meetings are full of simple, affectionate charm and a delighted observation of particulars. His American friends were touched by his genuine admiration for their work and, in turn, they recognised the American-inspired qualities in his poetry. The first chapter of ***Some Americans*** ends with the unanswered question why Tomlinson has remained in Britain when (as Wyndham Lewis suggested to him) he might have had much earlier recognition and a larger, more sympathetic, readership in the USA. Perhaps part of the answer is that Tomlinson is even more English than even he recognises. (pp. 68-9)

[In the second chapter] Tomlinson describes encounters with the founder-Objectivists, George Oppen and Louis Zukofsky. They are portrayed with deep affection. Tomlinson received craftsmen's and artists' encouragement from them—from Zukofsky in particular. (p. 69)

The making of poems as precise musical objects is what Tomlinson finds in the Objectivists, both confirming and, through Zukofsky, developing important (though not quite so central) facets of his own poetic. Lively portrayals of Oppen and Zukofsky conclude with a sympathetic analysis of the painful division which had grown between these former close friends and sensitive, proud writers.

Tomlinson's one meeting in 1963 with the painter Georgia O'Keeffe, described in his third chapter, reminds his readers that Tomlinson is a painter too. His appreciation of Miss O'Keeffe's work and of the desert landscapes of New Mexico in winter are written with a painter's sensitive eye. . . . (pp. 69-70)

In his final chapter—on memories of Italy and Ezra Pound—he creates a study in musical form and many styles. . . . **"Dove sta memoria"** is a brilliant piece in which Tomlinson's love of Italy—people, art, landscapes, and architecture—and modern poetry are woven in skilful prose, making one wonder why he has written so little in this genre before this.

All the positive qualities which Tomlinson has admired in his chosen Americans are to be found in the finely-wrought poems of ***The Flood.*** A sureness of poetic making combined with alternating joy in the world of the senses and sorrow that, inexorably, this world goes make this Tomlinson's most persuasive collection. Delighted senses and awareness of hurrying time are woven together in poem after poem. Although the locations change—from the poet's home terrain in a Gloucestershire valley, to New Mexico and Italy, then back to the Severn estuary and his home—it is time's passing which runs counter to evocations of place.

The first dozen or so poems move from winter to high summer in a landscape which Tomlinson knows as richly as ever Wordsworth knew his Cumberland. Indeed, Wordsworth and Coleridge are the writers of whom we are continually reminded. Tomlinson's poetic mode, like theirs, is one of imaginative possession of a terrain which is simultaneously of the mind's making and convincingly realised.There are several effective short lyrics here, including a truly haunting song ('Their voices rang'), but three longer poems—**"Snow signs", "For Miriam",** and **"The recompense"**—show Tomlinson completely in control of his medium. (pp. 70-1)

"Snow signs", alongside **"The flood", "The epilogue",** and **"Severnside"** at the end of this volume, is one of the most impressive achievements in contemporary lyric poetry. With a verbal music which Zukofsky would have delighted in, an eye for detail which vies with Marianne Moore's, the poem varies tone and measure so skilfully that it is difficult to quote from without giving a false idea of the whole. . . . **"The flood"** is perhaps not so complex as **"Snow signs",** but it is a superb evocation of home in winter flood and a recreation of the mind's self-making from the (literal) light of experience. It is also an artefact of mature craftsmanship. (pp. 71-2)

In ***Some Americans*** Charles Tomlinson has argued that English poets can learn from modern American poetics. He has also provided the most convincing introduction to American modernism for readers over here. In ***The Flood*** he has demonstrated this argument tellingly while showing above all that an original and masterly English imagination can transmute all its hard-won materials, from whatever source, into original English poetry. (pp. 72-3)

Alan Young, "Rooted Horizon: Charles Tomlinson and American Modernism," in Critical Quarterly, *Vol. 24, No. 4, Winter, 1982, pp. 67-73.*

WILLIAM H. PRITCHARD

The first fifteen poems from [***Notes from New York and Other Poems***] . . . are about visiting New York City, and are a delight. Manhattan by air, the World Trade Center, Madison Avenue, Verdi Square, and Hero Sandwiches are among the sights enjoyed. These are poems which no New Yorker would have thought to write, and they present their materials so as to make them fresh glimpses into the usual. . . . There is a fine calmness and inevitability about Tomlinson's lines which make no attempt to "work" on the reader, concerned as they are with, in Pound's phrase, the dignity of sheer presentation. But there is often wit in these quiet perceptions: "To cross a ferry that is no longer there, / The eye must pilot you to the farther shore," would surely be the way to begin "Crossing Brooklyn Ferry" if you were to rewrite such a poem, as Tomlinson has. **"In Verdi Square"** does charming things with that patch of turf known not so long ago as Needle Park and featured, before that, in Bellow's *Seize the Day:*

A minute garden
you must not enter
and whose birds (there are notices)
you are forbidden to feed:

Verdi surveys it all
stone cloak on arm
as if about to quit
his pigeoned pedestal:

without coming down
he knows perfectly well
which operas are in town . . .

and it goes on to bring off other nice effects, especially having to do with the square's presidor. It may be just my lack of imagination, but Tomlinson's poem made me think, for the first time, of Verdi Square in connection with—of all people—Verdi.

The poems in the later part of the volume are English in setting and more familiar as the sort of expertly practiced thing this veteran writer turns out. . . . The later poems seemed less memorable and relaxed than the New York ones. But the volume reminds us how much we take Tomlinson's art for granted. (pp. 339-40)

William H. Pritchard, "Aboard the Poetry Omnibus," in The Hudson Review, *Vol. XXXVII, No. 2, Summer, 1984, pp. 327-42.*

PETER PORTER

Mexico and England, as well as New York, are the venues for the poems in [***Notes from New York and Other Poems***]. . . . Despite the creed of 'seeing is believing' (the title of his first book), Tomlinson is a philosophical writer, a discerner of the shapes and essences which lie beneath the surfaces he describes. It might make more sense to reverse his dictum to 'believing is seeing.'

Thus New York, from the Verranzano Narrows to Verdi Square on 72nd Street is, for Tomlinson, a sort of conceptual city, as it might have been for a Renaissance theorist such as Alberti. He does not banish its denizens or subdue their oddity, but he is more interested in their almost geometric patterning than in their stories. In **"Lament for Doormen,"** he specifies the owners of apartments, Mrs Schwamm, Mr Guglielmi, and the Du Plessis family, then notes:

but the poetry of names
strikes little fire in the vestibule.
Spring: and the yellow cabs
go by each
with its Sun-King
inside and leave
doormen to the dark.

Tomlinson has developed a springy but relaxed adaptation of traditional blank verse which is beautifully at home when he also is at home—in Gloucestershire and the English countryside. Over the last 15 years, he has made an archive of some of the best writing about the changing landscape of England. This new book adds significantly to it.

Peter Porter, "Painting in Words," in The Observer, *June 17, 1984, p. 22.*

ROBERT GREACEN

Tomlinson's early poetry was largely influenced by American poets—Pound, Stevens, Marianne Moore—and to a lesser extent the English eighteenth century. Later, his painterly eye—he also paints professionally—focused on the world of nature ('It was a language of water, light and air / I sought . . .'). His concern has been to find a valid relationship between man and nature, and to translate Wordsworth, as it were, into twentieth-century terms. Travel accounts for much of Tomlinson's *oeuvre,* and some of his most successful poems have a North or South American provenance. **"Assassin"** recreates the death of Trotsky in Mexico as seen through the mind of the killer and is among Tomlinson's most impressive pieces: dramatic yet with the economy and exactness that characterize the poet at his best: 'The room / Had shrunk to a paperweight of glass and he / To the centre and prisoner of its transparency'. A consistently able technician, Tomlinson's Anglo-American idiom and width of range, geographical, natural and human, free him from any suggestion of insularity. ***Collected Poems*** represents a very considerable achievement for a poet still on the right side of sixty.

Robert Greacen, in a review of "Collected Poems," in British Book News, *November, 1985, p. 690.*

ROBERT GREACEN

Charles Tomlinson, poet and painter, brings together in [***Eden: Graphics and Poetry***] a collection of striking graphic images, a selection of over twenty poems and an essay entitled **"The Poet as Painter".** In both arts Tomlinson focuses on the world of nature, creating for himself 'a language of water, light and air'. He argues that the American poet Wallace Stevens .hit upon the basic fact that links poetry and painting when he observed that 'we live in the centre of a physical poetry' and that Stevens rightly saw the problems of poets as being largely the problems of painters. Not everyone may agree to this, though Tomlinson calls as witnesses to his views such heavyweights as Rainer Maria Rilke, D. H. Lawrence and William Carlos Williams. As painter, Tomlinson makes use of the surrealist devices of collage and decalcomania, and for the latter gives the 'recipe' outlined by Oscar Dominguez in the 1930s. In addition to analysing these techniques, Tomlinson explores the relationship between the visual and poetic impulses, and gives an account of their origin in himself during his childhood in the Potteries in Staffordshire. ***Eden*** is a finely produced book which will be appreciated by those who are interested in the theory and practice of poetry and painting.

Robert Greacen, in a review of "Eden: Graphics and Poetry," in British Book News, *January, 1986, p. 52.*

MICHAEL EDWARDS

Tomlinson's career of constant alertness, of forever becoming "awake to what is there", is exemplary, and in its way heroic. The effects are evident throughout this long overdue edition of his ***Collected Poems,*** which reprints all the volumes from ***The Necklace*** of 1955 to ***The Flood*** of 1981, along with a single poem from his 1951 pamphlet, ***Relations and Contraries.*** Regrettably, the publishers have not included his latest volume, ***Notes from New York,*** or provided an index.

Tomlinson's first widely noticed collection was ***Seeing is Believing,*** whose initial appearance in the United States, in 1958, remains as something of a reproach to the British poetry world. Its affirmative title still holds for his most recent poems, and also makes clear that the otherness of the places and objects to be encountered in his work is a matter not for disquiet, as in the Absurdism from which he distanced himself from the beginning, but for exhilaration. In such encounters, the self—which always needs to be justified in Tomlinson's poetry, where the English puritan tradition is still active—is experienced not (or not only) by introspection but by attention, as if the true self were less a private inwardness than a relation of inner to outer. The first line of the first poem is: "Wakening with the window over fields". The worth of the self depends on the quality of the looking.

The energy of Tomlinson's poems goes into perceiving. Perception is guided by a figurative intelligence and by a varied sense of human desire and of human impingement on the world: an awareness of both mystery and history. Similarly with his graphics. ***Eden,*** which also includes a selection of appropriate poems and the fine essay **"The Poet as Painter",** reproduces twenty-nine graphics from the 1970s, when Tomlinson was creating some of the freshest and most arresting visual images in the country. Largely based on decalcomania and collage, and relying on variations of black and white, they are governed by metamorphosis, the theme of Tomlinson's Clark Lectures. Yet with their density of foreground detail and the suggestion, beyond, of luminous space, they are, after their fashion, representational. By welcoming chance and by learning from Surrealism, they also seem to have made Tomlinson's writing more open to promptings from outside, and they suggest that a certain practice of Surrealism, which could have seemed anathema to the earlier Tomlinson, can actually be one way of deferring to what is beyond the will.

All the graphics explore the shifts between observing and imagining, and many of the poems too have that as their theme. . . .

Despite American and French influences, Tomlinson's way of seeing is very English; British empiricism does speak through these poems, but with subtlety and imaginative daring. Perception is enlarged by imagination, and the virtue of art is to move from "what is" to what "might be". That negotiation between the resistance of what is other and the transforming potential of the mind is also enacted in Tomlinson's language, which clarifies, I think, a fundamental question of rhetoric. His poetry is poetry in that it offers the pleasure of not calling a spade a spade: music is "a body one cannot see"; mushrooms, at the end of a poem about an almost magical quest, are "stepping stones across a grass of water". Yet the poetry also offers the pleasure of finding, for a spade, precisely the right word or combination of words, as if a perfect language were simply waiting to be learnt and applied. Most tellingly, Tomlinson also shows that the two impulses—to name accurately and to name anew—only appear to be contradictory. . . . Tomlinson has set up ["relations and contraries"] in his poetry between English and other writing, especially American. In volume after volume he has tacked between the two. His ''English'' poems are quickly recognizable. Some are based on a four-stress line—less a recovery of Anglo-Saxon measure, it seems, than a formal miming of natural alert speech—or even on the iambic pentameter. They may include rhyme or half-rhyme; their lines are sometimes alternately indented, and carry a visual suggestion of the couplet; their syntax can be highly elaborate. Other poems have an American appearance and movement, through a fastidiousness of diction, for example, encouraged by a reading of Marianne Moore, or through the importance given to the ends and beginnings of lines.

There are not quite, however, two distinct types of poem. Those that are English in their metre, and often their theme, may show an American ''cleanliness''; American short-line poems frequently advance through roving rhymes and assonances. . . . Even the triplets of many poems in ***A Peopled Landscape*** (1963), which look on the page like the triplets of William Carlos Williams, have a rhythm which is English, where iambs and the trochees into which they reverse play across the pattern:

> He [a fisherman] knows his net
> but knowledge
> must reassess its ground
> to comprehend
> the mystery of fact
> supple in sunlight
> teeming from the sound.

Tomlinson is his own master, changing what he finds, using various American lessons for English ends.

Although from the beginning Tomlinson has worked the English language for a new clarity in vocabulary, syntax and sound, and especially in the craft of the line, the reader also meets throughout the ***Collected Poems*** a kind of respect for the historical English that already exists. . . . In the ***Collected Poems*** one meets Pope, Coleridge, and Wordsworth (the Augustan-Romantic dialogue is central) as well as more recent Americans, and others, in a new guise. In the graphics one meets above all John Sell Cotman.

This is one of the ways in which Tomlinson speaks for England now, while also bringing an English eye to foreign poetry, painting, landscapes and history. He tells us something of what it is like to live on ''this island'', by testing the continuities between the industrial Midlands and rural Gloucestershire, and between English and foreign settings both urban and natural. He also writes a political poetry which opposes apocalyptic and revolutionary ''extremity'' in the name of the richness of circumstance, and of civility. (''Civil'', like ''civic'', is a recurring word.) His is a politics of right relationships within a whole larger than oneself (''reign'' and ''kingdom'' are among his metaphors), a whole which includes the stresses of history and of geography, along with neighbourhood, dwellings, objects and individuals. It is a politics unlikely to appeal to any avant-garde, whether of the left or of the right, especially as his civility also has a profound religious dimension; his writing continues the oldest and most elemental pursuit of poetry, the search, through a sense of awe and mystery, for a human way of being in a world other than human.

The ***Collected Poems*** presents three decades' work by one of the finest native English poets since Hardy. It is not a mirror of our distresses: instead it explores the sources of strength and wills an ideal, approaching it through the disciplines, audacities, renunciations, generosities of poetic technique. With ***Eden,*** the ***Translations,*** the *Oxford Book of Verse in English Translation,* ***Some Americans, Poetry and Metamorphosis*** and now this ***Collected,*** Tomlinson is available as poet, painter, translator, anthologist, autobiographer and critic; the time has come for us to take the measure of his presence.

Michael Edwards, ''American Lessons for English Ends,'' in The Times Literary Supplement, *No. 4329, March 21, 1986, p. 308.*

Yuri (Valentinovich) Trifonov

1925-1981

(Also transliterated as Iurii or Uri) Russian novelist, short story writer, and scriptwriter.

© Lütfi Özkök

A popular and respected literary figure in his homeland, Trifonov has been hailed by Western critics as perhaps the finest nondissident Russian writer of the post-World War II era. Trifonov's works chronicle the lives of the Moscow intelligentsia, focusing upon the complexity of personal relationships and the stressful nature of the urban Soviet lifestyle. In his fiction, Trifonov addresses what he perceives as the transformation from spiritual and ideological ethics to egoistic values induced by the pressures of contemporary Soviet life. His protagonists are often frustrated by the necessity to compromise their moral principles in order to live comfortably, and they feel further alienated by the insensitivity of friends and family members. Trifonov frequently poses the question of how one should live within the framework of *byt,* a Russian term denoting ordinary, everyday life. Geoffrey Hosking stated that Trifonov was "a kind of 'philosopher of everyday life,' focusing not on what appear to be the great issues of our time, but rather on the petty concerns which constitute the arena where, if at all, we actually do prove ourselves." Trifonov's fiction became increasingly controversial late in his career, as he angered Soviet literary censors with subtle social criticism, allusions to corruption in the party system, and unfavorable portraits of people in respected positions.

Trifonov's first novel, *Studenty* (1950; *Students*), which was awarded the Stalin Prize, depicts student life in the peaceful and relatively prosperous post-World War II period. This work centers upon the conflict between two scholars, one of whom represents socialist virtue, while the other strives for personal rewards. Adhering strictly to the tenets of Socialist Realism, Trifonov subordinates character development to discussions of social and political issues. Critics agree that Trifonov's next novel, *Utolenie zhazhdy* (1963), written after a ten-year period of travel in the Soviet Union and abroad, reflects a strong development of his artistic talents. The novel revolves around the struggle between proponents of the construction of a canal in Central Asia and representatives of the established bureaucracy, who attempt to obstruct the enterprise. The title, which has been translated as "The Quenching of a Thirst," refers to the desert's thirst for water and also to a metaphorical social thirst for truth and justice. In his next work, *Otblesk kostra* (1965), Trifonov reconstructs the life of his father, a hero during the Bolshevik Revolution who fell into disfavor with the Communist Party during the Stalin era. This documentary novel reflects Trifonov's knowledge of Russian history and utilizes his father's field notebooks, personal reminiscences, archives, and interviews with several survivors of the Revolution.

Beginning in 1969, Trifonov published a series of novellas in leading Soviet literary journals. In these stories, which are praised as among his most accomplished works, Trifonov dealt with the moral, political, and psychological conflicts of educated, city-dwelling Moscow professionals. Trifonov endeavored to present a realistic picture of Soviet life by abandoning the precepts of Socialist Realism and assuming an objective stance. He was consistently praised by critics for his meticulous attention to detail, masterful psychological portraits, and acute perceptiveness of urban life. *Obmen* (1969; *The Exchange*), the first of these novellas, revolves around an intended unlawful exchange of living quarters between a dying woman and her son's family and the son's abandonment of his family's spiritual ideals in favor of the materialistic values of his wife's family. In this work, Trifonov introduced the term *olukianit'sia,* derived from the surname of the wife's family, to describe materialistic Soviet urbanites who establish necessary social connections and evade laws in order to benefit within the restricted system. Trifonov's next novella, *Predvaritel'nye itogi* (1970; *Taking Stock*), consists mostly of the reminiscences of a middle-aged man who considers himself a failure when he realizes that his position as a successful translator constitutes little more than menial work. Pressured by his professional disappointments and the deterioration of his familial relationships, particularly his strained interaction with his son, the man flees to the rural region of Turkemia for refuge. This is one of several works in which Trifonov presents rural life, or *dacha,* as being more favorable than urban existence. Like *The Exchange, Taking Stock* portrays people who sacrifice ethical considerations for a comfortable existence. Trifonov's next major work, *Dolgoe proshchaniye* (1971; *The Long Goodbye*), focuses upon the politics of a Moscow theater company through the interaction of a young actress and a dramatist. In order to advance their careers, both characters compromise ethical principles, leading to the demise of their relationship. *The Exchange, Taking Stock,* and *The Long Goodbye* were published together in *The Long Goodbye: Three Novellas* (1978).

In the novella *Drugaia zhizn'* (1975; *Another Life*), Trifonov depicts the life of Sergei Troitskii, a historian who lacked the power and means to overcome injustice in everyday life. The story begins after the historian's death at the age of forty-two and is narrated by Troitskii's wife, who painstakingly attempts to understand her husband. Troitskii is perhaps Trifonov's most benevolent hero: he never sacrificed his moral principles for material advantages, yet he was never appreciated by his family or associates. *Dom na naberezhnoi* (1976; *The House on the Embankment*) is considered the best of Trifonov's novellas. This work explores the career development of Vadik Glebov, a successful literary bureaucrat, by examining his duplicitous behavior from childhood to maturity. Glebov plans to advance his career by association with a university department head whom he eventually betrays. This work was degraded by Soviet officials for its implication that the Soviet system facilitates opportunistic behavior as a means of gaining privileges from the party and government. *Another Life* and *The House on the Embankment* were collectively published as *Another Life. The House on the Embankment: Novellas* (1983).

Starik (1978; *The Old Man*) is regarded as Trifonov's most ambitious work for his analysis of the nature of truth and the importance of the past upon the present. In this story of war veteran Pavel Letunov, Trifonov employs historical allusions to suggest the need for present-day Russians to understand their country's recent history of revolution and civil war. Letunov searches for the truth about an incident that resulted in the trial and murder of a supposed revolutionary against whom he had testified without being certain of all the facts. Trifonov uses this story to present his belief that subsequent generations may never know the truth about their country's history if the people who actually lived during the turmoil cannot distinguish between a hero and an enemy of the state. Critics praised Trifonov's evocation of the chaos, power struggles, and suspiciousness of the Soviet civil war years.

(See also *Contemporary Authors,* Vol. 103 [obituary].)

N. N. SHNEIDMAN

One of the few Soviet writers who has tried to bypass the hurdles of literary censorship and editorial control and who is endeavouring to create a literature in which the ethical foundations of contemporary Soviet man are tested is Iurii Valentinovich Trifonov. He is presently one of the most widely read, discussed, and controversial Soviet writers.

Trifonov is by no means a newcomer to Soviet literature. His first published work appeared in 1947 and three years later he won a Stalin Prize for his novel ***Studenty. Studenty*** depicts student life at a Moscow institute in the immediate post-war period. The plot centres around a conflict and the juxtaposition of the two main protagonists and former childhood friends, Vadim Belov and Sergei Palavin. The first is an example of socialist virtue, while the second is a self-centred egotistic careerist. Palavin is exposed by his fellow students, including Belov, and he goes down to defeat. The novel is written in the spirit of the times. The characters can be easily distinguished as positive or negative heroes and their conflicts reflect the life of Soviet society of that period. The author does not endeavour to analyse in depth the psychological makeup of his heroes or the internal reasons for their actions. Personal relationships are treated in an unsophisticated manner and are secondary to the discussion of social and political problems. All solutions in the novel are black or white; one is usually positive or negative; actions are good or bad. In short, this is an exemplary product of socialist realism as was recognized by Soviet officialdom in awarding the book the Stalin Prize for literature.

In reflecting on his literary past, Trifonov calls the time when he wrote ***Studenty*** his apprenticeship period. He presently clearly sees its shortcomings and writes that "now I cannot read one line from it. I am even frightened to take it into my hands. If I would have the strength, the time, and, most of all, the desire, I would re-write the book from the first line to the last. But what for? There is no use returning to what has already passed. It was recently suggested that a second edition of ***Studenty*** be published; Trifonov claims, however, to have rejected this proposal.

The second period in the development of Trifonov's creative activity covers roughly ten years and deals mainly with the author's impressions from his travels in the Soviet Union and abroad. The major work of this period was the novel ***Utolenie zhazhdy*** which was written between 1959 and 1962. The action of the book takes place just after the Twentieth Party Congress at which Khrushchev denounced the "personality cult" of Stalin. The main conflict centres around the struggle of those who favour innovation in the construction of the Kara Kum Canal and those representatives of the old bureaucracy who stifle their initiative. A similar conflict exists in the editorial offices of the Ashkhabad newspaper in which the young narrator (Peter Koryshev) works.

The title of the novel has a double meaning. It refers to the thirst for water by the desert in Central Asia; a thirst which will be satisfied by the construction of the canal which in turn will bring new life to this desolate region. It also refers to a thirst for truth and justice which have been missing in this land for many years. This thirst, however, is not experienced in equal measure by all concerned. One protagonist suggests that there is a danger in taking too much food on an empty stomach—a hint that changes must be introduced slowly, step by step. In this there is an inherent fear of the new and a desire to hold on to the old and tested ways of life.

As a work of art, the novel is rather weak. Characterization is superficial; many conflicts are unresolved; the transition from the discussion of social problems to personal ones is not as smooth as one would desire. And yet, the novel is an important link in the development of Trifonov's art and in his investigation of the ethical foundations which guide Soviet man. This is particularly true of Koryshev's fellow journalist Zurabov who has much in common with Palavin from ***Studenty.*** Zurabov is not stupid, but he is a self-centred careerist and an opportunist without the convictions necessary to take a stand. He drifts along in life rather than being the master of his destiny. At work Zurabov usually sides with those who struggle for openness and truth, while behind their backs he is ready to coöperate with their opponents. He writes a malicious article in which he discredits the progressive leadership of the canal construction project with the sole purpose of appeasing the associate editor of the newspaper and his followers. People such as

Zurabov live in a spiritual vacuum; they lack the principles necessary to stand on their own feet. They usually become ethical cripples and fertile soil for the dissemination of evil.

The third period, the period of maturity, in the development of Trifonov's art begins in 1966 with the appearance of the stories **"Vera i Zoika"** and **"Byl letnii polden'"** published in *Novyi mir,* then still under the editorship of A. T. Tvardovskii. These stories were followed by **"V gribnuiu osen'"** (1968), ***Obmen*** (1969), ***Predvaritel'nye itogi*** (1970), ***Dolgoe proshchanie*** (1971), ***Drugaia zhizn'*** (1975), and **"Dom na naberezhnoi"** (1976). (pp. 335-37)

Most of Trifonov's works of the last decade have much in common but at the same time are distinctly different from his earlier writings. His main heroes are usually city dwellers, most of them well-educated professional people. The emphasis in these works is on the personal lives of the heroes while their work, their social and professional concerns are left in the background. Family problems, infidelity, narrow-minded egotism, the sacrifice of spiritual values for material well-being are a rule rather than an exception in these works. The actions and the relationships of the protagonists, outside the narrow circle of their immediate families, often express the same negative qualities which are best visible in the uninhibited situations of family life.

The Trifonov of the last decade is vastly different from the one who created ***Studenty*** and even ***Utolenie zhazhdy.*** The new Trifonov endeavours to present a truthful and realistic picture of Soviet life without minimizing the complexity of human relationships facing Soviet man. He has abandoned practically all the precepts of socialist realism by refusing to suggest positive solutions and by declining to make a clear choice. He continues in his new works to concern himself with ethical problems but no longer does he juxtapose his negative characters with positive ones, a contrasting device often used to elevate the positive hero and to make him appear in a better light than he really deserves. The new Trifonov treats his heroes with understanding and compassion. It is the approach of a writer who has learned to appreciate the limitations and shortcomings of man as well as his own imperfections.

Most of his recent plots are simple in themselves and deal with common problems and situations, but ones which are deeply rooted in Soviet reality and experience. The uninitiated western reader may have difficulty in deciphering the meaning of these narratives. Such, for example, is the essence of ***Obmen*** in which the main conflict centres around an intended exchange of living quarters, which are in great demand in Moscow. Dmitriev, his wife Lena, and their young daughter occupy a single room. Similarly Dmitriev's mother, Ksenia Fedorovna, has one room. Lena and her mother-in-law are not on speaking terms and yet, realizing that Ksenia Fedórovna has cancer and that her days are numbered, Lena urges Dmitriev to convince his mother to exchange their separate rooms for a two-room apartment. After their mother's death, the Dmitrievs could then retain the apartment instead of the single room they presently occupy. The exchange is by no means a simple operation. It involves a number of unlawful machinations and it requires the assistance of an outside operator. Dmitriev knows that what he is doing is unethical and even unlawful but all the same he goes ahead with the plan. Ksenia Fedorovna dies soon after the exchange has been consummated but Dmitriev himself comes down with an illness and is confined for several weeks to a hospital bed.

Dmitriev is Zurabov's blood brother; he pretends to be honest but acts in a manner which is most expedient to him at the given moment. There is nothing sacred to him if only in the long run things work out to his advantage. On one occasion, when Dmitriev visits his mother and tries to impress upon her about the mutual advantages of the exchange, Ksenia Fedorovna retorts: "You already made an exchange, Vitia. The exchange has occurred. . . . It was a long time ago." She obviously alludes to the change which has taken place in the character and behaviour of her son, who little-by-little gives up the spiritual values and the lofty ideals of his own family for those of his wife and her parents.

Trifonov has introduced a new term into Soviet literary criticism to describe such a process. It is called *olukianit'sia,* and is taken from the surname of Lena's parents. The Lukianovs represent a special breed of Soviet city dwellers. They are people who "know how to live," who have the necessary connections and manage to arrange their lives in a most useful and comfortable way. Such people often walk on the brink of the law, careful not to overstep it, but they completely ignore the unwritten moral laws on which the mutual cohabitation of people is based. The Lukianovs are no longer young. They were born and grew up in tsarist Russia and they could be regarded as remnants of the past. It is often said that their behaviour and actions are influenced by their bourgeois consciousness. Most characters in Trifonov's other recent works, however, regardless of their age, station in life, or social background, are also people who consider it a virtue "to know how to live" and who adhere to a peculiar code of ethics which is designed mainly to satisfy their personal needs.

Soviet critics view ***Obmen*** as a literary success. They suggest that "the importance of this story lies in its confirmation of a new, genuinely humane, morality." They claim that "due to his inner weakness and lack of principles, Dmitriev gives in to the pressures of his wife Lena who is the very embodiment of the lack of spirituality. By ascribing Dmitriev's behaviour and actions to his ethical shallowness and to Lena's lack of spirituality only, these critics are inconsistent with the requirements of Soviet literary theory, according to which social conditions are a moving force of social phenomena as well as of man's actions. ***Obmen*** is also highly regarded in the Soviet Union because the actions of Dmitriev and Lena can be considered as the shortcomings of individuals and are by no means characteristic of society in general. Such an interpretation is possible because in the background of the plot there is the noble family of Dmitriev's mother as well as Dmitriev's grandfather, who embodies all the lofty ideals of a dedicated revolutionary. Nothing of this kind can be encountered in Trifonov's works since 1969. The main subject of ***Predvaritel'nye itogi*** is the morality of representatives of the Soviet world of letters and higher education. In ***Dolgoe proshchanie*** we become acquainted with the unwritten laws of Moscow theatre life. Most of these conventions are base, unethical, and unjust; they work in favour of unscrupulous people, who have mastered the art of "how to live," but against those who have not yet learned to compromise with their conscience.

Trifonov's most recent works—***Drugaia zhizn'*** and ***Dom na naberezhnoi*** are artistically his most mature works. In the writer's own words, he "succeeded in expressing in them, as clearly as possible, the general phenomenon of life." A discussion of these works makes it possible to draw certain conclusions about the place of Trifonov in contemporary Soviet literature in general and about the development of his art in particular.

The picture of the main hero of ***Drugaia zhizn'***, Sergei Troitskii, is given through the eyes of his wife Olga. Sergei is an able and honest man who would never sacrifice his conscience for the tangible advantages of this world, but he is also a strange man who has difficulties in finding a place for himself in life. Sergei's life is further complicated by his family relationships. His wife loves him deeply but she is also terribly jealous. Olga suspects every woman in sight of a hidden relationship with her husband, trying, at the same time, to convince herself that she trusts him. Her suspicions and doubts, which are usually groundless, are subconscious. She follows Sergei everywhere so as to keep a constant check on him. It appears to her that she does this for his sake, for the sake of their love, but in essence she is driven to it by her irrational fear of another woman in her husband's life. One of Sergei's ostensible girl friends tells Olga: "If you drive your husband to death, that is your business. But I will destroy you if you do not leave me and my husband in peace." These words are prophetic. Sergei is driven to death at the age of forty-two. His "friends" at work, his wife's "love," and his inability to find a place for himself in life are the causes of his death. Before his death, when he is forced to resign his job at the institute because of his involvement in spiritualism, Sergei says that it is all for the better; that it is necessary to begin "a new life (*druguiu zhizn'*) for which there already remains little time." There is no need to worry. Sergei's tranquility is now unperturbed; his "new life" is now eternal.

The title of the story is symbolic and perhaps even pessimistic. It implies that it is difficult, if not impossible, to change man's nature; that there is no reasonable explanation why one human being has the inner capacity for happiness while another does not. It appears that the author does not believe in the possibility of a real change in the protagonists or in a new relationship between them. He concludes, therefore, that a true renewal is possible for Sergei only after his death.

The most important element in ***Drugaia zhizn'*** is Trifonov's ability to render convincingly the complexity of human relationships. Being a master of psychological analysis, he clearly demonstrates that excellent intentions are not enough to build a good relationship; that the irrational elements in human nature are often stronger than most reasonable convictions and decisions. He writes that "every marriage—is not a union of two people, as is presumed, but rather a union of collision of two clans, of two worlds." This union or collision becomes even more complicated because man strives all his life to understand his fellow man without realizing that he is unable even to understand himself. (pp. 335-41)

Trifonov's latest work, ***Dom na naberezhnoi*** is in many respects similar to the other works discussed in this paper. It is not difficult to see that Trifonov deals here with the same human material, similar problems, and the same time span as in ***Studenty.*** His approach to the events and his treatment of the heroes are, however, completely different. The evolution of Trifonov, the man and the writer, is most visible when comparing these two works. At the centre of ***Dom na naberezhnoi*** is the problem of ethics of the contemporary Soviet urban population; a problem which has been at the root of all Trifonov's works since ***Obmen.*** In ***Dom na naberezhnoi*** the author investigates the development of a literary bureaucrat. He follows the actions of his hero and the forces which influence his development from early childhood to maturity. Trifonov analyses the creation of a literary scholar who is without convictions or moral principles; a man of many different faces.

The hero of ***Dom na naberezhnoi,*** Vadim Glebov, grows up on a small street in Moscow. At school Glebov makes friends among the hoodlums as well as among the well behaved children who live in a nearby apartment house. After the war Glebov enrols in an institute to study literature. He learns that Professor Ganchuk, who lives in the apartment house and whose daughter Sonia had been his classmate, is now head of a department in the same institute. In childhood Sonia had been deeply in love with Glebov, but he hardly paid any attention to her. Now, a friendship with Sonia could help his professional advancement. Glebov begins to frequent the home of the Ganchuks where he becomes obsessed with the idea that all the material possessions accumulated by Sonia's parents could be his. He starts a love affair with Sonia without actually loving her. She is now included in his scheme of becoming the sole heir to the Ganchuks' wealth.

Glebov's calculations lead nowhere because at that very time the administration of the institute, represented by the most unworthy people in that institution, starts a campaign against the so-called cosmopolitans in literature which results in several good scholars and teachers being expelled. Ganchuk takes up their defence but he does not have to wait long for retribution. He is severely attacked by the bureaucrats and he is removed from his position, while Glebov is called upon to spy on his future father-in-law and to denounce him in public. The relationship of Glebov and Sonia, of course, breaks up. There is no place for her anymore in Glebov's calculations. She becomes ill and soon dies; so does her old mother who has been teaching German in the institute. At the end of the narrative, many years later in 1974, we encounter Glebov on his way to Paris to participate in an international congress of literary scholars, while the eighty-six-year-old Ganchuk visits the grave of his daughter and wonders about the absurdity of his existence: Sonia is dead while he is still alive and he wants to go on living.

The parallels and distinctions between ***Studenty*** and ***Dom na naberezhnoi*** are evident. There are many similar problems discussed in these two works but the solutions to them are completely different. In ***Studenty*** Professor Kozelskii is accused by his colleagues and students alike of formalism, aestheticism, and cosmopolitanism. The best people in the institute are against him. The main positive hero, Belov, is instrumental in helping to force Kozelskii out of the institute. The nature of the novel is such that Kozelskii appears to be in the wrong in that he hates Soviet literature and Soviet students. He is almost an enemy of the people. In ***Dom na naberezhnoi*** Professor Astrug is accused of similar transgressions but the best people in the institute stand up in his defence. They are unsuccessful in their endeavour, some are even penalized for this attempt, but they are bold enough to say what they think. In ***Studenty*** Kozelskii appears to be in the wrong, while in ***Dom na naberezhnoi*** the groundless nature of the conspiracy of the administration against Professor Ganchuk and his friends is emphasized.

Artistically Trifonov's latest works are vastly superior to works such as ***Studenty.*** In ***Studenty*** the characterization of the heroes was inadequate, the conflicts were resolved in an unconvincing manner, and journalistic clichés formed a major part of the narrative. In his latest works Trifonov creates real people with real problems. He presents the human relationship of his heroes in all its complexity and he creates in each work a special atmosphere which is characteristic of the given situation. It is often suggested that Trifonov's heroes are transparent, that we see through them, that the writer uses the X-ray technique to reveal their souls and minds. This approach is facilitated by the evolution of Trifonov's creative method in which there has been a transition from narration in the third person to narration in the first person. Trifonov claims that personal narration permits him to penetrate deeper into the souls of his characters. In many of his recent works there is a combination of narration in the first and in the third person. In ***Obmen,*** for example, the story concludes with a statement by the narrator who tells of his recent meeting with Dmitriev and of the latter's illness following the exchange. In ***Dom na naberezhnoi*** the narrator resides in the apartment house. He is in the background, however, appearing only from time-to-time to qualify the events and actions of the protagonists or to tell us something about himself. The presence of a narrator, who is almost an outsider to the main events in the plot, renders a sense of objectivity to the story and makes it more true to life.

Trifonov claims that his art is in the tradition of nineteenth-century classical literature. He feels that he is also indebted to the writers of the 1920's and 1930's and in particular to Andrei Platonov, Issac Babel' and Aleksei Tolstoi. He sees his place in contemporary Soviet literature as that of a continuator of the traditions of Anton Chekhov and of the writers of the 1920's. He asserts that he struggles for a very high level of expressiveness in his works. He strives to say much in very few words and he claims that a short work may often contain more meaning than a large novel. Trifonov suggests that "Chekhov's best stories are nothing but novels pressed together by the tremendous force of his art. While, at the same time, there are many long novels which are in essence stretched-out stories in which the action evolves around a single event, covering just a few days. It appears thus, that the novel and the story have equal potential for depicting life." Indeed, Chekhov's influence is evident in Trifonov's latest works. The lack of a direct social message, the atmosphere of mutual misunderstanding and inability to communicate, the predilection for understatement—so characteristic of Chekhov's stories—are all part of Trifonov's recent work.

The development of Trifonov the artist has been a slow process. In his literary youth he thought that in order to produce a good work of art the main thing was to find a good plot. Later he decided that appropriate words are just as important as a good plot. The mature Trifonov has come to the conclusion that "the main difficulty in writing prose is in finding ideas. . . . One must have something to say; to communicate something important to the reader." According to him, the most important aspect in writing is not how to build a phrase or how to find an appropriate conclusion to a story, but the ability to build a life and to create a fate which would be as truthful and real to life as possible. (pp. 341-44)

Trifonov is vulnerable to official criticism as much for what he says as for what he does not say. It might appear that the time is not yet ripe for a new Chekhov in contemporary Soviet literature. This does not mean, of course, that Trifonov has already reached the level of artistic mastery characteristic of his great predecessor. On the dull scene of contemporary Soviet literature, however, his recent works stand out from most other writing and give at least some promise for future artistic growth. (p. 344)

It is possible to conclude that the evolution of Trifonov the writer develops in step with the development of Trifonov the man. The Chekhovian approach to the treatment of human problems developed in him slowly and it became prominent only in the last decade. Indeed, in the "Author's Preface" to the English translation of ***Studenty,*** Trifonov notes that Sergei Palavin is "a 'negative' type whose attitudes are a harmful hang-over from an earlier period. . . . We are bound to remark them in order to remake them and take them with us into the bright future when communism will have been achieved." A quarter of a century later Trifonov has given up the idea of changing the "negative" hero. He does not divide his heroes anymore into "positive" and "negative." He alludes to the fact that no one is perfect and that many people have negative qualities which are necessary to counteract. He refuses even to acknowledge that Lena, the main culprit of ***Obmen,*** is a negative character; he says that she has good as well as bad traits of character, a fact which makes her even more human. The struggle between positive and negative characters in Trifonov's early works turns now into a struggle between the good and the bad qualities in man, into a struggle between goodness and evil. Trifonov is explicit in stating that it is possible to change a social order and the economic conditions of a people, but it is much more difficult to change the very essence of man. . . . Quoting Lermontov, who said that he presents problems but he is far from suggesting a remedy for them, Trifonov remarks that he also presents problems, mainly ethical problems, in the hope that they will teach people something, and will prompt people to think at least for a moment about their own shortcomings and behaviour. This is, according to him, the first step toward a moral regeneration of man.

The evolution of Trifonov's artistic method and his new approach to the treatment of his heroes are the result of the changes which have taken place in the Soviet Union in the post-Stalin period. In ***Studenty*** the message was explicit because no other literature was possible at that time. In ***Utolenie zhazhdy*** Trifonov again was in tune with the times as he paid tribute to the spirit of the Twentieth Party Congress and to the leadership of Khrushchev. Now, twenty-one years later, having realized that the post-Stalin reforms have changed the Soviet system and the essence of Soviet man very little and that one of the main shortcomings of Soviet society is the shallowness of the ethical values professed by most Soviet citizens, Trifonov has turned to a kind of literature in which there are few positive heroes, but in which there is a hidden call for self-perfection. This is a call for Soviet man to preserve his human face and his dignity. Trifonov's art has evolved in the mainstream of Soviet literature. Until the late 'sixties his writing very much reflected the situation existing in Soviet society in general, and in Soviet literature in particular. Trifonov's works appearing in the last decade, on the other hand, are an expression of the growing disparity between the theory of Soviet literature and the literary practice of the 'seventies as well as of the search for a new image of man in contemporary Soviet literature. (pp. 348-49)

A number of Trifonov's heroes spend their lives in a continuous search for happiness, for a meaning of life. But few actually attain the desired state of contentment and tranquility. People such as Sergei from ***Drugaia zhizn*** are subdued by daily life and by social pressures. They are unable to overcome the inherent contradictions between their individualistic natures and social convention. Others, like Dmitriev or Glebov, sacrifice spiritual for immediate material benefits, but it is doubtful whether the material well-being they achieve leads to true happiness. This leads to the conclusion that it is impossible to attain real happiness and contentment in life by adhering to social conventions which disregard basic spiritual values and ethical principles. Trifonov's works continue to be part of one of the main trends of contemporary Soviet literature in which the everyday life of the Soviet city-dweller is depicted. His works, however, are more controversial and perhaps artistically superior to those of other Soviet writers dealing with the same subject. The popularity of Trifonov among the Soviet readers can be ascribed to the controversiality of his topics as well as to his growing mastery in the genre to which he devotes most of his time. (p. 349)

> *N. N. Shneidman, "Iurii Trifonov and the Ethics of Contemporary Soviet City Life,'' in* Canadian Slavonic Papers, *Vol. XIX, No. 3, September, 1977, pp. 335-51.*

VERA DUNHAM

[Yuri Trifonov] is an important novelist in Russia, but it is doubtful that the Western reader will be inclined to respond to him as to a major writer. For one thing, Western taste makers seeking ''innovation'' are disappointed by both streams of Russian literature, domestic and émigré. Even Solzhenitsyn has been found old hat. And, indeed, together with Tendriakov and Shukshin, Rasputin and Belov, Zalygin and Aksionov, Trifonov resists experimentation. Such abstinence forms a curious bond between the good Russian prose writers. They echo Chekhov and Tolstoy. Yes, both.

Trifonov's prose is above all cognitive, exploratory. Ever since his first novel, ***Students,*** published in 1950 when he was 25 years old, he has explored the mores and carvings of Soviet philistinism, *meshchanstvo,* in its urban, professional, and specifically Moscovite recension. Writing in that first novel about the early postwar adjustments of young war veterans to student life—and doing that under Zhdanovite coercion—it is remarkable how much he managed to say. Middle-class dreams of prosperity and the thematic cluster of treason, careerism, and cowardice bind this early work to Trifonov's recent major achievement, ***House on the Embankment*** (1976) . . . , which has stirred up a good deal of controversy in Russia.

The damages of Stalinism live on in Trifonov's successful middle class and find their most chilling expression in Vadim Glebov, the protagonist of ***House on the Embankment,*** a jaded cunning nonentity, one of the most unsettling specimens under the author's microscope. Here, as elsewhere, Trifonov is an old-fashioned psychologist, a master of characterization, an even greater master of the space and interaction between the individuals he observes in their craving for love, status, and self-respect. His verbal texture is tight without being cryptic, rich without being overstuffed. Its purpose is singularly concrete, descriptive, centripetal. Abstaining rigorously from didacticism, from social problem solving, from generalizing, and especially from prettying things up, from everything Socialist realism demands, he is a chronicler equipped with a wondersome butterfly net for the meaningful detail. One might, therefore, think that his posture is that of detachment and objectivity. But he is really too Tolstoyan for that. Authorial values, entrusted to a clear-spoken narrator, are palpable in every paragraph. And it is his moral judgment, clear and strong, yet free of pompousness, that makes Trifonov an important writer. Thus, his centripetal stylization with its parochial folding unto itself turns out to be centrifugal after all.

It is difficult to summarize the plots of his stories because, in a way, they have no plots. He re-creates the way of life of Moscow engineers, writers, professors, actors and their families. What he writes about are family feuds, professionals who aspire to *kultura,* the trappings of their lives—ardently sought after tables with inlaid Empire medallions, fashionable rural antiques, pianos, TV sets, fur coats and automobiles. And yet what seems Russian in Trifonov's approach to his unprepossessing cast of characters and their pursuits is the emphasis on the need for love. . . .

Instead of belaboring Trifonov's craft and manner, one is tempted to simply string together the illuminating details of human conduct in his sober tales, of the longing and loathing for one another, and finger them like the worry beads that they are. Trifonov worries. And so should the reader, indigenous and alien alike.

He writes about ordinary citizens. Since he is no prophet, makes no demands on humanity at large, and is no partisan of a special cause, one keeps worrying about the exportability of his stories. Can the alien reader become interested in bland creatures from a remote and rather drab world? (p. 213)

He is especially sensitive to cruelties, sometimes lethal and sometimes petty, inflicted on others and on the self. One of his sufferers, convincing as all his weaklings are, is Gennady, the protagonist of ***Taking Stock*** [collected in ***The Long Goodbye: Three Novellas***]. A free-lance translator of verse, he goes to pieces when his unpleasant son calls his work rubbish. It happens to be exactly what he too thinks of his work, his abilities, and his life. The poisonous quarrels with his wife as well as with his son drive him from his home. Defeated and malevolent, he moves alone to Turkmenia. As a member of Trifonov's portrait gallery of failures, meticulously honest with himself, this character, in addition, holds the key to the author's work. In an essay, **"The Inexhaustible Beginning,"** Trifonov explains an important principle in his creative and ordering process:

> While working on the novella ***Taking Stock,*** I have radically changed, unexpectedly for myself, the destiny of the main hero. The original design called for his death. And I have been writing almost the entire novella keeping in mind this sad ending. But when there remained only three or four last pages to do, I suddenly understood that he must not die. I let him live. And I even sent him on his vacation. . . . And all this instead of lying dead in an urn of a crematorium. Don't you think it's a substantial change of destiny? But if you stop and think attentively, the purpose was to show not so much Gennady Sergeevich's destiny—although his destiny also!—but rather his *way of life* resulting from many different causes. Of course, death enters into the concept of a way of life as well. For people die their own way just as they live their own way. So, it would have been possible to close the tale with death. But it would have been a jolt breaking up the way of life, a sui generis catharsis, purification. Life without catharsis, however, answered the initial design better. And that's why Gennady Sergeevich was destined to linger somewhat longer in this world.

So, it is *byt* that matters, the way of life. In ***Taking Stock,*** this way of life, in no way conducive to freedom, growth, and metamorphosis, preordains the lukewarm reconciliation of a bickering couple, truly of one mind. And in all the flawed individuals, made masterfully vivid by Trifonov, it is, perhaps, the combination of paralysis of will and of honesty toward oneself, the self-deprecation growing out of self-knowledge that is so depressingly moving. . . .

Given the unchanged subservience of published literature in Russia to political purposes, and given the relentless and undiminished controls in the closeted space allocated to the writer, how is it possible that there is enough air for the heirs of Chekhov? (p. 214)

Vera Dunham, "The Discreet Charm of Soviet Reality," in The Nation, *New York, Vol. 227, No. 7, September 9, 1978, pp. 213-14.*

ENCOUNTER

[In] contrast with the wealth of knowledge now at our disposal about the historical, political and economic conditions which have determined the present state of the Soviet Union, on the whole we know very little about how the ordinary Russian lives and has his being; or about how far his way of life influences, if at all, the government which purports to represent him. Such knowledge of different peoples depends upon the free, continuous and uncontrolled communication between the inhabitants of the countries concerned which is normal and taken for granted in the Western world. Alternatively, perhaps, it might be the product of serious and exhaustive anthropological study of a people's manners and mores. But the Soviet Union is careful to keep both possible sources of knowledge under the strictest surveillance and control.

One is therefore grateful for the publication in English translation of three long stories [collected in ***The Long Goodbye***]; by the popular, successful and highly regarded novelist, Yury Trifonov; for popular fiction has always been one of our best guides, if only by implication, not only to how people actually live at any particular time and place, but to how they think they live.

Trifonov is neither a dissident nor a *samizdat* writer. He is a respected member of the Union of Soviet Writers and his novels and stories sell by the hundred thousand in the Soviet Union. It is also true, however, that in recent years his writings have aroused considerable controversy and criticism in the Soviet Union.

It is not difficult to see why this should be so. If one assumes, as many people do, that any good Russian writer today must necessarily be *samizdat* or dissident, and if officially tolerated must be a propagandist of Soviet ideology, a reading of these stories will prove somewhat disconcerting. Trifonov is by any standard a good writer, but what is equally surprising in an officially approved writer is that the picture his stories convey of Soviet life is both realistic and sombre and by implication constitutes a genuine criticism of it.

No doubt this is why his stories have in their turn aroused criticism. For in saying that Trifonov is a realistic writer one does not in the least imply that he in any way conforms to the official doctrines of Socialist Realism. Rather, as his translators suggest, he practises realism in the tradition of a Balzac, or of a Flaubert, *sans monstres et sans héros*. Trifonov has the same kind of eye for social detail, and the same sense of how much his characters are the creations, or the victims, of time and place and circumstances, and there is no trace in them of those idealised features of Soviet Man which have played so large a part in Soviet fiction.

If one speaks of the "heroes" of Trifonov's stories, it is not at all in the sense that, as Socialist Realism requires, they are representative of a state of affairs in which Soviet Man has realised all the potentialities of human nature when liberated from the chains of capitalism. They are simply the central characters of his stories, and as such are as much, or more, the victims of circumstance as anyone else. But they are differentiated by a peculiar common quality which arouses a particular interest in a Western reader and may tempt him to wonder how far they truly reflect the society which Trifonov so realistically describes.

Trifonov might well have used as an epigraph for these stories the opening lines of the *Inferno*:. . .

> In the middle of the journey of our life
> I found myself in a dark wood
> Where the straight path was lost

Each of his main characters is in the middle of a journey. Each finds himself in a dark wood in which somehow he has lost his way. Each wonders where he made his mistake, and what fatal error led him to where he is now.

These doubts are inspired by a moral dilemma, which springs directly out of a conflict between self-respect and the necessary compromises and accommodations which have to be made in order to come to terms with the conditions of Soviet life. There is no suggestion that Marxism-Leninism, or Soviet ideology, or visions of the bright future open to Soviet Man can provide any kind of answer to such a problem, or that alternatively, in the context of a communist society, it is strictly meaningless. Trifonov's heroes simply have the sense that somewhere along the way they have gone wrong, and that there is no guide, no Virgil, to lead them out of the labyrinth in which they find themselves. (pp. 24-5)

What is remarkable about these stories is that the kind of problems which trouble Trifonov's heroes are no different in kind from those of innumerable Western counterparts who equally vainly search for some justification for their lives. Thinking of the terrible sacrifices demanded of the Russian people in the last 60 years—of the Revolution, the Civil War, the famines, the Terror, the purges, World War II, the Gulag—one is driven to ask; did all that then go for nothing, so far as the way people actually live their lives is concerned?

What is equally disconcerting is that any intimations in these stories of the possibility of happiness spring not from the present achievements of the Soviet Union, but from a past in which it had not yet arrived at its contemporary position of power and, relatively speaking, prosperity, and Moscow had not yet become the Great Wen it is today. A strong air of nostalgia pervades these stories. Their heroes, now middle-aged, think back with regret to childhood days when country lanes outside Moscow were filled with the scent and colour of lilac, now obliterated by monstrous conglomerations of tower blocks, and to fishing expeditions along streams whose banks are now embedded in concrete to form part of the amenities of a Park of Rest and Culture. So, in our own country, might some conservationist deplore the destruction of London and its environs. Is this an illusion derived from the lost paradise of childhood everywhere? Or is it a genuine reflection of what Russians feel about their cities and their countryside?

Even more strangely, to Western eyes, it is not only the physical landscape of the past that provokes nostalgia; it is from the past also that come suggestions that there may be alternative ways of life to those of contemporary Soviet society. Thus, in ***The Exchange,*** Dimitriev's wife and her friend are enthusiasts and connoisseurs of Orthodox Russian Art. They envy the elderly maid, Nyura, because she has always possessed an ancient icon which hangs in the corner above her bed. But for them icons are *objets d'art;* for Nyura her icon is simply and purely an object of worship and she has neither thought nor care for its possible aesthetic or commercial value.

In the same way, in ***Taking Stock,*** the successful translator, in distant and provincial Turkmenistan, envies and admires the humble caretaker who has eleven children and has adopted a twelfth and continues a patriarchal way of life impossible to maintain in Moscow. Contemplating the love by which he is surrounded, the hero sorrowfully and bitterly compares it with the contempt which he has, rightly, earned from his worthless son.

Yet another curious sidelight on Soviet life is thrown by the parts played in these stories by the male and female characters. It is the men who are troubled, perplexed, distressed about the meaning and significance of their lives; it is the women who have no use for such vain and futile introspection. They are eminently practical, objective and clear-sighted in their whole-hearted efforts to combat and surmount the daily difficulties of Soviet life. They are the ones "who know how to live"; it is the men who do not or cannot accept what is required of them. But what then has happened to heroic Soviet Man of revolutionary legend?

It would be wrong to regard these stories as covering the whole spectrum of Soviet society. Trifonov's eyes are concentrated on a limited but important section of it, which we in the West would identify with the middle class, and in the Soviet Union comprises the middle and upper-middle range of the Soviet hierarchy; bureaucrats, technologists, approved representatives of the media, enjoying many privileges denied to millions of others, but excluded from the luxuries and amenities reserved for the highest ranks of Soviet society.

The working class plays no part in these stories or in the lives of its characters. They are not concerned with ideology or politics, except the intricate bureaucratic politics of their working lives, or indeed with anything that does not immediately and directly affect themselves and their families; the family indeed, especially in the person of mothers-in-law, has an influence on them which far exceeds any efforts of official Soviet propaganda to engage their interest. Outside this narrow ambit, they are cynics; it is only when they contemplate their own lives that uneasiness and doubt begin to arise.

They are indeed, if we are to believe Trifonov, very much like ourselves and perhaps this is the most surprising and interesting thing of all about these stories. (pp. 25-6)

R., "Column," in Encounter, *Vol. LIII, No. 2, August, 1979, pp. 24-6.*

PETER KENEZ

Uri Trifonov is a literary phenomenon. He is well thought of by the Soviet critical intelligentsia. A play based on his story, ***The Exchange,*** is the great popular success of the Moscow theater season. And his works, the most interesting to come out of the Soviet Union in years, are increasingly subversive. . . .

Few major writers have had such unpromising beginnings. Trifonov received the Stalin Prize for a novel, ***Students,*** in 1951, when he was only 26 years old. Since the book was among the very few products of Socialist Realism ever translated into English, it was, on occasion, used in American college courses as a horrifying example of the genre. Over the last two decades, however, he has found his medium, the short novel; he has developed a style of his own; and, most importantly, he now writes about real people in real situations.

Trifonov is not an experimentalist; there are few traces of modernism in his writings. His language is simple and his plots, while intricate, are unsurprising. His strength lies in his ability to create characters and place them in their family and social contexts. His description of the minutiae of Moscow life is marvelously evocative. His interest in character inevitably turns him into a moralist: It is through the choices his people make that they become understandable, real and meaningful to us.

As Trifonov has matured artistically, his characters have become more complex and their ethical dilemmas more difficult. In his moral concern, he somewhat resembles Dostoevsky. One of the major differences is that the 19th-century writer dealt with life-and-death issues, while Trifonov focuses on the ethics of everyday existence. Although the events are never extraordinary and the failings, weaknesses and betrayals of his characters are small-scale, the reader is never in doubt about what is right and what is wrong. The question is, rather, whether the characters will know, care or have the strength to do what is right.

The stories Trifonov published in the early 1970s, in the journal *Novy Mir,* provide a strikingly depressing description of modern urban Soviet life. The atmosphere is suffocating, and the characters to a smaller or larger extent are repulsive. The new Soviet man, educated or half-educated, is portrayed as being interested only in material possessions; he is completely without ideals. Traditional values and ties are disappearing and there is nothing to take their place. Corruption and hypocrisy are everywhere. And if the older generations, produced by harsh conditions, are weak or corrupt, the young are depicted as monstrous. A foreigner who wants to get the flavor of Moscow life, who wants to know the mentality of the citizens of the capital, could do no better than to read these stories.

In the last few years Trifonov has published two major works: ***Dom na naberezhnoi (House on the Embankment)*** and ***Starik (The Old Man).*** Both short novels appeared in the journal *Druzhba narodov*—the former in 1976, the latter in 1978—and are far more ambitious and effective than anything he has previously written. His earlier stories were valuable because they gave us a believable picture of Soviet reality. To be sure, they could be regarded as critical, but the criticism was constructive—materialism, faddishness and other unattractive traits were denounced. Thus the early works did no more than to hold a mirror to the society. In his two recent novels Trifonov has gone deeper: He is now concerned with nothing less than the creation of Homo Sovieticus, with the inevitability of betrayal, corruption and moral weakness in modern Russia. Being more profound, these works are also more political: Their interpretation of Soviet history calls into question the very legitimacy of the present system.

Of the two, ***House on the Embankment*** is the more affecting. It tells about the making of the career of a literary scholar, Glebov. We learn a great deal about this character, yet the author is not particularly interested in recounting his life. Trifonov's concern, rather, is to examine the exact moments when morally reprehensible choices are made. There is, of course, a large body of works in world literature dealing with the process of political corruption. The Soviet writer's contribution to this opus is his unique description of both the outside circumstances and of the mind of the person who is being seduced. His concentration on decisive situations, rather than on long-term developments, gives this brief novel the flavor of a short story. (pp. 12-13)

Trifonov uses an interesting literary device in presenting Glebov's character. The bulk of the novel is related by an impersonal narrator who sets out as good a case for Glebov as possible. We are willing to make allowances for his materialism and envy because he is poor and surrounded by luxury; we are willing to forgive his transgressions as we realize that he is merely an agent in the hands of truly malevolent forces. Sometimes, though, we hear another narrator—a classmate of Glebov, who loathes him. . . . He is not interested in extenuating circumstances: For him Glebov is a villain. Clearly both of the narrators represent Trifonov: As an artist he understands his character and appreciates the difficulties; at the same time, there is no doubt that whatever made Glebov into what he became, he is repulsive.

The Old Man, Trifonov's latest novel, is perhaps his best. The book successfully integrates two time frames: the present and the period of the Civil War. The sections dealing with current Soviet life take place in the summer of 1973 in a settlement of dachas outside Moscow. The atmosphere, the problems and the characters are typical Trifonov. Pavel Letunov, a 73-year old man, is spending the summer with his grown children and their families. The large Letunov family would like to acquire a larger dacha nearby that has just become empty through the death of its occupant, and this part of the plot revolves around the struggle for the dacha.

In Trifonov's depiction of contemporary society there are basically two types of Soviet men: the weak and the corrupt. Here we are given the contrasting figures of Ruslan Letunov, Pavel's son, and Kandaurov, a Soviet functionary, who also wants the dacha. Ruslan is weak: He loses his job, he drinks too much, he does not get along with his wife. Yet he is also an attractive person. Middle-aged and suffering from heart trouble, he nevertheless volunteers to fight a forest fire, endangering his life. Kandaurov, by contrast, is totally despicable. He uses others for his own purposes, is without scruples and is so corrupt that he cannot conceive that someone else might not be. While Ruslan has lost his job, Kandaurov is just about to accept an attractive assignment abroad.

Pavel Letunov is an unwilling fighter for the dacha. He attempts to use his influence only for the sake of his family and at their repeated urgings, but his mind is elsewhere. Specifically, he is preoccupied with an episode that occurred during the Civil War. His narrative of the distant past contains two distinct dramas. The first is the event itself. We become acquainted with the Cossack leader, S. K. Migulin, who, without becoming a Bolshevik, threw in his lot with them. He was a man of heroic proportions: an instinctive revolutionary, a fearless fighter and a charismatic leader. For all that, the Bolsheviks did not trust him. He was removed from his native Don, and when the need was so great that he had to be brought back, his enemies conspired against him.

Migulin is clearly based on F. K. Mironov, who was recently resurrected for us by Roy Medvedev. Trifonov is a good historian, and his reconstruction of the events and mood of 1919 is accurate. (pp. 13-14)

Other central characters include Danilov, Letunov's maternal uncle, and Shigontsev, both Bolsheviks. Danilov is a positive hero. He is totally devoted to his cause and sees the purpose of the Revolution as improving the life of the people. To him it is a contradiction in terms to perpetrate injustice in the name of revolution. Migulin and Danilov, naturally, trust and respect one another. Shigontsev, an old comrade of Danilov in exile, is dogmatic; he is willing to sacrifice anything and anybody in the name of misconstrued principles. It is people like Shigontsev who ultimately destroy Migulin.

The second drama, which is even more interesting than the first, involves Pavel Letunov's struggle with his memories. The young Letunov was present at Migulin's trial and had been in love with Migulin's wife, who was his childhood friend. When he was asked by the investigator whether he could entertain the thought that Migulin had participated in a counterrevolutionary rising, Letunov answered yes. It is this episode, festering in the back of Letunov's mind, that accounts for his great interest in the Migulin affair.

By intertwining the present and the past Trifonov makes some unpleasant points. He clearly does not like Shigontsev and his ilk, yet must admit that those people were genuinely motivated by high ideals and were willing to accept sacrifice for their principles. How very different the present is! Modern Soviet man can talk about world revolution only as a joke; he would not take ideology seriously even for a moment. Trifonov despises the materialism of his contemporaries, and in the age-old dispute between fathers and sons he wholeheartedly sides with the old. There is a basic and rather obvious irony here: Only Tsarism produced decent, strong and high-minded men.

Another aspect of the relationship between the two time periods is the relevance of the past for the present. Nothing is more important to the old man than knowing whether he had reason to suspect Migulin of counterrevolutionary tendencies. He searches for an answer to the question: Why did Migulin in August 1919 disregard orders and take his troops to the front? To be sure, he has private reasons for his curiosity, yet the truth is important not just for him alone, but for the entire Soviet society. In a crucial scene of the novel a casual visitor hits the nail on the head when he asks Pavel Letunov whether he feels guilty before the memory of Migulin. Letunov is overcome by emotion and answers passionately. No, he is not guilty before Migulin, but before all others, for not having revealed the truth.

Trifonov thus implies that there can be no overcoming corruption, no building a decent and healthy society without facing the past honestly, a most subversive notion in modern day Russia. What is more, Trifonov affirms again and again the responsibility of the individual for large and small crimes, and even for silence in the face of injustice.

That Trifonov could publish ***House on the Embankment*** and ***The Old Man*** is remarkable, for there certainly has been no general relaxation of censorship in the Soviet Union. Writers who recently attempted to bring out a fairly tame collection, *Metropol,* quickly found themselves in trouble; historians who treat Stalinism and the Revolution continue to concede nothing to truth. One can only speculate about Trifonov's ability to issue works that strike at the very heart of the regime. Maybe his considerable reputation is protecting him; maybe the fact that his writings only gradually became critical has misled the censors; maybe he has friends in powerful circles who come to his aid. Whatever the case, the Trifonov phenomenon shows that Russians are sometimes allowed to read some very subversive books. (p. 14)

Peter Kenez, "Trifonov's Russia," in The New Leader, *Vol. LXII, No. 17, September 10, 1979, pp. 12-14.*

CAROLINE DeMAEGD-SOËP

In contemporary Russian prose Iurii Trifonov is a pioneer in depicting the everyday life—*byt*—of the Russian intelligentsia. This interest is expressed in the themes, structure, and vocabulary of his Moscow stories. However, the word *byt* is seldom used, and Trifonov came to dislike the word. As he told us in Moscow, "I do not write about *byt* but about people's lives." The writer became annoyed by the fact that many Soviet critics and literary scholars define his short stories as *"proizvedeniia bytovogo zhanra"* (works in the *byt* genre). Many Western critics also stress the social aspects of his Moscow stories. Such an approach naturally means that the writer's purely artistic creativity is insufficiently appreciated! . . .

Trifonov thus categorically denied that the theme of his short stories can be defined as *byt*. Nevertheless it is fascinating to examine the evolution of his attitude towards the term. (p. 49)

In his treatment of *byt* Trifonov follows above all the Chekhovian tradition. This is especially noticeable in the way he treats the power of daily routine, people's mutual estrangement, indifference, and the real and the pseudo-intelligentsia. Trifonov, just as Chekhov did, is describing a period of stabilization in Russia. Trifonov's characters find it difficult to remember the war, but in apparently peaceful, contemporary Russian life the writer reveals forces which incite people to wage their own little wars anew every day!

Moscow is the central setting of the action and also determines the atmosphere of Trifonov's stories. In Moscow he unmasks the standardization characteristic of every modern large city and points to its "rapacious" character; a large city constantly expands its boundaries at the expense of nature. Trifonov also poses the problem of the village life sometimes led by the city intelligentsia. Indeed, the theme of the *dacha* plays an essential role in all of the Moscow stories. The *dacha* appears often as the symbol of true beauty, freshness, youth, and peace. For certain of Trifonov's heroes *dacha* life is in fact the sole refuge where they can escape from the difficult conditions of the city. Frequently the most beautiful moments in the lives of Trifonov's characters are experienced in the poetic atmosphere of the *dacha*. The latter symbolizes the "other life" for which Trifonov's heroes strongly yearn!

The transformation of man and human relationships under the pressure of the nervous bustle of city life is an important theme of the Moscow stories. (pp. 52-3)

The tearing pace of Moscow life affects the Muscovites most during their daily pursuit of elementary comfort. Trifonov depicts the many material problems of contemporary Soviet society down to the last concrete detail. In so doing he makes skillful use of *bytovaia leksika*. However, this depiction is intended to reveal the psychological state of the characters and this is at the heart of the stories' general human significance. In Trifonov's work it is in *bytovye* conflicts that people's varying characters and their outlooks on life are expressed. *Byt* in Trifonov's work is not merely bound up with the concrete problems of a flat, food, clothes, career, and travel abroad. The principal problem posed by the author is: "How must man live?" And above all: "How must man behave towards his fellowmen?" In a discussion with us Trifonov remarked that he considered the most important aspect of life to be the way in which people live together. For him the love of one's fellowmen is the most precious thing in our existence. The author has shown this conviction in a work where the remark is made that the love of one's fellowmen is "the oxygen" without which man cannot live. . . . (pp. 53-4)

In particular Trifonov points out the danger inherent in the loss of human contacts as a result of the new consumer ethic. However, he reacted just as strongly to the use of the term *meshchanstvo* (philistinism) with regard to his work as he did to *byt*. He remarked scornfully: "They say that my short stories are not only *'bytovye'*, but even *'meshchanskie'*." Nevertheless Trifonov unmasks philistinism, especially in intelligentsia circles. The author even coined a new term to denote the phenomenon: *olukianit'sia,* from the name of the petit bourgeois Lukianov family in the story ***Obmen*** (***The Exchange*** . . .). Here Trifonov depicts the unremitting hunt for greater material comfort. The hero, Viktor Dmitriev, reproaches his wife, Lena Lukianova, for wanting to obtain at any price his dying mother's room so as to exchange that room together with their own room for a large flat. Horrified by his wife's callous behavior, Viktor says bitterly: "You have some sort of spiritual defect. Some sort of underdeveloped feelings. Something . . . subhuman." . . . The author depicts Lena's possessive impulse as something animal-like. . . . Under pressure from his energetic wife, the weak-willed Viktor is driven to commit an act of which he disapproves and finally he compromises with his conscience and seeks salvation in resignation. (pp. 54-5)

In all of his Moscow stories Trifonov depicts the process of the sensitive, good-natured, but weak-willed intellectual who abandons his ideals under the pressure of everyday life and is reduced to frustration. He shows that many will not shrink from any quid pro quo, deceit, or treachery in the name of material and intellectual comfort. For this reason the term *"meshchanstvo"* must be viewed in the deeper meaning which the author gives to it. It is not merely an unbridled lust for possessions, but also a weltanschauung steeped in egoism and soullessness.

Trifonov makes frequent use of his *bytovaia leksika* to ironize about people "who have the ability to get their own way," . . . but who in fact reveal a "lack of intelligence and a truly piratical lust for acquisition." He calls them the "gentlemen of success." . . . For such people *byt* is no trial to bear but rather a kind of sport. They build up an indispensable circle of influential connections who can help them in their ascent of the social ladder. (p. 55)

Most conflicts in Trifonov's short stories are caused by the collision of these sober "energetic people" with the idealistic heroes, who are not at all adjusted to *byt*. They are distinguished by their rich spiritual interests and their striving for inspired creativity. However, their "sober" environment regards these people as "dreamers," "eccentrics," and "fantasts." They are said to have no "talent for living"! For Trifonov's idealistic heroes *byt* is a real trial. Chekhov too depicts the constant conflict between the idealist and his sterile environment. Trifonov's characters are so firmly rooted in prosaic *byt* that they form part of it and can no longer escape. In this then lies the tragic significance of Trifonov's work. However, the author also uses *bytovye* conflicts to reflect the indecisiveness and irresolute behavior of the idealistic hero. In his work the protagonists are repeatedly revealed as lacking the force required to oppose their own way of living. . . . But Trifonov, humane and understanding, also reveals the inexorability of *byt,* which is why the despondent, agonizing intellectual so frequently asks himself: "What is to be done?" or "Who is guilty?" He thus attempts to understand why he has behaved in his daily life in precisely such and such a way and not differently.

In the Moscow stories the question of "Who is guilty?" is given the most varied of answers. In ***Drugaia zhizn'*** (***Another Life*** . . .) Ol'ga, tormented by the premature death of her husband Sergei, searches for the causes: "Try to understand, there must be a meaning, somebody must be guilty, those near to you are always guilty." . . . In the case of Sergei, a gifted historian, his struggle with his colleagues of the research institute has apparently accelerated the fatal outcome. Ol'ga speaks of intrigues which Sergei's former friend, Klimuk, started in connection with her husband's dissertation: "If only he had reached an agreement with Klimuk then! . . . Everything would have turned out differently." . . . In fact Sergei was the victim of the unrelenting struggle between innovatory, honest, scholarly work and the unoriginal activity of scholars resembling Professor Serebriakov in Chekhov's play *Diadia Vania (Uncle Vania).* This age-old conflict is also portrayed in ***Dom na naberezhnoi*** (***The House on the Embankment*** . . .). Here there are no "guilty people" but the times are the guilty force. . . . (pp. 55-6)

In all of the Moscow stories Trifonov also depicts the protagonist's conflict with his conscience. In contrast to the revolutionary hero who acts in a social conflict, the conflict of Trifonov's contemporary hero is with himself. (p. 56)

Trifonov's stories illustrate the revival of psychological prose in present-day Soviet literature. The writer is also following in the Chekhovian tradition in that he gives a penetrating analysis of the emotional and spiritual state of his characters. He too structures his stories mainly in the form of an interior monologue. The narrator or protagonist analyses both his personal and his social life in order to understand his own personality. In so doing he sometimes ascribes the guilt for his failure to his own character, disposition, and upbringing. Moreover, the hero judges both his own behavior and that of other people from a well-determined moral standpoint.

Taking concrete *bytovye* events as a starting point, Trifonov shows far-reaching changes which take place in the spiritual world above all in his idealistic characters. The melancholy leitmotiv of "I have become a different person" runs like a thread through all the Moscow stories. Under the pressure of *byt* the good-natured, but also selfish and reticent hero usually turns into a prematurely aged man who suffers from all sorts of ailments. . . . Trifonov frequently penetrates the inner world of his characters like a psychiatrist establishing the correct connection between the psychic and the physical state of man. . . . By using an apposite medical terminology the author shows how every time his characters find themselves in a difficult situation they are stricken by some illness. Heart disease, high blood pressure, vegetative neuroses, fainting fits and such like all figure systematically in Trifonov's world. His ailing characters frequently look to nature for their salvation, or to a long journey, a dream, an illusion, or even to parapsychology.

But there is no remedy which can alleviate the ailments caused by dislocated relations between people. . . . The drama of many of Trifonov's characters lies precisely in the fact that to the extent that *byt* drains their living forces they are no longer able to have real relations with other people. The consequence is loneliness, misunderstanding, and an inability to help and to love. This failure is naturally felt most acutely in the relationship between husband and wife. (pp. 57-8)

But Trifonov also uses the term *byt* to render our general human condition. He depicts a series of characters who prove that not only *byt* acts as a brake, but also the temperament of certain characters who are not able to tackle effectively the daily struggle for existence. . . . In "egoism" Trifonov sees the greatest obstacle to human relations. He calls it "the oldest of all human illnesses" and depicts its nefarious consequences in many different forms. In ***Drugaia zhizn'*** the conflict between the spouses is caused not only by the differences in their characters and outlooks but also by what the author calls "the clash of two egoisms." . . . In ***Predvaritel'nye itogi*** a similar explanation of the family conflict is given and it is also noted that: "Every egoist has a way out. . . . To find a good person who will forgive him everything." . . . (p. 58)

In Trifonov's world forgiveness is an essential element of love. His ideal heroines are imbued with a spirit of all-forgiving love. They strive to save the man whom they love. . . . The women are also much more realistic and practical than the men and cope more effectively with daily routine. In the context of the theme of "love and *byt,*" which is treated by many contemporary Soviet writers, Soviet critics note that a man's value is determined by his attitude towards love: "soullessness" is regarded as the archenemy of true love. Trifonov also exposes the heartless insensitiveness of his heroes towards the woman they love. (pp. 58-9)

Trifonov sees in true love an exalting force which can oppose the draining power of routine. This vision coincides with Chekhov's conception of love, which is exemplified in "Dama s sobachkoi" ("The Lady with the Dog"). An echo of this story can be heard in ***Obmen*** where the protagonist, Viktor Dmitriev, says of his extramarital liaison with Tania: "It seemed to him that he had only become associated with that normal, truly human condition in which people should—and with time will—always live." . . .

Trifonov also sees in love a force which should permeate all humanity. The leitmotiv of love for one's fellowmen runs through all his stories and resounds clearly in the words: "It is possible to be ill, it is possible to do an unfulfilling job all one's life, but one must feel a man. For this one thing is necessary—an atmosphere of simple humanity. . . . Nobody can achieve this feeling by himself, autonomously, it arises from others, from those near to us." . . . (p. 59)

Trifonov often uses the verb "to pity" *(zhalet')* and we consider this word to be the key to an understanding of his weltanschauung. His vision is expressed in ***Drugaia zhizn':*** "All at once a love of one's fellowmen will appear, the ability to feel pity and compassion will emerge." . . . Sometimes the "restricted consciousness" of Trifonov's confused heroes reminds us of Dostoevskii, who is named more than once in Trifonov's stories.

His philosophical reflections about man's common lot gives Trifonov's work a general human significance. He does not judge people harshly because he understands the complexity of the human condition. . . . Trifonov makes us realize that man is not merely an enigma to his fellowmen, but also to himself. Ol'ga in ***Drugaia zhizn'*** expresses this melancholy thought: "To understand oneself for a start. Good heavens!

We do not have the strength, nor the time or perhaps we lack the ability, the courage.'' . . . Because of this human failing Trifonov opposes any form of contempt. In ***Predvaritel'nye itogi*** he says of one of Chekhov's characters: ''Professor Serebriakov is a man too. Why despise him so much? . . . People cannot be blamed for not being Leo Tolstois or Spensers.'' . . . Trifonov also reflects the relativity of all *bytovye* problems and conflicts when he says in ***Obmen:*** ''There is nothing in the world except life and death. And everything that is subordinate to the former is happiness but everything that belongs to the latter . . . is the destruction of happiness.'' . . .

A leitmotif of contemporary *byt* as depicted by Trifonov is the period of the revolution; it is most strongly exemplified in his late story ***Starik*** (***The Old Man*** . . .). In Trifonov's work a melancholy longing for Russia's revolutionary past can be felt in the appearance of many historical figures and motifs. Thus in his novel ***Neterpenie*** (***Impatience*** . . .) Trifonov turns his attention to the young idealists of the terrorist movement *Narodnaia Volia,* which was responsible for the assassination of Tsar Alexander II in 1881. However, for Trifonov's idealistic, powerless heroes Russia's revolutionary history is a spiritual refuge as it offers the possibility of escaping, albeit in thought only, from the grip of prosaic *byt*. For them the revolutionary is ''the true hero'' as he knows ''how man must live.'' Through the person of the revolutionary Trifonov also stresses the immense power of one's conscience. The answer to the question: ''How should one live?'' is found in ***Dolgoe proshchanie,*** where it is said of a revolutionary: ''He executed the will of his own conscience. . . . This is a tremendous strength.'' . . . (pp. 59-61)

The thematic richness of Trifonov's work in which *byt* and historic past are interwoven is determined by the complex structure of the Moscow stories. Present and past, daily occurrences and historic events are constantly alternating. By means of reminiscences the narrator or the protagonist continually compares past and present. . . . In the Moscow stories memory itself plays a capital role. The narrator constantly ponders on the significance of *byt,* history, life, and death, with the aim of reaching a definite conclusion. But the ''open finale'' in Trifonov's stories indicates that any conclusion is premature. Thus the hero, sadly reflecting on his past, so often says: ''If only . . .'' (Esli by . . .) but does not finish his thought.

The many suggestive thoughts and unfinished statements in Trifonov's work confirm that the author, like Chekhov, is relying on the reader as coauthor. Like Chekhov, Trifonov is a master of the art of objective depiction without a priori judgments, didactic declarations, and easy solutions. But Trifonov's work makes us understand that it is sometimes easier for a man to perform a historic deed than to live out every day in his prosaic existence of ''inexplicable and incomprehensible *byt*''! (p. 61)

Caroline De Maegd-Soëp, ''The Theme of 'BYT'—Everyday Life in the Stories of Iurii Trifonov,'' in Russian Literature and Criticism: Selected Papers from the Second World Congress for Soviet and East European Studies, *edited by Evelyn Bristol, Berkeley Slavic Specialties, 1982, pp. 49-62.*

JOSEPHINE WOLL

Tolstoy, Turgenev, Trifonov . . . Trifonov? Well, perhaps that's a bit of an overstatement. Yet of all the Russian novelists of the past 20 years, Yuri Trifonov is one of the closest to those two eminent forebears. He is nearly unknown to Western readers: Only three of his novellas have hitherto appeared in English (in a collection entitled ***The Long Goodbye***), and they were published by a press known mostly to specialists in Russian literature. . . . (An early novel, ***Students,*** which won a Stalin Prize more than 30 years ago, is also available in English in a Soviet edition.) But now . . . two of his last four works [are published in the volume ***Another Life. The House on the Embankment***], and English readers can judge for themselves if the genealogy rings true.

Less poetic in his prose style and exhibiting none of Turgenev's feeling for nature, Trifonov also is much less didactic than Tolstoy. The similarities, rather, are to be found in his manipulation of the stuff of everyday existence, and of history, to reveal the inner life of his characters and to answer the questions, ''What should men live by? How should man behave toward his fellow man?'' . . .

Born in 1925, Trifonov was the son of a Old Bolshevik killed during the 1930's purges, and a mother who spent years in the slave labor camps. As he pursued his craft, he inched steadily toward dealing honestly with the major subjects for a Russian of his generation and background: the evolution from Leninist Russia to Stalinist Russia; the Stalin years; the clash between idealism, integrity and honor, and pragmatism, opportunism and compromise. (p. 17)

Of the two novellas, ***Another Life,*** published in the leading literary journal *Novy Mir* in 1975, is deemed the more private; ***House on the Embankment,*** published the following year in *Druzhba Narodov,* mistakenly labeled a ''conservative'' journal, is seen as the more public. To some extent such distinctions are artificial in Trifonov's case. Unlike Turgenev, who reserved his most inward, emotional subjects for novellas and used the longer genre for treatments of social and historical issues, Trifonov shows a far greater degree of overlap.

What he gives us are people's lives—and that means an inextricable mixture of work, marriage, sex, children, friendship, and the periods involved. Nevertheless, in ***Another Life*** the refracting lens is a grieving widow's attempt to survive her loss by reviewing in her mind the life she and her husband shared. The theme of the past is there, as are her husband's conflicts with his colleagues, but the focus is personal: Olga can't conceive of another life for herself, can't begin a new life, until she comes to terms with her first one.

Like many of Trifonov's marriages or couplings, Olga's passionate and turbulent union with Sergei was a bonding between two very different people. She, a biologist, is practical and conventional; he, a historian, is fiercely independent, something of a loner, restless, lacking that gift of knowing how to get along so crucial to advancement in Soviet (or any other) society. Their professions reflect their differences: Olga is a materialist, and death means to her the end of a conglomeration of molecules, irreconcilable with life. She cannot understand the pursuit of history. . . .

Sergei believes that ''the individual is the thread stretching through time, the supersensitive nerve of history that can be teased out and separated—and from which one can then learn a great deal.'' This is certainly Trifonov's notion as well, although his canvas is fiction instead of fact. But he is less concerned with showing up the limits of Olga's imagination than in peeling back, layer by layer, the palimpsest of two oddly-suited people who live together in happy and unhappy love. Sergei's flirtation with parapsychology, coming at the end of his truncated life, is his last attempt to ''tease out'' the thread of other lives; it threatens the foundation of his relationship with Olga, a relationship that she, in her pain, romanticizes yet feels—and Trifonov concurs—can only be understood from the inside.

In ***House on the Embankment*** the author tries a slightly different approach, to give both the outside and the inside view; he mixes a third person and omniscient narrator with an occasional (and intrusive) first person voice. (In his posthumously published novel, ***Time and Place*** [published in Russia as ***Vremia i mesto***], he is more successful with this mixture.) The house of the title refers to an enormous apartment building in Moscow where big shots lived in the 1930s. This novella made the censors nervous: While almost all of Trifonov's works were published in editions of 100,000, ***House on the Embankment*** had a run of 30,000—by Soviet standards, for a writer of Trifonov's popularity, small indeed.

No wonder. It is a treatment of one man, Vadim Glebov, who in 1972 is prominent and successful, but whose past—in 1937, as a child living next door to the house on the embankment, and in 1947-48, as a graduate student in a literary institute—reveals a pattern of acquiescence to the exigencies of the times. What those particular times demanded was betrayal. And despite Trifonov's saying at one point that "the times were to blame," we are left with no doubt that Glebov's compliance, unwilling as it may have been, demands judgment.

Not that Trifonov judges presumptuously, or is unmindful of what the stakes were. He has no villains or gods; human frailty and foolishness are as apparent in his characters who do not cave in to pressure as in the ones who do. The climax for Glebov, the moment when he chooses, in Solzhenitsyn's words, to "participate in evil," comes during his graduate studies. His thesis adviser is Professor Ganchuk, a Civil War hero who had been an active participant in the literary battles that remained possible in the 1920s. Ganchuk's daughter Sonya is Glebov's lover (she is, incidentally, a Dostoyevskian Sonya, overwhelmed by pity for everyone, innocent, insulted, and injured). In the vicious era of the late 1940s, Ganchuk is selected for destruction and Glebov is invited—ordered—to participate in the beheading.

What is so impressive about Trifonov's handling of this difficult, delicate situation is his ability to display the warts of the victim in the very process of distinguishing between victim and victimizer. Ganchuk is dictatorial and self-righteous; he is free with terms like "petty bourgeois faker"; he regrets that when he had the chance in the 1920s he did not get rid of the man who now has the power to persecute him. Nevertheless, as Glebov sees clearly enough:

"The whole point was that [Ganchuk] was an absolutely honest and decent man, and to attack him implied an attack, as it were, on the very standard of decency itself." (pp. 17-18)

Glebov is the "individual thread stretching through time" that Sergei, in ***Another Life,*** believes to be the key to history. Through him Trifonov lays bare an epoch. Anyone who still wonders how Stalinism could have happened need only read ***House on the Embankment*** to find out. (p. 18)

Josephine Woll, "Plumbing the Soviet Psyche," in The New Leader, *Vol. LXVII, No. 3, February 6, 1984, pp. 17-18.*

RICHARD LOURIE

Russian literature isn't all vodka; it has its quiet beers as well. Yuri Trifonov's novellas are the latter. They are as formless and self-interrupting as conversation and make use of the telling detail a la Chekhov. Actually, in some ways Trifonov (1925-81) may be seen as a Soviet Chekhov, but whereas Chekhov, out of modesty, took an oblique approach to the dramatic, one suspects that Trifonov's avoidances derive from motives more complex and more entangled with history. . . .

[The two novellas published in ***Another Life. The House on the Embankment***] each begin with a sting that brings the past into the present. In ***Another Life*** it is the sudden death of Olga's husband, Sergei, a man in his early 40's, that sends her back into remembering and soul-searching. In ***The House on the Embankment,*** it is a chance meeting with a childhood friend that reveals how Glebov, a successful literary bureaucrat, got to the top. . . . Trifonov demonstrates that people like Glebov succeed in Soviet society because they can betray others so easily, because they are not burdened with a strong sense of themselves.

The weakness of this story, however, is that the author was unwilling to wear Glebov's skin and instead suggested what was in him by what might be called lyric sociology—evocative details in a social matrix to whose finest shadings Trifonov is sensitive. The problem is similar to that in the movie *Zelig*—how do you describe the inner life of the empty? But everything around the weak center works very well. Trifonov's specialty is the life of the Russian intelligentsia; he brings us into their homes, their book-lined studies, and into their childhoods with a sure sense of childhood's envies and adventures and the little sins that are the seeds of character. When Shulepa, Glebov's childhood friend, the boy on whom fate seemed to smile endlessly, is seen sporting an American aviator's leather jacket after the war, everything is excellently clear: How wonderful that jacket was in itself and how unlike the conditions of Soviet life, how Shulepa accepted it as his due and how Glebov instinctively, by virtue of that jacket, understood the injustice of the world. Such scenes are masterfully realized and lit by a warm compassion. . . .

Another Life is nearly flawless. A woman in her early 40's is suddenly widowed, and the death transforms her past. Trifonov knows we don't carry around clear, finished, detailed scenes in our memories. Memories are always partial and have very odd contours; he knows they tend to be dim except when lit by miniature details that have no special meaning of their own but illuminate everything else. Traces of the past alive in the present is a recurring motif in both novellas. And it is out of such traces that Trifonov constructs a widowhood—quite an achievement. . . .

Moving from the errands and arguments of daily existence to memory and then back again with perfect ease, Trifonov's portrait of Olga is free of the sort of "psychology" that sees life and people as problems to be resolved. The milieu is the minor intelligentsia, people trying to finish dissertations, working at the less important institutes. Even though Olga's husband had certain problems where he worked, they are less important here than in ***The House on the Embankment,*** where big prizes were at stake. This allows Trifonov to exercise his art more comfortably. We become absorbed in the widow's grief, her memories and questions, but we don't identify with her, which is the strength and beauty of the story; we are shown another person, someone else. And although there are guides to the stages and sub-stages of grief, Trifonov knows that grief persists until one day life replaces it with something new. . . .

[These] novellas are valuable works of literature, whose courage is only slowly revealed. By placing his story far in the background and by allowing himself to be absorbed in minutiae, Trifonov seems to say that our lives are made of small enduring traces, and all the rest, no matter how much harm it does us, really doesn't matter in the end.

Richard Lourie, "Tales of a Soviet Chekhov," in The New York Times Book Review, *March 18, 1984, p. 7.*

HARLOW ROBINSON

This ambitious novel [***The Old Man***] will probably surprise those who think of Yuri Trifonov as a writer of small-scale and minutely observed emotional detail—the "Soviet Chekhov," as many have described him. In ***The Old Man,*** one of the last works Trifonov completed before he died in Moscow in 1981 . . . , the walls containing Trifonov's cozy fictional world burst wide open. History—especially the bloody and complicated years of the civil war that followed the Russian Revolution—rushes in. It becomes, in fact, the protean and elusive protagonist.

In his best-known works (***The House on the Embankment, Another Life, The Exchange***), Trifonov only hints at events in the historical-political background. We see them primarily through changes in the Soviet middle-class domestic environment: larger or smaller apartments, newer or older cars, Western or Soviet clothing. The stage is the kitchen, or the bedroom, or the porch at the summer *dacha,* not the world "out there"—where neighbors are arrested in the middle of the night and hauled off to Siberia, and where wars rage and peasants starve. History is personal, even self-centered: What wine were we drinking the night we met? When did the snow first fall the year we married?

For Pavel Evgrafovich Letunov, the "old man" of the title of this novel, however, history—and memory—has a much wider significance. He must "find out" before he dies. What he is determined to discover is the truth about how he and his friends behaved during the chaotic years of the civil war, years so many times interpreted and reinterpreted by generations of Soviet historians and writers. Above all, he wants to find out about Migulin, a fiery and idealistic Bolshevik even before 1917, but later branded as a counterrevolutionary criminal for his individualistic tendencies as a military commander. Migulin was for a short time married to Asya, the great love of the old man's youth.

The old man's search for the truth leads him to newspapers, archives and telegrams of the war years (much of this material is reproduced in the novel). Eventually, after he has written an article "rehabilitating" Migulin, he receives a letter from Asya herself. They had lost each other for more than 50 years. Letunov hopes he will receive the final answer from her, the word that will deliver him from his own guilt about having considered Migulin a criminal. "I'm not blaming you—at the time that's what most people believed," she tells him. "People were in the throes of war and they saw things quite different from now, when they can evaluate everything calmly."

Trifonov contrasts the old man's concern with these historical and ethical issues to his neighbors' and children's petty "problems" of the 1970's—acquiring more living space and managing tedious infidelities. The people who surround him, Letunov realizes, are inconsequential, selfish and unprincipled. And yet isn't their moral flabbiness a result of the failure of the old man's generation to stand up to lies and distortions, like the ones that transformed the committed Communist Migulin from a hero into a villain and back into a hero?

All of this is a lot to cram into a relatively small novel. The material and characters seem sometimes undigested and fragmentary. Wandering between the civil war and 1973, the narration can be strangely jumpy and impersonal. The old man's search for the "facts" is related primarily from his viewpoint—in both the first and third persons—but his attention is so narrowly focused on Asya and Migulin that we don't find out enough about the old man himself. Detailed flashbacks to the Revolution and the civil war begin before we have become deeply enough involved with him to care about what he tells us. And other large chunks of the novel—involving the unseemly struggle over a vacant summer house—are told through the minds of characters only peripherally connected to the old man and his quest.

Yet in this disorganization and abdication of authorial responsibility, in this ambiguous narrative perspective, lies a brilliant statement of Trifonov's theme: the dangerously insecure grasp the dying Soviet generation has of its own constantly rewritten history. As Trifonov obviously understood, soon no one will be left who actually lived through the Revolution and civil war. What hope can there be that the younger generation will ever know the truth about its national past—and, even more important, its present—if even parents and grandparents who were eyewitnesses cannot distinguish between a hero and an enemy of the state?

Harlow Robinson, "Why Migulin Matters," in The New York Times Book Review, *February 3, 1985, p. 18.*

KAREN ROSENBERG

The Old Man, which appeared in the Soviet Union in 1978, follows the scattered thoughts of Pavel Evgrafovich Letunov, which are mainly about the Civil War in southern Russia in 1919. Rather than a historical novel, it is a novel about the search for historical truth and about the lies and omissions that even the well-intentioned prefer. The mystery that preoccupies the old man revolves around Sergei Kirillovich Migulin, who is based on an actual figure in the Civil War. Why did Migulin, a commander of the Red Cossacks, decide on his own to lead his men against the White General Denikin, an act which led to Migulin's arrest, a death sentence and a last-minute Dostoyevskian pardon? That is the question Letunov poses. But it may be a red herring, masking a more politically sensitive issue: Why did Moscow and most party workers at the front mistrust Migulin, and keep him idle when he itched to fight for the revolution, until he snapped and took matters into his own hands? Migulin's charisma, his resistance to domination by inexperienced and dogmatic political commissars and his protests against the forced requisition of grain made him suspect to many party functionaries.

Though Migulin was pardoned for his insubordination, he was later tried on charges of counterrevolutionary activity and executed. Letunov, who had known the commander in Civil War days, tried to rehabilitate his name in the 1960s. One summer in the early 1970s, he is still obsessed with the Cossack leader. Behind his fixation lies repressed guilt, but the reason for it cannot be divulged without spoiling the novel's surprise ending. Suffice it to say that the young Letunov was less sure than his older self about where he stood in the battle between Migulin and the Jacobin commissars. He had vacillated, carried away by the enthusiasms of the revolutionary era:

> Like lava it flows, that savage time, submerging and burying in its fire. . . . My God, and so few people were horrified; so few cried out! Because the lava blinds your eyes.

The scorching summer weather that threatens the old man's heart fuses with his memories of revolutionary hotheads to produce the image of history as a volcanic eruption. It's a metaphor that ignores human volition and moral choice, yet instead of condemning the old man for his blindness, Trifonov makes the reader empathize with him. Identifying with Letunov means recognizing that we too could lose our moral bearings and commit irrevocable crimes in the name of some great cause.

Trifonov reserves his scorn for another, Oleg Vasilevich Kandaurov, a careerist intellectual whose actions can't be excused by youth or misplaced idealism. As the Letunov children's competitor for a *dacha,* he pursues his selfish goals "right up to the hilt," a phrase that becomes increasingly sinister as the plot unfolds. Between the lines, one can read that a revolution that is cavalier in matters of fairness and justice is likely to create a society with similar shortcomings.

Letunov's Uncle Shura, an Old Bolshevik who objected, however futilely, to personal vengeance disguised as class struggle, stands for a better communist road not taken. A kindly father figure—some say, a fictional representation of Trifonov's own father—he is the only character in the novel who comes close to being the traditional positive hero of Socialist Realism. So it is surprising and significant that he fails to save the day. Shura's inability to shield Migulin from disaster suggests that in Trifonov's view, personal decency, while admirable, doesn't accomplish much in Soviet Russia, but he puts a politically acceptable opinion in Letunov's mouth: "The trouble was, there were no real commissars around." By hiding behind his protagonist, Trifonov leaves his novel open to contradictory interpretations.

Such camouflages and compromises have been attacked in *samizdat,* but not everyone is cut out for heroics. Trifonov's way of living with censorship may have made him peculiarly aware of weakness and ambivalence, and impatient with black-and-white characterizations. "They tried it while Migulin was still alive, shrieking out words like 'traitor' and 'betrayer'; and they're still trying it today, with cries of 'Leninist' and 'revolutionary,'" thinks Letunov. "If he could simply be explained in a single word I would not be sitting here in the middle of the night rummaging through papers." (pp. 184-85)

[Trifonov understands] the importance of memory and also its fragility. . . . The temptation to forget is great when the past is politically suspect or personally embarrassing, and when it doesn't even seem to make much sense. If official histories contain glaring omissions and distortions, then private recollections take on special value—as do the novels that explore and preserve them. (p. 185)

Karen Rosenberg, "Tickets to the Past," in The Nation, *New York, Vol. 240, No. 6, February 16, 1985, pp. 183-85.*

FERNANDA EBERSTADT

Perhaps because so little of "official" literature is translated in the West, Yuri Trifonov comes to us as something of an anomaly. Born in Moscow in 1925, the son of a Red Army commander in the civil war of 1918-21 who was executed in 1937 and expunged from party history, Trifonov seems in certain ways a throwback to an earlier era in the history of Soviet letters. His elegant, careful, and on the surface almost impassive novellas depicting contemporary urban life recall the work of writers like Ehrenburg and Leonid Leonov, who continued to produce and to publish even during the worst years of Stalinism but who managed to incorporate into the most correct monuments of socialist realism a suggestion of some of the truths of Soviet reality. It is this kind of layered, ambiguous fiction which the late Max Hayward called "the noblest type of collaboration."

Looking back at Trifonov's entire career (he died in 1981), one can detect an almost linear progress: an early novel, ***Students*** (1950), which won the Stalin Prize (and probably deserved it); another, ***Thirst,*** about the construction of a canal at Kara-Kum: a decade of near-silence spent in the State Archives, reconstructing the civil-war years in an effort to rehabilitate his father's name, the result of which was ***The Campfire Reflection*** (1965); then, throughout the 70's, "noble collaborations" in the form of novellas that are fresh, exquisite, memorable, but deliberately empty of hope or spiritual meaning; and, finally, his masterpiece, ***The Old Man.*** (A last novel, ***Time and Place,*** about a writer constrained by political circumstances from fulfilling his potential, [was published posthumously] in the Soviet Union.)

Of all the Soviet literary works available in translation today, Trifonov's novellas of the 1970's, collected in ***The Long Goodbye*** and ***Another Life/The House on the Embankment,*** are the most accessible, if only because their themes—domestic grievances, dissatisfaction at work, past infidelities recollected, all the compromises, grudges, and resentments of an unheroic middle age—are so dear to current taste. Indeed, these tales of urban disappointment and betrayal, delivered in a spare, delicately scented prose, are not only accessible, they must seem uncannily familiar to any reader of modern American fiction. No wonder they have elicited raves from American reviewers: Richard Lourie in the New York *Times Book Review* called Trifonov a Soviet Chekhov [see excerpt above]. . . . (p. 37)

Trifonov's fictional world is highly localized. It is a world of middle-aged Moscow professionals—academics, engineers, biologists, but more often employees at nameless institutes whose careers have been chiseled out of compromises and betrayals, men who are more absorbed by the task of finding a co-worker from whom they can cadge a loan or leaving the office early to visit a sick mother than they are by their work. The field of action is similarly constricted, the emotions muffled. These heroes of our time get caught in traffic jams or have trouble finding a cab, their wives nag them about getting their son into an elite school, they are snubbed in the street by a more successful colleague, they wonder whether they should buy a new mattress this year or next, they remember that the pipes in their summer home need fixing. Because the present is so gray and inadequate, much of the significant action here takes place in memory. In ***The Exchange,*** an act of submission to greed compels the protagonist to think back on his life to discover at what point he alienated himself from his own family and joined forces with his grasping wife and in-laws; in ***Taking Stock,*** a failed translator with a weak heart broods in a cultural-workers' resort over all the shabby betrayals in which he has acquiesced. Yet memory brings neither understanding nor resolution, only waves of self-pity.

The dangers inherent in these subjects are apparent. To read story after story about men dissatisfied with their dreary and compromised lives, about nebbish husbands whose wives made them do it, can become debilitating if there is no responsibility taken for actions, no effort to transcend circumstances, no higher authority invoked than self-interest, no knowledge gained from the exercise of memory. But Trifonov's own compassion for his characters is what saves these stories from such debility. Like a mother seeing her small child off to school, Trifonov lovingly pats his beleaguered academics' yellow briefcases and straightens their frayed ties, dabs black-market perfume behind their wives' pendulous ears, and sends them all off into the mean and meager world of his own making.

Moreover, despite the sense of emptiness that accompanies his heroes and heroines, Trifonov's novels are much more tightly peopled than one is used to in modern fiction. Not only parents and children, but also mothers- and fathers-in-law, aunts by marriage, cousins, and cousins-in-law live under the same roof, while neighbors, co-workers, ex-wives, and friends' widows clamor for attention.

The reader cannot but find himself engaged, too, by the jewel-like quality of Trifonov's writing: his delicate prose, his eye for choice detail, his intimate feel for light, location, change of season, weather, for physical appearance, sights observed from a train (the changing countryside around Moscow and the encroachments of urban blight are favorite themes, and well-suited to Trifonov's genteelly frayed, elegiac moods).

If it is above all for these almost peripheral rewards that his novellas of the 1970's are worth reading, nevertheless one feels that in them Trifonov is doing his talents an injustice. To judge from the heights he reached in ***The Old Man,*** the last novel to be published before his death, one might suppose that the failure of these novellas—which is a failure of daring—came from Trifonov's unwillingness to address directly their hidden subject: the nature of the political system which circumscribes these ordinary souls. In the novellas, it is as if Trifonov's characters were moving about under a tent; in ***The Old Man*** the tarpaulin is lifted, and one sees at last the black skies of socialism. (pp. 37-8)

In ***The Old Man,*** Trifonov's consummate virtues—his feel for character and especially for families, his eye for nature, his ear for idiosyncratic speech patterns—are brought to fruition in conjunction with the largeness of theme his abilities deserve. The book starts cold and gradually heats up. At first, Pavel Evgrafovich's crabbiness as an observer of present-day events, the abbreviated note form of his recollections, and his jumbling of time and place serve to exclude the reader, especially one unacquainted with the ins and outs of the civil war. As the narration proceeds, however, both past and present gain fullness and resonance, and the reader is drawn right to the heart of this story of thunderous events—of mutiny, massacres, battlefronts, sacked cities, military tribunals, and heroic men and women. Even Migulin—an autodidact of narrow intellect but immense principle, an opponent of Trotsky's draconian Cossack policies, an old soldier besotted with his young wife but unable to endure a life out of action—becomes both real and dear to us.

In this tale the reader may be surprised to find the role played by pity as an agent of redemption—surprised, since we are accustomed to thinking of this emotion as lying somewhere between condescension and contempt. Yet even Pavel Evgrafovich himself, a cantankerous old man in search of the truth, achieves at the last a transcendent pity for the people he has known, and thus a new humanity. This attachment to pity is a quality Trifonov shares with other Soviet writers, many of them of Jewish origin but Christian faith, who remind their readers again and again, as they describe the most cataclysmic events, that of Christianity's basic tenets, love of neighbor comes first, and that it is only through pity for his fellow-creatures that Soviet man [can, in Chekhov's phrase], "press the slave out of himself." Trifonov, to my knowledge, was neither Christian nor Jew, but that he should have come at the end of his life to express so clearly this traditional religious value seems in keeping with his final confrontation with Soviet history. (pp. 38-9)

Fernanda Eberstadt, "Out of the Drawer & into the West," in Commentary, *Vol. 80, No. 1, July, 1985, pp. 36-44.*

GEOFFREY HOSKING

[Yuri Trifonov] was well placed to reflect the changes taking place in the moral climate of the Soviet Union as brutal repression under Stalin and frenetic reform under Khrushchev gave way to stagnation and corruption under Brezhnev. His father was a pre-1917 Bolshevik, a leading figure in the Red Guards and a founding member of the Cheka; during the 1930s, he fell out of favour and perished—a victim of the tyranny he had ardently laboured to create. Trifonov himself thus grew up half in and half out of the élite, able to taste its privileges, without being secure in their enjoyment, at least until his position was consolidated by the award of the Stalin Prize for his first novel in 1951.

One of the themes of this first novel, ***Students,*** was the denunciation of a professor of literature to the authorities for some ideological error—an incident which recurs in ***The House on the Embankment.*** In the earlier novel, Trifonov gave an untroubled Stalinist account of the campaign. The implication was that the professor was simply a "survival" from the past and that the campaign against him was a worthy example of the vigilance of the true Soviet intellectual.

In the quarter of a century which elapsed before the publication of ***The House on the Embankment,*** Trifonov's views changed almost totally, and so too did his language and literary technique. One presumes that the reorientation started with the death of Stalin and with Khrushchev's subsequent revelations about his crimes. One may speculate (for we have no direct evidence other than his novels) that he began to re-evaluate his own student life of the late 1940s. Did he come to see himself as having been, by analogy, among his father's persecutors? At any rate, he went through a long period of crisis, during which he was unable to write. When he did re-emerge his writing was intensely subjective, full of anguish about moral issues. He undertook a painstaking re-examination of the early years of Bolshevik rule (***The Fire's Reflection,*** 1965; ***The Old Man,*** 1978), partly to rehabilitate his father, or at least to place his triumph and failure in historical perspective.

Most characteristic of Trifonov's late style, perhaps, were the series of short novels on the life of contemporary Moscow intellectuals which began with the publication of ***The Exchange*** in the last months of Tvardovsky's stewardship of the journal, *Novy mir,* in 1969. Here, too, the approach is partly historical, in that Trifonov surrounds his characters with families whose genealogy, whether humble or exalted, often stretches back before the revolution. Historical, too, in that the recent past weighs heavily on the interaction of those characters, and nowhere more so than in ***The House on the Embankment.*** As Trifonov himself has commented, "We mustn't pretend that nothing happened in our country. Because what happened is in our bones, our teeth, our skin."

But the predominant element in Trifonov's recent works is *byt* (as the Russians call the trivia of everyday life), which seems to hold characters in hopeless captivity. . . . This immersion in *byt* was Trifonov's major innovation, and one for which he has been much criticized in the Soviet press. And, indeed, *byt* is everything a self-respecting Soviet writer should *not* be concerned with. It is the humble here-and-now, the raw material to be transformed in the creation of a great future, and therefore not worthy of an artist's attention, unless carefully selected and illuminated by the radiant light of that future. Thus, at least, classical Socialist Realist theory. Trifonov had his own answer to such criticisms.

> *Byt* is the great test. One should not speak slightingly of it, as if it were a base side of human life, unworthy of literature. After all, *byt* is just ordinary life, the ordeal of ordinary life, where the morality of today manifests itself and is put to the test.

Trifonov is, in other words, a kind of "philosopher of everyday life", focusing not on what appear to be the great issues of our time, but rather on the petty concerns which constitute the arena where, if at all, we actually do prove ourselves. His approach is that of the moralist—one, moreover, whose outlook is formed, not by the class struggle or by historical expediency (as a Marxist morality should be), but by absolute values. At a first reading of his novels, it is easy to be misled about this, because these values are usually expressed by characters whose weakness and partiality are so patent that it is difficult to take what they say seriously. As one character comments subjectively on another, we begin to have the sense of a receding series of mirrors, none of whose images does justice to reality.

Yet the apparently fallible and biased judgments of individual human beings sometimes turn out to be confirmed by the structure of the novel as a whole, by the interplay of character, incident and narrative viewpoint. The intense subjectivity of Trifonov's stance is a sharp reaction against the Olympian objective narrators of Stalinist novels, who used to know exactly the intention and direction of "history" (the highest deity in the Stalinist universe) and so had a sure vantage-point from which to judge every personality and every act.

Getting this affront to Soviet *idées reçues* through censorship and the whole mechanism of literary control was a major achievement. How Trifonov accomplished it we do not know. No doubt his early Stalin Prize was a help, as was his relationship with such enterprising and politically astute editors as Tvardovsky of *Novy mir* and Baruzdin of *Druzhba narodov*. But one cannot discount the effect of his wilful ambiguity, the accumulation of subjective angles of vision. Some argue that censorship can be good for literature, because it compels writers to avoid direct statement and cultivate an allusive style which has its own subtle advantages. I am not convinced by the argument myself, but if there is a writer who seems to confirm it then it is Trifonov. . . .

To become a first-rate writer in Soviet conditions is exceedingly difficult; some would argue that it is impossible. If anyone has achieved it, then it is Yuri Trifonov. . . . His novels require close reading because of their density, their complex structure and surface ambiguity. He may at times appear despairing, but his refusal to offer solutions is a reaction against the "correct measures" which used to be required of a Soviet writer. As he once retorted to critics who accused writers like himself of failing to rise above the pettiness of the world they depict: "We are not the doctor, we are the pain."

Geoffrey Hosking, "'Byt' by 'Byt'," in The Times Literary Supplement, *No. 4314, December 6, 1985, p. 1386.*

JOSEPHINE WOLL

Yuri Trifonov, who died March 28, 1981, has been recognized for some time as one of the most important writers to be published within the Soviet Union. Inside Russia he has been popular for over thirty years, since the publication of his first novel, ***Studenty,*** in *Novyi mir* in 1950. But to Western readers and critics he seemed, for a long time thereafter, a writer orthodox in his approach to Soviet reality, and therefore not one meriting special attention, despite his undoubted gifts and his particular ability to distill and convey specific milieus. In the dozen years before his death, however, Trifonov published works that are subtle, complex, acutely perceptive and increasingly bold—and published them in unexpected places, and then in sizeable editions.

Why, in fact, he was published so regularly, and commonly in editions of 100,000, is a moot question. One negative reason may be his eschewal of all dissident activity; one positive reason may be that there are so few talented writers left in the Soviet Union that the authorities make concessions to those who remain, hoping to deter them from publishing abroad. It probably helps that Trifonov's style is not at all experimental: most of his works are written as compact, straight-forward narratives, with occasional flashbacks, altered time-sequences and stream-of-consciousness passages, devices that in no way trangress the bounds of stylistic acceptability current in Russia today.

In any event, no one except those at the top of the literary establishment in the Soviet Union can do more than guess at the reasons behind his continued publication. What is possible, and more profitable, is an exploration of what Trifonov achieved in his later works; particularly in the 1978 novella ***Starik (The Old Man).*** In ***Starik,*** and in his works written in the ten years preceding ***Starik,*** Trifonov takes his place in the 19th-century traditional mainstream of Russian writers, repeatedly exploring such questions as what men live by, how one defines the "right" way to live, how ideas and ideals are affected by reality. Sometimes he frames these questions in the past, such as his 1973 novel ***Neterpenie (Impatience),*** in which he took as his subject Andrei Zheliabov and the populist/terrorist movement of the 1870s and 1880s. In that work Trifonov focused on the route which led from idealism to terrorism, which transformed a group of young people into willing assassins and eager martyrs whose desperate impulse toward justice and freedom enabled them to justify the costs, both personal and societal, exacted. Sometimes Trifonov's plots are set in the present, among the sons and daughters of Russia's past. His contemporary characters are, almost always, intellectually dishonest, spiritually crippled and morally weak. Avid to barter their souls for material achievement, ready to dignify as compromise what is fundamentally betrayal, his modern Soviet man or woman is usually able to rationalize as harmless, or necessary, what he knows to be pernicious and destructive. Whether one looks at the husband in ***Obmen*** (***The Exchange,*** 1969), who yields his integrity to his wife's acquisitiveness, or at the wife in ***Dolgoe proshchanie*** (***The Long Farewell,*** 1971), who turns an impulsive act of sexual kindness into semi-prostitution in return for success, one finds Trifonov's characters caught in webs of self-deceit. Even when they acknowledge the price of the way they live, they can no longer refuse to pay it. Often, sadly, they don't even want to refuse.

In the novel and novellas mentioned above, past and present are discrete, impinging on each other only by implication. What marks off Trifonov's last works, the 1976 ***Dom na naberezhnoi,*** the 1978 ***Starik,*** and the posthumously published ***Vremia i mesto*** (1981) is the way in which Trifonov links the two. The past begets the present, which in turn reflects—and distorts—the past. The protagonist of ***Dom na naberezhnoi,*** first introduced in the early 1970s as a prosperous middle-aged scholar, is then given to us in previous incarnations: as the child who informs on friends, in the late 30s, in exchange for help for his family; as the young man who, after the war, abets in the destruction of his fiancee's family to save his own professional career. His own memory yields one image; a nameless childhood friend's yields another; Trifonov's omniscient narrator yields yet a third. The reader, endowed with this multiple vision, sees not only the facts of the past, and its atmosphere, but its consequences. We also see how memory can be used as a filter, a screen, justification and defense. Obliquely, without ever tackling Stalinism head-on, Trifonov shows us how one weak individual is affected by the climate of Stalinism (and, implicitly, how Stalinism depended on many such individuals), and how patterns of thought and behavior molded during those years lived on and influenced the post-Stalin era.

In ***Starik*** Trifonov again treats the relationship between past and present, as well as the role played by memory. His plot is twofold, one set in Moscow and its environs in 1973, the other set in the world of the Revolution and Civil War; both have the same protagonist, Pavel Evgrafovich Letunov. As an old man, in 1973, Letunov is embroiled in a dispute over acquiring a second dacha. His children and grandchildren urge him to use his influence to get the dacha, influence deriving from his status as a long-time Bolshevik. But while his family's happiness is important to him, the dacha affair is of little interest to Pavel Evgrafovich: his passion is reserved for the Cossack military officer, Sergei Kirillovich Migulin, who played an important—and controversial—role in the Civil War struggle for the Don region. While Migulin supported the Bolsheviks, the alliance was an uneasy one, and in 1920 he disobeyed Bolshevik orders by leading his regiment toward the front to fight the Whites. For this action he was tried and convicted of treason by a Revolutionary Tribunal, although his sentence of execution was repealed in view of his popularity among the Cossacks; about a year later, after a second arrest, Migulin was murdered. Pavel Evgrafovich was secretary of the first Revolutionary Tribunal which tried Migulin in 1920; he was also in love with Migulin's wife Asia, a childhood friend, and from these two involvements stems his obsession with the Migulin affair.

The action in ***Starik*** moves between two starkly different worlds, the summer colony near Moscow, with its various contenders for the dacha, and the Civil War struggle in the south, with additional reminiscences of pre-Revolutionary and Revolutionary days, and fleeting, elliptical references to the purge years of the 1930s. All are linked by the strange phenomenon of memory. The stories unwind and intertwine, from 1973 to 1914 to 1920 and back to the present, not in chronological order but as a necklace of events, thoughts, sensations, fears and perceptions strung together by memory, which in turn is triggered by equivalents of Proust's *madeleine:* the heat of two August evenings, one in 1973 and one in 1917, or the coincidence of two similar thoughts separated by fifty years. Indeed, the novel opens and closes with memory: it begins with a letter to Pavel Evgrafovich from Asia, after a hiatus in their relationship of some fifty years, and ends with his visit to her, several months later—a reunion of the only two people still alive who were intimately involved in the Migulin affair half a century earlier.

The palindromic structure of ***Starik*** seems to me a clue to Trifonov's central concern in the novel, a concern which I propose to examine in some detail. It is a recurrent theme in Trifonov's works, but nowhere does he scrutinize it so closely, or present it with such complexity, as in ***Starik.*** He is essentially concerned with the nature of truth and man's perception of truth—simple enough words that conceal a labyrinth of questions. Is the pursuit of truth important, and if so, why? Indeed, is there such a thing as objective truth, or is truth the proverbial elephant in the hands of the blind man? To what extent and in what ways do circumstance, point of view, emotional involvement, ideological commitment and historical exigencies influence one's perception of truth? All these questions are posed in ***Starik;*** through the combination of past and present Trifonov formulates answers far richer and more significant than either past or present could separately yield. (pp. 243-46)

Pavel Evgrafovich is spending the last years of his life in a quest for the truth of an episode, fifty years old, central to his personal history and to the history of his country. By understanding it, he hopes to understand himself; by understanding it, he hopes to understand the chromosomes extant in the newborn infant, Soviet Russia. He is making this immense effort not primarily because he is an old man, whose past is more real to him than his present (though, since he is a fully realized character, this common characteristic of old age plays a part in his search), but also because he believes, in a fundamentally simple way, that truth matters in itself. In this regard he stands practically alone in the novel: most of the characters are either indifferent to truth (in the sense that Letunov understands it) or are ready to accept easy definitions of it.

One such character is Kandaurov, the total pragmatist, a type familiar to us from other Trifonov works, who defines truth as self-interest. One of the contenders for the dacha, Kandaurov is the conspicuously successful Soviet man: he drives a blue Volga; he wears foreign-made clothes; he has just wangled a most desirable assignment to Mexico. Far from stupid, though almost entirely insensitive, he is enormously shrewd in knowing when and how to use influence, money, curses, threats and flattery to get what he wants. Even to his mistress, whom he loves, he lies as a matter of course. He assumes all people to be like him, and dismisses as cranks or irrelevancies those who don't seem to be. Kandaurov is not a monster; in some ways he is even likable. But he is all too recognizably a moral cripple. He jettisons the past whenever the past is inconvenient; he values no truth but the satisfaction of his desires; he believes in nothing but himself. In the end he is in effect dismissed from the novel, ironically thwarted by the fate and chance in which he has never believed.

A short step up from believing truth to be the present satisfaction of one's material goals is a certain kind of religious faith. Two characters, one from the past and the other from the present, exemplify this faith.

In 1919, in the chaos of civil war and an uprooted society, Asia's brother-in-law cannot find work: he bears an aristocratic name and descends from noble ancestors. His response is to turn to a distortion of Tolstoyism: not non-violent resistance to evil, but passive acceptance of it. Fifty-odd years later, in the summer colony, Pavel Evgrafovich's son-in-law offers a similarly passive brand of piety, together with a mystical explanation of an old man's ability to prognosticate the weather: "God speaks through him."

Pavel Evgrafovich has neither stomach nor patience for the kind of faith these men profess. Unlike his sister-in-law, who is incredulous that intelligent people can be taken in by such claptrap, Pavel Evgrafovich's intolerance does not stem from a knee-jerk rejection of God born of his atheistic, revolutionary past. Rather, the faith of Asia's brother-in-law, and of his son-in-law Nikolai Erastovich, offends him because it means passivity in the face of life. Their creed doesn't measure action against a moral standard of right and wrong (indeed, the son-in-law has forced his wife to undergo several abortions against her will); it is a sort of supernatural hocus-pocus that absolves man of responsibility. Thus it offends Pavel Evgrafovich's sense of participating in life, of being responsible for oneself and one's actions, of acting on and not just reacting to events. If Pavel Evgrafovich believes in God, it is a God who expects man to use all the powers of heart, mind, body and soul with which he is endowed, not One who countenances man's sitting on his hands and turning the rest over to Him.

More complex, and problematic, a form of truth is ideology. Not insignificantly, ideology appears only in the plot level dealing with the past: not even token adherence, not even hypocritical obeisance is paid by a single contemporary character to Marxism, Leninism, Bolshevism, or any other "-ism." Ideology, as a truth that defines life—or as a definition of life that serves as a truth—is entirely irrelevant to today's characters. In the Migulin story, in contrast, ideology plays a strikingly important role, as it does in the events preceding it (the immediate pre-Revolution period and the Revolution itself).

At no point in ***Starik*** does Pavel Evgrafovich ever question the inevitability, or desirability, of the October Revolution. His mother was an active Bolshevik; his uncle Shura spent years in tsarist prisons—both background and idealism inculcate in Pavel Evgrafovich a belief that the inequities and injustices of the tsarist system must be swept away. At the age of nineteen, Pavel Evgrafovich believes in ideological truth. When Asia's mother, deeply embittered by the havoc wreaked on her family by the Revolution, protests against the Revolution's inequities and injustices, Pavel Evgrafovich responds with "simple things" *(prostye veshchi):* dialectical materialism, permanent revolution, the eradication of enemies. His rhetoric hardly satisfies Elena Federovna, who has lost her husband to an epidemic, one son to the Reds, the other to the Whites, and seen her son-in-law condemned as an aristocrat, but for a while it satisfies Pavel Evgrafovich.

He is not alone. A number of characters, including several admirable ones, fall victim to the tendency to see ideology as total truth, replacing or including all other frames of reference. Through their commitment to a given ideology they obliterate distinctions they observe outside the ideological frame, so that the greys disappear, leaving only the black of "them" and the white of "us." Pavel Evgrafovich's mother, for instance, warns him to trust Asia's mother only up to a point, even though she has treated Pavel Evgrafovich like a son, because she is a member of the bourgeoisie. Asia's brother, Volodia, goes out at night and with revolutionary fervor beats up a boy—because his father has been labeled "counterrevolutionary." Volodia is not cruel, or lacking in moral scruple: just before the Revolution, he led a campaign at his school to spare a rat marked for dissection, simply because the rat had gained a name, had become Fedia instead of just a rat. And only a year after he beats the boy, Volodia is himself killed in the Civil War, wondering as he dies how innocent people can be executed "without a trial, without an investigation." Volodia is not a moral monster; he is an impressionable boy, caught up in what Pavel Evgrafovich elsewhere calls the "flow of lava" of the age. For a short while his vision is obscured by that "lava," that ideology cum rhetoric that become his truth, and in the name of which he betrays other forms of truth.

Many of the Bolsheviks involved in the Migulin affair are, like Volodia, caught in the lava; some of them are incapable of making distinctions under any circumstances, others are temporarily desensitized, still others put aside their scruples consciously, willfully. Truth, for them, is what serves the cause of the Revolution, and admits of no questioning, shading or challenging. They are contrasted with one man, Shura, the larger-than-life hero who embodies for Pavel Evgrafovich all the virtues, both revolutionary and human. Shura is devoted to the cause of establishing a just and equitable society in Russia, and is convinced that Bolshevism is the means to that end. At the same time Shura never loses his ability to see that the movement of history is grounded in the action of individuals, that ends may not justify means, that the fates of individual men and women are the stuff of which the new society will be made. For his reluctance to obliterate distinctions, for his caution that each suspected counterrevolutionary be carefully evaluated (since a man's life is at stake), he is viciously attacked by his colleagues, who accuse him of cowardice and threaten to try him for sabotage. Their response to his pleas for caution is to cite Danton on Louis XVI: "We won't try him, we'll kill him!"

It is not sentimentality that motivates Shura, nor only the sense that each human life is precious. Nor does he abjure judgments. But he wants those judgments to be based on truth, which is not always synonymous with fact, and he believes that truth must be discovered, not taken for granted. (pp. 246-49)

Ideological "truth" can also be a rationalization. Used as such in the Migulin story, it most often provides a convenient legitimacy to actions that really stem from characters' private emotional needs. This is the case with one Bolshevik, Bychin. As commander of a Cossack *stanitsa,* Bychin has arrested some forty people, among them the two sons of a schoolteacher named Slaboserdov. When Shura objects that this family is neither rich nor counterrevolutionary, Bychin responds, "They're harmful to the revolution." Only later do we learn that behind Bychin's ideological vigilance lies an old personal resentment against the Slaboserdovs. He wants the sons executed not, in fact, because of the alleged "harm" they might cause to the revolution, but because of a family quarrel that predates political developments. Shura recognizes this blurring of emotional and political needs, but cannot singlehandedly prevent Bychin from exploiting the revolution for his own purposes. Indeed, a delirious Shura calls out that Slaboserdov must be saved—but Bychin, and even Pavel Evgrafovich, can ignore that. In any event, it's too late. The sons are dead.

The emotion which motivates Bychin, and which permits him to murder two innocent men, is resentment over a past slight. And for willful blindness, his exploitation of laudable ideals for his own purposes, he incurs Pavel Evgrafovich's contempt. But Bychin is not the only character whose perceptions are dictated by emotions, and resentment is not the only emotion. Most of the characters in the book make judgments based on emotion, among them the most admirable, and among those—not coincidentally—most of the women.

A curious duality is at work here. On the one hand, emotion—especially love—becomes, for many of the women in ***Starik,*** a substitute for truth, just as ideology does for some of the Bolsheviks. Rather, not a substitute, exactly, but the only sort of truth which is important: they *choose* to make emotional truth the essential truth of their lives, they deliberately turn their backs on other definitions of truth. Thus most of the women are essentially apolitical; with the exception of Pavel Evgrafovich's mother, women's political loyalties in this book stem from alliances with men. Asia sees the entire Civil War struggle in the Don region in terms of Migulin's welfare. Her mother would happily damn all political "truths" if only she could have her family back together, alive and united. Rather like Pasternak's women (and indeed, much like Pasternak's understanding of truth in *Dr. Zhivago*), these women first love and then think, a sequence at the same time their limitation and their strength. Limited by love, they ignore facts, reject objectivity, deny two sides to every question. On the other hand, emotion endows these women with an almost animal-like intuition about truth. Strengthened by love, they pierce through the cobwebs of words, doubts, compromises and rhetoric woven by men. They see clearly who is on their side—that is, loving those they love—and who is not. (pp. 250-51)

This female instinct for emotional truth may not always be politically or historically correct, still less often "fair" (a word that in this context seems invented by a man). But repeatedly in ***Starik,*** the women are wiser than their men; their intuitions and judgments are sound. It is a man, Bychin, who wants the Slaboserdov sons to pay for their father's "sins." It is a woman, recalled in the flashback of a minor character, who says about the young son of a scoundrel: "The son is not to blame for his father."

It is, in a sense, apples and oranges—emotional truth and factual truth—and the two differing types of truth confront each other head-on in the climax of the novel's contemporary plot, when Pavel Evgrafovich and Asia finally meet. Pavel Evgrafovich makes the difficult journey to Asia's town because, he says, he must find out the truth about Migulin's treason. He has pored over the documents, interviewed the few surviving old men who knew Migulin, questioned Asia in his letters. But he still isn't satisfied, he wants to know more. Yet when they meet, after more than fifty years, Asia is silent. She has exhausted her memory's store of information, of factual truth. And she answers him flatly: "I've told you all I remember. I only know that I loved him as I've loved no one else in my whole life." . . . For Asia, that is not just all she knows. That is all she needs to know.

The allusion to Keats is not incidental. It is almost forced on one, because two views of truth are locked together in ***Starik.*** One is factual truth, the sort that can be found in documents, in transcripts, in texts. Pavel Evgrafovich values this sort because it cannot be distorted by time and memory. The other sort is emotional truth. In "Ode on a Grecian Urn" Keats suggests that the images on the urn, silent though they are, tell us more about what is depicted than any catalogue of facts could do. He implies that there is a truth beyond data which the urn conveys to us, which art immortalizes. Trifonov, similarly, shows us that Pavel Evgrafovich's documents are only a part of the truth of the Migulin story, that facts are only part of the truth of any story. There is truth, too, in Asia's memories and love. There is truth in the taste of the air in the south in 1920, a taste only Pavel Evgrafovich remembers. There is truth in the weight of Asia's inert, naked body which Pavel Evgrafovich holds in his arms after Volodia is killed. There is truth in the sound of revolutionary and Cossack songs coming from Migulin's prison cell as he and his "co-conspirators" await execution. There is even truth in the contradictory, Rashomon-like memories of the old men who recall Migulin for Pavel Evgrafovich. Trifonov has a vision of truth that encompasses all of these things, facts and emotion and memory together. He does not quite vouchsafe that vision to Pavel Evgrafovich. (pp. 251-52)

What Pavel Evgrafovich believes is hardly a new idea: "You shall know the truth, and the truth shall make you free." The present cannot be free to act and grow without an honest understanding of the past, mistakes and all. The truth of the Revolution and the Civil War in Russia (and, by implication, of all that followed) must be known to her people. It is, of course, impossible in the Soviet Union to present the whole truth. . . . (p. 255)

Without the truth of the past the present is built on a lie, and measures itself against false standards. What was of real value becomes confused with what was not; idealism and hypocrisy blur. And when, over time, truth is so consistently perverted, its very pursuit becomes valueless. So a society is built on lies: "kind" lies, "compassionate" lies, "white" lies, "necessary" lies—and no one can understand why Pavel Evgrafovich wants to learn the truth. In ***Starik*** the truth of the past, which in turn becomes the truth of the present, is an amalgam of memory, of documents, of impressions, of words and thoughts and sensations. Pavel Evgrafovich never claims that it will be comforting to know the truth. Merely that it is imperative. (p. 256)

Josephine Woll, "Trifonov's 'Starik': The Truth of the Past," in Russian Literature Triquarterly, *No. 19, 1986, pp. 243-58.*

Rex (Ernest) Warner

1905-1986

© Jerry Bauer

English novelist, essayist, nonfiction writer, translator, poet, editor, and author of children's books.

In his work, Warner explored the relationship between the individual and the state, focusing upon themes of responsibility and power among leadership figures and ordinary citizens. Warner investigated ancient and modern ideas pertaining to authority and individual freedom, drawing upon his knowledge of classical literature and history and his interest in twentieth-century political developments. During the 1930s, when Warner first gained recognition, he associated with such literary figures as W. H. Auden, Stephen Spender, and C. Day Lewis, with whom he shared Marxist and antifascist sentiments. Warner's novels of this era are political allegories in which his protagonists strive to overcome repressive forms of control representative of the World War II era. V. S. Pritchett, commenting on Warner's examination of the ideologies which influenced the 1930s, claimed that he was "the only outstanding novelist of ideas that the decade of ideas produced."

Warner cited the works of Franz Kafka as major influences on his allegorical novels. While critics frequently discuss Warner's use of Kafkaesque elements in these works, they note that he concentrated on social themes and ideas, while Kafka explored individual consciousness and the irrational nature of life. Warner's first novel, *The Wild Goose Chase* (1937), concerns three brothers who enter an unnamed country in pursuit of a mythical wild goose that symbolizes freedom and naturalness. Their quest leads them across a frontier, where an oppressed peasantry reside, and into a walled city, from which bureaucrats control the country. Warner develops allegorical implications by having the brothers encounter a series of characters who represent various ideas and personality types. While two of the brothers, who respectively embody human physical and intellectual attributes, blindly accept the degrading conditions imposed by the authoritarian government, the other brother, who represents the common man, strives to eliminate social repression in order to pursue individual freedom. *The Wild Goose Chase* and Warner's next novel, *The Professor* (1938), were praised for his use of symbolism and fantasy to temper his didactic presentation of ideas, although some critics argued that the philosophical debates intrinsic to his works are not conducive to novel form. Set in a country plagued by internal conflicts between communists and fascists and threatened by a hostile neighboring country, *The Professor* demonstrates Warner's interest in topical issues and strongly reflects the political situation in Austria during the 1930s. In this work, Warner suggests the limitations of liberal idealism in confronting irrational violence.

Warner's next book, *The Aerodrome: A Love Story* (1941), is regarded as his finest work. This novel centers on a young pilot who must choose between life in the disorganized village where he was raised and the powerful and efficient military complex recently built nearby. The corrupting influence of power, a recurring theme in Warner's work, is illustrated in *The Aerodrome* through the character of a dictatorial vice-marshal, who touts the stability and strength of the military installation at the expense of the unsettled social system of the village. As in several of his novels, Warner presents a melodramatic climax in which oppressive forces are symbolically destroyed. *Why Was I Killed?* (1943), like *The Aerodrome,* addresses issues related to World War II. In this work, a dead soldier returns to life to seek the meaning of his death by questioning people from different levels of society. Through this device, Warner develops a philosophical treatise on the nature of war. In *Men of Stones* (1949), Warner examines totalitarianism by depicting a megalomaniacal figure who rules an island society and promotes repression through religion and politics.

In his later novels, Warner speculates on the motivations of various significant historical figures. *The Young Caesar* (1958) is structured as an autobiographical memoir by Julius Caesar and depicts his maturation into a strong leader, while *The Imperial Caesar* (1960), which was awarded the James Tait Black Memorial Prize, portrays Caesar strengthening his authority while alienating both his subjects and his coterie. *Pericles, the Athenian* (1963) takes the form of a biography written by a friend of this statesman of Athenian democracy. *The Converts: A Novel of Early Christianity* (1967) offers an eyewitness account of the events surrounding St. Augustine's conversion to Catholicism. Warner also published a volume of poetry, *Poems* (1937), and a collection of essays, *The Cult of Power* (1946). His other literary endeavors include critical studies of the works of John Milton and E. M. Forster, as well as several nonfiction books in which he recreates the social and intellectual milieus of ancient Greece. Warner also translated works of Greek drama and history as well as tracts by such diverse figures as Julius Caesar, St. Augustine, and Plutarch.

(See also *Contemporary Authors,* Vols. 89-92, Vol. 119 [obituary] and *Dictionary of Literary Biography,* Vol. 15.)

HAROLD STRAUSS

There is an off-chance, just a chance, that ***The Wild Goose Chase*** will be remembered as a turning point for the literature of our day, for it successfully revolts against the methods of photographic realism and yet defends itself against the stigma of escapism. But whether it be praised or damned, whether it be remembered or forgotten, it proves that novelty still lies within the reach of novelists. For ***The Wild Goose Chase*** is a bold innovation, a fresh wind blowing across fallow land of the human imagination long untilled. And above all, it is a strange book to come out of England, where the novel, since Lawrence died, has been more noted for a niggardliness of spirit and an exactitude of craftsmanship than for the intemperate grandeur of its visions.

The author of this novel is a young man beset by visions of the first magnitude. . . . One can feel in every sentence of Rex Warner's work his contempt for the pedestrian accuracy of a Priestley and for the morbid photographic realism of a Farrell. One can feel his passionate dedication to those dreams and stirrings of the imagination which march far ahead of fact and science and social history, and indeed give them their impress.

There has been a small but growing group of critics who have been rebelling against the ugly and futile naturalism to which the social novel has become glued. It has been within our power to indicate what was false and morbid; we have been powerless, of course, to say clearly what should be done. That had to await the actual performance of a man such as Rex Warner. Thus, while in a sense we were prepared for Mr. Warner's work, it was unexpected, to say the least, that he should have turned to allegory for the accomplishment of his purpose. It is this use of allegory, a rigid and somewhat artificial device in contrast to the more natural epic method employed by a man like Jean Giono, which injects the element of doubt into our appraisal of ***The Wild Goose Chase*** as a literary landmark. . . .

Like all allegories, this novel escapes completely from time and place as we commonly know them. Its characters are personifications of social types and forces, and its theme is the quest for freedom. If that sounds forbidding, remember that it applies equally well to *Gulliver's Travels.* Once one has accepted the few conventions which Mr. Warner establishes, his narrative is as exciting and vivid as any product of realism. His people are flesh and blood. They are neither the moral calculations of Bunyan, nor the political calculations of Swift, nor the intellectual calculations of Cabell. The land in which they live is as earthy as Poictesme is evanescent. Were the reader not told that an allegorical meaning underlies each scene, he would frequently be unaware of the metaphorical nature of the narrative.

The difficulty is in the beginning. There is some hard going until one gets into the story, which opens in a town that differs from an ordinary English seaside town in that it lies near the frontier of a land which few men have explored. In this town there live three men, brothers, and to each has come the dream of hunting the Wild Goose, which may be taken as a symbol of freedom and naturalness. Everywhere the brothers see human life overlaid with stupidities and dishonest artifice; it is the honking of the great birds as they fly northward over the frontier that puts them to dreaming of a land where this is not true. One by one they set out—Rudolph, the windy empire builder and man of action; David, the supple and evasive intellectual; and George, the hero, an ordinary, forthright young man.

By a neat device it is George whose adventures we follow, although by occasional letters and encounters we are able to follow what happens to Rudolph and to David. George's first adventure is at the lonely castle of Don Antonio, a philosopher who, not daring to cross the frontier, has erected an ivory tower just on the near side of it, in which he leads a corrupt, fantastic, epicurean existence—an existence which the naturalness of George shatters. George then passes over the frontier, and comes at last to a rural district in which, though the fields are bountiful, the inhabitants live in a state of dire necessity because of the taxation and oppression of their conquerors, the strange men from the city.

In this rural community George meets with a variety of adventures. . . . The people of the farming community once were free. Now they are in a transitional stage, remembering freedom, unable to strike for it. They are the slaves needed to feed and clothe a planned Fascist economy, which is represented by the town. The town is the height of artificiality, the antithesis of the realm of the Wild Goose. (This is neatly parodied, for the people of the town venerate a stuffed goose.) In the town an invisible government regulates the least movement of every individual. When George wishes to make various protests to a responsible office, he is led from one authority to a higher authority, and from him to a still higher authority, and so on until he wearies. And he is no less wearied by the accomplished scientists who employ their amazing inventions for idiotic purposes, by the philosophers who quibble about inconsequentialities, by the decadent intellectuals of the Convent, and by the eternal chatter of the expert libertines who talk so much about sex that they have no time for its experience.

George's encounters with the inhabitants of this amazing city are so shot through with gusto and humor, so brilliant in their satirical implications, that one often forgets for a time their underlying allegorical meaning. But eventually, when George, in disgust, returns to the rural community to organize a rebellion against the corrupt city the fundamental theme of the book is brought forcefully to mind. Always George must put off his pursuit of the Wild Goose for some more immediate need. Thus, as we see it, the moral of the allegory is that naturalness and freedom can never be obtained by the individual until he has joined with his fellows to overthrow stagnant economic systems and to eradicate fascism.

In the brief space of a review, it is necessary to summarize George's adventures somewhat abstractly; yet it cannot be too much emphasized that the greatest achievement of ***The Wild Goose Chase*** is the robustness and concreteness with which it bodies forth a great dream. And finally, a word of admiration should be added for Mr. Warner's magnificently cadenced, eloquent prose style—a style that is as fresh and original as the narrative itself.

Harold Strauss, "To New Horizons in the Novel," in The New York Times Book Review, *January 23, 1938, p. 2.*

LOUISE BOGAN

It would be kind to call ***The Wild Goose Chase*** an extravaganza on revolutionary themes. Mr. Warner admires Kafka, and he has adapted a good deal of Kafkian detail and diffused Kafkian tone throughout his book. He also has read Swift. He fails where his masters succeed because, unlike them, he has no control over either his material or his emotions. He is not an artist gauging the first, or a mature human being with insight into the second. The two have collided on a level of his nature where extreme confusion holds, and the results are lamentable.

One element in Kafka's work which has not been thoroughly elucidated, and which bears on Mr. Warner's, is that in portions of Kafka's writing (notably in *The Trial*) he deals with the material of his own obsessions. . . . The development of the subconscious fantasy is continually being put through a checking process. Kafka is manipulating his nature and not being manipulated by it. Mr. Warner, on the other hand, with the best intentions in the world, gets nowhere because his subconscious nature, which he apparently knows nothing about, is manipulating him from the start.

Three brothers set out to find the wild goose ("freedom, naturalness"). One is ambitious. Another is an aesthete and a scholar. The third is "an ordinary young man." Their destination is an unknown country beyond a mysterious frontier. The peasants of this land are ground under by an insanely irresponsible and grotesquely heartless government whose seat is a fantastic modern city. The ambitious man and the scholar, both of whom are presented as perfect fools, accept the inhuman conditions put upon them by the government and are degraded by them. Not so the ordinary young man. He espouses the cause of the peasantry and enters the city determined to appeal to the king and change matters. No good comes of this plan. He then realizes that he cannot act alone, as a single adventurer. He returns to the countryside and works up a revolution which, although opposed by the police, spies, fiendish clergymen, and dreadful mechanical contraptions, finally, in a very bloody manner, succeeds. George—for that is the ordinary young man's name—then determines to create a new world according to the best Marxian formulas. The roof flies off the most horrid of the old institutions, and the wild geese are seen flying overhead.

The details thrown into this basic plan—and they are many—are so arbitrary, so futile, and so clumsy that they not only impede the story but often throw it violently off its track. If it suits the author's momentary convenience to erase someone from the plot or to change his or her nature overnight, the disappearance or the change is at once effected. Love affairs are dragged in by the heels, to point up George. Dreamlike events happen for reasons that remain obscure. Why Mr. Warner should have chosen, in the first place, to come out for revolutionary methods in terms of nightmare, it is difficult to discover. Through his poorly selected symbols the new world is made to seem as hideous as the old. All is translated into a phantasmagoria that the mind and emotions instinctively reject. (pp. 129-30)

Mr. Warner's book of verse, ***Poems,*** is better than his book of prose. Although rather smugly hortatory, and deriving from C. Day Lewis and Hopkins, it has moments of simplicity and beauty. It is curious that the author of ***The Wild Goose Chase*** should concern himself with poetry at all, since in his imaginary world poets are either idiots or frauds. But he has. (p. 130)

Louise Bogan, "Revolution in Wonderland," in The Nation, *New York, Vol. 146, No. 5, January 29, 1938, pp. 129-30.*

ELEANOR CLARK

For some time, particularly in England, people have been turning to the work of Franz Kafka: it was discovered suddenly that the obscure Austrian writer supplied a brilliant antidote to the current diseases of the novel. He was the impetus needed to free the imagination from the meaninglessness of fact, and give an integration, or rather *method* of integration, for the material of fiction. And it was he who opened up the blind alley of realism and made plausible once more the forms of allegory and myth.

The Wild Goose Chase, by a young Englishman of the Auden-Spender-Lewis group and inclination, is the first serious novel in English in which these forms and this impetus have been adapted to a truly modern content. More specifically, to the anti-public school, anti-bourgeois, vaguely and rather satirically pro-communist orientation that has lifted Mr. Warner's friends to the crest of the literary wave. (It should be said here that there is in Mr. Warner less public school and more communism than in any of his better known contemporaries, and that his work is of correspondingly greater interest.) The Kafka influence is direct and clear, and also curiously oblique. For Kafka the allegory, or release from common-garden conceptions of cause and effect, is a means of exploring certain logical and philosophic preoccupations. For Mr. Warner it satisfies a quite different need. He is not primarily interested in the common philosophical dilemma, though he poses one, but in the common social dilemma that balks the private search. And he has adopted a form that allows the presentation of the problem as a poetic concept, and a lyricism and clarity of satire that have been lacking in prose.

It allows also, and this is perhaps its central inspiration, a dream quality and situations created out of long neurotic fear, not lucid as in Kafka's imaginings. This is, in one aspect, the myth of young men growing up between wars and fearing desperately for their manhood. . . .

The key to this transformation of Kafka's usage is in a concept derived partly from psychoanalysis, expressed in one of Mr. Warner's poems: "by dying and by denying to believe and come alive." Three brothers set out on bicycles to find the Wild Goose, a symbol never clearly defined and one whose meaning emerges gradually through their adventures in the mythical country beyond the "frontier." It is those qualities which in the brutal present make the revolutionary, and which represent also a life beyond revolution. "It is the love of living, of delicacy, of strength," something to be found only through a "dying" of one's previous self. . . .

The story is refreshing; even, in its whole meaning, beautiful. Its weakness is one from which Auden and the rest also suffer and which is more apparent in Mr. Warner's unimaginative verse than in his rather too convincing allegory in prose. Many of his [pieces in ***Poems***] are inspired, as is the novel, by various dissatisfactions with things as they are and the realization that the poet's suffering is no good now as a private affair. But unfortunately this realization, honest as it may be, still smells of paint. "Now common words are sweetest and ordinary behavior / enchants the sense with its marvelous beauty." In practice, however, it is palm trees at night or the flight of lapwings "like uneasy ghosts slipping in the disheveled air" that inspire the poet's firmest work and his fine side-glancing images. When dealing with the upper classes he falls too easily into the sing-song advice from an undergraduate with which we are familiar, and "common words and ordinary behavior" are so remote still, so much more a question of conscience than of sensibility, that even his feeling for language fails in their service. One of the most moving and successful poems, **"Hymn,"** leads back to ***The Wild Goose Chase:***

Come then, you who couldn't stick it,
lovers of cricket, underpaid journalists,
lovers of nature, hikers, O touring cyclists,
now you must be men and women and there is a chance.

In the novel too it is the underpaid journalists, the sexless students, those who could write only book reviews, who are called out of their perfumed lairs to come and be alive. And it is they who are understood: the proletariat, bringer of new life, is present only by hearsay, and the true blood of the movement is all pastoral.

Eleanor Clark, "The Cabinet of Dr. Kafka," in The New Republic, *Vol. XCIII, No. 1209, February 2, 1938, p. 373.*

PETER MONRO JACK

It seems that each new poet from England has to be introduced from Oxford, that nest of singing birds, though they have left their nest and they don't precisely sing. [Rex Warner's ***Poems***] is the latest to appear in an American edition. . . . He is not the least nor the best of the poets. In particular he interests us with the frank and clear statement of the problems of the modern poet.

"How sweet only to delight lambs and laugh by streams," he begins, "to be a farmer's boy, to be far from battle." He would, any generation ago, have been a pastoral poet, and a good one, for he has a fine keen eye, especially for birds in motion—and I don't believe the revolution would be appreciably delayed if he stopped for a moment to give us more of them. . . . He recognizes only two kinds of living: to live as a "fungus" or else as one "in strict training for desperate war." Warner is not a satirist and he lets the fungi alone. He is not a militarist or athlete . . . , he is a teacher, a naturalist and poet: and his incitements to battle and pictures of war ("walls falling, the toppling of towers, disappearance of homes") are singularly unexciting, reminding me, if I may say so, of the much too tenorish aria in Mozart's "Il Seraglio": "Haste to Battle! None but Cowards Are Afraid!"

There are a few poems on Egypt, where Mr. Warner taught, and one on Nile fishermen shows what he can do with character, an interesting limitation. But it is the bird poems, to the tune of Gerard Manley Hopkins, that are most characteristic, and I don't think it much matters at the moment that they are derivative in style since their feeling is original. Hopkins's "The Windhover," with its sprung, exciting, alliterative rhythms . . . has clearly interested Warner to write of the Mallard. . . .

It is nothing comparable to Hopkins's technical mastery or spiritual intensity, but it is all done to much advantage, and we could do with more of it. But, sighing, Mr. Warner turns from them again to our present, our here and now that will seem to the happier future "sad, furious, fatal"—happier, that is, if those "fit for us among the masses" have regained the freedom we are losing.

Peter Monro Jack, "On Living in Training for Sudden War," in The New York Times Book Review, *February 6, 1938, p. 2.*

PHILIP BLAIR RICE

[***The Professor***] repeats the pattern of events leading up to the fall of Austria [to the Nazis]—although there are points of resemblance to Czechoslovakia—too closely for one to take seriously any other moral than that inherent in the events themselves. Yet Warner uses that pattern to describe the overthrow of a different kind of country and to illustrate the futility of characters quite dissimilar to the Austrian leaders.

The story begins during a crisis in a small European democracy. A powerful enemy, which is mobilized on the border and keeps its planes over the threatened country, has demanded a change of government and representation in the Cabinet for its puppet party, the National Legion. Shirted terrorists roam the streets by night, committing rape and murder. The feeble coalition government turns to Professor A, a non-political man, the world's greatest authority on Sophocles, who is summoned from his classroom to accept the chancellorship. His response to the crisis is to propose a plebiscite on the question of autonomy and to formulate an Economic Plan. While he is announcing his plebiscite to the country through a disconnected microphone, the Fascists make their putsch and the invader marches in. After a brief fugue, the Professor is captured, beaten, and finally shot upon his refusal to praise the new regime.

The author uses this plot for a satire on liberal ineptitude which, if it were more skilfully done, would have its pertinence. The Professor objects to the minor deceptions necessary to solidify the country; he is too doctrinaire in his liberalism to give the order to suppress the Fascist gangs even after they have raped his son's sweetheart, assassinated the ex-Chancellor, and made an attempt on his own life; he is unwilling to arm the workers who alone might have saved the day. But Warner has not taken enough pains with his principal character to make him plausible. The Professor is . . . an Oxford don, old style, with the addition of Social Democratic sympathies. The author has endowed him with a propensity to quote the Greek lyric poets and to go off on etymological disquisitions while the bombers are flying overhead, but neither this nor his senescent passion for a Garboesque Fascist spy suffices to make him more than a silhouette. Warner would be a more convincing spokesman of the people if he showed a sympathetic insight into any of his characters.

Imperfectly realized as it is, the novel has sufficient relevance to the tragic events of our day to keep the reader going in it, and there are scenes of a harassed populace into which the author does not intrude with his schoolboy pranks. At times, also, the satire achieves horror. . . . But the Communist policeman appearing miraculously in an assortment of false beards to rescue the Professor, together with the general Grade B Hollywood atmosphere, submerges what is genuine in the book.

Mr. Warner belongs to the coterie of young English writers whose leading spirit is the poet W. H. Auden, and he shares its symbols, ideas, and stock characters. Himself the author of a book of poems, Warner is, except for Christopher Isherwood, the only one of the group who so far has shown promise as a novelist. His first novel, ***The Wild Goose Chase,*** although it was structurally less unified than ***The Professor,*** was a much more brilliant and more veridical book. In it he used the devices of surrealism, of Kafka's fantastic novels, and of the movie thriller to sketch with a certain grotesque power the fascist state of the future. Here, however, Warner has used just enough of such machinery to destroy the narrative illusion, and too little to create a poetic equivalent of reality. What the book needs, besides some credible characters, is either more imagination or less. (pp. 238-39)

Philip Blair Rice, "News into Satire," in The Nation, *New York, Vol. 148, No. 9, February 25, 1939, pp. 238-39.*

CHRISTOPHER ISHERWOOD

Mr. Rex Warner is one of Kafka's first and most promising English pupils. As such, he must command our interest and attention. If his work sometimes seems immature, we should remember that he is attempting a supremely difficult medium, the satirical fantasy. There is nothing cheap or facile about his intention. And I think that ***The Professor*** is a very much better book than his earlier novel, ***The Wild Goose Chase.***

It describes the last week in the life of a great European classical scholar who has the misfortune to inhabit a small country strongly resembling pre-Anschluss Austria. The country is doubly threatened—from within, by the death-struggle between a fascist and a communist party; from without, by a powerful neighbor state which is preparing to annex it, in the sacred name of Order. At the peak of this crisis, the Professor is called upon to leave his university chair and become Chancellor. He is a highly respected national figure, and the only man, it is said, whom everybody can trust. In other words, he seems politically "safe."

But the Professor isn't as safe as he looks. For years, in the calm, theoretical atmosphere of his study, he has been working out a program of gradual socialism . . . , and now, he thinks, is the opportunity to put his ideas into practice. Upright, fearless and honest as the day, he does not doubt that all men are ultimately reasonable. . . .

His fate is the classic fate of the honorable theorist. From the first, everything is against him. His Cabinet is crooked and cowardly, his chief of police a traitor, the woman he loves is a spy. His only allies and true friends are the extremists, whose methods he deplores, and they cannot save him, for he will not listen to them in time. The country is, in fact, already sold out to its big neighbor. The military occupation, "by request," duly takes place. The Professor is arrested, has a chance to save his own life disgracefully, refuses it and gets shot, where most brave men are shot nowadays, in the back.

The best scenes in this novel have a weird, dreamlike quality which is perfectly suited to their subject matter. . . . But Mr. Warner seems less interested in the dramatics of his story than in the series of Platonic dialogues by which it is interrupted—and rightly so, since this is a book about ideas. Unfortunately it is just in these dialogues that the author's skill deserts him. The arguments on both sides are reasonably presented—reasonably, but rather flatly. The characters cease to be characters, and fade into the anonymous members of a debating society. Indeed, it would require the genius of a Thomas Mann to inform such discussions with life. Mr. Warner seems conscious of this weakness, for he ends each of these passages melodramatically. But melodrama is no solution.

Nevertheless, this is an absorbing and outstanding novel, about a vitally interesting subject—the fate of a liberal in the world of power-politics. The Professor is defeated, but he doesn't, ultimately, fail. Dead, he is still a formidable problem for his enemies, a problem they will never be able to solve. His gentle, persuasive voice will continue to be heard, long after the guns are silent, and the bombing planes have run out of gas. And because Mr. Warner succeeds in making us feel this, his story, though tragic, is heartening and inspiring as well.

Christopher Isherwood, "The Man of Honor," in The New Republic, *Vol. XCVII, No. 1266, March 8, 1939, p. 138.*

IRWIN EDMAN

There are books that in the guise of fiction are persuasive discourses in philosophy. Certain novels are not only pictures of life but commentaries on the issues life poses. ***The Return of the Traveller*** [published in Great Britain as ***Why Was I Killed?***] . . . is just such a narrative. It might almost better be described as a philosophical dialogue than as a novel—a conversation which in the speech of vividly imagined characters presents and indeed embodies ideas clearly defined. For what each character says about the most timely and tragically central theme of our era is made clear by a cleverly plausible flashback and prevision. Each life in this book, its past, present and future, explains each character's opinion.

But his opinion about what? This is the crux of this singularly beautiful book. For each person in the story is asked: "What is this war about?" The question is put in an urgent form. The spirit of a soldier killed in this war—felt as a presence rather than seen as an object—asks each of a variegated assortment of sightseers in an English cathedral: "Why was I killed?" . . . Each of the persons present—a pompous, smug but patriotic and sincere business magnate, a realistic skilled mechanic, seeking comfort, ease and security, his home-loving wife, a refugee scholar, a man who fought in Spain on the Loyalist side, a mother who has lost her son—each has a different answer to the question. It is presented hypothetically by a priest—the only one in the group who seems really to understand the dead soldier. The answers given and the personal history behind the answers constitute both the cluster of stories and the moral meanings of this book.

With varying degrees of uneasiness or confidence, brashness or sorrow, each character replies as his past and his destiny compel him to reply. The prosperous business man is prompt. For he is clearly committed to the view that the society he knows will always be, and that his countrymen—and indeed himself if necessary—will come to the succor of the nation he has comfortably known. "One would say to the soldier," he says, "You were killed for your country. Your country was in peril. You and many others answered the call. And this time as in the past you put up a mighty fine show. We are proud of you, sir." But he is uneasy after he has spoken, for he knows his response will not satisfy the dead. . . .

The man who fought in Spain has two answers. "You were killed," he would say to the dead soldier, "by the folly and incapacity of your own Government." He cites the non-intervention attitude toward the war in Spain. But he would tell him, too, that there was a deeper meaning to his death. He died, not to defend the old order, but to make a new world.

The woman in black has no reply in terms of grand causes or ideas, but in terms of human weakness, of sin and suffering. "I would tell him," she says, "that he died for the sins of the whole world. He meant no harm. Nor did we. But we all killed him and he killed himself."

The refugee scholar, with the memory of the concentration camp in his lined face, replies that "the solider defended us all, against obscene cruelties, against barbarism, against torture of the innocent. He defended us against evil. He defended civilization, culture, progress."

The dead soldier, inhabiting eternity, lives beyond all these separate human perspectives. As he listens to their answers he sees these people more clearly than they see themselves, for he sees the cramped, distorted lives which have made the substance of their imperfect replies. (p. 1)

The dead soldier feels how partial are the replies of each. (pp. 1, 27)

None can adequately explain his death to the soldier—and he begins to see why. At the moment of his own death he had had a vision, compounded of a sunlit valley, all happiness and peace, and his own body mangled among those of his fellows. He had seen "how unutterably splendid was the whole depth and array of life, how limitless were its horizons, how sweetly thrilling were its humblest aspects." But each of these people, in the cramped one-sidedness of his own perspective, has failed to grasp the meaning of life as a whole, the range and depths of its beauty and its degradation. And because so many have failed to see life whole, they have allowed—indeed, helped to bring about—the terror and dislocation, the shambles of war, almost as if war were an escape from life lived without the integrity of meaning.

There is a class of readers, doubtless, who will be repelled by the device, so often cheaply used, of a dead soldier reappearing to the living. But the author uses the device so subtly and delicately that it can scarcely put off even those allergic to the psychic and the supernatural.

The soldier had had a glimpse of the meaning of life, in its wholeness of beauty and horror, and in the wholeness of men for better or worse inextricably bound up in each other's fate. Only at the close of the book does he get a hint that his vision is seen by another. He sees it in the priest's eyes, hears it in the priest's words. This sense of the vast whole meaning of life, its union of blessing and burden, if shared by one other—one who is alive—may be shared by all. . . .

[Warner] was one of the group of radical poets of ten years ago in England who were hailing *the* or *a* revolution. He has grown beyond formulas and—though the form of his book is a fantasy—beyond mere fantasy now. He has plumbed to deeper issues than political ones, and has written in the form of a novel a dialogue on life and death that touches the basic anxieties and hopes of our time. And he has done it in a prose at once reticent and eloquent, and distinguished.

There are spots where the narrative sags a little, where the discussion is too measured and too slow. But the book belongs alongside Koestler's *Darkness at Noon* in the seriousness and intensity of the issues raised. It belongs, too, in the tradition of Plato's *Phaedo,* in its feeling for the way in which judgments of life are involved in discussions of death. It is not quite a novel, though it has the meat of several novels in it. It is something more, a human colloquy, tender, moving and profound, of the mortal perils and the immortal implications of a generation whose young men by the millions are dying in war. (p. 27)

Irwin Edman, "The Enigmas of Death and War," in The New York Times Book Review, *May 28, 1944, pp. 1, 27.*

NORMAN COUSINS

[For] a long time we had regarded Rex Warner as the possessor of tools of writing and thinking as efficient and proficient as are being used today by any novelist in the English language. In fact, he came pretty close to being our favorite contemporary novelist, largely on the strength of ***The Wild Goose Chase*** and ***The Professor,*** both of them novels of ideas, cool and discerning pieces of literary precision lacking in any of the metallic quality sometimes the automatic partner of impeccable craftsmanship. More than that: Warner was no showcase novelist; what he wrote he wrote because that was the only instrument available to him to help shape the ideas he felt so strongly. In ***The Professor,*** a powerful and intense piece of mature indignation against the weakness of one type of intellectual confronted by the engulfing presence of the wave of the future, to use a now-discredited and somewhat ancient metaphor, Rex Warner proved his ability to blend ideas with action. Thus we had the satisfying and fairly rare picture of a writer who could lend suspense and story structure to a philosophic novel.

The Return of the Traveller is an extension of Warner's technique into the realm of the fictional essay, for although the book is announced and presented as a novel, it would be more accurate to describe it as a series of philosophic essays having more to do with war and peace in general than the particular war in which the globe is now involved. The advantage, of course, is that a pattern of universals takes shape which can serve as a basis for abstract discussion of human and material values, as with Greek dialogues. The disadvantage is that there is a corresponding sense of uneasiness and lack of fulfillment in considering the broad and central question inspiring the book: why must men fight and die *today?*

There are no definitive answers in this book, only a series of brief portraits of a small group of people to whom the question is put by a priest. In a reverse sequence technique the answers put up by each member of the group in the light of his own experience, delving into the individual lives just long enough to catch a sidewise but cross-section view of the forces and influences that shape their minds. It is significant that no one of them manages to provide the real, the reassuring answer. Significant because it is clear that Warner has used this group as his symbol of an imperfect humanity, a representative collection of well-meaning human beings who, in their failure to understand or comprehend the meaning of the forces strangling them, succeed only in intensifying and accelerating their doom.

We are back, then, to where we were when we began. Mr. Warner's soldier is given no satisfaction save the unbelievably full and "unutterably splendid" awareness of the meaning of life, with all its phenomena and all its glory, all its futility and all its misery. The reader's satisfaction must likewise be measured in terms of philosophical exploration rather than in terms of specific information or direct impressions.

Our own quarrel with the book is that the overtones and undertones of negativism are quite as inconclusive as the answers themselves. It seems to us that Mr. Warner has accumulated all the despair of history and compressed it into one book; as such, it is a first-rate accomplishment in philosophical reflection. But as a novel of and for *today,* we are afraid the book is lacking in much that is valuable or cogent. Certainly it lacks the biting urgency that identified ***The Professor*** with the immediate moment. There is a certain danger in becoming over-profound and over-philosophical; things that are real and simple sometimes vanish just because they seem too real and simple to be true. The search for the eternal verities can crowd out the immediate tangibles.

Norman Cousins, "Why Was I Killed?" in The Saturday Review of Literature, *Vol. XXVII, No. 24, June 10, 1944, p. 18.*

BEN RAY REDMAN

It is hard to believe that anyone could finish [***The Aerodrome***] without wishing to begin, as soon as possible, the others its author has written. There are talents that stand tall in the crowd, while there are others of notable stature that have nothing to do with crowds. Mr. Warner's talent is obviously of the second order.

Aiming at something that is not realism, ***The Aerodrome*** takes off from the firmest of realistic runways. It begins with a young man who has just celebrated his twenty-first birthday, lying face down in the mud of a marsh, drunk, shaken, and dismayed. A few hours earlier he has been told that the man and woman whom he has always called father and mother are not his parents. Suddenly he is rootless, lost in space, for he does not know who he is. He cannot be sure that he belongs to the village in which he has grown up, nor even to the country he has taken for granted as his own.

From this beginning, in which belief is won by a careful factuality of statement, by a way of writing eye-to-eye with the reader which recalls Bunyan and Defoe and Kafka, both narrator and listeners are launched on a flight of discovery. Together, the young man and we who accompany him learn, through successive revelations, what kind of person he is, and what kind of world it is he inhabits. And at the same time we are presented with a clarifying view of ourselves and our own world; for we have not read many pages of Mr. Warner's convincing prose before we realize that he is an accomplished allegorist who is speaking to us of great matters in terms of symbols and simplifications. Indeed, his subject matter is the most important one with which any writer of our day can deal.

The village in which Roy has grown up is old: the aerodrome, which has come into being a mile distant, is new. The one clings to the imperfections of the past, while the other aspires to perfections which can be found, if anywhere, only in the future. From the point of view of the Air Force, the villagers, with their rectory, their squire, and their pub, are contemptible. Their lives are muddled and their government is muddled, for both are based on a faith that nobody properly understands. As the air vice-marshal declares to a rising class of fliers:

> Those who exist under such a regime must be slaves, incapable of clarity and consistency either in thought or action, drunk or hopelessly in love when they are not touching their caps to an employer or performing in accordance with some outworn system of mechanical and often unnecessary task. And in the cities you will see even worse things.

It is one of the duties of the Air Force to defend this indefensible civilization. But there are other duties, as yet undisclosed to the majority of the airmen, which will be revealed in due course. Meantime, those who wear wings must learn to live free of past ties and future fears, to put aside parents and all others, and love itself, for the sake of an ideal of which the vice-marshal is the eloquent prophet; for, as he is even now willing to tell the rank and file, the Force aims at nothing less than becoming "a new and more adequate race of men." What he does not tell them, what Roy learns when he rises to one of the highest positions of trust at the aerodrome, is that science will soon make all but a few "controlling" figures unessential to the Force's secret program. Ordinary pilots can easily be discarded in favor of automatically managed robots. And Roy also learns from the vice-marshal that this program aims not at defense, but at transformation: that it is against the very "souls of the people themselves" that war will be waged. . . . (pp. 9-10)

This is the great plan, in the execution of which Roy almost participates. He acquires the airman's point of view, and learns to see the countryside as it appears from the sky, "where there is no feeling or smell of earth." But he is subject to other influences than the vice-marshal's, and these impel him to a fateful decision which profoundly shocks his commanding officer. The story of how he reaches this decision may be left in Mr. Warner's very able hands, and with it may be left Roy's whole personal story, involving his instructive love affairs with an unsophisticated girl and a highly sophisticated woman. There is no need to say anything here about the plot-threads of ***The Aerodrome,*** except to say that they are strong and well-woven. . . .

The game of attempting to establish precise correspondences between the details of allegory and those of reality is one that every reader of ***The Aerodrome*** may play for himself. It is possible that some persons will even be willing to accept this book, which was finished during the London blitz, as merely an indictment of Hitlerism, as merely an account of the rise and fall of the Nazi Lucifer. But, details aside, there would seem to be little doubt as to what Mr. Warner is talking about: talking wisely and well, in words that should command our attention. He is talking of the dilemma in which man finds himself, now that he has reached a point in his history when his old, untidy civilization appears to have become incapable of duration, while all the tidy and bright substitutes which can be imagined would seem to be laden with germs of cultural death. He is talking of imperfect civilization opposed to perfect barbarism; of man versus the science of his own creation; of the dignity of the blundering individual contrasted with the possible power of a mechanically efficient state. He is posing the fundamental questions of our time: How can we combine security and freedom? How can we eradicate the old evils without destroying the old goods? What shall we do to be saved?

He gives us no final answer, of course. But he states the situation beautifully, seeing it in the round. And, unless I mistake his meaning, he says that we may learn to live "together in confidence though never in certainty," not by virtue of planning from above, but by virtue of individual effort from below. . . .

Many books are called important. I sincerely believe that this one is important, at least for our quickly passing day. (p. 10)

Ben Ray Redman, "What Shall We Do to Be Saved?" in The Saturday Review of Literature, *Vol. XXX, No. 2, January 11, 1947, pp. 9-10.*

IRWIN EDMAN

[The novels of Rex Warner are] in several respects as distinctive a genre as they are distinguished literature. Reading any page at random, one knows at once that this is writing of an elegance, music and compression rare enough at any time, and particularly in our own. Secondly, each of Mr. Warner's books has been a spiritual parable, and his novels have been vehicles for the expression of moral themes central to our time. (p. 4)

[In ***The Aerodrome***] Mr. Warner once more makes a story the image of a set of ideas. The tale is that of the gradual occupation of a traditional English village (with its pub, its church and its manor house) by a streamlined and efficient aerodrome. The lives of the villagers, dominated inefficiently and complacently by the Squire, the Rector and the publican, are contrasted with the lives of the aerodrome, dominated by the clear, ruthless will of the Air Vice Marshal.

The narrative is given through the mouth and feelings of a young man who, having been brought up in the rectory in the village, comes to be a member of the Air Force. Through his eyes the transformation both in the village and in his own soul is shown . . . the passage from the loose humanity of the old village to the inhuman clarity and power of the aerodrome.

The story itself, although obviously manipulated almost too symmetrically to illustrate the author's points, is full of moments of tenderness, violence and suspense. The writing is full of music and imagination, and it conveys almost nostalgically the English landscape, the flavor of local life in the dart-playing drinkers at the pub, the very feel of the air in a quiet English country twilight. And evoked, too, as only a poetic mind can evoke it, is the new idea of "clean" power, of clarity, of resolute order, of detached and disinterested efficiency such as the aerodrome embodies. Not only the style but the incidents are moving: the young love, reckless and ardent, of the hero, Roy, for Bess, the barmaid; his strange, half-jealous friendship of the young airman whom he knows before his own entry into the Air Corps; Roy's admiration, mingled with fear and resentment, of the Air Vice Marshal, all resolution, lucidity and discipline. (pp. 4, 35)

The book can hardly be classed as great fiction, for the chief characters, especially the Air Vice Marshal, seem illustrations of a thesis rather than living beings. The aerodrome and its life, too, are too much a geometric parable, and even the village, for all the sprawling and half-drunken life, is reduced to a formula: the pub, the rectory and the manor. The hero, the narrator of the tale, is a likable enough young chap, but his self-analysis and his analysis of the moods and meanings of the other characters are altogether too philosophical to be quite believable.

There is a special sort of suspension of disbelief necessary in reading a book of this kind. As a philosophic pilgrimage, as a latter-day "Everyman," it is a success. It cannot be, it perhaps need not be, accepted in the ordinary sense as a novel. It is really a moral dialogue thrown into narrative form. It is humanity versus power, sprawling life versus death-dealing regimentation. In an age of atomic energy, it is a parable worth reading, and for its poetry and insight worth enjoying. Rex Warner is a sort of English Koestler, both more poetic and more calm. (p. 35)

Irwin Edman, "Microcosm of Power," in The New York Times Book Review, *January 12, 1947, pp. 4, 35.*

MARK SCHORER

The Cult of Power consists of eight essays, several of them very slight, hardly more than organized notations, and at least one of them, **"Dostoievsky and the Collapse of Liberalism,"** a third of the book, considerably ambitious. Nearly all of them illuminate the two chief considerations which arise from Mr. Warner's novels—his persistent theme, and his literary method.

The theme of the novels—from the first, ***The Wild Goose Chase,*** to the last, ***The Aerodrome,***—has been the relation of the individual to the state. Warner's "individual" has been conceived as of two generally opposite kinds—the man whose motive is love and whose desire is to transform the state in the image of justice, and the man whose motive is will, his desire to transform the state in his own image.

The title essay of the present book begins with the tragic hero. In the universe of tragedy, individual violence is never effective, individual power never final, for a larger force—"God, Necessity, Law, Social Conscience"—is active above and beyond individual control; in this sense "all tragedy is religious." . . .

Mr. Warner reminds us always that "individualism" is a term which contains cruel and crucial contradictions, that both the humane and the ruthless individualist arise from the state of mind we call "liberalism," and that in times of social disorder we are likely to turn to the second in place of the first. And he recommends not "bogus religious revivals," but—I do not know with what degree of hopefulness—"the actual practice of general justice, mercy, brotherhood and understanding."

In four other essays, he is concerned with the same general problem and arrives at the same general proposal. He examines Dostoievsky to lay before us as the central contrast of his work the same difference between the "religious" humane and the egoistic aggressive. This is a penetrating essay with a concrete substance. But in **"May 1945," "On Freedom of Expression"** and **"The Study of the Classics,"** Mr. Warner writes again in the abstract, and invites little more than our assent, which he already has—the desire to exclaim "How true!" That is precisely our feeling at the end of his novels—where "love" is likewise recommended; we assent without being moved. I have the impression, stronger than ever after reading these essays, that Mr. Warner's experience of modern life—and his theme is of course the major problem *in* modern life—is a purely intellectual experience.

The impression finds some support in the method which Mr. Warner chooses for his novels, a method which he calls "allegorical." Allegory is the device in fiction most congenial to purely intellectual schematizations; it is also the easiest way to escape the shackles of ordinary realism. Mr. Warner, like many modern novelists, has been intent on giving us more of what is "real" than realism can give—and this is, unquestionably, the intention which will ultimately prove to separate the serious mid-century novelist from the trifling novelist. Like Dostoievsky, Mr. Warner would say, "Arid observations of everyday trivialities I have long ceased to regard as realism—it is just the reverse"; and to this end he has written his novels in a special vein of fantasy and bulwarked them here with his essay on **"The Allegorical Method"** and, less substantially, with two others called **"On Reading Dickens"** and **"Notes on the Language of Aeschylus."**

Early in his career Mr. Warner announced, "The only modern novelist I like is Kafka," and his novels have consistently emulated the tone of somnambulistic logic which is characteristic of Kafka. But Kafka is not an allegorist in the way that Mr. Warner is—and, when he emulates Kafka's tone, he is merely intellectualizing a technique which in the original expresses a vision of experience. Kafka's novels and stories cannot be paraphrased back into other, simpler statements, certainly not into one to one, point by point equivalents. One cannot say of the insect in "Metamorphosis," for example, that it *represents* something else; it simply *is* something. But in Warner, we can always translate. The Professor, in the novel of that name, is the Well-Intentioned Liberal; in ***Return of the Traveller,*** Sir Alfred is the Deluded Tory, "the Man from Spain," the Enlightened Radical, and so on. This is allegory.

Yet it is a definition with which Mr. Warner is not content. Dostoievsky and Dickens are allegorists too, he says, and they are greater than "the purer allegorists, like Kafka," because they "combine the realism of observation with the super-realism of allegorical imagination." But if Kafka's novels of neurotic sensibility are somewhat bare in their want of sensuosity and immediacy, Mr. Warner's are plainly diagrammatic; and to extend the definition of "allegory" to mean "symbolism" does not alter the fact.

All this is worth saying not because one wishes to denigrate the high seriousness of Mr. Warner's novels, or of his thinking about modern life and modern fiction. It is worth saying rather for the very reason that he has chosen for his novels the most serious possible theme—and that, in these essays, he has obliquely meditated upon his theme and his literary problem with both seriousness and intelligence. Still, he wishes for more in others and leaves us wishing for more in him than "pure allegory."

Mark Schorer, "Essays on Sundry Dilemmas of Modern Man," in The New York Times Book Review, *September 14, 1947, p. 4.*

LLOYD MORRIS

The Cult of Power is a collection of eight brief, pregnant essays as notable for their implications as for the sense of imminent peril, of desperate moral urgency, to which they are a response. For, although they illuminate the author's fiction, it is scarcely likely that he wrote them to do so. They are lucid, calm, reasonable and persuasive; but their tone is deceptive. It is impossible to resist the conclusion that they were written under the stress of an awareness that time, for all of us, is fast running out, and that even for the creative artist there may not be enough left to deliver his message in his chosen medium.

Mr. Warner's eight essays explore, in life and in literature, the conflict between liberty and authority, innovation and tradition, the individual and society in the guise of the state, which our age has found no way of resolving, though it has twice afflicted our civilization with unprecedented catastrophe.

The problem, as Mr. Warner points out, is as old as human history, but in our day it has become crucial because of the acknowledged bankruptcy of our traditional values and our failure to discover others upon which a "new order" can be successfully raised. It is not because we are deficient in scientific ability, he reminds us, that the elements of our life are not yet organized scientifically; it is because we are not certain why we want to live at all. This condition of spiritual vacuum and moral anarchy accounts, in his view, for our present plight. In the title essay he traces the degradation of a movement of intellectual skepticism to its final result in the emergence of the power-addict and the man-God "leader" who temporarily is able to furnish the masses with a system of ideas by which they can regulate and give significance to their lives. In an essay on **"Dostoievsky and the Collapse of Liberalism"** he discusses the antithetical doctrines of Dostoievsky and Karl Marx who, anticipating our crisis two generations before our day, strove to meet the impending vacuum and anarchy with new values in terms of which the social order might be reorganized. . . .

Readers of Mr. Warner's earlier books will require no invitation to secure, and to ponder, ***The Cult of Power.*** Those who have not yet made his acquaintance are earnestly exhorted by their reviewer to do so. For in ***The Cult of Power*** they will find a clarification of the issues which today press heavily on all of us. It is a book of genuine importance and its author may yet prove to be one of the most valuable interpreters of our times.

Lloyd Morris, "The Perennial Conflict," in New York Herald Tribune Weekly Book Review, *September 28, 1947, p. 10.*

BEN RAY REDMAN

Three years ago when I reviewed Rex Warner's ***The Aerodrome*** [see excerpt above] . . . I said that the author's subject was the most important one with which a writer of our day could deal, that he was asking—at a crucial moment of human history—no less a question than: "What shall we do to be saved?" In ***Men of Stones*** he is still concerned with the same question, but, if I read him correctly, he is even farther from reaching a definitive answer than he was at the conclusion of his earlier allegory. The quest, however, continues to provide Mr. Warner's readers with a steadily fascinating literary experience, for this new novel, although it is less substantial and at times less satisfying than its predecessor, has been created out of the same stuff as ***The Aerodrome,*** in the same style, with much of the same ingenuity and art.

It takes us to a nameless European country, which has recently suffered from bloody civil wars and subsequent ideological purges; to a beautiful island, dominated by a magnificent medieval castle, now a prison; and into the company of the prison's Governor, his beautiful and amorous wife, his younger brother—who has survived the rigors of a concentration camp by feeding on human flesh—and several other interesting if less unusual characters. Traveling to this island with Mr. Goat, who is a member of a Cultural Mission from a foreign country, the reader shares this young man's involvements with the Governor's wife, the Governor's philosophy, and the Governor's plans to become an earthly surrogate for God the Father. Mr. Goat's business on the island is to stage a production of *King Lear,* a task proposed to him by the Minister for Public Instruction, a practical politician who is intent upon persuading the outside world that the government of which he is a distinguished member is less brutal and intolerant than its enemies and surviving victims would have the world believe. (pp. 19, 29)

The incidents of this drama help to keep the reader's interest keen, but incidents are important in Mr. Warner's scheme only in so far as they evoke or justify or permit the expression of ideas. . . .

The eloquent central figure of ***The Aerodrome*** was, and is, the Air Vice Marshal, commander of a force dedicated to the transformation of mankind. The eloquent central figure of ***Men of Stones*** is the Governor, self-dedicated, single-handed save for his prisoner-disciples, to a similar change. Both men are uncompromising authoritarians, contemptuous of the individual and average man. (p. 29)

To Mr. Goat, who professes Christianity, the Governor points out the discrepancy between Mr. Goat's beliefs and practice, and suggests that he would do well to change his principles when he is so obviously incapable of living in accordance with the precepts of his faith. To Captain Nicholas, savant and *bon vivant,* who holds that the foundations of a good life may be found in the very history which the Governor is destroying, "in poets and philosophers, in wine, in love," the Governor replies that 3,000 years of poetry and philosophy and love have brought us to "the age of the concentration camp and of the atomic bomb." To Marcus, who is seeking a power "which, while it does not prevent misery, condoles with the miserable," the Governor says bluntly that no such power exists. The younger brother, however, once he has had his revelation, is proof against the elder brother's arguments: it is enough for him to know that love and pity and goodness really exist in the real world, even though they are not triumphant.

Marcus finds individual serenity and happiness. But it is the Minister for Public Instruction who has the last word, a word that obliterates the Governor's authoritarian dream, lights again the fires of civil war, and gives new impetus to the old cycle of evil. Is this, then, Mr. Warner's present conclusion: that the "practical" politician will always have the last (that is to say, temporary) word, and that the eternal recurrence of human folly and evil is ineluctable, save by those who escape through individual faith or dreams? Take it as you will—***Men of Stones*** is a book to read with pleasure, and to ponder in as much tranquility as life today allows. (pp. 29-30)

Ben Ray Redman, "Transforming Mankind," in The Saturday Review of Literature, *Vol. XXXIII, No. 7, February 18, 1950, pp. 19, 29-30.*

CHARLES J. ROLO

[Rex Warner's] boldly imaginative novels—***The Wild Goose Chase, The Professor, The Aerodrome***—have tackled the largest issues of the past two decades. Warner's last book dramatized the pragmatic advantages of the philosophy of power and its terrible perversion of human life. In ***Men of Stones*** . . . , Warner again focuses on the authoritarian idea, but now the argument advances further into theology.

This politico-religious novel, so immensely of our time, is attired in the vestments of weird melodrama. The setting is an island prison of an unnamed European country which has just emerged from civil war; and the novel's dominant figure is the prison Governor, a satanic, spellbinding genius who aspires to "organize the Good Life throughout the world" by making himself a new incarnation of God. "The Good Life, the good citizen," he says, "are by-products of faith," but faith has been destroyed in the name of progress, leaving man burdened with uncertainty and guilt—"Mankind is happy only in submission to a superior power." Like the executioner in Kafka's story, *The Penal Colony,* the Governor argues that men worship "precisely that which is not bound down to standards of thought and behavior which are familiar to them." By a program of arbitrary cruelty and arbitrary benevolence, he has succeeded, before the novel opens, in becoming God to his prisoners. And now he is almost ready to set this band of disciples free to proselytize throughout the world. . . .

If I understand the book rightly, it dramatizes the belief that the source of evil is man's ambition to be more than man, his *hubris* or overweening pride; that evil is inescapable; and that it is the ground stuff of philosophies of power—all of which looks rather like the doctrine of original sin. Warner has a good deal more to say which I won't attempt to paraphrase, since the crux of a novel is not its ideas but the effectiveness of their symbolic presentation.

Men of Stones, I'm afraid, left me with awkwardly mixed feelings. The novel's theme is arresting, its conception audacious, and it has stretches of brilliant argument, an undercurrent of excitement, and a powerfully suggested atmosphere of the bizarre. But the book is seriously flawed. High expectations are aroused in the first encounters with the Governor; then Warner loosens his grip by introducing, at mid-point, a considerable subplot centering on Marcus. And thereafter the book tends to become diffuse; its meaning is blurred by seeming irrelevancies. Granted this weakness, ***Men of Stones*** remains one of the more interesting of the recent novels.

Charles J. Rolo, in a review of "Men of Stones," in The Atlantic Monthly, *Vol. 185, No. 4, April, 1950, p. 88.*

MAX COSMAN

Mr. Warner has ever been concerned with arbitrary power. But he has been particularly interested in those who have seized it. He did not, of course, have to look far for baneful exemplars. (p. 643)

In any novel of his, then, attention has more often than not been focused on the dictatorial creature of the narrative. Perhaps it was inevitable that such Wells-Kafka characters of his as Rudolph in ***The Wild Goose Chase,*** Colonel Grimm in ***The Professor,*** the Air Vice-Marshal in ***The Aerodrome,*** the Governor in ***Men of Stones,*** being symbolic rather than full-bodied, should sooner or later give way to someone who did not have to be contrived, someone perhaps the very archetype of usurpers of power at any time—say Caesar himself.

So it has turned out. The expected study is now before us. Called a novel, either because it strains biographic fact through an assumed consciousness, or, seen from another view, because it comes in the guise of an autobiography set up for the occasion, ***The Young Caesar*** is bound to please all, and especially those who enjoy fictionalized historic figures. Like its predecessors in kind, *I, Claudius* and *The Ides of March,* or the recent *Memoirs of Hadrian,* it has authentic insight into personality and poetic deployment of record. Like them again, despite its muted dramatics, it has something else: that admiration which is given to those who in good or evil are larger than life.

The nature of the kingpin, the violent self-asserter, "the moral anarchist," to use the term Mr. Warner employs in his essay [**"The Cult of Power"**], is well-realized in Caesar. He is the thorough skeptic even as he serves the gods in the highest of religious offices. He rebels against venerable standards even as he urges a synthesis between them and new ones. He proclaims his adherence to necessity, to efficiency, even as he disregards both if they are invoked by anyone else. Gifted, audacious, extravagant, sentimental and cynical too, he gives himself to others, asking in return no more than they submit utterly to him. His colossal callousness, his inhumanity in the last analysis, can be seen when he sums up his activities for a certain period: he has stormed more than eight hundred cities, subdued three hundred nations, fought against as many as three million men. How satisfied he is, how detached in this recapitulation! Not a word about the appalling actualities of enslavement and slaughter, not to mention the ignoble looting that it represents!

Lack of authorial comment—this is the limitation in a novel in first person—is compensated for by Mr. Warner in the only way possible to him: he lets acts condemn pretensions. . . .

In ***The Young Caesar*** he has finally given universal form to his thesis that in the long run man has very little to gain from the megalomaniac as ruler. (pp. 643-44)

Max Cosman, "Moral Anarchist," in Commonweal, *Vol. LXVII, No. 25, March 21, 1958, pp. 643-44.*

JOSEPH G. HARRISON

In his two-volume fictionalized autobiography of Caesar, Rex Warner enables us pleasantly and profitably to broaden our acquaintanceship with one of history's major figures. In his first book, ***The Young Caesar,*** the author brings his man through boyhood, youth and early manhood to the verge of those Roman world-shaking events which are now recorded in ***Imperial Caesar***. . . .

Rex Warner's forte, as he proved in ***The Young Caesar,*** is his ability to recreate in convincing form the atmosphere and activity of 2,000 years ago. True, there is a great deal of the author in this book, particularly in those pages which deal with Caesar's self-explanation and soliloquizing, but seldom is the reader's credibility strained. Perhaps Caesar neither spoke nor thought exactly as the writer makes him do, but the reader is nonetheless left with what seems to be about as faithful a reproduction of imperial Roman thought as is reasonable from this distance.

Perhaps, again, there are historians who will feel that Mr. Warner has not been critical enough of Caesar's fatal action against the Roman Republic and that consequently Caesar emerges a bit too well from these pages. The debate over Caesar's action has been going on since the last half of the first century, B.C. with little agreement among the scholars. Mr. Warner would seem authorized to adopt his own interpretation of the event.

In short, an unusually well written and authoritative novel on one of history's greats.

Joseph G. Harrison, "The Atmosphere of Caesar's Rome," in The Christian Science Monitor, *June 16, 1960, p. 11.*

THE TIMES LITERARY SUPPLEMENT

[In ***Imperial Caesar***] Mr. Rex Warner continues the first-person narrative begun in ***The Young Caesar***. . . .

It is a difficult form, and perhaps Mr. Warner has not quite overcome its difficulties. Everything must be told in the past tense, and there is heavy-footed irony in Caesar's speculations as to whether he will be assassinated before he has completed his programme, and his assurance that, among many doubtful characters, at least the upright Brutus is completely to be trusted. But the reader's chief difficulty, as the lively narrative unfolds, is to remember that throughout this long book it is Caesar talking, and talking to himself.

This book would not excite a reviewer to argument if it were not exceptionally vivid and convincing. Mr. Warner's scholarship guarantees an accurate account of all the crises of the Civil War, and his portraits of Pompey and Cicero are acute and convincing. If Caesar did not think himself faultless a great many Caesarians did, or they would not have fought so strenuously. It is especially gratifying to see the half-forgotten hero Crastinus receiving his share of praise. Here is a thrilling, if one-sided, account of the chief turning-point of European history.

"Supreme Heads," in The Times Literary Supplement, *No. 3053, September 2, 1960, p. 557.*

DARSHAN SINGH MAINI

Of all the contemporary English novelists who have graduated to fame or recognition since the Pink Decade, perhaps none describes so straight and pure a literary line as Rex Warner. He has not only kept his ideological target in view, adjusting the sights accordingly, but has also followed his peculiar technique with the unsleeping devotion of an ascetic. This has necessarily limited the scope of his readership, for the method of fantasy and allegory, which characterises nearly all his work, demands from the reader 'the additional sixpence', to use the words of E. M. Forster. . . . (p. 91)

But the allegories of Mr. Warner do not have [the] universal or communal bedrock [of song and myth, of fable and folklore], for they invite readers not into an emotional and mystic partnership, but into a *camaraderie* of ideas, and ideas, as we know, are hardly the thing which would draw a crowd. In fact, where ideas are the sole *raison d'être* of a writer's work, as in the case of Mr. Warner, the novel is hardly the form suitable for expression. There is, however, a way in which his work may be said to acquire a sort of transferred universality. His appeal to the intelligentsia is at bottom a fight on behalf of the common man, in whose revolutionary potentialities, he has . . . great faith. What made him, therefore, restrict the area of his appeal is probably the belief that battles are won and lost, not in the mills and the streets, but in the minds of thinking men and women. Thus, it is they who have to be won over to the humanist ideals; the working classes have an instinctive regard for the beauty and holiness of life, and can always be salvaged through the actions of an intelligent and organised leadership.

If he is not as popular as George Orwell or Arthur Koestler, who are also *ad hoc* novelists—his understanding of contemporary politics, particularly of totalitarianism, is no less acute and penetrating, while his poetic sensibility is far richer than either's—it is because he has refused to descend to the journalistic level. He has not compromised his art and his vision. For one thing, he has no need to shout, for he has no bad conscience of a 'heretic' or a 'renegade'. He has not many skeletons in his ideological cupboard. This does not mean that his views have remained static over the years, or his political antennae have become too feeble to register changes. No creative artist—and Mr. Warner is one of the finest writers in the English language today—could sustain himself without a dynamic world-view. Only, unlike most of his contemporaries, he has ripened without the dramatics of a *volte face*.

His first novel, ***The Wild Goose Chase,*** 1937, is in a way perhaps the most important work of Mr. Warner, not because it is in any sense a great book or even one of his best specimens, but because it is something of a political and literary manifesto. It contains within its amorphous frontiers nearly all the important ideas he has developed since then. His later work, though more pleasing and powerful, is nevertheless a variation on the same theme in the same style. This is not to say that he repeats himself. It is as if he scattered with a prodigal hand all his ideological seeds at a single throw, and has since been gathering the crop in separate harvests. For there is hardly any novelist of ideas in contemporary English fiction who has followed a studied political and literary attitude with as much vigilance and purity of design as Rex Warner. His severely classical temperament (and he is a well-known Latin and Greek scholar) has imposed a rigorous discipline on his writings. He thus moves within a given, defined framework, and though this robs his work of that rotundity and multitudinousness of life which we find in great fiction, it nevertheless gives a tone of finality to what he has chosen to do.

A novelist of ideas is primarily interested in the kinetic power of thought. His interest in characters and situations is only a recognition of the fact that ideas by themselves can achieve little. This is true of Mr. Warner's novels, for he is concerned essentially, not with the jostling crowds in the streets or with the three-decker families in the homes, but with the political forces and compulsions which seize peoples and nations, and blow them about. His subject is therefore not men but man, not the abstract or metaphysical man, but the sociological and chiefly the political man. This naturally gives his books a sectional, esoteric interest. As works of fiction, these thin and spare volumes are a light-weight affair, but as political studies, they are instinct with a consuming, ideological passion. What they lose in breadth and length, these explosive, one-dimensional books gain in depth and power.

This preoccupation with politics, as we know, was a leading intellectual passion in the 'thirties. . . . Of the new, crusading, bourgeois young men in England who elected to chase the Communist siren on the one hand, and to destroy the hydra-headed Fascist monster on the other (the two were facets of the same problem at that time), Rex Warner was one. More than any other contemporary writer, he realised that the fight against Fascism was a fight against a dark, medieval, obscurantist tyranny, which was infinitely more dreadful, hideous and paralysing than any tyranny man had experienced before. Few understood as well the psychological side of this fatal fascination which Fascism exercised over the minds of volatile youth as he did.

What were the emotive compulsions behind this surrender? What were the logistics of this nightmare? He did not outline the case-history of a dictator . . . , but dramatised in a symbolical manner the 'mystic' pull which dictators exerted over their victim-votaries. (pp. 92-4)

But even more important than the dictator's career or his overwhelming influence over his people is the pernicious nature of the view of life he represents. Fascism, we are told by Mr. Warner, is a completely 'integrated' philosophy of life within its own phoney framework. It denied history and tradition; violated not only human institutions, but human nature as well. It had its own grim rituals and ceremonies, its own dark dogma and mystique, its own rigid hierarchies and the 'leader-principle'. The danger lay, not in its instruments of torture . . . but in its determined bid to violate the sanctity of life, to deify brute force and create a 'brave new world' of blond, Nordic youth drunk with power. It was the dreaded prospect of this insensate hate, which appalled Mr. Warner most.

Vander, the Fascist propagandist in ***The Professor,*** the Air Vice-Marshal in ***The Aerodrome*** and the Governor in ***Men of Stones*** represent the ultimate in 'the cult of power':

> 'Why is our propaganda more successful than yours?' asks Vander and replies in the same breath: 'Partly because our aims are definite, sensible and within reach instead of being vague, intellectualized and extending into infinity; but more still because, we appeal to the dark and vital and real forces in human nature. . . . '

Elaborating his credo of blood and bluster, he adds:

> Power over others is the normal flowering of personality, and women are conquered, not persuaded into lust. . . .

And this view of life and love is further explored in ***The Aerodrome,*** where the A.V.M. is the winged god of the new, pragmatic, cynical philosophy. Addressing the new recruits, he says:

> For good or evil, you are yourselves poised for a brief and dazzling flash of time between two annihilations. Reflect please, that 'parenthood', 'ownership', 'locality' are the words of the future. And so is 'marriage'! These words are without wings. I do not care to hear an airman use them.

Continuing his peroration, he declaims that parents are

> people who are unimportant in themselves, but who have served in most cases as channels or conduits through which you have all in varying degrees been infected with the stupidity, the ugliness and the servility of historical tradition.

This utterly bestial view of life is carried a step further in ***Men of Stones*** where the Governor, a palaeolithic figure of Satanic pride and grandeur stands for the fascist mystique of 'the *Fuehrer* principle', which when pushed to its logical extreme results in the Mumbo-Jumbo of 'man-god'. And this is his 'apocalyptic' Word:

> I model myself rather upon God the Father than upon God the Son. The actions of the Father are often unpredictable and often seem unjust to us. They are always powerful and overwhelming. His children are most happy when they are most utterly in submission to his will. . . .

(pp. 95-6)

I have quoted at some length from Mr. Warner's books to prove that his crusade against Fascism was more than a fight against a political creed. It was essentially an assertion of the humanist values which were threatened with total extinction by the Fascists. No artist, if he had to keep his vision alive could prevaricate or sit on the fence. There was no neutral or midway path, for truth is always partisan. To fight against Fascism was to fight for the preservation of man's culture and heritage. A poem, a novel or a play became as much of a political act as the shouldering of a rifle, or manning a barricade. Courage was not simply a matter of the solar plexus, it was also a matter of intellectual integrity, of spiritual inviolability. Thus amongst the artists who donned the gloves and came out openly into the ring was Rex Warner.

However, unlike most others at that time, he did not strip himself naked. On the contrary, he put on a fanciful, *bizarre* garb, which instead of coming in his way, permitted him to land his blows right on the target. For the method which he applied was not one of direct, frontal, sledge-hammer blows, but that of oblique, poetic and symbolic sleight of hand. Perhaps Mr. Warner realised that any crude, straight attack on Fascism was likely to yield little results. By its very nature—its cynical pragmatism and violence—totalitarianism was bound to succeed where the adversary fought with weapons already perfected by it. Thus the best way out at that time was to deal with the menace on the ideological or spiritual plane. A recourse to fantasy and allegory, incidentally a common feature of a great deal of contemporary political fiction, was thus something of an intellectual necessity.

This, however, did not prevent him from putting the full steam on. Only the action was transferred to a no-land and the characters became symbols. Indeed all his novels except ***Escapade*** are a series of long, sustained, passionate arguments worked out in a prose which is at once noble, majestic, evocative and electrifying. There is not only limpidity and clarity as in George Orwell, or power and passion as in Arthur Koestler, but also a strong poetic verve and a turn for a highly original, metaphorical language. It must not be forgotten that Mr. Warner is also a poet in his own right. Indeed I doubt, if any living writer in English can give his ideas such a broad sweep as he can do. . . . In Rex Warner, ideas take wings and soar above, rushing the reader along in a frenzy or ecstasy of language. All other fictional ingredients such as character, plot, humour etc. fade away for the moment, or are subordinated to long, overwhelming dialogues, which swollen with thought, go hurtling along at a breathless speed, The reader is indeed intoxicated with the pure wine of ratiocination. No impurities are tolerated. The idea, polished and licked into a shining diamond, proceeds along its course with the certitude and grandeur of a musical *finale*.

However, it is never a one-sided political harangue. On the contrary, opposing views or ideas are marshalled out in all their intrinsic vigour and beauty. The two protagonists: George and the King in ***The Wild Goose Chase,*** the Professor and Vander in ***The Professor,*** Roy and the Air Vice-Marshal in ***The Aerodrome,*** Charles and his bourgeois-liberal friend in ***Why Was I Killed?,*** Marcus and the Governor in ***Men of Stones,*** look at each other from across a yawning gulf of ideas. Each is allowed the liberty of his views. Each follows his own logical track with the precision of a clock. What 'message' he has to give is put down in the idiom of his choice. The author seems to stand outside the ring, watching the two fierce birds pluck each other's plumage in a fine frenzy. He identifies himself first with the one, and then with the other keeping the balance in the middle. This fascinating duel between ideas follows a contrapuntal pattern. Each idea is opposed by a counter-idea in order to achieve a polarity of vision. This stereoscopic method is an integral part of Mr. Warner's polemics, and proceeds, I think, from a dialectical understanding of reality. This does not mean that he follows an objective, eclectic, middle attitude, achieving synthesis between the two extremes. He certainly allows full time and space to both the sides in the manner of a presiding judge, but that does not preclude him from having his own private opinions. He is not only fully convinced of the rightness of his own views expressed through the anti-Fascist protagonist, but is also fully aware of the wrongness of the adversary's position, even though he gives him a long rope to reach the end of the tether.

This is seldom done in an ironical vein. . . . Mr. Warner is . . . usually in dead earnest when he elaborates the totalitarian doctrine from the point of view of Fascism. Humour or irony here is out of place. Except in that delightful though slender mock-heroic fantasy ***Escapade*** where the comedy has truly Dickensian patches, he seldom permits himself the luxury of a laugh or smile. He allows both sides to hit up a tall score, but his own sympathies are never in doubt. . . . Fascists prove the beastliness of their creed in the novels of Rex Warner. Not only are they usually defeated in the end in a violent, symbolic manner—the sudden dissolution of the steel city in ***The Wild Goose Chase,*** the explosion of the A.V.M's aircraft in ***The Aerodrome,*** the blowing up of the rock castle in ***Men of Stones***—they also reveal their Caliban nature in the daily doings of their life. Above all, Mr. Warner's undying faith in the humanist ideals, his essential optimism (in spite of the tragic end of ***The Professor***) reveal his progressive and revolutionary *Weltanschauung*. (pp. 97-100)

[Warner's] thought has apparently been moulded by three powerful influences: Marxism, Hellenism and Kafka-Dostoievsky spiritualism. It is strange and even baffling that philosophies as apart as those of Marx and Kafka should be made to yield a synthetic vision, but this is what primarily Mr. Warner has sought to achieve. Marxism is the philosophy of earth and daylight, of action and aggressive optimism; Kafka stands for the terror of the Unknown, for Existentialist *Angst,* for nightmarish visions and abysmal animal sin. One regards the present world as the only reality, the other regards it as a dream and a shadow. One professes to achieve happiness through corporate human endeavour, the other talks of the eternal restlessness of the human spirit. . . . One seeks to establish a materialist heaven on earth, the other draws our attention to the hell that's all around us. Thus it would appear incongruous to yoke the two together in an unnatural wedlock. (p. 100)

What Mr. Warner has therefore done (at least in his earlier novels) is to cloak Marxist thought in Kafkaish robes. Gradually however, the frame turns into the picture, and though the Marxist view is not abandoned, the Kafka-Dostoievsky view of human nature is accepted as an inescapable reality. What distinguishes him from the ex-Communists is his refusal to regard Stalinist tyranny as an inevitable part of the Marxist programme. Also, there is no tendency to equate Communist violence with Fascist violence. In his critical writings, he has questioned some aspects of Marxism, . . . but in his novels, the enemy is always totalitarianism of the Fascist brand, for insensate gratuitous hate is a characteristic not of Communism but of Fascism. He is not blind to the excesses of the Communists but their violence is regarded as a means to a higher end. . . . Mr. Warner's Marxism was always different from that of the commissars. A spiritual streak is visible even in his first novel, ***The Wild Goose Chase*** which may aptly be described as a 'Marxist *Pilgrim's Progress*'. Indeed the symbol itself is an echo of the Holy Grail *motif,* and his hero is more of a Socialist Galahad than of a militant revolutionary. This mystic *motif* is again to be found in ***Men of Stones*** where Marcus returns to his Fascist homeland in search of a mysterious picture which sheds tears of blood when the people are in a spiritual travail. Thus Mr. Warner, like his mystic pilgrims, is an eternal seeker after truth, which in the first novel seems to stand for beauty and strength, in the second for pity and compassion. We can see here the progress of a true humanist who has come to regard compassion as the highest virtue in the scale of human values.

In his essay on Dostoievsky . . . he refers to the spiritual hiatus created by Marx, and feels that the betrayal of the Socialist dream may partly be accounted for by the absence of God from the scheme of things. Man, he believes, does not live by bread alone, and a proper distribution of wealth by itself cannot solve all his problems, much less bring about universal happiness. That organised religion has nearly always played a reactionary rôle in the affairs of man, Mr. Warner would grant, though he would also say that just as Stalinism is no excuse for condemning Marxism out of hand, the abuse of religion by the priests and other vested interests is similarly no justification for its abolition or suppression. The true aim of religion as indeed of Socialism is to extend the frontiers of man's happiness, not through material goods only, but through the establishment of a moral order also.

As for the influence of Kafka, it may be noted that the inexplicable, nightmarish inhumanity of the rulers in Kafka's novels like *The Castle* and *The Trial* is as wanton and gratuitous as the senseless tyranny of the Fascists. Thus the framework of Kafka adjusted suitably to the needs of contemporary political trends in Western Europe fitted in perfectly with Mr. Warner's design. (pp. 100-03)

An allegorical fantasy requires a highly inventive mind which is at once poetical and logical, a mind such as we find at work in a *Kubla Khan,* a *Don Quixote,* a *Pilgrim's Progress,* a *Moby Dick,* a *Zuleika Dobson,* a *Brothers Karamazov,* a *Bleak House* etc. It reveals a dialectical unity between dream-work and brain-work. The truth of fantasy is the truth of poetry; it is strange and irrational. . . . It moves within the confines of its own logical orbit; its aberrations are essentially tangential. It works within a closed circle, and spins round on its own pivot. Thus the political phantasmagoria of Warner's novels could only be conveyed effectively through a poetical and symbolic technique. For when the baffling reality of life eludes the naturalistic grasp, fantasy steps in. . . . It serves to heighten and dramatise the issue in rendering the idea. Whereas in *Animal Farm* and more particularly in *1984* this technique serves as a pragmatic and utilitarian weapon, in the case of Mr. Warner, it is the very basis of his work, and springs from an integral, organic, poetical design. For finally, the effectiveness of an allegory or a fantasy depends upon the truth of the writer's point of view. (pp. 103-04)

By comparing his technique with the technique of such allegorists as Dickens, Dostoievsky, Melville or Kafka, I do not mean to place him in their category. For Mr. Warner's world is a very small world indeed. Not only does he operate in a limited field, his talents as a novelist are also limited. For one thing, his characters are his ideas walking on stilts. They are mere symbols—figures that inhabit a dreamland, and seldom walk out into the noon-day of palpable reality. They do not have the universality, width and power of Dickensian or Dostoievskyan characters. Again, his melodramatic plots (a weakness he shares with Dickens), though a part of his dramatic plan, nevertheless remain a clumsy piece of machinery. Nor has he the apocalyptic genius of Dostoievsky or the comic vision of Dickens. The only time he came anywhere near achieving that Dickensian effect is in his little novelette ***Escapade*** which is simply a flighty piece as mockingly gay as it is delightfully irresponsible. . . . ***Escapade*** is only a slender tale, not a political novel as such, and it is in that *métier* where Mr. Warner's achievement lies. There the comic muse is seldom in attendance, though the predicament of Mr. Goat in ***Men of Stones*** certainly has comic overtones. However, in novels like ***The Professor, The Aerodrome*** and ***Why Was I Killed?,*** there is a sepulchral seriousness, unrelieved by any light interludes. Perhaps all humour shrivels up in the dread presence of Fascism. It might even be sacrilegious to introduce it.

I finally come to the third, and perhaps the most lasting, if not vital influence in Mr. Warner's work, namely, Hellenism. One of his most lovable and human characters is the Professor who incidentally was a Greek and classical scholar. . . . The archetypal Greek myths (***Men and Gods*** is Mr. Warner's own account of some of these) seem to have left a permanent imprint on his mind. Again, Plato's theory of the shadow-world of ideas, and his use of the allegory to achieve *chiaroscuro* effects have had a lasting influence on Mr. Warner's thought and technique. In **"The Allegorical Method,"** he refers to 'the overt and the more or less occult' types of allegory in Plato. He has also been undoubtedly influenced in his language and the contrapuntal use of it by Aeschylus in whose method (as he tells us in **"Notes on the Language of Aeschylus"**), he finds 'the exact balance of the opposite points of view'.

But perhaps more important than all these Greek influences is the essentially classical temperament of Mr. Warner. There is always a cool, quiet centre at the heart of a storm, and this is precisely the impression conveyed by his novels, where the events rush the reader along at a terrific pace. For always, there is a feeling of a calm island nestling inside. This may be due to the fact that the humanist *motif* is perpetually there in the texture of his work. Against all the violence and frenzy of the totalitarian world, there is the serene joy of living, born of an indestructible faith in the miracle of life. Violence always spends itself, but the white dream of peace lasts for ever. (pp. 104-06)

Darshan Singh Maini, "Rex Warner's Political Novels: An Allegorical Crusade against Fascism," in The Indian Journal of English Studies, *Vol. II, No. 1, December, 1961, pp. 91-107.*

ANGUS WILSON

'What a record of confusion, deception, rankling hatred, low aims, indecision. One is stained by any contact with such people.' So the Air Vice-Marshal speaks of traditional English society in his final appeal to Roy, the hero of ***The Aerodrome,*** to abandon his mother and join the New Society represented by the Air Force. I can think of no more concise and apt phrases to describe what those of us who were young in the nineteen twenties and thirties felt about the social order which found its leaders in Baldwin, MacDonald and Neville Chamberlain. To our disgust and scorn for the muddle and complacency of our elders the last sentences of the Air Vice-Marshal's speech had the strongest siren appeal—'I urge you to escape from all this, to escape from time and its bondage, to construct around you in your brief existence something that is guided by your own will, not forced upon you by past accidents, something of clarity, independence and beauty.' By 1941 some inkling of the death of the spirit that lay behind this siren song of a clean, aesthetic society, unencumbered by muddled human emotion, had reached all but the most blind of us. . . . There was no inhuman short cut to human bliss. On the other hand, the revelation of what totalitarian utopianism (of all kinds) meant in terms of human deformity, of the cutting off of all sources of human warmth, did not reconcile us to the cruelties caused by the evasions, incompetences and callous hypocrisies of English society between the wars. We were poised ready to jump forward both from our crumbling heritage and from our fallen false gods. It is this strange, frightening, liberating moment of 1940 that Rex Warner catches exactly in the ending of his allegory ***The Aerodrome***. This exciting, simply and beautifully told adventure story is the history of every socially, morally conscious liberal-minded man in those decades between the wars. And for most of them, as for Roy, the escape from the nightmare illusions of totalitarianism came from the superior force of human love. The ordered utopias crashed to the ground because, as Roy realizes at a vital moment in ***The Aerodrome,*** they were not consistent with 'the infinite implications of all love'.

This, of course, is only to explain why ***The Aerodrome*** was the best and most exciting adventure story for all who, like me, were young when the last war started. Like all good allegories it has poetry and inventiveness, speed of narrative and great simplicity of language; like very few allegories it also has in its small cast of characters at least six or seven memorable, living people. The author in his conventional disclaimer of sources for characters remarks how unnecessary such a statement is, for 'I do not even aim at realism'. Yet realism of a very frightening kind is exactly what he achieves. We live in his living world and, even now over twenty years later, I do not find it easy to lay down this haunting book and dismiss that world by looking out at 'reality'. (pp. 9-11)

Mr. Warner's concern for love (physical love that transcends lust) will give ***The Aerodrome*** a metaphysical strength that was perhaps subordinate in the admiration of my political generation. But I do not think that the political symbolism of ***The Aerodrome*** will be any the less powerful for those who have squatted at rocket sites. . . . In any case it is high time that this thrilling story should be widely enjoyed again. (p. 11)

Angus Wilson, in an introduction to The Aerodrome: A Love Story *by Rex Warner, Little, Brown and Company, 1966, pp. 9-11.*

SAMUEL HYNES

There are really two Rex Warners. One is the distinguished present-day classicist, the author of historical novels of Greece and Rome, and an admired translator of Sophocles and Euripedes. His achievement is certain, and his reputation secure. Still, one may regret a little that his present dignity and stature have somewhat obscured his earlier, less sedate self. The earlier Rex Warner was a young Marxist of the thirties, a friend of Auden and the intellectual left, one of the most original novelists of his generation. Between 1935 and the end of the forties he wrote five fantastic novels that are quite unlike anything else in English; in them he did what Auden did for poetry—he found new forms in which to make political ideas at once artful and urgent.

If literary reputations were rationally arrived at, Warner would be resting securely on those five extraordinary inventions. As it is, the books have not been much noticed, and all have been out of print for years. Their failure to establish themselves may be explained in various ways: they appeared just before and during a distracting war; the ideas they dealt with were overtaken by time (who needs a warning against Fascism when the Germans are bombing London?); they were modern and difficult at a time when tired air-raid wardens wanted to re-read Trollope.

The critics also contributed their bit by calling Warner an English Kafka. To say this is to deny Warner's originality, and to make his novels unnecessary. . . .

To read Warner's early novels in the order in which they were written is to live through the political ordeal of the thirties and the war years, and to feel the rising anxiety, the hope, and the despair of British radicals as they watched Fascism and war spread over Europe. But more than this, the novels record the effort of a rich, poetic imagination to find ways of realizing this experience. The books are not realistic because realism could not compass the irrationality and violence of the time; the appropriate form for nightmare must be nightmarish.

What Warner wanted was novels that would be at once vivid and didactic, that would make ideas real. He found what he needed in a number of symbolic models; in Swift's voyages, in the parables of Kafka, in folktales, in science fiction and, nearest at hand, in the poems or plays of Auden. The journeys and tales provided patterns of action, and Kafka set the tone.

Auden added a symbolic geography of mountains, cities and frontiers, and a cast of contemporary allegorical characters: the airman, the surgeon, the orator, the clergyman, the revolutionist. Marxism pointed the moral: the class struggle, the threat of Fascism, the decadence of bourgeois society—though Warner, like Auden, was too intelligent and too imaginative to be orthodox. The five novels combine these elements in various ways, but are alike in this, that they defy realism, and compel symbolic reading.

The Aerodrome, first published in 1941, is Warner's third novel, but it is wisely chosen to introduce the young Warner to a new generation of readers. It is less ideological than either ***The Wild Goose Chase*** (1937) or ***The Professor*** (1938), and it is more controlled in its symbolic form. The theme is still a political one, but it is a general theme of political morality—the conflict between the cult of power and the human need for freedom. . . .

The crisis for the hero is his choice between the two—the mess and loneliness of freedom, or the security and inhumanity of power. It is the great political issue of our century, and this novel is a brilliant symbolic statement of it.

The reissuing of ***The Aerodrome*** is an encouraging sign that the young Warner is coming into his own at last, but it must be followed by the rest of the group, including ***Why Was I Killed?*** (1944) and ***Men of Stones*** (1949). The five together certainly deserve a permanent place in the literary history of our time.

Samuel Hynes, "Superman Had Wings," in The New York Times Book Review, *November 20, 1966, p. 80.*

THE TIMES LITERARY SUPPLEMENT

Anyone who has read the *Confessions* of Augustine of Hippo, will know that it requires a bold imagination to attempt a portrayal, from the outside as it were, of that passionate, contradictory, deviously philosophical, and profoundly learned man. This Mr. Rex Warner has done [in ***The Converts***], and if without complete success, at least with a beautifully realized recreation of the fermenting centre, in space and time, of Europe's first great creative crisis. . . .

The narrative is presented through the occasional reflections of Augustine's younger friend and sometime pupil, Alypius, later to become bishop of his birthplace, Thagaste in Tunisia, and a noted dispenser of justice, but at this time newly arrived in Rome to study law. From him we learn much of the detail of urban life in fourth-century Africa, how rich a contribution to the development of Christian culture came from this region, how little of vitality Rome had left to offer. While all this is beautifully done, and the regional fragmentation and mutual indifference within the crumbling empire vividly conveyed, there are disadvantages in this second-hand mode of presentation. The author is limited by the perceptions and sensibility of the narrator.

Alypius is almost exasperatingly uncritical, even apologetic, about others, permanently self-deprecating, phlegmatic, and abject in his subjection to Augustine. But much of the passion and agony of Augustine is lost. Alypius is unable to reproduce for us the brilliance, humour and energy of Augustine's conversations, but only the earnestness proper to himself. Within these limitations, tension and pace are unavoidably slackened, and at times the reflections become repetitive and vague. On the other hand, the very "negative capability" of Alypius's compassion allows him to see, perhaps more acutely than he himself realizes, into the torment of Augustine's domestic triangle. He also sees that Augustine's obsession with, and abhorrence of, sex is rooted in his inescapable relationship with his saintly mother. Similarly, in spite of his friend's infatuated excuses, a slightly repulsive impression involuntarily emerges of the young Augustine's inverted narcissism in expecting to be loved, and in searching, if disappointed, for the fault in himself. The most serious flaw in this method is that the climax of revelation and conversion, seen in the dulled mirror of Alypius's mind, seems inevitably disappointing and unconvincing.

Nevertheless, it is right that these criticisms should be levelled rather at Alypius than at Mr. Warner, who has made of this character so real and representative a creature of his time that the reader can readily be seduced into accepting that these "reflections" are authentic documents.

"Under Augustine's Thumb," in The Times Literary Supplement, *No. 3404, May 25, 1967, p. 433.*

SAMUEL HYNES

The British critic V. S. Pritchett once described Rex Warner as "the only outstanding novelist of ideas whom the decade of ideas produced." The decade he was talking about was the 1930's, and the novels he had in mind were Warner's political allegories—***The Wild Goose Chase, The Professor,*** and the recently republished ***The Aerodrome.*** Times have changed since then, and the kind of novels that Warner writes has changed, too. Nevertheless, Pritchett's remark still holds true; Warner is still our only outstanding novelist of ideas.

By trade and by inclination he is a classicist; he has been a distinguished translator of Greek tragedy, and a skillful reteller of classical myths. It is not surprising, then, that in recent years he has taken the subjects of his novels from the classical period, has written two novels about Caesar and one about Pericles. These scrupulous, rich studies of great political leaders are formally remote from the early fantastic allegories; still, one can see in them the same philosophically inclined mind at work, and on the same central theme.

What that theme is can be found in the title that Warner gave to a book of his essays; he called it ***The Cult of Power.*** Warner has always been concerned with the problem of power—its nature and its human costs. He began writing novels at a time when it would have been difficult not to be concerned with the uses and perversions of authority; for the 1930's was the decade in which modern power first showed itself monstrous.

Warner was the only English novelist of that time who succeeded in turning the threat of Fascism into literature. He could do so because his theme was greater than the immediate political issue: he saw behind it to the deep human conflicts—the conflict of freedom with fear, of individualism with the state, of authority with human feeling. More recently, in his classical novels, he has found occasions for the same concerns. In Caesar and in Pericles he found heroes who combined personal sensibility with extraordinary power, and who could therefore serve to dramatize the issues that have held his imagination. . . .

In his new novel [***The Converts***] he has moved on in time to the point where classical and medieval history meet, and has once more chosen as his subject the life of a man of power—this time Saint Augustine. In this case, the theme is power with a difference: the power is the power of faith, and the conflict lies between the world and the spirit. But because it is set in fourth-century Rome, ***The Converts*** is also a novel about politics; for in that watershed time political power and religious belief were not separable. The great men who appear in the story—Augustine, Ambrose, Jerome—were holy men and leaders of the church. They were also political figures who shaped the destiny of the empire—and, in a sense, Augustine's conversion was a political act.

To tell the story of that conversion is to retell Augustine's *Confessions,* and one might doubt the judgment of a writer who would choose to compete with that great book. But the author has avoided the obvious dangers of the subject. The *Confessions* is not really a biography—it is a meditation on a few spiritual events. Warner has turned that meditation into experience, while maintaining the focus on spiritual issues. . . . The novel follows Augustine's own narrative, but it places the spiritual matter firmly in its secular, political setting, in the struggle for power in Rome and in the church.

Reviewers of Warner's other historical novels sometimes complained that the plots lacked action, and that the books were not so much novels as meditations. One might say something similar about ***The Converts:*** that it is less a life of Augustine than a monologue on the theme of conversion. . . . The book is a novel of ideas, the playing of a fine intelligence upon the theme of faith and its consequences. There are more ideas than action, perhaps; but in a novel like this the ideas are the action.

The Converts is not a book that will hold the restless reader with vivid settings, flamboyant characters or thrilling adventures. But anyone willing to respond seriously to serious ideas will find it compelling enough, and in more than an historical sense. For the record of a great man's struggle for the power of faith in a crumbling, doubting world is surely a story worth the telling now.

Samuel Hynes, "The Power of Faith," in The New York Times Book Review, *July 30, 1967, p. 26.*

Tennessee Williams

1911-1983

(Pseudonym of Thomas Lanier Williams) American dramatist, short story writer, poet, novelist, scriptwriter, and autobiographer.

Along with Arthur Miller, Williams is generally considered one of the two greatest American dramatists since World War II. His stature is based almost entirely on works completed during the first half of his career, as his later dramas are generally regarded as less cohesive than his early plays. Williams earned Pulitzer Prizes and New York Drama Critics Circle Awards for *A Streetcar Named Desire* (1947) and *Cat on a Hot Tin Roof* (1955) and also received New York Drama Critics Circle Awards for *The Glass Menagerie* (1944) and *The Night of the Iguana* (1961). Williams's lyrical style and thematic concerns have played major roles in defining contemporary American theater. By combining symbolic and poetic elements of expressionism with the psychological credibility of the realist tradition, Williams conceived a distinctly American drama which transcends barriers of class, manners, and language.

Recurrent in Williams's work is the conflict between reality and illusion, which he sometimes equates with a conflict between truth and beauty. Many of his thematic concerns revolve around human sexuality: sex as life-affirming, contrasted with death and decay; sex as redemptive, contrasted with sex as sin; sex as an escape from the world; and sex as a way of being at one with the world. Williams followed D. H. Lawrence in attaching a cosmic significance to sex, and audiences and critics initially considered his preoccupation with sex and violence to be perverse. Williams's protagonists are usually lonely, vulnerable dreamers and misfits who confront stronger, more ruthless characters in their search for moral values in a chaotic world. Williams typically reveals the attractive and unattractive qualities of both types of people, demonstrating his understanding of the strength as well as the fragility of the human spirit. While Williams's vision of human nature and the world is usually bleak, he sometimes offers comfort in the form of a transitory moment of human communication—the type which Blanche DuBois in *A Streetcar Named Desire* ironically refers to as "the kindness of strangers."

Williams's insight into lonely, outcast characters, as well as the warring influences of puritanism and liberality demonstrated in his plays, is often traced to his family life. Williams's most explicit reworking of his family situation occurs in his first major drama, *The Glass Menagerie*. Set in St. Louis, where the Williams family lived after 1918, the play is narrated by Tom, whose dreams of being a writer are frustrated by his family's financial dependence upon him. Tom's sister, Laura, is crippled physically and emotionally and resembles Williams's older sister, Rose, who was institutionalized for schizophrenia for much of her life. Tom's mother, Amanda, is a fading Southern belle who lives in the past. The play begins with Amanda persuading Tom to bring to the house a "gentleman caller" whom she hopes will marry Laura and provide for her future. Recognizing the futility of such a gesture, Tom brings home a man who is already engaged, destroying Amanda's dreams and causing Laura to retreat more deeply into her fantasy world, which is symbolized by her miniature glass animal collection. As the play ends, Tom, like his father, leaves his family to pursue his own destiny.

Williams established his international reputation with *A Streetcar Named Desire,* which is widely considered a classic of contemporary drama. The play begins with the arrival of Blanche at the home of her sister, Stella, and Stella's husband, Stanley, a crude working-class man who feels threatened by Blanche's gentility and flirtatious behavior. Unbeknownst to Stanley, Blanche has witnessed the loss of her family's Southern estate and the suicide of her young husband; thus, she comes to Stella and Stanley seeking comfort and security. Blanche clashes with Stanley, however, and in a brutal act of physical assertion, Stanley rapes her, precipitating her withdrawal from reality and her eventual commitment to a sanitarium. Blanche and Stanley illustrate dichotomies and conflicts which recur throughout Williams's plays: illusion versus truth, weakness versus strength, and the power of sexuality to both destroy and redeem. Williams does not, however, allow either character to become one-dimensional or to dominate audience sympathies. Stanley's brutality is balanced by his love for Stella, his dislike of hypocrisy, and his justifiable anger at Blanche's mockery of him and her intrusion into his home. Blanche's hypocrisy—her attempts at pretentious refinement despite her promiscuity—is recompensed by the audience's knowledge of her past ordeals and by her gentleness and capacity for love. Williams's skillful balancing of Stanley and Blanche and the qualities each represents, both in dialogue and plot and on a symbolic level, have earned the admiration of critics and scholars. David Sievers deemed Blanche "no less a tragic figure than Antigone or Medea," and Jacob F. Adler called her "a stunning, vivid, complex creation, the sort of character that only a genuinely great writer can produce."

Although none of Williams's later plays attained the universal critical and popular acclaim of his best-regarded early works, several dramas from the 1940s and 1950s are considered significant achievements. In *Summer and Smoke* (1948), Williams continues his exploration of the tension between the spirit and the flesh, and in *The Rose Tattoo* (1951), one of his lightest plays, he celebrates the life-affirming power of sexuality. *Cat on a Hot Tin Roof,* which is set on a Mississippi delta plantation, revolves around lies and self-deception. This play involves some of Williams's most memorable characters: Brick, a homosexual, who drinks to forget his guilt over the death of a lover; Maggie, his wife, who struggles "like a cat on a hot tin roof" to save their marriage; and Big Daddy, whose impending death from cancer prompts his family to compete for the inheritance. Such plays as *Suddenly Last Summer* (1958) and *Sweet Bird of Youth* (1959), which make use of violence and black comedy, reflect Williams's traumatic emotional state during this time, when he began to abuse alcohol and drugs. *The Night of the Iguana,* which Williams said is about "how to get beyond despair and still live," was his last play to win a major prize and gain critical and popular favor.

Williams continued to produce plays until his death, but critical reception became increasingly negative. Many of Williams's later dramas consist of experimental revisions or adaptations of his earlier plays and short stories. In *Orpheus Descending* (1957), a revision of Williams's first play for Broadway, *Battle of Angels* (1940), a modern-day Orpheus attempts to save a woman from her tyrannical husband and the deathlike existence of a small Southern town. Although a failure on Broadway, the drama was successful off-Broadway, and John Gassner deemed it "one of the most chaotic contemporary works of genius." *The Two-Character Play* (1967), later revised as *Out Cry* (1973), reflects the influence of Luigi Pirandello and Samuel Beckett in its portrayal of two siblings who are declared insane by their theatrical troupe and abandoned to perform a play which seems to reflect the desolation of their lives. The drama has been faulted for its minimalist dialogue and overt symbolism but is recognized by some critics as a sustained exercise in theater and has continued to interest directors and performers. Williams's final plays, *Clothes for a Summer Hotel: A Ghost Play* (1980) and *Something Cloudy, Something Clear* (1982), were commercial failures. Since his death, Williams's later plays have undergone substantial critical reevaluation, and several of these works are now regarded as important additions to Williams's canon.

Although known principally for his dramas, Williams also produced several volumes of fiction and poetry. Williams stated in *Where I Live: Selected Essays* (1978) that the "atmosphere of hysteria and violence" which informs his first published story, "The Vengeance of Nitocris" (1928), "sets the keynote for most of what has followed." Williams's short story collections, which, like his dramas, often center on disillusioned or frustrated characters, include *One Arm and Other Stories* (1948), *Hard Candy* (1954), *The Knightly Quest: A Novella and Four Short Stories* (1966), and *Eight Mortal Ladies Possessed* (1974). The posthumously published *Collected Stories* (1985) elicited warm praise from critics, who detected the influence of Magic Realism in Williams's writing and lauded those pieces which reveal themes and elements of his plays. Robert Phillips declared: "Had he written nothing else, Williams's stories would be sufficient evidence of his bid for fame." Williams also wrote two novels, *The Roman Spring of Mrs. Stone* (1950) and *Moise and the World of Reason* (1975). Williams's poetry, like all of his work, is of a personal and confessional nature. His verse is collected in *In the Winter of Cities* (1956) and *Androgyne, mon amour* (1977).

(See also *CLC*, Vols. 1, 2, 5, 7, 8, 11, 15, 19, 30, 39; *Contemporary Authors,* Vols. 5-8, rev. ed., Vol. 108 [obituary]; *Dictionary of Literary Biography,* Vol. 7; *Dictionary of Literary Biography Yearbook: 1983;* and *Dictionary of Literary Biography Documentary Series,* Vol. 4.)

GERALD WEALES

"I began writing verse at about the time of puberty," Tennessee Williams wrote in **"Preface to My Poems—Frivolous Version"** . . . , his introduction to **"The Summer Belvedere"** in *Five Young American Poets* (1944). . . . In ***Memoirs*** (1975), after a doggerel couplet on the implacability of time, Williams commented, "From the above you can see why I never made much of a mark for myself as a poet." . . . The characteristic note of self-deprecation . . . is the proper one for his career as a poet. . . . Williams has been writing poems which persist in sounding like literary exercises, enlivened occasionally by a sudden, startling line or an impressive central image, too often ambushed between conception and creation.

Williams's verse, like his fiction, has always been peripheral to his main work as an artist, his plays, and this is nowhere more obvious than in the making of ***Androgyne, Mon Amour.*** If Williams were not very much alive—about to burst on Broadway with ***Vieux Carré***—the new volume might be considered a posthumous collection. It has that look about it—as though someone had said, let's see if we can find enough uncollected early stuff to go with the recent Williams poems and maybe we'll come up with a book. In 1956, when Williams put together his first poetry collection, ***In the Winter of Cities,*** he used most of the poems from **"The Summer Belvedere."** Now, ***Androgyne, Mon Amour*** has picked up all the discards except the Blake-sounding **"Morgenlied,"** which someone may be saving for the next collection. Most of the **"Belvedere"** pieces in ***Androgyne*** are of minimal interest. **"Dark Arm, Hanging over the Edge of Infinity"** is an exception, less for itself than for what has happened to it. Williams, whose plays can testify to his fondness for revision, took the central section of **"Dark Arm,"** mixed it with lines from **"The Marvelous Children"** and fashioned the first poem in ***Cities,*** **"In Jack-O'-Lantern's Weather."** Now, the other two sections of **"Dark Arm"** are printed alone, a simple poem full of double entendre in which the speaker's black lover falls asleep in mid-manipulation but awakens to fill the heavens with "the sound of shattering glass!" (*vs.* Stanley's "colored lights"). The missing section never really belonged in the poem, an object lesson to precariously set stanzas and lines elsewhere in Williams's work.

Aside from the **"Belvedere"** borrowings, ***Androgyne*** picks up other poems from the 1940s, some of which—**"The Harp of**

Wales" and **"A Liturgy of Rofes"**—might better have been left [out]. . . . The poems, then, date from 1941 (**"Dark Arm"**) to 1976 [**"Androgyne, Mon Amour"**]; the new and the old lie side-by-side in the volume, with no recognizable chronological, thematic or stylistic connection. There are autobiographical elements in some of the poems—people and events familiar to anyone who has read ***Memoirs***. . . . Many of the later poems touch on or deal directly with the death of Frank Merlo, the man Williams seems to have loved most deeply, but even these lack a clear poetic voice. In **"His Manner of Returning,"** in which the poet, at one remove, imagines Merlo back in his Key West garden, the choice of the second person is presumably a device meant to heighten the tension between the trivial, the formal and the anguish and guilt they cover; instead it is a device that looks like a device, that pushes the reader away from what is, after all, one of the more effective poems in the volume.

In discussing voice in relation to a poem like **"His Manner,"** I may seem to be suggesting that I want to hear the poet's own voice, unencumbered by distance or art. That is not the case. It is simply that Williams, as a playwright, has a remarkable ear, an ability to create a character out of verbal nuance (think of Maggie's opening soliloquy in ***Cat on a Hot Tin Roof,*** Alexandra's swimming into consciousness in ***Sweet Bird of Youth***). No exact equivalent can be expected outside a dramatic monologue, but surely every successful poem cuts its own verbal shape on the air. Williams works a variety of genres—lyric, narrative, ruminative, doggerel ballad—but in none of them do the outlines hold. In **"The Lady with No One at All,"** for instance, he presents a woman who goes boating with an invisible lover, a sister to the early Williams heroines, but lines like, "It is an hour when desolation is most inclined to assail her," weigh the lady down with a tendency to overexplain and a languor that is not her own. The poetic voice is never sure whether it is simply observing, archly ironic or sentimentally sympathetic.

The poems have a heavy burden of infelicity . . . , an extra ration of favorite words (*apparition* wins hands down), a tongue-tripping dedication to adverbs fenced off by commas. They have a penchant for cliche ("unremembered, sheltering dreams of a mother") and significance through reiteration ("the magisterial tick of a watch, of many, so many watches"), as these two lines from **"Young Men Waking at Daybreak"** indicate. Williams can come up with an interesting image—the beggar as giver in **"A Mendicant Order,"** the outstretched hand offering, not asking—and then talk it to death. Some of the later poems—the "Fear is a monster . . ." verse from ***The Two-Character Play*** and **"Turning Out the Bedside Lamp"**—have the advantage of briefness (neither of them go astray tonally or thematically), but their subjects—that fear takes many forms, that death is both frightening and attractive—are so conventional that something more surprising than journeyman work is needed to give them new force.

Most of the Williams themes can be found in ***Androgyne, Mon Amour***—his familiar approaches to sex, love, time, death, loss—but only the hungriest Williams fan is likely to find sustenance in the volume. (pp. 32-4)

Gerald Weales, in a review of "Androgyne, Mon Amour," in The New Republic, *Vol. 176, No. 23, June 4, 1977, pp. 32-4.*

WILLIAM A. H. KINNUCAN

If ***Tennessee Williams' Letters to Donald Windham*** does nothing else, it vindicates the skeptic.

Following so comparatively close upon the heels of Williams' ***Memoirs,*** the publication of these letters by novelist Donald Windham somewhat naturally arouses the reader's suspicions: what are the collector's motives? Not surprisingly, Mr. Windham's introduction never directly addresses itself to this important question. Instead, it succeeds in opening up a veritable Pandora's Box of related problems, contradictions, and ambiguities.

The first three pages of the introduction consist largely of a character sketch of the fledgling dramatist Windham met upon arriving in New York in 1940. . . . To this sketch Windham adds the first of many troublingly unequivocal statements which are to appear throughout the rest of the collection: ". . . I gradually discovered that the emotions of the various characters [Williams] portrayed were always his own." In turning, at last, to the letters themselves, Windham writes: "To read them is to know why I liked him," thus striking the same self-congratulatory note which will later echo in such assertions as the one in which he claims to have given Truman Capote the title for *Breakfast at Tiffany's*.

Such relatively minor annoyances as these pale in the light of the fundamental contradiction which informs the greatest portion of the introduction and indeed Windham's editorial technique throughout the collection. On the one hand, Windham maintains that the letters of the 1940s, which comprise a good three-quarters of the collection, "are a running account of what (Williams) was doing and thinking, frequently day by day—a gold mine of biographical information." Unwittingly pitted against this assertion, on the other hand, are Windham's repeated and judgmental references to those characteristics of Williams which make him, in Windham's words, "an impossible documenter." Specifically, he often speaks of Williams' "transference." One supposes that Windham is referring to Williams' ability to project his own guilt, need for condemnation, and the like onto the people to whom he was writing or speaking. Though the concept is never clearly defined or illustrated, Williams, we are told, is simply not to be trusted. (p. 38)

The reader can, of course, transcend Windham's editorial presence in the ***Letters,*** though some considerable effort is required. The letters themselves provide us with only the sketchiest biographical outline, but they profit from having been written during those interesting years when the playwright's star was definitely on the rise. Furthermore, it matters very little how self-conscious a letterwriter Williams was: in contrast to the ***Memoirs,*** Williams' epistolary poses are breaths of spring air.

As with any collection of letters, there is a good deal of chaff here. Williams has never played the Pollyanna, and because the medium allows him to be at his graphic best, many of the letters provide a playground for the prurient. (Careful readers may want a Dictionary of Sub-Culture Lingo at hand.)

On the whole, however, the letters display a remarkable range of emotions and information. In addition to scenes of backstage drama with Williams' many producers, directors, associates and lovers, we catch glimpses of Gore Vidal, Truman Capote, Christopher Isherwood, Leonard Bernstein, and Greta Garbo. Because he was and is so mobile, the settings change with as much rapidity as do the descriptions of them bubble with vitality and charm. Best of all, perhaps, is the chatty humor with which he adorns a good bit of his correspondence. . . . Editorial motives aside, these letters often make entertaining and informative reading. (p. 39)

William A. H. Kinnucan, in a review of "Tennessee Williams' Letters to Donald Windham: 1940-1965," in The New Republic, *Vol. 178, No. 5, February 4, 1978, pp. 38-9.*

STEPHEN GRECCO

Considered by many to be America's finest living playwright, primarily because of the poetic quality of his dramatic work, Tennessee Williams has also carved out a minor reputation as a writer of fiction and poetry. ***Androgyne, Mon Amour,*** his second book of collected verse . . . , regrettably will add little to his stature as a poet. . . . (p. 467)

Given the explicit nature of his autobiography, one can only wonder if Williams has anything more to be candid about. The answer, happily, is No. Only a handful of the poems are actually new—[**"Androgyne, Mon Amour"**], for instance—and many go back to the 1940s. But true to his tragic heroes and heroines, Williams is very much the guilty Puritan, determined to seek in his own sensational way a kind of absolution from what he hopes will be a properly shocked albeit totally forgiving public.

The book's title, like the figure on the jacket of a nearly nude young man painted by the author, is presumably meant to scandalize, yet its similarity to *Hiroshima, Mon Amour,* a film that deals with another kind of "impossible love" and whose dominant image is also that of death, suggests that Williams may have had the Resnais/Duras work in mind while putting together his collection. That Williams equates the deviant with the catastrophic is certainly not original, nor is the idea that such transgressions must often be paid for in horrible ways. The old men of **"Old Men Go Mad at Night"** lose their sanity for reasons that will surprise no one familiar with the Williams canon; and Mathilda, an erstwhile prostitute in **"Cider Hill,"** dies trying to make a comeback. None of this, however, is really vintage material; but it just might sustain the devotee until the real thing comes along. (pp. 467-68)

Stephen Grecco, in a review of "Androgyne, Mon Amour," in World Literature Today, *Vol. 52, No. 3, Summer, 1978, pp. 467-68.*

SELDEN RODMAN

What do Dylan Thomas, Tennessee Williams, and Allen Ginsberg have in common? All three were (are) poets in the broad sense of the word. All three were figures of the avant garde, expressing in their different ways revolt against the "Victorian" morality and "capitalist" class structure still quite firmly dominating the Establishment at the times of their comings-of-age. All three were sexual misfits, two of them very openly flaunting their homosexuality and using it as a symbolic key to the "alienation" that their works focused on to the exclusion of all other values. Other artists in other times (perhaps *most* other artists) have been as neurotically incapable of adjusting to family life and society, but never until now had neurosis itself been accepted consciously as the burden of the work of art. Never before had the artist assumed (or pretended to assume) that his hang-ups provided the key to artistic excellence or the good life. (p. 1094)

[Williams' and Ginsberg's] successes seem to have enclosed them so deeply within their enlarged egos that they were quite content to turn out stereotypes. The stereotypes of Williams' later plays—deviates and studs, the castrated and the castrators—began to take over, his friend Windham thinks [as he states in ***Tennessee Williams' Letters to Donald Windham***], around 1948, when the dramatist stopped writing about sympathetic characters caught in inescapable situations and yielded to self-dramatization. "It is because he cannot face his own actions that he denounces lying and mendacity in others. He has to blame the world (as Brick does in ***Cat***) and present it as a place where you cannot live without money (as Maggie does) in order to cancel his guilt." The following year, when, as the letters show, Williams was in the process of abandoning his friends to luxuriate in his fame, the playwright put it this way: "Ordinarily my ratio of concerns is something like this: 50 per cent work and worry over work, 35 per cent the perpetual struggle against lunacy . . . 15 per cent a very true and very tender love for lover and friends." That last figure, he goes on to say, has now dropped to 1 per cent. Windham, the only lifelong friend Williams had, and once his "conscience," is about to be asked to withdraw his name from a play they wrote together and accept a lower share of the royalties.

From then on, Williams writes Windham only to explain the things he intends to do for him (and never does). Which is not to say that even these morally bankrupt letters are devoid of the gaiety, wit, and occasional brilliant self-analysis that gave the earlier letters their charm. Playwriting, unlike poetry, is a semi-communal art. Many hands are involved, craftsmanship develops through the rehearsals and performances, compromise shapes the final product. If Williams' plays themselves are never tragedies, that is because there are no heroes with whose betrayal or fall from grace one can identify; but in the ***Letters*** there *is* such an undoing, and Donald Windham has had the insight to trace it with compassion all the way. (p. 1095)

Selden Rodman, "Three Neurotics," in National Review, *New York, Vol. XXX, No. 35, September 1, 1978, pp. 1094-95.*

JACK SULLIVAN

[In ***Where I Live: Selected Essays,*** it] scarcely matters that **"A Summer of Discovery"** tells us little about ***Night of the Iguana,*** which it purports to introduce. What this 1961 reminiscence of a 1940 "aborted flirtation with the dark angel" during a despairingly drunken summer in Mexico does tell us about is an impulse toward life that glows most luminously during "desperate intervals." In that sense, it could serve as an introduction to almost any Williams play.

Most of the other essays in this collection are similarly loose-jointed. The foreword to ***Sweet Bird of Youth,*** for example, could actually serve as (among several other things) a fascinating foreword to his early horror fiction for *Weird Tales* magazine: As Williams sees it, the "atmosphere of hysteria and violence" in these youthful shockers "sets the keynote for most of what has followed."

Williams is temperamentally impatient with the essay form . . . , and the weaker essays have a listless abstractness that will jar anyone used to his customary intensity. But the better ones—such as his famous **"On a Streetcar Named Success"**; the wonderfully jaded 1972 description of obnoxious interviewers; and the moving tributes to Carson McCullers, William Inge, and Tallulah Bankhead—are in Williams's authentic voice. Especially high-powered is his account of the trauma of sudden success, of being "snatched out of virtual oblivion" and thrust into an expensive Manhattan hotel where his dinner was rolled into his room "like a corpse." He is at his best when simple and anecdotal—the "unregenerate romanticist," as he calls himself, unregenerately obsessive about his past.

Jack Sullivan, in a review of "Where I Live: Selected Essays," in Saturday Review, *Vol. 5, No. 30, December, 1978, p. 54.*

JACOB H. ADLER

Williams *aficionados* will have read most of [the pieces in ***Where I Live: Selected Essays***] before, but it is good to have them all in one place, and indeed to have a chance to reread them and to make comparisons. The idea of what it is to be a "romantic," for example, occurs from early (the first essay in the volume is from 1944) to late (the last is from 1978). Likewise, Williams has a style, and the style remains much the same through the years. It can be succinct and precise: "... the theater, which is the charlatan of the arts, is paradoxically the one in which the charlatan is most easily detected." ... It can also ramble, and Williams can be aware that it rambles: "This is a long excursion from a small theme into a large one which I did not intend to make, so let me go back to what I was saying before." ... Some of it is sentimental, but much of it is remarkably pointed and true.

Autobiographical fragments occur frequently, and they are especially interesting in the light of Williams' actual ***Memoirs.*** In one essay, for example, first printed in 1952, Williams describes his adolescence in St. Louis just as it is presented in ***The Glass Menagerie***: the dismal apartment in the dismal inner city, the poverty, the feeling of displacement not only from moving out of the rural Deep South to a big city but also from moving out of middle-class comfort into something approaching squalor. Yet the ***Memoirs*** make it clear, with pictures to demonstrate, that there were times when the family lived in nice houses in nice neighborhoods—and even, on occasion, had servants. Like ***The Glass Menagerie,*** too, one would know from the autobiographical fragments that Williams had a sister, but never that he had a younger brother. And there are interesting contradictions. . . . [One passage] suggests that writing ***Camino Real*** was a euphoric experience. Yet when ***Camino Real*** was revived, Williams wrote (1960): "I wrote this play in a time of desolation: I thought, as I'd thought often before and have often thought since, that my good work was done. . . . And so it was written to combat or to purify a despair that only another writer is likely to understand fully." . . . Memories can be contradictory. (pp. 96-7)

There are other occasional inconsistencies, of which I will mention only one. In speaking about violence in the Foreword to ***Sweet Bird of Youth,*** Williams said that he had produced only five plays which were not violent, and included ***Summer and Smoke*** among the five. Yet ***Summer and Smoke*** involves a murder, and it is even onstage, as the violence in ***Sweet Bird*** and some of the other plays is not.

But probably the major interest in going through [***Where I Live: Selected Essays***] is in comparing Williams' remarks with actual plays. For example: "[If] asked about a theme, I . . . say, 'it is a play about life' . . . You can . . . extend that . . . and say it is a tragedy of incomprehension. That also means life. Or you can say it is a tragedy of Puritanism. That is life in America." . . . This was published in 1948, long before some of the plays to which it so interestingly applies were written. Incomprehension is a major element in ***Menagerie*** and ***Streetcar,*** of course. But one thinks also, for example, of the memorable scene in ***Cat on a Hot Tin Roof*** between Brick and his father, in which the incomprehension is partially dissipated, or of the similarly dissipated incomprehension between Hannah and Shannon in ***Night of the Iguana.*** And given a reasonably broad definition, Puritanism, too, can be found in ***Cat*** and ***Iguana,*** and, indeed, just about every play.

Then there are the remarks about Williams' depiction of women, such as: ". . . I would say that frustrated is almost exactly what the women I write about are not. What was frustrated about Amanda Wingfield? Circumstances, yes! But spirit? . . . Was Blanche . . . frustrated? About as frustrated as a beast of the jungle! And Alma Winemiller? What is frustrated about loving with such white-hot intensity that it alters the whole direction of your life?" . . . One may quarrel here with Williams' apparent definitions of both *frustration* and *love* (does being a fighter mean one is not frustrated? Does accepting an assignation mean one is in love?), but beyond this one may think of the bitter frustration and its happy—and loving—conclusion for Serafina in ***The Rose Tattoo***; of Maggie's battle to end frustration in ***Cat***; of Hannah's virginal, impoverished, but unfrustrated state in ***Iguana.***

Or one more, from endless examples: "I prefer a play to be not a noose but a net with fairly wide meshes. So many of its instances of revelation are wayward flashes, not part of the plan of an author but struck accidentally off." . . . Williams' plays are obviously not given to strong unified construction, and this statement at a minimum shows recognition of the fact, and may or may not help explain it. (He frequently assumes, as he does here, that what is true for him is true for other writers—a quite unsafe assumption.) There are scenes one remembers from all the best of his plays which are no necessary part of any causal sequence but which are indeed instances of revelation, Blanche with the young boy, for example. And this statement of Williams may even help explain his attitude toward directorial changes, a matter which he discusses in detail in his essay, **"Author and Director: a Delicate Situation"** (1957).

Unfortunately, this collection of essays lacks an index, but on the whole, in spite of some moments of mistaken memory, contradiction, false romanticism, and self-pity, the essays are revealing, interesting, insightful. (pp. 97-9)

Jacob H. Adler, "New Books on Southern Playwrights," in The Southern Literary Journal, *Vol. XII, No. 1, Fall, 1979, pp. 96-102.*

JEFFREY WALKER

[Williams's four collections of short stories] reveal worlds very similar to those of Capote and O'Connor. His characters resemble those in his plays. In fact, many of the stories were early versions of the ideas he later used in works for the stage: **"Portrait of a Girl in Glass"** for ***The Glass Menagerie; Three Players of a Summer Game*** for ***Cat on a Hot Tin Roof;*** **"Man Bring This Up Road"** for ***The Milk Train Doesn't Stop Here Anymore;*** and **"The Night of the Iguana"** for the play of the same name. In all of his work, Williams portrays both adolescents and adults who are disillusioned and frustrated. They are men and women who are different, and because of their eccentricities have a need to see the world clearly. They succeed, but end up recognizing the horror that is present. As characters lost in time, they tend not to belong to their own world or to any other. Like his Southern contemporaries, Williams's stories become portraits of a generation that views itself as displaced.

One Arm and Other Stories (1948) is Williams's first collection. **"Portrait of a Girl in Glass"** exemplifies the people in his fictional world. Laura is a girl who "made no positive motion toward the world but stood at the edge of the water so to speak, with feet that anticipated too much cold to move." She needs to be "shoved . . . roughly forward" to overcome her fear of the world. As the story comes to a climax, she never does. Similar tales of meandering in and out of life make up the major stories in ***One Arm.*** In **"The Field of Blue Children,"** two loners briefly meet, love, and drift away from each other into their own world; in [**"One Arm"**], a young man finds himself penned "in a corner and only waiting for death"; in **"The Malediction,"** Lucio finds a cat, Nitchevo, wounded and dying. He sees in the cat's eyes a reflection of his own life: "They were full to the amber brims with all the secrets and sorrows the world can answer our ceaseless questioning with loneliness—yes. Hunger. Bewilderment. Pain. They wanted no more."

In ***Hard Candy: A Book of Stories*** (1954), Williams's second collection, similar themes and techniques appear. Throughout, the individual's confrontation with a truth too painful to bear is the highlight of the action. In ***Three Players of a Summer Game,*** Brick Pollitt, former athlete and current alcoholic, is driven by his wife Margaret to a condition that turns him into a wreck of a man. Margaret controls Brick: "It was as though she had her lips fastened to some invisible wound in his body through which drained out of him and flowed into her the assurance and vitality that he had owned before marriage." By the end of the story, Brick has given in to Margaret's hammerlock on his life and is "no longer a human, but a babbling and goggling wreck." He has become her "boy" and she his conqueror. Other stories reveal the same emphasis on the unlived life that is not worth living. In **"The Vine," "The Important Thing," "The Resemblance Between a Violin Case and a Coffin,"** and **"The Mattress by the Tomato Patch,"** Williams's protagonists are all afflicted by their loss of innocence and inability to face reality.

By the time his third collection, ***The Knightly Quest: A Novella and Four Short Stories*** (1961), was published, Williams's craft had diminished. His best fiction by this time had already been written, his best plays already produced. ***The Knightly Quest,*** the novella, is a strange story of Gewinner Pearce, who returns home after years of travel to discover that great changes have taken place. The Project, a top-secret government plan, obsesses the town, and the Laughing-Boy Drive-In has been built directly across from the Pearce family mansion, having been given a ninety-nine-year lease by Gewinner's brother. The story is almost farcical as it follows the antics of Gewinner and the townspeople responding to these changes. Gewinner, for instance, is launched into space on a knightly quest, a part of the story made unbelievable by Williams's treatment of the entire incident. The other stories are more vintage Williams as they explore earlier themes.

It is clear that Williams's reputation as a major American literary figure rests in his dramatic achievements. Yet the early stories are important, too, especially as the best of them mirror the themes of his most remarkable plays, for they establish his place in the Southern renaissance. (pp. 24-5)

Jeffrey Walker, "1945-1956: Post-World War II Manners and Mores," in The American Short Story: A Critical History, 1945-1980, *edited by Gordon Weaver, Twayne Publishers, 1983, pp. 1-34.*

RUBY COHN

Sex, South, and violence brought Tennessee Williams to a Broadway which then allowed him no deviations. From ***A Streetcar Named Desire*** (1947) set in New Orleans to ***Sweet Bird of Youth*** (1959) set in Florida, Williams usually wrote true to type. Even though ***The Night of the Iguana*** (1961) garnered his fourth (and final) New York Drama Critics Circle Award, Williams was edged out for the Pulitzer Prize, a more responsive barometer to current climate. ***Night*** started his descent from popularity, as his Lord Byron had prophesied in ***Camino Real*** (1953); "There is a passion for declivity in this world!" (p. 336)

In the 1960s Williams began to stray from the triad that endeared him to Broadway. Although many of his characters continue to be Southerners, his settings are not necessarily in the South. Although sex continues to be frankly discussed and dramatized, it often goes unconsummated. Violence is muted or even absent; the explosive scenes of his earlier plays simmer down to an atmosphere of resignation. Never one to rest on his laurels—or magnolia—Williams during the 1960s and 1970s moves into new territories, fashions new kinds of characters, experiments with new forms. . . . Opposing most viewpoints in print, I think that three major Williams plays date from the last decade of his life; perhaps he sometimes worked simultaneously on ***The Two-Character Play, Vieux Carré,*** and ***Clothes for a Summer Hotel,*** which were produced in that order.

The final version of ***The Two-Character Play*** was published in 1976, and two earlier versions were published in 1969 and 1973. Other, unpublished revisions may exist among Williams's scattered papers, but the three printed versions show a movement toward economy of language within an increasingly ambiguous and inclusive context.

From the first, ***The Two-Character Play*** is cast in the old baroque form of a play within the play—Williams's only venture in that form. The play within Williams's play is called "The Two-Character Play," and it contains major elements of Williams's drama when he was Broadway's golden boy. It is set in a small town in the American South. Its two characters, brother and sister, Felice and Clare Devoto, are perhaps incestuous lovers. Violence accounts for the deaths of the siblings' parents; their father, having been threatened by their mother with commitment to an insane asylum, has shot first her and then himself. The siblings are not only orphaned, but also destitute because suicide voids collection of life insurance. And the siblings are not only destitute, but also ostracized by the townspeople. . . . In this play within the play, with its family resemblance to earlier Williams plays, brother and sister are so introverted and fearful that they do not dare to leave their Victorian home, which is bordered by sunflowers as high as the house. During the course of the play within the play, the two characters dramatize their isolation as a fugitive kind—to use an old Williams phrase—or as unnatural creatures—to use the phrase of this play. Fantasy is their heritage—in the form of iridescent soap bubbles—and fantasy may be their fate—if they can impose an ending on this play written by Felice. At the same time, violence is their heritage, and violence may be their fate, for their father's revolver is within their grasp.

Violence, fantasy, sex, South mark the Williams landscape, and "The Two-Character Play" is typical Williams also in that autobiography is transmuted to fiction. Like Williams, who has often been criticized for drawing his plays from his life, Felice Devoto draws upon *his* life to write his "Two-Character

Play.'' It is as though Williams has synopsized critical clichés about his plays and recast them in the form of a short play. Moreover, in each successive version, the plot of the inner play grows more compact. (pp. 336-37)

Affected by Pirandello and Beckett, Williams embedded his typical Williams play in an absurdist frame, so that real and role overlap increasingly. Unlike the inner play [''The Two-Character Play''], the frame play [***The Two-Character Play***] is set in a theater in an unspecified country, on a cold evening as opposed to the sunny afternoon of the inner play. Again there are two characters, brother and sister, Felice and Clare, actors in a repertory company on tour. When the frame play opens, Felice . . . is penning—to be precise, penciling—a monologue opposing fear to its near homonym fire. Clare interrupts him, unsteady from sleep or drugs. Expecting a press conference, she is surprised and disappointed to find only her actor/playwright/brother. She recognizes the partial set for ''The Two-Character Play,'' and she sulks because that is not on their program. Felice then shows her a cablegram from the rest of their company. Declaring that the two are insane, the company has left for home. The abandoned siblings have no choice but to play ''The Two-Character Play,'' if they are to play at all. (p. 338)

Occasionally, they improvise, or call for a line, or interrupt the text to comment on their actual situation. . . . When Felice leaves the stage for a moment, Clare ruminates that she knew ''The Two-Character Play'' would be her brother's last work. She briefly recalls their glorious moments of touring, and Felice returns to announce that they are locked into this foreign theater. They are ''confined''—the word they hesitated to use in the play within the play. Shivering but fearless, they return to ''The Two-Character Play.'' They run swiftly through key scenes, but a new action starts when Clare points the revolver at Felice. We cannot tell (as earlier, at less climactic moments) whether they are in or out of ''The Two-Character Play'' as she drops the gun, unable to shoot. It is the turn of Felice, but he too fails to shoot. He drops the revolver, and each of them raises hands toward the other. ''As they slowly embrace, there is total dark in which The Curtain Falls.'' An embrace is, of course, a traditional ending, but *their* embrace is a way of facing a slow death—the unalterable circumstance of absurdist drama.

As early as ***Streetcar*** Blanche says to Mitch: ''And sometimes—there's God—so quickly.'' But the remark is not developed, and not until ***Suddenly Last Summer*** (1957) does Williams blend his own extremist characters into a metaphysical quest—in the same decade that Adamov, Beckett, and Ionesco were creating the theater of the absurd. Williams evidently read or saw them late, and Beckett alone seems to have moved him. It is Beckett's bleak hue that shades the endgame atmosphere of Williams's frame play. It is Beckett's grim, funny gamesmanship that Williams shares in ***The Two-Character Play,*** titled ***Out Cry*** in its second published version. In a fragmented world where none of the old rules hold, both playwrights convey that all we can do is act roles which will screen for a time our existential loneliness. So all of us are locked into theater—for the minimal warmth of dialogue. And the play we play is decided by the language we speak on the set where we are thrust—in Williams's case, lyrical English in a changing South. With a new self-consciousness about his art in a wider context, Williams worked for a decade at what may be his masterpiece, the 1976 ***Two-Character Play.***

While putting the finishing touches to ***The Two-Character Play,*** Williams began a very different unappreciated play, ***Vieux Carré.*** First glance shows that not only the *carré* is *vieux*. Like ***Streetcar, Vieux Carré*** is set in the old French Quarter of New Orleans—722 Toulouse Street, to be specific. As in ***Glass Menagerie,*** one of the characters is a writer through whose memory the play's action is filtered. Like ***The Two-Character Play, Vieux Carré*** is the product of drastic revision, but rather than discontinuous tinkering through a decade, this revision expands a one-acter written nearly forty years earlier—the 1939 ***Lady of Larkspur Lotion.***

The early title is a mocking reference to a forty-year-old whore who uses Larkspur Lotion, ''a common treatment for body vermin.'' In a boardinghouse on the Vieux Carré, the ''Lady'' inspires contrasting attitudes in the other two characters—the scorn of the hard-nosed landlady Mrs. Wire, and the compassion of the nameless Writer, who introduces himself as Mr. Chekhov. In ***Vieux Carré,*** Williams retains the place and time of the main action—the Vieux Carré in 1938-1939, when one could buy ''[m]eals for a quarter in the Quarter.'' He develops the money-hungry landlady, rejuvenates the Writer, and totally transforms the Lady into a young fashion designer of good education with ''some—blood thing'' draining her life away. To these characters, Williams adds a stripshow barker who is the fashion designer's lover, a tubercular homosexual painter, two starving ladies of good family, an old black maid, and a clarinet player. In spite of the relatively large cast, the landlady realizes: ''There's so much loneliness in this house that you can hear it.''

Besides loneliness, ***Vieux Carré*** dramatizes crises in the lives of this group of people. The rapacious landlady dementedly confuses the young Writer with her long-lost son, and the two old ladies exist on pickings from garbage cans. The tubercular painter is carried to the state hospital to die, and the fashion designer learns that her death is near, whereupon her lover deserts her. The Writer leaves, joining the clarinet player, who has never been admitted to the boardinghouse on the Vieux Carré. The boardinghouse tenants were given life through the Writer's memory, but the play closes: ''They go when you go. . . . This house is empty now.''

When the house is full, we witness the disintegration of its inhabitants. Less insistently than Tom of ***Glass Menagerie*** (1944), this Writer also introduces us to his neighbors and then slips into his own play as an involved character. In 1944 the narrator/character technique was relatively new, filtered through Thornton Wilder's 1938 Stage Manager and Williams's course with Erwin Piscator in 1940. By 1977-1978, when Williams wrote ***Vieux Carré,*** the technique was as well-worn as some of the typical Williams characters, but it is therefore right for a play set in New Orleans of 1938-1939—racist, sexist, and unselfconscious in its seediness.

In the 1939 ***Lady of Larkspur Lotion,*** the Writer facetiously gave his name as Mr. Chekhov, but it was not until the late 1960s (in ***Confessional***) that Williams was attracted to the Russian dramatist's forte—the group protagonist. The attraction returns in ***Vieux Carré,*** and although Williams falls short of Chekhov's mastery, he nevertheless weaves lives skillfully into a temporary pattern dissolved by the Writer's departure. Like *The Seagull,* too, ***Vieux Carré*** ascribes to artists privileged threads in this pattern. . . . By play's end, death will claim the old painter and the young fashion designer in the Vieux Carré, but into the unknown West go the young Writer and the clarinet player, whose name is Sky. Against an old Williams background, the playwright newly dramatizes the fate of art. Though some artists may die on Vieux Carré, art lives on in other places and other media. (pp. 338-41)

In sharp contrast, the setting for Williams's last major play is threatened by fire which destroyed an actual insane asylum in 1947. It is one of several reasons that Williams subtitles ***Clothes for a Summer Hotel*** "a ghost play." The main reason is that Williams dramatizes historical characters who are dead—ghosts. Williams himself cites "chronological licenses" as the ground of ghostliness. This is the first time that he not only bases a full-length play on actual people, but houses them in an imaginative structure where they can at once live through and look back on their lives. . . .

Despite "chronological licenses," the beginning and end of ***Clothes*** are centered on Scott Fitzgerald's visit to his wife, Zelda, in her hilltop asylum. Scott has been summoned from Hollywood by Zelda's doctor because of a marked improvement in her condition. Boarding a plane at once, Scott is dressed in summer clothes inadequate for the windy North Carolina hill. As husband and wife peep at each other before meeting, they are appalled at what they see: the once handsome Scott is gray and bloated; the once lovely Zelda is fat and bedraggled. A millionaire friend, Gerald Murphy, joins the celebrated writer, speaking partly in the grim present and partly in their bright past, and introducing the subject of Scott's repression of Zelda's writing. When husband and wife meet, wind howling, Williams plays the present against the past. (p. 341)

The scene changes to 1926, with Scott so absorbed in his writing that he pays scant attention to Zelda. They quarrel about Scott's prettiness and Zelda's ambition: "What about *my* work?" Left to be merely "a dreamy young Southern lady," Zelda openly takes a French lover, Edouard. A handsome, efficient, and traditional French lover, Edouard (played by the same actor as the Intern) is dismayed by the imprudence and intensity of Zelda's passion. He disappoints her when he admits that he has grown old, "weighted down with honors." He is horrified when she tells him at a Murphy Riviera party that she swallowed a bottle of sleeping pills when he left her. . . . The stage action zigzags between Scott's impatience with Zelda's doctors and Hemingway's disruptive presence at the 1926 party. Hemingway refuses to admit his attraction to the feminine loveliness of Scott; Hemingway knows that he will betray his friends, especially Scott, when he comes to write *A Moveable Feast*. Scott mulls over the loneliness of all three writers in Williams's play—Hemingway, Fitzgerald, and Zelda.

The last scene returns to Zelda in Highland Hospital. The Intern/Edouard urges her to say goodbye to her husband, who shivers in his summer clothes. Zelda speaks a long monologue about her unsatisfied creativity, her romantic fantasies, her fearlessness at the prospect of death. . . . As she enters the iron gates of the asylum, Zelda flings a last defiant challenge at the husband who has drained her life for his art: *"I can't be your book anymore! Write yourself a new book!"* (pp. 341-42)

It is uncertain whether ***Clothes for a Summer Hotel*** was inspired by Williams's reading of Zelda Fitzgerald's 1932 novel, *Save Me the Waltz,* or Hemingway's 1964 *A Moveable Feast,* or Nancy Milford's 1970 biography, *Zelda,* or some quite different association. It *is* certain that Williams depended on these works for his material—especially the Milford biography. Broadway reviewers sneered at this literary background—"Almost everything of interest and value in the play is contained in one of those books, and is better in its original form," wrote John Simon. The original forms, however, are not theater, and Williams created theater, marking theme and characters as distinctively his own.

As in many other Williams plays, the protagonist of ***Clothes*** is a suffering Southern lady, but this lady is named Zelda Fitzgerald, who died in a fire in her insane asylum. Williams makes ominous use of his setting—its black gates, its howling winds, and intermittent lights resembling flames. He manipulates time to reflect Zelda's hallucinations. He portrays all three writers sympathetically, although they were ruthless to one another.

Williams incorporates Hemingway's pathetic Fitzgerald from *A Moveable Feast,* but his Scott is both loving and repressive, a generous man but a selfish artist. Williams adheres closely to Zelda's life as painstakingly researched by Milford, but he creates a more dramatic portrait of a gifted woman who rebels against the behavior code of a Southern lady. Zelda actually charged that there was a homosexual attraction between her husband and Hemingway, which Williams exploits to dramatize the betrayal of their friendship. Perhaps Williams's most subtle invention was to blend Zelda's French lover into an Intern in the asylum—a living reminder of her failed rebellion and an emotional outlet for her fantasies. In this late play, Williams deftly creates extreme but sympathetic characters who are ghosts of our culture.

In theme ***Clothes*** asks with other late Williams plays: what is the price of artistic creation? The answer is human betrayal. Hemingway betrays friendship, Zelda betrays marriage, and Scott betrays his own humane impulses. Not only is marriage a "monumental error," but so also are friendship and other durable relations—among artists. Obsession with creation drives some artists to drink, some to drugs, and others to insanity.

All three late Williams plays probe the cost of creation. In ***The Two-Character Play,*** brother and sister are abandoned, but they support each other in continued play within a meaningless cosmos. Art survives beyond ***Vieux Carré,*** even if its artists die. And ***Clothes for a Summer Hotel*** resurrects three celebrated American writers as ghosts who can look back on lives misspent for art, without which there would be no art. The famous novelists are not triumphant; they rarely justify themselves; they are little more than instruments to fill demanding blank pages. Having fulfilled the same demand from his adolescence on, Williams dramatized it in these three strikingly dissimilar late works for which he garnered no prizes and little praise. But like the play within the play of ***The Two-Character Play,*** Williams's artistry has no ending. (pp. 342-43)

Ruby Cohn, "Late Tennessee Williams," in Modern Drama, *Vol. XXVII, No. 3, September, 1984, pp. 336-44.*

ALLEAN HALE

In the year of the ***Iguana,*** 1962, Tennessee Williams was enshrined on the cover of *Time* as "barring the aged Sean O'Casey, the greatest living playwright. . . ." He had won two Pulitzer prizes, four New York Critics Circle awards, had had seventeen New York openings in sixteen years. Yet by 1969, after ***In the Bar of a Tokyo Hotel,*** *Time* had him "on the sickbed of his talent" while Stefan Kanfer . . . dispatched him as having no talent, having suffered "infantile regression," being a burned-out cinder.

With the success of ***Small Craft Warnings*** ten years later, *Time* had to dust off its old story and declare with no reservations that Tennessee Williams was "the greatest living playwright in the western world." It was as if he had been away during that decade, or dead, although occasionally phrases like "aging master" and "living legend" floated back from exotic ports. . . . The author said from Singapore that he was fighting to recover from a mental breakdown. Depression over a string of failures, the loss of his companion of fourteen years, his bouts with drugs and drink had led to a hospitalization he referred to as "the loony bin" and to cruising China seas. The real man was on a trip through *Dragon Country,* "the country of pain." . . . [***Dragon Country,*** a book of plays] published during this period, should have been a clue that the author was alive, working, and sane. (pp. 201-02)

Williams' new direction was outward bound. The settings were existential, and he seemed to be going metaphysical, experimental—and oriental.

A hint of Japanese first shows in ***The Night of the Iguana,*** which Williams wrote in 1959. The stage directions seem peculiar for a New England spinster in a play laid in Mexico. . . . [Hannah] "stands motionless as a painted figure . . . a gold-lacquered Japanese fan . . . open in one hand. . . . Her attitude has the style of a Kabuki dancer's pose." In classic Japanese theater the dancer strikes such a pose to illustrate a moment of extreme tension, and the word *hana* (flower) is a term for the spiritual effect of Noh drama, "Hannah," referred to as a "female standing-up Buddha," may also suggest *Hannya,* the female ghost-mask of a Noh play; Williams' Hannah is holy ghost whose mission is to drive out Shannon's demon before it drives him over the cliff. (p. 202)

The Milk Train Doesn't Stop Here Any More, written in 1962, was a very occidental title which again hid oriental mysticism. The play, laid in Italy, calls for folding screens handled by stage assistants who function "in a way that's between the Kabuki Theatre of Japan and the chorus of Greek theatre." They should be dressed in black, Williams adds, to represent invisibility—although now and then they have short lines that serve as cues to the principal performers, and "they sometimes take a balletic part in the action." The principal, Flora Goforth, wears a Kabuki wig and her guest wears samurai robe and sword.

Such orientalisms went unnoticed as the public, coming to see a play about "one of the theater's great all-time bitches" and her male prostitute, as *Time* described it, was shocked to find it was about dying. The playwright called it an allegory; pressed for an explanation of his new religious bent, he brought out a copy of the *Bhagavad-Gita* and said that a trip to the Orient had left him deeply impressed with eastern philosophy. But the play died and Williams' next, ***Slapstick Tragedy,*** a double-bill produced off Broadway in 1966, ran only seven performances. Its first half, ***The Mutilated,*** was about death *and* resurrection. Its second, ***The Gnädiges Fräulein,*** was so incomprehensible that few reviewed it. . . . ***The Two-Character Play*** was introduced in London in 1967 and failed. British reviewers could make no sense of it, saying it would take a psychoanalyst to interpret the enigma. It was about insanity and ended with one character staring into a gun. In Williams' last long play, ***In the Bar of a Tokyo Hotel,*** the protagonist, tortured to madness, does die on stage.

The critics smelled death easily enough: ***Tokyo Hotel*** was, to summarize the quotes: more deserving of a coroner's report than a review—an open letter announcing esthetic impotence . . . Not a play but a blueprint, a charade, a series of monologues in a bar between a drunk and a nymphomaniac. Its prevailing mood was torpor, the characters weren't real, Williams had lost his celebrated ability to construct scenes. It was tasteless, banal, confusing, incomplete—and none of the characters finished their sentences!

While critics were calling him disoriented, the author fled to the Orient. Later he remarked with almost saintly mildness that the critics hadn't taken the trouble to understand ***Tokyo Hotel.*** He might have said that before condemning the play they should at least have been seated in the right theater—a Noh theater, as I believe he had tried to tell them in the title. Williams customarily used a simple form of free association or word play which works much as in the game of charades: "Tokyo" implies "Japanese," "hotel" can also be "house"; in this instance not a guest house but a playhouse, a theater. He had used "hotel" as "house of life" or "house of death" in previous ***Dragon Country*** plays (in ***Two-Character Play*** as a metaphor for life, death *and* the theater). (pp. 203-04)

A distinctive feature of the open-stage Noh playhouse is that it resembles the gateway to a shrine, the *Torii* of Japanese prints: two upright posts topped by crosspieces, one straight, one concave. (Noh originated as religious ritual performed before a temple.) "In the bar" was the phrase critics pounced on, making quick analogies to alcoholism; but a bar can also be a gate and "in the bar of a Tokyo hotel" could translate simply "inside a Japanese playhouse." "Bar" also evokes "crossing the bar" and combined with hotel-as-house-of-death becomes *At the Gate of the House of Death,* a play in a very different mood. (p. 204)

Even before the sixties Williams had been casting about for a new medium. He was through with violence, with frustrated fluttery ladies, through with Broadway. Before ***Iguana*** he'd remarked that "nobody writes my kind of play any more." In 1956 Beckett's *Waiting for Godot* was something absolutely new on the American scene. . . . Williams, criticized for melodramatic, talky, overcrowded plays, saw that the new drama was spare, abstract, with few actors on an empty stage. Pinter and Beckett explored silence. Ionesco and Genet were using improvisation, pantomime, clowns, the surreal, to say that life was absurd. All were influenced by Antonin Artaud's revolutionary manifesto, *The Theater and Its Double* . . . , which urged an end to theater as entertainment, a return to its spiritual origins: to magic, to language as incantation, to metaphysical truth. (pp. 204-05)

Whatever path would have led Williams to Noh, it had elements that suited his talents: the central monologue, the lyric language, the imagery, the fantasy, the theatrical effects. It resembled Greek theater, on which he had always drawn. It avoided his weakness, plot construction, since it was virtually plotless. Its minimal set and cast suited the way theater was moving. Its somberness suited his depressive mood. Noh presents some universalized human passion at a moment of crisis and suggests transcendence to a balanced existence; this aspect especialy applied to Williams, who in the sixties was wrestling with a crisis both artistic and emotional. Noh is centered on an idea, not a personality. Its characters are abstractions of that idea; its symbols, costumes, even its prescribed structure subtly reinforce it. To a westerner, watching a Noh play is like listening to a three-hour oratorio without knowing its score. Noh combines music, narrative, and dance movement in a form much like our opera or ballet but is the opposite of our drama.

Non-representational, anti-real, its action outside of the climactic dance is confined to symbolic gestures: a pose, the handling of a fan. . . . Noh is mood. Evocative, dreamlike—also repetitive, cryptic and static, words often applied to Williams' ***Dragon Country*** plays. (pp. 205-06)

[Williams' next work] was called ***The Two-Character Play.*** Noh plays are specifically two-character plays, although the two may have assistants. The primary character, the *shite,* is a supernatural being who always wears a mask. The secondary, the *waki,* is real, unmasked and is often a priest or pilgrim journeying to some famous shrine where a mystery will be revealed. Here the pilgrim meets the *shite* who is disguised as an ordinary person—a fisherman, or a beautiful lady—but who later reappears in his true form—a legendary warrior, a serpent. So Hannah with her spirit lamp is Shannon's guiding spirit masked as a New England spinster; Chris Flanders is the Angel of Death masked as a poet. The idea of masking reappears in the possibility that the two characters in [***I Can't Imagine Tomorrow***] and ***Tokyo Hotel*** may be one sex, male masked as female. This could be given homosexual meaning, but it also fits the Noh convention of males playing all roles. (pp. 206-07)

Two-Character Play was an experiment in staging metaphysics. The London production effectively used mirrors to enhance the illusion/reality theme as the "real" play shifts to the play-within-a-play. A brother and sister, two actors deserted by their troupe, are condemned to act out their "Two-Character Play" in a locked theater which has become their prison. Mirror images of each other and of their parents, they are also prisoners of the childhood trauma that conditioned them when Father shot Mother then killed himself. Like Noh pilgrims they return to the significant scene to find out: must they re-enact the crime? Their image is a monstrous sunflower, a misfit in the conventional garden as they are misfits in their world (and as Williams saw himself and his sister—the artist and the insane—as "freaks"). Here Williams simply transplanted the symbolic flower of his own childhood (on the Sunflower River in Mississippi) to oriental soil. In Japan the chrysanthemum, also called sunflower, represents immortality and is considered sacred. Allusion is piled on allusion to undergird the meaning of a play which on the surface seems another ***Glass Menagerie,*** forty years after.

In the Bar of a Tokyo Hotel, Williams' last long play of the sixties, is the most oriental in its deviousness because it appears to be the most straight. Williams later said he wrote ***Tokyo Hotel*** while on drugs. This may help explain the hallucinatory quality of this split-personality play. It can be decoded as Freud might have unraveled a dream for it contains all the disguises of dreamwork: condensation, puns, free association, substitution of opposite meanings (religion is disguised as obscenity). Williams was by nature an intuitive writer but to maintain two consistent allegories, one Christian, one oriental, under the surface of a third realistic play is a tour de force.

The opening action clues "This is a Noh play" when the barman raises a metal shaker to signal the start of the scene, recalling the shoulder drum raised by the Noh drummer who sets the play's rhythm. The barman here is cleverly condensed into orchestra, chorus and stage assistant as well; he pointedly repeats and explains to show that he is the chorus. If "bar" is the gate of the house of Death, he is the gatekeeper. He is also the impartial observer, judge at the bar of judgment where a victim, Mark-the-Target, is on trial. This is another two-character play and Mark is the pilgrim seeking enlightenment. In her circle of light, Miriam sits before the bar wearing a fantastic hat of cockfeathers. Her preening neck, croaking voice, and incessant pecking at her husband Mark emphasize "cock" as her image. "Cock" also suggests sex and Miriam is animal sex, a bitch in heat. "Crock" is what she calls her alcoholic husband, so the play is set up on the surface as a *Virginia Woolf*-type brawl. But "crock" metaphysically is "clay"—man as a spiritual vessel in the hands of the divine potter. Cock vs. Crock, carnal vs. spiritual: Williams has restaged his flesh-spirit duel of ***Summer and Smoke*** and ***Streetcar*** in the Orient. (pp. 207-08)

I believe that Miriam, far from being a life force as has been suggested, is the oriental death principle, the Yin: the earthly, negative, female, cold and dark elements. Mark is the Yang: heavenly, positive, active, male, light. One represents terrestrial matter, the other creative power, equal halves in the circle of existence. Together they created all natural phenomena and they must be in balance in man's nature for him to be whole. Miriam describes the Yin-Yang symbol in her lines "convex demanding concave." She confronts Mark with the possibility that they are halves of the same person, that the artist is tied to the animal. (The idea of two halves becoming one occurs also in ***Two-Character Play.***) Reviewers upset by the play's incomplete sentences failed to hear them as musical phrases. Moreover, ***Tokyo Hotel*** is about incompletion. Mark is the artist who can never complete his work and who, because he gave his life to art, cannot be complete as a human being. If Miriam and Mark are halves of one person, there is no need to complete sentences.

Reviewers did note that the terror in this schizophrenic play was real. In 1969, when Williams thought he was dying, he became a Catholic. In these Noh plays, when he feared he was going mad, he may have been searching for absolutes in Buddha or Tao. The quality of ***Tokyo*** is suffering and the subject is art; Williams at his most withdrawn was writing about the artist's fear of not being able to separate himself from his material. To capture the pure light Mark thinks he sees ahead he has to break with reality. This, Miriam points out, is to go insane. But what in Freudian terms is a psychotic break may be in eastern mysticism a merging with the cosmic unconscious: Zen's satori—total enlightenment. So the artist is the supreme gambler, prisoner to the judgments of time. Meanwhile an artist must remain productive; to slap down Mark's aspirations as constantly as Miriam does is to put him in Hell. (pp. 208-09)

[For the one-act plays which make up ***Slapstick Tragedy,*** Williams specified sets] "as delicate as Japanese line drawings." Both plays have music and a chorus but the contrast between them points to the most ancient origins of Japanese drama. ***The Mutilated*** depicts a religious miracle, an act of magic. ***The Gnädiges Fräulein*** is counter-magic, part pantomime, part clown-show, with actors masked as birds and the Gracious Lady a juggling acrobat. So in Japan before the seventh century A.D., the priest chanted his spells while a variety of stunts and animal acts went on around him. The religious strain evolved into Noh, the secular into *kyogen,* the farcical interludes between the serious Noh plays.

Fräulein is a sadistic farce set in Cocaloony Key (Williams' Key West). The Fräulein, a has-been performer now blind in one eye (as Williams was) but still eager to earn her keep in the rooming house of life, is compelled to rush to the docks whenever the boat whistle blows and bring home a fish. As she runs she is bloodied by the attack of savage cocaloony birds (like Williams struggling under attack to bring in a new play). Harold Clurman noticed that the pelican bird-men looked remarkably like critics but couldn't bring himself to smile at the play's black humor: "I was too conscious that its author was in pain." Most would agree with Foster Hirsch's assessment: "a sad, overwrought play . . . Williams was having his nightmares in public." Writer Donald Newlove gave its one rave review, seeing a Christian parable with the Fräulein in her fright-wig aureole as the Virgin and calling the playwright a tragicomic genius. No one noticed the oriental touches. (pp. 209-10)

Cranes, sunflowers, demons, bird-men? These conjure up a new and scholarly Williams with an Encyclopedia of Oriental Folklore at his side. He called himself "a sloppy writer" who "absorbed" information. His friends saw him as a quick study who never missed a nuance. Reams have been written about Williams' personality, his sex life—very little about his working methods or education as a playwright. Even in his ***Memoirs,*** Williams resisted explanations. "I feel the plays speak for themselves," he wrote. "And my habits of work are so much more private than my daily and nightly existence." (p. 210)

Tokyo Hotel's failure seemed to mark the end of Williams' secret experiment and he did not enlighten those who called the sixties his "stoned age." He may have absorbed some oriental tranquility along with his celebrated cure in a St. Louis hospital but from then on his emphasis changed from death to survival and his writing headed back to earth. When he rewrote ***The Two-Character Play*** for a Chicago opening in 1971 it was called ***Out Cry*** and was significantly different from the original. Definitely no-Noh, Williams called it "my Bangkok version," chuckling. Sex instead of sunflowers; symbolic mirrors and shifts in reality gone. . . . It wasn't as interesting as the original script but Williams, who sat on the back row the night I saw it, laughed enthusiastically and led the applause. (p. 211)

[Williams] sometimes remarked that ***Tokyo*** was not as bad as the critics had said. In his ***Memoirs*** he mentions "a turn in my work in the sixties toward a new style and a new creative world with which the reviewers and the audiences found it very hard to empathize." He told a reporter . . . : "Actually, I wrote two or three of my best plays then, even if they were a little weird: ***In the Bar of a Tokyo Hotel*** . . . and the two-character play sometimes called ***Out Cry.*** In these, I began experimenting with writing in incomplete sentences."

Upon his death in February 1983, . . . critic Walter Kerr wrote his epitaph: "He was the greatest American playwright. Period." Most of the many obituaries dismissed his sixties plays as products of his declining years. Only actor Hume Cronyn maintained that ***The Two-Character Play*** was "monumental in the 20th century." Few have yet read ***Tokyo Hotel,*** which Donald Newlove called "his great crucifixion play" and playwright Lanford Wilson predicted that, when understood, "will blow your mind."

Will these experiments all remain closet drama, as were the final works of Strindberg, Yeats and Claudel? Will they someday be studied by scholars as Williams' Noh period? Or can it be that in 20 years these personal plays which ask such serious questions about life and art and were written off as "regression" will be performed as the playwright's most significant work? If so, let us hope that Tennessee Williams, in some mystical reincarnation, can be in the theater. (pp. 211-12)

Allean Hale, "Tennessee's Long Trip," in The Missouri Review, *Vol. VII, No. 3, 1984, pp. 201-12.*

MICHIKO KAKUTANI

Afflicted by a "morbid shyness," a fear of desiring or loving anything or anyone too much for fear of losing them, Williams tried, throughout his life, to break out of his "solitary confinement" by writing—by transforming his fears, his anger, his longings and his guilt into words, and the words into characters who might in turn transform the singular into the plural, the personal into the universal. He wrote every morning of his adult life—even when reeling from drugs and alcohol and loss—and he left behind an astonishing body of work, including the 49 stories [in ***Collected Stories***].

Some are intriguing, provisional studies for the plays; some are grotesque explorations of sexual desire and its consequences, suffused in an air of violence and hysteria; some are simply schematic renderings of stray fantasies and emotions. But taken together, they form, as Gore Vidal points out in his introduction, "the true memoir of Tennessee Williams." Where the author's ***Memoirs*** offered only a dull, scurrilous record of his sexual exploits and social meanderings, these stories provide a shimmering, expressionistic mirror of his emotional and imaginative life.

Although the earliest story in this volume, **"The Vengeance of Nitocris"** (1928), written when he was 16, foreshadows the mature Williams's taste for quick, brutal conclusions, the tale—which portrays an Egyptian princess's efforts to avenge her brother's death by flooding a banquet hall with the waters of the Nile—reels under the weight of its alien subject matter and its mannered, breathy prose. . . . By the time ***Battle of Angels*** was produced in 1941, though, the playwright had succeeded in forging his rhapsodic love of language into a distinctive lyrical voice, and he'd discovered, too, that his subject matter lay not in the exoticism of far-off times and places but in the familiar, if exotic, regions of his own heart.

"The Field of Blue Children" (1967) presents an elegiac portrait of the author as a young poet, yearning for love and beauty and eager to apprentice himself to the angel of Art, and its self-portrait is fleshed out further by subsequent stories in this volume. **"Portrait of a Girl in Glass"** (1943), a prose version, in essence, of ***The Glass Menagerie,*** and **"The Resemblance Between a Violin Case and a Coffin"** (1949) offer softly-lit reminiscences of his thwarted childhood and that of his beloved sister, Rose. **"The Angel in the Alcove"** (1943) presents a somewhat surreal account of his life among the down and out in New Orleans, and **"Two on a Party"** (1951-52) celebrates the adventures he and Marion Black Vaccaro enjoyed traveling together on the road.

In a sense, of course, Williams was always writing about himself, exploring his own psyche through the prism of his creations, and even the stories that do not seem overtly autobiographical are strewn with bits of personal history. His strained relationship with Frank Merlo is mirrored in the squabbling of two aging lesbians in **"Happy August the Tenth"** (1970), and the death of his first love, Kip, surfaces again and again in the untimely deaths of young men in such tales as **"Violin Case," "The Kingdom of Earth"** (1954) and [the novella] ***Three Players of a Summer Game*** (1951-52).

Three Players, it turns out, is a kind of early version of ***Cat on a Hot Tin Roof,*** though readers will no doubt be surprised at the stark differences between the story and the play. Big Daddy, that towering presence of authority based on Williams's own father, is nowhere to be seen in the tale, nor is Big Mama or their son Gooper. Maggie is an almost subsidiary character here; her role as the frustrated wife is taken, more or less, by the widow of a young man who was befriended by the moody, alcoholic Brick. In fact only Brick—and his dilemma as a closet homosexual—can be clearly discerned in the bare bones of ***Three Players.*** The stories **"Night of the Iguana"** (1948) and **"The Yellow Bird"** (1947), a precursor of ***Summer and Smoke,*** similarly lay out the histories and temperaments of their central characters . . . but only hint at the shape that the narratives of their lives will later assume.

Besides providing valuable clues to the working methods of a writer who was continually revising his own oeuvre, the stories in this volume are also illuminating—and in some cases, richly satisfying—in their own right. They are, by turns, disturbing, moving and funny; and they help amplify Williams's tragic vision, for like the plays, they underline his preoccupation and insight into the conflicts of the human heart. . . . The frightened young spinster in **"Completed"** (1973), the mutilated male hustler in **"One Arm"** (1945), the desperate hooker in **"In Memory of an Aristocrat"** (1940), indeed nearly all the people in these stories, belong to that same gallery of the dispossessed—the lost, the frail, the lonely, the innocent and the damned—that Williams delineated with such fierce eloquence and compassion in his plays.

Michiko Kakutani, "Conflicts of the Heart," in The New York Times, *November 9, 1985, p. 15.*

REYNOLDS PRICE

The unalterable fact of [Williams's] immense contribution to dramatic literature—from ***The Glass Menagerie*** in 1944 through ***The Night of the Iguana*** in 1961—is currently all but sunk in the closer reality of his disastrous late plays and the public spectacle of a runaway life. If the great plays are inadequately remembered and honored, how much more so the stream of related work Williams published or left—two interesting, eccentric novels, ***The Roman Spring of Mrs. Stone*** and ***Moise and the World of Reason;*** his disordered but hilarious and often touching 1975 ***Memoirs;*** and this enormous ***Collected Stories,*** composed of four published volumes, along with some previously unpublished or uncollected short fiction. . . .

Even [Williams's] greatest admirers have condescended to the stories, finding them of interest only insofar as they foreshadow characters, plots and themes for his plays. Readers' tallies will be different, but given this chronologically arranged and presumably ultimate collection, any fair account of Williams's fiction must surely agree that six or eight pieces are of an invigorating individual mastery. For me, **"Portrait of a Girl in Glass,"** which prefigures the plot and entire cast of ***The Glass Menagerie,*** is as self-contained and piercing as the play. And the novella ***Three Players of a Summer Game,*** which invents Brick and Maggie Pollitt of ***Cat on a Hot Tin Roof,*** is a more complex and profound achievement than the play based on it. Admittedly, pieces like **"Man Bring This Up Road"** (which led to the play ***The Milk Train Doesn't Stop Here Anymore***) and even **"The Night of the Iguana"** are little more than unsatisfactory sketches for eventual large plays. But the chief pleasure that this collection offers so abundantly is specifically the pleasure of brief mastery. . . .

Williams's genius—and it was as large a genius as America has produced—was for condensed and pressurized experience and expression. Plays, which seldom ask more than three hours of our lives, and stories were natural functions of his understanding, his essential metabolism. (Inexplicably, his brief poems rarely jell.)

How good are the stories? How likely to give present and enduring pleasure and guidance "in this dark march toward whatever it is we're approaching"—to quote his heroine Blanche DuBois? First, as in most lifelong compendiums, there is the expected portion of botched apprentice work—though his first published piece, **"The Vengeance of Nitocris,"** . . . may prove a genuine hoot for party performers. And even in the awkward early prose, there are almost always moments of startling power—fragments of the explosive vision that Williams will eventually mold into incandescent bombs.

The apprenticeship slides almost imperceptibly into art with the stories of the late 1930's and early 40's—**"The Field of Blue Children," "The Mysteries of the Joy Rio"** and **"Portrait of a Girl in Glass."** The first successes, we now know, proceeded more or less directly from events of his own youth and early manhood. By the mid-1940's to early 50's, he was attempting stories that, while still grounded in personal experience, abound in the kind of magic realism so widely believed to have originated in Latin America—stories like the outrageous but dead-serious **"One Arm"** and **"Desire and the Black Masseur."**

But the large successes of this middle period are still those grounded in Williams's own gypsy youth—**"The Resemblance Between a Violin Case and a Coffin"** (another story about his tragic sister, Rose) and ***Three Players of a Summer Game*** (from his boyhood in Mississippi and Tennessee). They move with a leisurely, even archaic, nobility of pace and tone through unblinking scrutiny of those few tendencies of human nature that empowered him—the irreparable damage one person can inflict on his or her companions, the tyranny and persistence of physical desire, the pathos and peculiar grace of the walking wounded.

The scrutiny continued with no pause through his remaining harried years—the latest story is from 1977—but by the 1960's the careful, grave stride had changed to an often frantic, occasionally hilarious surreal dash through unearthly landscapes peopled by cartoon-bold but empty allegorical figures. The novella-length ***Knightly Quest*** is the most nearly successful example of this final manner. The promise of a Kafkaesque parable set in a secret weapons factory is quickly sabotaged by an air of reckless and random invention. Something has come loose in the writer's life and gaze; a still comic but now desperate cry of rage at human folly flaps wildly through the jagged actions and generally drowns whatever communication was intended—though perhaps none was. As with so many aging artists, the late work is far more a dialogue with the self than with an audience. Perhaps the public and critical rejection of his last plays had convinced Williams he had no audience. The final vision is desperate, incommunicable, sealed.

But the youthful and middle years are here in dignified plenty. Even at the sad, rejected end, Williams knew his own worth—he'd made a whole world. These stories, fruits of labor in the mouth of hell, confirm this and give the lie to his detractors.

Reynolds Price "His Battle Cry Was 'Valor!'," in The New York Times Book Review, *December 1, 1985, p. 11.*

SEYMOUR KRIM

It is trite to say at this late date, but Tennessee Williams obviously wrote to survive. To quote his own telling line in one of the first-person stories [in ***Collected Stories***], he practiced "a religion of endurance" by means of his work, and the further removed it was from the public hoopla that greeted his plays and films the more we can see the almost desperate nature of his literary need. Here are stories about bewildered, helpless, very human losers—stories that are both unfalteringly understanding and pitiless, cutting far beneath the public image of the bright-eyed and ingratiating Tennessee that we recall from TV talk shows. Knowing these stories now in their entirety—the climate of iron loneliness, the entrapment of desire, the futile beating of fists or hearts against what expressionlessly lies waiting—we can easily understand why Williams often dissembled in public with the armoring of drink or drugs. Like his colleague Eugene O'Neill, he knew what the pits of hell were all about. But it's one thing to experience those pits and quite another to own the craft that will snare them in all their unholy glory.

The astonishing thing about Williams the short story writer is that he found his style by the time he was 17 (that is no misprint) when he wrote the first story in this collection, entitled **"The Vengeance of Nitocris"**.... The narrative itself is full of sweeping theatrical effects that were ultimately to serve him better on the stage than the page, but what is uncanny is the simplicity and poise of the prose itself, which was never to change. Whether he was writing about ancient Egypt, as in this first story, or a Midwestern college town as in **"The Field of Blue Children"** (1939), he was always direct, clear, unaffected and unafraid to confront what most of us don't want to see.

One overpowering impression emerges from all these stories put together: Tennessee Williams (1911-83) knew more about the hidden life of far-flung America than any of us really suspected. He was a vagabond for many years before his smashing Broadway success in the 1940s, knowing working-class as well as bohemian environments from Mississippi all the way north to Provincetown, Massachusetts, spanning both coasts as well, and the fruit of all this knocking around dominates his early and perhaps freshest work. Here are salesmen, waiters, hobos, male and female hookers, slightly crazy young poets (using the bottled-up young Tennessee himself) and lonely young women who go to college or work in libraries. Few male writers can identify so convincingly with the less blunt sensibilities of the other sex—the artistic revenge, if you will, of that "sissy" tag that was hung on Williams by his father. . . . (pp. 3, 11)

One gets the feeling that unlike his peers in the American short story, Williams never consciously set out to write "masterpieces" as did, say, Katherine Anne Porter. Theater was his first public art while prose and poetry were almost his private compulsion, as necessary as breathing but hidden away from all the status-conscious pressures that besiege the craftsman who has everything riding on this form. Nevertheless Williams, especially in his pre-celebrity period, turned out stories that are the equal of any American writing done in his lifetime—pieces like **"Twenty-seven Wagons Full of Cotton," "The Accent of a Coming Foot," "Desire and the Black Masseur," "The Dark Room,"** and **"Something About Him"** have every chance of edging their way into permanence. The classic Williams story of this period has a purity of language and an unusual emotional depth, often with no reprieve, that simply humbles our standard responses. But as so often happens, Williams lost touch with his most basic materials after he became famous, and many of the stories from the late '50s to the end have that blowzy, international-set air that we can get from innumerable others.

One beauty, however, is **"Two on a Party,"** written just before this last, sagging period set in. It tells the story of a burnt-out gay writer and an alcoholic nymphomaniac who cruise different U.S. cities together, each helping the other get what they need. . . . Their fragile happiness, which we know can't last, is as good a symbol of what Williams stood for as any he ever created—that every real person is a cripple of some kind, and the only true enemies are the self-appointed "whole people" who enforce a superficial and finally brutal version of reality on the more helpless.

Without a doubt, sadly, there are too many unnecessary stories in this handsomely produced book—especially with the falling-off in the last two decades before Williams' death—but it has the look and feel of a true labor of love, an artifact created in honor of an extraordinary individual. One day there will be a much tighter *Selected Stories,* but this original, grand gesture, in every sense, is the one to keep close. (p. 11)

Seymour Krim, "The Public Playwright and the Private Storyteller," in Book World—The Washington Post, *January 12, 1986, pp. 3, 11.*

ROBERT PHILLIPS

Did any major American artist suffer the abuse and neglect accorded Tennessee Williams? His last play to be well-received in this country was ***The Night of the Iguana***—produced in 1961. After that, until his death in 1983, he could do nothing right in the critics' eyes. Yet the plays streamed forth: Over a dozen more full-length plays were unsuccessfully mounted. . . .

Through all this, Tennessee Williams rose every morning and continued to write. What most don't realize is that, in addition to his plays, he wrote stories, and had done so since the late 1930s. Their copyright dates extend from 1939 to 1982. In his lifetime four story collections were published. But they were not noticed like the best and worst of his plays. Now, finally, we have his ***Collected Stories***—a hefty volume of fifty pieces and nearly 600 pages. What it makes apparent is that had he written nothing else, Williams's stories would be sufficient evidence of his bid for fame.

The anonymous editor . . . has reprinted all the stories from the earlier four collections, plus uncollected and unpublished stories, including Williams's first published effort. . . . It should be said that Williams has not been entirely served by the inclusion of every story; some of the early ones are quite awful, and so is their prose ("Hushed were the streets of many peopled Thebes . . ."); some of the very last stories read like masturbatory daydreams. . . . Another late story, **"Miss Coynte of Green,"** is racist and sexist. Even Miss Coynte's surname is, I take it, intended as a crude pun.

But between the early and late stories there is an abundance of wonderful, moving, and original fiction. Williams began to hit his stride with **"The Field of Blue Children"** (1935), about seventy pages into the book. It is a portrait of the artist as a young poet, and deals with matters of art and love. **"The Mysteries of the Joy Rio"** is an authentic ghost story. **"Portrait of a Girl in Glass"** deals with the themes and characters of ***The Glass Menagerie,*** and is as successful a story as the play was a play. It is one of several attempts by Williams to portray the pathetic figure of his sister Rose.

Other stories prefigure plays: **"The Night of the Iguana,"** ***Three Players of a Summer Game,*** **"Man Bring This Up Road,"** and **"The Kingdom of Earth"** are early versions and variations on ***Iguana, Cat on a Hot Tin Roof, The Milk Train Doesn't Stop Here Anymore,*** and ***The Seven Descents of Myrtle.*** These often are quite different from the plays. It is as if, having created living characters, Williams could let them go on acting independently of any confines of plot. In ***Three Players of a Summer Game,*** for instance, Gooper and his family, Big Mama and Big Daddy, are nowhere to be seen, and Maggie is relegated to a bit part. But Brick and his many problems are explored in a manner which just possibly surpasses the play. "For love I make characters," Williams once wrote, and his characters do exceed the boundaries of the boards or the page.

The ***Collected Stories*** reveal that Williams had several very different fictional modes—the nostalgic, the naturalistic, the comic, and the fantastic. Yet each is underpinned by the same piercing psychology, compassion, and black humor that marked his best theatrical works. This is a book I will keep and revisit. It belongs on the shelf with Eudora Welty's and Flannery O'Connor's collected stories. . . . The anonymous editor also found a previously uncollected intimate memoir, **"The Man in the Overstuffed Chair,"** which is placed as a prologue. It goes a long way toward explaining the roots of Tennessee Williams's particular strange genius.

Robert Phillips, "Evidence for Fame," in Commonweal, *Vol. CXIII, No. 5, March 14, 1986, p. 156.*

W. KENNETH HOLDITCH

[When Williams died in 1983, he had] outlived the time when his success as the country's premier dramatist was at its apex, had survived to see a succession of plays and productions disparaged by many critics and rejected by the theater-going public, who in earlier, happier days had so extravagantly praised and cherished his works that he had become one of the most financially successful major writers in American literary history.

To many of the critics—and in drama they sometimes seem to be a more vicious lot than in other areas of literature—this decline in popularity demonstrated a failure of the author's powers, a descent into self-parody which some of them almost gleefully chronicled during most of the last two decades of his life. Richard Gilman, for example, in 1966 wrote a tasteless attack . . . entitled "Mistuh Williams, He Dead." So discouraging to Williams were the bad reviews and vituperative critiques that his reliance on drugs grew, his paranoia increased, and he struggled at times against an almost suicidal depression. In 1975, he had to be dissuaded by a friend from calling his memoirs "Flee, Flee This Sad Hotel."

In a very real sense, it is surely true that the failure of some of those later plays—***Out Cry, Vieux Carré*** and ***Clothes for a Summer Hotel*** among them—was to a large extent the result of changes in the theater in the United States rather than of the waning powers of the aging author. In a 1979 article . . . ("Surviving With Grace: Tennessee Williams Today") [see *CLC*, Vol. 19], I predicted that even though the dramas of the past decade had been judged by many critics to be inferior, the creator of ***The Glass Menagerie, A Streetcar Named Desire,*** and ***Cat on a Hot Tin Roof*** might yet "surprise and astound us with magic." That hope has unfortunately proven to be overly optimistic, if one judges solely by the quality of the later plays in performance; but it cannot be denied that every effort of the final years of his life contained touches of that distinctive dramatic magic, and many of the new works represented startlingly original experiments. The question remains as to what extent failures of various productions resulted from inadequate staging and direction or from the fact that audiences and critics expecting yet another well-made play in the pattern of ***Menagerie*** and ***Streetcar*** were unable to adapt to the avant garde quality of what Williams was now writing. A performance of a play is, after all, the result of a collaborative effort; one can read the script, certainly, but only when properly trained and directed actors in a felicitous stage setting voice the language as the author intended with appropriate actions and gestures can the work be realized. In the 1970s and early 1980s, Tennessee Williams was no longer blessed with the guiding hand of such a directorial genius as Elia Kazan, who had known not only how the earlier masterpieces should be brought to dramatic life, but how to work sympathetically with the sensitive artist in need of his expertise and guidance. It seems probable that some imaginative future director can provide a suitable staging for such late works as ***The Red Devil Battery Sign*** and ***A House Not Meant To Stand,*** which are, if not of the high quality of the early dramas, nevertheless worthy of attention as unique creations of one of America's foremost playwrights. (pp. 892-93)

In terms of published reminiscences and memoirs, Williams seems to have been unwise to have always depended on the kindness of friends in confiding aspects of his private life. The fact that at a certain point in his career he chose to reveal, in interviews and in the 1975 ***Memoirs,*** details of his sexual history and other intimate facts seems to have been interpreted as a license by [various writers and critics] . . . who have felt free to "tell all" about the man with whom they had been, in varying degrees, close. Further, each seemed determined to outdo the others in the shock value of the material he chose to reveal and to make himself the center of attention in a narrative purportedly about Williams. Comparison of the various efforts makes all of them suspect, since the same incident may be related in quite different ways by different storytellers. What all these "reveal-all" chroniclers share is a lack of propriety, a lack of sensitivity not only to the friend but also to the reading public. Gore Vidal, for example, in his otherwise impressive critical introduction to the recent ***Collected Stories*** of Williams, relates a hitherto unpublished personal fact about the Reverend Walter Dakin, the dramatist's maternal grandfather, that might serve some purpose in a biography of the author but here constitutes nothing more than a gratuitous bit of gossip. Besides throwing a dubious light on all the accounts this inclination to disclose salacious details complicates the task of the serious biographer who must sift through the accumulated spiteful trivia to find whatever truth may be hidden there. (pp. 894-95)

The most recent addition to [Williams'] published body of work is the ***Collected Stories.*** . . . There are forty-nine pieces of short prose fiction, most of which have appeared in a variety of magazines over a fifty-year period, the first in 1928, the last in 1978. There are also several previously unpublished stories found among Williams' papers after his death which the editor wisely included, since they reflect motifs, interests, characters, settings, and episodes subsequently employed in plays. One of the most intriguing entries is the first, **"The Vengeance of Nitocris."** . . . This bizarre piece of Gothic fiction in highly stylized language ("Hushed were the streets of many peopled Thebes."), showing the influence of his childhood reading of Poe and others, retells a story found in Herodotus. Nothing here indicates the works of genius that were to follow, beginning a decade later, other than the youthful fascination with language and the strong elements of Romanticism.

Even the reader familiar with the earlier volumes of stories will be amazed, examining this collection, to realize how much short fiction Wiliams managed to produce between bouts of playwriting. Without doubt, his final reputation in literature will rest on the plays, but had they never been written, his standing as a fiction writer would have been by no means negligible. The range of types of stories is wide: there are the grotesque protrayals of men and women engaged in actions society would judge abnormal (**"Desire and the Black Masseur,"** for example); broadly humorous depictions of human foibles (**"The Yellow Bird"**); touching rites-of-passage stories in which sensitive, artistic young men and women struggle to adapt to a world they little understand; and, interestingly, several works that identify Williams as a skillful practitioner of what has come in recent years to be termed "Magic Realist" fiction. Here in narrative form appear the outcasts, the haunted and desperate characters of the same type as those in the dramas. Indeed, the reader meets many of the same people here as in the plays (Amanda, Tom and Laura, Brick and Maggie, Hannah Jelkes, Flora Goforth, for example), although in slightly different guises. Like Faulkner, Williams seems to have used the short story as a testing ground for characters and situations, and thus these works become interesting reading not just for their individual virtues, but as glosses on the plays. ***Collected Stories*** opens with a preface entitled **"The Man in the Overstuffed Chair,"** a touching autobiographical piece in which the author makes peace with Cornelius Coffin Williams, the deceased father against whom he had since youth held bitter feelings. (pp. 900-01)

Can the best of [Williams'] plays be considered as poetry or only as dramatic literature, and which aspect is more important? What is the true quality of the plays of the last two decades; do they represent a decline in the powers of their creator, or are they good works waiting for significant productions to reveal their power? Of what value are the other writings of Tennessee Williams—novels, short stories, poems—which have been for the most part overshadowed by the dramas? (p. 902)

[Williams' work] straddles two disparate disciplines, theater and literature, which are often not especially compatible in the academic world. . . . [Scholars of literature] have to a surprising extent ignored the writings of Williams. The reason for such neglect, other than the fact of his central works' overlapping of the two disciplines, is not clear. Critics in the field of drama, on the other hand, have concentrated on mechanical aspects of production and technical elements of the plays rather than on plot, character, and the component parts of Williams' often very poetic language. . . . Clearly, the field is open, and given the "publish or perish" atmosphere of many universities today, it will no doubt soon be filled with critics.

Whatever unpublished scripts, poems, or stories may yet be discovered and printed; whatever dramatic productions of the plays, those already acclaimed and those as yet unacknowledged, may lie ahead, one can say, without much fear of being proven wrong, that Tennessee Williams' reputation as one of the two major American dramatists is firmly established and will survive. It is tragic that he should have died at a time when, after a long period filled with unsuccessful stagings of late works, his power to endure as a major figure in world theater must often have seemed to him doubtful—a time when myriad loose ends both in his life and in his literary and theatrical careers led him into discontent and misery, although they never forced him to stop working. But, as he himself wrote in 1945 in the short story **"One Arm,"** "death has never been much in the way of completion." It remains for scholars, producers, directors, audiences, and readers to supply for a life full of such powerful creative energy the only truly happy ending. (pp. 902-03)

W. Kenneth Holditch, "Surviving with Grace: Tennessee Williams Tomorrow," in The Southern Review, *Louisiana State University, Vol. 22, No. 4, Autumn, 1986, pp. 892-906.*

Appendix

The following is a listing of all sources used in Volume 45 of *Contemporary Literary Criticism*. Included in this list are all copyright and reprint rights and acknowledgments for those essays for which permission was obtained. Every effort has been made to trace copyright, but if omissions have been made, please let us know.

THE EXCERPTS IN CLC, VOLUME 45, WERE REPRINTED FROM THE FOLLOWING PERIODICALS:

Agenda, v. 19, Summer & Autumn, 1981; v. 19-20, Winter-Spring, 1982; v. 23, Autumn, 1985 & Winter, 1986. All reprinted by permission of the publisher.

America, v. 138, April 22, 1978 for a review of "New Collected Poems" by James Finn Cotter; v. 148, January 29, 1983 for "Poets Then and Now" by James Finn Cotter. © 1978, 1983. All rights reserved. Both reprinted with permission of the author.

The American Book Review, v. 4, September-October, 1982; v. 5, May-June, 1983. © 1982, 1983 by *The American Book Review*. Both reprinted by permission of the publisher.

The American Poetry Review, v. 10, May-June, 1981 for "Castles, Elephants, Buddhas: Some Recent American Poetry" by Dave Smith; v. 10, July-August, 1981 for "A Generation of Silver" by Mary Kinzie; v. 11, March-April, 1982 for "The Overdefinition of the Now" by Mary Kinzie; v. 14, September-October, 1985 for "Frederick Garber: Geographies and Languages and Selves and What They Do" by Frederick Garber. Copyright © 1981, 1982, 1985 by World Poetry, Inc. All reprinted by permission of the respective authors.

The American Spectator, v. 19, November, 1986. Copyright © *The American Spectator* 1986. Reprinted by permission of the publisher.

Analog Science Fiction/Science Fact, v. LXV, July, 1960 for a review of "The Star Conquerors" by P. Schuyler Miller; v. LXXV, June, 1965 for a review of "Star Watchman" by P. Schuyler Miller; v. 99, March, 1979 for a review of "Colony" by Edward Wood. Copyright © 1960, 1965, 1979 by the Condé Nast Publications, Inc. All reprinted by permission of the respective authors./ v. CI, November 9, 1981 for a review of "Voyagers" by Spider Robinson; v. 106, January, 1986 for a review of "Privateers" by Tom Easton; v. 106, May, 1986 for a review of "The Astral Mirror" by Tom Easton; v. 106, June, 1986 for a review of "Voyagers II" by Tom Easton. Copyright © 1981, 1986 by Davis Publications, Inc. All reprinted by permission of the respective authors.

The Antioch Review, v. 38, Winter, 1980; v. 42, Summer, 1984; v. 43, Fall, 1985. Copyright © by the Antioch Review Inc. All reprinted by permission of the Editors.

Art in America, v. 74, April, 1986 for "Eric Bogosian at the American Place Theater" by Patrick Amos. Copyright © 1986 by Art in America, Inc. Reprinted by permission of the publisher and the author.

Artforum, v. XXIV, November, 1985. Copyright 1985 Artforum International Magazine, Inc. Reprinted by permission of the publisher.

The Atlantic Monthly, v. 185, April, 1950./ v. 224, September, 1969 for "Plotter and Plodder" by Charles Nicol. Copyright 1969 by The Atlantic Monthly Company, Boston, MA. Reprinted by permission of the author.

Best Sellers, v. 35, March, 1976; v. 45, November, 1985. Copyright © 1976, 1985 Helen Dwight Reid Educational Foundation. Both reprinted by permission of the publisher.

Book Week—The Sunday Herald Tribune, September 13, 1964; January 31, 1965; August 29, 1965. © 1964, 1965, *The Washington Post.* All reprinted by permission of the publisher.

Book World—The Washington Post, September 20, 1970 for "More Tales from the Homer of Wall Street" by Richard Freedman. © 1970 Postrib Corp. Reprinted by permission of *The Washington Post* and the author./ June 6, 1976; December 17, 1978; September 23, 1979; July 13, 1980; February 15, 1981; September 27, 1981; December 20, 1981; February 28, 1982; September 5, 1982; February 27, 1983; June 5, 1983; September 4, 1983; May 20, 1984; July 22, 1984; September 16, 1984; October 21, 1984; November 18, 1984; December 16, 1984; July 14, 1985; October 6, 1985; January 12, 1986; May 11, 1986; June 8, 1986; June 22, 1986; July 27, 1986; August 24, 1986; September 28, 1986. © 1976, 1978, 1979, 1980, 1981, 1982, 1983, 1984, 1985, 1986, *The Washington Post.* All reprinted by permission of the publisher.

Booklist, v. 81, February 1, 1985. Copyright © 1985 by the American Library Association. Reprinted by permission of the publisher.

The Booklist, v. 72, October 15, 1975; v. 72, January 1, 1976; v. 72, July 1, 1976. Copyright © 1975, 1976 by the American Library Association. All reprinted by permission of the publisher.

Books, August 27, 1961. © 1961 I.H.T. Corporation. Reprinted by permission of the publisher.

Books and Bookmen, n. 342, March, 1984 for a review of "Blood and Guts in High School Plus Two" by Cosmo Landesman. © copyright the author 1984./ v. 19, October, 1973 for a review of "A Distant Likeness" by Piers Brendon; v. 22, July, 1977 for "A True Simplicity" by George Barker; v. 23, November, 1977 for "Memento Mori" by James Brockway; n. 356, June, 1985 for "Master of Sudden Death" by Ronald Blythe. © copyright the respective authors 1973, 1977, 1985. All reprinted by permission of the respective authors.

Boston Review, v. XI, February, 1986 for a review of "Peru" by Richard Marius; v. XI, December, 1986 for a review of "Anagrams" by Matthew Gilbert. Copyright © 1986 by the Boston Critic, Inc. Both reprinted by permission of the respective authors.

Brick: A Journal of Reviews, n. 20, Winter, 1984. Reprinted by permission of the publisher.

British Book News, May, 1984; June, 1985; November, 1985; January, 1986. © *British Book News,* 1984, 1985, 1986. All courtesy of *British Book News.*

The Canadian Forum, v. L, November & December, 1970. Reprinted by permission of the publisher.

Canadian Slavonic Papers, v. XIX, September, 1977 for "Iurii Trifonov and the Ethics of Contemporary Soviet City Life" by N. N. Shneidman. Copyright ©, *Canadian Slavonic Papers,* Canada, 1977. Reprinted by permission of the publisher and the author.

The Changing World, 1947.

Choice, v. 10, March, 1973; v. 14, April, 1977; v. 16, July & August, 1979; v. 19, January, 1982; v. 22, October, 1984. Copyright © 1973, 1977, 1979, 1982, 1984 by American Library Association. All reprinted by permission of the American Library Association.

The Chowder Review, n. 14, Spring-Summer, 1980. Copyright 1980. Reprinted by permission of the publisher.

The Christian Science Monitor, June 16, 1960; May 2, 1968; May 7, 1970; October 11, 1983; April 9, 1986; June 9, 1986. © 1960, 1968, 1970, 1983, 1986 The Christian Science Publishing Society. All rights reserved. All reprinted by permission from *The Christian Science Monitor.*/ September 25, 1952. Copyright 1952, renewed 1980, The Christian Science Publishing Society. All rights reserved. Reprinted by permission from *The Christian Science Monitor.*

Commentary, v. 79, March, 1985 for "The Custer of Our Dreams" by Wayne M. Sarf; v. 80, July, 1985 for "Out of the Drawer & into the West" by Fernanda Eberstadt; v. 80, September, 1985 for "One Cheer for E. M. Forster" by Joseph Epstein. Copyright © 1985 by American Jewish Committee. All rights reserved. All reprinted by permission of the publisher and the respective authors.

Commonweal, v. XXIII, November 15, 1935./ v. LXVII, February 28, 1958; v. LXVII, March 21, 1958; v. LXIX, February 13, 1959. Copyright © 1958, 1959 Commonweal Publishing Co., Inc. All reprinted by permission of Commonweal Foundation/ v. CXIII, March 14, 1986; v. CXIII, May 23, 1986; v. CXIII, October 24, 1986. Copyright © 1986 Commonweal Foundation. All reprinted by permission of Commonweal Foundation./ v. LIII, February 9, 1951; v. LVIII, May 8, 1953. Copyright 1951, renewed 1979; copyright 1953, renewed 1981, Commonweal Publishing Co., Inc. Both reprinted by permission of Commonweal Foundation.

Critical Quarterly, v. 23, Summer, 1981; v. 24, Winter, 1982; v. 26, Spring & Summer, 1984. © Manchester University Press 1981, 1982, 1984. All reprinted by permission of the publisher.

Critique: Studies in Modern Fiction, v. 7, Winter, 1964-65; Copyright © 1964, Helen Dwight Reid Educational Foundation. Reprinted with permission of the Helen Dwight Reid Educational Foundation, published by Heldref Publications, 4000 Albemarle Street N.W., Washington, DC 20016.

Daily News, April 4, 1986. © 1986, New York News, Inc. Reprinted with permission of the publisher.

Dance Magazine, v. LVIII, January, 1984; v. LX, May, 1986. Copyright 1984, 1986 Dance Magazine, Inc. Both reprinted by permission of the publisher.

Delta, n. 59, 1979.

Encounter, v. LIII, August, 1979; v. LVI, February & March, 1981; v. LVIII, May, 1982; v. LXI, December, 1983. © 1979, 1981, 1982, 1983 by Encounter Ltd. All reprinted by permission of the publisher.

English Studies, Netherlands, v. 42, 1961. © 1961 by Swets & Zeitlinger B. V. Reprinted by permission of the publisher.

Essays in Criticism, v. XXXIII, October, 1983 for "Geoffrey Hill's 'The Mystery of the Charity of Charles Peguy': A Commentary" by Henry Hart. Reprinted by permission of the Editors of *Essays in Criticism* and the author.

Exquisite Corpse, v. 2, May-July, 1984. Reprinted by permission of the publisher.

Extrapolation, v. 25, Summer, 1984. Copyright 1984 by The Kent State University Press. Reprinted by permission of the publisher.

Fantasy Review, v. 8, March, 1985 for "Bova's Short Fiction: A Balanced Collection" by Keith Soltys; v. 9, June, 1985 for "Predictable but Unbelievable" by Lawrence I. Charters; v. 9, March, 1986 for "Bova's Latest—Predictably Upbeat" by Bill Collins; v. 9, April, 1986 for "On the Brink of Godhood?" by Rick Osborn. Copyright © 1985, 1986 by the respective authors. All reprinted by permission of the respective authors.

fiction international, v. 15, 1984. Copyright © 1984 by the editors. Reprinted by permission of the publisher.

The Georgia Review, v. XXXIII, Fall, 1979; v. XXXIV, Summer, 1980. Copyright, 1979, 1980, by the University of Georgia. Both reprinted by permission of the publisher.

The Hudson Review, v. XXVI, Summer, 1973; v. XXVII, Summer, 1974; v. XXXIV, Winter, 1981-82; v. XXXVII, Summer, 1984; v. XXXVIII, Autumn, 1985. Copyright © 1973, 1974, 1981, 1984, 1985 by The Hudson Review, Inc. All reprinted by permission of the publisher.

The Indian Journal of English Studies, v. II, December, 1961 for "Rex Warner's Political Novels: An Allegorical Crusade against Fascism" by Darshan Singh Maini. Reprinted by permission of the author.

The International Fiction Review, v. 7, Winter, 1980. © copyright International Fiction Association. Reprinted by permission of the publisher.

Irish Literary Supplement, v. 3, Fall, 1984. Copyright © 1984, *Irish Literary Supplement.* Reprinted by permission of the publisher.

Journal of the Karnatak University, v. VIII, 1974.

Kirkus Reviews, v. XLVI, June 15, 1978; v. XLVII, June 15, 1979; v. LIV, August 15, 1986; v. LIV, September 1, 1986, Copyright © 1978, 1979, 1986 The Kirkus Service, Inc. All rights reserved. All reprinted by permission of the publisher.

Library Journal, v. 98, September 1, 1973 for a review of "When the Sky Burned" by Robert L. Middleton; v. 101, June 1, 1976 for a review of "The Multiple Man" by Henri C. Veit; v. 103, May 15, 1978 for a review of "A Good Journey" by Brian Swann; v. 106, June 1, 1981 for a review of "Household Saints" by Donna L. Nerboso; v. 111, April 15, 1986 for a review of "The Ego Is Always at the Wheel" by David Sowd. Copyright © 1973, 1976, 1978, 1981, 1986 by Reed Publishing, USA, Division of Reed Holdings, Inc. All reprinted from *Library Journal,* published by R. R. Bowker, Co., Division of Reed Publishing, USA, by permission of the publisher and the respective authors./ v. 106, March 15, 1981. Copyright © 1981 by Reed Publishing, USA, Division of Reed Holdings, Inc. Reprinted from *Library Journal,* published by R. R. Bowker, Co., Division of Reed Publishing, USA, by permission of the publisher.

The Listener, v. 78, July 6, 1967; v. 83, April 30, 1970; v. 113, April 25, 1985. © British Broadcasting Corp. 1967, 1970, 1985./ June 14, 1973 for "Bailey's Bridgelessness" by Susan Hill. Copyright © 1973 by the author. Reprinted by permission of Georges Borchardt, Inc./ v. 96, November 11, 1976 for "No More Nannies" by Naomi Lewis; v. 97, June 2, 1977 for "Pass Marks" by Paddy Kitchen; v. 100, September 7, 1978 for "Writers and War" by Ronald Blythe; v. 106, October 15, 1981 for "'His Is a Talent Not to Amuse, but to Abuse'" by Peter Kemp; v. 115, April 17, 1986 for "In or Out?" by Vernon Bogdanor; v. 116, October 2, 1986 for "Culture with a K." by Jim Hiley. © British Broadcasting Corp. 1967, 1970, 1976, 1977, 1978, 1981, 1986. All reprinted by permission of the respective authors.

London Magazine, n.s. v. 21, June, 1981. © *London Magazine* 1981. Reprinted by permission of the publisher.

London Review of Books, June 17-30, 1982 for "Kelpers" by Claude Rawson; October 4-17, 1984 for "Rumba, Conga, Communism" by Neal Ascherson. Both appear here by permission of the *London Review of Books* and the respective authors.

Los Angeles Times Book Review, January 23, 1983; November 6, 1983; December 9, 1984; August 11, 1985; July 13, 1986; September 14, 1986; September 21, 1986. Copyright 1983, 1984, 1985, 1986, *Los Angeles Times*. All reprinted by permission of the publisher.

Maclean's Magazine, v. 98, November 4, 1985. © 1985 by *Maclean's Magazine*. Reprinted by permission of the publisher.

The Magazine of Fantasy and Science Fiction, v. 51, November, 1976 for a review of "Millennium" by Joanna Russ; v. 61, November, 1981 for a review of "Voyagers" by Algis Budrys. © 1976, 1981 by Mercury Press Inc. Both reprinted by permission of *The Magazine of Fantasy and Science Fiction* and the respective authors.

The Malahat Review, n. 35, July, 1975 for "Craft and Ceremony: 'Some Notes on the Versecraft of Robert Graves'" by Robin Skelton. © *The Malahat Review* 1975. Reprinted by permission of the author.

Meanjin, v. 30, September, 1971 for "'Beware of the Past': James McAuley's Early Poetry" by Chris Wallace-Crabbe; v. 44, March, 1985 for "True Stories: Women's Writing in Science Fiction" by Philippa Maddern. Both reprinted by permission of the respective authors.

Michigan Quarterly Review, v. XXI, Winter, 1982. Copyright © The University of Michigan, 1982. Reprinted by permission of the publisher.

The Midwest Quarterly, v. XXVII, Spring, 1986. Copyright, 1986, by *The Midwest Quarterly*, Pittsburgh State University. Reprinted by permission of the publisher.

Minority Voices, v. 3, Fall, 1979. Copyright 1979 by The Paul Roveson Cultural Center, Pennsylvania State University. Reprinted by permission of the publisher.

The Missouri Review, v. VII, 1984. Copyright © 1984 by The Curators of the University of Missouri. Reprinted by permission of the publisher.

Modern Age, v. 23, Spring, 1979. Copyright © 1979 by the Intercollegiate Studies Institute, Inc. Reprinted by permission of the publisher.

Modern Drama, v. XXVII, September, 1984. Copyright *Modern Drama*, University of Toronto. Reprinted by permission of the publisher.

Modern Fiction Studies, v. 32, Spring, 1986. Copyright © 1986 by Purdue Research Foundation, West Lafayette, IN 47907. All rights reserved. Reprinted with permission of the publisher.

Mundus Artium, v. XII & XIII, 1980 & 1981. Copyright, 1981 Rainer Schulte. Reprinted by permission of the publisher.

The Nation, New York, v. 146, January 29, 1938; v. 148, February 25, 1939; v. 152, January 25, 1941./ v. 189, November 14, 1959; v. 203, July 4, 1966; v. 211, September 7, 1970; v. 221, December 13, 1975; v. 227, September 9, 1978; v. 234, March 20, 1982; v. 234, April 3, 1982; v. 236, April 23, 1983; v. 236, June 11, 1983; v. 240, February 9, 1985; v. 240, February 16, 1985; v. 240, May 18, 1985; v. 243, October 25, 1986; v. 243, November 15, 1986; v. 243, November 22, 1986. Copyright 1959, 1966, 1970, 1975, 1978, 1982, 1983, 1985, 1986 *The Nation* magazine, The Nation Company, Inc. All reprinted by permission of the publisher.

The National Observer, January 20, 1969. © Dow Jones & Company, Inc. 1969. All rights reserved. Reprinted by permission of *The National Observer*.

National Review, New York, v. XXX, September 1, 1978. © 1978 by National Review, Inc., 150 East 35th Street, New York, NY 10016. Reprinted with permission of the publisher.

New Directions for Women, v. 14, May-June, 1985. v. 14, July-August, 1985. © copyright 1985 New Directions for Women, Inc., 108 West Palisade Ave., Englewood, NJ 07631. Both reprinted by permission of the publisher.

New England Review and Bread Loaf Quarterly, v. 9, Autumn, 1986. Copyright © 1986 by Kenyon Hill Publications, Inc. Reprinted by permission of the publisher.

The New Leader, v. XLIII, October 31, 1960; v. LVII, March 4, 1974; v. LXII, September 10, 1979; v. LXIV, June 1, 1981; v. LXVI, July 11-25, 1983; v. LXVII, February 6, 1984; v. LXVII, August 20, 1984. © 1960, 1974, 1979, 1981, 1983, 1984 by The American Labor Conference on International Affairs, Inc. All reprinted by permission of the publisher.

New Letters, v. 48, Fall, 1981 for "Differences of Opinion" by Robert Dana. © copyright 1981 The Curators of the University of Missouri. Reprinted by permission of the publisher and the author.

New Mexico Humanities Review, v. 6, Fall, 1983. Copyright 1983. Reprinted by permission of the publisher.

The New Republic, v. XCIII, February 2, 1938; v. XCVII, March 8, 1939; v. 127, October 6, 1952; v. 137, October 14, 1957./ v. 147, December 15, 1962 for "The Healthiness of Sick Comedy: 'Beyond the Fringe'" by Robert Brustein. © 1962 The New Republic, Inc. Reprinted by permission of the author./ v. 160, June 7, 1969; v. 175, December 18, 1976; v. 176, June 4, 1977; v. 178, February 4, 1978; v. 190, May 28, 1984; v. 191, July 9, 1984; v. 192, March 25, 1985; v. 193, September 16 & 23, 1985; v. 194, May 5, 1986; v. 196, March 30, 1987. © 1969, 1976, 1977, 1978, 1984, 1985, 1986, 1987 The New Republic, Inc. All reprinted by permission of *The New Republic*.

New Statesman, v. 71, March 25, 1966; v. 73, June 2, 1967; v. 79, April 17, 1970; v. 99, January 29, 1980; v. 99, March 28, 1980; v. 102, October 16, 1981; v. 112, August 29, 1986; v. 112, November 7, 1986. © 1966, 1967, 1970, 1980, 1981, 1986 The Statesman & Nation Publishing Co. Ltd. All reprinted by permission of the publisher.

The New Statesman & Nation, v. XLIV, November 1, 1952.

New York Herald Tribune Book Review, October 1, 1950; September 21, 1952. Copyright 1950, 1952 I.H.T. Corporation. Both reprinted by permission of the publisher./ May 26, 1957. © 1957 I.H.T. Corporation. Reprinted by permission of the publisher.

New York Herald Tribune Weekly Book Review, September 28, 1947. Copyright 1947 I.H.T. Corporation. Reprinted by permission of the publisher.

New York Magazine, v. 16, October 31, 1983; v. 19, February 3, 1986. Copyright © 1983, 1986 by News America Publishing, Inc. Both reprinted with the permission of *New York* Magazine.

New York Mirror, October 29, 1962. Reprinted by permission of the publisher.

New York Post, April 4, 1986; June 27, 1986. © 1986, News America Publishing, Incorporated. Both reprinted from the *New York Post* by permission.

The New York Review of Books, v. VI, June 23, 1966 for "Fiction a la Mode" by Roger Shattuck. Copyright © 1966 Nyrev, Inc. Reprinted by permission of Joan Daves for the author./ v. VIII, February 9, 1967; v. XXVI, February 8, 1979; v. XXXI, May 10, 1984; v. XXXI, June 28, 1984; v. XXXIII, May 8, 1986; v. XXXIII, December 18, 1986. Copyright © 1967, 1979, 1984, 1986 Nyrev, Inc. All reprinted with permission from *The New York Review of Books*.

The New York Times, October 31, 1935; January 11, 1941; January 18, 1951; April 12, 1953. Copyright 1935, 1941, 1951, 1953 by The New York Times Company. All reprinted by permission of the publisher./ December 30, 1967; November 5, 1968; July 26, 1969; February 17, 1973; November 26, 1975; September 15, 1977; April 29, 1983; March 6, 1985; March 30, 1985; June 26, 1985; September 13, 1985; November 9, 1985; January 21, 1986; February 7, 1986; April 2, 1986; April 4, 1986; April 12, 1986; June 27, 1986; July 17, 1986; October 18, 1986. Copyright © 1967, 1968, 1969, 1973, 1975, 1977, 1983, 1985, 1986 by The New York Times Company. All reprinted by permission of the publisher.

The New York Times Book Review, January 23, 1938; February 6, 1938; May 28, 1944; January 12, 1947; June 1, 1947; September 14, 1947; January 6, 1952. Copyright 1938, 1944, 1947, 1952 by The New York Times Company. All reprinted by permission of the publisher./ October 21, 1956; January 27, 1957; January 12, 1958; February 1, 1959; January 31, 1960; March 20, 1960; September 25, 1960; July 23, 1961; September 13, 1964; January 31, 1965; March 7, 1965; September 25, 1966; November 20, 1966; May 21, 1967; July 30, 1967; November 3, 1968; August 31, 1969; May 24, 1970; November 26, 1972; February 25, 1973; April 4, 1973; April 29, 1973; March 7, 1976; April 11, 1976; August 29, 1976; May 22, 1977; December 31, 1978; June 24, 1979; October 7, 1979; February 3, 1980; February 8, 1981; March 1, 1981; July 12, 1981; November 8, 1981; December 20, 1981; March 7, 1982; April 18, 1982; May 2, 1982; August 1, 1982; March 20, 1983; April 3, 1983; May 22, 1983; June 12, 1983; August 14, 1983; September 4, 1983; September 25, 1983; January 1, 1984; March 4, 1984; March 18, 1984; April 22, 1984; April 29, 1984; August 12, 1984; October 14, 1984; December 16, 1984; December 23, 1984; December 30, 1984; January 20, 1985; February 3, 1985; April 7, 1985; April 28, 1985; June 22, 1985; August 18, 1985; August 25, 1985; September 1, 1985; September 19, 1985; October 13, 1985; December 1, 1985; February 2, 1986; February 23, 1986; April 6, 1986; May 4, 1986; May 18, 1986; May 25, 1986; July 27, 1986; August 31, 1986; September 28, 1986; October 19, 1986; November 2, 1986; November 30, 1986. Copyright © 1956, 1957, 1958, 1959, 1960, 1961, 1964, 1965, 1966, 1967, 1968, 1969, 1970, 1972, 1973, 1976, 1977, 1978, 1979, 1980, 1981, 1982, 1983, 1984, 1985, 1986 by The New York Times Company. All reprinted by permission of the publisher.

The New Yorker, v. XXXVI, April 2, 1960; v. LXII, August 4, 1986. © 1960, 1986 by The New Yorker Magazine, Inc. Both reprinted by permission of the publisher./ v. LXI, February 3, 1986 for "Winning Losers" by Brendan Gill; v. LXII, April 14, 1986 for "Airborne and Earthbound" by Brendan Gill; v. LXII, September 22, 1986 for "The Great Paraguayan Novel and Other Hardships" by John Updike. © 1986 by the respective authors. All reprinted by permission of the publisher.

Newsday, June 27, 1986. © Newsday, Inc. 1986. Reprinted by permission.

Newsweek, v. XCII, October 30, 1978; v. CVII, March 24, 1986; v. CVII, May 12, 1986. Copyright 1978, 1986, by Newsweek, Inc. All rights reserved. All reprinted by permission of the publisher.

The North American Review, v. 269, September, 1984. Copyright © 1984 by the University of Northern Iowa. Reprinted by permission from *The North American Review.*

The Observer, August 8, 1965; March 2, 1969; July 17, 1983; June 17, 1984; September 2, 1984; September 18, 1986. All reprinted by permission of the publisher.

The Ontario Review, n. 19, Fall-Winter, 1983-84. Copyright © 1983 by The Ontario Review, Inc. Reprinted by permission of the publisher.

Pacific Sun, v. 18, July 18-24, 1980 for "Unending Search for Knowledge" by Rita Fink. Copyright © 1980 the author. Reprinted by permission of the author.

Parnassus: Poetry in Review, v. 7, Spring-Summer, 1979. Copyright © 1979 Poetry in Review Foundation. Reprinted by permission of the publisher.

Partisan Review, v. 47, 1980 for a review of "Uncertainties and Rest" by J. D. McClatchy. Copyright © 1980 by *Partisan Review.* Reprinted by permission of the author.

Plays & Players, v. 29, December, 1981. © 1981 Brevet Limited. Reprinted with permission of the publisher.

Poetry, v. CVIII, September, 1966 for "British Chronicle" by Richard Howard; v. CXXXVII, November, 1980 for "Chords and Keys" by Ben Howard; v. CXL, September, 1982 for a review of "Hard Words" by J. D. McClatchy; v. CXLV, December, 1984 for a review of "Opening the Hand" by Paul Breslin; v. CXLVII, February, 1986 for a review of "New Selected Poems" by Vernon Shetley; v. CXLIX, March, 1987 for a review of "Sapphics Against Anger and Other Poems" by David Shapiro. © 1966, 1980, 1982, 1984, 1986 by the Modern Poetry Association. All reprinted by permission of the Editor of *Poetry* and the respective authors./ v. LXXX, April, 1952, for "The Poetry of Kathleen Raine" by Evan Owen. Copyright 1952, renewed 1980 by the Modern Poetry Association. Reprinted by permission of the Editor of *Poetry* of the Literary Estate of Evan Owen.

Poetry Australia, n. 72, October, 1979. © South Head Press 1979. Reprinted by permission of the publisher.

Poetry Review, v. LVI, 1965 for "Gascoyne in Retrospect" by Derek Stanford; v. 68, January, 1979 for "Seeing as a Faith" by John Cassidy; v. 70, December, 1980 for "Houses of Choice" by Anne Stevenson; v. 72, April, 1982 for "Charles Tomlinson" by Michael O'Neill. Copyright © The Poetry Society 1965, 1979, 1980, 1982. All reprinted by permission of the respective authors.

Poetry Wales, v. 7, Summer, 1971 for "The Poetry of Roland Mathias" by Jeremy Hooker; v. 21, 1985 for "Roland Mathias: 'The Strong Remembered Words'" by Jeremy Hooker. Both reprinted by permission of the publisher and the author.

Prairie Schooner, v. XXXI, Winter, 1967. © 1967 by University of Nebraska Press. Reprinted from *Prairie Schooner* by permission of the University of Nebraska Press.

Publishers Weekly, v. 196, October 20, 1969; v. 203, June 25, 1973; v. 205, January 21, 1974; v. 210, December 6, 1976; v. 213, June 19, 1978; v. 219, May 8, 1981; v. 227, May 24, 1985. Copyright © 1969, 1973, 1974, 1976, 1978, 1981, 1985 by Xerox Corporation. All reprinted from *Publishers Weekly,* published by R. R. Bowker Company, a Xerox company, by permission./ v. 229, March 7, 1986; v. 230, August 22, 1986; v. 230, August 29, 1986. Copyright 1986 by Reed Publishing USA. All reprinted from *Publishers Weekly,* published by R. R. Bowker Company, a Reed Publishing company, by permission.

Punch, v. CCXLIX, August 18, 1965; v. 278, March 12, 1980. © 1965, 1980 by Punch Publications Ltd. All rights reserved. Both may not be reprinted without permission.

Quadrant, v. VIII, October-November, 1964 for "Reasonable, Decorous, and Epic" by Norman Talbot. Reprinted by permission of *Quadrant,* Sydney, Australia and the author.

The Review of Contemporary Fiction, v. 6, Summer, 1986. Copyright, 1986, by John O'Brien. Reprinted by permission of the publisher.

Rocky Mountain Review of Language and Literature, v. 36, 1982; v. 40, 1986. Copyright © 1982, 1986 by the Rocky Mountain Modern Language Association. All rights reserved. Both reprinted by permission of the publisher.

Russian Literature Triquarterly, n. 19, 1986. © 1986 by Ardis Publishers. Reprinted by permission of the publisher.

Saturday Review, v. XLIII, September 24, 1960; v. XLVIII, February 6, 1965; v. XLVIII, July 17, 1965; v. LIII, August 29, 1970; v. LIV, March 6, 1971; v. 3, April 17, 1976; v. 5, December, 1978; v. 6, December, 1979; v. 9, April, 1982; v. 9, May-June, 1983. © 1960, 1965, 1970, 1971, 1976, 1978, 1979, 1982, 1983 *Saturday Review* magazine. All reprinted by permission of the publisher.

The Saturday Review, New York, v. XXXV, January 26, 1952; v. XXXV, September 20, 1952; v. XXXVI, July 25, 1953; v. XXXVI, October 3, 1953; v. XXXVII, July 10, 1954./ v. XLI, January 11, 1958. © 1958 *Saturday Review* magazine. Reprinted by permission of the publisher.

The Saturday Review of Literature, v. XXVII, June 10, 1944; v. XXX, January 11, 1947; v. XXXIII, February 18, 1950; v. XXXIII, October 14, 1950. Copyright 1944, 1947, 1950 *Saturday Review* magazine. All reprinted by permission of the publisher.

School Library Journal, v. 15, July, 1968; v. 16, November 15, 1969; v. 18, September, 1971; v. 19, January 15, 1973. Copyright © 1968, 1969, 1971, 1973. All reprinted from *School Library Journal*, published by R. R. Bowker Co./A Xerox Corporation, by permission.

Science Fiction & Fantasy Book Review, v. I, April, 1979. Copyright © 1979 by The Borgo Press. Reprinted by permission of the publisher./ n. 7, September, 1982; n. 12, March, 1983; n. 18, October, 1983. Copyright © 1982, 1983 by Science Fiction Research Association. All reprinted by permission of the publisher.

Science Fiction Review, v. 5, August, 1976 for "Starschlocked" by Richard E. Geis; v. 7, November, 1978 for a review of "Colony" by Orson Scott Card; v. 14, August, 1985 for a review of "Orion" by Elton T. Elliott; v. 14, November, 1985 for a review of "Privateers" by Elton T. Elliott; v. 15, May, 1986 for a review of "Voyagers II: The Alien Within" by Gene Deweese. Copyright © 1976, 1978, 1985, 1986 by the respective authors. All reprinted by permission of the respective authors.

The Sewanee Review, v. LXXV, Spring, 1967; v. XCII, January-March, 1984. © 1967, 1984 by The University of the South. Both reprinted by permission of the editor of *The Sewanee Review*.

The Small Press Review, v. 13, November, 1981; v. 16, August, 1984. © 1981, 1984 by Dustbooks. Both reprinted by permission of the publisher.

Southerly, v. 32, December, 1972 for "The Wounded Hero: James McAuley's Collected Poems, 1936-1970" by R. F. Brissenden; v. 44, 1984 for "Patience and Despair: James McAuley's Pessimism" by Peter Kirkpatrick; v. 45, 1985 for "The Late Poems of James McAuley" by Noel Macainsh. All reprinted by permission of the publisher and the respective authors.

The Southern Literary Journal, v. XII, Fall, 1979. Copyright 1979 by the Department of English, University of North Carolina at Chapel Hill. Reprinted by permission of the publisher.

The Southern Review (Louisiana State University), n.s. v. II, Winter, 1966 for "Southerners and Jews" by Louis D. Rubin, Jr.; v. XIV, April, 1978 for "'Sassenachs, Palefaces, and a Redskin: Graves, Auden, MacLeish, Hollander, Wagoner, and Others'" by James K. Robinson; v. 17, Summer, 1981 for "Reciprocals" by Wyatt Prunty; v. 22, Autumn, 1986 for "Surviving with Grace: Tennessee Williams Tomorrow" by W. Kenneth Holditch. Copyright, 1966, 1978, 1981, 1986, by the respective authors. All reprinted by permission of the respective authors.

Southwest Review, v. 63, Winter, 1978 for "William Humphrey's Blue Heaven" by Bert Alman; v. 64, Winter, 1979 for "'The Old Voices of Acoma': Simon Ortiz's Mythic Indigenism" by Willard Gingerich; v. 68, Winter, 1983 for "A Patch of Vacancy" by Sandra Prewitt Edelman. © 1978, 1979, 1983 by the respective authors. All reprinted by permission of the publisher.

The Spectator, v. 191, September 4, 1953; v. 193, October 1, 1954; v. 197, August 31, 1956; v. 198, January 18, 1957./ v. 204, March 4, 1960; v. 218, June 2, 1967; v. 238, June 4, 1977; v. 247, July 18, 1981; v. 253, December 8, 1984; v. 257, July 19, 1986; v. 257, October 4, 1986. © 1960, 1967, 1977, 1981, 1984, 1986 by *The Spectator*. All reprinted by permission of *The Spectator*.

Steinbeck Quarterly, v. XIV, Winter & Spring, 1981. All rights reserved. Reprinted by permission of the editor-in-chief.

Studies in Short Fiction, v. 22, Summer, 1985. Copyright 1985 by Newberry College. Reprinted by permission of the publisher.

Texas Studies in English, v. 37, 1958 for "The Poetry of Kathleen Raine: Enchantresses and Medium" by Hazard Adams. Reprinted by permission of the publisher and the author.

Theatre Arts, v. XXV, March, 1941./ v. XXXV, March, 1951. Copyright 1951 by John D. MacArthur.

Time, New York, v. 106, December 8, 1975; v. 110, October 3, 1977; v. 127, April 14, 1986; v. 128, December 8, 1986. Copyright 1975, 1977, 1986 Time Inc. All rights reserved. All reprinted by permission from *Time*.

The Times, London, February 28, 1980; July 17, 1986; September 25, 1986. © Times Newspapers Limited 1980, 1986. All reprinted by permission of the publisher.

The Times Educational Supplement, n. 3541, May 11, 1984. © Times Newspapers Ltd. (London) 1984. Reproduced from *The Times Educational Supplement* by permission.

The Times Higher Education Supplement, n. 283, March 25, 1977. © Times Newspapers Limited, 1977. Reprinted by permission of the publisher.

The Times Literary Supplement, n. 2819, March 9, 1956./ n. 3053, September 2, 1960; n. 3057, September 30, 1960; n. 3259, August 13, 1964; n. 3311, August 12, 1965; n. 3404, May 25, 1967; n. 3423, October 5, 1967; n. 3536, December 4, 1969; n. 3555, April 16, 1970; n. 3589, December 11, 1970; n. 3631, October 1, 1971; n. 3721, June 29, 1973; n. 3726, August 3, 1973; n. 3831, August 15,

1975; n. 3890, October 1, 1976; n. 3924, May 27, 1977; n. 3957, January 27, 1978; n. 3995, October 27, 1978; n. 4014, February 29, 1980; n. 4019, April 4, 1980; n. 4035, July 25, 1980; n. 4062, February 6, 1981; n. 4085, July 17, 1981; n. 4089, August 14, 1981; n. 4093, September 11, 1981; n. 4124, April 16, 1982; n. 4132, June 11, 1982; n. 4198, September 16, 1983; n. 4200, September 30, 1983; n. 4204, October 28, 1983; n. 4219, February 10, 1984; n. 4254, October 12, 1984; n. 4259, November 16, 1984; n. 4276, March 15, 1985; n. 4286, May 24, 1985; n. 4307, October 18, 1985; n. 4310, November 8, 1985; n. 4314, December 6, 1985; n. 4329, March 21, 1986; n. 4338, May 23, 1986; n. 4349, August 8, 1986; n. 4356, September 26, 1986; n. 4368, December 19, 1986. © Times Newspapers Ltd. (London) 1960, 1964, 1965, 1967, 1969, 1970, 1971, 1973, 1975, 1976, 1977, 1978, 1980, 1981, 1982, 1983, 1985, 1986. All reproduced from *The Times Literary Supplement* by permission.

TriQuarterly, n. 56, Winter, 1983 for a review of "Saint Augustine's Pigeon" by Fred Shafer. © 1983 by *TriQuarterly,* Northwestern University. Reprinted by permission of the publisher and the author.

The Twentieth Century, v. 165, June, 1959 for "The Restoration of Symbols" by Elizabeth Jennings. © *The Twentieth Century,* 1959. Reprinted by permission of the author.

Twentieth Century Literature, v. 14, January, 1969. Copyright 1969, Hofstra University Press. Reprinted by permission of the publisher.

USA Today, July 18, 1986. Copyright, 1986 *USA Today.* Excerpted with permission of the publisher.

VLS, n. 4, February, 1982 for "Professor of Desire" by Sally O'Driscoll; n. 15, March, 1983 for a review of "Hungry Hearts" by Stephen Harvey; n. 25, April, 1984 for "Blame It on the Cha-Cha: Cabrera Infante's Carnal Knowledge" by Enrique Fernández; n. 44, April, 1986 for a review of "Bigfoot Dreams" by Jan Hoffman; n. 53, March, 1987 for "Text and Violence: Kathy Acker Strikes Again" by C. Carr. Copyright © 1982, 1983, 1984, 1986, 1987 News Group Publications, Inc. All reprinted by permission of *The Village Voice* and the respective authors.

The Village Voice, May 31, 1983 for "Three Ways to Sunday" by Eliot Fremont-Smith; v. XXXI, February 25, 1986 for "Kesh Flow: Ursula Le Guin Sees the World" by Jacqueline Austin; v. XXXI, March 25, 1986 for "Havana Vice: A Cautionary Tale" by Enrique Fernández; April 29, 1986 for "Child's Play" by Walter Bode; v. XXXI, July 29, 1986 for "Race Case" by Rob Nixon. Copyright © News Group Publications, Inc., 1983, 1986. All reprinted by permission of *The Village Voice* and the respective authors.

The Virginia Quarterly Review, v. 57, Spring, 1981; v. 59, Spring, 1983. Copyright, 1981, 1983, by *The Virginia Quarterly Review,* The University of Virginia. Both reprinted by permission of the publisher.

Voice of Youth Advocates, v. 5, February, 1983. Copyrighted 1983 by *Voice of Youth Advocates.* Reprinted by permission of the publisher.

The Wall Street Journal, December 24, 1984. © Dow Jones & Company, Inc. 1984./ October 22, 1984 for "The Cold War at 50 Fathoms" by John R. Alden. © copyright 1984 by the author. Reprinted by permission of the author./ August 18, 1986 for "Pentagon Pet Lets the Soviets Have It Again" by Mark Zieman. © Dow Jones & Company, Inc. 1986. Reprinted by permission of the author./ January 3, 1983; October 1, 1986. © Dow Jones & Company, Inc. 1983, 1986. All rights reserved. Both reprinted by permission of *The Wall Street Journal.*

West Coast Review of Books, v. 10, January-February, 1984; v. 10, September-October, 1984; v. 10, November-December, 1984. Copyright 1984 by Rapport Publishing Co., Inc. All reprinted by permission of the publisher.

Western American Literature, v. XIII, November, 1978; v. XIV, May, 1979; v. XVII, Winter, 1983; v. XIX, November, 1984; v. XXI, August, 1986. Copyright 1978, 1979, 1983, 1984, 1986, by the Western Literature Association. All reprinted by permission of the publisher.

Western Humanities Review, v. XXXVIII, Winter, 1984. Copyright, 1984, University of Utah. Reprinted by permission of the publisher.

Wilson Library Bulletin, v. 60, November, 1985. Copyright © 1985 by the H. W. Wilson Company. Reprinted by permission of the publisher.

Women's Wear Daily, April 4, 1986. Copyright 1986, Fairchild Publications. Reprinted by permission of the publisher.

World Literature Today, v. 51, Winter, 1977; v. 52, Summer, 1978; v. 54, Summer, 1980; v. 57, Spring, 1983; v. 58, Winter, 1984; v. 58, Summer, 1954; v. 58, Autumn, 1984; v. 59, Winter, 1985; v. 59, Spring, 1985; v. 59, Summer, 1985; v. 60, Winter, 1986. Copyright 1977, 1978, 1980, 1983, 1984, 1985, 1986 by the University of Oklahoma Press. All reprinted by permission of the publisher.

The Yale Review, v. XLVII, Autumn, 1977 for a review of "New Collected Poems" by Helen Vendler. Copyright 1977, by Yale University. Reprinted by permission of the author.

THE EXCERPTS IN CLC, VOLUME 45, WERE REPRINTED FROM THE FOLLOWING BOOKS:

Buckley, Vincent. From *Essays in Poetry: Mainly Australian*. Melbourne University Press, 1957.

Bucknall, Barbara J. From *Ursula K. LeGuin*. Frederick Ungar Publishing Co., 1981. Copyright © 1981 by The Ungar Publishing Company. Reprinted by permission of the publisher.

Canary, Robert H. From *Robert Graves*. Twayne, 1980. Copyright © 1980 by Twayne Publishers. All rights reserved. Reprinted with the permission of Twayne Publishers, a division of G. K. Hall & Co., Boston.

De Maegd-Soëp, Caroline. From "The Theme of 'BYT'—Everyday Life in the Stories of Iurii Trifonov," in *Russian Literature and Criticism: Selected Papers from the Second World Congress for Soviet and East European Studies*. Edited by Evelyn Bristol. Berkeley Slavic Specialties, 1982. Copyright © 1982 by De Maegd-Soëp. All rights reserved. Reprinted by permission of the publisher and the author.

Elsom, John. From *Post-War British Theatre*. Routledge & Kegan Paul, 1976. © John Elsom 1976. Reprinted by permission of Routledge & Kegan Paul PLC.

Fontenrose, Joseph. From *John Steinbeck: An Introduction and Intrepretation*. Barnes & Noble, 1963. © copyright, 1963 by Barnes & Noble, Inc. All rights reserved. Reprinted by permission of the publisher.

Foster, David William. From *Augusto Rao Bastos*. Twayne, 1978. Copyright 1978 by Twayne Publishers. All rights reserved. Reprinted with the permission of Twayne Publishers, a division of G. K. Hall & Co., Boston.

Grubb, Frederick. From *A Vision of Reality: A Study of Liberalism in Twentieth-Century Verse*. Barnes & Noble, Inc., 1965. © Frederick Grubb 1965. Reprinted by permission of the publisher.

Heine, Elizabeth. From an introduction to *Arctic Summer and Other Fiction*. By E. M. Forster, edited by Elizabeth Heine and Oliver Stallybrass. Holmes and Meier Publishers, 1981. Introduction copyright © 1980 by Elizabeth Heine. All rights reserved. Reprinted by permission of Holmes & Meier Publishers, Inc., 30 Irving Place, New York, NY 10003.

Howe, Irving. From a foreword to *In Dreams Begin Responsibilities and Other Stories*. By Delmore Schwartz, edited by James Atlas. New Directions Books, 1978. Copyright © 1978 by New Directions Publishing Corporation. All rights reserved. Reprinted by permission of the publisher.

Jones, Glyn. From *The Dragon Has Two Tongues: Essays on Anglo-Welsh Writers and Writing*. J. M. Dent & Sons Ltd., 1968. © Glyn Jones, 1968. All rights reserved. Reprinted by permission of Laurence Pollinger Limited for the author.

Keane, Patrick J. From *A Wild Civility: Interactions in the Poetry and Thought of Robert Graves*. University of Missouri Press, 1980. Copyright © 1980 by The Curators of the University of Missouri. All rights reserved. Reprinted by permission of the publisher.

Kirkman, Michael. From *The Poetry of Robert Graves*. The Athlone Press, 1969. © 1969 Michael Kirkman. Reprinted by permission of the publisher.

Levant, Howard. From *The Novels of John Steinbeck: A Critical Study*. University of Missouri Press, 1974. Copyright © 1974 by The Curators of the University of Missouri. All rights reserved. Reprinted by permission of the publisher.

Levin, Bernard. From *The Pendulum Years: Britain and the Sixties*. Jonathan Cape, 1970. © 1970 by Bernard Levin. Reprinted by permission of the author. In Canada by Jonathan Cape Ltd.

Lisca, Peter. From *The Wide World of John Steinbeck*. Rutgers University Press, 1958. Copyright © 1958 by Rutgers, The State University. Reprinted by permission of Rutgers University Press.

McAuley, James. From *A Map of Australian Verse: The Twentieth Century*. Oxford University Press, Melbourne, 1975. Copyright © 1975 by Oxford University Press, Inc. Reprinted by permission of the publisher.

McDowell, Frederick P. W. From *E. M. Forster*. Revised edition. Twayne, 1982. Copyright © 1982 by Twayne Publishers. Reprinted with the permission of Twayne Publishers, a division of G. K. Hall & Co., Boston.

Phillips, Robert. From a forward to *The Ego Is Always at the Wheel*. By Delmore Schwartz, edited by Robert Phillips. New Directions, 1986. Copyright © 1986 by Robert Phillips. All rights reserved. Reprinted by permission of New Directions Publishing Corporation.

Schmidt, Michael. From *An Introduction to Fifty Modern Poets*. Pan Books Ltd., 1979. © Michael Schmidt 1979. Reprinted by permission of the publisher.

Skelton, Robin. From an introduction to *Collected Poems*. By David Gascoyne, edited by Robin Skelton. Oxford University Press, London, 1965. © Oxford University Press 1965. All rights reserved. Reprinted by permission of the publisher.

Snipes, Katherine. From *Robert Graves*. Frederick Ungar Publishing Co., 1979. Copyright © 1979 by The Ungar Publishing Company. Reprinted by permission of the publisher.

Stanford, Derek. From *The Freedom of Poetry: Studies in Contemporary Verse*. The Falcon Press Limited, 1947.

Summers, Claude J. From *E. M. Forster*. Frederick Ungar Publishing Co., 1983. Copyright © 1983 by The Ungar Publishing Company. Reprinted by permission of the publisher.

Thurley, Geoffrey. From *The Ironic Harvest: English Poetry in the Twentieth Century*. Edward Arnold, 1974. © Geoffrey Thurley 1974. All rights reserved. Reprinted by permission of the Literary Estate of Geoffrey Thurley.

Thwaite, Anthony. From *Twentieth-Century English Poetry: An Introduction*. Heinemann Educational Books, 1978. © Anthony Thwaite. Reprinted by permission of the publisher.

Timmerman, John H. From *John Steinbeck's Fiction: The Aesthetics of the Road Taken*. University of Oklahoma Press, 1986. Copyright © 1986 by the University of Oklahoma Press. Reprinted by permission of the publisher.

Trussler, Simon. From *The Plays of John Osborne: An Assessment*. Victor Gollancz Ltd., 1969. © Simon Trussler 1969. Reprinted by permission of the author.

Walker, Jeffrey. From "1945—1956: Post-World War II Manners and Mores," in *The American Short Story: A Critical History, 1945-1980*. Edited by Gordon Weaver. Twayne, 1983. Copyright © 1983 by Twayne Publishers. All rights reserved. Reprinted with the permission of Twayne Publishers, a division of G. K. Hall & Co., Boston.

Waterman, Andrew. From "The Poetry of Geoffrey Hill," in *British Poetry Since 1970: A Critical Survey*. Edited by Peter Jones and Michael Schmidt. Carcanet Press, 1980. Copyright © 1980 Carcanet New Press. All rights reserved. Reprinted by permission of the publisher, Carcanet Press.

Wilson, Angus. From an introduction to *The Aerodrome: A Love Story*. By Rex Warner. Bodley Head, 1966. Introduction Copyright © 1966 by The Bodley Head Ltd. All rights reserved. Reprinted by permission of the publisher.

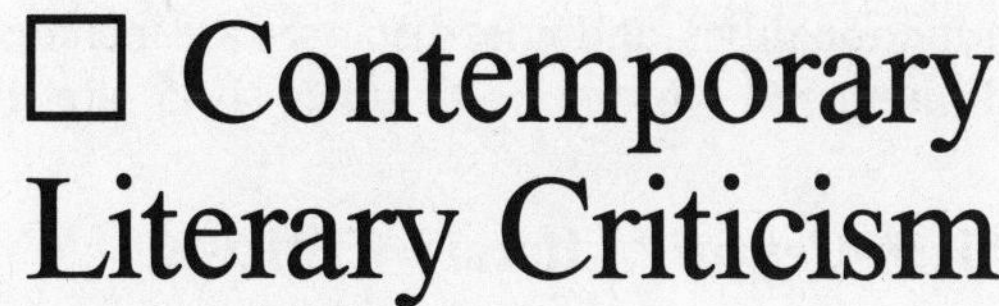

☐ Contemporary Literary Criticism

Cumulative Indexes
Volumes 1-45

This Index Includes References to Entries in These Gale Series

Contemporary Literary Criticism

Presents excerpts of criticism on the works of novelists, poets, dramatists, short story writers, scriptwriters, and other creative writers who are now living or who have died since 1960. Cumulative indexes to authors, nationalities, and titles discussed are included in odd-numbered volumes. Volumes 1-45 are in print.

Twentieth-Century Literary Criticism

Contains critical excerpts by the most significant commentators on poets, novelists, short story writers, dramatists, and philosophers who died between 1900 and 1960. Cumulative indexes to authors, nationalities, and titles discussed are included in each new volume. Volumes 1-24 are in print.

Nineteenth-Century Literature Criticism

Offers significant passages from criticism on authors who died between 1800 and 1899. Cumulative indexes to authors, nationalities, and titles discussed are included in each new volume. Volumes 1-16 are in print.

Literature Criticism from 1400 to 1800

Compiles significant passages from the most noteworthy criticism on authors of the fifteenth through eighteenth centuries. Cumulative indexes to authors, nationalities, and titles discussed are included in each new volume. Volumes 1-5 are in print.

Children's Literature Review

Includes excerpts from reviews, criticism, and commentary on works of authors and author/illustrators who create books for children. Cumulative indexes to authors, nationalities, and titles discussed are included in each new volume. Volumes 1-13 are in print.

Contemporary Authors Series

Encompasses five related series. *Contemporary Authors* provides biographical and bibliographical information on nearly 88,000 writers of fiction, nonfiction, poetry, journalism, drama, motion pictures, and other fields. Each new volume contains sketches on authors not previously covered in the series. Volumes 1-121 are in print. *Contemporary Authors New Revision Series* provides completely updated information on active authors covered in previously published volumes of *CA*. Only entries requiring significant change are revised for *CA New Revision Series.* Volumes 1-21 are in print. *Contemporary Authors Permanent Series* consists of updated listings for deceased and inactive authors removed from original volumes 9-36 when these volumes were revised. Volumes 1-2 are in print. *Contemporary Authors Autobiography Series* presents specially commissioned autobiographies by leading contemporary writers. Volumes 1-5 are in print. *Contemporary Authors Bibliographical Series* contains primary and secondary bibliographies as well as analytical bibliographical essays by authorities on major modern authors. Volumes 1-2 are in print.

Dictionary of Literary Biography

Encompasses three related series. *Dictionary of Literary Biography* furnishes illustrated overviews of authors' lives and works and places them in the larger perspective of literary history. Volumes 1-62 are in print. *Dictionary of Literary Biography Documentary Series* illuminates the careers of major figures through a selection of literary documents, including letters, notebook and diary entries, interviews, book reviews, and photographs. Volumes 1-4 are in print. *Dictionary of Literary Biography Yearbook* summarizes the past year's literary activity with articles on genres, major prizes, conferences, and other timely subjects and includes udpated and new entries on individual authors. Yearbooks for 1980-1986 are in print. A cumulative index to authors and articles is included in each new volume.

Concise Dictionary of American Literary Biography

A six-volume series that collects revised and updated sketches on major American authors that were originally presented in *Dictionary of Literary Biography.* Volume 1 is in print.

Something about the Author Series

Encompasses two related series. *Something about the Author* contains heavily illustrated biographical sketches on juvenile and young adult authors and illustrators from all eras. Volumes 1-49 are in print. *Something about the Author Autobiography Series* presents specially commissioned autobiographies by prominent authors and illustrators of books for children and young adults. Volumes 1-4 are in print.

Authors in the News

Reprints news stories and feature articles from American newspapers and magazines covering writers and other members of the communications media. A cumulative index to authors and a list of surveyed periodicals are included in each volume. Volumes 1-2, both published in 1976, are in print.

Yesterday's Authors of Books for Children

Contains heavily illustrated entries on children's writers who died before 1961. Two volumes only. Volumes 1-2 are in print.

Literary Criticism Series Cumulative Author Index

This index lists all author entries in the Gale Literary Criticism Series and includes cross-references to other Gale sources. For the convenience of the reader, references to the *Yearbook* in the *Contemporary Literary Criticism* series include the page number (in parentheses) after the volume number. References in the index are identified as follows:

AITN: *Authors in the News,* Volumes 1-2
CAAS: *Contemporary Authors Autobiography Series,* Volumes 1-5
CA: *Contemporary Authors* (original series), Volumes 1-120
CABS: *Contemporary Authors Bibliographical Series,* Volumes 1-2
CANR: *Contemporary Authors New Revision Series,* Volumes 1-20
CAP: *Contemporary Authors Permanent Series,* Volumes 1-2
CA-R: *Contemporary Authors* (revised editions), Volumes 1-44
CDALB: *Concise Dictionary of American Literary Biography*
CLC: *Contemporary Literary Criticism,* Volumes 1-45
CLR: *Children's Literature Review,* Volumes 1-13
DLB: *Dictionary of Literary Biography,* Volumes 1-58
DLB-DS: *Dictionary of Literary Biography Documentary Series,* Volumes 1-4
DLB-Y: *Dictionary of Literary Biography Yearbook,* Volumes 1980-1986
LC: *Literature Criticism from 1400 to 1800,* Volumes 1-6
NCLC: *Nineteenth-Century Literature Criticism,* Volumes 1-16
SAAS: *Something about the Author Autobiography Series,* Volumes 1-3
SATA: *Something about the Author,* Volumes 1-48
TCLC: *Twentieth-Century Literary Criticism,* Volumes 1-25
YABC: *Yesterday's Authors of Books for Children,* Volumes 1-2

Author Index

Braine, John (Gerard) 1922-1986 .... **CLC 1, 3, 41**
See also CANR 1
See also CA 1-4R
See also DLB 15
See also DLB-Y 86

Brammer, Billy Lee 1930?-1978
See Brammer, William

Brammer, William 1930?-1978 ..... **CLC 31**
See also obituary CA 77-80

Brancati, Vitaliano 1907-1954 .... **TCLC 12**
See also CA 109

Brancato, Robin F(idler) 1936- ..... **CLC 35**
See also CANR 11
See also CA 69-72
See also SATA 23

Brand, Millen 1906-1980 .... **CLC 7**
See also CA 21-24R
See also obituary CA 97-100

Branden, Barbara 19??- ..... **CLC 44** (447)

Brandes, Georg (Morris Cohen) 1842-1927 .... **TCLC 10**
See also CA 105

Branley, Franklyn M(ansfield) 1915- .... **CLC 21**
See also CANR 14
See also CA 33-36R
See also SATA 4

Brathwaite, Edward 1930- .... **CLC 11**
See also CANR 11
See also CA 25-28R
See also DLB 53

Brautigan, Richard (Gary) 1935-1984 .... **CLC 1, 3, 5, 9, 12, 34** (314), **42**
See also CA 53-56
See also obituary CA 113
See also DLB 2, 5
See also DLB-Y 80, 84

Brecht, (Eugen) Bertolt (Friedrich) 1898-1956 .... **TCLC 1, 6, 13**
See also CA 104

Bremer, Fredrika 1801-1865 ..... **NCLC 11**

Brennan, Christopher John 1870-1932 .... **TCLC 17**
See also CA 117

Brennan, Maeve 1917- .... **CLC 5**
See also CA 81-84

Brentano, Clemens (Maria) 1778-1842 .... **NCLC 1**

Brenton, Howard 1942- .... **CLC 31**
See also CA 69-72
See also DLB 13

Breslin, James 1930-
See Breslin, Jimmy
See also CA 73-76

Breslin, Jimmy 1930- .... **CLC 4, 43**
See also Breslin, James
See also AITN 1

Bresson, Robert 1907- .... **CLC 16**
See also CA 110

Breton, André 1896-1966 ..... **CLC 2, 9, 15**
See also CAP 2
See also CA 19-20
See also obituary CA 25-28R

Breytenbach, Breyten 1939- .... **CLC 23, 37**
See also CA 113

Bridgers, Sue Ellen 1942- .... **CLC 26**
See also CANR 11
See also CA 65-68
See also SAAS 1
See also SATA 22

Bridges, Robert 1844-1930 .... **TCLC 1**
See also CA 104
See also DLB 19

Bridie, James 1888-1951 .... **TCLC 3**
See also Mavor, Osborne Henry
See also DLB 10

Brin, David 1950- .... **CLC 34** (133)
See also CA 102

Brink, André (Philippus) 1935- .... **CLC 18, 36**
See also CA 104

Brinsmead, H(esba) F(ay) 1922- .... **CLC 21**
See also CANR 10
See also CA 21-24R
See also SATA 18

Brittain, Vera (Mary) 1893?-1970 .... **CLC 23**
See also CAP 1
See also CA 15-16
See also obituary CA 25-28R

Broch, Hermann 1886-1951 ...... **TCLC 20**
See also CA 117

Brock, Rose 1923-
See Hansen, Joseph

Brodsky, Iosif Alexandrovich 1940-
See Brodsky, Joseph
See also CA 41-44R
See also AITN 1

Brodsky, Joseph 1940- .... **CLC 4, 6, 13, 36**
See also Brodsky, Iosif Alexandrovich

Brodsky, Michael (Mark) 1948- .... **CLC 19**
See also CANR 18
See also CA 102

Bromell, Henry 1947- .... **CLC 5**
See also CANR 9
See also CA 53-56

Bromfield, Louis (Brucker) 1896-1956 .... **TCLC 11**
See also CA 107
See also DLB 4, 9

Broner, E(sther) M(asserman) 1930- .... **CLC 19**
See also CANR 8
See also CA 17-20R
See also DLB 28

Bronk, William 1918- .... **CLC 10**
See also CA 89-92

Brontë, Anne 1820-1849 .... **NCLC 4**
See also DLB 21

Brontë, Charlotte 1816-1855 .... **NCLC 3, 8**
See also DLB 21
See also DLB 39

Brontë, (Jane) Emily 1818-1848 .... **NCLC 16**
See also DLB 21, 32

Brooke, Frances 1724-1789 .... **LC 6**
See also DLB 39

Brooke, Henry 1703?-1783 .... **LC 1**
See also DLB 39

Brooke, Rupert (Chawner) 1887-1915 .... **TCLC 2, 7**
See also CA 104
See also DLB 19

Brooke-Rose, Christine 1926- ...... **CLC 40**
See also CA 13-16R
See also DLB 14

Brookner, Anita 1938- .... **CLC 32, 34** (136)
See also CA 114

Brooks, Cleanth 1906- .... **CLC 24**
See also CA 17-20R

Brooks, Gwendolyn 1917- .... **CLC 1, 2, 4, 5, 15**
See also CANR 1
See also CA 1-4R
See also SATA 6
See also DLB 5
See also CDALB 1941-1968
See also AITN 1

Brooks, Mel 1926- .... **CLC 12**
See also Kaminsky, Melvin
See also CA 65-68
See also DLB 26

Brooks, Peter 1938- .... **CLC 34** (519)
See also CANR 1
See also CA 45-48

Brooks, Van Wyck 1886-1963 ...... **CLC 29**
See also CANR 6
See also CA 1-4R
See also DLB 45

Brophy, Brigid (Antonia) 1929- .... **CLC 6, 11, 29**
See also CAAS 4
See also CA 5-8R
See also DLB 14

Brosman, Catharine Savage 1934- .... **CLC 9**
See also CA 61-64

Broughton, T(homas) Alan 1936- .... **CLC 19**
See also CANR 2
See also CA 45-48

Broumas, Olga 1949- .... **CLC 10**
See also CANR 20
See also CA 85-88

Brown, Claude 1937- .... **CLC 30**
See also CA 73-76

Brown, Dee (Alexander) 1908- ..... **CLC 18**
See also CANR 11
See also CA 13-16R
See also SATA 5
See also DLB-Y 80

Brown, George Mackay 1921- .... **CLC 5**
See also CANR 12
See also CA 21-24R
See also SATA 35
See also DLB 14, 27

Brown, Rita Mae 1944- .... **CLC 18, 43**
See also CANR 2, 11
See also CA 45-48

Brown, Rosellen 1939- .... **CLC 32**
See also CANR 14
See also CA 77-80

Author Index

Author Index

Author Index

Author Index

Author Index

Author Index

Author Index

Author Index

CLC Cumulative Nationality Index

Nationality Index

CLC Cumulative Title Index

Title Index

Title Index

Title Index

Title Index

Title Index

Title Index

Title Index

Title Index

Title Index

Title Index

Title Index

Title Index

Title Index

Title Index

Title Index

Title Index

Title Index

Title Index

Title Index

Title Index

Title Index

Title Index

Title Index

Title Index

Title Index

Title Index

Title Index

Title Index

Title Index

Title Index

Title Index

Title Index

Title Index

Title Index

Title Index

Title Index

Title Index

Title Index

Title Index

Title Index

Title Index

Title Index

Title Index

Title Index